An Introduction to Christian Ethics

An Introduction to Christian Ethics

History, Movements, People

Harry J. Huebner

BAYLOR UNIVERSITY PRESS

Cover Design by Stephanie Milanowski
Book Design by Diane Smith

Library of Congress Cataloging-in-Publication Data

Huebner, Harry John, 1943–
  An introduction to Christian ethics : history, movements, people / Harry J. Huebner.
  688 p. cm.
  Includes index.
  ISBN 978-1-60258-063-3 (pbk. : alk. paper)
  1. Christian ethics. I. Title.
  BJ1251.H83 2012
  241--dc23
                          2011032167

BAYLOR
UNIVERSITY

Printed in the United States of America on acid-free paper with a minimum of 30% PCW recycled content.

My students
past – present – future

The Author's Prayer

If aught in this book was said through lack of knowledge, or through weakness of faith in thee or of love for humanity, I pray thee to overrule my sin and turn aside its force before it harms thy cause. Pardon the frailty of thy servant, and look upon him only as he sinks his life in Jesus, his Master and Saviour. Amen.

Walter Rauschenbusch,
For God and People: Prayers of the Social Awakening

The Disciple's Blessing

Then turning to the disciples, Jesus said to them privately, "Blessed are the eyes that see what you see! For I tell you that many prophets and kings desired to see what you see, but did not see it, and to hear what you hear, but did not hear it." (Luke 10:23-24)

The Seer's Charge

When I saw him, I fell at his feet as though dead. But he placed his right hand on me, saying, "Do not be afraid; I am the first and the last, and the living one. I was dead, and see, I am alive forever and ever; and I have the keys of Death and of Hades. Now write what you have seen. . . ." (Rev 1:17-19)

TABLE OF CONTENTS

PART IV
CRITICAL RESPONSES TO TWENTIETH-CENTURY CHRISTIAN ETHICS

ACKNOWLEDGMENTS

Books, even books that I write, are among my closest friends. As such they are special gifts to me. This is, in part, because I could not write books by myself. Nothing I have ever written has been truly my own; that is true in several ways. This book is born in the awareness that I have been given great ideas and life-models from the time that I began reading. Each author has become a friend of sorts. I honor these donors not by naming them here, as is customary in books like this, but by writing about them at some length.

As a teacher, I have become aware that in my students I was given eager minds and hearts waiting to devour what I had received from others. My first nod of gratitude, therefore, goes to my students, to whom this book is dedicated. They are the inspiration and the motivation for the book. It is a genuine honor to give to them what was given to me.

Writing a book, especially one of this magnitude, takes time and energy. Parts of this project have been in my computer for some twenty years and have survived interim administrative appointments and other writing projects along the way. It would never have seen light of day had not many people repeatedly urged me to bring it to fruition. Certainly the encouragement sometimes came with the tone of "just get it done already," but it also, on occasion at least, came with the intent to persuade me that it too could become a gift for others. For both kinds of prodding, I am grateful.

I owe an enormous debt of gratitude to my colleagues at Canadian Mennonite University (CMU) in Winnipeg, especially those in the Biblical and Theological Studies Department. I am profoundly grateful for almost daily encouragements that came from some, for those who read chapters and gave helpful critical suggestions, those who were willing to take on additional assignments because I requested repeated writing leaves, and those in administration who were willing to have me spend a disproportionate amount of my workload on writing. These are truly special friends, in the classical sense of that term, meaning that they held me to the discipline necessary to accomplish a task. Within this large group of supporters there are those who deserve special mention: Earl Davey, Irma Fast Dueck, Paul Dyck, Adolf Ens, Dan Epp-Tiessen, John J. Friesen, Gerald Gerbrandt, Titus Guenther, Chris Huebner, Waldemar Janzen, Sheila Klassen-Wiebe, Karl Koop, Gordon Matties, Justin Neufeld, Cheryl Pauls, David Schroeder, Sue Sorensen, George Wiebe, and Gordon Zerbe. There are really few academic joys greater than writing in the company of others who know its many struggles and help make them bearable by also knowing how to participate in the passion that drives us to write. I truly count myself among the blessed to be able to call CMU my home institution.

Special thanks goes to Margaret Franz who, out of sheer loyalty and friendship, logged countless hours at the painstaking work of copyediting. She did this not as an obligation but out of interest and passion to make a given text a better text.

Then there are those whose friendship extends far beyond the content of this project and exactly because of this sustained me—whether they read chapters or not. I thank them for the engagement of mutual *Menschlichkeit*. So often they offered strength precisely because they diverted my attention away from my work, reminding me that life is more than ceaselessly typing on a computer keyboard. For without diversion we would all succumb to the distortions of life that inadvertently seek to wedge their way into our routines. Such friends remind us of what is most important—love, peace, justice, silence, God, people, rest—both through their presence and in their naïve insistence on the ordinariness of life, like eating, playing, and beholding beauty. They are diverters from the temptations to narrowness, which all too easily have us stray from openness to God's love.

Among these diverters, I include my grandchildren. It is a quirk of time—perhaps testimony to my tardiness—that all seven of my current grandchildren were born during the gestation of this book. Their births themselves were disruptions of the most wonderful kind. And today their pleading requests to play with the model train, or go to the playground, or read a story, or their insistence that I join them at the cottage, while perhaps inconvenient at the time, are absolutely indispensable diversions in helping me remember that I am not really my own. In their disruptions they teach me something important about ethics—for "a little child shall lead them" (Isa 11:6b) is not just a quaint and sentimental saying, but an invitation to a discipline of openness, to a beyond which one cannot configure the contours of in advance.

During the writing of much of this book I have been involved in two religiously focused dialogues: one with Roman Catholic scholars from St. Paul's College in Winnipeg, and another with Shia Muslims from Iran. Both groups of scholars have in different ways reminded me of the geography of faith, that is, the particularity of our time and place. They have helped me to see that the religious quest is indeed extremely large and diverse and that I am but a speck in this quest. They have shown me that humility is truly the only posture appropriate before both God and the other.

The writing of this book was made possible by generous research grants from my university, not only once but several times. Hence, I was able to ask student research assistants to help with the collection of material and with indexing. I am grateful to Jonathan Dyck, Annalee Giesbrecht, Aaron Janzen, and Joshua Paetkau and thank them for their conscientious work.

The CMU library staff was generous beyond the call of duty in assisting with interlibrary loans, finding difficult-to-locate articles and books, researching material, ordering books, and so on. A special thank you to Wes Bergen, John Dyck, Tamara Dyck, and Vic Froese.

It may seem strange to thank my home church congregation, Charleswood Mennonite Church, for its role in an academic writing project, but it is not inappropriate for one who sees the nature of Christian ethics as I propose. For I believe that being faithful disciples is impossible apart from a community of friends seeking to be brothers and sisters in Christ and to one another. Only openness to a redeeming God can make of us an *ecclesia*. Together we have been on this journey, both as I have been ministered to and as I have been permitted to test my words with their spirit of truth. For unless my theology can be "for them," it is not likely to be theology for anyone.

Profound gratitude goes to my family— Agnes and the clan of children and their spouses. Preoccupation with this project has, on occasion, meant that I was unavailable to them, preoccupied with things much less enjoyable. I know that to be my loss. I thank them for making me feel that it was also their loss. I am grateful for their love, encouragement, nudging, and even pressure to get it done. I thank Agnes for her ongoing support and sacrifice and for proofreading several chapters. Thank you to Chris for cheering me on both as a colleague and a son.

I thank Baylor University Press for being willing to work with me on this project. Special thanks to Carey C. Newman, director of Baylor University Press, for his patience and grace in light of my repeated requests for extensions. I thank him for his commitment to this project. There is no greater gift to a writer than to have a publisher with dedicated people devoting their skills to the birthing of a cherished manuscript.

Above all else, I thank God for daily sustenance, the spirit of grace, and the gift of time. I know all too well that if there be any goodness, beauty, or truth in the words below, it is so because of what is given from their true source. And if there should be a blessing that flows from these pages, to even a single reader, it is not because of what is said but because, through special grace, what

was said has been transformed into a message by the one whose Word insists on breaking into flesh again and again.

No doubt this book will also disappoint some who will feel unfairly represented or perhaps not represented at all. I really have no defense to offer other than my own limitations. Nevertheless, I will sincerely confess my unspeakable joy of having been able to enter into the "world" of so many wonderful Christian ethicists. My lament is that I was unable to tarry with them longer.

I now invite the reader to linger with these words. This book is intended as a textbook and is therefore not a fast read. Read slowly, ponder, absorb, cherish the words, the ideas, the challenges of thought, the tensions, and even the quarrels. But better still, especially where the ideas and practices of authors represented in this book inspire you, read, not my words only, but read the books of the authors represented. If these pages can achieve that, they will have brought forth fruit.

PREFACE

The idea of another book on Christian ethics can hardly be met with great enthusiasm. There are quite enough around already. The plethora of books might suggest that the task of finding a text for a Christian ethics course is an easy one. But quite the opposite is true. As a teacher, I have found it challenging to choose a satisfactory resource which introduces students to the subject matter of Christian ethics. It seems irresponsible to plunge first-time ethics students into the subject via a focus on moral issues. For what guides students in the determination of what makes something a moral issue? Moral issues don't just happen; they are the products of social imaginations. So the study of Christian ethics must devote as much attention to the socially constructed world, the home of moral issues, as to the issues themselves. Moreover, our generation is not the first to discuss the matter of what makes for the good Christian life. Much can be learned from fellow Christians both present and past. Much, that is, not only in regard to what they believe the practical import of the Christian life to be, but much also in why the corpus of Christian ethics comes to us today in the way that it does. This study then does not begin with ready-made assumptions of what Christian ethics is, or what the issues are, but rather it seeks to tell the story of why Christian ethics has come to be what it is.

The value of this book, if there be any, lies in the rationale which undergirds it, a rationale which may well be somewhat contentious. My own teaching experience has taught me that in addition to the problems of beginning with moral issues, there are two other ways not to teach a course in Christian ethics: the first is to focus on moral decision-making, as if students can thereby learn how to do it well. Christian ethics is not first of all—not even significantly—a logical skill, which one can learn as though nothing else matters. Therefore, this approach is bound to fail in teaching students very much about how Christians ought to live. A second common approach is to teach students different moral theories. It is common pedagogy to iterate different methods available so that students may select from among them the approach which best suits them or makes most sense to them. Here the assumption is that in the process students will learn the rational skills to evaluate among competing approaches to ethics. But this approach fails because it does not recognize that Christian life and thought have a far more complex relationship than is often thought. It assumes that people will do what they *think* is right. But we all know that there are forces in this world, even within ourselves, that keep us from doing what we think is right. Teaching Christian ethics, therefore, has as much to do with learning what these forces are, how they control our lives, and how we can overcome their power in our lives than it does with proper thinking. Alas, Christian ethics is not primarily about methodology. The world is not best understood via theories, as many modern scholars allege, but via stories, which have the power to make theories intelligible.

This book should be seen as an attempt to renarrate the understanding of Christian practice, paying attention to the story of Christian life and thought and to how contemporary Christian ethicists give expression to it. It attempts to do this in four sections: first, the history of ethics. This series of chapters describes the vast sociocultural entanglements of the Christian understanding of life. It focuses on the major epochs from Greek thought to the nineteenth century. It is of necessity a general survey and does not pretend to be comprehensive. Yet such a survey is important to help students learn to see that context matters. Second, we will take a brief side-glance and ask how ethics has been understood by the academic disciplines that claim it by analyzing what four disciplines of study—philosophy, sociology, psychology, and theology—have said about the nature of ethics. This section is intended to familiarize students with the scholarly language of ethics. It is not intended to suggest that these are the only areas of study that could help make Christian ethics intelligible; one could easily think of others like anthropology, political studies, and the natural and biological sciences. Yet the four chosen disciplines are necessary to make the language of ethics intelligible. The last set of chapters (the bulk of the book) focuses on specific theologians who have had significant impact in framing the terms of contemporary ethical discourse. Since ethics is an "embodied practice," it is important to examine the writings of specific Christian scholars as contextualized in their own time. Students learn at least as much about Christian ethics by learning to follow particular persons' lives—their practices and their thoughts—as they do by clarifying their own thoughts. These scholars are divided into further broad sections. Part III attends to several mainline, early twentieth-century theologian-ethicists who set the agenda for the contemporary discussion. Part IV presents selective critics who have made alternate (to the mainstream) proposals, including general critics of the tradition

in which Christian life gets cast and specific critics like liberation theologians, feminist scholars, and peace theologians.

In summary, the book has a fourfold, distinctive character. First, its person-oriented focus. It does not present Christian ethics by abstractly discussing disembodied social issues like abortion and euthanasia or ethical theories like utilitarianism or situation ethics. Instead, it invites readers into real lives—lives which are just as multifaceted and filled with ambiguities and questions (perhaps even more so) as their own. Second, although the approach is person-oriented, this book also takes history and other disciplines seriously. The story of ethics demands such an approach, as Christian ethics is largely unintelligible without narrating the language of the tradition. Third, it approaches the matter of criticism in a distinctive way, in that authorities other than the author of this book offer the critical engagement. Almost half the book is a critical response to the formulations of the mainline tradition. Fourth, this volume includes a specific Canadian contribution to the discussion of ethics, one not found in textbooks written by American authors, namely, chapters on J. S. Woodsworth, who embodies a radical, christocentric faith as a Canadian Member of Parliament; and George P. Grant, whose criticism of Western society has a uniquely Canadian bent.

It is hoped that this book might convince the reader that Christian ethics fails when it simply tries to be *realistic* about living the Christian faith and it also fails when it belittles the complexities of *embodying* the life of Christ in this multifaceted world. For if ethics is too preoccupied with realism, it is restrained from seeing "the whole new world" that the Apostle Paul speaks of that is available to us "in Christ" (2 Cor 5:17); and if ethics sees life in overly simple terms like quandaries and issues that come to us prepackaged, we may well come to believe what the prophets warned against, that by our power and by our hands we have come to control the terms in which to understand the good. There will no doubt be some ethicists presented in this book who do a much better job than others of avoiding both temptations. It is hoped that those the reader finds most convincing might become the impetus for living a good life. My prayer is that the reader may, in these complex times, find here some compelling life-models; but even more, I pray the reader may become convinced that ethics has less to do with doing the right thing and more to do with joining the right group through which to engage the world—the church. For this step is vital in order to be not "conformed to this world, but transformed by the renewing of your minds, so that you may discern what is the will of God—what is good and acceptable and perfect" (Rom 12:2).

Harry J. Huebner
Canadian Mennonite University
January 2012

Introduction

WHAT IS CHRISTIAN ETHICS?

A British philosopher once said, "It is bet-ter to be clearly wrong than confused." Clarity is an important virtue, especially for books that are to serve as introductions to students for whom the topic is new and laden with confusion. And the study of ethics certainly can be confusing. Yet a commitment to clarity does not imply the avoidance of difficult materials. Rather, it means that the assumptions made, the conclusions drawn amid the many twists and turns in the arguments, and the entangled historical/sociological processes are exposed as plainly as possible. In an introductory text, it will also mean that sometimes only general synopses of arguments and processes—as opposed to the detailed minutiae—can be presented.

Recently my librarian sister-in-law observed that I was "constantly sitting at the computer" so she inquired what I was doing. I said that I was attempting to write an introductory textbook for my students in "Christian ethics." "What moral issues are you writing about?" she wondered. I said, "None." This surprised her. "Isn't this what ethics texts usually do?" she asked. This is not an uncommon perception. Nor is it inaccurate. Yet it is not the focus of this study.

What then is the objective of this inquiry, and why do we need another study dealing with matters pertaining to Christian ethics? The answer does not arise from a conviction that no good resources currently exist in the field. Rather, there are very few studies which deal with the topic from a sufficiently inclusive perspective such that first-time

Christian ethics readers receive the necessary overview. Ethics books that focus on the historical and systematic contexts for Christian ethics while providing analyses of the thought of representative Christian ethicists are extremely rare. Most are polemical, advocating that Christian ethics be understood in a particular way, in contradistinction to other approaches. This approach gives students an example of how one theologian works at matters of Christian practice, which can be very valuable, but it is insufficient as a general introduction. Some include selections from the formative ethicists without much analysis or interpretation. Others deal with social issues and/or personal dilemmas. These are all valuable resources, but they fall short because they fail to show the extent to which Christian ethics is an embodied practical discipline requiring the learning of a specific language, skills, and social customs lived by ordinary people. The above-mentioned approaches all abstract Christian ethics from its rightful place within community, tradition, and personhood and lodge it primarily within an intellectual context.

This study proposes to view Christian ethics as the social embodiment of Christian convictions within individuals, communities, and traditions. It is a theology book which claims that every theology is a sociology. It holds that Christian ethics functions simultaneously to shape the life-forms of these individuals–communities–traditions and is the product which results from the relational dynamics of experience and criticism operating on life and sacred texts.

It is an exceedingly daunting task to do justice to the historical, social, and systematic dynamics in Christian ethics as well as present representative thinkers in the field. It is especially difficult to do this all in one book. The scope is extremely large. It must therefore be selective—especially when presenting the history of ethics and when choosing contemporary Christian ethicists. I will seek to be clear about my principles of selection but of necessity must curb the urge to be exhaustive. Introductions sample the literature; they do not argue novel theses. The plan will therefore be to address fewer subjects more thoroughly instead of treating them all.

It will be noted that this study is person-focused. This is atypical, and herein lies its benefaction, if there be any. I have been compelled into this project largely because of a growing conviction that ethics cannot be properly understood apart from people whose lives are shaped by it and who in turn form an ongoing self-critical and interactive body which serves to give ongoing refinement to its convictions. It is because I believe Christian ethics should not be divorced from social history and personal story that I have become convinced that teachers of Christian ethics need to pay more attention than they sometimes do to biography and related disciplines like the humanities and the social sciences. We especially need to give serious attention to the social/psychological contexts in which scholars make moral pronouncements.

Not only does this project arise out of convictions about the nature of Christian ethics, it also springs from views about the nature of Christian education. Just as I believe that Christian ethics, properly perceived, entails biography and communiography, so I believe that Christian teaching should be community- and person-centered. For a Christian teacher, it is hardly satisfying to see students merely become good thinkers; Christian education requires more, namely, that students also become good persons. I concur with educators like James William McClendon Jr., Stanley Hauerwas, Alasdair MacIntyre, Charles Scriven, and Michael Goldberg, to name a few, who all argue that the Enlightenment ideal, which was to teach students to think clearly and distinctly (a project initiated by the seventeenth-century French philosopher René Descartes) thereby enabling them to critique for themselves all biased standpoints, is bogus. Christian education involves the whole person, the intellect as well as the character. Indeed, it involves the whole community.

Christian education generally, and this study in particular, suggest that students ought to learn (become educated) to model their lives after others. This is extremely hard to do if no lives are presented for students to emulate. But even when this is done, a basic question remains: which examples should we as Christians model our own life after? The general answer is, of course, Jesus Christ. But if this were the full answer, Christianity would be reduced to mere mysticism with no community of any moral significance. To claim the moral significance of tradition and community is to claim the moral imperative of modeling ourselves after our best moral exemplars, who in turn model their lives after Jesus Christ. But the question still remains: who are they?

This study will not answer that question definitively. However, it will present the reader with several examples of Christian pilgrims struggling to be faithful. Yet, if students see only a smorgasbord of options to choose from based on their newfound awareness of available choices, they will have missed the point. This book will succeed only if its central assumption becomes convincing, namely, that Christian ethics is at bottom a matter of social embodiment and not merely an intellectual pursuit. That is, it is an invitation to its readers to become members of a community of believers and through its practices participate in the disciplines of becoming a good person. This book alone will make no one a good person. Only the practices within a well-formed Christian community can do that.

Since biography is not insignificant for my view of ethics, it is perhaps important to tell the reader something about myself. I was born into a Mennonite family and grew up under the influence of devout Christian parents and the larger extended family. Later, I enthusiastically, albeit not uncritically, embraced my cultural and religious heritage as my own. To some degree I had no choice in the matter because this very culture had already made me who I was. But to some degree I did have a choice. Insofar as I chose, I gave my inherited Christian tradition the power to mold me into a distinctive person. It could be said that I allowed the virtues of my tradition to take hold of me as I began to see how living by their tutelage promised to make me a good person. All this occurred in the context of the 1960s, when it was in vogue to reject tradition and fight the establishment.

Of course, I too resisted my heritage. But I did that only to return with a second naïveté to re-embrace it. My return happened partly because of a thorough disillusionment with what the alternative "liberal education system" attempted to teach me, namely, that clear thinking alone can disclose what is true and good. I eventually came to consider this idea to be shallow and untrue. In this respect, the culture of my original upbringing was more truthful. Grounded in a radical discipleship theology, my tradition taught me the opposite—one cannot really think clearly about things unless one does so from a particular social place because there is no place to stand that affords the universal point of view. In fact, the very quest is an oxymoron. In effect, I was taught that tradition precedes knowledge and that therefore it also precedes ethics.

A word must be said about the relationship between theology and ethics. McClendon has challenged the assumption popularized by the systematic theologians of this century that one must first get one's thinking about God (theology) straight before one can talk about what one ought to do (ethics).[1] He goes on to critique the assumption made by systematic theologians that the proper logical order begins with "foundations," moves to "doctrine," and then finally to "ethics." McClendon is not advocating an opposite logical order that he acknowledges would lead to an ethical reductionism. He is claiming instead that there is no logical ordering among these three aspects of systematic theology. There may, however, well be a temporal ordering. And so, he argues that chronologically Christians should begin with ethics. He raises this sobering thought: might it not have made a big difference if the early church at Nicaea in 325 CE, instead of addressing only the metaphysical (foundational) niceties of Christology, had also "devise[d] a strategy by which the church might [have] remain[ed] the church in light of the fateful political shift."[2]

It is also important to make the point about the interrelatedness of theology and ethics from the opposite end. In our day, it may well be a greater temptation to claim ethical superiority over theology in a problematic way. For many Christians, it is easier to talk about human rights and justice than it is to talk about God. A "commonsense Christianity" is often derived from what we already claim to know independently of the content of the Christian story from a conscientious focus on such notions as "relevance" and "meaningfulness."[3] Logically speaking, beginning with ethics is no less a problem than beginning with theology. Theology and ethics are logically interdependent. This may well suggest that "theological ethics" is a more proper designation for the enterprise before us than "Christian ethics."

[1] See James William McClendon Jr., *Ethics: Systematic Theology*, vol. 1 (Nashville: Abingdon, 1986).

[2] McClendon, *Ethics*, 42. See also Stanley Hauerwas, *The Peaceable Kingdom: A Primer in Christian Ethics* (Notre Dame, Ind.: University of Notre Dame Press, 1983), 99–115; and Michael Goldberg, "Discipleship: Basing One Life on Another—It's Not What You Know, It's Who You Know," in *Theology Without Foundations: Religious Practice and the Future of Theological Truth*, ed. Stanley Hauerwas, Nancey Murphy, and Mark Nation (Nashville: Abingdon, 1994).

[3] See Alister E. McGrath, "Doctrines and Ethics," *Journal of the Evangelical Theological Society* 32, no. 2 (1991): 145–56.

> **Ethics:** A discipline that focuses on behavior, virtues, values, judgments, structures, and so on, in an effort to understand their nature and function as it seeks to guide human beings to a well-formed, good life.

WHAT IS CHRISTIAN ETHICS?

This study will not assume that ethics is best understood as an enterprise of decision-making by individuals caught in moral dilemmas, not even when these decisions are influenced by values passed on through families and cultures. Nor, on the other hand, is ethics simply the acceptance and propagation of the tradition into which we are born. Ethics—personal and social—is the delicate, critical embrace and expression of the good which, albeit perhaps in a cumbersome manner, is expressed through a particular culture and is learned in the socialization process of its members. Of course, no tradition is pure enough to be perpetuated unchanged. In fact, an unchanging tradition would be a mere abstraction from social reality and hence could not deliver an ethic at all. As someone has said, "If we do what our forbearers did the way they did it, we have not yet done what they did." Yet individuals are not strong enough and not good enough to be Christian on their own. They require the power of the interplay among reason, experience, and tradition to teach them the concrete social expression of goodness. They also require

> **Christian Ethics:** A discipline of thought and action that spells out the practical import of Christian convictions on daily life. It makes concrete how our theological beliefs about humanity, the world, and God can help us to be the kind of people who are committed to following Jesus.

the discipline imposed by the community for attaining the skills of right living.

This means that there will inevitably be a struggle between the individual and the tradition regarding matters related to the basics of life, such as rules and principles, ideals and virtues, convictions and values, and so on. In addition, we must acknowledge the struggle among competing traditions. It is in this multifaceted interaction that acceptance, refinement, and the continuation of tradition happens. It is in this process that people come to understand the good and acquire the will and power to appropriate it.

Yet it should be acknowledged that these dynamics often occur at a very subtle level. It is important to note that the rituals and festivals that shape us into people of particular practices are largely inherited from preceding generations. Our task, first of all, is to understand the contextual meaning of these events and second, to evaluate them in relation to their life-sustaining qualities as we participate within them. The temptation is to evaluate them from an objective "disinterested" perch. But this is impossible, for we live in the very world we critique.

The common assumption about *Christian* ethics is that it is best learned by studying ethics generally. Many ethicists would hold that if something is right, it is right for everyone, not only for Christians. Notice that this approach assumes there is no significant distinction between ethics generally and Christian ethics. But this contentious assumption is being challenged by many current scholars.[4] Although the structure of different ethical approaches may well be similar, the difference in content between Christian and, say, hedonistic ethics, is significant. Moreover, failing to appreciate the moral determination of culture and tradition often leads ethicists to prematurely focus on specific cases as they believe the relevant moral content originates from the situation itself.

---

[4] Most notable is Alasdair MacIntyre, *After Virtue: A Study in Moral Theory*, 2nd ed. (Notre Dame, Ind.: University of Notre Dame Press, 1984); and his *Whose Justice? Which Rationality?* (Notre Dame, Ind.: University of Notre Dame Press, 1988).

The approach that underlies this study holds that the qualifier "Christian" is far more determinative than is commonly assumed.[5] When we have come to know what Christianity is, we have also come to know what Christian ethics is. This may sound like a simple truism, but in light of the contemporary discussion in both theology and ethics, it is a rather controversial claim. Many Christian theologians treat theology as a belief system and never get to a discussion of what impact it has for a way of life. And many Christian ethicists talk about ethics as if it were an independent discipline of thought, unrelated to theological notions of grace, salvation, kingdom of God, Jesus, Holy Spirit, or, for that matter, the biblical story. Both approaches assume that ethics is simply grounded in proper thinking about practices and human conduct. They treat ethics as a generic science, suggesting that we can come to know what is right and good by focusing on the logic of ethics itself. This would make "Christian ethics" redundant because the "Christian" would add nothing to what is already included in "ethics."

Hence, there is every reason to be skeptical of an unqualified ethic. And in this study we will assume that the qualifier "Christian" is determinative in shaping the content of Christian ethics. Stanley Hauerwas and others have pointed out that we should learn from the early Christians. They did not have an ethic; they were an ethic. They were a people who lived their beliefs. They believed that Jesus was the one who showed them the godly way of life. Hence, Christians neither have nor lack an ethic in the sense that it is somehow an optional possession. To speak about Christian ethics is to speak about what kinds of people Christians try to become, given their convictions as Christians.

Generally speaking, it should be noted that we are the kind of people we are not because of the decisions we make but rather we make the decisions we do because of the kind of people we are. Of course, the relationship between our identity and our decisions does not flow only in this one direction, yet if the "Christian" in Christian ethics is to be morally significant, the relationship must flow primarily in the way suggested. We become the kind of people we do for a host of factors that are as unobtrusive to us (and hence as hidden from us) as the air we breathe. We are socialized into being certain kinds of people. We come to behave the way we do because we have absorbed, usually over a long period of time, from the people we trust, such as parents, friends, and teachers. We are continuously doing what we have adopted, often without even noticing that we are doing so.

It follows from what has been said that Christian ethics has a specific source—goodness—and the content of goodness is given in the biblical narrative. And before we can affect the Christian story we must first allow it to affect us. The same could be said of any other narrative. Hence, to identify our task as a study of "Christian ethics" (or "theological ethics") is to have specified its scope. It should be noted that those who speak of ethics generally are also drawing on a specific source, only they pretend not to. Most often this source is something general like nature, the situation, or common beliefs, which, when examined more carefully, are found to be specific aspects of the dominant culture.

Ethics on the view proposed is like a game: hockey, baseball, soccer, basketball. When someone invites you to play baseball you immediately know that there are rules to which you must submit yourself. The specifics governing your behavior while playing one game are quite different from those of other games. Now suppose someone asked you to just play. This is, of course, nonsense. If you were to accept the invitation and go somewhere (notice even the place—arena, open field, living room, gym, playroom—is already determinative), you would no doubt end up playing a particular game, or perhaps some combination, in which a new specific game would be created. A game without a qualifier

---

[5] See Hauerwas, *Peaceable Kingdom*, 17–24.

cannot be played. Similarly, ethics without a qualifier does not exist.

Perhaps some examples of the practical import of viewing Christian ethics as a distinctly Christian enterprise may be helpful. As a teacher of Christian ethics, I am occasionally consulted on "what to do" in a particular "situation." Recently I got a phone call from a woman who said she was forty years old, a happily married mother of three children, and pregnant. She asked if I would tell her whether it was morally justifiable in her situation to have an abortion. She went on to explain that having a child at this point in her life would seriously disrupt the routine of the entire family. Moreover, it was still very early in the pregnancy so no one but her husband and her doctor would need to know about the pregnancy and the abortion. And her doctor had already consented to perform the operation. Her name revealed that she was from an ethnic Mennonite background, so I asked whether she wanted me to consider the matter with her from the standpoint of the Christian faith. From her rather hesitating response, I surmised that she found this to be a strange question. Yet I could not be sure what part of the question she found strange. Was it that I had suggested that we think through it together, or was it that I had suggested that the Christian faith be the basis for doing so? Her response was something like, "Well, I found myself with this moral dilemma and I thought that since you teach ethics you would no doubt have come across this kind of situation before. I just wanted your opinion on what you thought was the right thing to do in this situation. I thought it might help me make my own decision."

I tried as gently as possible to tell her that my whole effort in teaching Christian ethics was to get students to see that there was no such thing as the "right decision coming from the situation." This is the prevalent modern myth about ethics. So while I could help her to think through what it might mean for a Christian to find herself in such a situation, or indeed, as an exercise, I could probably help her think through what it might

mean for a Muslim or Jew or a utilitarian or hedonist to think through such a problem. Yet I could not just help her generally with "the right thing to do in this particular situation." Her response was that I was making the matter unnecessarily complicated and she hung up.

On another occasion, I was asked if I would represent the liberal perspective on homosexuality in a public debate at a local Christian college. This request upset me, quite apart from the realization that it falsely pegged me as a liberal. The approach behind this request seemed to reduce an important social issue to mere amusement. I said that I might be able to do this as an intellectual fiction, but why would a serious institute of learning want to play mind games with a public concern as important as this? I told them that I had no interest in discussing this matter other than from the standpoint of what it might mean for a community of people which is seriously trying to be Christian—the church—to respond to someone who claimed to be gay or lesbian. If they wanted me to speak to it on this basis I would be glad to do so. My claim was that the issue here is the content of the Christian faith regarding this matter, not the liberal opinion and the conservative opinion and perhaps the literalist biblical view, or heaven knows what other interesting perspective we could bring to bear on the subject. That seemed to me more like a strange attempt to entertain. If someone wished to evaluate my interpretation of the basic Christian convictions and how I see them addressing the matter at hand, that, of course, was fair game. But as a mere intellectual exercise I was not willing to do it. I never did go!

With these examples, I wish to emphasize the importance of Christian theology for the study of Christian ethics. It does not follow that we will pay no attention to general ethical issues and concepts. It would be inadequate for a study of Christian ethics to focus only on "Christian" content, ignoring that it has come to be intermeshed conceptually and linguistically with the larger discipline of studies called ethics. Moreover, Christian ethics must give answers to questions of how to live and what to do in our modern world, and therefore, it cannot be a reclusive discipline. Understanding our world and the context of ethical debate generally are crucial to this study. In fact, it is largely in relation to the other approaches that we can come to see in what sense Christian ethics can be Christian. It is therefore important that we come to understand the sociological, psychological, and philosophical language of ethics and that we learn the history of thinking about the many different approaches to ethics. Nevertheless, we should not forget that the task of understanding Christian ethics is largely a task of learning Christian theology.

Another matter must be addressed here. It is sometimes argued that we must make a distinction between individual (personal) ethics and social ethics because the two are quite different and should not be confused. Of course, there are basic differences, yet fundamentally they ought not to be separated in any morally significant way. The reason is that it is impossible to separate one's personal theology from one's public theology. This means that to say things like "For me this is right but for you it may not be" is really nonsense, unless, of course, we are members of very divergent communities.

Focusing the Christian ethical enterprise in the manner we have advocated means we must understand it as a discipline of studies which examines the theological belief structure and the life it shapes. This cannot be different for the individual in private life than it is for the individual or the community in public life. Such a distinction would demand two theologies and ultimately two gods. And this is theologically intolerable.

THE LANGUAGE OF ETHICS

Much of what is involved in an introduction to any subject matter is learning a new language. Each discipline of studies has its own technical jargon which is an attempt to uncover a world hitherto hidden from students. It could be argued that this is all any good

introductory course does and thereby merely provides the tools necessary for further, more in-depth study of the material. We should remind ourselves that, in a field of studies like ethics, it may well be less a process of learning a new language than a process of redefining terms we are already using. This makes a study of ethics different from, say, a study of nuclear physics or computer science.

A place to begin to learn the language of ethics is with a distinction between descriptive and evaluative language. For example, to say a car is good is to speak differently about the car than saying the car is white "White" is a descriptive word, and "good" is an evaluative word. Yet to say a car is good invokes a different use of "good" than when we say a person is good. Used in reference to cars and other objects, "good" is a nonmoral evaluative term while "good" used in reference to persons and human actions is usually, although not always, a moral and hence an evaluative term. (An exception would be when we call someone a good swimmer.)

> **Descriptive Language:** Language that is used to describe objects or people that does not inherently carry positive or negative evaluative freight. Most of the language we use in daily discourse is descriptive language.

There is, of course, a whole family of moral terms: good, bad, ought, worthy, right, wrong, and so on. Yet it should be emphasized that these terms are only sometimes used as moral terms. They can also be used in contexts which are not moral. For example, to say that "The tornado *ought* to strike any second" makes the term "ought" a nonmoral term. To say that I have one *good* eye and one *bad* eye is to use these terms in a nonmoral sense. Even saying that a person is a *good* sprinter employs the term "good" in a nonmoral sense, although it is used in reference to a person. What determines whether a term is a moral term is the context in which it is used. If the context is such that

Evaluative Language: Language that is laden with value like moral, legal, and aesthetic language. Words like "beautiful," "illegal," "right," and "wrong" are all evaluative words. It should be noted that legal, aesthetic, and moral terms are all subsets of evaluative language.

it is intended to convey moral freight, then we say that it is a moral term. If not, then it is either a descriptive term or evaluative yet nonmoral.

But what is "moral freight?" Perhaps we can get our clues from the nonmoral realm. If I say that someone is a good sprinter, I mean that the person measures up to the commonly accepted standards of sprinting, such as form, speed, and endurance. Since there are clear standards, it becomes possible to use evaluative language regarding sprinting. If there were no standards, one could not use such language. Similarly, when saying of someone that she/he is a good person, which would be an example of using "good" to convey moral freight, one assumes that there are accepted standards of personhood. Granted, these are often difficult to identify. In fact, it is impossible to develop a list of standards that would be universally accepted. This is why there can be no unqualified ethic.

Legality: The legality of an act is determined solely on the basis of whether a law of the country in which it was committed has been broken. In democratic countries, laws are made by consenting legislators. However, what is legally right may be morally wrong.

However, within every well-defined culture there are convictions about what makes for a full human life. For example, in our North American society, we believe that it is impossible to be fully human unless we are free, have basic human rights, can determine our own destiny, and so on. We make certain assumptions about how a society ought to be

constructed to ensure that such a "good life" is possible. Education, independence training, and the opportunity for free expression are all very important to us. We believe a democratically organized society is best able to produce a qualitatively good life and therefore develop charters, constitutions, contracts, declarations, and other powerful social forces and symbols to ensure society will be structured so as to guarantee the possibilities of the good life. And we call anything that threatens such a society or persons within it bad, and we call actions and people that promote such a society good.

We need to remind ourselves that not everyone in a given nation operates with the same moral framework. This means that there will be disagreement between public morality and the morality of certain groups or even of individuals within society. For example, Christians, by and large, believe God rules the world and is calling a people—the church—into existence to live in peace and harmony as a sign of the reign God wills for all of humanity. Hence, there is usually a difference between public morality and Christian morality. The standards of excellence are different; the process of learning to become a good person is different, and so on. Christians believe, for example, that the biblical story is, generally speaking, the yardstick by which the quality of life for Christians gets measured. We also believe that worship and devotion to God, the one who created us in the first place and the one who can mold us into a new people, are the means of becoming good. Granted, there is a great deal of diversity among Christians on these matters as well. Yet it is important to note that it is precisely this theological diversity that lies at the roots of the many debates we have about what constitutes the good life.

It is also important to point out several of the different conceptual frameworks in which we commonly use evaluative and yet not moral terms. For example, there is the legal "world," which shares much of the same language with ethics, yet legal language is not moral language. To say that something is legally right is not necessarily to say that it is morally right. Take for example the matter of greed. Laws in our country do not forbid personal greed, provided it is exercised within the framework of the law. However, within a Christian community, we believe that greed destroys peace and harmony among people, and hence greed is a vice. Or consider the issue of abortion. In Canada and the United States, abortions, under certain conditions, are legal. Yet many Christians believe that abortion is murder. Although societies generally attempt to make laws on the basis of a public morality, public morality and Christian morality are not synonymous.

> **Aesthetics:** Realm of evaluative language that pertains to the arts. To judge a painting or sculpture or a piece of music as good is to make a judgment in keeping with the standards of artistic taste and not morality.

There are also other areas of evaluative judgment like aesthetics and etiquette. Paintings and sculptures can be judged good or bad. You can pass food in the wrong direction at the dinner table, or (apparently) wear the wrong kind of clothes to a particular social function. But these are not moral evaluations. One can make these judgments because there are presumably known standards for such things. One can give the right answer in a spelling contest or take a wrong step in a dance. Indeed, any rule-governed structure like games or organized societies or mathematical or scientific disciplines occasion the possibility for evaluative language. The reason you can use the wrong word in a sentence or have a wrong answer in a mathematics test is because both language and mathematics are governed by a set of well-accepted rules. We know what belongs, or fits, and what does not. There is a "logic" that governs such things. Moral language is like this as well. When there are no longer accepted rules governing the behavior of certain groupings of people, or when we forget

> **Moral Language:** Evaluative language which assesses people's actions, thoughts, character, and speech in terms of convictions which are believed to be of the nature that make us good or inhibit our becoming good people. These beliefs are imbedded in a conceptual scheme about human nature, the world, and ultimate reality.

the social contexts or "narratives" which give our lives meaning, then moral language ceases to be meaningful. Or, as appears to have happened in current North American society, when the rules become ambiguous, everyone becomes shy about using evaluative language. In this context, we tend to lose confidence in our abilities to defend our use of such language. Meaningful evaluative language assumes an understanding of a rule-governed structure. Moral language assumes a conceptual scheme with convictions about what makes a person good, structures that foster such goodness, and symbols and signs that allow for its expression.

I conclude this introduction with a story to help students become aware of how they themselves think morally. Furthermore, it is intended to point out the close interconnections between how we live and how we rationalize our actions. It raises questions about the role of the past and our own personal convictions in determining how we structure our lives. It highlights the nature of ethics and, perhaps most of all, the place of Christian ethics within a multicultural society.

There are well over one million children living in single-parent families in Canada. Most of them are living with their mothers, whose marriages resulted in divorce. The following is an account of three mothers living in different parts of Canada, ranging in ages from 23 to 45 years. Their stories were told on Peter Gzowski's "Morningside" show, CBC Radio, Monday, January 7, 1991.

Janice, Erin, and Gloria have one, two, and three children respectively. One of them said that she had children because, although she wanted to be a mother, she did not want to be a wife. She liked most things about mothering but hated most things about having a husband. Another said that her biological time clock was ticking away, and she had always wanted to be a mother. Although she was open to being married, no one was coming along who looked promising, and at 32 years of age she decided to have a "test-tube" baby. She was still not opposed to marriage, but it just so happened that the right man had not come along. The other woman said that when she found herself pregnant, she made the decision to have the baby and raise it on her own because she rejected the options of abortion on the one hand, and getting married to the father of her child on the other. She also was not entirely closed to marriage but was not actively interested nor was she looking.

All agreed that the likelihood of raising their children on their own was greater than average in any event, given the divorce rate in Canada; therefore whether to get married first to have children or have children independently of marriage was not a significant matter for them. All also spoke of the wonderful support structures they had from friends and extended families. None regretted the decision to become single parents and raise their children in this manner.

Although this is not the place, most would agree that we cannot really understand what is going on in this discussion without a major sociological, psychological, and historical analysis. Equally important, I would suggest, is that we also need a moral analysis. This, I suspect, is a much more contentious claim. I do not mean that we should find ways to simply condemn these changes; rather that with these important social shifts, it is important to ask basic questions about what makes for a good life.

Christian ethics is committed to giving an account of life in terms of what is sustainable, beautiful, and good. Over the years, answers to these questions have varied, but such an account has always been deeply embedded in the storied lives of people. We now turn to the task of discerning these stories.

PART I

RENARRATING CHRISTIAN THOUGHT
AND PRACTICE

Chapter One

GREEK ETHICS

Greek ethics is not easy to summarize in one short chapter. It should also be said at the outset that really there is no such thing as Greek ethics in the sense that Greek thinkers all agreed with one another. There is a variety of views among the different writers. There may well be some common threads that can be discerned among the variety, but these will not be the focus of this chapter. Instead, it is important to gain an appreciation for the multiplicity of an imagination that has ruled much of the Western intellectual world over the centuries. This chapter will focus briefly on three major contributors of this period: Plato, Aristotle, and Epictetus.

First, something must be said about the social and intellectual circumstances in which the early Greeks, especially Plato and Aristotle, found themselves. It is interesting to note that theirs was a context which shared some common features with our own culture. It can be significant, therefore, to read their writings as though they speak to our own times. Learning how scholars of an earlier time dealt with some of the same questions and struggles we have today may well give us some important "new" insights. I say this not to suggest that the solutions to our modern problems lie with the thought of Plato and Aristotle, but because it could well be helpful to let intellectual giants of more than two millennia ago speak a word of critique to current popular thinking.

CONTEXT

It is important to understand the social/political as well as the intellectual contexts of the early Greeks. First, let's examine the social context. Athens during the fifth century BCE was embroiled in a struggle between a democracy (Athens) and a military oligarchy (Sparta), not unlike some of the struggles our own world has seen of late. This resulted in a prolonged war called the Peloponnesian War (431–404 BCE). Athens lost this particular war, but the debate raged on over whether the old oligarchy or the new democratic system of government was better. The dispute was essentially over the choice between maximizing individual freedoms on the one hand and structuring a morally good society on the other hand. Democracy was rooted in freedoms of the individual, and some feared this would result in an immoral society based on what people wanted (that is, rule by the ignorant masses), whereas an oligarchy, while sacrificing some individual freedoms, nevertheless appealed to a model where the wise rulers, knowing the good, would be given the power to implement it.

At one level, this seems like a relatively harmless debate, but some very important issues are at stake here. The Greeks knew that how society gets organized politically, that is, how the polis is structured, depends on what it believes about itself morally. To say it in another way, the form of our political organizations tells us something about who we believe we are. The debate over proper political organization really has to do with what it means to be human, what virtues we hold and cultivate in order to become fully human, and how good character gets shaped. For example, is unlimited freedom an essential characteristic of being human? If so, a society that inhibits freedom is considered evil. Does morality have a source outside of human beings to which we must submit, or is its source within human consciousness? The interrelationship of metaphysical and ethical issues is inevitable in theorizing about what kind of society we should promote.

Not only was the Peloponnesian War about the shift from the old political order to the new, but, as a way of dealing with this shift, it had a distinct effect on defining what being human is all about. And this should not be surprising. The way we in fact live will determine the kind of people we become. Hence, if there is no philosophy of life that informs our way of thinking, then we merely become what we in fact do.

This war, like all wars, was a cruel tutor of human character. Thucydides, the great Greek historian said, "War is a teacher who educates through violence; and he makes men's character fit their condition."[1] He gave a stirring description of the level of cruelty men stoop to in war. What especially troubled Thucydides was that the twenty-seven years of almost continuous warfare had changed the notions of private and public virtue as though they were nothing more than a fleeting fancy. The old ideals of what it meant to be human had disintegrated, and a new understanding of humanity had crept in almost unnoticed.

What was this new view of humanity that so upset Thucydides? W. T. Jones summarizes it as follows:

The new type of man who was developed under the pressures of war was egotistical, irreligious, and violent. He was a cynic who believed that might makes right, who rejected all the old loyalties and the old virtues unless they were expedient, that is, unless they helped him accomplish his own private ends.[2]

The change that had taken place was a shift in thinking from the permanency of traditional beliefs to a manner of interpreting life that suggested beliefs and virtues had their source within human beings. "Man hath forgotten God," it was said.

The social/political turmoil of this period was also the occasion for serious debate. This takes us to the second important context for an understanding of Greek ethics—the intellectual milieu in which Plato and Aristotle found themselves. Some scholars were rationalizing the move to greater autonomy as a good thing. It freed the individual from enslavement to tradition. The Sophists, prominent in the middle of the fifth century, were one example of a group of scholars who attempted to give intellectual justification for a move to individualism.

Sophists, such as Protagoras and Thrasymachos, are characters in Plato's dialogues. It needs to be said that Plato saw them as his chief antagonists, so they do not get very good press in his writings. Nevertheless, Plato goes to great lengths to elaborate their views. What did the Sophists believe?

They believed that the world was intelligible in and of itself and could be fully known by us as we experience it via the human senses. In other words, the world did not require principles outside of itself to be understood. What you see is what there is. The Sophist's criterion of knowledge was based upon empirical reality as experienced. Frederick Copleston calls them "Encyclopaedists" employing a method of reason which he designates as "empirico-inductive."[3]

These itinerant professors traveled from city to city to teach the art of rhetoric. In order to be a political leader in ancient Greek society, you had to be able to speak well. This could

---

[1] Quoted from W. T. Jones, *A History of Western Philosophy* (New York: Harcourt, Brace, 1952), 3.
[2] Jones, *History of Western Philosophy*, 19.
[3] Frederick Copleston, *A History of Philosophy*, vol. 1, pt. 1 (Garden City, N.J.: Doubleday, 1962), 102–3.

help you to be noticed; it could help you win lawsuits and generally to convince people. However, such teaching quickly got the Sophists into trouble. They were seen by many as hostile to the traditional virtues and even as encouraging people to make the unjust appear just.[4] The fact that they extracted payment for their instruction did not help either.

Their philosophy was a major change from the way of the tradition because it equated virtue entirely with expedience and success. Sophists promoted the idea that no one view of reality is either true or false; it is only that one is more expedient than the other. To argue that empirical reality is all there is to this world meant that no appeal could be made to goodness apart from what was apparent. This led Protagoras to make perhaps the most famous of the Sophists' statements: "Man is the measure of all things, of those that are, that they are, of those that are not, that they are not."[5]

Plato points out that by reducing the source of all knowledge to sense perception, the Sophists end up with a relativistic epistemology. Thrasymachos, as portrayed in Plato's The Republic, advances the argument that what is right is directly associated with one's own self-interest, that is, with pleasure. The law of the state is just because there is a sovereign—the "stronger," as he puts it—in whose interest it is to have loyal citizens and in whose power it rests to implement laws. Justice therefore gets defined, by Thrasymachos, as "the interest of the stronger."[6] Today we would characterize this view with the phrase "might makes right." On this view, one should obey laws only if one is forced to, unless, of course, obeying them is in one's interest. Hence, the Sophist tradition became associated with skepticism, cynicism, relativism, and a rejection of the very possibility of ultimate truth and goodness.

Plato found this way of thinking intolerable, and he devoted his entire life to articulating a way of thinking which challenged Sophism. He ended up with a profoundly different model. Even today when we speak of *moral absolutes*, which, admittedly we do not speak of very often, we are invoking the philosophy of Plato. But before we explain Plato's response to the Sophists, we must say something about Socrates.

Socrates (470?–399 BCE) has been given the venerable place in the history of philosophy as the earliest antagonist of Sophist relativism. As tradition spawned by Plato's *Apology* has it, he began as a Sophist himself but changed his views radically after his encounter with the Delphic oracle where he received the message that he was the wisest living human being. After this, Socrates began to teach the kind of knowledge that makes for the good life. Unfortunately, we have no writings by Socrates and so we are compelled to rely exclusively upon those who interpret him. Although the tradition is not in total agreement, we will rely primarily upon Plato's account of Socrates.

The "Socratic Method" of teaching is itself interesting. It took the form of a dialogue where Socrates would begin by confessing his ignorance and proceed by asking questions of clarification. For example, when someone would inadvertently use the word "justice," he would inquire into its meaning. A definition would be given, and Socrates would tinker with what seemed like minor clarifications at first but eventually the whole definition would come unraveled and would be abandoned by the original advocate.

His quest for "universal definition" was the strategy for refuting the relativism of the Sophists. Truth is not mere expedience; it is a fundamental given, which human beings can come to know through proper reflection. Moreover, for Socrates, knowledge and virtue were essentially connected. He taught that if anyone knew the good that person would also do it. In other words, he did not

[4] Copleston, *History of Philosophy*, 104.
[5] As quoted in Copleston, *History of Philosophy*, 108.
[6] Plato, "The Republic," in *The Dialogues of Plato*, vol. 1, trans. B. Jowett (New York: Random House, 1937), 603.

believe anyone did evil knowingly. Evil is done out of ignorance, not moral weakness or malice. Everyone acts in accordance with an understanding of what is right, but everyone does not always know the truth. Virtue is therefore to be identified with knowledge, meaning that it becomes impossible to act contrary to what one knows to be right.

This view got Socrates into a difficult situation at the end of his life. He was criticized for his teaching and was charged with negatively influencing his students toward the state. The death penalty was demanded. Popular belief has it that his accusers assumed he would go into exile before the trial, but that kind of expedient action was the very thing Socrates had taught against. "We are to live by the truth, not by self-interest," he had taught. So while his friends attempted to convince him to escape, he refused. In Plato's *Crito*, Socrates says that "we ought not to retaliate or render evil for evil to any one, whatever evil we may have suffered from him." And from this follows the inescapable and self-incriminating rhetorical question: "Ought a man to do what he admits to be right, or ought he to betray the right?"[7] So Socrates accepted the power that the state had over him and died voluntarily, participating in his death.

PLATO (427–347 BCE)

Plato was born into a prominent political Athenian family. His early education came from within the political establishment. Yet, because of his disillusionment with the existing political regimes, and perhaps especially because of his anger at their treatment of Socrates, he forewent his rather natural destiny into politics and instead devoted his life to teaching and writing. He is responsible for setting up what could well be called the first European university, which lasted for some nine hundred years. Plato is often considered the greatest philosopher who ever lived.

Plato's thought went through significant changes during his life. Unfortunately, space does not permit much attention to the development of his thought; instead we will focus primarily on his theory of knowledge and metaphysics generally and how that relates to ethics as it gets expressed in *The Republic*. This book was probably written over a fairly long period of time. So Plato's thought here corresponds roughly to the middle and later periods of his development.

One of the puzzles, much discussed by the pre-Socratics, was that of change—any change—political, social, and physical change. We all encounter change, but how is it to be accounted for? Is change all there is, or is there something permanent which undergirds it and makes change itself intelligible? If change is all there is, then the Sophists are right in maintaining that perception is final, and knowledge is sense perception. However, this idea is better put the other way around: if perception is the only source of knowledge, then change is all there is. Plato believed that the Sophists were not right about this and that there must be something more basic in terms of which change can be explained. Here he sided with his mentor, Socrates.

Plato's accounts of change as well as his theory of justice entail postulating the existence of two realms: one that is in a constant state of flux (the empirical world) and the other, which is permanent (the intellectual world). These two realms of reality are very different, yet they are not unconnected. In fact, it is precisely their interconnectedness that can explain change. Change is intelligible because the permanent aspect of an object of knowledge does not change while the empirical does. Consider an example. This book changes with each successive chapter that gets written, yet it still remains this book. There is no fear that it will turn into a tree with the next chapter. It is not an entirely new reality every time something changes about it, yet it is in fact something quite new and different. If perception is all there is, then there would be nothing to connect one reality to another. There could be no understanding of change at all; there would only be different unrelated

---

[7] Plato, "Crito," in *The Dialogues of Plato*, 1:433–34.

perceptions. Moreover, this book is a book in the same sense that other books are books. Difference and sameness are both necessary for this particular book to exist as an object of our knowledge. The difference can be accounted for via perception; the sameness must be accounted for intellectually.

Plato drew some important conclusions from this relatively simple insight. He began by saying that it is not possible that a book, or any other object of knowledge, can be understood as the Sophists thought—on the basis of sense perceptions alone. If this were our only means of access to reality, then we could never come to know anything. As soon as one considers a class of objects, one is in fact acknowledging something in virtue of which these objects are the same that itself is not an item of sense perception. Hence, one is acknowledging that the knowledge of something requires that the mind have access to "ideas" without which it would be impossible for us to know what there really is.

This kind of thinking begins to unpack what has been called Plato's theory of forms. This theory divides the world into two realms: the world of sense perception and the world of "ideas." Plato uses two illustrations to explain what he means by this and how it is possible for us to have knowledge on the basis of this theory. The first is the Divided Line Analogy.

Physical World		World of Forms	
A	**B**	**C**	**D**
shadows	things	forms	The Good
"Appearances"		"Reality"	

What Plato is attempting to demonstrate with this illustration is that in order for us to know something we must make the distinction between what something really is and what it appears to be; hence the vertical line dividing the two realms. It is, after all, the reality of an object—the object's being what it really is—that makes it possible for us to know it to begin with and for it to appear to us. But when it appears to us, it does so in its physical manifestation. This empirical manifestation is not to be confused with the real thing. The real thing is the *idios*, the idea or form, which makes it possible for it to appear at all. As a philosopher, Plato is interested in understanding the reality itself—the forms. And only careful rational thinking can reveal the content of such reality to us.

The myth (allegory) of the Cave adds another important element to the overall explanation of his theory which the Divided Line only hints at, namely, the *fire*, also called the *sun*. With this additional symbol, Plato is suggesting that the lower ideas owe their existence to a higher, ultimate idea—the Good—without which there would be nothing and we would know nothing. What we perceive with our senses, far from being all there is, as the Sophists taught, is but a reflection of real objects, which in turn owe their existence to an even higher reality, the Good.[8]

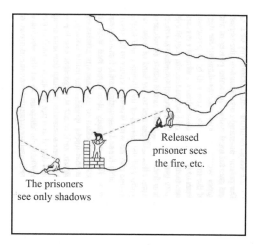

Released prisoner sees the fire, etc.

The prisoners see only shadows

It is important to take note of some of the other aspects of this image. Notice that the people, the masses, are prisoners shackled to

---

[8] The illustration of The Cave is adapted and taken from Forrest E. Baird and Walter Kaufmann, eds., *From Plato to Derrida*, 5th ed. (Upper Saddle River, N.J.: Prentice Hall, 2008), 121.

look only straight ahead at the big screen of images, which owe their existence to the light of the fire shining on the real objects. They are unaware of either the light or the objects which it illuminates on the big screen.

Most people are happy in the cave because they believe it is the real world. So they make the best of it. Yet, sense perception and sensual pleasure are wrongly seen as ultimate, and therefore, this is the life of ignorance. There is a way out of the cave, but it is not easy. The very idea of wanting out will be ridiculed because it is implicitly an indictment on those who believe the cave is the real world. Socrates is the best example of someone who left the cave and as a result got himself into serious trouble.

The way out of the cave is the way of reason fostered by education. Learning the truth about the real world entails coming to see the empirical world for what it really is: unreal. But whether we do this depends on several things. First is our willingness to be taught by a wise person who knows the truth; if we refuse this, we are condemned to a life of ignorance. Second, our native capacity to learn will dictate if we are intelligent enough to understand what is required; if not, we will be condemned by fate to live in ignorance. And third, we require a teacher who is a philosopher—one who knows the truth and is willing to teach us.

What does all this have to do with ethics? Two things must be said. First, to understand the world as it really is, is to see it as good. This follows from Plato's explanation of the forms and their relation to the ultimate form of the Good. This also gives us the standards for every good thing. Something is good insofar as it is real. In other words, evil is non-being, and good is reality.

Yet, how precisely does this help us to understand ethics? According to Plato, we know something to be good insofar as it participates in its true form. This is how we judge good from bad things. For example, a good teacher is one who does what teachers *qua* teachers do. A bad teacher is one who does not. In other words, a good teacher is a "real"

teacher, one who embodies the real characteristics (virtues) of a teacher. Hence, we can only judge a teacher to be good if we know what a teacher is. A good child is one who does what a child as child does, namely, learn from the instruction of parents. A good father does what a real father would do. And so on. Notice that in order for us to know what a good "X" does, we must first know what "X" is. To put it differently, for Plato, ethics presupposes metaphysics. Once we know what something is, we also know the Good.

The second implication for ethics is that this approach commits us to the task of searching for universal definitions. This is important because universal definitions disclose to us the essence of things insofar as they identify the essential properties an object must have to be what it is.

To determine what constitutes a good human being requires trying to get our minds to understand the form of humanness as illuminated by Goodness, rather than accepting as normative the variety of physical representations of the human being. That is, you cannot determine what it means to be human by asking a representative sample of human beings how they understand themselves. Not even an exhaustive empirical description of what can be observed about how humans behave will accomplish this. This is what the Sophists believed, but all they would come to know is how humans *appear* to be, not how they really are. Plato insists that we must go behind this to the definition of humanness.

Plato does not answer the question of the nature of humanness as precisely as we might like and, if one takes his writings as a whole, he does not even seem to be entirely consistent. Yet in *The Republic* he advances a view of human essence, and it turns out to be parallel to his view of the state. The Ideal Person and the Ideal State have similar structures, he argues. Hence, a just person and a just state are simultaneously explained.

Here is how Plato proceeds to do this. The human being consists of body and soul. The body is the physical manifestation of a soul.

The soul is what makes a person a real person, and the body gives a person temporal and spatial existence. So clearly, the enquiry into the structure of the soul is more important for Plato than is a determination of bodily characteristics.

What is the structure of the soul? Reason tells us, says Plato, that it has three aspects: the rational, the "appetitive" or passionate, and the spirited aspect. We are quite familiar with the rational side to our being, so that needs little explanation. By passion or appetite, Plato means that which drives us, like hunger, sex, basic desires, and so on. By spiritedness, he means something like spunk or gusto—our drive to accomplish a task. One might cite as an example the courage it takes to do the morally right thing. These different aspects function in harmony with one another in order to make up the person.

Each aspect of the soul is subject to a virtue in order for it to function as it should: wisdom is to govern reason, temperance or self-control rules passion, and courage determines the proper functioning of the spirited aspect. The fourth cardinal virtue that Plato identifies is justice. Justice is the virtue guiding all aspects of the soul so that they remain in proper relationship one to another, each doing what it ought to do. It should be clear that there is an important hierarchy of governance within this tripartite division. The wisdom of reason is the highest in rank, then the courage of spiritedness, and then temperance of the passions.

All of this then ultimately leads to an explanation of what it means to be a good person. A good person is a real person—one who lives a life which does not suppress the real aspects of his/her being; one who knows the good and lives in accordance with it; one who allows for each aspect of the soul to be brought under the sovereignty of the respected virtue and in proper relation with the hierarchy. For Plato, Socrates was a prime example of a good person. He exemplified all

the cardinal virtues: Socrates was wise, he was courageous, he was temperate, and he was just. This is so because he was temperate with his passions, courageous in spirit, and wise in his reason.

Plato's ethic is "eudaemonistic," meaning that happiness derives from the pursuit of the Good. Happiness comes from the life of reason, which shows us the virtues we ought to live by in order to be "full" human beings. Happiness and the pursuit of virtue are inseparably connected for Plato.

Remember that for Plato the structure of the soul (*psuche*) and the structure of the state (*polis*) are parallel. Hence, this view of the soul also sets up the model for him to define a just state, which is, after all, the stated objective of *The Republic*. Notice that this soul-state parallelism means that for Plato there was no structural distinction between personal ethics and social ethics.

Plato's ideal state consists of three classes of people: the guardians who are the rulers because they are wise, the military class which protects the people because they are strong, and the masses. People are not all endowed with the same gifts and natural talents. But this does not mean that all cannot be good. Being good will take on its own expression as we practice the virtues subject to the class we are in. Rulers are to be governed by the virtue of wisdom, the military by the virtue of courage, and the masses by the virtue of temperance. Justice exists when each class submits itself to the appropriate virtue as well as to the hierarchy of virtues. Notice how this relates to the tripartite division of the human soul. Frederick Copleston summarizes Plato's view of justice as follows: "As the individual is just when all the elements of the soul function properly in harmony and with due subordination of the lower to the higher, so the State is just or righteous when all the classes, and the individuals of which they are composed, perform their due function in the proper way."[9]

---

[9] Copleston, *History of Philosophy*, 255.

It is worth summarizing what Plato says about the definition of justice in *The Republic*. Over against Thrasymachos, who defended the superiority of "effectiveness" over "excellence," Plato has given a rationale for "excellence over effectiveness." To put it another way: Thrasymachos argued that *techné* (from which our English word "technology" comes) is a skill which allows anyone who is able and willing to use it to bring about his or her personal interests. Plato has shown that this is immoral and that it is "apparent" only to the ignorant who deny the virtues. Those who have genuine wisdom and knowledge will use *techné* for the service of the Good; that is, just as they will use their skills to act in keeping with goodness in spite of personal consequences. Socrates remains the paradigm!

ARISTOTLE (384–322 BCE)

Aristotle was Plato's student and learned much from him. Like Plato, he came from a prominent family and hence was sent to the academy at age seventeen. After he finished his studies he became a teacher. Undoubtedly his most famous student was Alexander the Great. For seven years, until the young prince was twenty years old, Aristotle attempted to impart his view of morality and politics to the would-be emperor. Some have argued that he was not very successful. Nevertheless, from early in his life, Aristotle believed that philosophy must be practical.

After Plato died, Aristotle gradually dissociated himself from the "otherworldly" flavor of Plato's thought. This does not mean that he was any less concerned about combining metaphysics with ethics; he only proposed a more practical way of relating the two as he became increasingly convinced that Plato's theory of ideas was impractical. He believed Plato's metaphysics concentrated too much on a transcendental realm of being and consequently found no way of speaking meaningfully about the empirical world. "How can it make sense to speak of the 'cause' of things as existing in another realm totally distinct from the things themselves," he asked. Aristotle became convinced that Plato had set up an impossible metaphysical dualism.

Aristotle's view was oriented toward the empirical world, yet he was no Sophist. He also used Plato's language of forms, even if he changed the meaning somewhat. He believed that individual objects consisted of a union of form and matter. It was the philosopher's job to sort out how these were related. And he saw this relationship in terms of what he called the "four causes" for something being what it is. In his *Physics,* and later in his *Metaphysics*, he explains these "causes." First, in order to understand an individual object, we must understand the material of which it consists (the material cause); second, we must know how it came to be (the efficient cause); third, we must learn the purpose for which it exists (the final cause); and finally, we must understand its form or shape through which it fulfils its purpose (the formal cause). Notice how this is a substantially different account of reality than Plato gives. There is no appeal here to a transcendent realm, only the mind working on objects of experience. Aristotle thought of this world as real in a way that Plato did not.

Aristotle's view on metaphysics is important for understanding his ethics. When is something good? Plato's answer was that something is good insofar as it participates in its own essential form, and ultimately in the form of Goodness. But since the forms and Goodness themselves exist in another realm, there could, frankly speaking, be nothing good in this world. For Plato, this-worldly reality is implicitly evil. Aristotle believed that with this view you end up in a quest for being good that has you directed away from this empirical world—in a flight from this world. Aristotle offers a different answer to the question, "when is something good?" He argues that everything has a form which is its purpose or fulfillment. To say this differently, everything has an end (*telos*) toward which it "tends." This end or purpose is its good; it is what it would be if it were fully what it was. This applies to simple objects as well as to complex reality. For objects, the end is easy to identify. For example, we all know that the *telos* of an eye is to see. So if an eye sees well, it fulfills its purpose and is therefore called a good eye; if it does not, it is a bad eye. The end of a human being is admittedly much more difficult to articulate because humans are more complex than eyes. But if we want to understand what it means to be a good person, this is the very thing we must do. It is important to notice here that Aristotle agrees significantly with Plato's view. For Aristotle, goodness is also understood as something that an object does not fully possess as it is in itself, but it is good insofar as it participates in its perfection. The difference is that, for Aristotle, the perfection of an object is not outside of the empirical world.

Aristotle thought he could identify the *telos* for humans: *happiness*. Happiness, says Aristotle, is desirable in and of itself, not for the sake of something higher than itself. Everything else we choose is unlike happiness in this respect. We choose honor, pleasure, reason, and every virtue only partly for themselves; we really choose them for the sake of happiness. Happiness is never chosen for something else, and therefore it is the final and true *telos* of humanity and of all human activities.

What is more difficult for Aristotle to explain is what happiness actually is. After much discussion, happiness turns out to be the exercise of the human soul (reason) in accordance with the virtues that make life complete and beautiful in all its possible functions. And this remains an ongoing process. For Aristotle, ethics is an imprecise science. People do not become good by getting their thinking straight first and then living that way. Both thinking and acting require training to be perfected. We are only able to move toward the good from where we happen to be in life. And the way to do this is by beginning to cultivate both right thinking

and right living from where we are. In fact, what happens is that the two inform each other. We often come to understand things more clearly only after we begin to live in a particular way, and vice versa.

One of Aristotle's major contributions to ethics is his clarification of the meaning of virtue (*arete*). From what we have just said about the close relationship of thought and action, it should not surprise us to find that he speaks of both intellectual and moral virtues. He puts it this way: "Virtue, then, being of two kinds, intellectual and moral, intellectual virtue in the main owes both its birth and its growth to teaching (for which reason it requires experience and time), while moral virtue comes about as a result of habit, whence also its name *ethike* is one that is formed by a slight variation from the word *ethos* (habit)."[10] It is also significant to note that both the intellectual virtues and the moral virtues are discussed in his treatment of ethics, which is further testimony that for Aristotle thought and action belong together.

In his *Nicomachean Ethics*, Books II–V, he discusses the nature of moral virtue. Here, he defines moral virtue not as a passion or a faculty but a *state of character*.[11] Virtue is what makes a person good; it determines good behavior. This is relatively difficult for us moderns to understand. We tend to think that we are made good by the values we have, which in turn inform the choices we make. As the modern psychologist, Lawrence Kohlberg, suggests, virtue-formed character inhibits our freedom to act as we desire. Moreover, it gives society an arbitrary heteronymous standard of judging people's behavior. He suggests that the character we have is created by the behavior we have freely chosen. On this view our actions themselves are left without "outside" moral guidance.[12]

Aristotle's relationship between character and virtue is the opposite of Kohlberg's. That

---

[10] Aristotle, *Nicomachean Ethics*, bk. 2, in *The Basic Works of Aristotle*, ed. Richard McKeon (New York: Random House, 1941), 952.

[11] Aristotle, *Nicomachean Ethics*, 957.

[12] See chap. 11, below for a fuller treatment of Lawrence Kohlberg's view on the virtues.

is, for him virtue determines character. And how does it do this? Through the exercise of virtuous activities. Aristotle puts it this way, "we become just by doing just acts, temperate by doing temperate acts, brave by doing brave acts."[13] It is insofar as just behavior becomes habitual that we are just; temperate behavior becomes habitual that we are temperate, and so on. And this requires the same training as an athlete requires.

A few comments of explanation. As we have seen, Aristotle makes a distinction between something (an object or person) as it happens to exist as a matter of empirical fact and what that same thing could be if it were fully what it is intended to be. And it is the virtues that move human beings from one to the other. This makes it analogous to an athlete. A hockey player, for example, can only become a good hockey player if he or she reaches the full potential (telos) of the game, and this can only happen if he or she learns the skills of the game so well that all the moves become habitual.

One of the most difficult tasks for any virtue theorist is to answer the question of what it means to be human. After all, virtues are really only the skill that makes a person a full human being. Hence, what a particular virtue theorist holds to be virtues, will be directly related to what that person's understanding of being human is. This is why the specific virtues proposed by Aristotle may be quite different from, say, the Christian virtues. Aristotle and Jesus Christ had quite divergent views of what it meant to be human. Yet one thing is basic: virtue theorists assume that human beings have the capacity for good and that through virtuous activities can become good people.

One of the themes in Aristotle's virtue theory is the concept of sophrosyne (moderation). Virtue is seen as the mean (mesotes) between excess and deficiency. Both excess and deficiency are vices. A truly virtuous person

would not, for example, go overboard with respect to being courageous or honest. The virtuous person would know how to choose between foolhardiness and cowardice and between lying and legalistic description. Virtues are not derived from a priori principles of logic but from the cultivated activities of a wise person. To live virtuously is to do what makes sense in the tension between excess and deficiency. This "Golden Mean" characterizes all the virtues—courage, temperance, justice, pride, friendliness, and so on. In their extreme, all are vices; in their mean, they are virtues. Consider the following examples:[14]

VICE (Excess)	VIRTUE (Mean)	VICE (Deficit)
Too much fear	Right Attitude	Too little fear
Cowardice	Courage	Foolhardiness
Profligacy	Temperance	Insensitivity
Prodigality	Liberality	Illiberality
Vulgarity	Magnificence	Meanness
Vanity	Self-respect	Humility
Obsequiousness	Friendliness	Sulkiness
Injustice	Justice	Injustice

In Book V of Nicomachean Ethics, Aristotle gives a further analysis of the concept of justice. Recall that Plato presented a view of justice which suggested that as long as people took their place within the ideal state defined by the philosopher-king justice would be done. Aristotle took a slightly different approach. He argued that justice is divided into two kinds: distributive justice, which has to do with how the state divides its goods among its citizens, and "rectifying" or retributive justice, which has to do with how people relate to one another and especially with how they are to be "justly" treated when they violate the norms of proper behavior.[15] Both aspects of justice are important, and the two should not be confused. Furthermore, both are measured in relation to the virtues

---

[13] Aristotle, Nicomachean Ethics, 952.
[14] This chart is taken from Jones, History of Western Philosophy, 221.
[15] Aristotle, Nicomachean Ethics, bk. 5, 1005–6.

and in relation to the well-being (happiness) of the well-formed human being.

There are many more themes we could explore in Aristotle's ethics, but space does not permit us to continue. We must move on to our last topic related to Greek ethics, Stoicism. We acknowledge some major omissions of Greek—ethical thinking during this period. Nothing has been said about Epicureanism and neoplatonism, two important later Greek schools of thought. We choose Stoicism as a representative of post-Aristotelian ethics because it was in vogue during the writing of the New Testament. In fact, it has been argued that the Apostle Paul, finding himself with no clear ethical guidelines from the radical life and teaching of Jesus, borrowed freely from the Stoics.[16] This argument will be examined in greater detail later in this study, and our examination of Stoicism here will provide us with a basis for later comparison.

STOICISM

Stoicism is a Hellenistic philosophy that attempted to bring into harmony the human will and the will of nature. Stoics believed the order of the cosmos was the normative order of all life, including human life. Hence, as long as your own life was in accord with the laws of nature, then all was as it ought to be. A story is told of a prominent Stoic who saw his slave steal his lamp. He was so caught up with the need to harmonize himself with the will of nature that he shouted after the slave, "I give this lamp to you."

Stoicism enjoyed a long history of popularity among the Greeks and Romans. Its earliest forms began around 300 BCE with such thinkers as Heraclitus of Ephesus and Zeno of Citium. The latest forms of Stoicism ended some time around 180 CE with the Roman emperor Marcus Aurelius.

The Stoic we will examine here briefly is Epictetus (50–138 CE). He, like all Stoics, believed that the source of our ethics rested in reason and the nature of things. This was not unlike Plato and Aristotle, but it got expressed quite differently. He writes in dialogue form and is easy to understand. Let me quote some of his short dialogues.

> A good man is expected to conserve his composure under all circumstances whether he is a father, son, brother, or average citizen. The principal danger to a man's correct behavior results from his failure to achieve his desires, and to suppress his aversions. Even philosophers don't expect a man to be undisturbed by passion in the same sense that a statue is. Therefore, a good man must train himself in proper behavior, so that he will respond correctly to all his responsibilities in life.
>
> The three main goals of a good man's training are the following: 1) He should perform his duties willingly and cheerfully. 2) His desires and aversions should be within control of his will. 3) His mind, his judgment and his actions must be in accordance to reason.
>
> The principal and most difficult of the above requirements of the good man is that concerning his temper and his passion, because if either anger or passion possesses a man, his reason will have failed him. Without reason, a man ceases to be a man and becomes another animal.[17]

This passage is clear in its emphasis that passion and anger can destroy our moral character. Therefore we ought not to obey them. Our duty is derived from reason. Let us look at another short dialogue on "duty."

> EPICTETUS: The duties of a man to his family, friends and country are measured by his relationship to each. For example is a certain man your father? In this relationship the son is expected to submit to the father, accepting his reproaches patiently. Then, when his father is old, to provide for him.
> SCHOLAR: But supposing the father is a bad father. What then?
> E.: Is the natural tie of the son to a *good* father? No, but to a father.
> S.: Well, what should my relationship be to a bad brother?
> E.: Preserve your own just relationship to him.

---

[16] For an analysis of this argument, see John Howard Yoder, *The Politics of Jesus:* Vicit Agnus Noster, 2nd ed. (Grand Rapids: Eerdmans, 1994), 162–92, and in chap. 2 below.

[17] This is a section from Epictetus, "Training for the Philosopher," in *Epictetus: A Dialogue in Common Sense*, trans. John Bonforte (New York: Philosophical Library, 1974), III-2.

Don't consider what *he does*; but remember what *you* must do to keep your own will in conformity with nature. Neither your brother nor anyone else can hurt you, unless you allow him to do so.

Therefore, you will only be hurt if you consent to being hurt. In this manner, if you accustom yourself to thinking of your own proper relationship to your family, your friends and your country, and act accordingly, your relationship to each will always be correct.[18]

One final quote from a section titled "Grief."

EPICTETUS: The will of nature may be learned from certain matters upon which we are all agreed. For example, if a neighbor's boy breaks a cup, or a glass, or some similar minor object, we casually say, "Accidents like that are bound to happen."

Therefore, whenever your own cup, or glass is accidentally broken, your reaction should be just as casual as when your neighbor's cup was broken. Now let us apply the same logic to more important matters, such as the death of your neighbor's wife or child. Hearing this news, most persons will say, "Well, that's really too bad, but after all, we are all mortals and sooner or later death is bound to come to us all."

However, if a member of your own family is accidentally killed, then comes the grief, the lamentation and cry of, "O! How wretched am I!"

When we are faced with a family disaster, we should always remember how we were affected when a similar occurrence happened to our neighbor.[19]

These three portraits—of Plato, Aristotle, and Epictetus—must suffice to show both the variety and the similarity within the ancient Greek imagination. There is no doubt that their thinking was extremely influential throughout the entire Christian tradition. In fact, some might argue that the theological-ethical diversity within the church is itself a reflection of the diversity of thinking within Greek thought. Certainly it would not be too difficult to trace a bipolar debate throughout Western thought between those who adopted a more Platonic and those who embraced a more Aristotelian worldview. Some of these dynamics will be exposed in later chapters.

---

[18] Epictetus, "Duty," in *Dialogue in Common Sense*, E-30 (emphasis in original).
[19] Epictetus, "Grief," in *Dialogue in Common Sense*, E-26.

Chapter Two

BIBLICAL ETHICS

Two issues relate to the topic of biblical ethics. One has to do with content, that is, what can be said about the character of ethics in the Bible. This is similar to explaining the nature of Greek ethics, for example. The other has to do with how Christians today might relate to the ethics of the Bible, that is, how does the Bible furnish us with a guide for moral living? While the first is analogous to our study of ethics in other eras, the second is not. The difference is that, for Christians, the Bible is no ordinary book; it is canon, or authoritative Scripture. This chapter will consider each question in turn and, since there is much literature on both questions, it will need to be highly selective.

THE NATURE OF BIBLICAL ETHICS

To speak of the content of biblical ethics is a complex matter. To begin with, it suggests that there is something distinct and unified to talk about. Yet biblical scholars tell us that there is not one story that holds together the entire body of literature we call the Bible; there are many stories, teachings, commandments, and a variety of genres: stories, laws, history, poetry, oracles, proverbs, letters, and so on. This variety does not easily make for a single unified narrative, let alone a single ethical thrust. Yet, while the Bible is a collection of diverse books,[1] it is also more than that. Scholars generally concur that there are important themes and key events that give focus and structure to the biblical understanding of faithfulness under God, and these themes and events have broad interconnections. For example, the New Testament does not make any sense without the Old Testament, or the Epistles without the Gospels, or the prophets without the Torah, even if the nature of these continuities can be debated. In this section, I will begin by identifying some key themes in the Bible in an effort to present what might be called the biblical moral imagination.[2]

To raise the question of the biblical moral imagination is to inquire about the moral vision or the overall moral landscape of loosely connected traditions. In other words, it requires that we discern how the biblical writers disclose to their readers the deepest convictions of their characters and communities. Questions like these present themselves: What governed the people's everyday affairs? What language did they use to give account of their identities, their goals and aspirations, and indeed their failings and shortcomings? What practices shaped their self-understanding? How did they give a rationale for these practices? And, even more basic, what is their view of God? How is the biblical character of God portrayed? How does the Bible view God's

---

[1] The word "Bible" comes from the Greek words *ta biblia*, meaning "the books."

[2] See Harry Huebner, "Justice and the Biblical Imagination," in Harry Huebner and David Schroeder, *The Church as Parable: Whatever Happened to Ethics?* (Winnipeg, Manitoba: CMBC Publications, 1993), 120–46. This section borrows heavily from that essay.

agency; that is, how does God act? What is the relationship between God's agency and that of the people of Israel? How does the story of Jesus relate to this overall vision? What is the biblical view of the church?

Covenant and Call

A remarkable characteristic of the biblical people of Israel is their sense of history and memory. This is largely what shaped the moral identity of the people of ancient Israel. They were who they were because they kept alive a distinct memory. They did this not only by memorization and recitation of specific sacred texts and not only by retelling their stories, but by rehearsal and re-enactment of important events of the past. For example, when they celebrated the Passover it was a practice that had the effect of shaping a people of gratitude and, as such, of recommitment to faithful living. It was an act that reminded them—took up residence in their moral imagination and in their social existence—that they were brought out of the land of Egypt where they were slaves, not by their own hand but by the hand of God. In other words, this festival, and others like it, re-created them into liberated people, and it set them free for God. The mere observance of the event shaped them into a specific moral community. The Deuteronomist writes:

> Observe the month of Abib by keeping the passover to the LORD your God, for in the month of Abib the LORD your God brought you out of Egypt by night. You shall offer the passover sacrifice to the LORD your God, from the flock and the herd, at the place that the LORD will choose as a dwelling for his name. You must not eat with it anything leavened. For seven days you shall eat unleavened bread with it—the bread of affliction—because you came out of the land of Egypt in great haste, so that all the days of your life you may remember the day of your departure from the land of Egypt. (Deut 16:1-3)[3]

Notice that the command in this text is for the people to observe a ritual lest they forget who they are. Here we are not dealing with a typical command to commit or not commit a specific moral action like truth-telling or stealing. Such prohibitions are also given in the Bible, but they are derivative of a more fundamental identity, one that is best cultivated by a people re-enacting their stories. The basic moral imagination finds roots in the practices of worshipping God, who liberated the people from slavery and therefore deserves to be praised. The meaning drawn from these rituals was concrete and ongoing from one generation to the next.

> And when your children ask you, "What do you mean by this observance?" you shall say, "It is the passover sacrifice to the LORD, for he passed over the houses of the Israelites in Egypt, when he struck down the Egyptians but spared our houses." (Exod 12:26-27)

The exodus story is fundamental in the shaping of the people of Israel. As a storied people, they emphasized both its context and its specific implications. The context was the call of Abraham, the exodus, covenant law, and finally, the land. Listen to the liturgical response the people recited after bringing their offerings to the altar at the temple:

> A wandering Aramean was my ancestor; he went down into Egypt and lived there as an alien, few in number, and there he became a great nation, mighty and populous. When the Egyptians treated us harshly and afflicted us, by imposing hard labor on us, we cried to the LORD, the God of our ancestors; the LORD heard our voice and saw our affliction, our toil, and our oppression. The LORD brought us out of Egypt with a mighty hand and an outstretched arm, with a terrifying display of power, and with signs and wonders; and he brought us into this place and gave us this land, a land flowing with milk and honey. So now I bring the first of the fruit of the ground that you, O LORD, have given me. (Deut 26:5-10)

It is clear from the way the story gets told that God's granting of liberation from slavery has the effect of creating a moral identity.

> Now therefore, if you obey my voice and keep my covenant, you shall be my treasured possession out of all the peoples. Indeed, the whole earth is

---

[3] It should be noted here that the final canonical text is, of course, based upon various traditions from different times and settings, and so its formation is more complex than it might appear in my presentation.

mine, but you shall be for me a priestly kingdom and a holy nation. (Exod 19:5-6)

It is equally clear that the divinely liberated community is committed to a specific way of life in the land to be given by God. The existence of such a "priestly kingdom" is spelled out in the revelation to Moses at Mount Sinai in what we have come to know as "The Ten Commandments." This is perhaps the most famous piece of biblical literature today, although it should not be taken out of the context of other laws. It is also referred to as "The Decalogue."

> Then God spoke all these words: I am the LORD your God, who brought you out of the land of Egypt, out of the house of slavery;
>
> 1. You shall have no other gods before me.
> 2. You shall not make for yourself an idol . . .
> 3. You shall not make wrongful use of the name of the LORD your God . . .
> 4. Remember the sabbath day, and keep it holy . . .
> 5. Honor your father and your mother . . .
> 6. You shall not murder.
> 7. You shall not commit adultery.
> 8. You shall not steal.
> 9. You shall not bear false witness against your neighbor.
> 10. You shall not covet your neighbor's house. . . .
>
> (Exod 20:1-17, selected and numbered)

What is important to remember here is that the moral imperatives are not derived from some general source of rational insight, but from a liberating God who helps a people understand themselves as redeemed and gifted people;[4] a people characterized by the memories of liberating activities that they are called to enact in their festivals. In effect, the message to them is: "You are liberated people and here is how divinely liberated people live." They are capable of being such people because they train themselves daily in living by a set of practices. The logic here suggests that they were only capable of worshipping a liberating God when they lived in

a particular moral manner; but it is also true in reverse that they could only live this way when they worshipped a liberating God. To say it generally, ethics and theology were so intertwined that Israel could not have one without the other, nor did one have logical priority over the other.

Stories and the Imagination

The moral identity of the people of Israel was cultivated in many ways. In addition to re-enacting festivals, they also told different kinds of stories—stories that are not historical narration but function more like theological imaginings or myths. One such story touching directly on the understanding of the moral imagination comes from the accounts of creation in Genesis, particularly the story of the so-called "fall." What is especially interesting for our purposes is to note that in the second account of creation (Gen 2:4ff), Adam and Eve were asked not to eat of the "tree of the knowledge of good and evil" (Gen 2:17).[5]

This account is worth reflecting on briefly. When Adam and Eve acquire the forbidden fruit of the knowledge of good and evil, they become sinners. This sounds odd to our modern ears! It seems to imply that moral knowledge—our knowledge of good and evil—is what makes us sinful. And this goes counter to the best insights of all of Christianity, which has always seen it as the Christian task to seek good and overcome evil.

Whatever might be the historicity of this account of creation, it is fascinating to ponder why the story gets framed this way. Why the prohibition? Gordon Kaufman, a contemporary American theologian, reflects on this story as follows:

> It is in terms of the good/evil distinction that man's moral autonomy—and thus his freedom *from* God—becomes possible. The good/evil

---

[4] The reader will notice my repeated use of the term "gifted" in reference to people in somewhat unusual ways. I do not mean "talented" but rather "people who have been given something." In German, the verb is *beschenken*, as opposed to *begeben*.

[5] This is not to suggest that the Genesis text is making a sharp distinction between moral knowledge and knowledge in general. I suspect that this distinction may be considerably less clear than it is to contemporary scholars.

dichotomy serves as a kind of internal compass enabling men to chart their course, to decide and act and set purposes without reference beyond ourselves to the transcendent Lord of history. So they become their own masters, and the question of God's purpose for them drops out as superfluous. It is on the basis of "knowledge of good and evil" that every autonomous humanistic culture is created. Through this knowledge, as the serpent has claimed, man becomes his own lord: ". . . when you eat of it your eyes will be opened, and you will be like God, knowing good and evil." (Gen 3:5)[6]

Karl Barth puts it in very similar terms: "When man thinks that his eyes are opened, and therefore that he knows what is good and evil, when man sets himself on the seat of judgment, or even imagines that he can do so, war cannot be prevented but comes irresistibly."[7]

If we follow the theologizing of Kaufman and Barth on these passages, we see that the punch line of the creation account is that the origin of sin is human hubris. To say it differently, human beings do evil when they claim on their own to have knowledge without God—when they claim on the basis of their own resources the power to name meaning and purpose for themselves.

It is instructive to observe a divinely liberated people giving an account of the origin of the universe in the terms they do. The story begins with the creation by God of all that is, including Adam and Eve. The reason there is order rather than chaos, or indeed, something rather than nothing, is because God is Creator! God gives life! The initial relationship between God and Adam and Eve is idyllic—a garden. It is important to note that the original state of God's creation is peaceful. It is created not out of conflict as, for example, in the Babylonian creation story,[8] but *ex nihilo* (out of nothing), a radical gift from God; only by the word of God speaking creation into being.[9] This theme is especially prominent in the pattern of liturgical repetition presented in Genesis 1, where the text reads over and over, "And God said, 'Let there be . . . And it was so.'"

Within the creation story we have a reciprocal openness between the different parts of creation, symbolized by intimate interaction between Adam and Eve, between them and the animals, between the animal kingdom and other aspects of nature like the rocks and the soil. Adam and Eve's nakedness represents this openness—they were fully exposed to each other, the elements, and to God in an uninhibited and joyous manner. They "were not ashamed." God is clearly the one who is in charge—albeit God's authority is presented as gift. God is not just the origin of life but the giver and ongoing sustainer of life. God's authority is not a threat to the life of the people, the animals, or the rest of creation. For all that existed, existed by the creative word of God. God's authority makes all things good.

As long as the relationship between Adam and Eve remains open to God and to each other, life is reported as good and beautiful. The problems begin when Adam and Eve's openness to God was put into question. "Did God say that he is the only giver of life?" "Is not life apart from God good?" "Can we not determine our own destiny apart from God?" This questioning of the very meaning

---

[6] Gordon Kaufman, *Systematic Theology: A Historicist Perspective* (New York: Charles Scribner, 1968), 354 (emphasis in original).

[7] Karl Barth, *Church Dogmatics* (Edinburgh: T&T Clark, 1956), 4.1:451.

[8] The Babylonian poem "Epic of Creation" (also called *Enuma Elish*), speaks of war between the gods, Marduk and Tiamat. Marduk wins the battle, and Tiamat's body is severed into two halves which become heaven and earth. After Marduk structures the planets and other heavenly bodies, he creates the city of Babylon. Then Tiamat's husband is destroyed and from his blood humankind is created. (Taken from Thorkild Jacobsen, *The Treasures of Darkness: A History of Mesopotamian Religion* [New Haven, Conn.: Yale University Press, 1976]).

[9] The creation *ex nihilo* thesis is more widely accepted within the theological tradition and by some (Gerhard von Rad), but not nearly all, biblical scholars. For the latter, "creation out of chaos" is a more common view. This debate, while interesting, goes far beyond the scope of this chapter.

of creation as rooted in and flowing from God, or, we might say, as participating in the Creator, is challenged not only with words but with action; and sin is born.

The subsequent stories of Cain and Abel (Genesis 4), the flood (Genesis 7), and the Tower of Babel (Genesis 11) bear out dramatically the disastrous consequences of rejecting God. Not only is God excluded from the lives of the people, but God becomes the enemy—the one who is ultimately wrong because the people are right. And the people usurp the moral throne of God.

The retelling of this story was for the people of Israel an expression and affirmation that their own existence is best seen as a gift from God . . . again! That is, they have been rescued from the fall. The fall is there in the sense that it serves as warning and as threat. While the original state of creation is no longer accessible to them in that life "in the garden" is not theirs to enjoy, life in communion with God still is. But this requires a re-viewing and a re-acting of how they understand themselves. To distance themselves from the immorality of the "generation of Noah" means to let God be giver-God again. For they see themselves as people chosen through Abraham and rescued from bondage in Egypt by God's hand. This God, who is without a name, asks only to be referred to as "I AM" (Exod 3:14).[10] "I AM" is clearly not done creating, albeit, after the fall, God's creative activity is seen as taking place through the people God has chosen—a people who, like the people of the garden, were at once both faithful and rebellious. Jeremiah reflects on this history as follows:

[Thus says the Lord of hosts] . . . this command I gave them, "Obey my voice, and I will be your God, and you shall be my people; and walk only in the way that I command you, so that it may be well with you." Yet they did not obey or incline their ear, but, in the stubbornness of their evil will, they walked in their own counsels, and looked backward rather than forward. (Jer 7:23-24)

From the beginning, it is clear that God is also the giver of promises. This is a central characteristic of the God of Abraham.

Now the LORD said to Abram, "Go from your country and your kindred and your father's house to the land that I will show you. I will make of you a great nation, and I will bless you, and make your name great, so that you will be a blessing. I will bless those who bless you, and the one who curses you I will curse; and in you all the families of the earth shall be blessed." (Gen 12:1-3)

God's Gifts of Peace and Justice

As we have seen in the exodus story, when the object of God's grace is the slaves of Egypt, God gives freedom. In the desert when the people are hungry, God gives manna and quails. God gives the law so the people will remember who God is and who they are expected to be. And God gives land, the place of rest and security.[11]

The land that I gave to Abraham and Isaac I will give to you, and I will give the land to your offspring after you. (Gen 35:12)

The biggest threat to gifted people is forgetfulness. In their forgetting, they act unjustly. When people forget the primary relationship to the giver God, they cease seeing themselves as gifted people and become concerned about their security. The tendency to forget is directly related to the people's sense of their own autonomy. The more self-sufficient people become, the more they rely upon something other than an open relationship with the giver of life, and hence, the easier it is to forget.

---

[10] But Moses said to God, "If I come to the Israelites and say to them, 'The God of your ancestors has sent me to you,' and they ask me, 'What is his name?' what shall I say to them?" God said to Moses, "I AM WHO I AM." He said further, "Thus you shall say to the Israelites, 'I AM has sent me to you'" (Exod 3:13-14). Although extensive speculation on the significance of recounting God's self-disclosure merely in terms of "being" is unwise, it is nevertheless noteworthy, especially because it supports our earlier comments on seeing all of reality in terms of its rootedness in the being of God.

[11] I have found the writings of Walter Brueggemann especially helpful in showing that the people of Israel are gifted people. I will use several of the same passages of Scripture that he cites. See esp. *The Land* (Philadelphia: Fortress, 1977), and *The Prophetic Imagination* (Philadelphia: Fortress, 1978).

Hence, forgetting and injustice go hand in hand in the biblical narrative.

> Take care that you do not forget the LORD your God, by failing to keep his commandments, his ordinances, and his statutes . . . When you have eaten your fill . . . then do not exalt yourself, forgetting the LORD your God, who brought you out of the land of Egypt, out of the house of slavery, who led you through the great and terrible wilderness . . . Do not say to yourself, "My power and the might of my own hand have gained me this wealth." (Deut 8:11-17)

The prophets are among those who help people not to forget. Their task is to remind God's children who they are, and hence, what they ought to do in light of what they have been given. It then follows that they are to take care of their neighbor, to love kindness and walk humbly, to not live by coercion or exclusive concern for security.

> Thus says the LORD: Act with justice and righteousness, and deliver from the hand of the oppressor anyone who has been robbed. And do no wrong or violence to the alien, the orphan, and the widow, or shed innocent blood in this place. (Jer 22:3)

> Thus says the LORD GOD: Enough, O princes of Israel! Put away violence and oppression, and do what is just and right. Cease your evictions of my people, says the LORD GOD. (Ezek 45:9)

Gifted people live by being givers to others and not hoarders of God's life. Gifted people know of no other God but the giver of life. Gifted people know that the meaning of life rests not on what they can own or possess, but on what they give because of what they have received. Hence, the prophets can say that if you do not turn from your ways of ungiftedness, then you will be destroyed, for ungiftedness leads to hoarding and hoarding to injustice and the life of injustice cannot be sustained.

One of the ways memory and giftedness were brought together was through the Sabbatical year and the year of Jubilee. In Leviticus 25, we read about how justice can be sustained over an indefinite time period when it is patterned after the flow of God's creation. One might call this Sabbatical justice. For the people of Israel, the creation story sets up a model of work and rest, or, one might say, work with the recognition that God gives the blessing. We have already seen how one of the serious threats to this storied people is forgetting that God delivered them and thinking that, "my power and the might of my hand have given me this wealth." Yet this logic is but to re-enact the fall.

The Sabbatical year and the year of Jubilee have several provisions: Every seventh year the soil should be left fallow; every seventh year prisoners should be liberated; every seventh year debts should be forgiven; and every fiftieth year known as the Year of Jubilee (after seven times seven years) everyone should be permitted to return to the original property of their families. Notice that this is a form of structured remembering that liberation and social redemption are at the center of the lives of people who have themselves been released from bondage and are therefore committed to the liberation of all people. To say this another way, the pattern of work and rest apparent in divine creation is the life pattern of the people. For when people rely on the might of their own hands (rather than on God's redemptive hand), they will enslave others, even the soil; whereas, openness to God's redemption places control and security into the hands of Creator God.[12]

We have already noted that the God of Abraham is a God of promises. With a long history of Israel's forgetting whose they were and their subsequent disobedience, a new hope for justice comes in the form of a new promise of one who will come to move the covenant made at Sinai toward even greater peace and justice. Although the vision for a

---

[12] An exercise I have used with students in the past is to have them rewrite the rules of the board game "Monopoly" according to the Jubilee provisions. When they report back on the experience, they invariably comment on how the game never ends. That, of course, is the point of these provisions—it is a way of ensuring that there are no winners and losers; justice is perpetual.

new future is not a single unified one, there are many allusions to a new age coming. For example:

> The days are surely coming, says the LORD, when I will make a new covenant with the house of Israel and the house of Judah. It will not be like the covenant that I made with their ancestors when I took them by the hand to bring them out of the land of Egypt—a covenant that they broke, though I was their husband, says the LORD. But this is the covenant that I will make with the house of Israel after those days, says the LORD: I will put my law within them, and I will write it on their hearts; and I will be their God, and they shall be my people. No longer shall they teach one another, or say to each other, "Know the LORD," for they shall all know me, from the least of them to the greatest, says the LORD; for I will forgive their iniquity, and remember their sin no more. (Jer 31:31-34)

There is also talk of a new king ("the Anointed One") who will come, and the reign of this king will unite the tribes of Israel and bring Jerusalem to shalom again. This is especially so after the end of David's rule when suffering and darkness overcome the people and the glory days of the Davidic rule cannot be forgotten. Not that David is seen as a perfect king, but the covenant God made with David (2 Samuel 7) leads Israel to hope for a fulfillment of the promise of a new righteous king. We read about this in the words of the prophet Isaiah.

> The people who walked in darkness have seen a great light; those who lived in a land of deep darkness—on them light has shined. . . . For a child has been born for us, a son given to us; authority rests upon his shoulders; and he is named Wonderful Counselor, Mighty God, Everlasting Father, Prince of Peace. His authority shall grow continually, and there shall be endless peace for the throne of David and his kingdom. He will establish and uphold it with justice and with righteousness from this time onward and forevermore. The zeal of the LORD of hosts will do this. (Isa 9:2, 6-7)

It is naturally tempting for Christians to make the immediate and simple connection to the Christ event. While not dismissing the connection here, that is not my point. The point in these texts is that of purification and the restoration of holiness. It was clear to all, and especially the prophets, that the life of the covenant people was marred with sin. The idyllic life of "the garden" was not available to them. But the imagined memory of such a life and the yearning for a peaceable kingdom were not gone. And they believed that Creator God was continuing to create the kingdom of peace and justice.

Before I proceed to an examination of New Testament ethics, I offer a few reflections on the story so far. A remarkable upsurge of interest in Old Testament ethics can be noted within Old Testament scholarship since the 1970s.[13] Some of these relatively recent studies follow strictly historical and sociological interests in searching for ethical norms and practices in specific biblical times and contexts. While these studies contribute to our understanding of ancient Israel, scholars pursuing such research generally refrain from drawing normative conclusions for Christian ethics. In an introduction to Christian ethics, we are therefore more interested in those studies that attempt to discern the ethical teachings of the canonical Old Testament with a view to their relevance for New Testament ethics and for the nature of obedience to God within the Christian church. The difficulty of this task lies in coming to terms with the vast array of Old Testament texts found in diverse genres (such as law, poetry, proverbs, prophetic oracles, and most prominently, narrative).

One study that is particularly compatible with what has been said earlier in this chapter is offered by Waldemar Janzen.[14] Janzen eschews the selection of any one Old Testament genre (e.g., law), ideal (e.g., justice), body of literature (e.g., prophecy), or favorite text (e.g., the Ten Commandments) as an organizing principle for comprehending

[13] A bibliographical essay offering brief characterizations of a good number of pertinent works in English can be found in Christopher J. H. Wright, *Old Testament Ethics for the People of God* (Downers Grove, Ill.: InterVarsity, 2004), 415–40.

[14] Waldemar Janzen, *Old Testament Ethics: A Paradigmatic Approach* (Louisville, Ky.: Westminster John Knox, 1994).

obedient living. Instead, he discerns five distinctive but related perspectives on the God-willed life; he calls them paradigms, or models of ethical imagination. They are composite intellectual constructs resulting from the impacts of many texts of every genre. The priestly paradigm, for example, is the inner vision shaped by the concern for holiness, deposited now in texts of many genres (laws, rituals, stories, psalms, and so on) as central to faithful living. Another perspective, emphasizing the wise life, leads to the wisdom paradigm. The royal paradigm embraces the vision of justice, and the prophetic paradigm models obedience to God's word to the point of suffering. Embracing these four paradigms in a comprehensive way is the familial paradigm, that is, the composite inner image resulting from the search for what it means to be human. The paradigm that embraces the four others in their emphases on holiness, wisdom, justice, and obedience is a vision of God-intended humanness, defined by a particular understanding of life (all life as analogous to life in families), land (the equitable distribution of the means of sustenance), and hospitality (the guide to interhuman responsibilities, preferred here to justice as projecting grace and being less encumbered by legal associations than justice).

In Israel, claims Janzen, these paradigms, though part of the vision of the God-pleasing life for *all* Israel, were associated with special carriers: the priests, the sages, the king and his officials, the prophets, and ultimately, the clans and families of Israel as they worshipped and told their stories. The paradigms found their literary repositories in the literature of these various carriers, but their impact on people was made not by any one specific biblical text or character but by the cumulative input of such texts or characters toward a holistic inner vision that guided life. In other words, the paradigm was not Abraham, or a certain law, or an advice stated in a proverb; it was the holistic vision to the shaping of which such individual characters or texts had contributed.

In his last chapter, Janzen establishes a bridge between the ethical paradigms of the Old Testament and the so-called "offices" of Jesus as king, priest, prophet, sage, and God-imaging human. It is through these paradigms that we learn to see the manifold ways in which God is the giver of all that sustains life.

The Ethical Teaching of Jesus

I shift now to the ethics of the New Testament. The reader might expect a new section, but that is intentionally avoided to symbolize continuity rather than disjunction. There are two overriding themes we need to address here; one has to do with Jesus as the new, and for Christians, primary source of moral guidance, and the other emphasizes the church as the primary locus of faithful Christian existence. Both are crucial for the formation of an early Christian understanding of ethics.

Jesus did not see his message as marking a rupture with the past, but spoke instead of fulfillment. While he said, "You have heard that it was said to those of ancient times . . . But I say to you . . ." (in Matthew 5 several times), which suggests discontinuity, he also said:

> Do not think that I have come to abolish the law or the prophets; I have come not to abolish but to fulfill. For truly I tell you, until heaven and earth pass away, not one letter, not one stroke of a letter, will pass from the law until all is accomplished. (Matt 5:17-18)

The latter suggests continuity. This tension between the old and the new is never fully resolved in the ministry of Jesus. Yet it is important to remember that Jesus was born a Jew, he studied Judaism, and he remained a Jew all his life. He knew the tradition perhaps better than anyone else.

His public ministry, as recorded in Luke's Gospel, begins with a reading from the Hebrew Scriptures—Isaiah 61:

> The Spirit of the LORD is upon me, because he has anointed me to bring good news to the poor. He has sent me to proclaim release to the captives and recovery of sight to the blind, to let the oppressed

go free, to proclaim the year of the LORD's favor. (Luke 4:18-19)

The French pastor and theologian, André Trocmé, has suggested that Jesus is here serving notice that he is reintroducing the institution of the Jubilee year—the year of the Lord's favor."[15] Other scholars, especially John Howard Yoder, have relied on Trocmé's work to show how, throughout his ministry, and especially through his parables, Jesus emphasized Sabbatical-Jubilee justice and spelled out the specific difference it makes to live in a jubilary mode.

Another theme prominent in the teaching of Jesus is the extension of the covenant to include both Jews and Gentiles. This is perhaps the most radical departure from his tradition. For Jesus there was only one family of God and on earth only two kinds of people: those who see their lives as fully under the sovereignty of God and those who do not. The concern to open the covenant to Gentiles is already made clear in the narrative following the Nazareth synagogue reading. Initially Jesus was well received by the people in the synagogue, but they became outraged and sought to kill him after he recounted for them how, during the famine in Israel in Elijah's time, Elijah had helped not the widows of Israel but "a widow at Zarephath in Sidon," a Gentile; and how during the time of Elisha, there were many lepers in Israel but Elisha healed none of them except Naaman the Syrian, another Gentile. Jesus was adamant that God's grace cannot be hoarded.[16]

The theme of opening the covenant to include the Gentiles receives emphasis in Jesus' parables as well, for example, the prodigal son story. The setting for the story in Luke 15 is one where Jesus has been challenged to respond to the charge, "This man receives sinners and eats with them" (Luke 15:2). Notice that a distinction is introduced between those inside and those outside the kingdom of God. And Jesus takes the bait and tells his hearers about insiders and outsiders.

The story is a simple one. Father-God has two sons. The difference between the two is that while one accepts the gifts of the father, the other rejects them. One chooses to remain within the family, the other chooses to "de-father" himself by requesting his inheritance prematurely. But the loving father-God responds with exactly the same graciousness to both.

According to the ancient Palestinian culture, the father would have been justified in disowning and even killing the younger son because of his audacious request.[17] After all, in requesting his inheritance out of season, the son was declaring his impatience for his father's death. Yet the father never wavers in his desire to have his son restored to full fellowship. Instead of punishing him for making an unjust request, the father simply grants it.

At no point in the story is there ever any coercion used in an effort to change the son's behavior. In fact, the story emphasizes that it is the father's love for his son that ultimately makes it possible for his son to return. When he does return, there is full restoration of sonship. When the son attempts to work himself into the good graces of his father with a "face-saving speech," the overbearing compassion and extravagant love that the father showers upon him results in the son's fortuitous amnesia. Clearly, the restoration of the relationship is not dependent on what the son brings to the father, but on what the father gives to the son.

Meanwhile, the older son—the insider—is expected to respond to his brother like the father responded to the son. "But we had to

---

[15] See André Trocmé, *Jesus and the Non-Violent Revolution*, rev. and ed., Charles E. Moore (Maryknoll, N.Y.: Orbis, 2004).

[16] It should be noted that this theme is there from the very beginning of the Abrahamic covenant story. Perhaps nowhere is it more pronounced than in the story of Jonah, where Jonah shows extreme anger to God for showing grace to the Ninevites.

[17] I am relying for my interpretation of this parable upon Kenneth Bailey's study, *The Cross and the Prodigal: The 15th Chapter of Luke, Seen Through the Eyes of Middle Eastern Peasants* (St. Louis: Concordia, 1973).

celebrate and rejoice, because this brother of yours was dead and has come to life . . ." (Luke 15:32). The expectation of being in relationship with the father is that you reflect the same character of graciousness and compassion in response to your siblings—insiders and outsiders.

In the parable, father-God is compassionate and gracious toward his children. Justice here is not about desert or merit, but the justice of father-God is grounded in grace and giftedness, that is, in forgiveness. Forgiveness, of course, is fundamentally unjust from the standpoint of merit. Forgiveness is not deserved; forgiveness is not fairness; forgiveness ignores the natural balance between pleasures gained and pleasures sacrificed. The justice of God is rooted in *agape* which, when confronted with sin, springs forth in forgiveness, not because it must as if it were a moral demand, but because the very nature of *agape* entails the desire to restore and heal what is broken. And this translates into the concern about the closed covenant because one symbol of brokenness was the division between Jews and Gentiles. God has only one family!

The surprising thing, and I suspect a frustration for the religious leaders of his day, is that Jesus reaches back to the teaching of his tradition to justify his views on opening the covenant to include the Gentiles. Clearly, the tradition has room for this reading as we have already seen. Luke records another parable (Luke 10:25-37) that Jesus tells in response to a question from a lawyer. Jesus is asked, "Teacher, what must I do to inherit eternal life?" And Jesus responds by asking how the lawyer himself would answer. And the lawyer in his reply relies on the traditional Shema text from Deuteronomy 6:4 that every Jew would have known from memory: *Shema Yisrael Adonai Elohenu Adonai Echad* (Hear, O Israel: The Lord is our God, the Lord alone). And the words following the Shema are what Luke quotes the lawyer as saying:

> You shall love the LORD your God with all your heart, and with all your soul, and with all your strength, and with all your mind; and your neighbor as yourself. (Luke 10:27)

Jesus responds to the lawyer with approval even though this answer combines two commandments—love of God and love of neighbor—that are not always combined in the tradition, albeit both are clearly part of Judaic faith. And when the lawyer inquires further about how "neighbor" should be understood, Jesus tells the parable of the good Samaritan.

The story is about a man traveling from Jerusalem to Jericho who was robbed and left on the roadside to die. A priest and a Levite passed by but did not help the man. Then a Samaritan arrives on the scene (Samaritans were outsiders and not liked) and with extraordinary generosity, mercy, and hospitality, he helps the man, seeing to it that he is nurtured back to health. Then Jesus asked, "Which of these three, do you think, was a neighbor to the man who fell into the hands of the robbers?" And after the lawyer's answer, Jesus said, "Go and do likewise." Not only is Jesus here breaking down the insider/outsider division but he lauds the outsider for exemplary behavior, and all of this on the basis of interpreting the ancient law.

It is interesting that in the Gospel of Luke we find the story of Mary and Martha immediately following the good Samaritan parable (Luke 10). In medieval interpretation, these two stories were often treated together. Notice that the good Samaritan story addresses only the love of neighbor part of the great commandment. The story of Mary and Martha was thought to address the love of God.

Mary, in opening herself to the love of God "sat at the LORD's feet and listened to what he was saying" (Luke 10:39). Jesus, in chiding Martha, could not have been critical of her acts of hospitality that he praises elsewhere in his ministry, but only of her failure to recognize that work not modeled on the creation paradigm with Sabbath rest as part of the rhythm is in danger of not sustaining life. The rupture of spirituality and ethics, so common in the modern and postmodern worlds, does not have its root in the biblical exposition of the Shema tradition.

While Jesus teaches and embodies qualities like neighborliness, hospitality, forgiveness, *agape*, and inclusiveness, the mode of moral training is following after the Master, which also goes by the name of discipleship.[18] In other words, knowing is only half the story; the other half is learning to own and live by these qualities. Hence, discipleship is really a process of formation. Says Klassen-Wiebe:

> The formation of [the] disciples into faithful followers, who will continue the mission to which Jesus called them even after his resurrection and ascension, is an important thread of the story and one that intertwines closely with the main story line of Jesus, the protagonist.[19]

Luke tells us that Jesus had many disciples and of these he chose twelve whom he also calls apostles (Luke 6:12-16). He gave special instructions on what they should do.

> Then Jesus called the twelve together and gave them power and authority over all demons and to cure diseases, and he sent them out to proclaim the kingdom of God and to heal. He said to them, "Take nothing for your journey, no staff, nor bag, nor bread, nor money—not even an extra tunic. Whatever house you enter, stay there, and leave from there. Wherever they do not welcome you, as you are leaving that town shake the dust off your feet as a testimony against them." They departed and went through the villages, bringing the good news and curing diseases everywhere. (Luke 9:1-6)

Somewhat later, Luke records Jesus' appointment of the seventy. Although he does not call "the seventy" either disciples or apostles, Jesus gives them virtually the same instructions as the twelve received—to proclaim peace, to cure the sick, and announce the kingdom of God as present (Luke 10:1-12). It is clear from the words of Jesus according to Luke that followers of Jesus were intended to emulate the master—do what Jesus himself did. The model of ethics in the New Testament, like in the Old Testament, was not a careful thinking through of what made sense in light of bringing qualities like love or kindness into engagement with present realities,

but rather living in emulation of the Master who has already been shown to be faithful.

One of the most difficult areas of modeling for the disciples relates to the cross. Jesus was forthright in his teaching here, saying, "If any want to become my followers, let them deny themselves and take up their cross daily and follow me" (Luke 9:23). It is difficult to know what the disciples would have understood with this teaching. Yet, since the context was Jesus foretelling his own death and resurrection, it could not have escaped the hearer that following Jesus meant being ready to suffer.

In Matthew 16, this story is narrated slightly differently. An exchange takes place at Caesarea Philippi between Jesus and his disciples (Matt 16:13-28). When Jesus asks his disciples, "But who do you say that I am?" (Matt 16:15) Peter answers, "You are the Messiah, the Son of the living God." Jesus replies to him:

> . . . And I tell you, you are Peter, and on this rock I will build my church. . . . I will give you the keys of the kingdom of heaven and whatever you bind on earth will be bound in heaven, and whatever you loose on earth will be loosed in heaven. (Matt 16:18-19)

This is a rare time when Jesus talks about the church (*ekklesia*), and it is interesting that the context is one where Jesus' own identity as Messiah is announced and where his suffering and death are foretold.

It is also interesting that Peter, the rock on which Jesus will build his church, seems unusually dull, for only a few moments later this "rock" gets placed in the company of "Satan" and called a "stumbling block" by Jesus in a rather harsh rebuke.

Indeed, the cross is a hard teaching. Yet the cross-resurrection stands at the center of the gospel ethic because it represents Jesus' fierce commitment to love of enemies, his dogged determination not to use violence as a means to get out of tough spots, and his total trust

---

[18] For a helpful "narrative-critical" reading of Luke's presentation of discipleship, see Sheila Klassen-Wiebe, "Called to Mission: A Narrative-Critical Study of the Character and Mission of the Disciples in the Gospel of Luke" (Ph.D. diss., Union Theological Seminary, Richmond, Va., 2001).

[19] Klassen-Wiebe, "Called to Mission," 1.

in God as the agent of deliverance. It turns out the logic here is also in continuity with the tradition: Moses said to the Israelites, "Do not be afraid, stand firm, and see the deliverance that the Lord will accomplish for you today; for the Egyptians whom you see today you will never see again. The Lord will fight for you, and you have only to keep still" (Exod 14:13-14). In other words, deliverance (resurrection) clearly lies not in our own hands, but in God's—as radical gift. Creator-God can, will, and does provide and re-create.

The ethic of Jesus therefore turns on the same radical faith as does the ethic of Moses. Do not worry, do not resist an evildoer, love your enemies, and the other injunctions Jesus speaks about in the Sermon on the Mount (Matt 5–7)—all derive from the simple conviction that our heavenly Father knows what we need and will provide for us (Matt 6:32-34).[20] The risk of faithfulness is therefore commensurate with the strength of our conviction that life is a gift from God.

While Jesus disassociated himself from the religious leaders of his day, he nevertheless embraced the vision of Abraham and Moses and the tradition of his storied people. The Zealots' attempt to violently overthrow the Roman occupiers, the Pharisee's defense of the establishment religion status quo, and the Essene's withdrawal inclination which lead them to be interested in purity (their own and their religion's), were all ways that Jesus rejected. Indeed, the way of the cross that he modeled was to stand firm in the presence of evil and not yield to its demands. For as Moses showed in Egypt, Gideon at the hill of Moreh, Elisha at Dothan, and many others throughout the tradition of Israel, the source of goodness and justice lies in the hands of God, the miraculous deliverer, and we participate in God's deliverance only by God's grace.

Paul and the Church

After Jesus' resurrection and ascension, the disciples found themselves in a strange spot. Their Master was gone and they were on their own. But they did what they had been taught: preached, taught, and healed. For they were convinced that Messiah had come. They taught in the synagogues and also to the Gentiles. But zealous Pharisees saw this "religious sect" as heresy and started persecuting it. Saul of Tarsus, who later became known as Paul, was one such Pharisee.

But Saul/Paul experienced a major transformation on his way to the city of Damascus, where he was on a mission to hunt down Christ's followers, also called people of "The Way." The practice was that they were abducted and brought to Jerusalem, where they would be tortured and often killed. On this occasion Saul/Paul was confronted with a bright light and a voice saying, "Saul, Saul, why do you persecute me?" (Acts 9:4). And when Saul enquired whose voice it was, the reply came: "I am Jesus, whom you are persecuting. But get up and enter the city, and you will be told what you are to do" (Acts 9:5-6). Paul was struck with blindness and did not eat for three days; then Ananias, a disciple, was sent to lay hands on him and restore his sight. After a few days, Saul/Paul began to proclaim Jesus as Messiah in the synagogues.

After that, Paul was enemy number one to the Jewish leaders, nor was he well received by the Hellenists. Yet he was not deterred. He taught and he wrote letters to groups of Christ-followers in several cities. When he spoke, he preached a new humanity and an ethic of unity in Christ, as he heard that Jesus himself had done.

> But now in Christ Jesus you who once were far off have been brought near by the blood of Christ. For he is our peace; in his flesh he has made both groups into one and has broken down the dividing

---

[20] This, of course, does not suggest that for Jesus there is no tension between his teaching and the tradition of Moses. After all, Jesus pits the two against each other ("You have heard that it was said . . . but I say to you . . . " Matt 5). Yet Jesus also says, "Do not think that I have come to abolish the law or the prophets; I have come not to abolish but to fulfill" (Matt 5:17). My point here is that Jesus and Moses are best understood in continuity rather than discontinuity.

wall, that is, the hostility between us. He has abolished the law with its commandments and ordinances, that he might create in himself one new humanity in place of the two, thus making peace, and might reconcile both groups to God in one body through the cross, thus putting to death that hostility through it. So he came and proclaimed peace to you who were far off and peace to those who were near; for through him both of us have access in one Spirit to the Father. So then you are no longer strangers and aliens, but you are citizens with the saints and also members of the household of God, built upon the foundation of the apostles and prophets, with Christ Jesus himself as the cornerstone. In him the whole structure is joined together and grows into a holy temple in the Lord; in whom you also are built together spiritually into a dwelling place for God. (Eph 2:13-22)

The specific qualities that Paul upholds as exemplary for the Christian life are humility, gentleness, patience, love, grace, and so on. And especially when speaking to Gentiles, he contrasts their existing life with a new life in Christ.

Now this I affirm and insist on in the Lord: you must no longer live as the Gentiles live, in the futility of their minds. They are darkened in their understanding, alienated from the life of God because of their ignorance and hardness of heart. They have lost all sensitivity and have abandoned themselves to licentiousness, greedy to practise every kind of impurity. That is not the way you learned Christ! For surely you have heard about him and were taught in him, as truth is in Jesus. You were taught to put away your former way of life, your old self, corrupt and deluded by its lusts, and to be renewed in the spirit of your minds, and to clothe yourselves with the new self, created according to the likeness of God in true righteousness and holiness. (Eph 4:17-24)

Everywhere Paul preaches moral instructions to those who will live "in Christ." In his letter to the Romans:

Owe no one anything, except to love one another; for the one who loves another has fulfilled the law. The commandments, "You shall not commit adultery; You shall not murder; You shall not steal; You shall not covet"; and any other commandment, are summed up in this word, "Love your neighbor as yourself." Love does no wrong to a neighbor; therefore, love is the fulfilling of the law. (Rom 13:8-10)

His language is important to note. The moral imperatives are grounded in two notions: one is discipleship and the other is participation in Christ. Not only are followers of Christ to do as Jesus did, but to do so requires a mode of being in Christ in such a manner that their very identity is to be given shape by the identity of Christ. Paul speaks of the Christ-disciple relation in two directions: we are to be in Christ and Christ is to dwell in us. For example, he says: "I have been crucified with Christ; and it is no longer I who live, but it is Christ who lives in me" (Gal 2:19-20). Either way, the moral imperative is lodged in a metaphysical relationship, one where our being and Christ's being are interconnected, albeit certainly not identical.

Paul also addresses how disciples should live in relation to institutions such as marriage and family (Eph 5:22–6:9; Col 3:18–4:1), state (Rom 13:1-7), and others. In each case, Paul stresses the importance of "being subject" to authority figures. On the surface this sounds like a rather conservative "don't rock the boat" response to possible structural injustices such as slavery, dictatorships, and male domination. Moreover, it has been argued that the reason Paul made such conservative moral pronouncements is because the radical ethic of Jesus—turning the other cheek, walking the second mile, loving enemies—simply was not a viable social ethic, and Paul therefore was forced to borrow from the Stoics, a standard social ethic at the time with which Paul would have been familiar. But as scholars like John Howard Yoder have pointed out, Paul's ethic is emphatically not a borrowing from the Stoics; rather Paul is precisely attempting to exemplify the ethic of the cross-resurrection for those wanting to follow Jesus.[21] And in doing so, he is trying to steer a path around two popular alternatives:

---

[21] See John Howard Yoder, *The Politics of Jesus:* Vicit Agnus Noster, 2nd ed. (Grand Rapids: Eerdmans, 1994), esp. chap. 9, "Revolutionary Subordination," 162–92.

rebellion toward unjust structures and a silent acquiescence to injustice.

Yoder's argument is similar to the interpretation Walter Wink has given to Jesus' injunction to turn the other cheek and walking the second mile (Matt 5).[22] "The Third Way" reading of these sayings advocated by Wink is that they represent challenges to the status quo by confronting unjust power practices. For example, the one who is turning the other cheek is, in effect, saying, "I challenge you to treat me as an equal." This is so because the backhanded slap on the right cheek is the slap of insult and the openhanded slap on "the other" would be between equals. Hence, far from being a mere acceptance of abuse, it is, like the cross, an act of standing up to abusive powers, even when it causes suffering.

The ethics of cross-resurrection is unlike much of what we are used to, so careful thought needs to be given to Paul's language in order to see how he was counseling the early church "disciples" of Jesus in what it means to embody the ethic of Jesus. And he is constantly presenting the church as a body of believers participating in the very body of Christ and therefore living an ethic counter to the mainstream; a counterethic because it is born out of a countersoteriology and a counterpolitic—counter, that is, to the world in which he was speaking and writing.

This countercommunity called church is the body in which discipleship training, or moral formation, takes place when the Master is no longer present in the way he was to the first disciples. Guided by the Holy Spirit, this "body of Christ" practices the disciplines that can make us faithful—holy communion, binding and loosing, baptism, marriages, funerals, gift discernment, relating to one another in the mode of gift exchange, and so on. Paul and the other teachers, such as Peter and John, address all of these disciplines and

many more, and in the process they make clear how deeply political the body called church really is—political in the sense that it aims to live by a different vision than standard politics.

When Paul wrote his letters to the churches, and perhaps even more so when they were read publicly, the sense of this being a counterpolitic could not have been starker. The Jewish German philosopher Jacob Taubes states it dramatically when he calls Paul's letter to the Romans a "declaration of war on the Caesar." Speaking of the salutation in the letter, Taubes says:

> I want to stress that this is a political declaration of war, when a letter introduced using these words, and not others, is sent to the congregation in Rome to be read aloud. One doesn't know into whose hands it will fall, and the censors aren't idiots. One could, after all, have introduced it pietistically, quietistically, neutrally, or however else; but there is none of that here. This is why my thesis is that in this sense the Epistle to the Romans is a political theology, a *political* declaration of war on the Caesar.[23]

The ethics of Jesus and Moses are radical counterethics to the mainstream—whether that is in Egypt, Rome, or North America today. For both Jesus and Moses, ethics is embodied in a people: for Moses the people of Israel and for Jesus and Paul a new body called the church, one which seeks to bring together people that have been divided—Jews and Greeks, men and women, slave and free, rich and poor, and so on. How well the church has done in achieving this goal of a united humanity is open to judgment.

THE BIBLE AND CHRISTIAN ETHICS

At the beginning of this chapter, I indicated that I would address two questions under the topic of biblical ethics: one dealing with content and the other asking how Christians today might claim the Bible as authoritative

---

[22] Walter Wink speaks about "The Third Way" in several of his writings. The most recent is in *Jesus and Nonviolence: The Third Way* (Minneapolis: Augsburg Fortress, 2003).

[23] Jacob Taubes, *The Political Theology of Paul*, trans. Dana Hollander, ed. Aleida Assmann (Stanford, Calif.: Stanford University Press, 2004), 16 (emphasis in original).

in constructing a viable and faithful understanding of Christian ethics. I turn now to the second question.

It is hard to know where to turn for help on how to come to terms with the variety of moral guidance offered in the Bible. Many scholars, primarily theologians and ethicists, have offered models.[24] It is impossible to present them all in this chapter. Yet one essay that turns up, perhaps more than any other, is written by a contemporary American ethicist, James M. Gustafson. So I use this essay to begin the reflection on how the Bible might furnish us with moral guidance.

Gustafson's Summation

In Gustafson's essay titled "The Place of Scripture in Christian Ethics: A Methodological Study,"[25] he presented four ways of using the Bible as a basis for Christian ethics. At the time he wrote the article, he applied his analysis of biblical ethics to the American invasion of Cambodia. For those of us less familiar with that war, we might well use the current wars in Afghanistan and Iraq as references. Let me summarize Gustafson's four ways.

First, a common way of reading the Bible to glean from it moral guidance for today is to read it as offering *moral law*. Gustafson shows that two issues are involved when one approaches the Bible this way: the content of the law and its application. In Jewish religion the process of identifying the law (Torah) is relatively simple, but how that translates into everyday practice is extremely complex. The Mishna and the Talmud contain judgments by rabbis, giving readings of how the Torah is to help the faithful come to concrete decisions. It is, after all, important to be clear on what it means to steal, or to lie, or to keep the Sabbath. And it is not always obvious how one is to understand neighbor (hence the

question by the lawyer to Jesus), or enemy, and so on. There is an added complication when we get to the New Testament. Jesus is then read as introducing a "new law," sometimes identified as the "law of grace," but it is hard to see precisely how grace can be a law. There is also the attempt within contemporary Christian ethics to define the new law as the "law of love," and here Jesus' own words lend support when he says that the whole Torah can be summed up in "love of God and love of neighbor."

To think about war from the standpoint of this approach points out many of the difficulties with it. First, one might want to respond by saying that to evaluate war from the standpoint of love (especially love of enemies) makes all war immoral. But then, just-war theories hold love to be crucial in determining how war is to be conducted. Second, the distinction is sometimes made between the public and the private realms; then it is argued that love relates to the private and not to the public realm. Third, the argument is made that when assessing an action on the basis of love one should consider humanity as a whole and not only a particular individual. Then it can be argued that a particular war is more loving because it may well maximize love for all by destroying a few lives to save many. All of this is to show that this approach demands careful interpretations at many levels in order to know what "love" means in a particular case. Of course, some would argue that this approach permits us to justify anything, if it can be successfully argued that "love of enemy" can be made consistent with killing the enemy at all.

Gustafson's second way of reading the Bible is to find *moral ideals* that adherents should strive to attain. Those theologians who emphasize the kingdom of God as central to

[24] Although there are far too many to give an exhaustive list, here are a few examples: A. Verhey, "The Use of Scripture in Ethics," *Religious Studies Review* 4 (1978): 28–39; D. H. Kelsey, *The Uses of Scripture in Recent Theology* (Philadelphia: Fortress, 1975); E. L. Long, "The Use of the Bible in Christian Ethics: A Look at Basic Options," *Interpretation* 19 (1965): 149–62; W. C. Spohn, *What Are They Saying about Scripture and Ethics?* (New York: Paulist, 1984); Jeffrey S. Siker, *Scripture and Ethics: Twentieth Century Portraits* (New York: Oxford University Press, 1997).

[25] James M. Gustafson, "The Place of Scripture in Christian Ethics: A Methodological Approach," *Interpretation* 24 (1970): 430–55.

biblical interpretation find particular favor with this approach. The logic goes something like this: the Bible shows us the general direction in which God wants things to go—liberation, fulfillment of peace and justice, and so on—and the faithful are called to do what they can to move history in this direction. Proponents of the Social Gospel sometimes align themselves with this view.

The main difficulties with this approach are two: first, do we know enough and are we powerful enough to move history in the direction we think it should go? Reinhold Niebuhr refers to the notion that the direction we wish history to go is often not the direction it goes as the "irony of history."[26] The second difficulty relates to moral agency. To what extent is it our task as mere mortals to seek to move history forward in our favorite directions? And most certainly we are not all agreed on which direction that ought to be, which itself causes conflict. Yet the latter is a much-favored approach. On this model, the current Middle East War or any other war can quite easily be justified. Just-war logic is built on the notion that sometimes moral ideals justify what appear to be immoral means.

The third way Gustafson suggests the Bible can be read is slightly more complicated. Here, our relationship to the Bible, morally speaking, is seen as an analogic one. We determine which situations in the biblical account are *analogous to our current situations* and then we have a basis for acting in response to such situations. For example, Jesus tells the parable of the unforgiving servant (Matt 18:23-35), and whenever we find ourselves in an analogous situation we should do likewise. In fact, this is the very advice Jesus gives to the lawyer after he tells the story of the good Samaritan in Luke 10:37.

This approach presents its share of difficulties because analogic thinking is fraught with imprecisions. What, for example, is the current Middle East War analogous to? A few years ago in a Vancouver-based Christian newspaper called *Christian Info News*, Benno Friesen, a Mennonite Conservative Member of Parliament, argued this way in relation to the 1991 Persian Gulf War in which allied forces drove Iraq out of Kuwait. His point was that freedom and justice were at issue in that war. He concluded this from drawing the analogy with the story of the good Samaritan. "Here is a small, almost totally defenseless nation [Kuwait] lying on the roadside, wounding and bleeding."[27] He believed allied nations were called to be the "good Samaritans" coming to rescue Kuwait and bind up its wounds. For Friesen, this analogy justified the war as a war of liberation.

As this example shows, it all depends on which analogy is invoked in the particular case in question. And choosing the analogy gets much harder when we think of the many problems that confront us in the advent of contemporary technology: climate change, stem-cell research, cloning, computer technology, genetic engineering, and so on. The major problem with this approach is its inherent temptation to seek those biblical events and stories that support our convictions about what is right, which we know in advance of reading the Bible.

Gustafson calls the fourth way of reading the Bible the *conglomerative* approach. It suggests that there is validity in all of the methods discussed—moral law, moral ideals, and analogies to significant events/stories—and that it is unwise to rely on only one approach. Hence, our task is to appeal to all methods and to choose the one most appropriate.

While this approach has the advantage of not being reductionist, which is the weakness of each of the others, it nevertheless has its own difficulties. It also lends itself to giving biblical authorization to what one believes to be right independently of the Bible. On the one hand, this approach explains all too well why there is so much diversity within the Christian community regarding issues such as war; after all, one can pick whatever model

---

[26] See Reinhold Niebuhr, *The Irony of American History* (Chicago: University of Chicago Press, 1952, 2008).

[27] Debra Fieguth, *Christian Info News*, II, no. 2 (27 January 1991): 1. Fieguth was the editor of the newspaper.

best suits the position one wishes to defend. On the other hand, why should one assume that there is only one faithful approach? Each approach has some validity when it is brought to proper use.

Nevertheless, the overall approach that Gustafson brings to the biblical text is an abstract one. The assumption seems to be that with the correct intellectual tools and analyses it will be possible to discern the single or complex strand of moral guidance. What this chapter has shown, if anything, is that the Bible displays far too great a variety for this approach to be helpful. What seems to be called for is not a model of reducing the multifaceted text to a single strand but a model showing how to live morally responsible lives embracing the variety within our moral source book. So I default to the church.

I suggest that what the Gustafson approach as well as many other approaches lack is a discerning community. After all, to invoke a moral law or analogy may be exactly what is needed to be faithful in a particular setting—not because it severs the individual's or group's interests, but rather because it is the Christian thing to do. However, for the latter determination to be made requires the faithful functioning of the "body of Christ." And this points to an even deeper issue underlying all the above approaches; namely, that very few of us possess the qualities necessary to read the Bible as Scripture. The approaches Gustafson puts forward all assume that if individuals on their own read the Bible they are able to understand what it calls them to do. But is this really the case?

Stanley Hauerwas has summarized the problem well:

> Most North American Christians assume they have a right, if not an obligation, to read the Bible. I challenge that assumption. No task is more important than for the church to take the Bible out of the hands of individual Christians in North America. Let us no longer give a Bible to every child. . . . Let us rather tell them and their parents that they are possessed by habits far too corrupt for them to be encouraged to read the Bible on their own.[28]

In other words, the problem here is not so much a hermeneutical problem—what does the Bible say?—as it is an ecclesiological problem: can the church create in its members virtues that will help us become the kind of people the Bible is calling forth? There are approaches that take church seriously in this very way.

Contrasting Approaches

I will look at two contrasting approaches that seek to read the Bible from the standpoint of the community called church.

First, the American Old Testament scholar, Brevard Childs, in his book *Biblical Theology in Crisis*, includes a chapter titled, "Biblical Theology's Role in Decision-Making."[29] Here, he gives attention to how his canonical approach to the Bible impacts our understanding of ethics today. For Childs, one of the most important aspects to any reading of Scripture has to do with theology. That is, what is the larger theological framework in which God's will can be understood?

Childs argues that in the Bible the will of God has been made known through the narrative accounts of the people responding to God. Yet God also gives us the responsibility to discern that will at every moment. In fact, God's will is not something abstract, but it becomes clear only within the concrete involvement of real-life situations. For example, it is clear that the Bible communicates that we should love our neighbors. But a debated point even within the Bible itself is the matter of who our neighbor is. The will of God to love neighbor becomes concrete only when the command and a specific neighbor

---

[28] Stanley Hauerwas, *Unleashing the Scriptures: Freeing the Bible from Captivity to America* (Nashville: Abingdon, 1993), 15.

[29] Brevard S. Childs, *Biblical Theology in Crisis* (Philadelphia: Westminster, 1970). See also his more recent work, *Biblical Theology of the Old and New Testaments: Theological Reflection on the Christian Bible* (Minneapolis: Fortress, 1992), esp. chap. 10, "The Shape of the Obedient Life: Ethics," 658ff.

come together. It is precisely in this process that the Bible functions as Scripture.

One of Childs' main contributions to this discussion has to do with his view on what the Bible actually is. He does this by reminding us of how it came to be Bible. The formation of the canon tells us that the community of believers held that it was the entire *corpus*, now called the Bible, that reveals the will of God to us. Hence, the proof-texting approach of "using the Bible" to support a view which one believes independently of the Bible is not valid. The Bible is the church's book in that its contents shape the church because the church has selected it. "To the query: 'What does God want from me/us?' the Christian replies: 'Read the Scriptures.' Yet the context of the canon serves to remind its users that the Bible does not function as Scripture apart from the community of believers."[30]

Childs reminds us that there is ethical pluralism in the Bible; hence, with this approach it is not easy to find quick answers to difficult moral problems. For example, there are different views expressed toward sexuality in Proverbs 7 and in the Song of Songs. The biblical view must take into account both views and not resolve the tension on merely one side of the matter. The faithful answer to moral issues that require response from us today must be found as one wrestles with what the biblical text as a whole says about what God wills from human beings. The pluralism within the modern world is also reflected within the Bible. To resolve the tensions that arise out of this too easily is but another form of unfaithfulness resulting from a failure to read the entire Bible as Scripture.

Second, Richard Hays, an American New Testament scholar, has helped us understand how the Bible can give us moral guidance.[31] In his work, Hays focuses especially on New Testament ethics although, much like this chapter has sought to do, he stresses the unity rather than the diversity of the biblical story. Focusing particularly on the New Testament expression of this story, he summarizes the biblical moral imagination as follows:

> The God of Israel, the creator of all that exists, has acted (astoundingly) to rescue a lost and broken world through the death and resurrection of Jesus; the full scope of that rescue is not yet apparent, but God has created a community of witnesses to this good news, the church. While awaiting the grand conclusion of the story, the church, empowered by the Holy Spirit, is called to reenact the loving obedience of Jesus Christ and thus to serve as a sign of God's redemptive purposes for the world.[32]

He goes on to suggest that there are four overlapping operations in the faithful reading of the text in order for it to become normative theology for us: the descriptive, the synthetic, the hermeneutical, and the pragmatic tasks.[33] The descriptive task involves reading the texts as carefully as possible in order to attend to the message of each individual New Testament witness. The synthetic task includes placing the different individuals side by side to determine whether they are coherent. However successful this latter process might be, there is still the more difficult hermeneutical task, which seeks to bridge the cultural distance between the text and us. The last task is the pragmatic one. It involves the embodiment of the scriptural imperatives within today's Christian community.

When Hays puts these tasks to work, he begins by identifying three focal images that can guide us in our own moral discernment: community, cross, and new creation. He sees

---

[30] Childs, *Biblical Theology in Crisis*, 131. See also Phyllis Bird, *The Bible as the Church's Book* (Philadelphia: Westminster, 1982).

[31] See Richard B. Hays, *The Moral Vision of the New Testament: Community, Cross, New Creation: A Contemporary Introduction to New Testament Ethics* (San Francisco: Harpe Collins, 1996), and *New Testament Ethics: The Story Retold*, J. J. Thiessen Lectures (Winnipeg, Manitoba: CMBC Publications, 1998).

[32] Hays, *New Testament Ethics*, 26.   [33] Hays, *New Testament Ethics*, 23.

these as pillars for understanding the New Testament story. First, he sees *"The church [as] a counter-cultural community of discipleship, and this community is the primary addressee of God's imperatives."*[34] In other words, the Bible's emphasis is the forming of a covenant people, and so the primary locus of moral understanding is not the individual but the community called church. Second, *"Jesus' death on the cross is the paradigm of faithfulness to God in this world."*[35] And third, regarding the new creation's focal image he says, *"The church embodies the power of the resurrection in the midst of a not-yet-redeemed world."*[36] He proposes that these three images be seen as lenses that help us see more clearly the unity of the New Testament moral vision.

When Hays turns to the hermeneutical operation, he speaks of "metaphor-making" which, of course, is an act of the imagination. He says, *". . . whenever we appeal to the authority of the New Testament, we are necessarily engaged in metaphor-making, placing our community's life imaginatively within the world articulated by the texts."*[37]

For the pragmatic task, Hays asks what the church might look like as an "embodied metaphor." On this model, the task of the church is literally the embodiment of the text—the Word. He relies on the Apostle Paul's Epistle to the Corinthians: "you are a letter of Christ, . . . written not with ink but with the Spirit of the living God, not on tablets of stone but on tablets of human hearts" (2 Cor 3:3).[38] Hays freely acknowledges that to see the pragmatic task in this light leads him back to the hermeneutical operation, for *"right reading of the New Testament occurs only where the word is embodied."*[39] So for Hays, the only way that the New Testament can help us to be faithful is for us to learn to read and embody it in the community called church. "Until we see God's power at work among us we do not know what we are reading. Thus, the most crucial hermeneutical task is the formation of communities that retell the story by seeking to live under the word."[40]

One final word on the topic of biblical ethics. It is important to acknowledge that the move toward a fuller engagement of ethics and the Bible does not come only from biblical scholars but also from some contemporary ethicists. Brevard Childs and Richard Hays are among those who have done much to inspire modern ethicists to take the Bible seriously in developing a viable Christian ethic. Here, Hans Frei, George Lindbeck, Stanley Hauerwas, John Howard Yoder, James William McClendon Jr., Nicholas Lash, and Stephen Crites are among the most common names. Because several of these ethicists will be discussed later in our study, we need not attend to them here.

---

[34] Hays, *New Testament Ethics*, 28 (emphasis in original).
[35] Hays, *New Testament Ethics*, 29 (emphasis in original).
[36] Hays, *New Testament Ethics*, 30 (emphasis in original).
[37] Hays, *New Testament Ethics*, 33 (emphasis in original).
[38] Hays, *New Testament Ethics*, 36.
[39] Hays, *New Testament Ethics*, 37 (emphasis in original).
[40] Hays, *New Testament Ethics*, 38.

Chapter Three

EARLY CHURCH ETHICS

W e are tempted to think that, because the early church was small and a politically irrelevant minority, its views should not be taken seriously. Moreover, is it not usually the most mature forms of thought that best express the views of a particular position? Certainly it could be argued that this early theology is not very advanced, measured from the perspective of theology several thousand years later. If we look at the early church from this vantage point, we are glad that we have reached a more sophisticated understanding of Christian theology generally and Christian ethics specifically.

The other extreme is to view the early church as the near-perfect embodiment of the Christian faith because it was closest to the real thing. In this view, the early Christians become the model for later Christians and it is then said that Christendom has fallen away from this idyllic posture.

Between these two extremes lies another that holds greater promise. The theology and life of the early Christians are important because of their proximity to the source, culture, and language of the original message. It is reasonable to believe that their expression of the Christian faith is less encumbered and hence more focused than a faith thousands of years later. Yet the fact that we live two thousand years on this side of their history with many cultural and intellectual changes means that a simple imitation of their way of life is not possible, nor would it be desirable. So something akin to a translation is called for here: a linguistic

and cultural reappropriation on our side of the great chasm. Yet to understand their interpretation of Christian ethics is extremely valuable, even if we cannot emulate it simply.

THE APOSTOLIC CHURCH

I have divided this chapter into two parts: the apostolic and the post-apostolic church, a somewhat arbitrary division based on sources. By "apostolic church" I mean merely the view of the church we glean from the canonical sources and by "post-apostolic church" the view we receive from writers beyond these sources. Hence, the material of the first part of this chapter overlaps with the previous chapter. I will pick themes and references here that I did not deal with in the last chapter.

The apostolic writings are filled with invitation and admonition to live particular moral lives—for distinct reasons. Listen to the letter the Apostle Paul sent to the church at Ephesus:

Finally, be strong in the Lord and in the strength of his power. Put on the whole armor of God, so that you may be able to stand against the wiles of the devil. For our struggle is not against enemies of blood and flesh, but against the rulers, against the authorities, against the cosmic powers of this present darkness, against the spiritual forces of evil in the heavenly places. Therefore take up the whole armor of God, so that you may be able to withstand on that evil day, and having done everything, to stand firm. Stand therefore, and fasten the belt of truth around your waist, and put on the breastplate of righteousness. As shoes for your feet put on whatever will make you ready to proclaim the gospel of peace. With all of these, take the shield of faith, with which you will be able to quench all the flaming arrows of the evil one. Take the helmet of salvation, and the sword of the Spirit, which is the word of God. (Eph 6:10-17)

Notice the emphasis on *perseverance*, a key moral quality. This is perhaps the replacement virtue for what the Greeks call courage. Perseverance is different from courage in that it assumes a tangible given to the moral life that is in tension with the mainstream; hence, special efforts will need to be exerted to remain faithful. Courage is a virtue required to bring about a challenging goal.

The biblical view of the world is that all kinds of powers in this world are vying for our loyalty. In light of this, the writer is suggesting that we put on God's armor, which is the kind of protection we will need in the battle to avoid being seduced by the powers of evil. What kind of defensive weaponry is envisioned as the armory of God? Paul speaks of truth, righteousness, the equipment of peace, and faith. These are the protectors of faithfulness found in the word of God. So we are invited to read, study, and meditate on it and to place ourselves under such power.

At the beginning of the fifth chapter in Ephesians, the same theme is expressed in another way. "Therefore be imitators of God, as beloved children. And live in love, as Christ loved us and gave himself up for us, a fragrant offering and sacrifice to God" (Eph 5:1-2). So what is to be the guide for living the Christian life? A life of divine imitation: a life different from mainstream culture, hence requiring careful cultivation of habits unlike those seen in the common social realm.

It is important to reflect briefly on how discipleship and the faithful Christian life are understood here. This is not first of all about learning to make right decisions or about seeking to bring about just goals. It is rather about becoming particular characters. *Character building* is the second moral quality of the early church, closely associated, of course, with perseverance.

The text speaks of forming characters capable of withstanding the temptations of competing ways of life that might look appealing to us on the surface. The way of Christian faithfulness suggested here contains a rigorous discipleship training process that literally molds people into distinctive moral people—people with characters capable of participating in the very spirit of God, thereby reflecting that spirit to others. Another way of saying this is that it is training for the life of virtue. For it is the habitual practice of virtues that keep us from going astray, or from being ensnared by the evil one.

It is important to point out that the Christian virtues are not the same as the Greek virtues. Hence, the Christian model person will look different from the Greek gentleman. In Galatians 5 we have an interesting summary of virtue-like qualities that are called the fruits of the Spirit. Before the specific "fruits" are identified, the "offense of the cross" (v. 11) is referred to as that which especially bothers unbelieving Galatian thinkers and makes the Christian faith unacceptable to them. But for the writer of the letter, it is precisely the cross that is to be the center of the Christian moral life. What does this mean? He spells it out by calling his hearers to first "become slaves to one another" (v. 13), then to "love your neighbor as yourself" (v. 14), and finally to "live by the Spirit" (v. 16). Living according to the cross of Christ has specific social expressions tied to some measure of reversal of standard power models.

The cross names a third moral quality of the early church: *witness*. At stake here is a particular view of moral agency. The cross-resurrection relationship is itself a model for how the early Christians presented themselves to one another and to society around them. It is a form of presentation that says what we are doing is not all that is being done. In other words, God is at work in this world bringing it to justice and peace long before we are. And our way of participating in God's overall project is to live faithfully to God's expression of love, even love of enemy. According to this view, when there is injustice or a state of unpeace, it is ultimately not our task to restore it; it is God's task and God will bring it about whether we suffer and even die in the process or not. Our task is to remain faithful through patient perseverance, fidelity of character, and open witness. This is a unique view of moral agency that sounds somewhat strange to foreign ears, and it certainly was strange to the unbelieving Galatians.

Paul lists the fruits of the spirit as follows in Galatians 5:22: love, patience, faithfulness, joy, kindness, gentleness, peace, generosity, and self-control. Notice the absence of the Greek cardinal virtues of wisdom, courage, temperance, and justice. One should, however, be careful not to make too much of this absence since this is but a selection of a larger list of Christian virtues mentioned elsewhere in the Bible. We have already seen how perseverance is much like courage, and certainly wisdom and justice are important Christian virtues. Yet it is important to emphasize that the model of cross-resurrection places distance between our actions and the outcome of God's cause. Since it is not our agency alone that brings about justice, the training of habits that bring justice about by the most efficient and effective means possible are not the focus for the early Christians. Instead patience, gentleness, and peace, virtues which focus on keeping us faithful, are much more important.

Living by these virtues shapes people's characters in specific ways. Some examples are spelled out in Ephesians 5 and 6 that speak of how to live as disciples within the household. Wives are told to submit to their husbands, husbands are told to love their wives, children are told to obey their parents, fathers are told not to provoke their children to anger, slaves are told to obey their earthly masters, masters are reminded that they too have a Master who is in heaven.

Much debate has focused on this particular passage of Scripture. One of the main issues of debate has been whether this view of ethical relationships is uniquely Christian in the sense that its source lies with Jesus or whether it is an adaptation or borrowing from the dominant cultural ethic of Stoicism. David Schroeder has compared these "Household Codes" (*Haustafeln*) with the ethics of the Stoics and has challenged the mainline thesis that Paul is borrowing directly from Stoic ethics in order to tell early Christians how to live.[1] Martin Dibelius' defense of the "borrowing thesis" arises from his conviction that Jesus' ethic of "turning the other cheek" and "giving all to the poor" was too radical to form the basis of a viable social ethic.[2] So Paul, when he was faced with the task of giving responsible moral advice to the early Christians, had no choice but to go elsewhere than to Jesus. For the purposes of Christian ethics, the question of whether Jesus was seen as the reliable model for Christian living by writers such as the Apostle Paul is crucial because at issue is whether the cross-resurrection model was viable for early church theologians like Paul. Hence, the Dibelius thesis warrants some attention.

First, as we have seen with Paul and with Epictetus earlier,[3] the language of *submission* functions to elaborate the understanding of ethics for both men. Yet how agents are to submit is different for each. Epictetus calls for the son to submit to his father because he is the father; that is, the subordinate party must submit to the super-ordinate party. This idea is essential for Stoicism and in the standard power paradigm—the powerful demand respect and submission simply because of their status. For Paul and the early church, the logic is different. Because the ethical basis is Jesus Christ and the cross and resurrection, the power paradigm is turned upside down. Hence, in Paul's Household Codes, you have wives called to be submissive and you have husbands called to love their wives "as Christ loved the church and gave himself up for

---

[1] See David Schroeder, "Die Haustafeln des Neuen Testaments, Ihre Herkunft und ihr theologischer Sinn" (Ph.D. diss., University of Hamburg, 1959).

[2] For a further discussion of Martin Dibelius' "borrowing thesis," see John Howard Yoder, *The Politics of Jesus*: Vicit Agnus Noster, 2nd ed. (Grand Rapids: Eerdmans, 1994), 164–65.   [3] See 23ff.

her" (Eph 5:25). That is, the call is for *mutual* submission, and with that we see a transvaluation of ethics.

Second, perhaps the greatest difference between the two ethics (Stoic and Pauline) is that the early church considered the subordinate parties—women, children, and slaves—to be *moral agents*. But in Stoic literature, these persons are not addressed as moral agents and what they do or do not do is a reflection on their dominant partner, to whom they are bound. They themselves are not morally responsible and to consider them such would have required a different understanding of what it meant to be a human being. In Christ, however, all have been set free, including women, children, and slaves. In Christ all are held to be God's children, and hence all are moral agents, accountable for their actions. In Christ, who we are is given definition by who Jesus is, and that is common to both men and women, the powerful and the weak. Paul seeks to make this idea intelligible by emphasizing that Jesus was our model not by the power and status he accrued to himself but by what he gave up and how he surrendered to God (cross-resurrection)—the power to effect radical change. And this every person, regardless of status, is able to do.

Third, the *ground* of the moral imperatives is different. Within Stoicism the ground is "the nature of things," whereas in the Household Codes it is the revelation received in Christ Jesus. The justification clauses mentioned in Ephesians are: "out of reverence for Christ" (5:21), "as Christ does" (5:29), "in the Lord" (6:1), and "as you obey Christ" (6:5). The explicit intention of the writer is to anchor the way of life for early Christians in Christ. This is different from the rationale provided in Stoic ethics. Here "fatherness" and "sonness" and "citizenness" determine what it means for someone to be responsible. For example, if you are a father then . . . is what you must do. If you are a son, then . . . is your duty. In other words, your ethic is derived from your status or station.

These differences demonstrate a disjunction between the ethics of the early church and the ethic of the dominant mainline culture. The reason underlying these differences was that the early Christians believed Jesus Christ had begun a new reign, one in which God Almighty was calling all of the faithful to gather together under a new way of life. This new way of life was characterized by discipleship and faithfulness to the life that was begun in Jesus and to the cross-resurrection that was modeled by him.

Why was Jesus seen as so important? Because he was believed to be the one from God—the Messiah. If Jesus had died a natural death like anyone else and simply disappeared from the scene, any earlier convictions about Jesus' messianic identity would probably have waned. But because he was raised from the dead, reappeared again to his disciples, and ascended into heaven, there was no doubt for his disciples that he was the one come from God. Jesus, therefore, is given the power to call people to a new way of life. One description of that life is seen in these words from Paul:

> Let love be genuine; hate what is evil, hold fast to what is good; love one another with mutual affection; outdo one another in showing honor. Do not lag in zeal, be ardent in spirit, serve the Lord. Rejoice in hope, be patient in suffering, persevere in prayer. Contribute to the needs of the saints; extend hospitality to strangers. Bless those who persecute you; bless and do not curse them. Rejoice with those who rejoice, weep with those who weep. Live in harmony with one another; do not be haughty, but associate with the lowly; do not claim to be wiser than you are. Do not repay anyone evil for evil, but take thought for what is noble in the sight of all. If it is possible, so far as it depends on you, live peaceably with all. Beloved, never avenge yourselves, but leave room for the wrath of God; for it is written, "Vengeance is mine, I will repay, says the Lord." No, "if your enemies are hungry, feed them; if they are thirsty, give them something to drink; for by doing this you will heap burning coals on their heads." Do not be overcome by evil, but overcome evil with good. (Rom 12:9-21)

Paul believed that the one who raised Jesus from the dead was now fashioning a new community called the body of Christ.[4] This was the conviction of the apostles and the early Christians.

The body of Christ names the fourth moral quality of early church ethics—*the church*. The Apostle Paul's passion for the church was at the center of his view of the Christian life. It seems that he could not imagine how one could remain Christian without the support, the prayers, the worship, and the love shown by those who gathered regularly and sought the power of God's sustaining grace. The church as moral body went in two directions: perseverance, character, and witness flowed to the individual through the church, but equally important, the church embodied these qualities. This made the church itself a political body, with a constitution, a structure, and a set of practices different from the politics of Rome.

It is not surprising therefore that Paul was concerned about much more than personal ethics. Nor should it surprise us that his political ethic employs Jesus' cross-resurrection as a model here as well. Right after the words on how Christians ought to love one another (Rom 12:9-21), Paul writes the following on how we should see the governing authorities and our posture in relation to them.

> Let every person be subject to the governing authorities; for there is no authority except from God, and those authorities that exist have been instituted by God. Therefore whoever resists authority resists what God has appointed, and those who resist will incur judgment. For rulers are not a terror to good conduct, but to bad. Do you wish to have no fear of the authority? Then do what is good, and you will receive its approval; for it is God's servant for your good. But if you do what is wrong, you should be afraid, for the authority does not bear the sword in vain! It is the servant of God to execute wrath on the wrongdoer. Therefore one must be subject, not only because of wrath but also because of conscience. For the same reason you also pay taxes, for the authorities are God's servants, busy with this very thing. Pay to all what is due to them—taxes to whom taxes are due, revenue to whom revenue is due, respect to whom respect is due, honor to whom honor is due. (Rom 13:1-7)

The history of interpretation of this passage of Scripture is so vast that we cannot here pretend to do justice to its meaning. Yet a few comments are in order. First, we notice that submission language is used here as it is in other cases where Paul talks about how Christians ought to live. Second, whatever one says about the state, it is ultimately under God's sovereign rule. Hence, governing authorities are not morally autonomous. Third, as followers of Christ, Christians are called to relate to the state, as did Christ, in open subjection to the power it has even to execute its people. Fourth, whether states are just or unjust is not addressed here, so it appears not to matter. What does matter is that Christ followers are not justified in using violence against the state, nor—especially if one reads this passage together with the passages on love both before and after this passage—are they justified in doing the violence of the state. In summary, although Christians are morally concerned about the same kinds of issues—related to peace and justice, for example—their way of seeking the fulfillment of such goals is vastly different from those of the state. The church stands as witness to an alternative political reality that cannot be imposed on subjects because its very essence is a gift, and its posture is as sign and invitation to the peace of Christ.

THE POST-APOSTOLIC CHURCH

With the death of the apostles—many of them martyred because of clashes with the governing authorities—the early church was faced with the challenge of articulating its

[4] The notion of the "body of Christ" is an image not to be misunderstood. Of course, the church is not literally the body of Christ, and yet it is that. New Testament scholar Richard Hays has used the expression, "embodied metaphor," to describe the church. See Richard B. Hays, *New Testament Ethics: The Story Retold*, J. J. Thiessen Lectures (Winnipeg, Manitoba: CMBC Publications, 1998), 35ff. We participate in Christ but are not fully faithful. Hence, there is a distinction to be made between the community as it is and the community as it would be if we were fully faithful.

faithfulness to Jesus.[5] It was, of course, true, as the Scriptures had warned,[6] that many would be the temptations to capitulate to ways of thinking and living that were different from the teachings of the apostles. And so vigilance, perseverance, fidelity of character, and a stance of witness to the saving power of Jesus Christ were constant emphases, just as they had been with the apostles.

A major struggle for the early Christians had to do with how to live in a world that was structured in accordance with an ethic they could not accept. The world was violent, they were not; the world was greedy, they were not; the world used power to get what it wanted, they could not; the world ordered itself on the premise that you get what you deserve, they understood what they had as gifts; the world protected itself from enemies and killed them when they needed to, the Christians sought to love their enemies. In virtually every respect, they found themselves out of sync with the world around them.

Perhaps the earliest teaching of the post-apostolic church is a document called the *Didache*. It appeared some time around 100 CE. It was thought to be a summary of the "Teaching of the Twelve Apostles." It shows how the apostolic teaching differentiates these "Two Ways."

1. There are two Ways, one of Life and one of Death, and there is a great difference between the two Ways.
2. The Way of Life is this: "First, thou shalt love the God who made thee, secondly, thy neighbour as thyself; and whatsoever thou wouldst not have done to thyself, do not thou to another."
3. Now, the teaching of these words is this: "Bless those that curse you, and pray for your enemies, and fast for those who persecute you. For what credit is it to you if you love

those that love you? Do not even the heathen do the same?" But for your part, "love those who hate you," and you will have no enemy.
4. "Abstain from carnal and bodily 'lusts.' If any man smite thee on the right cheek, turn to him the other also," and thou wilt be perfect. "If any man impress thee to go with him one mile, go with him two. If any man take thy coat, give him thy shirt also. If any man take from thee what is thine, refuse it not"—not even if thou canst.
5. Give to anyone that asks thee, and do not refuse, for the Father's will is that we give to all from the gifts we have received.[7]

Nowhere was this tension between the two worlds more glaring than in their relationship to the state. Caesar demanded total loyalty for himself, but loyalty of Christians lay alone with Jesus. This resulted in direct clashes and serious hardship for the early Christians. And in line with a tradition they had inherited from the earlier apostles, they too understood themselves as martyrs. This ought to be seen in both the generic sense of being *witnesses* to Jesus Christ (the Greek term "martur" [μαρτυρ] means "witness"), and in the common meaning of the term to die for one's religious convictions.

One of the powerful stories of the early church is the martyrdom of Polycarp, who lived approximately 69–155 CE, was the bishop of Smyrna, and died as a martyr when he was eighty-six years old. I tell the story of his death because it highlights the early Christian understanding of faithfulness to Jesus. The issue for them was quite simple: it had to do with convictions about who saves—can Caesar save us or only Jesus Christ? This is important because it ties together the notions of soteriology and ethics that often get broken apart in Christian theology. That is, how you express your Christian life has

---

[5] This is not the place to discuss the intricacies around the martyrdom deaths of the many apostles; some of these are reported in the Bible, but most are mentioned only in other texts. Tradition has it that most of the first disciples and apostles were martyred. If we add together the biblical accounts and the larger tradition, we have the following list: John the Baptist, Peter, Andrew, James, Philip, Bartholomew, Thomas, Matthew (possibly), Jude, Simon the Zealot, Matthias, and Paul. Certainly this suffices to show the weight of the strong martyrdom tradition in the early church.

[6] E.g., "See to it that no one takes you captive through philosophy and empty deceit, according to human tradition, according to the elemental spirits of the universe, and not according to Christ" (Col 2:8).

[7] From Kirsopp Lake, ed., *The Apostolic Fathers* (London: Harvard University Press, 1970), 1:309.

everything to do with what you believe about who is ultimately able to deliver salvation.

The story of the martyrdom of Polycarp is recorded for us by Eusebius of Caesarea, the Roman historian from whom we receive much early church history. He claims to have received it as a copy of a letter written by the church of Smyrna to the church of Philomelium.

The story is narrated in the context of martyrdom more generally. The early church understood itself as bearing testimony or giving witness to the saving power of Jesus Christ. That is, the threat of death is of no consequence to or has no power over those who confess the saving power of Jesus Christ, because in Christ death itself has been overcome. The martyrs saw themselves as participating in the cross-resurrection event of Jesus Christ. In fact, martyrdom became an honor for many early Christians precisely because it made the identification with Jesus immediate. This did not mean that they saw Jesus merely as a martyr, but in their martyrdom they were being utterly faithful.

Since martyrdom was a public act and as such a public challenge to the gods of Rome, at one such event—the martyrdom of Germanicus—the people began to chant, "Away with the Atheists; let Polycarp be sought out!"[8] To understand this chant we need to remember that the Christians were denying the Roman gods and hence they could be called atheists. Moreover, Polycarp was asked for because he was the most famous of the teachers who persuaded people to leave the Roman gods.

Polycarp heard about the people's demand for his life but continued unperturbed in his work. Eventually, his friends convinced him to move to the country, where they thought he would be safe. "There he stayed with a few [friends], engaged in nothing else day and night than praying for all men, and for the churches throughout the world, according to his usual custom."[9] And while he was praying he had a vision that during his sleep the pillow under his head was on fire. And so he prophesied that he would be burned alive.

When the authorities came to search for him he was betrayed by one of his servants. (Notice throughout this story the parallelism with the account of the suffering and death of Jesus.) His persecutors had little difficulty finding him. Once they did, Polycarp refused to flee any more, saying, "The will of God be done."[10] When his persecutors arrived at his hiding place, he immediately addressed them, offered them food and drink, and then requested that he be given time to devote himself to prayer. They agreed and he prayed without ceasing for two hours. Some of his accusers were deeply moved. As soon as he stopped praying, they sought to persuade him, "What harm is there in saying, Lord Caesar, and in sacrificing with the other ceremonies observed on such occasions, and so make sure of safety?"[11] But Polycarp refused and was dealt with violently on the way to the stadium ". . . where the tumult was so great, that there was no possibility of being heard."[12] The story continues as follows:

> Now, as Polycarp was entering into the stadium, there came to him a voice from heaven, saying, "Be strong, and show thyself a man, O Polycarp!" No one saw who it was that spoke to him; but those of our brethren who were present heard the voice. And as he was brought forward, the tumult became great when they heard that Polycarp was taken. And when he came near, the proconsul asked him whether he was Polycarp. On his confessing that he was, [the proconsul] sought to persuade him to deny [Christ], saying, "Have respect to thy old age," and other similar things, according to their custom, [such as], "Swear by the fortune of Caesar; repent, and say, Away with the Atheists." But Polycarp, gazing with a stern countenance on all the multitude of the wicked

---

[8] "The Encyclical Epistle of the Church at Smyrna, Concerning the Martyrdom of the Holy Polycarp," in *The Ante-Nicene Fathers*, ed. Alexander Roberts and James Donaldson, American ed. vol. 1, *The Apostolic Fathers with Justin Martyr and Irenaeus* (Grand Rapids: Eerdmans, 1975), 40.

[9] "The Encyclical Epistle," 40.

[10] "The Encyclical Epistle," 40.

[11] "The Encyclical Epistle, "40.

[12] "The Encyclical Epistle," 41.

heathen then in the stadium, and waving his hand towards them, while with groans he looked up to heaven, said, "Away with the Atheists." Then, the proconsul urging him, and saying, "Swear, and I will set thee at liberty, reproach Christ;" Polycarp declared, "Eighty and six years have I served Him, and He never did me any injury: how then can I blaspheme my King and my Saviour?"

And when the proconsul yet again pressed him, and said, "Swear by the fortune of Caesar," he answered, "Since thou art vainly urgent that, as thou sayest, I should swear by the fortune of Caesar, and pretendest not to know who and what I am, hear me declare with boldness, I am a Christian. And if you wish to learn what the doctrines of Christianity are, appoint me a day, and thou shalt hear them." The proconsul replied, "Persuade the people." But Polycarp said, "To thee I have thought it right to offer an account [of my faith]; for we are taught to give all due honour (which entails no injury upon ourselves) to the powers and authorities which are ordained of God. But as for these, I do not deem them worthy of receiving any account from me."[13]

At this point, the proconsul threatened him with the wild beasts that he had at hand waiting for him. Polycarp challenged him to bring them on. Then the proconsul threatened him with fire if he did not repent, but again Polycarp encouraged him to commence the proceeding. After he spoke, the ". . . multitude of both the heathen and the Jews . . . cried out with uncontrollable fury . . . This is the teacher of Asia, the father of the Christians, and the overthrower of our gods, he who has been teaching many not to sacrifice, or to worship the gods."[14] They called for the lions but were told the show involving the wild beasts was over and the animals would not be called back. Then they requested that Polycarp be burned alive.

Wood was gathered and preparations were made for the fire. And as they prepared to nail him to the wood so he would not escape, as was the custom, Polycarp said, "Leave me as I am; for He that giveth me strength to endure the fire, will also enable me, without

your securing me by nails, to remain without moving in the pile."[15] His request was honored, and Polycarp was placed on the fire, praying to God.

> I give Thee thanks that Thou has counted me worthy of this day and this hour, that I would have a part in the number of Thy martyrs, in the cup of thy Christ, to the resurrection of eternal life, both of soul and body, through the incorruption [imparted] by the Holy Ghost. . . . Wherefore also I praise Thee for all things, I bless Thee, I glorify Thee, along with the everlasting and heavenly Jesus Christ, Thy beloved Son, with whom, to Thee, and the Holy Ghost, be glory both now and to all coming ages. Amen.[16]

When Polycarp was placed into the fire, an amazing thing happened—his body was not consumed and he was not injured. Of course, this perplexed his persecutors, and so they called an executioner to pierce him with a dagger. As the dagger entered his body, a dove flew out from the wound and a great quantity of blood gushed forth and extinguished the fire. Nevertheless, Polycarp died from his dagger wound.

When the Christians requested his body for burial, they were denied, ". . . lest forsaking Him that was crucified, they begin to worship this one."[17] Of course such a notion was thought absurd by the Christians. They could never forsake Christ, for he was the one who made martyrdom possible and necessary. Martyrdom had no meaning in itself, but only in relation to the one who was able to save them. "For [Jesus] indeed, as being the Son of God, we adore; but the martyrs, as disciples and followers of the Lord, we worthily love on account of their extraordinary affection toward their own King and Master, of whom may we also be made companions and fellow-disciples."[18] The body of Polycarp was then burned and the ashes were given to the Christians.

I recount this story here at some length to emphasize that martyrdom was a way of life

---

13 "The Encyclical Epistle," 41.
14 "The Encyclical Epistle," 41.
15 "The Encyclical Epistle," 42.
16 "The Encyclical Epistle," 42.
17 "The Encyclical Epistle," 42–43.
18 "The Encyclical Epistle," 43.

for the early Christians. To say this differently, they saw their task as being a *witness* to the saving power of Jesus Christ, which required enormous *perseverance* and *character*. And for them this meant to take up the cross and follow him. It is impossible to understand the ethic of the early church without seeing it in this light.

Martyrdom is but another way of expressing Christians' total otherness to the world without the God of Jesus Christ, and along with this their alternative moral character. And when they were confronted, their stance was witness; this meant they refused to defend themselves because they surrendered their defense to the one who raised Jesus from the dead. For example, Polycarp was able to say:

> But He who raised Him from the dead will raise up us also, if we do His will, and walk in His commandments, and love what He loved, keeping ourselves from all uprighteousness, covetousness, love of money, evilspeaking, falsewitness; "not rendering evil for evil, or railing for railing," or blow for blow, or cursing for cursing, but being mindful of what the Lord said in His teaching: "Judge not, that ye be not judged; forgive, and it shall be forgiven unto you; be merciful, that ye may obtain mercy; with what measure ye mete, it shall be measured to you again;" and once more, "Blessed are the poor, and those that are persecuted for righteousness' sake, for theirs is the kingdom of God." (*Polycarp, Bishop of Smyrna, ca. 100*)[19]

Virtually every early church "theologian" up to about 300 CE understood the Christian faith to mean that one's defense belonged to God and hence one could not participate in violence or in any form of killing—neither abortion nor capital punishment nor war. The Christian church was the kind of community that organized its life in accordance with the life, death, and resurrection of Jesus, and that meant concentrating on *giving* life—setting people free to live—not on taking life.

The sheer volume of material on this theme from the early church fathers is impressive. One after the other, they state what it means to follow Jesus and the themes of peace as discipleship are always there. I take the liberty to quote at some length some of the writings of these theologians.

> Thou shalt love Him that created thee: thou shalt glorify Him that redeemed thee from death. Thou shalt be simple in heart, and rich in spirit. Thou shalt not join thyself to those who walk in the way of death. Thou shalt hate doing what is unpleasing to God: thou shalt hate all hypocrisy. Thou shalt not forsake the commandments of the Lord. Thou shalt not exalt thyself, but shalt be of a lowly mind. Thou shalt not take glory to thyself. Thou shalt not take evil counsel against thy neighbour. Thou shalt not allow over-boldness to enter into thy soul. Thou shalt not commit fornication: thou shalt not commit adultery: thou shalt not be a corrupter of youth. Thou shalt not let the word of God issue from thy lips with any kind of impurity. Thou shalt not accept persons when thou reprovest any one for transgression. Thou shalt be meek: thou shalt be peaceable. . . . Thou shalt love thine neighbour more than thine own soul. Thou shalt not slay the child by procuring abortion; nor, again, shalt thou destroy it after it is born. . . . Thou shalt not call things thine own; for if ye are partakers in common of things which are incorruptible, how much more [should you be] of those things which are corruptible. (*Barnabas, an Alexandrian Jew, ca. 100*)[20]

> [W]e who were filled with war, and mutual slaughter, and every wickedness, have each of us through the whole earth changed our warlike weapons,—our swords into ploughshares and our spears into implements of tillage,—and we cultivate piety, righteousness, philanthropy, faith, and hope, which we have from the Father Himself through Him who was crucified. (*Justin Martyr, a Gentile born A.D. 100, ca. 130*)[21]

> We have learnt not only not to strike back and not to go to law with those who plunder and rob us, but with some if they buffet us on the side of the head, to offer the other side of the head to them

---

[19] Polycarp, "The Epistle of Polycarp to the Philippians," in *Ante-Nicene Fathers*, 33.
[20] Barnabas, "The Epistle of Barnabas," in *Ante-Nicene Fathers*, 148.
[21] Justin Martyr, "Dialogue with Trypho," in *Ante-Nicene Fathers*, 254.

for a blow, and with others if they take away our tunic to give them also our cloak.

For it is not enough to be just (and justice is to return like for like) but it is incumbent on us to be good and patient of evil.... For when they know that we cannot endure even to see a man put to death, though justly, who of them can accuse us of murder or cannibalism? ... And when we say that those women who use drugs to bring on abortion commit murder, and will have to give an account to God for the abortion, on what principle should we commit murder? (*Athenagoras, a Christian Greek philosopher, ca. 175*)[22]

In peace not in war we are trained. War needs great preparation, but peace and love, quiet sisters, require no arms, no expensive outlay. Various peoples incite the passions of war by martial music; Christians employ only the Word of God, the instrument of peace....

If you enroll as one of God's people, heaven is your country and God your lawgiver. And what are His laws? ... Thou shalt not kill.... Thou shalt love thy neighbour as thyself. To him that strikes thee on the one cheek, turn also the other. (*Clement of Alexandria, ca. 180*)[23]

For those who before were quite perverse and who let [*sic*] no evil work undone, now that they have come to know and to believe in Christ and as soon as they have embraced the faith, have changed their manner of living, and they adhere to the strictest demands of righteousness. (*Irenaeus, disciple of Polycarp of Smyrna, ca. 185*)[24]

Shall it be held lawful to make an occupation of the sword, when the Lord proclaimed that he who takes the sword shall also perish by the sword? And shall the son of peace take part in battle when it does not become him even to sue in law? ... How shall a Christian man wage war, nay, how shall he even be a soldier in peacetime, without the sword, which the Lord has taken away? ... Christ in disarming Peter ungirt every soldier. (*Tertullian from Cathage, first theologian to write in Latin, ca. 200*)[25]

No longer do we take the sword against any nation nor do we learn war anymore since we have become the sons of peace, for the sake of Jesus who is our leader. (*Origen from Alexandria and Palestine, ca. 225*)[26]

We could go on to cite statements from Hippolytus, Minucius Felix, Cyprian, Maximilian, Arnobius, Lactantius, Martin, Bishop of Tours, and others well into the fourth century to show that an overwhelming number of early church fathers led the charge in favor of peace and pacifism and hence opposed actions like abortion, violence, and other worldly customs.

An important factor in all of this is their view of ecclesiology, which is more presupposed than spelled out. Yet it is important for understanding their view of ethics. First, there is the *authority* issue. In the church, Christ and his teachings are the authority. There must be no diffusing of this authority with Caesar or with anyone else. Second, there is a sharp *dualism* between church and world, or, put more narrowly, Christ and Caesar. The two simply do not have anything in common. Caesar sheds blood, the church does not; the world is idolatrous in that it worships Caesar, money, and power, the church worships the one and only true God who, in Christ, told us that it is wrong to want to be Lord and exercise power. The polarity is real and at every point calls forth a different ethic. It is only when the church sees itself over against the world and Caesar that it can understand itself as church. Third, embedded within the body of the church are the moral qualities of the apostolic teaching that sustain the church's identity: *perseverance*, *character*, and *witness*.

This separatist ecclesiology is important for understanding the ethics of the early church. It means that the church does not first of all understand itself abstractly and theologically and then ask what kind of ethic it should embrace. Its ethic is its being. The early church, as Stanley Hauerwas reminds

[22] Quoted from William R. Durland, *No King But Caesar? A Catholic Lawyer Looks at Christian Violence* (Scottdale, Penn.: Herald, 1975), 73.

[23] Durland, *No King But Caesar?*, 74–75.

[24] Durland, *No King But Caesar?*, 75.

[25] Durland, *No King But Caesar?*, 76.

[26] Durland, *No King But Caesar?*, 77.

us, does not have an ethic; it is an ethic.[27] Its ethic is revealed when its theology is expressed, and its theology is seen aright when its ethic is lived.

Yet we should not think that the early church was a static entity for three hundred years. It changes in many respects as it comes to view the world and the state with greater and greater favor. This has a profound effect on its ethical self-understanding because it gradually shifts the focus from self-identity to a form of global identity.[28]

As the state becomes more tolerant of Christians, the Christians experience less and less persecution. Somewhere around 170, Tertullian reports that there are a few Christians in the army. Yet he has a strong argument with tradition on his side that it is wrong for Christians to be so involved. Christians have never been in the army before because it is inconsistent with what they are called to be. This inconsistency is not due to the specific nature of this particular army; for example, that it is a form of idolatry, and hence another army which is not idolatrous could be joined by Christians. Tertullian argues that it is wrong because of what armies do and what Jesus says Christians cannot do. But as persecution lets up and as more and more second- and third-generation Christians know less and less of persecution, the people become less critical of the state and of the world. Hence, it is easier to see how participation in the army is not inconsistent with being a Christian.

In addition, the church sees part of its task as making the Christian faith intelligible to the non-Christian world around it. Hence, it begins to use the language of the world. For example, it starts expressing Christian ideas in terms of Greek philosophical notions such as wisdom. This leads to the Christian language becoming intermixed with the language of the world. While this change is inevitable and even necessary in order to give a faithful account of its faith, nevertheless it had the effect that the church began to see itself as less different.

With less distance between church and world, the greater the loyalty to the powers of the state. From here it is just a small step to thinking that bringing about God's kingdom can indeed be a joint effort. This will be the topic of our next chapter.

---

[27] Stanley Hauerwas, *The Peaceable Kingdom: A Primer in Christian Ethics* (Notre Dame, Ind.: University of Notre Dame Press, 1983), 99.

[28] John Howard Yoder traces this shift in his *Christian Attitudes to War, Peace and Revolution: A Companion to Bainton* (Elkhart, Ind.: Co-op Bookstore, 1983).

Chapter Four

MEDIEVAL CHURCH ETHICS I

Admittedly it is a highly selective process to decide which movements/symbols/writers to highlight in this rich period of church history. The options are extremely vast. One chapter can hardly suffice for even a token presentation of its impact on our thinking about ethics today. To help somewhat, the "Medieval Church Ethics" discussion is divided into two chapters. This chapter focuses on Constantine and Augustine, the next on Thomas Aquinas and late medieval thought. Even so, we cannot give this period of history the attention it deserves.

CONSTANTINE (272/4–337)

A great deal of controversy centers on Constantine, the great Roman emperor. Some see his rule as a watershed in the concept of the church: before there was, and after there was not, a faithful church. Not only the church is at stake here, but some argue that because of the church's apostasy, so-called "orthodox theology," which was largely formulated after Constantine—indeed some of it even led by Constantine—is not a reliable expression of biblical theology.

Others believe that the church survived because of the work of Constantine. Had it not been for the turn to favorable status of Christians, the persecution experienced prior to Constantine could well have destroyed the church. Hence, he is heralded as a great defender of the faith and as a great man of God.

We need to leave many of the intricacies of this debate for another time, as our focus here is quite specific. Our goal is to understand what shifts, if any, took place in the understanding of faithful Christian living, in other words, the concern for Christian ethics.

I begin with Constantine's conversion to Christianity. Even here there is controversy. Was it authentic, or was it merely an effective ploy to enhance his chances of military victory and unifying the empire? Admittedly, this is a difficult question to settle, and certainly it is presumptuous to question the veracity of anyone's conversion. Nevertheless, it is important to examine the view of the Christian faith that underlies this very interesting figure. It is especially significant to determine how it relates to the theology of the early church and how it affected the way the Christian life is framed. At the same time, it must be said that what really matters here is not the man but the impact of the ecclesiological shift associated with his thought and political theology.

The early Roman church historian Eusebius of Caesarea gives the standard account of Constantine's conversion. It should be said at the outset that Eusebius' panegyric of Constantine's life presupposes that it was the will of God that Constantine become the "prince and sovereign" of the empire.[1]

---

[1] For this story I will rely on Eusebius, "The Life of Constantine," in *The Nicene and Post-Nicene Fathers of the Christian Church*, 2nd ser., vol. 1, ed. Philip Schaff and Henry Wace (Grand Rapids: Eerdmans, 1976), 481ff.

The context for the story is that in 308 Constantine was considering the "liberation" of Rome from a "tyrant" named Maxentius. Says Eusebius of Constantine: "Life was without enjoyment to him as long as he saw the imperial city thus afflicted, and [he] prepared himself for the overthrowal of the tyranny."[2] Hence, he contemplated how this might be done since his army was no match for the enemy. Here is a lengthy excerpt from Eusebius' account.

> Being convinced, however, that he [Constantine] needed some more powerful aid than his military forces could afford him, on account of the wicked and magical enchantments which were so diligently practiced by the tyrant, he sought Divine assistance, deeming the possession of arms and a numerous soldiery of secondary importance, but believing the co-operating power of Deity invincible and not to be shaken. He considered, therefore, on what God he might rely for protection and assistance. While engaged in this enquiry, the thought occurred to him, that, of the many emperors who had preceded him, those who had rested their hopes in a multitude of gods, and served them with sacrifices and offerings, had in the first place been deceived by flattering predictions, and oracles which promised them all prosperity, and at last had met with an unhappy end, while not one of their gods had stood by to warn them of the impending wrath of heaven; while one alone who had pursued an entirely opposite course, who had condemned their error, and honored the one Supreme God during his whole life, had found him to be the Saviour and Protector of his empire, and the giver of every good thing. Reflecting on this, and well weighing the fact that they who had trusted in many gods had also fallen by manifold forms of death, without leaving behind them either family or offspring, stock, name, or memorial among men: while the God of his father had given to him, on the other hand, manifestations of his power and very many tokens: and considering farther that those who had already taken arms against the tyrant, and had marched in the battle-field under the protection of a multitude of gods, had met with a dishonorable end (for one of them had shamefully retreated from the contest without a blow, and the other, being slain in the midst of his own troops, became, as it were, the mere sport of death); reviewing, I say, all these considerations, he judged it to be folly indeed to join in the idle worship of those who were no gods, and, after such convincing evidence, to err from the truth; and therefore felt it incumbent to honor his father's God alone.
>
> Accordingly he called on him with earnest prayer and supplication that he would reveal to him who he was, and stretch forth his right hand to help him in his present difficulties. And while he was thus praying with fervent entreaty, a most marvellous sign appeared to him from heaven, the account of which it might have been hard to believe had it been related by any other person. But since the victorious emperor himself long afterwards declared it to the writer of this history, when he was honored with his acquaintance and society, and confirmed his statement by oath, who could hesitate to accredit the relation, especially since the testimony of after-time has established its truth? He said that about noon, when the day was already beginning to decline, he saw with his own eyes the trophy of a cross of light in the heavens, above the sun, bearing the inscription, CONQUER BY THIS. At this sight he himself was struck with amazement, and his whole army also, which followed him on this expedition, and witnessed the miracle.
>
> He said, moreover, that he doubted within himself what the import of this apparition could be. And while he continued to ponder and reason on its meaning, night suddenly came on; then in his sleep the Christ of God appeared to him with the same sign which he had seen in the heavens, and commanded him to make a likeness of that sign which he had seen in the heavens, and to use it as a safeguard in all engagements with his enemies. At dawn of the day he arose, and communicated the marvel to his friends: and then, calling together the workers in gold and precious stones, he sat in the midst of them, and described to them the figure of the sign he had seen, bidding them represent it in gold and precious stones. And this representation I myself have had an opportunity of seeing. . . . The emperor constantly made use of this sign of salvation as a safeguard against every adverse and hostile power, and commanded that others similar to it should be carried at the head of all his armies.[3]

---

[2] Eusebius, "Life of Constantine," 489.
[3] Eusebius, "Life of Constantine," 489–91 (emphasis in original).

Some reflections: first, we note that the "reasons" for becoming a Christian are utilitarian. Which god has worked better in the past and therefore which god is it better to worship today *in order to achieve the desired military-political ends?* This is a rather peculiar motive/rationale for becoming Christian. God, on this account, is seen as a power source at the emperor's disposal, which, upon proper appeasement, can net the emperor vast personal benefits. This bears virtually no resemblance to the biblical and early church view, where God was revered because God was Creator, Savior, and Sustainer of the universe. In God lay the victory; therefore it was right and proper for God's sake, not for your own, to be willing to die for God's cause, as many early Christian martyrs did. For Christians of the early church, it was wrong to kill enemies, not to mention plotting to aggressively destroy them. These Christians believed that Jesus meant what he said when he told his disciples to love their enemies.

Second, assuming the authenticity of the vision, it is peculiar that it would not have occurred to Constantine that "CONQUER BY THIS"[4] meant something entirely different than the meaning he assigned to it. His interpretation was only possible in the absence of the larger narrative of Jesus Christ, which gives the cross specific meaning. If he had understood the cross via the Christianity of the early church, he could not possibly have concluded from such a vision that he was to use it as a weapon to kill his enemies in the name of Christ. This is not because the cross had nothing to do with how one relates to enemies but because it gave the opposite answer. The early Christians would have read "CONQUER BY THIS" to mean, like Jesus had said to his own disciples, and indeed as Jesus endured in his own life, that they too were now being asked to "take up the cross and follow him." That is, rather than seek the

death of enemies they, like Christ, were to be willing to die in their stead, should it come to that. Constantine's reading of the sign was a military reading from the start. He seems not to have had the linguistic and conceptual skills to see that which he had never seen before, namely, the power of God in Jesus Christ. He understood there to be only one power, namely, military power. So if the cross was to help him, it could do so only as a weapon of war.

Third, we should take note that in the end the sign becomes a "sign of salvation." (Eusebius says, "The Emperor constantly made use of this *sign of salvation*.") Perhaps this should not be surprising, given that Eusebius sees Constantine as a great servant of God. Nor, of course, is it inappropriate to link the cross with salvation. Yet it is interesting to see how Constantine understood salvation. Again it is abstracted from the biblical story. Constantine saw salvation primarily in terms of "liberating" his people from "dictators"; perhaps more accurately, the overthrowing of emperors whom he judged to be dictators. Of course, salvation as "liberation from oppressive rulers" is not foreign to the Bible either. However, the paradigmatic biblical liberation story, the exodus, was an act of a liberating God, not the violent acts of a military commander. Since Constantine had no way of knowing about a God who liberates supramilitarily, he seems to have had available to him no other interpretation of salvation but that of violent overthrow. Hence, for the first time in the Christian church, but certainly not the last, war became a way of salvation. This is something that the Christians of the first centuries would not have seen as consistent with the teachings of Jesus.

It is not surprising that the Eusebius account spells out how the conversion of Constantine resulted in new-style military escapades. When he entered Rome and drove

---

[4] In Latin "In hoc signo vinces" and in Greek, "εν τούτωι νίκα." The Greek is significant because Constanine used it as his motto in the Milvian bridge battle, and the Greek letters chi (X) and rho (P), the first two letters from the name of Christ (Χριστός), were brought together to form the image of the cross called the *Labarum*. According to tradition, this cross was used extensively in military battles.

out the tyrant Maxentius, he sent him fleeing across the Milvian bridge, which collapsed from the weight of his equipment, destroying Maxentius' entire army. Eusebius describes this event in all the splendor and style of an Old Testament holy war.

> For as once in the days of Moses and the Hebrew nation, who were worshippers of God, "Pharaoh's chariots and his host hath he cast into the sea, and his chosen chariot-captains are drowned in the Red Sea,"—so at this time Maxentius, and the soldiers and guards with him, "went down into the depths like a stone. . . ."[5]

Notice how the good/evil dichotomy gets set up in Constantine's favor. Having found the "right god" means that he automatically succeeds in battle over the one he sees as God's enemies. And when you fight God's enemies, your victories are God's victories. Again, this form of human identification with divine agency is in tension with the understanding of divine agency in the early church. Embracing the doctrine of the incarnation and the church as body of Christ, they were content to be agents of God's salvation by giving voice to the great acts of God, in the manner of Matthew 5:16: ". . . let your light shine before others, so that they may see your good works and give glory to your Father in heaven." And when it came to violence as a mode of dispute resolution, they saw the cross-resurrection of Christ as the model.

Constantine took full advantage of the "power of the gospel" to promote his own military and political goals. After the liberation of Rome, he

> immediately ordered a lofty spear in the figure of a cross to be placed beneath the hand of a statue representing himself, in the most frequented part of Rome, and the following inscription to be engraved on it in the Latin language: BY VIRTUE OF THIS SALUTARY SIGN, WHICH IS THE TRUE TEST OF VALOR, I HAVE PRESERVED AND LIBERATED YOUR CITY FROM THE YOKE OF TYRANNY. I HAVE ALSO SET AT LIBERTY THE ROMAN STATE AND PEOPLE, AND RESTORED THEM TO THEIR ANCIENT DISTINCTION AND SPLENDOUR.[6]

Eusebius reports how Constantine was heralded as *the* new great agent of God's mercy and grace.

> Thus the pious emperor, glorying in the confession of the victorious cross, proclaimed the Son of God to the Romans with great boldness of testimony. And the inhabitants of the city, one and all, senate and people, reviving, as it were, from the pressure of a bitter and tyrannical domination, seemed to enjoy purer rays of light, and to be born again into a fresh and new life.[7]

The political theology of the Constantine event resolves at least one side of the earlier tensions between the state and church. As we saw in the previous chapter, polarity between the church and the state was perceived to be categorical on both sides. This was so because both demanded ultimate loyalty; both were politically interested. This polarity now morphed into a synthesis. The two realms were no longer incompatible, but complementary. Whereas the Christian minority had formerly lived in a hostile pagan state, with Constantine and his "Christianized" state, church and state became one. From that point on, Christians and non-Christians were pushed to coexist in one moral realm, where the emperor is both ruler and bishop.

In 313 CE the Edict of Milan was issued by Constantine and Licinius. It resolved

> to grant both to the Christians and to all men freedom to follow the religion which they choose, that whatever heavenly divinity exists may be propitious to us and to all that live under our government.[8]

Constantine's goal was to unify the empire. And to do so he saw it as his task to unite the Christians behind his leadership. Becoming Christian himself (although he was only baptized just before his death in 336) gave him status and power within the church; this, in turn, allowed him to influence its

---

[5] Eusebius, "Life of Constantine," 493.
[6] Eusebius, "Life of Constantine," 493 (emphasis in original).
[7] Eusebius, "Life of Constantine," 494.
[8] Eusebius, "The Church History of Eusebius," in *Nicene and Post-Nicene Fathers*, 379.

direction, to some extent even its theology. For example, he called and presided over early church councils, like the Council at Nicea (325), which produced the Nicean Creed. He helped work out theological differences within the church, and he issued more and more edicts giving favored economic and social status to Christian institutions.

Eventually, the union of church and empire was made official in 389 by Emperor Flavius Theodosius, and the persecution of Christians stopped. There was now no theological quarrel between the church and empire, and so the church took on an important new role. Yet when the empire becomes Christian, it requires that a distinction be made within the church itself; that is, between those who are Christian by conviction and those who are Christian by virtue of birth into a Christian state. So gradually, new definitions of faithfulness were formulated having important ecclesiological implications. One dichotomy that was invented fell between the "religious" and the "laity." The state gave special exemptions to the clergy that the laity did not enjoy. Why? Because it was beneficial to the state. Clergy were exempt

> from all public duties, that they may not by any error or sacrilegious negligence be drawn away from the service duty to the Deity, but may devote themselves without any hindrance to their law. For it seems that when they show greatest reverence to the Deity, the greatest benefits accrue to the state.[9]

This new language of the church bears little resemblance to the self-description of the early church. When everyone is a member, then the theology of the "Two Ways" no longer works very well. Yet ecclesiological dualism is not so easily overcome. One of the ways it now finds expression is with the distinction between the visible and the invisible church. This is the first element of the Constantinian shift. For the early Christians, the church was visible, that is, it was a socially and publicly constituted counter-body

that everyone could see. After Constantine, everyone understands that the socially embodied church—the visible church—is not the true church in the sense that it is not the community of the faithful and committed. So where is the true church to be found? It is internal, hidden in the hearts of men and women for God alone to see. It is not any kind of social embodiment at all. It is a disembodied aggregate of individuals known only to God. In terms of sociopolitical governance, the "true church" does not exist.

Closely related is a second important shift. For early Christians, the church was itself a political body in that it addressed issues pertaining to economics, governance, power, and enemies. Now the church and state tacitly agreed to a kind of division of labor where the church as worshipping community dealt with the spiritual and personal and the state with the physical and political. Hence, the church in effect lost its political relevance and relegated that task to the state.

This leads to a third ecclesiological shift, namely, that God is now seen as governing the world through the emperor and not through the church's faithful. This had a profound impact for how to understand the movement of history—the faithful no longer have a direct role in this process. The "true church" is irrelevant with regard to how the world moves forward. Its "political" function is replaced with a purely religious purpose. Devoutly religious Christians have no pertinent advice to give to their leaders that comes from their commitment to following Jesus; political leaders should listen to them in this regard only as it pertains to their individual spiritual life.

Fourth, a distinction is now generated between the clergy and the laity. Insofar as one can speak of a visible church at all, it now becomes associated with the church hierarchy: clergy of the church who administer the sacraments and provide other important religious exercises. And, as we have already seen, "the religious" live by one ethic and the

---

[9] Eusebius, "Church History," 383.

laity by another. This dualism seems to rest on an inherent contradiction of the Constantinian synthesis that affirms that everyone is Christian by law yet confesses at the same time that not everyone is Christian by conviction. Constantine's state needed Christians who did not live by the ethic of Jesus, that is, who did not take their faith to have political relevance and uncritically obeyed the political authorities.

Fifth, when Christianity gets extended to all peoples of the Roman Empire, the source as well as the standard for evaluating the source must come from elsewhere than the Bible and the insights of the worshipping community. To say this differently, when a particular (biblical) imagination gets universalized, appeals for sustaining it also become universal, like common sense, reason, nature, human nature, and so on. Such sources are reminiscent of Greco-Roman Stoicism, but not of Christianity. In the end it must be said that Constantine was more Stoic than he was Christian. Christian communities that meet regularly for worship learn the meanings of their symbols by retelling the stories in which they function. In the absence of these stories, their meanings get badly misconstrued. Their employment "out of context" so distorts their true character that, although it may well have minimal appeasement value to the faithful, nevertheless, their use cannot long survive unless they are given a new theological home, and thereby a new meaning.

Let me summarize the ethical import of the Constantinian shift by placing ourselves within his world. The ruler of the nation is now one of us and we feel a Christian duty to give him advice; to do that we need to think about ethics from his perspective. Yet, to quote John Howard Yoder:

> [W]e cannot tell him to be like Jesus or do what Jesus said. We can't give the emperor the guidance of a pre-Constantine ethic; that won't work. Why won't that work? Because he couldn't stay in

power, and staying in power is necessary. We want him to stay in power because we would rather have him in power than one of the others. And a ruler does after all what needs to be done. God wants him to stay in power, in order to rule the world, even if to do that means accepting a non-Jesus ethic. It is better that that be done by one of us than by someone who isn't one of us.[10]

This shift has far-reaching implications for moral reasoning. Whether an act is right or wrong now is not directly determined by reference to Jesus, but by considerations like "What would happen if the emperor did it?" or "What would happen if everyone did it?" In other words, we are now more interested in whether history comes out right for us and through us than we are in the question of being faithful to Jesus. And, of course, we set ourselves up as the judge both of how history is, in fact, moving and whether it is moving in the right direction—both at best dubious human competencies. Pre-Constantinian Christians could not have understood such a thing. And for us, this shift demonstrates the fracture of what for the early Christians was necessarily connected: ethics and the worshipping community.

The yearning for faithful Christian living goes on, however. And one of the great thinkers to struggle intently with the matter of Christian faithfulness within both the givenness of historical contingency and the profound love and mystery of God is the great theologian-philosopher Augustine.

SAINT AUGUSTINE (354–430)

Augustine lived and wrote while seeing the workings of a Christian Empire up close. This empire was both the nest in which he hatched his theological eggs and the foil against which he formulated many of his ideas. Says Rowan Williams:

> Constantine had made the Christian religion fully legal in 313, and Theodosius had made it the official creed of *imperium Romanum* in 389. Yet Augustine in *The City of God* treats the Empire as

---

[10] John Howard Yoder, *Christian Attitudes to War, Peace, and Revolution: A Companion to Bainton* (Elkhart, Ind.: Co-op Bookstore, 1983), 49.

doomed, and justly so, as a "city" built on violence and oppression whose long-deserved nemesis has at last come. For Rome had fallen to the Goths in 410, and Augustine is writing those who regard this as a catastrophe for the church. . . . Whatever the social order, the church is still on a pilgrimage and the "Christian Empire" is as transitory and ambiguous a phenomenon as any other social form. Augustine lived to see the near-total collapse of Roman authority in the province of Africa; he died as the barbarians began the siege of Hippo. To him, as to most sensitive Christians in Africa and Western Europe, any notion of the Empire as a sacral kingdom under divine protection would have been painfully absurd.[11]

Augustine wrote many treatises, sermons, biblical commentaries, books, and responses to specific issues in the church. Two of his most famous books are *Confessions* and *The City of God*. *Confessions* is unique as a genre of books. In it, Augustine puts into words his own personal adventures of faith with the conviction that the hand of God is everywhere at work in his life, even when he does not see it. While an autobiography of sorts, it is so much more than a chronology of personal events; for it gives expression to the conviction that human beings find their own true identities, and therefore their purpose and well-being, in God. As he puts it, "*Noverim te, noverim me*" (I would know you [God], I would know myself). The story of his life, as is the story of everyone's life, is for him the homecoming of a wandering child; for only in God do we find our true home.

The notion that all that is finds its true identity in ultimate goodness and beauty—God—is of course reminiscent of neoplatonism. Yet Augustine moves considerably beyond the rationalism of Greek thought. For him, desire and passion are as determinative in shaping who we are as is human reason, since human beings long for God precisely because God has become present

to us, touching us in the flesh. He says, "You called, and cried aloud, and forced open my deafness. You gleamed and shine, and chase away my blindness. You exhaled odours, and I drew in my breath and do pant after You. I tasted, and do hunger and thirst. You touched me, and I burned for Your peace."[12] In other words, we are driven to God, whether we are committed Christians or not, by the passion within us, which is itself rooted in God. And Augustine's entire life story gets cast within this paradoxical tension of a "united" passion and reason.

Augustine was born in a small city called Tagaste in the North African province of Numidia (today Souk-Ahras, Algeria). His mother, Monica, was a devout Christian and his father, Patricius, until very late in his life, was not. His mother's tireless efforts to bring her son into the Christian fold was eventually to be realized, but not until he was thirty-two years old.

When Augustine went to Carthage at the age of fifteen to study rhetoric, he began a fifteen-year live-in relationship with his first mistress. From this relationship, he received a son in 372 when he was a mere eighteen years old. They named him Adeodatus, Latin for "the gift of God." Adeodatus proved to be an important source of strength and support to Augustine. He was a dialogue partner in several of his writings (for example, *The Teacher*), and they were baptized together in 387.

All his life, Augustine was a serious truth-seeker. Initially he was greatly inspired by the philosophical writings of Cicero (106–43 BCE), the Roman philosopher and statesman. For nine years (373–382), he was a follower of Manichaeism, a Persian dualistic philosophy popular at the time. But when Manichaeism collapsed into undeniable contradiction for him, Augustine resorted to

---

[11] Rowan Williams, *The Wound of Knowledge: Christian Spirituality from the New Testament to Saint John of the Cross* (Cambridge, Mass.: Cowley, 1990), 101.

[12] Augustine, *Confessions*, bk. X, chap. XXVII, para. 38, included in *Nicene and Post-Nicene Fathers*, 1st ser., vol. 1, trans. J. G. Pilkington, ed. Philip Schaff (Grand Rapids: Eerdmans, 1974). Quoted here from a revised edition for *New Advent* by Kevin Knight, available online at http://www.newadvent.org/fathers/1101.htm.

skepticism. Not until 383, when Augustine went to Rome, did he begin a serious struggle with the Christian faith.

It was a year later, at Milan, where he came under the influence of neoplatonism (especially Plotinus). In Milan he was given a promising position as professor of rhetoric in the New Academy. Yet the most profound influence came from another source, the great bishop, Ambrose (340–397). He speaks of the powerful sermons he heard the bishop of Milan preach. It was here that his doubts about Christianity began to resolve themselves. He recounts the story of how it all came to a head one day in 386. He was having one of his many deep, spiritual struggles in the company of a friend, Alypius. But this time the results of his struggle were amazingly different from other times. He recounts it in vivid detail.

> But when a profound reflection had, from the secret depths of my soul, drawn together and heaped up all my misery before the sight of my heart, there arose a mighty storm, accompanied by as mighty a shower of tears. Which, that I might pour forth fully, with its natural expression, I stole away from Alypius; for it suggested itself to me that solitude was fitter for the business of weeping. . . . I flung myself down, how, I know not, under a certain fig tree, giving free course to my tears, and the streams of mine eyes gushed out, an acceptable sacrifice unto thee. And, not in these words, yet to this effect, spake I much unto thee,—"But thou O Lord, how long?" "How long, Lord? Wilt thou be angry for ever?" . . . I was saying these things and weeping in the most bitter contrition of my heart, when, lo, I heard the voice as of a boy or girl, I know not which, coming from a neighboring house, chanting, and oft repeating, "Take up and read; take up and read." Immediately my countenance was changed, and I began most earnestly to consider whether it was usual for children in any kind of game to sing such words; nor could I remember ever to have heard the like. So, restraining the torrent of my tears, I rose up, interpreting it in no other way than as a command to me from Heaven to open the book, and to read the first chapter I should light upon. . . . So quickly I returned to the place where Alypius was sitting; for there had I put down the volume of the apostles, when I rose thence. I grasped, opened, and in silence I read that paragraph on which my eyes first fell—"Not in rioting and drunkenness, not in chambering and wantonness, not in strife and envying; but put ye on the Lord Jesus Christ, and make not provision for the flesh, to fulfil the lusts thereof" (Romans 13:13, 14). No further would I read, nor did I need; for instantly, as the sentence ended—by a light, as it were, of security infused into my heart—all the gloom of doubt vanished away.[13]

Not long after this momentous experience, Augustine's mother died with joy in her heart. It was as though her life was now complete, and she could go in the peace and assurance of the salvation of her son. On Easter eve 387, at the age of thirty-two, Augustine was baptized by Bishop Ambrose. It was a special joy for him to be baptized with his son, Adeodatus, and his close friend, Alypius.

Augustine was as intense about his Christian faith as he had been about his other beliefs. Shortly after his baptism, he returned to Tagaste in North Africa, where he established a small religious community. In 391 he was ordained as priest, and only a few years later (395), he was named bishop of Hippo (now Annaba, Algeria), a post he held until his death in 430.

Augustine was a prolific writer. There is hardly a theological topic he does not address, always seeking to give intelligent answers to questions of the faithful. He speaks of his conversion experience as having "renewed his whole mind." It is important to inquire in what way this happened. Clearly his thoughts are now different from before, but interestingly, they are also different from those expressed by early church theologians. His unique style and theology emanate from his specific background and the set of philosophical issues he felt needed to be addressed. Cicero's Roman philosophy, neoplatonism's Greek thought, Manichaeism's Persian ideas were all to be "overcome" in order to embrace

---

[13] Augustine, *Confessions*, bk. XIII, chap. XII. Quoted from "The Confessions of St. Augustin," in *Nicene and Post-Nicene Fathers*, 127–28.

Christianity. Yet, this very struggle left an imprint on him. For example, in the early church the operative question was, "Does this come from Jesus and the Scriptures?" If not, it was not Christian. In other words, Jesus and the Bible were the only norms. One might say that it was largely an internal hermeneutic. The task of the early church writers was not to figure out how biblical understanding related to other forms of thought but rather to gain the courage to live as disciples of Jesus in a time when that was not the norm—they were separatists and not integrationists. Augustine's context was different. For example, his context was no longer one where the Empire and the social environment were hostile to Christianity. Moreover, his struggle with skepticism required a kind of *rationalization* that needed to answer why a way of thinking based on Jesus' life and teaching *made more sense* than other alternatives. His battle with Manichaeism required an interpretive scheme with superior rhetoric and logic to the available alternatives. And for this, neoplatonism proved a helpful framework.

Two matters of general importance for Christian ethics warrant comment here. The first has to do with how source relates to content. Here Augustine learned much from his bishop. Ambrose saw no difficulty in relying on other sources for his articulation of the Christian life. Says Roland Bainton about Ambrose, "His tract *On the Duties of the Clergy* was a free reworking of Cicero's *De Officiis*."[14] Cicero was a Roman philosopher whose ethical source and content was nature and not Jesus and the Bible. Moreover, Ambrose was one of the first to make a distinction between the ethics of some and the ethics of all. For example, he argued that individual Christians should not defend themselves by killing another person, and clerics should not, under any circumstance, participate in war, but neither logic was extended to the population at large acting under the authority of the state.

Yet we should be careful not to conclude that Ambrose and Augustine did not rely upon the Scriptures. No early church theologian quotes Scripture more often than Augustine. What is important is the manner in which he reads and "uses" the Bible. It is not merely an ancient book for him; it connects with this world and its problems and its interpretations. Or, to say it differently, the word of God is incarnate in Jesus Christ; God becoming present *in this world* meant that this world was fundamentally infused with the being of God. It also meant that the content of the Christian faith is housed in human social and intellectual forms. All this suggests that there is no pure content and no pure form.

The second comment has to do with Augustine's view of Christian faithfulness. Just as theology is not done in a vacuum, so faithfulness is nonsense without context. This can be seen in the biblical narrative itself. For example, when the Israelites asked Samuel for a king so they could be "like other nations" (1 Sam 8:5), Samuel saw this as unfaithfulness. And, of course, it clearly was not the model of obedience for either Samuel or the Lord, according to the narrative. Yet in the end the Lord said, "Listen to their voice and set a king over them" (1 Sam 8:22). A concession perhaps, but the suggestion is that the goals and expressions of faithfulness were possible this way as well. Similarly, Augustine never wavered in his belief that, while the "Christian Empire" may not be the best context for the Christian life, faithfulness was nevertheless possible within it, even if now it had to take on different forms.

To understand Augustine's account of the Christian faith we need to examine how he resolved the issues that stood in the way of his conversion, namely, Manichaean dualism.

Mani (ca. 216–276), a Persian philosopher who attempted to amalgamate Zoroastrianism, Buddhism, Christianity, and Gnosticism, had argued that the universe was

---

[14] Roland H. Bainton, *Christian Attitudes Toward War and Peace* (Nashville: Abingdon, 1960), 90.

governed by two contending forces (realms or powers): light and darkness. Originally they were, and ontologically they are, separate and independent realms, but in our lives these forces are mixed and sometimes difficult to sort out. The Manichaeans drew heavily from Greek Gnosticism and held that matter is evil and spirit is good. Redemption therefore comes via flight from the body (matter) and is fulfilled in the mystical union with the great light, God. In real life, such redemption is only gradually attainable; hence, there are two classes of people: those who have not yet reached spiritual perfection and those who have. The latter (the elect) live by strict moral discipline; they are vegetarian, celibate, and abstain from alcoholic drink. Their life is devoted to teaching the way of truth. They become one with the great light upon death while those who have not yet attained this level return to earth to continue the road to perfection.

Augustine eventually rejected Manichaean thought as heresy, even though a remnant of the dualism of light and darkness remained with him throughout his writings. It is noteworthy that it was neoplatonism that helped him see the irrationality of Manichaeism. Neoplatonism teaches that the supreme Good, knowledge of which alone can give life its meaning, is God. Hence, only insofar as we turn to God are we able to find true happiness. Knowledge of the physical world is nothing in comparison to knowledge of God.

Augustine accepted the basic dualistic philosophy of neoplatonism while rejecting the ontological dualism of Mani. That is, Augustine found it unacceptable to embrace a dualism that postulated the independent existence of two opposites: good and evil. He now saw that this postulate was in tension with the view that God was the creator of all that is. It forced him either to accept that God did not create all, or that God created evil—both are intolerable to Christian belief. A good God cannot create evil; an omnipotent God cannot have rival creators.

The dualism of neoplatonism presented a resolution for Augustine's struggle because it was not a metaphysical dualism. Plato and the Platonists viewed evil as negative, as privation or the absence of good. That is, evil as an ontological entity did not exist. Something was evil only insofar as it did not participate in the good, or did not do so fully. The Platonists did not say that something was evil because it participates in badness. That would have required the idea of badness (evil) to exist. It did not! Evil was nonbeing! Yet, similar to Mani, the Platonists (as did Augustine to a degree) also associated evil with the material and goodness with the spiritual-intellectual. Ideas were good. Things were good insofar as they participated in goodness. This is because matter tended away from the ideal and ideas tended toward it.

Yet Augustine went further than most Platonists in two ways. First, he argued that ideas are good because they exist in the mind of God. They become ours through illumination (that is, by becoming light to us) via God's graciousness toward us. Hence, all illuminating knowledge is knowledge via God. God alone is the teacher of truth because God is Truth. Notice the universality inherent in Augustine's epistemology, which is a significant shift from the way the early church Christians understood their faith. The early Christians knew what they knew because it made sense to them via the particular story of Jesus, not via a more general epistemology.

Second, and this is really the ground for his epistemology, for Augustine all that is—creation as such—exists only insofar as it participates in God, the Creator. This does not mean that God is somehow immanent, visible in created matter, touchable in the objects and animals around us, for God is beyond being—transcendent—and remains ineffable even though knowable in part. But it does mean that all animals from the smallest ant to the highest human form and all objects and items of matter are properly understood only when they are seen to be more than they appear to be, namely, as given to us by the one who willed this world into existence. So reality is gift and to understand it only in re-lation to itself is anathema for Augustine. In this way he sought to give expression to the Apostle Paul's notion of the Christian doing all and seeing all "in Christ."

We should notice that the way Augustine has set up his rejection of Manichaean meta-physical dualism leads him to a new way of speaking about the Christian life. How is he now to account for evil acts? If evil has no positive reality, how is it to be conceived? Perhaps the most significant shift Augustine introduces into the language of Christian eth-ics is the concept of human will.[15] When the will is directed away from God, and toward things like self-interest, money, or anything else material, it is evil; when it is directed to-ward God, it is good. This makes sense be-cause God alone is good, and this is also why humility (openness beyond self) is good and pride (love of self) is the core of evil. In other words, a good will is a will directed to God; a bad will is a will directed away from God.

Augustine goes on to say that we are natu-rally inclined toward God, even though we are prone to turn away and seek other av-enues of life. Whenever our will is in tune with God's, we are in harmony with our own innermost being, whether we can see this or not, and happiness will be ours. However, when we turn away from God, we also turn away from our own essence and evil comes our way. Our will is free, but if it is not subject to the love of God, it destroys us. We are free to turn to God or to turn away from God. In the former is life; in the latter is death. Hence Augustine can say, *dilige, et quod vis fac* (love and do what you will).[16]

We need to explore further Augustine's thesis that the will is morally primary. At first

blush one wonders whether he really means that evil stems only from a bad will and nothing else. Is it not proper to enquire what causes the will to be bad? Can the will's be-ing badly trained or misinformed not be the cause of it acting badly? For Augustine, ap-parently not! Speaking about wicked people, he says:

> If the further question be asked, What was the ef-ficient cause of their evil will? there is none. For what is it which makes the will bad, when it is the will itself which makes the action bad? And consequently the bad will is the cause of the bad action, but nothing is the efficient cause of the bad will.[17]

This is a new formulation of how human beings are understood morally. Augustine's explanation of why we do bad things is not in terms of lack of knowledge, or bad rea-soning, or lack of discipline, as it seemed to be with the early Christians, but in terms of a will directed to the self (pride) and away from God. And this way of speaking about the moral life had direct implications for how Augustine spoke of the virtues. The Greeks, as we have seen, believed that the virtues were necessary to direct, discipline, or shape (cause?) the will, because without ongoing habit-forming practices, the will remains weak and is prone to wander into evil. Au-gustine spoke of the virtues in a different way. With the primacy of the will disconnected from reason and discipline and directed only to God, Augustine thought of the virtues not as human skills but as themselves fundamen-tally related to God.

> For although some suppose that virtues, which have a reference only to themselves, and are de-sired only on their own account, are yet true and genuine virtues, the fact is that even then they are

---

[15] J. Philip Wogaman says, e.g., "To Augustine, there is no evil outside the will" and again, "Augustine, thus, grounds Christian ethics in the moral will, not in the goodness or evil of objects outside the will. The will is good or bad in accor-dance with what it worships and loves. A will directed by its love for God is good, while a will directed by love of self and lesser goods is evil—even though these lesser goods are not, in themselves, evil" (*Christian Ethics: A Historical Introduction* [Louisville, Ky.: Westminster John Knox, 1993], 51, 53).

[16] Quoted from Vernon J. Bourke, *History of Ethics*, vol. 1 (Garden City, N.Y.: Image Books, 1968), 83.

[17] Augustine, *City of God*, bk. XII, chap. 6. Quoted from "St. Augustin's City of God," trans. Rev. Marcus Dods, in *Nicene and Post-Nicene Fathers of the Christian Church*, 1st ser., vol. 2, ed. Phillip Schaff (Grand Rapids: Eerdmans, 1977), 229.

inflated with pride, and are therefore to be reckoned as vices rather than virtues.[18]

Hence, since the role of the virtues is to please God, the virtues are themselves products of the will of God. To say it differently, the will chooses the virtues; the virtues do not shape the will, as the Greeks had emphasized. The virtues cannot govern the will in the service of God. That would violate the primacy of the will. This leads Peter Lombard, twelfth-century scholar, to paraphrase the so-called Augustinian definition of the virtues as follows: "Virtue is the good quality of the mind, by which we live righteously, of which no one can make bad use, which God works within us, but without us."[19]

By speaking of Christian ethics in this way, Augustine introduced a new set of problems: namely those associated with the will. Particularly important is the relation between the human and divine wills. It should be pointed out that will-language is not only the new language of human goodness; it is also the language of God's goodness. That is, goodness must be understood as that which God wills. For our wills to be good then, requires that they be "in" God's will. Obviously God's will is morally superior to ours, hence authoritative. Moreover, God foreknows our wills. So how then does Augustine connect God's goodness and foreknowledge with our freedom to will?

Sorting out the thorny issues around this cluster of questions occupied an inordinate amount of Augustine's energy. It also pits his view of the Christian life against an alternative view espoused by his contemporary Pelagius (ca. 354–418?),[20] whose theology was judged as heretical when Augustine's view received the stamp of orthodoxy. If we

are to understand the controversy between Pelagius and Augustine properly, we must give at least brief attention to the thought of Pelagius.

Pelagius was a "British monk" who struggled, on the one hand, with the demands of the holy life as presented in the Sermon on the Mount, and on the other hand, with how he saw it lived around him. He felt that the "Christian Empire" promoted the idea of "pagan Christians" who, after baptism, too easily lapsed "back into their old, comfortable habits of self-indulgence and careless pursuit of Mammon."[21]

Pelagius took the Christian life very seriously. In fact, he gave up his career and became an ascetic devoted to the task of living as a disciple of Jesus. As he puts it, "A Christian is one who is not merely such in name but in works, who in all things imitates and follows Christ."[22] Pelagius understood himself as anything but a heretic. He accepted with deep devotion the theology of the church councils. He saw his work as explicating orthodoxy, but he took issue with the notion that humans should see themselves as unable to do what God in the Bible asked them to do, like living a holy life.

His theology holds a central place for the notions of the righteousness of God and the possibility of humans living in accordance with what God requires of us. A righteous God would not demand more of us than we are able to give. So if God expects us to live righteously (for example, to obey the Ten Commandments, to sell all we have and give to the poor, to turn the other cheek, to love and forgive our enemies, and so on), it must be possible. And when we do sin, we will be held accountable. The only way to escape

[18] Augustine, *City of God* in *Nicene and Post-Nicene Fathers*, 2:418–19.

[19] Quoted from Vernon J. Bourke, ed., *The Essential Augustine* (Indianapolis: Hackett, 1974), 149–50.

[20] These dates cannot be verified. After the Pelagian doctrine was condemned as heretical at a Council of Carthage in 418, Pelagius disappeared, and it is thought that he died shortly after.

[21] B. B. Rees, *Pelagius: A Reluctant Heretic* (Woodbridge, Suffolk: Boydell, 1988), 20.

[22] Pelagius, *Liber de vita christiana*, chap. 6 in *Patrologiae, Cursus Completus*, Series Latina, ed. J. P. Migne (Paris, 1844ff.), 40, col. 1037. Quoted from Bernhard Lohse, *A Short History of Christian Doctrine: from the First Century to the Present*, trans. F. Ernest Stoffler (Philadelphia: Fortress, 1985), 109.

the consequences of sin (death) is through repentance and God's forgiveness, which, when sought, is *graciously* given.

It is important to note that Pelagius spoke highly of God's grace, albeit in a manner different from Augustine. Bernhard Lohse summarizes the difference nicely.

> For Pelagius grace means, on the one hand, that we are endowed with reason and on the other that we have been given the law. It is grace that we are able by nature to fulfill God's law. In Pelagius, therefore, grace is associated with creation, while in Augustine it is associated with redemption. Beyond this, Pelagius understands grace to be something more, namely, the forgiveness of sin.[23]

One of the doctrines that Pelagius rejected was that of original sin. He simply could not believe that the sin of Adam was transmitted to successive generations via the carnal acts of past humanity. This kind of thinking, he believed, was inspired by Manichaean dualism that held matter to be evil. He believed that it was definitely inconsistent with a Christian theology proclaiming the *embodiment* of God in Jesus and the divine origin of the *material* world. For Christians, matter cannot be viewed as evil, and he saw Augustine's theology to be in danger of heresy at this point. Moreover, righteous God would not hold us accountable for the sins of others, even though the sins of past generations may affect our own propensity to sin.[24] The task of Christians was to pray and meditate and in various other ways discipline themselves to be the kind of people who, through their way of life, bear witness to their allegiance to Jesus the Christ.

An important teaching for Pelagius was the Patristic notion of watchfulness (*nepsis*). In a "Letter to Demetrias," he counsels a fourteen-year-old woman who, while engaged to be married, took the vows of chastity. In this letter he stressed that Christians need to cultivate disciplines that protect them from the temptations to evil.

> All your care and attention must be concentrated on keeping watch, and it is particularly necessary for you to guard against sin in the place where it usually begins, to resist temptation at once the very first time it appears and thus to eliminate the evil before it can grow and spread.[25]

Augustine saw the theology of Pelagius as heretical because it relied too heavily upon *human* (natural) reason and merit. This is not to say that Augustine relied less upon reason, however. In fact, there are those scholars who draw an association between him and Descartes, the father of modern rationalism, although clearly that is a stretch.[26] But he did reach different conclusions from those of Pelagius. The differences can be seen in at least three areas.

First, the sense in which he argues that our wills are free is different. Augustine was greatly troubled by Pelagius invoking his name for support of the thesis that human wills are unconditionally free. According to Augustine, the theory of free will espoused by the Pelagian heretics "leaves no place for the grace of God, since they hold it is given in accordance with our merits."[27] One might well forgive Pelagius' (mis)reading of Augustine given his repeated emphasis on the primacy (the uncaused nature) of the will.

---

[23] Pelagius in *Short History of Christian Doctrine*.

[24] For further discussion on this, see Pelagius in *Short History of Christian Doctrine*, 108.

[25] B. B. Rees, trans., "Letter to Demetrias," in *The Letters of Pelagius to his Followers* (Woodbridge, Suffolk: Boydell, 1989), 26:3. See also Deacon Geoffrey Ó Raida, "Pelagius: To Demetrias," http://www.brojed.org/pelagius.html, for an analysis of Pelagius' thought.

[26] See, e.g., Augustine, *The Teacher* and *On Free Will*. Although in the latter, at one point, he seeks to demonstrate "that there is something above reason," bk. II, 14, the argument is still made on the basis of the assumption that "each of us has his own private rational mind," bk. II, 15. These quotes are taken from *Philosophy in the Middle Ages: The Christian, Islamic, and Jewish Traditions*, ed. Arthur Hyman and James J. Walsh (Indianapolis: Hackett, 1973), 38. Moreover, in Augustine, *City of God*, bk. XI, 26, he is sometimes taken to be foreshadowing Descartes' famous dictum *cogito ergo sum* (I think therefore I am) with his own *si . . . fallor sum* (if I am mistaken, I am).

[27] *Retractations*, bk. I, chap. 9, no. 3. Quoted from *Philosophy in the Middle Ages*, 65.

Nevertheless, Augustine's view of the human will as free is only properly understood when it is seen "within" the will of God. Because of the sin of Adam and Eve (original sin), the human will has been permanently distorted. Left on our own, we are condemned to evil acts. We cannot do good on our own. To be able to choose freely between good and evil therefore requires the grace of God. Only in this way can we do good acts and only in this way can we be free.

Second, and closely connected to the first, because our wills are made good by the grace of God, the God-human relationship is most properly characterized by God's love—grace—to us. Hence, we cannot will this relationship; instead God wills it. There simply could not be a God-human relationship at all (again because of original sin) if it were not for a gracious God, who comes to us in spite of our sinfulness. This leads directly to the doctrine of predestination. The only thing we can do is to respond positively or negatively when God comes to us. We can open ourselves to God's grace, or we can close ourselves to it. If we do the former we will live at peace with God, with each other, and with ourselves; if we do the latter we will not. But we can never merit God's grace.

Third, God, who is eternal, does not have knowledge from the standpoint of time but only from the standpoint of eternity. Hence, God already foreknows all of our actions, past, present, and future. Yet this does not mean that our actions are not our own. God's foreknowledge and predestination are essential because without God we can do no good. This both ensures our freedom—since without God we could choose only evil—and positions our understanding of our own goodness and freedom. Our worth is not derived from our meritorious actions (we cannot do any good on our own) but from the grace of God, who enables us to have a good will.

With Augustine's influence on the African bishops to be vigilant for correct theology, they collectively appealed to church authorities, and by 418 the Carthage councils pronounced Pelagianism as heresy. This decision

had the effect of making Augustine's theology—and not Pelagius'—the norm for the church.

Another of Augustine's legacies is his formulation of a theology of history. He does not provide us with a philosophy of history in the manner of Georg Hegel in the nineteenth century, but he does speak to questions like: How can we understand God's rule in the world? How are we to see God's kingdom? And his answer invokes the metaphor of two cities: the city of God—also sometimes called Jerusalem—and the earthly city—also called Babylon. The city of God identifies all those who are elected of God and are in his will, and the earthly city identifies those who are not. He puts it this way:

> Accordingly, two cities have been formed by two loves: the earthly by the love of self, even to the contempt of God; the heavenly by the love of God, even to the contempt of self. The former, in a word, glories in itself, the latter in the Lord. For the one seeks glory from men; but the greatest glory of the other is God, the witness of conscience. The one lifts up its head in its own glory; the other says to its God, "Thou art my glory, and the lifter up of mine head" (Ps. 3:3). In the one, the princes and the nations it subdues are ruled by the love of ruling; in the other, the princes and the subjects serve one another in love, the latter obeying, while the former take thought for all. The one delights in its own strength, represented in the persons of its rulers; the other says to its God, "I will love Thee, O Lord, my strength" (Ps. 28:1). And therefore the wise men of the one city, living according to man, have sought for profit to their own bodies or souls, or both, and those who have known God "glorified Him not as God, neither were thankful, but became vain in their imaginations, and their foolish heart was darkened; professing themselves to be wise" (Rom. 1:21-25),—that is, glorying in their own wisdom, and being possessed by pride,—"they became fools, and changed the glory of the incorruptible God into an image made like to corruptible man, and to birds, and four-footed beasts, and creeping things." For they were either leaders or followers of the people in adoring images, "and worshipped and served the creature more than the Creator, who is blessed for ever" (1 Cor. 25:28). But in the other city there is no human wisdom, but only godliness, which offers due worship to the true

God, and looks for its reward in the society of the saints, of holy angels as well as holy men, "that God may be all in all."[28]

Augustine's neoplatonic dualism is strongly evident here. In respect to matters true, religious, and moral, the heavenly city (*De Civitate Dei*) is our authority, yet the earthly city is our habitation for the time being. We must make the best of it while we are here, that is, do what we can to make it as tolerable as possible knowing all the while that our true citizenship is in another city. It is important to note that for Augustine these two cities exist "indistinguishably from the beginning of the human race to the end of the world, through the changing ages and destined to be separated at the last judgment."[29]

This way of speaking about the kingdom of God has important implications for an understanding of the church and Christian ethics. First, the church, which bears a special relationship to the city of God but, of course, is both visible and invisible. The visible church is intermingled with both those who have renounced the love of self for the love of God and those who have not. For baptism within the church (the outer sign of church membership) is no guarantee of salvation. The invisible, that is, the "real church" is known only to God. In the end, members of each will receive their just rewards, and only a few will come to see God. Yet it is important to note that the visible church—that body that can be seen in its concrete practices and politics—bears a relationship to the true church much like Plato's Republic to the ideal state, namely, one of "participation" in something beyond itself. And such participation can only be marked by practices that point beyond themselves known as sacraments.

Second, consider the implication of Augustine's thought on Christian ethics. As he saw it, God is present in this world, actively bringing into existence the reign of peace and justice for all. Even in places where we may have given up, or in acts we may write off as outside of God's grace, God is still present and redeeming what is not whole. For example, God may well be working through the executioners bringing about good.[30] Christian ethics has to do with participating in God's activity of redemption in this world. Hence, Augustine is able to justify Christian participation in activities that would at first blush seem unbecoming a disciple of Jesus. Furthermore, as is suggested by the notions of the visible and invisible church, God's rule is mysterious, which means that our own moral obedience participates in divine mystery. But how is this participation to be understood?

For Augustine, although the church is clearly imperfect, it already enacts the truth of the city of God through the practice of the sacraments. Sacraments are visible signs of the invisible reality of God's presence and activities. Augustine had a particular understanding of sign, which related closely to Plato's theory of forms, where the material world is a "manifestation" of invisible ultimate reality. Sacraments are signs of the truth and, as such, both reveal and veil truth. As signs, they are revelatory and participate in that to which they point. In this way they are also "objective," meaning they are effective in their revelation on account of Christ and not on account of either the ministrant or the recipient. That is, they are effective *ex opere operato*, which means they are still valid even if an unholy minister administers them. This is because the sacrament is not a human

---

[28] Augustine, *The City of God*, bk. XIV, chap. 28. Quoted from *Nicene and Post-Nicene Fathers of the Christian Church*, 2:282–83.

[29] *On Catechizing the Uninstructed*, 21, 37, in Bourke, *The Essential Augustine*, 227.

[30] Actually Augustine makes a much stronger point in *On Order* (2.4.12), an early writing on the problem of evil (probably written in 387). Here he argues that executioners are necessary for the greater good. However, it is unclear whether he still held this view at the end of his life even though he would clearly maintain that God can create good out of the acts of the executioner, as horrible as those events may be. For a further discussion see John M. Rist, *Augustine: Ancient Thought Baptized* (Cambridge, Mass.: Cambridge University Press, 1994), 207–8.

word/act but emphatically Christ's word/act. Augustine argues this against the Donatists who deny that sacraments are effective when administered by an unholy minister.

We can see, therefore, that Augustine's Christian ethics is inherently connected to sacramental theology. This is largely possible because he has adopted a structure of metaphysics and ethics that is similar to Plato. Even though it is quite different in content, nevertheless he is able to speak of goodness and our participation in it by holding a relationship of the material reality to the Trinity in a matter analogous to Plato's relation between objects and the Good.

We must now try to pull the many strands of Augustine's thought together for the purposes of understanding how Christians should behave. It seems that he has moved rather far from the content of Plato's *Republic*, the Aristotelian polis, and the early church community conceptions of ethics. For Augustine there seems to be no explicit community shaping the moral life; there is only the interaction between God and the self. And all people are deeply affected by the sting of original sin. We cannot escape its grasp on us by ourselves since the will (the locus of action) has been corrupted and the community of truthful believers cannot help us because we know not who they are. But God chooses to save us; we can be freed from this enslavement and can respond positively. When we do, we are changed, attitudinally and motivationally. That is, the change is an inner one of spirit, not necessarily an outer public one.

The value of the claim that God's rule is invisible is readily apparent—for who can say precisely where God is at work? But Augustine may well be pushing this claim too far. He seems to be suggesting that, as far as God is concerned, the inner alone matters. Outer appearances are unimportant. He puts it thus: ". . . when philosophers themselves become Christians, they are compelled,

indeed, to abandon their erroneous doctrines, but not their dress and mode of living, which are no obstacle to religion."[31] And since externals are unimportant, Augustine believes he has found a medium for uniting the church. Whether you are rich or poor, whatever your lifestyle is, indeed what you do, is not relevant to the faith. These are all issues that divide us. What you believe, what your thoughts and attitudes are, how you do what you do, how you are inwardly disposed to God are the important things. But when Jesus speaks of the faithful followers, he puts it precisely in terms of outward signs such as wealth: selling what you have and giving it to the poor; that is, Jesus speaks about what Augustine would call irrelevant externals.

This has left some ethicists to suggest that Augustine may not have left Manichaeism as far behind as he might have. True, he rejected the *metaphysical* independence of good and evil, which enabled him to affirm the supremacy of God, but he substituted an alternative dualism which one might call trajectory dualism: movement toward God—good—and movement away from God—evil. And by associating the latter with matter—acts, body, earthly city—and the former with spirit—attitude, soul, heavenly city—he still ends up with a reformulation of an old dualism with some new implications for the Christian life.

Such reasons have led Roland H. Bainton, respected Yale University church historian, to suggest the following:

The inwardness of Augustine's ethic served to justify outward violence, because right and wrong were seen to reside not in acts but in attitudes. Such a distinction had proved very useful in explaining the apparently unchristian deportment of the patriarchs of the Old Testament. Elijah, for example, was warranted in calling down fire from heaven because at the same time he had love in his heart, whereas the disciples were rebuked for wishing to do likewise against the Samaritans because the wish was prompted by vengeful intent. Killing and love could the more readily be squared

---

[31] Augustine, *City of God*, bk. XIX, chap. 19. Quoted from *Nicene and Post-Nicene Fathers*, 2:423.

by Augustine because in his judgment life in the body is not of extreme importance. What matters is eternal salvation. The destruction of the body may actually be of benefit to the soul of the sinner.[32]

Actions are now evaluated on the basis of information which is not public. I cannot judge another's action as wrong because I am privy to the inner disposition of only my own soul. Above all, I cannot know whether God willed another person to do whatever that person is doing. Right and wrong are, on Augustine's model, determined on the basis of private intentions and not public behavior. Hence, the Christian life is as mysterious as is God's rule. In principle it cannot be sorted out. The very attempt to do so would be to presume to know God's will. This makes *Christian* ethics a very difficult enterprise and tends to give credence to the notion that we ought to do what *makes common sense,* albeit, we ought to do it with a Christian disposition.

One issue of common moral concern which Augustine discussed throughout his writings was that of war and peace. He was not the first Christian theologian to argue that Christians could/should participate in war under certain conditions. Bishop Ambrose, who was a military man before he became a bishop and therefore found it easy to believe that defending the faith and defending the empire could be complementary acts, had already given a Christian rendering of some of Plato's and Cicero's thoughts on war. Although Augustine nowhere gives a systematic treatment of a just war, most would agree that he was the first to give the notion of a just war its official sanction.

Augustine does not say that Christians should do as the pagans do when it comes to war. In fact, he says the very opposite. Wars are always lamentable, but they are

sometimes necessary. He intended the just-war theory to put controls on wars by establishing rules, making them less violent, and determining when wars were necessary. Nevertheless, for the Christian and for the empire, this theory had a profound impact. It should not go unnoticed that by the year 416 it was illegal for anyone who was not a Christian to be in the military. Christians were simply better warriors.[33]

The just-war theory has a rich history and has been refined many times by ethicists after Augustine. I will present the theory here as found in Augustine's writings.[34] According to Augustine, the code of conduct within war (*jus in bello*) and the justification for declaring war (*jus ad bellum*) are qualified by six conditions in order to be just. First, and most general, is the requirement that a war should be just in its intention. To say this differently, a war can only be justified if the will which governs it is a good will. The intention cannot be to seek revenge, or to appease one's anger, or to amass control of large territory, but to seek peace and justice. War must be seen as a last resort and a necessary evil, never as a first option or as a good thing. In fact, leaders should bemoan the necessity of needing to declare even a just war. There should be no gloating or reveling in victory. Says Augustine, advising Count Boniface, governor of the province of Africa:

> Peace should be the object of your desire. War should be waged only as a necessity and waged only that through it God may deliver men from that necessity and preserve them in peace. For peace is not to be sought in order to kindle war, but war is to be waged in order to obtain peace. Therefore even in the course of war you should cherish the spirit of a peace maker.[35]

Second, a just war must be waged on the basis of a proper inward disposition, namely Christian love. Augustine has already shown

---

[32] Bainton, *Christian Attitudes,* 92.

[33] See, e.g., Jean-Michel Hornus, *It Is Not Lawful For Me To Fight: Early Christian Attitudes Toward War, Violence, and the State,* rev. ed. (Scottdale, Penn.: Herald, 1980), esp. the chapter "Christian Soldiers and Soldier Saints," 118–57.

[34] For a detailed elaboration of the just-war theory, see Yoder, *Christian Attitudes to War,* 67–71.

[35] Quoted from Bainton, *Christian Attitudes,* 96.

that the intent of an act is more important than the act itself. Hence there is, for him, no tension between the Sermon on the Mount teaching to love our enemies and a summons to kill them.

> If it is supposed that God could not enjoin warfare, because in after times it was said by the Lord Jesus Christ, "I say unto you, That ye resist not evil: but if anyone strikes you on the right cheek, turn to him the left also," the answer is, what is here required is not a bodily action, but an inward disposition.[36]

And again:

> You may chastize but it is love that does this, not cruelty. You may strike but you do it for disciplinary reasons because your love itself does not permit you to leave the other person undisciplined. At times what comes from love and hatred seems self-contradictory. Hatred sometimes comes out in sweet tones and love in harsh ones.[37]

Third, the object of a war must be to vindicate justice. Although Augustine did not define clearly what he meant, nevertheless, he believed that wars of aggression could not be justified while attacks on the state could. In addition when states were unjustly restricted, such as being denied passage to important trade routes, war could also be justified.[38]

Fourth, a war can be declared only by a legitimate authority. This rules out all civil wars and rebellions by people taking matters of political justice into their own hands. Augustine believed the state had the God-ordained function to provide peace and security in a way that no one else did. They were therefore God's representatives in matters of national security and peace. So if wars were declared by anyone else it would be wrong.

> A great deal depends on the causes for which men undertake wars, and on the authority they have for doing so; for the natural order which seeks the peace of mankind, ordains that the monarch should have the power of undertaking war if he thinks it advisable, and that soldiers should perform their military duties in behalf of the peace and safety of the community. When war is undertaken in obedience to God, who would rebuke, or humble, or crush the pride of man, it must be allowed to be a righteous war; for even the wars which arise from human passion cannot harm the eternal well-being of God, nor even hurt His saints; for in the trial of their patience, and the chastening of their spirit, and in bearing fatherly correction, they are rather benefited than injured. No one can have any power against them but what is given him from above. For there is no power but of God, who either orders or permits.[39]

Fifth, the conduct of war must be just. Many of the rules which govern proper conduct for warfare were common to those of earlier traditions. "Faith must be kept with the enemy. There should be no wanton violence, profanation of the temples, looting, massacres, or conflagration. Vengeance, atrocities, and reprisals were excluded, though ambushes were allowed."[40] Says Augustine:

> What is the evil in war? Is it the death of some who will die in any case, that others may live in peaceful subjection? This is mere cowardly dislike, not any religious feeling. The real evils in war are love of violence, revengeful cruelty, fierce and implacable enmity, wild resistance, and the lust of power and such like; and it is generally to punish these things, when force is required to inflict the punishment, that, in obedience to God or some lawful authority, good men undertake wars.[41]

Sixth, only soldiers can fight in war. It stands to reason from what Augustine has said thus far regarding the proper functions of different aspects of a God-ordained state structure that each would require training proper to the execution of its role. Soldiers therefore need to be trained to handle the job of killing properly. For example, ordinary citizens could not do a task of this nature without passion, hatred, and anger. Only soldiers, with much discipline, can kill enemies from

---

[36] Augustine, *Reply to Faustus the Manichaean*, in *Nicene and Post-Nicene Fathers*, 4:301.
[37] Quoted from Wogaman, *Christian Ethics*, 58.
[38] See Bainton, *Christian Attitudes*, 96, for further discussions on this point.
[39] Augustine, *Reply to Faustus the Manichaean*, in *Nicene and Post-Nicene Fathers*, 4:301.
[40] Bainton, *Christian Attitudes*, 97.
[41] Augustine, *Reply to Faustus the Manichaean*, in *Nicene and Post-Nicene Fathers*, 4:301.

the disposition of Christian love. Likewise, those belonging to a religious order should not be soldiers because they have devoted themselves to the special tasks of fulfilling the function of the church and not the state. God wants them to pray, heal, and lead in worship. They should be exempt from such earthly matters as marriage, private property, and war.[42]

With the aid of these six qualifiers, Augustine sought to bring together his two most passionate Christian convictions. On the one hand, transcendent God invites us to mysteriously participate in the New Jerusalem by putting on the dispositions which Christ spoke of in the Sermon on the Mount and which the Apostle Paul preaches about in his epistles. On the other hand, we are bound by the human fate of this-worldly "Babylon-existence," which limits all our efforts at Christian perfection and hence requires our constant repentance for our own sins and God's gracious forgiveness. Our participation in the maintenance of public justice, peace, and security often requires violence because of the reality of sin in this world, but it ought never to stem from hatred, revenge, or anger.

In summary, the genius of Augustine's view of the Christian life was the introduction of the will and its attachment to inner intentions and convictions. Granted, he differentiates the two realms of morality by way of city imagery, which sounds inherently social and not merely individualistic,[43] yet he presents a view of the Christian life which has made it easy for those who came after him to cultivate the mystical and spiritual in a manner that has neglected the establishment of viable, peaceful, socio-political institutions of justice. Rightly or wrongly, Augustine's writings have been used to "depoliticize" the gospel. Yet we should not be too quick to dismiss his contributions to a vision of morality. After all, he introduced a radically new understanding of the very notion of politics. The real contribution of the monastics, whom he inspired and who so dominated the medieval expression of Christian faithfulness for centuries after Augustine, was an attempt at teaching by alternative example. So perhaps the discipleship ethics of the early church was not so much replaced as it was recast and reconceived.

---

[42] See Bainton, *Christian Attitudes*, 98.

[43] It should be acknowledged, however, that the view that Augustine presents an individualistic understanding of both the state and the church is being challenged. For example, John Milbank says, "Augustine, in particular, has been interpreted as foreshadowing Protestantism and liberalism. It is contended that he invents an individualistic understanding of both the Church and the state, because, on the one hand, he interprets the state as merely a compromise between individual wills for the satisfaction of material conveniences, and, on the other, he understands the Church, the Civitas Dei, as the collection of the elect true believers, known only to God. This contention, is, however, almost totally erroneous" (*Theology and Social Theory: Beyond Secular Reason* [Cambridge, Mass.: Blackwell, 1990], 400).

Chapter Five

MEDIEVAL CHURCH ETHICS II

At the conclusion of the previous chapter, it became clear that Augustine's theology played a significant role in laying the groundwork for a long tradition within the Christian church called *monasticism*. Although proper historical analysis of this tradition would require study of the linkage between medieval monasticism and much earlier ascetics such as John the Baptist, Augustine's thought had a lasting impact, especially within some Eastern Christian traditions. Today we still find strong monastic orders and desert monasteries in places like Egypt and Palestine, where the daily rituals, voluntary poverty, and mystical theology resemble the fifth century.

Although Augustine himself was not a reclusive monk, his life's story, especially the manner in which he tells it, is often seen as an example of a monastic style of religious exercises.[1] In his *Confessions*, we notice again and again a triadic movement in his pattern of resolving spiritual struggles. First, he withdraws from the worldly influences around him; second, he turns inward to his own soul; and third, he calls on transcendent God to resolve his struggle. This ritualized pattern is basic to monastic spirituality.

There are two kinds of early ascetics, the *anchorites* and the *cenobites*.[2] The anchorite monks were primarily concerned with

their own salvation and with keeping themselves pure from evil around them. They felt that they needed to withdraw from the influences of the sinful world in order to be Christian. Among them you find the desert hermits, the extreme of whom practiced lifetime seclusion and voluntary confinement to small cells with minimal human contact. The cenobites, on the other hand, were communal monks. Although they also understood themselves as separatists, and their lives were devoted to being apart from the sinful world around them, they were nevertheless apart as a community and not as individuals. Their view of salvation was to live in an alternative *society*, structured on Christian–discipleship–of–Jesus practices. This could only be accomplished through separation from the world, albeit community separation. At the same time, the separation was not only intended as a way of saving themselves; it was also a way of teaching the world what it meant to follow Jesus. How else would the world understand but via the distinctiveness of such a life made visible by an alternative society?

One might wonder whether monasticism with its strong emphasis on discipleship was not in tension with Augustine's teaching on salvation by grace. That is, was the monastic tradition not much closer to

---

[1] See, e.g., Vernon J. Bourke, *The Essential Augustine* (Indianapolis: Hackett, 1974), 150.

[2] For a helpful discussion of these two forms of monasticism, see esp. C. H. Lawrence, *Medieval Monasticism: Forms of the Religious Life in Western Europe in the Middle Ages* (London: Longman, 1984). See also J. Philip Wogaman, *Christian Ethics: A Historical Introduction* (Louisville, Ky.: Westminster John Knox, 1993), 63–74, for a general discussion of the ethical significance of monasticism.

77

works-righteousness than to salvation by grace? Was it really necessary to "leave" this world in order to please God? Strictly speaking, the monks might well have said no. However, the monastic life permitted a foretaste of heavenly existence which this world can never know. Hence, while it was not necessary to leave the world, separation was the manner of claiming a greater portion of salvation than one could claim by remaining in the world.

Renunciation and discipline were key to both the anchorites and the cenobites. Voluntary poverty was, for example, seen as the lived expression of the faith that our well-being does not reside in material possessions. Chastity and celibacy were lived expressions of the faith that salvation entails the cultivation of the gifts of the spirit and not the flesh and that the Christian church does not grow biologically but by conversion. The recognition of the power of "the flesh" (the material world) led monks and nuns to commit themselves to a life of rigorous discipline. Cultivating the Christian virtues comes only with constant repetition and diligent habit-forming consistency. Hence, monasteries are places with many rules and rigid routines. The anchorites and cenobites disagreed over which virtues and rules are most important and how best to cultivate them. For example, St. Basel of Caesarea (330–379), who was a cenobite, says, "If you live alone, whose feet will you wash?"[3] However, on the renunciation of the world, all ascetics were agreed.

SAINT BENEDICT (CA. 480–550)

For centuries the Rule of Saint Benedict has been the norm for Western monasticism. Although Benedict, an Italian, was inspired by the Egyptian and Palestinian ascetics, and in this respect was not that different from many other abbots and hermits, it was the popularity of his Rule, especially in Europe, that has earned him his central place in the history of monasticism. The most significant impetus for his prominence was the publication of two books by Pope Gregory the Great: the *Life of St. Benedict*, his biography, and *Dialogues*, his hagiography.

C. H. Lawrence summarizes Gregory's portrayal of Benedict's life thus:

> Gregory tells us that Benedict was born in central Italy in the province of Nursia—the conventional date of 480 is pure surmise—and was sent to Rome for his education in liberal letters. But distressed by the debauched life of his fellow-students, he abandoned the schools, "knowingly ignorant and wisely untaught", and fled with his nurse to the village of Afide, some twenty miles away. From there he withdrew to the solitude near Subiaco, a deserted spot in the Sabine Hills, where he lived in a cave for three years. During this time he was supplied with bread by a monk named Romanus from a nearby monastery, who also instructed him in the practice of the ascetical life. Gradually disciples settled around him, and he organised them into groups of twelve, appointing an abbot over each group. Finally he migrated to the hilltop of Monte Cassino that towers above the Via Latina midway between Rome and Naples. And there he built a monastery for a fully coenobitical community, which he directed for the rest of his life.[4]

Benedict believed that discipleship was the key to the Christian life. Only when you cultivate the practices of following Jesus can you acquire the skills of a person who can "love the Lord your God with all your heart, and with all your soul, and with all your strength and with all your mind; and your neighbor as yourself" (Luke 10:27). This does not happen through pure will, as suggested by Augustine. Benedict's monastery was thus set up where teaching was done by abbots who had small groups of disciples they trained in obedience and discipleship. He says of his abbots:

> [W]hen anyone receives the title of abbot he ought to preside over his disciples with twofold manner of teaching: that is, to show forth all that is good and holy by deeds even more than by words, so as by his words to set the commandment of the Lord before the more intelligent disciples: but to those hard of heart and to those of less capacity to show forth the divine precepts by his deeds.

---

[3] Quoted from Lawrence, *Medieval Monasticism*, 9.

[4] Lawrence, *Medieval Monasticism*, 19.

And all things that he has taught the disciples are contrary to the divine precepts, let his own deeds indicate are things not to be done; lest preaching to others himself be found reprobate.[5]

The Benedictine Rule consists of many strict precepts. The intent, however, is clear: the formation of a character worthy of the name Christian. Observe the following sample of the regulations that he calls the instruments of good works.

In the first place, to love God with the whole heart, the whole soul and the whole strength. Then one's neighbour as if oneself. Then, not to kill. Not to commit adultery. Not to steal. Not to covet. Not to utter false witness. To honour all men. To do as one would be done by. To deny oneself that one may follow Christ. To chastise the body. Not to embrace delights. To love fasting. To relieve the poor. To clothe the naked. To visit the sick. To bury the dead. To help in tribulation. To console the sorrowing. To become a stranger to worldly deeds. To prefer nothing to the love of Christ. Not to carry anger into effect. Not to prolong the duration of one's wrath. Not to regain guile in one's heart. Not to make a false peace. Not to abandon charity. Not to swear, lest perchance one forswear. To utter only truth from heart and mouth. Not to return evil for evil. Not to do injury, but to suffer it patiently. To love enemies. Not to curse in return those who curse one, but rather to bless them. To bear persecution for righteousness. Not to be proud. Not to be given to much wine. Not to be gluttonous. Not given to much sleep. Not to be sluggish. Not to be given to gambling. Not to be a detractor. To put one's hope in God.[6]

This list goes on and on. Obedience and humility are basic virtues of Christian character that are closely interrelated. Proud people have difficulty with obedience because they cannot believe that it is worth serving anyone other than themselves. Yet Benedict remembered the words of Jesus: "For those who want to save their lives [proud people] will lose it, and those who lose their lives for my sake [humble people] will find it" (Matt 16:25, insertions added).

Benedict learned much from Augustine, especially in his association of sin with pride. However, his understanding of the Christian life is also significantly different, with two main differences. First, pure will alone cannot be the locus of Christian moral action. Regular training of the will is equally important. This concept is closely related to the second difference, namely, Benedict's insistence upon the unity of inner disposition and outer actions. We can already see this unity implicit in the above quotations; however, he makes it explicit in several of his writings, including in his elaboration of the twelve steps of humility. For example:

The seventh step in humility is if he not only with his mouth denounce himself as inferior to all and more worthless, but also believe it in his inner consciousness, humbling himself. . . . The twelfth step in humility is if a monk not only be humble in heart, but also always in his very body evince humility to those who see him.[7]

This unity of the inner and the outer is important for Christian ethics. Without it, as is the case with Augustine, the church remains invisible and God is taken to work mysteriously in the world through individual consciences and pure wills. But then the church as an alternative social-moral community plays no role in God's agential purposes. With the unity of the inner and the outer, as with the cenobitic monastics, God's rule is visible in an alternative social reality. This community plays a crucial moral role both in molding its members to becoming Christian disciples as well as in providing a contrasting model to the world. The world could never know itself as world if it were not for an alternative social reality—the church—which it is not.

HILDEGARD OF BINGEN (1098–1179)

It is important to note that not all medieval ascetics were monks. The monastic

---

[5] Quoted from Waldo Beach and H. Richard Niebuhr, eds., *Christian Ethics: Sources of the Living Tradition*, 2nd ed. (New York: Ronald Press, 1973), 153.

[6] Beach and Niebuhr, *Christian Ethics*, 153–54.

[7] Beach and Niebuhr, *Christian Ethics*, 156–57.

movement also produced several prominent women theologians/nuns. Hildegard is but one example.

Hildegard was a Benedictine abbess who exerted significant influence upon the church in her time through the presentation and interpretation of her many visions. These visions began when she was age three and "saw such a great light that my soul quaked."[8] The visions continued throughout her entire life.

At the young age of seven, Hildegard entered the cloister in a house in Disibodenberg, now Germany, built by Count Stephan of Spanheim for his daughter Jutta, who had also taken the vows of chastity and was rejecting all offers of marriage. Here Hildegard was "enclosed," which meant that she made the commitment to stay in her cell for the rest of her life.[9] For us moderns this seems like an immoral thing for parents to do to a seven-year-old child. Yet this act was a concrete way of turning your child totally over to God in order to have her experience the bliss of godliness while on earth. As it turned out, Hildegard gradually moved out of her cell and at the age of fifteen became a Benedictine nun. Later, after Jutta died, she became the abbess in a double monastery consisting of both monks and nuns.

In her mature writings, Hildegard became progressively more interested in wholeness and unity of all reality. She taught that all is created and ordered by God, which means that everything stands in complementary relation to everything else. Nothing exists in and for itself since it is but part of God's creation. The problems of life—sin—result from each part of the whole breaking away from its inseparable connectedness to the other. For example, the body has its own desires, and if it is not reined into proper relationship by the spirit it will destroy itself. Spirit and body are not to be separated because they are a unity. In fact, even the arrangement of the organs in our body has spiritual significance. Just as God is one (unity) in three (the Trinity) so we are in relation to one another and indeed to all of creation. Here is an example of the unity of man and woman.

> For man is the work of God perfected, because God is known through him, and since God created all creatures for him, and allowed him to embrace the true love to preach and praise him through the quality of his mind. But man needed a helper in his likeness. So God gave him a helper, which was his mirror image, woman, in whom the whole human race lay hidden. It was to be brought forth in the power of God's strength, just as the first man was produced by him. And the man and the woman were thus complementary, so that one works through the other, because man is not called "man" without woman, nor is woman without man called "woman". For woman is the work of man, and man the form of woman's consolation. Neither can exist without the other. And man signifies the divinity of the Son of God; woman his humanity.[10]

Hildegard is not saying that every man must marry a woman and every woman a man. After all, she is speaking as one who has taken the vows of chastity to be godly. Her attempt is rather to give expression to the view of ontological relatedness from which no person can escape. Autonomous self-understanding is the root of all pride; humility is the precondition of godliness.

SAINT FRANCIS (1182–1226)

Saint Francis of Assisi, originally named Giovanni Francesco Bernardone, was born to a wealthy Italian merchant family. As a young man he lived a rather worldly life. Then, while a prisoner of war, suffering from a serious illness, he resolved to become a disciple of Christ and to change his way of life. Once out of prison he immediately began working with lepers and impoverished church communities. This identification with poverty so angered his wealthy father that he eventually disinherited him.

---

[8] Quoted in Sabina Flanagan, *Hildegard of Bingen: A Visionary Life* (London: Routledge, 1989), 25.

[9] See Flanagan, *Hildegard of Bingen*, 30–31 for a description of the ceremony of enclosure.

[10] As quoted in Flanagan, *Hildegard of Bingen*, 149.

Yet Francis was not deterred in his resolve to follow Christ. One day in 1208, he received a distinct calling, via Matthew 10:5-14, to take the vows of poverty and to serve the Lord with gladness, preaching that "the kingdom of heaven is at hand." That same year he gathered twelve disciples, who immediately made him superior; thus was born the First Order of the Franciscans. Only a few years later (1212), the Second Order was established by a well-known nun named Clare.

Francis' writings, as did his life, inspired many. In his *The Little Flowers of St. Francis*,[11] he speaks of the life of true Christian discipleship, which consisted of a rigid prayer routine and a conscientious discipling commitment. He writes:

> The grace of God and the virtues that flow therefrom are a way and a ladder that leadeth to heaven; but vices and sins are a ladder and a way that leadeth to the depths of hell. Vices and sins are a venomous and mortal poison, but virtue and good works are a salutary medicine.[12]

Notice the close connection between good works and grace in the above quotation. Unlike Augustine, Francis made no distinction between the inner and outer when speaking of the Christian life. Christian love was both an inner disposition as well as an outward action. He believed that the distinction led to an intolerable justification of evil in the name of Christian love. As he puts it explicitly, quoting Brother Giles approvingly:

> I would choose rather to be in the secular state, continually and devoutly desiring to enter into holy Religion, than to be cloaked in the religious habit without the exercise of good works.[13]

While Francis emphasizes the importance of good works in ways that Augustine before him and Luther after him would find objectionable, it is nevertheless important to note that his is not a simple works righteousness.

That is, good works do not make a person good before God; instead God enables and indeed requires good works of all disciples. God is the source of human good works and being in tune with God is therefore the basis upon which good can be done. Hence, prayer is at the center of the Christian's life. Without it the Christian life is impossible.

> Prayer is the beginning, the middle and the end of all good; prayer illuminates the soul, and enables it to discern between good and evil. Every sinner ought to pray daily with fervour of heart, that is, he should pray humbly to God to give him a perfect knowledge of his own misery and sins, and the benefits which he has received and still receiveth from the good God. But how can that man know God who knoweth not how to pray? And for all those who shall be saved, it is needful above all things that, sooner or later, they be converted to the use of holy prayer.[14]

It is indeed this unity of the spiritual and the ethical so characteristic of St. Francis' writings that many of us today repeat in our worship services. The following prayer has made it into the worship resource book of the place of worship for this author.

> Lord, make me an instrument of your peace. Where there is hatred, let me sow love; where there is injury, pardon; where there is doubt, faith; where there is despair, hope; where there is darkness, light; where there is sadness, joy. O Divine Master, grant that I may not so much seek to be consoled, as to console; to be understood, as to understand; to be loved, as to love. For it is in giving that we receive; it is in pardoning that we are pardoned; it is in dying that we are born to eternal life.[15]

It is not possible here to examine the writings of all the important medieval writers. For example, we must forego the rich insights of the mystics[16] and the attempted Augustinian revival by St. Anselm of Canterbury (1033–1109). Nor will we examine the very painful era for the Christian church during

---

[11] St. Francis of Assisi, *The Little Flowers of St. Francis*, trans. Dom Roger Hudleston (London: Burns Oates, 1953).

[12] Quoted from Beach and Niebuhr, *Christian Ethics*, 162.

[13] Beach and Niebuhr, *Christian Ethics*, 173.

[14] Beach and Niebuhr, *Christian Ethics*, 170.

[15] Quoted from *Hymnal: A Worship Book* (Newton, Kan.: Faith and Life, 1992), prayer no. 733.

[16] Three examples of late medieval mystics are Bernard of Clairvaux (1090?–1153), Meister Eckhart (1260?–1328?), and Catherine of Siena (1347–1380).

which the Crusaders used violence and political expansionism as a means of proselytization. These would be fruitful discussions in a study more narrowly concentrated on the history of this period. Instead, we must shift our attention to the most influential philosopher/theologian of the late medieval period: St. Thomas Aquinas.

SAINT THOMAS AQUINAS (1225?–1274)

Thomas was born into a noble family in Roccasecca, Italy. He received his early education in a Benedictine monastery and at the University of Naples. While at the university, and in the year of his father's death (1243), he joined the Dominican order. His mother was so strongly opposed to her son's involvement in this religious order, which lived by begging from the wealthy, that she got his brothers to kidnap and confine him to the family castle for over a year. But to no avail. When he was released, he continued his studies in philosophy and theology in Paris and later in Cologne. In 1250 he was ordained as a Dominican priest, and two years later he began teaching at the University of Paris. When he completed his doctorate in 1256, he was appointed professor of philosophy at this same university and taught there for most of his life, interrupted only by occasional lecturing at the papal court in Rome.

Thomas' thought must be placed within the context of the broader thinking of the church at the turn of the millennium. The theological foundations of the church at this time were those set by Augustine six hundred years earlier. This was the dominant Catholic theology. Granted, the ascetics set themselves apart from the rest of Christian society because they insisted on greater continuity between the inner (dispositions) and the outer (actions) than Augustine's "two cities" theology provided. But their views were not a serious challenge to the mainstream because their way of life was not seen to be for all Christians, in part, no doubt, because of their insistence on celibacy. In the main, however, Augustine's rejection of the metaphysical dualism of good and evil, which required the repudiation of the ontological independence of each, was uncontested dogma for the medieval church. In God all things have their being, and from God's perfect will comes the disclosure of what is right and wrong to the human imperfect will. Says Wogaman of this period of history:

> Augustine's analysis of the moral will, with its conception of pride as the essential sin, had become the basis of much of the church's moral discipline, along with its corresponding emphasis upon the virtue of humility. It had established a positive view of and relationship to the state, notwithstanding the collapse of the central Roman authority soon after the triumph of Constantinianism. Such theological, philosophical, and ethical beliefs were not without their internal tensions. But the intellectual accomplishments of early Christian thought had succeeded in laying the foundations for a remarkably unified theological/social/moral worldview among medieval Christians. That worldview was so broadly shared that there was little stimulus for bold, creative thinking.[17]

In the thirteenth century, several stimuli "for bold, creative thinking" emerged which contributed to the discontentment with the status quo and the onset of a new form of theological inquiry. First, a new intellectual climate of critical scholarship was taking shape. This is evidenced by the fact that universities flourished during this time, which contributed to the questioning of the status quo. Second, Aristotle, whose thought had remained untranslated during the medieval period, was now being rediscovered via translation into Latin. And Aristotle was generally seen as a philosophical rival to Augustine. Third, Muslim scholarship, especially through Averroes and his interpreter Siger de Bradant, was presenting a view of Aristotle which undermined the theological approach of the Roman Catholic Church,

---

[17] Wogaman, *Christian Ethics*, 82–83.

namely, that knowledge was based upon revelation and not on natural reason. Fourth, there was a growing concern for the integration of all knowledge and of all reality. The dualisms of the supernatural and the natural, the inner and the outer, the Christian life as understood and lived by the ascetics and the Christian life of the ordinary church member, spiritual knowledge and empirical knowledge, faith and reason were all being rethought. To say this another way, the division between Plato and Aristotle and the church's unilateral identification with Plato's otherworldly realism through Augustine's two-kingdom theology was no longer being taken for granted.

This rethinking was driven by several forces. One such force was the concern for the *practice* of Christianity (Christian ethics). The Christian life is not adequately characterized in terms of aspirations focused only outside this world, or, indeed on the spiritual dimensions of human reality. After all, God created *this* world; God loves *this* world; God became paradigmatically present in *this* physical world in the person of Jesus Christ and does so again and again in faithful witness. This theme is intrinsic to the biblical story from Genesis to Revelation. It is not hard to see, therefore, that on the one hand, the Augustinian suspicions of matter and flesh, which he learned from neoplatonism, and on the other hand, the incongruity of the inner and the outer, propelled serious thinkers to take another look at how theology is to be done.

Thomas is, of course, the foremost of such thinkers, even though his involvement in this development was not entirely of his own choosing. The papal authorities felt that they could not leave the Islamic commentaries on Aristotle unchallenged. It threatened the integrity of their approach to theology specifically and to the Christian faith generally. The lot fell to Thomas to defend the faith. He did so by forging a new synthesis between Aristotle's approach to knowledge and philosophy generally and the traditional medieval understanding of theology.

There are several aspects of Aristotle's philosophy which Thomas incorporates into his understanding of the Christian faith. Two of the most basic are the teleological view of reality and the language of the virtues. It is important to look at both before we discuss his view of law.

Thomas believed that the doctrine of divine creation implied that everything is created for a specific purpose or end (*telos*, in Latin *finis*). Since this is so, whether something is good or not is determined by whether it fulfils its *telos*. That is, if it does the job well for which it was created, it is good; if not, it is evil. Thomas summarizes his argument about the relationship between goods and ends as follows: "Therefore the end of a thing is its perfection. But the perfection of a thing is its good. Therefore everything is directed to good as its end."[18]

We know this *telos*–good relationship intuitively with regard to things we create. For example, a good car is one that does the job of being a car well, a bad one does not; a good computer is one that does well the job it was created to do, a bad computer does not.

Of course, it is possible for people to argue that there is no such thing as a good car or a good computer, period. For example, those sympathetic to the view of the Luddites, the early nineteenth-century anti-technology group, may well put forth such an argument. They could argue that the inherent end of computers (the possibility of virtually unlimited access to information, the possibility of virtual universal and instantaneous communication, the necessity to quantify knowledge in electronic bytes, and so on) is superseded by higher ends like peace, economy of resources, respect for privacy, and tranquility for the entire human community, with which computer ends are intrinsically incompatible.

---

[18] St. Thomas Aquinas, *Summa Contra Gentiles*, III, chap. XVI. Quoted from Anton C. Pegis, ed., *Basic Writings of Saint Thomas Aquinas* (New York: Random House, 1945), 2:26.

This example raises the matter of a hierarchy of being and consequently of the hierarchy of ends. According to Thomas, nothing but God is purely good. Everything else is merely relationally good. That is, God is the end (*telos*) of all being. There is no *telos* in relation to which God can be judged good or bad. He puts it thus:

> Now there is but one supreme good, namely God. . . . Therefore all things are directed to the highest good, namely God, as their end. . . . Therefore the supreme good, namely God, is the cause of goodness in all things good. Therefore he is the cause of every end being an end, since whatever is an end is such in so far as it is good. Now *the cause that a thing is so is itself more so.* Therefore God is supremely the end of all things.[19]

Everything other than God is only relationally good; that is, not good in itself but good in relation to something else and ultimately to God. Let me explain with still another example. An atomic bomb can be a good bomb if it does its job well as intended by its designers. So when nuclear engineers speak about whether this or that bomb is good or bad, they are merely speaking about how well it does what it is designed to do. Clearly on this account, some bombs will be better than others. Yet when Japanese social theorists reflect on whether "Little Boy" (the bomb dropped on Hiroshima on August 6, 1945) and "Fat Man" (the bomb dropped on Nagasaki on August 9, 1945) were good or bad, they are hardly speaking about their effectiveness. They are evaluating them in relation to a higher end; in fact, the effectiveness which made them good for the designers makes them bad in relation to this higher end of well-being for Japanese society.

Thomas' hierarchy of being has God on top—that is, he agrees with Augustine's rejection of Manichaean dualism, saying "evil is not a real essence,"[20]—then angels, whose being is entirely spiritual, then human beings, who exist both spiritually and physically, then animals, who are physical beings with sensations, then vegetation, which lives and grows, and finally inanimate matter. At each level, there is the possibility of assessing goodness both in relation to the ends of the object itself as well as assessing it in relation to that which is higher. In other words, something like a bomb may be good in relation to its own internal end but evil because of its conflict with the ends of vegetation, animals, humans, and God.

Thomas speaks specifically about the *telos* of human beings. Like Aristotle, he calls it happiness (*eudaemonia*). What happiness is and wherein it consists preoccupies much of his time. Certainly it is no more associated with mere pleasure for Thomas than it was for Aristotle. To define happiness, Thomas goes through a long litany of examples of wherein happiness does not consist: carnal pleasures, honors, glory, wealth, worldly power, goods of the body, the senses, acts of the moral virtues, acts of prudence, and the practice of art.[21] When speaking positively, he states that happiness consists in "contemplating God" or alternatively, "the contemplation of the truth."[22]

The significance of this explanation can be seen only when it is compared with Augustine's view of the autonomy of the will. As we have seen, according to Augustine, one can know the good and one's passions can be well-disciplined, yet one can will evil and hence do evil. And nothing can determine the will; the will is autonomous and determines all else. In other words, act has priority over being. For Thomas this is clearly not the case. For him, being and knowing the truth are primary. He would ask why we would love God (act of the will) if it were not for our beliefs about who God is. Or why would we do good, if doing good did not make sense? Act and being are intimately associated.

According to Thomas, the will is not a higher power than the intellect because the

---

[19] Aquinas, *Summa Contra Gentiles*, 27 (emphasis in original).
[20] Aquinas, *Summa Contra Gentiles*, 12.
[21] Aquinas, *Summa Contra Gentiles*, 51–59.
[22] Aquinas, *Summa Contra Gentiles*, 59–60.

intellect causes the will to act. It is the intellect that first assesses something as good before the will can act on it. In his words:

> The suggestion put forward . . . that the will is a higher power than the intellect, as being the latter's motive power, is clearly untrue. Because the intellect moves the will first and *per se*, for the will, as such, is moved by its object, which is the apprehended good; whereas the will moves the intellect accidentally as it were, in so far, namely, as the act of understanding is itself apprehended as a good, and on that account is desired by the will, with the result that the intellect understands actually. Even in this, the intellect precedes the will, for the will would never desire understanding, did not the intellect first apprehend its understanding as a good.[23]

The implications of Thomas' argument are significant. As we saw in the previous chapter, Augustine had difficulty viewing the virtues as shaping Christian character because of his insistence on the autonomy of the will. In his view, the will chooses the virtues. This meant that the radical freedom of the will, determined only by God, should not be harnessed by the forces of knowledge, or reason, or tradition, or character, or virtue, or anything. All can come in the way of doing the good. For Thomas, it is different. Since the *telos* of humanity (happiness) is the contemplation of God or the knowing of the truth, it follows that human beings must cultivate the life appropriate to this knowledge. That is, our wills must be trained to act in a particular manner just like an athlete in a game trains his/her will in such a way that the body habitually makes the right moves (determined by the *telos* of the game). Hence, for Thomas there is great significance to the virtues that shape character out of which actions flow.

Before we examine Thomas' treatment of the virtues, it is important to make clear that Thomas' view of happiness is not exactly like Aristotle's. In some respects, here he is much closer to Augustine, for whom happiness is centered in God. But as we shall see, he must also be differentiated from Augustine at this point, who calls Aristotle's view imperfect or temporal happiness and contrasts it with perfect happiness. Thomas acknowledges that, since Aristotle was a pagan, he could not have known that true knowledge of God is what defines our *telos*. Knowledge of God, according to Thomas, is the most perfect and complete form of knowledge, and it is our attainment of this knowledge that can make us good. Yet to reach this level of happiness fully in the natural life is not possible. This is only possible in another life. Thomas puts it thus:

> [T]he more our mind is raised to the contemplation of spiritual things, the more it is withdrawn from sensible things. Now the divine substance is the highest term to which contemplation can reach: hence the mind that sees the divine substance must be wholly freed from the senses, either by death or by rapture. Wherefore it is said in God's person (Exodus 23:20): *Man shall not see me, and live.*[24]

Yet this quote can be misleading. While it is true that Thomas believes that happiness becomes complete in the soul's union with God—its Creator—at the end of human physical existence, nevertheless, in this life happiness and knowledge cannot avoid a relation with the material and therefore with the sensible world. In other words, for Thomas the natural and the supernatural are not in nearly as great a tension as they are for Augustine. Thomas puts it this way: "Since therefore grace does not destroy nature, but perfects it, natural reason should minister to faith as the natural inclination of the will ministers to charity."[25]

It is important, therefore, to recognize that, just as divine knowledge is a gift—an act of divine grace—for Augustine, so it is for Thomas. The latter, however, emphasizes that it is precisely the perfecting work of grace upon nature that requires a role for the virtues.

[23] Aquinas, *Summa Contra Gentiles*, 51.
[24] Aquinas, *Summa Contra Gentiles*, 82 (emphasis in original).
[25] St. Thomas Aquinas, *Summa Theologica* I, Q. I. Art. 8. Quoted from Pegis, *Basic Writings of St. Thomas Aquinas*, 1:14.

Thomas accepts Aristotle's general designation of virtues as "good habits." To say that "human virtues are habits"[26] means that they are the qualities that guide our power to act (will) in such a manner as to make us good. These "powers of the soul,"[27] whether acquired or infused,[28] are, however, the powers of God acting in us and through us. Hence the intellect, through which "contemplation of God" happens, is the vehicle of God's perfecting activity in our lives. To say this differently, as we come to know God, we come to know the *telos* of ourselves and all other creation. The virtues are the powers to become that which we truly are and to see all other reality for what it truly is.

Regarding the general definition of virtue, however, Thomas is in essential agreement with Augustine. He accepts that virtue is "a good quality of the mind, by which we live righteously, of which no one can make bad use, which God works in us without us."[29] However, in his *"I answer that"* discussion of this definition, he states that it would be better to substitute "habit" for "quality."[30]

Thomas follows Aristotle in naming several kinds of virtues. The *intellectual* virtues that perfect the powers of our minds are: wisdom, which enables the mind to "rightly judge and order all truth";[31] science (knowledge), which "perfects the intellect";[32] and understanding (intuition), which discerns first principles. The *moral* virtues that perfect the appetitive part of the soul toward the realization of its *telos*, are: prudence, whereby the will is ordered by reason; temperance, which controls the passions; fortitude, which empowers us to act on the courage of our convictions; and justice, which is the power of the proper ordering of relationships and the distribution of goods and services. The *theological* virtues

that are known by the special revelation of God's grace are: faith, which is the power whereby "the intellect apprehends what it hopes for and loves";[33] hope, which enables us to overcome the powers of the natural and empowers us to know and to strive after the supernatural; and charity, which is the power that contemplates and does the good.

To oversimplify somewhat, it could be said that the intellectual virtues govern the intellect in its pursuit of truth and knowledge ("the good of the intellect is truth"[34]); the moral virtues, which Thomas calls cardinal or principal, govern the pursuit of goodness generally; and the theological virtues govern the pursuit of the spiritual union with God. However, to segregate the relative functions of the virtues in this manner is an oversimplification because Thomas wants to emphasize their interconnectedness and their unity—not their separateness. Happiness, the true end of human life, is only possible when these virtues work in harmony, not in competition. Only in this manner are all aspects of the human being perfected. The tendencies to separate the contemplative from the active or the moral from the spiritual do not have their roots in Thomas. Yet we should not lose sight of the fact that in his discussion of the *cardinal* virtues,[35] he is unambiguous in citing the moral virtues. This is significant because it means that there can be no such thing as pure knowledge abstracted from goodness, or indeed mystical union with God that legitimates the suspension of the ethical. The cardinality of the moral virtues prohibits this.

In concluding our discussion of Thomas and the virtues, a word must be said about his view of the relationships among sin, grace, and good works. It would be a mistake

---

[26] Aquinas, *Summa Theologica*, Q. 55. Art. 1, 2:413.

[27] Aquinas, *Summa Theologica*, Q. 56. Art. 2, 2:420.

[28] "Acquired virtues" such as prudence, temperance, fortitude, and justice are habitual acts which govern dispositions in accordance with natural law, and "infused virtues" such as faith, hope, and love are the powers of God helping us to share in the divine grace.

[29] Aquinas, *Summa Theologica*, Q. 55. Art. 4, 2:416.

[30] Aquinas, *Summa Theologica*, Q. 55. Art. 4, 2:417.

[31] Aquinas, *Summa Theologica*, Q. 57. Art. 2, 2:432.

[32] Aquinas, *Summa Theologica*, Q. 57. Art. 2, 2:432.

[33] Aquinas, *Summa Theologica*, Q. 62. Art. 4, 2:479.

[34] Aquinas, *Summa Theologica*, Q. 62. Art. 4, 2:432.

[35] Aquinas, *Summa Theologica*, Q. 62. Art. 4, 2:466–67.

to think that Thomas has a weak view of sin and therefore a weak view of divine grace. That is, he is not saying that mere human determination to live by the virtues—which reason and God disclose to us—can make us good. At the same time, original sin has not so utterly distorted our God-given human capacities to reason, will, and act such that our agential involvement in good work is forever thwarted. Rather, God's infusion of divine grace, especially through the theological virtues, is at work perfecting our distorting capacities. That is to say, happiness—the human *telos*—is a gift from God, in which human beings can participate already in this world. Insofar as grace perfects nature, nature itself becomes good.

Thomas is perhaps best known for a theory of ethics called "natural law." This theory is falsely caricatured as "whatever is natural is good." Yet it is evident from what has been said already about Thomas' teleological theory of goodness and his theory of virtue that he believes the good and the natural are in intimate relation.

There has been some confusion among scholars on how to relate Thomas' virtue theory of ethics with his natural law theory. After all, ends-language embraces a teleological view of obligation and law-language a deontological one. (Contemporary dichotomies of moral ordering are read back into history with great peril!) Consider, for example, the ambivalence in Wogaman's transitional paragraph from Thomas' virtue theory to moral law theory:

> A second way of viewing human good is found in Thomas's reformulation of moral law. It is perhaps inevitable that even an end-directed ethic like Thomas's would also have to be stated in prescriptive form—for that had been the recognizable form

of most moral teaching for many centuries. The general form of his ethic remains teleological, however. Law does not exist for its own sake but rather as a means to natural and supernatural ends.[36]

The most common interpretation of Thomas has been to give natural law priority over virtue theory. And in so doing natural law theory is viewed as:

> [T]he belief that there exists in nature and/or in human nature a rational order which can provide intelligible value-statements independently of human will, that are universal in application, unchangeable in their ultimate content, and morally obligatory on mankind.[37]

This interpretation would put Thomas in continuity with the Stoic and the Roman naturalists and assumes that we can, by appealing to reason alone, come to know and do the good. Such a reading of Thomas makes it difficult to understand the harmony he wants to bring to grace and nature. Moreover, it makes his theory of virtue largely irrelevant.

Some recent scholars have argued that this represents a misreading of Thomas; it is a case of projecting onto a philosopher's position a theory that comes from a different era.[38] The proper reading of Thomas, it is then suggested, is from the standpoint of the priority of the virtues, particularly the cardinal virtue, prudence.[39] As Daniel Mark Nelson puts it:

> [R]ather than relying on the intuitions of synderesis [habitual knowledge of moral principles] and applying them syllogistically to circumstances, prudence depends on education into the customary judgments of society about what human goods in particular are appropriate and about how they are to be achieved.[40]

It is not possible for us to enter the details of this debate here although the arguments

---

[36] Wogaman, *Christian Ethics*, 88.

[37] Paul Sigmund, *Natural Law in Political Thought* (Cambridge, Mass.: Winthrop, 1971), viii. Quoted from Daniel Mark Nelson, *The Priority of Prudence: Virtue and Natural Law in Thomas Aquinas and the Implications for Modern Ethics* (University Park: Pennsylvania University Press, 1992), 3.

[38] Examples of scholars who are suggesting this alternative reading of Thomas are Karl Rahner, Alasdair MacIntyre, Stanley Hauerwas, and Daniel Mark Nelson.

[39] See esp. Nelson, *Priority of Prudence*.

[40] Nelson, *Priority of Prudence*, 145 (definition of synderesis inserted).

are compelling and warrant serious consideration. Yet here I will merely point out that Thomas' comparatively brief discussion of natural law comes after a lengthy treatment of the virtues. This alone suggests that he believed that his teleology and virtue theory were to serve as the theoretical framework into which his comments on law were to be placed.

Nevertheless, Thomas' teaching on natural law is very important. I begin this discussion of natural law by noting that, according to Thomas, there are four kinds of law: eternal law, natural law, human law, and divine law.[41] Regarding *eternal law* he says,

> Now it is evident, granted that the world is ruled by divine providence . . . that the whole community of the universe is governed by the divine reason. Therefore the very notion of the government of things in God, the ruler of the universe, has the nature of a law. And since the divine reason's conception of things is not subject to time, but is eternal . . . this kind of law must be called eternal.[42]

Eternal law is therefore to be understood as divine wisdom directing all actions and movements such that all things seek their due ends.[43] Since eternal law belongs to divine being, we cannot know it as it is in itself. However, the imprint of eternal law is within us all, meaning, we can all learn to know it as humans know it. "It is therefore evident that the *natural law* is nothing else than the rational creature's participation of the eternal law."[44] That is, natural law (*lex naturalis*) is our appropriation of eternal law through the process of *learning* the eternal law; that is, by the practice of participation in the divine wisdom. But how do we do this? By learning the language of faith whereby eternal law becomes self-evident! Speaking of propositions that reason holds to be self-evident, Thomas says this:

But some propositions are self-evident only to the wise, who understand the meaning of the terms of such propositions. Thus to one who understands that an angel is not a body, it is self-evident that an angel is not circumscriptively in a place. But this is not evident to the unlearned, for they cannot grasp it.[45]

Natural law, therefore, cannot be abstracted from the language of faith; it is the explication of that language.

What does our "participation of the eternal law" (that is, natural law) teach us about our own human natural ends? Generally speaking, it tells us that we ought to act in keeping with our *telos*. Moreover, the first principle of practical reason is "*Bonum est faciendum et prosequendum, et malum vitandum*" ("Good is to be done and promoted and evil is to be avoided").[46] That is, our reason tells us that we must be what we in essence (according to divine reason) are.

More specifically, natural law tells us three things about ourselves. First, there is an "inclination to good" which we have in common with everything else, namely the inclination to self-preservation. The second, "inclination to good" is procreation and species perpetuation. And the third is "to know the truth of God, and to live in society."[47]

This does not mean that these three natural ends can be fulfilled in any manner whatsoever. On the contrary, it is the virtues that guide the fulfillment of these ends. As he says, "[T]here is within every man a natural inclination to act according to reason; and this is to act according to virtue."[48] That is, how we preserve our lives, how we perpetuate our race, and how we come to know God are all guided by the virtues.

The third kind of law Thomas calls *human law*. These are the laws made by humans that govern our societies and are necessary as

---

[41] For a helpful summary of Thomas' view of natural law, see D. J. O'Connor, *Aquinas and Natural Law* (London: Macmillan, 1967).

[42] Aquinas, *Summa Theologica*, Q. 91. Art. 1, 748.

[43] Aquinas, *Summa Theologica*, Q. 93. Art. 1, 763.

[44] Aquinas, *Summa Theologica*, Q. 91. Art. 2, 750 (emphasis added).

[45] Aquinas, *Summa Theologica*, Q. 94. Art. 2, 774.

[46] Aquinas, *Summa Theologica*, Q. 94. Art. 2, 774.

[47] Aquinas, *Summa Theologica*, Q. 94. Art. 2, 775.

[48] Aquinas, *Summa Theologica*, Q. 94. Art. 2, 776.

training toward "the perfection of virtue."[49] Thomas puts it this way:

> [A] man needs to receive this training from another, whereby to arrive at the perfection of virtue. And as to those young people who are inclined to acts of virtue by their good natural disposition, or by custom, or rather by the gift of God, paternal training suffices, which is by admonition. But since some are found to be desolate and prone to vice, and not easily amenable to words, it is necessary for such to be restrained from evil by force and fear, in order that, at least, they might desist from evil-doing, and leave others in peace, and that they themselves, by being habituated in this way, might be brought to do willingly what hitherto they did from fear, and thus become virtuous.[50]

Human laws are derived from natural law. They are the application of natural law to a particular time and place. As such, human laws change. Human reason often produces something better than the status quo that human laws should seek to accommodate.

For Thomas, customs—or we might say tradition—can acquire the force of law. Quoting Augustine positively, he says, "The customs of God's people and the institutions of our ancestors are to be considered as laws. And those who throw contempt on the customs of the Church ought to be punished as those who disobey the law of God."[51]

The fourth kind of law is *divine law*, which is enacted by God and made known to us by revelation. It might seem that natural and human laws are adequate for directing human conduct. But Thomas gives four reasons why this is not so. First, since we are ordained to an end of eternal happiness, no natural or human laws are adequate to bring about such an end. Second, since human beings disagree and can err in judgment, divine direction is necessary. Third, human beings can only make laws in those areas where they are competent to judge, and these are predominantly outward actions; God alone can judge interior acts. And fourth, we cannot possibly have laws for all evil deeds. Divine law is required

so that "all sins are forbidden."[52] Divine law is therefore important to ensure that moral laws as we understand them in and through our human conditioning are never reduced to mere human mores.

Thomas set for himself a truly remarkable task. He tried to show that the natural order, which the Greeks had discovered and to which we as humans were subject, such that we could come to know the good and live in harmony with the created order, was in fact congruent with the Christian life ordered in divine reason. God's revelation and proper reason were not enemies, but partners. Faith and reason needed each other. To come to see this is to see that we do not create the law, the law creates us; we do not discover the truth; the truth discovers us. And when we are thus discovered and created, we can come to know ourselves as we are known by the one who created us.

DUNS SCOTUS (1265/6–1308)

Duns Scotus is usually regarded an obscure High Middle Ages thinker who has little new to contribute to medieval thought. But he is rather important because around his name and others, such as William of Ockham (1285–1349), a veritable intellectual revolution is said to have taken place. This revolution had to do with how we think of *being* as such, or one could say, it had to do with understanding reality itself, both empirical and ultimate. One might think that such a discussion is not germane to ethics because it does not immediately tell us what to do, but on the contrary: here is where the shift from understanding ourselves as *participating in transcendent reality* to a *distant imitating of the transcendent* (or obeying God's will/law) takes place. This move from participation to imitation is, as we will see, rather important for Christian ethics and is often thought of as beginning the slide into the nineteenth-century secularist renditions of power and will.

[49] Aquinas, *Summa Theologica*, Q. 95. Art. 1, 783.
[50] Aquinas, *Summa Theologica*, Q. 95. Art. 1, 783.
[51] Aquinas, *Summa Theologica*, Q. 97. Art. 3, 803.
[52] Aquinas, *Summa Theologica*, Q. 91. Art. 4, 753.

Scotus was a nickname that meant he was a Scot. His family's name was Duns. He was ordained as a Franciscan priest early in life, studied theology and philosophy at Oxford, and later became a lecturer on the writings of Peter Lombard. Like Thomas, Scotus was an Aristotelian who had much to say about natural theology. Yet in criticism of Thomas, he questioned the notion of the analogy of being (*analogia entis*). And here is the beginning of the intellectual revolution.[53]

As we have seen, with Aquinas as with medieval thought in general, all that exists participates in God. For human beings, this means that we yearn for communion with God, whether we know it or not. Yet God is beyond all things and hence cannot be spoken of with language as it ordinarily functions. While God can be "read" from the world—since ordinary reality participates in God—nevertheless, God as God remains hidden and is inscrutable. Knowledge of God comes to us primarily via revelation, that is, self-disclosure, yet it is not as though this knowledge is incompatible with reason or transcends it, for, according to medievalists, reason's charge is to make sense of revelation.

For Thomas, God is the very basis of all that is, the one in terms of whom all else has its existence; hence, God cannot exist like all else exists. Therefore, while we can still speak of God, it is possible to do so only when our language functions analogically and not literally nor univocally.

In Scotus' reconception of the language of God, he concluded that as a term encompassing all that is, including God, "being" must function the same way (univocally) whether ascribed to God or to any other being. If this were not so, he argues, our God-language (theology) would be incomprehensible

nonsense. But this rather innocent sounding shift implies that, in an important way, God is as we are; not in that we share God's attributes, but that for theology to make sense, "being" cannot function one way when ascribed to God and another when used of humans.

This way of casting the matter is radically different from the tradition. For Thomas, the Creator exists in profoundly different ways from creatures. Creatures have being only insofar as they participate in God, that is, only to the extent that God gives them being; whereas God simply exists, owing God's being to no one! If we are to believe Scotus, the difference between God and us is a matter of degree—we ascribe to God what we ascribe to creatures although God has these qualities infinitely and we do not. Phillip Blond summarizes Scotus' view nicely. "Duns Scotus, when considering the science of metaphysics, elevated being (*ens*) to a higher station over God, so that being could be distributed to both God and his creatures."[54] James Smith deduces from this saying, "the result is that the vertical suspension of creation from the Creator is unhooked, and because being is 'flattened,' the world is freed to be an autonomous realm."[55]

So a fundamental shift has taken place with Scotus—in effect a new metaphysical language is born that foreshadows both the Enlightenment distinction of fact and values and nineteenth-century nihilism. The language of the univocity of meaning has so "flattened" our conception of reality that God is now one among many other beings. While still the most important being—and an infinite, all-powerful, and all-knowing being—nevertheless, God is no longer the one who grounds all that is, but is seen as an inscrutable and ultimate force, one who relates

[53] It is important to identify a body of literature that I am drawing on called radical orthodoxy. There are far too many authors to mention but two are necessary: John Milbank, *Theology and Social Theory: Beyond Secular Reason* (Oxford: Blackwell, 1990); and Catherine Pickstock, *After Writing: On the Liturgical Consummation of Philosophy* (Oxford: Blackwell, 1998); and "Duns Scotus: His Historical and Contemporary Significance," *Modern Theology* 21, no. 4 (2005): 543–69. For an extensive bibliography on Radical Orthodoxy, see James K. A. Smith et al., "Radical Orthodoxy: A Selected Bibliography," available to download from the website *Radical Orthodoxy Online* at http://www.calvin.edu/~jks4/ro/.

[54] Quoted from James K. A. Smith, *Introducing Radical Orthodoxy: Mapping a Post-secular Theology* (Grand Rapids: Baker, 2004), 97.   [55] Smith, *Introducing Radical Orthodoxy*, 97.

to the world through the imposition of divine will.

Before I summarize the implications of this shift for Christian ethics, it is important to point out that historical change often happens quite slowly. And so it is here. The effects of this intellectual shift certainly were not immediately evident, but seeds were sown which came to fruition in their own time. Some are taking hold only today, more than fifteen hundred years later. Also, it is a sobering thought that, as we will see, what was eventually to render Christian ethics an altogether dubious enterprise comes from within the church itself. Now to the implications of the shift from Thomas' analogy of being to Scotus' univocity of being.

First, as already hinted at above, God can now be seen as an almighty power, an absolute and singular will. That is, God does what God does. This view has the distinct effect of producing distance and even fear into the God-human relationship. In its extreme form, it suggests that God is at war with God's own creation, seeking to tame it and to bring it under dominion once more.

Second, a specific view of law now becomes the primary metaphor of God's rule. Of course, law has always been important for understanding God's rule, but it can be interpreted in many different ways; for example, as Thomas understands it, that is, where nature and law are kept together and God's will/law is "natural," or God as the ultimate sovereign who imposes God's will using divine imperatives to tame a hostile and evil world. This latter view, where God has both the power and the right to impose law on the people, now becomes more and more prevalent.

Third, the univocity of being makes possible a view of the world where reality is understandable in its own right, that is, in reference to itself. You can now fully know something without locating it in divine reason. Everything carries its own meaning rather than receiving its meaning as gift—in

and through God. This has implications for ontology in general and especially for human nature. Our wills are now our own, derived from our own nature, and naturally in conflict with God's (foreign) will. We can now see and understand ourselves as apart from God, that is, as autonomous beings, rather than as viewing our wills and nature as participating in God's being and will.

Fourth, faith and reason now divide without a common source; they are separated realms of knowledge. As we have seen, for Thomas, faith and reason or reason and revelation must be held together because they both belong to the same intellectual world. It was not as though faith was subjective and arose from an act of will and reason was objective; nor as though faith gave us religious knowledge via revelation and reason gave us knowledge of the empirical world apart from God with the aid of philosophy. This view of a division between faith and reason now makes possible a major rupture between theology and philosophy, giving rise to philosophy as an autonomous academic discipline. This fracture also gives rise to the view popular in our day that sees religion as grounded in emotions, hence producing fanatical ideas and behavior, which the objective, secular, and sober reason of the state must hold in check. In this view, one must conclude that true salvation is made possible only by the sober reason of the state, for human beings really need to be saved from the tyranny of religion.[56]

Fifth, this new view of the world opens up the possibility of justified violence in a new way. With the denial of *analogia entis* (the analogy of being) came the loss of the mystery of being, and a new drive emerged for control and domination, along with a quest for absolute knowledge. That is, if one insists on complete understanding or total certainty as a basis of knowledge and is uncomfortable with change and surprise and with control lodged elsewhere than in our own hands,

---

[56] For an elaboration of this argument, see William T. Cavanaugh, "A Fire Strong Enough to Consume the House," *Modern Theology* 11, no. 4 (1995): 397–420.

then one is required to use violence to foreclose the ambiguities of meaning and new possible understandings that come with life under God. The principle of univocity ultimately requires an epistemology of violence—a quest for the subjugation of truth itself. It should therefore not surprise us that an epistemology based on pure reason—the driving force of philosophy in the Enlightenment—replacing the metaphysics of participation and mystery with an a priori knowledge that produces an imperative for mastery. At the risk of getting too far ahead of our historical trek, perhaps an irony could be noted here since an important theme of the Enlightenment is also that of peace and security. The Enlightenment notion of peace is grounded, not on the gracious acceptance of difference or the gifts of God's redemption in which we all participate, but on the coercive principles of universal reason, that is, a further flattening of all social reality.[57]

Sixth, as the medieval metaphysics of participation is weakened, so is the power of sacrament. After all, sacrament is only possible when we see this world as participating in God, for a sacrament is a visible sign of participation in divine, mysterious-invisible reality. Historically, sacrament has been crucial for the understanding of Christian ethics. Consider the following sacraments: baptism is a visible declaration of a human being's participation in Christ; the Eucharist is a visible sign of nourishing our bodies in the act of partaking of the feast of God's abundant grace; marriage is a visible participation in an intimate human union drawing two human beings into God's goodness, generosity, and redemption; and so on. The sacraments have to do with how we understand who we are in Christ and how our ethic flows from our identity. With the weakening of a metaphysic of participation, and hence of sacrament, comes the potential reversal of the relationship between our identity and our action. For this change makes thinkable the notion that who we are is formed not by God but by what we do. And what we do derives from our own wills.

I have chosen to end this chapter with both a backward glance and a forward peek. Many of the shifts that were identified here have extremely broad implications for how we read intellectual history generally and Christian ethics specifically. These implications involve debates that are not readily settled, and I raise them here with all-too-brief comments as signposts for the road ahead. We will encounter them again as we make our way through the historical material yet to come. They are issues that do not belong in the dustbins of history, for we will see them deeply embedded in the contemporary debates about the meaning of Christian ethics.

---

[57] See esp. Immanuel Kant's work called, "To Eternal Peace," in *Basic Writings of Kant*, trans. Carl J. Friedrich, ed. Allen W. Wood (New York: Modern Library, 2001), 435–75.

Chapter Six

RENAISSANCE AND REFORMATION ETHICS

Grouping history into intelligible constructs is, of course, a work of the human mind. History does not come ready-made in classical, medieval, and Enlightenment periods. One of the dangers of historical construction is that it can reduce diversity and diminish difference for the sake of simplicity and neatness. We need to remind ourselves that history remains contingent and is always fraught with complexities that do not lend themselves to easy organization. Often there are smaller movements or diverse forces within larger ones. So it is with the periods called the Renaissance and the Reformation. They are not neat divisions; one does not simply follow the other. In fact, the former encompasses the latter. This makes it difficult to know which to treat first. One could start with either. We will be somewhat arbitrary and begin with the Renaissance.

THE RENAISSANCE

It is not clear whether it is useful to think of the Renaissance as an intellectual construct at all. It certainly is not a single, monolithic event. It is difficult to give precise dates for this era, although it is often thought to span the fourteenth to seventeenth centuries. It also had diverse incarnations in different parts of the world, such as Italy, Britain, Germany, and France. Moreover, there are important and interesting writers in this period, like Dante Alighieri (1265–1321), Desiderius Erasmus (1466–1536), Niccolò Machiavelli (1469–1527), Thomas

More (1478–1535), William Shakespeare (1564–1616), and John Milton (1608–1674), to name only a few. And many artists make this among the richest aesthetic periods of all time: Sandro Botticelli (1445–1510), Leonardo da Vinci (1452–1519), Michelangelo (1475–1564), and Raphael (1483–1520) are, again, only a few examples.

The word "Renaissance" suggests a reaching back to a former age—one worthy of restoration, or at least worthy of offering new insights. Renaissance thinkers were especially interested in rereading works from classical antiquity, where they found a message that they saw in tension with a narrow transcendentalism stressed in medieval Christianity. They also found problematic the unnuanced church-state collusion. This did not mean that they wanted to reject Christianity; rather, they saw in it a neglect of the human condition, which they believed the church as church needed to address. Perhaps one could say that many of the Renaissance writers struggled with a too-simple bifurcation between the physical and the spiritual, the human and the divine, the church and the state. On the one hand, the church was declaring its own war—the Crusades, inaugurated by Pope Urban II in 1095—and on the other hand, small sects within the church embracing the peace vision of the New Testament found it necessary to withdraw from matters political. It should be no surprise that, during the Reformation period when these debates became most intense, the ultimate outcome was the division of the church itself.

Many Renaissance writers saw their convictions deeply rooted in the rumors of an earlier golden age when the ingenuity of the human mind opened up a world of wisdom and goodness and with these the hope for peace and justice. This was occasioned in part by the translation of Greek and Arabic texts into Latin, and, although there were other factors, it became a time when Hellenistic and Arabic scholarship regained intellectual respectability in Western Europe. Hence, new resources were brought to bear in the assessment of life in general—including the life of the church.

Writers drew directly from both Greek and Roman writers, as did Machiavelli in his critique of government. Dante, in his great Christian allegory *The Divine Comedy*, draws from the classical Roman poet, Virgil. As Dante seeks to escape the deadly powers of sin by climbing "a beautiful mountain," he meets Virgil, who promises to lead him safely on the right path. Here are Dante's words as he first meets the one who will become his master and guide him on his perilous journey:

> Canst thou be Virgil? Thou that fount of splendour
> Whence poured so wide a stream of lordly speech?
> Said I, and bowed my awe-struck head in wonder;
> Oh honour and light of poets all and each,
> Now let my great love stead me – the bent brow
> And long hours pondering all thy book can teach!
> Thou art my master, and my author thou,
> From thee alone I learned the singing strain,
> The noble style that does me honour now.[1]

Dante heralded a vision of universal peace where the state would work with the church to preserve what was born from the Christian narrative. Although the late medieval sectarian pacifists, for example, the Waldensians, Franciscan Tertiaries, a branch of the Hussites, and the Cathari, held up this vision as they understood it from the texts of the Christian tradition, they abrogated their responsibility—according to Dante—precisely because they withdrew from the world they wished to save. Dante represented a more holistic view.[2] Yet both were mournful at the church's amnesia of its own just-war logic and practice. For lament over needing to kill in self-defense had been replaced with the zeal and lust for combat common in the Crusades. Both Dante and the pacifist sects sensed that something was seriously wrong when the church's involvement in the capture of Jerusalem could be described with the following words of Raymond of Agiles:

> Some of our men (and this was more merciful) cut off the heads of their enemies; others shot them with arrows, so that they fell from the towers; others tortured them longer by casting them into the flames. Piles of heads, hands, and feet were to be seen in the streets of the city. . . . But these were small matters compared to what happened at the temple of Solomon, a place where religious services are ordinarily chanted. What happened there? To tell the truth, it will exceed your powers of belief . . . men rode in blood up to their knees and the bridle reins. Indeed it was a just and splendid judgment of God, that this place should be filled with the blood of unbelievers, when it had suffered for so long from their blasphemies. . . . How [the people] rejoiced and exulted and sang the ninth chant to the Lord. . . . "The Lord made this day, and we rejoiced and exulted in it," for on this day the Lord revealed Himself to His people and blessed them.[3]

This kind of militarization of Christianity, namely, aggressively seeking to slaughter the infidel, seemed to be fueled by the same lust for power that motivated the barbarians and had nothing whatsoever to do with Christian convictions. Such actions were seen as an insult not only to Christianity but to humanity itself. And so, while the promise of a Christian way was fading, a new hope for humanity gets articulated; a hope not outside of God's grace but also not one without critique of the church's sins. And this hope, for Renaissance writers like Dante, could be rekindled in part by reading about the classic vision of

---

[1] Dante Alighieri, *The Divine Comedy*, trans. Dorothy L Sayers (Middlesex, UK: Penguin, 1949), 73.

[2] See Roland H. Bainton, *Christian Attitudes Towards War and Peace: A Historical Survey and Critical Evaluation* (Nashville: Abingdon, 1960), 118–21.

[3] Quoted from Bainton, *Christian Attitudes*, 112–13.

goodness and beauty. For if the church does not provide for the happiness of humanity, it cannot be the church. Hence, the words of a Christian humanist proclaiming the dignity of the human spirit in harmony with Christian confession:

> O great liberality of God the Father! O great and wonderful happiness of man! It is given to him that he chooses to be that which he wills . . . he will be an Angel and a Son of God.[4]

Two writers of this period are of special interest to the study of Christian ethics: Desiderius Erasmus and Thomas More. Both sought to empower the Christian faith and specifically energize the church to greater faithfulness with a renewed interest in Bible study, the church fathers, and the classical tradition. They admired each other; Erasmus even dedicated his *In Praise of Folly* (1511)[5] to More. Both were critical of the abuses of power they saw within the leadership of the church. And unlike the Protestant Reformers, both Erasmus and More remained faithful to the Catholic Church until their deaths, believing reform was possible and desirable from within the church. Hence, they had grave difficulty with people like Luther and Calvin and their perceived need to separate themselves from the Catholic Church.

Desiderius Erasmus (1467?–1536)

Erasmus "of Rotterdam" is perhaps the best-known "Renaissance humanist" and Catholic theologian of his time. Although he was born out of wedlock, his parents, especially his father, cared for him until they died when he was seventeen years old. Despite the poverty of his family, Erasmus received a good education in several schools run by monks. It was here that he encountered the classics

and began to learn the meaning of Christian piety. This led him to say later in life that "perfect piety . . . joins us together with God . . . so that we are made one with him."[6] It is interesting that Erasmus, the humanist, used the language of piety to express his understanding of the faith, but he saw complementarity in his Christian and humanitarian convictions. Perhaps this is why at a young age he had considerable trouble with the strict rules of the monastery and with the demeanor of some of his teachers. For he felt that "Christian piety" as an expression of a relationship with God could not easily be quantified, especially not by legalistic rules.

In spite of his qualms about rules, in 1492 Erasmus entered an Augustinian monastery at Steyn. Here he continued to learn Greek and Latin and to develop a love for the classics. He did not see a necessary tension between the classics and the teaching of Christ. In fact, he thought that the needed reforms in the areas of church, society, and even in theology could come only if there were a synergistic relation between Christianity and classical literature. Why? Because this would be a way of bringing the rich faith of the gospel into contact with the best of the world. The world too was God's, in his view.

With the goal of reforming the church, Erasmus developed the notion of the "philosophy of Christ."[7] He believed education was crucial because, like Socrates, he held that "no one does evil knowingly." So if you educate people well, both about matters of the faith and about affairs of the world, you will create a virtuous society.

He wrote several books to make clear how Christians should live. He did this using satire and featuring foolishness in *The Praise of*

---

[4] Giovanni Pico della Mirandola (1463–1494), *On the Dignity of Man*, para. 3 and 5. Available at the website: http://www.mcah.columbia.edu/arthumanities/pdfs/arthum_raphael_reader.pdf.

[5] Tradition has it that the title is a play on Thomas More's name. The word for "folly" in Greek is "moria" which appears in the title, "Moriae Enconium." Erasmus describes More as "a man for all seasons"; the contemporary drama and film by that name was made popular in 1966.

[6] Quoted in Dale Schrag, "*Encomium Pietatis*: Teaching for Community," in *Mennonite Education in a Post-Christian World: Essays Presented at the Consultation on Higher Education, Winnipeg, June 1997*, ed. Harry Huebner (Winnipeg, Manitoba: CMBC Publications, 1998), 88.

[7] See William R. Estep, *Renaissance and Reformation* (Grand Rapids: Eerdmans, 1986), 84.

Folly, andadaga he freely gave advice on the kind of education that would make a good prince in *The Education of a Prince*. He used literary devices and many other techniques to expose the seductions that were keeping the ordinary people, as well as the leaders of society and church, in dark ignorance. And in this, his objective was not that different from classic writers like Plato.

Erasmus believed with the likes of Augustine—no doubt this he absorbed in his monastic training—that everything is related to Christ. All that is has value in Christ. He was critical of the Scotists for undermining the Thomistic connection of nature and theology and exposed their efforts at developing a whole edifice of knowledge without once referring to Scripture. In Scripture we learn that all truth finds its center in Christ.[8]

Several offers were extended for Erasmus to go to Rome and become part of the church hierarchy, but he rejected them all. As he saw it, structured religion had a way of tempting disciples into a kind of formalism that could too easily lead to unfaithfulness. He saw Christianity essentially in terms of discipleship. That is the way the Christian life is talked about in the Scriptures, where it means an essential connection, continuity, and imitation of the life and teachings of Jesus.

Erasmus was one of the first humanists who was passionate in his opposition to war. Roland Bainton says, "on no subject did Erasmus speak so often and with such passion."[9] He believed there to be practical alternatives, like arbitration and compromise, to resolving conflicts and suggested as a final court of appeal that the matter be presented to "an impartial judiciary made up of bishops and magistrates."[10] He was appalled at the Crusades. He deplored even a just war against the Turks, for he believed that they too were human beings. War was altogether inconsistent with the message of the gospel. In his *Adagia* he says:

> The end and aim of the faith of the Gospel is conduct worthy of Christ. Why do we insist on those things which have nothing to do with morality, and neglect the things which are like pillars of a structure—once you take them away the whole edifice will crumble at once? Finally, who will believe us, when we take as our device the Cross of Christ and the name of the Gospel, if our whole life obviously speaks of nothing but the world?[11]

It is interesting to see how Erasmus seeks to hold together the very thing that Reformers like Luther found necessary to separate, namely, the church and world. For Erasmus the world ought never to be understood on its own terms as the world. and its institutions and structures are best understood through Christ and his body: the church.

Thomas More (1478–1535)

More was a somewhat controversial figure. As a writer, lawyer, and British statesman, he, like his Dutch friend Erasmus, retained a deep loyalty to the church and a commitment to the betterment of humanity. He was a constant advocate for the poor, and he had some distinct ideas about the reform of the church. The Catholic scholar, G. K. Chesterton, has said that More "may come to be counted the greatest Englishman, or at least the greatest historical character in English history."[12] Ironically, after being knighted and serving in many stately capacities as House speaker, ambassador, and chancellor of England, he was executed for treason by the very state he had so diligently served.

This is clearly not the place for a detailed narration of events surrounding More's trial and ultimate beheading. At one level, the issue was King Henry VIII's divorce of Catherine of Aragon—More refused to sign a

---

[8] See Estep, *Renaissance and Reformation*, 85.

[9] Roland H. Bainton, *Erasmus of Christendom* (New York: Scribner, 1969), 119.

[10] See Estep, *Renaissance and Reformation*, 91.

[11] Quoted from Estep, *Renaissance and Reformation*, 92–93.

[12] Cited in R. W. Chambers, *Thomas More*, The Bedford Historical Series (London: Jonathan Cape, 1938), 373.

letter asking the pope to annul the marriage. But far more important for More was the question of who has ultimate authority in the church, the king or the pope? While More was willing to accept Parliament's power to name Anne Boleyn the new queen of England, the Act of Succession to which More was to swear allegiance contained, in its preface, language implying that the king was the supreme head of the Church of England. This language the Catholic More could not accept because for him the primacy of the church and the authority of the pope were fundamental articles of faith. So in his own words, he was martyred for "the faith of the Holy Catholic church."[13]

More was a social visionary. His novel, *Utopia* (1516), popular to this day, describes a peaceful imaginary island, and the story served as a critique of his own society. As he saw it, the world was a place for peace and the acceptance of difference. Yet, while he emphasized the importance of difference, he placed clear limits on this notion. For example, since atheists have no court of appeal higher than themselves in matters of truth-seeking, they could have no ontological base for order and community. And for More, a mere like-minded aggregate of people is not yet a community. Hence the voice of an atheist necessarily needed to be given diminished authority. Individual freedom was not his concern; shaping a disciplined people was. In *Utopia*, More sought to bring together his Catholic commitment to monasticism, his influence by classical philosophy—for example, Plato's *The Republic* rooted in the universal Good—and his reading of the post-Pentecost vision in Acts.

More had serious difficulties with Protestantism because it fragmented the church in ways he thought were unnecessary. Not only this, mainline Protestants were also separating what the Catholic Church had sought to hold together, namely, the salvation of the physical and the salvation of the spiritual. More had some intense exchanges with Martin Luther, which resulted in full-length books, especially his commissioned response to Luther's *On the Babylonian Captivity of the Church*. More thought of Luther as a heretic, hence a threat to both church and society. The Protestant Reformation movement was far from a simple threat for More. In fact, as chancellor, he had several Lutherans executed and many more imprisoned and tortured. He sought to preserve the unity of the church at all costs.

Tradition has treated More well, despite his being martyred. He was beatified by Pope Leo XIII in 1886 and canonized in 1935. As recently as 2000, Pope John Paul II declared him the "heavenly Patron of Statesmen and politicians."[14]

Much of what is said under the banner of the Renaissance has impact on questions of Christian ethics: the nature of the church, how it relates to institutions of society, how to live as faithful Christians, issues of peace and war, and even more generally, the self-understanding of who we are as human beings. For how we understand our place in life, how we perceive ourselves under God and in relation to others and our involvement in shaping history, are all important ethical matters. What we do and what we can find justification for, ultimately, come from how we understand our very being—as individuals and societies.

THE REFORMATION

The major Reformers like Martin Luther and John Calvin rarely talked about ethics as an independent discipline of study or even as a separate theological category. Ethics, for them, was the practical expression of sound theology. They took it as self-evident that what one believed about God, Christ,

---

[13] For a helpful account of More's life and thought, see Kenneth D. Whitehead, "The 500th Anniversary of the Birth of Saint Thomas More (1478–1978)," http://www.ewtn.com/library/MARY/TOMOR500.HTM. I am also drawing general information from Wikipedia articles on Thomas More.

[14] From "Thomas More," *Wikipedia*, last modified March 29, 2011, http://en.wikipedia.org/wiki/Thomas_more.

salvation, and so on, had implications for how one ought to live. Christian ethics ought to be seen as the process of spelling out what those implications are, but it was not to be distinguished from the larger theological task.

This is entirely as it should be and very close to the way it was suggested that ethics be understood in the introduction to this book with the claim that theology is ethics, and ethics theology. For the Reformers, however, the notion of Christian ethics is problematic in another way. Ethics focuses on what Christians must do in order to be good Christians, and mainline Reformers saw this as the central mistake of the Roman Catholic Church. In fact, it is precisely this way of speaking about becoming good Christians that is largely what required reformation, according to Luther and Calvin. Both believed that the only way we can become good is as a result of God's grace. They believed that theology had to do with the primacy of God and the depravity of humankind, not how we can learn to be good. Theology is all about what God has done for us and not about what we must do for God.

We should not conclude from this, however, that the Reformers said nothing about the Christian life. Quite the contrary. In many respects, Luther's reformation quest was rooted in his intense belief that the life of Christians was not Bible-based. Note, for example, one of his Ninety-Five Theses: "86. Again: Since the pope's income today is larger than that of the wealthiest of wealthy men, why does he not build this one church of St. Peter with his own money, rather than with the money of indigent believers?"[15] Granted, there were issues other than wealth here, like how salvation is properly understood, yet wealth distribution was not irrelevant to Luther's concern. The emphasis of the Reformers was that when we properly understand the biblical teaching of what it means to be Christian, we will understand why the notion of "moral obligation" is problematic. The issue for Luther was really all about God's power (ability) and ours.[16] And on this matter, humans are simply far less significant than God. So if ethics is primarily about us, and theology is primarily about God, then Christians should be more concerned about theology than ethics.

In this section on the Reformation, I will seek to make sense of the similarities and differences among the three main actors: Martin Luther, John Calvin, and the Anabaptists. I will do this by devoting a section to each.

Martin Luther (1483–1546)

Luther was born to a peasant family in Eisleben. His parents managed to provide a good primary and secondary education for their son, and at age seventeen, he entered the University of Erfurt. Here he received a bachelor's degree in 1502 and a master's degrees in 1505. The summer of 1505 was tumultuous for young Martin. The plan, and certainly his father's wish, had been for him to study law. But something happened that took him in a very different direction (biographers are not agreed on exactly what happened). Several things were on his mind during this summer—the death of a friend (although not a close friend) caused him to think about the afterlife and the last judgment, and pressure from his father to marry scared him half to death. Amidst his inner turmoil, he had an encounter with a violent thunderstorm on July 2, 1505. A bolt of lightning struck the ground near him, and he was caught in a state of panic and terror and thrown down with a force sufficient to injure his leg. Some biographers say he was also

---

[15] Quoted from John Dillenberger, ed., *Martin Luther: Selections from His Writings* (Garden City, N.Y.: Doubleday, 1961), 499.

[16] "Now, if I am ignorant of God's works and power, I am ignorant of God himself; and if I do not know God, I cannot worship, praise, give thanks or serve Him, for I do not know how much I should attribute to myself and how much to Him. We need, therefore, to have in mind a clear-cut distinction between God's power and ours, and God's work and ours, if we would live a Godly life" from Martin Luther, "Bondage of the Will," in Dillenberger, *Martin Luther*, 179.

rendered unconscious. In any event, before he quite knew what was happening to him, he burst out with these words, "Do thou help, St. Ann; I will become a monk."[17]

Luther interpreted the lightning as a direct call from heaven ("intimidation from heaven," he later calls it), and he saw his involuntary response as a vow to take up the religious life. When he reflected on this experience, he said this was a forced decision made under extreme "consternation." "I became a monk against my will and desire."[18] Nevertheless, at the time, Luther felt bound by "the vow" he had made, so he abandoned his studies, sold his books, and on July 17, 1505, barely fifteen days after uttering the words of promise, he knocked on the door of an Augustinian monastery and requested permission to become a monk. At age twenty-two, a new life began for him.

Luther was an obedient novice and practiced the religious rituals with diligence. He reflects on his early years thus:

> I was a good monk and kept my orders so strictly that I could claim that if ever a monk were able to reach heaven by monkish discipline I should have found my way there. All my fellows in the house, who knew me, would bear me out in this. For if it had continued much longer I would, what with vigils, prayers, readings and other such works, have done myself to death.[19]

He did not find peace with God, however. He could not help but see himself before an angry God who demanded obedience and in whose presence he could not do anything but obey.[20] That lesson he had already learned from the lightning bolt. He did not want to be in a monastery—God had put him there against his wishes. How could an angry God bring peace to a troubled soul? Indeed it did not happen! Nevertheless, he became a monk in 1506, and a year later was ordained to the priesthood.

Luther was now bound for a life of theological study and teaching. There were many new universities in Germany at the beginning of the sixteenth century, mostly staffed by monks. Shortly after he entered the monastery, Luther was assigned to Wittenberg to study and teach. His first work assignment was to teach Aristotle's *Nicomachean Ethics*.

Luther had many doubts during this stage of life. The Wittenberg cloister was, for him, a sad place. Biographer Hartmann Grisar writes: "Luther says of his monastic life: 'My heart trembles and flutters, when I meditate on how God may be merciful to me. Often have I been frightened at the name of Jesus, and, when I looked upon Him as He hung on the cross, He was as lightning to me.' He was often compelled to say: 'I wish there were no God.'"[21] Yet in his early years Luther was quiet about his inner turmoil. On October 19, 1512, Luther received his doctorate and was given the position of "biblical lecturer" and immediately began teaching the Psalms and, soon thereafter, the Epistle to the Romans.

Even early in his teaching career he sought to disassociate himself from the traditional ecclesial observances of the church and the self-righteousness of scholars whose writings defended these practices. He was altogether disgusted with the scholastics. He called them "swine theologians." More specifically, Aristotle was "that buffoon who has misled the church" and Aquinas was "the source and foundation of all heresy, error and obliteration of the Gospel."[22] In contradistinction, he

---

[17] Martin Luther, *Tischreden*, Weimar ed., IV, Nr. 4707. Quoted in Hartman Grisar, S. J., *Martin Luther: His Life and Work*, trans. Frank J. Eble (Westminster, Md.: Newman, 1954), 38. Saint Ann, according to Erik Erikson, was Luther's father's patron saint, see Erikson, *Young Man Luther: A Study in Psychoanalysis and History* (New York: Norton, 1962), 92.

[18] Quoted from Grisar, *Martin Luther*, 38.

[19] Quoted from Michael Mullett, *Luther* (London: Methuen, 1986), 23.

[20] It is interesting to notice here how distant God seems to Luther and indeed how wholly other and even strange God is. This is in stark contrast to Augustine and Thomas. Indeed, one wonders whether the influences of Scotus' and Ockham's doctrines of univocity make this distanced view of God more readily intelligible for Luther.

[21] Grisar, *Martin Luther*, 49.

[22] Quoted in Denis R. Janz, *Luther and Late Medieval Thomism: A Study in Theological Anthropology* (Waterloo, Ontario: Wilfrid Laurier University Press, 1983), 3.

saw himself as an enlightened student of the Apostle Paul and Augustine.[23] From the very beginning of his teaching career, Luther portrayed himself as one disenchanted with the theological convictions he inherited from the church.

At the heart of Luther's Reformation thinking was the recovery of sound doctrine on the basis of authoritative biblical sources. Only this, he believed, could sustain true faithfulness and new life. In his *Lectures on Romans* (1515/1516), we see already the principal outline of his later theology. He emphasizes *sola gratia, sola fides, sola scriptura,* human resignation to the sovereignty of God, and the depravity of human beings. Human beings are not really free to do good; our freedom usually gets us to do evil.

Luther's new theology, not to mention his provocative and audacious style, earned him many enemies, but no one in his order in Wittenberg could compete with him as an orator. Inferior efforts only increased both his audacity and tenacity. Many sensational disputations took place, where the doctrines, practices, and indeed the authority of the church were put in question, and where his new theological theme—the primacy of God's grace—was asserted.

On October 31, 1517, Luther issued a public invitation to a disputation over indulgences. It is generally believed that he did this by nailing ninety-five theses on the door of the All Saints Church (Castle Church) in Wittenberg. Regardless of how he made his theses public, for Luther the issue was this: an indulgence was a remission, purportedly obtained from God, from the penalties of sin through the payment of money. The practical side of this practice was that it was used by preachers as a way of raising money. It literally paid to convict people of their sins! In Luther's day, this practice was a means of

raising funds for the building of Saint Peter's Church in Rome. It is not hard to see that this practice would be in direct opposition to Luther's conviction that God does not consider our actions meritorious according to our labors or our money. No payment of money could possibly earn God's favor. Hence, he considered indulgences unbiblical and heretical.

Although the Ninety-Five Theses were originally in Latin, they were immediately translated into German and were widely read. The many debates and public disputations eventually led to an investigation by Roman ecclesial authorities, who condemned Luther's teachings and excommunicated him from the church. On April 17, 1521, he appeared before Emperor Charles V at the Diet of Worms. The Archbishop of Treves, John von Eck, asked Luther to retract the teachings of his book(s), which had been placed on a table before him. Luther responded with a speech defending his basic convictions. When he was finally forced to answer clearly whether he recanted or not, he said:

> [Since] I am not convinced [of your arguments] by proofs from Scripture or clear theological reasons, I remain convinced by the passages which I have quoted [in my book] from Scripture, and my conscience is held captive by the Word of God. I cannot and will not retract, for it is neither prudent nor right to go against one's conscience. So help me God, Amen![24]

It is a matter of dispute whether Luther added the words, "Here I stand, I can do no other," or whether they were inserted later. In any event, with the Emperor's response, "A single friar who goes counter to all Christianity for a thousand years must be wrong,"[25] Luther was made an outlaw.

The Emperor had intended to give Luther safe passage back to Wittenberg. However, because his life was in danger, it had

---

[23] Luther also says: "Plato can assert neither that God cares about us nor that he hears and helps the needy. He stays within the limits of metaphysical thought like a cow staring at a new gate." And again, "Philosophers and Aristotle are not able to understand or define what the theological man is, but by the grace of God we are able to do it, because we have the Bible." Both quotes are taken from Paul Althaus, *The Theology of Martin Luther,* trans. Robert C. Schultz (Philadelphia: Fortress, 1966), 10.

[24] Quoted from Grisar, *Martin Luther,* 185.   [25] Quoted from Mullett, *Luther,* 41.

been prearranged to have him kidnapped by friends and given a secret hiding place. He was taken to Wartburg and given a new identity: Squire George. At Wartburg he wrote some tirades against the pope and against the "Transactions at Worms." However, his major project at this time was the translation of the Bible. Luther was not happy at Wartburg; his heart was in Wittenberg.

Wittenberg was in turmoil. Disgruntled students and peasants were attacking churches and priests. There was a general state of confusion and disorder. The government issued a strict warning to the bishops not to tolerate riots, and the Elector Frederick was given instructions to restore calm. It was then that Luther chanced his return, believing he could assist in re-establishing order. Yet there was a problem: how would the local city authorities be disposed to having an outlaw return to town? Fortunately, they needed help.

On March 6, 1522, Luther arrived in Wittenberg, and the following Sunday he began his preaching. For eight successive days he preached. Given his powerful oratory skills, he was able to restore order to Wittenberg.

From 1522 until his death in 1546, Luther spent his time refining his "reformation theology." This is not the place where all the refinements can be treated. Instead, I will address briefly those aspects of his theology that pertain most directly to Christian ethics: God/election, good works, orders of creation, law/gospel, anthropology, sin, and the two kingdoms.

God/Election: Luther's reform efforts were all about changing the theological center of gravity from anthropology to theology, or from Thomas' natural law to Augustine's revealed theology. His cry to "Let God be God" was echoed by a corresponding plea, "Let humans be human." His emphasis on the primacy of God allowed him to interpret all of theology—indeed all of the Christian life—from the standpoint of the mercy and grace

of God toward us and our utter sinfulness and depravity in the face of God.

Two theological concepts are at the core of his writings: "justification"—the restoration of the relationship between God and humans—and "sanctification"—the resultant holy life. Both focus on God. And with these two concepts lies the essence of his conception of the Christian life. In other words, ethics has little to do with our efforts of obedience; it has everything to do with our being justified by God's grace. He says:

> God shows mercy out of his great goodness and hardens out of no wickedness, so that he who is saved has no basis for glorifying in any merit of his own, and he who is damned no basis for complaining of anything except what he has fully merited.[26]

This emphasis on the absolute sovereignty of God is fundamental for Luther. He did not derive this from some speculative process of rational reflection but by his reading of Scripture. And it was precisely here where his criticism of medieval theology was the sharpest; as he saw it, Thomistic theology was not based on the reading of the Scriptures but on an understanding of natural law.

It is interesting to reflect on the fact that both Thomas and Luther embraced the basic tenets of Augustine, and yet Luther is scathing in his critique of Thomas. They clearly took different paths from Augustine. Thomas developed, somewhat with the aid of Aristotle, the notion of a natural theology, and Luther did not. But Thomas was able to do that because he accepted Augustine's teaching that all of creation participates in the being of the Creator. Hence, the natural (creation) was not separate from God for Thomas like it was for Luther. Thomas was a medievalist in a way that Luther was not. For Thomas the natural and the revealed, reason and revelation, the natural and the transcendent, were not discontinuous but bore a particular relationship to one another

---

[26] Martin Luther, "Lecture on Romans," in *Luther: Lecture on Romans*, The Library of Christian Classics, vol. 15, trans. and ed. Wilhelm Pauck (Philadelphia: Westminster, 1961), 276.

and so, as the natural participated in God, one could, given proper hermeneutical care, read revelation from natural law. This Luther could not accept.

As Luther saw it, the sovereign will of God revealed in Scripture is fundamental for understanding the Christian life. Sin is the rejection of God's will, and righteousness is the unequivocal acceptance of God's will. According to Luther, only after we subject ourselves totally to God's will, even to the point of saying, "If I am damned, alright, let me be damned," can we be saved. God elects the saints and the sinners. This is the prerogative of God, and we must accept what God elects.

Good Works/Christian Liberty: This is what Luther says regarding the place of good works in the Christian faith.

> So then, why does man take pride in his merits and good works? They can not in any way please God, because they *are* good and meritorious, but only because God elected from eternity that they would please Him. We do the good only on the basis of gratitude, because our works do not make us good, but our goodness or, rather, the goodness of God makes us good and our actions as well. For what we do is not good in itself, but only because God reckons it to be so. Our deeds are good or not good only to the degree in which God does or does not regard them so. Hence, our reckoning or nonreckoning is worth nothing.[27]

He says further, "it is grace which enables man voluntarily to do good works; and if he lacks it (grace), he is unwilling to do them (good works)."[28] And again:

> The following statements are therefore true: "Good works do not make a good man, but a good man does good works; evil works do not make a wicked man, but a wicked man does evil works." Consequently it is always necessary that the substance of a person himself be good before there can be any good works, and that the good works follow and proceed from the good person, as Christ also says, "A good tree does not bear evil fruit, nor can a bad tree bear good fruit." (Matt 7:18)[29]

This theology of good works is related to the notion sometimes called the Protestant work ethic.[30] At first, this seems like a contradiction. If good works are given such a low position within the Christian faith, and God's grace such high esteem, then how could this underwrite a work ethic? That is, how could it produce people who think it so important to work hard? To answer this question we must notice that, although good work does not produce favor with God, it is nevertheless a sign of God's favor. Hence, good work is evidence of God's blessing on us. This produces an incentive to demonstrate that God is gracious to us. Moreover, whether we do right or wrong is only secondarily important because it is after all God's election which determines this. We are therefore set free to do honest hard work without guilt of becoming rich or fear of doing wrong by becoming successful. Not only are the negative impediments lifted, the positive incentive is that good works demonstrate God's blessings upon us.

Luther further developed this teaching by making reference to the notion of *Beruf* (a calling). He was critical of the medieval tradition that also spoke of a calling, but here it meant a call from God to become one who would renounce the mundane world, withdraw from it, and live a life enslaved to rules, hoping thereby to win God's favor.[31] He argued that rather than faithfulness, this represented the opposite: it was a tendency toward work-righteousness, and it represented a failure to meet one's temporal obligations. He believed that Christians had obligations in both the spiritual and temporal realms. Hence, he speaks of ordinary vocations as callings; temporal obligations, which are not governed by rules but by grace, are manifested via labor adequate to the development of the natural

---

[27] Luther, "Lecture on Romans," 266.
[28] Luther, "Lecture on Romans," 392.
[29] Martin Luther, "Freedom of a Christian, 1520," in Dillenberger, *Martin Luther*, 69.
[30] See esp. Max Weber, *The Protestant Ethic and the Spirit of Capitalism*, trans. Talcott Parsons (New York: Charles Scribner's Sons, 1958).   [31] See Weber, *Protestant Ethic*, 80–81.

order of things. Christians are indeed free, nay obligated, to be the best farmers, doctors, bank managers, nurses, teachers possible. Voluntary poverty is out; free to be successful in worldly vocations is in!

Orders of Creation: According to Luther, God has created the world organized into stations or orders (in German, *Stand).* One sees many different stations. Luther lists examples like fathers and mothers, married people, servants and maids, lords and subjects, pastors, and so on. Sometimes he speaks about them as though they can be grouped into three main groups: family, religious vocations, and secular vocations. These stations are not "man-made;" they are God-created and "man-revealed." Given these different stations God has ordered, we find that each of us is in many of them at the same time; that is, I am a father, a husband, a teacher, a citizen, and so on. In fact, these stations are interrelated and build on each other. Moreover, they are necessary in order for the world to exist. He says at one point that "these stations must remain if the world is to stand."[32]

These stations are divinely instituted and are intended to serve God and the world in such a way as to make this world a more godly place. Each person is called to participate in a particular *Beruf* (vocation). This is the contribution each Christian is to make in being faithful to God's call. We are to fulfill our duties in relation to our calling. How? By giving concrete expression to the love of God in Christ Jesus in the particular station in which we happen to be involved. The different stations all have the same value. None is better than the other. Hence, there are no special stations—other than the ministry perhaps—which Christians are called to.

Law/Gospel: Luther speaks about the "old law" and the "new law." By "old law" he means that law which guided the people's behavior before Christ and by "new law" he means the law of the gospel. The new law is different in content from the old, and it is also different in nature. It is not a law of works like the old law. It is a law of faith, which is given by the grace of God through Jesus Christ. The old law was necessary because it curbed the powers of the flesh, but the new law goes much further in that it frees us from fleshly desires. Luther states the difference between the two as follows:

> The old law says to those who are proud in their righteousness: you must have Christ and his spirit. The new law says to those who humbly recognize that they lack all righteousness and who seek Christ, "Behold, here is Christ and his spirit!" They, therefore, that interpret the Gospel as something else than "Good News," do not understand the Gospel. Precisely this must be said to those who have turned the Gospel into a law rather than interpret it as grace, and who set Christ before us as a Moses.[33]

Hence, as a result of the gospel of Jesus Christ, law as heteronymous obligation ceases to be a functional concept for Christians. The gospel is to compel us not by obligation but by spirit. Like Augustine before, if the inner attitude was right the outward act could not be wrong. If justification was effected, sanctification was bound to follow. But the outward act could well vary in different situations. This is precisely why the Christian life could not be governed by law. Law regulates outward behavior; gospel regulates inner spirit. Hence, for the Christian the guiding question must be, "What is the form of love applicable in this situation—to endure injustice and to demand justice?"[34]

Anthropology: Since God is ultimately sovereign and omnipotent, we are absolutely dependent upon God. Moreover, morally speaking, we are completely impotent. Our nature and will are so totally corrupt that there is no way back to God on our own

---

[32] Quoted from Paul Althaus, *The Ethics of Martin Luther,* trans. Robert C. Schultz (Philadelphia: Fortress, 1972), 37.

[33] Luther, "Lecture on Romans," 199.

[34] Heinrich Bornkamm, *Luther's Doctrine of the Two Kingdoms in the Context of His Theology,* trans. Karl H. Hertz (Philadelphia: Fortress, 1966), 9.

initiative. All depends upon God. Hence, God inflicts tribulation on us so that we will see our condition and recognize that our only way out is by accepting the salvation which comes from God. Salvation can come "only by grace through faith" and not by any "works, lest we should boast."

As we have already seen, Luther has learned much from Augustine, and he used his dualistic anthropology to articulate his own criticism of a Thomistic naturalism. Our spiritual selves are governed by the grace of God and our natural selves by fleshly desires. Or as Luther puts it, "Nature . . . sets before itself no other object than the self. . . . That is what it means to have a 'perverse' and 'wicked' heart. *Grace* puts God in the place of everything else it sees and seeks only what is God's and not its own . . . ."[35] Our natural self is in love with itself and must be crucified with God, and our spiritual nature must be cultivated.

It is no doubt clear by now that Luther believes that human beings are utterly sinful. What may not yet be clear is how he understood the nature of sin. The primary view of sin is as concupiscence. Moreover, sin is original and independent of our actions. By sin as concupiscence Luther meant something more than Augustine. Augustine had distinguished between proper self-love and perverted self-love, and he called the latter concupiscence. Luther called all self-directed love sinful. Sin is exactly identical with humans seeking their own egotistical will, because this will is always opposed to God's will. "This concupiscence is always in us, the love of God is never in us, except insofar as grace has been given us a beginning of it."[36]

This sin is an independent force: ". . . not I that do it but the sin that dwells within" (Rom 7:20). Over this force we can have no control, yet God can. And unless God exercises this control in our lives, we are doomed to destruction by the power this sin has in our lives. But sin is also original. There is an original power or proneness to evil and

the loathing of the good that is natural. This characteristic makes sin an independent force—independent of our actions and God's power. It is simply part of being human and extends back to Adam. The reason for this is at least partly due to the fact that we are first born of the flesh before we can be born of the spirit. As Luther puts it:

> Due to original sin, our nature is so curved in upon itself at its deepest levels, that it not only bends the best gifts of God towards itself in order to enjoy them, nay, rather, "uses" God in order to obtain them, but it does not even know that, in this wicked, twisted, crooked way, it seeks everything, including God, only for itself.[37]

This sin is never completely overcome in our lifetime, and so the Christian life remains a struggle. Faith does not transform the whole person all at once. *Simul justus et peccator* (simultaneously justified and sinner) is a basic Reformation doctrine. Hence, individual righteousness is seen as intermixed with individual sinfulness, much like Augustine's use of the wheat and the tares parable for the nature of the kingdom. In fact, as we will see, this intermixture of good and evil is a dominant theme also in the understanding of Luther's two-kingdoms doctrine.

Luther's Two Kingdoms: Luther's division between the two kingdoms had its roots in the human body. We are beings with both physical and spiritual dimensions, and we cannot simply shed one aspect of our existence and embrace only the other. At least, this is not possible in this spatiotemporal world. Hence, we have to find ways of living with both dimensions under the dominion of God.

The two kingdoms are the kingdom of God in which the rule of Christ's love is normative and the "kingdom" of the worldly authorities, whose task is to curb the power of evil by whatever means necessary. The secular government would not be necessary if the world consisted only of *true* Christians, since they live by the inner spirit of Christ's love, which

---

[35] Luther, "Lecture on Romans," 219–20.
[36] Luther, "Lecture on Romans," 129.

[37] Luther, "Lecture on Romans," 159.

makes both law and justice superfluous. Yet this is not so generally, and even most Christians do not live by their Christian calling consistently.

Christians live in two worlds. In the one you "suffer injustice toward yourself as a true Christian" and in the other you "tolerate no injustice toward your neighbor."[38] These two realms of government are distinct. In the one, you have rule by the uncoercive word of God, and in the other you have rule by the coercive power of government. In the one, forgiveness and sacrifice prevail; in the other, punishment and self-defense are operative. In the one, you deal with sin redemptively; in the other, you deal with it coercively and with violence if necessary. Both kingdoms are absolutely essential in this world, belonging together side by side. In fact, they require each other. Luther puts it this way:

> For this reason these two kingdoms must be sharply distinguished and both be permitted to remain; the one to produce piety, the other to bring about external peace and prevent evil deeds; neither is sufficient in the world without the other. For no one can become pious before God by means of the secular governments, without Christ's spiritual rule. Hence Christ's rule does not extend over all, but Christians are always in the minority and are in the midst of non-Christians.[39]

Why does Luther insist so strongly on the point that we must live in both? Because we all have commerce with institutions outside the church; we live in houses bought on the market; we are citizens of the state; we pay taxes; and so on. We live in both kingdoms and we act in both, just like we all live as physical and spiritual beings.

But how are we to act in both? Before we answer this, we need to make one additional point. Both kingdoms are ordained by God, and God acts in both in keeping with God's grace and love. This is what binds the two together. Bornkamm puts it thus:

Among all the contrasts between the two kingdoms which Luther lists—kingdom of God/worldly kingdom, gospel/law, the faithful/the infidels, spiritual/secular, for one's self/for others, the Word of God/the sword, and so forth—he never says "kingdom of love/kingdom without love." Love encompasses both.[40]

Luther suggests that, since both are ordained by God, each has is own operative ethic derived in relation to what is appropriate in each realm. In the church, sin can be dealt with through forgiveness because people are already under the conviction of the Holy Spirit. In the world, where this is not so, sin cannot be dealt with in this manner. Here, sin needs a more powerful enforcer, like the sword. Hence, to the question of whether Christians should bear the sword, Luther answers:

> You have now heard two propositions: The one is that the sword can have no place among Christians, therefore you cannot bear it among Christians and against Christians, who do not need it. The question, therefore, must be directed on the other side, the non-Christians, whether as a Christian you may there bear it. Here the other proposition applies, that you are under obligation to serve and further the sword by whatever means you can, with body, soul, honor, or goods. For it is nothing that you need, but something quite useful and profitable for the whole world and for your neighbor. Therefore, should you see that there is a lack of hangmen, beadles [constables], judges, lords, or princes, and find that you are qualified, you should offer your services and seek the place, that necessary government may by no means be despised and become inefficient or perish. For the world cannot and dare not dispense with it.[41]

For Luther, the basic question determining one's actions rests on which realm one is acting in. If one is acting as a citizen of the state, then one is required to use the sword; if one is acting as a member of the church, then this would be inappropriate. It is not that one sphere is more important than the other; they just have different functions

---

[38] Quoted from Bornkamm, *Luther's Doctrine*, 7.

[39] Martin Luther, "Secular Authority: To What Extent it Should be Obeyed" (1523), in Dillenberger, *Martin Luther*, 371.

[40] Bornkamm, *Luther's Doctrine*, 9.   [41] Luther, "Secular Authority," 374–75.

in this world. Both are under God's rule of grace and love. And these functions are confused at great peril. For example,

> If any one attempted to rule the world by the Gospel, and put aside all secular laws and the secular sword, on the plea that all are baptised and Christian . . . what would happen? He would loose the bands and chains of the beasts, and let them tear and mangle every one. . . . Just so would the wicked in the name of Christian . . . say that they were Christians subject neither to law nor sword, as some are already ranting and raving.[42]

Luther's view of the Christian acting in the two kingdoms could be illustrated as follows:[43]

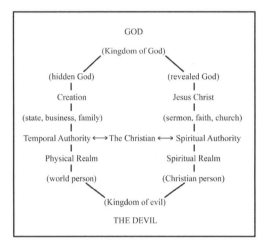

Several comments are in order. First, as this diagram suggests, Luther is really distinguishing among four realms: the kingdoms of God and evil, (*regnum Dei* and *regnum diaboli*) and the realms of the physical (temporal) and the spiritual. Jürgen Moltmann puts it this way: "Just as this conflict between the two kingdoms dominates world history, it also dominates the personal life of the Christian as the *continual conflict of the Spirit against the flesh*, justice against sin, life against death, faith against unfaith."[44]

Second, Luther believed that God's love could be expressed in two ways: directly and indirectly. He calls the latter the strange work of love or God's second hand. An act can be an act of love, even though it may not look much like it on the surface. What makes an act divine is the hidden intention of God. The use of violence, even causing death, may not look like love, but it can be. Third, this same distinction between the inner intention and the outer act also applies to humans. As Wogaman explains: "In a justified war, [Luther] writes, 'It is a Christian act and an act of love confidently to kill, rob, and pillage the enemy'—though he promptly follows this with admonitions to offer mercy to those who surrender and not to harm the innocent."[45] Fourth, it is important to recognize that the basis of the Christian life for Luther resides in the legitimating autonomy which both the temporal and the spiritual realms have been given by God. The danger is always to measure the one by the other (for example, ruling the world by the Sermon on the Mount and ruling the church by the laws of the state). Each realm has its own sovereignty under God. That is, both realms are willed by God, and each is known via its own route: one by the revelation of God through Christ Jesus and the other through the natural knowledge of the orders of creation.

Luther succeeded in dividing the world into two morally independent realms. The details of this discussion proved extremely contentious for the contemporary Thomists and also for the Anabaptists some years later. Even John Calvin, who agreed with much of what Martin Luther had to say, found this radical moral dualism untenable.

John Calvin (1509–1564)

Calvin was born in Nolan, France, yet most of his reform activities came out of Geneva.

---

[42] Luther, "Secular Authority," 370–71.

[43] This illustration is adapted from Jürgen Moltmann, *Following Jesus in the World Today: Responsibility for the World and Christian Discipleship*, Occasional Papers, no. 4 (Elkhart, Ind.: Institute of Mennonite Studies, 1983), 23.

[44] Moltmann, *Following Jesus*, 23 (emphasis in original).

[45] J. Philip Wogaman, *Christian Ethics: A Historical Introduction* (Louisville, Ky.: Westminster John Knox, 1993), 114.

He was one of the few Reformers who did not arrive at his theological position from inside the priesthood. He says of his early years:

> Ever since I was a child, my father had intended me for theology; but thereafter inasmuch as he considered that the study of the law commonly enriched those who followed it, this expectation made him incontinently change his mind. That is the reason why I was withdrawn from the study of philosophy and put to the study of the law, to which I strove to devote myself faithfully in obedience to my father. God, however, in his hidden providence, at last made me turn in another direction.[46]

Although he received an education at the University of Paris that prepared him for the priesthood, at the time he was much more interested in humanism than in reform theology. In 1532 he published a book on the Roman Stoic philosopher Seneca, called *Commentary on the De Clementia*. Yet Calvin was not a blind admirer of Stoicism, even in his early years. It was the Stoic's love for truth and their commitment to a scientific method of inquiry that made them interesting. His biographer, François Wendel, says that "Towards the end of his sojourn in Paris, we must imagine Calvin to have been like one of those Catholic humanists . . . for whom the establishment of good literature was infinitely more important than any attack upon Roman dogmatics. That tendency became even more marked in the following years."[47]

Despite Calvin's own claim that his conversion to Luther's Reformation project was sudden, we have no exact date for the event. Wendel puts it somewhere in the first half of 1534. In the beginning, Calvin's reform vision was broader than Luther's. He could not see why the Reformation could not include an Erasmus as well as a Luther.[48] However, it did not take long before he became more exclusive. Eventually he came to call those who were only halfway committed to the reform movement, Nicodemites.[49] Shortly after his conversion, however, he was forced to leave the University of Paris when the newly elected rector, Nicholas Cop, his close friend and associate, declared his support for Martin Luther.

Calvin's career as a Reformer began in earnest when he was appointed Reader in Holy Scripture to the church in Geneva. Soon after, he was commissioned to preach sermons, and "he was always a professor." Wendel identifies "four domains" in which Calvin did original work: exegesis, dogmatics, preaching, and reconstitution of the church.[50] And in Geneva the most original of these, certainly the most contentious, was his re-conception of the church. It was also the most important for understanding his view of the Christian life.

Ecclesiology: Although we cannot here recount the details of his ecclesial reconstruction, nevertheless a few things are important for our study of Christian ethics. The political structure of Geneva at the time consisted of four chief magistrates (syndics) and several councils. During Calvin's time in Geneva, the elections and appointments to these councils were going through transition, and power was being decentralized. Calvin supported this change.[51] Given these political reforms, Calvin thought it timely to inject his own proposals for a renewed church structure.

On January 16, 1537, he submitted to the Geneva councils a series of *Articles* presenting his ideas. Here he sought to hold together a complicated tension between the church defined by its faithful members and hence

---

[46] Quoted from François Wendel, *Calvin: The Origin and Development of His Religious Thought 1509–1564*, trans. Philip Mairet (London: HarperCollins, 1963), 21.

[47] Wendel, *Calvin*, 20–21.

[48] Wendel, *Calvin*, 42.

[49] Wendel, *Calvin*, 47.

[50] Wendel, *Calvin*, 50.

[51] See Wendel, *Calvin*, 50ff. and esp. Williston Walker, *John Calvin: The Organizer of Reform Protestantism* (New York: Putnam, 1906).

by the kingdom of Christ—an ecclesiology not that dissimilar from the Anabaptists—and the church that extended to include all Genevans, a view of church rejected by the Anabaptists. Calvin believed, with the mainstream, that the wheat and the tares cannot be separated in this life and hence both also exist in the church.

But Calvin had a difficult time with his reforms. Both the mainstream and the radicals, for quite different reasons, made it difficult for him. The biggest challenge, however, was with the magistracy (city council heads). Against the odds, in March of 1537 his *Articles* were accepted. Yet this was not enough for Calvin. He moved forward with more specific reforms, but was unsuccessful a year later when he demanded all Genevans sign the *Confessions*, which was a kind of summary of his *Catechism*. This failure was the beginning of the end for Calvin in Geneva. A further run-in with the magistracy over liturgical practices—the problem being that the liturgical forms were changed without consultation with Calvin and the other preachers—left Calvin outraged at infringement of the church's authority. When he and the other preachers refused to comply, they were ordered to leave Geneva. Subsequent efforts at reconciliation were not successful.

Although Calvin's immediate wish at this point was to go to Basel, he actually ended up in Strasbourg, where he again preached and took active leadership roles in the church. And he seemed quite content to remain there since he felt God was blessing his ministry. Back in Geneva, the departure of Calvin and his fellow pastors left the church in a state of disorganization and dissatisfaction. Eventually, his supporters in Geneva were able to convince the authorities to have Calvin return to bring about a lasting peace. So an official delegation was sent to Strasbourg on October 20, 1540, to convince Calvin to return to Geneva.

On September 13, 1541, now thirty-two years old, Calvin arrived back in Geneva

with a single-minded mission. Says Wendel, "On the day of his arrival he presented himself before the Magistracy, and straightaway, with almost feverish haste, demanded the setting-up of a commission of pastors and advisers which was to draft 'regulations for the Church and Consistory'—a design, that is, for the ecclesiastical constitution."[52]

Calvin believed that if Geneva was to be a theocracy, it needed to show it, that is, it needed to be structured in accordance with the word of God. And so there was naturally a tension between the civil powers and the powers he wished to preserve for the church, especially on matters such as frequency of communion, selection of pastors, and—perhaps most explicitly—matters of discipline. Originally, Calvin wanted the body that was to oversee matters of correct doctrine and right morals to consist of the pastors and twelve councillors appointed with the agreement of the pastors.[53] But this was not permitted because the magistracy also held jurisdiction over moral matters. Here was a clear clash between the temporal and spiritual realms. So Calvin needed to relent, and this caused him much pain and anguish.

Calvin could not give up on his overall vision of the church as the body of Christ. Christ was Lord and Master over the church, and this clearly had direct implications for both the personal morals as well as for church governance. Regarding the latter, he believed the Lord had instituted four church ministries: pastors, teachers, elders, and deacons. But in working out the precise powers of these roles, he encountered many tensions with the civil authorities.

Church Doctrine: Calvin saw himself as the defender of orthodoxy and, as such, he was as interested in doctrine as in ecclesial governance. And in his view, these were complementary to each other. I have focused my analysis on church governance in part to show how important that is for Christian ethics. But, for Calvin, church doctrine was equally important, for he clearly believed, as

---

[52] Wendel, *Calvin*, 70–71.   [53] Wendel, *Calvin*, 72.

we have stressed earlier, that what we believe affects what we do.

It is noteworthy that both Luther and Calvin began their theological careers with a commentary on the Epistle to the Romans. This fact alone has significance, in that Romans gives priority to concepts like grace and the sovereignty of God. It also links Luther and Calvin with several other theologians for whom Romans has had a major formative influence, for example, Augustine and Karl Barth.[54]

If Calvin and Luther managed to change anything in terms of approach to theology, it was their emphasis on the role of Scripture. *Sola scriptura* became the new *modus operandi* for the Reformation movement. That is, their first critique of the Roman Catholic Church was that it did not base its theology squarely enough on the revealed word of God—tradition and nature were too prominent in its theology. In their view, this is what needed changing and this is what they set out to change. And when they viewed theology from this new standpoint, the revelation of the grace of God became overwhelming. Then, as Calvin puts it: "Man's only righteousness is the mercy of God in Christ, when it is offered by the gospel and received in faith. Men are asleep in their sins, and flatter and deceive themselves by a false idea of righteousness."[55]

Although history since the Reformation has led Lutheranism and Calvinism on somewhat divergent paths, Luther and Calvin were initially agreed on virtually every aspect of theology.[56] Whether on the orders of creation, law/gospel, anthropology, or the sacraments, the difference was more nuance and emphasis than substance. It is therefore not necessary to recount their theological tensions.

Yet emphasis does make a difference. And perhaps more than at any other place the difference comes at two key points related to Christian ethics. As Roland Bainton suggests, for Luther all theology was rooted in God's forgiveness of human sin, whereas for Calvin the center was the sovereignty of God.[57] Their other point of difference was the way they spoke about the state. Around these two themes I will explore Calvin's thought further.

The Sovereignty of God and the State: Calvin was overwhelmed by the majesty of God. God directs the affairs of this world so that God's purposes—not ours—are met. And so obedience to God was the cornerstone of faithful living. Obedience was every bit as important to Calvin as it was for the Anabaptists, only, as Bainton puts it, "for the Anabaptist the obedience was directed to Christ and for Calvin to God."[58]

Another way of saying this is to contrast it with Luther's view of the state. Calvin rejected the way Luther portrayed divine governance of the world. There cannot be two ethics under God, even though there are two very different kinds of people: those for whom God is sovereign and those for whom God is not. Given that there are two kinds of people, there may well be people living by different norms, yet all people of this earth are called to live under God's rule. Calvin got this notion from the Old Testament, where God as ultimate king rules all people. God is seen as king, and all earthly kings and all people are bound by God's rule.

Calvin's notion of a theocracy suggests that there cannot be the same tension of realms that there were for Luther, for example, between the revealed way of Jesus and the natural way of creation. Moreover, reason and revelation must coincide. Hence, there were not two or more standards operative for different stations in life; there was but one norm emanating from God for all of

---

[54] In fact, although it should not be overemphasized, one can draw parallels between most theologians in which the book of Romans figured centrally as a force of theological formation. For example, Augustine, Martin Luther, John Calvin, and Karl Barth share very similar approaches to theology, and all were heavily influenced by the book of Romans.

[55] John Calvin, "The Epistle of Paul the Apostle to the Romans," in *Calvin's New Testament Commentaries*, trans. and ed. Ross Mackenzie (Grand Rapids: Eerdmans, 1960), 5.

[56] See Roland H. Bainton, *The Age of the Reformation* (New York: Reinhold, 1956), 48ff.

[57] Bainton, *Age of Reformation*, 48.   [58] Bainton, *Age of Reformation*, 49.

life. One might say that this emphasis made Calvin both more Roman Catholic in that he insisted on the unity of reason and revelation and more Anabaptist in that he emphasized radical obedience.

Calvin's view of church and state is much more difficult to illustrate than Luther's. But the illustration below helps point out some pertinent differences.

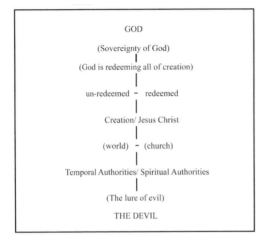

The diagram seeks to make several key points. First, the good news of the gospel is that God is redeeming all of creation. Second, the reality of this world is that the power of sin (the lure of evil) distracts even the faithful from obedience to God. But in spite of this, God's will is not thwarted. Third, the main dualism that exists here is between the redeemed and the unredeemed. All are subject to God's law, yet not all obey. And it is the task of the redeemed to hold the law of God before the entire world. Yet our own righteousness is found in God and not within ourselves. For Calvin says:

> Since the soul is regenerated into a heavenly life by that saving knowledge of God in Christ, and our life itself is formed and regulated by holy exhortations and precepts, we display our enthusiasm for ordering our life in vain, if we have not first shown that the origin of all righteousness for men is to be found in God and Christ.[59]

Fourth, the other dualism represented here is between the church and the world. The church gathers to worship, receives the sacraments, and praises God. Yet the distinction is not sharp and not at all clearly visible. On the one hand, the church is where the sacraments are administered; on the other, it does not consist only of the chosen ones. As Bainton says, Calvin "equated the church with the entire community in Geneva."[60] However, this is not entirely true either, in that if someone was excommunicated from the church, it did not follow that this person was immediately banned from the town. Neither did this person have longevity in town. So, to say the least, the distinction between church and world was fuzzy.

Fifth, God's norms for life must be realistic and drawn from the entire Bible. This does not mean that all will see why a society must be structured in this way, and not all will be able to live the life of self-sacrifice that is called for. But it is those who read the Bible who will come to see how a society under God should be structured. It is therefore important for Calvin that governments are just because if they are not, then Christians are not to participate in them. In fact, then they ought to rebel against them. Also, if the government is too lax in dealing with sin, the Christian ought to push it to become harsher so that sin may be crushed. But when the government is just, Christians ought to give it full support and participate in it fully.

I said earlier that Calvin was perhaps both somewhat Catholic and somewhat Anabaptist. It is important to point out where his teachings are in tension with both. For Roman Catholics, there were two kinds of Christians: those who were to be absolutely obedient to Christ—the counsel of perfection—and those who lived with the cares and demands of the world. Calvin did not accept this distinction. All Christians were called to be totally obedient to God, even when this created tension with obedience to Jesus

---

59 Calvin, "Romans," 262.   60 Bainton, *Age of Reformation*, 50.

Christ. This makes him sound more Anabaptist. Yet, regarding the Anabaptists, who sought radical obedience to Christ and the purity of the church, Calvin disagreed because for him the wheat and the tares could not be so easily separated. And so in this regard he was again more Catholic.

Radical Reformers

Obviously, the Reformers were not agreed on how to reform the church. The so-called Radical Reformers (of which the Anabaptists are a part) felt that what Luther and Calvin were about was fine to a considerable extent but did not go far enough. Particularly with respect to the nature of the church, how Christians live faithfully in this world, and how they relate to the state, the mainline Reformers were still far too bound to the tradition, in the view of the Radical Reformers.

The Anabaptist emphasis was not a mere political add-on; it was in fact deeply imbedded in their reading of the call of Christ. They believed the way that Luther and Calvin legitimated Christian involvement in the world/state undermined the critical posture of the gospel of Jesus Christ, hence rendering the church apostate. They saw the Roman Catholic Church as half right—the monastic view of faithfulness was in keeping with Jesus' call to discipleship. And they saw the Protestant Reformers making precisely the wrong move by seeking to bring monasticism into the world. Such a move destroyed the radical view of faithfulness that monasticism had right. But given the problematic ecclesiology grounded in the Catholic dualism of religious/laity, the Anabaptists, in effect, sought to bring the entire church into the monastery. While this idea of course required them to adjust the concept of monastery, it nevertheless connected them more closely theologically with early church ecclesiology. In turn, this afforded them a posture of radical separation and critique of both world and empire.

The Radical Reformers' theological differences with the mainline Reformers focused primarily on Christology and ecclesiology. Because they understood Jesus as one who called for radical discipleship, they saw the church as a body that needed to pay careful attention to its identity. They believed that the church's very being, like that of the monastery, was its ethic. Hence, they found themselves sorting out their own convictions in relation to both the Catholic and the Protestant theologies.[61]

One should not pretend that there was a monolithic theology among the Anabaptists, for clearly there was much debate among them. Nevertheless, there are some early documents that state the difference from mainline theology rather sharply. Let me quote extensively from one such document, the Schleitheim Brotherly Union (1527).[62]

> The articles which we have dealt with, and in which we have been united, are these: baptism, ban, the breaking of bread, separation from abominations, shepherds in the congregation, the sword, the oath.
>
> I. Notice concerning baptism. Baptism shall be given to all those who have been taught repentance and the amendment of life and [who] believe truly that their sins are taken away through Christ, and to all those who desire to walk in the resurrection of Jesus Christ and be buried with him in death, so that they might rise with him; to all those who with such an understanding themselves desire and request it from us; hereby is excluded all infant baptism, the greatest and first abomination of the Pope. For this you have the reasons and the testimony of the writings and the practice of the apostles. We wish yet resolutely and with assurance to hold to the same.
>
> II. We have been united as follows concerning the ban. The ban shall be employed with all those who have given themselves over to the Lord, to walk after [Him] in His commandments;

---

[61] Walter Klaassen, *Anabaptism: Neither Catholic nor Protestant* (Waterloo, Ontario: Conrad, 1973).

[62] This quotation comes from a translation by John Howard Yoder in his *The Legacy of Michael Sattler* (Scottdale, Penn.: Herald, 1973), 36–41.

those who have been baptized into the one body of Christ, and let themselves be called brothers or sisters, and still somehow slip and fall into error and sin, being inadvertently overtaken. The same [shall] be warned twice privately and the third time be publicly admonished before the entire congregation according to the command of Christ (Mt. 18). But this shall be done according to the ordering of the Spirit of God before the breaking of bread, so that we may all in one spirit and in one love break and eat one bread and drink from one cup.

III. Concerning the breaking of bread, we have become one and agree thus: all those who desire to break the one bread in remembrance of the broken body of Christ and all those who wish to drink of one drink in remembrance of the shed blood of Christ, they must beforehand be united in the one body of Christ, that is the congregation of God, whose head is Christ, and that by baptism. For as Paul indicates, we cannot be partakers at the same time of the table of the Lord and the table of devils. Nor can we at the same time partake and drink of the cup of the Lord and the cup of devils. That is, all those who have fellowship with the dead works of darkness have no part in the light. Thus all who follow the devil and the world, have no part with those who have been called out of the world unto God. All those who lie in evil have no part in the good.

So it shall and must be, that whoever does not share the calling of the one God to one faith, to one baptism, to one spirit, to one body together with all the children of God, may not be made one loaf together with them, as must be true if one wishes truly to break according to the command of Christ.

IV. We have been united concerning the separation that shall take place from the evil and the wickedness which the devil has planted in the world, simply is this; that we have no fellowship with them, and do not run with them in the confusion of their abominations. So it is; since all who have not entered into the obedience of faith and have not united themselves with God so that they will to do His will, are a great abomination before God, therefore nothing else can or really will grow or spring forth from them than abominable things. Now there is nothing else in the world and all creation than good and evil, believing and unbelieving, darkness and light, the world and those who are [come] out of the world, God's temple and idols, Christ and Belial, and none will have part with the other.

To us, then, the commandment of the Lord is also obvious, whereby He orders us to be and to become separated from the evil one, and thus He will be our God and we shall be His sons and daughters. . . . Thereby shall also fall away from us the diabolical weapons of violence—such as sword, armor, and the like, and all of their use to protect friends or against enemies—by virtue of the word of Christ: "you shall not resist evil."

V. We have been united as follows concerning shepherds in the church of God. The shepherd in the church shall be a person according to the rule of Paul, fully and completely, who has a good report of those who are outside the faith. The office of such a person shall be to read and exhort and teach, warn, admonish, or ban in the congregation, and properly to preside among the sisters and the brothers in prayer, and in the breaking of bread, and in all things to take care of the body of Christ, that it may be built up and developed, so that the name of God might be praised and honored through us, and the mouth of the mocker be stopped. . . .

VI. We have been united as follows concerning the sword. The sword is an ordering of God outside the perfection of Christ. It punishes and kills the wicked, and guards and protects the good. In the law the sword is established over the wicked for punishment and for death, and the secular rulers are established to wield the same.

But within the perfection of Christ only the ban is used for the admonition and exclusion of the one who has sinned, without the death of the flesh, simply the warning and the command to sin no more.

Now many, who do not understand Christ's will for us, will ask: whether a Christian may or should use the sword against the wicked for the protection and defense of the good, or for the sake of love.

The answer is unanimously revealed: Christ teaches and commands us to learn from Him, for He is meek and lowly of heart and thus we shall find rest for our souls. . . .

Second, is asked concerning the sword: whether a Christian shall pass sentence in disputes and strife about worldly matters, such as the unbelievers have with one another. The answer: Christ did not wish to decide or pass judgement between brother and brother concerning inheritance, but refused to do so. So should we also do.

Third, is asked concerning the sword: Whether the Christian should be a magistrate if he is chosen thereto. This is answered thus: Christ was to be made king, but He fled and did not discern the ordinance of His Father. Thus we should also do as He did and follow after Him, and we shall not walk in darkness. For He Himself says: "Whoever would come after me, let him deny himself and take up his cross and follow me." He himself further forbids the violence of the sword when He says; "The princes of this world lord it over them etc. but among you it shall not be so." . . .

VII. We have been united as follows concerning the oath. The oath is a confirmation among those who are quarrelling or making promises. In the law it is commanded that it should be done only in the name of God, truthfully and not falsely. Christ, who teaches the perfection of the law, forbids His [followers] all swearing, whether true or false; neither by heaven nor by earth, neither by Jerusalem nor by our head; and that for the reason which He goes on to give: "For you cannot make one hair white or black." You see, thereby all swearing is forbidden. We cannot perform what is promised in swearing, for we are not able to change the smallest part of ourselves. . . .

The theology represented here is deliberately written to be in contrast to the mainline Reformers and Roman Catholic theology. The differences lie in four main areas: Christology, ecclesiology, sin, and the state. I will examine each briefly.

Christology: For the Christians at Schleitheim, Jesus was emphatically the final and ultimate revelation of God. Hence, Jesus was the absolute authority and could therefore not be given partial authority shared by a God of creation whose natural self-disclosure was somehow at variance with Jesus. This is not to say that they held that the world/state and the church were governed by the same ethic, but it meant that *they as disciples of Jesus* could not participate in anything other than what Jesus called for, whether they found themselves in the worldly stations or in the church. There was only one authority

for Christians and that was Jesus. And in this they viewed themselves as orthodox.

We might ask why the Anabaptists saw fit to locate their christological differences in this way. After all, did not the church of Augustine/Thomas, Luther, and Calvin assert with equally strong conviction their allegiance to orthodox theology—for example, the full divinity and humanity of Christ (Council of Chalcedon, 451)? The answer, in part, is that Anabaptists believed that when it came to grounding an ethic, which for them was the same as being the church, Jesus was often placed over against Creator God. At least the words and ways of Jesus were not seen as the sole moral authority for all in the church, only for the monastics. For the Anabaptists, the affirmation of the dual nature of Christ was important because it made him both worthy of following (divinity) and made it possible for all Christians to do so (humanity). The conclusion they then reached was that Jesus was divinely authoritative for their lives and that the perfection of Christ was for all Christians.

Ecclesiology: The Anabaptists' understanding of the church was at odds with both the mainline Reformers and the Catholics in that they rejected the view of church expressed by *corpus christianum.* The language they used for church was the "perfection of Christ" and the new "body of Christ" consisting of all baptized believers who had repented of their sins and were committed to walking the path trod by Jesus Christ. The baptism of infants was rejected because that presupposed a *corpus christianum* ecclesiology and threatened the very identity of the church as people of discipleship. They believed that when you baptize everyone, then the church becomes indistinguishable from the world. In this, one might say that the Anabaptists reverted to a pre-Constantinian ecclesiology of full obedience to Jesus Christ for all Christians in all matters. For them, faithfulness to the way of Jesus meant separation from the ways of the world, along with strong spiritual training which kept the seductive powers of the world at bay. Only these steps could keep the church pure. Only this disciplined body could worship God in spirit and in truth.

Sin: One of the sharpest differences between the mainline theologians and the Anabaptists had to do with how sin was conceived and responded to. It was not that sin was defined all that differently, but there was a different view of how to undermine its destructive power. The mainline Reformers had emphasized the importance of the power of sin and the need to deal with it decisively and violently if necessary. The Anabaptists took a different approach. Sin was to be dealt with the way Jesus dealt with it—by giving up your life for it. In the church it meant using the ban—that is, disassociating yourself from sin so that you do not give it more power than it already has. In the world it meant virtually the same thing—that is, separating yourself by refusing participation. Only in this way could sin's power be undermined.

As we have seen, the Anabaptists were not unique in their practice of excommunication; Calvin advocated the same practice. Yet the underlying theologies were different. For the Anabaptists, separation from sin in order to avoid further seductions was the key basis for excommunication; a close second reason was the purity of the church. For Calvin, since he did not believe separation from sin was possible and hence, thought the church could not be pure because within it were both the wheat and the tares, these could not be the bases. For Calvin, discipline/punishment for unrepentant sinners was far more important.

The State: Because of the differences listed above, it is not surprising that the Anabaptists had a profoundly different view of the state. They could not imagine Christians participating in the kinds of activities that authorities within the state felt were necessary for its existence. Hence, they could not hold government offices that required them to use violence. And certainly true Christians could not participate in any government-sponsored use of the sword. The Anabaptists believed that this disassociation with violence was something that the early church had right.

Their view of the state, in contrast with those of Luther, Calvin, and the Catholics, may be illustrated with the diagram below.

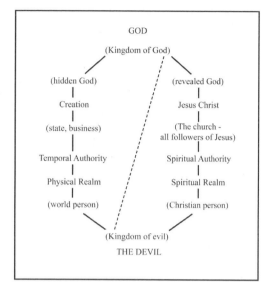

Several comments on this illustration: First, "the Christian" does not figure as an individual but is a constituent of the body called the perfection of Christ. As such, he or she acts on behalf of the church. Second, the church is wholly under the spiritual authority and hence, its members are never under the temporal authority alone. The Anabaptists believed that Christ had inaugurated a new rule that was already a sign of the Parousia; that is, it was a sign of the passing of a world that did not have the moral goodness to last forever. Christians were invited to embody that rule, and in that embodiment the church was to sign what the world was to become eventually. Hence, it was in its very existence an ethic, and its faithfulness was not best understood as providing for the world good moral counsel on the world's terms.

Third, the dualism of the Anabaptists was different from that of the others. The Catholics distinguished between the pure Christians (the monastics) and other Christians working in the world. Calvin and Luther tended to lodge the dualism of the physical and the spiritual right within the individual Christian person. The Anabaptists did neither. This does not mean that the Anabaptists saw themselves as having no dealings in the physical realm, but even in that realm they were under the authority and rule of Christ. They simply did not accept the physical/spiritual distinction in the way that the mainline Reformers did.

Fourth, the diagonal perforated line in the diagram is intended to show that, while there is a strong ideological separation, a geographical separation is much more difficult to maintain. In fact, a geographical separation is not even desirable. It is not that existing structures of governance and business are evil in themselves and should be shunned. In fact, many Anabaptists were personally involved in such structures. But the effort was to seek to pattern every structure after the way of Jesus. To say this differently, for the Anabaptists, salvation was not just a spiritual-personal matter; it was also a physical-structural matter. Even businesses could be saved. Hence, the extent to which they could participate in the structures of the world depended not so much on them being in the world, as it depended on which structures permitted them to do so as faithful followers of Christ.

Fifth, rooted in this theological imagination the Anabaptists saw their moral stance primarily as one of witnessing to the way of Jesus. Such witness, of course, made martyrs of many of them. Here they again identified with the early Christians. Whether they were martyred or not, however, did not depend as much on them as on the powers around them who had the authority to kill them. They were only to be faithful, and this sometimes resulted in being killed.

Being martyred was a way of bearing witness to their convictions—what they knew and what they did not know. They did not know how to move the current state of violence and injustice to its overcoming, for they knew that they were not in charge. But they also knew that while their persecutors believed they were in charge, it was indeed a belief that would be proven false. How did they know that? Through the revelation of the one who himself sacrificed his life rather than destroy his persecutors. And often in perfect silence, every martyr shouted this conviction loudly to anyone who had the ears to hear it. This was their moral posture.

In summary conclusion to this section on the Reformation, the reader should note how thoroughly ecclesiology and Christology determine Christian life, that is, ethics. In other words, to ask how a Christian should act presupposes the question of how one is ecclesiologically situated. If you are a Catholic and in the monastery, you will get one answer, if a Lutheran or a Calvinist, another, and if you are an Anabaptist, you will often get still another answer.

Before I leave this chapter, I want to raise one other matter that has to do with the so-called Wars of Religion, the name that has been given to hostilities that began in 1562 and ended with the Edict of Nantes in 1598. It is important to mention these wars because of the way this part of history gets narrated, especially in our generation; it has directly to do with the church and violence. Today, modern analysts tell us that it is secular society and particularly the secular state that has overcome the violence of warring religious factions. And the state has done this with the introduction of tolerance and respect for the individual, whereby religion is reduced to a private matter.

In an article written by William Cavanaugh on the subject of these wars,[63] he challenges the conventional interpretation offered by secular liberalism. For example, liberal social philosopher Jeffrey Stout says that "liberal principles were the right ones to adopt when competing religious beliefs and divergent conceptions of the good embroiled Europe in the religious wars. . . . Our early modern ancestors were right to secularize public discourse in the interests of minimizing

---

[63] William T. Cavanaugh, "'A Fire Strong Enough to Consume the House': The Wars of Religion and the Rise of the State," *Modern Theology* 11, no. 4 (1995): 397–420.

the ill effect of religious disagreements."[64] Cavanaugh believes that this way of narrating the matter puts it backward.

This way of stating the issue suggests that the church itself is the problem people need to be saved from and that the state, grounded in secular reason, is the mode of this salvation. But if this reading is correct, then the very notion of Christian ethics is anathema.

Cavanaugh does not exonerate the church for its role in the wars, but he gives an entirely different reading of the events. He suggests that what was going on during this time was the very creation of religion itself. The notion of religion—an entirely new way of understanding the church—was necessary to satisfy "the State's need to secure absolute sovereignty over its subjects."[65] And the only way to do this is to reduce the church to "a set of privately held beliefs without direct political relevance."[66]

This change is certainly among the most serious challenges to the church and to Christian ethics, and indirectly how the Reformers play into this dynamic. For all of them—Luther, Calvin, and the Radical Reformers—although in different ways, granted to the state an independence that eventually led to its autonomous self-understanding and from that to seeing itself as agent of salvation. We do well to remind ourselves that there is something inherently violent about this way of casting religion and the church. For this is but an imposition of a secular rationality that cannot see the world as participating in God's grace. It seems then that the road to secular reasoning opened up by Duns Scotus and William of Ockham just two centuries earlier runs right through the Renaissance and Reformation. Yet its most significant formulation is yet to come with the writers of the Enlightenment. To that discussion we now turn.

---

[64] Quoted in Cavanaugh, "Fire," 398. Taken from Jeffrey Stout, *The Flight from Authority: Religion, Morality, and the Quest for Autonomy* (Notre Dame, Ind.: University of Notre Dame Press, 1981), 241.

[65] Cavanaugh, "Fire," 398. [66] Cavanaugh, "Fire," 398.

Chapter Seven

ENLIGHTENMENT ETHICS

The Enlightenment is the period of intellectual history which covers roughly the seventeenth and eighteenth centuries; some scholars will want to include the later part of the sixteenth and perhaps even the beginning of the nineteenth century. In other words, the boundaries are not well defined. Moreover, to think that there is a monolithic ethic that characterizes this era is also a mistake. Our chapter heading is therefore somewhat misleading but is intended to designate an approximate time frame in which a diverse group of thinkers adopted a similar foundational approach to the quest for knowledge. This approach marks a distinct shift away from a heavy reliance on tradition, which was characteristic of medieval thought. And this move led to a fundamental change to the way in which ethics came to be understood in the modern era.

It is important to carefully examine the underlying philosophical arguments of this shift because contemporary folk are often considered children of the Enlightenment in the sense that we have inherited the thinking that gets hammered out in this period of thought. In other words, our current skepticism about all things ethical and our inability to find ways to resolve moral disputes finds its logic right here.

In this chapter, I will examine some of the changes that took place, especially pertaining to Christian ethics. We have already noted that the church's understanding of ethics went through changes as it moved from the early church to the end of the

medieval period. Hence, some Christians began to wonder whether a reversion back to a pre-Constantinian ecclesiology and Christology was necessary. Compared to the theological shift that took place as a result of the Enlightenment response to medieval thought, the Constantinian shift may yet be seen as minor.

Some argue that the Enlightenment revolution is so profound and so radical that we are not able to grasp its significance properly from this side of the event. Something so serious has been lost that attempting to understand it is virtually impossible because the very canons of understanding that preceded it are no longer in place.

Alasdair MacIntyre, in *After Virtue*, puts forward such a "disquieting suggestion" with a hypothetical analogy constructed in reference to the natural sciences. He asks the reader to engage in the following thought experiment:

Imagine that the natural sciences were to suffer the effects of a catastrophe. A series of environmental disasters are blamed by the general public on the scientists. Widespread riots occur, laboratories are burnt down, physicists are lynched, books and instruments destroyed. Finally a Know-Nothing political movement takes power and successfully abolishes science teaching in schools and universities, imprisoning and executing the remaining scientists. Later still there is a reaction against this destructive movement and enlightened people seek to revive science, although they have largely forgotten what it was. But all they possess are fragments: a knowledge of experiments detached from any knowledge of the theoretical context which gave them significance; parts of theories unrelated either to the other bits and pieces of theory which they possess or to experiment; instruments whose use has been forgotten; half-chapters from books, single pages from articles, not always fully legible because torn and charred. Nonetheless all these fragments are reembodied in a set of practices which go under the revived names of physics, chemistry and biology. Adults argue with each other about the respective merits of relativity theory, evolutionary theory and phlogiston theory, although they possess only very partial knowledge of each. Children learn by heart the surviving portions of the periodic table and recite as incantations some of the theorems of Euclid. Nobody, or almost nobody, realizes that what they are doing is not natural science in any proper sense at all. For everything that they do and say conforms to certain canons of consistency and coherence and those contexts which would be needed to make sense of what they are doing have been lost, perhaps irretrievably. . . . The hypothesis which I wish to advance is that in the actual world which we inhabit the language of morality is in the same state of grave disorder as the language of natural science in the imaginary world which I described. What we possess, if this view is true, are the fragments of a conceptual scheme, parts which now lack those contexts from which their significance derived.[1]

Whether MacIntyre has overstated the case is not our concern here. He does, in a most convincing manner, make the case for the importance of understanding the impact of the Enlightenment for our conception of ethics. His "disquieting suggestion" forms the backdrop as we inquire what happened to the way we have been led to think by the Enlightenment, and how it has impacted our understanding of ethics.

RENÉ DESCARTES (1596–1650)

Descartes was born in La Haye en Touraine, France. At age ten he entered the Royal Jesuit College at La Fleche, where he studied for nine years in the general areas of humanities, theology, and philosophy. At twenty-two, he

became especially interested in mathematics and gravitational physics. He spent much of his adult life teaching in universities and tutoring royalty. He lived in France, the Netherlands, and Sweden. While he was teaching at the Utrecht University, he developed a relationship with a servant girl, Helene Jans, with whom he fathered a daughter, Francine. He died of pneumonia in Stockholm, Sweden, where he was at the time the tutor of Queen Christina. It is said that Christina demanded the teaching sessions take place early in the morning, to which Descartes was unaccustomed because of his practice of morning meditation in bed, and that this may have contributed to his death at age 53.

Descartes is sometimes called the Father of Modern Philosophy, which emphasizes that he began an approach to philosophy that marked a break from the past. His concern was primarily epistemology, that is, how can we know what there is. And his answer provided a foundational approach to knowledge that emphasized certainty based not on tradition, but in the mind. Mathematics was his model for this approach. Who can doubt that two plus three equals five or that the sum of the interior angles of a triangle is equal to 180 degrees? Descartes believed these were indubitable truths and as such were models in other areas of knowledge, especially philosophy and religion. This did not mean that he doubted the truths he had received via tradition, but, while he accepted many of his important beliefs on faith, not all people do. And they were his concern. He says it thus:

> I have always thought that two topics—namely God and the Soul—are prime examples of subjects where demonstrative proof ought to be given with the aid of philosophy rather than theology. For us who are believers, it is enough to accept on faith that the human soul does not die with the body, and that God exists; but in the case of the unbeliever, it seems that there is no religion, and practically no moral virtue, that they can

---

[1] Alasdair MacIntyre, *After Virtue: A Study in Moral Theory*, 2nd ed. (Notre Dame, Ind.: University of Notre Dame Press, 1984), 1.

be persuaded to adopt until these two truths are proven to them by natural reason.[2]

We should note that this approach makes profoundly different assumptions from the one guided by the motto: *fides quaerens intellectum* (faith seeking knowledge). In effect, Descartes turns tradition-based knowledge on its head. With the traditional approach, objects of faith were the primary given (a gift), and understanding was the secondary given arising from faith. With Descartes, rational understanding is the starting point and faith the conclusion. Of course, it does not take much reflection to wonder whether faith under Descartes' approach actually remains faith in the traditional sense or whether it morphs into something altogether different.

To explain Descartes' thought I will identify five focal points.

Doubt

First, doubt. Doubt plays a special heuristic role in Descartes' philosophy. He says:

> Some years ago I was struck by the large number of falsehoods that I had accepted as true in my childhood, and by the highly doubtful nature of the whole edifice that I had subsequently based on them. I realized that it was necessary, once in the course of my life, to demolish everything completely and start again right from the foundations if I wanted to establish anything at all in the science that was stable and likely to last. . . . So today I have expressly rid my mind of all worries and arranged for myself a clear stretch of free time. I am here quite alone and at last I will devote myself sincerely and without reservation to the general demolition of my opinions.[3]

While the role that doubt plays in Descartes' philosophy is methodological and is not itself the occasion for a personal epistemological crisis, nevertheless it makes the point that only indubitable propositions should be accepted as true; that is, only those claims which, when doubted, become absurd. He says:

> I will suppose that everything I see is spurious. I will believe that my memory tells me lies, and that none of the things that it reports ever happened. I have no senses. Body, shape extension, movement and place are chimeras. So what remains true? Perhaps just the one fact that nothing is certain.[4]

But no! He continues:

> So after considering everything very thoroughly, I must finally conclude that this proposition, *I am, I exist*, is necessarily true whenever it is put forward by me or conceived in my mind.[5]

He goes on to spell out what he means with concluding that *I am, I exist*. (Elsewhere he speaks in the argument form *cogito ergo sum*—I think, therefore I am.) He intentionally does not want this to be understood as an inference. So stating it as an argument is somewhat misleading. The way he wishes it to be understood is as a self-evident and indubitable truth—as incapable of being doubted by any rational person.

Metaphysical Dualism

Descartes' *cogito* leads him to metaphysical conclusions; especially, he makes the following comments: "But what then am I? A thing that thinks. What is that? A thing that doubts, understands, affirms, denies, is willing, is unwilling, and also imagines and has sensory perceptions."[6] He intentionally rejects the classical definition of human identity as "rational animal" because that would require knowledge of what an animal is and such knowledge is acquirable on empirical grounds, which cannot be trusted. Notice the implication: as a thinking thing, he renders the knowing subject autonomous from all material contexts (traditions) and even all other subjects. Knowledge is purely the result of the activities of an individual's

[2] René Descartes, from the dedicatory letter to *Meditations on the First Philosophy*, as cited in *From Plato to Derrida*, ed. Forrest E. Baird and Walter Kaufmann, 5th ed. (Upper Saddle River, N.J.: Prentice Hall, 2008), 377.

[3] Descartes, from the opening paragraph to "First Meditation" of *Meditations on the First Philosophy*, as quoted in Baird and Kaufmann, 384.

[4] Descartes, "First Meditation," 387.

[5] Descartes, "First Meditation" (emphasis in original).

[6] Descartes, "Second Meditation," 388.

rational mind. The mind has primacy over the body and, because of his quest for certainty patterned after mathematics, is more easily known than the body.

Yet, for Descartes, the mind and the body interact as disparate entities. That is, the mind does not cease to be mind when it acts on body and the body does not cease to be body when it acts on mind. The issue of whether two different substances could actually interact was a serious issue for philosophers of this time. Baruch Spinoza (1632–1677), a Jewish philosopher, argued that this was not possible and not necessary because there was only one substance—God. And all that is, is of God! But for Descartes, there were two fundamentally separate substances.

This dualism has grave implications for the Christian doctrine of the incarnation, which claims that the fundamentally other substance becomes body in Jesus Christ. And as we have seen, in medieval times the platonic doctrine of *participation*—the notion that body participates in mind—was used to explain the connection. But with Descartes, the separation is made total and unbridgeable, except insofar as interaction takes place. But one does not participate in the other.

Clear and Distinct Ideas

Descartes claims that "I am certain that I am a thinking thing," and then he asks rhetorically, "Do I not therefore also know what is required of my being certain about anything?" His answer is quick to follow: "So I now seem to be able to lay it down as a general rule that whatever I perceive very clearly and distinctly is true."[7] In other words, his whole "edifice of knowledge" gets built up from the starting point (foundation) of a self-evident knowledge claim that "I am; I exist" and then by adding only self-evident truths after that.

Descartes pushes the "metaphysical doubt" principle very hard, even to the point of imagining an "evil genius" who is deceiving him

into believing that the conclusions he reaches, like his existence as a thinking thing, are in fact uncertain. He believes the only way out of this problem is to prove that God exists and is not a deceiver. The existence of God therefore becomes a necessary piece of the overall quest for certainty. But since it is his system that "proves" the existence of God, who in turn is to ensure the soundness of the system, one cannot help but wonder about the veracity of his approach.

Existence of God

For Descartes, the existence of God could be rendered certain in the same manner as all other knowledge. But first, his definition of God and a summary of his logic:

> By the word "God" I understand a substance that is infinite [eternal, immutable], independent, supremely intelligent, supremely powerful, and which created both myself and everything else (if else there be) that exists. All these attributes are such that, the more carefully I concentrate on them, the less possible it seems that they could have originated from me alone. So, from what has been said it must be concluded that God necessarily exists.[8]

Descartes has many ways of showing the impossibility of God not existing, but this is not the place to present them all. All of them seem in one way or another to come down to the notion that necessity of existence flows from the idea of God, or, to say it differently, that God as defined above cannot be thought of as not existing. For Descartes, God's essence and existence cannot be separated. As he puts it:

> [I]t is quite evident that existence can no more be separated from the essence of God than the fact that its three angles equal two right angles can be separated from the essence of triangle, or that the idea of a mountain can be separated from the idea of a valley.[9]

Hence God's existence is necessary because his nonexistence cannot consistently be thought. Or to say this another way, God's

---

[7] Descartes, "Third Meditation," 392.
[8] Descartes, "Third Meditation," 396.

[9] Descartes, "Fifth Meditation," 406.

existence is necessary because of the structure of our mind. Or perhaps more cynically, God is the product of human thought.

Edifice of Knowledge

The change of knowledge paradigms wrought by Descartes is profound. The only kind of knowledge that counts after Descartes is "certain" knowledge. Knowledge that can be doubted is not legitimate. But in order for us not to doubt what we claim to know requires that it be wrapped up so tightly that several important conclusions follow: not much can be known, partial knowledge is not knowledge, faith seeking knowledge is nonsense, and, perhaps most important of all, anyone who doubts Descartes' canon of knowledge is not really human. For a fully formed human being is a thing who thinks right, that is, just like Descartes thinks.

The quest for universal, indubitable knowledge is essentially a quest for ultimate control. For one who is able to explicate for all people the limits of the human mind sets the terms by which we have access to reality. This, of course, is the direct opposite of the notion that knowledge comes to us by revelation (as a gift), which we may receive gradually and tenderly.

Slavoj Žižek, a Slovenian philosopher, in a public lecture, refers to rabbits who do not need differential calculus to be happy nor do the rabbits know that they do not need it.[10] For rabbits this is an unknown unknown;[11] that is, they do not know that they do not know, yet they are happy. Descartes presents us with a view of the autonomous subject who finds the realm of the unknown at once threatening and hence denies its existence. We must know, and we must know conclusively. Perhaps humans should confess their kinship with rabbits in this sense: not all is

knowable and not all that is known is known for certain.

Perhaps the reader will wonder what Descartes' rant about certain knowledge has to do with ethics. The implications may still be hidden. Yet having plucked the subject of ethics out of the community/tradition that shaped it and placed it and all knowledge at the mercy of autonomous reason, Descartes started the route toward a radical subjectivity that will take hold only later. Moreover, the notion of ethics barely figures in his writings, nor is this a surprise. Ethics has its roots in a tradition, or a particular religion, which Descartes' universal reason cannot appreciate. The details of the implications of Descartes' approach will become clearer as we examine other scholars who follow his lead.

THOMAS HOBBES (1588–1679)

Hobbes was born in Wiltshire, England. In his adult years he spoke about being born "a twin with fear." There were several reasons for this: one was that his mother delivered him prematurely when she heard of the impending Spanish Armada invasion; another was that he lived during great political and social upheaval—for example, a civil war, the execution of Charles I—and he was forced to flee from England. It should perhaps not surprise us that in his writings he was concerned about matters of peace and security.

Hobbes made significant contributions to many areas of knowledge, like history, physics, geometry, and philosophy generally; but his primary legacy is in the area of political theory. He is most commonly associated with developing the underpinnings of Western political philosophy and especially with the notion of the social contract.

In an attempt to get at the "first principles" (basic presuppositions) of a political society,

---

[10] See Slavoj Žižek's lecture on violence organized by the *International Journal of Žižek Studies*, Paul A. Taylor, ed. available at http://zizekstudies.org/video/video_issue.html, accessed May 7, 2011.

[11] Žižek invokes the distinctions made famous by Donald Rumsfeld between the known knowns, known unknowns, unknown knowns, and unknown unknowns. Rumsfeld, American Defense Secretary, made these distinctions on February 12, 2002, at a Department of Defense news briefing ("News Transcript," U. S. Department of Defense, http://www.defense.gov/transcripts/transcript.aspx?transcriptid=2636, accessed March 31, 2011).

Hobbes suggests that we abstract from civil society, as we know it, all established institutions, an approach not all that different from Descartes' radical doubt. What we are left with is a state of nature.

In this state of nature, we have two unlimited rights: the right to protect ourselves and others using any means necessary and the right to things, that is, the right to possess, use, and enjoy all one needs. Both are "natural rights," which are derived from natural laws. To say this differently, according to Hobbes, it is as natural for us to protect ourselves and possess as many things as we can use as it is for a stone to roll down a hill.

As a result of these two basic natural rights, Hobbes says, "in the nature of man we find three principal causes of quarrel. First, competition; secondly, diffidence (mistrust); thirdly, glory."[12] The natural state of man is therefore a state of quarrel or war.[13] In such a state, individuals depend only upon themselves—their strength and wits. Hence, in a state of nature there can be "no industry . . . no arts, no letters, no society, and which is worst of all (there is) eternal fear and danger of violent death."[14]

There can be no moral values in a state of nature. In this state, "the notions of right and wrong, justice and injustice, have no place. Where there is no common power, there is no law, where no law, no injustice. Force and fraud are in war the two cardinal virtues."[15]

The state of nature is therefore not a desirable state. And nature itself, through the use of reason, leads us out of this state of violence. Our natural faculty of reason suggests "convenient articles of peace upon which men may be drawn to agreement. These articles are they, which otherwise are called Laws of Nature."[16] And because we fear death in our natural (lawless) state, we are led to act reasonably and to accept these Laws of Nature.

Hobbes mentions nineteen such Laws of Nature, of which we will only consider his first three, the most basic ones.

First Law of Nature

"Every man ought to endeavor peace as far as he has hope of obtaining it, and when he cannot obtain it, that he may seek, and use all help and advantage of war."[17] Hobbes refers to this law as the most fundamental law of nature. It has two parts: the first part says, "seek peace and follow it," and the second part points to our absolute right to self-preservation and says "defend yourself at all costs."

Second Law of Nature

"That man is willing, when others are so too, so far forth, as for peace and defense of himself he shall think it necessary to lay down his right to all things, and be contented with so much liberty against other men, as he would allow other men against himself."[18] This law is based on the preceding law, presupposing our fundamental right to self-preservation, which is of greatest interest and advantage for every individual. Hence, Hobbes again speaks of certain inalienable rights that no one lays down; for example, the right to defend one's own life.

This law essentially involves a mutual transference of rights (other than the inalienable rights). And this Hobbes refers to as a *contract*.

Most contracts, however, involve a trusting relationship where individuals within the contract are left to perform their part of it at all times. This Hobbes calls a covenant.

---

[12] Thomas Hobbes, *The English Works of Thomas Hobbes*, vol. 3, ed. William Molesworth (London: Bohn, 1839–1845), 112.

[13] Of war, Hobbes says, "For war consisteth not in battle only, or the act of fighting; but in a tract of time, wherein the will to contend by battle is sufficiently known: and therefore the notion of *time* is to be considered in war, as it is in the nature of weather. For as the nature of foul weather lieth not in a shower or two of rain; but in an inclination thereto of many days together: so the nature of war consisteth not in actual fighting; but in the known disposition thereto, during all the time there is no assurance to the contrary. All other time is peace" (*English Works*, 113).

[14] Hobbes, *English Works*, 113.

[15] Hobbes, *English Works*, 115.

[16] Hobbes, *English Works*, 116.

[17] Hobbes, *English Works*, 116–17.

[18] Hobbes, *English Works*, 118.

Covenants are a very crucial basis for the formation of any state.

Third Law of Nature

"That men perform their covenants made."[19] These laws of nature, although inevitable to the rational person, do not in themselves guarantee peace and security. There is a danger that human beings may not keep this covenant. A person may decide that some other action is of greater advantage and pursue it, even though eventually it will prove harmful, or a person may simply be irrational. To ensure that we keep the covenants we make, Hobbes says that people need a "common power to keep them in awe, and to direct their actions to the common benefit."[20] This common power, which is either one person or an assembly, is what Hobbes calls a sovereign.

What are the powers of the sovereign? Unlimited and categorical. For peace and harmony to reign, there must be an ultimate power over citizens, who has absolute authority.

"Covenants without the sword are but words and of no strength to secure a man at all."[21]

Hobbes has now provided his theory of the state. He has uncovered our inalienable natural rights; he has developed the Laws of Nature that follow from these basic rights, when our goal is peace and security; and he has empowered an authority to enforce these laws. He has created for us "that great Leviathan, or rather, to speak more reverently, of that mortal God, to which we owe under the immortal God, our peace and defense."[22]

Hobbes relates his discussion of the state to the biblical notion of the kingdom of God. He says two things: first, when Jesus speaks of the new kingdom where peace, love, forgiveness, and harmony reign, this kingdom is not of this world but rather a culmination of human efforts at the end of time. Second, when Jesus speaks of the kingdom as a present reality, he means the kingdom of the Israelites. Jesus' mission, according to Hobbes, was to restore the old kingdom and not to begin a new one. Jesus came to identify God's kingdom with the political kingdom. So Christians should submit unquestioningly to the will of the sovereign, until such a time as the kingdom of love, peace, and justice is brought about by God . . . which will be at the second coming of the Messiah . . . because it is the sovereign who heads God's kingdom on earth.[23] Hence, there are not two kingdoms on earth, the church and the state, but one, the political kingdom. The new kingdom of heaven exists in our hearts and will come into existence when and where God wills it.

For purposes of brevity, I will not present the political theories of either John Locke (1632–1704) or Jean-Jacques Rousseau (1712–1778). Although there are some important differences among these scholars, all agree with the idea of the social contract, though Rousseau perhaps more than any other works out the details of this notion. The quarrel among them is over the state of nature and especially its understanding in relation to private property. Locke argues that the original state was good, yet he finds it necessary to contend that a society built on reason is better. How does reason help us structure society? He offers an example in his famous statement on private property:

> Though the water running in the fountain be everyone's, yet who can doubt but that in the pitcher it is his who drew it out. His labour has taken it out of the hands of nature, where it was common and belonged equally to all her children and hath thereby appropriated it to himself.[24]

---

[19] Hobbes, *English Works*, 130.
[20] Hobbes, *English Works*, 157.
[21] Hobbes, *English Works*, 154.
[22] Hobbes, *English Works*, 158.
[23] Hobbes, *English Works*, 476–81.
[24] John Locke, *Two Treatises of Government*, ed. A. C. Fraser (Oxford: Oxford University Press, 1894), §27.

Rousseau, on the other hand, freely admits, contrary to both Locke and Hobbes, that virtually all ills in life are due to a politically planned society and that is because emotion rather than reason that makes for the happy life. He offers an example of how a particular form of reason—the kind that is self-evident to Locke, for example—messes us up. He says:

> The first man, who, after enclosing a piece of ground, took it into his head to say, "This is mine," and found people simple enough to believe him, was the true founder of civil society. How many crimes, how many wars, how many murders, how many misfortunes and horrors, would that man have saved the human species, who pulling up the stakes or filling up the ditches should have cried to his fellows: Be sure not to listen to this imposter; you are lost, if you forget that the fruits of the earth belong equally to us all, and the earth itself to nobody![25]

Seven years after uttering these words, Rousseau too tries his hand at structuring a society that is to lead people to both security and freedom. He begins his *Social Contract* with the words, "Man is born free, and everywhere he is in chains," and in this study he seeks a correction to Hobbes' view of the state.[26] In brief, he rejects Hobbes' view of submitting ourselves to a sovereign in exchange for peace. Instead, he proposes that we submit ourselves to each other and to the general will of the people, and this general will itself becomes the sovereign. This is much closer to what we today understand as democracy in Western societies.

Descartes, Hobbes, and company have profoundly shifted the basis of ethics generally and Christian ethics particularly. First, by locating all knowledge within abstract reason, there is now no distinction between ethics in general and ethics based on a particular tradition like Christianity. In fact, their very project is an effort to obliterate that distinction. Second, the "reason" invoked here is a foreign operation when judged from

the standpoint of classical and medieval thought. Both classical and medieval reason held together goodness and reality or, if you like, metaphysics and ethics. With Descartes and Hobbes, that unity is severely strained, and social morality is now lodged within the consent of the majority of ordinary people. And with David Hume, the linkage of morality and religion/metaphysics gets broken asunder even further.

DAVID HUME (1711–1776)

Hume was born in Edinburgh, Scotland, into a deeply religious family. His lawyer father died when David was only two years old, so his devout Christian mother raised him. As a young child he embraced the piety of his mother—it is said that he would often make lists of his sins in order not to miss any when he sought forgiveness. But he left behind the pious life and his religious belief when he entered university at the unusually early age of twelve.

At university Hume began with the study of law but soon changed to philosophy, with an interest in economics and history. He was most impressed with the writings of John Locke and George Berkeley, and he himself made major contributions to empiricist philosophy. Hume never married and, due to his atheism he struggled to gain a university teaching chair. He began his writing career when he was still young and wrote his most influential book, *A Treatise of Human Nature*, at the age of twenty-six.

Hume was the first Enlightenment philosopher to develop a thoroughly naturalistic philosophy. Prior to Hume, the notion that human minds were reflections of the divine mind underwrote the assumption that how our minds disclose reality to us was not unrelated to the manner in which God had created it. Of course, as an atheist Hume rejected this notion; even further, he was skeptical about whether our representations

---

[25] Jean-Jacques Rousseau, *Discourse on the Origin of Inequality* (1754), chap. 3, pg. 1, part 2.
[26] See Jean-Jacques Rousseau, *Social Contract* (Harmondsworth, UK: Penguin, 1968).

of the world were indeed as the world really was in itself.

Hume was a radical empiricist, who had little room in his system for anything that looked like traditional ethics. As we have seen, John Locke, Thomas Hobbes, and Jean-Jacques Rousseau were united in their effort to unhook social morality from an ontological source. This meant that, although natural reason still disclosed all this to us, nevertheless, morality was now largely separated from natural knowledge. This was a very significant departure from the way of thinking about "the Good" which had characterized the whole medieval period and even the Reformers. Majority consent now determined the good, which would have been a travesty to the ears of Plato, Aristotle, Augustine, Thomas, Luther, Calvin, and the Radical Reformers, where what was given by God determined the good to which people were called to be subservient.

Yet what Locke, Hobbes, and Rousseau had begun lacked thorough philosophical completeness, and it was Hume whose rigid naturalistic philosophy entrenched this view firmly in a consistent epistemology. He did this by inventing a new dualism: a dualism about how we come to know things and a dualism about what there is to know. The history of thought, as we have seen, is no stranger to dualisms. Yet the very thing that the Greeks and medievalists had tried to keep together despite their dualisms, Hume broke apart. For Plato, for example, the highest form of *reality* was the Good, and it was the Good in virtue of which all else had its being. So the two worlds—what is good and what there is—were separated precisely to show how they were united. Hume's dualism of facts and values shows their absolute separation because for Hume they have fundamentally different ontological sources. According to Hume, the chasm between these two realities cannot be bridged epistemologically, metaphysically, or logically.

For Hume, "fact" designated that which is, and "value" designated human judgments about what is. Valuing can only be done by a valuer. Human beings are intrinsically valuers. We make judgments about what is on the basis of our own view of things, our wants, interests, passions, and desires. In other words, values are entirely subjective while facts are objective. Notice how this is also the undergirding assumption of the social contract theory, albeit, not fully spelled out, where valuing, as the basis for seeking consent, was primary.

As Hume saw it, facts were not logically relevant in establishing moral conclusions. As he puts it:

> In every system of morality, which I have hitherto met with, I have always remarked, that the author proceeds for some time in the ordinary ways of reasoning, and establishes the being of a God, or makes observations concerning human affairs; when all of a sudden I am surprized to find, that instead of the usual copulations of propositions, *is*, and *is not*, I meet with no proposition that is not connected with an *ought*, or an *ought not*. This change is imperceptible; but is however, of the last consequence. For as this *ought*, or *ought not*, that expresses some new relation or affirmation, 'tis necessary that it should be observed and explained; and at the same time that a reason should be given; for what seems altogether inconceivable, how this new relation can be a deduction from others, which are entirely different from it.[27]

In other words, it is because "ought" judgments are entirely different sorts of sentences than factual statements that the former can never flow logically from the latter. In fact, this "leap" in logic is later given its own name, the "naturalistic fallacy."

The distinction between facts and values has been referred to as Hume's Guillotine, suggesting that Hume has cut the world into two. And so he has! But think about the significance of this for ethics. The link between ultimate reality and morality has now been radically broken. What is can be known apart from metaphysical goodness, and what

---

[27] David Hume, *A Treatise on Human Nature* (New York: Oxford University Press, 1978), bk. 2, part 1, sect. 1 (emphasis in original).

is good—our "values"—can now be known apart from any ultimate source. For valuing has its basis in the passions and not in reason. Why do we act or why do we hold something to be valuable? Hume's answer is the passions, not reason or tradition. This view has little ring of orthodoxy left. That which Aristotle, Plato, Augustine, and Aquinas saw as necessary to overcome in order for human beings to be good, has, with Hume, become the cornerstone of ethics—namely passion and subjective values.

Hume was not the only philosopher to promote a radical chasm between fact and values. The French philosopher, Denis Diderot (1713–1784), was largely in agreement with Hume that we are moved to action not so much by reason as by feelings and passion. As Hume suggests in his *A Treatise on Human Nature* and Diderot in his *Le Neveu de Rameau*, the notion of a human nature is a myth; one that was invented by the Greeks and perpetuated by the medievalists. So what is good for us is determined not by what is given us, a *telos*, but by our own desire and passion.

IMMANUEL KANT (1724–1804)

The German philosopher, Kant, was born in Königsberg, which at the time was the capital city of Prussia. He grew up in a pietist household and so would have learned the strict demands of the Christian life. Although he never traveled far from home, he saw fit to develop a philosophy that he based upon "universal" reason. As he saw it, this meant that all thinking people would agree with him.

Perhaps his most popular essay is "*Beantwortung der Frage: Was ist Aufklärung?*" ("Answer to the Question: What is Enlightenment?") written in 1784. Here he sought to characterize his own revolutionary age, one that he believed heralded a new era of knowledge and world peace. In this essay, he spoke of the tensions that derived from two

of his basic convictions. On the one hand, he shared Hobbes' view that the state should be given considerable powers to regulate the lives of individuals and that individuals had the obligation to obey the state. Yet on the other hand, he characterized this new age as: "*Sapere Aude*! Have the courage to use your own intelligence!"[28] He went on to say that "All that is required for this enlightenment is freedom . . . the freedom for man to make *public use* of his reason in all matters."[29] By "public use of reason" he meant what a scholar does in presenting his or her reason to the "reading public." There is also a private use of reason which restricts one, say, within a "civic post or office." Here one must remain "purely passive in order that an artificial agreement with the government for the public good be maintained or that at least the destruction of the good be prevented."[30] So in an important sense, freedom is in tension with itself, or, perhaps better put, freedom has its limits.

Kant argues further that this private/public tension lies deeply within every individual. He uses the example of the clergy. Clergy have the obligation to teach church doctrine to their congregations. And so they are not free! But they are also scholars and as such they are free and even obligated to communicate to the public their thoughts concerning erroneous points in church doctrine. For what you do and say in private is one thing; what you say in public falls under the domain of universal reason. He writes:

> As a priest (a member of an organization) he is not free and ought not to be, since he is executing someone else's mandate. On the other hand, the scholar speaking through his writings to the public which is the world, like the clergyman making public use of his reason, enjoys an unlimited freedom to employ his own reason and to speak in his own person. For to suggest that the guardians of the people in spiritual matters should always be immature minors is a nonsense which would mean perpetuating forever existing non-sense.[31]

---

[28] Immanuel Kant, "Answer to the Question: What Is Enlightenment?," in *Basic Writings of Kant*, trans. Thomas K. Abbott, ed. Allen W. Wood (New York: Modern Library, 2001), 135.

[29] Kant, "Answer," 136 (emphasis in original).

[30] Kant, "Answer," 137.

[31] Kant, "Answer," 138.

Kant, like Hobbes and Rousseau, was concerned about establishing a view of the state that would guarantee peace and security. And he believed this to be possible. But, perhaps unlike the political theorists who preceded him, he saw the problem not so much with ensuring the rights of individuals within the state as with the logic that grounds the relations between states. Therein lies the problem of war, and a key problem here was the standing army. In an essay, "Perpetual Peace" (1795), he argued that if we were rational about our relation to other states we would realize that standing armies will gradually disappear.[32] Why? Because "standing armies incessantly threaten other states with war by their readiness to be prepared for war. States are thus stimulated to outdo one another in number of armed men without limit."[33] And this leads inevitably to war. He says that on occasion war is even preferred over peace because of the army's readiness.

To get to a desired state of peace among nations then, Kant believed that the world needed a kind of federation of free states, which he called a *Völkerbund* or a union of states. This was not to be an all-out *Völkerstaat*, a state of nations, but it was still to be a significant union. What Kant was interested in, and what he thought reason dictated, was an authoritative forum for rational debate. He argued that if a state says:

> "There shall be no war between myself and other states, although I do not recognize a higher legislative authority which secures my right for me and for which I secure its right," it is not easy to comprehend upon what ground I would place my confidence in my right, unless it be a substitute [*Surrogat*] for the civil social contracts, namely a free federation. Reason must necessarily connect such a federation with the concept of a law of nations, if authority is to be conceived in such terms.[34]

Kant saw fit to contrast this world union of states with a peace treaty; a peace treaty seeks to end a particular war, whereas the world union seeks to end all wars forever. This did not mean that Kant was espousing pacifism, but it did mean that, as he saw it, universal pacifism was the more rational approach and war was irrational. And a rational people (the eventual goal of the Enlightenment) would eventually come to see this and then bring a cessation to all wars.

What he says about peace applies equally to hospitality. For "*hospitality* (good neighborliness) means the right of a foreigner not to be treated with hostility when he arrives upon the soil of another. The native may reject the foreigner if it can be done without his perishing, but as long as he stays peaceful, he must not treat him hostilely."[35]

The point to be noted here is that for Kant reason determines moral action. His supreme faith in reason and the rationality of all people is astounding. And he comes by this conviction not arbitrarily but with a philosophical *tour de force*. In the process of working out his thought, he managed to solidify several important dualisms; facts and values (he agreed with Hume), what there is (*noumena*), and what we can know (*phenomena*), pure reason and practical reason, and so on. On all of this his ethics is grounded.

Kant argued that there are two kinds of reason: pure reason and practical reason. Pure reason gives us knowledge of the phenomenal world—the world as mediated through our senses and our categories of understanding. Of the world as it is in itself (*noumena*), we can have no knowledge. In other words, what we know is due to the categories with which our mind and senses mediate knowledge to us. The analogy of a fishing net is helpful here—it would be foolish for a fisher who uses a net with three-inch square netting to be surprised at the catch of fish all larger than three inches in diameter. It would be equally foolish for the fisher to claim that there are no fish smaller than three

---

[32] Kant, "To Eternal Peace," trans. Carl J. Friedrich, in *Basic Writings*, 437.
[33] Kant, "To Eternal Peace," 437.
[34] Kant, "To Eternal Peace," 447.
[35] Kant, "To Eternal Peace," 448–49.

inches in diameter in the sea. Similarly, that we see all objects in time and space is not because of how the world is but because of how we are. And that we understand only events that have a cause, for example, is not because of how the world is but because causality is a category through which our mind filters all our knowledge. Knowledge that we can claim to have with certainty (Kant calls this metaphysical knowledge) is derived from the workings of the rational apparatus called pure reason. Such knowledge is at once necessarily true (a priori) and tells us something about the world as we will experience it (synthetic knowledge).

Practical reason is the other kind of reason Kant envisions. This gives us regulative principles for living. Here Kant was also in search of synthetic and a priori principles. Although he accepted Hume's two realms of fact and value, he nevertheless believed that it was possible to show that valuing had a rational source and was not merely grounded in passion and desire. Why? Because valuers are rational beings. This implied, for Kant, that one could name an unconditional universal duty (categorical imperative) that was binding on all human beings. It is of the nature of reason that it produces universal and consistent principles. Hence he went on a search for that one categorical principle that could be the ground of morality and the universal human duty.

And he found it. He states this principle in several different ways, but always in terms of universalizability and as an imperative. For example, "Act according to a maxim which can at the same time make itself a universal law."[36] In other places, "Always act so as to treat human beings, whether in your own person or in that of others, as an end, and not as a means."[37] What he intends is that you should never treat another person as though that person were a mere instrument of your own will. Reason is superior to and

independent of will—*contra* Hume—and hence one's justification for acting must appeal to it. This protects ethics from degenerating into mere power dynamics.

Kant gives several examples of how the categorical imperative provides us with moral guidance; hence a duty to act concretely. Here is his case against suicide:

> A man reduced to despair by a series of misfortunes feels wearied of life, but is still so far in possession of his reason that he can ask himself whether it would not be contrary to his duty to himself to take his own life. Now he inquires whether the maxim of his action could become a universal law of nature. His maxim is: From self-love I adopt it as a principle to shorten my life when its longer duration is likely to bring more evil than satisfaction. It is asked then simply whether this principle founded on self-love can become a universal law of nature. Now we see at once that a system of nature of which it should be a law to destroy life by means of the very feeling whose special nature it is to impel to the improvement of life would contradict itself, and therefore could not exist as a system of nature; hence that maxim cannot possibly exist as a universal law of nature, and consequently would be wholly inconsistent with the supreme principle of all duty.[38]

Some important questions arise in relation to Kant's view on ethics. Why should reason be equated with universalizability? That is, why is reason not seen as the capacity to see the good and then to embody it in a manner that does not violate its goodness? But Kant connects universalizability with reason and then goodness with rationality. Hence, something can be good only if it is good for everyone. But why, we may ask, could we not say of a potential action that, although it would not be right for everyone, it is right at this particular time, place, and context? That is, hospitality, generosity, humility, love, and so on, all need to be contextualized in order for them to retain their goodness.

Kant's solution to the problems of Hume's and Diderot's insistence that the basis of

---

[36] Kant, "Fundamental Principles of the Metaphysics of Morals" (1785), trans. Thomas Abbott, in *Basic Writings*, 194.
[37] See Kant, "Fundamental Principles," 178.
[38] Kant, "Fundamental Principles," 179.

morality is desire and passion fails not because it emphasizes reason but because it does so on the basis of the dualism of fact and value. That is, if metaphysics (what is real) and epistemology (what we can know) are not essentially linked, then the task of reason is to *produce* the good rather than to unveil its nature. The difference between Enlightenment thought and the classical thought of Plato and Aristotle is not that the former heralded a new capacity of reason which the latter failed to see; the difference is that the Enlightenment made reason autonomous and the classical thinkers made it subservient to a higher master, namely, ultimate reality. Here the task was to uncover what has been given us mortals to see, even if only dimly, and then to "put it on" in the quest to allow it to shape us into characters capable of being good.

It seems that Kant's system begs two important questions, namely, whose reason and what has it to do with what is really good? In the end, his approach suggests that we "do not do anything which is irrational, in the sense that we would not consent to having someone else do." But are there not maxims that we can consistently will that are not necessarily good? For example, "Let all people do what they think is good, provided that it harms no one else." Surely the mere fact that we are able without inconsistency to will this maxim does not make it a good moral maxim!

It is important to summarize briefly what is at stake when viewing where Enlightenment thought has taken us. We have identified four concerns with the Enlightenment approach to ethics generally and with Christian ethics in particular. First, what we see from the Enlightenment scholars is that ethics is now thoroughly lodged in reason alone. What this means is that ethics is no longer based in ultimate reality, but instead in a mere human capacity. This is the reversal of classical and medieval thought, in that there we found the

Good as the ultimately real and reason as the means to help us gain access to the Good and determine the extent to which any particular could participate in it. After the Enlightenment, there is no Good in itself, but only goodness insofar as an autonomous subject wills it and, for Kant, wills it universally. Now humans create goodness, but goodness does not create humans.

Second, for Enlightenment thought there is no such thing as human nature, or a *telos* in terms of which we can judge our own character, and no virtues which shape our characters. In fact, "virtue language" has altogether given way to "value language." To say this differently, just like for John Locke, we know nothing at birth, one could say that we are nothing at birth. We are only what we create ourselves to be. Our actions do not flow from "who we are" but "who we are" is determined by what it is that we do. This is reminiscent of twentieth-century existentialism. As Jean-Paul Sartre summarizes:

> [E]xistence comes before *essence*—or, if you will, that we must begin from the subjective. . . . What do we mean by saying that existence precedes essence? We mean that man first of all exists, encounters himself, surges up in the world—and defines himself afterwards. If man as the existentialist sees him is not definable, it is because to begin with he is nothing. He will not be anything until later, and then he will be what he makes of himself. Thus there is no human nature, because there is no God to have a conception of it. Man simply is.[39]

Third, for the Enlightenment philosophers, tradition is a problem. Since our knowledge and understanding come from reason, tradition becomes the enemy. Tradition represents a force that gets us to repeat patterns of behavior by habit and custom without careful thought. This can be said differently by noting that the reason of the past from which these customs arise is not to be trusted—such reason must be subjected to the new, better reason of the autonomous subjects.

---

[39] J. P. Sartre, "Existentialism Is a Humanism," in *Existentialism from Dostoevsky to Sartre*, ed. Walter Kaufmann (New York: Meridian, 1956), 289–91 (emphasis in original).

For when reason becomes autonomous, even if it gets universalized as with Kant, tradition becomes unnecessary, nay, even repudiated.

Fourth, the result of this way of approaching ethics is emotivism. Moral disputes are now impossible to resolve because they are either based on values arising from passion and desire, or values put forth by the rational mind willing universally. In either case we are left with a morality stripped of the capacity to form a people of character.

This leaves a rather dire legacy for the nineteenth and twentieth centuries. It is not that the challenge has not been taken up by several thinkers, but the search for a viable quest for a model of Christian ethics is not easily found once virtually all the props have been removed. Yet to this quest we now turn.

Chapter Eight

POST-ENLIGHTENMENT ETHICS

In this chapter the designation, "post-Enlightenment," names the period of history that has its beginnings in the nineteenth century and is inaugurated by the writings of people like Georg Hegel, Friedrich Schleiermacher, and Arthur Schopenhauer. Immanuel Kant died in 1804, and that marked a transition of sorts. It is not that the mantra of Kant's essay "What is Enlightenment?" changes from "Dare to Reason" to something else, but reason itself gets reconceived in important ways; that is, history, subjectivity, and will become categories through which human reason itself gets unpacked. That said, among the most important shapers of ethics in the nineteenth century are the Utilitarians, Kierkegaard, Marx, and Nietzsche. However, to do justice and set the stage for the issues of their day, we must briefly present the ideas of Hegel, Schleiermacher, and Schopenhauer.

GEORG W. F. HEGEL (1770–1831)

Hegel was born in Stuttgart, Germany. His father was a government worker; his mother, although she did not have a profession, took care of the family and taught young Hegel Latin. Unfortunately, she died when he was only eleven years old. He was born into a family with one sister and one brother. Hegel was extremely bright, yet did not divulge his scholarly potential in school, even though, upon graduation, he received a scholarship to enter Tübingen University to study theology. Theology was too narrow for him. He was far too interested in other subjects like literature, philosophy, and the classics. His broadened interest was due in part to the influence of two important friends: the poet Johann Hölderlin and the philosopher Friedrich Schelling. Perhaps even more significant was his early awareness and conviction that the dynamics within history could not easily be subsumed under a single perspective.

After five years at Tübingen, Hegel began to write, not in order to gain standing in any university but to clarify his own ideas. Since he had inherited some money from his father's estate, he was able to devote himself to writing and minimal teaching without drawing a salary.

In 1799 he joined his friend Schelling at the University of Jena, where he began work on one of his famous books, *The Phenomenology of Mind*, which was published in 1807. Once his money ran out, Hegel was forced to find work and became a newspaper editor for a short period of time. But always he was writing books. In 1816 he became chair of philosophy at the University of Heidelberg, and here his *Philosophy of Right* was published in 1821. Hegel married a woman twenty-one years his junior in 1811, and together they had two sons.

As someone who uttered abstract-sounding thoughts like "What is real is rational—what is rational is real," Hegel's influence in nineteenth-century thought and beyond is truly remarkable. He set in motion a trajectory of interpreting the world that was either accepted and modified by people like

Karl Marx, vehemently opposed by Søren Kierkegaard, or embraced quite uncritically and even unconsciously by others to this day. Nobody can ignore his thought. Not only is his thought important, abstract though it be, Hegel's global impact through concrete political movements like twentieth-century German nationalism and, through his closest disciple Karl Marx, is hard to measure.

It is important to note that Hegel is every bit as concerned with reason as Kant and the other Enlightenment thinkers, yet Hegel's understanding of reason could not be more different. The Enlightenment thinkers held to a view of things where the paradigm for understanding reason was human nature. In other words, for people like Kant, reason was derived from the unchanging structure of the mind. Hegel introduced a radical departure from the reason of Kant in that he saw the nature of the mind influenced by forces like desire, interests, and will. Spirit and matter are not fundamentally at odds with each other but intersect in ever-new ways. And as he saw these dynamics change over history, he also saw that the rational explanation of the world changed. What was once rational is no longer so.

For Hegel, history itself became the dominant category of logic, reality, knowledge, and ethics. He realized, for example, how Greek culture changed because of the impact of Socrates and Plato. People now thought differently because the mythological narratives of Greek society met their critics and questioners. Public debate, that is, logic at work, changed the culture! He also saw that Christianity brought about a new understanding of the world and our place within it. In fact, he describes the change that Christianity brought about as a revolution. "The supplanting of paganism by Christianity is one of those remarkable revolutions whose causes the thoughtful historian must labor to discover. . . . How could a religion have been supplanted after it had been established in states for centuries and intimately connected with their constitutions?"[1] What is Hegel's answer to the question he asks? He rejects the usual answer, which he says is "intellectual enlightenment" or "fresh insight," for, he says, "the heathens too had intellectuals."[2]

His own answer, although somewhat convoluted, is instructive. It is not as though Christianity was convincing because it provided a better intellectual explanation of things, it was convincing because it provided a better existential account of human life. In the coming of the Messiah, the promise of the fullness of life was being offered as a gift and this made it possible for human beings to come to grips with their own moral failures in ways not earlier conceivable. It was not that they were now justified in being morally weak (this was Nietzsche's critique), but they were assured of the outcome of peace and justice, despite the fact that they continued to mess up.

Hegel's answer is instructive because it suggests that history is in a perpetual state of change. But it is important to note that for Hegel the change is not random. There is a meaning and a goal to history. One way of understanding his philosophy of history is to say that there is both a push and a pull that governs it. The push is alienation; that is, human beings will not tolerate being alienated so every possible resolution will be pursued, and the pull is freedom, which he also calls *Geist*. In other words, *Geist* pulls history into an overcoming of alienation.

In alienation Hegel identifies an inescapable human condition. There is a seemingly endless separation between our strivings and what is already ours, which puts us in a constant state of unhappiness. The genius of Christianity is that it offers an avenue to overcome this alienation through participating in the divine. Christianity makes it possible to have what we most deeply desire even

[1] Georg Hegel, "The Positivity of the Christian Religion," quoted from *Hegel Selections*, in *Early Theological Writings*, ed. M. J. Inwood (New York: Macmillan, 1989), 76.   [2] Hegel, "Christian Religion," 76–77.

when it is impossible for us to achieve it on our own. We do this by projecting onto God our earnest strivings, hoping that they may come back to us as gift.[3]

For Hegel, this movement of history is governed by what he calls logic, that is, it is a development of mind, or *Geist*. The word "Geist" is hard to unpack. It can be translated as both mind and spirit. What he is seeking to name is not individual *Geist* but not mere collective, societal *Geist* either. Nor is it just the logic that wins the day—the spirit of the times, like consumerism or certain fashions. Rather, it is something like social and political sense-making—sense-making that minimizes alienation. So the freedom that is the goal is not the freedom of individuals doing their own thing but the freedom to participate in the activity of social-political rationality. This is not the pure reason of Kant, nor is it the mere random dynamic that comes from open and free public debate. It is instead something like logic and truth interacting and becoming truth in all its fullness.

Although Hegel does not use the term, what he is describing is a kind of historicism—a process of historical logic unfolding, a process he also calls "dialectic." His dialectic sometimes gets explained in terms of a triadic formula: thesis, antithesis, and synthesis. Hegel himself does not use this formula to describe it, but he talks about abstract, negative, and concrete. It is not hard to see how this might work since it is the way public discussions are often structured today. For example, in formal debates we believe it to be insightful to hear the interaction between two opposing positions on a particular subject, the assumption being that there is truth on both sides and the "further" truth emerges through such engagement.

Given that Hegel did not see history as random; he saw it as a process with an end, and the end of history is pure knowledge. It is hard to know how to explain this concept, but he sees pure knowledge as the union of subject and object; that is, when that which is known is known as it really is, or when the knower and the known meet. According to Kant, this is the overcoming of the break that is not overcomable, between the phenomenon and the noumenon. This is even sometimes seen as the philosophical equivalent to the incarnation of Christ—where full humanity and full divinity become one.

It might be hard to see how Hegel's thought has any immediate bearing on Christian ethics, but the major impact here is that he unleashed a new category—history—which requires an entirely new way of understanding how to live. This gets worked out in the thought of people like Karl Marx and Ernst Troeltsch and eventually meets with an emphatic "no" in Karl Barth.

FRIEDRICH SCHLEIERMACHER (1768–1834)

Although Hegel and Schleiermacher were writing and teaching in Germany at the same time, their approaches to life were quite different. For Hegel the dominant notions were history and logic; for Schleiermacher experience was central.

Schleiermacher was born the son of an army chaplain. As a youth he attended a Moravian school at Niesky, Germany, where he said he learned to be a "true lover of Jesus." After theological studies and an extensive study of the works of Immanuel Kant, he became a preacher at a Calvinist church. But his preaching was short-lived. Soon he made his way to Berlin where his Enlightenment convictions ran up against a dimension of human existence he thought was being neglected. What was officially called romanticism was less a philosophy than a style and a disposition. But it was a reaction to the narrow intellectualism of the Enlightenment and an affirmation of the affective side of human life.

---

[3] It is interesting that for Ludwig Feuerbach, a disciple of Hegel, the first half is all there is—hence God is merely human projection.

In Berlin, Schleiermacher wrote his first book. He called it *Reden über die Religion* (1799) (literally *Addresses about Religion*; later translated as *On Religion: Speeches to its Cultured Despisers*).[4] The book, as the title suggests, was an attempt to address those who despised religion because, as Schleiermacher believed, they misunderstood what it really was. In his *Speeches*, he sought to redefine religion so that the educated would find it acceptable. Eventually, in 1806 he became a professor at Halle. Here he wrote several other books but throughout remained committed to the notion that religion and the intellectual life should never be broken apart, and, decidedly, that the intellectual should never dominate as it had in the Enlightenment. It should also be said that throughout his life Schleiermacher was influenced by Plato (he translated two volumes of Plato's works). This is significant because Schleiermacher, in some ways similar to the Renaissance writers, was seeking a broader understanding of religion than he saw at work in the nineteenth century.

Perhaps Schleiermacher's main contribution has to do with the way he formulated the core of religion. He believed that with the Enlightenment, human beings had forgotten what religion was about: the human heart and the thirst for God. Religion was not about true dogma and petty theological debates for it was about "experience, not given to cold analysis, but to be lived in and enjoyed."[5] Mackintosh takes Schleiermacher to be saying the following:

> You reject the dogmas and propositions of religion. Very well, reject them. They are not in any case the essence of religion itself. Religion does not need them; it is only human reflection on the content of our religious feelings or affections which requires anything of the kind, or calls it into

being. Do you say that you cannot [do] away with miracles, revelation, inspiration? You are right; we are children no longer; the time for fairy tales is past. Only cast off as I do faith in everything of that sort, and I will show you miracles and revelations and inspirations of quite another species. To me everything that has an immediate relation to the Infinite, the Universe, is a miracle; and everything finite has such a revelation, in so far as I find in it a token or indication of the Infinite. What is revelation? Every new and original communication of the Universe to man; and every elemental feeling to me is inspiration. The religion to which I will lead you demands no blind faith, no negation of physics and psychology; it is wholly natural, and yet again, as the immediate product of the Universe, it is all of grace.[6]

As we can see, Schleiermacher was emphatic that, in order for religion to be understood and accepted by the critics, it needed to be redefined. Religion is not a science or a morality, nor is it about reason, or conscience or will, but it is about *feeling*. More specifically, it is about the feeling of absolute dependence, which is a universal feeling. Hence, religion finds itself more in kinship with psychology than with either philosophy or history. In our quest for religious understanding, therefore, we must look to self-consciousness of the infinite rather than to cognitive knowledge. This is not to suggest that the focus of religion is not God, but rather that the route to one's understanding of God has to do with the sense of one's own limitations, the sense of the giftedness of existence, absolute dependence, and so on. And access to such awareness is by a feeling, or intuition, not reason or history.

ARTHUR SCHOPENHAUER (1788–1860)

It is interesting that while Schopenhauer's writings were completely disregarded during

---

[4] Friedrich Schleiermacher, *On Religion: Speeches to Its Cultured Despisers*, trans. John Oman (New York: Harper and Row, 1958). It is important to note that Schleiermacher is participating in a significant historic shift, namely, from a discussion of the Christian faith to a discussion of religion in general. The notion of religion in general was popularized in the nineteenth century and is significantly different from the Christian faith.

[5] H. R. Mackintosh, *Types of Modern Theology: Schleiermacher to Barth* (London: Fontana, 1969), 48.

[6] Mackintosh, *Types of Modern Theology*, 48.

the first half of the nineteenth century, he became enormously influential on the writers of the latter half of the century; especially on thinkers like Friedrich Nietzsche, Sigmund Freud, and Ludwig Wittgenstein. And his romanticism saw new appeal in the second half of the twentieth century.

Like other philosophers, Schopenhauer was interested in understanding the world in which he lived. And certainly he had not shed the Enlightenment notion of system building. He felt, like Kant, that it was necessary to identify an underlying reality to the given phenomenal world we all experience. Yet he was not satisfied with Kant's answer that we could know nothing of the *noumenal* world. He believed that it was possible, on the basis of rational reflection, to say at least something about what lies beneath our phenomenal knowledge.

In his reflections, he argued that although our senses and our mind give us differentiated knowledge, there must be something undifferentiated that undergirds this knowledge. So far, Kant would probably agree! Yet Schopenhauer believed that Kant had not pushed hard enough on the matter of knowing things in themselves. For the one reality that we know immediately, that is, in a way unmediated by the senses and the mind, is ourselves (echoes of Descartes?). Even though we do not know ourselves fully, because much of what we do is done unconsciously, we know ourselves differently from the way Kant suggested we can know other objects (a foreshadowing of Freud?).

All of this was an attempt to move beyond Kant's metaphysical agnosticism and to make a claim about ultimate reality. When Schopenhauer speaks of the one undifferentiated reality, he does so with the word "will," which to our ears sounds somewhat strange. "Will" connotes intentionality that Schopenhauer does not necessarily wish to convey. Scholars have suggested that what he is trying to get at is something more akin to energy, in

that matter is but a manifestation of will or energy.[7]

The world as Schopenhauer saw it was a terrible place. He saw prisons and hospitals, and animals devouring each other and concluded from this that life was a pathetic nightmare. He was completely pessimistic about making it anything other than this. After all, each individual is in some way identical with this one reality, and so the nightmare enveloped not only society at large but each person within it.

So what does he say about morality? Ultimately we must turn against reality because it is horrible and evil; we must deny its power (or will) over us, and turn to beauty, love, and compassion for the other. Aesthetic contemplation, in the sense of desiring not the object itself but that which the object represents—something like Plato's Idea—is a step that makes possible the overcoming of the appalling reality we call the world.

Schopenhauer was one of the very early public atheists, and also one who learned deeply from the Eastern traditions. His turn to nothingness and the overcoming of being—or as he calls it, asceticism, in the sense of seeking to overcome the suffering and pain that is a given in the world—is the only way out. Much of this thinking had its origin in Eastern philosophies, and his influence on Nietzsche was, as we will see, readily apparent.

JOHN STUART MILL (1806–1873)

Unlike Hegel, Schleiermacher, and Schopenhauer, Mill offers a philosophy with immediate connections to ethics. Yet he is only properly understood under their influence since the roles of history, feeling, and will figure heavily in Mill's thought.

Mill was born in London, and was the eldest of nine children. He grew up in a home where education was regarded very highly. He read Plato at age six and began studies in Greek and Latin even earlier. He was homeschooled by his father, who, Mill says, was a

---

[7] It is surprising how much Schopenhauer anticipated what modern science was later to confirm.

stern taskmaster and showed no signs of feeling. This, he intimates later, contributed to his problems with depression at age twenty. Hence, he says, he needed to "teach himself to feel as his father had taught him how to think."[8]

The beginning of the nineteenth century was a time when the popular approach to ethics was being articulated by Jeremy Bentham (1748–1832). Mill's father, a philosopher in his own right, was a staunch Bentham supporter. Bentham says that the political theorist and natural philosopher/theologian, Joseph Priestley, taught him the phrase "the greatest happiness of the greatest number." In his work, *An Essay on the First Principles of Government and Liberty*, Priestley suggests that in the world of politics it is the majority of members who determine what is right and wrong. In other words, the democratization of values is the ground of morality. Bentham agrees and adds, "Priestley was the first (unless it was Beccaria) who taught my lips to pronounce this *sacred truth*: that the greatest happiness of the greatest number is the foundation of morals and legislation."[9]

Bentham's claim, of course, is an unprecedented "sacred truth," one which could never have been uttered a few centuries earlier, for it would have been considered "blasphemy" and certainly neither sacred nor true. Notice that in Bentham's take on the subject, there is no reference to an autonomous good from which right and wrong can be derived; no transcendence (God or Idea) in relation to which goodness receives its sense. Only the most immediately subjective, albeit collective, feelings of pains and pleasures are referenced. Hume's argument that the passions are the domain of morality is here brought to full expression. Yet the Utilitarians were

dissatisfied with leaving ethics entirely to the relativism of the feeling subject. While they rejected a transcendent ground, as the Christian tradition had held, their basic principles shifted to the utterly concrete. They held that there could be empirical determination for right and wrong, but this was possible only if there were measurable qualities like pain and pleasure that became the ground of morality. Hence, Bentham spent his energy developing a hedonistic calculus (sometimes called felicific calculus)[10] designed to measure pain and pleasure in order to render objective determinations of right and wrong actions.

Mill ate heavily from the tree of Bentham's Utilitarianism. He was perhaps not as mathematical as was Bentham, yet he embraced his underlying principles with vigor and enthusiasm. He said:

> The creed which accepts as the foundation of morals, Utility or the Greatest Happiness Principle holds that actions are right in proportion as they tend to promote happiness, wrong as they tend to produce the reverse of happiness. By happiness is intended pleasure, and the absence of pain; by unhappiness, pain, and the privation of pleasure.[11]

Mill published *On Liberty* in 1859 and *Utilitarianism* in 1861, the former in the same year as the publication of Darwin's *On the Origin of the Species*. I mention Darwin here because it helps to historically situate Mill. This was the age of empirical investigation, and scholars like Bentham and Mill found a way to render ethics in empirically verifiable language. They saw this as a major contribution toward the betterment of both the individual and society.

For Bentham and Mill, grounding moral behavior not in intrinsic qualities or transcendent ideals but on consequences was a revolutionary and progressive idea. Only if extrinsic value—utility—justifies our moral

---

[8] Forrest E. Baird and Walter Kaufmann, eds., *From Plato to Derrida*, 5th ed. (Upper Saddle River, N.J.: Prentice Hall, 2008), 922.

[9] Jeremy Bentham, *Common Place Book*, in *The Works of Jeremy Bentham*, vol. 10 (Edinburgh: William Tait, 1843), 142 (emphasis added).

[10] Bentham spoke of variables and vectors like intensity, duration, purity, and extent, among others, and sought thereby to develop measurable units to determine amounts of pleasure and pain. He believed that the better able we became to calculate actual amounts of pain and pleasure, the better able we would be to assess the rightness and wrongness of actions.

[11] J. S. Mill, "Utilitarianism," in Baird and Kaufmann, 927.

behavior can there be a built-in protection against abuse. That is, only when happiness itself is the object of morality does it become impossible to sacrifice people to the cause of the right. But, of course, this all depends on how the notion of happiness gets unpacked. In other words, if happiness is a predefined, abstract, human notion, imposed upon the meaning of human existence, then individuals in their freedom-quest may well find that oppressive. Whereas if the free individual and collectively free society are permitted to determine the nature of happiness itself, then not. It is this very delicate balance that Mill seeks to develop, and in this process he is both associated with and differentiated from Aristotle.

His relation to Aristotle is via the notion of happiness as an end of moral action. Like Aristotle, Mill's understanding of happiness is eudemonistic; that is, it has to do with the fulfillment of basic human needs. Yet for Aristotle, these needs are determined by what it means to be human; that is, they are intrinsic to human beings *qua* human beings. Whereas for Mill, these needs are determined by clear-thinking human beings who have come to know through empirical associations what makes us happy.

What are the basic human needs as Mill sees them? Among others, he identifies things like cultivating friendships, refining our intellectual capacities, enjoying beautiful aesthetic experiences, having free association with others, and so on. The fulfillment of these qualities is what makes us happy. Notice that he is not talking about immediate satisfaction that might come from activities like parties, eating good food, or drinking beer. The cultivation of our basic qualities requires a certain level of intellectual maturity, which is only possible in a highly developed civilized society. For example, a child might

think that raiding the cookie jar and indulging without limit is fulfilling a need, but this is clearly not so and should not be tolerated. Similar reasoning gets Mill to exempt "barbarians" from his kind of ethic.[12] Only when individuals and societies have progressed to the point where they are morally and intellectually "enlightened" enough to be able to take responsibility for their liberties can Utilitarianism work. (Notice the assumptions of a Hegelian historicism.) This is so because Mill's moral account is not rooted in an intrinsic human *telos*—as was Aristotle's—but in a happiness attainable only by those who have already become educated and civilized so they can handle human freedom. In other words, at the base of Mill's ethics lies an overt optimistic and a progressive view of moral development guided by enlightened self-awareness and utility.

As we have already noticed, for Mill the pursuit of our basic human qualities is impossible without maximum human liberty. But how is human freedom to be maximized? Mill seeks to steer a path between freedom of the individual as individual and the lesser freedom of the individual as social being. Let me clarify with an example. In every society with cars, people are forced to drive on either the right or left side of the roads—people are not free to choose on their own. Authorities are justified in coercing individuals to restrict their liberties insofar as it is a matter of protection of others in public. In other words, there is a principle that limits our freedom, which is sometimes called the "harm principle," and which limits the individual's exercise of liberties that may bring harm to others. Yet outside authorities do not have the right to interfere with human liberties insofar as it is a matter only for the good of the individual. In fact, individuals are free to harm themselves if they so desire. Mill says,

---

[12] He says, for example, "Despotism is a legitimate mode of government in dealing with barbarians, provided the end be their improvement, and the means justified by actually effecting that end. Liberty, as a principle, has no application to any state of things anterior to the time when mankind have become capable of being improved by free and equal discussion. Until then, there is nothing for them but implicit obedience to an Akbar or a Charlemagne if they are so fortunate as to find one" (Mill in *On Liberty*, ed. Elizabeth Rapaport [Indianapolis: Hackett, 1978], 10).

"The only part of the conduct of any one, for which he is amenable to society is that which concerns others. In the part which merely concerns himself, his independence is, of right, absolute. Over himself, over his own body and mind, the individual is sovereign."[13]

It may appear so far that Mill has collapsed morality entirely into legality. But this is not so. He is clearly eager to establish a utilitarian basis for a politically structured society, but he wants to go one step further and speak as well about a utilitarian basis for society, beyond what is legally regulated. We need legally binding laws that are enforced for purposes of protection (and that will limit our freedoms somewhat), but we also need mechanisms whereby we do not do harm to one another beyond that. For example, am I free to invade another person's private space at my discretion even when I do not violate any legal laws? I might do this by coming into a person's presence and seeking to start up a conversation. Yet this may well inhibit his/her personal freedom. Mill is not advocating a world of restricted social interaction; in fact, he encourages us to maximize it. So he does not wish to regulate such behavior with legally binding laws. Yet this may create problems regarding the clash of our liberties.

The way Mill advocates that we protect our liberties in the social realm is through the notion of social rights.[14] That is, you are morally (note, not legally) unjustified in exercising your freedom in ways that violate another's social rights. So as long as I have not violated your rights in the exercise of my freedom, which I do when I get drunk and make a public disturbance (Mill's example), or, we could add, which I do when I enter your space when you have clearly told me not to, I have done nothing wrong. And

whenever I do such things, I need to be coerced to surrender my liberties.

Mill also makes the point that, on utilitarian principles, all citizens are required to contribute to society. We need to bear our fair share of society's costs, for failing to do so harms everyone.

SØREN KIERKEGAARD (1813–1855)

With the life and thought of Kierkegaard, scholarship is brought to another level. In a general sense, Kierkegaard's thought might be seen as following Mill's ethical "subjectivism"; after all, Mill grounded ethics in the subjective qualities of pain and pleasure. Yet Kierkegaard was no Utilitarian. He was opposed to the very logic that led people like Mill to their conclusions, yet Mill was not Kierkegaard's chief antagonist; that honor belongs to Hegel. Hegel was the problem for Kierkegaard because he reduced everything, including the individual, to the process of thought: logic. Such a move was anathema and even diabolical for Kierkegaard. In response, he sought to interject a radical subjectivity into religion and ethics, arguing that truth itself is subjective. Mill had introduced pain and pleasure as the ground of ethics precisely in order to objectify ethics. For Kierkegaard there was no such objective ground. In other words, what the great scholars so far had missed, according to Kierkegaard, was the element of lived experience, or individual existence. Existence is unlike thought in that it carries with it no necessity; it is by definition contingent and unpredictable.

In Kierkegaard's language, terms like "paradox" and "absurdity" are used to describe his notion of subjectivity. Not only is his language different, his convictions also deeply affect his style of writing. He blurs the boundaries between poetry and cognitive

---

[13] Mill, *On Liberty*, 9.

[14] Mill speaks about social rights extensively, especially in chapter 4 of *On Liberty*, but it is far from clear exactly what he has in mind. This is obviously long before the articulation of the Universal Declaration of Human Rights (England did have a bill of rights, but that did not really address the social rights of which Mill was speaking), but from his comments it is something like this that he had in mind. Yet it seems that "social rights" were more socially located than the Universal Declaration is.

language and he writes many of his works under pseudonyms. He says about the latter: "My role is the joint role of being the secretary and, quite ironically, the dialectically repudiated author of the author or the authors."[15] For Kierkegaard it is not only (perhaps not even primarily) important *what* is said, but the emphasis should be on *how* it is said. And to this end, his self-proclaimed task is "to make difficulties everywhere."[16] Yet he does not seek to make his writings obtuse as if that is somehow in itself a virtue; rather, he believes that life is nuanced in ways that do not admit of simple depiction.

His emphasis on lived experience gets Kierkegaard to weave his own life's story into his thought, sometimes in overt ways, but mostly through veiled accounts. It is therefore important to give serious attention to his biography.

He was born in Copenhagen, Denmark, when his father was fifty-six years old. His father, Michael, played more than a casual role in the young Dane's life. Michael educated young Kierkegaard at home and was a rigorous teacher, exposing him to classical literature and languages. His father also taught him religion, but when Kierkegaard reflects on this part of his education, he speaks less than fondly about it. This is partly due to a passion that accompanied his father's religious convictions, a passion that Kierkegaard found difficult to understand and even more difficult to handle emotionally. Religious fathers were not supposed to have doubts and struggles, but his father did. His father did not have a straightforward, happy existence; certainly it was spiritually checkered.

Father Michael retired at an unusually young age—barely in his forties—from a successful wholesale grocery business. This came at the same time as the death of his first wife, and there may well have been a connection between these two events that has not been recorded. Within less than a year, however, he married his wife's maid, who was pregnant with his first child. In 1813, Søren was born, the last of seven children. (The first marriage had been childless.)

The Kierkegaard children were all physically frail, and several of them died young. Kierkegaard himself had a deformed body. There was also plenty of psychological trauma and melancholy to go around. His brother had to resign as bishop because of his struggles with insanity; one of his nephews committed suicide. Another nephew wrote from an insane asylum, "My uncle was Either/Or, my father is Both/And, and I am Neither/Nor."[17] (Presumably the uncle reference is to Kierkegaard.)

Yet by far the biggest psychological trauma that Kierkegaard alludes to again and again, albeit in veiled ways, has to do with the sins of his father's past—sometimes referred to as a family curse and sometimes as the great earthquake. In one of his journal entries he says: "The dreadful case of a man who when he was a little boy suffered much hardship, was hungry, benumbed with cold, stood upon a hummock and cursed God—the man was not able to forget this when he was eighty-two years old."[18] It is thought that Kierkegaard is here speaking of his father and this revelation seems to have come to him on his twenty-second birthday.

Kierkegaard prided himself in never overtly divulging "the secret" of this curse to his readers. Yet he did reveal it indirectly, through metaphorical sleight of hand and the retelling of classical myths. He also did it in another way: the power of his father's "curse" weighed so heavily on his heart that the way he narrated his life or, for that matter, life in general, is with constant reference to this darkness.

---

[15] Said in his *Concluding Unscientific Postscript*, quoted from *The Essential Kierkegaard*, ed. Howard V. Hong and Edna Hong (Princeton, N.J.: Princeton University Press, 2000), ix.

[16] Kierkegaard, *Postscript* (emphasis in original).

[17] Quoted from Walter Lowrie, *A Short Life of Kierkegaard* (Princeton, N.J.: Princeton University Press, 1970), 27. Other biographical details also draw from this work.   [18] Lowrie, *Short Life*, 71.

When his father disclosed his own sexual sins and how he believed that God had condemned the family for his sins, Kierkegaard was emotionally crushed. "This man who was his father had violated his mother when she was a virgin. His mother! Horrible! His father had seduced a servant girl who was entirely dependent upon him."[19]

Up to this time in his life Kierkegaard had lived the life of hedonistic revelry—parties, spending lots of money, drinking—but this now came to an abrupt end. Shortly after his father's disclosure, Kierkegaard had a Christian conversion experience. He then returned to his studies in theology in preparation for becoming a Lutheran pastor. In a remarkable turn of events, he was able to make peace with his father before he died, shortly after Kierkegaard's twenty-fifth birthday. But Kierkegaard never became a pastor because his disgust for the church made that quite impossible.

It was also during this time that Kierkegaard became engaged to marry seventeen-year-old Regine Olsen. This was not a happy story either. Right after she agreed to marry him, he gives the following rather peculiar description of his mood: "Immediately I extended the relationship to the whole family. My virtuosity was especially directed towards the father, for whom, by the way, I always had a great liking. But inwardly—I saw that I had made a mistake. A penitent as I was, my *vita ante acta*, my melancholy, this was enough. I suffered indescribably in that period."[20]

Why did he consider the engagement a mistake? Why the suffering? This is not easy to answer. It may be as simple as his confession that he "is not capable of making a girl happy" but, since nothing is ever simple for Kierkegaard, it is not likely the whole story. It seems that he found himself in a position where he could neither tell her the truth nor tell her a lie. For to lie would be inauthentic and to tell her the truth would be to initiate

"her into terrible things, my relationship to my father, his melancholy, the dreadful night which broods in the inmost depths, my wildness, lusts and excesses."[21] Perhaps there was yet another level of struggle. Kierkegaard's psychological and theological reflections are quite intertwined. We note, for example, that he has Johannes de Silentio say in *Fear and Trembling* that he was not able to make the movements of the knight of faith (religious person), but perhaps Kierkegaard was not even able to make the movements of the ethical person. He was comfortable within the aesthetic realm where he knew how to relate to Regine, but to marry her was to become a husband, which required a life bound by moral obligations like truth-telling and fidelity, something he was not able to do. Whatever was at work within the heart and mind of young Kierkegaard, after a few months he broke off the engagement. He was twenty-eight years old and had just published his dissertation, *The Concept of Irony*. He ended up never marrying. Regine Olsen, however, married her former teacher, Fritz Schlegel, and they lived a happy life together. After this, Kierkegaard threw himself into his writings, even though he was not happy.

In his philosophical-theological writings, Kierkegaard makes it clear that he finds Hegel's historical concept of the spirit unacceptable. For Hegel, history itself was a category of reason and as such it subsumed the thought of individuals into itself. Kierkegaard found this notion abhorrent in that it relegated to history a power it could not have and to the individual an impotence he could not accept. For example, he says, "What I really lack is to be clear in my mind *what I am to do*, not what I am to know, except insofar as a certain understanding must precede every action. The thing is to understand myself, to see what God really wishes *me* to do; the thing is to find a truth that is true *for me*, to find *the idea for which I can*

---

[19] Lowrie, *Short Life*, 75.
[20] Lowrie, *Short Life*, 136.
[21] Lowrie, *Short Life*, 137–38.

live or die.[22] This Hegel's "system" did not provide.

As we have seen, Hegel believed that the truth of history was born out of the struggle of opposing ideas that were themselves constitutive of every idea. He called this process by the Greek name "dialectic." Kierkegaard found Hegel's dialectic completely useless, not only because it could not give him guidance on how to live but also because it supposed that the human spirit was constantly evolving and becoming more intelligent and better able to understand life in general. This quest for impersonal objective truth was for Kierkegaard an altogether false pursuit. This did not mean that he rejected the notion of dialectic, however, but he makes it personal; perhaps better, existential. In other words, the dynamic of conflict and struggle may well occur in history, but what is important is that it occurs within each of us as well. And to understand this dynamic helps us to know how to live.

The individual's struggle—a dialectic—as Kierkegaard saw it, occurs on at least two levels: first on the level of micro-decisions but secondly, and more importantly, on the level of macro-decisions about the kind of life one wants to live. Kierkegaard talks about the second level in terms of realms: the aesthetic, the ethical, and the religious realms. Each person is faced with the decision about which realm he or she wishes to operate in. It is important to say something about each of these realms, but perhaps the most important thing to say immediately is that for Kierkegaard there is no rational basis for making the decision of which realm to claim for oneself.

The *aesthetic life* is one of pleasure or satisfaction. We all crave satisfaction, which can come to us in different ways. One way is through sensual gratification. Among Kierkegaard's favorite operas was Mozart's *Don Giovanni*. The opera is based on the legend of Don Juan, a free spirit who seduces women in unprecedented numbers. But as the opera suggests, sexual pleasure is not the only route to satisfaction. People can receive great satisfaction from making something beautiful: a piece of art, a beautiful building, delicious baked goods, and so on. But the problem with the aesthetic way of life is that it invariably ends in boredom. Repetition, a common theme in Kierkegaard's work, cannot sustain the satisfaction that is craved by the human spirit.

An alternative to living in the aesthetic realm is the *ethical life*. Kierkegaard differentiates sharply between these two realms, even though the Utilitarians see pleasure as the ground of the ethical. The ethical life, as Kierkegaard sees it, promises to deliver what the aesthetic ultimately could not (human fulfillment); and so it is an attractive alternative, even though for Kierkegaard it also clearly lacks a rational basis. The difference between the aesthetic and the ethical is like the difference between the lover and the married. The life of the former is characterized by passion, pleasure, enjoyment, and recreation, and the latter by duty and obligation.

Kierkegaard accepts the traditional rendering of the ethical as the rational—this he learns especially from Kant, where the categorical imperative (the obligatory) is conflated with the rational; that is, never do anything whereby you treat yourself as a special case; more positively, always do what reason tells you to do. Kierkegaard makes clear that once a person has made the choice to opt into the ethical realm, then doing what is rational follows, but *whether or not* to choose the ethical way of life cannot be based upon reason. That can only be done via a rationally unwarranted leap.

While the life of the ethical is laudable—in fact it may even be possible to be fulfilled within the ethical (Socrates may well be such an example)—it nevertheless has its limitations. Ethical people eventually suffer from

---

[22] Søren Kierkegaard, in *The Journals of Søren Kierkegaard*, ed. Alexander Dru (London: Oxford University Press, 1938), 15 (emphasis in original).

fatigue. They get weary of doing good. And so the ethical life, like the aesthetic, has difficulties in delivering the quality to human existence that we all seek. And fortunately there is another choice we can leap into: the *religious life*. And when we choose this option, we are brought into a realm that transcends both the aesthetic and the ethical. It is, like the others, not a choice that has a rational basis, but also like the others, it holds out the promise of giving quality to life.

Kierkegaard works out the religious life in his *Fear and Trembling* under the pseudonym Johannes de Silentio. Here the biblical story of Abraham and the near-sacrifice of Isaac is the model story. As Kierkegaard reads the story, Abraham is called by God to sacrifice his "miracle son," given to him by his "barren" wife. Clearly the sacrifice of a child is a violation of any ethic. Abraham's willingness to do this indicates that he was not acting within the ethical realm. In the end, Abraham sacrifices a lamb and not Isaac, but he is able to do all these things in complete openness and obedience to God's call. Kierkegaard calls Abraham the "knight of faith" because he was able to act in the religious realm by suspending the ethical and the aesthetic, for had either been the highest authority for Abraham he would not have been able to hear God's call and act in complete faithfulness.

This understanding of the religious way of life is difficult to express simply. Kierkegaard puts it thus: "Faith is the paradox that the single individual as the single individual is higher than the universal . . . that the single individual as the single individual stands in an absolute relation to the absolute."[23] In other words, before God we stand not under the "universal" demands of ethics, but we opt out of ethics altogether—he calls it the "teleological suspension of the ethical"—and in

openness to God we are called to live the life of faith which to ordinary human beings will appear absurd. In fact, if one were to really follow Kierkegaard carefully, one would notice that his point is that the religious life is really not speakable, since the very act of saying it is to objectify what is best grasped only subjectively. It is not by accident that *Fear and Trembling* is penned by John, "the silent one." Of course, we may think it ironic that it takes many words for Kierkegaard to talk about what was in principle ineffable, but this irony did not escape Kierkegaard either.

So how does Kierkegaard help us understand Christian ethics? In a way, he helps us a lot, and in a way, not much at all. He is adamant that the traditional formulation of ethics is not significant for those seeking to be Christian. In fact, it is an impediment. Furthermore, when he reflects on the state of the church in Denmark he is unrelenting in his indictment. He repeatedly says that it has nothing whatsoever to do with the Christianity of the New Testament. For example, "The religious situation in our country is: Christianity (that is, the Christianity of the New Testament—and everything else is not Christianity, least of all by calling itself such), Christianity does not exist—as almost anyone must be able to see as well as I";[24] and again, "'Christendom' is . . . the betrayal of Christianity; a 'Christian world' is . . . apostasy from Christianity."[25] In other words, the church, in its collusion with the state and Danish society has forfeited its identity with the New Testament notion of church, and hence has ceased to be the faithful church.

One might expect from his tirade against the Danish church that he would give an account of the faithful church. But not so! About the church as a moral community he has nothing positive to say at all. While he may well be right in speaking out against

[23] Søren Kierkegaard, *Fear and Trembling and Repetition*, ed. and trans. Howard V. Hong and Edna H. Hong (Princeton, N.J.: Princeton University Press, 1983), 55–56.

[24] Søren Kierkegaard, "The Religious Situation," March 26, 1855, in *Attack upon Christendom*, trans. Walter Lowrie (Princeton, N.J.: Princeton University Press, 1946), 29.

[25] "Salt," March 30, 1855, in *Attack upon Christendom*, 33.

the hypocrisy and dishonesty of the Danish state-church, nevertheless it seems that he has removed the religious so far from the ethical that the New Testament vision of the social form of the church—where Jews and Gentiles, former enemies, can live together in one body of Christian unity—completely escapes him. Thus, he is left with an understanding of the Christian life about which very little can be said, and about which the church as church seems largely irrelevant.

KARL MARX (1818–1883)

Marx is no doubt the most influential figure in the nineteenth century, although he was not during his lifetime. Literally a quarter of the earth's population has been in some way affected by his views on economics and politics.

He was born in Trier, Germany (Prussia). His father, Herschel Mordechai, and his mother, Henriette Pressburg, both came from a long line of rabbis. But his father became a Lutheran in order to keep his job as a lawyer in Trier. At age seventeen, Marx entered law school at the University of Bonn, and a year later he enrolled in the more prestigious Faculty of Law at the University of Berlin, where he studied for four years. While at the University of Bonn, Marx became engaged to Jenny von Westphalen, daughter of the prominent Baron von Westphalen. They married in 1843, a marriage initially opposed by both families. During the early years of their marriage they lived well, in part because of a significant inheritance that came from his father's estate. But that resource soon ended, and thereafter they lived with very meager means. They had seven children together, but several of them died young.

During his early student years, Marx joined the Young Hegelians, also known as Left Wing of the Hegel movement.[26] It seemed to him that Hegel had many basic ideas right.

He was fascinated by the notion that history was governed by a logic and a goal. This notion never left him, even though he radically redefined the essence of that logic.

As a Young Hegelian, Marx was enamored with Ludwig Feuerbach (1804–1872), especially his portrayal of religion. Feuerbach had extended Hegel's philosophy and offered a psychological explanation for the origin of religion. Feuerbach says: "Man—this is the mystery of religion—projects his being into objectivity, and then again makes himself an object to this projected image of himself thus converted into a subject."[27] The idea of "religion as human projection" makes the Christian object of worship a product of the human imagination. This notion, coupled with a specific use of Hegel's thought, proved powerful in shaping Marx's own view of religion as well as history.

Marx's search for a career led him to journalism. In 1842 he became the editor of *Die Rheinische Zeitung*. But this lasted for less than a year, and the paper was shut down. Following this he moved to France.

It was in Paris where Marx met Friedrich Engels and became a communist. But his time in Paris was also brief; in 1844 he moved to Brussels and then after a few years to England, the home of Engels. It was during his time in England that Marx began to develop his materialist concept of history. It was also here where he and Engels were invited to write the *Communist Manifesto* that became a blueprint for the worker's revolution that began in Europe in 1848.

While in London, Marx raised his family with extremely meager resources that came largely from Engels' cotton business and weekly articles that Marx published as a foreign correspondent for the *New York Daily Tribune*. During this time, Marx was also involved in writing major works on political economy; eventually, in 1867, he published

---

[26] The Right Wing Hegelians were those who believed that the Hegelian synthesis had largely been achieved with the existing Prussian state. The Left Wing Hegelians thought that what Hegel had set in motion was a process that was far from complete, and that a more basic revolution was necessary to bring about a fully just society.

[27] Ludwig Feuerbach, *The Essence of Christianity*, trans. George Eliot (New York: Harper Torchbooks, 1957), 29–30.

his first volume of *Das Kapital.* Volumes 2 and 3 were published after his death by Engels.

During the 1870s, Marx's health began to decline. He died in 1883 and is buried at Highgate Cemetery in North London. Said his closest friend, Engels, in a eulogy at his funeral attended by family and only a few friends: "On the 14th of March at a quarter to three in the afternoon, the greatest living thinker ceased to think. He had been left alone for scarcely two minutes, and when we came back we found him in his armchair, peacefully gone to sleep—but for ever."[28]

Marx's thought literally began where Hegel's left off. He was thoroughly Hegelian in that he agreed that reality is in constant historical movement, governed by a dialectical interplay of tensions. Marx also accepted (from Hegel) that there was a goal to this historical process, and that the goal was the overcoming of conflicting forces within history. But until that goal is reached, human beings will experience alienation. All of this comes directly from Hegel. But Marx took one important additional step, and that made all the difference.

Marx read the insights of Hegelian logic through the lens of political and economic dynamics in a way not done by Hegel. His famous statement that "Philosophers have only interpreted the world; the point is to change it"[29] symbolized what he did differently. He saw that if thought could not access justice and goodness, as Kant and Hume had argued, then there is indeed very little importance to be associated with thought itself. In fact, herein lay the problem with philosophy, as he saw it. The philosophers spent time in contemplation for contemplation sake. But this was entirely useless because *it produced nothing.*

Hegel may have been brilliant in injecting into thought the process of history, a quite revolutionary idea in its own right, nevertheless, history governed by reason—mind or *Geist*—was not yet that radical. Indeed, the evidence suggests that Hegel had overindulged in the fruit of the Enlightenment: abstract reason. The problem with Hegel's approach, therefore, was that, although it might well give us a resolution to the conflicts of disassociated ideas at the intellectual level, it did not bring justice about at the material level. For that to happen, the forces and dynamics of material reality needed to be recognized in ways that Hegel's philosophy did not. For example, Marx saw that material forces like food, employment, shelter, health, and so on were in fact engines in determining the direction of history. And unless these realities were recognized, history could not be understood properly, and even more important, could never lead to justice. In sum, Marx developed a materialist philosophy of history, while Hegel had an idealist philosophy of history. The logic was very similar, but the content was vastly different.

As a result of Marx's materialist philosophy, the relationship between thought and action was now reversed. Action itself now becomes a dominant category of thought. Not desire/passion (Hume), not reason (Kant and Hegel), not choice (Kierkegaard), but action forms the basis of truth and justice. It might be said that for Marx revolution becomes the way to truth. Or, to put it more poignantly, action determines thought. For Marx the superstructure (how we think) is determined by the substructure (how we live) and what one does has primacy over how one thinks.[30]

For Marx, human beings were significant agents in the determination of history. In

---

[28] From Friedrich Engels, "Speech at the Graveside of Karl Marx" given at Highgate Cemetery, London, March 17, 1883, quoted from *Reader in Marxist Philosophy*, ed. Howard Selsam and Harry Martel (New York: International Publishers, 1963), 188.

[29] The 11th thesis of the edited edition by Engels, *Theses on Feuerbach*, which first appeared in 1886 as an appendix to Friedrich Engels, "Ludwig Feuerbach and the End of Classical German Philosophy," in *Die Neue Zeit.*

[30] Marx managed to turn Hegel on his head. Hegel believed that the substructure, i.e., how we live and what we do, was determined by the superstructure, i.e., how we think. For Marx this was the ultimate tragedy of modern philosophy—it had

fact, we are in large measure the shapers of our own destiny. While it is true that economic forces control us, it is also true that we can create different economic realities and hence take our futures into our own hands. Of course, in order to be able to say this consistently, Marx had to denounce religious ideology. Such an ideology was itself too Hegelian. Any belief in a supernatural reality (a superstructure), necessarily subjects us to a structure limiting our freedom to act and determining for us how we ought to live. Hence, reaching back to his friend Feuerbach, he proclaimed religion an illusion from which we should try to free ourselves. He saw how it was being used by the wealthy in society to underwrite an unjust social structure. It was being used to keep people from changing their lot of alienation. In this way, it had become the "opium of the people."[31] Note that what Marx is doing here is explaining religious ideas not on the basis of an appeal to truth (superstructure), but on the basis of how we act in society (substructure)—that is, on the basis of its "cash value." Insofar as religion sought to maintain an unjust status quo it needed to be overcome.

Marx tried hard to be consistent. Yet he overtly held some views in tension. He believed that although we as human agents are free to better our economic and political conditions, we are still bound by the necessary outcome of history. And this is a good thing. Marx argued that the laws of history are as natural as the laws of nature.[32] The outcome of history—a classless society—was therefore as inevitable as it is for copper to

expand when heated. This was so because of the way things are, not because of our actions or desires. His challenge is to get everyone on board the train of historical inevitability and to get them to stop resisting the movement toward the resolution of conflict and the establishment of justice. Hence, his call for revolution was not so much a call, which if it went unheeded would end in failure, but one that alerted people to the inevitable.

Marx has been enormously influential in determining the context for ethical discussion in the East as well as the West. He has in fact convinced many of us that we are in control of our destiny and that this control makes it possible for us to add quality and freedom to our lives. Marx has shown us that we have power, which we did not know we had, and if we use it properly, we can enhance human freedom. It is perhaps ironic and indeed sad that some nations that have gone through a Marxist revolution have done so through totalitarian regimes and thereby have eroded much of the freedom and even justice that Marx envisioned. Although Marx was a revolutionary, the accompanying bloodshed of totalitarian Marxist states seems on the face of it inconsistent with his best thinking. Yet his influence in setting the terms of discussion for much of the world today is undeniable.

FRIEDRICH NIETZSCHE (1844–1900)

Nietzsche was born in a small German (Prussian) village named Röcken. He was named after the Prussian king, Kaiser Friedrich Wilhelm IV, on whose birthday he was born. He

---

given us a false logic of history. He argued the very opposite, namely, how we think is determined by the fact that we need to eat and have the means to clothe ourselves and to provide shelter for our families.

[31] Here is his full comment in context: "Religious suffering is, at one and the same time, the expression of real suffering and a protest against real suffering. Religion is the sigh of the oppressed creature, the heart of a heartless world, and the soul of soulless conditions. It is the opium of the people. The abolition of religion as the illusory happiness of the people is the demand for their real happiness. To call on them to give up their illusions about their condition is to call on them to give up a condition that requires illusions. The criticism of religion is, therefore, in embryo, the criticism of that vale of tears of which religion is the halo." Quoted from "Introduction to a Contribution to the Critique of Hegel's Philosophy of Right," in *Deutsch–Französische Jahrbücher* (February 1844), 1.

[32] Friedrich Engels said at his "Speech at the Graveside of Karl Marx" (1883) that, "Just as Darwin discovered the laws of evolution in organic nature, so Marx discovered the law of evolution in human history," *Reader in Marxist Philosophy*, 188. This was a time in history when evolution was in the air; Charles Darwin (1809–1882), who died one year before Marx, published his first edition of *On the Origin of the Species* in 1859.

came from a loyal church family; his father, his uncle, and his grandfather were all ministers in the Lutheran church.

For the first few years of his life, Nietzsche lived with his parents and younger sister. Both his father and younger brother died before he was six years old. After his father's death, the family was required to leave the parsonage and he, his mother, and sister moved into an extended-family living arrangement.

During his adolescence, Nietzsche attended a boarding school in Pforta. Here he distinguished himself as a fine student and became interested in music, giving leadership to a music and literature club.[33] It was his early interest in music that led him to explore the works of Richard Wagner (1813–1883) who was a major source of inspiration, especially in Nietzsche's early work, *The Birth of Tragedy*.

In high school his bouts with severe headaches began. This was disconcerting for him since his father had died of what at the time was called "softening of the brain," which was often connected with mental illness, from which his father also suffered. Nietzsche was prescribed medication for his headaches, which unfortunately resulted in nausea, so for most of his life he suffered from either headaches or nausea.

After high school, Nietzsche attended the University of Bonn and studied theology and philology (linguistics). A year later, in 1865, he discovered the work of Arthur Schopenhauer, *The World as Will and Representation* (1819). This book made an immediate and enormous impression on him, and "will" (or "desire," or "effort") became a central concept in his philosophy, even though this required a reinterpretation of Schopenhauer. Other themes in Schopenhauer caught his attention as well: Schopenhauer's pessimistic view of the world, his atheism, and his view of music as an art form unlike others, one that has an immediate connection with will. In his *The Birth of Tragedy*, Nietzsche argued that

music exists beyond language and hence, he believed, was not limited by the structure of language. (Remember that he was a philologist.) Music is higher than all other art forms in that it does not represent anything outside of itself and so is pure will expressing itself.

In his early twenties, Nietzsche became personal friends with three people who were to influence his work in immeasurable ways: Richard Wagner, Hermann Brockhaus (1806–1877), and Franz Overbeck (1837–1905). I have already commented on Wagner's influence. Brockhaus was an orientalist who did work in Zoroastrian religion. This was Nietzsche's initial gateway into the thought of Zarathustra, the prophet of Zoroastrianism. Overbeck, who lived in the same house as Nietzsche for several years, became a somewhat unlikely friend. He was a theologian at the University of Basel, specifically a professor of New Testament and church history. He believed there could be no Christian theology, properly speaking, because there is an unbridgeable chasm between the view of objective knowledge fashionable in nineteenth-century European academia and the original religion of Jesus Christ.

Nietzsche traveled widely—actually "traveled" may not be quite accurate since he often stayed in other cities for extended periods of time, usually with friends. Switzerland, France, and Italy were all countries where he lived for longer periods, but of course, Germany was his home. In each place he threw himself into the local culture, both absorbing deeply from it and working feverishly to understand it. With this type of nomadic existence, it is surprising that he brought to publication as much as he did.

In his mid-twenties, while Nietzsche was a student at the University of Leipzig, one of his professors, Friedrich Ritschl "was so impressed with Nietzsche's work that he . . . recommended him for a chair of classical philology at the University of Basel."[34] Nietzsche was given the position as associate

---

[33] Nietzsche was himself involved in composing music for piano, choir, and orchestra, although this part of his career never flourished.   [34] Baird and Kaufmann, *From Plato to Derrida*, 1011.

professor without having written a doctoral dissertation, but the university gave him a doctorate—gratis—and within a year he was appointed full professor. All of this was testimony to his extraordinary brilliance and respect within the academic community. But this did not mean that he had a long tenure of university teaching. Barely seven years later, he stopped teaching altogether and threw himself into writing as much as his health permitted.

Nietzsche's writings have had a profound impact on other scholars, especially in the twentieth century. And his influence has extended far beyond his primary field of philosophy and linguistics to English literature, psychology, religion, sociology, cultural studies, and so on. Yet his work is hard to summarize. He does not have a system, although there are those who would argue that his *The Will to Power* and *The Transvaluation of All Values* are attempts at such. Also he is often polemical in his writing, giving a clearer view of what he does not believe than what he does believe; add to this that he changes his views on whom he supports and whom he attacks. For example, both Schopenhauer and Wagner are admired at the beginning of his career and maligned at the end.

Nietzsche is a remarkable figure in that he saw clearly the consequences of Enlightenment thought. He, more than anyone else, was able to draw the dire conclusions for religion and ethics even while some scholars were still blissfully unaware of what had happened. However, the problem is that he often states the consequences of the failure of intellectual history so starkly that readers have a hard time believing that he is serious, or that the situation is so grave.

Nietzsche was willing to confront nineteenth-century cultural reality head-on, so that it was no longer possible to believe in the traditions of religion and morality. Hence, in the name of honesty, he thought it appropriate to proclaim their death and, along with this, the end of the intellectual assumptions that underwrote them. Consistently, he states that the transcendent reference presupposed by both religion and morality is vacuous. Hence, given the nineteenth-century way of thinking about the world and involvement in it, no longer can belief in God and heteronomous goodness be sustained. It is therefore up to us as human beings to create our own values and our own ultimate realities.

Listen to his piercing words taken from a piece he entitled "The Madman" found in his *The Gay Science*:

> Have you not heard of that madman who lit a lantern in the bright morning hours, ran to the market place, and cried incessantly, "I seek God! I seek God!" As many of those who do not believe in God were standing around just then, he provoked much laughter. Why, did he get lost? said one. Did he lose his way like a child? said another. Or is he hiding? Is he afraid of us? Has he gone on a voyage? or emigrated? Thus they yelled and laughed. The madman jumped into their midst and pierced them with his glances.
>
> "Whither is God" he cried. "I shall tell you. *We have killed him*—you and I. All of us are his murderers. But how have we done this? How were we able to drink up the sea? Who gave us a sponge to wipe away the entire horizon? What did we do when we unchained this earth from its sun? Whither is it moving now? Whither are we moving now? Away from all suns? Are we not plunging continually? Backward, sideward, frontward, in all directions? Is there any up or down left? Are we not straying as through an infinite nothing? Do we not feel the breath of empty space? Has it not become colder? Is not night and more night coming on all the while? Must not lanterns be lit in the morning? Do we not hear anything yet of the noise of the gravediggers who are burying God? Do we not smell anything yet of God's decomposition? Gods too decompose. God is dead. God remains dead. And we have killed him. How shall we, the murderers of all murderers, comfort ourselves? What was holiest and most powerful of all that the world has yet known has bled to death under our knives. Who will wipe this blood off us? What water is there for us to clean ourselves? What festivals of atonement, what sacred games shall we have to invent? Is not the greatness of this deed too great for us? Must not we ourselves become gods simply to seem worthy of it? There has never been a greater deed; and whoever will be born after us—for the sake of this deed he will be part of a higher history than all history hitherto."

Here the madman fell silent and looked again at his listeners; and they too were silent and stared at him in astonishment. At last he threw his lantern on the ground, and it broke and went out. "I come too early," he said; "my time has not come yet. This tremendous event is still on its way, still wandering—it has not yet reached the ears of man. Lightning and thunder require time, the light of the stars requires time, deeds require time even after they are done, before they can be seen and heard. This deed is still more distant from them than the most distant stars—*and yet they have done it themselves.*" It has been related further that on that same day the madman entered divers churches and there sang his *requiem aeternam deo.* Led out and called to account, he is said to have replied each time, "What are these churches now if they are not tombs and sepulchres of God?"[35]

When we read these words, we need to remind ourselves that Nietzsche, coming from a family of ministers, was familiar with Christianity and the church, and so he was quite aware how disruptive his claim about the death of God really was. It is also important to remind ourselves that his attack is on Christianity and its history and not necessarily on the figure of Christ.

George P. Grant (1918–1988) summarizes the point of Nietzsche's stinging words when he says:

We have been taught to recognize as illusion the old belief that our purposes are ingrained and sustained in the nature of things. Mastery comes at the same time as the recognition that horizons are only horizons. Most men, when they face that their purposes are not cosmically sustained, find that a darkness falls upon their wills. This is the crisis of the modern world to Nietzsche.[36]

Nietzsche addresses the "crisis of the modern world" in an immediate and direct manner. Now that the Enlightenment edifice of knowledge—indeed all of Western thought—is no longer credible, what can we do, and how shall we think? He accepts that our knowledge and our values are not given to us from anything outside of ourselves—there is

in fact nothing there—so we are left to create them for ourselves. His entire enterprise is about how we go about doing this momentously difficult task of creating. And he suggests that the process involves two specific turns: first, it requires a demolition—a task of deconstruction, as it has come to be called; and second, it requires a constructive task—a new way of thinking to replace the old. The first task involves showing how Christianity has misled us and how a false ethic has been derived from it—he calls it a genealogy—and the constructive process entails formulating an understanding of life that does not rely on false crutches.

It is important to say, however, that it is not Christian morality alone that is the problem for Nietzsche; that is but exhibit A. He is every bit as critical of Greek ethics, of Socrates, Plato, and Aristotle; moreover, he is also critical of the ethics of the masses evident in common German society because these derive from the metaphysical assumptions of those who have misled us. All must be rejected and replaced with something better.

But why, we might ask, is Nietzsche so opposed to Christian morality? The simple answer is that it teaches the very thing that we have come to see as false—that there is something outside of ourselves on which to base our lives. For Nietzsche this is not just metaphysically false; it is also existentially false. That is, to teach people that they should turn the other cheek, or have compassion on the sick, or pity the weak—as Christianity does—teaches the sick and the weak that their well-being comes from outside themselves. And that is inauthentic and serves to perpetuate weakness. It is interesting that Nietzsche may well accept compassion and love for a strong, independent person, but not if it celebrates weakness. What is authentic is to learn to stand on our own, to assert our own true humanity, our power as human beings, and to live life to its fullest. Indeed, his indictment

[35] Friedrich Nietzsche, *The Gay Science*, in *The Portable Nietzsche*, ed. Walter Kaufmann (New York: Viking, 1968), 95–96 (emphasis in original).
[36] George P. Grant, *Time as History* (Toronto: Canadian Broadcasting Corporation, 1969), 31.

here is rather sweeping, in that it debunks all of morality—since traditional morality always refers to some sort of outside rules or duties, or claims something universal to which we should subordinate ourselves. Hence, all forms of nonreligious morality, starting with the Greeks, through Kant and the Utilitarians, are inauthentic. All must go, and Nietzsche is adamant that he does not wish to replace this debunking with an alternative universal system. Such a move would have the same problem. (This way of speaking about morality should be reminiscent of Kierkegaard, except that Kierkegaard still retained God; for Nietzsche, God too had to go.)

One might risk a specific comparison with Kierkegaard. For Kierkegaard, the "knight of faith" stands alone before God and is not subject to traditional moral laws and duties. Similarly, the authentic person for Nietzsche stands alone (in his case all alone and not before God) and certainly should not be subjected to the morality of the masses. It is important to state that Nietzsche had as much contempt for democracy as he had for Christianity. The heroic person was a law unto himself.

Furthermore, also not unlike Kierkegaard, Nietzsche's contempt is extended to include reason itself. Only Nietzsche attacks it at its source: Euripides, Socrates, and Plato. And according to Nietzsche, it all comes apart here because the post-Socratic Greeks explicitly rooted reason in an objective, independent, metaphysical source, which Nietzsche claims cannot exist.

In his work, *The Birth of Tragedy*, Nietzsche argues for a rebirth of the pre-Socratic view of the world. Here Nietzsche contrasts two art forms: the Apollonian and the Dionysian, named after two Greek gods: Apollo, god of the sun, representing harmony of the type we find in ancient Greek architecture and culture; and Dionysus, god of wine and ecstasy, represented by the activities we might find at drunken cult festivals. Greek tragedy brings these two art forms together and as such brings pleasure to its audience, while challenging them to clear self-understanding. Tragedy can take us into the depths of human existence, yet it cannot easily resolve the tension there. That is because the tension is resolved with false structures like reason. Hence, music is its most authentic expression, especially music of the kind composed by the early Wagner! For Nietzsche, this art form offers a kind of authenticity ritual.

For Nietzsche, Dionysus is a special kind of salvation symbol and an important contrast to Christianity. Dionysus' existence is not limited to himself but exists eternally in the essence of life and the hope for its recovery. In other words, Dionysus' existence is ensured through eternal living of other authentic people.

Nietzsche contrasts this view of salvation with the Christian view, which he sees as a flight from this life to another life outside of earth, that is, heaven. He puts it this way:

> Dionysus versus the "Crucified": there you have the antithesis. It is *not* a difference in regard to their martyrdom—it is the difference in the meaning of it. . . . It is a problem of the meaning of suffering: whether a Christian meaning or a tragic meaning.[37]

As he sees it, Christianity renounces life on earth, and Dionysus affirms life on earth. And he is seeking to point to an understanding of life that affirms the meaning of the earth. For example, in his *Thus Spoke Zarathustra*, he puts the following words into the mouth of Zarathustra:

> Behold I teach you the overman. The overman is the meaning of the earth. Let your will say: the overman *shall be* the meaning of the earth! I beseech you, my brothers, *remain faithful to the earth*, and do not believe those who speak to you of otherworldly hopes! Poison-mixers are they, whether they know it or not. Despisers of life are

---

[37] Friedrich Nietzsche, *The Will to Power*, 542–43, quoted from David Toole, *Waiting for Godot in Sarajevo: Theological Reflections on Nihilism, Tragedy, and Apocalypse* (Boulder, Colo.: Westview, 1998), 19.

they, decaying and poisoned themselves, of whom the earth is weary: so let them go.[38]

His is no mere intellectual rant against Christian ideas; Nietzsche's solution has to do with concrete human existence. He is convinced that Euripides (480?–406 BCE) destroyed the Dionysian art form with his obsession with the rational explanation of everything, an obsession that is still being played out in the late nineteenth century. Yet there is evidence of its demise. He believed that he was seeing within European culture the decay of a hope in rational scientific knowledge. Science will never be able to explain the mystery of life to us, human beings will never be satisfied with a denial of this life, and the rational quest will never be able to deliver the fulfillment of our most basic pursuits. Nietzsche believed that there lies within the German spirit the potential for a vitality that he is calling for even though much of German culture is also still in a state of denial and false hope.

It is important to mention here that Nietzsche was not only not a proponent of democracy, he was expressing a fear that democracy would destroy civilization as we know it. For example, he saw all too clearly that the reason Western civilization had come this far was precisely because we have not heeded the teachings of those who wish to laud the weak and the ignorant. Just look around! It is in fact the strong ones, the intelligent ones, the powerful ones, who have dominated; and it is out of the interplay of the strong that we have come to contemporary civilization. And democracy, an arrangement where everyone has an equal voice—the intelligent as well as the stupid, the strong as well as the weak, that is, where the herd rules—such a social structure is the very threat that he is naming in his writings.

To see Nietzsche's alternative to democracy, we must explore two other themes in his work: the will to power and the overman. As we have already seen, Nietzsche was influenced by Schopenhauer's concept of will. While Schopenhauer believed that will and desire were tainted with evil, Nietzsche believed that will was good. Will for Nietzsche was the affirmation of desire and self-assertion; hence, the denial of the will was the denial of self. Affirmation of will is important because it is able to eradicate what is weak within us. Hence, it is a will to power. And this works both within the individual and within society as a whole. Society too needs to celebrate the strong, the healthy, and only in this way can it give rise to the aesthetical quality of life—the beautiful.

The will to power is directly related to Nietzsche's comments on the overman. His teaching on the nature of humanity centers on the cultivation of what is strong and beautiful within the self, which leads to his teaching of the notion of the last man. The last man is the arrival of humanity, both individual and collective, that has gone through the process of the re-evaluation of values. The last man is the free spirit, the unrepressed spirit, the one who is able to affirm self, who does not allow the self to be pulled down by all that is not good within society. That is, there is no resentment in this person, and this person is characterized by a generous spirit. There are even those who have drawn similarities between the last man and the Christian character.

The writings of Nietzsche are obviously important for Christian ethics. We cannot do a thorough analysis and here carry this discussion into the twentieth century, but it would be a fruitful exercise to explore the post-Nietzschean contemporary writers through scholars like Michel Foucault (1926–1984), Jacques Derrida, (1930–2004), and Gilles Deleuze (1925–1995), to mention only a few. The influence of some of these writers, as well as the writings of Nietzsche himself, will be seen more clearly when we examine the writings of contemporary ethicists later in this book. But this will need to suffice for our comments on Nietzsche.

---

[38] Friedrich Nietzsche, *Thus Spoke Zarathustra*, in *The Portable Nietzsche*, 125 (emphasis in original).

It is difficult to know where to end this chapter. Since no specified time frame is designated—it references *post*-Enlightenment—theoretically everything *after* the Enlightenment is relevant. There are at least two influential thinkers who deserve to be mentioned briefly; they are Ludwig Wittgenstein and Martin Heidegger.

LUDWIG WITTGENSTEIN: (1889–1951)

Wittgenstein was born in Vienna, Austria. His family was wealthy and socially prominent; his father was in the steel business, and his mother was a concert pianist. Wittgenstein was educated at home and was poised to become an engineer. In 1908, after studying engineering in Germany, he left for England to study aerodynamics at the University of Manchester. While in England, his interest in mathematics drew him to Cambridge, and especially to the philosopher Bertrand Russell, who had just co-authored, with Alfred North Whitehead, their mammoth three-volume *Principia Mathematica*.[39] In it, they sought to lay the philosophical foundations of mathematics, which Wittgenstein found fascinating. The story is told that when Wittgenstein read Russell's book he went straight to him and asked whether he (Russell) thought him (Wittgenstein) to be an idiot or not. For if not, he could become a philosopher but if so, he would need to remain an aeronautical engineer. Russell asked him to write a paper as background to answering this question, and upon reading it, he confirmed that Wittgenstein was not an idiot. So Wittgenstein threw himself into philosophical studies.

The only book Wittgenstein published during his lifetime was *Tractatus Logico-Philosophicus*,[40] published in German in 1921. Several other books of his have been published posthumously, the most important of which is *Philosophical Investigations*, first published in 1953. In 1929 Cambridge University gave him a doctorate for his *Tractatus*. And in 1939 he became professor of philosophy at Cambridge.

Wittgenstein is significant for our purposes because his philosophy has a direct bearing on ethics. His early writings make ethical discourse meaningless, and about which philosophy must be silent; the later works show in what way it can be meaningful discourse. But the later Wittgenstein is only understandable in relation to the Wittgenstein of the *Tractatus*. We need to examine that work first.

The early Wittgenstein believed that he had found a way to solve all of philosophy's problems. He thought he had done so because he had shown how language works. And how was that? Language consists of statements that function as pictures of the world. This is known as the "picture theory of meaning." This view of language assumes that "the world is a totality of facts"[41] and language consists of corresponding propositions picturing these facts. So when language is properly unpacked—a job for the philosophers since by "language" here he does not mean simple ordinary language—we are able to see the world as it is, much like a picture depicts reality. Individual words name objects, and when they are put together they portray reality. But this means that of those things that cannot be stated as facts, where words don't seem to name objects, there is really nothing that should be said. In other words, if language does not picture or name anything, it is not meaningful. This includes such things as ethics and religion. So the last proposition of the *Tractatus* is, "What we cannot speak about, we must consign to silence."[42]

[39] Alfred North Whitehead and Bertrand Russell, *Principia Mathematica*, 3 vols. (Cambridge: Cambridge University Press, 1910–1913).

[40] The book was named after Benedictus Spinoza's *Tractatus Theologico-Politicus*.

[41] Ludwig Wittgenstein, *Tractatus Logico-Philosophicus*, trans. D. F. Pears and B. F. McGuiness (London: Routledge Kegan Paul, 1972), prop. 1.1.

[42] Wittgenstein, *Tractatus*, prop. 7.

Wittgenstein soon realized that this rather anemic view of language was unable to account for the rich way that language helps us see the world. In his *Philosophical Investigations*, he acknowledges that words do not function only to name objects but also more like tools. So we must ask how words are used or how they function in particular cases. This changes much for Wittgenstein. For example, now it is not reality that determines our language but our language enables us to see reality. The structure of our language—grammar—actually determines how we come to know the world. This has monumental implications. For example, now ethics and religion can no longer be dismissed as meaningless; rather, they are ways of imagining the world. So when we use religious language, we are using language to disclose a world to us. Religious language, like every language, is governed by a set of rules and cannot be used any which way. In fact, language functions much like a game or a form of life, both expressions he uses. In sum, language discloses worlds to us—the worlds that we inhabit.

Wittgenstein's later philosophy has led us into a different way of conceiving ethics and religion: no longer as meaningless gibberish, but rather as extremely important life-giving discourse. To give a concrete example, given Wittgenstein's view of language as disclosing reality to us: it is now possible to ask people to imagine a language that would give an account of what it might look like for us to live under the conviction that Jesus is Lord. Wittgenstein was a philosopher and did not see it as his task to develop the grammar of any ethic, Christian or otherwise, but he did make it possible for those following his lead to do so. He saw it as his role to be the philosopher, and the "aim in philosophy" is "To shew the fly the way out of the bottle."[43]

MARTIN HEIDEGGER (1889–1976)

The writings of Martin Heidegger are important for Christian ethics in several ways: first, he pronounced the end of modernity and with this the freedom to recover the meaning of human existence;[44] and second, he gave one of the earliest critiques of modern technological culture. But to understand how he did these things, we need some background.

Heidegger was born in a small town called Messkirch in southwest Germany. He grew up in a Catholic family and attended a Catholic boarding school. Because his family was poor and he was preparing for the priesthood, Heidegger's schooling was paid for by the church. After high school, he became a Jesuit novice, but this did not last long and soon he was discharged. He then entered Freiburg University to study theology and philosophy. We are told that in 1911 he underwent a personal crisis that resulted in the abandonment of his intention to pursue the priesthood once and for all. Instead he threw himself into the study of philosophy full-time.[45]

Heidegger began his philosophical studies with the reading of Edmund Husserl's *Logical Investigations*, and this work figured heavily in his dissertation, which he completed in 1913. To become eligible to teach in a German university, he also needed to write a *habilitation* (qualifying) thesis. He did that on Duns Scotus. This choice of topic is significant because it shows that for him theology and philosophy were thoroughly intermixed.

For some years, Heidegger taught at Freiburg University as an assistant to Edmund Husserl. During this time he officially broke with the Catholic Church. In 1923 he went to teach at Marburg University as an associate professor. This is where he became friends with Rudolf Bultmann and Hannah Arendt. It is also here where he wrote his

---

[43] Ludwig Wittgenstein, *Philosophical Investigations* (New York: Macmillan, 1958), para. 309.

[44] Heidegger is considered an existentialist, somewhat in the tradition of Kierkegaard, and was a major source of inspiration for J. P. Sartre.

[45] For more details on his life, see Michael Inwood, *Heidegger* (Oxford: Oxford University Press, 1997), 1.

most important book, *Being and Time*, first published in 1927. In this book, Heidegger reacted against the phenomenology of Edmund Husserl (1859–1938). So it is important to say just a few things about his nemesis.

Husserl was another philosopher who thought he had solved all of philosophy's problems. He believed that his approach made clear the basis for understanding all that could be understood. In his quest, he was able to bring Descartes, Kant, and even the early Wittgenstein to their consummation. And as one might expect, given this agenda, he shares in their mathematical approach to knowledge, the underlying assumption of which is that we are subjects knowing objects.

As we have seen, during the Enlightenment, the major agenda centered on the existence of the external world. Husserl believed he had solved this problem by focusing on what he thought could be known with certainty, namely our *awareness* (or consciousness) of objects. He believed that our awareness of objects and the objects of our awareness were in fact the same thing. This may sound odd, but here is what he meant: our consciousness of objects was not something we could be wrong about because it was uniquely ours. That is, it is ours in an immediate way—it is what our mind gives us. In fact, the very essence of the mind is such that it is always directed towards objects; it is always aware of something. He calls this intentionality. For example, consider the book you are currently reading. You are aware of it; you hold beliefs about it, think it too large, whatever. Whether the book is as you are aware of it is not of interest to Husserl. He "brackets" that question out of order. All you have is you and the object of your consciousness—subject and object; the mind and that of which the mind is aware.

Heidegger dedicated *Being and Time* to Husserl, but he believed him to be fundamentally mistaken about his basic assumptions. Not only Husserl, but the whole Western philosophical tradition was mistaken about the subject-object model of human consciousness. Heidegger believed that we are not primarily subjects with minds that are conscious of objects around us. To think of ourselves this way misrepresents subjects in two important ways. First, as subjects, we are ourselves among other subjects and objects and are affected by them. This means that we are not autonomous as the subject-object dichotomy assumes. The very separation Husserl presupposes is therefore not possible in the way he and others believed. Second, awareness, or consciousness, of objects plays little role in most of what we do. He uses the example of a hammer to illustrate. A skilled carpenter uses a hammer without really paying much attention to what he is doing. He can have a conversation while hammering, listen to the radio, reflect on the previous night's party, or whatever. But there is no subject-object consciousness in the way that Husserl and others presupposed. In fact, for the really skilled carpenter, the hammer in effect becomes an extension of the hammerer; or we may say that the object becomes inseparable from the subject. And it is like this with much of what we do: driving a car, walking down a path, typing on a keyboard, milking a cow, and so on. In other words, our activities are often not determined by our consciousness of them at all, for much of what we do is set by the way we have been socialized from very young. Of course, when something goes wrong—when the hammer breaks—then it becomes an object of our consciousness. But that is not the first level of human awareness.

Why is this important? Heidegger believes that he has shown that we understand the world best when we see it as "ready-to-hand," meaning that we connect to the world without theory, or without inference; like the (un)awareness of the hammer. And the revolutionary nature of this insight is not easily overstated. The Enlightenment's preoccupation with the existence of the external world, and Kant's agnosticism on *noumenal* reality (things in themselves), are mocked by Heidegger's disbelief that this could ever have been a serious concern. As he sees it, our primary mode of being is "being-in-the-world."

The autonomous subject—as mind stuck inside an internal world—is anathema to him, because we are always already situated beings. "*Dasein*" (literally, being-there) is his untranslatable word for this.

It is here that we begin to see how being is related to time. Human existence in the world, *Dasein*, is always situated in a given time and space. And in any particular time we are present-into-the-future. That means, we live in an in-order-to manner; we are engaged in activities open to and anticipating a future. For example, we are students in order to gain an education, or teachers in order to teach students, and so on. And we are not the first in the world to be such. There is a past, present, and future to all human actions. But equally important, we are not the only ones who are involved in in-order-to activities. We live in communities with other people. Being, or how we exist, is only intelligible if we understand ourselves in our relationship to the world around us as both participants and recipients. Hence, activities that have no future cannot be meaningful activities for us; and activities that are not essentially socialized activities are not meaningful either. We learn to talk, for example, in order to communicate, and others are necessary in order for talking to have significance. Similarly, we buy things, eat food, behave in public, and these are all activities that fit into a web of socialized practices. We live in socialized worlds. And one of the great world-forming activities of *Dasein* is language. We are always putting worlds together through the process of social articulation. This is the imagination through which Heidegger looks at his world.

According to Heidegger, one of the problems associated with our technological age—note the connection of being with particular time—is anxiety. Technology teaches us that, on the one hand, nothing is given and, on the other, that everything is possible. This is deeply troubling for human existence. But this is not the only danger with technology. By far the greatest threat of technology for human authenticity is that it has the power to redefine us and thus can master the very essence of human existence. There is very little that can stop this movement except the human spirit itself, for our essence is our existence.[46]

Heidegger addresses the problem of technology directly in a booklet called, *The Question Concerning Technology*. It is fascinating that, while Heidegger died before the advent of the personal computer, he anticipated its awesome power and potential to reconceive our identity. He talked about the power of the "language machine" (*Sprachmaschine*), and he saw it as dangerous because he believed that, if permitted, it would control the world of language itself. Remember how important he thought language was in defining human existence. He says that human beings will always insist that we are in control of our machines, but once the machine takes us and our language into its management—as it tends to do and as we in our current generation see many examples of—then the machine has become our master and we its slaves. This is what he calls the "essence of technology"; its insidious power to literally transform the way we think, the way we speak, and even the way we desire and will. In other words, technology has the power to transform our very existence. And since what we do flows from who we are and how we understand ourselves, technology determines our ethic.

We could well go on and discuss other important ideas in Heidegger's work, but we will draw our discussion to a close here. Perhaps it is fitting to end the post-Enlightenment section with a word about technology and its impact on us. After all, this is the world which we inhabit, and this is the world in which we must learn faithful Christian existence. To that larger task we now turn.

---

[46] J. P. Sartre, in his formative essay on existentialism, "Existentialism Is a Humanism," speaks about "existence preceding essence" in the case of human beings who are free to define themselves. Sartre is one of Heidegger's closest protégés. See Baird and Kaufmann, *From Plato to Derrida*, 1138–44.

Excursus

PART I

This section began with a presentation of Greek ethics. The reader may wonder why we would begin a book on *Christian* ethics with a non-Christian source. The answer is that throughout church history Christian ethics has been in such intensive and sustained engagement with Greek philosophy that it is impossible to understand it without the ideas of Plato and Aristotle. With the Greek philosophers, we saw a presentation of ethics that placed the standard and criteria of goodness outside the human being. In other words, in order to discern what is good, one did not look inward, but to reality itself—indeed ultimate reality. Although they developed it differently, both Plato and Aristotle argued that reason was the process that disclosed the source of goodness.

The early church also looked for the ground of ethics outside the human being. And yet the source was not abstract reality but the concrete person, Jesus Christ, who was seen as the manifestation of ultimate personal reality—God. And the access to this source was given through encounter with, and participation in, the life, death, and resurrection of Jesus Christ. This put the early church at some distance from both the approach and the content of Greek thought.

Yet these worlds were not kept apart for long. With the advent of Constantine and the declaration of the empire as Christian, the church was soon brought into the mainstream in ways unfamiliar to the early Christians. Indeed, this produced a new way of conceiving of Christianity itself.

By far the most influential early church thinker was Augustine. We saw that Augustine became a Christian in part because of the insights that neoplatonism provided. It may sound strange, but Christianity became intelligible to him via the thought of a pagan philosophy. Yet for him this was not a mere expedient merging of the two worlds through carelessness about the Christian faith; rather he sought an intentional philosophical and theological engagement that in turn brought about both a new philosophy and a new theology. For Augustine it was inconceivable for there to be anything in this world that did not participate in God, and with this conviction both the sinfulness of human beings and the attainability of human goodness were important tenets of belief. And he deduced these convictions from his reading of both the Scriptures and the Greek philosophers.

Throughout the Middle Ages, theology and philosophy were intermixed. Faith and reason, as well as reason and revelation, were not separated as distinct ways of understanding. Faith was in a constant quest of seeking rational articulation. Augustine and the other medieval theologians also believed that the church and state could not be simply separated as two independent realms, even as they could also not be simply identified. Morally speaking, church and state had everything to do with each other; they needed and depended on each other. Yet neither was *sui generis*, and both were properly understood in their separated roles only under God's ordering of a just world.

Augustine emphasized that the religious communities were able to devote themselves fully to the Counsels of Perfection and so expressed the high demands of Christian discipleship best. Yet all the church was under the mandate to be faithful to the call of Christ. Even the state and the larger public could not be left to live by their own standards. There were principles by which the state as state needed to conduct all its affairs as it sought to rule justly. This logic resulted in the formulation of the just-war theory. This theory was an effort throughout the Middle Ages to bring to bear standards of peace and justice for a political structure that did not embrace discipleship as an explicit standard but was still called to live under God's sovereignty.

While it is tempting to draw a sharp distinction between Augustine and Thomas Aquinas, I have presented them in substantial continuity. It is true that their philosophical tentacles go back to different Greek origins—Augustine relied more on Platonic sources and Thomas more on Aristotelian sources—nevertheless their reading of the Christian faith is similar. Both affirmed the continuity of faith and reason and the belief that reality cannot be read properly without seeing it as created and sustained by God; both emphasized the virtues, the just-war theory, a similar view of church and state, and so on. Yet it is also true that Thomas' view of the natural world was more positive than Augustine's. This made it possible for Thomas to speak of being good *in this world* in ways that, due to the predominance of human sin, Augustine was more reluctant to do.

We saw a major theological shift at the end of the Middle Ages with Duns Scotus and William of Ockham. While there were differences between Augustine and Thomas on matters of how to unpack the nature of the Christian life, both embraced the notion that all that exists in this empirical world participates in the divine. Hence, nothing that is created is understandable in relation to itself

alone, or even in relation to other empirical reality. Goodness and right action cannot be understood apart from being related to God's being. And God's being is only understandable with analogical language, which protects both the otherness of God and, peculiarly, also the "otherness" of the created world.

With the emphasis on the univocity of being, as introduced by Scotus and Ockham, it became possible to reconceive the world in such a way that created reality was understandable in relation to itself. The being of God and the being of empirical reality, it was now argued, are both intelligible because of what they have in common, namely, being—they both exist. Although God is clearly greater, better, more powerful, and so on, than any created reality, and still has moral authority, nevertheless, God's being is intelligible because we understand what it means for us to be. With this "participation in," God loses his meaning and power. This innocent sounding shift has the impact of "flattening" our reality; understanding it not in terms of what it could become or what it would be if it were fully real, but rather as fully real in the manner it is given to us empirically.

Whether causally connected or not, this shift was followed by the Renaissance's emphasis on humanity with a focus on the value and beauty of the natural world, and the Reformation that sought a new way of conceiving of the world theologically—new, that is, in relation to the theology of the Middle Ages. But the Reformers—including Calvin and Luther—and the Radical Reformers had a hard time giving expression to the Christian life without resorting to a dualism of those in Christ and those not. Notice that participation language is now reserved for only a few. The tensions between faith and reason, reason and revelation, church and world, secular and sacred, facts and values, all have a way of asserting themselves even if not yet in their fullness.

Not until the Enlightenment did these tendencies unravel more fully. The foundation of all knowledge now gets lodged in a reason that is available to every mind by a search internal to the mind. What our senses and our reason give us to understand is all that can be known about the world. Reason and revelation now became exclusive alternatives. Revelation cannot be trusted because it has no objective base; reality is divided between facts and values, the former being knowable and the latter being a mere subjective quality and private to the individual; religion, ethics, aesthetics are all relegated to the private sphere, where in principle disputes cannot be settled; and so on. This means that the metaphysical link between reality and ethics was entirely broken. Whereas earlier what was good was a measure of the extent to which an object was connected to its full reality, now what is good is a subjective and unverifiable assessment of an object or action.

While we saw an effort by Kant to lodge ethics and religion within the category of reason alone, it is not surprising that all he is able to muster is a very formal-sounding principle that everyone should do what is rational. A reason devoid of lodgment within ultimate reality now seeks to "make sense" of a world that stands in stark independence before us. And the only access possible is given via our senses and the universal categories of the mind. Now ethics generally, and especially Christian ethics, are subjective and private enterprises, and hence "unintelligible" in the traditional sense.

The nineteenth and twentieth centuries show some efforts at giving responses to this death knell. Nietzsche and Marx are both examples of this effort, seeking to move forward without questioning the verdict; others like Hegel and Kierkegaard are not so convinced and seek to start over once again—Hegel with the category of history and Kierkegaard with the individual. Yet the church as a moral community, teaching us to see the world anew and shaping characters capable of reading the world as divine gift, seems all but lost. Writers like Wittgenstein and Heidegger offer some hopeful signs that ethical discussion can again become intelligible, but the true test will come with a look at the specific, contemporary ethics/theologians. And after a brief interlude where we look at the contributions to Christian ethics of four disciplines of study, we will begin the examination of these ethicists.

PART II

A DISCIPLINED INTERLUDE

Chapter Nine

PHILOSOPHY AND ETHICS

Philosophers interested in ethics have considered it their task to analyze ethical arguments and to clarify the usage of ethical language. They begin by subdividing the field of ethics into three kinds of inquiry: descriptive ethics, normative ethics, and metaethics. Each, they argue, deals with the subject matter of ethics from a different perspective.[1]

Descriptive ethics is an approach to ethics in which the social and human sciences engage. Psychologists, sociologists, anthropologists, and historians consider it important to describe and explain what people hold to be right, wrong, good, and bad, and how such beliefs have shaped and affected their understanding of themselves and their social organizations. Here, questions like the following are asked: "How does one society differ from another morally?" "What are the conditions that have led to these differences?" "What can be said about moral development in light of what we observe about the social and psychological changes in human beings?" Some philosophers, particularly those in the Anglo-American analytic tradition, do not consider discussion of

> **Descriptive Ethics:** A subdiscipline of ethics in which the goal is to successfully describe the morality of a given group of people. This is of interest to anthropologists and sociologists, but not to philosophers.

these questions to fall under the domain of philosophy proper. They believe that philosophers should do only two things: first, engage the issue of whether something is or is not right (wrong) and how this can be established; and second, inquire about what moral terms mean. They believe that philosophers should not be concerned with what people hold to be right or wrong, because people can be mistaken about such things. To say this in another way, these philosophers are more interested in the justifiability of moral statements and the meaningfulness of moral language than they are in understanding how people in fact think and act. Descriptions of how people in fact think are left to history and the social sciences.

There is, of course, validity to the philosophers' concern to get beyond the merely descriptive to a sound basis in the search for moral answers. Yet, simultaneously, it is surely myopic to ignore history and the human and social sciences that serve to show how moral convictions become concretely meaningful. In the final analysis, a well-rounded understanding of ethics must seek ways of properly accounting for the ethical systems of diverse peoples. This study will seek to do this by devoting the next two chapters to a look at ethics through the eyes of the social and human sciences.

Normative ethics is the subdiscipline of philosophical ethics that deals with a cluster

---

[1] For a presentation of ethics in this way, see William K. Frankena, *Ethics* (Englewood-Cliffs, N.J.: Prentice-Hall, 1963).

Normative Ethics: A subdiscipline of ethics in which the goal is to determine the best theoretical framework for the evaluation of morality. Hence, it is concerned about showing what makes certain actions wrong or right.

Epistemology: A subdiscipline of philosophy which examines issues pertaining to knowledge and truth. It is derived from two Greek words "*episteme*" meaning knowledge and "*logos*" meaning "word of." Literally, "the study of knowledge."

of issues that the average person normally holds to be ethical matters. Here, the debate centers on what should be the moral position regarding specific social problems. For example, normative ethics deals with how we settle matters related to wealth distribution, human rights, euthanasia, and abortion, to mention a few examples. The issue here is over what we hold to be good and how we move from our understanding of the good to the justification of actions or rules.

Therefore, in normative ethics we discuss questions like: "Is war ever justifiable, and if so, under what conditions, and if not, why not?" "Is love a basic moral virtue, and if so, why?" "What kind of persons ought we to be?" "How can we make society more just?"

Metaethics is a subdiscipline of philosophical ethics where reflection takes place around the structure of moral thought, specifically about the nature of moral language. Metaethicists are concerned about the kinds of thinking ethicists are engaged in when they discuss matters of normative ethics. Hence, they are interested in the nature of moral justification and the meanings of moral terms. Metaethics is really more an epistemological inquiry (that is, how we come to know something) than it is an ethical quest. It considers issues like: "Under what conditions are moral knowledge claims legitimate?" "What are the meanings of moral terms like good, bad, right, wrong, obligatory, and how do these terms function in giving us moral knowledge?" "Is it philosophically legitimate to argue to moral conclusions based

Metaethics: A subdiscipline of ethics in which the goal is to analyze the meanings of ethical terms such as "right" and "wrong" and to evaluate the nature of moral justification.

on purely factual knowledge?" "Is the source of our knowledge about the world and our knowledge about what is good and bad the same or is it different?" and so on. These are all matters metaethicists claim must be settled in order to complete the task of ethical investigation.

In the remaining pages of this chapter, I will present and discuss the arguments philosophers have advanced in both the normative and metaethical subdisciplines.

NORMATIVE ETHICS

This is an aspect of the ethical inquiry that focuses particularly on establishing a defensible theory of obligation. If we try to answer why it is that we ought to do something and what it is we ought to do, or why it is that we ought to be a particular kind of person and what that would be, or why we should act on a particular virtue and what that virtue is, we are engaging in a normative ethical enterprise. For example, why should I or should I not be concerned about the environment? The basic answer will be because it is or is not the right thing to do. But if we ask why it is or is not right, we must come up with a rationale that can potentially convince others of this position.

The rationale that undergirds our sense of moral obligation is of particular interest to normative ethicists. Philosophers have suggested that when we analyze the arguments that normally convince rational human beings about moral obligation, they divide into two general approaches, called deontology and teleology.

A *deontological theory* of moral obligations attempts to answer the moral "why question" by referring to the *nature* of the act or rule or virtue which might be known intuitively

Deontological Theories of Ethics: Theories of normative ethics which argue that the rightness or wrongness of a moral action is determined by the inherent moral value of the action itself or by an intuition or rational principle which makes its rightness or wrongness self-evident. These theories ignore the consequences of actions as criteria for the moral assessment of actions and rules.

or which is based on moral reasoning or on a command given by an ultimate authority. If we apply this logic to war, it would look as follows: since war involves killing people and since it is always wrong to kill people, war is morally wrong. Or, Jesus commands us to love our enemies, and therefore we should not kill them. Or, some would argue that it is intrinsically right to protect ourselves and hence, defensive wars are permissible, perhaps even obligatory. Or, it could be argued that God commands the faithful to fight in particular wars to protect the truth, or righteousness, or justice, or even God, and hence we must fight. These are all deontological justifications for the moral conclusion that war is or is not morally justifiable. They are such because they focus on the nature of the act, rule, or command and not on the *consequences* of acts.

The term "deontological" comes from two Greek words *deon* and *logos* meaning "duty" and "word" respectively. Hence, etymologically, "deontological" means "theory of duty."

Historically, Immanuel Kant is the best known deontologist, as we have already seen. Kant argued that one's duty is determined on the basis of correct reasoning. That is, we know it to be irrational to treat human beings as anything other than ends in themselves, and therefore we can never justify harmful actions toward others. We cannot justify actions or moral rules in terms of a higher good than the human being. There is no higher good because each person is already of ultimate worth. Hence, Kant stated

his categorical imperative as follows: "Act so that you always treat human beings as ends in themselves and never as means" or, the more common version: "Act so that you can wish the maxim on which you act to become a universal law of human conduct."[2]

Categorical Imperative: A general rule of moral conduct that Immanuel Kant believed applied to everyone, which said that we should always "Act so that the law upon which we act applies universally to all people." In effect, do not treat yourself as a special case.

Consider another example of deontological justification that is quite different from Kant's. Modern pietists use this reasoning when they argue that given that God has commanded "Thou shalt not kill" (we know this from reading God's Word) and that abortions are acts of killing, we can never morally justify acts of abortion. This is a form of deontological moral reasoning because it argues from a specific rule to a moral judgment.

Teleologists employ a very different view of moral justification. They argue that the rightness or wrongness of an action or rule is determined not in reference to the action or rule itself, as Kant and modern pietists would have it, but in relation to the amount of good or evil that is brought about by a particular action or by living in accordance with a specific rule. Another way of putting it is to say that teleologists evaluate moral behavior by the extent to which an action or rule participates in nonmoral goodness like happiness or pleasure.

Let me provide two examples. Suppose you are asked by a friend who is suffering from a terminal illness to assist in his suicide. If you say, "No, that's murder," you are a deontologist. If you evaluate the request based on how much better it would be for your friend and/or for everyone else involved, you are a teleologist. Or, suppose you are asked

---

[2] For a more detailed discussion of Immanuel Kant's approach to ethics, see chap. 7 above.

advice from a friend who is considering ending a marriage relationship. As a teleologist you would ask whether a divorce participates in the greater good. If more good (however goodness is defined and philosophers do not agree) can come from a divorce, then what can be the rationale for remaining married, say the teleologists. Deontologists would reject the moral force of this question by pointing to the importance of more primary concerns like "You ought not to break your promises" or "What God has joined together let no one put asunder." Teleologists would claim such factors to be superseded by other matters pertaining to ends.

> **Aristotle's Teleology:** The belief that moral value is derived from the *telos* of being. Right action is determined by the extent to which we move from being-as-it-exists-empirically to being-insofar-as-it-is-what-it-essentially-is.

It is important to distinguish between two kinds of teleologists. The one is closer to deontology than the other. Classical teleologists, like Aristotle, are quite different from modern teleologists, like John Stuart Mill and Jeremy Bentham. All use the term in its etymological sense which, like "deontology," is derived from two Greek words *telos* and *logos*. *Telos* means "end" and hence "teleology" literally means a theory of ends. Yet the sense in which *telos* is *understood* by these two schools of thought is quite different. For Aristotle the *telos* of something is inherent in its being. For Mill *telos* is the definition of goodness defined by valuing human beings.

Let me illustrate. Aristotle would argue that the *telos* of a watch is given by its being a watch; that is, it is inherent in the meaning of watch. The *telos* of a watch is to tell time. This is the way "watch" is defined. Hence, if a watch tells time well, it is a good watch; if it does not tell time well, it is a bad watch. Notice that whether a watch is good or bad (evaluative terms) depends on how well it fulfills its *telos*, which is given by the watch

> **Mill's Utilitarianism:** A teleological theory of ethics which states that the rightness or wrongness of a moral action is determined by the amount of utility, that is, happiness, produced for the greatest number of people. Also sometimes called "ethical universalism" or "consequentialism."

being what it is. This same logic is applied to humans. Insofar as we take our place in the world as human beings, and do that well, we are good; insofar as we step outside the role of human being, we are not good. So for Aristotle's ethic, once we know what human beings are, that is, once we know the definition of being human, we can derive from this what it means to be good. Notice how Aristotle makes metaphysics (issues of what really is) and ethics (issues of what we ought to do) inseparable.

The teleology of John Stuart Mill, better known as utilitarianism or consequentialism, works quite differently. Here, human beings set goals and objectives for themselves or for society and in so doing presuppose their right to define what is good. Furthermore, their actions that move toward the realization of these goals are now deemed good and those that do not are deemed not good. For example, if the nonmoral content of goodness is taken to be happiness, then whatever produces the greatest amount of happiness for the greatest number of people is good.

The difference between these two teleologies centers in the source and definition of goodness. Mill's view of goodness is rooted in human aspirations, and the consequent actions that naturally flow from such aims. Aristotle's approach presupposes an independent realm of being that gives status to goodness andexists independently from valuing humans. Whereas for utilitarianism

> **Metaphysics:** A subdiscipline of philosophy that studies theories of reality in an effort to determine which is the most defensible explanation of being. Plato and Aristotle were philosophy's first great metaphysicians.

the most important moral question is, "How can we get from where we are to the goals that we project to be good?" for Aristotle it is, "How can we come to know what is good and then submit ourselves to its power over us?" If you like, we can say that Aristotle's view pushes us to concentrate on knowing what is and Mill's view leads us to focus on what we must do to bring about our desired ends.

It is actually quite surprising that two such different approaches to ethics have come to be called by the same name. This has resulted in untold confusion on the topic. In this study, we will endeavor to avoid such confusion by using the term "consequentialism" or "utilitarianism" to designate the teleology of John Stuart Mill and the term "teleology" for Aristotle's theory.

Although many philosophers like to think that the teleology/deontology distinction is exhaustive, there are several other theories of ethical justification that do not fit neatly into these two camps. We will look at only three of the most common.

First, let us consider *existentialist ethics*. This view is popular among moderns. As a theory, it is the polar opposite of Aristotle's view of teleology. As we just noted, Aristotle believed that the *telos* was independently given and our appropriation of it could come only through discovering or learning its content. Existentialists believe that there is no such thing as a given *telos* and that goodness is derived from a creative process of human consciousness called valuing. They claim that what makes it possible for there to be something called goodness and morality is our ability to hold something dear, to appreciate it, to confer on it significance and worth. That is to say, existentialists believe that human existence and human freedom are the fundamental realities and therefore

> **Existentialism:** A modern philosophy of life that rejects classical thinking by arguing that how we should live (our existence) comes before (in fact determines) our essence. Alternatively, since there is no such thing as a human essence, what-we-do cannot be derived from who-we-are. This philosophy is the polar opposite of Aristotle's.

we are the creators of goodness. Goodness for them is not an independent reality that shapes us. This would inhibit our freedom. We are the fundamental reality, and we create goodness.[3]

Existentialists also believe that there is no rational basis for choosing one set of values over another. Therefore, the individual is left to his/her own devices in this process. Moreover, the primary immoral act, given this model, is the inauthentic act of heteronymous moral determination—inauthentic because it denies the autonomy of the self and presupposes the submission of self to an outside moral standard. Since freedom and the right of self-valuing are the fundamentals for existentialists, imposition and submission are the basic evils.

According to some philosophers, "existentialist ethics" is in fact an oxymoron since existentialism is a view of radical autonomy and ethics is at least in some measure an infringement on individual freedom. Nevertheless, it remains an apt description of much of what today goes under the banner of "ethics," whether it is a contradiction or not. It should also be said that philosophers like Søren Kierkegaard and Jean-Paul Sartre have cited contradiction as a basic category of human life. Hence, even if there were a contradiction here, it would not be seen negatively by these writers.[4]

---

[3] For a carefully nuanced definition of existentialism, see J. P. Sartre, "Existentialism Is a Humanism," in Walter Kaufmann, ed., *Existentialism from Dostoevsky to Sartre* (London: Penguin, 1975), 345–68.

[4] Although both Kierkegaard and Sartre have been called existentialists, to bring them together in one sentence can be misleading. As we have already seen in chap. 8 above, Kierkegaard was a passionate Christian and believed that a particular version of existentialism best expressed the Christian faith; Sartre was an atheist and believed that the very notion of existentialism was incompatible with belief in God. Yet it is true that both affirmed the significance of the category of the absurd.

Responsibility Theory of Ethics: H. Richard Niebuhr's approach to ethics, which repudiates both teleology and deontology, arguing that to decide what to do on the basis of what is good or what end to pursue is problematic. We are primarily responders and as Christians are called to respond to God's action upon us.

A second alternative model to deontology and teleology is called *responsibility ethics*, and it has been made popular by an American theologian, H. Richard Niebuhr.[5] Niebuhr cites the symbol of response as primary for the understanding of Christian ethics. The reason for this is relatively simply. Niebuhr advocated a radical monotheism and the primacy of God acting upon us. This was his starting point for theology and especially for ethics. Therefore, the central ethical question for us has to be couched in terms of our response to God's primary action.

Niebuhr argues that deontology is limited because it attempts to understand human beings via the symbol of law. In this model, our primary identity is as "citizens." Although not entirely false, because this symbol can handle many of life's experiences, it is, nevertheless, inadequate because Christian existence cannot be fully explained as life under the law, particularly not in light of the Protestant emphasis on grace. He concludes therefore that the deontological model is problematic.

For Niebuhr, teleology is also not adequate. Its dominant symbol is "man-the-maker," as he calls it. We understand ourselves best, this view assumes, when we understand ourselves as artisans or technicians, as makers or actors, even as creators. But this is inadequate for Christians because we wish to see ourselves as beings under God, that is, as the created and the acted upon—as having been brought about. Teleology assumes a view of freedom that simply is not true to our experience. We are who we are, first of all, not because of what we produce but because of

what we have received. We are fundamentally not free to create ourselves. We have been created!

Niebuhr suggests that we understand ourselves best via the symbol of responsibility. The primary question for us as Christians cannot be, "What is the basic law of life under which we must live?" nor is it, "What is the goal that I must seek to bring about?" but rather "How can I respond to God's actions upon me?" or, "How can I respond in everything so as to respond to God's loving and redemptive activities in this world?" For Niebuhr, therefore, the chief moral quest is to "fit" ourselves into God's activities which are always already under way.

Narrative Ethics: An approach to ethics which has its roots in H. Richard Niebuhr and is more fully developed by ethicists like Stanley Hauerwas, who argue that ethics is better understood in the context of story than via the traditional models of deontology or teleology. Narrative ethics is based on an understanding of character, that is, on "being" rather than on "acting" and "decision making."

A third normative ethical theory that does not fit neatly into the deontology/teleology mold can be called *narrative ethics*. H. Richard Niebuhr paved the way for narrative ethics in a chapter in his book *The Meaning of Revelation*, "The Story of Our Life." Yet this approach has gone far beyond what Niebuhr spoke about. Niebuhr made the point that our life is shaped at least as much, if not more so, by encounters with others than by sound argumentation. He reminds us that what kept the early Christians faithful was not philosophical arguments for God's existence or the rationalization of moral ends or rules of obligation, but rather the "simple recital of the great events connected with the historical appearance of Jesus Christ and a confession of what had happened to the community of

[5] See esp. H. Richard Niebuhr, *The Responsible Self: An Essay in Christian Moral Philosophy* (New York: Harper & Row, 1963).

disciples."[6] This act of retelling the Christian story succeeded in shaping a community—a people with a story—which lived a distinctive life.

After Niebuhr, scholars like Hans Frei, George Lindbeck, Stanley Hauerwas, and others have all argued for the importance of understanding our moral existence in terms of the multifaceted dynamics of a narrative, rather than via the more restricted symbols connected with deontology and teleology.[7] Life is shaped by both laws and ends, by principles and rules, by decisions and goals, by doing what is right and knowing the good. Understanding why we do what we do is best achieved by asking the larger questions of who we are than the more narrow ones of what we must do. And this can only be done by knowing the story that defines us. In any event, we all know that changing people's views about how to live happens more readily by invitation into a well-articulated narrative, one that can handle and make sense of life's complex experiences, than by telling them what they ought to do based on fancy arguments.

Later in this book, we will examine in more detail several theologians/philosophers mentioned in this section on narrative ethics. Now we must look at the philosophical discussion surrounding the other subdiscipline of ethics called metaethics.

METAETHICS

Metaethics is a subdiscipline of philosophical ethics concerned with the clarification of moral terms and the adequacy of theories of justification. This has usually taken the form of analyzing the meanings of moral terms and asking whether in fact they function differently from ordinary nonmoral terms. In addition, it entails the examination of moral propositions by asking what it is that they convey and how they do so. This has involved

> **Cognitive and Noncognitive Statements:** A cognitive statement, since it asserts something, is capable of being true or false. A noncognitive statement, since it is taken not to assert anything, is not capable of being true or false.

important distinctions philosophers have invoked that they claim are essential for understanding how ethical language functions. It needs to be remembered that metaethics is a reflection upon the discipline of ethics and therefore has many elements in common with epistemology.

In recent decades, metaethical discussion has centered on a debate between two schools of thought, each claiming that moral language functions one way and not the other. These two schools of thought are called cognitivism and noncognitivism. The meanings of the terms "cognitive" and "noncognitive" are relatively simple. A cognitive statement is one capable of being true and false, and a noncognitive sentence is incapable of being either true or false because it asserts nothing. An example of a cognitive statement is an assertion like "This book is green" or "Socrates is mortal." These are cognitive sentences because they make verifiable assertions. An example of a noncognitive sentence is "Shut the door." Noncognitive utterances, like "Shut the door" or "What a slob!" or "How old are you?" are meaningful utterances, yet they do not assert anything factual. Hence, they cannot be said to be either true or false.

In order to clarify the issues in the debate between these two schools of thought, one saying that ethical language is cognitive and the other saying it is not, I will summarize the claims made by each. Ethical cognitivists claim that moral language functions no differently from nonmoral factual language, albeit the meanings of moral terms may well

---

[6] H. Richard Niebuhr, *The Meaning of Revelation* (New York: Macmillan, 1941), 32.

[7] See, e.g., Hans Frei, *The Eclipse of Narrative* (New Haven, Conn.: Yale University Press, 1974); George Lindbeck, *The Nature of Doctrine: Religion and Theology in a Postliberal Age* (Philadelphia: Westminster, 1984); and Stanley Hauerwas and L. Gregory Jones, eds., *Why Narrative? Readings in Narrative Theology* (Grand Rapids: Eerdmans, 1989).

> **Ethical Cognitivism:** An approach to ethics which believes that ethical statements are like most other statements in that they assert something and hence are capable of being true or false (cognitive statements).

be more varied and contentious. Yet not all ethical cognitivists agree. One group is called definists or ethical naturalists. They claim that when someone says something like "Polluting the environment is morally wrong" what is meant is that these acts are such that they are in fact disapproved of by significant moral agents. Yet even the ethical naturalists disagree about which moral agents must approve to make an act right. Some will contend that society's disapproval is what makes actions wrong; others that God's disapproval is required; some that only the disapproval of the person making the claim is meant; and still other ethical naturalists will argue that such statements imply the disapproval of an ideal moral observer who knows every relevant matter pertaining to the specifics in question. In all cases, this group of cognitivists believes that moral terms have definable meanings and that when we use moral propositions, we are in fact asserting something cognitively meaningful. Hence, such statements can be shown to be either true or false in much the same way as any other factual statement.

A different group of ethical cognitivists call themselves ethical nonnaturalists, and claim that moral terms are not definable in other terms. They are also called nondefinists. This group argues that the very effort to define moral terms in nonmoral terms is logically untenable since it assumes that one can define something in terms of what it is not. How can it ever be successful to define something that has moral meaning in terms of

> **Definism/Naturalism:** A subbranch of ethical cognitivism which believes that moral terms are in principle definable in nonmoral (natural) terms, and hence can be shown to make an assertion which is verifiable.

something else that has no moral meaning? This, they say, will always be fallacious. The name they give to this fallacy is the naturalistic fallacy.

> **Naturalistic Fallacy:** The name given by the intuitionists to the mistake that naturalists make when they try to define moral terms in natural terms. Because they are using natural terms, it is argued, they can never be successful in correctly defining moral terms.

This group of ethical cognitivists argues that moral terms are in fact simple terms and hence are unanalyzable, meaning that they cannot be defined further. They are like other simple terms in the English language, such as "yellow." You do not come to know the meanings of terms like yellow by first learning their definitions, that is, by knowing other terms and putting them together to discover the meanings of more complex terms. You come to know them by example, that is, by being shown yellow objects, for instance. They are knowable through experiencing and then intuiting the meanings of what you have experienced. This approach to ethics has been called intuitionism or ethical non-naturalism.

> **Non-naturalism/Intuitionism:** A subbranch of ethical cognitivism which believes that moral terms are not definable in nonmoral (natural) terms or in any other terms, for that matter. Nevertheless, moral statements do make assertions, which make them verifiable. This view is also called nondefinism.

Now let us examine the metaethical thinkers who disagree with the ethical cognitivists, namely the ethical noncognitivists. Ethical noncognitivists disagree with the naturalists and the nonnaturalists (both cognitivist positions) because they believe that they make false assumptions about the nature of moral language. Noncognitivists claim that while

> **Ethical Noncognitivism:** A metaethical theory which says ethical statements are unlike ordinary true/false statements in that they are neither true nor false. Hence, ethical statements are really not statements at all but are emotive utterances. This view is also called emotivism.

> **Logical Positivism:** A view of philosophy made popular at the beginning of the twentieth century which suggests that unless a statement is in principle verifiable it is not worthy of philosophical consideration. Moreover, logical positivists considered ethics (as well as religion and metaphysics) to fall within the realm of nonverifiable discourse and hence outside the scope of philosophy.

moral utterances may look like ordinary statements asserting that something is good, bad, right, wrong, this is in fact an illusion. When we look carefully at how moral language functions, they argue, we realize that they are but emotive utterances intended to get others to express similar sentiments. For example, when someone says that "lying is wrong," they are expressing a negative emotion or sentiment about lying with the hope that the hearers will accept this sentiment for themselves. Hence, although moral utterances have enormous power and influence in that they can change people's minds about important matters, nevertheless, there is no factual ground upon which moral disputes can be resolved. Some noncognitivists, particularly logical positivists, claim that although normative ethics may be interesting, it does not fall within the domain of philosophy because there is no conceivable rational ground upon which anything can be settled. It is analogous to literature and poetry, they say, which may both be quite valuable, but outside the realm of philosophical analysis from which truth and understanding can come.

The historical development of ethical noncognitivism is interesting and illuminating. The major impetus for the embrace of ethical noncognitivism came from the logical positivists in the first half of this century with scholars like A. J. Ayer.[8] Logical positivists advocated the "verification criterion of meaningfulness," which claimed that no statement was cognitively meaningful unless it could be empirically verified, either directly or indirectly. Since moral language could not meet these conditions, it was seen as cognitively meaningless.

With logical positivism as the latest tool of conceptual clarification, several ethicists took up the task of discussing in what sense moral language then could be meaningful discourse. The earliest among them were scholars like C. L. Stevenson and R. M. Hare,[9] who argued that ethical discourse could still have meaning in two senses. First, it does convey some factual content and hence moral disputes can frequently be settled by recourse to those factual matters. Second, there is a nonfactual component to moral language. If the dispute were merely over this evaluative component, which, of course, is hardly ever the case, then there could be no hope for resolution of disagreements.

Philosophers of this early stage of the debate accepted the exclusivity of the fact/value distinction and held that it was logically unwarranted to move from factual premises to value conclusions. This they had inherited from the Enlightenment thinkers, particularly from the Scottish philosopher David Hume. Given this conviction, they believed there could be no logical connection between one's moral sentiments and one's factual knowledge. Or, to say it differently, there could never be a moral conclusion derived from premises that could be shown to be factually true.

---

[8] See esp. A. J. Ayer, *Language, Truth and Logic* (New York: Dover, 1952).

[9] See C. L. Stevenson, *Ethics and Language* (New Haven, Conn.: Yale University Press, 1944); and R. M. Hare, *The Language of Morals* (Toronto: Clarendon, 1952).

Yet this raised some very important questions for other philosophers who tended to be sympathetic to the basic noncognitivist thesis. Can we not say that someone who would hold that torturing little children is morally justifiable because he/she enjoys it, is, to say the least, not being "morally rational?" Surely the mere description of the horror warrants the conclusion that the perpetrator is engaged in wrongful behavior and therefore should stop doing it. In other words, the factual premises (that is, the mere *description* of the horror) warrants the moral conclusion (that is, he/she *ought* to stop the torture).

This type of thinking got some noncognitivists, for example, Stephen Toulmin, and Kurt Baier,[10] to argue that there were in fact "good reasons" for why we should have certain moral sentiments with respect to certain things. Moreover, people who did not have certain moral sentiments regarding certain acts or events were making some kind of mistake of reason. But now the debate centered on the nature of the mistake that is made when a person accepts the facts of a case but not the "appropriate" moral conclusion. Some argued that the mistake was logical, some that it was linguistic, and still others that it was a type of pragmatic contradiction. But it is important to note that however the mistake is identified one thing is being affirmed here, namely, that moral claims are not without factual bases. This gets very close to affirming some sort of ethical cognitivism.

Fact/Value Distinction: David Hume, a Scottish philosopher during the Enlightenment period, argued that there is a distinction of logical realms between facts and values. Hence, one cannot logically move from one to the other. It is always making a logical mistake, so Hume claimed, to argue from factual premises to a moral conclusion. This is sometimes referred to as the is/ought distinction or problem.

In fact, some will argue that these "noncognitivists" have come full circle and are really better classified as ethical cognitivists.

Let us consider some illustrations of this latter point. If I say, "I promise to visit you on Thursday of this week," I am morally obliged to do so. The factual statement is simply the description of the promise. Hence, from the factual statement we can infer a moral conclusion, which is that I ought to visit you this week on Thursday. Consider another example. Suppose Joe is playing a game of baseball. Suppose also that he does not understand the rules very well. It is his turn to bat. He tries hard to hit the ball, because he has come to understand this to be an important objective of the game. He tries three times and the umpire yells, "You're out!" His response is that he wants another attempt because he is sure that he will be successful if he were given a fourth try. The umpire insists that Joe leave the batter's box, and all the spectators would agree that he *ought* to go. So from the mere *fact* that he has tried to hit the ball three times and missed each time, we can infer, given the context of baseball, the conclusion that he *ought* to leave the batter's box.

It is hard to know how to assess the work of these philosophical ethicists in their endless quest for analysis. Have they really helped to make things more clear? Or have they merely helped to clarify the muddle of the Enlightenment's problematic habits? Notice that while the noncognitivists began with the revolutionary claim that you cannot get from facts to values (they surely learned that from Hume) and hence there can be no resolution of moral disputes, the latest version of noncognitivism demonstrates that we actually must make some sort of logical move from descriptions to prescriptions if there is to be anything resembling ethics at all. This contention, however one wishes to precisely formulate it, basically affirms that there is something fundamentally problematic with

---

[10] See Stephen Toulmin, *An Examination of the Place of Reason in Ethics* (Cambridge: Cambridge University Press, 1950); and Kurt Baier, *The Moral Point of View: A Rational Basis of Ethics* (Ithaca, N.Y.: Cornell University Press, 1958).

the way the ethical agenda has come to us through the Enlightenment philosophers. And this may well be the most valuable learning from the above analysis.

The issues behind the debate are important. They are directly related to the matter of whether moral disputes are resolvable or not. And this is a matter that affects us all. Think back to your own moral discussions with others. How would you interpret these discussions? Are they merely reducible to conflicting opinions or personal values, or are they in principle resolvable on some rational ground? If you believe the former, you adhere to some version of noncognitivism, and if the latter, then you are some kind of cognitivist.

It is not surprising that philosophers of the past few decades have, however, not found the language of cognitivism and all that useful in carrying the discussion forward. More and more are turning to the language of moral realism, the language of the classics, and especially virtue theory. This is not the place to give a full presentation of this position especially since more will be said about this approach later in our study.

Chapter Ten

SOCIOLOGY AND ETHICS

Sociology is the inquiry into the nature of society. It examines the forces which shape society's beliefs, institutions, behavior, manner of organization, patterns of defense from danger, religious structures, structures of power and authority, and so on. It inquires about how the individual fits into these social complexities and is especially interested in the many different, but related, social "units" that make up a given society, like the family, religion, school, the economy, business, and politics.

Sociologists of the nineteenth and twentieth centuries have been concerned about the social "break-up" of the old society and the alternative structures that have emerged. How have dynamics like industrialization, democracy, technology, and education affected the stability and/or disintegration of society? Have they produced greater freedom or alienation? How have they changed our view of authority and power, improved—or not improved—the quality of life, and so on?

It is commonly thought that sociologists are engaged in a purely descriptive pursuit as they go about their investigations, but this really is not so. They express what they find in theoretical constructs, which are efforts to explain not only what is seen but why and how what was seen makes sense. This process has resulted in a variety of theories of social differentiation. The great sociologists

of the nineteenth and twentieth centuries, like Auguste Comte, Ferdinand Tönnies, Max Weber, Karl Marx, Karl Mannheim, and Emile Durkheim, to mention only the most obvious, do not agree on the theoretical structures that best account for why society as a whole works the way it does, and why we as individuals act within it the way we do. Nor do they agree on the central "unit-ideas" of sociology.[1]

Although virtually all sociologists see morality as an important cultural dynamic, they are not agreed on its role. For example, does ethics shape society or is it the other way around? It makes a profound difference—the first gives ethics an important social role and the other does not. When most of us "ordinary" people see what is happening around us, we do not pay much attention to matters like how the computer shapes our character, or how Internet and cell phone communication affects our understanding of what we hold to be right or wrong, or how our urban existence affects our view of social organization, or how social forces make us good or bad people. We do not often think of the impact on our understanding of ethics when we reflect on how profoundly different we are, morally speaking, from our grandparents and great-grandparents. We do well, therefore, to analyze what sociologists are telling us about how social reality has changed and what difference that has

---

[1] The notion of a "unit-idea" will be further discussed when we look in more detail at the work of Robert A. Nisbet, *The Sociological Tradition* (New York: Basic Books, 1966).

made for the moral identity of society generally and for individuals specifically.

In their effort to analyze what social forces are at work in shaping us into the kinds of people we are, sociologists do not like to admit that they are engaged in a discussion about whether we are now better or worse off than we were. In other words, as I have already suggested, they want to be descriptive scientists. Nevertheless, such an "evaluative" process is often implicit in their "descriptions" of modern societies. For example, in a famous study, *Habits of the Heart*, which appeared in 1985, a noted American sociologist, Robert Bellah, led a team of social investigators in the task of establishing how "America" had changed since Alexis de Tocqueville's *Democracy in America* of some 150 years earlier.[2] Bellah would readily admit that their study is full of evaluative claims about the impact of growing individualism in American society, and how this threatens the very notion of a healthy society. I will say more about their work later in this chapter, but for now I cite it as a reminder that, since few sociologists are neutral about their interests in a strong and viable social structure, their "moral" concerns are often readily apparent. Of course, they still tend to think it important to be "value free" in the sense that they seek to adopt a disinterested manner of research in order to protect the relative objectivity in obtaining their results. Nevertheless, most remain morally interested and hence are not purely descriptive. Of course, this ought not to be seen as a critique of their trade; rather it is a critique of the inherited view of scientific inquiry, which assumes that it is possible as a detached study of the facts. Especially when the object of study is ourselves, such an approach is out of human reach.

There is no doubt that our study of Christian ethics relates closely to sociology. Sociology analyzes the factors that make us into the kinds of social beings we are. It might

be said that sociology seeks to give an account of why we do what we do. Ethics is concerned about what is good and how cultivating habits of goodness can guide us into becoming good people. If our behavior can be explained entirely in sociological terms, then it would seem that ethics is somewhat irrelevant. One important intersection between ethics and sociology has to do with what might be called a sociology of morals, where we ask: What has been the sociological development that has led us to view morality the way we do today? That is, why do we believe, while other societies do not, that individual freedoms and rights are our most treasured goods?

In 2008 and 2009, I traveled to the Islamic Republic of Iran to participate in inter-religious dialogue and cultural exchange activities. In that society, it is wrong to drink alcoholic beverages, for men and women to shake hands, and for women to be seen in public without wearing the hijab. These behaviors are considered wrong and not left purely to the discretion of the individual conscious to comply. Hence "morality police" enforce such behavior in much the same way that we enforce car parking patterns in our cities. Iranian society as a whole is seeking to shape a moral-religious people, and as such it restricts certain actions, including public inter-gender relations, and cultivates others, like prayers five times a day, appropriate clothing, and so on. Of course, in North America we also seek to form certain kinds of people, but we focus mostly on respecting each other's rights and freedoms and property rights. What we call "morality" is relegated to the private domain in which we officially do not permit society or any other social structure to tell us what to do. How have we come to be like this? What has changed in our understanding of society to make us this way?

In order to understand ourselves morally,

---

[2] See Robert Bellah et al., *Habits of the Heart: Individualism and Commitment in American Life* (Berkeley: University of California Press, 1985); and Alexis de Tocqueville, *Democracy in America*, trans. and ed. Richard D. Heffner (New York: New American Library, 1956).

it is important to determine how we came to be this way, and why we think it is "good" for us to permit no one but ourselves into the process of defining "good." And might this in fact be a grand illusion, in that our society is far more determinative than we think in defining what is good for us? The process of social analysis will not help us to understand what Christian ethics is, but it will help us see the context in which we are seeking to be Christian.

MODERN SOCIAL ANALYSTS

The old social order,[3] like any other, was held together with both intellectual and social-moral glue. Social reality always has both an intellectual imagination that undergirds the existing social structures and a reality that emerges from or is in some other relationship to the world of ideas. When one changes radically, the other is bound to change also. In the seventeenth and eighteenth centuries, both the intellectual superstructure and the social substructure went through profound changes. This gets even the nineteenth-century English poet, Matthew Arnold (1822–1888), to weigh in with a lament that the old fixed world has given way to a social void. He perceives his society to be:

> Wandering between two worlds, one dead,
> The other powerless to be born.[4]

In this section, through the process of reviewing the "breakup," I will refer to some of the material the reader has already seen in previous chapters. This is to situate the issues and therefore identify the overall project of sociology itself. It will be an attempt to show that the unraveling of the old intellectual world produced a radically new social agenda.

As we have seen, Thomas Hobbes (1588–1679), John Locke (1632–1704), and Jean-Jacques Rousseau (1712–1778) were among the first social thinkers who, when theorizing about the nature of society, thought differently from the way of the ancients. The old order had been sustained by a fixed structure of thought which assumed that divine reason reflected the order of things. Everything had its proper place, from the family, to the church, to the state, and so on. God and the natural-rational order were fundamental, and ours was the task of coming to understand them as given and place ourselves under their tutelage. In this process of understanding, we come to see social reality for what it really is. If you like, the social substructure was determined by the intellectual superstructure.

Hobbes and Locke introduced a social philosophy quite different from this. They argued that, metaphysically speaking, nothing is given and that the way we structure ourselves socially is but a reflection of how we understand ourselves and how we rationalize our own projections for desired relationships. We all have natural human rights, which are inalienable, and these we want to protect at all costs by structuring a society that guarantees them. The way this is done is by entering into a "social contract," an implicit covenant we make with one another and with an absolute authority. This contract sometimes requires us to give up certain rights in order that the overall social structure is protected.

Hence, what it is that we ought to do is no longer justified in reference to participation in the givenness of reality, or indeed ultimate reality, but on the basis of the contracts we make with one another. This is a significant change from the way of thinking found in the old order.

As we have seen, Immanuel Kant (1724–1804) went even further and, through his "Copernican Revolution," revolutionized the world of thought itself. What we used to

---

[3] By the "old order" I do not mean what is euphemistically called the "good old days," but I mean the premodern period. This could also be called the "presociology" period, not that there was no social analysis before this time—social analysis has existed since the beginning of intellectual reflection—but as a social science, sociology came into its own only in the nineteenth century.

[4] From Matthew Arnold, "Stanzas from the Grande Chartreuse" (1855).

think was at the center is now replaced with something else, like Copernicus changed the paradigm for conceiving of heavenly bodies. We used to believe that independent reality was at the center of our understanding of truth and was the arbiter of all thought. But Kant suggests that the human mind is at the center. He argues that what we come to call knowledge is determined by the structures of the mind rather than the structures of reality. This is now an almost complete reversal of the old order of thought.

For ethics and religion, Kant's conclusions had profound consequences. Both were now placed entirely within the contexts of reason alone.[5] Philosophers who succeeded him have struggled with this conclusion to this very day.

Georg Hegel (1770–1831) was the first to do so.[6] In his *Early Theological Writings*,[7] he argued that reason, instead of illuminating life for us, actually alienates human beings from life. Life must be lived, not thought. Thinking objectifies things and hence God, for one, and life, for another, cannot be fully grasped through the categories of thought; they can only be captured through categories of living relationships. To say this differently, both can only be "understood" in the *action* of love.

Canadian theologian/sociologist Gregory Baum writes a helpful chapter on Hegel's early thought in his book, *Religion and Alienation*,[8] in which he points out the social and moral consequences that Hegel foresaw in Kant's philosophy of an "objectified God." This, he argues, emanates from a false application of reason to life and points the way to a sociology of religion.

First, when we objectify God, God becomes the stranger and object. If God exists only over and above history, in the heavens, and not in history itself, then God is irrelevant to us because we exist in history. This is what Hegel calls bad infinity. Second, Hegel says that this results in a conception of a stranger God who cannot exist as the source and definition of life. This, according to Hegel, is what Jesus discovered. For Jesus, God existed in acts of human reconciliation, that is, in the mystery of human love that can never be expressed as merely a truth of the mind and is always expressed in "love of God and neighbor."

Baum also points out, via Hegel's essay, "The Spirit of Christianity and Its Fate,"[9] what implications follow from the reduction of life to universal reason. The reader should note a possible connection here with earlier challenges to ethics that were brought about by both the Enlightenment fact/value distinction as well as the late medieval univocity-analogy dichotomy. It may well be that what the early Hegel was struggling with was the result of the false chasms that were created by these dualisms. For he shows in this essay how a theology rooted in an "objectification of God" alienates us from nature, from ourselves, and from each other. Such alienation has implications, not only for our self-understanding, but also for an understanding of how we have come to justify our actions.

It becomes more apparent what Hegel means when we examine each of these alienations more carefully. First, alienation from nature: if God is viewed as object to be found only outside this world, then it is

---

[5] See, e.g., Immanuel Kant, *Critique of Practical Reason*, trans. Lewis White Beck (Indianapolis: Bobbs-Merrill, 1956); and *Religion Within the Limits of Reason Alone*, trans. Theodore M. Greene and Hoyt H. Hudson (New York: Harper, 1960).

[6] Hegel is an interesting philosopher to name as someone who in his early life was critical of Kant's rational reductionism. After all, as we saw in chap. 8, Kierkegaard levels the same charge against Hegel. Although we cannot discuss the issues here in detail, at least part of the debate between Kant and Hegel involved different understandings of reason. Hegel was particularly critical of Kant's ahistorical and universal rationality, as what he preferred was a historicized rationality. It might be said that Hegel had more fully accepted the disintegration of the old order and paved the way for what became the great sociological tradition. Nevertheless, his "encyclopedia of knowledge," which characterized his later philosophy, according to many philosophers and sociologists alike, was every bit as problematic as was Kant's.

[7] Georg W. F. Hegel, *Early Theological Writings*, trans. T. M. Knox (Philadelphia: University of Pennsylvania Press, 1948).

[8] Gregory Baum, *Religion and Alienation: A Theological Reading of Sociology* (Toronto: Paulist, 1975).

[9] Georg W. F. Hegel, "The Spirit of Christianity and Its Fate," in *Early Theological Writings*, chap. II, 182–300.

proper for us to turn away from the environment in order to find God. When this world is not really our home, it is easily seen as a source of fear and danger. In fact, it then can become an enemy for us—an enemy that must be conquered and ruled and even destroyed. We might say that Hegel foresaw the makings of what we today call the environmental crisis. In objectifying God, we make God into a power at our disposal in the conquering of our fears and our enemies, or bad infinity to Hegel. Good infinity sees God in nature and in other people. Our real encounter with God is therefore possible through our encounter with nature and through our encounter with other people. Knowing God is not in the final analysis rooted in a mental act called *understanding*, but in a human encounter called *love*, and therefore in the possibility of reconciling what is broken apart by fear and distance. In fact, destroying nature or other people, or generally bringing suffering upon creation, in whatever form, is an act of blasphemy against God.

Second, if we view God as object, then we will be alienated from ourselves. If God is outside and above history, then our source of life comes from outside us and is foreign to us. Our freedom can only be seen in terms of an outside "ought" that comes to us over against us. But this can never be experienced as freedom, only as alienation from our deepest sense of identity. On the other hand, good infinity connects God intrinsically to our being by intimately connecting God with us. This is the experience of freedom from alienation and an experience of the deepest sense of love. It is simultaneously the greatest sacrifice because it is a way of giving up ourselves to another; but because the other is God, we receive our freedom back again in the form of an act of love. Love is able to put back together what has been broken apart within us.

Third, if God is object, alienation from other human beings is bound to follow.

Inability to embrace the *love of God* is fundamentally part of the inability to embrace each other. If we are unable to see the mystery of God's creative love in other human beings, they become objects for us. Objects are always at our disposal. Hence, if we see God as object who relates to us in God's power over us, then we will see the art of mastery as the stuff of life itself. On this model, we will relate to others in our mastery over them. Domination is then the highest form of relationships. But when dominion, and not communion, is the center of our understanding of life, conflict becomes normative, and violence and war the only means of keeping order and peace.

Why do we objectify God if it leads us to alienation from nature, others, and self? Hegel's answer is that eighteenth-century rationalism teaches that objective knowledge can save us from the tyranny of religious superstition. So we have come to believe that when we do not feel like loving our neighbor we can rationalize (objectify) the moral injunction away. We can "justify" our actions to an objectified God, one who exists as an object of our mind. But deep inside, we know this to be a false account of life because it cannot overcome our experienced alienation. The good life, based upon "good religion," is something else. As Baum puts it:

> Hegel recognized good religion, i.e., religion that was capable of de-alienating human life. For if the divine mystery is present in and through the finite reality—Hegel thought that this was in fact revealed by Jesus Christ—if, in other words, the divine is present in nature, present in one's own personal depth and in the community at large, then religious openness to God will lead to reconciliation.[10]

For Hegel, "bad religion," that is, religion based on the objectification of God, other, and self, underwrites the structures for domination in society—domination is then the key to security, peace, and unity. But good religion, one based on love and reconciliation,

---

[10] Baum, *Religion and Alienation*, 16.

sets up the very possibility for community, true peace, and harmony. The early Hegel believed that intellectuals at the beginning of the nineteenth century needed to work especially hard not to be seduced into the false reason of Kant.

As we saw in chapter 8 above, Hegel's intellectual pursuits soon took him in the directions of idealism where historical reason became the key force of history. So he is hardly a mentor that the sociological tradition can claim as its own. And yet he was profoundly significant in shaping the sociological agenda. As we also saw, it was Karl Marx (1818–1883) who thoroughly embraced Hegel's historicism, yet lodged the forces that moved history forward not in abstract reason but in social struggle.

The French social philosopher Auguste Comte (1798–1857), sometimes considered the father of sociology, was also, like Marx, influenced by a Hegel-style historicism. He sought to integrate the rationalism of science and social observation and believed that he saw an evolutionary movement in larger history from the beginning to the present that explained social and intellectual development. As the human mind gained more knowledge, he argued, history could be seen to move through three stages: the theological (or theocratic), the metaphysical, and the positive (scientific).

The theological stage interprets life as emanating from divine will. The highest form of this stage is monotheism (lower forms are atomism and polytheism) because it presupposes a universe governed by a single will. The metaphysical or philosophical stage follows the theological and is intellectually more advanced because it substitutes abstract ideas for divine will and shows how natural law is the ruling power. But the final and, of course, the highest stage, which Comte believed his generation was finally able to get glimpses of, was positive science. Our scientific knowledge has already shown us that there can be no first cause or ultimate personal will that gives this world intelligibility; there are only relationships and comparisons which allow us to see correctly what is in fact materializing before us and, on the basis of this knowledge, what is to come. This data must be gathered together and put into proper scientific formulations so that society may become intelligible to us.

Comte was a positivist, believing that all knowledge properly so-called should be based on pure facts derived from observation and experimentation. The data that is derived from this process is then compared with other data. With this process he believed he could prove that just as there is a hierarchy of historical stages (theology, philosophy, science), so there is a hierarchy within the sciences, beginning with mathematics and moving to astronomy, physics, chemistry, biology, psychology, and eventually to sociology. Sociology for Comte was the new "Queen of the Sciences."

Comte's positivist formulation of this new social science was not met with overwhelming agreement, even from his peers. Most sociologists believed that you could not do sociology in this way since, like history, it deals with contingencies and no necessary laws can be deduced from contingent events. There are real changes in society that simply do not fit the neat categories that Comte proposes.

One such rival was Max Weber (1864–1920). Weber rejected the positivism of Comte and made a careful distinction between the method of the natural science and that of social science. Weber went beyond both Comte and Marx and abandoned the search for laws that govern social changes and instead looked for rational associations that served as plausible explanations of social changes. In other words, history does not come with meaning; we place our ideals and purposes upon history. In this sense, Weber is often considered the founder of modern sociology. I will say more on Weber later.

Emile Durkheim (1858–1917) is another French social analyst of note, and sometimes also a contender for the title of "father of modern sociology." Like Marx, he grew up in a Jewish family; his father was a rabbi, and he was destined for the same role. But Durkheim soon became convinced that religion was in fact a product of society, in that every society sought to worship a symbolic representation of itself. And so he became a prophet of a different kind, arguing that with the advance of science the religious symbolic interpretation of the world would soon disappear.

Durkheim, like most sociologists, saw a sharp divide between traditional and modern societies. Traditional societies consisted of a collection of independent social units not immediately connected by concrete social structures. What united these units into a single coherent society was a tradition of symbolic rituals. Gregory Baum summarizes Durkheim's answer as follows: ". . . the social bond was the common symbol system. Social solidarity was created through sharing in the same rites, values, dreams and myths."[11]

Modern societies, on the other hand, are characterized by social interdependence brought about by a complex "division of labor."[12] The social and economic units of a modern society rely on each other for the creation of social order. In modern societies, specialization makes us good at only one thing, but a society needs many functions to work well. Again, Baum summarizes: "Durkheim tried to show that the social laws operative in modern society were in fact creating a profound social bond and establishing values of a new kind, values that enabled people to transcend egotism and acquire a truly social commitment."[13] The early Durkheim believed that modern society no longer required symbols for social cohesion. We participate in each other's lives through interconnected work and not through common rites; people find their meaning in their work! Yet the later Durkheim began to question his own conclusions, especially when he analyzed the social phenomena of suicide.[14] In this study, he came to realize the important connections

between social reality and human consciousness. And with this he saw a greater role for religion in both social formation and for giving symbolic meaning to human life.

The ideas of Weber and Durkheim are important for our understanding of ethics, and we will return to them later in this chapter. But first we need to present the two social revolutions without which nineteenth- and early twentieth-century sociology is largely unintelligible.

TWO SOCIAL REVOLUTIONS

Much of what we have heard from Weber and Durkheim was a response to the major social revolutions of their day. More than any other social events, they represent the breakup of the old social order. It is important therefore that we give them brief attention.

The Industrial Revolution and the French Revolution were taking place alongside the momentous intellectual upheaval we have already spoken about in previous chapters. All of these changes had a major impact on society and its structures. Of course, the intellectual and social changes were interwoven in countless and complex ways that we will not be able to unpack in this short chapter. Nor will we be able to present the many dynamics of these two social revolutions. Yet a few words are in order.

In many ways the Industrial Revolution had its origins in the early stages of the Renaissance and the Enlightenment. Yet the eighteenth century is normally the date given for this revolution, and it began in Britain. Changes took place that revamped economic structures: an agriculturally based economy became an industrial-based economy. What changed specifically was the means of production. Goods that were once made in small villages and even in family workshops were soon made in factories; efficiency was enhanced by specialization and coordination

[11] Baum, *Religion and Alienation*, 126.
[12] See Emile Durkheim, *The Division of Labor in Society*, trans. George Simpson (New York: Free Press, 1933).
[13] Baum, *Religion and Alienation*, 126.
[14] See Emile Durkheim, *Suicide: A Study in Sociology*, trans. John A. Spalding and George Simpson (Glencoe, Ill.: Free Press, 1951).

of labor; new technologies were developed,[15] and so on. Of course, this brought about many important social shifts, the most important of which was the movement of population from the rural areas to the cities, where ever-larger factories were being built. The sheer volume of production increased dramatically, producing a wealthier nation and many very wealthy entrepreneurs.[16] Businessmen grouped together and created large companies. It also had other effects like production of ever-more-sophisticated military weapons and machinery.

These changes brought about significant economic prosperity, especially to those who already had financial means. It brought about overall health benefits, mobility, and greater ease in communication, all benefits for the upper class. But these changes also had some negative results. In some cases, the lower class did not enjoy any of the benefits but was forced to endure hard labor and many hours of work with little leisure time. And there were major environmental costs: pollution poured from factories, much land was reserved for industrial purposes, urban sprawl further took over the natural habitat, and so on. Whatever gain there was to members of the human race, it was of no benefit to wildlife and plants.

Sociologists focused on specific themes related to this revolution that they felt had the greatest social impact. American sociologist Robert Nisbet, in his formative book, *The Sociological Tradition*, suggests five such themes: "the *condition of labor*, the *transformation of property*, the *industrial city*, *technology* and the *factory system*."[17]

It is important to note that the notion of the *working class* becomes, for the first time in history, a category of moral and social analysis. Why was this? Says Nisbet, "[I]t was the undoubted degradation of labor, the wrenching of work from the protective context of guild, village, and family, that was the most fundamental, and shocking, characteristic of the new order."[18] Conservative and liberal sociologists alike were agreed in their indictment of capitalism because it represented a dismantling of the old order and the positive virtues that went along with it.

The second important theme to emerge from the Industrial Revolution was property. Sociologists debated the value of property. All seemed bothered by the notions of large-scale industrial property, or the impersonal property of shares bought on the market, or property of the type the speculators were interested in. Yet in the end, the Marxists and the conservatives disagreed on the value and role of private property—Marx wanted to abandon the very concept itself, and the others did not.

Likewise urbanism, technology, and the factory system became important categories of social debate during this time. Industrialization moved the people to the city with the promise of prosperity. Yet the conservative sociologists saw disaster in this move. The rural setting provided a natural rhythm to life based on the cycles of nature, which could not be found in the city. The fear was that this lack would cause alienation. In the city, human beings became enslaved to the machines in large factories. This was dehumanizing.

The second major social revolution of the late eighteenth century is called the French Revolution and is usually dated 1789–1799. It also had a profound social impact, especially upon the "old political order." Sociologists like Robert Nisbet also call it the "democratic

---

[15] Examples of new technologies during this time are the steam engine (1712–Newcomen and 1775–Watt), which hastened the construction of the steamboat in 1807 and steam locomotives in 1801; and the threshing machine in 1758. In addition, the iron, coal, and textile industries all grew rapidly.

[16] The British government permitted economic development to prosper with little interference. It should also be acknowledged that during this time the Scottish economist/philosopher Adam Smith wrote an important book advancing the free-market economy. See Adam Smith, *The Wealth of Nations* (New York: Collier, 1902).

[17] Nisbet, *The Sociological Tradition*, 24 (emphasis in original).

[18] Nisbet, *The Sociological Tradition*, 24.

revolution."[19]

The French Revolution is, of course, compared with the American Revolution (1775–1783), for example, by sociologists like Alexis de Tocqueville, who in 1831 visited America and in 1835 published his famous *Democracy in America*. Without getting into this debate over the comparative sociological importance of these two revolutions, it is important to note first, that the American Revolution preceded the French Revolution; second, the American Revolution was an independence movement before all else; and third, both revolutions created profound political and social change, whether for the old world or for the new world.

It has sometimes been said that what the Industrial Revolution was to English society, the democratic revolution was to the French. From the Declaration of the Rights of Man to the passing of unparalleled laws ensuring the rights and freedoms of human beings, this revolution strove in a unique manner to liberate the people from the authoritarian structures of the old world order—structures like the church, aristocracy, guilds, and the monarchy. Alexis de Tocqueville wrote:

> No previous political upheaval, however violent, had aroused such passionate enthusiasm, for the ideal the French Revolution set before it was not merely a change in the French system but nothing short of a regeneration of the whole human race.[20]

What was so revolutionary about this change was that it completely refashioned the people's self-understanding and altered the structures that had previously defined them. We will discuss only two examples, the family and the church.

The notion of *family* went through profound changes. Indissolvable marriages were seen as contrary to reason in the late eighteenth century. Hence, marriage was made a civil contract between two consenting adults, much like the social contract of Jean-Jacques Rousseau, Hobbes, and Locke. What was the result of the change in views of family? Again I quote Nisbet:

> That the relaxation was not unwelcome in some quarters may be inferred from the fact that in the sixth year of the Republic the number of divorces in Paris exceeded the number of marriages. But there was more to follow in reform of the family. Strict limitations were placed upon paternal power, and in all cases the authority of the father ceased when the children reached legal age. In 1793 the age of majority was fixed at twenty-one, and in the same year the government decreed the inclusion of illegitimate children in matters concerning family inheritance. The attitude of the legislators was plainly hostile to the customs governing the solidarity of the old family.[21]

This change in the family structure directly affected other aspects of society. The way property was now viewed, for example, significantly changed as a direct result. Large estates could no longer be passed on intact via inheritance. Fathers were obliged to break them up and pass on the property in equal parcels to all their children. This was another way in which the family as a social power structure was weakened.

In the area of education, an equally major shift took place, also related to the change in the social place of the family. It was customary in the old world for the family and the church to take care of the job of education. But during this time, education became a duty of all citizens and hence, was wrested from the control of the family and the church. This had the obvious effect of reducing the role of both the family and church and strengthening the power of the state. And this of course was not an accident. Napoleon is quoted as saying, "for so long as people are not taught from their childhood whether they are to be Republicans or Monarchists, Catholics or free-thinkers, the State will not form a nation."[22]

We can well see from even discussing only briefly the implications of the changing view of family how such a relatively small social

---

[19] Nisbet, *The Sociological Tradition*, 31.
[20] Tocqueville, *Democracy in America*, 34.

[21] Nisbet, *The Sociological Tradition*, 37.
[22] Quoted in Nisbet, *The Sociological Tradition*, 38.

change ripples throughout society to affect other significant changes. This is certainly also true of the church. The family and the church were strongly linked institutions in the old world, and as the social power of one faded, so did the power of the other. Nisbet puts it starkly: "At the outbreak of the revolution there was no manifest wish to abolish Christianity, but there was plainly desire to regulate it completely. If there was to be a church, it must reflect the character of the new political order."[23]

While the historical fact of the reduction of the church's social power is important, it is equally important to notice the logic used to make this a reality. Nisbet quotes a member of the Assembly who argued that only persons and states have natural rights; corporations have rights only insofar as they are derived from the law which gives them rights.

> Individuals exist before the law, and they hold rights drawn from nature that are imprescriptible, such as the right of property; all corporations, on the other hand, only exist by law, and their rights are dependent on the law. . . . The destruction of a corporate body is not a homicide.[24]

Napoleon's comment and the comments by the member of the Assembly are very profound, the significance of which we should not overlook for our interest in ethics. The explicit suggestion that the state can only be strong when individualism is strong or when the shaping power of other institutions move in the same direction as the shaping power of the state has major moral implications for how morality and society are related. If the strength of the nation state relies on the weakness of other social institutions such as family, church, and private education, then how are we going to be able to speak about Christian ethics? This will need to be addressed later in our study. For now it must suffice to point out that at the beginning of the nineteenth century these were some of the dynamics of the great ideological and social revolutions which coalesced into the restructuring of a brave, new world.

RETHINKING THE REVOLUTIONS

The nineteenth century was preoccupied with rethinking. Not only did this happen in other scholarly disciplines like philosophy and theology, it happened in social theory as well. The sociologists focused their rethinking in several areas sometimes called unit-ideas. A unit-idea is what sociologists divide society into. These are the tools of analysis, much like normative ethics and metaethics are the component ideas of philosophers thinking about ethics. In this section, I will examine several such unit-ideas. With each we will choose one or two sociologists as representatives, even though there are clearly many more who have participated in the discussion.

The early sociologists seemed to have different concerns that guided their work. Emile Durkheim, for example, was interested in giving an account of the nature of society itself: what were the unifying forces, what would last as a significant force and what would not? Weber seemed more interested in giving an account of the interrelationship of social dynamics so that we could understand our own roles in helping to move history forward.

Max Weber, as we have already seen, was the foremost sociologist reflecting on the power and nature of industrialized Europe. And he made an explicit connection between Christian ethics and capitalism.[25] And because Nisbet does not include ethics as one of the five unit-ideas of sociological analysis, I will first present Weber's thesis on how Christian ethics has functioned in the area of economic development before I address Nisbet's unit-ideas.

Weber's book, *The Protestant Ethic and the Spirit of Capitalism* (1904–1905), is of special interest for a study in Christian ethics.

---

[23] Nisbet, *The Sociological Tradition*, 38.
[24] Nisbet, *The Sociological Tradition*, 39.
[25] See Max Weber, *The Protestant Ethic and the Spirit of Capitalism*, trans. Talcott Parsons (New York: Scribners, 1958).

One might say that this was his response to the new reality brought on by the Industrial Revolution as he sought to bring into interaction two key social forces: the economic dynamics and religious convictions.

In exploring the relationship between the ethics of Protestantism and the emergence of European capitalism, Weber observes that there seems to be a shift in the centers of economic power away from the Catholic countries like France, Spain, and Italy to Protestant countries like England, Scotland, Germany, and Holland. He was interested in exploring why this might be; that is, what were the social dynamics that bring about such a shift? And he identified religious beliefs as specific social forces that were instrumental in this change.

His thesis that religious convictions and practice might be influencing economic reality is particularly interesting because it represents a reversal of the Marxist thesis, where ideological thought like religion is determined by economic realities—not the other way around. It is therefore noteworthy that Weber's project is decidedly anti-Marxist.

It is important for us to be clear on what Weber is saying. He is not suggesting that Protestantism caused the rise of capitalism—capitalism was well established already—but rather he is stating an observational link between a certain branch of Protestantism and the flourishing spirit of capitalism. Mainline Lutheran teaching was that people were saved by grace alone and works did not matter. Catholic teaching had a strong emphasis on the church and such notions as simplicity, voluntary poverty, and the irrelevance of material possessions for salvation. As Weber saw it, the only alternative was Calvinism and a different theology.

Weber is clear about his understanding of capitalism. He points out that it sees profit as a virtue and hence as an end in itself. On the face of it, this might seem to be incompatible with Christian virtues altogether. But

not so, says Weber! Protestantism generally is more positive than Catholicism regarding the religious character of a worldly *calling*, which already makes a social and economic difference; nevertheless, this is only half the answer to the question Weber is asking. The other half comes from Calvinism specifically. Calvin had argued for predestination, that is, who is and who is not saved and damned has already been determined by God, and there is nothing that we as humans can do about it. Yet we are in deep psychological need for clues on whether we are saved. Being blessed in material matters is one such clue. So people work hard to assure themselves of this evidence. And this hard work fits well with the rise and promotion of capitalism.

It is important to note here that Weber was not interested in the ethics that Calvin taught or that the church adhered to. Rather, he was merely interested in "the influence of those psychological sanctions which, originating in religious belief and the practice of religion, gave a direction to practical conduct and held the individual to it."[26]

We turn now to some unit-ideas that Nisbet discusses, beginning with *community*. It changes in important ways in the nineteenth century, and most sociologists do not leave this notion undiscussed. A whole book was written on the topic by one sociologist: Ferdinand Tönnies (1855–1936).

Tönnies was a German sociologist and founder of the German Society of Sociology. Like some of the other early sociologists, he shows considerable longing for the old order when community was a stronger social reality. In his book, *Gemeinschaft und Gesellschaft* (*Community and Society*),[27] he identifies two ideal types which help us understand the different ways in which people see themselves as collectives. By "*Gemeinschaft*" Tönnies meant what we normally mean by community. By "*Gesellschaft*" he meant something that is more difficult to define. It was something akin to "society" in the sense of a

---

[26] Weber, *Protestant Ethic*, 97.
[27] Ferdinand Tönnies, *Community and Society*, trans. Charles Loomis (New York: Harper Torchbook, 1963).

professional "society." Although Tönnies was talking about the old and the new orders, and thereby suggesting that the old order was best characterized by community and the new by society, he was also doing something more. These ideal-types are helpful for understanding any group of people. We do well to examine them more closely.

Gemeinschaft is a term that is closely associated with family. You enter a *Gemeinschaft* by virtue of birth, that is, naturally. It is something given to you; you receive it, you do not create it. In a *Gemeinschaft* one experiences kinship, friendship, place, and so on, because meaningful "co-existence," or "com-unity," is brought into being. The "we" experience is more powerful than the "I" experience. Community shapes people, not primarily the other way around. In a community of this kind, people have a natural place; honor is real; authority is well defined. People rely on one another and have their moral characters shaped by adopting the story of the community as their story. Morality is not defined by the choices that get made; rather choices are made because the community shapes the people that make them. Moreover, such communities are by nature intergenerational.

Tönnies is giving us an ideal-typical sketch of the Middle Ages. While he is not saying that this view of collective identity is forever gone, he is saying that the modern era is characterized by another form of collective identity: *Gesellschaft*. (Remember that ideal-types can admit exceptions.)

Gesellschaft is therefore a contrast term to *Gemeinschaft*, intending to highlight the impact of the industrial and democratic revolutions on modernity. For Tönnies, *Gesellschaft* symbolized the way people understand themselves in nineteenth-century, industrialized Europe. If *Gemeinschaft* is a term rooted in family, *Gesellschaft* is a term related to the notion of "free association." In this model, the individual is more important than the group, and a collection of individuals defines the

group. You become a member of a collective group by voluntarily making the decision to do so, not by accident of birth. A *Gesellschaft* is created for a given purpose; it is not a generic group like a *Gemeinschaft*. This means that a *Gesellschaft* is held together not by the bonds of a long tradition but by contract. The people of *Gesellschaft* are defined by skills, roles, and functions they share in common, and by that which can be more expediently achieved by being together.

Tönnies speaks about the difference in the sharpest tone as follows:

> The theory of the *Gesellschaft* deals with the artificial construction of an aggregate of human beings which superficially resembles the *Gemeinschaft* insofar as the individuals live and dwell together peacefully. However, in *Gemeinschaft* they remain essentially united in spite of all separating factors, whereas in *Gesellschaft* they are essentially separated in spite of all uniting factors.[28]

Tönnies' analysis of society regarding community is most profound. It remains helpful in understanding tensions within our own society. And it is especially helpful for understanding contemporary discussions in Christian ethics. Those promoting a discussion of narrative or character ethics want to invoke a strong sense of *Gesellschaft*, which other ethicists will accept as having little basis in social reality. We will encounter this debate when we consider specific ethicists.

Nisbet's second unit-idea of sociology is political power, also called *authority*. No society can survive without political authority, and the French Revolution had raised the question of the nature of political authority in fresh ways. Power/authority has not always been understood in the same manner. Certainly the nineteenth century did not produce a single, unified understanding. Two of the most basic and most divergent answers are given by Alexis de Tocqueville and by Karl Marx. Tocqueville believed that in societies characterized by strong people-power there is a strong threat to freedom;

---

[28] Tönnies, *Community and Society*, 64.

you need political power to guarantee freedom. Marx believed the opposite. For him, political power is equivalent to alienation. Nisbet summarizes the difference between these two great scholars aptly: "Tocqueville believed that there was more personal freedom under aristocracy than under democracy—where public opinion becomes, in his view, more despotic than the medieval Inquisition. For Marx there was no real freedom under aristocracy."[29]

Weber offers an instructive analysis of authority. His formative essay on the topic of the politics and the state, "Politics as a Vocation" (1918),[30] was originally delivered as a lecture to Munich University students at the end of World War I (1918) and in the context of the German Revolution (1918–1919). The debates among the students, and ones that typified the Revolution, were intense and wide-ranging: on the powers of the states, on democratization, on whether rapprochement or military victory was the best route to peace, and so on. In this heated atmosphere, Weber opens his lecture with the comment that "This lecture, which I give at your request, will necessarily disappoint you in a number of ways." And then he proceeds to talk about the nature of the state, ethics, and models of authority.

He asks how the state can be appropriately defined from a sociological point of view. His answer:

> Ultimately, one can define the modern state sociologically only in terms of the specific *means* peculiar to it, as to every political association, namely the use of political force. . . . If no social institution existed which knew the use of violence, then the concept of state would be eliminated, and a condition would emerge that could be designated as "anarchy," in the specific sense of this word. Of course, force is certainly not the normal or the only means of the state—nobody says that—but force is a means specific to the state. Today the relation between the state and violence is an especially intimate one. . . . Today, however, we have to say that a state is a human community that (successfully) claims the *monopoly of the legitimate use of physical force* within a given territory. . . . The state is considered the sole source of the "right" to use violence. Hence, politics for us means striving to share power or striving to influence the distribution of power, either among states or among groups within a state.[31]

It is clear from Weber's account that the earlier "social contract" philosophers' view of the state is accepted. And he is not shy about drawing the conclusions for ethics. He asks boldly, "What relation do ethics and politics actually have?"[32] In his meandering answer, it is clear that politics knows of no "absolute" ethic like that of the Sermon on the Mount. Whereas the Sermon on the Mount says "'Resist not him that is evil with force,' for the politician the reverse proposition holds, 'thou *shalt* resist evil by force,' or else you are responsible for the evil winning out."[33] An ethic of politics is an "ethic of responsibility" or an ethic of compromise because politics is all about responding to situations. That is, politics is about viable *means* to peace and justice, given the obstacles in the way. Hence, pacifists discredit both politics and peace. Weber argues that pacifists are willing to sacrifice just ends for peaceful means and thereby they discredit not only politics but peace itself because as an absolutist ethic it is insensitive to violent consequences.[34]

Another important discussion in this lecture is the nature of authority, often called models of leadership and influence. He identifies three distinct models, all "ideal types." The first is *tradition-based authority*, which was the model of a "sacred tradition" like feudalism or a patriarchal structure. Of

[29] Nisbet, *The Sociological Tradition*, 133.

[30] Max Weber, "Politics as a Vocation," in *From Max Weber: Essays in Sociology*, ed. H. H. Gerth and C. Wright Mills (New York: Oxford University Press, 1946).

[31] Weber, "Politics as a Vocation," 77–78 (emphasis in original).

[32] Weber, "Politics as a Vocation," 118.

[33] Weber, "Politics as a Vocation," 119–20 (emphasis in original).

[34] See esp. Weber, "Politics as a Vocation," 120.

course, this model cannot change unless the tradition itself changes radically, which is what happened through the social revolutions of the nineteenth century. This is the authority of a *Gemeinschaft* and does not work well in a *Gesellschaft*.

The second model Weber identifies is *charismatic authority*. This is the authority of an extraordinary "gift of grace" given to a leader. Biblical prophets are examples of this kind of authority; warlords might be others; an elected political leader can have this gift. This does not mean that the patterns of such a leader are erratic or lack routine; in fact, charismatic authority can be quite compatible with the tradition-based authority model.

The third model is more difficult to name because it is not lodged in a person first of all but in a structure of laws. It might be called *legal-rational authority*. This model places authority not in individuals but in states or constitutions themselves. Hence, it is the system that has the authority, and individuals who know the system derive their authority from that.

Weber uses these models to show how authority shifts over time. It is not that there is a gradual movement from one model to another, but different models are clearly evident, especially in the shift to modernity.

Another unit-idea of sociology is religion, or, as Nisbet calls it, *the sacred*.[35] There are many interesting social perspectives regarding the analysis of religion. We will look briefly at three distinctions made by the nineteenth-century sociologists: between religion and magic, between church and sect, and between ideology and utopia.

Emile Durkheim was the first to make the comparison between religion and magic. Durkheim, although not himself religious, adopted a minority position, arguing that religion did not derive from magic but was a primary phenomena. Max Weber, on the other hand, accepted the more standard view of the anthropologists that religion did indeed derive from magic. Yet both held that they had quite distinct characteristics, regardless of their origins. Religion creates community; magic does not. Magical rites are not social but particular or even individual. Religion is expressed in worship to God as an act of surrender to another. Magic attempts to find ways of gaining power over the gods in order that they may assist the person in achieving his/her objectives. The religious pastor/priest speaks and acts in the name of the community, and the magician speaks/acts in his/her own name.

Weber emphasized that the basic distinctions rest in the fact that religion applies reason to life and magic does not. Hence, religion makes life meaningful, whereas magic can at most make life tolerable or enjoyable, but because it is built on irrational powers it can never produce meaning. It is the process of "rationalization" that is responsible for magic becoming religion in society.

Weber also distinguishes between taboos and religious ethics. Taboos irrationally—in the sense that they cannot be grasped by reason—regulate human behavior ritualistically. As he sees it, religious ethics appeals to rationality and hence has a higher degree of generalization and is concerned about the good life for all. Hence, it is not a taboo but an ethic.

The second dichotomy under the unit-idea of the sacred is church and sect. Ernst Troeltsch (1865–1923)[36] spoke of the nature of the church from a social science perspective in his *The Social Teaching of the Christian Churches*.[37] He made a distinction between two different forms of the church: church and sect. Troeltsch says both are represented in Catholicism and in Protestantism.

---

[35] It is interesting how language itself already portrays important shifts. In earlier times the "church" would have been an important social unit. "The sacred" is something different, in that it identifies *the idea of the religious within individuals;* the church is a social body. That "the sacred" can be measured as a social unit at all is already significant.

[36] I devote an entire chapter to Ernst Troeltsch later—see chap. 13—so will not say much about him here.

[37] Ernst Troeltsch, *The Social Teaching of the Christian* Churches, trans. Olive Wyon (New York: Macmillan, 1931).

Troeltsch puts the distinction as follows:

The church is that type of organization which is overwhelmingly conservative, which to a certain extent accepts the secular order, and dominates the masses; in principle, therefore, it is universal. i.e., it desires to cover the whole life of humanity. The sects, on the other hand, are comparatively small groups; they aspire after personal inward perfection, and they aim at a direct personal fellowship between the members of each group. From the beginning they are forced to organize themselves in small groups, and to renounce the idea of dominating the world. Their attitude towards the world, the State, and Society may be indifferent, tolerant, or hostile, since they have no desire to control and incorporate these forms of social life; on the contrary, they tend to avoid them; their aim is usually either to tolerate their presence alongside of their own body, or even to replace these social institutions by their own society.[38]

This distinction is important for an understanding of Christian ethics. It employs the same logic as Weber in drawing a sharp divide between an ethic of the Sermon on the Mount and an ethic of the state-world. In other words, biblical ethics cannot be relevant to any form of political governance, and pacifists are a discredit to both peace and politics. We will have occasion to come back to this distinction when we present the specific Christian ethicists. Certainly Christian ethicists are sharply divided as to whether this is a helpful distinction.

The third dichotomy under the unit-idea of the sacred, is best made by Karl Mannheim (1893–1947). He distinguishes between ideology and utopia in an effort to define how sociologists understand religion. Gregory Baum summarizes this distinction as follows:

Religion (or any symbolic language) is ideological if it legitimates the existing social order, defends the dominant values, enhances the authority of the dominant class, and creates an imagination suggesting that society is stable and perdures. By contrast, religion is utopian if it reveals the ills of the present social order, inverts the dominant values of society, undermines the authority of the ruling groups, and makes people expect the downfall of the present system.[39]

In essence, this is a parallel distinction to the church-sect distinction that Troeltsch makes. Only the implication is even stronger: any religion that stands in critique of or outside of society in its own self-definition is utopian and therefore irrelevant. The implications of this logic for Christian ethics are profound, and we will see them reverberate throughout as theologians seek to find a language to express how then we are to live.

IMPLICATIONS FOR SOCIAL ETHICS

This chapter would not be complete without a few comments on the implications of the above sociological analysis for our own generation. But that, of course, could be another major study. I will restrict myself to commenting on only five areas: individuation, language, freedom, power, and technology.

Individuation

Sociological studies like *Habits of the Heart* have amply documented the "tyranny of individualism" rampant in our North American society. Their quote from Matthew Arnold's, "To Marguerite–" (1857), "We mortal millions live *alone*,"[40] has intense echoes for today. We are even more individualistic, more fragmented as a society; our identity is characterized less by *Gemeinschaft* and more by *Gesellschaft*; we are less religious and more secular than in the previous century. The very notion of "citizenship in society" has become all but meaningless since society is little more than an aggregate of collectives—organizations, interest groups, families, and so on—and our primary allegiance is to a smaller group.

All of this leaves us with a rather weak sense of *social* ethic as ethics, if meaningful at all, takes on an ever-greater individual face. This has implications in many areas; there is

---

[38] Troeltsch, *Social Teaching*, 331.
[39] Baum, *Religion and Alienation*, 102–3.

[40] Bellah, *Habits*, 281 (emphasis in Arnold's poem).

virtually no agreement among individuals about anything ethical since moral authority is itself individuated; universities today consist of independent and unrelated disciplines of learning—that is, knowledge has become individuated; churches have spiritually-attuned individuals with little loyalty to the identity of a tradition as defined by the people they comprise and as such they lose the power to shape their members; family identities are less significant in shaping individual members; and so on. But the most basic implication of this theme is that we no longer conceive of any common standards of goodness—good is itself individuated.

Language

As we have seen, moral language has changed dramatically. The language of goodness has largely lost its meaning for moderns. Right and wrong hardly function as intelligible discourse anymore. And along with these, we no longer speak of character, virtues, and human nature. These losses are products of the move toward individuation. When the standards of goodness, right, and wrong are lodged within individuals, or even groups, then such terms cannot be used for making moral pronouncements. Yet there is one kind of moral language that we still speak, and that is the language of contract. In personal relationships, it is expressed as "rights language" and is only intelligible within a contract—tacit contracts like social contracts or contracts made between individuals or groups. The latter explains why there is so much attention paid today to professional ethics. Rights language is intended as a clarification of responsibilities and as setting limits to and protecting our freedom. Ethicists later in this study will debate many of these issues.

Freedom

We have seen in the works of Marx, de Tocqueville, Tönnies, and Weber their characterization of the nineteenth century as a quest for human freedom. That search has persisted in our day. Yet the pursuit of freedom tends to function in a unique way today. We no longer believe that the moral life will set us free; instead, we believe that freedom is the moral life. So acts are often judged to be right or wrong insofar as they are done freely, so that anything imposed is wrong. This makes ethics in the traditional sense unintelligible since ethics there required an authority; an ought, in relation to which we were asked to give up the desire of freedom; for example, if as a pacifist, I am not free to use violence to resolve conflict. The pivotal role of freedom is in part why there is a reluctance today to consider self-identity in terms of moral character.

Power

As Friedrich Nietzsche foresaw in the modern move from external moral authority to internal meaning, what remains is the repudiation of outside institutions and the affirmation of self. Such self-affirmation is an assertion of power not weakness, for what the self cultivates is the strength and beauty from within. The motto becomes, "we can do anything that we set our minds to." This is not, strictly speaking, a denial of ethics, but it is a shift to an ethic of "the will to power." But such an ethic has little resemblance to the ethics of the Christian tradition.

Technology

It is an understatement to say that the twentieth century has seen profound technological changes. The advance of technology could not have taken place had it not been for the parallel changes in understanding freedom, power, and the individual. The philosophy underlying technology is that we can bring about virtually anything we want; we have the freedom, the power, and the will to do so. And once there is no external good that governs our will, the slogan "if it is possible, it is necessary" becomes operative. And then, as Martin Heidegger suggested, nothing is given and everything is possible.[41] So

---

[41] See 152ff.

it is virtually impossible to regulate on moral grounds things like stem-cell research, cloning, genetic modification research, nuclear research, and so on. Moreover, this philosophy of technology teaches us to think that we are in control not only of our own lives but of history itself. On this model, our ethic is largely stated in terms of bringing about goals and objectives. Yet when our goals and objectives are developed on the basis of our own interests, how can we know them to be good? And if there is no external *telos* to guide us, it is not surprising that we often experience the irony of: the very good thing we wanted to bring about we managed not to bring about. This topic too is the concern of contemporary ethicists.

The agenda is long, and it is time to move on. In tracing the observations of the sociologists we must acknowledge that the signs of hope for a viable Christian ethic are not many. Yet this cannot deter the search.

Chapter Eleven

PSYCHOLOGY AND ETHICS

Psychology is an important discipline of study for Christian ethics. Among other things, psychologists analyze human behavior.[1] They are interested in finding out why people do what they do. And an answer to this question will naturally be of interest to Christian ethicists since they ask the same question. Psychologists also alter people's behavior, by administering drugs or by other means. Ethicists wonder to what extent drug-induced behavior, or behavior resulting from a chemical deficiency, is morally responsible behavior.

We need to note, however, that when psychologists ask this "why" question they are usually searching for something other than what ethicists are looking for when they ask it. To highlight the difference, consider the distinction between explanation and justification. The response to the question "Why does Jane do X?" might be given in terms of her desire, her disposition, personality traits, moods, and so on. Then it would be a psychological *explanation*. Or, the response could be given in the form of a moral *justification* like, "she is a generous person; she believed it was the right thing to do; she thought it would bring about good," and so on. These are vastly different answers. Yet the two answers remain related, since, if psychology can give a definitive account of

people's behavior, what is there for ethicists to say?

Modern psychology tends to function like a science in that it looks for law-like generalizations that govern human behavior. It is called a behavioral science because it deals with the behavior of the individual. Some psychologists have called modern psychology the "gospel of modernity,"[2] meaning that it presupposes the givenness of a singular human psyche common to all people regardless of their cultural settings. Just like copper expands when heated in India in the same way as it does when heated in identical ways in Canada, so, it is assumed, the behavior of Asians and can be explained in reference to the same psychological "laws" as the behavior of North Americans. Alvin Dueck, who questions this and several other assumptions of modern psychology, notes with some dismay that many universities outside of North America use the same introductory psychology textbooks as do American universities, as if culture and place do not matter.

There is another sense in which psychology is the "gospel of modernity." As we saw in the chapter on sociology and ethics, modern society is in love with the individual, and this has translated into a way of casting religion and ethics with a distinct individual

---

[1] Of course, psychologists address other subjects as well, like perception, motivation, cognition, interpersonal relationships, and so on. Many of these topics intersect with the study of human behavior but cannot be given attention in this brief chapter.

[2] See Alvin C. Dueck, *Between Jerusalem and Athens: Ethical Perspectives on Culture, Religion, and Psychotherapy* (Grand Rapids: Baker, 1995), 51.

bias. For example, the authors of *Habits of the Heart* referred to an American woman named Sheila Larson who, when counseling a dying patient, said, "'if she looked in the mirror' she 'would see Jesus Christ.'"[3] The quest for a view of self that is free of external constraints has proven to be fertile ground for psychology, and this has made the traditional understanding of Christian ethics and Christianity itself all but unintelligible.

It will not surprise the reader to hear that psychologists have not all given the same explanation to the question of why people do what they do. In this brief chapter, only a few answers will be given by major psychologists.

SIGMUND FREUD (1856–1939)

Freud was born to Jewish parents in the Austrian empire. His mother was the second wife of Jakob Freud, a wool merchant. Freud was born when his mother (Amalia) was twenty-one years old and his father was forty-one.[4]

Freud was an outstanding student by high school, and upon graduation he studied medicine with a special interest in physiology. In his early life, he became convinced that living organisms were simply complicated chemical and physical interactions, and what we call personality is but a set of neurological functions. These are views that he later abandoned. After medical school and further study in Paris and Berlin, he returned to Vienna. Here he married Martha Bernays, daughter of a Jewish rabbi.

Early in his life he believed that hypnosis was a promising cure for his patients, but he abandoned that approach in favor of what came to be known as the "talking cure." This was the basis of his psychoanalysis, and it consisted of patients talking through their problems.

Freud himself suffered from psychosomatic ailments. For example, he had "exaggerated fears of dying and other phobias."[5] Based on self-analysis, especially of his dreams, he gave an explanation he believed plausible to account for his feelings and behavior. Reflecting on his own childhood, he became aware of the intense hostility he had for his father and the childhood sexual attraction he had for his mother. Moreover, he became convinced that these early familial relationships offered explanations, not only of his own anxieties and behavior, but also those of his patients.

In 1938 Nazi Germany invaded Austria, which was followed by acts of anti-Semitism. This led to the Freud family's decision to leave Austria and relocate to London so Freud could "die in freedom."[6] The following year he decided to die. Having smoked cigars all his life, and struggling with oral cancer, he came to see his life as completely devoid of meaning.[7] So he called on his doctor and personal friend, Max Schur, to deliver on an earlier promise to help him end his life when it became unbearable. After several doses of morphine, Freud's life came to an end on September 23, 1939.

Freud believed that human behavior was complex; it could not be simply explained in terms of doing what we hold to be right. The only way to understand human behavior was in terms of the structure of the personality. Gerald Corey describes Freud's view as follows:

> From the orthodox Freudian perspective humans are viewed as energy systems. The dynamics of personality consist of the ways in which psychic energy is distributed to the id, ego, and superego. Because the amount of energy is limited, one system gains control over the available energy at the expense of the other two systems. Behavior is determined by this psychic energy.[8]

---

[3] Robert N. Bellah et al., *Habits of the Heart: Individualism and Commitment in American Life* (New York: Harper & Row, 1985), 235.

[4] Information on Freud's life and ideas is readily available in many places. For my comments I am drawing especially from Peter Gay, *Freud: A Life for Our Time* (New York: Norton, 1998); Gerald Corey, *Theory and Practice of Counseling and Psychotherapy*, 4th ed. (Pacific Grove, Calif.: Brooks-Cole, 1985); and "Sigmund Freud," *Wikipedia*, last modified April 1, 2011, http://en.wikipedia.org/wiki/Sigmund_Freud.

[5] Corey, *Theory and Practice*, 95.

[6] Gay, *Freud*, 588.

[7] For a vivid account of Freud's death see Gay, *Freud*, 629ff.

[8] Corey, *Theory and Practice*, 97.

According to Freud, the id was the biological component of the personality, the ego was the psychological component, and the superego the social component. To say more, the id is our personality at birth—characterized by biological instincts. It is illogical, amoral, and instinctual according to the natural desire for pleasure.[9] It acts wholly at the unconscious level. The ego is "the 'traffic cop' for the id, superego, and the external world."[10] It is the rational monitor of the id's instincts and the superego's idealistic tendencies. The ego is realistic, and it seeks to not permit the id or superego to harm the personality. If the ego is the rational monitor, the superego is the moral monitor that strives for perfection and excellence. It represents the ideals, traditional values, and the good; it appropriates tradition and society within itself. As such, it can generate feelings of pride and self-love or feelings of guilt and inferiority.[11] According to Freud, our personality is the locus for the dynamic interplay of these three energy systems acting on our instincts, our rationality, and our moral ideals.

An important overlay on this three-part view of personality is Freud's view of consciousness. He identified several different levels of consciousness. He called the conscious level that which we are aware of at any particular time. This includes one's perceptions, thoughts, memories, feelings, moral ideals, and so on. This roughly corresponds to the activities of ego. Then there is the preconscious level—closely related to the conscious level and sometimes associated with the superego. This is what we can easily retrieve into consciousness when we need to; for example, memories we are not currently aware of, past thoughts, feelings, and so on. So far, most psychologists would agree. Freud's more radical assertion was that these two levels form but a tiny part of the human personality. The largest part, like the submerged portion of an iceberg, is the unconscious. This is the id and the level of which we are not aware. What is especially important here is that, according to Freud, the unconscious id determines much of what we say and do. While it cannot be known directly, the id can be known indirectly. We can come to know it through analyzing dreams, observing slips of the tongue, and by noting what people divulge under hypnosis. The unconscious works, in part, like a repository of unhappy thoughts, feelings, experiences, motivations, and needs. Because these are part of the unconscious, we are not aware of them, yet they determine our behavior and moods. The exercise of psychotherapy is to delve into the unconscious and bring to consciousness those factors that are affecting our behavior; in this way alone can we make positive decisions.

Closely related to this tripartite understanding of the personality is the feeling of anxiety. When the needs or demands of each level of consciousness cannot be harmonized by the ego, anxiety results. For example, when our natural drives like hunger or sexuality are so strong that the superego cannot reconcile it with its understanding of what is right and good, the ego becomes anxious.

Freud identifies a specific anxiety for each level of consciousness. He calls the anxiety associated with the ego "realistic anxiety." This is the fear resulting from a perceived threat to one's well-being, loss of a job, bad medical report, being chased by a bear, being called upon to perform a task, and so on. Here the threat comes from outside the self. Superego anxiety, or "moral anxiety," comes from within. This is the anxiety associated with guilt and shame and the fear of punishment. It comes as a result of feeling judged for an action, being caught in an indiscretion, feeling bad about one's own inadequacies, and so on. "Neurotic anxiety" is the anxiety associated with the id. It has no ostensible internal or external cause. This is what Freud was most interested in. It is a nonrational and amoral anxiety, yet it is so real that it can cause one

---

[9] Corey, *Theory and Practice*, 97.
[10] Corey, *Theory and Practice*, 97.

[11] Corey, *Theory and Practice*, 98.

to feel like one's world is coming apart, or one is going crazy.

Freud believed that if he was successful in gaining access to neurotic anxieties and was able to determine their causes, neurotic persons could be restored to health. Failing that, people were left with natural self-defenses called defense mechanisms. Corey lists twelve such defense mechanisms, many of which have made it into common parlance, like repression, denial, regression, and rationalization. While defense mechanisms are normal, there are times when they are unable to overcome our anxieties, and then, thought Freud, psychotherapy is the only option.

Freud's analysis of the personality makes it possible for him to map out the stages of human development which several other psychoanalysts, such as Erik Erikson, for example, have built on. He believed that human beings go through several distinct stages as follows:[12]

- Oral stage—first year of life
- Anal stage—ages 1–3
- Phallic stage—ages 3–6
- Latency stage—ages 6–12
- Genital stage—ages 12–18
- Adulthood—ages 19 and higher

This is not the place to comment on each of these stages, yet it is important to note that for Freud these stages have powerful effects not only at their particular age level but throughout the entire life. Consider the phallic stage, for example. We have already seen how Freud analyzed his own adult life with reference to his childhood experiences. But, we might ask, why should that be relevant for understanding everyone's life? Freud supplies the answer.

We are all born of mothers, and we all have biological fathers. Most of us grow up with both our mothers and our fathers. Hence, some of the relational dynamics of our young lives are common to us all. Freud felt that it was therefore possible to extrapolate from these common experiences to a model story which, if we were willing to accept, would make us all well-formed people. It is the job of the therapist to help individuals do this.

What is this common "story?" It is the story of King Oedipus who killed his father and married his mother. This Greek myth becomes a kind of salvation myth for Freud, which means that when people are able to successfully tell their own stories in terms of this story they are able to live full lives. Hence, Freudian therapy uses this model to help people who cannot cope with their lives.

But how can a story from Greek mythology be meaningful to you and me, you ask? Freud believed that the meaningfulness of human existence was integrally tied to experiences of close relationships. The primary relationship of children is to their parents. This involves experiences of nourishment, refuge, and tenderness to the mother and fear and hostility to the father. The reason for the hostility to the father is because the father's primary relationship is to the same person as the child's. Hence the mother becomes the savior and the father the threat. This, thinks Freud, is simply the way it is, and ours is the option to accept it and come to a greater knowledge of the self or fight it and be forever miserable. By accepting it, we are able to see our relationships to ourselves and others colored by this primal set of relationships. This will liberate us from the false understanding of ourselves and set us free to be truly human.

The details of Freud's psychoanalytic model are much more complex than can be described here, but it is important to note some key themes. First is the role of symbols in his explanation of human behavior, and the second closely related theme is the role of a model story in developing a healthy self-concept. As we have already noted, Freud did not accept the scientific positivism of his day and instead stressed the importance of the symbolic. The dynamics of the unconscious were simply not quantifiable even though

[12] See Corey, *Theory and Practice*, 103–4 for a more detailed account.

they could be pointed to with the aid of symbols and stories.

One area where Freud sees a wealth of potential symbolic knowledge for understanding the unconscious is dreams. In his book, *The Interpretation of Dreams*,[13] he argues that dreams reveal our deepest desires and therein lies the secret to understanding why we do what we do. Yet normally, dreamers do not understand the significance of their dreams. Since these dreams symbolize powerful processes which shape our behavior, only a well-trained therapist is able to interpret them in such a way that they can be understood properly.

Dreams reveals the otherwise hidden world in which we live without being fully aware of it. Health comes from finding peace with this world. Freud believed that people live in worlds of symbolic meanings, that is, in imaginations. Healthy people live with this world peacefully because they know how their life fits together. Unhealthy people are unable to do this. So, both knowledge of the world and meaning within this world are required in order to live a healthy existence.

Freud was a fascinating scholar and set the stage for much in psychotherapy that came after him. Psychologists like Carl Jung (1875–1961), Alfred Adler (1870–1937), and Erik Erikson (1902–1994) have not always agreed with him, but none could have done their work without the pioneering work of Freud. His ideas should not be too easily discounted.

As a Christian, I might find his primal story difficult to accept as the universal story; nevertheless, I suspect he is right when he speaks about living by symbols within a meaningful narrative imagination. It is easy to find Christian theologies that do this very thing. For example, American fundamentalist Christians often give an account of salvation in terms of Jesus dying for our sins individually. By accepting this story and making it their own, they are freed from the powers of sin that bind us. In this way, it is possible for them to become whole and healed people. Liberation theologians usually see the exodus story as normative and hence give a different account of salvation. Each of these "model stories" has direct implications for understanding Christian ethics; liberationists would hold social issues like oppression and freedom as paramount, and fundamentalists see as primary issues of individual ethics—abortion, marriage, homosexuality, and so on.

Regardless of how one reads the Christian narrative, one cannot escape the Jesus event itself. In some way, for Christians, Jesus is the model human being, and in his life and story we have our salvation. Most Christians confess that Jesus reveals to us *who we are*. Hence, the struggle of Christian existence in one way or another entails the dynamics of making the Jesus story our story. This may well be more Freudian in form than many Christians would like to believe.

BEHAVIORISM

Behaviorism is another approach to psychology. It builds on the assumption that there can be a science of human behavior on par with other sciences. Hence, it is in tension with approach of Freud whose reaction to scientism led him to see human behavior in symbolic terms, not capable of precise quantification.

B. F. Skinner (1904–1990) is probably the best known of the modern behaviorists. He grew up in the eastern United States and attended school in New York City. His initial interest was in English literature, and he aspired to become a writer. After completing his undergraduate studies, he became interested in human behavior and attended Harvard University to study psychology. After teaching at a few other universities, he eventually received a teaching post at Harvard and taught there for the rest of his career.

---

[13] See Sigmund Freud, *The Interpretation of Dreams*, trans. Joyce Crick (Oxford: Oxford University Press, 1999).

Although Skinner wrote twenty-one books, his most popular are *Walden Two* and *Beyond Freedom and Dignity*.[14]

Other American behaviorists are J. B. Watson (1878–1958) and E. L. Thorndike (1874–1949); and some well-known Russian behaviorists are Ivan Pavlov (1849–1936) and V. M. Bekhterev (1857–1927). They all argued that human beings learn behavior patterns just like other living organisms, which makes it possible to deduce laws from the observation of this behavior.

Generally speaking, their answer to the question "why do we do what we do?" is that we are conditioned to do so—mostly unconsciously. This may sound like Freud, but it is quite different. The forces that determine our behavior are not childhood relationships and attachments that can only be disclosed to us through dreams and other indirect probing, rather, our behavior is determined by the reinforcements we have received from others for our past behavior.

Although there are variations among the behaviorists, their basic tenet is that when, under controlled conditions, we correlate the responses of animals and humans with certain features of their environment, we observe a repeated pattern between stimuli and responses. This happens with such regularity that it allows us to predict with great accuracy what responses will follow from specific controlled stimuli. Hence, the conclusion is reached that all behavior is learned from interactions with our environment.

This idea has profound implications for ethics. Consider a simple example: a child can be taught to manipulate the environment at an early age. Mother feeds the child whenever the child cries. Hence, the child learns that when it wants to eat it cries, which "trains" a child to be calculating. "I can get what I want; all I have to do is find the appropriate item in my environment to manipulate to my advantage." On the other hand, if a child is allowed to cry and is fed on a schedule unrelated to the child's behavior, the child will "learn" no such traits. The child will develop a passive orientation. Hence, whether we are aggressive or passive has nothing to do with morality—matters of right or wrong or matters of personal *moral* training—but is a matter of what behaviorists call operant conditioning.[15] What we used to think were trainable virtues—honesty, patience, kindness, gentleness, mercy—now turn out to be conditioned traits determined for us by how others have responded to us!

Some behaviorists are so passionate about their scientific discoveries that J. B. Watson, the author who originally inspired Skinner to study psychology, once said that if he were given a dozen healthy infants and if he were allowed to create his own special environment for them, he could shape any one of them into any kind of person he wanted.[16]

Behaviorism and its sophisticated forms of operant conditioning have several distinct uses in society. For example, it can be used to retrain people who exhibit undesirable behavior. In other words, all behavior can be modified; abnormal behavior can be made normal. Yet while the theory might be used to change behavior, it is not able to define what normal behavior is. This remains a problem.

It is important to identify several assumptions of behaviorism. First, it assumes the thesis of determinism. It should not be surprising that behaviorism, as a science of behavior, rejects human freedom. It should therefore also not be surprising that it is antagonistic to ethics. Ethics without some

---

[14] B. F. Skinner, *Walden Two* (New York: Macmillan, 1962); *Beyond Freedom and Dignity* (New York: Knopf, 1971). Other important books by Skinner are *Science and Human Behavior* (New York: Macmillan, 1953); *Analysis of Behavior*, with J. G. Holland (New York: McGraw-Hill, 1961); and *Technology of Teaching* (New York: Appleton-Century-Crofts, 1968).

[15] Skinner's view of operant conditioning is a more sophisticated view of what Pavlov did with his dog. Rewarding an animal with food for desired behavior will reproduce that behavior. Then that behavior can be modified by further rewarding some aspects of it and not others. In other words, Skinner found a way of operating on the environment with greater control than did Pavlov with his classical conditioning.

[16] See J. B. Watson, "Psychology as the Behaviourist Views It," *Psychological Review* 20 (1913): 158–77.

modicum of freedom is anathema. Second, it rejects a view of consciousness that accepts the self-transcendent capacity of human beings. In other words, if we are able to "step outside ourselves" it would, in principle, be impossible to control the environment enough for a stimulus to produce a desired response. The environment would itself be an object of our consciousness. This may well make Sigmund Freud more convincing as a general approach to human consciousness than behaviorism, not because he is right in all its details, but because it is less straightforwardly reductionist.

HUMANISTIC PSYCHOLOGIES

It should not be surprising to find that there are psychologists who are dissatisfied with both the psychoanalytic or behaviorist account of how we can be well-formed human beings. Abraham Maslow (1908–1970), Carl Rogers (1902–1987), Viktor Frankl (1905–1997), and Rollo May (1909–1994)[17] all rejected the psychoanalytic approach because of its heavy reliance on the unconscious, and they rejected behaviorism because of its excessive emphasis on the environment as a determinant of human behavior. One alternative is an approach to psychology sometimes called humanism, which emphasizes that human beings are free to make choices. These choices, for which they must bear full responsibility, create them into particular persons.

It is important to emphasize that there are many different kinds of humanist psychologies. Most of what goes under modern counseling theories today relies on some version of this school of thought. I will present only some of the basic presuppositions.

One of the key beliefs is that *self-actualization* is the best way to describe what it means

to become fully human. Human beings all have certain needs. The overall need is for the actualization of the self, that is, be all we can be. Yet this general need breaks down into several more specific needs—the need to belong, to be loved, the need for self-expression, for creativity, for friendship, and so on.

Whereas the other two approaches to psychology emphasized the objective side of being human, that is, what is out there that makes us human, this model emphasizes the subjective dimension, that is, how we are involved in making ourselves human. Having a healthy self-image and being capable of honest self-evaluation and feeling good about oneself are all important qualities of this approach. Moreover, since the self is central, listening becomes a dominant concern—listening to others and to yourself. Since each person is unique, and each person has special gifts, there is no talk here of a scientific basis for understanding human behavior. The fundamental assumption is that each person is "OK" and that for healing resources one must look inside and not outside.[18]

While the humanist approach addresses some of the difficulties of the other two models, especially as it relates to our interest in Christian ethics, it raises some concerns as well. An ethic based on a humanist view of a good person would, at best, result in a kind of "democratization of ethics," that is, what is good and right is based on the observation of what the majority of people in fact hold to be good and right. Perhaps even this is too generous, and this approach leads directly to ethical egoism. After all, if an outside imposition of human nature is rejected or seen as self-alienating and not as self-actualizing, then the notion of being human is entirely self-determined. Insofar as this view rejects

[17] Classification becomes difficult here. Frankl and May are sometimes called "existential psychologists," and Rogers is sometimes identified as having the "person-centered" approach. (See, e.g., Corey, *Theory and Practice*). Although distinctions could obviously be made within this grouping, in this short chapter I lump them together for brevity's sake.

[18] One study that makes this explicit is Thomas A. Harris, *I'm OK—You're OK: A Practical Guide to Transactional Analysis* (New York: Harper & Row, 1969). Transactional Analysis is an approach made famous by the psychologist Eric Berne (1910–1970), that emphasizes the client's role in naming the directions and goals of the therapeutic process, thereby increasing the client's ownership in altering the course of his or her life.

all reference to a heteronymous ought to which the self is subject, it is hard to see how ethics can function as a meaningful notion.

STAGES OF MORAL DEVELOPMENT

One might think from the discussion so far that psychologists do not engage the subject of ethics. But that is not so. One of the common topics in psychology involves moral development. As we have already seen from our study of Freud, seeking to identify stages of development is important to psychologists. In relation to ethics, the question is whether decisions and views of what is right and wrong can be tied to psychological development theory. Most will say that they can.

Lawrence Kohlberg (1927–1987) is an American psychologist who believed that it is possible to observe moral development in the normal life cycle of a human being. Although not the only psychologist studying moral development, he is one of the best-known for his views on the subject.[19]

Kohlberg was born into a wealthy family in New York. His family, of Jewish background, was cosmopolitan and international—his father was an importer and his mother was a chemist. Kohlberg was the fourth and youngest child. He had a good elementary and secondary education, and upon graduation, which coincided with the end of World War II, he joined the Marine Corps and served briefly in Europe. His interest in moral development arose in part from his revulsion at the Holocaust. He said:

> The Holocaust is the event in human history that most bespeaks the need for moral education and for a philosophy that can guide it. My own interest in morality and moral education arose in part as a response to the Holocaust, an event so enormous that it often fails to provoke a sense of injustice in many individuals and societies.[20]

Kohlberg took his college education at the University of Chicago and, upon graduation in 1958, he received a teaching post at Yale University and eventually at Harvard University. His research interests were in moral education and moral development. Once, after many years of research in American schools, and after writing extensively about moral development theory, he visited several kibbutzim in Israel. Here he was surprised by the level of moral behavior and attributed this to the closeness of the community. This prompted him to become involved in starting a new school in Cambridge called the "Cluster School," which was designed for senior high school students. This school stressed "ethical relationships" as an important part of the learning experience. Through involvement in this project, he got to interact with his critic and colleague, Carol Gilligan, and they worked together in setting up "ethical communities" that focused on the moral development of children, prisoners, and others.

Kohlberg's life ended in tragedy. After a long illness that resulted in depression, he eventually found life unbearable. On January 19, 1987, his body was found in Boston Harbor, an apparent suicide.

Kohlberg is most famous for his six stages of moral development, which he formulated from substantial research in American schools. He had become disillusioned with the way the public school system taught children about moral matters. He claimed that schools were teaching morals as a "bag of virtues." That is, he believed that schoolchildren were being taught honesty, truthfulness, justice, as if these were somehow valid virtues attempting to guide them into an expression of the good life. He felt this approach was unhelpful and ineffective and believed there were no honest children or dishonest

---

[19] For the sake of brevity, I will consider only the work of Lawrence Kohlberg in this section. It needs to be said, however, that there are several other psychologists who have done considerable research on the topic of moral development, and, although there are detailed differences, there is general overall agreement on structure. Others are the Swiss psychologist Jean Piaget (1896–1980) and the contemporary American psychologist Elliot Turiel.

[20] Lawrence Kohlberg, *The Philosophy of Moral Development: Moral Stages and the Idea of Justice* (San Francisco: Harper & Row, 1981), 407.

children, only honest and dishonest acts. This meant that we should rethink teaching of morality to focus on acts and decisions, not on virtues.

One researcher summarizes Kohlberg's objections to the "bag of virtues" approach as follows:

> Arbitrariness exists in composing the list of virtues, depending upon the composition of committees to develop such a list, their agreements and inconsistencies. Virtue words are relative to cultural standards that are psychologically vague and ethically relative (e.g., the inability to agree on the meaning of "self-discipline"). Moreover, by labeling a set of behaviors with positive or negative traits does not in itself show that it is of ethical importance but represents an appeal to social conventions. Additionally, longitudinal research findings raise doubts whether childhood personality traits are stable or predictive over time and stages of development . . . research suggests that various character traits do not stand for consistent personality traits but are merely evaluative labels.[21]

Kohlberg set out to develop an alternative approach to teaching about moral matters. In order to arrive at his method, he did research on how children think, presenting children with moral dilemmas and then asking for their responses. For example, one of the dilemmas was as follows:

> A woman was near death from cancer, and there was only one drug that might save her. It was discovered by a druggist who was charging ten times what the drug cost him to make. The sick woman's husband could only get together $1000, which was half of what the drug cost. He asked the druggist to sell it cheaper or to let him pay later. But the druggist said no. So the husband got desperate and broke into the man's store to steal the drug for his wife. Should he have done that? Was it actually wrong or right? Why?[22]

Each child was then asked what action should have been taken by the husband and why. The reasons were tabulated, and Kohlberg discovered that they fell into a threefold structure of levels. The first he called the *preconventional level*, the second he called the *conventional level*, and the third the *postconventional level*. Each level is determined by the kind of rationale the children gave for their decisions. Kohlberg also showed that each level could be further subdivided into two stages. His model looks as follows:[23]

I. PRECONVENTIONAL LEVEL

STAGE 1. PUNISHMENT ORIENTATION: At this stage rules are obeyed to avoid punishment. Authority is heeded because it has the power to implement what is being commanded.

Response to example: "He shouldn't steal the drug because he could get caught and sent to jail."

STAGE 2. HEDONISTIC ORIENTATION: At this level the child conforms in order to obtain rewards. Right action is determined by how well it fulfils my needs and how well it fulfils your needs. "You scratch my back; I'll scratch yours."

Response to example: "It won't do him any good to steal the drug because his wife will probably die before he gets out of jail."

II. CONVENTIONAL LEVEL

STAGE 3. "GOOD BOY" ORIENTATION: In this stage the child attempts to do what wins approval. Approval is won by being nice.

Response to example: "He shouldn't steal the drug because others will think he is a thief. His wife would not want to be saved by thievery."

STAGE 4. AUTHORITY ORIENTATION: At this level the child is committed to upholding law and order. Right behavior consists in doing one's duty, regardless of the consequences.

Response to example: "Although his wife needs the drug, he should not break the law to get it. Everyone is equal in the eyes of the law, and his wife's condition does not justify stealing."

STAGE 5. SOCIAL CONTRACT ORIENTATION: At this level the person appeals to the rational and consensual grounds for society's rules. Mutual consent is what gives people rights and obligations. Rules are therefore recognized to be relative to the people in question, but they are made for the benefit of the people concerned.

---

[21] John Martin Rich and Joseph L. DeVitis, *Theories of Moral Development* (Springfield, Ill.: Charles C Thomas, 1985), 90.

[22] Quoted from Dennis Coon, *Introduction to Psychology: Exploration and Application*, 3rd ed. (New York: West, 1983), 453.

[23] Quoted from Coon, *Introduction to Psychology*, 453–54.

Response to the example: "He should not steal the drug. The druggist's decision is reprehensible, but mutual respect for the rights of others must be maintained."

STAGE 6. INDIVIDUAL PRINCIPLES ORIENTATION: At this point the person appeals to universal principles which are general, self-chosen and comprehensive. Here high value is placed on justice, dignity and equality.

Response to example: "He should steal the drug and inform the authorities that he has done so. He will have to face a penalty, but he will have saved a human life."

Kohlberg found that people move through these stages at different rates and at different ages. But generally speaking, there is a correlation with age as follows: stages 1 and 2 typify the way young children respond to moral dilemmas; stages 3 and 4 are typical of older children and adults. Only about twenty percent of the adult population operates at stages 5 and 6, and in fact, Kohlberg claims that only about ten percent are at stage 6 consistently.

It is interesting to note that Kohlberg is explicitly evaluative about these stages. It is clear that he considers the last stage to be morally superior to others. But what would be his basis for concluding this? Is he himself claiming to be operating at one of these levels? Or is he at yet a higher stage? And what argument could he advance which would suggest that one stage was morally better than the other?[24]

Much has been written about Kohlberg's stages of moral development, and it is impossible to survey that material here. It is important, however, to note some shifts that have taken place in the way that moral thinking itself has developed, given Kohlberg's work; that is, shifts away from the traditional way of thinking about ethics to his "new" way. According to Kohlberg, "virtues thinking" is unhelpful and ineffective. Why? Because the the virtues approach presupposes a

particular view of the good life for which we ought to train ourselves. But he believes that such a qualitative view of life cannot be sustained in the modern world; hence, there is really nothing for which we should be training ourselves. In fact, his view of morality is an inversion of the traditional model. Where earlier an understanding of the good life was presupposed and virtues were required to bring about such a life, with Kohlberg, the people and their values shape the view of life. This means that morality is both an *expression* of what people do and a *definition* of the norms. Hence, no serious evaluative reflection can occur about how a child or adult responds to particular moral dilemmas. Each response is as good or bad as any other. In other words, all responses are morally neutral. Yet it seems that Kohlberg himself did not believe this. After all, he wanted to claim that one kind of response was morally superior to another. Yet the basis for this is not evident.

ETHICS AND PASTORAL CARE

Another area of overlap between psychology and Christian ethics, which is especially important for the church, is pastoral care. Counselors usually presuppose a view of psychology, or combination of views, when engaging in Christian counseling. For example, they make these assumptions when they analyze a person's "problem" and in their response when trying to be helpful. The more reflective counselors have a view of what they are doing when they engage in the act of counseling. Are they therapists, are they listeners, or are they priests? Their answers to these questions all presuppose a view of psychology as well as ethics.

There are not many researchers who have done sustained work on the interrelation of ethics and pastoral care. This is itself surprising because one would think morality would be one of the more important concerns of a

---

[24] For helpful critical reflections on Kohlberg's theory, see R. S. Peters, "Moral Development: A Plea for Pluralism," in *Psychology and Ethical Development: A Collection of Essays on Psychological Theories, Ethical Development and Human Understanding* (London: Allen & Unwin, 1974), 303–35.

pastoral counselor. After all, most situations have moral implications of one sort or other. Perhaps this lack of concern for ethics is because ethics itself has for so long been seen as the reason people have difficulty coping with life and so people need to be rescued from it. In other words, ethics is the problem, and counseling is seen as the means whereby "guilt"—the product of ethics—is overcome.

Don S. Browning is one scholar who has written on this subject. In his book, *Religious Ethics and Pastoral Care*, he begins his study by citing a specific case discussed at a conference where pastors gathered to examine the nature of pastoral care. I quote this case at length.

> The case of Jim and Betty Farr, as we shall call them, involved a situation of marital strain and tension. As they brought their problem to their minister, it appeared on the surface to center around Betty's problem with alcohol. The couple, in their early forties, had two teenage children. She had come from a vaguely Catholic background. He was from German stock, with equally loose relations to the Lutheran tradition. At the time, the Farrs were occasionally attending a local Lutheran church. They had met in California where both had gone as young adults in order to escape what each perceived as a rather dreary life at home. They had met while Jim was working on a Ph.D. in chemistry. Betty had helped put her husband through school.
>
> By way of preparation for the psychological interpretation to follow, the seminar received the following information concerning the developmental backgrounds of the Farrs. Mrs. Farr was one of several children. Her childhood memories centered around her mother's constant criticism of her and coldness toward her. This criticism seemed always to have existed and to have been aimed more at Betty than at the other children. When Betty was an early teenager her mother became ill and eventually died. Betty began at that point to play a much more responsible role in the family. Her siblings began to depend upon her, and her father praised her lavishly for her newfound dependability.
>
> Mr. Farr's early memories centered around a significant family trauma that occurred when he was about six years old. His father, who had been a rather dashing and successful businessman, suddenly lost everything in the Great Depression. Jim's father and mother both reacted to the attendant social demotion with depression and increasing detachment. Jim remembers his mother becoming sick shortly thereafter and remaining sick until her rather early death. Both Jim and Betty seemed old for their years, constricted in affect, and generally depressed.
>
> The minister, whom we shall call Peter Spicer, was a more-than-middle-aged pastor. As he developed the case for members of the seminar, he came across as deeply imbued with his rich Lutheran liturgical tradition. But in spite of these marks of ecclesiastical self-consciousness, he had for some years also been involved with psychology and counseling and saw these as important aspects of his ministry. Indeed, it was interesting to note that Pastor Spicer—and for that matter all the seminar participants—found it easier to develop a psychological interpretation of the Farrs than to interpret the case from a theological-ethical point of view.[25]

The pastor was then asked to give both a psychological- and a theological-ethical interpretation of this case. The pastor's psychological interpretation was as follows: he relied on a psychoanalytic approach to show that both Jim and Betty had defects in their self-representations, resulting from traumatic childhood experiences. Betty had no doubt developed an oedipal, or perhaps pre-oedipal, relation with her father, despite the fact that this type of relationship normally comes much earlier in childhood than the date of her traumatic loss of her mother. This explained her current "narcissistic" needs.

Jim's personality deficiency was clearly pre-oedipal. His self-image was shattered by the trauma of seeing his father lose prestige. At the time that he was identifying with his father, his father lost his own identity. So he, with his father and mother, retreated into a "mode of detachment." Since both had the same problem, neither could provide the other with what was most needed: a reassurance of their mutual self-worth.

---

[25] Don S. Browning, *Religious Ethics and Pastoral Care* (Philadelphia: Fortress, 1983), 20–21 (emphasis in original).

The pastor's theological–ethical interpretation was much less complex. He began by saying that through his relationship with Jim and Betty he was trying to show them the love God had for each of them. This would affirm them in their humanness and that would address the problem as he saw it— lack of self-worth. His reference to Scripture was 1 Corinthians 13:12-13: "For now we see in a mirror dimly, but then we will see face to face. Now I know only in part; then I will know fully, even as I have been fully known." The pastor mentioned that marriage "was not the most important thing." He demonstrated no "theology" of marriage, sexuality, or interpersonal relationships. He did say that the growth of both Jim and Betty as individuals was a good goal to pursue. His recommendation to them was that they come to his church so they could remain in contact with him. He also suggested that they see a professional counselor to work at "old wounds" that go back a long way. He recommended that Betty attend Alcoholics Anonymous sessions, which she did.[26]

Browning points out that the pastor in this case does not take ethics seriously. Insofar as he does, he could be called an ethical egoist, or perhaps a utilitarian. Browning himself then reflects on this example using other models of pastoral counseling.

He refers specifically to Seward Hiltner and Howard Clinebell; both are prominent scholars in pastoral counseling, yet both are reluctant to push the relationship of ethics and pastoral counseling. Hiltner argues that the solutions to people's problems should be drawn out from the creative potentialities which each person brings to the table. He claims that counseling is inherently "eductive" and that healing ways come from within the clients themselves. Browning points out that

Hiltner, in his *Preface to Pastoral Theology*,[27] makes the distinction between ethics, which he says is "logic centered" and pastoral theology which he says is "operation centered." The two approaches are difficult to integrate. This, says Browning, leads Hiltner to adopt a "situation ethics" approach to counseling. Browning is not convinced.

Howard Clinebell, according to Browning, only minimally discusses the relationship between ethics and pastoral psychology.[28] Although a church minister should always do what he/she regards as right, integration gets little attention in his writings.

Finding a paucity of work in the area, Browning seeks to provide a model for integration. He begins by stating that for such a model to be Christian, it must be based on the church community. He speaks of the church as a "community of moral discourse." For his understanding of church, he relies on Avery Dulles,[29] especially his model of church as herald and servant.

In developing this model, Browning identifies "five levels of practical moral thinking." Each of these is a response to a specific question. The questions are: first, what kind of world or universe constitutes the ultimate context of our action? Second, what are we obligated to? Third, which of all our human tendencies and needs are we morally justified in satisfying? Fourth, what is the immediate context of our action and the various factors which condition it? And fifth, what specific roles, rules, and processes of communication should we follow in order to accomplish our moral ends?[30] Browning then suggests that each of these questions leads to a different level of moral thinking; the first, a metaphorical level; the second, an obligational level; the third, a tendency-need level; the fourth, a contextual-predictive level; and the fifth,

---

[26] These responses are summaries of Browning's report on the case study, Browning, *Religious Ethics*, 21–24.

[27] Seward Hiltner, *Preface to Pastoral Theology* (New York: Abingdon, 1959).

[28] See Howard Clinebell, *Basic Types of Pastoral Care and Counseling: Resources for the Ministry of Healing and Growth* (Nashville: Abingdon, 1984).

[29] See Avery Dulles, *Models of the Church* (Garden City, N.Y.: Image Books, 1987).

[30] Browning, *Religious Ethics*, 53.

a rule-role level. By correlating these levels, he endeavors to show how practical theology and religious ethics intersect.

Although Browning has embarked on a commendable task, there are distinct deficiencies with his approach. It is hard to see how he has been successful in bringing *Christian* ethics and pastoral care together. The church, which was supposed to be the context for his work, served no relevant role in the end.

A more promising approach in the task of bringing ethics and pastoral care into creative interaction is found in the work of Alvin Dueck.[31] Dueck begins with the rejection of the Enlightenment view of the autonomous self, which he believes is in principle incompatible with "ethical discernment and religious character."[32] This is because the Enlightenment produced a notion of individual consciousness that was singular and could not handle plurality; hence, individual autonomy was the beginning and end of human identity and morality and religion are always threats. In contrast, Dueck, referring to the Russian writer Georges Gurdjieff and the work of P. D. Ouspensky,[33] argues that "the self is a plurality."[34]

Dueck maintains that the notion of the self as a plurality changes everything because it leads to a communal understanding of self rather than an autonomous view. One in fact has many selves. He gives the example of Michael, who is at once a psychology professor, a son, a therapist, a lover, an executive, and so on. Each of these selves has slightly different patterns of behavior and hence slightly different personalities, yet all are resident in one person. How can one understand health and illness on this model?

Relying on the work of Gurdjieff, Dueck speaks of a communal relationship within the self; a kind of "congregation within" the self. And here he makes overt connections with the Christian faith and especially with the church. He first reminds the reader that Christians see God as three in one (a plurality of self), and that Jesus and Paul often speak of the battle that rages within us—among the different selves. But even more important, he likens the ethic of the reign of God that governs the church to the ethic that governs the self. He says that ". . . by analogy the ethic that governs the church is also appropriate to the internal congregation."[35]

Although Dueck does not spend many pages elaborating his view of the relationship of Christian ethics and psychology, we have with his approach a serious effort of reading the view of self through the nature of the church. And this is only possible with a radical rejection of the Enlightenment view of the autonomous self, which modern psychology has so unequivocally adopted. Although this chapter cannot further explore the interesting implication of this view, one sees in this unusual and courageous approach a new kind of hope; a hope for the possibility of a holistic, unified view of psychology and ethics.

---

[31] See Dueck, *Between Jerusalem and Athens*, esp. 201–17.
[32] Dueck, *Between Jerusalem and Athens*, 202.
[33] See, e.g., P. D. Ouspensky, *In Search of the Miraculous* (New York: Harcourt Brace Jovanovich, 1949).
[34] Dueck, *Between Jerusalem and Athens*, 202.
[35] Dueck, *Between Jerusalem and Athens*, 213.

Chapter Twelve

THEOLOGY AND ETHICS

The reader may wonder whether devoting a chapter to theology and ethics in general does not prejudge the overall project, especially since the entire book deals with this relationship. Moreover, some of what needs to be said on this topic has already been said in other chapters. Nevertheless, there are important themes that warrant exploration here. By looking at theology as a discipline of thought and asking how Christian ethics is situated within it, we treat theology on par with philosophy, sociology, and psychology. When we elaborate the thought of contemporary theologians in subsequent chapters, these themes will be revisited in more detail.

This chapter will focus on only a few theological concepts and will ask: What difference does thinking theologically make for shaping and understanding how we ought to live in this world? It is highly selective and treats only the following themes: theological method, Christology, ecclesiology, and eschatology.[1]

A word of caution about language. I am not intending to suggest that ethics and each of the theological themes mentioned are independently intelligible. Precisely the opposite will be argued! As was emphasized at the beginning of this book,[2] theology is best conceived as ethics, and Christian ethics as theology. The focus here will be on showing how this mutual interdependence shapes a wholesome understanding of the Christian life and thought. The conjunctive formulation of our headings, including the chapter title, is therefore misleading and technically inaccurate.

THEOLOGICAL METHOD AND ETHICS

American Baptist theologian, James William McClendon Jr.[3] has made the point that theological reflection should begin with ethics rather than the way it often conceives of its task—leaving ethics to the last consideration in an enterprise shaped by an otherwise independent logic. McClendon argues that one cannot think right unless one lives right; and so ethics is a good place to start when writing a systematic theology book. A difficulty, however, one which McClendon acknowledges, is that one cannot live right unless one thinks right also. This only shows how interconnected theology and ethics really are, and how important it is to properly conceive of the theological project itself.

A helpful study on the nature of theology is found in George Lindbeck's work.[4]

---

[1] Other themes could have been chosen, like soteriology, sin, creation, hermeneutics, reign of God, pneumatology, spirituality, Trinity, and so on. The choice of four is deliberately selective.

[2] See esp. "Introduction," 1ff.

[3] See esp. James William McClendon Jr., *Systematic Theology: Ethics* (Nashville: Abingdon, 1986).

[4] See esp. George A. Lindbeck, *The Nature of Doctrine: Religion and Theology in a Postliberal Age* (Philadelphia: Westminster, 1984).

Lindbeck was born in 1923 and spent his early years in China and Korea with his parents, who were Lutheran missionaries. His graduate work was at Yale University, the Pontifical Institute of Medieval Studies in Toronto, and at Ecole Pratique des Hautes Etudes in Paris. He graduated from Yale with a doctorate in 1955, by which time he had already been appointed as a professor at Yale Divinity School, where he taught until his retirement in 1993. He is known especially as a medievalist and ecumenist, with special interest in Lutheran-Roman Catholic dialogue.

Lindbeck believes that the way theology is done usually arises from the prevailing view of knowledge, which is not unique to theology but to the intellectual enterprise generally. Hence, as the view of knowledge changes, so does the approach to theology. He argues that after the Enlightenment we have three available options: we either continue with the Enlightenment approach of universal certainty, accept the "existential" model based on subjective experience, or develop a third approach which has affinities with the pre-Enlightenment, medieval view of knowledge. He favors the third option.

He identifies the two historically dominant approaches as *cognitive-propositional* and *experiential-expressive*, and his proposed model he calls *cultural-linguistic*.[5] Each approach has parallel approaches in ethics. I will present a brief explanation of each model.

Cognitive-Propositional Model

This model suggests that when we write and think theologically we are attempting to *describe* God and the world. Hence, theology is seen as a quantificational inquiry supplying us with information about ultimate reality. This suggests that our theological statements are either true or false. On this model, doctrine is seen as a description of objective reality, which we believe because it is literally true. Hence, Christian faithfulness is closely associated with theological correctness, like the virgin birth, or the Trinity, or bodily resurrection, and so on, because it describes the content of the faith.

Theological disagreement takes on a distinct form with this approach. Either one or the other is right and the other therefore wrong, or both are wrong. Two incompatible beliefs cannot both be right, and so there can be no "reconciliation without capitulation."[6]

This method of theology carries with it a parallel approach to ethics. Some also see ethics as a cognitive discipline. Moral statements are what they appear to be: true or false statements describing the objective world. This approach is sometimes called natural law ethics but should not be confused with the views of Thomas Aquinas. The argument here is as follows: just like physical laws of the universe, like "water boils at 100 degrees Celsius," and "unsupported rocks roll down hill," are true descriptions of objective reality, so moral laws, like, "lying is wrong," or "premarital sex is wrong," are true descriptions of an objective moral order. We can come to know the content of these laws through rational reflection on the nature of reality—just like in natural science—and then live our lives under their sovereignty—just like in natural science. To disobey moral laws of the universe has death-like consequences, just like jumping out of a ten-story building in defiance of the laws of gravity.

Experiential-Expressive Model

This is the approach made popular by the post-Enlightenment rejection of universal rationality and the cognitive-propositional method of theology. It says that theological statements are in fact not cognitively true or false at all. That is, they do not convey verifiable information. They are qualitatively true or false like poetry and fiction. We therefore need to recognize that the "same thing" can be said in many different ways. On this model, says Lindbeck, theology

---

[5] Lindbeck, *Nature of Doctrine*, 31–32.

[6] This is a phrase used frequently by Lindbeck, e.g., *Nature of Doctrine*, 16.

interprets doctrine as noninformative and non-discursive symbols of inner feelings, attitudes, and existential orientations. This approach highlights the resemblances of religion to aesthetic enterprises and is particularly congenial to the liberal theologies influenced by the Continental developments that began with Schleiermacher.[7]

Hence, in this model, theology is the attempt to express the content of a common religious "feeling of absolute dependence" (Friedrich Schleiermacher).[8]

In this approach it is an error to assume that there is an independently real object that is being described when doing theology. The proper focus of theology, it is alleged, is human experience, feeling, and inclination. It is therefore not impossible that people of diverse religious backgrounds may be talking about the same faith, even though they express it quite differently. God is seen as being within each of us, and therefore what is more important than careful argumentation about the correctness of theological statements is the cultivation of listening skills so that we may hear the other's expression of God within. God-realization and self-realization tend to merge into the same thing.

In this model, theological disagreements look different from the previous model. Serious theological debate is rare. How can I disagree with the way you express your "feeling of absolute dependence?" Of course, my views could change as a result of an engagement with another person. Such dialogue can be enriching and educational if it is done with genuine respect for the other. But there can be no compelling reason for why I should change my mind. And theological doctrine becomes altogether unimportant on this view.

This model of theological discourse has parallels in ethics. As we have seen earlier, ethical noncognitivism or emotivism is a popular approach to ethics that believes ethical language is noncognitive and moral utterances are merely expressions of emotion, not vehicles of truth.[9] Hence, as in theological debate, there can be no resolution of moral disagreements because there is no basis upon which to settle disputes.

Cultural-Linguistic Model

Lindbeck proposed a third model which, he argues, is a better way of accounting for how theological language functions. The name he gave this approach is cultural-linguistic. He learned from Ludwig Wittgenstein[10] that theological language, like all language, has meaning only within certain well-defined contexts. Hence, theological learning is essentially language learning. And since one cannot learn to just speak but must learn to speak a language such as English or French, so one cannot come to know God without learning a particular God-language. Hence, learning to know God is learning to know how God-language functions.

To explain what Lindbeck is saying, I offer an anecdote. When I watched my first football game and knew nothing about the sport, what I saw was utterly meaningless activity. I saw everything my buddies saw, who understood the rules and objectives, that is, they knew the context of the game, and everything made sense to them; but nothing made sense to me. I could not tell when something was "out of order" nor could I tell when anything significant was accomplished. All I saw were isolated items of behavior—mostly of people piling on top of each other time and time again. I could not imagine how people could enjoy doing something like this, or, for that matter, why people would pay money to watch it. Had I known the language, I would have been able to participate in the

---

[7] Lindbeck, *Nature of Doctrine*, 16.

[8] See esp. Friedrich Schleiermacher, *On Religion: Speeches to its Cultured Despisers*, trans. John Oman (New York: Harper & Row, 1958).

[9] See chap. 9 above, "Philosophy and Ethics."

[10] For a fuller discussion of the thought of Ludwig Wittgenstein, see 151ff.

imagination of football. And only then could I have understood the event.

The language of football can open up a new world of meaning, and to some degree this has happened even to me since I am writing this chapter while watching a Super Bowl game. So can the language of theology open up a whole new world of meaning. The more fully one understands how this language functions, the more thoroughly one understands the "game."

We all know that just because we learn the language of football, it does not follow that we understand hockey. Just like with football, we cannot understand hockey without learning its language. And so it is with religions, says Lindbeck. To come to understand a religion other than your own, you must learn its language. Religions are not fully understandable via a foreign language.

Additionally, in any sport, it is possible to learn a lot *about* it by learning the language, but to come to know the sport fully requires learning to play it. And so it is with religion, says Lindbeck. Remember, he calls his approach the cultural-linguistic approach. There is a difference between knowing what Christianity is all about and practicing the Christian faith. The difference is analogous to watching and playing football.

Lindbeck draws on Wittgenstein's notion of "language games" and their interrelationship with a "form of life." Ways of life are undergirded by ways of thinking. Our imaginations about theology are expressed through rituals, actions, institutions, and so on. We learn to live what we think and we learn to make sense of how we live. Lindbeck sees his model as the integrated reciprocal relationship of experience-thought and religion.

Theological statements, in Lindbeck's model, function not to describe reality or merely to express subjective views; rather, they serve as rules for understanding and living. Theological language functions more

like a language game where one can say, within a rule-governed context, what is or is not the case, or what ought or ought not to be done, while outside this context such claims are largely meaningless. Within a Christian framework, one kind of language makes sense, while within a Muslim context it does not. This is like a game; within football the language of "downs" has meaning and "strikes" does not.

The connections with ethics here is fairly obvious. In this model, it is easy to see how Christian ethics is theology. What one believes about God, Jesus, church, and so on, will determine how one lives. The word "God" functions as the term that designates ultimate reality giving life its ultimate quality. God is the author and culminator of my life. To call Jesus Messiah means that, although a historical person, he embodies God in all fullness. Hence, he gives concrete social and personal expression to life in general and also to my life. When Christians use the languages of God and Jesus Christ, they are making affirmations about their view of life and how it ought to be lived. In this way, theology and ethics become inseparable.

We need to be careful not to confuse Lindbeck's claim with those of the neo-Kantian theologian Albrecht Ritschl's (1822–1889).[11] That is, Ritschl is reductionist in a way that Lindbeck is not. Ritschl sees theology in terms of its "relational value" for the Christian family. Lindbeck affirms the truth of theological statements but, when he unpacks their meaning, he shows not only how theology functions linguistically but also how significant their regulative functions are. They shape culture. An example we might draw on here comes from John Howard Yoder, when he says that if we do not believe in the divinity and humanity of Christ—classical doctrines of the orthodoxy creeds—then Christian ethics is anathema. That is, if Jesus is not human, he can hardly be an example for *humans* to

---

[11] See, e.g., Albrecht Ritschl, *The Christian Doctrine of Justification and Reconciliation: The Positive Development of the Doctrine*, 3rd ed., trans. H. R. Mackintosh and A. B Macaulay (Clifton, N.J.: Reference Book Publishers, 1966).

follow, and if he is not divine why would his life be of any greater normative importance to us than any other mortal's? Believing in Jesus Christ, while a theological affirmation, is simultaneously an ethical affirmation about how one ought to live.

Lindbeck's analysis of the three approaches to theology has opened up the possibility of better understanding why there is a diversity of approaches to theological ethics. Why do some ethicists argue for the universality of moral values and seek to impose them on society in general; some for ethics as a personal matter between the individual and God; and others for a view of discipleship ethics with a strong ecclesiology? Lindbeck shows the limits of both a traditional objectivist-cognitivist and a modern subjectivist-noncognitivist view of theology in much the same way as the philosophers do in the debate between ethical cognitivists and noncognitivists.[12]

Although this is not the place to evaluate Lindbeck's model, it is possible to see some big challenges he must deal with. One of the questions which begs to be answered is to what extent his approach leaves us without any ability to speak about transcontextual reality. Or is this not possible at all? Some will argue that his approach ultimately leads to a form of contextualism that is in tension with a biblical view of the world. Nevertheless, one asset of Lindbeck's approach is that it makes clear how theology needs a practicing community to make it intelligible—an important parallel to the claim that Christian ethics without the church is unintelligible.

CHRISTOLOGY AND ETHICS

A contentious topic among Christian ethicists is how Christology informs ethics. That is, what does our belief about Jesus Christ have to do with our view of how we ought to live? It should really go without saying that Jesus is the norm for *Christian* ethics; what

else could make ethics Christian? Yet most Christian ethicists have found the life and teaching of Jesus to be "too radical" for contemporary moral existence.

John Howard Yoder, in his *The Politics of Jesus*,[13] has summarized several ways mainline Christian ethicists have found of making Jesus' life and teaching irrelevant to their ethical construction. I list them here, but since I will have occasion to return to Yoder in a separate chapter, I will not discuss them in detail.[14] Each rationale has adherents in contemporary Christian ethics, and all are premised on the belief that to live as Jesus did is both impractical and irresponsible.

First, the argument is put forward that Jesus was under the false belief that the world was soon to pass away. Hence, the ethic he advanced was but for a short "interim" period. Since Jesus was wrong about this—the world did not pass away—those of us on this side of his error must find other ways of structuring our lives. After all, it is one thing to give to the poor all that you have if you believe the world will end soon; it is quite another to do so when you need to worry about the kid's education and your own retirement. Second, as a simple rural figure, Jesus can hardly help us live in modern, complex societies. A village sociology cannot be the basis of a post-industrial, urban society. Third, Jesus lived in a world over which he had no control and for which he therefore needed to assume no responsibility. In our world, especially in a democracy, we, the people, are the ones who must take responsibility for finding relevant answers to complicated and intricate, moral dilemmas. To refuse to participate in a situation because it could compromise our ideals is irresponsible. Yet it was quite appropriate for Jesus, because his voice had no effect in any case. His world was simply different. Fourth, Jesus' message was not intended as an *ethic* to begin with because his

---

[12] See chap. 9, "Philosophy and Ethics," above.

[13] John Howard Yoder, *The Politics of Jesus:* Vicit Agnus Noster, 2nd ed. (Grand Rapids: Eerdmans, 1994), esp. 4–8.

[14] See chap. 32 below.

was primarily a *spiritual* message, intended to address our inner dispositions. For us to draw specific ethical conclusions from what he said and did is therefore not appropriate. Fifth, Jesus was a radical monotheist (a la H. Richard Niebuhr),[15] and this relativizes ethical considerations to specific situations. How? It calls us to open ourselves to God in every situation so that God can show us what to do. Hence, it is impossible to develop an ethic at all, let alone one based on the discipleship of Jesus, because God can and does call us to violate every ethical system we design. Sixth, Jesus had a specific mission to accomplish, which was to give his life as a sacrifice or ransom for our sins, and this is why he did what he did and not because he wanted his followers to do as he did. For us to imitate his actions is therefore misguided.

These are the six reasons Yoder cites which theologians have given for why we must go elsewhere in establishing a basis for Christian ethics. Where else then do they go? Yoder identifies nature, reason, creation, and reality as alternative moral logics.[16]

I will add one other common reason why some scholars believe that Jesus cannot be morally relevant. This arises from a view which holds that God and Jesus reveal different imaginations. God as Creator is concerned for the entire creation and hence an ethic based on Creator God will entail a defense for all of creation and will be an ethic for everyone. On the other hand, Jesus reveals an ethic which is but for the faithful remnant: people who are signs for the rest of the world. On this logic one arrives at an ethic for only a few dedicated people, who, as Jesus followers, can be radical. Hence, a Christian ethic which is concerned with all of society cannot be based on Jesus but must be derived from Creator God, which is different.

This is not the place to discuss each of these arguments in detail. Actually, our entire study will do this. At this point, I will focus on what it means to say that Jesus is morally relevant—especially what it might mean when accepting a view of theology integrated with ethics as outlined earlier. I will use as a general guide ethicists who have a commitment to making intelligible the notion of "discipleship of Jesus" for the contemporary world—theologians like John Howard Yoder, Stanley Hauerwas, and Dietrich Bonhoeffer.[17] I will not discuss these writers in detail since each receives focused attention later in the book, but I will draw generally on their thought.

When we bring a discipleship ethic together with Lindbeck's theology, we could say that faithful Christians seek to enter the cultural-linguistic imagination of Jesus. That is, we seek to make his "story" our "story," which involves thinking like he did and living like he did. In simpler terms, it means being his followers and pupils; that is, being open to his teachings. Of course, this is no easy task given the cultural distance between us, and so it requires careful translation and often the learning of a new language. Yet at all times it holds before us the challenge of becoming people worthy of the name of the Christ.

Discipleship learning is more than mere head learning. It involves learning to use theological discourse to describe how to see life, one's own and life in society. But it also entails the embrace of a form of life—a community of character shaped by the virtues which emanate from the God-character, Jesus Christ. Such learning involves a "renewing of the mind" and "presenting the body as a living sacrifice," language used by the Apostle Paul in Romans 12.

---

[15] See H. Richard Niebuhr, *Radical Monotheism and Western Culture* (New York: Harper, 1960).

[16] Yoder, *Politics of Jesus*, 19.

[17] See Yoder, *Politics of Jesus*; Stanley Hauerwas, *The Peaceable Kingdom: A Primer in Christian Ethics* (Notre Dame, Ind.: University of Notre Dame Press, 1983), and *A Community of Character: Toward a Constructive Christian Social Ethic* (Notre Dame, Ind.: University of Notre Dame Press, 1981); McClendon, *Systematic Theology: Ethics*; and Dietrich Bonhoeffer, *The Cost of Discipleship*, trans. R. H. Fuller (New York: Macmillan, 1949).

When discussing the idea of being disciples of Jesus, it is important to address the moral-theological imagination that Jesus invites us into. Whom are we to follow? To what are we asked to commit?

I respond to these questions under five headings. First, cosmology. How did Jesus understand the world? From what we read in the Gospels it seems like Jesus believed that all of life was rooted in God. God gives life; God wills to shape life and receive it back. Life is good because it is given by God. Such an orientation has far-reaching implications. It means that Jesus had a distinct view of evil and its place in the world. Of course, evil has power, but it can never be the last word. Since God is good, evil is temporary and will not reign ultimately. If it were not so, God would not be God. The power of God's goodness is ultimate, and therefore evil's power will be undermined. So Jesus responded to evil by not allowing it to sway his path, even when the evil powers sought to kill him. But how does Jesus have the power to do this? It comes from God. God gives the faithful the power to persevere in the face of evil, even when they are fully within its grasp. We know this from the many stories which speak of unexpected return to wholeness and healing.[18]

Second, Jesus' view of the "kingdom coming" is spoken of in unusual ways. His kingdom "strategy" was something that he *proclaimed*: "[The Spirit] has sent me to proclaim release to the captives, and recovery of sight to the blind, to let the oppressed go free . . ." (Luke 4:18). In other words, justice is spoken into being, or more accurately, the kingdom comes with a proclamation that the power of God's justice rules; the power that has kept all the captives, the blind, and the oppressed, "down" is not ultimate; it will pass away. God will liberate, and this is the good news of the kingdom. Similar justice logic seems to be at work when Jesus rejects

the temptations of using power from the top down to bring about his kingdom's goals.[19] That form of power is radically different from the power that Jesus embodies. The power of Jesus to change injustice to justice and evil to good seems lodged in the power of Creator God to re-create and restore what is broken.

Third, and closely related to the idea of justice as proclamation, is the notion that Jesus saw faithfulness to the rule of God coming through loving invitation—"follow me!"[20] For people to learn to understand justice means learning to understand living by invitation, not by force. How does this teach disciples how to live? Through imitation and modeling; for the godly form of life, which is the ethic of Jesus, is "incarnation." Hence, Christian ethics on this "discipleship" approach is all about embodiment. This is why the Apostle Paul can speak of the church becoming the very body of Christ. If the rule of God is incarnation, then mercy and forgiveness are its expression. The response to those who are caught in evil's grasp must be to break the cycle, and that can only happen with a fundamentally other power of God's grace: forgiveness.

Fourth, since the rule of Christ is incarnation, it follows that for Jesus the moral life was in essence not about making decisions in response to personal dilemmas. This had nothing to do with him avoiding difficult situations; Jesus actually had a knack for getting into moral and political trouble. Rather his moral self-understanding centers in two things: giving expression to the love of God (incarnation) and resisting the temptations to take matters into his own hands. He could do this because he believed that God's love was ultimately powerful—the same love from which creation itself flowed. Therefore, even death could be redeemed to life. Because of this conviction, Jesus could concentrate

---

[18] See, e.g., the stories of "The Lost Son" (Luke 15:11-32), "The Good Samaritan" (Luke 10:25-37), and esp. the cross-resurrection story.
[19] See Luke 4:5-8.
[20] There are many examples of Jesus using the language of following: Luke 5:27; Matt 4:19; Mark 2:14; and so on.

on embodying the love of God regardless of consequences.

Fifth, it is out of this imagination that one can understand Jesus' teaching on the love of enemies. All five of the above relevance arguments lead directly to the somewhat unpopular position in contemporary ethics called pacifism. And it is not surprising that each of the theologians I have been drawing from have referred to themselves as such. The issue of pacifism is therefore another way of articulating the divide in contemporary ethics. To clarify further, I look briefly at two different ways of claiming the theological imagination of Jesus.

Recently, during a discussion with someone about the war in Iraq, he told me of the great dedication of a soldier friend of his who was willing to give his life for peace and justice, and how that reminded him of the sacrifice Jesus had made on the cross. Just as Jesus was unselfishly willing to give up everything for obedience to the call of God, so his soldier friend was willing to make "the supreme sacrifice" for the higher cause of peace and justice.

It is worth reflecting on this analogy. Are the two really acting out of the same imagination? Jesus lost his life for what he knew *he could not do* because of his faithfulness to God, and the soldier was willing to give up his life doing what he thought *he must do* in faithful obedience to a just cause. To put it differently, the soldier was willing to sacrifice his life while seeking to accomplish what he believed to be just; Jesus gave up trying to accomplish his goal because he saw no way of doing so without violating the justice of God's ultimate love. For Jesus the matter is put incarnationally; for the soldier it is put instrumentally.

Participating in either of these ways of thinking might result in a martyr-like death, but they emanate from profoundly different—actually opposite—theological imaginations. What is morally praiseworthy is not that someone died for a cause, but rather whether the imagination that leads to the willingness to sacrifice my life is rooted in the incarnational imagination of Jesus Christ.

Although much more could be said about Christology and ethics, I must now move on to a closely related theological topic of the church and ethics.

ECCLESIOLOGY AND ETHICS

The emphasis on discipleship and incarnation suggests that the church is integral for Christian ethics. It is interesting to note that all three of the theologians referred to earlier—Yoder, Hauerwas, and Bonhoeffer—have argued that without the church Christian ethics is anathema. The reason for this assertion is that if ethics is the embodiment of the new kingdom inaugurated by Jesus Christ, then it is a community of character which trains its members to be particular kinds of people. Hence, the church is that community which seeks to be God's people.

There are several important characteristics of the church which help to make its expression as ethics clear. The first is worship. Worship is the most important life-forming event for Christians, since it is the act of opening ourselves to God's creative powers. We saw earlier that Jesus was able to be faithful because he opened himself to the power of God's redeeming love; the same is true for the body of Christ.

Readers may think that it rather unusual for an ethicist to begin with worship. Often there is a tension between the church that sees itself as a moral community and the church that sees itself as a worshipping community. One is seen as centering on God and the other on self and world; alternatively, the worshipping congregation is concerned about spiritual matters and the moral community about social matters. This dichotomy is, however, misguided for theologians who believe the church to be central for ethics. For them, the worshipping community *is* the moral community.

The second characteristic of the church for those who hold a close association between church and ethics has been expressed with the call to let the church be the church.[21] What is really at stake here is the identity of the church; that is, how the church is formed and what is its primary task. Just as important is the identity of moral agent. And the affirmation is that these two are connected in a distinct way. The shaping of a moral community as well as moral individuals takes place when they gather to open themselves to God's transforming power over them in the presence of each other. To let the church be the church suggests that we do not define it, rather it defines us. Its primary task is to be what it is: the body of Christ. Therein lies its identity and, as Christians, ours lies in the church.

The church is the community in which we seek to open ourselves to God's story by telling and retelling this story and by finding our place within that story. It is the community in which we can be honest about our sinful nature, and our perpetual desire to step outside our limits and control things in the direction of our own interests. Here we train ourselves to give up greater and greater control to God, which can free us from the need to manipulate outcome. This, in turn, can help us to love even our enemies because whether they kill us or not is not the ultimate issue here; trust in God is.

A closely related third characteristic of the church is that it *is* a social ethic. Stanley Hauerwas makes the distinction between the church *having* a social ethic and the church *being* a social ethic.[22] In the first model, the church is seen as having a position on war, on feminism, on the environment, on poverty, and so on. This way of conceiving the church makes it possible to separate between what the church is and what it believes and does. It suggests that the church has an identity apart from what it believes and does. On the contrary, the church is what it believes.

Hence, the church is to concentrate on cultivating those virtues which make it worthy of the name Christian.

Hence, the fourth characteristic of the church highlights its virtues, which define both itself and its members. The virtues of the church are most clearly expressed in the stories of Israel; of the life, death, and resurrection of Jesus; and the story of the church itself. In the Bible we read about God seeking to teach the children of Israel that they were to live as gifted people. Because God gifted them with life, food, land, and so on, God's people too are called to live as gifted people to the poor, the stranger, and the weak. What does gifted existence imply? Be patient, God's grace takes time to be received. Be gentle and compassionate as your heavenly Father is compassionate. Love one another. The divine message and reality is that where there is no mercy there is no life. So we are to be merciful people. God rules the world by mercy. God rules the world by the cross. The church is invited to a life expressing this rule.

Hauerwas lifts out one virtue for comment—patience—in order to emphasize its importance for shaping a Christian people.[23] Patience is a basic prerequisite for other virtues like compassion, mercy, and nonviolence, and perhaps especially for people who follow Jesus' invitation to take up the cross and follow him. To be people of the cross requires the art of learning to do nothing. Not doing anything can at times be as significant as doing something, especially for people committed to peace. Jesus exhibited enormous patience on the way to the cross, loving his enemies. Moreover, it must also be emphasized that it is possible for us to be patient because our life is a gift from God—it is being received and hence it is worth waiting for. We could not be patient if we did not believe

---

[21] See, e.g., the chapter "Let the Church Be the Church," in John Howard Yoder, *The Original Revolution: Essays on Christian Pacifism* (Scottdale, Penn.: Herald, 1971), 107–24; and Hauerwas, *Peaceable Kingdom*, esp. 99ff.

[22] See Hauerwas, *Peaceable Kingdom*, 99–102.   [23] Hauerwas, *Peaceable Kingdom*, 102ff.

in the fundamental givenness of life and the graciousness of God.

Notice that this is the opposite view to Kohlberg's, or, for that matter, to the humanist and behaviorist psychologists, who would have us believe that who we are comes from within ourselves. Christian ethics based on the church requires us to believe that who we are is determined by the story we embrace and the kind of virtues this story invites us to embrace. And it trains us to be virtuous through the corporate act of preaching, teaching, praying, and other rituals. We constantly need to be reminded that our life is rooted in God; we constantly need to be reminded of the kind of people we are.

Just like Jesus is made irrelevant for many contemporary Christian ethicists, so the church is often seen as irrelevant for Christian ethics. This is because ethics is usually based on decisions made in personal dilemma situations. The model that I have sketched from the three theologians who hold to the relevance of Jesus for Christian ethics also argue that not only is the church not irrelevant but it is central to Christian ethics.

ESCHATOLOGY AND ETHICS

A related theme and one that links closely to Christology and ecclesiology is the idea of history: what drives it, how do we participate in it, how are we to understand its meaning, and how are we to understand the relationship of history and the establishment of the kingdom of God? This bundle of questions is what theology refers to as eschatology. To relate eschatology to ethics focuses especially on the question of our role in moving history in the right direction.

There are three theological perspectives on the question of the human role in moving history forward. I will address each briefly.

First, the so-called conservative tradition tells us that this process does not really involve us at all. God is working out this relationship, and it will be brought to fulfillment whenever God deems appropriate, and by whatever means God chooses. Human beings are not involved; it is none of our business. Therefore we should stay out of it and concentrate on the more immediate moral matters at hand like family values, sexuality, abortion, and so on.

Second, the so-called liberal position says that the work of God on earth is done by human beings. We are called to bring about the kingdom of peace and justice—what Jesus calls the new kingdom—which is shown to us in the story of Israel and Jesus. This vision suggests that faithful Christians are called to "Christianize the social order."[24] That is, we are to make the world Christian.

The third position is critical of both the conservative and liberal views. It emerges from the view of the church that we have presented above. It says that Christians are not called to Christianize the world but nor are they to consider their role in the kingdom to be irrelevant. They are called to be the church. How is this relevant in the world's peace and justice? The theological conviction behind this view is that God's preferred will is to rule the world via the faithful incarnate expression of God's truth in the church. So by being the faithful church, we are open to being part of the divine agency in bringing about the kingdom. To understand this presupposes a unique view of history.

This view of eschatology sees the relationship between events in history as not necessarily related by the law of cause and effect, as they are normally understood. There are many biblical symbols that express a different paradigm; for example, moving from slavery in Egypt to the exodus, and from hunger in the desert to bread. The primary New Testament symbol for this "logic of history" is the relationship of cross and resurrection. What do all these have in common? In each case it is not the antecedent event that

---

[24] See, e.g., Walter Rauschenbusch's book by this name *Christianizing the Social Order* (Waco, Tex.: Baylor University Press, 2010).

produces (causes) the next event. Rather, the fundamental relationship between each of these couplets involves the blessing of God as primary agent. If we look more closely at the cross-resurrection event, we can say that the relationship between them is one of incarnation-faithfulness-God's blessing rather than cause-event.

On this latter model, the relationship between our faithfulness and God's triumphant victory is of a specific nature. The role of the church is that of the faithful servant community speaking/living the truth of God's mercy as proclamation. We cannot move history in the direction of God's kingdom by force, nor by threat, but by faithfully proclaiming the work of God and inviting all who are willing to hear and to participate.

In conclusion, we have seen that each of the four themes explored—theological method, Christology, ecclesiology, and eschatology—make distinct contributions to the larger discussion of Christian ethics. And clearly theological orientation makes a big difference. The field of theology, as with philosophy, sociology, and psychology, is much too large to be adequately covered in this short chapter, but it is important to point to the rich potential for more in-depth exploration that can only come with careful reading of specific theologians. To that process I now turn.

Excursus

PART II

These four chapters should be read as a systematic and "disciplined" summary of the contemporary state of affairs in matters pertaining to ethics. The reader should see them as the stage for the future of discussion within the academic study of ethics. And the picture is not promising. There is little evidence in any of the four disciplines of the potential for ethics being a viable study offering society anything like a vision for the good life. Instead, everywhere there is the tacit assumption that "the good life," as traditionally understood, is like the dinosaur: a relic of the past. With some writers, this is met with lament, while others greet it with delight.

UTILITARIANISM AND EMOTIVISM

Throughout the section we have seen that conclusions were being drawn from the logic of the Enlightenment. The philosophers, in offering an analysis of the state of normative ethics, almost universally reject the notion that there is something independent of human beings that makes us and society good. Instead, insofar as we can speak of goodness at all, it is either somehow based upon an indefinable sense of duty—deontology, which is the legacy of Immanuel Kant—a view not widely adhered to among current philosophers, or goodness is defined by the instrumental value that is brought about for

society—utilitarianism, the legacy of John Stuart Mill.

In truth, scholars today are less inclined to speak of the good and the right and more inclined to speak of fairness. What seems fair is thought to be more accessible and intuitive than traditional moral language. What is fair has to do with just distributions of things we value—money, property, pleasure, and so on—and just deserts—punishments, reward, praise, and so on. Hence, we have the language of distributive and retributive justice. This leads directly to the language of human rights. Such rights are extended to all humans and are pitted against the scarcity of resources and against the tension between liberty and equality. All of this is the context for the debate on justice.[1] Of course, this is but an underwriting of a form of political realism called democracy; and in a democracy there is little "good" of which one can speak, apart from the democratization of the values that people hold.

There are also those philosophers who wish to return to virtues and character language—scholars like Alasdair MacIntyre and Stanley Hauerwas—but they do so precisely because they understand that the current conception of ethics, in terms of human rights and utilitarianism, is utterly bankrupt as a base for Christian ethics.

---

[1] An example of this logic today is found in John Rawls, *A Theory of Justice* (Cambridge, Mass.: Harvard University Press, 1977); and also his volume, *Justice as Fairness: A Restatement*, ed. Erin Kelly (Cambridge, Mass.: Harvard University Press, 2001).

The metaethical discussion makes the point about the paucity of ethics in yet another way. The philosophical analysis of ethical language is conducted on the assumption of the fact-value distinction. From here it is but a simple truism that ethical language, which is the language of values, not facts, cannot be cognitive language and hence, neither true nor false. Nothing is being asserted, only expressed. While this is an explanation for why moral disputes are irresolvable—an experience familiar to all of us—it is simultaneously an expression for the failure of the discipline of ethics in general.

SOCIETY

Sociologists of the nineteenth and twentieth centuries give a vivid description of how society has changed. Few are more blatant than Robert Bellah and his group in their portrayal of the effects of individualism in contemporary society. Together with earlier sociologists, like Ferdinand Tönnies, who present the results of revolutionary changes brought about in the nineteenth century, they suggest that the notion of society as a unified identity has become unintelligible. What we call society today is but an aggregate of individuals or groups, each with opinions or a set of values. What is good is now derived from contracts we make with one another and rights that derive from these contracts. But the collective sense of goodness rooted in reality outside of social realities is gone. This has implications for important social institutions such as family, church, state, school, marriage, and so on; the implications being that we are permitted to create them to our own liking; and the same applies to what is right and wrong.

The work of Max Weber, Ernst Troeltsch, and Karl Mannheim on the view of religion and church is especially noteworthy for our interests. Weber's view that Christian ethics and politics have little to do with each other exempts politics from a critique that emanates from Christian peacemakers. Troeltsch's distinction between church and sect likewise declares irrelevant any critique of society and state that has its origins in a discipleship ethic. Mannheim's ideology-utopia dichotomy all but insulates the status quo social order from any outside appraisal. It should therefore not be surprising that contemporary Christian ethicists have felt that discipleship ethics holds little potential to address today's ills. When Jesus' radical teachings and the church's counter-cultural stance are seen as relevant to the world, society, and the state, then it becomes a challenge to understand Christian ethics, on one hand, and Jesus and the church on the other.

THE INDIVIDUAL

Modern psychology, like the other disciplines, has also challenged the traditional understanding of ethics. This has resulted in a significant shift in language. For example, the traditional way of speaking about ourselves was in terms of *character* shaped by *virtues*. Hence, we could talk of ourselves as honest or patient or kind. This was possible because we were taught to understand ourselves as participating in a social reality which cultivated such virtues because they were characteristic of the good life. In this way, we opened ourselves to becoming honest, patient, and kind. Modern psychology has reversed this way of speaking about ourselves. We do not live by virtues anymore: we cannot get ourselves to believe in an objective good to which we should commit. So instead of thinking of ourselves as honest or kind people, we think of ourselves as people who are free to act honestly or kindly or not. All of this suggests our focus has shifted away from being to acting and from faithfulness to freedom.

We now see ourselves as *personalities* instead of *characters*. Personalities are shaped by factors like parental relationships or environmental stimuli. Personalities have distinct *needs* and *goals*, both of which are determined by the *values* we freely choose. Each person, of course, has his/her own set of values for which no one but that person is responsible.

As a result, most moral language itself has become taboo. The language of obligation is no longer useable. *Ought*, *should*, and *wrong* are all met with strange responses when used. Why? Because all of these words imply an infringement on personal freedom.

THE CHURCH

Emotivism, the church-sect distinction, and the flourishing of the individual have combined to make practically impossible an ethic in which the church functions at all. An ethic based on Jesus is seen as too radical, and so of course an ethic based on the "body of Christ" is equally "irresponsible." Hence, much of what goes by the name of Christian ethics has sought ways of thinking that relegates both Jesus and the church to the sidelines. We will see in our subsequent chapters that finding ways of understanding the relevance of Jesus and church will be a constant battle among contemporary ethicists.

All of this is to say that developing a Christian ethic that arises out of our convictions about Jesus and the church will be a serious challenge. The theologians who we will examine in the remainder of the book will attest to that. We will find those—Ernst Troeltsch and the Niebuhrs—who will argue for an ethic of responsibility. We will also find those—Dietrich Bonhoeffer and John Howard Yoder—who will present a pacifist and discipleship ethic. And of course there will be many who will present nuanced mediating positions.

The examination of the four disciplines has served to highlight the fundamental issues before us; the remaining chapters should be read as addressing these issues.

PART III

SELECTED TWENTIETH-CENTURY
CHRISTIAN ETHICISTS
•
Section A
Early Responses to the Nineteenth Century

Chapter Thirteen

ERNST TROELTSCH
(1865–1923)

The significance of Ernst Troeltsch for Christian ethics is profound, albeit somewhat indirect. It is not that he had a clearly worked out approach to ethics, but he did have a distinct theological strategy that brought theology and ethics into harmony. In fact, he is one of the first modern theologians who believed that ethics and theology were so closely interconnected that you cannot have one without the other. That is, he would not have disagreed with the convictions expressed in earlier chapters of this book that theology is ethics and Christian ethics is theology.[1] Moreover, he also proposed that the Enlightenment separation of facts and values makes all knowledge, and hence both theology and ethics, impossible. One of his central concerns was to show a way to bring theology, ethics, and metaphysics into unity. His most general answer to the question of how this was possible comes through the articulation of a different way of thinking which he called historicism. History as a category of knowing, doing, and being is the "integrating principle" of his thought.[2]

Shortly before his death in 1922, Troeltsch was asked to write an autobiographical article clarifying his own thought. He begins it thus: "I have no system, properly speaking, and in that I am different from most other German philosophers."[3] But Troeltsch well understood that he could not operate entirely without a systematic framework, nor did he pretend that his method was without presuppositions. Hence he continued in the same article:

> Of course I keep [a system] in the back of my mind, as a basic presupposition, but only to correct it constantly as a result of specific research. I cannot display the system in such an unfinished condition. I can only explain the sequence of my books—which in the case of a systematically orientated person is in itself a kind of system.[4]

By the time he reaches the end of this article, he speaks yet more positively about systems. "Naturally the philosopher needs a system; the system is what makes him a philosopher. His reader, too, or whoever else wants to understand him, must be able to discern his systematic orientation, because only thus can the presuppositions and directions of thought taken by the author be intelligible. . . . The system is what makes comparison with other philosophers possible."[5] Yet Troeltsch's system was unlike that of most philosophers. He tried hard not to let abstract presuppositions determine the content of his theology. The method he used

---

[1] E.g., see chap. 12, "Theology and Ethics."

[2] This chapter draws from Harry Huebner, chap. 2, "The Intellectual Development of Ernst Troeltsch," in *The Continuity of Axiology and Epistemology: An Examination of the Presuppositions of Ernst Troeltsch's Historicism* (unpublished Ph.D. diss., University of St. Michael's College, Toronto, Ontario, 1981).

[3] Ernst Troeltsch, "My Books," in *Religion in History*, trans. James Luther Adams and Walter Bense (Minneapolis: Fortress, 1991), 365.

[5] Troeltsch, "My Books," 377.

[4] Troeltsch, "My Books," 365.

and the content which it yielded served as mutual checks upon one another, which is the key to his unsystem-like system.

Troeltsch was a historicist through and through.[6] This is reflected in his writings both by the theology he propounds and the method he uses in doing so. But equally important, this is also the approach which characterizes his own intellectual development. The description of his method as "it dissolves all dogma in the flow of events and tries systematically to do justice to all phenomena..."[7] can equally well be applied to the evolution of his own thought. It is his attempt to "do justice to all phenomena" within the realm of his own experience as well as within history which results in an intellectual achievement of "continuous development" rather than "a set of dogma." Truth, as he saw it, was not static but was continually evolving.

Troeltsch was attempting to answer the same question the Enlightenment philosophers had struggled with—namely, what is the basis of our thinking and acting? He rejected the passion/desire of Hume, the reason of Kant, the choice of Kierkegaard, and the power of Nietzsche. There had to be something more which would explain why each of the above were thought to be answers. This "more" is what he thought could be found only if one took a long-range historical view of thought. In this respect, he was thoroughly Hegelian.

Troeltsch's intellectual development brings together a wide range of knowledge, especially from three related areas: philosophy of history, theology, and the sociology of values. While some general connections can be made with respect to the chronology of these emphases, they do not fall neatly into any kind of successive order. All one can really say is that there are major periods in Troeltsch's career where he concentrates more heavily upon one aspect than upon another.

EARLY INFLUENCES

Troeltsch was a Protestant (Lutheran) theologian, born in Augsburg, Germany. Perhaps somewhat unusual for a German academic, he had a very broad range of academic interests: theology, philosophy, sociology of religion, and history. While Christian ethics may not have been a narrow focus, he was constantly seeking ways to make the "ethics of Jesus" relevant. But from the start, Troeltsch did not mean that Jesus gave the command that we must obey, rather that Jesus pointed us in a direction of relative embodiment of the love of God and neighbor which we must seek to emulate in our way in our time. This, he believed, was the best way of understanding the relevance of Jesus, and it required a rethinking of both theology and Christian ethics.

Several important factors form the context for Troeltsch's choice to study theology. From his earliest recollection, the question of knowledge was for him an historical one. In this he identifies himself with the philosopher, Wilhelm Dilthey (1833–1911). Yet he grew up in a family preoccupied with natural science and medicine, his father being a physician. Furthermore, he received his early schooling in a humanistic *Gymnasium* (high school) at a time when Darwinism was popular. All this had a double impact upon him. On the one hand, his early studies and his family led him to a naturalistic and materialistic interpretation of the world; on the other hand, his historical instincts suggested to him that there was a different dimension to reality: the historical. This double awareness helped to bring about an early consciousness of the interrelationship of theology, philosophy, and the problem of values. Speaking of

---

[6] "Historicism," or "*Historismus*," as Troeltsch called it, was a philosophical approach which assumed that all human knowledge and experience must take into account the fact of historical change and hence, even truth could not be spoken of outside of this framework. This was a direct result of beginning with the category of history as his methodological building block.

[7] Ernst Troeltsch, *The Absoluteness of Christianity and the History of Religions*, trans. David Reid (London: SCM Press, 1972), 47.

these early influences, he says: "Metaphysics and history were in fact the two extremely significant areas that simultaneously and jointly aroused my interest. This led almost automatically to the systematic study of religion, which places both sets of problems in intimate cross fertilization."[8]

Little is known about Troeltsch's family life. He married late in life because he was preoccupied with studies and getting himself set up to teach in university in his younger years. When he was thirty-six years old, he married the "daughter of an officer and landowner in Mecklenburg"[9] named Maria. Twelve years later, they had their only son, Ernst Eberhard.

It is noteworthy that Troeltsch was friends with Max Weber, and the Troeltsch and Weber families lived in the same house for several years. The friendship, however, ended when Weber accused Troeltsch of unjustly compromising when Troeltsch, as a reserve officer in the First World War, made a decision to permit a professor from Alsace to visit French prisoners of war in a military hospital under Troeltsch's supervision.[10] But intellectually they learned much from each other in their research in the sociology of religion.

For one year of his life (1888–1889) he was an assistant Lutheran minister in Munich, where he was ordained in the St. Matthäus Church.[11] Yet this did not last, as his passion for theology prevailed. He studied theology because he believed that it was only there that the metaphysical and historical questions were being asked—albeit even there they were not asked all that directly. First, (1884) he studied Lutheran theology at Erlangen. But the theologians there were less than impressive to Troeltsch, because they did not give attention to the basic philosophical questions he considered to be of greatest importance. He considered these theologians as belonging to another age—antiquity.

The theology that fascinated Troeltsch most was historical theology, but even that was never to be seen as an end in itself. In fact, theology was always only a means. "The end was the penetration of the religio-metaphysical consciousness."[12] Since the Erlangen theologians were not very helpful in this pursuit, Troeltsch turned to the philosophers. Here his teacher, Gustav Class, was of greatest help. Class, a Leibnizian philosopher sympathetic to German idealism, pointed Troeltsch to Rudolf Lotze (1817–1881), who in turn led him to Kant, Fichte, and Schleiermacher. "But," says Troeltsch, "Lotze was the controlling spirit at first . . . In those formative years I read his books again and again."[13]

It is instructive to note some of the main tenets of Lotze's idealist philosophy, since it finds recurrent expression in Troeltsch's own thought. First, it can be said that Lotze's method was shaped by his response to three great schisms: "The schisms between science and Christianity, which was known at that time as the conflict between science and religion; the schism between religion and feeling; and the schism between knowledge and value."[14] Lotze argued that all of these schisms resulted from a faulty dualistic interpretation of reality. The world is best understood holistically and not dualistically or pluralistically. To this end, the second methodological tenet stresses his view that all philosophical systems must remain open and undogmatic. Reality is far too complex to be understood dogmatically and absolutely.

[8] Troeltsch, *Absoluteness of Christianity*, 47.

[9] Hans-Georg Drescher, *Ernst Troeltsch: His Life and Work* (Minneapolis: Fortress, 1993), 99.

[10] See Drescher, *Ernst Troeltsch*, 125.

[11] Drescher, *Ernst Troeltsch*, 33.

[12] Troeltsch, "My Books," 367.

[13] Troeltsch, "My Books," 367.

[14] Rubin Gotesky, "Rudolf Hermann Lotze," in *Encyclopedia of Philosophy*, vol. 5, ed. Paul Edwards (New York: Macmillan, 1967), 87. It is also noteworthy that the problem of integration, particularly of knowledge and value, is not something Troeltsch considered to be important late in life only, but was something he encountered at the beginning of his career.

It was probably Lotze's influence at Göttingen that attracted Troeltsch there as a student. Unfortunately, Troeltsch was never able to study under him since Lotze had already left for Berlin before Troeltsch got to Göttingen. There, Troeltsch met two other teachers who influenced him immensely: Albrecht Ritschl (1822–1889) and Paul de Lagarde (1827–1891). From Ritschl he learned the independence of religion from nature, metaphysics, philosophy, and history; while from Lagarde he learned the opposite: that Christianity belongs properly among the history of religions—hence, history and philology must become prominent tools for the interpretation of Christianity. Both scholars were to have great influence on Troeltsch's thought. The fact that their thought is so diverse also shows itself in Troeltsch's theology. But even at Göttingen Troeltsch admits that he learned more from the philosophers than from the theologians, particularly in regard to theological method. The most influential of all philosophers was Dilthey; from him, Troeltsch learned that the life of the spirit over against the natural world determined the reality of history. Dilthey taught him the distinction between *Geisteswissenschaften* (historical science) and *Naturwissenschaften* (natural science), which emphasized the difference between the approaches of history and natural science. The latter emphasizes universality, while the former emphasizes individuality. The latter is deterministic; the former is not.

As a result of Troeltsch's encounter with Dilthey, the problem of the relationship between history and nature began to exert itself upon his mind with great force. It is a problem that lies at the very heart of his thought from early in his life to his death. The implications are worked out in two larger groups of issues: first, the relationship between religion and intellectual history, in which Troeltsch had to deal with the question of how religion is fairly expressed in different cultures and—for him especially—the modern world; and second, the relationship between religion and ethics, in which he had to develop a new way of dealing with the Enlightenment problem of the fact-value dichotomy. I will discuss both issues.

RELIGION AND HISTORY

Troeltsch's writing career began with his doctoral dissertation, *Reason and Revelation in Johann Gerhard and [Philipp] Melanchthon* (1891). The significance of this work is often debated, but it is important for our purposes in two ways. First, in this essay, Troeltsch sets the historical record straight by demonstrating that the Protestant Germans, especially the Lutherans via Melanchthon and Gerhard, had remained thoroughly medieval in their thinking. They differentiated themselves from the Catholics only in that they introduced a new emphasis upon the gospel. Why was this important? The standard belief was that the Protestant Reformation was the beginning of the modern era adopting a different way of thinking than the old (Catholic) era before it. Troeltsch argued that, contrary to this belief, Protestant theology is much more closely associated with medieval thinking than is usually thought.[15]

The significance of this conclusion is twofold: first, it allowed Troeltsch to present a new periodization of history where the Enlightenment and not the Reformation was the watershed between medieval and modern life and thought. Second, this explained, for Troeltsch, why both Protestantism and Catholicism had so tenaciously adhered to supernaturalism, a principle which relegated Christianity to a realm beyond history. Any serious integration of Christianity with post-Enlightenment thought would require a change. The notion of a modern,

---

[15] Albrecht Ritschl and Wilhelm Herrmann had both been arguing the modernity of Protestant thought. With this, Troeltsch consciously disagrees although he was not entirely alone. "Dilthey grappled with this theme at the same time and came to exactly the same conclusions, although neither of us knew anything of the other at that time" (Troeltsch, "My Books," 368–69).

supernatural Christianity is a contradiction in terms, and so for Christianity to be relevant to this world would mean that it must be historically, not dogmatically, understood.

The second way in which his dissertation is important for us is that it foreshadows the theological-philosophical concerns which remain of central importance throughout Troeltsch's career. The relationship between reason and revelation belongs to a larger set of issues having to do with the relationship of religion and philosophy generally, or, with religion and intellectual history. How is what we hold to be true regarding religion related to what we can determine to be true by philosophical reflection and/or historical investigation? If religion is wholly subordinate to philosophy, then religion is no more than a human enterprise; if there is no relationship at all, then religion is unintelligible. Already in his first work, Troeltsch can accept neither alternative, and this unhappy dilemma leads him directly to a development of his own philosophies of religion and history, where he deals specifically with the question of how we can adequately speak of knowledge if both reason and revelation, both facts and values, are determined by history. These problems are intrinsically related to the ever-changing social-cultural-historical conditions in which the human mind seeks to make knowledge claims.

After his doctoral study, Troeltsch plunged into a more careful examination of some of these major problems. The ones he treats first arise directly out of his continued double-sided relationship to Ritschl. He explains this as follows:

> [T]rained in the school of Ritschl, I learned very early that two elements were united in the impressive teaching of this energetic and great scholar; a distinct conception of traditional dogma by means of which modern needs and problems were met, and just as decided a conception of the modern intellectual and religious situation, by means of which it seemed possible to accept and carry

forward the teaching of tradition, understood in the Ritschlian sense. The question arose, therefore, quite naturally, first, whether this conception, were true to dogmatic tradition in its actual historical sense, and, second, whether the present situation was being interpreted as it actually is. Then it became clear that from both sides a certain process of assimilation had been completed which did not correspond with actual facts and which did not permit the real contrast to appear in its full actuality. Thus, I found myself confronted by a double task; to make clear to myself both the ecclesiastical, dogmatic tradition of Protestantism in its own historical sense, and the intellectual and practical situation of the present day in its true fundamental tendency. Hence the double nature of my researches—the analysis of early Protestantism and the analysis of the modern world.[16]

All his life, Troeltsch grappled with the question, "How is it possible for Christianity to be integrated with the modern world?" He identifies three main adversaries of Christianity: natural science, neo-humanism, and positivism. He believes that these three influences have shaped the current period of history into an epistemological skepticism, especially for *religious* knowledge, because all suffer from a false dichotomy between knowledge and value. All stress cognition at the expense of valuation, and hence they lose the ground for the possibility of their own evaluation. Moreover, Troeltsch is convinced that his articulation of historicism provides a solution to this problem.

For him the task of bringing Christianity into the modern world is first of all an epistemological matter that asks how we can think or know in a way that is true to our historical nature without rendering Christianity meaningless in the process. To put this differently, how can we bring into dialogue the modern scientific approach, which is based on observation and reason, with Christian theology, which historically has been based on revelation? His answer is that we have to find a new way of thinking about theology not based solely on revelation, that

[16] Ernst Troeltsch, *The Social Teaching of the Christian Churches*, vol. 1, trans. Olive Wyon (New York: Harper & Row, 1960), 19.

is, we must deny the dogmatic approach to theology.

To develop this answer, Troeltsch gives an attentive ear to neo-Kantianism. Kant's critical idealism and Christianity belong together for him as do critical idealism and the quest for knowledge generally. He puts it thus: "Idealistic metaphysics and Christian belief are essentially inter-related . . . they do not overlap in any way but they belong together."[17] The reason for this connection is obvious. Idealism does not make the fact-value distinction in the characteristic way. It holds that what we can know has been constituted within our own consciousness—at least in part—in accordance with the structure of the mind.[18] Our quest for knowledge therefore simultaneously entails discernment of direction and value. To say this differently, all knowledge is always "in order to" knowledge; there is no pure valueless knowledge. And since Christianity, science, philosophy, and psychology all have interests in making this a good world, we can work together in this task. There is no implicit distinction of realms, which makes the quest for knowledge and the quest for the good inseparable quests.

Troeltsch now adds another important component to his thought. He argues for the "sovereignty of the spirit over nature" by relying on Dilthey's thought and in this way defends the notion that the human spirit is free. Nature is determined by laws; the spirit is free. We are "governed" by the freedom of the spirit, which only Christianity, idealistically understood, can properly account for. Notice that this implies a very broad understanding of Christianity. All of science, the arts, and culture are subsumed under the concept of the Christian spirit unfolding as it should. Troeltsch is here very close to the Hegelian dialectic.[19]

Although Troeltsch defends an *historical*, that is, an empirical, understanding of Christianity, he leaves no doubt that Christianity is the absolutely final religion. He means by this that it is by far the best in being able to give an account of the empirical expressions of the free human spirit. What is required at every new age is its defense against the onslaught of new isms. Although his view later changes slightly, in 1894 he puts it this way: "Hence we believe with good evidence, that Christianity has always been and will always be the truth, which frees us from the burden of the world and the pain of sin."[20]

We should take care to notice the logic here, for Troeltsch speaks of a general "religious idea," which has many specific expressions: Judaism, Christianity, Islam, Buddhism, Hinduism, and so on. When he begins his thinking this way, he next needs to ask which one of these many specific religions best accounts for or best expresses the religious idea. And this is an empirical, not a dogmatic, question to which the answer is Christianity.

Identifying religion's task in this way necessitates the introduction of the concept of development. That is, truth is not static but dynamic. Hence, the truth of Christianity is not the same today as it was when Jesus lived it. Yet it can still be either true or false depending on how faithfully it expresses the spirit of the religious idea. At this point, Troeltsch borrows heavily from Hegel, even though he is here critical already of Hegel's identification of religious development with intellectual development. But the language is nevertheless unmistakably Hegelian, as is seen in such phrases as "[t]he inner dialectic of the religious idea. . . ."[21]

While Troeltsch's appeal to Schleiermacher and Hegel is evident, his purpose for doing

---

[17] Ernst Troeltsch, "Die christliche Weltanschauung und ihre Gegenströmungen" [The Christian Worldview and its Counter Currents], 227–327 (1894/1895), in *Gesammelte Schriften* (hereafter *Gesammelte*) II, 248–49. Partial unpublished translation made available by James Luther Adams.

[18] See the discussion of Kant's philosophy, 126ff. above.

[19] See the discussion of Hegel's thought, 131–33 above.

[20] Troeltsch, *Gesammelte* II, 327.

[21] Troeltsch, *Gesammelte* II, 200, et passim.

so is twofold. First, it sets religion on a new footing. As Hans-Georg Dresher summarizes, "We have then an inquiry into religion, freed both from rationalizing constructionism and from any reduction to moral concepts."[22] Second, Troeltsch was attempting to harmonize knowledge and value in a new way, as anyone advocating a historical basis for knowledge must. How is what we can know about the development of any religion finally to be judged? From outside this historical development as the dogmaticians do? Emphatically no! But from within history itself. How is this done? By a historical investigation of how well the fundamental concepts of religion—which he identifies as God, world, soul, and redemption—find concrete expression in the lives of people.

Troeltsch argues that when he applies this test to the great historical religions, Christianity clearly emerges on top. He says:

> The inner dialectic of the religious idea points in the direction of the perfectly individual and therefore universal religion of redemption. It can only be that, because it is perfectly spiritualized and moralized. . . . The strictest scientific objectivity shows Christianity to be most profound, the most powerful and the richest expression of the religious idea. . . . In the personality of its founder and prophet it has the most living and adaptable basis. In this it reverences the guarantee and model of its truth and yet depends not on external and mechanical authority but on the purely religious and moral significance of Jesus and his inner conversion with God.[23]

In other words, the judgment of the validity of Christianity is an empirical and inductive one, not a dogmatic one.

In 1898 Troeltsch wrote an article, "Über historische und dogmatische Methode in der Theologie" ("Regarding Historical and Dogmatic Method in Theology")[24] as a reply to Professor Friedrich Niebergall (1866–1932) and his teacher Julius Kaftan (1848–1926) on the subject of theological method.

It is devoted to setting himself in sharpest opposition to the dogmatic theological method as expressed by Kaftan and Niebergall. The difference between the two methods is one of principle, and hence cannot be reconciled. While the historical method begins with the relativity of historical scholarship, the dogmatic method begins beyond history, with supernatural revelation. Hence, the conclusions of the former are relative, tentative, and concrete, while the conclusions of the latter are dogmatic, absolute, and abstract. While the historical method views history as a realm of the creative interrelationship between God and the human spirit, the dogmatic method sees human beings as utterly sinful, and hence is forced to make the distinction between human history (worldly/secular) and God's history (*Heilsgeschichte*). While the historical method is open to ever-new categories of understanding the historical/religious process, the dogmatic method is interested in developing dogma which will help it in understanding a supernatural God through divine revelation. In the historical method, religion and ethics must necessarily remain relative to history and must be evaluated relative to their historical embodiment.

Troeltsch's main objective in this paper is to show that the historical and dogmatic methods are incompatible. In doing so, he is faced with immense theological problems at every turn. The most obvious problems relate to how it is possible on the basis of the historical method to develop an ethic. Does not the reality of historicism render ethics relative, impossible, and irrelevant? Is not the task of Christian ethics necessarily dogmatic? Obviously, Troeltsch answers these questions negatively. In fact, he wants to argue that it is precisely historicism that gives Christian ethics its integrity because this approach makes it concrete and relevant.

---

[22] As quoted in John Powell Clayton, ed., *Ernst Troeltsch and the Future of Theology* (Cambridge, Mass.: Cambridge University Press, 1976), 8.

[23] Troeltsch, *Gesammelte* II, 200.

[24] Appears in Troeltsch, *Gesammelte* II, 729–53.

Before I summarize his thought on Christian ethics further, I need to explain his historical method in greater detail. It is, after all, not only a method for Christian theology, but also for ethics. In explaining this approach he says:

> The historical method itself, by its use of criticism, analogy, and correlation, produces with irresistible necessity a web of mutually interacting activities of the human spirit, which are never independent and absolute but always interrelated and therefore understandable only within the context of the most comprehensive whole.[25]

It is worth reflecting briefly on this statement. First, Troeltsch mentions three criteria which make historical knowledge possible. Second, these criteria acting on the human spirit make history, and therefore Christianity and ethics, intelligible. Third, the objective is "the most comprehensive whole." In other words, universal knowledge is the ultimate goal here. Christianity and ethics must be able to give an account of the whole of history. This is, of course, a monumental undertaking, and it is easy to see why Troeltsch could not embrace anything dogmatic.

The three criteria or principles that shape the operation of Troeltsch's historicism are important. First is the principle of criticism. In the realm of history, all statements of knowledge are probable statements. Clearly some are more probable than others; however, historical statements are never absolute but always contingent. This means the debate is always on; there is always criticism involving "analysis, correction, and transformation."[26] The process never ends and is always open to the future for new insights and discoveries. The process is also all-encompassing; that is, every tradition is considered and is part of the critical debate; every interpretation of things is brought to the bar of historical critique. Christianity and ethics are not protected by a favored tradition with authority beyond historical critique. What makes sense makes sense before the bar of reason as such.

The second principle focuses on analogy. Although Troeltsch does not explicitly say so, one cannot help but think of this notion in conjunction with Dilthey's views on empathy. Dilthey argues that what makes knowledge of history possible at all is the human capacity for empathetic understanding. For example, we can understand territorial wars of the past because we can understand them today, or we can understand other religions insofar as we understand our own. This does not eliminate difference; instead, analogy is what makes difference intelligible. One cannot appreciate the full impact of this principle until one puts it to the test on some of the difficult affirmations of the Christian faith, like miracles, the sinless nature of Jesus, and the resurrection. Where do these notions have analogues in our current experience? And if they don't, must we simply dispense with them? Troeltsch does not answer this question directly but says that "fewer and fewer historical 'facts' are regarded as exempt from the exigencies of the analogical principle; many would content themselves with placing Jesus' moral character and the resurrection in this category."[27] Given this way of responding, it seems that he is suggesting that all events claimed in any religion must have analogues in ordinary empirical history; otherwise the religion is not intelligible.

The third principle is called correlation or relationism. This is the recognition that all events in history are interrelated; that is, political, philosophical, personal, and institutional forces are all interconnected and none is intelligible without relation to the others. Hence, biblical events, for example, cannot be understood apart from their correlation with other events around them, so he lauds the Bible scholars who have begun to investigate "general political, social, and intellectual history of antiquity."[28] This does

---

[25] Ernst Troeltsch, "Historical and Dogmatic Method in Theology," in *Religion in History*, 15.

[26] Troeltsch, "Historical and Dogmatic Method," 13.

[27] Troeltsch, "Historical and Dogmatic Method," 14.

[28] Troeltsch, "Historical and Dogmatic Method," 15.

not mean that there are no unique forces in history, but even so, "these unique forces also stand in a current and context comprehending the totality of events, where we see everything conditioned by everything else so that there is no point within history which is beyond this correlative involvement and mutual influence."[29]

Troeltsch identifies several consequences of this historicist methodology. First, it "brings a measure of uncertainty to every single fact . . . the historical link between original fact and present influence must remain at least partly obscure."[30] Second, all evaluations and judgments must be done in relation to the whole and cannot transpire from a trans-historical point. This means that the evaluation of Christianity is identical to the evaluation of Greek and Roman culture. There is no fixed essence to Christianity. In other words, Christianity must be evaluated on the basis of its involvement in general history along with every other truth force.

Troeltsch summarizes the consequences of historicism as follows:

> Obviously, this is how the historical method works. It relativizes everything, not in the sense that it eliminates every standard of judgment and necessarily ends in a nihilistic skepticism, but rather in the sense that every historical structure and moment can be understood only in relation to others and ultimately to the total context, and that standards of values cannot be derived from isolated events but only from an overview of the historical totality.[31]

The reader will notice that this way of speaking about theological method has direct implications for ethics. In this approach, there can be no universal, trans-historical values or standards, but all values are situated within the relativities of history. So the challenges for constructing a Christian ethic are huge.

RELIGION AND ETHICS

From what has been said so far about Troeltsch's theological method, it should be clear that his approach to ethics will not fall neatly into one of the traditional categories—utilitarianism, deontology, narrative ethics, and so on. In some ways, his work is in direct continuity with the Enlightenment project; for example, he accepts the language of values as the language of ethics; he accepts the quest for universality as the only way to formulate the truth and value quests, hence, Christian ethics is for everyone; and he rises to Kant's challenge of "dare to reason," hence, universal rationality is a given. Yet in some ways, he is also critical of the Enlightenment, partly, I suspect, because of the influence of Hegel and German idealism. For him the separation of subject and object as the model of knowledge is problematic because the subject is always involved already in framing the historical object. This is the whole point of historicism; it is from the beginning a theology of the involvement of the subject.[32] Likewise, he is incessantly preoccupied with the agenda to overcome the knowledge-value dichotomy because the resultant problems with positivism and scientism make historical knowledge impossible. For Troeltsch there can be no objective science without subjective commitment.[33] All of these are ways he seeks to move beyond the Enlightenment.

Readers might be inclined to be less than charitable regarding Troeltsch's affirmation of historical relativism. "Relativism" seems to be a bad word, but when I read Troeltsch I cannot help but be reminded of the language of the Apostle Paul: "If I have . . . all knowledge . . . but do not have love, I am nothing. . . . Now I know only in part; then I will know fully . . ." (1 Cor 13:2b, 12b). Two of Troeltsch's themes are expressed here: the

[29] Troeltsch, "Historical and Dogmatic Method," 15.
[30] Troeltsch, "Historical and Dogmatic Method," 17.
[31] Troeltsch, "Historical and Dogmatic Method," 18.
[32] For an interpretation of Troeltsch from the standpoint of involvement, see Benjamin A. Reist, *Toward a Theology of Involvement: The Thought of Ernst Troeltsch* (Philadelphia: Westminster, 1966).
[33] This theme is argued by Gregory Baum in "Science and Commitment: Historical Truth According to Ernst Troeltsch," in *Philosophy of Social Science* 1 (1971): 259–77.

inability to know fully and the continuity between knowledge and value (love). Troeltsch is certainly right to argue that such assertions have major implications for both epistemology and ethics, and hence on how we think, teach, and learn.[34]

For Troeltsch, ethics was admittedly a challenging intellectual inquiry, and he spent the last twenty years of his career attempting to work out the obstacles to a viable ethic. Since there are no anchors in history on which values can be based, one must accept that they are generated by life itself. But to make such a claim *simply*, that is, without all sorts of qualifications, rightfully makes thoughtful theologians and ethicists extremely nervous. For, if values arise from life itself, how can one ensure against an endless drift of values where human desires reign supreme? Clearly, this is not the result Troeltsch intends, and so the stakes are rather high for him to show that this is not the implication of historicism.

Already in 1895, four years before "Historical and Dogmatic Method in Theology," he wrote an article titled "Atheistische Ethik" ("Atheistic Ethics").[35] But the bulk of his work comes later with such essays as "Grundprobleme der Ethik" ("Fundamental Problems Regarding Ethics") (1902),[36] "Englische Moralisten" ("English Moralists") (1903),[37] and *Politische Ethik und Christentum* (*Political Ethics and Christianity*) (1904).[38] The problem of ethics and historicism preoccupies Troeltsch even to his last set of lectures (1923), where he gives three presentations under the general heading of "Der Historismus und Seine Ueberwindung," which literally translated is, "Historicism and Its Overcoming" but has been published under the somewhat strange title, *Christian Thought: Its History and Application.*[39]

Troeltsch's struggle with historicism is about holding the relative and the absolute together, which, of course, sounds like an oxymoron. The only way this is even a meaningful assertion is to historicize both concepts, which is what Troeltsch does. He defines "relative" to mean relative to history and "absolute" to mean historically absolute.

The best example of how Troeltsch holds the relative and the absolute together is his argument in the book, *Die Absolutheit des Christentums und Religionsgeschichte* (*The Absoluteness of Christianity and the History of Religions*) (1902). I will show later how he makes analogous moves when he addresses the relevance of Jesus for ethics in our day, but it is important to see how he does this with respect to Christianity since it will have direct relevance to the ethics discussion.

In *Absoluteness of Christianity*, Troeltsch is concerned with showing how Christianity, understood as a historical phenomenon, can still be absolute. As one would expect, he rejects the two traditional approaches. First, the supernatural apologetic is inadequate

---

[34] This is not the place to discuss the implications of historicism on the question for learning and pedagogy, but the implications are substantial. For a discussion of this topic, see my essay, "Learning Made Strange: Can a University be Christian?" in *God, Truth, and Witness: Engaging Stanley Hauerwas*, ed. L. Gregory Jones, Reinhard Hütter, and C. Rosalee Velloso Ewell (Grand Rapids: Brazos, 2005), 280–308.

[35] In Troeltsch, *Gesammelte* II, 525–51.

[36] In Troeltsch, *Gesammelte* II, 552–672. The section, "The Ethic of Jesus," which is part of "Grundprobleme der Ethik" (*Gesammelte* II, 629–39), has been translated by Walter Bense and appears in *The Unitarian Universalist Christian* 29, no. 1–2 (1974): 38–45. Another part has been translated by Donald Miller and appears in *The Shaping of Modern Christian Thought*, ed. Warren F. Groff and Donald Miller (Cleveland: World, 1968), 230–44.

[37] Troeltsch, *Gesammelte* IV, 374–429.

[38] This essay has been translated by Walter Bense and appears in Ernst Troeltsch, *Religion in History*, 173–209.

[39] The lectures in this volume are "The Morality of the Personality and of the Conscience," "The Ethics of the Cultural Values," and "The Common Spirit," in Ernst Troeltsch, *Christian Thought: Its History and Application* ed. Baron F. von Hügel (London: University of London Press, 1923). The story of how this book came by its odd English title is interesting. It was translated by several British scholars because these lectures were to be delivered at several universities in England (London, Oxford, and Edinburgh), but Troeltsch died suddenly before the scheduled date of delivery. Together with the editor, Baron F. von Hügel, the translators agreed that Troeltsch was not successful in "overcoming" historicism and hence decided that the title should not imply that he did. Hence, a title remains mute on Troeltsch's thesis.

because it relies upon miracles to ". . . confirm the reality of what all religious thought demands, namely, the manifestation of religious truth and of a power for life that in principle lies beyond all human fallibility and impetus."[40] Second, the evolutionary apologetic, which argues that Christianity is the most highly evolved religion, is rejected because it argues that "Christianity is . . . identical with [the] principle of religion that is everywhere implicit and that comes to complete explication only in Christianity. . . ."[41] Both are inadequate because they maintain an arbitrary separation between knowledge and value. He maintains further that "both the evolutionary and the orthodox schools of thought desire to obtain this normative value by placing Christianity as a matter of principle in a unique position. They are not content with a *de facto* supremacy and ultimacy. . . ."[42]

He then spells out and defends this *de facto* supremacy, which he modifies only slightly at the end of his life.[43] His argument is that, as a thoroughly historical phenomenon, Christianity is at once individual and relative. "Absoluteness" can therefore not mean abstract universality. It must somehow be brought into unity with historical relativity. To say it differently, historical Christianity must somehow be harmonized with historical religious certainty.

How can this be done? Troeltsch answers this question in two stages. First, "Christianity is the highest religious truth that has relevance for us, a truth on the basis of which an evaluative understanding rooted in religious faith and developed with reference to the religions of the world might be organized."[44] This is a kind of individual absoluteness. He calls it "naive absoluteness," which for the individual becomes the "focal point" around

which all else is interpreted and integrated. Troeltsch cites Jesus as an example of such naïve absoluteness.

> The naïve absoluteness of Jesus is simply his faith that he had been sent by the Heavenly Father and his certainty that just as the will of the Father is the only truth by which human behavior should be governed, so the promise of the Father is the only salvation. The justification for his claim is that it flows from the purest and most powerful religious ideas in a way that encounters the inner man most deeply and compellingly.[45]

The second stage of his answer is: "Christianity is the highest realm of religious life and thought that has validity for us."[46] In this stage of his argument, he puts forward the view that Christianity has a universality which integrates all of human knowledge—including other religions—into its own self-understanding precisely because Christianity is a historical religion which demands the rationalization of all of history from beginning to end. Therefore, all historical phenomena must be subsumed under it. This view of absolutism he calls "rational absolutism."

It is worth pondering these answers further. Troeltsch often has subjective and objective poles to his arguments. And so it is here. The subjective pole, or as he calls it, naïve absolutism, is the position of subjective certainty—the view that maintains as Luther did, "Here I stand, I can do no other." But objective absolutism is different; it puts the three principles of criticism, analogy, and correlation to work and shows how Christianity can bring into a comprehensive whole all of historical reality. Interestingly, he lodges the task of bringing it all together directly with the church:

> [T]he church carefully gathers all the tiny sparks together on her own sacred hearth, where they

[40] Troeltsch, *Absoluteness of Christianity*, 52.
[41] Troeltsch, *Absoluteness of Christianity*, 50.
[42] Troeltsch, *Absoluteness of Christianity*, 51.
[43] He said in 1923, "Such was the conclusion I reached in the book which I wrote some 20 years ago, and from the practical standpoint at least, it contains nothing which I wish to withdraw. From the point of view of theory, on the other hand, there are a number of points which I should wish to modify today, and these modifications are, of course, not without some practical effects" (Troeltsch, *Absoluteness of Christianity*, 21).   [45] Troeltsch, *Absoluteness of Christianity*, 147–48.
[44] Troeltsch, *Absoluteness of Christianity*, 107.   [46] Troeltsch, *Absoluteness of Christianity*, 107.

grow into a mighty flame. Everything true and noble that is conceived in metaphysics, cosmology, psychology, ethics, of statecraft, she draws to herself as a fragment and expression of her own truth and cultivates as an essential part of her own heritage. Thus all the great problems of mankind, and all skill in theoretical thinking, are claimed on behalf of the church, and it is by the church, and particularly because of her supernatural foundation, that they are rightly comprehended and brought to an authentic conclusion. Church philosophy constitutes the rational absoluteness of Christianity, just as the doctrines of the incarnation, revelation, and ecclesiology constitute the supernatural.[47]

Troeltsch's argument for the comprehensive whole should be familiar to present-day, liberal readers. It is the view that responsible Christianity integrates with everything—every area of knowledge, from the natural sciences, to the humanities, and social sciences, and even facets of culture. Today we hear examples of this from many quarters, examples like, "The Christian faith must be expressed in post-modern language," and "There cannot be any tension between what science teaches us about the earth and the theology of creation." Troeltsch would whole-heartedly agree.

Yet the argument in *Absoluteness of Christianity* goes far beyond the view over whether Christianity is the greatest religion. In fact, Troeltsch acknowledges later in his writings that "this book contains the germ of everything that is to follow."[48] Perhaps he makes that statement because in this book he refines the methodology for all his further inquiries. And this is important for our investigation into what he says about ethics.

Troeltsch identifies the underlying problem of historicism with the concept of "normative knowledge." For Troeltsch, all knowledge is normative in two senses. First, there is no purely factual knowledge; knowledge is always laden with values and power,

and hence should be used responsibly.[49] And second, the task of Christian theology is to harmonize all knowledge under the normative vision of the kingdom of God. He says, for example:

> What theology is concerned with is not the history of religion in general but *normative* knowledge acquired through the scientific study of religion. Only this can have meaning for theology. This normative knowledge is not one of many chimaera-like possibilities that hover far off in the distance. It is within reach, and by a practical consensus among wide-ranging circles of influence in our present-day culture, it leads naturally in the direction of Christianity.[50]

We see from all of this that for Troeltsch ethics is a very broad concept; it does not simply name the realm of human moral behavior or social activism. Rather, all knowledge, all institutions, all disciplines of study, the world of politics, everything, is laden with values, and Christianity has a perspective on all of this. It is therefore not surprising that his discussion of the absoluteness of Christianity is thoroughly bound up with his view of ethics.

In 1902, the same year as the publication of *Absoluteness of Christianity*, Troeltsch also published an essay titled, "Grundprobleme der Ethik" ("Fundamental Problems of Ethics"). Here, Troeltsch is critical of the ethics of Wilhelm Herrmann (1846–1922) and Immanuel Kant. For Herrmann, who relies heavily on Kant, the New Testament has only a subjective ethic of the personality. But for Troeltsch, there is also an objective ethic grounded in Jesus' understanding of the kingdom of God. Such an ethic is fundamentally linked to social reality such as the family, state, humanity, and so on. And Troeltsch is critical of Herrmann for not addressing any of these important social institutions. The problem with Kant, as Troeltsch sees it, is that ethics is a purely formal concept.

---

[47] Troeltsch, *Absoluteness of Christianity*, 153.

[48] Troeltsch, "My Books," 370–71.

[49] As we can tell, he speaks about knowledge in language similar to that of Friedrich Nietzsche. Although he works hard at avoiding the nihilistic conclusions of Nietzsche, he frequently cites him approvingly in other areas.

[50] Troeltsch, *Absoluteness of Christianity*, 25–26.

This is inadequate because Christian ethics must find its true meaning not in any formal imperative but in the objective good of the kingdom.

Troeltsch could not tolerate an abstract-universal ethic. In fact, for him, this is a contradiction in terms. Ethics must be utterly concrete. On the one hand, it is a guide for interpersonal relationship and personal behavior; this is its subjective side. On the other hand, it is a guide for the establishment of a just society, forming just social institutions and structures; this is its objective side. Both are particular, and the good of the kingdom should be embodied in both.

Troeltsch saw his own society threatened by "natural egoism, inertia, sensualness, and reduction to the merely given and the immediately factual."[51] This, he argues, leads to a deterioration of objective cultural values. Given these destructive forces, he argues that:

> [T]he family becomes merely an orderly form of sexual desire. . . . The nation-state becomes merely the police protection of material prosperity or an arena of honorable greed. Corporate manufacture and production becomes a mere competitive struggle and a hunt for the dollar. Art turns into mere entertainment and caprice. Science becomes a way to pass the time and a kind of idleness. Religion is then mere revelry and dogmatism. The principles of subjective morality can do nothing to stave off this deterioration.[52]

Troeltsch argues for the relevance of Jesus precisely at the point of helping us see how this deterioration can be avoided. In his, "The Ethics of Jesus," a section in "Grundprobleme der Ethik," he summarizes his position as follows: "The quintessence of Jesus' ethic lies in the content of the moral will and not in its form, and this content is not something that can simply be taken for granted but a task that continues to assume new forms."[53]

What does he mean? First, Troeltsch suggests that what Jesus willed should guide our wills. Second, it is the *content* of the will, namely, its end, that guided Jesus and therefore should guide us. Third, the form, that is, the *way* the end was sought in Jesus' life and in ours, is not normative. In other words, *what* Jesus sought is normative for us; *how* he sought it is not.

In this section of the essay, Troeltsch emphasizes that the *subjective* ethic of Jesus is love. However, this is not the Golden Rule, "Do unto others as you would have them do unto you." Such a humanistic formulation cannot be the center of Jesus' ethic. Instead, "For Jesus, love has a foundation wholly different from this, namely, gratitude toward the Lord who has forgiven all their large debt . . . [to the] perfect goodness of the Father who lets the sun shine upon both the just and the unjust, and who requires his children to be similarly mild and good . . . that is, love's foundation is the common recognition of the divine purpose."[54]

The best illustration of Jesus' "love ethic" comes in his response to the question about the greatest commandment in Matthew 22:37-39. Love of God and love of neighbor nicely encapsulate Troeltsch's subjective and objective poles. As he puts it, "the requirement to love God implies nothing other than the requirement to act out of the individual purpose of the value of the soul, which is to be attained through love and surrender to God, while the requirement to love the neighbor implies nothing other than the requirement to act out of the social purpose of the building of a community of all children of God."[55]

When Troeltsch finally comes to speaking about the *objective* side of Jesus' ethics, he says the following:

> The objective character of this ethic is obvious. It is the specifically religious ethic, the highest and most consistent type of the religious ethic on the basis of prophetic personalism and theism.

---

[51] Troeltsch, "Grundprobleme der Ethik," *Gesammelte* II, 620.
[52] Troeltsch, "Grundprobleme der Ethik," 620.
[53] Troeltsch, "The Ethic of Jesus," in *Unitarian Universalist Christian*, 44.
[54] Troeltsch, "The Ethic of Jesus," in *Unitarian Universalist Christian*, 39.
[55] Troeltsch, "The Ethic of Jesus," in *Unitarian Universalist Christian*, 39.

Moreover, Jesus himself annunciates this fact most clearly. The goal of action and the motive for action is the Kingdom of God. But of course the Kingdom of God is not the relationship among men attained through a common recognition of the law of autonomy as a law implanted in our breasts by God; this is a modern abstraction, wholly removed from the naïve realism of the ancient world. Rather, it is a wonderful gift of God, something completely objective, the community of men in complete peace and complete love, which are both realized in a complete surrender and submission to the perfectly revealed rule of God, under the specific guidance and protection of God; a kingdom in which God will be seen and in which the merciful will receive mercy.[56]

Troeltsch has a particular reading of Jesus' understanding of the kingdom. The kingdom is spoken of as eschatological, but in a particular sense. Jesus did not envision something that was to happen in the faraway future, but something that was imminent. It was to happen—in fact, it was already happening—in this time and space. And it made radical demands on its citizens, like giving away your wealth and not resisting evil. Moreover, it was possible for Jesus to preach these radical moral demands because God was leading the charge and was realizing the kingdom goals imminently.

But such a radical ethic could not be sustained over time. As Walter F. Bense says, explaining Troeltsch's argument, "But now—actually, ever since the passing away of the first generation of Christians, and along with them, of the expectation of an imminent kingdom—such radicalism is no longer appropriate."[57] The radical teachings of Jesus served the purpose of firmly establishing the goals of the kingdom, but what was needed

for the next generation, Bense explains, was "*a more comprehensive and less strictly religious ethic,* for the development of a *relatively* Christian culture, for a *synthesis* between the religious goal and the immanent values of the world."[58]

The cultural synthesis, which brings the ideals of the kingdom into an integrated whole with the concrete realities of human culture, has taken place ever since the early church. Troeltsch identifies three models of this synthesis in church history and characterizes them as follows. First, the Orthodox and Roman Catholic churches have divided the church into two parts: the religious orders who live by the "evangelical counsels of perfection," and the masses of Christians who live primarily by natural law. Second, the Reformation Protestants distinguished between the morality of the person and the morality of the office (or vocation), which is like the Catholic distinction because the latter are also to live by a form of natural law known as "orders of creation." Third, modern Protestantism seeks a synthesis via the notion of "the sanctification of the world," which is about the process of creating a "Christian culture."

Troeltsch is critical of all three attempts at the cultural synthesis. The first two distinguish between the faithful ones who are irrelevant to culture (the religious orders) and the relevant ones who have forgotten about the ideal goals of the kingdom (the masses).[59] Modern Protestantism with its goal of sanctifying the social order, while on the right track, must work harder at the task of replacing the "naïve realism of the ancient world" with a "sophisticated modern idealism," as Bense

---

[56] Troeltsch, "The Ethic of Jesus," in *Unitarian Universalist Christian*, 41.

[57] Bense, "The Ethic of Jesus," in *Unitarian Universalist Christian*, 22.

[58] Bense, "The Ethic of Jesus," in *Unitarian Universalist Christian*, 22 (emphasis in original).

[59] The reader should notice here the implicit operation of Troeltsch's church-sect-mysticism distinction. E.g., the sects, among which he would include the Radical Reformers and their offspring, do not even register for Troeltsch because they would be like the religious orders, simply off the map of the cultural synthesis agenda. Hence, he would perceive them to be entirely irresponsible, socially and ethically speaking. The mystics are likewise irrelevant to the cultural synthesis. And this leaves the "church-type" with the task of bringing the kingdom goals into the cultural realities to the extent that contemporary culture will permit.

puts it.[60] What this means is that we, as individuals and as organizations, should be enlightened about the workings and forces of the contemporary world and into that world inject and seek to realize the ideals of the kingdom. In other words, the challenge is to seek to make the world as holy as the world permits itself to be.

In the end, for Troeltsch, the Christian ethic is an exercise in cultural synthesis or, as he also calls it, an ethic of compromise. In the last chapter of his last book, Troeltsch addresses the relationship between politics, patriotism, and religion. He spells out this relationship around the principle of compromise. Compromise, for Troeltsch, leads to justice precisely because it insists upon taking seriously two realities, in this case politics and religion, which in their ideal forms are incompatible. The creative integration of religion and practical life is what Troeltsch identifies as the innermost meaning of the Christian gospel. It is likewise the task of every Christian and Christian community.

This is not to argue that in such an ethic there can be no principles or ideals. But in themselves they are ethically unimportant.

Their ethical significance is derived from their application to actual cultural settings, and it is important to name some implications in this approach. The position that some churches take to be pacifist or anti-abortion, for example, or any position that has led to martyrdom, must be judged as morally irresponsible on Troeltsch's approach. Why? Because it holds to the belief that ethical norms come from elsewhere than what makes practical, historical sense. In other words, it is a failure to integrate facts and values—and that renders values meaningless. Historicism is to be lauded for its efforts at pushing the embodiment of the gospel that Jesus preached, but it must be questioned at the point of putting the culture and the gospel on a common footing. For the gospel that Jesus preached (the kingdom of God) was already encultured. And as such, Jesus' teaching of love of neighbor embodied a critique of his own culture. Yet it is important to note that, in framing the question of ethics in terms of a relationship between Christ and culture, Troeltsch set the agenda for Christian ethics for a very long time.[61]

---

[60] Bense, "The Ethic of Jesus," in *Unitarian Universalist Christian*, 24.

[61] It is interesting to compare two very different books by this title, written more than fifty years apart: H. Richard Niebuhr, *Christ and Culture* (New York: Harper & Row, 1951); and Graham Ward, *Christ and Culture* (Oxford: Blackwell, 2005).

Chapter Fourteen

KARL BARTH
(1886–1968)

Karl Barth began his theological career by embracing nineteenth-century liberal theology of which Ernst Troeltsch was an exponent. Yet it did not end there. In fact Barth's theological journey can be seen as a profound rejection of the liberal theology he inherited from his teachers. In order to appreciate Barth's approach to ethics, it is important to understand his view of theology, which he has described as a "theology of the Word." He, like Troeltsch, held theology and ethics so closely together that there could be no Christian ethics without a Christian theology, but their approaches were profoundly different.

It is also important to note that the debate between liberals and conservatives in Europe at the turn of the century was not the same as a similar debate in North America. For example, the European conservatives had little trouble with the form-critical approach to biblical interpretation. They employed both lower and higher criticism which, in North America, was rejected by the conservatives. It is perhaps correct to characterize the European liberal-conservative distinction as being on a continuum, whereas in North America the two tend to embrace more radically different approaches to theology.[1] Nevertheless, it should be stressed that in both cases the liberals were more open to accepting the methods and insights of modern scholarship than the conservatives.

HIS LIFE

As we saw with Troeltsch, it is impossible to separate a scholar's life from his thought, so it is important to narrate briefly how Barth came to be what some have called "the Protestant angelic doctor."

Barth was born in Basel, Switzerland, on May 10, 1886. His father, Johann Friedrich Barth, was at the time a minister in a Swiss Reformed Church as well as on the faculty at a local seminary. Later, his father became a professor of church history and New Testament exegesis at the University of Bern, where he placed himself in overt opposition to the liberal theology of the day. Barth's mother, Anna Katharina Sartorius, was also from a preacher family. Her father was a pastor who embraced the orthodoxy of Calvinism. Theology and church ministry seem to have been Barth's destiny from the beginning, and certainly he grew up in a committed Christian family. His brothers, Peter and Heinrich, both became reputable scholars— theologian and philosopher, respectively.

Although Barth was born in Basel, he grew up in Bern, the capital of Switzerland. Here, at the University of Bern, he began his

---

[1] I say this even though Ernst Troeltsch has claimed the radical discontinuity between dogmatic and historical theology as the dividing chasm of liberalism and conservatism in Europe. And as we will see later, to some degree at least, Barth embraces dogmatics in opposition to natural theology. However, it is still the case that Barth's "Evangelical" theology is seen by many North American conservatives as too liberal. For a discussion of the conservative/liberal controversy in North America, see William E. Hordern, *A Layman's Guide to Protestant Theology* (New York: Macmillan, 1968).

studies in theology at the age of eighteen. At first his father pushed him into conservative theology courses, but that did not last long. Soon Barth encountered Kant's philosophy and Schleiermacher's theology, both voices of theological liberalism. He found their writings intellectually liberating. In 1906 Barth enrolled in the University of Berlin, Germany, and there took classes from Adolf von Harnack and Julius Kaftan. Clearly Harnack was the inspiration, especially his book of lectures, *Das Wesen des Christentums* (*The Essence of Christianity*).[2]

It was also during this time that Barth read Wilhelm Herrmann's *Ethik*, which impressed him enormously. Although his father initially resisted Barth's eagerness to study with Herrmann, in 1908 Barth enrolled in the University of Marburg, where Herrmann was a teacher. Here he sat at the master's feet and became a disciple. During his time at Marburg, he also studied under the biblical scholars and the neo-Kantian philosophers. Even here, Barth began to raise questions about their approaches to scholarship; nevertheless, the overriding response was one of embrace—the critique was to come later. It is interesting that Barth "never pursued doctoral studies in theology,"[3] and it is amazing that this never deterred him in his university teaching career. His authentication as a scholar came from his preaching, lectures, and his writing, especially his *Epistle to the Romans*.

Given his strong commitment to the church, it is hardly surprising that Barth was ordained to the ministry (by his father) in 1908. After a two-year stint as an assistant pastor in Geneva, he became the leading minister of the Reformed church in the village of Safenwil in northern Switzerland. Here he served for ten years, 1911–1921. While he was in Safenwil, he renewed his friendship with Eduard Thurneysen, who was now a pastor in a neighboring village, Leutwil. They had been fellow students at Marburg.

Barth and Thurneysen became part of a movement called Christian Socialism because they felt it tied in closely with what they were preaching every Sunday. They saw the vision inherent in socialism as closely connected to the biblical vision of the kingdom of God.

Church ministry was very important to Barth. Here is what he says about his vocation as a minister:

> Once in the ministry, I found myself growing away from those theological habits of thought and being forced back at every point more and more upon the specific *minister's* problem, the *sermon*. I sought to find my way between the problem of human life on the one hand and the content of the Bible on the other. As a minister I wanted to speak to the *people* in the infinite contradiction of their life, but to speak the no less infinite message of the *Bible*, which was as much of a riddle as life.[4]

In 1913 Barth married a talented, young violinist named Nelly Hoffmann. She was barely twenty years old when they married, and he was twenty-seven. She was a confirmation candidate in his first class as a minister in Safenwil, and they became engaged when she was only eighteen years old.[5] Her father, a lawyer, had died when she was very young, and so she had been raised entirely by her mother. A year after their marriage, they had their first child, a daughter. Over the next seven years, they had four sons. One of their sons, Markus, also became a theologian.

On August 1, 1914, the First World War started. This sparked an immediate crisis for Barth in two ways. First, "the war raged through all my sermons, until finally a woman came up to me and asked me for once to talk about something else."[6] The second

---

[2] Adolf von Harnack, *What Is Christianity? Lectures Delivered in the University of Berlin during the Winter Term 1899–1900*, trans. Thomas Bailey Saunders (New York: G. P. Putman's Sons, 1904).

[3] David L. Mueller, *Karl Barth* (Waco, Tex.: Word, 1972), 17.

[4] Karl Barth, *The Word of God and the Word of Man*, trans. Douglas Horton (New York: Harper & Row, 1957). Quoted from Mueller, *Karl Barth*, 19 (emphasis in original).

[5] Eberhard Busch, *Karl Barth: His Life from Letters and Autobiographical Texts*, trans. John Bowden (Philadelphia: Fortress, 1976), 93.

[6] Busch, *Karl Barth*, 81.

crisis was much deeper. Barth reflects on an event that shook him to the core shortly after the war began:

> [N]inety-three German intellectuals issued a terrible manifesto, identifying themselves before all the world with the war policy of Kaiser Wilhelm II and Chancellor Bethmann-Hollweg. For me it was almost worse than the violation of Belgian neutrality. And to my dismay, among the signatories I discovered the names of almost all my German teachers (with the honorable exception of Martin Rade).[7]

Barth saw this act as a symbol of the utter moral failure of theology. He began to believe that the ideology of integration of theology with culture made theology powerless in the face of an ideology of war. And he saw in this manifesto how easily the Christian faith could turn "into intellectual 42 cm cannons."[8] And if such heresy was possible for thinking intellectuals, how much easier might it be for the masses! Shaken to the very foundation of his being, he wrote a private letter expressing his critique of the state of Christian scholarship to Martin Rade who, without Barth's permission, published the letter. So now the critique of his former teachers was public, and it would only grow more intense in the years to come.

After his ministry at Safenwil, Barth began his tenure of teaching: first at Göttingen from 1921 to 1925, at Münster from 1925 to 1930, and then at Bonn from 1930 to 1935. All of these teaching posts were in Germany. But in 1935, because he refused to swear allegiance to Adolf Hitler, it was no longer possible for him to teach in Germany so he went to Basel, Switzerland, where he taught until his retirement in 1962, at the age of seventy-six. Each of these universities represents different writing projects—from his *Epistle to the Romans* in 1922 to his *Church Dogmatics*, written mostly during his years in Basel.

The monumental output of Barth—his *Church Dogmatics* alone is thirteen volumes and an estimated six million words—would not have been possible without some diligent support from a valuable assistant and trusted friend, Charlotte von Kirschbaum. He first met "Lollo," as he called her, while teaching in Göttingen. She was thirteen years younger than Barth, a Red Cross worker trained in secretarial skills. She became interested in Barth's projects and was eager to help him with his research and writing. Barth says she was his "faithful fellow-worker. She stayed by my side and was indispensible in every way."[9] They worked together for many hours a day, traveled together, took vacations together, and for at least three decades she literally became part of the family and lived in the Barth household.

While this arrangement was of great benefit to Barth personally, it clearly put great stress on other family members, not the least of whom was his wife, Nelly. Says Eberhard Busch, his biographer and personal assistant for the last few years of Barth's life after Charlotte became ill:

> [Charlotte's] readiness to throw in her lot with Karl Barth in this way was, of course, a risk for her: she put herself in an extremely unprotected position. Many people, even good friends, and not least his mother, took offence at the presence of "Lollo" in Barth's life, and later even in his home. There is no question that the intimacy of her relationship with him made particularly heavy demands on the patience of his wife Nelly. Now she had to retreat into the background. Nevertheless, she did not forsake her husband. . . . it was very difficult indeed for the three of them to live together. Barth himself did not hesitate to take the responsibility and the blame for the situation which had come about. But he thought it could not be changed. It had to be accepted and tolerated by all three. The result was that they bore a burden which caused them unspeakably deep suffering. Tensions arose which shook them to the core. To avoid these, at least to some extent, was one of the reasons why in future Barth and Charlotte von Kirschbaum regularly moved to the Bergli during the summer vacation.[10]

---

[7] Busch, *Karl Barth*, 81.
[8] Busch, *Karl Barth*, 81.
[9] Busch, *Karl Barth*, 185.
[10] Busch, *Karl Barth*, 185–86. ("Bergli" was a summer house on Lake Zurich where Barth spent many hours writing.)

Regardless of the difficulties of the arrangement, adjustments were made by all concerned and it continued until 1965 when "Lollo" was diagnosed with a "brain disease" and could no longer assist him in his writing. She was eventually admitted to a nursing home and died ten years later in 1975.

Barth died not having finished his *Church Dogmatics*. And perhaps this was as it should be or as it needed to be. He did not consider himself as having the last word on theology. He said, "I see . . . the *Church Dogmatics*, not as a conclusion but as the opening of a new conversation."[11] But he did die writing. The lecture he was preparing for delivery was left in mid-sentence. He was found in his bed by his wife on the night of December 10, 1968, with the music of Mozart—his favorite composer—playing in the background. It was to have been his wake-up call.

LIBERAL THEOLOGY

Barth's thought goes through an interesting process of change. As we have seen, he begins as a liberal but then becomes liberalism's chief critic later in life. It is important to understand what exactly he was up against in early twentieth-century European theology and what he saw as the main issues.

Ernst Troeltsch, who died in 1923 at the height of his career, was one of the dominant spokespersons for liberal theology. His was an example of an attempt to capitalize on the progress that had been made in all areas of theology in the nineteenth century. Troeltsch's effort was to articulate an approach to theology which, in many respects, would approximate the methodology of science. This new scientific theology spread its tentacles in many directions.

First, biblical studies were affected. The study of biblical interpretation received much attention in the nineteenth and twentieth centuries. Great strides were made in finding ways of reading the Bible with the aid of techniques intended to get at what the authors were *really* saying. The art of literary criticism and the approach of historicism set new standards for students of the Bible.

Second, the historical school of religions became the dominant form of religious studies. For Christian theologians, this meant studying Christianity from the standpoint of what it means to be religious, or how Christianity participates in the religious idea. Hence, one studies Christianity in relation to other religions, the assumption being that you can best understand it when you understand it comparatively, by determining what makes it both the same and different from Judaism, Hinduism, Islam, and so on. The theory is that once you have understood the differences then you have understood the essence of Christianity. The more traditional approach assumes that you can understand Christianity best in relation to itself, that is, by studying how each facet has meaning in relation to the others.

The third component of liberal theology is that it believes Christianity is inseparably related to culture. That is, one understands Christianity best when one sees how it answers the questions, issues, and concerns of the local culture. It is, after all, an embodied and lived faith. So culture becomes the idiom of theology. Contemporary art forms, particular language, the needs and experiences of the people—all form the cradle of theology.

This approach led quite naturally to a fourth dimension of liberal thought, namely, theology's reduction to philosophy. The intellectual relationship between Martin Heidegger, the philosopher, and Rudolf Bultmann, the New Testament theologian and "disciple" of Heidegger, is an example of this dynamic. Heidegger developed an anthropology quite apart from any Christian content. Although he speaks of faith, hope, optimism, possibility, meaning, existence—all of which have to do with basic human experience and reality, and hence with theology—he seldom makes reference to God and never to the Bible and Jesus. In Bultmann's reliance on Heidegger,

---

[11] Busch, *Karl Barth*, 488.

he tended to accept that theology was informed by philosophy and not only by biblical revelation.

A fifth dimension of liberal thought was another kind of reductionism, namely, from theology to ethics. This was especially evident in the thought of Albrecht Ritschl and played special havoc with the church because it redefined it as a purely social force in society. This places worship in juxtaposition to ethics and truncates both. Moreover, when theology becomes ethics, then Christianity and civilization become virtually synonymous. Hence, mission work is relegated to places that are "uncivilized," and the gospel is in danger of confusion with cultural enlightenment.

Each of these dynamics played a role in the formation of Barth's thought. But what made them particularly powerful was that they were embodied in some spirited teachers.

BARTH'S TEACHERS

Two of Barth's teachers are worth specific mention, Harnack and Herrmann. Adolf von Harnack (1851–1930) was a church historian teaching at Berlin who considered one of the chief errors of Christianity to be its excessive reliance on orthodox doctrines. His major study, *Outlines of the History of Dogma*,[12] convinced him that the "essence of Christianity" lay not in dogmatics but in history. In this he agreed with the theology of Ernst Troeltsch. History and dogma (insofar as one can speak about dogma at all) are inseparable. Dogma is dangerous because Christianity is not a speculative religion but a lived faith.

With this as his basis, Harnack, in a lecture series delivered in 1899 and 1900 at the University of Berlin and later published as *Wesen des Christentums* (*What Is Christianity?*), suggests that there are three essential components to the religion of Jesus which are of permanent value. All the rest is due to cultural contextualization. As James D. Smart summarizes it:

> To reach the simple essence of Jesus' religion . . . the historian had to strip away the temporary expressions of it that concealed what was of permanent value. The Jewish forms in which it first clothes itself, and then the Hellenistic ones that followed, did not belong to the essence, but Harnack was confident that "anyone who possesses a fresh eye for what is alive and a true feeling for what is really great" will have no difficulty in distinguishing the essence from the temporary elements. "The Christian religion is something simple and sublime: it means one thing and one thing only: eternal life in the midst of time, by the strength and under the eyes of God."[13]

Harnack specified three essential elements of Christianity or, as he says, the teachings of Jesus: First, the kingdom of God and its coming; second, God the Father and the infinite value of the human soul; and, third, the higher righteousness and the commandment of love.[14] All the rest is dispensable and due entirely to the powerful cultural forces, like the Greek philosophical tradition or Judaism. The process of developing a speculative theology with the aid of the Trinity, incarnation, or the two natures of Christ, which was already begun by Paul because of his embrace of Greek thought, should never have been given the seriousness which elevated these items to the status of correct doctrine. It was the religion of Jesus—consisting essentially of the Lord's Prayer and the Sermon on the Mount—which alone are central. The miracles, eschatology, the mythical representations, and the doctrinal formulations in the New Testament are all dispensable.[15] But Harnack, like Troeltsch before him, insisted on the uniqueness and absoluteness of Christianity in relation to the other world religions. Also like Troeltsch, absoluteness was determined on the basis of historical, not speculative, reason.

Wilhelm Herrmann (1846–1922) was a teacher at the University of Marburg, where

---

[12] Adolf von Harnack, *Outlines of the History of Dogma*, trans. Edward Knox Mitchell (Boston: Starr King, 1957).

[13] James D. Smart, *The Divided Mind of Modern Theology: Karl Barth and Rudolf Bultmann 1908–1933* (Philadelphia: Westminster, 1967), 31.   [15] Smart, *Divided Mind*, 32.

[14] von Harnack, *What Is Christianity?*, 55.

Barth studied, who made a greater impression on Barth than did either Harnack or Troeltsch. Herrmann considered himself a conservative and hence, served as somewhat of a check against the liberalism of Harnack and Troeltsch. Yet, like Harnack, he argued that the creeds did violence to the soul of every person. Nothing should be confirmed as true until it is true for that person. Christianity is fundamentally concrete, and to affirm church creeds *universally* is to abstract the faith of the church in a way it ought not to be done. Christianity is a religion of the human spirit not of dogma.

So why then did he consider himself a conservative theologian? Because the liberals did not take seriously enough the authority of Scripture, especially as it finds its basis in special revelation. They felt that everything could be understood from our side of the great divide between God and us. Liberals did not see the full implications of the failures to stress that God comes down to us first. This is the very tenet that was to become the point of departure for Barth's theology later in his life.

Herrmann affirmed the transcendence of God and hence, the notion of special revelation through Jesus. This led him to argue that a science of religion was impossible. Such a science is a way of constructing religious thought on the basis of empirical necessity and common understanding—on cultural and human-determined knowledge—not on the basis of special revelation. Since the latter is an essential component of Christianity, you cannot understand Christianity through a scientific approach. God chooses to reveal whatever knowledge God wants us to know. We are not called on to figure it out as we do through scientific understanding. This would limit God's power of revelation to our scientific categories of understanding.

In his *Ethik*[16] (*Ethics*), which first appeared in 1905 and was revised four times (this is significant because it shows how much it was being read and discussed, not because it points out how inadequate earlier editions were), Herrmann is seen as relying essentially on Kant and Schleiermacher for his ethical beginnings. God is revealed via goodness and can be known through human conscience. For example, children see God for the first time in the goodness of their parents, and this shapes their own conscience into a moral power for the future. Yet in Jesus we see a perfect goodness which no human being can match. Hence, we always remain morally dependent upon Jesus for the shaping of our morality. And how does Jesus shape our lives? We can be confronted by the person of Jesus through the reading of Scripture and an opening of our lives to Jesus.

EARLY THEOLOGY OF BARTH

There are several themes in Barth's early theology I will comment on briefly: first, his early response to liberalism; second, his friendship with Thurneysen; third, his response to World War I; fourth, his *Epistle to the Romans*; fifth, the Barmen Declaration; sixth, his *Nein* to Emil Brunner; and seventh, his view of the state.

Early Thoughts on Liberalism

Barth began theologizing as a liberal. Yet it is fair to say that even in the early stages of his thought he was not entirely happy with this theology. He wrote two articles in the beginning of his career that demonstrate this. The first article, written when he was twenty-three, he entitled, "Modern Theology and Work in the Kingdom of God" (1909).[17] He had been asked why so few students educated as liberals go into foreign mission work, and this article was his reply. So why is it the case? Is it because they do not know what they believe? Is it because they have no belief? Or is it because they cannot distinguish between matters of faith and matters

---

[16] Wilhelm Herrmann, *Ethik* (Tübingen: JCB Mohr Paul Siebeck, 1913).

[17] First published as, "Moderne Theologie und Reichsgottesarbeit," in *Zeitschrift fuer Theologie und Kirche* (Tübingen: JCB Mohr Paul Siebeck, 1909), 317–21.

of society/culture? His answer is that liberal students take far more time to formulate their faith than conservative students. This, he says, is so for two reasons: first, liberals demand that students think for themselves, and that the salvation that they find is for themselves. Consequently, they do not know what they have to say to people in other cultural contexts. Second, the historical-scientific approach exposes all knowledge as relative. This leads to a kind of insecurity on the part of liberal students.

The second article appeared a year later and was titled, "The Christian Faith and History" (1910).[18] Here Barth challenges the dominant liberal theologians, Friedrich Schleiermacher (1768–1834) and Albrecht Ritschl (1822–1889). Both had assumed the close interconnection between culture and theology. Barth argues that given their theology, which he was at this stage not willing to abandon entirely, we must find ways of keeping God from disappearing out of history. In order for us to do theology properly, we have to find meaningful ways of talking about God acting in history. How do we do this? Barth answers: through the "experiences of God, direct consciousness of the presence and activity of the superhuman supernatural and therefore absolute transcendent life power."[19] The historical Christian faith must be in some kind of continuity with a transhistorical reality. Otherwise it is simply baseless human projection.

At this early stage in his writing career, Barth does not yet fully understand the impact of his claims. The radicalness was to be stated only later. Yet already here he is clear about the agenda of theology for modernity. If the historical approach of the liberals cannot find ways of speaking meaningfully about God acting in history, then all we are really talking about is sociological theory. And, for theologians, that is not enough.

Influential Friendship

Barth's ten-year stint of ministry as a pastor in a church at Safenwil, Switzerland, had a profound effect on his theology. He tells an interesting story about an event that resulted in his radical shift away from liberalism. Through Thurneysen he met an evangelist, Christoph Blumhardt, whose father had once healed a girl of demon possession. The son was now conducting healing services based on the power of a personal God who wills to heal the peoples of this world. One day Barth was a participant in a meeting where Blumhardt was engaged in an act of faith healing. When Barth reflects on this, he says that liberal theology has no way of explaining this event. It has no categories for understanding how this kind of event is possible. Why is this? Because liberal theology begins with ordinary, cultural reality, and in our day we don't talk about demon possession. Hence, neither can there be talk about faith healing. These two things go together, and our culture is destroying a theology of the presence of God.

Barth maintained that theology must be able to account for "Jesus the conqueror," one who can heal our ills, just as readily as any ancient theology. This reality cannot be dispensed with by history. To do so would be to dispense with the gospel itself. The Jesus of the gospel is just as apropos for us today as he was two thousand years ago.

World War I

The First World War had a very profound impact on Barth's theology. Chief among the reasons for this was the support for the war given by his former liberal teachers of theology. Says James Smart:

> How far all these influences had reached by Sept. 4th, 1914, one cannot say exactly, but we know that on that day one theological era came to a decisive end for Barth and another era began. War had been underway for one month when a

---

[18] First appeared as, "Der Christliche Glaube und die Geschichte," in *Schweizerische Theologische Zeitschrift* (Tübingen: JCB Mohr Paul Siebeck, 1912) in two installments, 1–18; 49–72.

[19] Smart, *Divided Mind*, 48.

Manifesto appeared in Rade's *Die christliche Welt*, signed by a whole array of German theologians, to give a religious validation to the Kaiser's war. On the Manifesto were the signatures of Barth's most respected teachers. In a letter to Thurneysen that day he wrote: "The unconditional truths of the Gospel are simply suspended for the time being and in the mean time a German war-theology is put to work. . . . Here is sufficient proof that the 'truths' were nothing more than a surface varnish and not an inmost possession of this *Christliche Welt* Christianity. It is truly sad. Marburg and German civilization have lost something in my eyes by this breakdown, and indeed forever." . . . "Disillusioned by their conduct, I perceived that I should not be able any longer to accept their ethics and dogmatics, their biblical exegesis, their interpretation of history, that at least for me the theology of the nineteenth century had no future." A failure in ethics revealed in him a bankruptcy in theology.[20]

With liberal theology's support for the war, Barth saw the final collapse of whatever hope there was in liberal theology. Christianity and Western culture had in fact become one and the same thing. And this was a desecration to Christ. Christianity is always a judgment on culture, and this war was God's judgment on human sin. But even more important for Barth as a theologian, this war was God's judgment on liberal theology: the complicity between culture and religion.

Barth begins to see no alternative but to separate himself from the theology of his teachers. The next phase of his thought therefore consists of a parting of the ways with liberal thought. His theology now begins the slow, 180-degree turn away from the approach that starts with human experience toward an approach that begins with God's revelation. This marks a fundamentally different way of doing theology. All the issues change with this approach. Liberals spoke of the human predicament, human sin, human faith, and the religious experiences, but were

unable to give satisfactory answers to these issues. Why? Because their answers came from within history. The answer to the human predicament lies beyond history—in God. In other words, Barth's alternative to liberal theology was to let theology be theology (word of God), not anthropology (word of man).

Epistle to Romans

In 1919 the first edition of *Römerbrief* (*Epistle to the Romans*)[21] appeared. As with Augustine, Luther, and Calvin, for whom the book of Romans also served as a launching pad for their theology, for Barth this commentary served to give expression to the absolute sovereignty of God. Here lay the answer to liberal theology!

When Barth began his commentary on Romans in 1916, he was at a point of theological crisis. He had simply taken for granted that he would do theology in the mode of Schleiermacher. That is, theology was all about how to say what needs to be said in a culture that determines the form for saying it. But if this was no longer adequate, where should he turn for new theological beginnings?

As he was discussing this dilemma with his friend Thurneysen, they decided to turn to the Bible and reread the Old and New Testaments. Says his biographer of Barth's resolve, "[I] began to read the book of Romans as though I had never read it before. I wrote down carefully what I discovered, point by point. . . . I read and read and wrote and wrote."[22] He continues his reflection on this process thus: "At this time I was still in the process of coming out of the eggshells of the theology of my teachers."[23] But in all of this he opened himself to listening, as he had never listened before, to the voice of Paul, and what Paul was saying about the truth of the biblical testimony.

---

[20] Smart, *Divided Mind*, 67.

[21] Karl Barth, *Römerbrief* (Bern: G.A. Bäschlin, 1919); ET, Karl Barth, *The Epistle to the Romans*, trans. Edwyn C. Hoskyns (London: Oxford University Press, 1968).

[23] Busch, *Karl Barth*, 99.

[22] Busch, *Karl Barth*, 98.

And what did he hear in this process? He heard both the voice of God and the voice of modern culture; and they were vastly different. The theology of culture was saying: "Everything had always already been settled without God."[24] But the Apostle Paul tells us that the more zealous people become in their work for God, the more they are a hindrance to God's ways. "Our 'movements' . . . stand directly in the way of God's movements; our 'causes' hinder his cause, the richness of our 'life' hinders the tranquil growth of the divine life in the world . . . the collapse of our cause must demonstrate for once that *God's* cause is exclusively *his own*. That is where we stand today."[25]

It is interesting that during the time of his writing of *Epistle to the Romans*, Barth was also very actively involved in the movement of Christian Socialism. In fact, his involvement was so intense that many people in his church felt this was a hindrance to his ministry, and he became known as a "comrade pastor." At one point, the church sought to ban him from his political activity but, of course, that did not work. I mention this here because it was not as though his emphasis on the priority of God's act meant that we should do nothing politically. Instead it meant a careful discerning of where God was at work, and from there to seek to humbly participate in what God was already doing.

In 1918 he finished his commentary, but he had a hard time finding a publisher. No mainline publisher would accept it. However, eventually, it was published; only two years later, he began to revise it, and in 1922 the second edition was published. In the second edition, he emphasized even more strongly the biblical teaching of the sovereignty of God and the doctrine of revelation. For Barth had come to believe that the liberal tradition was simply not able to acknowledge God as God.[26] That is, liberal theology had become humanist.

What was the approach that would let God be God? Barth called it the *dialectical* approach or *crisis theology*. This was an effort to juxtapose God and human beings over against each other. Robert Willis quotes Thomas Torrance to explain this approach as follows:

> Theological thinking is inescapably dialectical because it must be a thinking by *man* not from a centre in himself but from a centre in *God*, and yet never seeks to usurp God's own standpoint. It is dialogical thinking in which man remains man but in which he meets God, listens to him, answers him, and speaks of him in such a way that at every point he gives God the glory. Because it is dialogical, it can only be fragmented on his side, for it does not carry its co-ordinating principle in itself, but derives it from beyond itself in God's Word.[27]

Barth calls this *crisis theology* because the word "crisis" in Greek means separating, dividing, or judgment. Hence, this kind of theology points to a radical transcendence of God. God is "wholly other" and unknowable on our initiative. And yet, God can be known in Jesus Christ because of God's act of self-disclosure. Jesus Christ is transcendence in history—an oxymoron, or paradox—and certainly nothing liberal theology can explain; every effort at explanation ends in reductionism. Crisis theology is also judgment since it affirms the unequivocal sinfulness of this world. The world stands in need of redemption, and only God can redeem it. No human being can escape the crisis this places us in. We are damned; only God can save us. We cannot know God unless God takes the initiative.

Two scholars of great influence on Barth's thinking during this time were Franz Overbeck (1837–1905) and Søren Kierkegaard (1813–1855). From Overbeck he learned that Christianity and history were in fundamental opposition to each other. Listen to some of Overbeck's claims.

[24] Busch, *Karl Barth*, 99.
[25] Busch, *Karl Barth*, 100 (emphasis in original).
[26] Busch, *Karl Barth*, 119.
[27] Robert E. Willis, *The Ethics of Karl Barth* (Leiden: E. J. Brill, 1971), 23 (emphasis in original).

Whoever seeks to represent Christianity as a historian does so only against the will of Christianity. . . . History is an abyss into which Christianity is cast wholly against its will. . . . Historical Christianity, that is, Christianity subject to time, is something absurd.[28]

To this, Barth responds approvingly by saying, "Relentlessly he [Overbeck] puts us before the choice: if Christianity, then not history; if history, then not Christianity."[29]

An ahistorical Christianity was, of course, not Barth's original invention. Kierkegaard, before both him and Overbeck, had already propounded the errors of historical Christianity. Barth learned much from Kierkegaard, who had advocated a dialectical theology of his own, the unknowability of God, the sinfulness of human nature, paradox, and the absurdity of the incarnation. None of these emphases were new to Barth. Yet Barth was not an existentialist, at least not in the mode of Kierkegaard. And the place where this finds clearest expression is in his affirmation of the historical reality of the one unhistorical event—Jesus Christ. This is where time and eternity, life and death meet, and hence this is where we find the source of knowledge.

Jesus was the *word* of God made flesh in history. It is in Barth's more mature theology that this notion gets spelled out in detail. The notion of the centrality of the word of God required a whole new orientation to theology. This is what Barth set out to do in his *Church Dogmatics*, the first volume of which appeared in 1932.

But before the *Church Dogmatics* appeared, Barth had some other work to do. He was now actively teaching at Göttingen (1921–1925) and was beginning to think about his treatise on Dogmatics.[30] His first volume on "Dogmatics" (which he later abandoned) appeared in 1927 and was called *Christian Dogmatics*. And part of the reason

for abandoning that project was his other writing on the great Catholic philosopher, Anselm. That study came out in 1930. I will say more about this later in the chapter.

Barth's teaching career took him from Göttingen to Münster (1925–1930), to Bonn 1930–1935), and eventually to Basel in 1936. It is important to acknowledge that university appointments were at the time civil servant jobs. This meant that the Ministry of Cultural Affairs made the appointment. This is important because it meant that, unless one was somewhat sympathetic to the views of the state, it was difficult to have a teaching post at the university. It is this very issue that got Barth to move to Switzerland in 1936.

Barmen Declaration

In the spring of 1934, Barth was teaching in Bonn, Germany, and lecturing on his *Church Dogmatics*. But he was also traveling. He tells the story that while in Paris on vacation he attended a Strauss operetta. He marveled at the "infinite number of possibilities open to a woman of moving her arms and even more her legs, wiggling, enticing, beckoning and frolicking in all directions." And "I thought again of the old question, 'Why doesn't the church at least try to be as good at what it does as the children of the world with their singing, miming and dancing.'"[31]

As this story indicates, Barth loved imagery and metaphor. He had a very rich view of theology, seeing it as a study of how the church thinks and acts. For all the heady intellectualism one finds in his *Church Dogmatics*, theology is theology of the church. Hence, Barth was always preaching in the church, heavily involved in conferences where the church talked about the importance of theology, and active in the local congregation. Here is what he says about theology during this time:

---

[28] Quoted from Thomas W. Ogletree, *Christian Faith and History: A Critical Comparison of Ernst Troeltsch and Karl Barth* (Nashville: Abingdon, 1965), 84.

[29] Ogletree, *Christian Faith*, 85.

[30] Barth's lectures at Göttingen have been collected into a volume titled, *The Göttingen Dogmatics: Introduction in the Christian Religion*, vols. 1 & 2, ed. Hannelotte Reiffen, trans. Geoffrey W. Bromiley (Grand Rapids: Eerdmans, 1991).

[31] Busch, *Karl Barth*, 243–45.

Of all disciples [sic] theology is the fairest, the one that moves the head and heart most fully, the one that comes closest to human reality, the one that gives the clearest perspective on the truth which every disciple seeks. It is a landscape like those of Umbria and Tuscany with views which are distant and yet clear, a work of art which is as well planned and as bizarre as the cathedrals of Cologne or Milan. . . . But of all disciplines theology is also the most difficult and the most dangerous, the one in which a man is most likely to end in despair, or—and this is almost worse—in arrogance. Theology can float off into thin air or turn to stone, or worst of all it can become a caricature of itself.[32]

During the spring of 1934, Barth was invited to address the Reformed Church Convention in the Bergkirche in Osnabrück. Here he openly warned the church not to permit people representing the interests of the state to diffuse the truth of the triune God. He was adamant that the state needed to hear the critique and judgment that had its roots in the voice of God, and at every turn he saw the danger of the church's accommodation to the subtle and not so subtle political interests.

Thoughts like this did not endear Barth to the German Christians or to all those who were loyal to Adolf Hitler. Barth's critique of the church's lack of resistance was noticed by notables like the Minister of Cultural Affairs, who at one point put him under "city arrest."[33] Also, two of his sons, Markus and Christoph, felt pressures from the state and were urged to relocate.

Barth firmly believed that the church's resistance to the direction of the state had been rather pathetic. The fledgling "Confessing Church" had been ineffective and weak in its witness. So the decision was made to hold the first "Confessing Synod of the German Evangelical Church" on May 29–31, 1934 in the Reformed Church of Barmen-Gemarke.[34]

In preparation of the theological theses for the Synod, two Lutheran theologians, Thomas Breit and Hans Asmussen, met with Barth two weeks before the event. Barth tells the story of the process as follows: "The Lutheran Church slept and the Reformed Church kept awake."[35] In other words, while the two Lutherans took an afternoon nap, Barth says, "I revised the texts of the six statements, fortified by strong coffee and one or two Brazilian cigars. . . . The result was that by that evening there was a text. I don't want to boast, but it was really my text."[36]

This text that was presented to the 138 delegates, and a slightly revised version, called the Barmen Declaration, was accepted on May 31, at 11:30 a.m. Since the text is not that long, I quote the main portion here.

In view of the errors of the "German Christians" of the present Reich Church government which are devastating the Church and also therefore breaking up the unity of the German Evangelical Church, we confess the following evangelical truths:

1. "I am the way, and the truth, and the life; no one comes to the Father, but by me" (John 14.6). "Truly, truly, I say to you, he who does not enter the sheepfold by the door, but climbs in by another way, that man is a thief and a robber. . . . I am the door; if anyone enters by me, he will be saved" (John 10:1, 9).
   Jesus Christ, as he is attested for us in Holy Scripture, is the one Word of God which we have to hear and which we have to trust and obey in life and in death.
   We reject the false doctrine, as though the church could and would have to acknowledge as a source of its proclamation, apart from and besides this one Word of God, still other events and powers, figures and truths, as God's revelation.

2. "Christ Jesus, whom God has made our wisdom, our righteousness and sanctification and redemption" (1 Corinthians 1:30).
   As Jesus Christ is God's assurance of the forgiveness of all our sins, so, in the same way and with the same seriousness he is also God's mighty claim upon our whole life. Through him befalls us a joyful deliverance from the godless fetters of this world for a free, grateful service to his creatures.

---

[32] Karl Barth, *God in Action: Theological Addresses*, trans. E. G. Homrighausen and Karl J. Ernst (Manhasset, N.Y.: Round Table, 1963), 39–40. This translation is from Busch, *Karl Barth*, 244.

[33] Busch, *Karl Barth*, 245.

[34] Busch, *Karl Barth*, 245–46.

[35] Busch, *Karl Barth*, 245.

[36] Busch, *Karl Barth*, 245.

We reject the false doctrine, as though there were areas of our life in which we would not belong to Jesus Christ, but to other lords—areas in which we would not need justification and sanctification through him.

3. "Rather, speaking the truth in love, we are to grow up in every way into him who is the head, into Christ, from whom the whole body [is] joined and knit together" (Ephesians 4:15, 16).

The Christian Church is the congregation of the brethren in which Jesus Christ acts presently as the Lord in Word and sacrament through the Holy Spirit. As the Church of pardoned sinners, it has to testify in the midst of a sinful world, with its faith as with its obedience, with its message as with its order, that it is solely his property, and that it lives and wants to live solely from his comfort and from his direction in the expectation of his appearance.

We reject the false doctrine, as though the Church were permitted to abandon the form of its message and order to its own pleasure or to changes in prevailing ideological and political convictions.

4. "You know that the rulers of the Gentiles lord it over them, and their great men exercise authority over them. It shall not be so among you; but whoever would be great among you must be your servant" (Matthew 20:25, 26).

The various offices in the Church do not establish a dominion of some over the others; on the contrary, they are for the exercise of the ministry entrusted to and enjoined upon the whole congregation.

We reject the false doctrine, as though the Church, apart from this ministry, could and were permitted to give itself, or allow to be given to it, special leaders vested with ruling powers.

5. "Fear God. Honor the emperor" (1 Peter 2:17).

Scripture tells us that, in the as yet unredeemed world in which the Church also exists, the State has by divine appointment the task of providing for justice and peace. [It fulfills this task] by means of the threat and exercise of force, according to the measure of human judgment and human ability. The Church acknowledges the benefit of this divine appointment in gratitude and reverence before him. It calls to mind the Kingdom of God, God's commandment and righteousness, and thereby the responsibility both of rulers and of the ruled. It trusts and obeys the power of the Word by which God upholds all things.

We reject the false doctrine, as though the State, over and beyond its special commission, should and could become the single and totalitarian order of human life, thus fulfilling the Church's vocation as well.

We reject the false doctrine, as though the Church, over and beyond its special commission, should and could appropriate the characteristics, the tasks, and the dignity of the State, thus itself becoming an organ of the State.

6. "Lo, I am with you always, to the close of the age" (Matthew 28:20). "The word of God is not fettered" (2 Timothy 2:9).

The Church's commission, upon which its freedom is founded, consists in delivering the message of the free grace of God to all people in Christ's stead, and therefore in the ministry of his own Word and work through sermon and sacrament.

We reject the false doctrine, as though the Church in human arrogance could place the Word and work of the Lord in the service of any arbitrarily chosen desires, purposes, and plans.

The Confessional Synod of the German Evangelical Church declares that it sees in the acknowledgment of these truths and in the rejection of these errors the indispensable theological basis of the German Evangelical Church as a federation of Confessional Churches. It invites all who are able to accept its declaration to be mindful of these theological principles in their decisions in Church politics. It entreats all whom it concerns to return to the unity of faith, love, and hope.[37]

This Declaration drew another line in the sand. In reality it was a critique of the German Christian alliance with Hitler's political agenda. In practice, it made Barth's tenure at German universities a lot more precarious.

---

[37] Quoted from Arthur C. Cochrane, ed., *Reformed Confessions of the 16th Century* (Philadelphia: Westminster, 1966), 332–36.

Response to Emil Brunner

Barth was not yet finished with his critique of theological liberalism. In September/October of the same year as Barmen, Barth wrote an amazing polemic against his friend Emil Brunner, specifically in response to his work on *Natur und Gnade* (*Nature and Grace*).[38] Barth entitled his response with one word, *Nein!* (*No*).[39] It becomes clear in his "Angry Introduction" that Barth is actually theologically very close to Brunner. And perhaps this, along with Brunner's critique of Barth, is what made the response so visceral. The two did remain friends through it all and, as we will see, Barth's extreme juxtaposition of grace and nature softens in his mature years.

But in this response, Barth believed that Brunner's approach to theology threatened the church. What was Brunner's approach? He was trying to work out the continuity of nature and grace in such a way that we do not see nature without grace and a grace that is unnatural. Of course, this language was reminiscent of Thomistic theology. And so Brunner identified the task of theology as follows: "To find a way back to a legitimate natural theology."[40] In essence, it was this sentence that Barth responded to with an emphatic "No." He saw Brunner as identifying with the bankrupt theology of German liberalism. Barth believed that this was not the time to champion a natural theology, for unless we look outside of nature for an assessment of German culture, there can be no critique at all. Now is the time for God to break into the politics of Germany and exercise judgment.

It is interesting that Barth reports that he wrote his response to Brunner while on vacation in the city of Rome in the dawn between five and six a.m.[41] In this Roman Catholic place, he was reminded of the theology of Thomas Aquinas, and especially his doctrine of the *analogia entis* (analogy of being), which affirmed analogous continuity between the world of grace and nature, that is, between Creator and creation.[42] And Brunner's effort to find a way back to a true *theologia naturalis* is to affirm what was for Barth a false continuity. Barth states this in another way: "We must learn again to understand revelation as grace and grace as revelation, and therefore turn away from all 'true' or 'false' *theologia naturalis*."[43]

We do well to ask further why Barth is so upset at natural theology. Barth understood by "natural theology" a way of knowing God via means other than Jesus Christ, that is, through nature. And such an approach makes it possible for human beings to claim knowledge of God through abstract speculation and permits "natural" culture without judgment. And this is abhorrent! The only alternative is an answer from the revelation of God in Jesus Christ.

It is impossible to assess the significance of this debate in this short chapter. But it is not an overstatement to say that it is on this very debate between Brunner and Barth that the possibility of a Christian ethic hinges.[44] For if we read Barth to be maintaining a completely unbridgeable dichotomy between nature and grace, then it would seem that

---

[38] Emil Brunner, *Natur und Gnade: Zum Gespräch mit Karl Barth* (Tübingen: JCB Mohr, 1935).

[39] The full title is *Nein! Antwort an Emil Brunner* (Zurich: Theologischer Verlag, 1935).

[40] Busch, *Karl Barth*, 248.

[41] Busch, *Karl Barth*, 248.

[42] It is important to recall Thomas' claim about natural theology and the *analagia entis* (see chap. 5 above). His view was twofold: there is an absolute chasm between God and humans. And so there can be no literal bridge. Second, there can, however, be an analogical bridge; otherwise all knowledge of God would be impossible in principle. So the *analogia entis* is intended precisely to protect God's otherness. And for the strict Thomists it was "univocity" that threatened to either make God like us, only greater, or unknowable altogether. Neither alternative is theologically tolerable.

[43] Quoted from "Introduction to Barth's *Nein*," Karl Barth Society of Amherst website, last modified May 21, 2007, http://barthamherst.blogspot.com/2007/05/introduction-to-barths-nein.html.

[44] For a more thorough analysis and response to Barth on the relation of nature and grace, see my as yet unpublished lectures, "Christian Ethics: In Christ in the World" (presented at Associated Mennonite Biblical Seminary, February 17 & 18, 2010).

the only good one can claim is the good that does not touch this earth. And then one is inclined to wonder why the incarnation was not anathema to him. But clearly Barth affirms the incarnation, and so we need to be careful how we read him at this point. There are signs in Barth's more mature theology that he may have overstated the God–human (Creator–creature) dichotomy in his earlier work. After all, Barth talks rather positively about Roman Catholic theology later in life, to the point when he feels it necessary to caution, "Do not worry, I am not going to become a Roman Catholic!"[45] Although Barth is not able to speak positively about the *analogia entis*, he does use language that suggests that the natural secular world in some ways participates in the divine, when he speaks of "secular parables of the truth."[46] Moreover, he develops some strong relationships with Catholic theologians and the Vatican.[47] Even Pope Pius XII spoke of Barth as the most important theologian since Thomas Aquinas.

View on State, War

As with each of these subtopics, it is impossible to do justice to Barth's rich and nuanced thought. But a few things must be said. In his *Epistle to the Romans*, he offered a rich reading of Romans 13:1-7, in which he argued that Paul's view of the state should be seen as a limit and that therefore this passage should not be used as the central plank in a Christian doctrine of the state. On this reading, Christians should not see obedience to the state as somehow apart from or outside the obedience to God in Jesus Christ. In fact, as Rowan Williams makes clear, for Barth "Romans 13:1-7 is meant as a gloss on 12:21 ('Be not overcome of evil . . .')."[48]

Issues like how to participate in political matters, such as war, for example, were not ethical issues in the sense of being derived from theological beliefs. No, they were first-order theological convictions themselves. They were expressions of the conviction that Jesus is Lord. A good example of this is found in a statement of ten theses which were adopted by several churches in Germany and were presented to the German Evangelical Church Synod in April 1958. It turns out that these statements were written by Barth himself.[49]

1. *War* is the ultimate means of political confrontation between peoples and states, a means that is in all its forms questionable and ambiguous.
2. *Churches* of all lands and ages up to the present day have maintained that preparation for and employment of this means, for particular good and less good reasons, are not admissible.
3. The prospect of a future war waged with the use of modern means of annihilation has created a new situation, in face of which the *Church cannot remain neutral*.
4. War in the form of *atomic* war means the mutual annihilation of the peoples involved as well as of innocent people of other nations not involved in the conflict between the two parties.
5. War in the form of atomic war is therefore manifestly *useless as a means of political confrontation*, because it destroys the preconditions for such engagement.
6. The church and the individual Christian can therefore only say *No* in advance of any war waged as an atomic war.
7. Even the preparation for such a war is in all circumstances a *sin against God and neighbor*, and no Church, no Christian can share in the guilt of this.
8. Thus we demand in the name of the gospel, *that there be an immediate end* to all preparation for such warfare in our country and state, with no regard for any other considerations.

---

[45] Busch, *Karl Barth*, 481. Barth's engagement with a Catholic theologian, Hans Urs von Balthasar (1905–1988) is fascinating. See esp. Edward T. Oakes, *Pattern of Redemption: The Theology of Hans Urs von Balthasar* (New York: Continuum, 1994), 45–71.

[46] Quoted in Eugene F. Roberts Jr., *Thomas Aquinas and Karl Barth: Sacred Doctrine and the Natural Knowledge of God* (Notre Dame, Ind.: University of Notre Dame Press, 1995), 185.

[47] In 1966 Barth was invited to Rome to participate in talks regarding the Second Vatican Council. This speaks to his stature in the Roman Catholic Church.

[48] Rowan Williams, *Wrestling with Angels: Conversations in Modern Theology*, ed. Mike Higton (Grand Rapids: Eerdmans, 2007), 153.   [49] See Busch, *Karl Barth*, 431.

9. We call on all those who are serious in their wish to be Christians to *refuse* to cooperate in preparation for atomic warfare, unconditionally and in all circumstances.

10. An opposite viewpoint or a neutral stance on this question is *indefensible in Christian terms*. Both would mean the denial of all articles of the Christian faith.[50]

The reader should pay particular attention to the "grammar" in these words. It would, for example, not be "morally wrong" to participate in atomic war, it would be a sin. Why? Because it would violate "the articles of the Christian faith." Throughout Barth's writing, the Christian was always called to live as a Christian, that is, in keeping the convictions of the church.[51]

BARTH'S CHURCH DOGMATICS

In the early 1930s, Barth worked on another important project, namely, a book on Anselm.[52] This book is often viewed as a side interest for Barth, but he claims otherwise in the preface to the second edition:

Only a comparatively few commentators, for example, Hans Urs von Balthasar, have realized that my interest in Anselm was never a side-issue for me . . . Most of them have completely failed to see that in this book on Anselm I am working with a vital key, if not the key, to an understanding of that whole process of thought that has impressed me more and more in my *Church Dogmatics* as the only proper one to theology.[53]

This quotation shows a struggle within Barth that, while he was rejecting natural theology and affirming dialectical theology in its place, he was also presenting a positive theology that was able to speak about the knowledge of God and about the good creation. *Fides quaerens intellectum* (Faith seeking understanding) and *credo ut intellegam* (I believe in order that I might understand), the phrases Anselm made popular, were really what Barth was seeking to do in his *Church Dogmatics*. Over and over, he says the only way the theologian can speak as theologian is to presuppose that God has acted and revealed to us what we know. The larger task is to make this knowledge intelligible.

Like many theologians and philosophers before him, Barth was attempting to both maintain the chasm between Creator and creation and find a bridge so that we mortals were not hopelessly stuck on this side of the divide. But finding a way to do that would require another dramatic shift. In 1927 Barth wrote *Christian Dogmatics in Outline* (also called *Prolegomena*), which was intended as the first of a multivolume work. He eventually abandoned this project, and a completely revised first volume appeared in 1932, with a new title, *Church Dogmatics*. What happened? Here is William Nicholls' account:

Again Barth has scandalized the theological public. Not only would he write dogmatics, he would now write ecclesiastical dogmatics, dogmatics linked to the church and to its confession, instead of the academic community and to free inquiry. In the preface to the first volume . . . he says that his aim in revision had been to remove from his writings any trace of dependence upon existentialism and any other philosophy. Theology is to depend wholly on the Word of God. Thus it necessarily becomes an activity of the church. But this repudiation of philosophical support should not mislead us. Barth now intends to speak *more* rationally than before, not less so.[54]

Hans Urs von Balthasar (1905–1988) argues that it was Barth's gradual acceptance of the importance of analogy in theological thought that underlies this shift. He believes

[50] Quoted from Williams, *Wrestling with Angels*, 151–52 (emphasis in original).

[51] For further discussions on Barth's view on the state and war, see esp. George Hunsinger, ed., *Karl Barth and Radical Politics* (Philadelphia: Westminster, 1976); and John Howard Yoder, *Karl Barth and the Problem of War* (Nashville: Abingdon, 1970).

[52] The full title is *Anselm: Fides quaerens intellectum, Anslem's Proof of the Existence of God in the Context of his Theological Schemes*, trans. Ian W. Robertson (London: SCM Press, 1960).

[53] Barth, *Anselm*, 11. I owe much of this "Catholic reading" of Barth to Oakes, *Pattern of Redemption*, 60–61.

[54] William Nicholls, *The Pelican Guide to Theology*, vol. 1, *Systematic and Philosophical Theology* (Harmondsworth: Penguin, 1969), 108–9. Quoted from Oakes, *Pattern of Redemption*, 61 (emphasis in original).

that Barth's absolute divide between creation and Creator became less and less distinct during his career.[55] Says von Balthasar:

> It is characteristic of Barth that he came to a balanced christology earlier than he did to a balanced doctrine of creation. It is from Christ himself that he will eventually learn that it is a good thing to be a creature, that not to be God is not a disaster or a contradiction in terms but a good in and of itself.[56]

Barth himself says that he comes within "a hair's length nearness to Catholic theology."[57] Why? Because in struggling with how transhistorical Creator-God is revealed in the divine/human Jesus Christ and how Christ shapes our human existence, he has been forced to articulate a kind of natural theology. Thus it is both possible and impossible for him to speak of theological ethics.

BARTH'S THEOLOGICAL "ETHICS"

It is of course misleading to inquire at the end of Barth's work about his theological ethics as if it were a new topic. As is quite clear by now, he speaks everywhere about how Christians who confess Jesus as Lord must live—that was his passion from the very beginning. And throughout we have seen his conviction that liberal theology is unable to answer the question of Christian ethics because it begins with culture. For Barth, ethics and theology do not separate into distinct inquiries; dogmatics is ethics, and to separate them is to have already succumbed to the notion that there is a source of goodness that is other than God.[58]

Barth writes several important documents that focus specifically on the question of Christian ethics. To these I will now turn briefly.

"Obeying the Commandments"

Barth presented a little-known lecture at a Christian student conference at Aarau in 1927 called "Das Halten der Gebote" ("Obeying the Commandments").[59] Here he spoke about the "so-called ethical problem," which is the matter of deciding what to do. Notice that he does not frame the ethical question in terms of the classical philosophical language of being and virtues. Why did he reject this approach? Because it assumes that there is a "natural" essence to being human which can be known through speculative philosophy and from which we can know the good of humanity. And this approach makes the word of God irrelevant.

What then is the answer to the question as he puts it? *Follow the command of God.* In his words:

> The thesis which shall be presented and explained in this lecture is as follows: Regarding the so-called ethical problem, which is always both an old and a new question: What are we then to do? . . . No answer can be given except this: *Follow* the *command*, understand both ideas in their plainest and deepest meaning, as they are to be understood in the Bible. . . . Ethical truth thereby distinguishes itself from both mathematical truth, and the truth perhaps discovered in metaphysical speculation, in that it is never immediately evident, but only *becomes* evident in the specific situation of the individual, in which we all really find ourselves. . . . Ethical truth, as it becomes evident in a given situation, is not general truth. It is rather the truth of the Church, and it is that as the very particular truth which emerges at the moment of our decision.[60]

What is evident here is that at the very beginning ethics has its center in God. And this means, as Barth saw it, that human decisions are in fact always wrong; they can only

---

[55] See Oakes, *Pattern of Redemption*, 61.

[56] Quoted from Oakes, *Pattern of Redemption*, 62.

[57] Quoted by von Balthasar in Oakes, *Pattern of Redemption*, 62.

[58] See esp. "Dogmatics as Ethics," in Karl Barth, *Church Dogmatics*, I:2 (Edinburgh: T&T Clark); and "The Command of God," *Church Dogmatics*, II:2.

[59] This essay appeared in *Theologische Fragen und Antworten: Gesammelte Vorträge*, vol. 3 (Zürich: Evangelische Verlag A. G. Zollikon, 1957), 32–53.

[60] Barth, *Theologische Fragen*, 32–33. Quoted from Robert E. Willis, *The Ethics of Karl Barth*, 41n5, and 42nn1–2 (emphasis in original).

be made right by the grace of God. We live and obey only to the extent that God's hand is upon us.

Ethics

In 1928, after lecturing in Münster on the topic of ethics, he published a two-volume book by that title,[61] in which he further clarifies that ethics is neither about human subjectivity, as it was for Kierkegaard, nor about cultural objectivity, as it was for Ernst Troeltsch.[62] Again he states that it is the primacy of God's activity that forms the nexus of our moral self-identity. What does this mean? He says:

> The Word of God is the Word of God only in act. The Word of God is *decision*. God *acts*. Only with reference to this reality which is not general but highly specific can theological ethics venture to answer the ethical question. Its theory is meant only as the theory of this *practice*.[63]

In emphasizing the primacy of God's act, he has set the theological framework for Christian ethics as that of creation, reconciliation, and redemption. For this is how God acts! And our actions are best seen as our participation in what God is doing. So Barth speaks about theological ethics in terms of *calling* under the subject of the "Command of God the Creator," *justification* by faith under the subject of "Command of God the Reconciler," and *conscience* under the subject of "Command of God the Redeemer." In each of these sections of his book, Barth elaborates how we can understand ourselves in and participate in—even if sinfully—the overall economy of what God is doing in this world.

Church Dogmatics

The third writing that Barth devotes specifically to the topic of Christian ethics is the last volume of his *Church Dogmatics*.[64] The language of ethics here is still the language of "the command of God." He says, for example, "Our task is that of Christian ethics as an attempt to portray Christian life under the command of God."[65] Furthermore,

> [T]he first step of this life of faithfulness to God, the Christian life, is a man's baptism with water, which by his own decision is requested of the community and which is administered by the community, as the binding confession of his obedience, conversion, and hope, made in prayer for God's grace, wherein he honors the freedom of this grace.[66]

Barth was not only concerned about the primacy of God's act; he was also interested in getting the human condition right. We are sinners! We live in a fallen world. The world is structured and governed by fallen powers. And while we might revolt against the disorder of the world, we cannot change it. And in the midst of this fallen creation, we have, in Christ, been given the hope of a new creation. While we acknowledge our own complicity in the plight of the world—for we too are fallen—we ask God for redemption—ours and the world's. So we *pray* and we *work*. But when we work for wholeness and peace, we do so in a particular manner.

This is but to say that Barth pays attention to the "grammar of doing."[67] When we pray "Thy kingdom come" and work "in the kingdom" we situate ourselves as moral agents in a unique way. He says:

> The unity of God and man in Jesus Christ guarantees the fact that God and man and man and God

---

[61] Karl Barth, *Ethik I & II* (Zurich: Theologische Verlag, 1928/29).

[62] See John Webster, *Barth's Moral Theology: Human Action in Barth's Thought* (Grand Rapids: Eerdmans, 1998), 42.

[63] Webster, *Barth's Moral Theology*, 48 (emphasis in original).

[64] See Karl Barth, "The Christian Life," *Church Dogmatics* IV: 4: *Lecture Fragments*, trans. Geoffrey W. Bromiley (Grand Rapids: Eerdmans, 1981).

[65] Barth, "Christian Life," 49.

[66] Barth, "Christian Life," 47.

[67] The phrase comes from Webster, *Barth's Moral Theology*. It is the title of chapter 8.

belong together, and are in fellowship with one another. In him the covenant has its irrevocable basis. In him it cannot be broken. . . . God unconditionally precedes and man can only follow. The free God elects and wills. The free man must elect and will what God wills and elects. God is the giver and man the recipient. Man is an active and not an inactive recipient, and even in his activity he is still a recipient.[68]

There is no doubt that for Barth human moral agency is intelligible only insofar as God in Christ both constitutes us as moral agents and provides a model for how it's done. For in the human reception of divine grace God acts. And in this receptive act we are moral agents.

---

[68] Barth, "Christian Life," 29.

Chapter Fifteen

DIETRICH BONHOEFFER
(1906–1945)

Dietrich Bonhoeffer was executed by the Nazi Schutzstaffel (SS) when he was thirty-nine years old. By then, he had already exerted considerable influence on the European theological scene, especially in Christian ethics. Although Bonhoeffer read the works of Karl Barth and Ernst Troeltsch, his theology took a somewhat different turn. The basis of this shift lay in a new emphasis on Christology and ecclesiology.

Perhaps even more so than with Troeltsch and Barth, Bonhoeffer's personal life, public life, and intellectual life were of one piece. Because of the positions he took against both the German church and the state, he was compelled to give a theological account of his actions. Hence, his life's story is a good example of "theological existence" and how he lived the life of a "storied" person.

FAMILY LIFE

Bonhoeffer was born in Breslau, Germany, on February 4, 1906, into an upper-class, non-churchgoing, Christian (Lutheran) family. He had a twin sister, named Sabine; three older brothers; and three other sisters. His father, Karl, was a physician and an authority on neurology and psychiatry who created a reputation for himself by being strongly opposed to the Freudian interpretation of psychology. His mother, Paula (von

Hase), in addition to running a household of eight children, was a historian and was heavily involved in homeschooling the children. The Bonhoeffers were reluctant to give their children's minds over to others, yet the children regularly took the state examinations and did very well. As it turned out, this schooling arrangement made possible an accelerated form of learning in Dietrich's case, which meant that he was ready for university studies at an earlier age than usual.

The family did not attend church regularly, but that did not mean the children were not trained in Christian practices. Bonhoeffer's mother was a devout woman of Moravian background.[1] And so the children prayed before meals and were told Bible stories. At bedtime they said common prayers like, *Müde bin ich, geh zur Ruh.*[2]

Dietrich Bonhoeffer's decision as a young child to become a minister and theologian was somewhat unusual, and it took a while for the family to take him seriously. But after convincing his family that he really did not want to become a musician, despite showing real talent in the area, he threw his lot to theology when he was a mere fifteen years old. And he never looked back. Eberhard Bethge, the famous Bonhoeffer biographer, wonders whether the initial motivation for his vocational choice may have been to gain

---

[1] The Moravian Church had its beginning in Bohemia (now the Czech Republic) with the pre-Reformation martyrdom of Jan Hus in 1415. The church's motto is: "In essentials unity; in non-essentials liberty; in all things love." Originally the church was known as "Unitas Fratrum," meaning "The Unity of the Brethren."

[2] Eberhard Bethge, *Dietrich Bonhoeffer: Man of Vision, Man of Courage*, trans. Eric Mosbacher, et al. (New York: Harper & Row, 1967), 21.

some independence from the family.[3] Regardless, once he opened himself to the study of theology, it seemed to take hold of him and move him forward.

In the Bonhoeffer household, the standards of learning and general discipline were extremely high. Father was clearly the authority. Children did not speak at mealtimes unless they were spoken to. Yet they were often challenged on serious matters of politics and academics and expected to answer clearly and correctly. Bethge suggests that by today's standards we would say the Bonhoeffer children had an "authoritarian" upbringing.[4]

In 1912, when Bonhoeffer was six years old, the family moved to Berlin, where his father was appointed professor of psychiatry. This meant that young Bonhoeffer felt the influence of academics even more directly with professors and other professionals making frequent appearances in his household. Professors tended to live in close proximity to each other and so on Wangenheimstrasse, the street on which the Bonhoeffers lived, there were regular meetings of theologians like Adolf von Harnack, Ernst Troeltsch, and Friedrich Meinecke. It is said that Harnack took a special liking to Bonhoeffer and that they had many theological talks, especially as Bonhoeffer grew older.

During this time, Bonhoeffer also got to know war firsthand. When the First World War began in 1914, he was a mere eight years old. But when the German Revolution began in November 1918, Bonhoeffer was old enough to be drawn into the debates over the conflict. Bethge says that it was this conflict that "corresponded with the awakening of Dietrich Bonhoeffer's interest in politics."[5] It was at this time that he joined the Boy Scouts, which created numerous occasions for intensive debates on political matters.

During his last years before university, Bonhoeffer made many friends and read voraciously. His reading included the classics like Greek and Roman philosophy, Schleiermacher's *On Religion*, Tönnies' *Gemeinschaft und Gesellschaft*, and works by Max Weber.[6] Although he did not read much in theology at that time, he nevertheless showed eagerness in studying it firsthand.

Bonhoeffer entered university at the age of seventeen and fell in love with the world of theology and philosophy. His father had attended Tübingen, and so it made sense for him to do so as well; there he joined a Swabian fraternity called *Igel* (Hedgehog), again following the footsteps of his father.

At Tübingen he encountered the biblicist Adolf Schlatter, who, in a new way, was seeking to get at what the Bible actually said. His assumption was that the content of the Bible was very important for structuring present-day life. Bonhoeffer liked this emphasis and was an admirer of Schlatter's, studying the Psalms and Old Testament theology with him. But he soon felt the need to study systematic theology. He believed that one cannot simply go from the Bible to the present and pretend that nothing happened in between; rather, he believed one has to go through the discipline of systematic theology to bring the content of the Bible into the contemporary world. The Bible must be *interpreted* in order to be understood in our world.

During his second semester, Bonhoeffer threw himself into the study of dogmatics. This brought him into a class with Professor Karl Heim, who was intent on bringing contemporary scientific knowledge into the study of theology. Here Bonhoeffer got to study Schleiermacher's *On Religion* under the tutelage of a master. He loved the history of religion, philosophy generally, and especially epistemology and logic.

After his first year at Tübingen, Bonhoeffer had the rich experience of a study semester in Rome and Africa. Here he encountered the Roman Catholic Church and Islam. The two left somewhat opposite impressions, impressions that remained with him throughout his

---

[3] Bethge, *Man of Vision*, 23.
[4] Bethge, *Man of Vision*, 6.
[5] Bethge, *Man of Vision*, 17.
[6] Bethge, *Man of Vision*, 27.

life. He was struck with the enormity of the Catholic Church, its buildings, organizational structure, and its theology. At the same time, he was caught by the fracture and almost impossible challenge of uniting a broken church, especially between the Catholics and the Protestants. With Islam, he was caught by the idea that there is no "church" counterpart that can separate itself from anything, which contrasts with the Christian assumption of the separation of realms—that religious life is distinct from everyday life, including from matters of the state, for Catholics as much as for Protestants. From the Muslims, he learned the opposite—there is *one* realm, life! Ordinary life, including the state, is seamless with personal piety.

Clearly the overwhelming impression of this trip—one that lasted his entire life—was the importance of ecclesiology. A few years later, when he was pastor in a church in Barcelona, he preached a sermon on 1 Cor 12:26ff in which he emphasized the difference in understanding of church between the Catholics and Protestants. Bethge records these words from his sermon:

> There is a word that when a Catholic hears it kindles all his feelings of love and bliss; that stirs all the depths of his religious sensibility . . . that certainly awakens in him the feeling of home; the feeling that only a child has in relation to its mother, made up of gratitude, reverence and devoted love. . . . And there is a word that to Protestants has the sound of something infinitely commonplace, more or less indifferent and superfluous, that does not make their heart beat faster; something with which a sense of boredom is so often associated. . . . Woe to us if that word does not become important to us soon again, does not become important in our lives. Yes, the word to which I am referring is "church," the meaning of which we have forgotten . . .[7]

In 1924, when Bonhoeffer was eighteen years old, he moved from Tübingen and enrolled at the University of Berlin. He was a student there for three years and encountered a whole new set of instructors: Adolf von Harnack, with whom he studied church history; Karl Holl, a Luther scholar; Reinhold Seeberg, an expert in systematic theology, who would later become his *Doktorvater*; and Adolf Deissmann, a New Testament scholar. This was the theological cradle that would nurture Bonhoeffer's Christology and ecclesiology.

In 1925 Bonhoeffer began to read Karl Barth's theology in earnest. He had a cousin, Hans-Christoph von Hase, who was studying at Göttingen where Barth was lecturing, and so he had access to the early notes that eventually became Barth's volume on *Christian Dogmatics* in 1927. Moreover, he was well aware of the debate between Harnack and Barth in *Christliche Welt*, which put in radical opposition the scientific theology of Harnack and the dogmatic theology of Barth. Bonhoeffer embraced Barth's early version of the notion that theology could not be rooted in human experience but must instead be lodged in the majesty of God. But Bonhoeffer also saw a danger here. The danger had to do with Barth's inability to *really* make the church the starting point for his theology, contrary to Barth's own convictions. To speak of revelation as the absolute beginning is still to set up the issue as an epistemological problem, when it really was a soteriological one. Of course Barth struggled with this issue himself,[8] but it is noteworthy that Bonhoeffer believed that early in Barth's work, his ecclesiological weakness was already evident because of Barth's overemphasis on the otherness of God.

EARLY INFLUENCES

Before I present Bonhoeffer's writings in more detail, I will summarize in broad stokes three important influences. Whether negatively or positively, each served to crystallize his conviction that the church is at the center of theology.

---

[7] Bethge, *Man of Vision*, 42.

[8] See chap. 14 above.

European Liberal Theology

Bonhoeffer, like Barth, was opposed to liberalism because it did not have a proper emphasis on the sovereignty of God. In other words, it did not understand the God–human relationship properly, nor could it speak adequately of the time-eternity and life-death tensions.

Yet, it must also be emphasized that Bonhoeffer was positively influenced by liberal thought. His teachers, many of whom also taught Barth, were liberals, and from them he learned that Christianity is not something speculative or abstract, but fundamentally concrete and sociological. And of this he never let go. At the same time, he was a "student" of Barth in that he read avidly everything of his that he could get his hands on. And very quickly he developed a love-hate relationship. Barth was right in emphasizing the sovereignty of God, but he did so in a way that abstracted God too much. Bonhoeffer believed that God lives in the hearts of men and women who open themselves to the power of God's redemption in the social spaces that they occupy. Moreover, in Christ, God was embodied in the concrete reality of this earth. So while God was radically transcendent, God was also radically immanent. Such was the double-sided impact of Bonhoeffer's teachers; a tension that followed him through his entire life.

Yet Bonhoeffer clearly rejected the methodology of the liberals. He believed that they began with the wrong questions, which focused either on the needs of the individual or of culture; and overriding these needs was the need to know. These emphases had the effect of relegating both Christ and the church to the sidelines.

Bonhoeffer's issue with liberal theology was anything but cosmetic. For him, as for Barth, revelation was key. But for Bonhoeffer, Christ was the model of revelation. Revelation must be concrete; it must find expression in the social reality called church. This necessarily binds all theological knowledge to the contingencies of time and space, namely the concrete social reality called church.

Ecumenical Discussions

The ecumenical movement began shortly after the turn of the century, around 1910, and it culminated in the founding of the World Council of Churches in 1948. Bonhoeffer was involved in this process at its early stages.

Ever since Bonhoeffer's first visit to Rome, he had held church unity in high regard. It is not that he believed that all the churches should be the same in worship styles, polity, or even theology, yet he believed that in Christ we can have the unity of what has been broken apart—Jews and Greeks, males and females, masters and slaves could be made one in Christ. Division and hostility in the church are matters of lament and tragedy. And so he saw it as a biblical mandate to work at unifying what was divided by sin.

Bonhoeffer began his formal involvement in ecumenical discussions in 1931, and in 1934 he became a member of a subgroup of the World Alliance of Churches called "Life and Work." This had many side benefits for him. He could now travel abroad and meet other church leaders, and he did, using every opportunity to study the international church on these occasions.

Ecumenical dialogue in the 1930s had many political overtones, both in the Alliance itself and from outside national interests. Bonhoeffer had been appointed as one of the youth secretaries of the World Alliance. The Alliance felt that Bonhoeffer's appointment was a special coup, in light of the fact that Karl Barth was reticent about joining the ecumenical council; the Alliance believed it had landed a younger version of Barth, who was a key theological voice in Germany.

In September 1931, a conference was scheduled at Cambridge, England. In the summer prior to the event, the German branch of the Alliance held a preparatory conference at Hamburg. On the opening day of this meeting, the local newspaper published a statement under the heading "Protestant Church and International Reconciliation."[9] Bethge quotes a portion of this article reflecting the effort to impose the intransigent nationalistic divisions onto the church.

> [T]here can in our opinion be no understanding between us Germans and the nations which were victorious in the World War; we can only show them that while they continue the war against us, understanding is impossible . . . it should be undeservedly recognized that Christian and churchly understanding and cooperation on questions of *rapprochement* between the nations is impossible as long as the others conduct a policy lethal to our nation.[10]

This kind of bellicose language made Bonhoeffer more and more skeptical of the notion of a state church. In anticipation of attending the Cambridge conference, he wrote: "On 15th August I am being sent for three weeks to England to attend the Cambridge conference. What shall we say to the Americans about cooperation between the churches? Surely we shall not talk such nonsense as Hirsch did recently . . ."[11]

At this conference, the youth delegates were granted full participation for the first time. This obviously gave the youth a much stronger voice, and Bonhoeffer's position as youth secretary now made him part of the inner circle of the World Alliance. He was granted jurisdiction over Germany and other parts of Europe. This meant he got to attend the meetings of the executive committee of "Life and Work," which had the added benefit that he made frequent visits abroad.

Issues Regarding Church

The third major early influence also had to do with church. Bonhoeffer struggled with the question of faithfulness in the German Church. The ambivalence was over how a state church could satisfy the demands of both Christ's radical call and the state's protectionist interests. This same issue had already led Barth to Barmen, where the distinction between *Die deutsche Christen* (German Christians) and *Die Bekennende Gemeinde* (the Confessing Church) was crafted.[12] Bonhoeffer was a strong supporter of the Barmen Declaration and the Confessing Church and, as we will see in his writings, did what he could to give them credibility.

A lot hinged on the issue of the Confessing Church, which made supporting it far from simple. First, Bonhoeffer was throwing his energies behind uniting the broken church, so how could the founding of a new church in Germany—dividing it further, as it were—be justified? And yet he believed that ecumenical dialogue could not happen within the national church. This was an irresolvable struggle for him. Second, his livelihood literally was at stake over ecclesiology. For example, the ability to teach at a university depended on church membership and views of church. The Confessing Church had no legal status, and so its members could not get jobs as a civil servants teaching in universities. Some professors were able to hide their church affiliation in order to avoid confrontation, but this option presented difficulties. Bonhoeffer was caught in this process because he identified openly with the Confessing Church.

As is evident from the foregoing, church was at the center of Bonhoeffer's passion. As he saw it, to be the church was to be in Christ in the world. Hence, there could be no abstract, *Christian* ethic. The Christian life is embodied, and hence it is always expressed at a particular place in a particular time. It will be no surprise to learn that during these early years Bonhoeffer was engaged in an intensive writing project on the nature of the church.

[9] Bethge, *Man of Vision*, 148.
[10] Bethge, *Man of Vision*, 148 (emphasis in original). The full newspaper statement was signed by Professor D. P. Althaus, Erlangen, and Professor D. E. Hirsch, Göttingen.
[11] Bethge, *Man of Vision*, 149.
[12] See pp. 248–50 above.

EARLY WRITINGS

In the fall of 1925, at the age of nineteen, Bonhoeffer began his doctoral dissertation under the directorship of Reinhold Seeberg, at the University of Berlin, which he described as "half historical and half systematic."[13] The title of his dissertation would be "Sanctorum Communio: *A Dogmatic Enquiry into the Sociology of the Church*."[14] It is said that when Karl Barth read it he called it a theological miracle. Bonhoeffer was only twenty-one years old when he finished.

There is an interesting story about how Bonhoeffer came by his dissertation advisor. He wrote a paper for Harnack, who was very impressed and suggested that this was of doctoral quality and that Bonhoeffer should study under him and write a dissertation on the subject. Bonhoeffer was not swayed by the praise. He wrote another paper for another professor who responded similarly. When he wrote a paper for Reinhold Seeberg, he received major critique. Bonhoeffer then asked to study under Seeberg.

In his dissertation, Bonhoeffer sought, on the one hand, to accept the Troeltschean emphasis on sociology and show that the church is always embodied in social reality, while, on the other hand, to accept the emphasis of Barth's otherness of the church. To say this differently, Bonhoeffer was critical of Barth because he felt that his emphasis on revelation made it extremely difficult to take the church seriously as the body of Christ within social reality; and he was critical of Troeltsch in that he had made the church so thoroughly sociological that Christ had become little more than a moral ideal, an impossible one at that.

In "Sanctorum Communio," Bonhoeffer argues that we are never alone. God is always with us. Moreover, insofar as we live without acknowledging God's presence, we are not fully human. That is, we find our humanity only in relation to God, and the church is where this is made possible. Hence, the church is not a place where we escape our humanness or where we transcend it. Rather, it is the space where we become human; where, in Christ, we enter fully into humanity by entering into the presence of God.

This naturally gets Bonhoeffer into theological tension with the Barthian notion of transcendent God. For Bonhoeffer the church is both an ordinary and extraordinary place, for we meet God there not in God's otherness but in God's encounter with the fully human. God wills to become present in this world both through the community as a whole and via those persons who welcome such presence—those who make themselves vulnerable to losing their ordinary selves in order to risk finding themselves in God's presence. This act of "self-discovery" is best modeled for us by Christ.

When Bonhoeffer talks about *ordinary* humanity he means *sinful* humanity. Even in the church, sin is not overcome. Augustine, Luther, Calvin, and Barth are all right in emphasizing that we are fallen human beings—imperfect and always in the tension between good and evil. He says:

> The world of sin is the world of "Adam," the old humanity. But the world of Adam is the world Christ reconciled and made into a new humanity, Christ's church. However, it is not as if Adam were completely overcome; rather, the humanity of Adam lives on in the humanity of Christ. This is why the discussion of the problem of sin is indispensable for understanding the sanctorum communio.[15]

Clearly Bonhoeffer does not see the church as a place without sin and the world as a place only of sin. Yet when we participate in the "body of Christ," we open the door for God's participation within our lives. We

---

[13] Bethge, *Man of Vision*, 57.

[14] The dissertation was first published in 1930 and is now translated and published as *Dietrich Bonhoeffer Works*, vol. 1, Sanctorum Communio: *A Theological Study of the Sociology of the Church*, trans. Reinhard Krauss and Nancy Lukens; German ed., Clifford J. Green (Minneapolis: Fortress, 1998). Bonhoeffer used the phrase *Sanctorum Communio* (community of saints) in an effort to get at the earliest view of church. He cites Jerome (347–420) as the first Latin church father to use it, 122.

[15] Bonhoeffer, Sanctorum, 107.

are then willing to be taken where God's redemptive path will lead us, and are no longer against God in the good/evil battle. God is in us because we are in Christ.

Two things are important regarding Bonhoeffer's view of sin and salvation. First, Bonhoeffer is critical of the modern notion of individual salvation because salvation is always corporate; it always has a social dimension. This is so because sin is both corporate and individual and we are not best understood as *individual* moral agents. As he says it, we are "collective persons."[16] He reflects on the call that came to the people of Israel:

> The call comes not to the individual, but to the collective person. The people must do penance as the people of God. It was not the individual but the people who had fallen into sin. Thus it is the people who must be comforted (Isa. 40:1). *Where peoples are called, God's will for their purpose in history is at work*, just as where individuals are called they experience their history. . . . God is concerned not only with the nations, but has a purpose for every community no matter how small, every friendship, every marriage, every family. . . . There is not only the culpability of individual Germans and individual Christians, but also the culpability of Germany and the church. It is not enough for individuals to repent and be justified; Germany and the church must likewise repent and be justified.[17]

Bonhoeffer is concerned not to speak of justice and peace in a way that fails to recognize that both are embodied in institutions, which means that injustice and violence are often structural. Hence, individual repentance alone, as important as that is, cannot bring about peace and justice.

Bonhoeffer's concept of the church is unique in several ways. He speaks of it as follows:

> The concept of the church is conceivable in the sphere of reality established by God; this means that it cannot be deduced. *The reality of the church is a reality of revelation, a reality that essentially must be* either believed or denied. Thus

an adequate criterion for judging the claim of the church to be God's church-community can be found only by stepping inside it, by bowing in faith to its claim.[18]

Bonhoeffer recognizes that there are really two concepts of church in the New Testament: one which he calls the "prototype of the Roman Catholic church"[19] found in Jerusalem primarily with Jewish Christians, and the other more Lutheran, developed by Paul for Gentile Christians. The Jerusalem church was ordered and hierarchical, while the Gentile church, or the *ecclesia*, or individual congregation, was where the word is preached and the Spirit discerned.

Yet whichever view of church is practiced, the church exists as an act of God in Jesus Christ. "It is the new humanity in the new Adam. It has been created in a real sense only by the death of Christ."[20] This means that the church in one sense is already complete and in another it is still being actualized through the Holy Spirit. As he says it, "The church is the presence of Christ in the same way that Christ is the presence of God,"[21] already and not-yet at the same time.

Bonhoeffer's image of the church borrows from Ferdinand Tönnies' distinction between *Gemeinschaft* and *Gesellschaft*.[22] In other words, it is best understood as a *Gemeinschaft* where the I-concept is shaped by the identity of the group and not as a *Gesellschaft*, which is an aggregate of individuals, each with an independent identity. Hence, the church is itself a corporate identity—in effect a collective person. It is that insofar as the church exists in Christ from whom its being and character are derived. And so the church acts and can be held accountable just like an individual moral agent can. Perhaps even more important, individual members of the church-community act not on their own behalf but on behalf of the community.

Bonhoeffer summarizes the relation of Christ and the church as follows:

---

[16] Bonhoeffer, Sanctorum, 118.

[17] Bonhoeffer, Sanctorum, 118–19 (emphasis in original).

[18] Bonhoeffer, Sanctorum, 127 (emphasis in original).

[19] Bonhoeffer, Sanctorum, 135.

[20] Bonhoeffer, Sanctorum, 137–38.

[21] Bonhoeffer, Sanctorum, 140–41.

[22] See chap. 10 above.

The relationship of Jesus Christ to the Christian church is thus to be understood in a dual sense. (1) *The church is already complete in Christ, time is suspended.* (2) *The church is to be built within time upon Christ as the firm foundation. Christ is the historical principle of the church.* Time belongs to him, the vertical direction as it were.[23]

Bonhoeffer emphasizes the unique Christian understanding of love.[24] Although the command to love is not specifically Christian, yet Christian love has distinct qualities. First, it is not a human possibility. Second, it is possible only through faith in Christ and through the gift of the Holy Spirit. Third, Christian love is purposeful in a particular way. "The purpose of love is exclusively determined by God's will for the other person, namely, to subject the other to God's rule."[25] Fourth, Christian love loves the real neighbor; it is embodied in both act and being. And fifth, Christian love knows no limits.

It is not that Bonhoeffer's ethic can be summarized merely as "doing the loving thing," for we do not know what love is except through Christ. In other words, it is not sufficient to see love as a rule or principle for one can know love only when it is embodied. It is not surprising, therefore, that he distinguishes himself from Troeltsch and Weber who see primarily two options for understanding church sociologically: on the one hand, they interpret Christian "sects" as holding to the view that love is an ideal that only the segregated pure can practice because it cannot be lived in the sinful world and, on the other hand, they see the "church" as being able to practice love in the real world only as a compromise to Christ's teaching. Neither one is Christian love. Bonhoeffer puts it as follows:

[T]he sanctorum communio, the Christian community of love as a sociological type, is dependent upon the word of God, and it alone. According to the promise in Isa. 55:11, it is present within every historical form in which the word is preached. The distinction between church and sect suggested by Weber and Troeltsch is untenable both historically and sociologically. Based on the efficacy of the word, we must believe the sanctorum communio to be present even within the sociologically unique type of the Roman Catholic church. Striving to attain the true church and pure doctrine is inherently necessary.[26]

The act of embodying Christian love is a precarious practice for Bonhoeffer, and it is only partially possible, and certainly its expression is owned by no group of Christians. The notion of embodied love can gain intelligibility only as it is properly placed within the *being* of Christ; in other words, only as we come to understand it within the unity of act and being.

Bonhoeffer's work on the church flowed naturally into his second major book called *Act and Being*,[27] which served as his qualifying dissertation for university teaching. This is a deeply philosophical work in which he relates his claim about theology as ecclesiology to some major philosophical writers popular in Germany at the time, especially Martin Heidegger. He puts it this way: "This entire study is an attempt to unify the concern of true transcendentalism and the concern of true ontology in an 'ecclesiological form of thinking.'"[28]

It is important to realize what is at stake in this book. Bonhoeffer believes that, in order to get Christian ethics right, we need to bring to unity two questions that are often separated: "What should we do?" and "Who are we?" The existentialists tend to argue that our identity (who we are) is formed by what we do. That is, we are nothing in ourselves (but free) and in our actions we define

---

[23] Bonhoeffer, Sanctorum, 153–54 (emphasis in original).

[24] Bonhoeffer, Sanctorum, 167ff.

[25] Bonhoeffer, Sanctorum, 168.

[26] Bonhoeffer, Sanctorum, 270–71.

[27] *Akt und Sein* was first published in 1930 and most recently has been translated and republished as *Dietrich Bonhoeffer Works*, vol. 2, *Act and Being: Transcendental Philosophy and Ontology in Systematic Theology*, trans. H. Martin Rumscheidt, eds. Hans-Richard Reuter, German ed.; and Wayne Whitson Floyd Jr., English ed. (Minneapolis: Fortress, 1996).

[28] Bonhoeffer, *Act and Being*, 32.

ourselves.[29] In other words, if you persist in stealing you become a thief. In this model, act determines being. In the opposite model, being determines act. Here, what you do is determined by who you are. This means that if you are a pacifist, you cannot go to war. How one understands the relation of act and being is crucial for ethics; certainly it is so for Christian ethics.

In *Act and Being*, Bonhoeffer criticizes Rudolf Bultmann (1884–1976), a Lutheran New Testament scholar at the University of Marburg, and he further nuances his critique of Karl Barth. He sees Bultmann as being too Heideggerian. Martin Heidegger, a German existentialist philosopher of *dasein* (literally, being there), was for Bultmann a significant source for understanding the New Testament.[30] Heidegger believed that act and being could find unity through a philosophical analysis of *dasein*. Bultmann argues that we understand theology best when we take the existentialist anthropology of Heidegger seriously. The problem with this, says Bonhoeffer, is that Bultmann shortchanges the power and reality of Christ in the process. Why? Because Bonhoeffer holds that it is Jesus Christ, and not philosophy, that defines for us who we are and how we ought to live. We cannot, without careful biblical-theological scrutiny, accept a definition of ourselves from humanistic philosophy.

Barth is criticized for his formalistic interpretation of the freedom of God. Bonhoeffer shows that for Barth God is radically free to do what God wills to do. To this Bonhoeffer replies with a nuanced "No!" Of course God is free in the sense that God's actions are not determined by forces outside of God, say, human forces. But we know God as one who has already acted decisively, for example, in creation and in the incarnation of Jesus Christ. To say now that God is *radically* free without qualification means that God could

act in ways inconsistent with Jesus Christ. And that would make Christian theology impossible. Instead, Bonhoeffer believes that God's *acts* have shown us God's *being*! God has acted freely, and through revelation we now see God's character. In other words, God has freely limited God's freedom by self-disclosure in Jesus Christ.

According to Bonhoeffer, Barth is in danger of making God morally irrelevant for human existence. God is morally relevant in revelation, which has both the effect of helping us see the good and of seeing God's freedom as qualified. To see God as absolutely free in Barth's sense is to see no moral guidance there.

It is important to understand Bonhoeffer's reading of theological history here. He relates his critique of Barth's view of the freedom of God to the theological shift that took place with William of Ockham and Duns Scotus.[31] That is, during the thirteenth century, the God-human exchange was reconceived. The suggestion was made by Ockham and Scotus that God does what God does (God is radically free), and hence reality is understandable independently from God. After all, on earth we have natural laws. God and time-space reality are now understood in their mutual otherness. Hence, there is no *participatory* relationship between this-worldly reality and the being of God. The effect of replacing the analogy of being with the univocity of being was to turn the incarnation into an intangible mystery and the church as the body of Christ into a mere symbol. Moreover, it made it especially easy to affirm human control over time-space reality instead of seeing the world as rooted in divine being and *received* as a gift of divine grace. And with the diminution of grace and the affirmation of possession and power as metaphors of being comes the justification of violence.

---

[29] This is the language of J. P. Sartre in "Existentialism Is a Humanism," in *Existentialism from Dostoevsky to Sartre*, ed. Walter Kaufmann (New York: World Publishing, 1956), 287–311.

[30] See 152ff. above for a brief discussion of Martin Heidegger's philosophy.

[31] Bonhoeffer, *Act and Being*, 82. See also 89ff. above for a description of the shift in theological thinking introduced by these thinkers.

Bonhoeffer's ecclesiology demands that we view the church as that body through which God wills to bring about the kingdom. This does not limit the power of God; instead it explains the freedom of God. It is a strengthening of both the immanent dimensions of the God/human relationship—underemphasized by Barth and overemphasized by the liberals—as well as the transcendent dimension—which is overemphasized by Barth and underemphasized by the liberals.

As Bonhoeffer sees it, our actions and representations are significant for God's redemption of this world. To say this was especially important in Germany at this time because, as Bonhoeffer believed, political propaganda was moving things in a direction away from God's redemptive ends. Bonhoeffer thought that this direction could be reversed by exerting as much divine-human effort as possible. He feared that Barth's theology would lead to a less active expression of God's will in the German context.

In all of this, the church was key for Bonhoeffer's theology. He believed that philosophical analysis alone could not give an account of *dasein* that would unite act and being. Only the visible church can do that. How? Seeing the church as the body of Christ defines both the church and us, for the mode of being within the church is revelation; standing between heaven and earth in openness to God in Christ. "Christ is in the community of faith as the community of faith is in Christ."[32] Who we are and what we do are therefore not read from our own natural selves but from God in Christ. In this way, "revelation happens in the community of faith"[33] meaning that, not only do we come to know God and the world, we come to know both who we are and what we must do "in Christ." This is the unity of act and being. For seeing ourselves in Christ's body is to see both our true selves (who we are) and hence what we must do.

The last section of *Act and Being* deals with the understanding of human beings "in Adam" and "in Christ." He begins with Luther's words that "by faith alone we know that we are sinners."[34] Bonhoeffer believes that sin is not something that human beings can get out of—the church community is not perfect. We all exist "in Adam."

To explain the manner in which we exist "in Christ" he again resorted to Luther. "Seek yourself only in Christ and not in yourself, and you will find yourself in Him eternally."[35] As he has argued, the problem of the philosophical understanding of *dasein* is that we understand ourselves only in relation to ourselves. "The solution to this problem comes as humanity orients its gaze towards Christ."[36] For "being in Christ, as being directed towards Christ, sets Dasein free. Human beings are 'there' for and by means of Christ . . ."[37] Being "in Christ" in the church-community is the model of Christian ethics for Bonhoeffer.

The two books, Sanctorum Communio and *Act and Being*, were pivotal in getting Bonhoeffer launched in his theological agenda. He was now set to take the German theological world by storm. And yet he writes about this time in his life in a rather unusual way. He speaks about "something happening," the details of which remain shrouded; something that had a profound impact on his life. He says in a letter to a friend:

> Then something happened, something that has changed and transformed my life to the present day. For the first time I discovered the Bible . . . I had often preached, I had seen a great deal of the church, and talked and preached about it—but I had not yet become a Christian. . . .[38]

Bonhoeffer does not let us know many details, nor does he tell us exactly what he means by becoming "a Christian." He elaborates by saying that in the past he used "the doctrine of Jesus Christ" for "personal advantage" and that in his past life he had been

---

[32] Bonhoeffer, *Act and Being*, 111.
[33] Bonhoeffer, *Act and Being*, 113.
[34] Bonhoeffer, *Act and Being*, 136.
[35] Bonhoeffer, *Act and Being*, 150.

[36] Bonhoeffer, *Act and Being*, 150.
[37] Bonhoeffer, *Act and Being*, 153.
[38] Bethge, *Man of Vision*, 154.

"quite pleased with himself." All this changed now. He goes on to say:

> Then the Bible, and in particular, the Sermon on the Mount, freed me from that. Since then everything has changed. . . . I suddenly saw as self-evident the Christian pacifism that I had recently passionately opposed . . .[39]

It is not clear what to make of Bonhoeffer's confession here. But whatever we might say, there is in his life after *Act and Being* evidence of an intensification of his commitment to be and act in Christ. We should be cautious not to make too much of his language, however, since he says in 1944, reflecting on his entire life, "I don't think that I have ever changed very much, except perhaps at the time of my first impression abroad and under the first conscious influence of father's personality."[40]

He was ordained to the ministry in 1931 as soon as he was eligible, that is, once he reached the age of twenty-five. He saw preaching as the all-important theological event because it was the proclamation of the love and peace of Christ, in the very body of Christ.

During 1930 and 1931, Bonhoeffer visited the United States, particularly Union Theological Seminary in New York. He attended classes and gave several lectures. He was fascinated with what was going on in the United States. One of his interests was the black population. American ethicist Paul Lehmann says that Bonhoeffer had a remarkable "identity with the Negro community, so that he was received there as though he had never been an outsider at all."[41]

The American church remained a puzzle to him. The church was not supported by the state, yet it was thriving. It was not a confessing church, as was emerging in Germany, and yet it had hot theological debates. People were insisting on the separation between church and politics, and yet there were many Christians in politics. There was a great emphasis on tolerance, and yet American Christians resisted the ecumenical movement. Some of these things frustrated him.

Bonhoeffer liked the American students—their freedom of expression and inquisitive nature. At the same time, he was discouraged by what he saw happening with democracy. He believed that the temptations of American democracy were so subtle that the church was easily seduced by them. Moreover, he thought that Americans did not take theology as seriously as did Germans. On his return home he wrote to a friend:

> Looked at from across the Atlantic, our standpoint and our theology look so local, and it seems inconceivable that in the whole of the world just Germany, and in Germany just a few men, have understood what the Gospel is. And yet I see a message nowhere else.[42]

Bonhoeffer had an opportunity to make several side trips while in the United States. He went to Philadelphia, the home of the Quakers, and to Cuba. He traveled to Mexico with someone who would become a dear friend, Jean Lasserre, the well-known French, Christian pacifist. He got to know Lasserre well in their ecumenical collaboration and particularly at the ecumenical conference in Fanø, Denmark, in 1934.

SECOND PHASE OF LIFE AND THOUGHT

When Bonhoeffer returned to Germany from the United States in 1931, Germany was in a state of serious political upheaval. There was resentment regarding the unjust settlement (toward Germany) after World War I.[43] There were feelings of deep humiliation, which in turn gave rise to an ardent nationalism. In

---

[39] Bethge, *Man of Vision*, 155.

[40] Eberhard Bethge, *Dietrich Bonhoeffer: A Biography: Theologian, Christian, Man for His Times*, rev. ed. Victoria J. Barnett (Minneapolis: Fortress, 2000), 203. We should remember that these comments were made to close personal friends and one speaks differently in private than in public.

[41] Quoted in Bethge, *Man for His Times*, 155.

[42] Bethge, *Man for His Times*, 166.

[43] In the aftermath of World War I, Germany felt compelled to sign the Treaty of Versailles. This placed severe restrictions upon Germany, including loss of territory, limiting the size of their armed forces, reparation payments, and so on.

addition, there were major economic problems like poverty and unemployment. People were becoming more and more determined to rectify the felt injustice. This was not unrelated to a struggle for identity of a new national self. The power and popularity of the National Socialistic movement increased substantially, and its eloquent leader, Adolf Hitler, was able to fan the flames of nationalism into solidarity for his cause.

In July 1931, Bonhoeffer visited Barth. This meeting took place when Barth was forty-five and Bonhoeffer merely twenty-five years old. The meeting was cordial and very positive for both men. Bonhoeffer had great respect for Barth, and they met on several other occasions as well. Whatever disagreement there was between them, Bonhoeffer always believed his own theology came "from within, not without, the Barthian movement."[44] This is said despite the fact that on occasion he could state his disagreement rather emphatically.

In 1932 Bonhoeffer gave a series of lectures including "The Nature of the Church" and "Is there a Christian Ethic?" He also taught a course on "Creation and Sin" which, a year later, resulted in the book *Creation and Fall*. At this time the mainline church and the government of Germany were becoming increasingly anti-Semitic, not only covertly but also officially with new state legislation.

In January 1933, Hitler was installed as the chancellor of Germany. In February of that year, Bonhoeffer gave a radio address on the topic, "Changes in the Concept of Führer." In the speech, he warned the German people of the immorality of the state's actions and of coming disasters. He called what was happening in his country idolatry because it was a total abrogation of the sovereignty of God and believed that Germans were claiming power for themselves which they had no rights to. They were acting in ways that assumed they had ultimate control over history and its vindication of injustice. In the

process, they excluded the right of an entire segment of society (the Jews) from the state's protection from injustice. Bonhoeffer never made it through the speech. He was cut off while he was on the air, and after that he was considered an enemy of the regime.

During that same year, Bonhoeffer did what he could to speak out against heresy in the churches. He published pamphlets, "The Aryan Clause in the Church" and "The Church and the Jewish Question". He reminded the churches of their identity as God's people, people who accept that all peoples of this world are God's people. He emphatically condemned as heresy the notion that Christians should be involved in creating a New Reich which was explicitly set over against the Jewish people. He was particularly upset with the practice of church leaders who invoked the blessing of God upon such practices by political leaders. In spite of his efforts, the church was effectively taken into the control and dominion of the government. Friends of Hitler were appointed bishops and then became the mouthpieces of the new regime. In April 1933, the "Aryan Paragraph" which made it illegal for any person of Jewish blood to hold public office, became law. Bonhoeffer was deeply depressed.

He was teaching at the University of Berlin where he began to notice that his theology had become suspect and he felt that he would not be there much longer. He also began to feel that the university was no place to train Christians. For example, in the university, you do not have a community of faith. There you talk of ideas and how people think; you do not focus on shaping a people. This concern was in keeping with a shift in language that was already taking shape in Bonhoeffer's mind and would be expressed more formally later, namely, that radical discipleship was a requirement of all Christians.

At the Fanø Ecumenical Conference in 1934, Bonhoeffer gave a speech which has become known as the "peace speech."[45] In

---

[44] Bethge, *Man for His Times*, 178.

[45] This speech has been published as "The Universal Church and the World of Nations." See Bethge, *Man for His Times*, 387.

it, he began with the church—the body that gathers in the name of Christ. The speech served as the sermon in a worship service. He struggled with the matter of how the church should align itself in the evident stampede to war in which Germany was at the forefront. He was unequivocal in his assertion that the international body called church must preach peace. Bethge describes the effect of this sermon as follows: "Never before . . . had he stated so distinctly that, for the disciple, the renunciation of force meant the renunciation of defence."[46] Then Bethge quotes Bonhoeffer directly, "[Christians] may not use weapons against one another because they know that in so doing they are aiming those weapons at Christ himself."[47] It was at this conference that Jean Lasserre presented the resolution brought forward from the Youth Conference on conscientious objection.[48] On the way home from Fanø, Bonhoeffer traveled via Bruay in the Artois, where Lasserre worked as a pastor among poor factory workers.[49]

Another pacifist influential on Bonhoeffer was Mahatma Gandhi. At the Fanø conference, he met a personal friend of Gandhi and for several years afterward desired to travel to India. Although this visit never took place, Bonhoeffer wanted to talk with Gandhi because, as he worked his way into the Sermon on the Mount, he saw ever more clearly the co-connections between pacifism and discipleship. He believed that Gandhi, although not Christian, had some important insights on both.

When he returned to Germany from Denmark, Bonhoeffer started an underground seminary in Finkenwalde, which was in effect a commune where work, worship, and study were the three modes of student life. This was also where several of his important

books took shape: his book on *Psalms*, *The Cost of Discipleship*, *Temptation and Fall*, and *Life Together*. During this time he was still teaching one course at the university, but most of his time was now spent at the "preacher's seminary."

Although there was serious political turmoil in Germany, this was a time when Bonhoeffer was at peace with himself. In 1935 he wrote:

> I now believe that I know at last that I am at least on the right track—for the first time in my life. And that often makes me very glad. . . . I believe that inwardly I shall be clear and honest with myself only if I truly begin to take seriously the Sermon on the Mount. That is the only source of power capable of blowing up the whole phantasmagoria [i.e., the Nazi illusion] once and for all.[50]

He continues to emphasize that Christianity's central focus should be the church-community. But this focus is now expressed by emphasizing the importance of Jesus Christ as Lord. And here the Sermon on the Mount in the Gospel of Matthew is the key biblical text. In other words, to say that Christ is Lord of the church is to place the accent on being in Christ in a particular way, to call yourself a Christ-ian is to name your master. This is the theme of *The Cost of Discipleship*, which was published in 1937.

In explicating his discipleship ethics, Bonhoeffer begins by speaking about "cheap grace" and "costly grace."[51] The former is what allows for a comfortable lifestyle; the latter does not, especially not in the context of injustice. The first two sentences of *The Cost of Discipleship* are: "Cheap grace is the deadly enemy of our Church. We are fighting to-day for costly grace."[52] Cheap grace allows us to deflect responsibility by believing that since we are not in charge—it all happens by

---

46 Bethge, *Man for His Times*, 388.
47 Bethge, *Man for His Times*, 387.
48 Bethge, *Man for His Times*, 391.
49 Bethge, *Man for His Times*, 392.
50 Bethge, *Man for His Times*, 205.
51 Dietrich Bonhoeffer, *The Cost of Discipleship*, trans. R. H. Fuller (New York: Macmillan, 1974), 45–60. *The Cost of Discipleship* was titled *Nachfolge* in German, which literally means "follow after."
52 Bonhoeffer, *Cost of Discipleship*, 45.

the grace of God—our actions do not matter. Costly grace affirms that our actions do matter, not because we matter, but because God and God's grace matter. When we embody the grace of God in the presence of other people, we are instruments of God's glorification. That matters ultimately. And this may prove costly, as it did for Jesus. Costly grace, says Bonhoeffer, is in essence the message of the gospel. The grace of Jesus is not cheap.

Discipleship ethics is derived from the belief that the church is the body of Christ. Bonhoeffer reflects on the difference between the first disciples who lived in the bodily presence of Jesus and the current disciples who do not. He says:

> The disciples enjoyed exactly the same bodily communion as is available for us to-day, nay rather, our communion with him is richer and more assured than it was for them, for the communion and presence which we have is that of the glorified Lord. Our faith must be aware of the greatness of this gift. The Body of Christ is the ground and assurance of that faith. It is the one and perfect gift whereby we become partakers of salvation. It is indeed newness of life. In the Body of Christ we are caught up into the eternity of the act of God.[53]

The church is a living body that bears testimony to the concrete humanity of the Son of God. As Bonhoeffer puts it, "The Body of Christ takes up space on earth."[54] The visible church is a suffering church. Suffering in this sinful world cannot be avoided. If it is avoided, then the church cannot be understood as the body of Christ.

Herein lies the essential danger with the state church, for it relies on the power of the state for its protection and in so doing it compromises its identity. A discipleship church exists in the kingdom of the resurrection. Here all earthly powers are broken, and the only power that exists is the power of God. And this is always a redeeming power.

Bonhoeffer sees this power confusion rooted in Luther's teaching of the two realms. For example, he says:

> Thus in his own way Luther confirms Constantine's covenant with the church. As a result a minimal ethic prevailed. Luther, of course, wanted a complete ethic for everyone, not only for monastic orders. Thus the existence of the Christian became the existence of the citizen. The nature of the church vanished into the invisible realm. But in this way the New Testament message was fundamentally misunderstood, inner-worldliness became a principle.[55]

In a similar vein, in 1932 to 1933, Bonhoeffer had critiqued Luther's orders of creation in his *Creation and Fall*. This, he said, was an unacceptable beginning point for ethics because it depreciated the transforming power of the resurrection which can create a whole new reality. Luther's "order of creation" thesis assumed that the way the world is, is the way it must be. People of the resurrection cannot see the world that way.

In *The Cost of Discipleship* Bonhoeffer also lays the groundwork for his view of pacifism. He says:

> The followers of Jesus have been called to peace. When he called them they found their peace. But now they are told that they must not only *have* peace but *make* it. And to that end they denounce all violence and tumult . . . [Jesus'] disciples keep the peace by choosing to endure suffering themselves rather than inflict it on others. . . . The peacemakers will carry the cross with their Lord, for it was on the cross that peace was made.[56]

It is hard to describe Bonhoeffer's later view of pacifism simply. It sounds so clear and relatively simple here, but it is anything but that. While he was always passionate about peace, he was not a pacifist who merely applied the principles of "Do not kill" and "Love your enemies." We might call Bonhoeffer an embodied pacifist, seeking to give expression

---

[53] Bonhoeffer, *Cost of Discipleship*, 263.

[54] Bonhoeffer, *Cost of Discipleship*, 277.

[55] Quoted from Dietrich Bonhoeffer, *No Rusty Swords: Letters, Lectures, and Notes, 1928–1936*, trans. John Bowden and Edwin Robertson, ed. Edwin Robertson (New York: Harper & Row, 1965), 324.

[56] Bonhoeffer, *Cost of Discipleship*, 126–27 (emphasis in original).

to peace and justice in a violent world in the name of Christ. With the knowledge that sin is both out there and within all of us, Bonhoeffer realized that the perfect expression of the peace of Christ is not an option that is often available to us. Hence pacifism for him did not mean "adopting nonviolence as an absolute principle in all circumstances," as Clifford Green summarizes.[57] It meant, rather, being present and "responding" to evil and injustice from deeply within the "peace of Christ." This is no different from the way Bonhoeffer approached Christian ethics generally. Ethics does not derive from theory or principles but from a person, Jesus Christ.

In 1939 Bonhoeffer was invited by Reinhold Niebuhr to go to the United States to teach. It was becoming evident that Bonhoeffer was on a collision course with the Nazi regime, and people like Niebuhr wanted to save him from inevitable harm. Yet Bonhoeffer refused, putting into practice what he had been saying about costly grace. The decision caused him much agony because personally he really wanted to leave Germany. Yet he believed that the Germans needed him more than ever. Hence, to leave at that time would have meant deserting his people. So he went to the United States for a short period of time but returned after a few weeks.

THIRD PHASE OF LIFE
AND THOUGHT

In 1939 Hitler invaded Poland and World War II began. Bonhoeffer had predicted this would happen, so when it finally did, his worst fears were realized. Now he worried even more about the eventuality of some of his other dire predictions about the lengths to which Hitler would go to realize his ambition. He thought it important to consult with others about his course of action, especially with friends outside of Germany, so he traveled to London to meet with Bishop George Bell, an Anglican theologian, the Bishop of Chichester, and a leader in the Ecumenical Movement.

At home, Bonhoeffer was experiencing severe political controls. In 1937 the Gestapo had dissolved the seminary; in July 1940, Bonhoeffer was forbidden to speak in public and was required to report regularly to the police. In 1941 he was forbidden to publish. Yet somehow, during all this turmoil, he was able to write some of his most seminal thoughts on Christian ethics.

Bonhoeffer's *Ethics*, as we have it today, is a posthumously published book of manuscripts written during the last years of his free life (1940–1943). It represents his most mature thinking after a tumultuous battle of resistance to the politics of National Socialism in the name of Christ and the church.

In *Ethics*, the way Bonhoeffer presents the case for Christian ethics becomes especially clear. As we have already seen about pacifism specifically, so it is with all other matters of ethics; principles, goals, and values cannot determine faithfulness for those bound to Jesus Christ. Only Christ and the church can ground the Christian life. But this means something quite specific; if Christ is the guide, then the Christian life can only be embodied in concrete social spaces as it was modeled by Christ himself. Embodiment does not admit of formulas or repeatable patterns. Theories cannot tell us how to live. This is the case with ethics, and in a similar way it is so for theology as a whole. Neither theology nor ethics are solutions for anything. For both, the temptation is to locate the good and God in a humanly manageable space. But that always destroys their power and their truth; neither the good nor God are locatable. Bonhoeffer gives an especially astute theological example of this in a letter later published as part of *Letters and Papers from Prison*:

> Belief in the resurrection is *not* the "solution" of the problem of death. God's "beyond" is not the

---

[57] Quoted from "Editor's Introduction to the English Edition," by Clifford J. Green, in Dietrich Bonhoeffer, *Dietrich Bonhoeffer Works*, vol. 6, *Ethics*, trans. Reinhard Krauss, Charles C. West, and Douglas W. Stott; English ed. Clifford J. Green (Minneapolis: Fortress, 2005), 15.

beyond of our cognitive faculties. The transcendence of epistemological theory has nothing to do with the transcendence of God. God is beyond in the midst of our life. The church stands, not at the boundaries where human powers give out, but in the middle of the village.[58]

In other words, only by seeing Jesus Christ present among us are we able to participate in his life and being; only then will we know how to live "in Christ." This is indeed a precarious matter, for it involves risk, interpretation, commitment, and radical action.

Two themes from his *Ethics* require special attention: the relation of penultimate to ultimate and his treatment of "the natural." His discussion of cheap and costly grace developed in *The Cost of Discipleship* is picked up in *Ethics* in a specific way. The penultimate/ultimate relationship is all about grace. God's grace justifying sinners is the ultimate; our participation in God's grace is always penultimate.

The relationship of penultimate to ultimate is both a historical-eschatological relationship[59] and also a transcendental-ontological one. One might say that it involves both our actions as well as our being. Hence, for Bonhoeffer, it serves as yet another way of uniting act and being. In other words, to understand Christian ethics properly, he believed that we must see ourselves as participating in something that is far bigger than we can grasp or even imagine. This is the case both in relation to what is to come (historical), as well as in relationship to what is already really taking place (being). To act and exist in Christ always involves much more than is immediately apparent. Thus he can say, "The past and future of the whole of life flow together in God's presence."[60]

Bonhoeffer uses the penultimate/ultimate dynamic to clarify how we are to see ourselves as participants in Christ's being/acting in the world. He says: "In Christ the reality of God encounters the reality of the world and allows us to take part in this real encounter. It is an encounter beyond all radicalism and all compromise. *Christian life is participation in Christ's encounter with the world.*"[61] At one level, the relationship between penultimate and ultimate is quite simple: the ultimate is what Christ does and the penultimate is our participation in that. On the other hand, it is complex since our actions and being always extend beyond themselves. He explains:

> What is this penultimate? It is all that precedes the ultimate—the justification of the sinner by grace alone—and that is addressed as penultimate after finding the ultimate. At the same time it is everything that follows the ultimate, in order to again precede it. . . . The penultimate does not determine the ultimate; the ultimate determines the penultimate. . . . What concerns us in all that has been said about penultimate things is this: prepare the way of the word.[62]

The logic of this dynamic relationship becomes clearer when he gives concrete examples. He speaks of feeding the hungry and responding to the needy and unjustly treated persons. He says:

> It would be blasphemy against God and our neighbor to leave the hungry unfed while saying that God is closest to those in deepest need. . . . If the hungry do not come to faith, the guilt is upon those who denied them bread. To bring bread to the hungry is preparing the way for the coming of grace. . . . To give the hungry bread is not yet to proclaim to them the grace of God and justification, and to have received bread does not yet mean to stand in faith. But for the one who does something penultimate for the sake of the ultimate, this penultimate thing is related to the ultimate.[63]

These are remarkable words. For Bonhoeffer, only Christ prepares the way. We, on the other hand, open ourselves to

---

[58] In a letter to Eberhard Bethge on April 30, 1944, he seeks to explain the sense in which Christianity is "religionless." Bonhoeffer, *Letters and Papers from Prison*, enlarged ed., trans. Reginald Fuller, ed. Eberhard Bethge (New York: Macmillan, 1971), 282.

[59] He uses the terms "*Letztes*" (last) and "*Allerletztes*" (very last). Bonhoeffer, *Ethics*, 146n.

[60] Bonhoeffer, *Ethics*, 147.

[61] Bonhoeffer, *Ethics*, 159 (emphasis added).

[62] Bonhoeffer, *Ethics*, 159–61.

[63] Bonhoeffer, *Ethics*, 163.

letting Christ prepare the way both in us and through us for others.

This way of presenting the matter of Christian ethics leads Bonhoeffer away from mainline Protestant theology and directly into traditional Catholic thought; if you like, to the natural. He is struggling here with the same issue as Barth; both found themselves pushed to some version of a "natural theology." Bonhoeffer says, "The concept of the natural has fallen into disrepute in Protestant ethics."[64] Again this is an issue of how to understand grace. But here the issue is how grace relates to nature. In his earlier work, he was still under the heavy influence of Barth's response to Brunner on the radical separation of nature and grace. Now he is much more sympathetic to Thomas Aquinas and his view that "Grace does not destroy nature, but perfects it."[65] This requires an adjustment to what it means to affirm God as both Creator and Savior, and human beings as both nature and spirit. And in both cases it raises again the question of the *analogia entis*; not that we can know God by looking at nature, but that nature is not understood properly without seeing it as participating in the divine.

Bonhoeffer believed that German Protestants especially had moved too far away from the doctrine that nature participates in the transcendent God and too far toward seeing God as a power resource at the disposal of human beings in their quest for peace and justice. For God is not a power separated from nature but a power present in nature redeeming (perfecting) it. And in following Christ, we are invited into what God is already doing.

With this logic as background, Bonhoeffer speaks of the notion of the responsible life. He says:

> By being responsible for Christ, who is life, before human beings, and only thus, I simultaneously take responsibility for human beings before Christ. I *simultaneously* represent Christ before human beings, and represent human beings before Christ.[66]

The last several years of his life saw Bonhoeffer deeply involved in a struggle against the Hitler atrocities. It is difficult to narrate this aspect of his life precisely because not everything is well documented. It is clear that he collaborated with the German Abwehr (a military intelligence organization) where his brother-in-law Hans von Dohnanyi worked. It is also clear that he served as a courier of documents to other countries. And he assisted in the escape of Jews to Switzerland. To what extent he was directly involved in the violent assassination attempts of Hitler is not known.

Bonhoeffer taught that Christ despises anyone who terrorizes other human beings. Christ is life; Christ cannot be for killing. And yet he finds himself drawn into a conspiracy to kill a tyrant. How can this be? He talks about "the willingness to take on guilt." Clearly his involvement in this conspiracy involves guilt, and he never seeks to *justify* such a thing, for it cannot be justified. But when a conscience that has been formed by faithfulness to Christ compels one to act in ways not faithful to his teachings, what then can one do? The alternatives are either nothing or something sinful. Yet both, he believes, involve guilt; for "nothing" permits evil knowingly, while "something sinful" commits it in an effort to overcome it. He says, "Those who act out of free responsibility are justified before others by dire necessity; before themselves they are acquitted by their conscience, but before God they hope only for grace."[67]

During the early 1940s, Bonhoeffer was able to see documents that revealed government plans to invade neighboring states. This upset him greatly and seriously challenged his commitment to pacifism. He earnestly

---

[64] Bonhoeffer, *Ethics*, 171.

[65] Thomas Aquinas, *Summa Theologica*, I, Q. I, Art. 8, reply obj. 2, trans. Fathers of the English Dominican Province (New York: Benziger Bros., 1947–48).

[66] Bonhoeffer, *Ethics*, 256 (emphasis in original).

[67] Bonhoeffer, *Ethics*, 283.

desired consultation, but no ethicist in Europe or North America could help him wrestle with his struggle from the standpoint of his view of the peace of Christ. On this matter he felt isolated. He remained firmly resolved that whatever his commitment to pacifism required of him in this desperate situation, escape was not one of them. Pacifists are as much resident in this sinful world as anyone else; there is no escape. Doing nothing was as sinful for Bonhoeffer as doing something violent.

In March 1941, he went to Switzerland to present a paper on "The Church and World Order." At this time he proposed to his British colleagues that Britain should offer peace to Germany and that would strengthen the resistance movement because it would provide an international peace link. But things did not work out that way. He again met Bishop Bell. He showed him plans to assassinate Hitler and disclosed the names of the people involved. The bishop was anguished.

When Bonhoeffer returned to Germany, he discovered that a major deportation of Jews from Berlin had taken place. He was now more resolved than ever that he should seek to stop Hitler. In 1943 he made a few more trips back to Norway and Switzerland for discussions and support for the German resistance.

It is puzzling to see how, during this difficult time, Bonhoeffer found time for a courtship, but he did. On January 17, 1943, he was engaged to Maria von Wedemeyer. Unfortunately their marriage never took place.

On March 13 and 21, there were two unsuccessful assassination attempts on Hitler's life. On April 5, Bonhoeffer's house was searched, and he was arrested and placed in Tegel prison. Several others from the Abwehr were arrested with him.

On July 20, 1944, there was another assassination attempt on Hitler's life and several documents implicating Bonhoeffer were discovered. Again, several people were arrested, including his brother Klaus and his brother-in-law Rüdiger Schleicher. On February 7, 1945, Bonhoeffer was moved to Buchenwald

prison. Eventually he was moved to Flossenbürg where he, together with his brother and brother-in-law, was executed on April 9, 1945. As he was led to his death, Bonhoeffer is recorded to have said, "This is the end—for me, the beginning of life."

CONCLUSION

I refer to some of Bonhoeffer's comments from prison to conclude this chapter. Two phrases in particular are often discussed: "the world come of age" and "religionless Christianity."

What Bonhoeffer means by "the world come of age" is that in our world we have displaced God from the universe. We must now understand ourselves as living in this kind of world, which is admittedly very dangerous. Moderns are seeking to create a world without God. Hence, they can see no limits or guidance. Technology and science have made possible idolatrous forms of existence.

In part, this is due to past bad theology, where God has been misunderstood as a God of the gaps. That is, in the past we thought of God as invoked whenever we could not otherwise explain something. But this has never been a true understanding of the God who saves us in Jesus Christ. God is incarnate in the body of Jesus Christ and in the church. So God is everywhere in forgiveness, love, and mercy. God is fundamentally in this world—everywhere. This means that we must embrace a Christianity that discards the traditions that tell us that God is otherworldly. The God of Jesus Christ is as fully in this world as is possible, willing even to die in the struggle to redeem the sinfulness of this world. The world has come of age and Christianity must now be seen as religionless; that is, Christianity is not a religious system of ideas, but a way of life in Christ.

Bonhoeffer explains these notions in what became his *Letters and Papers from Prison*. He writes on July 18, 1944, less than a year before his execution:

> Man is summoned to share in God's suffering at the hands of a Godless world. He must therefore really live in a Godless world, without attempting

to drop over or explain its ungodliness in some religious way or other. He must live a "secular" life and thereby share in God's suffering. He *may* live (as one who has been freed from false religious obligations and inhibitions). To be a Christian does not mean to be religious in a particular way, to make something of oneself . . . on the basis of some method or other, but be a man—not a type of man, a man that Christ creates in us. It is not a religious act that makes the Christian but participation in the suffering of God in the secular life. That is *metanoia*: not in the first place thinking about one's own needs, problems, sins, and fears, but allowing oneself to be caught up into the way of Jesus Christ, into the messianic event, thus fulfilling Isaiah 53. Therefore "believe in the Gospel," or, in the words of John the Baptist, "Behold, the Lamb of God, who takes away the sins of the world" (John 1:29). . . . This being caught up into the messianic suffering of God in Jesus Christ takes a variety of forms in the New Testament. It appears in the call to discipleship, in Jesus' table-fellowship with sinners, in "conversations" in the narrow sense of the word (Zacchaeus), in the act of the woman who was a sinner (Luke 7). . . . The only thing that is common to all these is their sharing in the suffering of God in Christ. That is their "faith." There is nothing of religious method here. The "religious act" is always something partial; "faith" is something whole, involving the whole of one's life. Jesus calls men, not to a new religion, but to life. But what does this life look like, this participation in the powerlessness of God in the world? I will write about that next time, I hope.[68]

Unfortunately next time did not come. His notion of the powerlessness of God, so promising in answering some of the outstanding questions we have of him, is not developed. Perhaps there is poetic irony here. After all, according to Bonhoeffer's teaching, theology and ethics are not about answering all the outstanding questions, but rather about living/dying in faith without final answers. Yet he tells us much about his view of God. The powerlessness of God implies that we are called to seek out where in the world there is suffering and go there and hang on the cross with the sufferer. This is the act of participation in divine suffering, and hence in this way we can bring the presence of God, the suffering One, to the suffering ones.

---

[68] Bonhoeffer, *Letters and Papers*, 361–62 (emphasis in original).

Chapter Sixteen

HANS URS VON BALTHASAR
(1905–1988)

Hans Urs von Balthasar was a pious, Swiss, Catholic scholar, and, as Blaise Pascal is known to have said, "Pious scholars are rare." Balthasar's life attests to his own stated claim that he desired to be a kneeling theologian rather than a sitting theologian. But clearly this did not mean that he had little to say, for it is alleged that he has written more than one hundred books and hundreds of articles.

We have already met Balthasar as an interlocutor with Karl Barth. There we saw him as one concerned with not letting Barth off the hook on his own affirmations of the word of God become flesh in Jesus Christ. Balthasar believed that it was precisely the somewhat absurd notion of the incarnation that required a radical yes from Christians to both God *and* the world. And in his debate with Barth, he sought to push him further in the direction of a theology of nature.

Perhaps a word is required on why I include Balthasar in this study of Christian ethics. He is neither an ethicist in any narrow sense, nor is he well known, especially not in the English-speaking world. Moreover, even in Roman Catholic circles, he has a somewhat checkered history. There are three reasons for his inclusion here: first, his place within the Catholic Church; he is today seen as a most important Catholic intellectual, and Karl Rahner is said to have called his achievements in the area of Catholic theology "really breathtaking."[1] His standing in the Catholic Church is evidenced by the fact that he was to have been elevated to the College of Cardinals although he died two days before it was to take place. Second, as a Catholic "cultural theologian"[2] he brings especially rich insights on aesthetics, that is, the study of the good and the beautiful, and so adds an immeasurably profound perspective on our subject of theological ethics. And third, although he is not as well known in North America as either Hans Küng or Karl Rahner, his rich theological read of culture is sorely needed in a theological wilderness where theology is not only strange language but most often considered as entirely tangential to Christian ethics. All of this is not yet to mention that Protestant-Catholic theological engagement is itself an issue of Christian faithfulness.

HIS LIFE

Balthasar was born in Lucerne, Switzerland, on August 12, 1905, into a noble family (hence the *von* in his name).[3] His father,

---

[1] S. Joel Garver, who teaches philosophy and theology at La Salle University in Philadelphia, reports this on his website, http://www.joelgarver.com/writ/theo/balt/bio.htm, accessed May 9, 2011.

[2] This is the designation given him by Thomas O'Meara, O. P., in "Of Art and Theology: Hans Urs von Balthasar's Systems," *Theological Studies* 42, no. 2 (1981): 272.

[3] Throughout this chapter and especially for the biographical aspects of Balthasar's story, I am relying on two excellent sources: Edward T. Oakes, *Pattern of Redemption: The Theology of Hans Urs von Balthasar* (New York: Continuum, 1997); and Peter Henrici, S. J., "Hans Urs von Balthasar: A Sketch of his Life," in *Hans Urs von Balthasar: His Life and Work*, ed. David L. Schindler (San Francisco: Ignatius, 1991).

Oscar Ludwig Karl Balthasar (1872–1946), was a master builder and constructed many grandiose buildings, including the St. Karli Kirche, one of the impressive, modern church buildings in Switzerland. His mother, Gabrielle Pietzcker, who died when Balthasar was only twenty-four years old, was the first general secretary of the Swiss League of Catholic Women. He had a younger brother, Dieter, an officer in the Swiss Guard, and an older sister Renée, who also joined a religious order: the Franciscan Sisters of Sainte-Marie des Anges.[4]

Balthasar's pre-university education matched his noble stock, being with both the Benedictines and the Jesuits. This prepared him well for his later studies. Before he arrived at the University of Zurich, he had already studied at universities in Vienna and Berlin. In Zurich he completed his doctoral work in German language and culture in 1928. He wrote a dissertation titled "The History of the Eschatological Problem in Modern German Literature."

One day while he was still in his early twenties he was on a retreat in the Black Forest led by a Jesuit. Here, while on a walk in the woods, he received a profound call. Later in life he reflected on this event as follows:

> Even now, thirty years later, I can still go to that remote path in the Black Forest, not far from Basel, and find again the tree beneath which I was struck as if by lightening. . . . And yet it was neither theology nor the priesthood which then came into my mind in a flash. It was simply this: you have nothing to choose, you have been called. You will not serve, you will be taken into service. You have no plans to make, you are just a little stone in a mosaic which has long been ready. All I needed to do was "to leave everything and follow," without making plans, without wishes for insights. All I needed was to stand and wait and see what I was needed for.[5]

This is an interesting account of a religious experience and is reminiscent of Augustine's and Martin Luther's conversions. Although it led in directions just as profound, it seems from the beginning to have been more open-ended—more like the call by Jesus to his disciples to leave what they were doing and follow. They too had no idea where faithfulness would take them.

On November 18, 1929, Balthasar sought entry into the Society of Jesus (Jesuits). The training process for becoming a Jesuit had him spend two years as a novice, then another two years studying philosophy near Munich, and after this another four years at the Jesuit theologate in Fourviere, France, (near Lyon), studying theology. Here he fell in love with theology and the church fathers under an inspiring teacher, Henri de Lubac. While Balthasar had earlier completed a doctorate in German literature, he never received a Ph.D. in theology or philosophy.

To join a religious order required renunciation, and one aspect of this was especially difficult for Balthasar: giving up his love for music. This was a sacrifice not only because of his desire to be nurtured by his awe-inspiring love of music but also because of his interest in German literature and culture. Yet he did make the sacrifice, and when he reflected on it later, he said that he was able to give away his records and players because he had memorized the entire works of Mozart.[6] And, of course, memory cannot be taken away.

After his ordination in 1937, Balthasar was assigned to work in Munich, putting his literary training to work at the Jesuit monthly, *Stimmen der Zeit*. But because of the impending war, Germany became a dangerous place. So the church offered him a choice between two positions: one in Rome as a professor of theology and the other in Switzerland as a student chaplain at the University of Basel. His reply: "I was glad to be offered the position in Switzerland that transferred me to direct pastoral work."[7]

---

[4] See Henrici, "Hans Urs von Balthasar," 8.

[5] Hans Urs von Balthasar, *Pourquoi je me suis fait pretre*, as quoted in Oakes, *Pattern of Redemption*, 2.

[6] Henrici, "Hans Urs von Balthasar," 8–9.

[7] Oakes, *Pattern of Redemption*, 3n5.

It is important to remember that during this time in Switzerland the Jesuits were not highly respected; they were merely tolerated. It is also interesting that "In reaction to Hitler's Germany, Catholics turned more and more to French Catholicism."[8] In other words, just like in the Protestant church of Barth and Bonhoeffer, what was happening in Germany raised serious challenges for the Catholic Church.

Balthasar soon worked his way into university life at Basel, adding work as an editor and translator to his regular duties. Student chaplaincy work afforded opportunities for many lectures and debates set up by student societies. He conducted many retreats for male students and eventually also for female students. The latter were a novelty and well received. His students were impressed with his poetic illumination of theology and also with his ability to sit down at a piano and play from memory Mozart's *Don Giovanni*. Even at this stage in life, he had published many articles and even books.

As student chaplain, he had the opportunity to interact with Protestants, and one of the Protestant theology professors at Basel at the time was Karl Barth. Often, when Balthasar gave public lectures, Barth was in attendance and vice versa. Balthasar's interest in theological exchange with Barth eventually led him to write a book on his theology.[9] Balthasar was greatly inspired and influenced by Barth's radical christocentrism, that is, his theology of the Word. But Balthasar wanted more from him; he wanted Barth to give a more charitable account of God's creation; he wanted a wholesome rendering of the sacraments—in effect, he wanted Barth's conversion. Balthasar believed that the changes necessary for Barth's theology were not capable of accommodation into a Protestant theological framework. But the change he sought from Barth was not to happen, even though Barth made some rather significant adjustments to his theology as a result of his encounters with Balthasar. And Barth freely acknowledged Balthasar's influence on his own thought.

In Basel, Balthasar also met a Protestant doctor, Adrienne von Speyr (1902–1967), who would end up exerting an enormous influence upon his life and theology. Von Speyr had married a Basel history professor named Emil Dürr in 1927. He died accidentally after only seven years of marriage. This tragedy resulted in another, namely, von Speyr's loss of faith in God. Two years later she married her husband's successor, Professor Werner Kaegi, with whom she stayed until her death. Together they lived in a beautiful home which would later also serve as a guesthouse for Balthasar.

Von Speyr was extremely devoted to her patients, especially the poor and those with psychological problems. She was bright, imaginative, and socially popular. But she was a Protestant who had lost her faith. Shortly after she met Balthasar, and with his guidance, she converted to Catholicism. The conversion was not popular with her Protestant friends and certainly not with her family. Almost immediately there were accounts of miracles and visions; these raised both curiosity and suspicion.[10] But Balthasar and von Speyr remained close friends.

It was not long after von Speyr's conversion that the Community of St. John was founded. At first this was only a women's group with three postulants, and was relatively unknown.

---

[8] Henrici, "Hans Urs von Balthasar," 15.

[9] See Hans Urs von Balthasar, *The Theology of Karl Barth* (San Francisco: Ignatius, 1992). For a discussion of the theological exchange between Balthasar and Barth, see chap. 14 above.

[10] Edward Oakes recounts one of the "most remarkable" stories told by Balthasar: "Another of Adrienne's unintelligible and hence troubling experiences took place at the coffin of a twelve-year-old only son of her admired and beloved friend, Professor Merke. She had prayed 'like crazy' at the bedside of the dying child; she had even offered God her own children in substitution. Yet when the boy died she again had prayed until the body moved and half sat up. Then suddenly a voice was heard as from heaven: why are you questioning my decision? The dead body immediately fell back and the nurse, amazed by it all, had to re-fold his hands" (my translation), cited in German in Oakes, *Pattern of Redemption*, 301n2.

This changed a few years later when Balthasar published a book which promoted the Community. It was becoming apparent that Balthasar was eager to promote both von Speyr's activities and her thought. In 1947 he was involved in setting up a publishing company called Johannes Verlag, for the expressed purpose of publishing von Speyr's works. It turned out that this move also was not without controversy. Yet, as we will see, the major issue centered on his involvement and promotion of the Community of St. John.

The bishop of Basel, Franziskus von Streng, had serious reservations about Balthasar's involvement in the Community of St. John.[11] Balthasar's efforts to have von Speyr's visions authenticated increased the strain. It was becoming clear to all that Balthasar's theology and work were moving in directions different from his order. So in 1948, when on a retreat under the direction of Father Donatien Mollat,[12] Balthasar made the decision to leave the Society of Jesus. After eighteen months in limbo, his departure from the Jesuit order was finally made official.

It might seem surprising that Balthasar's departure from the Jesuits was not more devastating to him. After all, this was his family, his spiritual home, his church. Henrici helps us to understand: "It was a question . . . of the conflict of 'his inner certainty, reached in prayer' and his obedience to the society, in other words, the conflict between obedience to the society and direct obedience to God."[13] This is a hard distinction for a Catholic priest to make since the two are normally not separated. Henrici goes on to explain that only after the death of von Speyr was it possible to tell how much her many healings, miracles, and visions helped Balthasar in his own spiritual and pastoral work. And of course, herein lay a significant tension with his order.

It is important to acknowledge that the connection between Balthasar's and von Speyr's work is neither mere coincidence nor convenience. As Balthasar saw it, it was necessarily linked. He said, "I want to try to prevent anyone after my death from undertaking the task of separating my work from that of Adrienne von Speyr. This is not in the least possible, either theologically or in regard to the secular institute now underway."[14] So after leaving the order, he threw himself into her work. Certainly this did not mean that he wrote less or that his theology suddenly changed, but it meant that much of his energy went into promoting her work.

It was because the Jesuits refused to take responsibility for the "secular institute" that Balthasar felt he had to leave the order. This probably would not have happened after the Second Vatican Council, when the rules on church order were less rigid. In any event, this move should be seen as more than a clash of strong wills; it was a dispute rooted in the theology of the church. The Catholic Church distinguished between a secular institute and a religious order. According to the Code of Canon Law #710, "A secular institute is an institute of consecrated life in which the Christian faithful, living in the world, strive for the perfection of charity and seek to contribute to the sanctification of the world, especially from within."[15] In a secular institute, individuals are consecrated persons professing chastity, poverty, and obedience, but they do not live in community with other religious individuals.

Both Balthasar and von Speyr believed that the time had come for the church to move beyond the "withdrawal" approach of the religious orders, to one that engages Christians more directly with the messiness of society's ills. The church needed to be "in the world" in an immediate manner if it was ever to

---

[11] See Henrici, "Hans Urs von Balthasar," 21.

[12] See Henrici, "Hans Urs von Balthasar," 21.

[13] Henrici, "Hans Urs von Balthasar," 21–22.

[14] Oakes, *Pattern of Redemption*, 3.

[15] See "Code of Canon Law," at http://www.vatican.va/archive/ENG1104/__P2F.HTM, accessed September 12, 2011.

effect serious change. This thinking threatened the church.

Henrici summarizes what was at stake in this dispute.

> The issue is the Church in the world, not a radiating of the Church's holiness into the profane world, but the leavening of the world from within in order to make visible God's glory which still shines in this world. The center of the Church, says von Balthasar, is where people usually see the periphery: her secular mission. That is why the defensive bulwarks must be razed to the ground and spacious boulevards built from the rubble. This mission of the Church in the world must be carried out by the laity, who live completely in the world. But, to be able to fulfill that mission they really must be "salt" and "leaven." They must live at the very heart of Christianity in the shame of the Cross, in prayer, and renunciation.[16]

This vision of living the gospel of Jesus Christ in the world is what the secular institutes were all about; and this is what the Community of St. John was trying to put into practice. And it is over this difference of interpreting the mission of the church that Balthasar left the Jesuit order.

After the separation, life was extremely difficult for Balthasar; he was not permitted to perform the functions of priest, which meant that he was forbidden by church law to celebrate mass publicly, to preach, or to hear confessions. Not only this, he had only a little sustenance from his publishing company and was literally put out on the street. So the Kaegis invited him to live at their house, and he became von Speyr's full-time spiritual director. Finally in 1956 one of the bishops in Switzerland allowed him to serve in church, which lifted the cloud. Then came Second Vatican Council and the "complete vindication of all that he had fought for as a theologian."[17]

Balthasar was by then in his early fifties and the dynamics around his life had taken their toll on his health. In the fall of 1957, he suffered extreme exhaustion which led him to believe he was having a nervous breakdown. But he recovered in six months, only to be struck with phlebitis the following summer. Then a few months later a form of leukemia struck him and left his limbs partially paralyzed. From this malady, he would never fully recover.

In addition, in the early 1950s, von Speyr had become physically sick and since Balthasar was by then her full-time advisor it meant that he was looking after a seriously ill woman while trying to complete his work on theological aesthetics. She would live for another ten years and die in 1967 of cancer of the bowel. The last three years of her life she was almost completely blind.

Von Speyr's death meant that Balthasar's life took on a new phase. He was now able to move around freely, and he spent much of his last twenty years getting von Speyr's work recognized by the church. This was also a time when he worked intently at his own theological writings.

Yet life was far from easy for Balthasar. Although he was blessed with an unusual amount of energy, weariness was constantly at his door. He had become an enormously popular Catholic theologian, and demands on him were extremely high. Henrici strings together a series of quotations from Balthasar during the 1970s: "With all the secondary chores (radio, lectures, endless mail), I scarcely get to read and work . . . (1974). . . . I'm free in principle, yet in practice less and less free for myself, because I am at everyone's beck and call—and you can't say No to everything (1976)."[18] Whatever spare time he had, he devoted to writing. Yet physical illnesses would come again, including cataracts that forced surgery on both eyes in 1980 and 1981.

Part of his sustaining energies, despite his many challenges, came from his friends. Henrici names three friendship groups: the *Communione e Liberazione* movement with which he became associated; the many doctoral students from around the world who

---

[16] Henrici, "Hans Urs von Balthasar," 24–25.

[17] Oakes, *Pattern of Redemption*, 5.

[18] Henrici, "Hans Urs von Balthasar," 40.

were writing dissertations on his theology and came to seek clarification of his insights; and the group of twelve international editorial teams that centered around his journal *Communio*. Although also taxing, each of these groups had ways of offering him inspiration and nourishment, helping to sustain him.

In the spring of 1988, Balthasar traveled to Madrid, Spain, for editorial meetings and a symposium on his theology. Upon his return, he learned he had been appointed cardinal by the pope. Although an embarrassment—because he thought himself unworthy—he accepted "out of obedience to the Pope." After a quick trip to Rome to be measured for his cardinal's robe, he wrote to a friend saying, "Those above seem to have a different plan."[19] However, while he was preparing for Mass, two days before he was to become cardinal, he died "gently."[20]

HIS THEOLOGICAL WORKS

In his written work, as in his life, Balthasar constantly sought to bring *Theologie und Heiligkeit* (*Theology and Holiness*) into unity. To say this differently, he sought to bring "sitting theology," that is, the work of the academic's careful intellectual scrutiny, together with "kneeling theology," the devotion of one in unimpeded openness to God. Still another way of saying it is, as he said in 1958: "I am trying to bring aesthetics and theology face to face. . . . A tremendous theme, but who would be up to it these days? Where has *eros* got to in theology, and the commentary on the Song of Songs, which belongs to the very *center* of theology?"[21]

Articulating this unity was Balthasar's life's passion, and he rooted it in the incarnation of Christ. While his language on occasion sounds Platonic, his is not Greek philosophy, which holds that all that appears on earth participates in an *intellectual form* beyond

the physical realm. His is distinctly Christian in that *in Christ*—an empirical, receivable person event—ordinary human beings can "see the form";[22] that is, the meeting of heaven and earth becomes evident. In that meeting, one that Greek philosophy held to be impossible, the beauty of the infinite infuses the finite with beauty. Hence, only in Christ can we truly understand this world. Only in Christ can Christian theology—creation, redemption, eschatology, and so on—become intelligible. The form of this theology is not derived from logical necessity but from contingent reception. Theology is the unveiling of the given Son of Trinitarian God, received into the world through open obedience of Mary, and embodied by the church through the Holy Spirit.

When Balthasar began his theology studies, he realized that something had gone wrong to make a "discipline" that is so rich and beautiful so stale and boring. So he set himself a task: to discover what had happened and to seek to bring theology to its potential luster. In the process, he felt that he needed to bring together what the modern academic mind had broken apart—religion, aesthetics, and ethics. (Actually, Balthasar's Trilogy outline is slightly different, albeit similar: aesthetics-beauty, dramatics-goodness, and logic-truth). The hope lay in the recovery of the imagination of the incarnation and the Trinity. In this project, we hear a consistent affirmation: truth is one, beautiful, and good, and any severing of this unity makes not only Christian theology vacuous, but all of life flat and without joy. This is what has happened, and modern culture is living the fruits of this "fall." He puts it poignantly:

> We no longer dare to believe in beauty and we make of it a mere appearance in order the more easily to dispose of it. Our situation today shows that beauty demands for itself at least as much courage and decision as do truth and goodness,

---

[19] Henrici, "Hans Urs von Balthasar," 41.

[20] Henrici, "Hans Urs von Balthasar," 41.

[21] As quoted in Henrici, "Hans Urs von Balthasar," 27 (emphasis in original).

[22] We should note that the first volume of Balthasar's Trilogy, *The Glory of the Lord*, is subtitled "Seeing the Form."

and she will not allow herself to be separated and banned from her two sisters without taking them along with herself in an act of mysterious vengeance. We can be sure that whoever sneers at her name as if she were the ornament of a bourgeois past—whether he admits it or not—can no longer pray and soon will no longer be able to love.[23]

In a further vivid depiction of what it means to live in a world without beauty, he points out that not only should beauty be joined to truth and goodness, but that without beauty, truth, and goodness nothing can compel us toward the *telos* of humanity.

> In a world without beauty . . . in a world which is perhaps not wholly without beauty, which can no longer see it or reckon with it; in such a world the good also loses its attractiveness, the self evidence of why it must be carried out. Man stands before the good and asks himself why *it* must be done and not rather its alternative evil. For this, too, is a possibility, and even the more exciting one; why not investigate Satan's depths? In a world that no longer has enough confidence to affirm the beautiful, the proofs of the truths have lost their cogency.[24]

Theology can be nothing if it cannot recapture the power and glory of the beautiful. So begins his theological project.

Before I consider his theological writings, I need to point out that, as Balthasar saw it, it was not his writings that were his major accomplishment; that honor went to his involvement in the many "foundations" set up to serve people. These were not all initiated by him, but he was drawn into them as a service. Usually, four are named:[25] the first was a kind of education-student society (*Studentische Schulungsgemeinschaft*) in which he taught theology and philosophy courses;

the second, the Community of St. John; the third, the publishing house called Johannes Verlag; and the fourth, a journal called *Communio: International Catholic Review*. Balthasar put enormous energy into each of these projects, because each was an *expression of* and hence a concrete *invitation into* the beautiful.[26] Where his writings spoke of theology, his foundations put it in practice.

Balthasar's main theological work can be grouped into three general areas: the Trilogy, his work on spirituality, and his numerous books on the church fathers.[27] It is, of course, impossible to consider his entire corpus in this brief chapter, so I will comment only on his Trilogy. Even here it is completely impossible to do more than give a general glimpse into his thought. It also needs to be said that his work is not best understood as a system; it is more like artwork, or literature, or even poetry. It points or signs beyond itself, seeking to illuminate something outside its grasp rather than describing what is within the intellectual clutches of the author. He loved creative expressions and metaphors; really, he was a master artist in a theological studio.

The Trilogy consists of fifteen volumes written between the years 1961 and 1987. Of course, a trilogy has three parts: First, *The Glory of the Lord* (*Herrlichkeit*), which consists of seven volumes on the topic of "theological aesthetics." Here, theology is brought before the beautiful by portraying proper Christian theology as one piece with aesthetics. In other words, Søren Kierkegaard was wrong—aesthetics, religion, and ethics are not either/or alternatives but complementary and interdependent.[28] Theology is not

---

[23] Hans Urs von Balthasar, *The Glory of the Lord: A Theological Aesthetics*, vol. 1, *Seeing the Form*, trans. Erasmo Leiva-Merikakis, ed. Joseph Fessio and John Riches (San Francisco: Ignatius, 1982), 18.

[24] Balthasar, *Glory of the Lord*, 19 (emphasis in original).

[25] See Balthasar, *Glory of the Lord*, 28ff.

[26] One can't help but notice the name "John" recurring again and again in Balthasar's life. This was no accident. He was moved by John, the beloved disciple, who "runs ahead" at the same time as he remains "in the office." This metaphor is, for Balthasar, a model for the church. Love must always run ahead and shape the office. See Henrici, "Hans Urs von Balthasar," 42–43. See also Balthasar's *Love Alone*, trans. and ed. Alexander Dru (New York: Herder & Herder, 1969).

[27] Balthasar wrote many more books that do not fit neatly in this threefold division, but these three are seen as his main works.

[28] Kierkegaard may have been right in his insistence on reading human existence theologically rather than rationally, ethically, or aesthetically, a view largely shared by Balthasar, but he gave insufficient nuance and hence a truncated reading of theology itself.

merely an intellectual exercise but one that also awakens our spiritual and aesthetic capacities, such that we are able to give an account of the whole person and indeed all of reality. Only by unveiling Christ as the beauty of God touching and adorning (that is, redeeming) all of creation can theology disclose the glory of truth.

The second part of the Trilogy is called the *Theo–Drama* (*Theodramatik*). This topic spans five volumes, and in it he brings action and contemplation into harmony. Here theology is placed before goodness. God acts, and we respond as in a drama directed by Christ. The relation of the good to right actions does not entail calculations of any kind but results from the interpretive artwork of the master director and the assigning of roles to actors who are called to give creative expression as they participate in bringing the "play" to the "stage."[29] I will say more about this later because it relates especially to Balthasar's portrayal of the Christian life.

The third part of the Trilogy is called *Theo–Logic* (*Theologik*), where in three volumes he seeks to bring theology before truth. It is one thing to present the theological aesthetics and the theo–drama as interesting and subjectively compelling (it all sounds very nice), but why (and how) should we take it to be true? It is fascinating to see how Balthasar goes about responding to this challenge. He does not resort to an abstract and universal reason; he stays within the Christian story. He explains through an Anselmic "logic" of "faith seeking understanding" how we can come to know the infinite Word through finite word. And, of course, this is but another way of expounding the two natures of Christ.

Shortly before he died in 1988, Balthasar wrote an unusually succinct essay, "A Résumé of My Thought."[30] He acknowledged the need to give a synopsis of his massive corpus, and his comments are instructive. He suggests that theology needs to recognize that human beings exist as limited in a limited world. Yet our rational capacity is unlimited in the sense that we are able to recognize our own finitude. In so doing, our minds are, in effect, able to step outside of our finitude, or, at least, recognize limits to our finitude. For example, we can conceive of nonbeing; we know that there are many things that do not exist that could exist; as well, we know that all things that do exist need not exist. All of this is but to say that we know that existence is contingent. Balthasar says, "Essences are limited but being (*l'etre*) is not."[31] There is, of course, nothing new in this insight. As Thomas Aquinas has reminded us, the essence-being dynamic is the source of all philosophical and religious thought, and it poses the question of Absolute Being.

How are human beings to negotiate this dynamic of essence and being? One could try to leave the distinction behind, which has been attempted by ancient scholars like Parmenides and Heraclitus; but that is futile. So as human beings we must affirm "an inescapable duality; the finite is not the infinite."[32] Plato did this; indeed all of Western philosophy has done the same. But for Balthasar the question is, "Why must Christians do this?" The summary of his answer is short and to the point: God is God and we are not.[33] This means that any attempt to *overcome* this duality represents a fall; a decline that calls for a road to salvation.[34] If salvation is to be salvation for finite humanity, which it must be in order to be salvation for us, then it cannot take us out of this world; rather, it must provide a way of being in this world in a "saved" way. This means that salvation is always a reclaiming of the duality. To say this

---

[29] Echoes of Shakespeare's "All the world's a stage . . ." from his *As You Like It* are obvious.

[30] This essay appeared in *Communio: International Catholic Review* 15 (Winter 1988). It is translated by Kelly Hamilton and reprinted in *Hans Urs von Balthasar*, ed. David Schindler, 1–5.

[31] Balthasar, *Communio*, 1.

[32] Balthasar, *Communio*, 2.

[33] See Balthasar, *Communio*, 2.

[34] It is not difficult to notice the resonance with the Genesis account of the fall in these words of Balthasar.

differently, for us creatures there is no way to behold God face to face but only as God in relation to God's creation; alternatively, there is no way to understand creation but only as creation in relation to creation's God.

We see here that Balthasar finds himself in the same theological canoe as Karl Barth; no *philosophy* can satisfactorily account for the meaning of human existence. For this we need theology! The Apostle Paul knew this when he talked about God creating humanity in order that we could commune in the divine. In the fourth century, Augustine developed this same theme. He said that we can know such "community" only when we open ourselves to seeing Being as "revealing himself from himself."[35] As human beings, we are capable of understanding such revelation because we are human *beings*. God (Being), who is the Creator of human beings, has created the eye and the ear, and so too God can see and hear. Similarly the one who has created language can speak to us, even through the disruptions of ordinary speech (Pentecost). Human reason must therefore be open to infinitude and, when it is, it can render "understandable" that which is only accessible by analogy. "Thus," he concludes, "there is no biblical theology without a religious philosophy."[36] And with this affirmation, we see that he goes beyond where Barth is able to go.

Balthasar says that it is at this point that the substance of his thought asserts itself. He calls his approach meta-anthropology, and wants to surpass both the cosmological and the anthropological sciences by making sense of the world and human beings in ways not available through natural science.

His thinking goes as follows: Human beings exist in encounter with others. The most fundamental form of this "dialogue" is love. In fact, we are brought to consciousness only in love—that is, only in relation with others—for we cannot just love, we must love someone. Consider the most primal human experience: love of mother. This love unveils for us our first glimpse of being; we see being as consistent, stable, that is, as one; we see through the love of mother that being is good, true, and beautiful. Only through the love of another being can we come to see the sustaining beauty of our own being.

Yet being has sense only if in the appearance we somehow also grasp the thing itself. In other words, beauty, goodness, and truth are not merely subjective appearances. They can reside in us precisely because they are real outside of us from which they come to us. Balthasar's theology, rooted in the incarnation and the Trinity, goes beyond the Kantian dichotomy of phenomena and *noumena*. Simply put, the infant comes to know the mother, not only the appearance of *the mother*. Yet he carefully points out that this does not imply identity of finite and infinite; it only rejects the absoluteness of the distinction. He goes on to argue that the one, the good, the true, and the beautiful are all transcendental attributes of being, meaning that they surpass the limits of what we can know as being.[37] So while there is an insurmountable distance between God and creation, there is, because of the reality of Jesus Christ, also analogy and the possibility of creaturely participation.

The possibility of encounter with the otherness of God is not because of who we are and what we are capable of but rather because of who God is and therefore *whose* we are. Balthasar suggests that God is the source of the plentitude of the true, the good, and the beautiful. All of creation participates in this plentitude, albeit only partially and in a fragmentary fashion, and only because it is given to us. This theological reading of God and creation suggests a rather unusual (for moderns, that is) understanding of reality: "it has an epiphany; in appearing it gives itself, it delivers itself to us; it is good. And in

---

[35] David Schindler, *Hans Urs von Balthasar*, 2.
[36] Schindler, *Hans Urs von Balthasar*, 2.
[37] See Schindler, *Hans Urs von Balthasar*, 3.

giving itself up it speaks itself, it unveils itself; it is true."[38] In other words, God, and through God, the world, appears. God appeared to Abraham, to Moses, to Isaiah, to Jesus Christ, and through them all, God appears to us. In Christ, God appears uniquely because the very one through whom God appears is the one who is appearing as God. And in God's appearance we come to see who we are and the world as it truly is. That is, Christ illuminates creation, redemption, eschatology, anthropology, and so on.

It is because God is love that we are invited into the dramatic unfolding of history. One might be able to conceptualize a view of God that would have no role for human agents in the divine purpose, but that view could not be made consistent with the God of Jesus Christ. Here God's hand is shown; love for the earth compels the most radical of gifts and the most radical alliance with sinful humanity.

As has already been pointed out, none of this can make any sense apart from the Chalcedonian affirmation of the two natures of Christ. Unless Christ is fully God, we could know him, at best, as an important prophet and teacher but not as the very embodiment of God's love on earth. And unless Christ is fully human, we could know him, at best, as an important sign from afar but not as the embodiment of God's love on earth. To know Christ as God's embodiment of love and beauty in time-space existence is to know him as one in whom our being is made complete.

Balthasar concludes his résumé with reflections on the uniqueness of the Christian faith. Christianity goes beyond Judaism and Islam. These two great, monotheistic religions are ultimately the same in that both are incapable of giving an account of why God created a world, given that God did not need to do so in order to be God. While both affirm the fact of creation, neither makes it *intelligible* in the Anselmic sense. How does Christianity do this?

Christian theology can only speak about creation from the point of view of the Trinity and the incarnation. In the Trinitarian affirmation, love is shown to be the quality that embraces both otherness and sameness. Divine love is already fully realized and expressed within the Trinity so, while God is not compelled to create, creation nevertheless flows as pure love that freely wills to relate to otherness. As for the incarnation, the Son's embodiment of the Father can take on created form without disgrace and without adding to or taking away from creation, and through redemption reclaim what was already given by God in creation. Hence, nature and grace are united, not in identity but in a relationship whereby nature is perfectible through grace.

LOVE ALONE AND THEO–DRAMA

By now, it will not be surprising to find that of his many books Balthasar does not have one exclusively devoted to Christian ethics. The reason for this, I suspect, is that he did not believe in it! Why not? Because it is not ethics that should guide a Christian in faithful living; it is theology. The Christian life consists in learning how to negotiate life under the directorship of Christ and the Holy Spirit; one could say that living as Christians is living in Christ. So the mode of learning how to live is set by learning how to see and hear God; seeing and hearing are the forms through which the Christian ethics enterprise gains intelligibility.

Balthasar's *Theo–Drama* and *Love Alone* are especially rich in painting a picture of the quality of human existence under God. In the *Theo–Drama*, as we have already seen, he develops first the framework and then the characters of abundant living.[39] The Christian life

---

[38] Schindler, *Hans Urs von Balthasar*, 4.

[39] A helpful navigation through Balthasar's work, esp. his Trilogy, is provided by Garver on his website. See http://www.joelgarver.com/writ/theo/balt.htm, accessed May 9, 2011. I am indebted to Garver's thoughtful road map through Balthasar's convoluted and massive project.

is a drama with actors, stage, playwright, director, and script. When he portrays the characters, he begins with human freedom and the freedom of God. Freedom is, of course, an especially thorny conundrum for moderns. Normally, it is held as a precondition for responsibility, and more and more it is also seen as the goal of ethics. In other words, whether an act is judged right or wrong is determined by two conditions: whether it is committed freely and whether it leads to freedom. But there is little real discussion on what freedom is. This is where Balthasar begins.

Balthasar presents a view where human actors are free only under the freedom and sovereignty of God. God is absolutely free, independent, and so on; humans have freedom in relation to God. We are not in charge of the drama; we are the actors in it.

It is important to remember that Balthasar also uses the drama metaphor to speak of the Trinity, where the Father is the author, the Son the actor, and the Holy Spirit the director. This shows that drama is not foreign or outside the divine reality, which is needed only to give account of the *otherness* of creation. Drama is the form of both ultimate and penultimate being; and the dramatics of finite existence participate in the dramatics of ultimate existence.

Both humans and God are free. Yet God is free differently from human beings. One way to understand God's freedom is via neoplatonism—as free only in relation to self and hence not free to enter into relations with others. A second view of freedom arises from Hegelianism in which God's freedom is dependent upon others. Both, according to Balthasar, are problematic.

His alternative, by now not surprisingly, is rooted in the Trinity, where God is both one and many at the same time. Each person of the Trinity is different from the other, and yet God is not different from himself. Hence, unity should not be seen as incompatible with

difference. It now becomes easy to see how God is at once in no need of the world and yet may choose out of love to create a world. Our freedom is under God and exists only within God's sovereign freedom. We are free because we emanate from God's gratuitous love; free, that is, to love and live in praise for what we have received. Another way of saying this is that when we are enslaved to God, we are enslaved to freedom; whereas when we are enslaved to sin, we are enslaved to unfreedom—reminiscent of both Johannine (John 8:31ff) and Pauline (Galatians 5) language.

In Balthasar's discussion of human freedom, he speaks of self-consciousness and language. We are different from animals in that we have language and hence have self-awareness. But the "I" of self-awareness under God is not the "I" of the Cartesian ego. This is so precisely because self-identity under God is self-identity in relationship to others, not self-identity apart from others. As Joel Garver puts it, "Where Descartes says 'I think, therefore I am' Balthasar would say, 'I am addressed, therefore I am.'"[40] In this way God is word (*Wort*) to us and we are response (*Antwort*) to God. According to Garver, then, we understand ourselves properly only when we understand ourselves as responses to a gift given to us. Balthasar quotes Nicholas of Cusa (1401–1464) who prayed, "How couldest Thou have given Thyself to me if Thou hadst not given me to myself before? . . . Thou hast given me the gift of freedom so that, according to my own volition, I may belong to myself."[41]

But then comes the problem of sin. Although we are all invited to be actors in the unfolding divine drama, the thwarting powers of sin are ever present. And so there can be little beauty or goodness apart from the salvation that comes to us in and through Christ, who lifts us back into the beauty of God. For in Christ there is identity of actor and role; in all other beings, sin makes

---

[40] Garver website.
[41] Hans Urs von Balthasar, *Theo–Drama: Theological Dramatic Theory*, vol. 2, *Dramatis Personae: Man in God*, trans. Graham Harrison (San Franscisco: Ignatius, 1988–1998), 288.

such identity impossible. This distance can be breached not because of our efforts made possible by God's love to us, but by the obedience of Christ, whose love takes him to the cross. What this means is that the same way that God created the world, not out of necessity but out of love, God also redeems creation, including sinful human beings. God "handed Christ over" (Rom 8:32) into the hands of sinners, knowing that the power of sin was not ultimate—it was the power of the corruption of creation, not its true essence. Its true essence, and therefore, true power, is rooted in the love of God, in whom creation, as well as the overcoming of sin's corrupting power, is lifted up. Hence, it is impossible for death to hold Christ captive, and it is equally impossible for death and sin to hold human beings captive.

Balthasar discusses the atonement theories advanced throughout church history, but he is reluctant to embrace any of them or to develop his own synthesis. Rather, he treats them as important metaphors that illuminate a reality too rich to be grasped by a single theory. What is to be illuminated is precisely the life that is possible in Christ. And the faithfulness of God's love in response to the obedience of Christ is the faithfulness of which every obedient human being is assured. The fear of abandonment is therefore overcome in the cross-resurrection event.[42] Because we can see ourselves aright only when we see ourselves in Christ, we can be assured of our own salvation in Christ. All of this is to say that there can be no Christian ethics apart from salvation.

When Balthasar speaks of the appropriation of salvation, there are two closely related themes that recur: Mary and the church. Mary is the model of both the personal Christian life and the church. He says, for example, that in Mary

> two things become visible: first, that here is to be found the archetype of a Church that conforms to Christ, and, second, that Christian sanctity is "Christ-bearing", "Christophorous" in essence and actualisation. To the extent that the Church is Marian, she is a pure form which is immediately legible and comprehensible; to the extent that the person is Marian (or "Christophorous," which is the same), the Christian reality becomes just as simply legible and comprehensible in him.[43]

Balthasar's view of Mary cannot be understood apart from his unique view of the feminine, and indeed, the sexes. In his *Theo-Drama*, under a section called "Man," he says:

> The beginning of the Bible devotes space to a phenomenology of the sexual; initially it is viewed in the sober framework of man's *creatureliness*. Nowhere is man more aware of his contingence than where each sex has to realize its dependence on the other; neither can be the whole human being on its own; there is always the "other" mode of being human, a way that is not open to its counterpart.[44]

In his third volume of the *Theo-Drama*, Balthasar has a long section titled "Woman's Answer," in which he shows how creatureliness and femininity are linked.[45] While in this view women and men are both feminine, nevertheless sexual difference is clearly important.[46] In reflecting on this image of feminine creatureliness, Balthasar says:

---

[42] For an inspiring presentation of the three days of Easter, see Hans Urs von Balthasar's *Mysterium Paschale: The Mystery of Easter*, trans. Aiden Nichols (Grand Rapids: Eerdmans, 1993).

[43] Balthasar, *Glory of the Lord*, 562. See also Lucy Gardiner, "Balthasar and the Figure of Mary," in *The Cambridge Companion to Hans Urs von Balthasar*, ed. Edward T. Oakes and David Moss (New York: Cambridge University Press, 2004).

[44] Hans Urs von Balthasar, *Theo-Drama*, vol. 2, *Dramatis Personae*, 368–69 (emphasis in original). It is interesting that Balthasar here, as he does in many others places, cites Karl Barth approvingly in his emphasis on the creatureliness of humanity.

[45] It will not be surprising that Balthasar's discussion of the feminine has created intense discussion within the Christian feminist community. One such example is Michelle A. Gonzalez, "Hans urs von Balthasar and Contemporary Feminist Theology," in *Theological Studies* 65, no. 3 (2004).

[46] For an analysis of Balthasar's views on sexuality see, e.g., Corinne Crammer, "One Sex or Two? Balthasar's Theology of the Sexes," in *Cambridge Companion*, ed. Oakes and Moss. Crammer has drawn a link here between Balthasar's view of sexual difference and that of the French writer Luce Irigaray.

[I]nsofar as every creature—be it male or female in natural order—is originally the fruit of the primary, absolute, self-giving divine love, there is a clear analogy to the female principle of the world. . . . if the creature is to be God's "image", it must be equipped with its own fruit-bearing principle, just like the woman (vis-à-vis the man). So we can say that every conscious creaturely being has a certain "mission" at a natural level . . . to be ready and open to receive the seed of the divine Word, to bear it and give it its full developed form.[47]

It is, of course, easy to see how in this theology Mary becomes the "archetype" of both the Christian life and the church. Lucy Gardiner explains:

In her faithful response at the annunciation, Mary represents the individual Christian and the contemplative aspect of Christian life which Balthasar so prizes. In the simplicity of Mary's (eventual) answer and acceptance, "Behold, I am the handmaid of the Lord; let it be with me according to your word" (Luke 1:38), Balthasar sees mirrored all that each one of us has to say and do in response to God.[48]

One cannot fairly present Balthasar's view of the church without talking about the Eucharist. Mary may be the archetype of the church, but clearly the Eucharist is the Christian's way to participate in the divine mission we are all called to in Mary's response to God. Healy's and Schindler's summary is helpful:

For in the gift of the Eucharist, Christ endows the Church with the "real presence" of his body and blood together with an inner participation in his mission to the world. If the mission of the Son is to redeem creation by means of an exchange . . . in which he offers himself eucharistically to the world and receives the world as gift from the Father, then the Church is called to enter into Christ's life and mission by *eucharistically receiving*

creation in its entirety as a gift that mediates and expresses the triune life—thereby confirming and fulfilling God's original plan for the world.[49]

As Balthasar read the world, that is, the ontological structure of the world, it could not be made intelligible apart from the church. This may seem like an odd thing to say, but he means it profoundly—the church precedes the world ontologically, epistemologically, and axiologically. Since all things are intrinsically ordered in Christ's divine love exchange, the whole world is so ordered. Christ must be understood as the concrete *analogia entis*; that is, in the union of the two natures of Christ, we have the concrete measure and language of every distance between God and humanity.[50] Hence, the church "pours itself out for the life of the world even as the world finds herself in the life of the Eucharist."[51]

SCATTERED SUMMATION

When it comes to asking how Balthasar's theology helps us understand Christian ethics, it is anything but neat and tidy. For just as truth, and indeed theology, is "symphonic,"[52] this music metaphor is equally apropos for the Christian life. Since Balthasar does not believe in abstract ethics—his commitment to seeing the world through the incarnation and Trinity prohibit this—he is compelled by his own logic into an ethic of the concrete. So what can be said without overreaching when one begins this way?

Marc Ouellet, S. S., tackles this question by enquiring into Balthasar's "foundations" of Christian ethics.[53] He begins with an analysis of his "Nine Propositions for a Christian Ethics"[54] which I draw from as well as add to

[47] Hans Urs von Balthasar, *Theo-Drama*, vol. 3, *Dramatis Personae*, 287–88.

[48] Gardiner, "Figure of Mary," 70.

[49] Nicholas Healy and David L. Schindler, "For the Life and the World: Hans Urs von Balthasar on the Church as Eucharist," in *Cambridge Companion*, ed. Oakes and Moss, 51 (emphasis in original).

[50] Healy and Schindler, "For the Life," 53.

[51] Healy and Schindler, "For the Life," 63.

[52] See Hans Urs von Balthasar, *Truth Is Symphonic: Aspects of Christian Pluralism*, trans. Graham Harrison (San Francisco: Ignatius, 1972).

[53] See Marc Ouellet, S. S., "The Foundations of Christian Ethics according to Hans Urs von Balthasar," in *Hans Urs von Balthasar*, ed. Schindler.

[54] Hans Urs von Balthasar, "Nine Propositions on Christian Ethics," in *Principles of Christian Morality*, ed. Joseph Cardinal Ratzinger, Heinz Schürmann, and Hans Urs von Balthasar, (San Francisco: Ignatius, 1986). My "affirmations" below are

my ten affirmations. Balthasar argues that the person can only be adequately understood on biblical and christological grounds. He sees Christ as the "supreme ethical norm" and says that "Christian ethics must be modeled on Jesus Christ."[55] Hence, the first affirmation of Balthasar's Christian ethics is that *Jesus Christ is the model*, meaning that he is the unique measure of divine love. For Balthasar Christ stands at the center of the Christian life.

The second affirmation is that for Balthasar there can be *no Christian ethics without the church*. The church is the embodiment of Christ in this world and "it is the church's task to gather the world together into a unity under the headship of Christ, thus offering the world that unity for which it is striving deliberately but clearly in vain."[56] And Mary, the servant of God, who in complete openness was able to say, "Here am I, the servant of the Lord; let it be with me according to your word" (Luke 1:38), is the archetype of the church. While Jesus Christ is the model, we cannot be like him in the way that we can be like Mary—bringing to birth the seed planted within us.

The third affirmation is about the nature of Christ. For any of his comments here to make sense, *Christ must be the unique Son of the Father* and not just a prophet or teacher. In other words, the incarnation and the Trinity stand or fall together. So there is no meaning to Christian ethics apart from the articulation of these two mysteries, and these mysteries can only be understood by expounding the two natures of Christ. For ethics, this means that Jesus Christ is not just someone we follow after; he is someone in whom we participate.

The fourth affirmation follows closely. If Christ is the supreme norm and model, then he is the *principal* actor in the "theo–drama," meaning that he distributes the roles for other actors.[57] To say this differently, Christ is in control of the outcome of the drama and *we are not in control.*

The fifth affirmation is best summarized with Balthasar's own words: "God does not recite the drama of the world as a soliloquy; he makes room in it for his human co-protagonists."[58] Just because Christ is in control does not mean that human beings are shut out of the action. In Jesus Christ, God and human beings encounter each other and hence *we are partners* in the dramatic unfolding of the new creation.

The sixth affirmation then addresses the nature of human beings. Who are we? This is not a philosophical or anthropological question for Balthasar, but a theological one. Why does this difference matter? It matters because the answer does not rest on the a priori structure of the person that we may glean from philosophical investigations, but on the a posteriori determination that is given in Christ.[59] In other words, we discover who we are when we look to Jesus Christ. *Christ defines for us what it means to be human.*

The seventh affirmation deals with the matter of analogy. Since we cannot be fully as Christ was, and yet Christ shows us who we are, how are we to see the connection between Christ and us? Balthasar's answer is "through analogy." There exists between Christ and the Christian, as between God and the creature, not univocity—sameness of language—but analogy. That is, both similarity and great dissimilarity must be affirmed.[60] Balthasar emphasizes that here is an analogy of being as well as an analogy of action and attitudes. In the process of participating in Christ, we, in effect, lose ourselves in something other than ourselves. Balthasar says it

---

not intended to follow closely Balthasar's essay. They cut across all of his thought. His nine propositions dealt with "'the accomplishments of morality in Christ (four propositions),' 'the Old Testament elements of the future synthesis (two propositions),' and 'fragments of an extra–Biblical ethics (three propositions)." Ouellet, "Foundations of Christian Ethics," 232.

[55] Ouellet, "Foundations of Christian Ethics," 232.

[56] Balthasar, *Truth Is Symphonic*, 97.

[57] Ouellet, "Foundations of Christian Ethics," 235.

[58] Ouellet, "Foundations of Christian Ethics," 233.

[59] See Ouellet, "Foundations of Christian Ethics," 237.

[60] See Ouellet, "Foundations of Christian Ethics," 237.

this way, "A human subject, inasmuch as he becomes a theological person by a unique call and mission, is simultaneously deprivatized, socialized, and made the location and bearer of community."[61] *When we live in Christ, we transcend our former selves, even though we cannot become Christ in all his fullness.*

The eighth affirmation relates to the uniqueness of Christian ethics. As Balthasar saw it, *Christian ethics is for Christians* because it presupposes the commitment of faith. Christian ethics is not a natural ethic within the bounds of universal reason to which Christian convictions add something. It is Christian from the start. There is here a model of participation in divine life that goes far beyond what the heart can see. Here Balthasar draws directly on Henri de Lubac.[62] The theological virtues are the modes of this participation. This results in an ethic that has to do with serving God in all things. This is not first of all the satisfaction of human desire but the satisfaction of God's desire. What is that desire? For the restoration of all creation! And from this perspective springs forth praise to God and service to broken humanity. That is, there is an inseparable unity between the love of God and the love of neighbor.

The ninth affirmation deals with hope and mystery. One of Balthasar's laments is that we have forgotten the notion of Christian hope because we have forgotten the notion of eschatology. Because we have substituted rationalism for hope, *we have forgotten the virtue of patience and waiting.* But Christian ethics, precisely because it is about love embodied in Jesus Christ, is not primarily about a teaching or a wisdom or an organization or a revelation; it is about hope in God, who wishes to give himself with complete freedom in the creative expression of his un-created love. Balthasar is critical of Western thought that believes it can disclose truth through Enlightenment reason and thereby

has done violence to a beauty that cannot be known apart from mysticism.[63]

Tenth, there is no recipe for Christian ethics. *Ethical discernment always involves struggle.* Yet the struggle is not first of all about principles; it is about human relationships. This again flows from his commitment to the incarnation, which implies another commitment, namely, to contingency. Balthasar gives the following example: "[Humanity] must not forget [the laws of] contingency, and, demand total disarmament, non-resistance or pacifism, in virtue of Christian charity and Christian communion by overlooking all political prudence."[64] In other words, whatever pacifism might name, it is untenable as a Christian ethic if it derives from an absolute principle like "do not kill" or "love your enemy." For the Christian, life is a drama; the danger is to see it as a computer program. And the solution for Christian ethics, as Balthasar sees it, "is to permit a multiplicity of realizations in the name of the one, sole commandment of love."[65] Of course, this is also not without its danger because it is hard to interpret the meaning of the commandment of love, especially on the periphery. And Balthasar realizes this. Yet this is the vulnerability of truth within the imagination of the incarnation and Trinity, from which there is no escape.

These ten affirmations are not intended to suggest that there is after all a systematic ethic in Balthasar's writings. Rather, they seek to paint a picture in a somewhat different way than either Balthasar himself or his interpreters, with strokes that may offer connections with the other writers in our study. Obviously much that is crucial in his thought is omitted in this summary; the hope is that some of his insights may have been captured.

CONCLUSION

Although it is not always explicit in his writings, Balthasar was an avid critic of the

---

[61] See Ouellet, "Foundations of Christian Ethics," 238.
[62] See Ouellet, "Foundations of Christian Ethics," 238.
[63] Ouellet, "Foundations of Christian Ethics," 248.
[64] Ouellet, "Foundations of Christian Ethics," 246.
[65] Balthasar, *Truth Is Symphonic*, 83.

modernist turn to a naturalist epistemology. Yet the language of his criticism is not always clearly understood. His language was unique and powerful; he refused to permit the almost insane pressures of "handing knowledge over to the world." But because there is but one world, and both God and we are in it, knowledge is sign; knowledge is gift; knowledge is precarious.

> [W]henever the relationship between nature and grace is severed (as happens . . . where "faith" and "knowledge" are constructed as opposites), then the whole of worldly being falls under the dominion of "knowledge", and the springs and forces of love immanent in the world are overpowered and finally suffocated by science, technology and cybernetics. The result is a world without women, without children, without reverence for love in poverty and humiliation—a world in which power and the profit-margin are the sole criteria, where the disinterested, the useless, the purposeless is despised, persecuted and in the end exterminated—a world in which art itself is forced to wear the mask and features of technique.[66]

From all that has been said, it is clear that for Balthasar the Christian life is inordinately rich because it is in Christ, and certainly it cannot be reduced to a formula on how to live. It is precisely this richness that makes it beautiful and vulnerable at the same time. When he says, "No one can really behold who has not also already been enraptured and no one can be enraptured who has not already perceived,"[67] he is saying that the Christian life cannot be lived unless we know whose we are. And from this we must conclude that he has no ethic—if by that term we mean a set of rules, goals, and virtues that determine our behavior. On the other hand, the richness of Balthasar's ethic is not easily surpassed because he refuses to let go of the notion that to live in Christ means to live in the world while living beyond the world— in the beauty of the infinite.

Perhaps there is no better end to this chapter than to let Balthasar speak one more time. "As far as Christianity is concerned, two things are clear: a faith that is based on the Incarnation cannot have recourse to flight from the world, and a faith that comes wholly from God's initiative is prohibited from 'hastening' salvation by its own efforts."[68]

---

[66] Balthasar, *Love Alone*, 114–15.

[67] Balthasar, *Glory of the Lord*, 10.

[68] Balthasar, *Truth Is Symphonic*, 185–86.

Chapter Seventeen

DOROTHEE SÖLLE
(1929–2003)

Dorothee Sölle[1] was a German theologian who wrote theology in a style different from the mainstream. Poetry, for example, was of one piece with her theological reflections. She was born at the beginning of a tumultuous era in Germany, and the events that transpired around her, especially during the early decades of her life, affected her deeply, not only personally but also theologically.

The fact that she was born in the same year as Anne Frank did not escape her. When she first read Anne's diary[2] in 1950, she was deeply moved and identified with her story in many ways—in personal ways, as when Anne writes about being told she was an "exasperating child" and writes of her "dreadful loneliness of adolescence"; and also in political ways, as when Anne writes of her alienation from her German-ness in Hitler's Germany.[3] For if Hitler and those supporting him were Germans, Sölle could not be!

Obviously, Sölle never experienced the utter despair and anguish of Anne Frank, but she experienced her pain with empathy and that made a big difference. She puts it this way: "It is something special to experience Anne Frank from the perspective of a German. The machinery of death to which she was delivered is one that my people conceived, planned, built, oiled, and serviced right to the bitter end."[4]

As is evident in her identification with Frank's story, Sölle too struggled deeply with being a German. When she read in Anne Frank's *Diary of a Young Girl* that "Hitler took away our nationality long ago," Sölle said she underlined the words to help her never forget them, and later wrote of her feelings about the passage:

> How often I wished that Hitler had also made me "stateless"! That I did not belong to the people I belonged to! Anne Frank's distinction between "these" Germans and others gives evidence of her ability to differentiate, to express herself with precision. But for me, a German, it is not quite so simple. In the end, all who did not put up resistance were implicated, entangled in the belief systems of "these" Germans, lending them a hand and sharing in the profits. Among those who "went along," in the broadest sense of the words, were all who had practiced the art of looking away, turning a deaf ear, and keeping silent. There has been much quarreling about collective guilt and responsibility, but my basic feeling is, rather, one of an ineradicable shame— the shame of belonging to this people, speaking the language of the concentration camp guards, singing the songs that were also sung in the Hitler Youth and the Company of German Girls. That shame does not become superannuated; it must stay alive.[5]

---

[1] In North America her name is also spelled "Solle" and "Soelle," and these spellings are used on some of the works cited here.

[2] See Anne Frank, *The Diary of a Young Girl*, trans. M. Mooyaart-Doubleday (New York: Modern Library, 1952).

[3] Dorothee Soelle, *Against the Wind: Memoir of a Radical Christian*, trans. Barbara Rumscheidt and Martin Rumscheidt (Minneapolis: Fortress, 1999), 14–15.

[4] Soelle, *Against the Wind*, 15.

[5] Soelle, *Against the Wind*, 15–16.

Sölle's faith, and indeed her theology, cannot easily be disentangled from the German catastrophe of Auschwitz. This context shaped her views on feminism, socialism, pacifism, and her activism. She opposed oppressions of all forms; she thought of herself as a liberation theologian, and she sought to give expression to a political theology that arose from the pain of her setting. That is why she called her theology "a 'post-Auschwitz' theology." She explained this further by saying, "I did not want to write one sentence in which the awareness of that great catastrophe of my people was not made explicit."[6]

In some ways, her theology is reminiscent of Dietrich Bonhoeffer's: ferociously committed to a form of incarnational "worldly Christianity," that does not let the reader forget the Christian call to speak the truth in love to places of power, violence, and injustice—to concrete places of pain *on this earth*. Perhaps her theology can be summarized in these words: "God's spirit makes us courageous and capable of truth. God wants to be born in us."[7]

HER LIFE

Sölle was born in Cologne, West Germany. She was the fourth in the Nipperdey family of five children; three brothers, Karl, Otto, and Thomas preceded her, and a sister, Sabine, was born after her.[8] Her family was middle-class and Protestant. Her father was a lawyer, who saw it to his advantage to be involved in neither politics nor religion. In the household, there was a strong emphasis on education and on the limited value of material possessions. In her own words:

> My parents were highly educated members of the German middle-class, who manifested a certain "enlightened" tolerance towards the church. It was in keeping with my bourgeois family background that I began my studies at the university in philosophy and in classical languages. Provoked by a number of friends who were Christians by choice and, even more so, by radical Christian thinkers such as Pascal, Kierkegaard, and Simone Weil, I found myself, after the fifth semester in an existential crisis that led me to take up theology.[9]

Sölle's primary and secondary education took place in the public schools in Cologne. By the time she was in high school, she had already become interested in theology and the church. This interest was perhaps unusual because her family did not attend church. Her personal faith quest initially took her to the Evangelical Church of the Rhineland, where her interest in matters theological was fostered.

Her university studies began in philosophy and ancient languages (philology) in 1949 at the Cologne and Freiburg universities. But two years later, she moved to Göttingen University, where she changed her focus to Protestant theology and German. Here, her teachers, included Friedrich Gogarten and Ernst Käsemann. In 1954 she received her doctoral degree from Göttingen in the area of literary criticism. Her dissertation was titled, "Studies in the Structure of Bonaventura's Vigils."

In 1954 she married painter-artist Dietrich Sölle, and they had three children, Martin, Michaela, and Caroline, before the marriage ended in divorce in 1964. Five years later, she married Fulbert Steffensky, a former Benedictine priest and a professor of religion and education at the University of Hamburg. During this marriage she had another daughter, Mirjam.

Her teaching career began in 1954 when she became instructor of theology and German at the high school (*Gymnasium*) for girls in Cologne-Mülheim. She taught for six years after which she was a research assistant at the Philosophical Institute of Aachen for two years. She then returned to the

---

[6] Soelle, *Against the Wind*, 16.

[7] Dorothee Soelle, *Theology for Skeptics: Reflections on God*, trans. Joyce L. Erwin (Minneapolis: Augsburg, 1995), 126.

[8] The material in this section relies heavily on "Dorothee Soelle," *Encyclopedia of World Biography*, 2004. Encyclopedia. com, http://www.encyclopedia.com/doc/1G2-3404706042.html, accessed May 10, 2011; and on her autobiography, *Against the Wind*.

[9] Soelle, *Against the Wind*, 34–35.

University of Cologne in 1962 to teach in the Institute of Germanic Philology.

In 1971 she wrote her *Habilitationschrift*[10] qualifying her to become a university professor, but she had difficulty securing a permanent professorship in a German university, partially due to her political activities. She did, however, lecture briefly (1972–1975) as part of the theology faculty at the University of Mainz.

In 1975 she accepted a teaching position as the Harry Emerson Fosdick Visiting Professor in Theology at Union Theological Seminary in New York City. She taught there for several months every year for thirteen years (1975–1987). Her reflections on coming to New York in 1975 are interesting:

> I arrived in an America that had just ended the Vietnam War and had finished with President Nixon. Unconsciously I looked at every man of the middle generation with the question, Were you in Vietnam? What did you do there? Vietnam had been such an elemental aspect of my own political and human biography. What was your position on the war in Vietnam? I could not put this question behind me, and even when it was unspoken, I judged many people in terms of it.[11]

During these years of traveling back and forth, she was constantly comparing German and American student culture. American seminary students came from a variety of backgrounds because they needed no theological training in their undergraduate programs to be admitted to seminary. So she found that they had nothing in common except that they tended to be older, and hence had more life experience.

Sölle states that it was impossible to assume that American students understood anything about the philosophy of Immanuel Kant or Georg Hegel, for example. Even more interesting was that when they came from Asian countries, they wanted her to engage Asian scholars. Her impression was that in America teachers were to take seriously where students came from in a way that was uncommon in her home universities. "Identifying with" students was not a high value in German universities, where students were required to rise to the level of the teacher. To say this differently, American education had much to do with offering students an interpretation of *their* place, rather than focusing on an interpretation of the great truths of history, that is, introducing them to a *new* place.

Sölle was impressed with American students' attempts to live what she called "an alternative life."[12] She noticed a "prevailing opposition against the culture of this country."[13] It was as if students had come to recognize the poverty of their own culture, its inability to answer the basic questions of human existence. Hence, she found here more cynicism than hope.

Despite these obvious differences, Sölle loved teaching in New York. She loved the free-spirited students, her colleagues, especially those who were doing theology "on the edge," and the generally open environment of American culture.

Throughout her life Sölle was an uncompromising pacifist. She was a critic of war in general, the nuclear arms race in particular, and oppressions of all forms in whatever parts of the world they occurred—Southeast Asia, South America, South Africa, and so on. And always, she was a critic of capitalism. Capitalism was founded on greed and competition with "the other," whereas Christian ethics taught generosity and love of the other.

Sölle received many honors during her lifetime, including an honorary doctorate from the Protestant Faculty at the University of Paris and the Droste Prize for poetry. She was awarded the Theodor-Heuss Medal, and in 1994, was named honorary professor of the University of Hamburg.

---

[10] A *Habilitationschrift* is a second research project of higher quality than the doctoral dissertation which is to qualify the writer to become a university professor.

[11] Soelle, *Against the Wind*, 58.

[12] Soelle, *Against the Wind*, 60.

[13] Soelle, *Against the Wind*, 60.

Many times she found herself in conflict with the political and legal establishments. For example, in 1985 on Hiroshima Day (August 6), she was involved in an action of civil disobedience protesting nuclear armament. The action took place outside the Pershing II missile base at Mutlangen. She was arrested and found guilty of "provoking arrest." A few years later, in 1988, she was involved in a protest outside the gates of the U. S. poison gas depot at Fishbach, Germany, and again found guilty of "attempting to provoke arrest."

Her passion for promoting peace and justice is evident not only in her writing and teaching, but also on the streets of cities and in nations across the world. She was always both a theologian and an activist. She was also both a mystic and a pragmatist—tensions that historically have been prone to breaking apart. But it is this tension that pushed her to reconceiving traditional theology toward one that was unable to justify dominance. For Christ was the one who was embodied contingently and provisionally in real history and hence must never be given finality in the sense of being an imposable power. She saw "Christ un-embodied" in contingent history as theological anathema; and Christ hoarded by a group or by a school of thought was apostasy. This placed her in direct opposition to Christian fundamentalism, which she referred to as a "Christofacistic religion."[14]

Sölle died very suddenly at the age of seventy-three. It was during Easter, and she was leading a conference on the theme, "God and Felicity" at Göppingen in southern Germany when she suffered a fatal heart attack. This was a truly sad occasion for many who had come to see her as a spokesperson for a theology that permitted their own liberation to take form, for she was remarkably skilled at gathering people into an imagination of Christian identity, responsibility, and freedom.

HER THEOLOGICAL ETHICS

Sölle had a passion for theology in a manner similar to that of Dietrich Bonhoeffer. Her first book, *Christ the Representative*, is subtitled *An Essay in Theology after the "Death of God"*. It is dedicated to her "Göttingen friends in hope of a reformation of the church." It is noteworthy that the German theologians we have studied emphasized the need for a new theology of church in order to properly understand the Christian life that Jesus invites us into. This was the case with the Protestants, Barth and Bonhoeffer, as is evident in the Barmen Declaration, but it was also the case with the Catholic theologian Hans Urs von Balthasar, who left the Jesuit order over the form of the church. Similarly, Sölle argues that Christian ethics and church renewal are of one piece.

The phrase "the death of God" names something quite specific for Sölle.[15] She points out that the significance of anyone's death is that it marks the point when a person no longer exists *for someone*. For example, the death of a mother means that she no longer exists for her children—"she is dead *for them*."[16] Sölle asks, "For whom, then, is God dead?"[17] In her answer, she suggests that the significance of the "death of God" is not that anything changes for the atheist, nor for those who simply reject the declaration as factually false and refuse to give it further sway. But there are those for whom this claim matters, namely, contemporaries who have had a profound theological "let down," like the Jews of Auschwitz and Christians

---

[14] One finds this phrase in Dorothee Soelle, *Beyond Mere Obedience: Reflections on a Christian Ethic for the Future*, trans. Lawrence W. Denef (Minneapolis: Augsburg, 1970).

[15] "Death of God" philosophy-theology goes back at least to Friedrich Nietzsche, and in North America it was made popular by writers like Thomas J. J. Altizer and William Hamilton. It espouses the position that in today's "secular" world, the notion of a transcendent God is no longer intelligible because this world is intelligible without reference to God.

[16] Dorothee Sölle, *Christ the Representative: An Essay in Theology after the "Death of God,"* trans. David Lewis (London: SCM Press, 1967), 11 (emphasis in original).   [17] Sölle, *Christ the Representative*, 11.

who believed that in Jesus we can find a personal salvation that heals all human pain. Sölle accepts that "God is dead" in the sense that the god of traditional theology must be overcome or at least must be rethought. Yet God is not dead in the sense that God was in Christ and Christ was in God, that is, in some sense Christ is still our representative. She sets for herself the task of developing a theology that recognizes both the reality and the incompleteness of the kingdom of God. For "if God is dead, Jesus ceases to concern us,"[18] but since Jesus continues to concern us we need to tie that concern to the quest for a political theology that will be *useless* as a justification for dominance and oppression, and *useful* as a theology of liberation.[19] That is, she seeks to write a "post-theistic" theology that can answer the complex questions intrinsic to human desire and the seduction of power.

Sölle poses the question of what we can still say that is meaningful about the old title given to Christ as "representative" since some things that have been said no longer have meaning for us. She puts it this way:

> Christ died for our sins in our stead. Representatively he reconciled us to God and revealed God's preeminent grace towards us. If . . . we . . . attempt here a new "doctrine of representation"—one which will keep constantly in view the new conditions briefly indicated by the term "post-theistic"—the justification for making such an attempt is provided by the obvious difficulties in which theology finds itself today.[20]

She examines two dominant answers to the difficulties that theology finds itself in: the seemingly unbridgeable tension between transcendence and immanence. These answers are that of German idealism, especially Hegel, and that of positivism. Finding both wanting, she develops her own view of Christology in dialogue with Bonhoeffer and Barth that she believes can more

appropriately answer how Jesus can represent both us before God and God among us.[21] Her concern is that traditional theology tends to divide on this question; either there is an overemphasis on God being beyond us—transcendent, distant, and irrelevant to human affairs—or God is "domesticated" by human interests. Both are problematic, and sorting out this tension is an essential task, especially for Christian ethics.

Her reading of both Barth and Bonhoeffer is that they overemphasize the move from above to below, in that both require a complete surrender of the life of human beings to another person.[22] And this, she suggests, leads to an "absolute responsibility" that fails to take into account the reality of human limits. Such a point of departure, therefore, leads to an inadequate view of representation; it leads not only to a truncated theological ethic in general but to an inadequate ecclesiology. She is critical of the notion which Bonhoeffer (and he learned it from Barth) puts forward that the church "stands at the point at which the whole world ought to be standing."[23] In addition, both further emphasize that the church is God's way of dealing with the world. She says in response to these claims, that "the Church's provisional character is consistently overlooked [by Barth and Bonhoeffer] because its representation is exclusively regarded as responsibility and not as self-eliminating provisionality."[24] Her concern here is that Barth and Bonhoeffer fail to take seriously that the church is a socially embodied reality and hence contingent, different from place to place, and not perfect.

Sölle names three concerns that arise from presenting the church in the manner of Barth and Bonhoeffer: first, the church is unable, on this basis, to protect itself from the temptation to absolutization; that is, its authority cannot be superseded, and hence there is no place from which it can be critiqued.

---

[18] Sölle, *Christ the Representative*, 12.

[19] See Dorothee Soelle, *Political Theology*, trans. John Shelley (Philadelphia: Fortress, 1974).

[20] Sölle, *Christ the Representative*, 14.

[21] Sölle, *Christ the Representative*, 16.

[22] See Sölle, *Christ the Representative*, 94.

[23] Sölle, *Christ the Representative*, 95.

[24] Sölle, *Christ the Representative*, 95.

Second, even though it may be true to say that the church represents to the world the model of faithful existence, nevertheless, the church also *depends* upon the world; that is, the church is not the "sum total of the world's hope,"[25] for the world too holds within itself the promises of God. Third, the church needs a view of eschatology in order to view itself as provisional. Provisionality names for her the precondition of the church's responsibility in concrete, social space. She says it this way, "Only as we are aware of [the church's] eschatological and provisional character can genuine responsibility be saved from a complacent superiority."[26]

Sölle's discussion of a proper understanding of Christ as representative takes place in dialogue with Jewish theology. She cites the theology of the Jewish scholar, Gershom Scholem,[27] who suggests that Christianity understands redemption as spiritual and invisible, while Judaism cannot understand it in terms other than political and social. For Jews, the test of Messiah's coming lies in empirical, social reality. This means that if the claim to messiahship is not grounded in evident social change, it is vacuous. Of necessity, therefore, given the current state of violence in the world, either the claim to the messiahship of Christ has been redefined in spiritual terms, or the Messiah has not come.

Of course, Sölle resists Scholem's rendering of Christianity as spiritual and apolitical, yet sadly she admits that there is much historical warrant for this interpretation of Christian theology. She says it is not difficult to show the disastrous implication of an apolitical theology because it leads directly to the notion of "the final Christ" giving Christians all the controls; all is already reconciled and all is absorbed in Christ. She says it this way: "That this final Christ is inevitably totalitarian is shown by the Church's anti-Semitism . . ."[28] In other words, when Christ is seen as final, then those who are not under Christ's allegiance are outside of God's redemption. If there is no provisionality to Christ, then those under Christ's lordship control God's redemption. Hence, "the final Christ" leads directly to "the triumphal church," which needs no future because all is already accomplished. But a future is precisely what suffering people need, and a future is what Christ provides. Living without a future is not the same as "living in postponement." The latter is what Jewish theology emphasizes; and it is but another way of speaking of living in hope. When living in hope, nothing can be done in a final way. Hope, then, necessitates a life of openness, vulnerability, and provisionality. In other words, the Messiah has come but not yet fully. She says, "this life in postponement, in provisionality, so far from having been ended for Christians by the Messiah, is the very thing which the representative makes possible."[29]

Christ is not best understood as the final Christ, but as the dependent Christ—dependent on both God and on us. Christ does not stand aloof but gets involved in human sin in a manner that costs him dearly. His suffering for us is not in our stead but by our side. In this way, it makes sin's overcoming both possible and concrete—concrete because it occurs in our space and possible because with Christ it happens in hope for a redeemed future.

Dianne L. Oliver provides a helpful four-point summary of Sölle's theological affirmations.[30] First, science, technology, and Auschwitz have shown us that God is replaceable. Science and technology have replaced God in offering explanations of how the world works; Auschwitz has shown us that

---

[25] Sölle, *Christ the Representative*, 96.

[26] Sölle, *Christ the Representative*, 96.

[27] See Sölle, *Christ the Representative*, 107. She cites specifically Gershom Scholem's *Judaica* (Frankfurt, 1963).

[28] Sölle, *Christ the Representative*, 109.

[29] Sölle, *Christ the Representative*, 111–12.

[30] Dianne L. Oliver, "Christ in the World: The Christological Vision of Dorothee Soelle," in *The Theology of Dorothee Soelle*, ed. Sarah K. Pinnock (New York: Trinity, 2003), 109.

God does not offer security and protection from harm. Hence, in many ways God is replaceable. God is only irreplaceable for those who love, for love is of God. God does not intervene in the world in direct, independent ways; God intervenes in the world through human compassion and love for others.

Second, this means the individual person is no longer to be thought of as unique before God but should be seen only in community. It is not our presence before God that defines our humanity but rather our presence in relation to other human beings. That is, it is not individual salvation that matters most; it is the salvation of all of humanity.

Third, Christ's sacrifice did not complete "the act of redemption once and for all,"[31] but Christ's redemption is provisional in the sense that it continues to take place through human agents. We are redemption to each other.

Fourth, the dialectic of dependency and responsibility exists both for God and for us. God is dependent on Christ and Christ is dependent on us. "Thus, God's future, kept open by Christ as representative, is linked with ours and our representation of God to one another."[32]

Sölle's radical immanentism—Christianity from below—is an extension of Bonhoeffer's "worldly Christianity" and "religionless Christianity." Yet it is doubtful that Bonhoeffer would be comfortable with the extent to which Sölle takes this view. For she is so emphatic on the denial of a theology that defers to God for solutions to the messes of this world that it is impossible for her to embrace a view of God as acting outside human agency. This, of course, is somewhat ironic because it requires an enormous faith in human responsibility, which is the very thing she has placed in question. However, her explanation for this human failure lies largely in the church's embrace of a faulty view of God as distant and independent of creation. Christian responsibility requires that this view of God must go.

God

In her book *Theology for Skeptics*, Sölle begins with personal experiences in trying to speak of God in different contexts. She reflects on an encounter with a taxi driver in Berlin after the opening of the Berlin Wall. The driver had become cynical of human intentions to do good. He believed that such efforts were in the end always self-serving. He called human beings a "design failure."[33] When Sölle tried to offer some signs of hope on the basis of her Christian faith, she failed. What the great mystic, Meister Eckhart, had promised her in his writings, namely, that God is "that which is most communicable"[34] proved wrong in this case. Or was she not using the right "language?"

This encounter prompted Sölle to become more critical in asking who we are talking about when we speak of God. And she holds out the notion that derives from the Reformation that everyone believes in God, only for most people the gods worshipped are idols and hence cannot deliver on the promise to answer our most basic needs. She came to believe that it mattered deeply that we learn to speak properly of the God of Jesus Christ.

Sölle concluded that the Western theological tradition has taught Christians the practice of speaking *about* God, when the proper mode of theological speech is *to* God. The latter requires that we place ourselves into God's presence before we say anything at all. And when we do speak, the only language appropriate is reverence, or better put, the language of worship and hope. She found this expressed concretely in another experience, this time with a friend who took her to the city slums. Here, unlike in her discussion with the taxi driver, she noticed complete openness to the "God encounter" by the slum dwellers. She saw now that her mistake with the taxi driver had been that she accepted his mode of theological discourse, that is,

---

[31] Sölle, *Christ the Representative*, 116.
[32] Sölle, *Christ the Representative*, 117.
[33] Soelle, *Theology for Skeptics*, 8.
[34] Soelle, *Theology for Skeptics*, 9.

descriptive analysis. After that, there was nothing more to be said, for God simply cannot be spoken about in that mode. God does not make sense logically. What did her friend do in the slums? He simply prayed with the people and asked that God's kingdom of justice might come. Everyone "understood" what he was saying and "identified" with the hope he expressed.

To illustrate the same point further, Sölle, recounts an occurrence at a conference where a group of women gathered to speak about religious matters. Here the question arose of whether God had been at Auschwitz. A woman in the group volunteered a response: "Auschwitz was willed by God." Everyone was shocked and wanted to know what she meant. The reply came forthrightly: "Quite simply," she said, "if God had not willed it, it would not have happened. Nothing happens without God." Then Sölle continues as follows with the logic of this all-too-common view of God:

> The Wholly Other God has so determined it, and though we cannot understand it we must accept it in humility. God's authority, lordship, and omnipotence may not be placed in doubt, it is not for us to inquire after God's providential will. The God who is completely independent from all God's creatures has willed everything that happens. God and God alone could have hindered it. But God's ways are not our ways.[35]

Sölle cannot accept this type of theology. She asks, "must we really speak in this way? God is mighty, we are helpless—is that all?"[36] She gives a counter story to this logic of God, which she embraces as an archway into her own theological imagination. She refers to another woman at the conference who said, "When I had understood Auschwitz, I joined the peace movement."[37] Sölle continues:

> In this statement I found a different God from the omnipotent Lord of heaven and earth who is completely independent of us. This woman had

understood that in the Nazi period in Germany God was small and weak. God was in fact powerless because God had no friends, male or female. God's spirit had no place to live; God's sun, the sun of righteousness did not shine. The God who needs people in order to come into being was a nobody.[38]

In other words, this woman did not hand responsibilities over to God and thereby justify her own inaction. Rather, she took on the *responsibility of God* by becoming God's hands and voice and thereby represented God's dream of peace in this concrete world. As Sölle puts it, "God needs us in order to realize what was intended in creation. God dreams us and we should not let God dream alone."[39]

These reflections are crucial in Sölle's task of re-imaging God. She believes it to be important to ask what images are appropriate to God so that human agents do not shirk their responsibilities. In other words, for her, theology is ethics! She suggests that there are two opposite poles that run through the Christian tradition on the question of imaging God: the "veneration of icons" and the "prohibition of images."[40] But both have problems. Imaging God is important precisely because human hope and participation in worship cannot be merely an intellectual process and hence cannot be satisfied with argument and theory. We need images that can help us identify with God concretely, that can help us place ourselves into spaces of peace, comfort, and justice.

Sölle addresses the association between the father image of God and the power of God. She states that there are only "twenty places in the Hebrew Bible where God is designated as father."[41] Moreover, the exodus tradition, which names God as "I am who I am" (Exod 3:14), suggests something quite different than an exclusive father image of God. She quotes French philosopher Paul Ricoeur who says, "[The Exodus] revelation of the name

---

[35] Soelle, *Theology for Skeptics*, 13–14.
[36] Soelle, *Theology for Skeptics*, 15.
[37] Soelle, *Theology for Skeptics*, 15.
[38] Soelle, *Theology for Skeptics*, 15.
[39] Soelle, *Theology for Skeptics*, 16.
[40] Soelle, *Theology for Skeptics*, 19.
[41] Soelle, *Theology for Skeptics*, 23.

signifies the annulment of all anthropo-morphic conceptions, all forms and shapes, including the form of the father. The name stands against the idol."[42] Similarly, Sölle also suggests that in the Synoptic Gospels the image of the "heavenly father" is not central; instead the central image is of the "kingdom of God."

Father imagery has historically been connected with a particular form of the adoration of power and by implication the valorization of the male. She says, "This masculinization of God, which in Christianity is extremely advanced, as it is expressed in purely anthropocentric language, always goes hand in hand with the deification of the male."[43] She confesses her difficulties with this as follows:

> My difficulties with the father, begetter, ruler, and controller of history deepened as I came to understand more precisely what it meant to be born as a woman, (that is, in the language of the tradition, "defective") and to live in a sexist society. How could I will that power be the central category of my life? How could I worship a God who was no more than a man?"[44]

Sölle does not deny that the father symbol for God is an acceptable mode of speaking about God, but when it becomes the dominant image it is what she calls "God's prison."[45] She suggests that divine mother imagery is every bit as appropriate in bringing out the goodness, beauty, and source of divine reality. She says, "People do not honor God because of God's power and lordship; rather they 'submerge' themselves in God's love, which is 'ground,' 'depth,' 'ocean.' "[46] She refers to the Hebrew notion of the Shek-inah of God as a way of uniting all of the multiple images that help us to understand God's indwelling and God's presence. She

says, "Perhaps the Shekinah, God's presence which accompanies the people into exile, is the form of God which reveals the most to us about God today."[47] The notion that God accompanies the people into exile naturally leads Sölle to a discussion of God's pain and ours, that is, the theme of suffering.

Suffering

To help her develop a theology of suffering, Sölle draws on the thought of Jewish writer and philosopher Elie Wiesel, and particularly his drama, The Trial of God.[48] In Wiesel's portrayal of the "Trial of Shamgorod," the theme of theodicy is exposed. The context is seventeenth-century pogroms in Russia, and in the play God is accused of letting innocent children suffer. Three drunken characters go around seeking someone willing to defend God. Finally, a stranger presents himself; he portrays God in the traditional ways: omnipotent, absolute, holy, and so on. The play develops in a way that the stranger takes on the mask of the devil. Says Sölle, "the clever theologian who defends God turns out to be the devil. He calls himself 'God's emissary. I visit creation and bring stories back to Him. I see all things, I watch all men. I cannot do all I want, but I can undo all things.' "[49]

Sölle believes that the traditional rendering of God must be overcome. In the past, attempts at developing a "justification for God" have sought to bring three qualities of God into harmony: omnipotence, love, and comprehensibility. So one "defense of God" is to say that God's ways are not our ways, and hence we should not seek to understand them. This absolves God (in our understanding) from responsibility for human suffering because God is then seen as loving and all-powerful but not comprehensible. A second

---

[42] Soelle, Theology for Skeptics, 22–23.
[43] Soelle, Theology for Skeptics, 25–26.
[44] Soelle, Theology for Skeptics, 16.
[45] Soelle, Theology for Skeptics, 27.
[46] Soelle, Theology for Skeptics, 28.
[47] Soelle, Theology for Skeptics, 34.
[48] Elie Wiesel, The Trial of God, trans. Marion Wiesel (New York: Schocken, 1979).
[49] Soelle, Theology for Skeptics, 62.

defense is to say that God's power is such that it is in conflict with love, and God simply must do things that are not in keeping with human notions of love. God loves in ways we do not. The third defense is that God is not omnipotent. God is infinitely more loving and desirous of overcoming evil than we are but is not powerful in the sense that we understand power. God cannot overpower evil.

Each of these views is represented by a group of scholars who find cogent arguments for their positions. Since the last line of defense is the one Sölle develops in her writings, she cites several scholars who have argued this position. From Judaism they are Elie Wiesel, Abraham Heschel, Hans Jonas, and Harold Kushner. From the Christian tradition, she cites Dietrich Bonhoeffer as coming close to this position.[50]

Sölle wants to wrest the discussion of God from the language of power. God's authority is intelligible to us not with the aid of traditional, patriarchal categories of omnipotence and hierarchy, but with the concept of presence. God is present with us in our pain and suffering. In this way, God does not redeem us from a distance but through his presence with us when we suffer. Here, Jesus Christ on the cross is the reality.

Sölle gleans much theology from her experience with suffering people. We have already seen her effort to develop a post-Auschwitz theology. She now draws on insights from others: slum dwellers in the cities and victims of oppressive regimes like in El Salvador. She resonates with liberation theologians like Jon Sobrino, Gustavo Gutiérrez, and Oscar Romero. She says, "Perhaps Oscar Romero helped the people in San Salvador most by calling those who had been murdered 'martyrs' and thereby giving the people the only illuminating and acceptable interpretation of unimaginable suffering."[51] For to call people martyrs is to place them into the providential care of God. And poor and oppressed people believe in God precisely because God can bring a measure of peace that no other healer can bring. Hence, poor people are ready for "good news," while rich people tend to be afraid of "good news."[52]

Sölle says, "The visit I made to El Salvador helped me understand the New Testament better. . . . in El Salvador the pains of the poor are also the pains of God. God suffers with them and transforms their pain."[53] The good news of the gospel in El Salvador is not that God stands outside of their suffering and from "beyond" pulls the strings of redemption, but that God stands with them in their suffering. As Meister Eckhart, whom she quotes again and again, has put it, "If my suffering is in God and if God suffers with me, how then can my suffering be misfortune?"[54]

As Sölle sees it, the story of Jesus Christ is the most important story of God's presence with us. She says that we may be able to doubt the success of Christ in overcoming pain and suffering in this world, but we cannot doubt his truth.[55] For in the end, success, overcoming, and victory are not the issue; loving presence is. And in divine presence, there can be earthly healing.

Throughout her writings, Sölle speaks of suffering. Her interpretation of the Christian faith is that it is all about overcoming suffering; and yet at its center is the story of the cross. So how is both the affirmation of suffering and its overcoming to be understood? In a book dedicated to the theme of suffering,[56] she raises two important questions. The first is, "What are the causes of suffering, and how can these conditions be eliminated?" And the

---

[50] Soelle, *Theology for Skeptics*, 65.

[51] Soelle, *Theology for Skeptics*, 69.

[52] See Soelle, *Theology for Skeptics*, 71.

[53] Soelle, *Theology for Skeptics*, 75–76.

[54] Soelle, *Theology for Skeptics*, 82.

[55] See Soelle, *Theology for Skeptics*, 96.

[56] Dorothee Soelle, *Suffering*, trans. Everett R. Kalin (Philadelphia: Fortress, 1975).

second question is, "What is the meaning of suffering and under what conditions can it make us more human?"[57]

In answering these two questions, Sölle emphasizes that much suffering is caused by ordinary natural conditions such as floods, crop failures, illnesses, earthquakes, and so on. About these not much can be done except insofar as human agents are involved in precipitating such events, and, of course, when they occur, in responding to their effects. But it is also the case that much suffering is caused by human beings inflicting pain on one another: war, greed, withholding food, crime, and so on. And this form of suffering can stop through the volition of human agents.

In *Suffering*, Sölle is critical of two views of suffering that have their roots in the traditional, theological imagination: "Christian masochism" and "theological sadism." And the two are intrinsically related. Christian masochism is the view that God's followers are called to submit to the decrees of God. And this submission causes suffering. The logic then continues that the suffering is endurable, even enjoyable, because it is for and from God. Christians who think like this can find pleasure in suffering, and as Sölle defines masochism: "Submission as a source of pleasure—that is Christian masochism."[58]

As she sees it, Christian masochism is not the worst perversion of the faith, since it can serve to keep followers pious. Worse is what she calls "theological sadism." When theologians develop a theology from the notion that God requires suffering for "self-satisfaction," then theology takes a deeply heretical turn. And this is the way many stories are cast: the sacrifice of Isaac, the sacrifice of Christ on the cross, and so on. Protestants are especially to blame for the turn to theological sadism.[59] She identifies the logic here as follows:

[T]hree propositions . . . recur in all sadistic theologies: 1) God is the almighty ruler of the world, and he sends all suffering; 2) God acts justly and not capriciously; and 3) all suffering is punishment for sin.[60]

By now it will not be surprising to find that Sölle does not accept this way of speaking about God. She does not believe that God causes suffering but that God wills to overcome all suffering. And God might call people into suffering only as a way to overcome it. Suffering is not punishment for sin. God suffers with us, and only in God's suffering with us can suffering itself be overcome. God is not the almighty ruler of the world, but, as we see in Jesus Christ, God permits himself to be killed on the cross because of his passion to overcome suffering.

In her discussion of suffering, Sölle makes reference to Fyodor Dostoevsky's *The Brothers Karamazov*, a novel that deals with evil in a manner similar to Elie Wiesel's *The Trial of God*. She reflects on the interaction between Ivan, the rationalist accuser of God, and Alyosha, who embraces the suffering ones. Ivan will not accept that the suffering of innocent children can serve any higher good purpose. Sölle narrates the interaction thus: "'It's not God that I don't accept, Alyosha, only I most respectfully return him the ticket.' To which Alyosha answers gently, looking down, 'That's rebellion.'"[61] Neither Ivan nor Alyosha wish to live as rebels, but neither of them like the suffering they see around them. Moreover, both reject the grand harmony often invoked to justify suffering. Sölle's reflections on the two different directions from which the brothers look at suffering is instructive:

Ivan rises against God who causes or allows such suffering. He wants nothing to do with his harmony. His gesture is that of accusation, of rebellion. Alyosha directs his attention not to the power above but to the sufferers. He puts himself beside

[57] Soelle, *Suffering*, 5.
[58] Soelle, *Suffering*, 22.
[59] See Soelle, *Suffering*, 22.
[60] Soelle, *Suffering*, 24.
[61] Soelle, *Suffering*, 174. Quoted from Fyodor Dostoevsky, *The Brothers Karamazov*, book 5, chap. 4.

them. He bears their pain with them. During this conversation he says almost nothing. He listens in agony as Ivan introduces examples of suffering he had assembled as witnesses against the compassion of God. Later Alyosha arises, goes up to Ivan, the rebel and insurrectionist, and kisses him silently on the lips.[62]

The kiss is also what Jesus gives the Grand Inquisitor in Dostoevsky's story. The kiss, ironically, becomes the real act of rebellion, not a rebellion against God but against a world that cannot imagine God other than in traditional ways. So Alyosha becomes Christ's brother, which means giving up on the metaphysical perspective of Christianity and shifting to the pain of this earth. Sölle says, "Ivan is metaphysically oriented in his rebellion, Alyosha earthly in his solidarity. . . . Both long for another world, one free of suffering. But what for Ivan is illusion is for Alyosha hope."[63]

War and Peace

Sölle was a pacifist and believed that pacifism represented not only an alternative way of thinking but an alternative way of acting. As she saw it, acts always flow from an imagination—a way of thinking and speaking. Pacifism, for her, is perhaps best described as a way of reimagining the world.

In 1980 Sölle preached a sermon on the text, "Blessed Are the Peacemakers" (Matt 5:9).[64] In the sermon, she speaks of a student named Rüdiger, and the story of his experiences in the *Bundeswehr* (the West German army). Rüdiger was a rebel, but one who was different from Ivan Karamazov. Shortly after he joined the army, he began to ask questions. He applied for a discharge several times on the grounds of conscientious objection to killing but was refused. Eventually, he was released and he studied theology. She

says, "If Rüdiger had not rebelled, he probably would have gone the normal route like everyone else. He would be 'dead' now, as he put it, which is to say he would be doing his job somewhere in an office or a plant."[65]

"Rebellion" is a key term for Sölle, because being a Christian peacemaker requires that one operate in another world and resist the power of the dominant world. She concludes her sermon with reference to the liberation struggle in Chile under the dictator Augusto Pinochet. She lets the Chilean rebels speak the benediction to her sermon: "Rebel! Don't cooperate with death! Choose life! . . . Don't let them steal away your soul."[66]

Sölle's view of the pacifist rebel is rooted in Christian hope; a hope that has surrendered the need for justification because it resides in mystery. Sölle puts it thus: "I have no political analysis of resistance to offer that justifies hope. We have to expect the worst, for a while. But I know from the tradition that sustains the struggling and suffering people of El Salvador that terror will not have the last word."[67] In this sense, pacifists literally do not know what they are doing because they do not know the outcome of their rebellion. While their hope is shrouded in mystery, they nevertheless know that they cannot justify the violence that most people around them can justify. They cannot stop wars, but they can speak for the peace of Jesus Christ. This manner of speech is not that of logical deduction but that of performance, shining a light in the darkness. Perhaps that is why Sölle felt it necessary to express pacifist theology in poetry.

CONCLUSION

Sölle was passionate in her efforts to present a theology of peace and justice that cannot itself be used to underwrite violence. In this,

---

[62] Soelle, *Suffering*, 175.

[63] Soelle, *Suffering*, 176–77.

[64] See Dorothee Sölle, "Blessed Are the Peacemakers," in *Of War and Love*, trans. Rita and Robert Kimber (Maryknoll, N.Y.: Orbis, 1983), 5–17.

[65] Sölle, "Blessed Are the Peacemakers," 6.

[66] Sölle, "Blessed Are the Peacemakers," 15.

[67] Sölle, *Of War and Love*, 99.

she has been an important voice in both Europe and North America, especially for fellow liberation theologians and peace activists. It is not difficult to be drawn into the beauty and power of her words that beg for healing a broken and violent world. It is easy to embrace her anger at Auschwitz. And yet there is also some resistance for those who love theology; resistance to her rejection of much rich traditional theology and her insistence of the necessity of forfeiting virtually all language of transcendence and metaphysics. While the challenge of peace in this world must entail the call to human responsibility, is it not the case that unless the warrant for this claim resides in the conviction that the project is larger than what we as humans can deliver, it lacks hope and promise? For if anything is evident from history, it is precisely the betrayal of humans in their responsibility and in their fickleness of commitment to peace. So while many will want to follow her, some will also resist.

Excursus

PART III-A

The chapters in this section, presenting the thought of early twentieth-century European theologians, might be viewed as only tangentially related to Christian ethics. This is, however, far from the case. It is easy to grant that these theologians may not think of themselves narrowly, or even otherwise, as ethicists. Yet if ethics, as I am suggesting throughout this book, is life lived by Christian convictions, then most certainly this is Christian ethics since all of the theologians have valuable insights for Christian living. Each of the scholars presented here have sought to bring into interaction three themes: Christology, ecclesiology, and the world. Yet they have done so quite differently. Troeltsch gave prominence to history and culture in a manner that Barth, Balthasar, and Bonhoeffer were not able to accept. They unanimously rejected the cultural relativism of early twentieth-century liberalism represented by Troeltsch's historicism because it so completely identified theology with culture that it could no longer be distinguished from anthropology. Sölle, although critical of Barth and Bonhoeffer, is perhaps most self-consciously an ethicist, however, at the expense of rejecting much of the theology of Barth and Bonhoeffer.

It is important to acknowledge that pacifism was an option for all but Troeltsch, but it is also important to acknowledge that only Sölle remained true to pacifist convictions to the end. (Bonhoeffer's views are admittedly complex on this issue.) One might wonder why this was the case. The most frequent explanation is that the tumultuous political situation in Germany at the time made pacifism impractical. But if that were an adequate answer it would imply that pacifism is possible only in a not-so-bad world, and that would make it theologically untenable in principle. For unless pacifism is credible in the world as it is, it cannot be a Christian calling. I suspect that for Barth and Balthasar it rather had to do with how to view the relationship between Christology, ecclesiology, and ethics.

CHURCH AND THE MORAL LIFE

The role of church in the thought of these theologians varies a great deal. All but Sölle were ordained, which is important to mention here, insofar as it points to their commitment to the church. And although Sölle was not ordained, she shared this commitment. Yet the church as the sanctified body of Christ shaping a people capable of living a life rooted in divine grace did not play as major a role in the mature thinking of either Troeltsch or Sölle as it did for Barth, Bonhoeffer, and Balthasar. For the latter three, theological ethics was church ethics in the sense that they were not doing ethics for everyone but for those who were disciples of Christ. They believed that the faithful church was a sign of what the world could be ultimately, once God's redemption was fully wrought. Hence, there was here an elastic tension in contingent time between the church and the world which housed it. The church was in effect the world's conscience and in part its standard so that the entire world could see through the church's being and activities the will and rule of God. This is why these theologians needed to work at reviving the church to its true calling, freed from its collusion with the less-than-benevolent interests and powers of the state. It is not by accident that both the Protestants—Barth and Bonhoeffer—and the Catholic—Balthasar—saw it as their tasks to reconceive the church toward this end: Barth and Bonhoeffer through their work at Barmen and their commitment to *Die Bekennende Gemeinde* (The Confessing Church), and Balthasar through his work with the Community of St. John. For them, without the faithful church, Christian ethics becomes anathema. And for Balthasar, an important caveat: without aesthetics and wonder, ethics becomes a dull logic. For both Troeltsch and Sölle, although in different ways, this view of church was problematic because it casts it in ways too detached from the real world. The church is a human-made, social structure, fully in the world and part of the world.

Hence, Troeltsch and Sölle serve as foils in this setting: Troeltsch preceded Barth, Bonhoeffer, and Balthasar and was critiqued by them, and Sölle followed them and became their critic. While Troeltsch was an ordained church minister and Sölle fought for church renewal, for both, the church was a socially embodied force for change different from the theologically nuanced body of Christ one finds with the other three. For Troeltsch and Sölle, the church was not invested with the defining power in shaping their ethic; it was rather their ethic that defined and critiqued the church. Ironically perhaps, for them, the historical Jesus was more important than the church, in that Jesus pointed to the ultimate ethic for all of humankind—an ethic that every individual and every nation should heed. The ethic of Jesus, therefore, was to find expression, as far as possible, in the world at large. While the church was an important instrument in bringing about the kingdom which Jesus inaugurated, it was a social force like many others.

One must be careful not to make the summary pigeonholes too neat, for clearly there are important differences between Troeltsch's historicism and Sölle's pacifism. For Troeltsch to adopt pacifism would have meant to relinquish an important social-political power which could move the world in the direction of the kingdom of God. Sölle, on the other hand, so abhorred the use of force, dominance, and power in the church and in the world—much of which she saw underwritten by traditional theology—that she brought to bear a view of liberation and a post-Holocaust German critique on both church and traditional theology. Hers was a theology from below because she did not trust Barth's dogmatics.

The logic of Troeltsch's approach bears clear resemblance to what the American theologian-ethicist Reinhold Niebuhr called Christian realism. Here the assumption is that the ethics of Jesus is a kind of ideal that we are to make as real as possible knowing well that it will be far from perfect. In this model, since Christian ethics is for everyone—non-Christians and Christians alike—the church is morally irrelevant.

INCARNATION AS ETHICS

We see with the five theologians that contemporary theology is born of a divided mind. In some ways, the division stems back to the Reformation debates between Catholic and Protestant theology. Here we see that Troeltsch is much more at peace with the straightforward argument from traditional Protestant assumptions inherited from theologians like Luther: distinctions about the church and world, the physical and the spiritual, and the political and the personal. Barth, Bonhoeffer, and Balthasar seem to want another crack at the larger Reformation debates.

Let me try to explain this as follows. The Reformers, both the mainline and radical, had drawn such a sharp demarcation between church and world that it seemed very little political freight was carried across the divide from the church to the world. It had become customary to think of the two as separate realms—as Luther put it, between the physical and spiritual realms.

This debate is renewed in the encounter between Barth and Balthasar, with Bonhoeffer involved in yet a different way. For all of them, the church was central to the way they conceived of the Christian life, even though they did not entirely agree on how. It was Barth who wrested the controls of history from human hands in his fight to let the church be the church. He reversed the approach to theology from the Troeltschean historicist-philosophical method to a *church* dogmatic, something that Troeltsch had repudiated because he believed the church could not tell us how to understand the world. For him, the relationship goes the other way. It is interesting that Barth learned this 180-degree turn away from Troeltsch's approach from the Catholic monk Anselm who, as a pre-Enlightenment philosopher, showed what it meant to not have a pure starting point, and that all theology was really "faith seeking understanding" or "believing in order to understand." In other words, there is no theology in general and there is no ethics in general, but there is the logic of the church, which is the logic of the Word made flesh. It was precisely this insight that freed Barth to write his *Church Dogmatics*, a fundamentally countercultural act. This is what set Barth apart from the liberals.

Yet Barth's "no" to Brunner in which he affirmed the chasm between nature and grace seems to get him off track on his own agenda; at least his friend Balthasar thought so and tried to get him to reconsider. One might have thought that beginning theology with "the revelation of the Word of God become flesh in Jesus Christ" would have kept him from making the categorical distinction between nature and grace. But Barth saw the world as so deeply fallen, so utterly depraved and Godless, that the only way to see Christ was to look beyond the world to an outside

that breaks into alien territory. The problem is that for him to push this claim comes close to making the incarnation impossible because Christ is the grace of God incarnate in a natural body. Barth may well have been right in seeing within the culture-theology synthesis of the early twentieth century a false copy of the *theologia naturalis* for which Thomas Aquinas is famous. Nevertheless, the version of natural theology that Barth was reacting to was a corruption of Aquinas' view; it was instead a form of secularism made popular by liberal Protestants. Aquinas never intended for nature to inform us of divine grace, but rather God's grace was actively transforming nature. As he put it, "Grace does not destroy nature but perfects it."[1] This would seem to be the very claim that Barth's "Word of God" theology should seek to embrace and one that a "Church" theology could build upon. And it seems that Barth recognized the overstatement of his claim (although he does not explicitly recant it) the longer his correspondence with the Catholic Balthasar continued.

But what is really at stake here for Christian ethics? In sum, it is the question of what it means to follow Jesus. Do we follow Jesus from a distance as wholly other than us? Or do we follow by participating in the one who helps us to understand our own true being? It is really Bonhoeffer's theology that helps us to understand the answer here. According to Bonhoeffer, Barth's Christ is still too much an object of knowledge, a command we must obey, before he is one we can participate in. In other words, the distance between us as knowers and Christ as the known is too great for Bonhoeffer. As he saw it, Christ and the church are both forms of embodiment, and hence only as we ourselves participate in the brokenness of Christ's body can God be made known to us. In other words, for him, the church was in effect a new monastic order—not that the church was a body that had within it monastic orders but as a

---

[1] Thomas Aquinas, *Summa Theologica* I, Q.1. Art. 8, trans. Fathers of the English Dominican Province (New York: Benziger, 1947–1948).

whole it was that mysterious body where all Christians participate in Christ and come to teach each other the meaning of faithfulness. Ironically, it was perhaps the failure of this very body of spirit-filled believers that led to the tragedy in his own life. For the hope for Christian ethics is that the light of redeeming Christ can come to shine through the ones who are themselves in Christ.

PART III

SELECTED TWENTIETH-CENTURY
CHRISTIAN ETHICISTS
•
Section B
Formative, Contemporary, Christian Ethicists

Chapter Eighteen

WALTER RAUSCHENBUSCH
(1861–1918)

Ernst Troeltsch, Karl Barth, Dietrich Bonhoeffer, Hans Urs von Balthasar, and Dorothee Sölle were all European theologians. With this chapter we move to North America. Yet, quite naturally, the influence of European thought on Walter Rauschenbusch was significant; he himself had German roots.

It will be noticed that thinking about Christian ethics in the United States takes on a unique character. I remind the reader that the time of Walter Rauschenbusch's life and work is largely prior to both Barth's and Bonhoeffer's. Of course, this makes it impossible for Rauschenbusch to draw on their thought, and, for whatever reason, Barth and Bonhoeffer did not engage Rauschenbusch's writings.

Rauschenbusch is perhaps the most important nineteenth-century, social ethicist in North America. He was the first to straddle the divide between European and American ethical thinking. He is associated with one of the most prominent movements in North American ethics—the Social Gospel Movement. This school of thought believed that the gospel of Jesus Christ was not properly understood as a gospel for individuals only. It was also a call for a whole new society—one in which peace and justice reigned. The gospel of Jesus Christ was the proclamation of the kingdom of God of

which the prophets of old had spoken. And a "kingdom" is nothing if not political and social, in this case with God as sovereign king and all the people as subjects. It is also from this movement that we get the phrase, "What would Jesus do?" which has become a popular test for personal faithfulness.[1]

Rauschenbusch's life did not start with a social reading of the gospel. In fact, it took a fair bit of coaxing by ordinary events before he was able to embrace this social reading of Scripture. His move from conservative preacher to social reformer is an unusual one, and the theological shifts he makes are important for understanding not only his own development but also the shaping of American Christian ethics.

LIFE AND THOUGHT

Walter[2] was born into a German immigrant family in western New York state, where his father, August, was working with German students at Rochester Theological Seminary. His mother, Caroline, and his two sisters, Frida and Emma, completed the family.

Rauschenbusch was greatly influenced by his father, who was a Lutheran pastor-missionary. His father stood in a long line of Lutheran pastors—five had preceded him. In 1936, when August was twenty years old, he had a dramatic conversion experience which got him to renounce his liberal

---

[1] See Charles Sheldon, *In His Steps: What Would Jesus Do?* (Chicago: J. C. Winston, 1937).

[2] Rauschenbusch was christened Walther, which is the German form of the name, and for a time his parents resisted the Americanization of his name.

training in German universities and embrace a form of pietism not uncommon in Germany at the time.

When the family moved to New York in 1847, fourteen years before Walter's birth, they had come in contact with the Baptists who had an influence on August's theology. He began to see that infant baptism was wrong and that it had misled Christians in their understanding of the church. The Baptists taught that the church should consist of those who renounced sin and the ways of the world and that required adult commitment and a sectarian ecclesiology. So in 1850 August was rebaptized by immersion in the Mississippi River and became a Baptist. This was a radical step for him as a Lutheran minister, and it was not received well by his family and friends back home. Later, his son wrote approvingly of this event: "It was a step that cost him dear; it cut his family to the quick; it completely alienated many of his friends; it rendered his entire future uncertain; but he followed the truth."[3] Walter's biographer, Paul Minus, adds, "Following the truth, regardless of the cost, became a hallmark of the elder Rauschenbusch's life, and generations of Baptist students were to admire him for it, but none more than his son."[4]

Given August's views on baptism and ecclesiology, it should not be surprising that he would find theological kinship with the sixteenth-century Radical Reformers. And certainly young Walter received the impetus for this learning from his father. The elder Rauschenbusch taught young Walter to read church history along the lines of Troeltsch's church-sect typology, and the Anabaptists

represented a kind of sectarian pietism that appealed to the elder Rauschenbusch.

The point is made by several Rauschenbusch interpreters that, because of his father's influence, young Walter considered himself "related to the mainstream of Anabaptist scholarship."[5] He too saw the Anabaptists'[6] view of the church as an expression of the reign of God on earth. Herein lay his critique of the mainline churches. He saw them as having so compromised with the world that they could no longer stand as a social alternative to it. Hence their view of faith was reduced to an internal spiritual reality only, while the social ills that plagued so many poor people were accepted with indifference. The Anabaptist model of church was the clear alternative, one that ought to be the model for restructuring the entire world. He writes:

> The Anabaptists believed in a religious transformation of social life. . . . The Anabaptist movement was a religious movement with social aims. The Anabaptists entertained the social revolutionary hope under Biblical guise. Christ was to come and rescue his poor and oppressed people, and, in place of the present reign of the wicked set up the reign of the saints. It was a passionate hope for speedy relief from intolerable oppression.[7]

Several other Anabaptist themes ran through Rauschenbusch's thought, including discipleship, love, and pacifism. On discipleship, he said, "To become a disciple means to learn to think of God and life with him as Jesus did, and to let all life be transformed by that new faith and knowledge."[8] Discipleship is clearly more than a relationship between Christ and the individual; it extends

---

[3] Quoted in Paul M. Minus, *Walter Rauschenbusch: American Reformer* (New York: Macmillan, 1988), 3.

[4] Minus, *American Reformer*, 3.

[5] Donovan E. Smucker, *The Origins of Walter Rauschenbusch's Social Ethics* (London, Ontario: McGill-Queens University Press, 1994), 32. Another biographer says, "Walther's lifelong passion for Anabaptism was evident in many of his papers." rom Christopher H. Evans, *The Kingdom Is Always but Coming: A Life of Walter Rauschenbusch* (Waco, Tex.: Baylor University Press, 2010), 37.

[6] Rauschenbusch defined Anabaptism broadly to include the Franciscans, Waldensians, Lollards, and Taborites, among others. See Smucker, *The Origins*, 32.

[7] Smucker, *The Origins*, 39. The quotation is taken from Rauschenbusch's article, "The Prophetic Character of the Anabaptist Movement," in *Rochester Democrat and Chronicle* (15 September 1903).

[8] Quoted in Smucker, *The Origins*, 44.

to the entire social order and indeed to all of history.

On love, he wrote: "Since love is the supreme law of Christ, the Kingdom of God implies a progressive reign of love in human affairs."[9] Love binds one to those that are unjustly treated in this world, and it is needed everywhere. But, he says:

> the severest task and the most urgent task of love today is in the field of business life. Unless love can dominate the making of wealth the wealth of our nation will be the ferment of its decay. There will be no genuine advance for human society until business experiences the impulse, the joy, the mental fertility of free teamwork. . . . Our age is asking leaders of the business world to take a great constructive forward step and to found business on organized love.[10]

His views on pacifism were more nuanced. He speaks differently about pacifism before and after joining the Fellowship of Reconciliation (FOR), a Christian pacifist organization. Smucker says of him:

> As for coercion in the social struggle, Rauschenbusch maintained a pragmatic pacifism during the period before he joined FOR. While not ruling out force in every instance, he believed that "force is not as effective as it looks . . . the slow conflict of opposing forces is God's method of educating a nation."[11]

After he joined the FOR in 1916, he gave a presentation in Boston in which he argued that war should always be seen as one of the great social evils, and love is the only principle that can bring about reconciliation to prevent war. And Jesus and war certainly remain in utter conflict.

It is important to ask how Rauschenbusch came by these radical views. His father was clearly only one influence; his education and personal faith development are others.

In March 1879, at the age of eighteen, Rauschenbusch was baptized in the First German Baptist Church in Rochester. Remembering

and recounting one's conversion experience were high priorities in Baptist pietist settings. Yet he writes about it only once. Given that he had from early childhood been enamored with the faith of his father—which did not mean that he was always a good boy—his own conversion story was less dramatic than some. He speaks of it as "the time of awakening for me" when, probably a year before his baptism, he said to himself, "I want to become a man; I want to be respected. . . ." With clear allusions to the biblical story of the prodigal son in Luke 15, he continues:

> This was my way of saying: "I am out in the far country, and I want to get home to my country, and I don't want to tend the hogs any longer." And so I came to my Father, and I began to pray for help and got it. And I got my own religious experience.[12]

Shortly after his baptism, he went back to Germany to study at the *Gymnasium* (high school) in Gütersloh and later at the University of Berlin. By this time, he had already decided to become a church minister, and so he enrolled in both theology and pastoral training courses. When he returned to the United States, he registered at the University of Rochester to complete his senior year and at Rochester Theological Seminary to study theology.

After graduation in 1885, Rauschenbusch became the pastor of the Second German Baptist Church in New York City. The church was situated at the edge of town in a rundown area known as "Hell's Kitchen." It was so named for its abject conditions—unemployment, poverty, wretched housing, malnutrition, disease, ignorance—and crime that went well beyond the average inner-city desolation. This was clearly not the kind of church Rauschenbusch had prepared for in his training for ministry.

About a year later, Rauschenbusch, now twenty-five years old, was ordained as a

---

[9] Quoted in Smucker, *The Origins*, 39.
[10] Quoted in Smucker, *The Origins*, 57–58.
[11] Smucker, *The Origins*, 60. The internal quotation by Donovan Smucker is from Rauschenbusch's, "The Ideals of Social Reformers."
[12] Quoted from Minus, *American Reformer*, 17.

Baptist minister. But this was not a process without anxiety. There were issues of orthodoxy over which both he and his parents were concerned. It was said that he had some "doubts and deviant attitudes" regarding the Old Testament and atonement.[13] Although the examinations were extensive and thorough, these matters did not become impediments, and he became an ordained minister in the Baptist church on October 21, 1886.

When he began his ministry, he questioned what his role as pastor was to be in the New York slums. His education had prepared him to preach the gospel not to be a social worker. Yet social work was what was needed here. So he read widely in social analysis and reform. He felt compelled to do what he could to improve the lot of his people. In 1889, he became the founder and editor of a newspaper, *For the Right*, a paper which was intended for the working people. His intention was to help them feel connected to one another so that together they might be empowered to help themselves out of their poverty. But it soon discontinued. A newspaper was not what his parishioners needed either; it was something else.

But what else would bring "salvation?" Indeed what was salvation? When Rauschenbusch first came to New York, he wanted to save the souls of those he addressed. But when he arrived and began to get to know the people by living with them, he saw that this was inappropriate and realized that his training was thoroughly inadequate. What was even more disconcerting for him was that he realized his passion for social justice came neither from his view of the church nor from his religious training but from his life in the slums where he met real, hurting people. He had no way of unifying into one imagination his task as a preacher and his task as

an empathetic social reformer. His evangelical passion and passion for justice remained disconnected.

Many of his friends urged him to give up his concern for social work and concentrate on what he had been called to do—preach the gospel. They told him that he was to do "Christian work." He replied as follows regarding his work with the poor:

> [T]he work was Christ's work . . . I went ahead, although I had to set myself against all that I had been previously taught. I had to go back to the Bible to find out whether I or my friends were right. I had to revise my whole study of the Bible.[14]

In 1888 Rauschenbusch became partially deaf because of an illness he did not attend to soon enough due to his energy-consuming work with his parishioners. Partly to facilitate his health and partly to further train himself as a pastor for the poor, he again returned to Germany on a study leave. Here he studied theology, and especially the New Testament. He identified himself with Friedrich Schleiermacher, Albrecht Ritschl, Ernst Troeltsch, Julius Wellhausen, and Adolf von Harnack—all liberals.

The German liberals proved to be a theological breath of fresh air for Rauschenbusch. His own work during this time reflected the same idealism and hope for profound social change that characterized much of German liberalism. He was greatly impressed with the liberals' passion for theological unity. He was convinced that the starting point for preachers should also be to bring together Christianity and secular culture, science and religion, faith and history, theology and sociology, the church and society. This is what his previous training had not given him, and this is why he was unequipped for a pastorate in the New York slums. As it

---

[13] As quoted in Minus, *American Reformer*, 53. In a letter to his parents on this matter of possible unorthodox theology regarding the Old Testament, Rauschenbusch writes, "I believe in the Gospel of Jesus Christ with all my heart. What this Gospel is, everyone has to decide for himself, in the face of God" (*American Reformer*, 53). Atonement was another matter. Just a year before his ordination, he had written an essay questioning the traditional and commonly adhered-to theories of "ransom" and "substitution" arguing that these metaphors see salvation as impersonal transactions. In response, he said, "we want something warmer, more living, something nearer to us," quoted from Evans, *Kingdom Is Always but Coming*, 39.

[14] Quoted from Robert T. Handy, ed., *The Social Gospel in America* (New York: Oxford University Press, 1966), 255.

turned out, liberalism saved him from giving up on the church.

His German teachers helped him find the unity of individual and social salvation in Jesus' teaching of the "kingdom of God," a theme which was prevalent in the entire Scriptures and would become the controlling impetus of his life's work. He puts it thus:

> So Christ's conception of the kingdom of God came to me as a new revelation. Here was an idea and purpose that had dominated the mind of the Master himself. All his teachings center around it. His death was suffered for it. . . . I found that this new conception of the purpose of Christianity was strangely satisfying. It responded to all the old and all the new elements of my religious life. The saving of the lost, the teaching of the young, the pastoral care of the poor and frail, the quickening of starved intellects, the study of the Bible, church union, political reform, the reorganization of the industrial system, international peace—it was all covered by the one aim of the reign of God on earth.[15]

The doctrine of the kingdom of God was, for Rauschenbusch, both a religious and a social concept. God, in a miraculous manner, was at work bringing into existence a just and peaceful society. This made the kingdom simultaneously present and future. While there could be no perfection on earth, there could be continual growth toward perfection. And the task of every faithful Christian was to participate in bringing this growth about.

Rauschenbusch's view of human nature was clearly optimistic. He believed that society was moving upward toward an ever-greater moral level. Human civilization, especially in the West, was evidence of this. Reflecting on this he said, "The swiftness of evolution in our own country proves the immense latent perfectibility in human nature."[16]

A formative discussion in which Rauschenbusch was involved was the historical Jesus debate. He believed that scientific biblical study was able to bring the master out of the past into the present, concrete, social reality. In this historical investigation, Jesus was presented as the first real man, the inaugurator of a new humanity, and hence a new kingdom.

In 1891 he became a leader in the rapidly developing Social Gospel Movement. While the movement was much larger than Rauschenbusch, he was very instrumental in giving it content. During this time, he gave many speeches and wrote many articles. He was active in his own church and especially in the Baptist Congress. In the early 1890s, he joined other young Baptist ministers to form the "Brotherhood of the Kingdom." This group was explicitly formed with the concern to give power and structure to Social Gospel theology. It served both as a united platform, somewhat like a political party (yet it was not involved directly in partisan politics), and as a support and testing body for Rauschenbusch to check where and how this theology could be applied socially.

During this busy time, when Rauschenbusch was giving his energy to promoting the Social Gospel Movement, he also got married. He met Pauline Ernestine Rother at a German Baptist Congress in 1889. She was a German teacher and active in the church. "She was a bright, brown-haired, blue-eyed woman, whose beauty was often accented by a flower worn in her hair."[17] They corresponded for two years and were married on April 12, 1893. Walter was thirty-two years old, and Pauline was twenty-nine. Together they had two children, Winifred and Hilmar.

In 1902 Rauschenbusch became professor of church history at his alma mater, the Rochester Theological Seminary. He was a passionate teacher and well-liked by his students. His subject matter was always historical, and he taught about the kingdom of God, the Bible, the church, and the social situation.

In 1907 Rauschenbusch published his first major book on the Social Gospel, *Christianity*

[15] Quoted in Handy, *Social Gospel in America*, 255–56.
[16] Walter Rauschenbusch, *Christianity and the Social Crisis* (New York: Macmillan, 1920), 422.
[17] Minus, *American Reformer*, 93.

and the Social Crisis, which analyzed the social issues that Jesus confronted and specifically how Jesus dealt with the people who were socially disadvantaged. He thought this book was radical and expected it to start a flood of criticism, since he broadened the notion of salvation to include all of society. In fact, he said he was ready to leave his teaching post if the negative fallout made it difficult to remain. But to his surprise, it was fairly well-received. It went through six printings in the first two years The churches loved it, as the book provided them with Christian answers to the deteriorating social conditions of the day.

Years later, in 1960, Martin Luther King Jr. referred to this book and said that it

> left an indelible imprint on my thinking. Of course there were points at which I differed with Rauschenbusch. I felt that he had fallen victim to the 19th-century "cult of inevitable progress," which led him to an unwarranted optimism concerning human nature. Moreover, he came perilously close to identifying the kingdom of God with a particular economic and social system—a temptation which the church should never give in to. But in spite of these shortcomings, Rauschenbusch gave to American Protestantism a sense of social responsibility that it should never lose.[18]

After the publication of this book, Rauschenbusch received many invitations to preach and speak, which gave him the opportunity to promote his ideas. He was clearly becoming the primary spokesperson for the Social Gospel Movement, although others like Washington Gladden (1836–1918) and Richard T. Ely (1854–1943) were also major figures.

In *Christianity and the Social Crisis*, Rauschenbusch argued that Jesus had explicit social aims that he inherited from the Hebrew prophets. Moreover, the church understood Jesus' claims in exactly this manner. It is not by accident that the early church at Jerusalem was a social community of justice—sharing everything in common. This was the true

form of the church. The fact that it lost its social character was due to other factors than the leading of God's spirit, like the church's hostility to the empire and the church's accommodation to the culture around it. In any event, now is the time when this can change. Rauschenbusch saw it as urgent that the gospel be given its proper social read, since the effects of the Industrial Revolution were destroying society, family, and other important social structures. The task of every Christian and the church collectively is to seize the moment and engage in "social evangelization." He says:

> Mankind is so closely bound together that no man lives to himself, and no man is saved to himself alone. The new salvation is contagious. Those who have wrought out a faith that embraces the salvation of all human relations, make it easier for others to reach the same unification of all relations in the great aim of the kingdom of God. There will be a *social evangelization*, consciously and unconsciously. The believers will win other believers.[19]

The theme of social evangelization became the center of his next major book, which he wrote in 1912, called *Christianizing the Social Order*.[20] In this book, Rauschenbusch contrasts what he calls social Christianity with personal religion. Personal religion is the religion of piety and spirituality. This, he says, is represented in Roman Catholicism by books like Thomas à Kempis' *Imitation of Christ* and in Protestantism by writings like John Bunyan's *Pilgrim's Progress*. While both are interesting and worthwhile studies, they do not represent the gospel of the New Testament.

Over against this tendency, he stressed that Christianity properly understood is a social religion into which every individual fits. It was not an anti-individual religion, but it was one that emphasized holism: the social environment and the individual. In fact, Christianity was first a social phenomenon before it was an individual one.

---

[18] Martin Luther King Jr., "Pilgrimage to Nonviolence," *The Christian Century* 77 (1960): 440.

[19] Rauschenbusch, *Christianity and the Social Crisis*, 352–53 (emphasis added).

[20] Walter Rauschenbusch, *Christianizing the Social Order* (Waco, Tex.: Baylor University Press, 2010).

It is important to remember that Rauschenbusch maintained a strong devotional and worshipful emphasis throughout his life. This is seen in several of his works; for example, *For God and People: Prayers of the Social Awakening* (1910),[21] is a wonderful book of prayers, in which he shows how the personal and the social intersect in meditation and worship. He also wrote many hymns and edited several books of church hymns, one being the *Evangeliums Lieder* (Gospel Hymns).[22] This is a special book for this author because we sang from it regularly in our worship services in the Crystal City Mennonite Church when I was a child. It is amazing to think that, while Rauschenbusch has the reputation of being a liberal theologian, he was so fervently evangelical in his music. It is a strong reminder that his pietist influence was never *replaced* by his emphasis on the social dimensions of the gospel; the two were held as complementary. He remained an evangelist all his life; however, his message broadened to include more than the individual.

During the last five years of his life, Rauschenbusch came out with five new books. In 1912 he published a little booklet called *Unto Me*; in 1914, *Dare We Be Christian?*; in 1916, *The Social Principles of Jesus*; and in 1917, *A Theology for the Social Gospel*. A book titled *The Righteousness of God* was posthumously compiled and edited from Rauschenbusch's notes by Max L. Stackhouse.[23] Each of these books represents a further working out of his theme that Christianity is a social gospel which demands a new world of justice emanating from the teachings of Jesus Christ.

As a person concerned with justice and peace, Rauschenbusch was deeply disturbed by the First World War. He had retained great love for Germany and as a U.S. citizen hoped sincerely that the United States would remain neutral. This did not happen. His death from cancer came only four months before the end of the war, on July 25, 1918. It was a cruel fate that he did not live to see the end of the war.

Before I reflect on specific characteristics of Rauschenbusch's Social Gospel ethic, I identify four main influences which Donovan Smucker suggests are a summary of his thought.[24]

1. Pietism. Rauschenbusch never ceased being an evangelist. Evangelism was in his blood and Jesus was always the focus of his teaching and preaching.
2. Sectarianism. He did not believe in mainline ecclesiology, which he believed was far too accommodating of the structures of society. He felt that social structures had to be transformed. To that extent, at least, the church stands over against mainline culture. This was the view of the sectarian left wing of the church. Hence, he found a prominent social role for the Baptist and even the Anabaptist church groups. Yet, while embracing sectarianism as a model, he also sought to overcome it in its early Anabaptist formulation. After all, he sought to make mainstream a model of church that had found it necessary to separate itself from both society and the views of church too compromised with society. In this sense, his effort to integrate a separatist view of church into greater society represents an impossibility.
3. Liberalism. Rauschenbusch was a strong advocate of European liberal theology, especially the Albrecht Ritschl and Ernst Troeltsch varieties. Both had identified theology with mainline culture. Both had criticized the heavy reliance of theology on metaphysics and the creeds, and in their place had emphasized theology's association with social ethics. This, felt Rauschenbusch, was right, and he did what he could to give expression to this view in the United States.
4. Transformationism. Rauschenbusch believed that human beings could be transformed from their self-centeredness to Christ-centeredness. He also believed that society could be so

[21] Walter Rauschenbusch, *For God and People: Prayers of the Social Awakening* (Whitefish, Mont.: Kessinger, 2007).
[22] *Evangeliums-Lieder 1 und 2* [*Gospel Hymns*]: *Mit deutschen Kernliedern*, selected and edited by Walter Rauschenbusch and Ira D. Sankey (Chicago: Biglow & Main, 1897).
[23] Walter Rauschenbusch, *The Righteousness of the Kingdom*, ed. Max Stackhouse (Nashville: Abingdon, 1968).
[24] Smucker, *The Origins*, 138–40.

transformed. He believed both because in the resurrection of Jesus Christ he saw the promise not only of personal transformation but also of socially dead cities.

SOCIAL GOSPEL ETHICS

In discussing Rauschenbusch's life I have already touched on several key tenets of Social Gospel ethics from the beginning of the twentieth century. What remains is to flesh out a few of these concepts.

The Kingdom of God Once More

In his first major publication, *Christianity and the Social Crisis* (1907), Rauschenbusch argues that Jesus was misunderstood throughout Christian history. While it may be true that "Jesus was not a reformer of the modern type"[25] since central to his emphasis was the religious life, nevertheless, "whoever uncouples the religious and the social life has not understood Jesus."[26] The social aims of Jesus have everything to do with his ethical teachings about the kingdom of God. The problem in our society and in the church is that we have come to see ethics as an individual matter only. But Christian ethics properly understood is fundamentally social. He says:

> All human goodness must be social goodness. Man is fundamentally gregarious and his morality consists in being a good member of his community. A man is moral when he is social; he is immoral when he is anti-social.[27]

In other words, when we see Christian ethics as only for individuals, we forget that we are corporate beings who constitute social realities. This makes intelligible the fundamental, moral virtue that Rauschenbusch finds in the ethical teaching of Jesus. He says: "The fundamental virtue in the ethic of Jesus was love, because love is the society making

quality. Human life originates in love."[28] Notice that love is not a subjective quality but a social or relational one; one without which society would be utterly fragmented and hence unjust.

Contemporary American ethicist Max Stackhouse reminds us that just as Bonhoeffer cautioned his readers against "cheap grace," so Rauschenbusch was critical of "cheap prophecy," a prevalent danger in his time and setting.[29] What will become of us (eschatology) is not a factor merely of calculating the numbers and proclamations found in apocalyptic biblical literature, but our future will be determined, at least in great measure, by whether we heed the call of kingdom-justice and exert whatever effort we can to change current injustices. Like cheap grace, cheap prophecy is all too often an excuse for inaction in the face of inequity.

Two key elements in Rauschenbusch's reading of the biblical kingdom of God were nature and history. Nature was associated with the biblical theme of land, via which he got his emphasis on the economic system, justice, class, sex, and so on; that is, matters of social and political import. These were topics that some church leaders would rather not talk about. And the biblical theme of history made possible the movement from current injustice to its overcoming. Theological history, or eschatology, although not worked out in detail, was an indispensable piece of his Social Gospel ethic. As Stackhouse puts it, for Rauschenbusch "the Kingdom of God is neither inevitable nor exhausted in history. It always stands as a transcendent future possibility, an eschatological possibility, even if it is partially manifest in the present. It is always 'already' and 'not yet.'"[30] Or, as Rauschenbusch says: "The Kingdom of God is

---

[25] Rauschenbusch, *Christianity and the Social Crisis*, 47.

[26] Rauschenbusch, *Christianity and the Social Crisis*, 48.

[27] Rauschenbusch, *Christianity and the Social Crisis*, 67.

[28] Rauschenbusch, *Christianity and the Social Crisis*, 67.

[29] See Max Stackhouse, "The Continuing Importance of Walter Rauschenbusch," Editor's Introduction to *The Righteousness of the Kingdom* by Walter Rauschensusch (Nashville: Abingdon, 1968), 14.

[30] Stackhouse, "Continuing Importance," 35.

always but coming; . . . you can never lay your hand on it to say 'It is here.'"[31] In this language lies the clue for how Rauschenbusch seeks to bring history and nature into unity—the *natural* state of injustice in its many forms can be and will be transformed through *history*. What he is not entirely clear about is whether the logic that governs this movement from here to there is a Hegelian dialectic, a Marxist dialectic, or a distinct theological understanding of history different from both.

Rauschenbusch does, however, make several insightful comments that move in the direction of a Christian theology of history/nature. Stackhouse identifies three. "First, history has been altered by the 'Kingdom event' of Jesus Christ."[32] What this means for Rauschenbusch is that in the coming of the Messiah the new reign has begun, and while not something we manage, we are invited, and indeed mandated, to join the movement. Second, the new kingdom is mediated by historically located persons. This does not make the kingdom either subjective or individual, but it makes every individual recognize his or her radical sociality in terms both of identity and responsibility. And third, the kingdom is mediated by the church. While not entirely clear what the precise relationship between the church and the kingdom of God is for Rauschenbusch, nevertheless the faithful church (the free church) participates in the kingdom of God which itself is much greater than its expression at any particular time. The kingdom is after all never fully present but has a future dimension beyond every social location.

Rauschenbusch was concerned about those theologians who viewed the theology of the Old Testament as dominated by law and the New Testament by gospel. Social ethics is always the first casualty of this kind of Christianity. If there is no law in the New Testament then what does it have to do with ethics? Rauschenbusch saw Jesus in continuity with the prophets of the Hebrew tradition. The kingdom which God was setting up in the days of the children of Israel was the same kingdom Jesus announced as "at hand" two thousand years ago,[33] and it is the very kingdom willed by God today.

Kingdoms have kings, people, and a politic or way of ruling. That is exactly the way the kingdom of God in the Old and New Testaments was understood. Hence, when Jesus spoke harshly to the rich and powerful this was a prescription for kingdom living. The new kingdom was intended as one of justice where there is no unjust wealth, or poverty, where the sick are cared for, and the imprisoned are set free, and so on. Salvation meant saying yes to this kind of world, and no to all others. This is why Rauschenbusch had such disdain for the theology that suggests one could personally participate in injustice and yet inwardly be saved. Such theology is sheer hypocrisy.

Clearly, Social Gospel ethics cannot be understood without reference to Jesus' teaching of the kingdom of God, and "being Christian" is unintelligible apart from a discipleship that embraces the politics of this kingdom. Rauschenbusch puts it succinctly:

> The kingdom of God is the first and most essential dogma of the Christian faith. It is also the lost ideal of Christendom. No man is a Christian in the full sense of discipleship until he has made the kingdom of God the controlling purpose of his life, and no man is intellectually prepared to understand Jesus until he has understood the meaning of the kingdom of God.[34]

Theology of Missions and Evangelism

Rauschenbusch's views on mission work and evangelism changed dramatically during his lifetime. He volunteered for traditional mission work right after graduating from seminary, but this was before he became convinced of the social message and power

---

[31] Stackhouse, "Continuing Importance," 35.

[32] Stackhouse, "Continuing Importance," 37.

[33] The full text in the NRSV reads: "Repent, for the kingdom of heaven has come near" (Matt 3:2).

[34] Rauschenbusch, *Christianizing the Social Order*, 49.

of the gospel. Once this occurred, everything changed. Evangelism and missions are now but new ways of spreading the Social Gospel. Neither mission work nor evangelism is abandoned, but both are refocused. He believed that it was grossly irresponsible to go into settings and seek to save only the souls of people. Their bodies and their social structures also must be saved. When this does not happen, the gospel being proclaimed is not Christian.

Rauschenbusch believed that evangelism in the style of Dwight L. Moody (1837–1899) was losing its appeal at the beginning of the twentieth century.[35] Moody represented the old evangelism. The new evangelism was based on a social awakening and revival. The old way was not wrong in that it talked too much about Jesus, God, and salvation; that is what evangelism is all about. It was wrong in that it did not root these notions in the biblical narrative. Jesus himself proposed fundamental social change as the sign of the age to come. Evangelism must incorporate this change into its gospel.

Mission work, evangelism, and salvation are always closely connected with a view of sin. Sin is what people are called to repent of. As Rauschenbusch saw it, the capitalist economic order was the major sin in North America and the Western world, and the Industrial Revolution was bringing it on. He has an impassioned section in *Christianity and the Social Crisis* on the Industrial Revolution, where he writes sarcastically about the era initiated by the inventions of the steam engine in 1769 and other "power machines." For example, he says about the harnessing of steam power: "If some angel with prophetic foresight had witnessed that epoch, would he not have winged his way back to heaven to tell God that human suffering was drawing

to its end?" Then responding, Rauschenbusch says, "Instead of that a long-drawn wail of misery followed wherever the power-machine came. It swept the bread from men's tables and the pride from their hearts."[36]

Rauschenbusch suggests that there are three forms of sin: sensuousness, selfishness, and godlessness.[37] However, each of these has important social dimensions that the tradition has disregarded. Traditional theology has made far too much of original sin, and although there is "a substance of truth in this unpopular doctrine of original sin . . . the old theology overworked it."[38] He says further:

> The theological definitions of sin have too much the flavor of the monarchical institutions under the spiritual influence of which they were first formed. In an absolute monarchy the first duty is to bow to the royal will. . . . Sin is not a private transaction between the sinner and God. Humanity always crowds the audience room when God holds court. We must democratize the conception of God; then the definition of sin will become more realistic. . . . We rarely sin against God alone.[39]

Clearly, capitalism and industrialism are the key sins for which we need to repent. These are the backbone of an unchristian economic order, and as such are powers that tempt good people to go astray. But they can be overcome. And the task of social evangelism is to redeem these sins. He says:

> An unchristian economic order tempts men and debases character, sets individuals and classes into unfraternal antagonism to one another, and institutionalizes widespread disloyalty to the common good. A Christian economic order would aid in training strong individuals by its assimilating influence, would place men in righteous relations to one another and to the commonwealth, and so promote the Christian purpose of giving all a chance to live a saved life. . . . A Christian order must be just. . . . A Christian economic order must offer to all members of the community the blessed influence

---

[35] Dwight L. Moody was in many ways like Rauschenbusch himself. He was an evangelist holding revival meetings in the inner city of Chicago. Like Rauschenbusch, he worked with Ira Sankey in his music ministry. But unlike Rauschenbusch, he did not preach a gospel of social reform.

[36] Rauschenbusch, *Christianity and the Social Crisis*, 214.

[37] Walter Rauschenbusch, *A Theology for the Social Gospel* (Nashville: Abingdon, 1978), 47. Originally published 1917.

[38] Rauschenbusch, *Theology for the Social Gospel*, 59.   [39] Rauschenbusch, *Theology for the Social Gospel*, 48.

of property rights. . . . Our economic order must work away from one-man power towards the democratizing of industry. . . . A Christian economic order must organize all workers in systematic and friendly cooperation, and so create the material basis for Christian fraternity. These fundamental demands of the Christian spirit are all simple and almost axiomatic, but they cut deep and are revolutionary enough to prove that they are really the laws of the Kingdom of God on earth.[40]

Rauschenbusch treats at some length the question of how the death of Christ atones for human sin. In his answer he characterizes atonement with the aid of three points: first that the death and resurrection of Christ "was the conclusive demonstration of the power of sin in humanity"; second, it was "the supreme revelation of love"; and third, it "reinforced prophetic religion."[41] Yet clearly the second point is the central one for him. He says:

> Jesus put love to the front in his teaching. . . . His death underscored all he said on love. It put the red seal of sincerity on his words: "Greater love hath no man than that he gives his life for his friends." Unless he gives it for his enemies too.[42]

For Rauschenbusch, love is the social glue and the salvation of society. As he puts it:

> Love is the social instinct of the race. In all its many forms it binds man to man. Every real improvement of society gives love a freer chance. Every genuine progress must be preceded by a new capitalization of love.[43]

In his beautiful little booklet on love, *Dare We Be Christian?*, Rauschenbusch spells out the social implications of a view of atonement based on self-sacrificial love. He says:

> We can watch the society-making force of love at work in the creation of new social organizations. Not even a little local trade union nor lodge nor church nor club can be made successful unless there are in its membership some individuals with

the higher qualities of enthusiasm and affection. Selfish interests are necessary, too, for durability, but love is the real chemical for amalgamation.[44]

Rauschenbusch was a strong supporter and promoter of the cooperative movement in the early twentieth century. "Cooperative organizations are a remarkable demonstration of a society-making power of love. . . . The next fifty years will see a long contest for survival and dominion between the capitalistic and cooperative type of organization. The former is strong through selfishness and possession; the latter through the resources of love."[45]

As is evident from these quotations, mission work and social action are not distinguishable for Rauschenbusch. The power of God seeks to transform both individual and social sins. Hence, to "Christianize the social order" is the task of the inspired evangelist.

Socialism and the Social Reformers

The socialist spirit is evident throughout Rauschenbusch's writing. He was influenced by the fact that the early church was a communist society, holding "all things in common" (Acts 2:44).[46] He did not find it hard to believe that private property was a major source of the social ills we find in Western society. He saw capitalism as a form of structured injustice. It guarantees the disparity between rich and poor. It leads directly to the rationalization for having "more" that creates untold social harm.

The great reformers had a lot to say about social change. Much of what they said, according to Rauschenbusch, was compatible with a Christian view of the economic order. In 1907 he gave a speech at the Conference of the Brotherhood of the Kingdom.[47] In it

---

[40] Rauschenbusch, *Christianizing the Social Order*, 372–73.
[41] Rauschenbusch, *Theology for the Social Gospel*, 267–74.
[42] Rauschenbusch, *Theology for the Social Gospel*, 270–71.
[43] Rauschenbusch, *Theology for the Social Gospel*, 270.
[44] Walter Rauschenbusch, *Dare We Be Christian?* (Cleveland: Pilgrim, 1914), 27–28.
[45] Rauschenbusch, *Dare We Be Christian?*, 29–30.
[46] The full text in NRSV reads: "All who believed were together and had all things in common; they would sell their possessions and goods and distribute the proceeds to all, as any had need" (Acts 2:44-45).
[47] This was later published in *The Kingdom* 1 (December 1907).

he challenged the churches to take seriously the writings of reformers and social philosophers like Leo Tolstoy and Karl Marx. Why? Because they knew something about how society works and what unjust structures in society looked like. From them we can learn about the evils of materialism that should give Christians pause. He says:

> The spiritual forces of Christianity should be turned against the materialism and mammonism of our industrial and social order. If a man sacrifices his human dignity and self-respect to increase his income, or stunt his intellectual growth and his human affections to swell his bank account, he is to that extent serving mammon and denying God. Likewise if he uses up and injures the life of his fellow-men to make money for himself, he serves mammon and denies God. But our industrial order does both. It makes property the end, and man the means to produce it. Man is treated as a *thing* to produce more things. Men are hired as hands and not as men. . . . Jesus asked, "Is not a man more than a sheep?" Our industry says "No."[48]

The echoes of Karl Marx are not hard to detect in these words, as Rauschenbusch explicates his understanding of the teachings of Jesus.

Rauschenbusch goes on to point out that the most fundamental institution of human existence, that is, the single most humanizing institution—the family—is a communist structure. He means by this that in the family, property and other goods are held in common. Public institutions are dehumanizing precisely because they do not model themselves on structures of love.[49]

Rauschenbusch distinguished between dogmatic and practical socialism. Socialism was by far the most powerful force for social justice in his day, and he also believed this to be the Christian mandate. Although he called himself a Christian socialist, it is important to understand in what sense he meant this. He was a mild, revisionist, evolutionary, and nondoctrinaire socialist. He never seemed tempted to run for public office in order to implement the changes he advocated. He was a prophet and not a politician. As a Christian, he obviously could accept neither Marx's materialistic philosophy nor his atheism. Yet he did accept much of his socialist view of justice.

The problem with doctrinaire socialism, as he saw it, was that it repudiated the very motivation—Christianity—that could bring about the just society of which it spoke. He agreed with the goal, but it was only possible to realize the goal if people were transformed by the power of God in Jesus Christ to become the kind of people who are capable of loving one another. So religion was not only not the "opiate of the people," it was the impetus and motivation for justice.

Although religion was to be a major force in achieving justice, it was not the sole social power. The state was important in this process as well. Rauschenbusch believed that the church should call and fully expect the state to implement the kingdom of God. This was the state's God-given task and responsibility. There were not two kingdoms, as he saw it, but one—God's. If the state could rule by a different set of policies than God's, then how could the kingdom ever be brought about? Yet the state is not necessarily run by people who are Christians. Hence it falls to the Christians to inform the state on the nature of the kingdom of God.

Actually, Rauschenbusch does not say much about the state in the abstract; he prefers to talk about the responsibilities of particular governments. He does not seem to have a "theory" of church-state relations. One might say that he comes closest to a kind of Calvinist theocracy, in that his view is not dualistic and he does not embrace a separatist, Christian pacifist position.[50] As he sees it, the individual Christian stands before a

---

[48] Rauschenbusch, *Christianity and the Social Crisis*, 369 (emphasis in original).

[49] Although Rauschenbusch does not make reference to the great sociologist Ferdinand Tönnies, similar distinctions to his *Gemeinschaft* and *Gesellschaft* seem to be at work in his thinking. See chap. 10 above.

[50] For his insightful comments about how to read Romans 13, see Rauschenbusch, *Righteousness of the Kingdom*, 246ff.

particular government as follows:

> This is the attitude of the Christian toward government: devoted assistance when government seeks the right; submission to troublesome burdens when they fall on him and do not compel a participation in wrong; passive resistance and public protest against compulsory participation in wrong-doing; and establishment of a genuine state when the previous one becomes a fraud, a class pretending to be a state. The judgment in every case lies with the individual conscience which, however, is bound before God to have sought all light and wisdom obtainable, and to act in concert with others wherever possible before he sets itself against public action.[51]

In many ways, Rauschenbusch did not care what form of government was in power; he cared what it did and did not do to promote the Christian order. After all, every government's role is to establish justice. During the time of his writing, he saw unbridled capitalism and industrialism as the adversaries of justice. And he saw practical socialism as helpful in pointing this out. Yet at bottom he was an evangelist with a social gospel.

The Role of Women

One of the problems with government is what he calls paternalism, or "grandmotherly legislation."[52] It has a tendency to offer help to needy people in the wrong way, such that the people needing help cannot learn to help themselves. "Socialism is not paternalism."[53] It offers help to its people in ways that people, through the help offered, learn to help themselves. This is because it respects both the special needs of the people as well as their special gifts. He singles out women as special examples:

> [T]he state must interfere on behalf of women. Experience has shown that women rarely organize in trade, and singly they are helpless. Moreover, their case differs from that of men in that they do not merely represent working capacity, but are the mothers of the race. When England declared it unfit that women work in mines, the usual objections were made both by mine owners and by the women; now everybody has acquiesced. But neither is it fit that young girls be kept standing all day in retail stores and enter marriage physically broken. Nor is it fit that nursing mothers work in factories while their babies are fed on artificial food at home, to die early or grow up puny.[54]

Some twenty years later, when he maps out the contours of his "Christianized social order," Rauschenbusch expresses his concern for women in our society in yet another way:

> Our first concern is for the weak. "Women and children first!". . . . Women . . . demand special protection because life springs from their bodies. They alone can exercise the sacred function of maternity, which is higher than the production of goods. Their capacity to bear and rear sound children is the most important physical asset of the race. Pregnant women should not be allowed to toil under the incessant strain of shopwork. Nursing the child with her own milk is part of a mother's duty to God, who made her breast the only fountain of pure and fit food for the babe. To take the sucking child from its mother's breast and harness her to a machine seems an indecency. For all women the hours of steady labor must be limited; night work and hazardous employment must be eliminated; we must see that these measures designed for their protection do not push the women of the poor farther into starvation. What the hours of labor in the cooperative commonwealth may come to be, we do not know. For the present an eight-hour day and a rest of forty consecutive hours at the week-end are the ideal of organized labor.[55]

Some might see these comments as themselves paternalistic, and in light of recent feminist developments they may well be. I quote them here at length to show how passionate and specific Rauschenbusch was about the implementation of what he called the "cooperative commonwealth." His passion was relentless in insisting that governments enact specific legislation in an effort to Christianize the social order.

---

[51] Rauschenbusch, *Righteousness of the Kingdom*, 249–50.
[52] From a speech presented in 1898 at the Baptist Congress. Quoted in Robert T. Handy, *The Social Gospel in America 1870–1920: Gladden, Ely, Rauschenbusch* (New York: Oxford University Press, 1966), 290.
[53] Handy, *Social Gospel*, 291.
[54] Handy, *Social Gospel*, 297.
[55] Handy, *Social Gospel*, 413–14.

Human and Divine Agency

The ethic of the Social Gospel centers on the task of making the world Christian. We have already said much about how Rauschenbusch envisioned the interaction between those committed to the vision of the Social Gospel and the powers that either deliberately or inadvertently perpetuate an unjust status quo. The clarion call to all Christians is to change unjust structures. But we have not heard much from him on a philosophy of social change. What are the means that Christians can use to bring about such change? Although he clearly desires the Social Gospel to be governed by the "social principles of Jesus,"[56] when it comes to asking whether Jesus is also a model of *how* we can move from an unjust to a just society, his answer is vague. To ask it sharply, with respect to the task of Christianizing the social order: what is God's role, what is the role of individual Christians, and what is the role of the church?

For Rauschenbusch, the world becoming Christian is already partly on the way. The social order, as he saw it in the United States and in the Western world at the turn of the century, is not unchristian, but "semi-Christian." We need to go further by doing more of the same thing, namely, more justice building. Yet we should not think that the Christianizing effort will be easy. It will take real social power to effect the changes required, because there is natural resistance to such change. So the question of acceptable means is very important.

Rauschenbusch emphasizes the power necessary to bring about social change as follows:

> The Lutheran and Calvinistic Reformation succeeded because they enlisted classes which were sufficiently strong politically and economically to defend the cause of Reformed Religion. It was only when concrete material interests entered into a working alliance with Truth that enough force

was rallied to break down the frowning walls of error. On the other hand, the classes within which Anabaptism gained lodgement lacked that concrete power, and so the Anabaptist movement, which promised for a short time to be the real Reformation of Germany . . . died a useless and despised death. In the French Revolution the ideal of democracy won a great victory, not simply because the ideal was so fair, but because it represented the concrete interest of the strong, wealthy, and intelligent business class, and that class was able to wrest political control from the king, the aristocracy, and the clergy.[57]

This is an instructive paragraph and it speaks directly to the matter of agency. For Rauschenbusch the only power that changes society is the social power that we see at work on a daily basis. Hence, if a Christian or the church becomes involved in bringing about change for justice, it is necessary to become adept at utilizing this form of power. Here is why pacifism is such a delicate matter for him. We may hear him opposing war on the one hand while saying very little about nonviolence as a means for bringing about justice. It seems that Rauschenbusch believed that once we have reached the new kingdom there will be no conflict, and hence no need to invoke violence for anything. All will live in love. But on how we get there, the path is not entirely clear.

Pacifism has to be a problem for Rauschenbusch because it places limits on the use of power; it is after all a denial of a violent use of power to bring about goals that cannot be attained peacefully. And in that case it is an affirmation that, although we can see no way to bring about justice nonviolently, this does not imply a capitulation to either the injustice or the use of violence. Why not? Because pacifists do not see themselves as the only agents of change in history. In fact, they do not even see themselves as being in charge; God is. This is an affirmation that we do not hear Rauschenbusch writing about.

---

[56] See Walter Rauschenbusch, *The Social Principles of Jesus* (New York: Association Press, 1916).

[57] Rauschenbusch, *Christianity and the Social Crisis*, 402.

For Rauschenbusch, Jesus was the founder of the purest religion possible; he was himself the purest religious spirit. Yet it was *what he pointed to*—the kingdom of God—that was normative for us. To say this differently, in Jesus we have seen what the goals of the kingdom of God are and have always been—peace, justice, eradication of poverty, equality, and so on—and now we must devote ourselves to the task of bringing these about. The goal has been made clear, and the task of accomplishing the goal is now ours. And regarding the means of bringing it about, Rauschenbusch seems to suggest that Jesus may not be our best model; after all, Jesus was himself not successful in realizing the kingdom of God.

CONCLUDING COMMENTS

Rauschenbusch makes a tremendous contribution toward the social interpretation of the gospel. No one before him had seen with such precision the social aspects of the New Testament. Hence, his social ethic is profoundly radical. At the same time, it may well be far less radical than it appears at first glance. Let me explain briefly.

I take his ethics to be radical at the point where he insists that salvation and ethics cannot be broken apart. Salvation is social, that is, communal, and hence, it is impossible for Christians to avoid issues of poverty, illness, lack of freedom, and so on. This is a most significant correction to mainline Christian thought.

Yet at another level, Christianity becomes associated with most of the values of modern culture, except perhaps the individual-based ones. And much of this hinges on his understanding of power and how social change is brought about. For Rauschenbusch, change happens from the top down, not the bottom up. One would have thought that with a strong focus on Jesus he would not have been able to say it this way. With Jesus the very reverse seems to be true. And if change comes from the top down, then peace and justice can only be brought about via imposition, that is, with the use of superior power. But is this not the basic belief of every responsible politician and other public officer in our countries—Christian or not? In this sense, his ethics is not that radical at all.

Moreover, it may well turn out that Rauschenbusch's view of a Christian economic order looks a lot like a revised version of what was already in place in his country. The kingdom of God aligned itself somewhat effortlessly with American-style democracy. Moreover, while one lauds the tremendous optimism that Rauschenbusch showed in the human spirit, and his beautiful passages on how to translate love into social justice structures, the reader is left with significant questions regarding the power of human frailty and sin. This is not to take away from his contribution to Christian ethics, only to point to areas where the task of comprehension is not complete.

Chapter Nineteen

JAMES SHAVER WOODSWORTH
(1874–1942)

Woodsworth is best remembered for his many contributions as a Canadian politician. He was a Member of Parliament in Ottawa for twenty-one years and was the founding president of a socialist political party called the Co-operative Commonwealth Federation (CCF).[1] In his early life, he was a Methodist Church minister, strongly influenced by the Social Gospel Movement, which had already gained significant momentum in the United States but was relatively unknown in Canada. It was his conviction that the gospel of Jesus Christ had concrete, social relevance and that it should therefore find expression in the world of politics. After all, politics is all about how a society is structured.[2]

The Social Gospel Movement came to Canada somewhat later than it did to the United States. Consequently, at the beginning of World War I, in 1914, this movement was just beginning to have influence in Canada. With Woodsworth, we have an example of how the gospel can have concrete implications for the official politics of a nation. In this respect, the Social Gospel Movement took on a different form in Canada than it did in the United States.

A major preoccupation of the Social Gospelers in Canada was the First World War.

They felt that the war was thrust upon them and that they were placed into structures with no choice of their own; structures that made it difficult to live by their Christian convictions. So they felt they had three options to choose from: opt out of society entirely and become a separatist church; develop an alternate vision—one based on justice and world peace; or adopt the popular view of the status quo churches and abandon as politically irrelevant much of the teaching of the gospel. Most could not find it within themselves to make the Social Gospel compatible with war; it was simply in contradiction with the gospel of Jesus Christ. And virtually all believed that a separatist church would be an abrogation of responsibilities. This led them into a direct conflict and debate with the dominant position held by both the mainline political parties and the churches. Pacifism was a defining issue during the early years of the CCF party, and for Woodsworth it was an issue all his life.

The Social Gospel Movement split in 1914 over the debate on which of the three options to choose. On the one hand, there were those who could not resist the strong momentum from the Protestant churches in Canada to pick up the World War I cause as a kind of crusade. After all, the totalitarian

---

[1] The Co-operative Commonwealth Federation (CCF) party was founded in 1932 in Calgary, Alberta. It was a coalition of western farmers, trade unions, and a few academics. Woodsworth became its first president in 1933. Its distinctive platform was universal health-care, old-age pensions, welfare insurance, family allowances, unemployment insurance, and other social welfare programs. In 1961 the CCF party became the New Democratic Party (NDP).

[2] This chapter is based in part on a lecture given by Professor Adolf Ens in my religious ethics class at Canadian Mennonite Bible College in Winnipeg, Manitoba in the autumn of 1987.

powers in Europe were engaged in autocratic and "evil" actions, and thereby threatening democracy and the rights of ordinary people. These things ought to be stopped. This group saw it as their Christian duty to participate in the great "crusade." They believed the defeat of the "enemies of democracy" could help prepare the world for the next stage in the building of the kingdom of God. J. S. Woodsworth is a clear exception to this strategy. He never once doubted his strong pacifist convictions. Wars are always immoral and ought to be denounced as evil. There was always a peaceful alternative no matter how grave the perceived injustice. This conviction brought with it much controversy at the beginning of his career, and it would be the conviction that ended his career in controversy.

EARLY PERSONAL YEARS

Woodsworth was born on a farm in Ontario in 1874 into a middle-class family. The house belonged to Peter and Esther Shaver, whose daughter Esther married James Woodsworth, the son of Richard and Mary Woodsworth. This brought together two people from quite different backgrounds; the Shavers, who changed the spelling of their name from Schaeffer to Shaver, were of German-Dutch background, and the Woodsworths were of British lineage. The Shavers had moved to Upper Canada from Pennsylvania in 1765, and here is where the two families met.

When Woodsworth's parents were first married, they lived for several years in the Shaver home in Ontario. His father, James, was from Yorkshire English Methodist stock and a minister of the Methodist church. As a minister, he moved his family from town to town as the church had need of him. He began his ministry in Ontario, but soon the family moved west. In 1882 they moved to Portage la Prairie, Manitoba, and three years later to Brandon, Manitoba.

Woodsworth was eleven years old when they moved to Brandon, where he loved to fish and swim in the Assiniboine River, and skate on frozen ponds in winter. He fell in love with the prairies. Later he says of the Brandon home, "Though built on puritan foundations there was nothing austere in its lines. Its hospitable doors were always open alike to friends and strangers. It radiated a genial warmth throughout the neighborhood."[3]

Parental influence and modeling, especially in leadership and authority, were keenly felt by the children. Woodsworth's father presented an orthodox piety that taught the children to believe that heresies were not uncommon and needed to be combated for the well-being of the church. Moreover, the Methodist Church in Canada had many middle- and upper-class members, and so renewal had little to do with changes in the social status quo but instead focused on inward disposition to stoke the fires of a new form of Puritanism. The social reading of the gospel that was taking place in the United States and offered a critique of wealth and capitalism had not yet taken hold of Methodism in Canada.

Woodsworth felt the call to church ministry at a young age, although not without a struggle. In 1891 he graduated from high school and entered Wesley College (later United College, and today University of Winnipeg). Here, he was encouraged by his professors to become a church minister; certainly, this is what his parents also wanted. Moreover, his interests lay in Christian ethics, and he had a strong desire to make a contribution to society. But from the start he struggled with what he saw as the "piety requirement." Methodist revivalism required its ministers to show evidence of a personal conversion experience accompanied by the requisite emotional expression. He was not easily given to such displays and notes in his diary during this time, "It appears to me that in my life I am looking within and striving to make my experience conform to those of men who are eminent for their high

---

[3] Quoted from Kenneth McNaught, *A Prophet in Politics: A Biography of J. S. Woodsworth* (Toronto: University of Toronto, 1971), 5.

Christian life rather than just allowing God to work out His own will in me in His own way."[4] Piety was partly the issue for him because he felt that it was disproportionately emphasized by the church at the neglect of issues like poverty and wealth, educational opportunities, and the social well-being of the disadvantaged, especially as he witnessed it in the inner city slums. These needs never made it to the sermon in church.

Yet this critical stance could not keep him away from a career in church ministry. He refused to reject the church for being less than perfectly faithful; instead he committed himself to the task of making it better. In 1898, he set out to study theology at Victoria College in Toronto, Ontario. Here he encountered scholars who enthusiastically embraced the latest tools of biblical criticism. He also ran across the work of Washington Gladden, a popular theologian of the American Social Gospel Movement. At the same time, he was a student of more than just the university; he studied with equal scrutiny the slums of Toronto. After his divinity studies in Toronto and on the counsel of his professors, he spent a year at Oxford, England, where he continued to "study" theology and philosophy, with a particular focus on Christian ethics. Yet while he got permission to attend the lectures of some professors at Oxford, he was emphatic that he was not there primarily to study; that, he said, he could do at home.[5] His particular preoccupation was an investigation into the social conditions of what was for him a new world, and he was especially interested in the slums of English cities.

He was both fascinated and frustrated by the modern world and its academy. He was not satisfied with the way the university was cut up into unrelated segments of knowledge. Case in point was the discipline of ethics. He noticed that theology never got to the study of ethics and ethics never to theology. So Christian ethics was in a kind of limbo.

He opined, "if Christianity is as universal as it claims to be it must combine in itself all morality—must allow for its highest development and be an essential factor in that development."[6] Theology, he believed, was so well poised to do exactly this important task of integration but instead wasted its energies on doctrine.

In 1900 Woodsworth returned to Canada and received his divinity degree from Victoria College. After returning home to Brandon, Manitoba, he was ordained in the Methodist church and served as minister in a number of congregations. Yet he continued to struggle with his theological convictions. On the one hand, he could not understand nor accept the doctrines of the Trinity or the two natures of Christ; on the other hand, he could not accept the church's divide between saving the individual and ignoring his or her social condition. While he was certain that "Jesus has given us a revelation of God which bears upon it the impress of truth and is witnessed to by our spiritual needs and experience,"[7] he simply suspended judgment on many traditional creedal affirmations of the church. He knew that this was a problem for his role as minister, and he even admitted to being "dreadfully heretical on many [theological] points."[8] So in 1902 there began a pattern that was to become all too common—he seemed always to be in the process of resigning from ministry. He had two main problems with being a church minister: one had to do with church doctrine and the other with preaching. One might wonder what is left, but he contended that the most important part of church ministry was the interaction with the people in order to help them be faithful Christian members of the congregation. He saw this as his primary role in a self-styled concept of ministry.

I speak of Woodsworth "being in the process of resigning from ministry" because he was rarely successful; ironically the church

[4] Quoted in McNaught, *Prophet in Politics*, 7.
[5] McNaught, *Prophet in Politics*, 10.
[6] McNaught, *Prophet in Politics*, 15.
[7] McNaught, *Prophet in Politics*, 20.
[8] McNaught, *Prophet in Politics*, 22.

would not let him resign. At one such attempt, they refused his resignation and instead made him a member of the placement committee. Now he was responsible for hiring ministers, and hence he was not able to resign. The next attempt had different specifics but the same end result. He handed in his theological reasons for disagreeing with church doctrine; the committee studied them and said they found them to be acceptable reasons and then refused to accept his resignation. So he remained a minister for a long time. In the 1902 effort to resign, he was offered a position as assistant pastor at the Grace Church in Winnipeg before he was able to offer his resignation, and he threw himself into this work with all his energies.

In 1904, when he was thirty years old, he married Lucy Lilian Staples from Ontario. He had met her at Victoria College when both were students there. Lucy was an educated woman with an undergraduate degree from Victoria and an honors degree from the Ontario Normal School.[9] Theirs was a happy marriage filled with love and mutual support. They had six children who would complicate the dynamics of Woodsworth's many moves.

Right after the wedding, the couple returned to Winnipeg, which was fast developing the reputation as the Chicago of western Canada. Here, Woodsworth picked up his duties as minister at Grace Church. This worked well for a while but soon proved to be quite difficult. His wealthy parishioners were becoming upset at his "radical" sermons that emphasized the corrupting powers of wealth. One finds comments like the following in his sermons: "The Kingdom of God is the kingdom of self-control—a kingdom of self-denial—and these are not virtues that are easily developed in a wealthy home."[10] This angered his well-to-do listeners. He was told by some who heard him that he was ruining his career and that he should stick to preaching the gospel and refrain

from pontificating on "ill-digested sociology."[11] He did not listen. He spoke of the "sins of indifference" that he saw in the wealthy, of the link between capitalism and war, and of the biblical call for Christian socialism.

In the summer of 1906, in part exhausted from the loneliness of his prophetic stance, he took a leave of absence from church ministry and together with his parents they sailed to England. This was a much-needed break and proved to be the occasion for him to clear his thinking theologically. He wrote that he was having more and more difficulty believing in any of the "supernatural" events spoken of in the Bible. He realized how problematic this was for his leadership work in the church. Again, he felt compelled to resign. However, while on his trip abroad, he received an invitation to take up a church in Revelstoke, British Columbia, that had become divided by conflict. He decided to accept the invitation and planned to hand in his resignation letter at the next conference. But for the meantime, he relocated to yet another church, this time in British Columbia.

CHURCH AND NEIGHBOR

Woodsworth's ministry at Revelstoke did not last long, and eventually he moved on from church ministry. In 1907 he became the superintendent of the All People's Mission in Winnipeg's North End. This was the place where immigrants were streaming into Canada from all parts of Europe, mostly from Eastern Europe. Here he worked with people of refuge whom Wilfred Laurier, then Prime Minister of Canada, had invited to Canada. The government of Canada had discovered that the "normal" immigrants who were coming into Canada were not useful for settling in the Prairies (that is, Alberta, Saskatchewan, and Manitoba). English immigrants just could not seem to make a go of it, so they looked for hardened East European immigrants from places like Poland and the

---

[9] A Normal School was a college where teachers were trained to teach, so named because the governments wanted to "normalize" teaching methods.

[10] McNaught, *Prophet in Politics*, 25.

[11] McNaught, *Prophet in Politics*, 24.

Ukraine. They were, according to church affiliation, Roman Catholic and Greek or Ukrainian Orthodox. That is, most of them were not Protestant and had not even heard of Methodists. These "strange" people made up the bulk of Woodsworth's congregation in Winnipeg's North End.

Woodsworth became more than an amateur student of sociology. He published books with titles like *Strangers within Our Gates*[12] and *My Neighbor*.[13] Both were attempts to understand society from the standpoint of being Christian, and both called Christians to "be Christian" in their relations with other people. The first book was explicitly focused on attempting to introduce the European immigrants so that they did not become second-class citizens.

In *My Neighbor* he challenged people to become involved in creating concrete, social structures and forces which would overcome the evils of ignorance and greed, two powers that did not foster community. He was overwhelmed by the negative effects of industrialization on community and neighborliness, especially on the city. In this study, he writes extensively about urbanization and urban planning. He was not romantic about the city, but he believed that cities could be built well or not so well. Cities don't just happen, they are created; the question is whether they are structured justly and peacefully or not. He struggled with what it meant to be neighbor in the "system" called city. He said:

> The whole system must be reckoned with . . . We must learn to be neighborly not only in the wilderness, or in the comparatively simple life of a country community, but in the crowded city with its many and complicated interests. How? Well, to discover that is the purpose of our present study.[14]

Woodsworth spent considerable time discussing the "Modern City" and the making of a just city. He analyzed the design and structure of older cities like Montreal and proposed careful thought on such matters as street layout, transportation, including rapid transit, planning of parks and playgrounds, water supplies, and so on, all with two objectives in mind: beauty and neighborliness. He fervently believed that Canadians in his time had "the grandest chance given to man—the youth of a new nation, with the inheritance and experience of an older one. If only our eyes can be opened in time and we have the good sense to learn from the experience of others."[15]

For Woodsworth, the church was presented with an important, twofold moral challenge: first it had the vision for beauty and community, and therefore needed to find ways to translate that into concrete, social terms; and second, it needed to address actual social injustices, which were always already present in the city. He said:

> Special attention should be drawn to the necessity of mission work in our cities. Here we have all sorts of conditions of men—the most needy isolated from those who might help them. The church must work out some new organization, and adopt special methods to accomplish this work. It would seem that institutional work is most effective. The effort must be not merely to preach to the people, but to educate them and to improve the entire social condition.[16]

Both books emphasize the theological truth he learned from his reading of Social Gospel literature, namely, that humans are communal beings and that our move toward individualism is going to destroy us. We must not let this happen. We understand ourselves best when we understand ourselves interdependently; as "neighbors." And for our cities to survive they must be built with community in mind.

Woodsworth believed that the government did very little to help the immigrants make a go of it in this new society. Language handicaps, not knowing the laws of the land,

---

[12] J. S. Woodsworth, *Strangers within Our Gates or Coming Canadians* (Toronto: University of Toronto Press, 1909).

[13] J. S. Woodsworth, *My Neighbor: A Study of City Conditions; A Plea for Social Service* (Toronto: Missionary Society of the Methodist Church, 1911).

[14] Woodsworth, *My Neighbor*, 21.

[15] Woodsworth, *My Neighbor*, 71.

[16] Woodsworth, *Strangers within Our Gates*, 256.

financial problems, and so on, made life very difficult for them. Since so many problems existed for the immigrants, they faced a virtual slum existence. One group that showed interest and concern for these people was the emerging labor movement. In the summer of 1909, Woodsworth began a regular column in the Winnipeg labor paper called *The Voice*. His intent was to attempt to write a weekday (as opposed to Sunday) sermon. This allowed him to make direct application of Christian convictions to social reality without invoking church doctrine and structures. And he took the opportunity to be critical of the church for not paying enough attention to the unjust conditions of the city. He warned that if the church did not take its responsibilities seriously, the government would need to intervene. But he also warned that in the process the church would become irrelevant and be replaced. These were the beginnings of his move to the initiatives and activities of the Labour Party.

During the course of his studies of society and his involvement with the labor movement, Woodsworth moved from what he called a negative religion. This was so in two senses: negative religion was filled with many "thou shalt nots," and he found himself constantly being critical of the church, that is, focusing on what the church was doing wrong or not doing at all. But now he sought to move to a positive religion, which was governed by the slogan "live and help live." One of his favorite sayings was, "While there is a lower class, I am in it, while there is a criminal element, I am of it, while there is a soul in jail, I am not free." This summarized his empathy for the marginalized people in society, and it summed up his view of ministry.

On one occasion, when he contrasted his work with a particularly narrow view of evangelism which emphasized the saving of souls, he wrote:

At least in this world, souls are always incorporated in bodies, and to save a man, you must save his body, soul and spirit. To really save one man, you must transform the community in which he lives.[17]

In 1913 Woodsworth resigned from All People's Church. This time his resignation was accepted because he was appointed secretary of a new national body called the Canadian Welfare League. This gave him national exposure, and he lectured across Canada, promoting his social concern for marginalized people. The interesting thing is that in the process of trying to understand the plight of the people, especially new immigrants, he developed a vision of Canada that would include all kinds of ethnic and national groups. Woodsworth was probably the first to have a truly multicultural view of Canada. This got him into some interesting situations. Once when he went as national secretary to Quebec to promote his vision of Canada, the editor of the most influential newspaper of Quebec, *Le Devoir*, Henri Bourassa (who eventually caused the defeat of Wilfred Laurier, and is the grandfather of a recent premier of Quebec) said Woodsworth was the first English-speaking Canadian who understood Quebec's vision of Canada. For Woodsworth, Quebec fit into Canada precisely because it was different from the rest of Canada, not because it was the same.

In 1916, two years into World War I, the Canadian Welfare League folded because no funds were available for this kind of work. However, the work the League had done was considered so important that the three Prairie Provinces—Manitoba, Saskatchewan, and Alberta—created a Bureau of Social Research. It was created to be the vehicle through which Woodsworth's work with the immigrants could continue. They asked Woodsworth to be its secretary, but after his first annual report, Woodsworth was fired, and the Bureau was closed.

The reason for Woodsworth's dismissal had to do with the war. At the end of 1916, director R. B. Bennet from the National Service Registration Board, the organization

---

[17] Grace MacInnis, *J. S. Woodsworth: A Man to Remember* (Toronto: Macmillan, 1953), 91.

responsible for war recruitment, wrote to Woodsworth that he should use his influence and organization to help in making the National Service Registration scheme a success. Woodsworth replied as follows:

> As I am opposed to that scheme, it would seem my duty as a citizen to state that opposition and the grounds on which it is based . . . (1) The citizens of Canada have been given no opportunity of expressing themselves with regard to the far-reaching principle involved in this matter. (2) Since "life is more than meat and body more than raiment," conscription of material possessions should in all justice precede an attempt to force men to risk their lives and the welfare of their families. (3) It is not at all clear who is to decide whether or not a man's present work is of national importance. It is stated that brewery workers in England are exempt. What guarantee have we that Canadian decisions will be any more sound, and who are the members of the board that determines the question of such importance to the individual? (4) How is registration or subsequent conscription, physical or moral, to be enforced? Is intimidation to be used? Is blacklisting to be employed? What other methods? Is this measure to be equally enforced across the country? For example, in Quebec, or among the Mennonites in the West? This registration is no mere census. It seems to look in the direction of a measure of conscription. As some of us cannot conscientiously engage in military service, we are bound to resist what—if war continues—will inevitably lead to forced service.[18]

This type of response was considered close to treason, and Woodsworth was fired from his job. The Bureau was closed on January 31, 1917. Following this event, Woodsworth had to make his living in whatever way he could, and he had severe difficulties finding decent work.

One of the obvious considerations for him was to go back to church ministry. But his difficulty with this option was that the churches too were being used as recruiting bases for soldiers. Ever since his studies in England, during which time the British were engaged in the Boer War in South Africa, Woodsworth had thought of war as "stupid." Now

he discovered that the Protestant churches were being used as recruitment grounds to enlist soldiers for the war and was outraged. He considered it to be a damnable perversion of the teachings of Jesus and speaks about a specific incident he witnessed in a letter to his wife Lucy.

> In the evening I went to St. James Methodist Church to a recruiting meeting. Really Lucy, if I weren't on principle opposed to spectacular methods, I would have gotten up and denounced the whole performance as a perversion—a damnable perversion, if you like—of the teachings of Jesus, and a profanation of the day and the house set apart for Divine Worship. War exhortations from the Hebrew prophets—it was significant that there was no New Testament lesson—war authors and hymns with war phrases, sung as war hymns. The national airs of the allied nations rendered by the organ. In the pulpit Sir [Thomas] Tait, the head of the Citizens' Recruiting Committee, Sir Wm. Peterson, president of the University, General Meighen, and Rev. Williams—a bad combination: business, the university, the army and the church! . . . A deliberate attempt was made through the recital of the abominable acts of the Germans, to stir up the spirit of hatred and retaliation. The climax was reached when the pastor in an impassioned appeal stated that if any young man could go and did not go he was neither a Christian nor a patriot. No! The climax was the announcement that recruiting sergeants were stationed at the doors of the church and that any man of spirit—any lover of his country—any follower of Jesus—should make his decision then and there! I felt like doing something desperate—forswearing church attendance—repudiating any connection with the Church.[19]

So he could not find the strength, nor lose enough personal integrity, to work for the church. He decided instead to move his family to the West Coast to a place called Gibson's Landing. There he worked at the shipyards. Woodsworth was a slim man, weighing only 135 pounds, but he managed to "throw his weight around" and become deeply involved in labor issues there.

In 1919, when the war was finally over, he was recruited once more by the national

---

[18] Published in the *Manitoba Free Press* on December 28, 1916. Reprinted here from MacInnis, *J. S. Woodsworth*, 97–98.
[19] MacInnis, *J. S. Woodsworth*, 104–5.

labor movement, this time as its publicist. That same year he went back to Winnipeg at the very time that a general strike was beginning to take place.

The strike began with a small, metal-workers union in the north end of the city, Woodsworth's old parish. And the other unions decided to act in solidarity with this union, which the company was trying to squelch. The labor situation was aggravated by the return of the soldiers from Europe, which created massive unemployment. Individual unions had virtually no power at the time, so all the unions agreed to strike together. For a few days, they managed to bring the city of Winnipeg to a complete standstill. Nothing functioned. The only paper that was printed was the strike bulletin, in which Woodsworth wrote frequently.

From the beginning of the strike, Woodsworth believed that the strikers were fighting for a just cause. Wages and the right for collective bargaining were the two main issues. He responded to the cry of the general public that they were asked to suffer as innocent victims as follows:

> "Why should innocent non-combatants suffer?" The general public has not been innocent. It has been guilty of the greatest sin—the sin of indifference. Thousands have suffered through the years under the industrial system. The general public have not realized. It did not touch them. They blame the strikers. Why not blame the employers whose arrogant determination has provoked the strike? Why not, rather, quit the unprofitable business of trying to place blame and attempt to discover and remove causes that have produced the strike and will produce, if not removed, further and more disastrous strikes?[20]

Woodsworth was an outspoken critic of both management and government for the way the strike was handled. The strikers were accused of attempting to overturn the government by force and establish a Soviet government. Woodsworth wondered why people could not simply believe that the strikers were after justice? This he said was the biggest hoax ever to be put over any people. Moreover, he was deeply frustrated by his own impotence. He said:

> When I came first, I thought that possibly I might do something to bring about a settlement, but that was impossible. I'm not saying that the strikers did nothing wrong. A strike is a serious weapon. But I do say that the strikers kept their heads far better than the business men.[21]

On June 23, 1919, Woodsworth was arrested on charges of seditious libel and put in a Winnipeg jail. Six specific charges were brought against him based on writings in newspapers about the strike, especially in the *Western Labor News.* Of the charges, it turned out that four were based on articles written by someone else; one article which was the basis of another charge was never published because the printing press was confiscated before the issue went to print. This left only two articles which resulted in the charges against him. One of these was a letter that asked for conciliation rather than conflict between the two parties, which could hardly be considered seditious libel. So the most serious charge, it turned out, resulted from a quotation from two passages of Scripture from the prophet Isaiah which Woodsworth printed without comment. They were:

> Woe unto them that decree unrighteous decrees, and that write grievousness which they have prescribed; to turn aside the needy from judgment, and take away the right from the poor of my people, that widows may be their prey and that they may rob the fatherless. (Isa 10:1-2)

> And they shall build houses and inhabit them; and they shall plant vineyards and eat the fruit of them. They shall not build and another inhabit; they shall not plant and another eat; for as the days of a tree are the days of my people, and mine elect shall long enjoy the work of their hands. (Isa 65:21-22)[22]

On June 29, the strike lost steam and was called off. Funds were running low, leaders had all been arrested, and families of

---

[20] MacInnis, *J. S. Woodsworth,* 134.
[21] MacInnis, *J. S. Woodsworth,* 135.
[22] Quoted from MacInnis, *J. S. Woodsworth,* 146–47.

workers were running out of food. Woods-worth was in jail for five days, after which he was released on bail. One of his colleagues, Fred Dixon, did go to trial. When Dixon was acquitted, the judge wrote Woodsworth a letter saying that the charges against him were stayed, which meant that they could be picked up at any later time. They never were, but neither was Woodsworth ever acquitted of the charges against him.

POLITICAL CAREER

In the 1921 federal election, Woodsworth ran in North Winnipeg, as an Independent Labour Party of Manitoba candidate. On December 6, 1921, he was elected to the House of Commons with a large majority. That night he said:

> Now my case has been tried by a larger jury and the verdict is one that I may well feel proud of. In fact, when the Meighen Government arrested me, it nominated me for Ottawa.[23]

There were two members from the Independent Labour Party elected in 1921, and from the Prairies there were about sixty-five members of a new party called Progressives. These Progressives were largely farmer candidates, and so the hope was that the two parties would be able to work together in Ottawa. But this was not to be. The farmers were committed capitalists, and Woodsworth was not.

Woodsworth had some idea about how Parliament worked but was unprepared for all the rules and protocol. It did not take him long to learn and use the system, however. Whenever a new session of Parliament begins, there is first the reading of the speech from the throne outlining the legislative proposals for the session. Then the throne speech is debated, and it is the only agenda on the table during the first several days, often for up to ten days.

Woodsworth waited until the first round of debate had passed and on the following day this brand-new Member of Parliament (MP) introduced two bills: one of them to amend the immigration act and the other to amend the criminal code. Both were attempts to right legislation which had been passed in 1919 in relation to the Winnipeg General Strike. At that time, Ottawa in just twenty minutes had passed an amendment to the immigration act that made it legal to deport without trial any noncitizen. People who had lived in Canada for eighteen years were suddenly, without warning, simply asked to leave as a result of that act. Woodsworth's second bill sought to amend the criminal code so it would no longer be possible to hold people under "emergency powers," as had been done during the Winnipeg General Strike.

Of course, a private member's bill does not stand much chance of passing, and Woodsworth's were not successful. Nevertheless, they were significant because Woodsworth had established himself as a no-nonsense politician. It showed the kinds of concerns he brought to Ottawa and the immediacy with which he would seek to act. He went to Ottawa to make Canada a more just society.

The place where he made his breakthrough in understanding how to work with Parliament related to an ore-miners strike in Cape Breton, Nova Scotia. In the aftermath of World War I, with a lot of labor available, companies had things going their own way. The British Empire Steel Corporation, attempted to take advantage of the situation by proposing a new contract to its union that would reduce wages by 37.5 percent from the previous contract. Of course, the union protested, and the negotiations went on for a while. Finally, a conciliation board was called in and a settlement was negotiated to reduce wages by 32.5 percent.

This reduction of income was a terrible hardship for the workers. Ottawa did nothing and simply allowed it to happen. So Woodsworth raised the matter in Parliament, asking how the government could allow such injustice to occur.

---

[23] MacInnis, *J. S. Woodsworth*, 149.

Woodsworth's actions were seen as an outrage by many MPs. What business did this new member from Winnipeg have in meddling in the affairs of eastern Canada? The member for Cape Breton was also upset. He said he had brought the matter to the attention of the authorities in Ottawa and been told that labor legislation was under provincial jurisdiction and so Ottawa had nothing to do with it. He felt he had done his duty.

Woodsworth's initiative resulted in a full-fledged debate on the Cape Breton strike in the House of Commons. Prime Minister Mackenzie King rose to say that the government did not interfere in provincial labor matters. Woodsworth had his reply ready. He asked, "What about 1919 in Winnipeg?" The press picked up this issue, and suddenly justice in Cape Breton was debated in Ottawa, which was heralded as a marvelous occurrence by the people of Cape Breton.

Woodsworth discovered from this event that if one played the "game" right, one could bring national attention to local problems and the plight of neglected groups in society. Within two days, Prime Minister King said Canadian officials had changed their minds and were sending a delegation to study the situation, which at least assured national attention for the issue.

In the same session, Woodsworth proposed a bill to repeal the military service act that allowed the government to conscript people for military service. His attempt was predictably unsuccessful, but every year when spending estimates for the military were presented, he would protest by raising the same proposal, seeking to reduce the power of the government to force people into the military.

In 1924 he proposed a bill to repatriate the Canadian Constitution from Britain. He argued that, as long as the Canadian constitution could be amended only by the Parliament in London, so long would Canada be an extension of British authority and therefore, part of British foreign policy.

Woodsworth wanted to know why Canada should be so tied to Britain, with all the risks this implies—particularly the risk to be drawn into its imperialistic wars? He continued this campaign to repatriate the constitution relentlessly until 1940 when Prime Minister King appointed the Rowell-Sirois Commission, which studied all the problems of federal-provincial relations. Their report brought ample evidence that Woodsworth was justified in his concerns and that constitutional changes were long overdue. Yet nothing happened.[24]

In 1929 Woodsworth supported a motion initiated by a member from Quebec to introduce family allowances. Woodsworth supported this bill because he argued that every child born in the country should have assurance of basic needs. Food, clothing, and health-care were basic human rights, and the government should have legislation to protect these rights. This bill was not passed at that time, but persistent work paid off until it was eventually passed in 1945.

In the 1920s, Woodsworth also began to argue for a national health plan, and such a plan eventually was passed during the Lester Pearson government in 1966. It too started with a dream that had its origin in Woodsworth's thinking about social justice grounded in gospel dreaming. The same thing can be said about the unemployment insurance bill. Even before the Great Depression in the 1930s, Woodsworth spoke about the urgent need for unemployment insurance legislation.

It was characteristic of Woodsworth to present his vision for just structures in Canada in the form of new legislation proposals. Of course he wanted them to succeed, but he never let long odds against the success of his ideas stop him from making the proposals. He presented them because they were the right thing to do. Hence, with many of these social programs that were implemented years after Woodsworth proposed them, it is

---

[24] The Canadian Constitution was repatriated many years later in 1982 by the Liberal government under the leadership of Prime Minister Pierre Elliott Trudeau.

difficult to say exactly how much influence he actually had. But this did not matter to him either. In many cases, his repeated presentations of the ideas made them sound both familiar and possible, and, more important perhaps, allowed them to develop a life of their own. In this way he was a "prophet in politics." Even so, he was generally on good terms with Mackenzie King, prime minister for most of Woodsworth's time in Ottawa.

In the 1925 election, a minority government was elected. Liberals and Conservatives had an equal number of seats along with a few Progressives and Independent Labour members who had also been elected. With a minority government, a third party has considerable power. Immediately after the election, the two Labour members, Woodsworth and Abe A. Heaps, approached both Mackenzie King and the leader of the Conservative party to ask what they would do with respect to unemployment insurance and an old-age pension.

Woodsworth and Heaps arranged to have dinner with Prime Minister King and told him that if he did not promise to introduce these two pieces of legislation, they would vote against the government. Immediately afterward, Woodsworth and Heaps drafted a letter to the Prime Minister for the record, which read:

Dear Mr. King:

As representatives of Labour in the House of Commons, may we ask whether it is in your intention to introduce at this session (a) provision for the Unemployed; (b) Old Age Pensions. We are venturing to send a similar inquiry to the leader of the Opposition.

Yours sincerely,

J. S. Woodsworth
A. A. Heaps[25]

King responded in a much longer letter in which he said:

With respect to amendments (a) the Immigration Act, (b) the Naturalization Act, and (c) the

Criminal Code, which were referred to at the time of our interview, I would say that having since taken up the proposed amendments with the Ministers concerned, I feel I am in a position to assure you that legislation on these matters will also be introduced in the course of the present session.[26]

The very next day, Woodsworth read the letter he received from the Prime Minister in the House of Commons for the record. Yet he never told anyone about the meeting with King. He did not see this as a game of one-upmanship; he just wanted it done.

In that session, the pension bill was presented; it was passed in the House but defeated in the Senate. The reason the Senate defeated it was because they felt that the pension would destroy the responsibility of families. They feared that if the bill became law, parents and grandparents would no longer be cared for by their children; and if this happened it could threaten the basic moral structure of society.

The next election in 1927 was fought on constitutional grounds, as the people were quite unhappy with the power of the Senate. In the end, Mackenzie King was re-elected; he then re-introduced the pension bill, which was passed by the Senate this time, although many still spoke against it.

Woodsworth was a pragmatist in Parliament. He might have argued that, since it seemed King was forever in power, he could have gotten more accomplished if he had joined the Liberals and sat where the real power was—in cabinet. He was invited to do just that by King several times, but he always turned it down. To one such invitation he said:

As a matter of fact I am firmly convinced that I can make greater progress as an Independent Labour member than I could as a member of the Liberal Cabinet. That was my position some years ago when there was a Liberal Cabinet and I had an opportunity of being a member of it.[27]

Woodsworth believed that he held power not as a member holding a powerful office

---

[25] MacInnis, *J. S. Woodsworth*, 188.
[26] MacInnis, *J. S. Woodsworth*, 189.

[27] MacInnis, *J. S. Woodsworth*, 185.

but as a Social Gospel, prophetic voice speaking truth to the powerful. He was elected continuously from 1921 until he died in 1942. When he died, his seat in Winnipeg North Centre was won by Stanley Knowles, who was defeated only once, and that was in the Progressive Conservative landslide led by John Diefenbaker in 1958. This seat was a stronghold for the CCF and later for the New Democratic Party (NDP) for many years, even after Woodsworth's death.[28]

WAR AND PACIFISM

Woodsworth gave many speeches on violence and war, always denouncing them as evil. His daughter says it this way:

> J. S. Woodsworth's hatred of war was a burning, passionate thing that flamed more fiercely every day he lived. War was a foul monster that killed and maimed human beings, that stripped them of humanity and left them as brutes. Not only did it destroy people and all that they had created, not only did it blot out their hard-won liberties, but it distorted the very ideas of right and justice upon which mankind was painfully trying to build a rational world. War was the hell that killed hope for the future. War was the ultimate evil.[29]

Perhaps one of the most succinct and famous of Woodsworth's antiwar speeches was given in the House of Commons in the 1935 session. Here he says:

> First I believe that military force is stupid; that it settles nothing and that it creates serious trouble. This conviction may be the result of Christian idealism, but it is confirmed by a study of psychology and a reading of history.
>
> Second, I believe that among the many causes of war the economic are the most fundamental, especially in modern times. Capitalism, social injustice, imperialistic expansion and war are inseparable. In my judgment war will not end until we destroy capitalism, with its social injustice and imperialism.
>
> Third, as a born individualist and an inheritor of pioneer traditions, I have an instinctive desire to keep myself and my country out of the troubles of other people. In this I think I am a fairly typical Canadian.
>
> Fourth, as a student of our complex industrial and social structure I realize that no individual can live to himself, or that no nation can live to itself. Self-sufficiency, independence, sovereignty and isolationism belong to the past. . . . I would emphasize that the mere declaration of neutrality is not enough. As I tried to point out the other evening, military defence does not seem to me to be an adequate defence. However, I do not think that mere disarmament will settle our problems.
>
> Fifth, in practice, political power with its military force is still largely in the hands of the predatory classes; hence national and international policies are dominated by anything but idealistic motives.
>
> Sixth, as an individual I refuse to participate or to assist in war, yet I am a citizen of a country which still relies upon force and as a public representative I must vote on alternative military policies.[30]

It is important to narrate Woodsworth's understanding of pacifism and opposition to war carefully. Pacifism, as he saw it, had everything to do with justice. He was not totally opposed to the use of force—in fact, he could be quite forceful in his own way—but he was opposed to war which legitimated the killing of enemies. He especially abhorred the alliance between capitalism and unjustified profiteering from the production of arms and the use of cheap labor to do so. War and capitalism were, in his view, natural allies. "He found it morally disgusting that anyone could recommend the principle of competition within a society and then reason that since this was a 'natural' principle, warfare between nations was also 'natural.'"[31] Such logic was spurious because it was wrong on both counts.

Woodsworth was not an "idealist pacifist" in the sense that he believed it to be practically unattainable. He used Jesus' teaching in the Sermon on the Mount to underwrite his pacifist convictions because he believed

---

[28] In 1958 the Diefenbaker Conservative Party took the seat for four years, but then it was retaken by the NDP. The NDP lost the riding again in the 1988 election, this time to the Liberal Party. In 1997 it went back to the NDP.

[29] MacInnis, *J. S. Woodsworth*, 99.

[30] MacInnis, *J. S. Woodsworth*, 230–31.

[31] McNaught, *Prophet in Politics*, 298.

that the teachings of Jesus were a basis for bringing about the greatest utility to human society.[32] He believed that violent resolutions of social problems were never permanent solutions because the repercussions of violence always fester. McNaught exposes the logic of this point with respect to the First World War. "Did the First World War assist social progress or did it merely create the causes of its successor; would not a second large war only create the causes of a third; and would not the steady advance of militarist preoccupation undermine completely the principles of brotherhood and cooperation which socialists should hold preeminent?[33]

It is not that Woodsworth was unwilling to take risks, but he believed that the far greater risk was of violent responses to conflict. For who knows where the hatred unleashed from violence may go next? His was the risk of peace, which meant that he placed his faith in what he called "moral force"—minimizing coercion, practicing justice, and extending forgiveness. Indeed, he saw this as the far lesser risk! Hence, the debate between him and the Prime Minister of Canada, Mackenzie King, was a real debate. While both saw war as evil,[34] nevertheless, Woodsworth was prepared to take the consequences of a peaceful, negotiated resolution to international conflicts, whereas King was not. Indeed, Woodsworth wanted Canada to remain neutral in all wars, no matter what the threats were. In fact, he proposed a motion to his party to that effect.[35] And in 1936 at a convention of the CCF party, this motion was debated and accepted. He was successful in making his party pacifist.

But this victory was not to last long. In 1937 Woodsworth introduced a motion in the House stating "that Canada would remain neutral in any war no matter who were the belligerents."[36] His motive here was his

particular concern that Canada would simply support the British government if it decided to go to war. Since there was no security agreement between Britain and Canada, he thought it wise to preempt the temptation to such agreement with this motion.

This motion unleashed a fierce debate in the House, in which Woodsworth, among other things, was called a communist. In the process, it became apparent that King's government was not forthcoming in what later proved to be its tacit alliance with Britain. This led to a heated exchange with the Minister of National Defence, Ian Mackenzie, where Woodsworth said, "Has Canada no opinion of her own? We ought to know that. Otherwise it is the case, as in the last war, of 'ready, aye, ready'. . . . Has the Liberal government taken that stand? If it has not I would like the Liberal government to say so."[37]

On September 3, 1939, the Second World War began; and Britain was now in the war. A special session of Canadian parliament was called. On September 6, the CCF National Council was called together to discuss its strategy in the upcoming debate. While delegates from British Columbia and Manitoba had already indicated their position for Canada's nonparticipation in the war, Saskatchewan delegates saw it differently. Hence, it quickly became clear that there would be a split on the question of whether the CCF party would continue to be a unified, pacifist party.

The September CCF council meeting was intense and fractious, and it was finally decided a subcommittee would be appointed that would draft a statement seeking to incorporate the opinions of the majority of its members. Woodsworth tried in vain to argue "that the mere discussion of any measure that could put Canada into the war"[38] would be a violation of previous CCF convention

---

[32] McNaught suggests that Woodsworth saw little tension between the teachings of Jesus and J. S. Mill's view on utilitarianism, *Prophet in Politics*, 299.

[33] McNaught, *Prophet in Politics*, 300.

[34] McNaught, *Prophet in Politics*, 301.

[35] McNaught, *Prophet in Politics*, 302.

[36] McNaught, *Prophet in Politics*, 302.

[37] McNaught, *Prophet in Politics*, 303.

[38] McNaught, *Prophet in Politics*, 305.

resolutions. When his motion to this effect was rejected, he saw the writing on the wall.

On September 7, the council debated the statement of compromise the subcommittee had provided, and when it came to a vote the position of neutrality was rejected. It was not as though Woodsworth did not have followers, but they were in the minority. After the result was announced, Woodsworth stood to address the group. Everyone knew what was coming. He tendered his resignation both from the office of president as well as from membership in the party.[39] Such a complete disassociation was hard for anyone in the party to accept. Although Woodsworth could not be convinced to stay on, the decision was made that he would present a minority position in the House against the case for Canada's participation in the war. The official party position would be presented by M. J. Coldwell.[40]

When Parliament met on September 7, it was made clear that Canada would join Britain and France in the war. Prime Minister King announced to the House that M. J. Coldwell had informed him "that when cooperation was necessary in so great a cause . . . the members of his party [would be] ready to do their part."[41] At that point everyone knew that Woodsworth had been deposed.

The Prime Minister was the first to speak, and he repeatedly referred to Woodsworth as a great moral-religious leader. But his major emphasis was that war was the great exception that men of moral ideals must sometimes make in the real world. When the time came for Woodsworth to make his minority speech, he did not mince words. He reminded his people that truth was always the first casualty in times of war, for then language becomes crudely political. He referred especially to the Prime Minister's reference to religion and morality, and said:

Well, I left the ministry of the church during the last war because of my ideals on war. Today I do not belong to any church organization. I am afraid that my creed is pretty vague. But even in this assembly I venture to say that I still believe in some of the principles underlying the teachings of Jesus, and the other great world teachers throughout the centuries. . . . War is an absolute negation of anything Christian. The Prime Minister, as a great many do, trotted out the "mad dog" idea; said that in the last analysis there must be a resort to force. It requires a great deal of courage to trust to moral force. . . . It requires a great deal of courage to carry out our convictions; to have peace requires both courage and sacrifice. . . .[42]

The conclusion was even more personal:

I said I wanted to state my conviction. Now you can hammer me as much as you like. I must thank the House for the great courtesy it has shown me. I rejoice that it is possible to say these things in a Canadian Parliament under British institution. It would not be possible in Germany, I recognize that . . . and I want to maintain the very essence of our British institutions of real liberty. I believe that the only way to do it is by an appeal to the moral forces that are still resident in our people, and not by another resort to brute force.[43]

When the vote was taken in the House and the speaker declared as carried the motion to move forward to war, Woodsworth rose and said, "There are some of us opposed to the main motion."[44] The speaker replied for the record, "Only one member rose."[45]

CONCLUSION

Woodsworth was a man of conscience. He was passionately committed to a truth that was in control of him, and he could not mess with it. He had the moral faith that it was possible to make Canada a pacifist nation, and as such it would be a great witness to all the world to the teachings of Jesus. But he felt alone. The church had abandoned him; his political party had left him; and leaders in the country were not about to support him either.

---

[39] McNaught, *Prophet in Politics*, 306.
[40] McNaught, *Prophet in Politics*, 307.
[41] McNaught, *Prophet in Politics*, 309.
[42] McNaught, *Prophet in Politics*, 311.

[43] McNaught, *Prophet in Politics*, 311–12.
[44] McNaught, *Prophet in Politics*, 312.
[45] McNaught, *Prophet in Politics*, 312.

This presented some major issues for him. One was how to deal with the issue of being a pacifist and representing a non-pacifist constituency. Another was living in a world that sees war as necessary. He was not afraid of compromise, but one has to know what to compromise on and what not to; for there are some matters of conscience one cannot compromise on and some that one can. He says:

> I find myself somewhat in a dilemma. . . . Under these conditions in the actual world of affairs, one must try to hold to his own convictions and keep ultimate objectives in view, and yet advocate measures which are recognized as merely ameliorative. One must accept half a loaf, or even support procedures which, though repugnant to one's principles, represent a real advance in public welfare and public morals.[46]

Woodsworth did not like the word "pacifism" much; it was too passive for the position he advocated. Peace was never a state of being for him, but a struggle.

While Woodsworth was deeply disappointed in the failure to convince his fellow MPs of his views on the absurdity of using military force to solve international conflicts, he was stoic about the acceptance of the many other "outrageous" ideas he presented to Parliament. It was his deepest conviction that the teachings of Jesus were meant as ways to govern societies, if indeed peace and justice were desired as goals. For that is the fundamental truth of the gospel.

---

[46] McNaught, *Prophet in Politics*, 229.

Chapter Twenty

REINHOLD NIEBUHR
(1892–1971)

Reinhold Niebuhr was no doubt the most influential ethicist in North America in the twentieth century. He is known for his criticism of a particular form of theological liberalism and for his development of an approach to Christian ethics called Christian Realism. Niebuhr believed that Social Gospel ethics of the type presented by Rauschenbusch and Woodsworth was too "idealistic," especially with respect to their views of human nature and historical progress. In an editorial in 1941, responding to liberalism's failure to deal with Hitler's invasion of Europe, he said:

> How blindly these apostles of love seek to make a success story out of the Cross. And what foolishness they make of the Cross. Only their foolishness is not the foolishness of God which is wiser than the wisdom of men. It is just foolishness. They think they can rob human life and history of its tragic note by just a little moral admonition.[1]

Religious conservatism, on the other hand, assumed a view of human nature that was too depraved and consequently made ethics impossible. In this view, humans could do nothing good. Christian Realism was an attempt to base an ethic on a view of human nature and the possibilities of change within a society without overstating human potentiality and without understating the power of sin and evil.

NIEBUHR'S EARLY LIFE

Gustav Niebuhr, Reinhold's father, came to the United States from Germany in 1881 when he was seventeen years old. He left Germany in part to escape military service. Two years later, he had a conversion experience in a Sunday morning church service, and not long after that he began the trek into church ministry. He was part of the Salem Evangelical Church in Freeport, Illinois, which was a German-speaking, ecumenically minded congregation. After studying at Eden Theological Seminary near St. Louis for two years, Gustav was ordained to the ministry in 1885 and sent to California to do missionary work shortly after. Here he married seventeen-year-old Lydia Hosto. In 1891, with two children in tow—Hulda and Walter—and Lydia pregnant with Reinhold, the family moved to Wright City, Missouri.

Reinhold Niebuhr was born in Wright City in 1892 when Walter Rauschenbusch was just beginning his theological writing. At the time, Niebuhr's father was a German-speaking, Lutheran pastor who readily mixed his Lutheran theology with Reformed theology. In other words, narrow denominationalism was not a family emphasis.

Niebuhr was strongly influenced by his father and says he was the first formative influence in his life. When Niebuhr was ten, he told his father that he had decided to become a church minister just like him

---

[1] From an editorial in *Christianity and Crisis* 22 (December 1941): 2.

because "you are the most interesting man in town."[2] And, of course, he kept his word.

Learning from his father meant something quite specific for Niebuhr. Gustav was a liberal after the style of Friedrich Schleiermacher, Ernst Troeltsch, and Adolf von Harnack, but he was also fervently evangelical. In a review of Harnack's *What Is Christianity?* in 1902, Gustav simultaneously praised Harnack for his work and offered these critical words:

> Like Schleiermacher in his time, [Harnack] feels impelled by the prevailing philosophy to declare as impossible a certain class of miracle, thereby limiting the omnipotence of God instead of defending the thoroughly Christian true-to-the-Gospel proposition that God the law-giver stands above all law, including the laws of nature.[3]

It is precisely this combination of the liberal commitment to integrate theology with culture and the fervor of the Christian faith that shaped the younger Niebuhr's style of theological ethics. The German proverb applies: "*Der Apfel fällt nicht weit vom Stamm*" ("The apple never falls far from the tree").[4] Reinhold realized this and accepted it gladly, and at age thirteen was confirmed by his father in the St. John's Evangelical Church and began his own journey into Christian ministry.

In 1907, at age fourteen, Niebuhr left the regular high school and entered Elmhurst College, which was specifically designed to prepare boys for Eden Theological Seminary, that is, boys who showed promise for Christian ministry. Three years later, he enrolled in the seminary, the same school his father had graduated from twenty-five years earlier. Upon graduation in 1913, Niebuhr was accepted into Yale Divinity School, which was unusual because, as Niebuhr himself put it, Yale had heretofore not accepted students from "second-rate denominational colleges."[5] Niebuhr would not fall short of the high academic standards at Yale.

In April of the same year, before he left for graduate studies in New Haven, Connecticut, his father died very suddenly of a diabetic attack. It was an utter shock to everyone. At the funeral the theme focused on the succession of leadership from Moses to Joshua. At one point the pastor looked to the front pew where the Niebuhr family was seated and said: "It gives me joy to know that the work our brother can no longer carry on will be continued by two of his sons."[6] The obvious reference was to Reinhold and his younger brother Richard. The torch was passed!

Needless to say, Gustav's death was especially traumatic for young Reinhold because he lost not only a father but also his closest theological mentor. But, as was the plan, in the fall of 1913 Niebuhr went off to Yale Divinity School to study theology.

At Yale he drank deeply from the fountain of liberal theology. His biographer, Bob Patterson says:

> He accepted the historical-critical method of biblical studies, rejected some traditional theological claims on the basis of their incredibility to the critical mind, assumed a religious optimism, championed individualism, accepted evolutionary categories, emphasized ethics, stressed the humanity of Jesus, and recognized the importance of toleration.[7]

From Yale he received a Bachelor of Divinity degree—equivalent to a master's degree in our time—but then discontinued his formal education and became a church pastor. He never received a Ph.D. although he was awarded eighteen honorary doctorates.[8] At Yale, as the liberals taught, he learned to be an integrationist. Long before it was academically fashionable for an institution of higher learning to insist on bringing together theory and practice, the resolve to develop a fully practicable faith seemed almost instinctively to push in on him. This meant that Christian

---

[2] Quoted in Bob E. Patterson, *Reinhold Niebuhr* (Waco, Tex.: Word, 1977), 20.
[3] Quoted from Richard Wightman Fox, *Reinhold Niebuhr: A Biography* (San Francisco: Harper & Row, 1985), 7.
[4] This is the phrase biographer Richard Fox uses to introduce young Niebuhr to his readers. See *A Biography*, 12.
[5] Fox, *A Biography*, 18.
[6] Fox, *A Biography*, 19.
[7] Patterson, *Reinhold Niebuhr*, 21.
[8] Patterson, *Reinhold Niebuhr*, 21.

theology had to be understood from the standpoint of ethics. This also meant that theology should not be viewed dogmatically, as Barth was suggesting, nor creedally, nor based on metaphysics. As Troeltsch and others had taught, theology and culture were thoroughly interwoven. After all, it was culture that let theology say what it had to say at a particular time. These liberal emphases never really left Niebuhr, even when he became critical of some of them.

It is interesting that his studies, and especially his passion for integration, led him to the conviction not to continue his studies. He put it this way: "my boredom with epistemology prompted me to forswear graduate studies and the academic career towards which it pointed."[9] So in 1915, he was ordained pastor of the Bethel Evangelical Church in Detroit, where he stayed until 1928, when he joined the faculty at Union Seminary in New York.

Detroit was a growing city with about 1.3 million people when Niebuhr arrived there. Henry Ford was "running the town" at the time with his car factories. Although Niebuhr's father may have been the most interesting man in another town, Ford was certainly the most powerful person in Detroit. Niebuhr ran headlong into conflict with Ford's policies of assembly-line work, poor working conditions for laborers, poor pay, and so on. Niebuhr said about his relationship to Ford, "I cut my eyeteeth fighting Ford."[10] Almost everything Ford did, Niebuhr despised.

As Niebuhr saw it, Ford represented the worst of the capitalistic system. And Niebuhr had learned enough from Rauschenbusch to know that capitalism and Christianity were not easily brought together. He intensely disliked the built-in protection that capitalism provided for the rich and the inevitable exploitation of the poor. So he put himself squarely against the injustices rampant in the "automobile city," and did so as an avowed socialist.

Niebuhr saw firsthand the human price of the capitalistic economic order. The part of town where he lived was rapidly industrializing. As a pastor, he had daily encounters with people caught in economic injustice and racial strife. It is here that Niebuhr embraced the slogan "courage to change," which was meant to challenge all Americans to take up the cause to transform unjust social structures. He saw this as a special task of church leaders and spokespersons; yet, in the process, , he discovered how difficult it really was to change society. Societal structures have a strong inertia, making it difficult to replace them with new ones. During this effort to change society, he said he "underwent a fairly complete conversion of thought which involved rejection of almost all the liberal theological ideals with which I ventured forth in 1915."[11]

It is important to understand this "conversion of thought." As we have seen, Niebuhr began his life as an ardent liberal but gradually became more and more aware of the limitations of liberalism. He was a supporter of Rauschenbusch's Social Gospel Movement because he saw in it a Christian base for social reform. Yet he began to see Rauschenbusch was wrong in trying to convince America to live by the Sermon on the Mount. Such a goal was naïve and patently stupid and symbolized much of what was wrong with liberalism generally. It is not possible to expect that the United States could live by the ethic of Jesus. Why not? Because it is neither practical nor realistic. In fact, to try to do so is in contradiction with itself. To have everyone live by the ethic of Jesus would require force, but the ethic of Jesus forbids the use of force. In general, this approach assumes an account of human nature and human will that is simply false. It takes power and force to make people do good things, and Jesus taught nonresistance. Rauschenbusch's view does not take seriously enough the social reality of sin. The power of sin will always

[9] Patterson, *Reinhold Niebuhr*, 21.
[10] Patterson, *Reinhold Niebuhr*, 24.
[11] Patterson, *Reinhold Niebuhr*, 25.

destroy our best intentions and thwart our best plans. So we cannot move forward with any sense of justice if we seek to do so only on the basis of love, peace, and goodwill. To find the courage to change with justice in mind will require that we find the courage to use force.

These were the years of the First World War, 1914–1918. In 1916 Niebuhr wrote an article in the magazine *Atlantic*, which was called "The Nation's Crime Against the Individual." Here he reflected on why soldiers so unselfishly give their full allegiance in time of battle. He suggested that it was because "loyalty and courage are made ultimate virtues for which men are honored."[12] While this may be laudable from the standpoint of the soldiers, the tragedy is that there is little regard for the ends which these virtues are to serve. He said: "The crime of the nation against the individual is not that it demands his sacrifice against his will, but that it claims a life of eternal significance for ends that have no eternal value."[13]

A year later, when the United States entered the war and President Woodrow Wilson convinced the American public that "making the world safe for democracy" was indeed a justifiable end, Niebuhr changed his mind.[14] Certainly fighting a war to end all wars was a laudable goal. Gradually, Niebuhr became a reluctant defender of the war, in part because he began to see this war's end as good.

Shortly after the United States became involved in the war, Niebuhr took a job with the church organization called the War Welfare Commission. It was intended as a pastoral service to soldiers, especially those from evangelical churches. He saw this as an important platform, for it would teach social responsibility. He believed thus:

[I]t was a position within the church from which he could exert strong pressure for greater Americanization. . . . Niebuhr became the most significant single soldier in the war to prove the synod's loyalty to America by discrediting its diehard adherents of the German name, the German language, and in a few cases the German cause.[15]

While he saw his role as important, it was nevertheless not without struggle. He bares his soul after visiting a number of war-training camps and says that while he can no longer bring himself to "associate with the pacifists," it was painful for him to realize he was now also "a priest of the great god Mars."[16]

In the early years of his life, Niebuhr was committed to pacifism. He was then an avid defender of the ethics of the Sermon on the Mount, and his powerful preaching bore witness to this. But gradually he began to see that the ethics of Jesus was too demanding for sinful people; this was so even for devout Christians. For example, following Jesus, as outlined in the Sermon on the Mount, would put a businessman out of business in no time and empty banks of money very quickly.[17]

During this time, Niebuhr was deeply moved by a young paperboy attending his catechism class who was orphaned because his father had been killed in an industrial accident.[18] The boy was trying hard to help his mother make ends meet. A laudable action! But there were mean, big boys in the neighborhood who on occasion would threaten to forcibly steal the money from him. The boy told Niebuhr that in such situations he could not just turn the other cheek as Jesus taught in the Sermon. So what was he to do?

Niebuhr reflected on what solution pacifism holds out in this context. And he could not see any! He believed moral responsibility

---

[12] Fox, *A Biography*, 46.

[13] Fox, *A Biography*, 47.

[14] Fox, *A Biography*, 47.

[15] Fox, *A Biography*, 50–51.

[16] Reinhold Niebuhr, *Leaves from the Notebook of a Tamed Cynic* (Louisville, Ky.: Westminster/John Knox, 1990), 19.

[17] See Niebhur, *Leaves*, 96.

[18] The story is referenced, e.g., in William E. Hordern, *A Layman's Guide to Protestant Theology*, rev. ed. (New York: Macmillan, 1968), 161.

required that force be used to overpower the bullies, which was the only way justice could be ensured. Hence, pacifism was no match for injustice.

This story became a symbol for Niebuhr of what was going on in the world. Pacifists assumed that evil was conquerable with love and that the ruling, moral law of history was love. It is not; justice is. Niebuhr argued that the situation of the paperboy was much like the international struggle between nations. It simply does not work to love the enemy and expect that love to bring peace. We must not be naïve in our thinking about enemies. We have a responsibility to respond to our enemies and the enemies of our friends in such a way that our security and theirs is enhanced, not weakened. When one is really honest, one must name pacifists as parasites. Why? Because theirs is a way of keeping themselves clean and alive at the expense of those who have the courage to do what is necessary when justice demands the use of violence.

Hence pacifism, as Niebuhr saw it, was an expression of liberal theology. It assumed that human nature was basically good, that sin was not very powerful, that society was gradually getting better, and so on. All these things were false. And in his preaching, he made sure that his hearers knew that the Sermon on the Mount was not a set of guidelines a society could live by; it was fine for individuals but not meant for society. Followers of the liberal tradition are simply naïve, and Christians deserve to know that the real world demands hard choices in the face of the power of evil.

It is important to remember that while Niebuhr was a sincere critic of pacifism, he was never a happy proponent of military power. He was profoundly aware of the temptations of nations and the abuses of military power. Because pacifism is so easily rejected by nations, Niebur believed, Christian ethics needed an alternative that was well worked out and realistic. Without a more pragmatic alternative, the Christian teaching of the cross and the love of Christ would be rendered entirely irrelevant. He was not about to let this happen.

Niebuhr continued as pastor at Bethel Evangelical Church until 1928. What began as a small congregation with sixty-five members had in thirteen years grown to more than seven hundred, and he was being pushed to move on. Henry Sloane Coffin (1877–1954), a Presbyterian minister and president of Union Theological Seminary in New York, was actively recruiting him. But becoming part of the Union faculty was not without controversy because Niebuhr did not have a Ph.D. However, in September 1928, he was appointed at Union Seminary as Associate Professor of Christian Ethics and Philosophy of Religion.

After just a few years of teaching, Niebuhr decided to run for a seat in the New York State Senate on a general, nondogmatic, Socialist Party of America ticket. The Seminary was not impressed, but since he was by this time a tenured professor and perhaps because Seminary officials were confident that the venture would not amount to much, they turned a blind eye. In any event, Niebuhr received a mere 1,480 votes.[19]

In the academic year 1930–1931, three foreign scholars became part of Union Seminary. Professor John Baillie, a Scottish theologian, came as a new faculty appointment in systematic theology, and two visiting graduate students came for a year of studies: Dietrich Bonhoeffer from Germany and Ursula Keppel-Compton from England. Each would have a unique impact on Niebuhr.

Professor Baillie (1886–1960) became Niebuhr's new theology colleague. Given Niebuhr's dislike of systematic theology, especially the variety that Barth was proposing, Baillie rescued theology from total irrelevance for Niebuhr. The virtue Niebuhr saw in Baillie's theology was that it began with human

---

[19] Fox, *A Biography*, 124. Fox says, "On November 4 [1930] Niebuhr got a miniscule 1,480 votes. The Democrat, Duncan O'Brien, got 20,271, and the Republican, Wilbur Murphy, 10,947."

knowledge and from there derived knowledge of God. This was the reverse of Barth's approach and quite amenable to Niebuhr.

Dietrich Bonhoeffer—then an impetuous, twenty-four-year-old, German, doctoral student—was entirely unimpressed with the intellectual stature of both the Union students and professors like Niebuhr. He said, for example, "The theological education of this group is virtually nil, and the self-assurance which lightly makes mock of any specifically theological question is unwarranted and naïve."[20]

The third visitor, Ursula Keppel-Compton, was an Oxford theological graduate, who would become Niebuhr's wife. She was a devoted Anglican and did not share Bonhoeffer's judgment of Niebuhr. She found him inspiring, shared his hesitation and critical stance toward the church, and "admired his enthusiasm for applying the Gospel to the social sphere."[21]

Before Ursula returned to England in May of 1931, she and Reinhold were engaged to be married. So in December the Niebuhr family traveled to England for the wedding. Niebuhr was thirty-eight years old; she was twenty-three. After the wedding, they returned to New York, where they lived for the rest of their married life. Together they would raise four children, one son and three daughters. An unfortunate consequence of Reinhold's marriage was that his mother, Lydia, could no longer live with him. This created considerable tension, especially between Ursula and Lydia, but so it had to be.

Ursula, who lived until 1997, was herself a theologian and professor. She founded the Religion Department at Barnard College in New York City and was its chairperson for many years.

Niebuhr remained at Union until his retirement in 1960. After this he wrote little scholarly material but remained active giving guest lectures at universities like Harvard and Princeton. He frequently commented on and wrote about current events and was politically active on a wide range of issues, including the Vietnam War (1955–1975) and nuclear disarmament. He had friends and hence influence in high political places. For example, Hubert Humphrey, U.S. vice president (1965–1969) under Lyndon Johnson and a presidential candidate in 1968, was a personal friend of Niebuhr. Yet his friendship did not lead him to blind allegiance, and when Niebuhr disagreed with politicians, they found out about it. For example, in 1966 Humphrey agreed with President Johnson's military escalation in Vietnam. To make matters worse for Niebuhr, Humphrey gave a major tribute to him at the twenty-fifth anniversary dinner for *Christianity and Crisis*. Even in this context, albeit with some embarrassment, Niebuhr let it be known that he disagreed with Humphrey's politics.[22] Two years later, during his presidential election campaign, Humphrey appealed to him for endorsement. Niebuhr wrote to his campaign manager: "despite our long friendship I *could not* endorse a candidate who is bound to the present futile policy in Vietnam."[23] Notice the appeal to realism in his rebuff.

It was Niebuhr's pragmatism that made him so appealing in Washington. There was always a Christian solution to every political problem. The Christian life was never just an ideal; it was always a culturally and politically real possibility. What was needed to get there was to think right and find ways to embody the ideal of Christian love in the midst of the vagaries of sinful reality. Niebuhr was never an uncritical enthusiast of American government policies because he knew too well the seductive forces toward moral obscurity that come with power dynamics within nations. But he was firmly committed to the task of sorting out the route toward justice. Perhaps what best sums up Niebuhr's approach to Christian ethics is his famous "serenity prayer" which most of us know as:

God, grant me the serenity to accept the things I

---

[20] Quoted in Fox, *A Biography*, 125.
[21] Fox, *A Biography*, 126.
[22] Fox, *A Biography*, 284.
[23] Fox, *A Biography*, 284 (emphasis in original).

cannot change; courage to change the things I can; and wisdom to know the difference.[24]

Niebuhr lived life to the fullest, at a pace that few could match. Although he suffered a heart attack in 1952, his health was generally good. But there came a time when his body was so ravaged by ill health that he no longer wanted to live, and his life ended peacefully at his home on June 1, 1971. He had been sick with pneumonia for some time and eventually his lungs gave out. Always the pragmatist, even in death, he arranged for his body to be donated to Harvard University for medical research.

THE LIBERAL LEGACY

Niebuhr himself often said that he was not a theologian. Whether we accept this self-designation is a matter for discussion, but there are those who admire him precisely because they believe that he got theology right. And discussion about whether he did or not is in part a throwback to the debate over liberalism in Europe—that is, between the "dogmatics" of Barth and the "historical" theology of Troeltsch. Niebuhr was certainly not a theologian in the style of Barth, but he was in the style of Troeltsch. The Niebuhrian, Gordon Harland, claims Niebuhr for theology when he says: ". . . if profound and continuous reflection on the meaning of the Christ event for man and history is the mark of the theologian then assuredly Niebuhr is a theologian."[25]

It is odd that both Barth and Niebuhr are sometimes called neo-orthodox theologians; all they really have in common is that they are both critical of what they call liberalism. But on what liberalism names, they disagree. For example, Niebuhr says that "the liberal culture of modernity is quite unable to give guidance and direction to a confused generation which faces the disintegration of a social system and the task of building a new

one."[26] But Barth would consider this a bare beginning of the critique necessary of liberalism and would say the task Niebuhr sets for himself is itself at the center of the liberal imagination. Hence, according to Barth's theology, Niebuhr remains firmly within the liberal tradition.

James Gustafson seeks to explain the tension between Barth and Niebuhr in another way. In his analysis of Niebuhr's Christian ethics, Gustafson reads Niebuhr on the basis of the distinction between two realms of discourse: the ethical and the theological. (Barth, of course, would reject this distinction itself.) He asks whether theological concepts are to determine what is written about ethics and whether ethical concepts ought to determine what is written about theology. He argues that, for Barth, theology is dominant over ethics, that is, the doctrine of God comes first and ethics follows. It works the other way around for Immanuel Kant, for example, who finds the need to say something about God because of what ethics demands. Gustafson suggests that theological ethicists must choose one framework over the other. Another way of naming this distinction is to say that for some ethicists the creation metaphor is dominant and for others eschatology or the language of apocalypse is most important. For Niebuhr, ethics determines theology. He is interested primarily in morality and politics and not in systematic theology. Notions like the Trinity, atonement, or eschatology are seldom discussed.

Gustafson develops four base points of ethics as a way to interpret Niebuhr.

1. No Self-conscious Methodology

Niebuhr was not methodologically self-conscious; we look in vain for a carefully defined, ethical methodology, at least one that adheres to a commonly accepted method.

[24] There has been some debate over whether Niebuhr is the author of this prayer or whether it comes from some more ancient sage. Niebuhr was vexed by the suggestion that it was not his, but he was much more upset by its commercial uses and never more so than when Richard Nixon used it to rally his "silent majority" in 1970. He intensely disliked Nixon. See Fox, *A Biography*, 290–91.

[25] Gordon Harland, *The Thought of Reinhold Niebuhr* (New York: Oxford University Press, 1960), 3.

[26] Reinhold Niebuhr, *Reflections on the End of an Era* (New York: Charles Scribner's Sons, 1934), ix.

If anything, he was a pragmatist. His was an ethic, to borrow a Weberian distinction, not of conscience but of culture. Niebuhr was interested in what made society a more just place. He was not fond of the distinction between deontology (law ethics) and teleology (ideal ethics). He did not see a tension between the two; for love is both the ideal and the law. Gustafson says, that for Niebuhr, "Love as agape is not a law applied to cases through secondary principles; for him this procedure would reduce the starkness of the tension, and thus the sense of judgment under which persons, institutions, and history stand."[27] For example, Niebuhr did not make much use of the just-war theory, which is sometimes seen as the principled expression of love in conflict; instead he spoke of justice as "love applied."[28] The tension that most governed Niebuhr's ethical writing was between the transcendent and the historical, that is, between the ideal and the real. The ideal is impossible and the possible is not ideal! We live in this world, not in another.

2. Interpretation of Circumstances

The second base point for Niebuhr, according to Gustafson, is the interpretation of circumstances. The real, unlike the ideal, is not given conceptually but is known empirically. It must be carefully examined and studied. The real is fraught with contingencies, and we learn from the Jesus story, especially the story of the cross, that the good life is not easily attained; it so often rebounds in death and suffering. Gustafson quotes Niebuhr: "Faith illuminates experience and is in turn validated by experience."[29] The revelation we see in Christ is not such that it can help us avoid evil in this world; it is a revelation of the way the world is—not perfect. Sin is a fundamental human given; it is in sin that love is applied.

3. Anthropology

The third base point of Niebuhr's theological ethics is anthropology; that is, what human beings are and what they are capable of. Gustafson says of Niebuhr's An Interpretation of Christian Ethics,[30] that it is "a Social Gospel book with respect to moral normativeness of the teachings of Jesus; its innovation is primarily in the interpretation of human agency."[31] Niebuhr is not preoccupied with the notion of salvation from sin; he is concerned with how it is possible for there to be moral and just political actions in history.

Gustafson points out that Niebuhr was popular with secular admirers precisely because one could take his ethic, which he based on biblical presuppositions, and apply them to history and politics without needing to accept any of those biblical presuppositions. This made Niebuhr's ethics appealing to a large base. But always, as is the hallmark of his approach, there is a warning of the optimism that tends to overextend moral possibilities.

4. Doctrine of God

The fourth base point of Niebuhr's theological ethics is the doctrine of God. Niebuhr is, of course, critical of Barth's excessive emphasis on the transcendence of God. At the same time, he is opposed to a radical immanence because it puts too much emphasis on the goodness of humanity. In fact, it is the space between these extremes that he wishes to claim for responsible, political ethics. His view of God is different from his brother Richard's view, in that the first question for Reinhold is not what is God doing. He believes that the story of God provides us with a transcendent norm, which can guide us and is ultimately the norm for judgment. But how it guides us is the task of human ethical discernment.

[27] James Gustafson, "Theology in the Service of Ethics: An Interpretation of Reinhold Niebuhr's Theological Ethics," in Reinhold Niebuhr and the Issues of Our Time, ed. Richard Harries (Grand Rapids: Eerdmans, 1986), 33.
[28] Gustafson, "Theology in the Service of Ethics," 34.
[29] Gustafson, "Theology in the Service of Ethics," 36.
[30] Reinhold Niebuhr, An Interpretation of Christian Ethics (New York: Harper & Row, 1935).
[31] Niebuhr, Interpretation of Christian Ethics, 39.

Gustafson concludes his essay by saying that "it is experience that validates faith and theology; it is for this reason I claim that in the end, for Niebuhr, theology was in the service of ethics. They are dialectically related, but in my judgment the weight is on ethics."[32] These words are not dissimilar from Bonhoeffer's words about Niebuhr at Union. Theology as theology had no value for Niebuhr. Theology was only valuable if it could help us find just responses to injustice.

NIEBUHR'S WRITINGS

His first book, *Does Civilization Need Religion?*[33] appeared in 1927, a year before he began teaching at Union. It represented his first effort at a sustained evaluation of Protestant liberalism. He argued that the liberal imagination was so much at home in the world that it had lost its capacity to critique modern culture. In fact, Protestant Christianity had become a mere extension of a natural hope, a natural progress, industrialism, technological development, and new social programs. It was impossible for it to offer any significant critique. Hence, he judged liberalism as bankrupt and hopeless.

While this may sound like Karl Barth's assessment of liberalism, Niebuhr resisted the return to orthodoxy. From the standpoint of what he came to call "Christian Realism," both orthodoxy and liberalism were inadequate—orthodoxy because it could not translate faith into practice and liberalism because it could not practice the faith it preached. To say this differently, orthodoxy was unhelpful because it offered a faith that was by definition an exercise of the mind and not a way of life for the modern world; it was a system of thought, a theology but not an ethic. Liberalism, on the other hand, had such a high ideal of culture that it could not practice the ideals that it believed in because it underestimated the power of countervailing forces like sin and evil. Both approaches failed because they

were unable to bring together the simplicity of the Christian teaching of love and justice with the complexity of the present conditions. Modern civilization needed a religion that could be lived. Niebuhr's entire writing career sought to show what such a pragmatic faith should look like.

In the early 1930s, a fascinating public debate ensued between Niebuhr and his younger brother Richard. In September 1931, Japan invaded Manchuria (Northeast China). This meant that Japan broke its own nonaggression pact, and such an openly belligerent act by a nation that was officially committed to peace was the occasion for serious soulsearching by Christian pacifists in America.

In March 1932, Richard Niebuhr, who was teaching ethics at Yale Theological Seminary, and Reinhold, teaching ethics at Union, squared off on the appropriate response to this invasion. Richard, according to Reinhold, represented the liberal, pacifist tradition; Reinhold, according to Richard, represented the liberal, Troeltschean tradition. Each saw the other's views as flawed.

In Richard's March 23 article in *The Christian Century*, "The Grace of Doing Nothing," he argued that in this particular case the right thing to do was nothing. He then raised the question of *how* we should do nothing; there are, after all, many ways of doing nothing—out of frustration, moral indignation, or as the communists might, believing that the revolution is inevitable anyway. Then he went on to say:

> But there is yet another way of doing nothing. It appears to be highly impracticable because it rests on the well-nigh obsolete faith that there is a God—a real God. Those who follow this way share with communism the belief that the fact that men can do nothing constructive is no indication of the fact that nothing constructive is being done.[34]

In other words, God is active in history redeeming the world, and Richard was critical of those with a view of moral agency that

[32] Niebuhr, *Interpretation of Christian Ethics*, 44.
[33] Reinhold Niebuhr, *Does Civilization Need Religion?* (New York: Macmillan, 1927).
[34] H. Richard Niebuhr, "The Grace of Doing Nothing," *The Christian Century* 49 (March 1932): 379.

assumed human beings were the only ones in charge. History's development is not best understood as the evolutionary betterment of society through human efforts alone. God acts to bring history to completion; and Richard believed this changed the stance of our moral agency. Among other things, what it called for was a new, radical Christianity uniting in love all Christians across the nations. He believed such loyalty lessened the lure of nationalism because it transcended national and class divisions. He was not clear on exactly how this could bring about peace and justice, but he spoke of the importance of repentance. He suggested that repentance named the classical way of speaking about doing nothing. Repentance and forgiveness were concrete forms of peacemaking applicable to the Manchurian situation because in effect "China is being crucified (though the term is very inaccurate), by our sins and those of the whole world."[35]

Reinhold was invited to respond to his brother's essay in the March 30 issue of *The Christian Century*, and his article was called "Must We Do Nothing?" He was uncharacteristically gracious but nevertheless made it clear that he disagreed profoundly. The nature of his disagreement is predictable; he interpreted Richard as making the claim that we can act in history from the standpoint of a "pure love ethic." He suggested that if this were required of us we could never act at all. He said, "I do not share his conviction that a pure love ethic can ever be made the basis of a civilization."[36]

Instead of love as the basis of international action, Reinhold advocated justice. Justice has to do with the balance of power and the interests of competing groups. This does not mean that love has no role in the process because without love, justice would degenerate all too quickly into violence. But love must be filtered through the principles of viability and sustainability; otherwise we would all end up crucified, as did Christ.

Reinhold went on to quarrel with Richard's eschatology, about which he said:

> What makes my brother's particular kind of eschatology impossible for me is that he identifies everything that is occurring in history (the drift toward disaster, another world war and possibly a world revolution) with the counsels of God, and then suddenly, by a leap of faith, comes to the conclusion that the same God who uses brutalities and forces, against which man must maintain conscientious scruples, will finally establish an ideal society in which pure love will reign."[37]

For Reinhold, it was precisely because we have no way of knowing whether, or if so, how, God acts in history, that *we* must act, and we must do so to the very highest moral standards possible. Ultimately, God will redeem us *out of history*, but for now we must learn to act within the confines and contingencies of history. According to Reinhold, the tragic side of history is simply inescapable since life's high ideals can never be realized this side of heaven.

The final installment of the debate came on April 6, 1932. In "The Only Way into the Kingdom of God," Richard wrote that he would "fire one more shot in the fraternal war between my brother and me over the question of pacifism."[38] It is important to note here that both saw this as a debate over Christian pacifism. Richard made the point that the fundamental question between the two of them was not activity or inactivity but whether human history is a perennial tragedy.

> For my brother, God is outside the historical processes so much so that he charges me with faith in a miracle working deity which interferes occasionally, sometimes brutally, sometimes redemptively in this history.[39]

For Richard, God is always in history, in the very structure of things, and in all that is. He was not impressed with Reinhold's effort

---

[35] H. R. Niebuhr, "Grace of Doing Nothing," 380.

[36] Reinhold Niebuhr, "Must We Do Nothing?" *The Christian Century* 49 (March 1932): 415.

[37] Niebuhr, "Must We Do Nothing?," 416.

[38] H. Richard Niebuhr, "The Only Way into the Kingdom of God," *The Christian Century* 49 (April 1932): 447.

[39] H. R. Niebuhr, "The Only Way," 447.

to make love realistic at the expense of re-shaping it into something other than itself. Richard believed that where we can find no way to embody the love of Christ we must patiently wait for the salvation of the Lord. God will redeem; life is not tragic. In the final analysis, life is not about "Christian perfectionism" or the "Christian ideal"; it is, according to Richard, about the human, God-given capacity for repentance, forgiveness, patience, and seeing.

In 1988, fifty-seven years after this debate, John Kelly summarized it as follows:

> H. Richard's "inactivity" presumed that God was in history, working out human salvation, and he concluded: "But if there is no God, or if God is up in heaven and not in time itself, it is a very foolish activity." Reinhold Niebuhr respectfully disagreed with his brother. . . . Recognizing that a society of pure love could never be realized in history, and that a gaping chasm would always separate "what is and what ought to be," Reinhold still believed that Christians were called upon to work actively for the cause of justice—"the highest ideal toward which human groups can aspire."[40]

Later in 1932, Reinhold wrote a book he wanted to call "The Ethics of Social Change," but it was published as *Moral Man and Immoral Society*.[41] Of course, this is Troeltschean language, and Niebuhr sought to show what difference it made for Christian ethics to take modern sociology seriously. Later he joked that a better title would have been "Immoral Man and Even More Immoral Society" because ultimately the ideal of Christian love is also impossible for individuals.

In this book, Niebuhr argues that there is a difference between individual and group ethics. As individuals we can be more responsible than we can be as groups. As individuals we can live more fully by the principle of love; as society we cannot. Groups are political, and as political beings they have to deal with power, that is, with competing wills and interests. No collective can escape the problem of power politics. Hence, it follows that in every society or small group one must make compromises in order to keep the peace. Within every group, the element of power makes the practice of ideal love impossible. Hence, each corporate ethic is unique, and no one specific ethic applies to another group.

Some have said that this book was as important for the American world as Barth's *Epistle to the Romans* was for Europeans.[42] It brought to "Christian America" an entirely new language of social justice. Niebuhr was drawing on current sociological and psychological insights to give an account of individuals and groups, and he found Protestant liberalism wanting. From this he concluded that social collectives were so fraught with dynamics of competing self-interests that the only way to achieve any semblance of justice is through a balance of power. As Niebuhr saw it, this was a good thing since it could serve to prevent the self-interests of the powerful from dominating the weak. Liberals of the Social Gospel movement have falsely believed love and justice are the same. They are not. In assuming that whatever moral ideals individuals are held to are also applicable to groups, liberals have made Christian ethics impractical and unintelligible. He argued that the love ethic Jesus taught simply cannot be applied when the "most significant moral characteristic of a nation is its hypocrisy."[43] Where sin is a fundamental given, as it is in any group or society, the love ethic of Jesus is not sufficient. Social Gospel ethics is simply wrong in this.[44]

---

[40] John Kelly, *The Christian Century* 105 (October 1988): 940.

[41] Reinhold Niebuhr, *Moral Man and Immoral Society: A Study in Ethics and Politics* (New York: Charles Scribner's Sons, 1932).

[42] See, e.g., Patterson, *Reinhold Niebuhr*, 32.

[43] Niebuhr, *Moral Man*, xxiii.

[44] It is interesting to note that, despite his claim to the contrary, Niebuhr himself draws deeply on Social Gospel logic that Jesus is ethically relevant only as a teacher of love whose example we should emulate. In the process, although inadvertently, he demonstrates where this logic leads. One wonders what difference it might have made had he seen in Jesus the Redeemer of our social sins.

It is not surprising that the logic of *Moral Man and Immoral Society* led Niebuhr to a complete break with pacifism. In January 1934, he wrote an article titled "Why I Leave the F. O. R."[45] The answer to why he left the Fellowship of Reconciliation—a pacifist organization—was that to live in society as though sin's power is easily vanquished is dangerous and unchristian.[46] He could no longer face the charge of Christian irresponsibility as the pacifists must. Sin should be aggressively eradicated in whichever way we can.

In his 1934 book, *Reflections on the End of an Era*,[47] Niebuhr continues the theme of responsible political morality. He speaks not only of American politics but of international economics as well. He is again critical of capitalist economics, which shows little capacity for justice. He reaffirms the mantra for Christian justice: remain practical politically and conservative theologically. This slogan was to see American society through the hard times of the 1930s.

In the spring of 1934, Niebuhr delivered the Rauschenbusch Memorial Lectures at Colgate-Rochester Divinity School in Rochester, New York. These were later published as *An Interpretation of Christian Ethics*. The topics of these lectures are instructive in that he treats systematically several of the issues he had named in his earlier writings—such as "The Ethic of Jesus," "Sin," "The Relevance of an Impossible Ethical Ideal," "Love and Forgiveness," and so on. Hence, these lectures served to summarize his theory of ethics up to this point in his career.

When speaking about the ethics of Jesus, he showed why it was impossible to embody his love ethic in current times. He says:

> The ethic of Jesus does not deal at all with the immediate moral problem of every human life—the problem of arranging some kind of armistice between various contending factions and forces. It has nothing to say about the relativities of politics and economics, nor of the necessary balances of power which exist and must exist in even the most intimate social relationships. The absolutism and perfectionism of Jesus' love ethic . . . has only a vertical dimension between the loving will of God and the will of man.[48]

Hence, the ethic of Jesus cannot be understood apart from an eschatology of Jesus that makes it irrelevant for us today. He continues:

> The ethical demands made by Jesus are incapable of fulfillment in the present existence of man. They proceed from a transcendent and divine unity of essential reality, and their fulfillment is possible only when God transmutes the present chaos of this world into its final unity.[49]

It is the sin of this world that makes it impossible to rule the world by the standards of the Sermon on the Mount. That rule is not of this world but for a different era.

Sin is a dominant theme in all of Niebuhr's writings. But he never roots his understanding of sin in the mere finitude of humanity. Rather it is the ever-present will to hide our finitude and to pretend to be more than human. For him, sin is therefore at the very root of liberalism—it is the effort to live the life of the ideal when all we are capable of is the life of the real. Sin is the temptation to play God. This tendency, or perhaps better-phrased, this temptation, is far more prevalent in our society than we like to admit. And Christians need to see that the effort to emulate Jesus' life is itself the equivalent of sin. Human beings simply cannot be as Christ was. And that is why pacifism is heresy.

---

[45] "Why I Leave the F. O. R." first appeared in *The Christian Century* 51 (January 1934). It has been reprinted in D. B. Robertson, ed., *Love and Justice: Selections from the Shorter Writings of Reinhold Niebuhr* (New York: Meridian), 254–59.

[46] He argues that those Christians who denounce pacifism are not less Christian but more so. He says, "If anyone would suggest that those of us who have thus renounced the pacifist position ought not any longer to regard ourselves as Christians, I would answer that it is only a Christianity that suffers from modern liberal illusions that has ever believed that the law of love could be made an absolute guide of conduct in social morality and politics." "Why I Leave," 258. For similar reasoning, see also his "Why the Christian Church Is not Pacifist," in *Christianity and Power Politics* (New York: Charles Scribner's Sons, 1940), 1–32.

[47] Reinhold Niebuhr, *Reflections on the End of an Era* (New York: Charles Scribner's Sons, 1934).

[48] Niebuhr, *Interpretation of Christian Ethics*, 23–24.   [49] Niebuhr, *Interpretation of Christian Ethics*, 35.

The Jesus ethic is still relevant, but it can only be so as an ideal that is impossible; that is, one which we are unable to attain fully, despite being able to get closer as individuals than we can as groups. The ideal of Jesus is important precisely because it is *the ideal* for us; *the real* is important because we must be morally responsible in this world. Sin names the failure to make this distinction and endeavoring to live a life made for heaven.

During this stage of Niebuhr's life, he seeks to juggle many demands: writing, teaching, formulating his theology precisely, remaining politically involved as a critic and strategist, and giving speeches everywhere in the United States and abroad.

In 1941 Niebuhr delivered the famous Gifford Lectures in Edinburgh, Scotland. They were subsequently published as *The Nature and Destiny of Man*, a massive study which sought to present a view of what it means to be human that arises out of the biblical theological tradition.

He begins the lectures with the sentence, "Man has always been his own most vexing problem."[50] He raises again the question of how we shall think of ourselves as human beings under God. The answer he gives is that we are sinners who live under the grace of God. We are finite, and God is infinite, and our greatest sin, as he has said before, is that we refuse to admit our "creatureliness."[51] In other words, we know ourselves properly only when we know ourselves under God, which limits us in ways that we want to resist.

These lectures elaborate a view of anthropology that underwrites his Christian Realism. The tendencies in the history of Western thought have been to speak of human nature in terms either of pessimism or optimism. Both are wrong. Humans are suspended between the two; we are not completely free, but we are somewhat free; we are not completely good, but we are not completely depraved either, and so on. "There is, therefore, no historic structure of justice which can either fulfill the law of love or rest content on its inability to do so."[52] Hence, he reaffirms that Christian ethics is paradox—namely, impossible possibility.[53]

The second theme in these lectures is the development of a theology of history, which he names the problem of human destiny. Since we cannot control history, we must act in it only in approximations of its ideal ends. He says, "There is no escape from the paradoxical relation of history to the Kingdom of God. History moves toward the realization of the Kingdom yet the judgment of God is upon every new realization."[54] His view of Christian history is that, although it can never be completed in time, it becomes tragic only because human beings seek to so complete it. That project must inevitably fail.

During this time, Niebuhr helped found and edit *Christianity and Crisis*, a periodical that was published for many years. During World War II, this paper was actively engaged in assessments of President Roosevelt's war efforts, and Niebuhr published several articles in which he discussed the evils as well as necessities of this war. What he said was instructive but by then no longer surprising. His argument was that Hitler was more evil than participation in the war. Some evils were simply greater than others. This is so because there are no perfect solutions, only relative ones. Hence, we must wage war on Hitler, since our failure to do so would represent our lack of concern for justice. If there were a clear nonviolent way that would ensure Hitler could be stopped, then, of course, that would be preferable; but there is no such option.

---

[50] Reinhold Niebuhr, *The Nature and Destiny of Man*, vol. 1, *Human Nature* (New York: Charles Scribner's Sons, 1941), 1.

[51] Niebuhr, *Human Nature*, 16.

[52] Niebuhr, *Human Nature*, 296.

[53] Although Niebuhr is clearly more interested in social ethics than is Kierkegaard, it is interesting how many allusions he makes in these lectures to Kierkegaard's work. The language of "paradox" is certainly reminiscent of Kierkegaard's *Fear and Trembling*.

[54] Reinhold Niebuhr, *The Nature and Destiny of Man*, vol. 2, *Human Destiny* (New York: Charles Scribner's Sons, 1941), 286.

During the next decade, Niebuhr was preoccupied with further refining a viable theology of history, and published several books on this theme.[55] All deal with the problems of how to disentangle the mixture of good and evil, such that we can make sense of history from the standpoint of the Christian faith. In the process, he makes two important points. First, God will eventually do the disentangling of history God's way, not our way. We are called to pursue whatever goodness is available to us. Second, he emphasizes again that evil inevitably results from our wrong use of our good capacities. Even when we have good intentions, evil still results. We are not in control of things as we tend to believe we are. We cannot therefore rely on the goodness of human actions.

He calls this view of history ironic. And he contrasts it with two other possible conceptions of history, namely, the pathetic view, which affirms that the ultimate meaning of history is pain and suffering, and the tragic view, which affirms that evil is necessary in order that good can be brought about. The ironic view of history, although it sounds like the tragic view, is not. It suggests that, while we do good in society, our doing good is always only at most a partial solution to the evil in society. It is never a complete solution. Evil is far too pervasive. Often the very good that we do ends up having the opposite effect. If we do not understand it in this manner, then we think of ourselves as something we are not—namely, overcomers of our own sinful capacity. This is our greatest temptation, and in so doing we re-enact the fall in Genesis.

In 1952 Niebuhr had a heart attack, and although it slowed him down, it did not stop him from writing more books at an exceptional rate.[56] And in each of them the theme was history. He was passionate about an emphasis on the theological language of "original sin" and on the consequences this had for human agency in history. Sin did not make our actions meaningless, but it situated them within history in proper perspective.

SUMMARY AND CONCLUSION

The phrase "Christian Realism" was not unique to Niebuhr. John C. Bennett used it as well.[57] This language was powerful in that it was able to impress people with the promise of the practicability of the Christian faith. It is therefore not surprising that although Niebuhr never held high political office, he was often appealed to by those who did; presidents like Jimmy Carter and Barack Obama have invoked his name in articulating their own political positions. Niebuhr's Christian Realism is seen by many as the way to be both realistic and Christian in politics.

I make three summary comments about Niebuhr's thought.

Importance of Justice

Perhaps the most important concept for Reinhold Neibuhr is justice. I believe one of the best definitions of Niebuhr's view of justice is given by Gordon Harland, who says justice is: "the relative social embodiment of love and as such it is an approximation of love. Justice is love finding a relatively complete expression in the world."[58]

Justice for Niebuhr is always more or less possible; it must take into account the powers that detract or enhance our ability to love. Justice is never unrelated to love, yet it

---

[55] See, e.g., Reinhold Niebuhr, *The Children of Light and The Children of Darkness* (New York: Charles Scribner's Sons, 1944); *Discerning the Signs of the Times* (New York: Charles Scribner's Sons, 1946); *Faith and History: A Comparison of Christian and Modern Views of History* (New York: Charles Scribner's Sons, 1949); and *The Irony of American History* (New York: Charles Scribner's Sons, 1952).

[56] Reinhold Niebuhr published *Christian Realism and Political Problems* (New York: Charles Scribner's Sons, 1953); *The Self and the Dramas of History* (New York: Charles Scribner's Sons, 1955); *The Structure of Nations and Empires: A Study of the Recurring Patterns and Problems of the Political Order in Relation to the Unique Problems of the Nuclear Age* (New York: Charles Scribner's Sons, 1959); *Man's Nature and His Communities: Essays on the Dynamics and Enigmas of Man's Personal and Social Existence* (New York: Charles Scribner's Sons, 1965).

[57] See John C. Bennett, *Christian Realism* (New York: Charles Scribner's Sons, 1941).

is always only a partial embodiment of love. Hence "to choose love is to seek justice, for failure to seek justice is to lose love, *not because justice is a secondary choice but is not a simple historical possibility. Agape transcends its own relative embodiment in justice.*"[59]

In his *The Irony of American History*, Niebuhr recaps as follows:

> Nothing that is worth doing can be done in our lifetime; therefore we must be saved by hope. Nothing which is true or beautiful or good makes complete sense in any immediate context of history; therefore we must be saved by faith. Nothing we do, however virtuous, can be accomplished alone; therefore we are saved by love. No virtuous act is quite as virtuous from the standpoint of our friend or foe as it is from our standpoint. Therefore we must be saved by the final form of love which is forgiveness.[60]

For Niebuhr, it is most important that we understand that this is earth and that we are not in heaven. Justice is seen within this tension. Sin is acting in denial of our finitude. It is a pretense that we are more than finite. Notice how this fits in with his definition of justice. Sin is our attempt to live beyond our capacities and embody love not properly constrained by the structures of our society.

Views on Pacifism

The second point I want to emphasize is that Niebuhr's Christian Realism is worked out in relation to his views on war and pacifism. It is important to note that he had great admiration for nonviolent, direct action. He was taken with Gandhi's work and, long before Martin Luther King Jr., Niebuhr made the following amazing prediction referring to a Gandhi-style campaign: "The emancipation of the Negro race in America probably waits upon the adequate development of this kind of social and political strategy."[61] He could say this because he knew the power of nonviolence. At the same time, he thought there was much confusion around this notion, and Christian Realism was his effort to sort out what is confusion and what is not.

The first confusion had to do with the belief that nonviolent resistance had anything to do with the teachings of Jesus. It did not. Jesus taught total nonresistance. Second, Niebuhr believed that there was confusion about the use of force; some pacifists believe that nonviolent resistance claimed the lack of force, whereas violent resistance was seen as using force. This he held to be false because both used force; hence, he preferred the distinction between violent and "nonviolent coercion."[62] Hence, says Richard Harries, "Niebuhr made two basic distinctions. First, between *non*-resistance and all forms of *resistance* and then between violent and nonviolent coercion."[63] Then he reasoned as follows: the life of nonresistance is simply not humanly possible; the life of nonviolent coercion, while possible, is irrelevant in a very limited number of political cases; that leaves the life of violent coercion that must always be engaged in with justice.

In the book *Christianity and Power Politics*, Niebuhr writes an essay called, "Why the Christian Church is Not Pacifist." In the article, he argues that the Christian churches are not pacifist because the Bible does not advocate pacifism as a way for Christians to live in this world. It advocates it only as a representation of the kingdom of God, which is not the kingdom of America, or any other society. Hence, you cannot advocate pacifism for the kingdom of America. This would not be biblical as pacifism is only for the kingdom of God. Thus, Niebuhr had to disassociate himself from Rauschenbusch's emphasis on christianizing the social order, which represents

---

[58] Harland, *Thought of Reinhold Niebuhr*, 23.
[59] Harland, *Thought of Reinhold Niebuhr*, 48 (emphasis in original).
[60] Reinhold Niebuhr, *The Irony of American History* (New York: Charles Scribner's Sons, 1952), 63.
[61] Richard Harries, "Reinhold Niebuhr's Critique of Pacifism and his Pacifist Critics," in *Reinhold Niebuhr and the Issues of Our Time*, ed. Richard Harries (Grand Rapids: Eerdmans, 1986), 105.
[62] Harries, "Critique of Pacifism," 105.
[63] Harries, "Critique of Pacifism," 106 (emphasis in original).

a naïve confusion between the kingdom of God and a particular state. These can never be the same. Pacifism is itself an unjust way of ordering a society. Pacifism does not help the paperboy. It does not get rid of the bullies.

A central element in his critique of pacifism has to do with the use of force. He says:

> Pacifists assume too easily, it seems to me, that all controversies are due to misunderstandings that might be solved by a greater degree of imagination. When the strong exploit the weak they produce a conflict that is not the result of ignorance but of the brutality of human nature. It may be that the strong can be convinced in time that it is not to their ultimate interest to destroy the weak. But they can hardly gain this conviction if the weak do not offer resistance in some form to oppression. It may be that this resistance may not need to express itself physically at all. It may express itself in the use of "soul force" advocated by Gandhi. But even as thoroughgoing a spiritual idealist as Gandhi has realized that the forgiving love of the oppressed lacks redemptive force if the strong are not made to realize that alternatives to a policy of love are within reach of the oppressed. Oppressed classes, races, and nations, like the industrial worker, the Negroes, India, and China, are therefore under the necessity of doing more than appeal to the imagination and the sense of justice of their oppressors.[64]

It is important to note that Niebuhr's critique of pacifism centers on the question of how sin is redeemed or rendered powerless in society. It is remarkable that he never once appeals to Jesus as a model for how the power of sin is undermined in real, social settings.

In this, as in other ways, Jesus is only Savior and not example. Ultimately, Niebuhr's only way of conceiving of overcoming the power of sin was via the use of force.

Political Realism and the Church

The third theological concept that we must briefly refer to in our concluding comment is the relationship between Niebuhr's view of political realism and the church. But there is not much to say because he says little about the church. This is all the more surprising because Niebuhr clearly held the church in very high regard and was a pastor for many years. Yet he never talks about the church as theologically significant; it plays no role in what makes Christianity "realistic." The arena of God's activity, and hence the arena of our own moral actions, is political-social reality. In fact, it is doubtful that Niebuhr ever saw the church as a moral agent. It seems that on this score he had learned the way of conceiving the matter entirely from Troeltsch.

It is difficult to know where to stop with the presentation of Niebuhr's ideas. Clearly, he has taken American culture by storm in setting the agenda for a contemporary account of Christian ethics. Yet even his brother disagreed with his way of putting the matter. As we move to consider other ethicists, we will surely notice both the strong affirmations and the strong critical responses to his thought.

---

[64] Reinhold Niebuhr, "Pacifism and the Use of Force," in *Love and Justice*, ed. D. B. Robertson (New York: Meridian, 1957), 249–50.

Chapter Twenty-One

HELMUT RICHARD NIEBUHR
(1894–1962)

We have already met the Niebuhr family through the older brother, Reinhold. Helmut Richard was also born in Wright City, Missouri. He was the youngest of four surviving children who were all prominent in their own way; sister Hulda, the oldest child, became an associate professor of religious education at the Presbyterian College of Education (now McCormick Theological Seminary) in Chicago; brother Reinhold was a popular ethicist at Union Theological Seminary in New York; and Walter, the oldest, was a businessman who is sometimes said to have been the financier of the family.

Richard Niebuhr lived in the shadows of his famous brother, Reinhold. Although, as we have already seen, he set himself apart theologically, he knew that he could not match Reinhold's influence and productivity. Yet this neither deterred nor inspired him. In many ways he was destined to follow father and brother into ministry and theological education. His father, Gustav, was a pastor and leader in the German Evangelical Church. Faith and piety were givens in the family; telling Bible stories was a regular practice. Father read the Bible in both Hebrew and Greek, impressing the children and giving them an appreciation for ancient languages at an early age.

When it came to close parental relationships, one senses differences among the children. It is often said that Richard found his father emotionally cold and distant, a stark contrast to Reinhold's account. This may seem strange, but it gets explained with language that portrays an unusually close bond between Gustav and Reinhold and a more distant relationship between father and the other children, especially Richard.

Richard attended the same theological college the Niebuhrs made famous—Elmhurst College in Chicago. This was a school patterned after the German *Gymnasium* and, while it offered a solid education in the classics, virtually nothing was taught in the social and physical sciences.[1] After completing the program at Elmhurst, he enrolled in Eden Theological Seminary in St. Louis, Missouri, where he graduated in 1915. During this time, Niebuhr struggled with why the students at Eden were required to speak German in an English-speaking country. He believed the school ought to focus on teaching the English language to its students. However, their churches still needed German-speaking preachers and, although with some reluctance, Niebuhr too followed the well-trodden route and became pastor of the Walnut Park Evangelical Church in St. Louis a year after completing his program of studies at Eden. He was the pastor there for four years.

During his first year at Walnut Park, the church was involved in a tragic experience when two of its people drowned after falling

---

[1] See Jon Diefenthaler, *H. Richard Niebuhr: A Lifetime of Reflections on the Church and the World* (Macon, Ga.: Mercer University Press, 1986), 5.

through thin ice while on a church retreat. The experience was significant in shaping Niebuhr's theology. It reinforced his theological convictions about the power and pervasiveness of evil. Evil and tragedy are everywhere in this world and ought never to be taken lightly. Evil strikes randomly and viciously; you cannot push evil out of your life into a distant corner. It is part of life itself. Even where God is, there is evil. In this world it is pervasive.

Yet what was said about the pervasiveness of evil also applied to redemption. Redemption too cannot be pushed into a corner. God's love and restorative will are universal and omnipresent. Good and evil must therefore be seen as intermixed, together at the same place and at the same time. There is neither perfect goodness nor perfect evil. Here Niebuhr and his brother were in agreement.

Niebuhr was a scholar and student even when he was a minister of the church. As was typical of many pastors in those days, while he served his church, he also studied theology part-time. Specifically, he enrolled in Washington University in St. Louis, where he became most interested in German poetry and also devoured the subjects of psychology and philosophy. He became especially eager to study the humanities and social sciences, and his interest in further learning took him to New York City in 1919, where he took courses at both Columbia University and Union Theological Seminary.[2] Later in 1919, he accepted a teaching position at Eden Theological Seminary in the area of theology and ethics.

During World War I and the following years, Niebuhr continued to wrestle with what it meant to be German in America. He began to teach his courses at Eden in the English language, and he preached in the churches also in English. In 1917, when the United States entered World War I, Niebuhr joined his brother Reinhold in the War Welfare Commission of the Evangelical Synod.

But he went one step further than his brother and enlisted as army chaplain.[3]

In 1920 Niebuhr married Florence Marie Mittendorff, and together they would have two children, Cynthia and Richard Reinhold, who also became a theologian. For a few years after their marriage, Niebuhr continued to teach at Eden. Then in 1922 he enrolled at Yale Divinity School as a Ph.D. student. Only two years later he completed his doctoral work, having written a dissertation titled "Ernst Troeltsch's Philosophy of Religion."

The work of Troeltsch was enormously significant to Niebuhr. Troeltsch had sought to integrate religion and sociology in a new and unique manner. That is, he saw that what was happening in this world and what we ought to believe as Christians had to be interconnected so our faith would not merely be a theoretical and dogmatic thought-structure. In other words, *how* we live in society, including how we organize ourselves as a church, is an important matter for Christian faithfulness. To simply repeat the faith in its old forms is to have not yet caught the power and truth of the faith.

While it is true that Troeltsch was a controlling influence on Niebuhr's thought, Karl Barth also made a powerful impression. In his theology Barth emphasized the opposite pole to Troeltsch's thought, arguing that we should not seek to understand the church primarily in relation to its social setting. This is not what gives the church its meaning and power. We should view the church, and indeed all of Christianity, by how skilled it is in *receiving* the one who comes to us from beyond our own best efforts.

Niebuhr said a strong yes to both these powerful theologians. In his 1941 work, *The Meaning of Revelation*, he exerts great effort to bring together the thought of Troeltsch and Barth. He believes that we understand the word of God only when we understand it as coming from God, and yet we know only

---

[2] Diefenthaler, *H. Richard Niebuhr*, 7.

[3] Diefenthaler, *H. Richard Niebuhr*, 9.

when we come to practice it in the present. He puts it as follows:

> Students of theology will recognize that Ernst Troeltsch and Karl Barth have been my teachers, though only through their writings. These two leaders in twentieth century religious thought are frequently set in diametrical opposition to each other; I have tried to combine their main interests, for it appears to me that the critical thought of the former and the constructive work of the latter belong together. If I have failed the cause does not lie in the impossibility of the task. It is work that needs to be done.[4]

His work on the meaning of revelation was published in 1941, and the struggle it represents permeated his entire life. He never tired of attempting to make the in-breaking reality of God's otherness both understandable and meaningful for personal existence and for modern culture. This was a lifelong preoccupation, and he was still engaged in it when he died suddenly in 1962 in the midst of writing what was to be his *magnum opus* on Christian ethics.

CHURCH, THEOLOGY, AND ETHICS

Niebuhr is set apart from other American ethicists of his time, including his brother, because the church functions theologically in his ethical work. This is especially evident in his early writing, although he claims it to be the case right to the end. Just two years before his death, he says: "My primary concern today . . . is still of the reformation of the church. I still believe that reformation is a permanent movement, that *metanoia* is the continuous demand made on us in historical life."[5] The church is important for Niebuhr because only a body that is in radical openness to God, who is actively redeeming this world, is able to participate in faithfulness. Only a worshipping community knows

reformation, and only a worshipping community can be faithful.

How does the faithfulness of the church relate to social ethics for Niebuhr? In a 1946 essay, "The Responsibility of the Church for Society," he answers this question. In general, his answer is that when the church takes itself seriously as church, it "becomes visible" as "the direct demonstration of the love of God and neighbor."[6] More specifically, he speaks of the church as "apostle, pastor and pioneer." As apostle, the church "exists for the purpose of announcing the Gospel to all nations and of making them disciples of Christ."[7] The church's pastoral role commits it to those in society who are hurting. "It responds to Christ-in-God by being a shepherd of the sheep, a seeker of the lost, the friend of publicans and sinners, of the poor and brokenhearted."[8] The church as pioneer concentrates on hearing the word of God, seeing God's judgments and God's resurrections, and responding by being drawn into God's work. A key act in all of this is repentance, not only of our own sins but of the sins of society. Yes, *the church is to repent for the sins of society*! He puts it this way:

> In ethics [the church] is the first to repent for the sins of a society and it repents on behalf of all. When it becomes apparent that slavery is transgression of the divine commandment, then the church repents of it, turns its back upon it, abolishes it within itself. It does this not as the holy community separate from the world but as the pioneer and representative. It repents for the sin of the whole society and leads in the social act of repentance.[9]

For Niebuhr, the faithful church will constantly review both its doctrine and practice. This is not because doctrine changes but because history does; for proper lived theology is always an integration of the word of God

---

[4] H. Richard Niebuhr, *The Meaning of Revelation* (London: Macmillan, 1960), xi.

[5] H. Richard Niebuhr, "Reformation: Continuing Imperative," *The Christian Century* 77 (1960): 250.

[6] H. Richard Niebuhr, "The Responsibility of the Church for Society," in *The Gospel, the World and the Church*, ed. Kenneth Scott Latourette (New York: Harper & Brothers, 1946), 132.

[7] Niebuhr, "Responsibility of the Church," 126.

[8] Niebuhr, "Responsibility of the Church," 129.

[9] Niebuhr, "Responsibility of the Church," 131.

articulated in a particular time. This means that the reformation of the church should be seen as an ever-present reality. Luther's original ninety-five theses were powerful not because they were novel but because they spoke the truth of faith into a time driven by the hope seen in new forms of faithfulness.

For Niebuhr, talk about who God is and how we structure our life under God's sovereignty is the essence of theology. God, as he liked to say, is "the center of value."[10] That is to say, God is the core of our thinking, being, and acting. God is that reality from which our understanding of everything else flows.

Readers will notice that Niebuhr's language sounds a lot like that of the American theologian Paul Tillich (1886–1965). Tillich defined God as the ground of being and value, or as "being itself," and he spoke of faith as "ultimate concern."[11] Niebuhr adopts this language and suggests God is the core around which we organize and integrate our lives. Hence, there is nothing out on the periphery which is not intimately connected with God, and when we speak of God we speak of the center of our existence—that which concerns us ultimately.

Niebuhr talks of God's presence to us in three ways: as Creator, Judge, and Redeemer. And these are always simultaneously present. This is what makes "God as transforming agent" intelligible. Hence for him, the best symbols for understanding God are the cross and resurrection. God is always at work in this world resurrecting crucifixions; that is, resurrecting that which is being crucified. "Cross" is the symbol of suffering, and "resurrection" is the symbol of overcoming suffering. Cross-resurrection was not just the way God was present in Jesus Christ, but it can also be so in our world today precisely because God was present in Jesus Christ in this manner, overcoming evil and even death. Christians see the world as fundamentally God's. God, who is Creator, Judge, and Redeemer transforms that which is evil into redeemed life. And since this is always in process and never complete, there is no such thing as perfection in this world.

Not only is Niebuhr unique as an American theologian thinking about life through the eyes of the church, his larger goal is to read all of life theologically. As an especially poignant example, he chooses to show how this is done in war. We have seen earlier how Dietrich Bonhoeffer struggled theologically with World War II as a German theologian; now we can observe an American theologian of German origin who will seek to do the same.[12]

During the Second World War, in 1942 and 1943, Niebuhr wrote a series of articles in *The Christian Century* reflecting on the nature of war. In these articles, he gave war a thick theological read, meaning that he showed how Christians might think theologically and ethically about it.

All his life, Niebuhr had strong pacifist leanings that were constantly challenged both by his brother's powerful rhetoric and by his own efforts to make sense of them.[13] As we saw in the debate with his brother in 1932, especially in his article, "The Grace of Doing Nothing," Richard's theology started with the view that God is at work in this world and that just because we could not think of anything to do did not mean that nothing was being done. Hence, the compulsion to act and control outcome was considerably lessened on his view of Christian ethics compared with Reinhold's. Ten years after that public debate, he felt compelled to engage in another round of critical analysis.

We do well to remember that the issue of war was for him deeply personal. It represented the agony of the soul to such an extent

---

[10] H. Richard Niebuhr, "The Center of Value," in *Moral Principles of Action: Man's Ethical Imperative*, ed. Ruth N. Anshen, (New York: Harper & Brothers, 1952), 162–75.

[11] See, e.g., Paul Tillich, *The Dynamics of Faith* (New York: Harper & Row, 1957), where he argues that faith is not about knowing in the face of uncertainty or about the will to believe, but faith is being ultimately concerned.

[12] See chap. 15 above.

[13] See esp. the 1932 debate in *The Christian Century* discussed in chap. 20 on Reinhold Niebuhr, above.

that he suffered personal depression over it. In 1944 he became seriously ill and required hospitalization from October to December. The problem as he saw it was that one could not decide for or against war in the abstract; it required concrete and personal agony of the kind that Jesus suffered in the garden of Gethsemane. Perhaps this is also why he had such a hard time making up his mind on pacifism; sometimes what he says is in its defense and sometimes not. For Niebuhr, pacifism too was not an issue over which to decide in the abstract.

In the two years prior to his depression, Niebuhr wrote three essays in which he wrestled with the problem of war theologically. His first article, "War as the Judgment of God," appeared in May 1942. He began by putting the issue this way:

> Pacifists have approached war as an action of the lower human self—the angry, hating self—and have tried to respond to it with the action of the ideal, rational self. Coercionists have looked on war as the action of aggressive nations and have summoned men of good will to resist those of ill will.[14]

But he sees this account as inadequate. In seeking to move beyond the two anemic alternatives, he again points out that the Christian view of history is based on the conviction that God is at work in all events in this world and that responsible human actions ought always to be measured by their response to what God is doing. Neither the pacifist nor the coercionist option as stated above does so! He reminds us that in the model he is proposing, "'What must I do?' is preceded by the question, "What is God doing?'"[15]

Niebuhr reminds the reader that the view of God at work in the world should not be foreign to Christians because that is the way the prophets and Jesus saw the world. When you begin the discussion of war with God, however, the questions change. Now we must ask: "Where does God stand in war; this particular war?" He suggests that had Isaiah simply looked at what the Assyrians were doing, or had Jesus considered only what the religious authorities and the Roman authorities were doing, and had they not asked what God was doing in all of this, the results would have been very different. Their only option would then have been to take matters into their own hands. To respond to God in the war, on the other hand, means that we are not responding primarily to the state or to the enemy but to a call of faithfulness to God.

Niebuhr asks specifically: "What does it mean to say that this war is a judgment of God on the nations or on all of us?"[16] He suggests it does not mean that war should be equated with hell; rather it means that wars are crucifixions.[17] Later he writes an entire article under that heading, so I will say more about it then. But minimally, to see war as crucifixion means for him that, as with Christ, war involves the death of innocents.

His focus on war as judgment highlights another theme; namely, war is the result of sin, again like the crucifixion. Yet this is not to say that war is either necessary or good. When Isaiah saw that Assyria was the rod of God, he did not mean by this that Assyria was not wrong before God; because that too was true. The justice of God cuts deeper. He puts it this way:

> This truth cuts both ways. It means that if a Hitler is seen to be the rod of God's anger he is not thereby justified relatively or absolutely; for he does not intend what God intends, "But it is in his heart to destroy and to cut off nations not a few." It also means that if the United Nations are the instruments of God's judgment on Germany, Italy and Japan, they are not thereby justified, as though their intentions were relatively or absolutely right. God does not act save through finite instruments but none of the instruments can take the place of God, even for a moment, either in their own view or in the view of the one who is being punished.[18]

---

[14] H. Richard Niebuhr, "War as the Judgment of God," *The Christian Century* 59 (1942): 630.
[15] Niebuhr, "War as Judgment," 630.
[16] Niebuhr, "War as Judgment," 631.
[17] Niebuhr, "War as Judgment," 631.
[18] Niebuhr, "War as Judgment," 631.

What are the consequences of this view of war for human actions? Niebuhr names three. First, it means that we should stop passing judgments on ourselves, our enemies, or our opponents. It is not a question of who is right; it is a question of what God is doing. In other words, what we should do is not determined by the relative good or evil done to us. Just because past wrongs have been done to us does not justify us to do wrong to others. Second, it requires the abandonment of "all thinking in terms of self as central."[19] He goes on to say that

> [T]o carry on the war under the judgment of God is to carry it on as those who repent of the self-centeredness and who now try to forget about themselves while they concentrate on the deliverance of their neighbors. . . . It is also to wage war in such a way that a decent—a just endurable if not a just and durable—peace can come out of it.[20]

Niebuhr singles out pacifists here, making sure they are not exempt from his critique. He says, "If nonparticipation by individuals and church is self-centered, as it often is, it is as destructive in the long run as self-centered participation."[21]

The third call for action is that when we see God in this war and respond to God's action, we respond in hope and trust. In other words, nothing is beyond the scope of redemption; not politics, not economics, nor any other aspect of life. "To recognize God at work in war is to live and act with faith in resurrection."[22]

While we can easily observe that Niebuhr does not provide details in his call for action, nevertheless, he has claimed that when Christians believe that God acts in history, it is inadequate to say either that war is the result of morally misguided leaders, or that war results merely from the amoral will to power. It is too bad if the correct theological

affirmation—God is in the war—messes up our neat dichotomies; but so be it.

The essay, "War as the Judgment of God," again resulted in a debate, but this time not with his brother. Virgil C. Aldrich, from the department of philosophy in the Rice Institute, Houston, Texas, responded with concerns about Niebuhr's comments.[23] Aldrich's concern has to do with the language of war as crucifixion. He pronounces: "A pox on your theological dramatization of the consequences of social mismanagement."[24] He argues that Niebuhr's theological dance only complicates the question of war, as he presumes to speak on behalf of God, when for Jesus—the true representative of God—war was a simple matter; it is born out of human sin and greed and we ought to get over it and learn to love our enemies.

In Niebuhr's response, he resists the charge of speaking on God's behalf. He says, "My problem is not that of looking with God on the world but of finding God in the world, or rather that of understanding how to stand in the presence of God as I stand in the presence of every individual event, good or evil."[25] In fact, he lays the charge of speaking from God's point of view at the feet of Aldrich. Niebuhr's counterclaim is that God is not subjective, as tends to be the case with Aldrich, but objective. Subjectivists "look for God's action within and will judge the world *with* him rather than be placed under the judgment of objective reality."[26] For Niebuhr to deny that God is in the war is simply to deny that God is God. And to

> look for God's judgment is to affirm as radical monotheists that there is no person, no situation, no event in which the opportunity to serve God is not present. It means that we do not relinquish hard and difficult situations to the reign

---

[19] Niebuhr, "War as Judgment," 632.

[20] Niebuhr, "War as Judgment," 632.

[21] Niebuhr, "War as Judgment," 632.

[22] Niebuhr, "War as Judgment," 632.

[23] See "Is God in the War? *The Christian Century* 59 (1942): 953–55. This title covers both Aldrich's response to the editor of *The Christian Century* and to Niebuhr's earlier essay as well as Niebuhr's response to Aldrich.

[24] "Is God in the War?," 953.

[25] "Is God in the War?," 954.

[26] "Is God in the War?," 954 (emphasis in original).

of irrationality and irreligiousness. The fight for the interpretation of war as divine judgment is, to my mind, a fight for rationality in religion and for consistency in man's ethical response to his environment.[27]

The next article came eight months later titled, "War as Crucifixion."[28] This is not a new thesis, but here he argues further that the crucifixion metaphor is much richer and truer in its disclosure of the place of war in God's economy than either the moral approach to war (the pacifists and the just-war theorists) or the amoral approach (a case of the survival of the fittest). For starters, the Christian account of the crucifixion acknowledges that the story is much bigger than the mere execution of three individuals. From the start, the crucifixion of Christ is presented as having cosmic justice proportions.

Niebuhr suggests that, even on the face of it, the crucifixion is like war in that three people charged with insurrection (war making) are being executed; and the point is not lost on those giving the account that there is a difference among them. All are revolutionaries, but only one is a peaceful revolutionary who refuses to kill his enemies. Had there been only the two executions all would have been ordinary, but there was Jesus, innocent of the charge and yet he is hung there with the others. Niebuhr points out that the crucifiers too are part of the mix of the justice-injustice dynamic; "war is like that—apparently indiscriminate in the choice of victims and of victors, whether these be thought of as individuals or as communities."[29]

War is like the crucifixion in yet another respect: "In its presence men must abandon their moral cynicism along with other peace time luxuries."[30] He means by this that the cross (like war) calls for the most serious and deepest of moral reflections; that is, it pushes for a deeper search for meaning and truth,

not a shallower one. Niebuhr pushes for the reader's consciousness to be shaped by the power of the crucifixion and its imagination, much like it did for the Apostle Paul.

> The crucifixion illuminated many things for him [Paul], but in particular it was the revelation of the righteousness of God which was distinct from the righteousness of the law, and which, when it became apparent, showed man's righteousness to be as unrighteous as his unrighteousness."[31]

In other words, in the presence of God we are sinners, and if we do not permit God's righteousness to save us from the consequences of our sins, then we will destroy ourselves and others, especially those who are weaker than we are. In this way, the crucifixion really helps us see the kind of universe in which we live. He says:

> The cross of Jesus Christ is the final, convincing demonstration of the fact that the order of the universe is not one of retribution in which goodness is rewarded and evil punished, but rather an order of graciousness wherein, as Jesus had observed, the sun is made to shine on evil and on good, and the rain to descend on the just and the unjust.[32]

This is the real order of things. Retribution simply is not life-sustaining; we do not get what we deserve, and hence, the moral universe is far messier than we like. But then we are not in charge; God is. Hence, despite evil, death, and war, God's plan prevails.

While there may be no single action that is the result of these reflections on war, nevertheless, in giving war a thick theological read, as Niebuhr has done in these three articles, he concludes as follows:

> There will be in [these reflections] no effort to establish a righteousness of our own, no excusing of self because one has fallen less short of the glory of God than others; there will be no vengeance in them. They will also share one positive characteristic: they will be performed in hope, the reliance on the continued grace of God in the midst of our graciousness.[33]

---

[27] "Is God in the War?," 954.

[28] H. Richard Niebuhr, "War as Crucifixion," *The Christian Century* 60 (1943): 514.

[29] Niebuhr, "War as Crucifixion," 514.

[30] Niebuhr, "War as Crucifixion," 514.

[31] Niebuhr, "War as Crucifixion," 514.

[32] Niebuhr, "War as Crucifixion," 514.

[33] Niebuhr, "War as Crucifixion," 514.

There are, of course, those who will say that Niebuhr's proposals here are hopelessly impractical, and perhaps even dangerous, in that they do not denounce the evils of war strongly enough. There are also those who will argue that the fundamental givenness of human sin and, hence of war itself, is disturbing. And, of course, there are those who will want more practical theology on how life can move from crucifixion to resurrection. And yet Niebuhr will resist, for he sees all human efforts to grasp control away from God as idolatrous. Perhaps the most significant contribution of his careful and passionate reflections is that he has placed the problem of war squarely into the arena of God's judgment and redemption. And in doing this, he has placed the morality of war into the body of Christ.

NIEBUHR'S MAJOR WRITINGS

Niebuhr wrote only one book before he was appointed associate professor of Christian ethics at Yale in 1931; it appeared in 1929 and was called *The Social Sources of Denominationalism*.[34] As one would expect from the title, it draws heavily on the sociology of religion made popular by Ernst Troeltsch.

In the book, Niebuhr is critical of the standard account of distinguishing between the plethora of denominations in North America in terms of doctrinal differences. The first problem with this explanation is that it is largely false because the divide more accurately evidences social and not doctrinal roots. But more important, the doctrinal description entrenches the division at the core of the church's identity, hence placing it beyond hope of redemption. Niebuhr believed that denominationalism was rooted in the ethnic realities of the churches; hence when analyzed properly, while still a problem, it now represented a "moral failure of Christianity."[35] He speaks about the fragmentation of the churches as follows:

[I]t fosters the misunderstanding, the self-exultations, the hatreds of jingoistic nationalism by continuing in the body of Christ the spurious differences of provisional loyalties; it seats the rich and the poor apart at the table of the Lord, where the fortunate may enjoy the bounty which they have provided while the others feed upon the crusts their poverty affords.[36]

The matter of denominationalism was a deeply personal issue for Niebuhr because his own church, the Evangelical Synod, was itself constantly being tempted by German ethnic protectionism. One sign of this was the pressure to retain the German language. Yet he believed that correct Christian doctrine demanded that the church be ecumenical, and this meant the Americanization of the churches in America.

Yet Niebuhr was not naïve; he knew that given the immigration realities in the United States at the time, church divisions were inevitable. It is natural for there to be nostalgic longing for continuity with the homeland. In fact, he predicted that, after some time, immigrant churches now kept apart by their ethnic attachment would eventually be drawn together.[37]

Niebuhr relied on the sociological tools he had learned from Troeltsch, namely, the typology of church and sect,[38] even though the ecclesial reality in North America was different from nineteenth- and twentieth-century Europe. While he was reluctant to name American denominations as simply church or sect ideal-types, he nevertheless saw the Lutheran and the Episcopalians as fitting more readily into the church-type and the Methodists and the Baptists fitting into the sectarian-type. The latter groups remained more sensitive to matters of social justice, especially during political and social crises, and the former identified more with the concerns of the state and the maintenance of the status quo. He found himself being critical of the church-types because they

---

[34] H. Richard Niebuhr, *The Social Sources of Denominationalism* (New York: Henry Holt, 1929).

[35] Niebuhr, *Social Sources of Denominationalism*, 25.

[36] Niebuhr, *Social Sources of Denominationalism*, 6.

[37] Niebuhr, *Social Sources of Denominationalism*, 214ff.

[38] See 186f. and 236 above.

seemed unable to offer critique of the state and mainline society. The sect-types, on the other hand, found it easier to oppose public policy because allegiance to Jesus put them at odds with much in society.

It was during this time in his career that Niebuhr sought to distinguish his approach to Christian ethics from the Social Gospel Movement associated with men like Walter Rauschenbusch and Washington Gladden. He published several articles on this topic, including "The Social Gospel and Liberal Theology"[39] and "The Attack upon the Social Gospel."[40] His concern about the Social Gospel was not that it incorrectly interpreted the gospel in social terms but that it had lost the power of grace in its preaching of social salvation. In other words, in Social Gospel theology, God is relegated to the sidelines, cheering on the faithful as they establish the kingdom of God on earth. Later, in his 1937 book, *The Kingdom of God in America*, he would summarize Social Gospel advocates as those who believed that "[a] God without wrath brought men without sin into a kingdom without judgment through the ministration of Christ without a cross."[41] In other words, the Social Gospel was too closely tied to the liberal philosophy that saw history driven by human effort seeking goodness. On occasion, Niebuhr contrasted this humanistic view with Karl Barth's theocentric view that God alone brings about the kingdom.[42] Niebuhr embraced neither Barth's nor the Social Gospel's exclusivism but sought to work out a mediating position that accounts for both divine and human agency.

In 1935 Niebuhr coauthored a book with Wilhem Pauck and Francis P. Miller called *The Church against the World*.[43] This is a significant work because it argues for letting the church be the church. Niebuhr is critical of the church's unholy alliances—with capitalism, nationalism, humanism, and so on—and as a solution he advocates withdrawal. He sees the dangers of the liberal tendencies which would have the church understand itself in terms of "'savior' of society rather than as 'the company of those who have found a savior.'"[44] We see in this view of church further evidence of a kind of sectarianism, as he cautions against the Social Gospel Movement's careless social reductionism of the New Testament gospel.

Niebuhr's ecclesiology is heavily nuanced and at times even paradoxical. He wants the church to withdraw from its compromising alliances on the one hand, but on the other, he, as much as does Rauschenbusch, wants to establish a new Christian, social order in America. And although he resists the church simply adopting American structures like capitalism, he nevertheless wants America to embrace the teachings of the Christian faith.

In *The Kingdom of God in America*, Niebuhr gives more attention to this question. It is interesting that here he talks of "Christianity in America" instead of "church" as he had done previously. This is a subtle shift but an important one. It now becomes easier for him to move, against his own better counsel, from Christianity as an embodied practice by a community of believers to Christianity viewed as a set of ideas. Although he still sees it as a reality which ought to be understood in relation to itself, it becomes progressively easier to leave behind a nuanced ecclesiology. Still, he praises the revivalists like Jonathan Edwards (1703–1758) who emphasized God's actions and sovereignty. What Niebuhr called for in this book was a kind of national conversion; a new birth of

---

[39] H. Richard Niebuhr, "The Social Gospel and Liberal Theology," *Keryx* 22 (1931): 12–13, 18.

[40] H. Richard Niebuhr, "The Attack upon the Social Gospel," *Religion in Life* 5 (1936): 176–81.

[41] H. Richard Niebuhr, *The Kingdom of God in America* (New York: Harper & Row, 1937), 193.

[42] The reference here is to an unpublished paper, "The Kingdom of God and Eschatology (Social Gospel and Barthianism)" cited in Diefenthaler, *H. Richard Niebuhr*, 49.

[43] H. Richard Niebuhr, Wilhelm Pauck, and Francis P. Miller, *The Church against the World* (New York: Willett, Clark, 1986).   [44] Quoted from Niebuhr et al., *Church against World*, 50.

sorts for the nation, only it would not have its impetus in human initiatives but in divine creativity. This meant that he was really not that critical of the aims of the Social Gospel; he was critical of the liberal philosophy that stood behind what its advocates were espousing.

Then came the Second World War, and we have already seen the toll that it took on Niebuhr. When he put his theology to work in *The Christian Century* he got into trouble, even with himself. But he and his theology persevered. He remained adamant that God acts in this world, evil is pervasive, and we live amid the relativities that history has dealt us. And in the midst of all this, he managed to come out with another book, seeking to be more intentional with a frequently referenced theme, namely, bringing the approaches of Karl Barth and Ernst Troeltsch into theological unity. The book was called *The Meaning of Revelation* (1941).

Niebuhr's approach to Christian ethics was different than his brother's, the other significant voice on the topic in the United States at the time. The difference centered on Richard Niebuhr's claim that God was at work in human affairs, like war, politics, and social reality generally. The onus was on him to make sense of this notion. How can it be known what God is doing? In other words, what is the meaning of Christian revelation?

In *The Meaning of Revelation*, Niebuhr begins with an affirmation of historical relativism and states that historical relativism is the only context in which we can talk about revelation because we simply cannot escape our time in history. He puts it this way:

> The problem and dilemma have been set by historical relativism. What has made the question about revelation a contemporary and pressing question for Christians is the realization that the point of view which man occupies in regarding religious as

well as any other sort of reality is of profound importance. This is doubtless an old conviction but it has been refreshed and given a new relevance by modern experience, especially by historical criticism and the self-criticism of theology.[45]

In other words, Troeltsch was right in saying that there is no ahistorical or dogmatic starting point for knowing God. And yet Barth is also right in that God breaks into history and discloses what history itself cannot produce. So he identifies the agenda of the book as: "How can revelation mean both history and God?"[46]

Niebuhr's answer to this question comes in a chapter titled, "The Story of Our Life." The language here is such that his thought is often associated with "Narrative Theology."[47] This is made evident by his claim that human beings do not just observe events but participate in them and make them meaningful. In clarifying this further, he finds the need to distinguish between internal and external history. External history is objective, impersonal, disinterested, and so on.[48] In this model, revelation cannot mean both history and God because God cannot be seen as a datum of objective history. Internal history, on the other hand, where the promise lies, is lived history, that is, an account of life by way of interpreted imagination, one could say, a story into which human beings can place themselves and feel at home. Such a history is not disinterested but is shared by a community with a common set of convictions—convictions about what saves. Only in this view can revelation mean both history and God. In fact, in this view of history, we can see what God is telling us about ourselves and about the culture in which we live. And that message will be in continuity with the larger story claimed by the tradition of convictions. This becomes the arena in which all truth of what God is doing gets sorted out.

---

[45] Niebuhr, *Meaning of Revelation*, 5.

[46] Niebuhr, *Meaning of Revelation*, 43.

[47] See, e.g., Stanley Hauerwas and L. Gregory Jones, eds., *Why Narrative? Readings in Narrative Theology* (Grand Rapids: Eerdmans, 1989), in which Niebuhr's essay is the lead article.

[48] See Hauerwas and Jones, *Why Narrative?*, 47.

In this model, we do not come to understand God by an examination of logical consistent reasoning; we come to understand by observing how God has acted in the past and from that knowledge judging how God is acting today in a particular, concrete situation in analogy with the past. In other words, this is a twofold process; it entails concentrating on the character of God gleaned from the story and simultaneously analyzing what is going on around us. When these two are brought together, we can know what God is doing and how we can participate.

In 1951 Niebuhr published *Christ and Culture*, which would become a popular textbook for undergraduate Christian ethics courses at colleges and universities in North America. This book employs Troeltsch's method of typologies, meaning it is not merely a summary of historical variations but a logical ordering of historical data according to types. Hence, each type is expressed in different times in history, although never in its pure form.

Niebuhr identified five Christ and culture types evident over the history of Christianity. This is far from a purely historical exercise for him; he is interested in exploring the different ways in which Christ has been integrated into cultures. "Culture," as he defines it, consists of "language, habits, ideas, beliefs, customs, social organizations, inherited artifacts, technical processes, and values;"[49] and, since the revelation of God is intelligible only amid the relativities of culture, what then can be said about Christian faithfulness in his time? He remains passionate about his conviction that ethicists have not found ways of saying enough.

He begins his analysis with two extreme types of relating Christ and culture, the first being "Christ against culture" and the second "Christ of culture." The first, he says, was the approach evident in primitive Christianity when early Christians separated themselves from Roman society. This type is also found in the monastic movements and in the sectarianism of Leo Tolstoy.

The "Christ of culture" type is the opposite extreme and accommodates to whatever culture happens to exist. This view is best seen in the early Christian Gnostics, European "cultural Protestantism," and Protestant liberals in North America. Here, Christ is viewed mostly as a moral teacher, whose teachings are integrated into the given culture to the extent possible. In this model, the tension between Christ and culture largely disappears, and little basis remains for a Christian critique.

The remaining three types—the synthesist, dualist, and conversionist—all hold common beliefs that the other two have not developed adequately. The beliefs are (1) Christian ethics must be *theocentric* and not *christocentric*. This will make a difference regarding the relevance of the radical teaching of Christ. For example, *God of creation* is concerned with all of the earth's people, not just with small groups who want to be radical followers of Jesus; (2) Sin is so pervasive that there is no escape from its power. Hence, you cannot "separate" yourself from culture even if you try. On the other hand, because the tension remains, you also cannot simply embrace this world without affirming some distance from it; and (3) God's grace is universal and cannot be restricted merely to a small group of people who want to display a radical faithfulness. Nor is it proper to rely only upon the powers within the culture itself; the grace of God comes from God. Hence some tension between Christ and culture must be affirmed. The three mediating options all seek to take these concerns seriously.

The synthesist model, also known as "Christ above culture" is best represented by the works of Thomas Aquinas and the Anglicans. This view is characterized by the notion that, although Christ is not opposed to culture, he does not simply bless it. In other words, the relationship is hierarchal where

---

[49] H. Richard Niebuhr, *Christ and Culture* (New York: Harper & Row, 1951), 32.

Christ, as it were, pulls culture to its highest possible level.

The dualistic model is also called "Christ and culture in paradox." Niebuhr says this view is best expressed by Martin Luther, the Apostle Paul, and Søren Kierkegaard. It holds that culture is indeed fallen but nevertheless is sustained by the graciousness of God as a provisional arrangement for a sinful world on this side of the Parousia. Hence, the relationship of Christ and culture is in tension and indeed paradoxical. It is an attempt to acknowledge that we experience good and evil in an intermixed fashion, never as clearly on one or the other side alone.

The conversionist model is also called "Christ the transformer of culture." This is a more hopeful view for society than the dualist view because it believes in the possibility of the redemption of the world. The dualist model holds that the world of culture cannot be redeemed and the conversionist model believes that it can.

The conversionist model acknowledges that God is the one who ordered and created this universe and is concerned about the whole of creation and history. What God wills is that the entire world be converted and transformed into a new reality. We, the Christian church, live as "signs of the time" pointing to another time when the kingdom will be fully established.

Although Niebuhr does not overtly commit to any of these models, nevertheless his strongest criticism goes to the separatists. He saw as inadequate any theology that required withdrawal from the world to obtain purity of the church. Given other comments about his passion for conversion of society, it is not hard to see that he favored the conversionist approach.

Niebuhr was an American theologian doing theology and ethics for Americans. He believed in the "American way of life," but he also saw its flaws and was committed to making it more Christian. This desire was seen in his books, *The Kingdom of God in America* and *Christ and Culture*, but it is also evident in his 1960 book, *Radical Monotheism and Western Culture*.[50] Here he worried that henotheism, by which he meant a kind of civic religion where people rely upon the nation for their well-being, was replacing faith in one God. He saw a tension between American democracy, something so good that it could hardly be criticized—that is, the will of the people—and the will of God. God can only be God on the basis of a radical monotheism. And when there are no other gods, there is no escape from the sovereignty of living God. Everything then comes under God's jurisdiction. God is radically at the center of all of life.

In the last decade of his life, Niebuhr's writing again focused on the church.[51] Throughout his life he saw himself as a church theologian. This is significant because many theologians during this time had moved into secular university settings where church-focused theology was replaced with a more generic variety. Niebuhr fought this tendency, even though the temptations were great for him also, especially given his passionate concern for christianizing America.

THE RESPONSIBLE ETHIC

Niebuhr died in the midst of preparing his *magnum opus*, which focused on bringing together his lifelong work in Christian ethics. He was only able to complete the first part of this project, which was originally given as the Robertson Lectures at the University of Glasgow in 1960. We know them as *The Responsible Self*.[52] This is Niebuhr's mature thought, in which he brings together many of the themes he developed throughout his

---

[50] H. Richard Niebuhr, *Radical Monotheism and Western Culture: With Supplementary Essays* (Louisville, Ky.: Westminster/John Knox, 1960).

[51] He wrote other books in the late 1950s on the church. E.g., *The Purpose of the Church and its Ministry: Reflections on the Aims of Theological Education* (New York: Harper & Row, 1956); and *The Ministry in Historical Perspective* (New York: Harper & Row, 1956).

[52] H. Richard Niebuhr, *The Responsible Self: An Essay in Christian Moral Philosophy* (New York: Harper & Row, 1963).

teaching. It is appropriate to conclude this chapter with this analysis.

Niebuhr begins these lectures with some interesting autobiographical comments on what it means to call himself Christian. These are especially significant words, as they come from a man who had struggled intensely, even to the point of personal illness, over matters of faithfulness. So after a lifetime of theological and philosophical reflections, he says:

> I call myself a Christian simply because I also am a follower of Jesus Christ, though I travel at a great distance from him not only in time but in the spirit of my travelling; because I believe that my way of thinking about life, myself, my human companions and my destiny has been so modified by his presence in our history that I cannot get away from his influence; and also because I do not want to get away from it; above all, I call myself a Christian because my relation to God has been, so far as I can see, deeply conditioned by this presence of Jesus Christ in my history and in our history. In one sense, I call myself a Christian in the same way that I call myself a twentieth-century man. To be Christian is simply part of my fate, as it is the fate of another to be a Moslem or Jew. In this sense a very large part of mankind is today Christian; it has come under the influence of Jesus Christ so that even its Judaism and Mohammedanism bears witness to the fact that Jesus Christ has been among us.[53]

In this book, Niebuhr seeks to develop an alternative model for Christian ethics, not different from what he has said in his other writings but different from the mainstream, philosophical models. Tradition tells us we must choose between the teleological and deontological models. He rejects that choice. Why? Because both are inadequate in providing a qualitative account of the Christian life consonant with the call of Christ.

The teleological view of ethics understands human beings as "man the maker";[54] the deontological model understands them as "man the citizen."[55] If we adopt the teleological way of thinking, which many Christians have,

then everything we do and think—in areas of education, justice, politics, legal matters, our understanding of anthropology, sin, and so on—everything will answer to the question, "What is the main goal of life?" For example, education will be shaped by the kind of person it wishes to produce; sin will be understood in terms of "missing the mark," and so on. This logic will also determine theological notions like salvation. If sin is "moving in the wrong direction" or "confusion about direction," then salvation will be clarity of direction, or resolution of the confusion, or moving in the right direction. Original sin, in this view, is seen as having so confused the direction that we no longer know the right path. And Jesus then restores the right path; he restores our vision.

The deontological view of ethics understands human beings differently. In this model, we are told that we are under God's law. Now sin is the breaking of God's law. The logic then unfolds as follows: God gave laws, and we are to obey them. Education, justice, anthropology are unpacked in terms of whether we are obeying the laws or the will of God. In this model, God commands and we obey; in the teleology model, God leads and we follow. Salvation, in the deontological model, is obeying the law of God, or obeying the ultimate law of life. God rules over us and we must find ways of obeying that rule.

We should note how this relates to Niebuhr's theme in *The Meaning of Revelation*, where he sought to bring together Troeltsch and Barth. Barth had distinct, deontologist leanings, while Troeltsch was a teleologist. Like in theology, so in ethics, both are important but neither is adequate. What is required is a new paradigm or symbol—responsibility.

Niebuhr acknowledges being influenced by psychologist George Mead, who led Niebuhr to ask questions about the nature of the self. He realized that the self is a complex reality. We find ourselves to be different selves in different situations: a friend, a citizen of a

---

[53] Niebuhr, *Responsible Self*, 43.
[54] Niebuhr, *Responsible Self*, 49.
[55] Niebuhr, *Responsible Self*, 51.

state, a husband, a church member, a father, and so on. How can we be the same person in all of these different situations? How can we have a united self?

These questions find no satisfactory answer on either the teleological or deontological models. That is, the matter is not solved by asking what law we are under. This leads to the unhappy position of having to admit that when we act in different contexts we find ourselves acting under different laws, hardly a satisfactory account of our experiences. The same could be said with respect to teleology logic.

In developing his "responsibility model," Niebuhr refers to a common example of being at the bedside of a suffering, dying person. Were you to ask, "What ought I to do?" or "What goal am I to pursue?" you would no doubt find yourself frustrated because no compelling answers can be given. There is often nothing we can do to change the situation.[56]

Niebuhr suggests that—rather than coming to this situation with a question involving goals or laws—we ask, "How can I respond?" Often the most redemptive and appropriate response is to do nothing but just be present. We all know this principle and practice it, but we cannot understand it ethically because we are trained to think in unhelpful, moral categories. In the situation of the suffering friend, our presence is already a response to things we cannot change. We are there responding to God's presence. God, the Redeemer, is present through our being there. This, in a nutshell, is Niebuhr's responsibility theory.

Systematically, his theory has four components.

1. The first component is the concept of *response* itself. Rather than asking about the right thing to do or the good we should pursue, we should ask what would be a fitting response.

2. The second component of his responsibility theory is *interpretation*. We do not respond involuntarily. In other words, there is a difference between a response and a reaction. Knee jerks are reactions because they are involuntary; responses require interpretation. We respond to an interpreted situation, one which we understand in a particular way. Frequently, two people interpret events differently and therefore they respond differently. "Response" and "interpretation" go together.

3. The third element in responsibility theory is that of *accountability*. By this, Niebuhr means we must realize that our response creates part of a chain of responses in an ongoing process. That is, our response is never final but, in fact, creates a whole new situation, which in turn invites further response. Other views of ethics based on decision-making in response to dilemmas, for example, suggest that our decisions can *solve* the problem. The reality is that we are always involved in responding; it is never finished, and hence we must be accountable for our response.

4. The fourth element of responsibility ethics is *social solidarity*. No one would be happy with a mere ongoing sequence of responses. Our responses must demonstrate some rational structure to actions upon us. That is to say, a Christian ethic forms the contexts in which we respond in such a manner so as to create a living, social solidarity. In other words, we are always involved in the creation of a society where peace and justice can flourish to the extent possible, despite the sinfulness of the world in which we live.

What might be said to be most important in Niebuhr's response theory of Christian ethics is what we are responding to. Not only are we responding to the interpreted situation but we are also responding to God's presence there. In order for ethics to be Christian, we must always respond to every situation so as to respond to God's action upon us. He puts it this way: "Christian teleology says: 'Remember God's plan for your life.' Christian deontology says: 'Obey God's command in all your obediences to finite rules.' Responsibility theory says: 'God is acting in all actions upon you. So respond

---

[56] Notice here the same theme reoccurring as in the "Grace of Doing Nothing," *The Christian Century* 49 (1932): 379; see chap. 20 above.

to all actions upon you as to respond to his action.'"[57] In other words, since God wants to redeem us in our concrete locations, responding to God's action upon us means we ourselves become agents of that redemption. We are in effect opening ourselves to God for healing to be brought about through human agents. This is the alternative theory of responsibility ethics which Niebuhr advances.

Niebuhr's approach to Christian ethics has been heralded by some as a new beginning in the pursuit of a viable, Christian ethic in North America, and it continues to be much debated all over the world. Just as it is impossible to present all the many nuances of his position, it is impossible to overstate the importance of his contribution to Christian ethics. The task he set for himself was extremely high, but always, he pointed beyond himself to Creator and Redeemer God as the one who would bring about goodness. All we can do is to respond to a thick reading of God's presence among us.

---

[57] Niebuhr, *Responsible Self*, 126.

Chapter Twenty-Two

MARTIN LUTHER KING JR.
(1929–1968)

Martin Luther King Jr. is a well-known peace activist who led the civil rights movement in the United States in the 1950s and 1960s. What is less known about King is that he was also a theologian who thought carefully about Christian ethics.[1] He carved out his own way of understanding what it meant to be a social reformer while being strongly influenced by people like Walter Rauschenbusch and Reinhold Niebuhr. What is especially interesting about King is that in his strategy for social change he adopted an approach quite uncharacteristic of either Rauschenbusch or Niebuhr. Of the many theologian-ethicists we have examined so far, we have seen that virtually all began as pacifists, but only J. S. Woodsworth retained the position until the end of his life. In this, King follows Woodsworth, but King did not find it necessary to leave the church to do so. It is important to ponder why that might be—perhaps it had less to do with the difference between Woodsworth's and King's views on pacifism and more with the counter-establishment church that shaped King's theology and informed his practice.

It is sometimes thought that King discovered a workable philosophy of social change for which he had no theology. This is not true. He was a trained theologian, and his practical views of how society could be changed grew out of that theology. Hence, King is of interest to us because he presents an unusual political theology and rationale for how to move from an unjust society to one that is more just.

KING'S LIFE

Perhaps even more than for other figures presented in this book, King's ethic is his life. His contribution to Christian theology could easily be presented by giving a detailed narration of his many actions, speeches, and political involvements. Hence, the sectional divisions of this chapter into his life and thought are quite arbitrary and serve a limited function.

King was born in Atlanta, Georgia, on January 15, 1929, where his father Martin Luther King Sr. was about to become the pastor at the Ebenezer Baptist Church. His mother, Alberta Williams, also came from a preacher family; her father was the long-time minister of the Ebenezer Church just prior to her husband.[2] King had an older sister, Willie, and a younger brother, Alfred.

An interesting story is told of how King got his name. In 1934 the family took a trip to Germany; there his father became so moved by the great reformer Martin Luther

---

[1] For an example of reading King as a serious Christian ethicist, see James William McClendon Jr., "Martin Luther King, Jr.: Politician or American Church Father?" in *Journal of Ecumenical Studies* 8, no. 1 (1971): 115–21. See also Herbert W. Richardson, "Martin Luther King—Unsung Theologian," in *New Theology*, ed. Martin E. Marty and Dean G. Peerman, no. 6 (New York: Macmillan, 1969), 178–84.

[2] Martin Luther King Sr. took over the leadership of the Ebenezer Baptist Church after his father-in-law, Rev. A. D. Williams, died in 1931.

that he changed both his name and that of his son from Michael to Martin Luther.[3]

King was born into the church. Growing up in a black, Baptist, Christian family where his father dealt with black leaders meant that he was involved from very early in a life that would constantly interact with theology, church, black politics, and experiences of racial prejudice. The impact of these factors in shaping the character and thinking of the young King cannot be easily overstated.[4] He followed in the footsteps of his father both in becoming a pastor—eventually in the same church as his father—and in adopting much of his thinking.

King attended Booker T. Washington High School in Atlanta, the first public, all-black high school in Georgia. It had opened in 1924, just five years before King was born. He skipped grades nine and twelve and so entered college at the age of fifteen. This meant that he was admitted into Morehouse College, the alma mater of his father, without having completed high school. There is never any indication that this proved a hardship for him. At Morehouse he earned a Bachelor of Arts degree in sociology and then entered a school for Baptist ministers, Crozer Theological Seminary in Chester, Pennsylvania. He graduated in 1951 with a Bachelor of Divinity degree, after which he enrolled in Boston University to study theology. He received his Ph.D. in 1955. His dissertation was titled, "A Comparison of the Conception of God in the Thinking of Paul Tillich and Henry Nelson Wieman." King was a bright student, which made it possible for him to complete his doctoral program in four years, finishing at age twenty-six.

In 1953 King married Coretta Scott (1927–2006) from Marion, Alabama. She had grown up in a segregated community and been bused to the closest black high school nine miles from her home. After high school, she attended Antioch College in Yellow Springs, Ohio, which was an all-white school experimenting with interracial education and so recruiting a few nonwhite students on full scholarships. Her older sister Edythe had been the first black student to attend Antioch. Scott studied music and while a student became active in the civil rights movement.

After two years at Antioch, she received a scholarship to study music, especially singing, at the New England Conservatory of Music in Boston. This is where she would meet King, since both were involved in civil rights activities. On June 18, 1953, they were married, with King's father officiating. They became parents of four children, all of whom became involved in the civil rights movement—Yolanda Denise King (1955–2007), Martin Luther King III (1957–), Dexter Scott King (1961–), and Bernice Albertine King (1963–).

In 1954 King was called to become pastor of the Dexter Avenue Baptist Church in Montgomery, Alabama. Here the couple ministered together; Martin preached and Coretta sang. But Montgomery would prove to be much more than a place to preach. This is where his civil rights campaign began in earnest.

In March 1955 Claudette Colvin, a black fifteen-year-old girl from Montgomery, refused to vacate her bus seat for a white woman, which was required by Jim Crow laws. She was kicked off the bus by the driver and arrested by the police. King and E. D. Nixon, leader of the National Association for the Advancement of Colored People (NAACP), investigated the incident and decided that this was not the best case to build a

---

[3] See Peter J. Ling, *Martin Luther King, Jr.* (New York: Routledge, 2002), 11.

[4] The story is told that one day his father accidentally ran a red light. Here is the exchange between the police and King's father: "'All right, boy, pull over and let me see your license.' 'I'm no boy,' replied the senior King. Pointing to the young Martin, he said, 'This is a boy. I'm a man, and until you call me one, I will not listen to you.' The policeman was so shocked that he wrote up the ticket nervously and then rapidly rode away." Quoted from William M. Ramsay, "Martin Luther King, Jr. and Civil Rights," in *Four Modern Prophets: Walter Rauschenbusch, Martin Luther King, Jr., Gustavo Gutiérrez, Rosemary Radford Ruether* (Atlanta: John Knox, 1986), 30.

protest around, partially because Colvin was fifteen, unmarried, and pregnant.

Then on December 1, the same year, Mrs. Rosa Parks of Montgomery, a forty-two-year-old, black housekeeper and seamstress, also said "No" to racial segregation by refusing to yield her bus seat to a white man. The bus driver demanded that she move; when she refused, she was arrested by the local police. This action was the spark that ignited a major campaign.

Rosa Parks' arrest triggered the Montgomery bus boycott. The NAACP and the Women's Political Council set December 5 as the day for blacks to refuse to ride the bus. King was urged to join the leadership of this event. At first he resisted, but he eventually gave himself to the project wholeheartedly. He got his church secretary to make multiple copies of a sign that read, "DON'T RIDE THE BUS," and it became a slogan across Montgomery. A staggering ninety percent of blacks in Montgomery did not ride the buses on December 5.[5]

On the very same afternoon, the Montgomery Improvement Association (MIA) was formed by a group of black church ministers and community leaders. King was named its leader. Says William Ramsay: "It was that night, in his initial speech as a civil-rights leader, that King first enunciated the concept he had been working out, the idea to which he was to dedicate his life: his faith in the power of active, loving, nonviolent resistance."[6]

The story of King's first day as leader of the MIA is told with some flair by Marshall Frady, one of King's many biographers.[7] After his somewhat reluctant acceptance of the leadership of the new organization, King knew that he would need to address the crowds in the evening meeting. What would he say? There was no time for supper. When they got close to the church where he was to speak, he saw thousands had gathered for blocks around the church (the estimate is more than four thousand people). As he surveyed the crowd, he sarcastically murmured to the driver of his vehicle, "You know, Finley, this could turn into something big."[8] Loudspeakers were set up for many blocks. As King and the other leaders entered the church, the people shouted and sang the old, gospel song, "Leaning on the Everlasting Arms."

After the singing and clapping subsided, King rose to speak: "We are here this evening for serious business."[9] As he spoke, the people responded in antiphonal rhythm with "amen," or "preach it," as is common in black gatherings. He continued, "You know, my friends, there comes a *time*, when people get tired of being trampled over by the iron feet of oppression . . ."[10] More thunderous clapping and shouts! Then with several more anaphoric evocations—"There comes a time . . .," "There comes a time . . .,"—he began with the meat of the matter. Remember that King did not personally know many people there. Most of them were strangers. He took a chance with his words:

> Now, let us say that we are not here advocating violence, we have overcome that. I want it to be known throughout Montgomery and throughout this nation that we are—a *Christian* people. . . . But the great glory of American democracy is the right to protest for right. . . . And if we are wrong, the Supreme Court of this nation is wrong. If we are wrong, God Almighty is wrong! . . . If we are wrong, Jesus of Nazareth was merely a utopian dreamer and never came down to earth! If we are wrong, justice is a lie. . . . And we are determined here in Montgomery to work and fight, until justice runs down like water and righteousness as a mighty stream![11]

Fascinating words! We should take note of at least four distinctive features:

1. He speaks out of a clear identity—"we are a Christian people." Even as a reformer, King

---

[5] See Ramsay, "Civil Rights," 33.

[6] Ramsay, "Civil Rights," 33.

[7] See Marshall Frady, *Martin Luther King, Jr.: A Life* (New York: Penguin, 2006).

[8] Frady, *A Life*, 33.

[9] Frady, *A Life*, 33.

[10] Frady, *A Life*, 34 (emphasis in original).

[11] As quoted in Frady, *A Life*, 35 (emphasis in original).

was unapologetically a pastor and leader of a church.

2. He speaks on the *assumption* that the ethic of Jesus' love of neighbor has conquered the impulse to violence in all his hearers.

3. His words show that the American dream and the Christian vision are not contradictory but overlap.

4. His language of overcoming is not precise strategy first of all but a biblical, prophetic proclamation of the peaceable kingdom in which all his listeners are a part. The cause of justice is God's cause!

These themes appear repeatedly in his speeches.

The civil rights revolution had begun. For 381 days, King led this boycott against the Montgomery public bus system. People walked to work, carpooled, biked, and found ways to get around without buses. King had become an important leader; the people rallied around him, and he could not let them down.

But where did King find the resources to provide such leadership? Theologically, he was a believer in the Social Gospel of Walter Rauschenbusch, who had pointed him to the teachings of Jesus and especially the Sermon on the Mount. This provided him with the intellectual certitude to continue the relentless battle of expressing love in the context of injustice and social evil, even though he thought Rauschenbusch was not careful enough in guarding against the prevailing liberal forces. Mahatma Gandhi's teaching of *Satyagraha* (which King often translated as "truth force" and "love force") gave him further insights on how to use nonviolence as a means of exposing injustice and demanding that the status quo be changed.[12] Yet neither of these sources gave him the emotional and spiritual resources to deal with the hatred and threats that came to him almost immediately after MIA was formed. For example, on

the evening of January 27, 1956, seven weeks into the boycott, the telephone rang and a voice said, "Listen, nigger, we've taken all we want from you; before next week you'll be sorry you ever came to Montgomery."[13] Two years later, when recounting the Montgomery boycott story in his own words,[14] he reflects on how he dealt with the emotional trauma and feelings of inadequacy after this phone call. He knew very well that if he did not show courage and strength in the face of this kind of persecution, the people he was about to lead would not have the courage to follow. He tells the story of his inner turmoil that night:

> I hung up, but I couldn't sleep. It seemed that all of my fears had come down on me at once. I had reached the saturation point. . . . The words I spoke to God that midnight are still vivid in my memory. "I am here taking a stand for what I believe is right. But now I am afraid. The people are looking to me for leadership, and if I stand before them without strength and courage, they too will falter. I am at the end of my powers. I have nothing left. I have come to the point where I can't face it alone." At that moment, I experienced the presence of the Divine as I had never experienced Him before. It seemed as though I could hear the quiet assurance of an inner voice saying: "Stand up for righteousness, stand up for truth; and God will be on your side forever." Almost at once my fear began to go. My uncertainty disappeared. I was ready to face anything.[15]

Three days later, on January 30, King's home was bombed. This was the first of many assassination attempts. Fortunately, no one was injured in the bombing, but it sent a sobering message about the high costs of trying to change a well-established, unjust, social order, especially one from which many people benefit. King had often preached that the cross was the price Christ paid for loving instead of killing his enemies; now he was beginning to see clearly that message was not

---

[12] See Ramsay, "Civil Rights," 34–35.

[13] Ramsay, "Civil Rights," 36.

[14] See Martin Luther King Jr., *Stride Toward Freedom: The Montgomery Story* (New York: Harper, 1958).

[15] Martin Luther King Jr., *Stride Toward Freedom: The Montgomery Story*, rev. ed., ed. Clayborne Carson (Boston: Beacon, 2010), 124–25. Also, it should be noted that these are, in part, the words that are displayed in "Dr. King's Kitchen" in the Civil Rights Museum in Atlanta.

a symbol of a distant possibility but a profound actuality of the cost of speaking truth to power.

King was plunged into a very steep learning curve. He had no formal training in the techniques of nonviolent direct action, nor was this the guide for his work. His teacher was Jesus and especially the Sermon on the Mount. Moreover, he was now a leader of a massive following of black people, many of whom had never heard of nonviolent love as a strategy for social change. As he preached nonviolence, the Ku Klux Klan rode through the streets of Montgomery in white, hooded robes and sought to break the resolve of the strikers. There were more bomb threats and bombing attempts. On one such occasion, two Klan members were arrested (upon signing confessions) for planting a bomb at King's house that did not explode. They were tried and acquitted. During the same time period, King was arrested, tried, and convicted of leading the boycott. He was sentenced to pay a $500 fine.[16] While King preached love of enemies, the white, Christian ministers in Montgomery remained silent. Apparently it did not occur to them that this was a Christian cause and not merely a black liberation movement.

Victory in the Montgomery struggle came on December 20, 1956, when the U.S. Supreme Court declared segregated buses in Atlanta and Montgomery to be unconstitutional. While celebrated with joy and praise to God, it was but a small victory in the larger scheme of things.

Nevertheless, important learning had taken place. Reflecting on the Montgomery bus boycott later in life, King says:

From the beginning a basic philosophy guided the movement. This guiding principle has since been referred to variously as nonviolent resistance, noncooperation, and passive resistance. But in the first days of the protest, none of these expressions was mentioned; the phrase most often heard was "Christian love." It was the Sermon on the Mount, rather than a doctrine of passive resistance, that initially inspired the Negroes of Montgomery to dignified social action. It was Jesus of Nazareth that stirred the Negroes to protest with the creative weapon of love.[17]

These comments are significant because in them we again see King as first a preacher, not a social activist or politician. And it is precisely his power of Christian rhetoric that made him an effective political voice.[18] He was a preacher who saw the entire black community as his church; and even more radically, he wished to make the entire American population his parish. Preaching was not an act of withdrawal or an act of setting a people apart, but an act of uniting what had been broken apart by hatred and prejudice.

In January of 1957, with the Montgomery boycott still very fresh on everyone's mind, King invited some sixty black leaders to a meeting at the Ebenezer Baptist Church in Atlanta. They had a vision: to form an organization that would—through the practice of Christian love—seek to desegregate the entire south. The discussion led to the formation of an organization called the "Southern Christian Leadership Conference" (SCLC).[19] King was chosen as leader, and he served in this role until his death in 1968.

The SCLC had a challenging time gaining support, even among the black churches and communities, because of potential threats like bombing, death to leaders, and economic hardship. There was also disagreement on how segregation should be challenged—legally in the courts or through boycotts, sit-ins, and marches on the streets. Add to this

---

[16] Frady, A Life, 36.

[17] Martin Luther King Jr., "Stride Toward Freedom," in A Testament of Hope: The Essential Writings and Speeches of Martin Luther King, Jr., ed. James Melvin Washington (San Francisco: HarperCollins, 1986), 447.

[18] See, e.g., Sig Polle, "The Nonviolent Rhetoric of Martin Luther King, Jr." (Ph.D. diss., University of Oregon, Eugene, 1990).

[19] The first name was "Negro Leaders Conference on Nonviolent Integration," then the "Southern Negro Leaders Conference," and finally SCLC. This information is taken from http://en.wikipedia.org/wiki/Southern_Christian_Leadership_Conference, accessed May 11, 2011.

that some black leaders believed the church's role was to address spiritual and not political matters. Nevertheless, the SCLC became the organization under which much of the important work of the U.S. civil rights movement was conducted.

In 1959 King resigned as pastor of the Dexter Avenue Baptist Church in Montgomery to join his father at the Ebenezer Baptist Church in Atlanta. It was a copastor arrangement because King was by then so heavily involved in the SCLC that he had little time for full-time pastoral duties.

In 1960 another organization, the Student Nonviolent Coordinating Committee (SNCC), was formed in Raleigh, North Carolina. This group was, in the words of Marshall Frady, "to act as a kind of commando strike force for deep-country operations."[20] Initially, the SNCC worked in harmony with the SCLC, and King gave it his full support, but there were clearly different styles and perhaps even different visions in the two groups, resulting in tensions between them. Many in the new group were impatient with what some perceived as King's restrained approach to change. Several felt less committed to nonviolence and were willing to use other means if and when peaceful ones proved ineffective. John Lewis was the leader of the SNCC for six years, until 1966.[21] He would later become a U.S. Congressman.

On November 8, 1960, John F. Kennedy won the American presidential race over Richard Nixon by a very narrow margin. Although King did not officially endorse either candidate, Kennedy went out of his way to court black voters. For example, when Judge J. O. Mitchell sentenced King to four months of hard labor three hundred miles from home, Kennedy made some strategic phone calls—to the King residence to console Coretta and to Georgia's governor to exert pressure to have King released. In a few days, King was free on bail.[22] Then on the last Sunday before the election, Kennedy had fliers sent to the black churches in the South that read, "'No Comment' Nixon versus a Candidate with a Heart, Senator Kennedy: The Case of Martin Luther King."[23]

Kennedy's narrow victory, attributable in part to the support of black voters,[24] gave the civil rights movement a much-needed entrée to Washington. Both President Kennedy and his brother Robert, who was U.S. attorney general from 1961–1964, publicly supported the civil rights movement.

King led several protest events in the early sixties; for example, in 1961 and 1962 the SCLC and the SNCC held a demonstration against racial segregation in Albany, Georgia. This event was not successful and drew virtually no national attention. By this time, it was a mark of failure if the event did not attract the national media. The media—especially television—were crucial components of the "power" of such actions.

In 1963 things changed. The campaign in Birmingham, Alabama, is usually touted as a model of success. Much was also learned from the not-so-successful campaign in Albany, including the importance of the careful targeting of a protest. In Birmingham, the effort specifically focused on desegregating stores.

George Wallace was the newly elected governor of Alabama, and in his inaugural address he had made his position against desegregation clear, shouting, "Segregation now! Segregation tomorrow! Segregation forever!"[25] So Birmingham became an important center for a campaign. The local head

---

[20] Frady, *A Life*, 72.

[21] Frady, *A Life*, 72.

[22] See Ling, *Martin Luther King, Jr.*, 73.

[23] Ling reports that "The margin of Kennedy's victory—just 112,881 votes out of over 68 million cast—was readily explained by the three-to-one preference for the 'candidate with a heart' among African American voters," 73–74.

[24] The point, of course, must also be made that the fact that Kennedy supported the Civil Rights Movement *cost* him votes. It is therefore difficult to be definitive on how the election was won.

[25] Quoted from Ramsay, "Civil Rights," 38.

of the SCLC was Rev. Fred Shuttlesworth, a black minister. His family had been beaten with chains, and he himself had been arrested eight times. He had won some minor concessions like restroom desegregation in downtown Birmingham but nothing significant.

The official responsible for enforcing segregation in Birmingham was Commissioner Eugene "Bull" Connor. He was known for his ruthless tactics. When King was asked to assist in the Birmingham campaign, he gladly accepted because he saw it as an opportunity to bring to the entire nation the serious problems of segregation in the South. He knew there would be major clashes and he anticipated that people would get hurt. This was not what he wanted, but with Connor in change of law enforcement, it was expected.

On April 2, 1963, a sit-in was organized. The demands were simple: the protesters were requesting services in places deemed off-limits for black people. Soon hundreds of them were arrested. The national media was there recording images that were shocking. Ramsay reports: "On television the nation saw the children marching up to the bared fangs of police dogs. Newspapers ran front-page pictures of Connor's police beating prostrate women. Fire hoses mowed down unarmed youths . . . and still they marched. Soon nine hundred children and young people had been arrested."[26] One month later, 3,000 African Americans filled the jails, and still crowds of 4,000 were protesting on the streets of Birmingham. Stores were boycotted, black shoppers refused to conduct business, and one day firefighters refused Connor's command to turn on the hoses.[27] Clearly the protest was working, not in the sense that major new laws were being enacted, but sentiment of people throughout the nation was beginning to change:

segregation is real, awful, wrong, and needs to change!

On Good Friday, April 12, 1963, King himself was arrested and held for twenty-four hours in solitary confinement.[28] Here he wrote his famous "Letter from Birmingham City Jail."[29] This letter, dated April 16, 1963, was a public response to eight white ministers who were appealing to blacks for patience, asking them to discontinue their protest and put their trust in the legal system. I have chosen to comment at some length on this letter because so much of King's theology of social change gets articulated in it, even if indirectly.

Among other things, the white clergymen complained that what was happening in Birmingham was as a result of "outside influence," intimating that it was inappropriate for King to give leadership to the protest in Birmingham. King responded with a reminder of the biblical mode of ministry. He alluded to the Old Testament prophets, who "left their villages and carried their 'thus saith the Lord' far beyond the boundaries of their home towns . . ."[30] He referred to the Apostle Paul, who "Left his little village of Tarsus and carried the gospel of Jesus Christ to practically every hamlet and city of the Greco-Roman world."[31] Turning to his own role as a minister of the church, he said, "I too am compelled to carry the gospel of freedom beyond my particular hometown."[32]

In his open letter, King also addressed the clergymen's concern about patience and implied that patience was a white man's luxury. He responded to their concern about the laws of the country being broken and reminded them it was dangerous for people committed to justice to obey unjust laws, especially laws that negatively impact others but from which they themselves benefit. His most penetrating response of all was to their concern that the activities in Birmingham were extreme.

---

[26] Ramsay, "Civil Rights," 38.

[27] Ramsay, "Civil Rights," 39.

[28] Ramsay, "Civil Rights," 39.

[29] Martin Luther King Jr., "Letter from Birmingham City Jail," in *A Testament of Hope*, 289–302.

[30] King, "Letter from Birmingham," 290.

[32] King, "Letter from Birmingham," 290.

[31] King, "Letter from Birmingham," 290.

He said:

> At first I was rather disappointed that fellow clergymen would see my nonviolent efforts as those of the extremists. . . . Oppressed people cannot remain oppressed forever. The urge for freedom will eventually come. This is what happened to the American Negro. . . . Was not Jesus an extremist in love—"Love your enemies, bless them that curse you, pray for them that despitefully use you." Was not Amos an extremist for justice—"Let justice roll down like waters and righteousness like a mighty stream." Was not Paul an extremist for the gospel of Jesus Christ—"I bear in my body the marks of the Lord Jesus." Was not Martin Luther an extremist—"Here I stand; I can do none other so help me God." . . . In that dramatic scene on Calvary's hill three men were crucified. We must not forget that all three were crucified for the same crime—the crime of extremism. Two were extremists for immorality and thusly fell below their environment. The other, Jesus Christ, was an extremist for love, truth and goodness, and thereby rose above his environment. So, after all, maybe the South, the nation and the world are in dire need of creative extremists.[33]

King then laid a heavy challenge on his fellow church leaders. He spoke of having traveled all over the southern states:

> Over and over again I have found myself asking: "What kind of people worship here? Who is their God? Where were their voices when the lips of Governor Barnett dripped with words of interposition and nullification? Where were they when Governor Wallace gave the clarion call for defiance and hatred? Where were their voices of support when tired, bruised and weary Negro men and women decided to rise from the dark dungeons of complacency to the bright hills of creative protest?"[34]

King concluded the letter by naming his love for the church: "Yes, I see the church as the body of Christ. But, oh! How we have blemished and scarred that body through social neglect and fear of being nonconformist."[35] King's theological ethics and his understanding of Christian practice arose deep from within his passion for the church—not the black church or the white church—but the Christian church. As such he found it inconceivable—not surprising, but ecclesiologically unimaginable—that fellow clergymen would stand *in critique of* a protest against oppression instead of *in solidarity with* hurting brothers and sisters in Christ.

The next major demonstration came in the heat of the summer, on August 28, 1963. This was the famous "March on Washington," where King delivered his historic "I Have a Dream" speech. This is perhaps the most famous speech of any contemporary public figure, and it is one that still stirs the emotions of listeners today.

The Washington march was officially called the "March on Washington for Jobs and Freedom." The context for this massive demonstration[36] was that the John F. Kennedy administration had proposed legislation outlawing segregation in schools, the workplace, and in public venues. In effect, this bill would invalidate the Jim Crow laws that had been so oppressive in the South. For most who attended the march, the event was seen as support for the passage of this legislation. But there were also those who feared that if the march turned violent it could undermine the promises in the new bill.

The precise purpose of the march was controversial even within the leadership circle.[37] Some saw it as an attempt to push President Kennedy beyond where he was

---

[33] King, "Letter from Birmingham," 296–98.

[34] King, "Letter from Birmingham," 299.

[35] King, "Letter from Birmingham," 299–300.

[36] Estimates of the number of people at the march vary from two to three hundred thousand. The website "March on Washington for Jobs and Freedom" states that "more than 2,000 buses, 21 special trains, 10 charter airliners, and uncounted cars converged on Washington. All regularly scheduled planes, trains, and buses were also filled to capacity." From http://en.wikipedia.org/wiki/March_on_Washington_for_Jobs_and_Freedom, accessed May 11, 2011.

[37] Several organizations were involved in giving leadership to this event, and their leaders were all given time to make speeches, including: A. Philip Randolph, president of the Brotherhood of Sleeping Car Porters, president of the Negro American Labor Council, and vice president of the AFL-CIO; James Farmer, president of the Congress of Racial Equality;

willing to go, to equal job opportunities and comparable wages, and others wanted to offer outright criticism for the narrowness of vision reflected in the bill. There were also some blacks like Malcolm X, a Muslim religious leader and his followers, who condemned the march altogether calling it a "farce on Washington." They believed that white violence and injustice were so deeply entrenched in the structures of American society that the nonviolent route to justice simply could not work.

One of the controversies around the march centered on the youngest of the speakers at the event, John Lewis. Lewis was the leader of the SNCC, and several of his colleagues and friends had helped him write his speech. The first draft included these words:

> The revolution is a serious one. Mr. Kennedy is trying to take the revolution out of the streets and put it into the courts. Listen, Mr. Kennedy. Listen, Mr. Congressman. Listen, fellow citizens. The black masses are on a march for jobs and freedom, and we must say to the politicians that there won't be a "cooling off" period.[38]

These sentences were excised at the urging of the more conciliatory voices in the leadership, who did everything within their power to make this event successful.

The crowning speech, of course, was King's "I Have a Dream." It was set up well with music from the likes of Joan Baez singing "We Shall Overcome" and "O Freedom," Bob Dylan's performance of "Only a Pawn in the Game," and Peter, Paul and Mary's popular "If I Had a Hammer." In this context of yearning for a new day, King gave his impassioned plea for justice. The speech concluded with these famous lines:

> I have a dream that one day every valley shall be exalted, every hill and mountain shall be made low, the rough places will be made plain, and the crooked places will be made straight, and the

glory of the Lord shall be revealed, and all flesh shall see it together. . . . And when we allow freedom to ring, when we let it ring from every village and every hamlet, from every state and every city, we will be able to speed up that day when all of God's children—black men and white men, Jews and Gentiles, Catholics and Protestants—will be able to join hands and sing in the words of the old Negro spiritual, "Free at last, free at last; thank God Almighty, we are free at last."[39]

These words pack a powerful punch, but their power lies not in their clear linear logic but in their rhetorical force in presenting an imagination of peace and justice that makes room for all Americans. It *painted a picture*, and in it everyone could find a place. It was first of all a proclamation of the word of the Lord, and at one level it simply urged the hearers to get on board God's justice train. For freedom is coming; we can fight it or we can support it and perhaps even hasten it. But its coming is inevitable, not because it is a law of history, but because the universe is in the hands of a God of justice. Everyone is invited to join in on what God is doing *now*.

In some ways, the event had its desired effect, despite the assassination of President Kennedy on November 22, 1963. The Civil Rights Act was passed on July 2, 1964, under President Lyndon B. Johnson's administration. Yet the passage of the Civil Rights Act of 1964 was more a launching pad of new initiatives than a culmination of the aspirations for justice.

In the next four-and-a-half years, King made many more speeches in strategic places in the South, seeking to hasten the liberation of an oppressed people. During this time, King spent frequent intervals in prison, received many threats and personal insults, endured much harassment, and suffered police brutality. But he also received some important public accolades, like the Nobel Peace Prize on December 10, 1964. More

---

John Lewis, president of the SNCC; Martin Luther King Jr., president of SCLC; Roy Wilkins, president of NAACP; and Whitney Young, president of the National Urban League. This information is taken from the "March on Washington for Jobs and Freedom," see n. 36 above.

[38] Taken from "March on Washington for Jobs and Freedom," see n. 36 above.

[39] Martin Luther King Jr., "I Have A Dream," in *A Testament of Hope*, 219–20.

and more, King was drawn into the struggle to overcome poverty (the Poor People's Campaign was started in 1967) and into criticism of the Vietnam War.[40] In the process of giving ongoing leadership to his suffering people, he became totally exhausted. Several times he collapsed into weeping in public;[41] he had long periods of depression, did not take care of his health, and became preoccupied with his own well-being. Frequent private meetings with women friends were also reported. His exhaustion was taking its toll. During this period he said, "I am tired of demonstrating, I am tired of the threat of death. I want to live. I don't want to be a martyr. And there are moments when I doubt that I am going to make it through. . . . I don't march because I want to. I march because I must."[42]

It is interesting to notice how he narrates his struggle; he speaks as if he is caught in a process that has a life and a power all of its own. He likens his struggle to the way of the cross.[43] His biographer, Marshall Frady, quotes him as follows:

> To be Christian, one must take up his cross, with all its difficulties and agonizing and tension-packed content, and carry it until that very cross leaves its mark upon us and redeems us to that more excellent way which comes only through suffering. . . . The cross is something that you bear and ultimately that you die on. . . . And that's the way I have decided to go.[44]

King's struggle to overcome poverty for his people and to help end the violence in Vietnam cost him much personal agony. He thought he could convince the Johnson administration to bring about changes on these fronts. But he was disappointed. He became more and more convinced that the gap between the vision of the nation and the vision of the church was vast and unbridgeable, and even the process of realizing the nation's own vision of justice seemed impossible. To say this differently, the possibilities of justice were limited when sought through the corridors of power politics. This was the weakness of the Social Gospel Movement. He was not deterred—not because of what he thought he could do but because of who God was—yet he felt that his strategy had to change. So he announced to the SCLC that they must find "new tactics which do not depend on government good will, but instead serve to compel unwilling authorities to yield to the mandates of justice."[45] Here he was clearly thinking of Gandhi's approach and his success in bringing about major changes against the political odds.

The Poor People's Campaign was very hard on King. One problem was its lack of focus, which made it difficult to know where action should take place and how to measure results. But he was determined to stay the course:

> I choose to identify with the underprivileged. I choose to identify with the poor. I choose to give my life for the hungry. I choose to give my life for those who have been left out. . . . This is the way I'm going. If it means suffering a little bit, I'm going that way. . . . If it means dying for them, I'm going that way.[46]

It was this resolve that took him to Memphis in April 1968. Black sanitation workers were on strike because the mayor refused to recognize their union and King had been invited to help. He was encouraged by his staff, Andrew Young, Rev. Ralph Abernathy, and

---

[40] On Vietnam he admitted lack of expertise, but he said, "I *am* expert in recognition of a simple eloquent truth. That truth is that it is sinful for any of God's children to brutalize any of God's other children. . . ." Frady, *A Life*, 188 (emphasis in original).

[41] Frady, *A Life*, 189.

[42] Frady, *A Life*, 189–90.

[43] Although King does not expand on the way of the cross as does John Howard Yoder, the similarity is striking. For both men, the cross represents the third way between that of quiet acceptance and violent revolution. In other words, it is the way to be "like Jesus" in the face of injustice opening up the overcoming of our plight to the possibility of God's resurrection. See especially, John Howard Yoder, "The Power Equation, the Place of Jesus, and the Politics of King," in *For the Nations: Essays Public and Evangelical* (Grand Rapids: Eerdmans, 1997).

[44] Frady, *A Life*, 190.

[45] Frady, *A Life*, 193.

[46] Frady, *A Life*, 191.

others not to go because, in relation to the larger goals of overcoming poverty, Memphis was seen as a detour. Moreover, an earlier protest in Memphis had turned violent, and King felt it had discredited his personal commitment to nonviolence. Add to this the efforts of his enemies, like FBI chief J. Edgar Hoover, who was doing everything in his power to undermine his efforts. King was depressed; even his preaching in Ebenezer was excessively focused on his sense of personal failure.

Nevertheless, on April 3, King and Abernathy traveled to Memphis and checked into the Lorraine Hotel; they were late because of a bomb threat on his plane. After a brief discussion, they decided the speech that evening to the group who had gathered at Mason Temple would be given by Abernathy instead of King. When Abernathy arrived at the church, a large group had gathered in spite of heavy rain and the media was covering the event. The situation called for King, and so he was summoned. He delivered one of his most famous speeches. The imagery was familiar—the land of justice is clearly visible, not as a present reality but one that is on its way. It has been promised by God who is faithful, and so it will come, even if not for everyone. Yet everyone is invited! The tone, of course, is ominously prophetic. It ends with these famous words:

> Well, I don't know what will happen now. We've got some difficult days ahead. But it doesn't matter with me now. Because I've been to the mountaintop. And I don't mind. Like anybody, I would like to live a long life. Longevity has its place. But I'm not concerned about that now. I just want to do God's will. And He's allowed me to go up to the mountain. And I've looked over. And I've seen the promised land. I may not get there with you. But I want you to know tonight, that we, as a people will get to the promised land. And so I'm happy, tonight. I'm not worried about anything. I'm not fearing any man. Mine eyes have seen the glory of the coming of the Lord.[47]

After King finished, he fell back exhausted and drenched in perspiration into the supporting arms of Abernathy, who helped him to his chair. This would be King's last public speech. At 6:01 p.m. the next day, April 4, 1968, King was shot as he stood on the balcony of the Lorraine Hotel. What was feared by all who were close to him had happened.

KING'S WRITINGS

Although King is not well known for his theological writings, he did write several books. Most were either a collection of his sermons and speeches or reflections on his experiences, especially his many campaigns.

His first written work was a Ph.D. dissertation, "A Comparison of the Conceptions of God in the Thinking of Paul Tillich and Henry Nelson Wieman." It was submitted to the systematic theology department at Boston University in 1955. The dissertation served to establish King as a credible theologian and to identify his interest in Christian ethics. He was never really interested in systematic theology in the sense that theology needed a theoretical framework, but he went to great lengths to show that Christian ethics must be grounded in theology. As he saw it, what Christians believe ethically is rooted in a specific conception of God. And hence, what was ethically possible depended on what one believed God to be doing in this world. In his study, he analyzed Tillich's notion that love and justice do not have separate ontological sources. Love alone is derived from the nature of God. Justice is a derivative concept dependent on love. In this he also followed the general thinking of Reinhold Niebuhr.

Yet King was also critical of Tillich and Wieman for speaking too abstractly about God. God was personal, had personality, and interacted with people in the world today, effecting changes, listening to prayers, and so on. His embrace of God's creative and redemptive activities in this world would

---

[47] Martin Luther King Jr., "I See the Promised Land," in *A Testament of Hope*, 286.

become a fundamental premise for every-thing that King uttered later in his speeches.

His first book, *Stride Toward Freedom*, ap-peared in 1958 and was significant for two reasons: first, it contained the story of the Montgomery bus boycott, and second, it of-fered hope of overcoming oppression to a subjugated people. These two reasons are closely related. The Montgomery boycott was a story of success in changing the law, and it employed a wholly new approach, with which the black community was unfamiliar. So far they had seen only two options before them: a Christian acceptance of suffering and an unchristian response of violent revolution. Most chose the former because of the futility of the latter. Montgomery represented a new, third way. Here is how King put it a few years after the boycott:

> I stand in the middle of two opposing forces in the Negro community. One is the force of compla-cency, made up in part of Negroes who, as a result of long years of oppression, are so drained of self-respect and a sense of "somebodiness" that they have adjusted to segregation; and in part of a few middle-class Negroes who, because of a degree of academic and economic security and in some ways they profit by segregation, have become in-sensitive to the problems of the masses. The other force is one of bitterness and hatred, and it comes perilously close to advocating violence.[48]

King was a preacher, so it is not surpris-ing that his next two publications were books of sermons. A little booklet of two sermons appeared in 1959 called *The Meas-ure of a Man*.[49] The sermons were "What is Man?" and "The Dimensions of a Complete Life." Perhaps it is not by accident that King moves from the question "who is God" in his dissertation to "who are we" in his ser-mons. In "What Is Man?" he emphasized that, while we are glorious human beings, we are nevertheless sinful. He sought to avoid

the tendency to deify human nature while at the same time emphasizing that we are marvelous creations. He rejected the liberal tendency to view human nature as basically good and gradually getting better. He was influenced by Reinhold Niebuhr's view that as individuals we have a greater capacity for goodness than as collectives. Yet he refused to believe that this meant that as commun-ities of people we were condemned to live in violence and oppression. While clearly sin had a stranglehold on us both individually and collectively, the power of God's grace in Jesus Christ was a power far greater than the worst kind of human sin. And so God's grace can empower us to greater heights than we can imagine.

His next book was a larger collection of sermons called *The Strength to Love*.[50] It ap-peared in 1963 and included the two sermons just discussed. In his dissertation, he had en-countered Tillich's conception of *agape*—the self-sacrificial love Jesus called us to—which he contrasted with *eros*—romantic love—and *philia*—the love of affection between friends. He emphasized that Jesus does not call us to "like" our enemies, he calls us to *agape* them. He embraced Tillich's description of *agape* which he described as follows:

> All love, except *agape*, is dependent on contingent characteristics which change and are partial, such as repulsion and attraction, passion and sympa-thy. *Agape* is independent of these states. It affirms the other unconditionally. It is *agape* that suffers and forgives. It seeks the personal fulfillment of the other.[51]

Agape is the core of Christian discipleship for King. It is not that he begins with love and moves to nonviolence later in life—his is an ethic of *agape* from beginning to end. Only *agape* is not seen as a narrow, indi-vidualistic concept; it is the grounding of a

---

[48] From "Letter from Birmingham City Jail," quoted in the editor's introduction to "Stride Toward Freedom," in *A Testa-ment of Hope*, 417.

[49] Martin Luther King Jr., *The Measure of a Man* (Minneapolis: Fortress, 2001).

[50] Martin Luther King Jr., *The Strength to Love* (New York: Harper & Row, 1963).

[51] Quoted in John J. Ansbro, *Martin Luther King, Jr.: The Making of a Mind* (Maryknoll, N.Y.: Orbis, 1983), 9 (emphasis in original).

political theology. In this he differentiates himself from both Walter Rauschenbusch and Reinhold Niebuhr. His sermons in *The Strength to Love* all display this theme, and it carries right through to the last sermons he preaches. Consider his last Christmas Eve sermon at Ebenezer Baptist Church, which later became part of the Canadian Broadcasting Corporation Massey Lectures called "A Christmas Sermon on Peace." Here he says:

Somehow we must be able to stand up to our most bitter opponent and say: "We shall match your capacity to inflict suffering with our capacity to endure suffering. We will meet your physical force with soul force. Do to us what you will and we will still love you. We cannot in all good conscience obey your unjust laws and abide by the unjust system, because noncooperation with evil is as much a moral obligation as is cooperation with good, and so throw us in jail and we will still love you. Bomb our homes and threaten our children, and, as difficult as it is, we will still love you. Send your hooded perpetrators of violence into our communities at the midnight hour and drag us out on some wayside road and leave us half-dead as you beat us, and we will still love you. Send your propaganda agents around the country, and make it appear that we are not fit, culturally and otherwise, for integration, and we'll still love you. But be assured that we'll wear you down by our capacity to suffer, and one day we will win our freedom. We will not only win freedom for ourselves; we will so appeal to your heart and conscience that we will win you in the process, and our victory will be a double victory."[52]

The words "strength to love" form the basis of everything King has to say about Christian ethics. He incessantly calls his hearers to open themselves to the only power that can sustain them and give them courage and strength to be the kind of people worthy of the name Christian—the love of God.

His next book, *Why We Can't Wait*,[53] was also published in 1963. Referring to the Kennedy assassination, he says:

We are all involved in the death of John Kennedy. We tolerated hate; we tolerated the sick stimulation of violence in all walks of life; and we tolerated the differential application of law, which said that a man's life was sacred only if we agreed with his views. This may explain the cascading grief that flooded the country in late November. We mourned the man who had become the pride of the nation, but we grieved as well for ourselves because we knew we were sick.[54]

This book contains King's famous "Letter from Birmingham City Jail," written in the same year. The letter is a response to church leaders who were begging him to change his tactics. His response was essentially that when you have lived with discrimination built right into the fabric of society, you cannot use that society's structure to fight injustice. The very system itself has to change for it is sick. While King believed in governments and structured order, he also believed that unjust laws should not be obeyed.

This is one of the rare places where King gives an account of nonviolent direct action and how it works. He makes clear that it is not nonviolence that will bring about the destruction of society, but the unjust response to it may. Nonviolence is grounded in *agape*, which is a unifying power; it does not destroy. Hence, if his movement results in injustice of any kind, it cannot be laid at his feet but at the feet of those who put down his movement violently. Violence and hatred separate; love and peace unite.

He describes how nonviolent action works. There are four steps to every nonviolent campaign: "(1) collection of the facts to determine whether injustices are alive, (2) negotiation, (3) self-purification, and (4) direct action."[55] Negotiation and ample opportunity for change are always present; at the beginning of the process, in the middle, and at the end. Even the goal of the direct action is to bring about a negotiated resolution.

---

[52] Martin Luther King Jr., "A Christmas Sermon on Peace," in *A Testament of Hope*, 256–57.
[53] Martin Luther King Jr., *Why We Can't Wait* (New York: Harper & Row, 1963).
[54] Taken from the editor's introduction to "Why We Can't Wait," in *A Testament of Hope*, 518.
[55] King, "Letter from Birmingham," in *A Testament of Hope*, 290.

King's last two books were published in 1967; another collection of speeches called *The Trumpet of Conscience*[56]—which included the Canadian Broadcasting Corporation's seventh annual Massey Lectures with King's strong critique of President Johnson's Vietnam War—and a book in which he outlines his view of what justice in the United States should look like, *Where Do We Go From Here?*[57] Most work published under King's name was done in collaboration with editors and the help of friends. He was too busy leading a campaign. He did not have the luxury of careful analysis and philosophical precision. In spite of this limitation, he compiled a substantial amount of written material and, because of his rhetorical gift, he presents powerful thoughts that paint a picture of the world as a place of overcoming and potential peace. Yet the overcoming is not based on strategic, human calculations and compromising actions shaped by expediency. Instead, his was an invitation into an imagination that was primarily driven by the grace of God and only secondarily involved human agency. Sinful human beings were invited into God's re-creating activities.

THEOLOGICAL ETHICS

In conclusion, I name several themes pertinent to King's Christian ethics which are somewhat scattered throughout his writings. This is not an attempt to systematize an unsystematic theologian but an effort to name the plethora of dynamics that shaped his thought and that he used as a theologian "on the way." There is no single, unifying strand in his theological ethics, unless it is that God loves us and that we are called to love others as God in Jesus Christ invites us to.

Liberalism

As was typical in his time, King was educated by liberals. These were the teachers in the schools he attended, both Crozer Seminary and Boston University. Walter Rauschenbusch's *Christianity and the Social Crisis* (1907) and *Christianizing the Social Order* (1912) made a profound impression on King. It was here that he first saw the possibility of reading the Bible as a book about the coming of a new kingdom of peace and justice in America. This was also where he learned that Christian churches have an obligation to work for social justice. And when he contrasted the vision of the biblical, peaceable kingdom in Rauschenbusch's work with what was being preached in most American churches, he saw a huge gulf.

We have already seen how the philosophy of personalism shaped his thinking. This is a school of thought rooted in the writings of Enlightenment philosopher Immanuel Kant, which was made popular by Edgar Brightman (1884–1953). Brightman argued that Kant's famous dictum, "Always act so as to treat human beings, whether in your own person or in that of others, as an end, and not as a means" implied that that every human personality is sacred and God-given. Hence, racism is sin!

This kind of thinking resulted in a high view of human freedom, equality, and a concern for individual human rights—all common liberal concerns. Yet King learned from Reinhold Niebuhr and others that there were limits to liberalism in general and to Rauschenbusch's Social Gospel in particular. Human sin was more powerful than liberals thought, and it had ways of leading matters in directions far beyond our control. King encountered this repeatedly, yet he did not turn in the Niebuhr direction of compromise in his language of Christian ethics. In distinction from Niebuhr, King went to the Sermon on the Mount because he saw the radical sayings of Jesus as politically relevant; Niebuhr did not. His view of church did not follow the Troeltschean church-sect model. He believed that the Black Baptist Church, which Niebuhr

---

[56] Martin Luther King Jr., *The Trumpet of Conscience* (New York: Harper & Row, 1967).

[57] Martin Luther King Jr., *Where Do We Go From Here: Chaos or Community?* (New York: Harper & Row, 1967).

would have named sectarian and hence politically irrelevant, formed the basis of seeing and changing what was politically wrong with America. In fact, it was the church in its distinct identity that was socially and politically relevant. King said, for example:

> Despite this prevailing tendency to conform, we as Christians have a mandate to be nonconformists . . . there are some things in our world to which men of goodwill must be maladjusted. I confess that I never intend to become adjusted to the evils of segregation and the crippling effects of discrimination, to the moral degeneracy of religious bigotry and the corroding effects of narrow sectarianism, to economic conditions that deprive men of work and food, and to the insanities of militarism and the self-defeating effects of physical violence. Human salvation lies in the hands of the creatively maladjusted.[58]

So while King began as a liberal, he did not end there. His was not a liberal theology of either the variety of Rauschenbusch or Niebuhr because it refused to think with the dichotomies that these theologians made popular.

Civil Disobedience

King was influenced by several writers who struggled with structured injustice. One was American writer Henry David Thoreau (1817–1862). From Thoreau's essay, "On the Duty of Civil Disobedience," King learned that resistance to an unjust system is not just permissible but is a moral duty. Thoreau said:

> Must a citizen ever for a moment, or in the last degree, resign his conscience to the legislator? Why has every man a conscience, then? I think that we should be men first, and subjects afterward. It is not desirable to cultivate a respect for the law so much as for the right. The only obligation which I have a right to assume is to do at any time what I think is right.[59]

Yet King was careful that his endorsement of Thoreau did not make him sound like an anarchist. King did not share Thoreau's

negative view of government when the latter said, "I heartily accept the motto; 'The government is best that governs least.'"[60] King believed that every government was beholden to God, and therefore was called to govern justly. Insofar as it did not, its citizens ought to cease obeying its commands. The Apostle Paul's admonition in Rom 13:1-7 to "be subject to the governing authorities" was a command to obey what God had instituted, and hence what obedience to God meant. This meant that only when governments ruled justly should they be obeyed. It simply made no sense, as King saw it, for a Christian—one who had given his/her allegiance to Jesus Christ—to simultaneously also give unqualified allegiance to the state. That would inevitably create a conflict of allegiances. Yet his was not a call for anarchy or revolution; it was a reminder to all of what was required of the state under God's sovereignty and by implication what was required of faithful Christians.

Mahatma Gandhi

Gandhi taught King that *ahimsa* (nonviolence) was a creative force useful for political change. King realized through reading Gandhi's work that ancient Eastern scholars already believed that love is more powerful than hatred; that mercy is greater than revenge; and truth more life-giving than deception. The reason that he could learn so readily from Gandhi, a Hindu, was that his words confirmed the words of the Sermon on the Mount. "Do not resist an evildoer" (Matt 5:39a) may sound passive, but it is not; it was spoken by one who had the profoundest understanding and practice of the power of truth that was exemplified over and over in his life. Hence, King could respond to a reporter's question, in March 1956 by saying: "I have been a keen student of Gandhi for many years. However this business of passive

---

58 King, *Where Do We Go*, 93.

59 Henry David Thoreau, "On the Duty of Civil Disobedience," in *Social and Political Philosophy*, ed. John Somerville and Ronald Santoni (New York: Doubleday, 1963), 283.   60 Thoreau, "Civil Disobedience," 282.

resistance and nonviolence is the gospel of Jesus. I went to Gandhi through Jesus."[61]

Hence, it was clear to King that Jesus' way of responding to evil was not passive non-resistance that is shy about the use of power, which is often attributed to him by Christian ethicists like Reinhold Niebuhr. What Gandhi did for King was help him understand the *power* of nonviolent, direct action, which he saw as complementary to the "way of the cross" lived and modeled by Jesus. King saw Jesus' language of the power of love and Gandhi's language of truth-force (*Satyagraha*) as the same family of languages.

Both Gandhi and Jesus proposed a model of social change that was built on suffering and patience. King embraced this model and, of course, experienced it. Once, when black residents asked the Alabama State Legislature to place their names on the voters' list so they could vote in the next election, there was a power confrontation of the two forces—violence and nonviolence.[62] The black petitioners lined the sides of the steps into the building and requested to speak with the governor. Members of security forces came out of the building and demanded that they retreat. The protesters refused and simply repeated their request: "We want to see the governor in order to be put on the voters' list." Eventually, the National Guard was summoned, and they forcibly removed the people from the steps; however, as soon as they were removed, others took their places and repeated the same request. All of this happened to the music of freedom songs. People were beaten and even killed, but the protest continued until the black petitioners met with the governor. In embodying a simple, moral truth and being willing to suffer the consequences of rejection, the power of nonviolence in this case was greater than that of violence.

King was convinced that for Christians concerned with bringing about justice, nonviolent, direct action and radical disobedience were necessary, especially when the system was structurally unjust. A sick society cannot be healed from within.

Christian Realism and Christian Hope

As we have already seen, while King followed Reinhold Niebuhr in his limited critique of liberalism, his was in many ways the theological antithesis of Niebuhr's Christian realism. King was a pacifist who sought to be politically relevant—a position Niebuhr scorned. Certainly King was no realist. Realism was not the solution to the ills of America; creative dreaming and acting out of the imagination embodied in Jesus Christ was.

In his speech to the Montgomery crowds in 1955, he said: "If we are wrong, Jesus of Nazareth was merely a utopian dreamer and never came down to earth! If we are wrong, justice is a lie . . ."[63] Although he never waxed theological about the incarnation, King believed that in Christ God had come all the way down and in doing so had definitively embodied the way for the new humanity. That way was defined by *agape* love. It was this same *way* of oneness in Christ that the Apostle Paul characterized in the words: "For [Christ] is our peace; in his flesh he has made both groups into one and has broken down the dividing wall, that is, the hostility between us" (Eph 2:14). It is in this promise that King saw the hope of overcoming.

King believed there was little hope in Christian realism because it required faith in existing, unjust systems. Hope must be found elsewhere. To place hope in the God of Jesus Christ is to place hope in the one who raised Jesus from the dead. In other words, as King so often preached, even suffering and death

---

[61] Quoted from David J. Garrow, *Bearing the Cross: Martin Luther King, Jr., and the Southern Christian Leadership Conference* (New York: Morrow, 1986), 75.

[62] This story is told in the video documentary, "King: A Filmed Record . . . Montgomery to Memphis," produced in 1970 by Richard Kaplan and Ely A. Landau, directed by Sidney Lumet.

[63] Quoted from Frady, *A Life*, 35.

will not undermine the hope that "we shall overcome."

King's view of evil was not that different from Niebuhr's. Both thought evil was radical, powerful, destructive, individual, collective, and structural. The pervasiveness of sin and evil was a common tenet to both. In fact, Niebuhr taught King not to rely upon an optimistic view of humanity. "They will kill you even if you love them. Love offers no guarantees." King was not optimistic, but he was hopeful because of what God did in Jesus Christ. He deeply disagreed with Niebuhr's interpretation of the limited power of love because in Christ love has overcome evil. In Jesus Christ we see that salvation is by grace (love); not by violence (Eph 2:8-10). That is the ground for Christian hope.

The American Dream

For King, Christian hope was possible because it could be concretely realized in a specific place and culture. Hence, his Christian vision could not be separated from the American dream, although the two are clearly not identical. America had a problem, and the solution was the Christian vision. It was not that the goal of "life, liberty, and happiness" was wrong; it was only that the collective imagination of the American people, and especially the leaders, was such that it could not be achieved or was attainable for only a few.

Toward the end of his life, in 1967, King gave a speech called "Where Do We Go From Here?" in which he spelled out the hope that the Christian vision holds for the realization of the American dream.

> [T]he movement must address itself to the question of restructuring the whole of American society. There are forty million poor people here. And one day we must ask the question, "Why are there forty million poor people in America?" And when you begin to ask that question, you are raising questions about the economic system, about a broader distribution of wealth. When you ask that question, you begin to question the capitalistic economy. . . You see, my friends, when you deal with this, you begin to ask the question, "Who owns the oil?" You begin to ask the question, "Who owns the iron ore?" You begin to ask the question "Why is it that people have to pay water bills in a world that is two-thirds water?" These are questions that must be asked. . . . I'm not talking about communism. What I'm saying to you this morning is that communism forgets that life is individual. Capitalism forgets that life is social, and the kingdom of brotherhood is found neither in the thesis of communism nor the antithesis of capitalism but in a higher synthesis. It is found in a higher synthesis that combines the truth of both.[64]

After these words, he told the story of how Nicodemus came to Jesus (John 3:1-10). And Jesus looked at him and said, "Nicodemus, you must be born again." King writes: "What I am saying today is that we must go from this convention, and say, 'America, you must be born again.'"[65] At the conclusion of the same speech, he says, "Let us be dissatisfied until that day when nobody will shout 'White power!'—when nobody will shout 'Black power!'—but everyone will talk about God's power and human power."[66]

King was convinced that in Jesus Christ we see the moral order of the universe. In other words, Christ has to do not only with part of reality but with all of it, even its very foundation. Furthermore, not only do we see the future of the vision but we also see the way to get to the goal—that is the way of the cross. He says:

> When our days become dreary with low-hovering clouds of despair, and when our nights become darker than a thousand midnights, let us remember that there is a creative force in this universe, working to pull down the gigantic mountains of evil, a power that is able to make a way out of no way and transform dark yesterdays into bright tomorrows. Let us realize the arc of the moral universe is long but it bends toward justice.[67]

[64] Martin Luther King Jr., "Where Do We Go From Here?" in *A Testament of Hope*, 250.
[65] King, "Where Do We Go?," 251.
[66] King, "Where Do We Go?," 251.
[67] King, "Where Do We Go?," 251–52. This speech, "Where Do We Go From Here?" was King's last SCLC presidential address; it was given in Atlanta on August 16, 1967, eight months before his death.

The details of "the way" do not get spelled out in King's speeches. This is in part, at least, because it is not ours to define clearly; for we are followers of the one who will lead us there. And with this approach, openness to possibilities and surprises are key characteristics. Nevertheless, the kingdom is coming to America and to the entire world.

Preaching as Ethics

King often said things like, "In the quiet recesses of my heart, I am fundamentally a clergyman, a Baptist preacher."[68] Such comments can easily be insufficiently attended to in seeking to understand who King was and what he did. Preaching is the best form we have of doing the very thing that ethicists and theologians are often not good at: using rhetoric that places hearers into a space from which they can see the coming of the Lord. What King seemed to get away with, that most leaders cannot, is that he could "preach" outside the walls of the church.

It is said that when President John F. Kennedy watched King's "I Have a Dream" speech on television in Washington on August 28, 1963, he exclaimed "He's damned good. Damned good."[69] King's wife, Coretta, had a different response; "the kingdom of God seemed to have come on earth."[70] What's interesting about these two responses is that they are two ways of naming the same reality. Good preaching does precisely that; it is able to address a diverse body and make it one by proclaiming the truth that can heal what is broken apart. And that itself is peacemaking.

Careful attention to King's sermons reveals in many of them a pattern of four parts: *proclaiming* a vision, often spoken of as a dream; describing and working at the task of *seeing* the new reality; reminding listeners of the *assurance* that we will get there; and naming the *way* of getting there—that it must be commensurate with the character of the vision, namely, peace. Rarely is there a detailed strategy or plan of *how* to get there—the speeches are actually amazingly general—always there is an appeal to the same power that the prophets appealed to, and always there is the plea of the human stance in the movement, which is endurance and peace.

King displayed an amazing capacity for patience, not a patience with unjust structures—hence his letter "Why We Can't Wait"—but the patience of God. God's agenda cannot be rushed, it cannot be fully known, and it cannot be usurped. However, it can be seen because it is transparent in Jesus Christ—peace and justice are coming.

Malcolm X

There is a fascinating interaction and dynamic between Malcolm X and King. They represent different views, not of what is wrong with America, but of how it ought to be fixed. Both favored revolution, that is, radical social change, but one advocated violent revolution and the other pacifism.[71]

Malcolm X (1925–1965) was born as Malcolm Little in Omaha, Nebraska, and like King, had a Baptist preacher father. Growing up, he suffered much from the endemic racism of the time. But here the similarity between the two men seems to end. Malcolm went to New York and there became involved in crime and wound up serving ten years in prison. While in prison, he educated himself and encountered Islam and the movement called "The Nation of Islam." His brother was already a member, and when Malcolm decided to join he threw himself into the study of the thought of its founder and leader, Elijah Mohammad. He learned much, but eventually Malcolm would have a falling out with

---

[68] Quoted from Richard Lischer, *The Preacher King: Martin Luther King, Jr. and the Word that Moved America* (New York: Oxford University Press, 1995), 3.

[69] Frady, *A Life*, 124.

[70] Frady, *A Life*, 124.

[71] See James H. Cone, *Martin and Malcolm and America: A Dream or a Nightmare* (Maryknoll, N.Y.: Orbis, 1991). For a fuller treatment of Cone's "Black Theology," see chap. 27 below.

his leader. But his cause to liberate Black America was not deterred.

Malcolm became a devout Muslim; he even went on a pilgrimage to Mecca in 1964. But like King, he had enemies because his message and vision were for a revolutionary change of the status quo. This threatened many. He was assassinated in New York on February 21, 1965.

Both King and Malcolm were passionate about justice for America. Both saw the problem of racism as deeply entrenched in the very fabric of the nation, meaning radical measures were necessary to bring about change. And yet they had very different proposals for how that change should happen. Malcolm believed that violence, and even all-out war, was required to bring about such change, and King believed that in Jesus Christ this change was already happening. All we needed to do was get on board with what had begun with Jesus and in this way present the truth of God's victory in word and action to the powers that saw it as judgment. The

alternatives between these two approaches could not be starker! And the utter tragedy that these two liberators were assassinated in their prime could not be sadder!

CONCLUDING COMMENTS

King's approach to theological ethics was unique in American history. It was different from Rauschenbusch's approach, in that Rauschenbusch did not see the extent of the structural entrenchment of evil. Niebuhr and Malcolm X both recognized the radical nature of evil and saw no alternative but the use of violence to overcome it. King asked the American people to be more radical than they were accustomed to in their understanding of Christian discipleship. For he was convinced that in Jesus Christ, the Messiah has come, and when we accept this, we live differently in a new world; we pronounce the new reality and live it in the face of evil, regardless of the consequences. For through the way of the cross "we shall overcome!"

Chapter Twenty-Three

JAMES MOODY GUSTAFSON
(1925–)

James Gustafson is the first in our lineup of ethicists still living at the time of this writing. He has been a major force in shaping the contemporary discourse of Christian ethics, especially through teaching, directing doctoral students, and working with institutes of applied ethics.

There are perhaps few prominent American ethicists more deeply influenced and shaped by the intellectual orientation of H. Richard Niebuhr. Gustafson did his doctoral work under Niebuhr's supervision, collaborated with him on research and writing projects, endorsed his books—he wrote the forewords to *The Responsible Self* and *Radical Monotheism and Western Culture*—and served as his junior faculty colleague at Yale for a few years. Like Niebuhr, Gustafson was skeptical of an approach he called sectarian, that is, a view of church that was shaped too heavily by a christocentric perspective. He preferred a more general approach, which he called "theocentric," believing it could address more adequately a greater variety of issues. Gustafson acknowledged his debt to Niebuhr at the beginning of his book, *Christ and the Moral Life*, writing, "I might well construe this book in terms of the subtitle of H. Richard Niebuhr's *The Responsible Self*, a study in 'Christian Moral Philosophy.'"[1]

Gustafson's interest in both philosophy and theology relates to the issue of scope. God is God over the entire world, meaning that all knowledge, indeed all of life, history, and nature must be brought under the dominion and sovereignty of God. And as he saw it, philosophy named that domain of inquiry better than theology. We saw this same concern fifty years earlier with Ernst Troeltsch, who eventually was led out of the theology faculty and into a philosophy department.

HIS LIFE

Gustafson was born in 1925 in Norway, Michigan. As the name suggests, this town had historical Norwegian connections. However, today's most prominent distinctive of Norway, Michigan, is its mines. Originally, the town had a Norwegian Lutheran Church with about forty Norwegian families, but, as the town website suggests, today they are all just "good Americans" and their Norwegian heritage seems a distant past.[2] In any case, "Gustafson" was a Swedish family name. Gustafson's father, John, even spoke Swedish occasionally, and so the Swedish tradition and culture was at least minimally cultivated by the family.

John Gustafson was a minister, so young Gustafson was exposed to theological discourse early. His mother's name was Edith Moody. Not much is known about the family specifically, and so one is left to surmise the

---

[1] James M. Gustafson, *Christ and the Moral Life* (Chicago: University of Chicago Press, 1968), 10.
[2] See http://www.norwaymi.com/images/files/Where%20Norway%20got%20its%20name(1).pdf, accessed May 11, 2011.

standard dynamics of an American Christian family during challenging economic times.[3]

Gustafson attended the local North Park Junior College; after graduating in 1944, he joined the U.S. army and served as an engineer for two years in Burma and India.[4] Upon his return from military service, he headed into university education. He graduated from Northwestern University in 1948 with a bachelor of science degree, then moved on to Chicago Theological Seminary and the University of Chicago, from which he earned a bachelor of divinity degree in 1951. From there, he went to Yale University, where he received his Ph.D. in 1955. Here he studied under, among others, H. Richard Niebuhr, who supervised the writing of his dissertation, "Community and Time in the Christian Church."

After earning his degree in 1951 and writing a thesis titled, "Max Weber's Methodology," Gustafson was ordained as a minister in the United Church of God, and he served as pastor of a church in Northford, Connecticut, for three years.[5] But even as a pastor, he was engaged in scholarly research and preparing himself for further study. Hence, no one was surprised when he left the post for graduate studies. During the last year of his doctoral studies, he was the assistant director of a large study funded by the Carnegie Foundation which focused on Protestant Theological Education in America. Niebuhr was the director and so the two collaborated.[6]

Immediately after graduating, Gustafson joined the faculty at Yale, becoming Niebuhr's junior colleague. He taught at both the Divinity School and the Department of Religion for seventeen years. In 1972 he left Yale for the University of Chicago Divinity School to teach theological ethics. From there he joined Emory University in a research post and spent ten years teaching faculty members from all departments and writing on Christian ethics. He retired in 1988 after forty-three years of teaching, research, and writing.[7]

In 1947 Gustafson married Louise Roos, and together they raised four children. In retirement they live in Rio Rancho, New Mexico.[8]

Gustafson's story is an interesting contrast with that of Martin Luther King Jr., in that King's life and thought were fully public and transparent. King was an activist; Gustafson was a scholar. Even when King wrote, he wrote about his activities, and many books and articles have been written about his life. Not very much has been written about Gustafson's life, other than that he was a university professor who taught and wrote books and articles. But the lack of public attention to his activities does not mean that Gustafson was uninvolved with practical matters. In fact, Gustafson has been far more involved than most North American ethicists in public debates on bioethics, ecology, war, human rights, and so on. He saw his role as helping the nation think through a Christian response to important social issues and conceived of himself as an analyst and agent of clear thinking. He too was committed to making America more Christian than it was, but both his style and his theology were different from those of King and Walter Rauschenbusch.

---

[3] Gustafson was three years old in 1929 when the Stock Market crashed, which was followed by the Great Depression of the 1930s.

[4] This and other information is taken from the biography on the web page that details the collection of Gustafson papers held by the Archives and Manuscripts Department, Pitts Theology Library, Emory University. "James M. Gustafson Papers, MSS 256," last modified February 1, 2006, http://www.pitts.emory.edu/Archives/text/mss256.html.

[5] "James M. Gustafson Papers."

[6] This work resulted in two publications under Niebuhr's name: H. Richard Niebuhr, *The Purpose of the Church and Its Ministry: Reflections on the Aims of Theological Education* (New York: Harper and Brothers, 1956); and H. Richard Niebuhr, Daniel Day Williams, and James M. Gustafson, *The Advancement of Theological Education* (New York: Harper and Brothers, 1957).   [8] "James M. Gustafson Papers."

[7] "James M. Gustafson Papers."

HIS WRITING

Gustafson has written twelve academic books, edited several others, collaborated on projects with other writers, and authored many articles in professional journals. In all of his work, we find a steadfast devotion to the "theocentric" perspective, which he learned from Niebuhr's thought, especially his work on radical monotheism.[9] Each of his books contributes to his overall project in a distinct way.

Treasure in Earthen Vessels

This book[10] was Gustafson's first after his appointment to the Yale Divinity School. It focuses on the church. In the preface, he identifies those scholars who have influenced him the most: James Luther Adams, Ernst Troeltsch, Max Weber, Wilhelm Dilthey, and Karl Mannheim. But of course, Niebuhr's influence exceeds all others.

Gustafson states that one of the purposes of the book is "to show that the historical and social relativities of the Church is part of its essential character."[11] Gustafson sees the church as an "earthen vessel" and it is only as an *earthen* vessel that it can be an effective agent of change in this world. He says, "The Church is *earthen*—of the stuff of natural and historical life. The Church is a *vessel*, it is useful."[12] In other words, the church is not perfect, and not best understood as a spiritual entity—it is in all respects a human and social institution. Hence, it should not be lifted out of, or separated from, this world.

Gustafson's analysis of the church can be likened most closely to that of Troeltsch's thought. Like Troeltsch, he emphasized the continuity of theology with sociology. Since we live in this world, how we live is given shape by the nature of this world. This means, of course, that Gustafson has significant difficulty with the theology of Karl Barth and his followers. For it is precisely this undifferentiated association of nature and grace to which Barth said no.

For Gustafson, to name the church "a human community"[13] means, at one level, that it is a natural community, one that is political, and has a common language, and a common theory of interpretation and memory and beliefs and actions. All of this is in general agreement with the theology of Barth and his followers like Bonhoeffer. And yet there is a profound disagreement here as well. As Gustafson makes clear, the theological starting point for Bonhoeffer is the opposite of his. He quotes Bonhoeffer's starting point as follows: "Only from the idea of revelation can one come to the idea of the Christian church."[14] As the subtitle in Bonhoeffer's *Sanctorum Communio*, suggests—"A Dogmatic Investigation into the Sociology of the Church"—sociology for Bonhoeffer is not a neutral science, and its proper revelation comes best from theological investigation. Hence, he can say: "The basic social category is the I-Thou relation."[15] For Gustafson, sociology is a science and as such is independent from theology and stands in conversation with theology as an academic discipline in its own right.

The church is a "natural community" in that it commemorates many of the same activities as those outside of the church—birth, marriage, death, and so on. These are all natural phenomena, meaning that they pertain to everyone, whether Christian or not, and therefore the church's function is to add religious significance to these natural phenomena. That is, the church does not define these

---

[9] See esp. H. Richard Niebuhr, *Radical Monotheism and Western Culture* (Louisville, Ky.: Westminster/John Knox, 1993).

[10] James Gustafson, *Treasure in Earthen Vessels: The Church as a Human Community* (New York: Harper & Brothers, 1961).

[11] Gustafson, *Treasure*, x.

[12] Gustafson, *Treasure* (emphasis in original).

[13] The title of the first chapter in this book is, "The Church: A Human Community."

[14] Gustafson, *Treasure*, 13n5.   [15] Quoted in Gustafson, *Treasure*, 13n5.

events because it has no special "ownership" of them. What he means by this is that the church ensures that these events never degenerate into their naturalistic functionality as expressed in the animal kingdom. Birth, for example, is an occasion for religious significance and is celebrated with baptism because that represents "the parents' desire for the preservation of the child's good estate through life and beyond death."[16] Similarly, the church meets a "natural need" in the case of death by offering consolation and assurance that all is well despite the pain of separation.[17]

Likewise, the church is a political community formally and informally. Formally, it is an organization with a constitution and a set of rules and operations and structures; informally, it is a set of practices and patterns of communication and behavior. This is important for understanding Gustafson because the politics of the church should not be lifted out of the human and social domains. The church is an institution like (not unlike) every other institution.

Gustafson is not suggesting that God no longer acts in history, but rather that the way God acts through the church is through a human community, a social and political community. He does not say this as a concession in the sense that it would be better otherwise, but asserts this as a positive attribute because the church has power and is effective precisely on the basis of its humanity, even its sinful humanity.[18]

Christ and the Moral Life

His first book was about the church; the second book was about Jesus Christ. In both, Gustafson is concerned about the structure of the moral life. This book is less a programmatic effort to clarify in what sense Jesus Christ is relevant for Christian ethics and more an analysis of how Christian ethics that

has been seen as Christocentric is limited. He serves notice here that a more comprehensive treatment of the moral life would call for a theocentric approach. He again relates his view to the "natural theology" of Thomas Aquinas, but even more so to that of Karl Barth. He suggests that, according to Barth, "not only one's view of man, but the task of theological ethics is to be governed by revelation, and not by independent views of man or ethics."[19] Then, referring to his own work, he adds, "Clearly this book is written from a different perspective."[20]

Gustafson uses chapter headings that all begin with "Jesus Christ" but have separate subtitles like: "Lord who is Creator and Redeemer," "the Sanctifier," "the Justifier," "the pattern," and "the teacher." He concludes the book with what he calls "A Constructive Statement." Here he identifies in what way Jesus Christ "does make, can make, and ought to make," a difference for the moral life. He suggests that one of the differences Jesus Christ makes for Christians is with respect to disposition and names two important dispositions central to the Christian life. First is the disposition to be hopeful, which is "grounded in trust in the goodness and power of God, a goodness and power that has a vaster time-and-space span than the particular experience of one man in one time, or a generation of men in one place."[21] Second, Gustafson says Christians ought to be "inwardly free, not bound by paralyzing fears and the necessity to justify themselves in the eyes of God or man."[22]

His summary of the constructive way in which Christ is the norm for Christian living is instructive. He says:

> Christ is the norm for the Christian's theological interpretation of what God wills that life should be among men; Christ is the norm for illumination of what the Christian ought to be and do in his actions; Christ is the central obligatory norm

[16] Gustafson, *Treasure*, 17.
[17] Gustafson, *Treasure*, 18.
[18] See Gustafson, *Treasure*, 111.
[19] Gustafson, *Moral Life*, 9.

[20] Gustafson, *Moral Life*, 9.
[21] Gustafson, *Moral Life*, 251.
[22] Gustafson, *Moral Life*, 253.

for those who would order their lives in disciple-ship to him.[23]

He illuminates this further in two ways, first with respect to the theme of humaniza-tion. "If God's will is that of humanization, Christians ought to be doing what God does; that is, they ought to be engaged in human-izing activity."[24] The second elaboration speaks to the options available to Christians. He says, "I would affirm that the Christian finds Christ to be a norm that illuminates his options and, insofar as he is loyal to Christ, deeply conditions his choice."[25] This does not mean that Christ prescribes the options for us nor that he dictates the choice. "Agency, the capacity to decide, to act, to initiate and respond, is not only our human condition, but it is such by creation, and I believe neces-sarily is respected by the providential power of God."[26] This has some significant implica-tions for how we should understand moral agency. It means that sometimes we need to think of ourselves as acting analogically in re-lation to what Christ did; sometimes we need to follow the command to love; sometimes we need think parabolically, and so on.[27] But always we ought to seek to bring to bear the "light of Christ." Gustafson says we ought to "Bring his light to bear upon the place where one's own life before God and the world is enacted."[28] Christ helps us to seek the light, but "Christ alone is [not] sufficient as a light, a norm, to shape one's decision in a given occasion."[29]

He goes on to warn the reader that Chris-tians ought not to consider themselves as somehow morally superior to those of any other position or group. Nor are we in any way to separate ourselves from the world as we seek to live by the light of Christ. "Rath-er [Christians] are impelled to share in the struggle of every man for whom Christ died, every man created by the Father who is known in Christ, every man under the lord-ship of Christ."[30]

Can Ethics Be Christian?

This book[31] begins with a story intended to highlight the sense in which ethics can be said to be Christian. The story recounts an experience which took place in a bar in a Manhattan hotel. Gustafson and his col-league went for some relaxing drinks after a hard day's work on a collaborative pro-ject. Here they encountered a drunken sol-dier ordering yet another drink. He gave the bartender a twenty-dollar bill but received change for only five dollars. Gustafson's col-league immediately intervened, insisting that the soldier receive his proper change. After an argument, the bartender gave the soldier his correct change. The soldier kept drink-ing, and it became clear that he would soon pass out. After talking to him, the colleague took the soldier's wallet from his pocket to determine his identity and place of residence. Then he led him out of the bar, hailed a cab, and gave ten dollars to the driver with a note explaining what he had done. He included his own contact information at the hotel in case someone wished to get in touch with him. He then went back into the bar and told the bartender that he would report the inci-dent to the hotel manager the next morning.

Gustafson makes the point that his col-league was not religious and not a Christian. And yet he realized that what was taking place in that bar was morally wrong—cheating is

---

[23] Gustafson, *Moral Life*, 265.

[24] Gustafson, *Moral Life*, 266.

[25] Gustafson, *Moral Life*, 268.

[26] Gustafson, *Moral Life*, 268.

[27] Gustafson spells out these options further in "The Place of Scripture in Christian Ethics: A Methodological Approach," *Interpretation* 24 (1970): 430–55.

[28] Gustafson, *Moral Life*, 269.

[29] Gustafson, *Moral Life*, 269.

[30] Gustafson, *Moral Life*, 270.

[31] James Gustafson, *Can Ethics Be Christian?* (Chicago: University of Chicago Press, 1975).

morally wrong and vulnerable people need protection! The experience that took place in that bar had all the markings of a moral experience and yet was not a Christian experience. In fact, Gustafson says his colleague "would find nothing particularly 'Christian' or even religious about what he did: its motives, its pattern of action, its consequences."[32] This then sets up the question of what difference it could have made had his friend been a conscientious Christian. After all, if a non-Christian can act in an exemplary fashion, even modeling behavior for Christians, then why be Christian or, as Gustafson pushes, what does it mean for ethics to be Christian?

This line of inquiry leads Gustafson to examine how we become moral beings. This is for him a highly psychological and sociological question but also a theological one. He gives the example of Mennonites, and says that, although not all Mennonites are the same, the general claim can be made that they "live with relative simplicity."[33] How can this be explained? His answer is that "individual members of the [Mennonite] community have been shaped by its ethos of loving service to those in need; there has been a coherence between the professions of faith and the style of life and activities of the community."[34]

Yet not all individuals who are part of the same socializing process are equally moral or moral in the same way because the relationship between religious living and moral activity are complex.[35] After all, there are all kinds of forces that impact the sort of persons we are becoming. "Religious persons are not 'clones' of Jesus Christ; they are not 'carbon copies' of what is most distinctive about his being. Rather, their experiences of the reality of God, their believing in God, occur in and through the individual and social aspects of their beings, through their personal and cultural experiences."[36]

So what is the move from the affirmation that God is love to becoming a loving person? In attempting to answer this question, Gustafson makes the point that it has everything to do with the understanding of the human condition. In other words, the power of sin is such that human dispositions and intentions are deeply affected by self-interest, which can never be overcome. This is true of the human condition in general—not just of Christians; nor is this a uniquely Christian account of the human condition. That is, the notions of grace and sin, while deeply Christian notions, best describe the human condition as such. This helps us understand his friend in the bar, who, while a virtuous person, was not a *Christian*, virtuous person. Nevertheless, the Christian affirmation of the reality of God ought to make a difference to the sort of person one becomes.

Gustafson finds it helpful to push the question, "Why be moral?" and he does not see this as a religious question, or even primarily a religious question. He invents a hypothetical conversation to explain what he means. He postulates asking his colleague why he did what he did. His colleague's answer is "that the bartender was dishonest and he believed in honesty." But why? Because human society cannot function well if persons are dishonest with each other." But why care about the well-being of human society? "Well, just because I do," could be his only answer.[37]

The more Gustafson writes, the clearer it becomes that he is pushing for a shift away from the concept some Protestants like Dietrich Bonhoeffer have based Christian ethics on—namely, *Nachfolge Christi* (following after Christ), which Catholics have preferred to call *imitatio Christi*. Gustafson is more comfortable with what he calls the "imitation of God."[38] This is the beginning of a turn he makes to what he will later call theocentric ethics. But here, by "imitation of God," he

---

[32] Gustafson, *Can Ethics Be Christian?*, 22.

[33] Gustafson, *Can Ethics Be Christian?*, 59.

[34] Gustafson, *Can Ethics Be Christian?*, 60.

[35] See Gustafson, *Can Ethics Be Christian?*, 63.

[36] Gustafson, *Can Ethics Be Christian?*, 64.

[37] See Gustafson, *Can Ethics Be Christian?*, 83f.

[38] Gustafson, *Can Ethics Be Christian?*, 114ff.

means something quite specific. Obviously, human beings cannot be God. He summarizes his idea as follows:

> God has done such and such for the well-being of creation; go and do likewise. God seeks justice for the weak and the fatherless; God seeks to maintain the rights of the afflicted and the destitute; God seeks to rescue the weak and the needy; God seeks their deliverance from the hand of the wicked. Go and do likewise. God has met man's deepest needs in love; men thus are to meet the deepest needs of their neighbors in love.[39]

Part of Gustafson's reason for moving from "imitating Christ" to "imitating God" stems from his fear of sectarianism. In other words, everyone is under the lordship of God but not everyone is under the lordship of Christ. Even his bar colleague can be seen as acting under what God wills, even though he is not a Christian. God is sovereign over all people of this earth; Christ is Lord only over those who confess him as Lord.

This shift from Jesus Christ to God as the ground for ethics helps him in coming to understand human, moral agency. He says the question, "'what is God enabling and requiring me (us) to be and to do?' is grounded in an affirmation of greater human autonomy, that is, in a view of persons and communities as agents."[40] This is not to suggest that Jesus is irrelevant to Christian ethics, but it is to affirm, as he says in another work, that "Jesus is not God."[41] Of course Christians follow Jesus Christ, but when Christians engage in the enterprise of Christian ethics, they move beyond Jesus Christ to God. Under God, we can speak a language of universality and rationality that is not available to us through Jesus Christ.

So can ethics be Christian? For Gustafson the answer depends on what we mean by "ethics." If one's ethical claims are justified on the basis of a narrow religious view—whether that be Christian or Jewish or Muslim—then not.

> If, however, that principle were justified on the ground that it is a universalizable principle, and therefore one on which presumably all rational persons can agree, the process would be in the realm of ethics. Indeed, the biblical language might be interpreted to mean that one ought to respect each person as an end in himself, or in some similar way, in order to cleanse it of its particular historical religious overtones.[42]

Hence, the sense in which it is intelligible to speak about ethics as Christian is threefold: first, is to recognize that our reason for being moral is not fundamentally a religious reason. Our religious convictions, of course, require that we be moral, but our being moral is not lodged within our religious convictions. Second, following closely from the first, to be moral agents is not the same as to be religious agents. To be a religious person has moral implications, but to be a moral agent does not require religious convictions. And third, the justification for our moral point of view is not distinctly religious, but our religious convictions help us to shape and to motivate our moral point of view.[43]

Gustafson's colleague in the bar displayed admirable moral behavior even though he lacked religious convictions. This is evidence to Gustafson that the moral realm is independent of the religious, even though the religious realm requires moral life. He recognizes the danger for this to be misinterpreted, and so he concludes his book as follows:

---

[39] Gustafson, *Can Ethics Be Christian?*, 116.

[40] Gustafson, *Can Ethics Be Christian?*, 157.

[41] James M. Gustafson, "The Sectarian Temptation: Reflections on Theology, the Church and the University," in *Proceedings of the Catholic Theological Society* 40 (1985): 93. The longer quotation is as follows: "Faithful witness to Jesus is not a sufficient theological and moral basis for addressing the moral and social problems of the twentieth century. The theologian addressing many issues—nuclear, social justice, ecology, and so forth—must do so as an outcome of a theology that develops God's relation to all aspects of life in the world, and develops those relations in terms which are not exclusively Christian in a sectarian form. Jesus is not God."

[42] Gustafson, *Can Ethics Be Christian?*, 169.

[43] See Gustafson, *Can Ethics Be Christian?*, 173.

If readers now ask, "If this is the case, then why be religious or Christian?" they have missed the basic point of the book. If one is Christian or religious in order to be moral, just as if one is Christian in order to be happy, the heart of religion is not yet grasped. The heart of religion is the experience of the reality of God, mediated through all sorts of other experiences.[44]

With this book, Gustafson has set the direction for his programmatic approach to Christian ethics. It now remains to be worked out in more detail. This is left primarily for his two-volume work, *Ethics from a Theocentric Perspective*.[45] I will analyze his thoughts on this subject under a separate heading.

In summary, Gustafson is concerned throughout his work with the question of ethical methodology, that is, metaethics. In other words, he asks repeatedly how ethics can be done in a manner that takes account of contemporary cultural forms and scientific knowledge. To this end, he makes many distinctions like the religious realm and the ethical realm, Protestant and Catholic ethics, theology and philosophy, teleology and deontology, faith and reason, church and sect, and so on. In the end, he wants to fudge some of these distinctions and bring them together under the sovereignty of God. He acknowledges that this gives him an instinctive bent to the Reformed tradition, even though he does not accept the ethics of that tradition uncritically.[46]

THEOCENTRIC ETHICS

From what we have seen of his work so far, clearly it is Gustafson's objective to present an alternative approach to Christian ethics intended to address the problems of contemporary ethics. His next two books take on that task explicitly. It is helpful to ask what contrasts with "theocentric ethics." Throughout his writings, Gustafson names two problems his approach will correct: the christocentrism of sectarianism and the anthropocentrism of contemporary ethics generally. So far, we have seen the strongest criticism directed at the "discipleship of Christ" ethics (christocentrism) common in Protestant thought. In his two-volume work *Ethics from a Theocentric Perspective*, Gustafson addresses the second problem, namely, that "man has become the measure in religion, theology, and ethics"[47] (anthropocentrism). He observes that, particularly where Protestantism has been prominent, Western culture has believed that God is there to fulfill human desires.

Gustafson is well aware that his effort to move away from an ethic emphasizing human fulfillment will be met with resistance. It is hard for us to accept that there may be something that is good in general but not good for us in particular. Yet it is so and should not be denied, even though the dangers in the theocentric approach should not be ignored. In warning against these dangers, he names a cause for "moral pause"[48] as follows:

> If man is seen more in continuity with the ordering of nature, and less in terms of the "grandeur" that is his as a result of his freedom, then it is easy to demean his value and significance. We need to be forthright about the moral perils that can result from going in this direction. . . .[49]

---

[44] Gustafson, *Can Ethics Be Christian?*, 179.

[45] James M. Gustafson, *Ethics from a Theocentric Perspective*, vols. 1 & 2 (Chicago: University of Chicago Press, 1981, 1984).

[46] See Gustafson, *Theocentric Perspective*, chap. 4, "A Preference for the Reformed Tradition," 1:157–93. Later in a panel discussion, he speaks about beginning his ethical project, as did his mentor H. Richard Niebuhr, by affirming that God is acting in every action upon us, that "It gets hard after that not to go to Calvin when Calvin says that God is not simply a determiner of a course of events, but the agent determining virtually the cause-effect sequence of every particular event in accordance with God's purposes." Harlan R. Beckley and Charles M. Swezey, eds., *James M. Gustafson's Theocentric Ethics: Interpretations and Assessments* (Macon, Ga.: Mercer University Press, 1981), 229. It needs to be said, however, that despite these words Gustafson does not wish to follow Calvin closely in his doctrine of predestination.

[47] Gustafson, *Theocentric Perspective*, 1:83.

[48] Gustafson, *Theocentric Perspective*, 1:99f.

[49] Gustafson, *Theocentric Perspective*, 1:99.

The shift from anthropocentrism to theocentricsm is necessary because it shows greater promise in overcoming the current problems of ethics. In basing an ethic on God, and not on human subjectivity, the "perils of ethics" are simply lessened. One such example relates to "ecological ethics." A tendency in our day arising from traditional formulations of Christian ethics is the romanticization of nature. But given what we currently know about the natural order, this is short-sighted. To simply let nature take its course, as if the natural is the good, is foolhardy. The natural can cause untold misery—mosquitoes cause malaria, parasites thrive in polluted water, there are earthquakes and droughts, and so on.[50] While the turn to theocentric ethics cannot be an uncritical one, it nevertheless is important to cultivate the larger good that moves beyond the concern for the individual. Gustafson says:

> The turn toward theocentric ethics requires that consideration be given to the "larger good," and even to the "good of the whole." This could, if not carefully developed, lead to the suppression of the well-being of the species, or of individuals, for the sake of the "whole." Grave issues have to be acknowledged."[51]

Gustafson also identifies a religious or theological pause. There is, after all, nothing more dangerous than a religious fanatic with access to weapons who gets his "instructions from God." Much evil can be done in the name of such a "theocentric ethic." History bears witness to such logic; slavery has been defended that way, the Crusades were rationalized on the basis of doing God's work, the ancient Hebrews conquered the Canaanites in the name of Yahweh, and so on.[52] The claim to know the moral law of God can result in much that is evil.

In spite of these "perils" implicit in a theocentric ethic, Gustafson is undaunted in his quest to move forward. His confidence springs from his view of God. If we view God aright, these problems can be avoided! The traditional view of God is personal and in the service of human well-being. This view must go because it is a recipe for confusing "my will" with "God's will." To protect against this confusion, a theocentric ethic focuses on the notion of the justice of God. God's justice is for the entire universe, not just for human well-being. This move prohibits the "use" of God for distorted personal purposes. He says:

> If God is "for man," he may not be for man as the chief end of creation. The chief end of God may not be the salvation of man. Man's place in relation to the universe has to be rethought, as does man's relation to God. The moral imperative that I shall develop in due course is this: we are to conduct life so as to relate to all things in a manner appropriate to their relations to God.[53]

This view will no doubt produce discomfort for many traditional adherents to the Christian faith, for it implies that human salvation is not the end of the Christian faith; God's concern for our salvation must be placed within a wider universal context. Says Gordon Kaufman in summary of Gustafson's position:

> Theocentric ethics, thus, does not depend particularly on maintaining a personal relation to God or Christ, or on commitment to biblical faith, or even on claims to some kind of definite or certain knowledge of God, though any or all of these may be in some ways involved for particular individuals or communities. A theocentric orientation is essentially a particular way of "construing" the ordering we actually find in human experience and in the world . . .[54]

Gustafson's own summary emphasizes that the Western moral tradition places

> man at the center of all valuation, or as the ultimate value, and sees all things in the service of man.

---

[50] His examples. See Gustafson, *Theocentric Perspective*, 1:105f.

[51] Gustafson, *Theocentric Perspective*, 1:106.

[52] His examples. See Gustafson, *Theocentric Perspective*, 1:107.

[53] Gustafson, *Theocentric Perspective*, 1:112–13.

[54] Gordon D. Kaufman, "How Is God to Be Understood in a Theocentric Ethics?" in *James M. Gustafson's Theocentric Ethics*, ed. Beckley and Swezey, 19.

The theological construal of the world that I have proposed fundamentally alters this view. It follows from that construal that there are occasions or circumstances in which a course of action that is apparently beneficial to the well-being of individuals or communities is not necessarily the right thing to be done.[55]

Of course, at one level this is not a very radical claim. Christian ethics has always held that human beings ought to obey God rather than earthly authorities, even when it causes personal suffering and discomfort. In this way, what Gustafson is saying is quite consistent with martyrdom ethics. Yet clearly Gustafson is not advocating a martyrdom theology. His theocentric ethics is cast quite differently!

One way of getting at what Gustafson is saying requires that we investigate the meaning of his concept of "construal." The self-understanding of his task as theologian involves engaging in a constructive or imaginative task of developing a coherent interpretation of God's relation to the world, perhaps better said, "God's enabling power." But on what basis can this be done? Here he compares himself to Karl Barth as well as to Catholic natural law ethics. Like Barth, Gustafson wants to begin with God. But he freely acknowledges that his difference from Barth is a difference of "how God and God's relation to the world are *construed*."[56] Barth rejects natural theology in a way that Gustafson does not, and Barth accepts natural law in a way that Gustafson does not. Barth sees God as "wholly other," and, while Gustafson also wants to see God as "Other," Gustafson claims to "know" God through natural and human means.[57] Because of his notion of revelation, Barth reads ethics, indeed the entire world, as inherently theological, whereas Gustafson "construes" knowledge of God and ethics through natural philosophy and the sciences. Hence, as he admits, he differs radically from Barth because for Gustafson

the discernment of the divine will is a human discernment, and any final judgment (whether morally right or not) is always a human judgment. Practical moral reasoning, based on resources Barth cannot legitimately include as well as on the kinds of "instruction" he does include, seeks to discern the will of God according to the maxim that we are to relate ourselves and all things in a manner appropriate to their relations to God. . . . Discernment is based upon human understanding of proper ordering and relationships, proper ends of human activities. It is not based upon hearing a particular command and obeying it.[58]

Whenever Gustafson compares his own thought to Protestant and Catholic theology, we see him more inclined toward Catholic theology because of his suspicion of a scriptural dogmatism common in Protestants like Barth and his attraction to the Catholic's embrace of natural theology. Natural theology, as Gustafson sees it, places human beings within the natural order and so can avoid the "turn towards the subject" as well as the "turn towards revelation" common in Protestant theology. Yet when Gustafson speaks of natural theology he does so quite differently from Catholics like Hans Urs von Balthasar, for example.[59] Catholic theologians do not speak of natural law without an appeal to the *analogia entis*, which unites nature and grace in ways that makes nature unintelligible in relation to itself. Nature becomes knowable only when it is perceived through the revelation of divine creation. Hence, the point could be made that Barth is more Catholic than Gustafson grants, and the manner in which Gustafson utilizes natural law is less Catholic than he thinks.

For Gustafson, everything is interpretation, which is but another way of emphasizing

---

[55] Gustafson, *Theocentric Perspective*, 2:5.

[56] Gustafson, *Theocentric Perspective*, 2:27 (emphasis added).

[57] If God were to be "wholly other" for Gustafson, he, like Barth, would need to admit knowing God only through God's self-disclosure. Yet this is not a move Gustafson is willing to make.

[58] Gustafson, *Theocentric Perspective*, 2:33.

[59] See chap. 16, above.

construal. He summarizes his theocentric approach via four base points as follows:

> These base points are: (a) the interpretation of God and God's relations to the world and particularly to human beings, and the interpretation of God's purposes; (b) the interpretation of the meaning or significance of human experience—of historical life of the human community, of events and circumstances in which persons and collectivities act, and of nature and man's participation in it; (c) the interpretation of persons and collectivities as moral agents, and of their acts; and (d) the interpretation of how persons and collectivities ought to make moral choices and ought to judge their own acts, those of others, and states of affairs in the world.[60]

No one would really disagree with Gustafson's emphasis that all of life is interpretation, but the primary question, given this claim, is, "What guides the interpretation?" And here Gustafson is less than fully clear. He is clear on what does not guide it: revelation in the Barthian sense, tradition, the authority of Scripture, the hermeneutical community called church, and so on. Saying it this way should not undermine the value of Gustafson's frequent reference to Scripture, tradition, church, and even to Barth, but these are of only general relevance in the construal of his view of responsible, moral existence. More important factors in the intellectual operation for Gustafson are human experience, science, natural philosophy, and reason. However, while naming the components of the operation, he is unclear on what rules govern this operation such that they will produce faithful, moral practices. This leads ethicist John Howard Yoder, who admittedly has a different approach to ethics, to say:

> My general objection [to Gustafson's approach] is that the rules distinguishing valid from invalid reconstruction need to be more clear. My objection here is that invoking the name of God specifically in favor of one's own project over against the others may be petitionary, self-contradictory, and impious.[61]

Gordon Kaufman, who substantially agrees with Gustafson's constructive theocentric project, nevertheless is worried that he ends up with a kind of stoicism or theological naturalism.[62] Although Gustafson speaks of God as Creator and Sustainer, he has failed to give an account of God that enables him to do so. Says Kaufman:

> The God he has described cannot be understood as significantly present in or working through those powers that have actually brought humans *qua their humanity* into being and that continue to sustain them in being. The God Gustafson describes—and which I would be inclined to call simply "nature"—is essentially the structure and order of inanimate being and of life that we find in the world around us (and also in our own existence).[63]

The web of debate into which Gustafson is cast involves profoundly basic questions, like "Who defines God?" and "What are the rules of the constructive process?" Although Gustafson is less than clear in answering these questions, he is firmly committed to the principle that the answers are to be found within a particular form of the human construal process where no transhuman or transcultural criteria are admissible. This naturally causes some readers to wonder how then his project can in principle overcome anthropocentrism. Certainly many Barthian theologians would see Gustafson's approach as a primary case *of* anthropocentrism in need of a theology of revelation that is open to the self-disclosure of God in Jesus Christ.

---

[60] Gustafson, *Theocentric Perspective*, 2:143. It is important to acknowledge that Gustafson sees himself not only giving an account of how Christian ethics works, but also giving a phenomenological description of the nature of ethics in general. He would argue that all sound approaches to ethics have these four points in common, albeit the first point would need to be modified to accommodate a nontheological ethic.

[61] John Howard Yoder, "Theological Revision and the Burden of Particular Identity," in *James M. Gustafson's Theocentric Ethics*, ed. Beckley and Swezey, 72n14.

[62] See also Robert Audi, "Theology, Science, and Ethics in Gustafson's Theocentric Vision," in *James M. Gustafson's Theocentric Ethics*, ed. Beckley and Swezey, esp. 181f.

[63] Kaufman, "How Is God to Be Understood," 28 (emphasis in original).

ASPECTS OF THE MORAL LIFE

In the second volume of his *Ethics from a Theocentric Perspective*, Gustafson considers several common topics of the Christian moral life: marriage and family, suicide, population, and bioethics. And for each, he suggests how his theocentric approach analyzes and discerns responsibly. I cannot, in this short chapter, present his thinking on each issue, hence I will select only one: marriage and family.[64] I make this choice in part because I find it laudable that Gustafson treats this subject as a matter of Christian ethics. After all, family is the context for moral formation, and the topic of family is often left to just the conservative voices. Moreover, other topics are far more popular in the lineup of contemporary social issues; perhaps this is because moral formation is not viewed as very significant by Christian ethicists today.

In discussing marriage and family, Gustafson begins, as is predictable by now:

> Our question is, What is God enabling and requiring us to be and to do as participants in the patterns and processes of interdependence in marriage and family life? Our response to this will be guided by the general answer, We are to relate ourselves and all things in a manner appropriate to our and their relations to God.[65]

Gustafson points out that many things have changed over the years with respect to the rights of spouses and children and thus, what constitutes a good marriage and a good family today must be measured with these "moral advancements" in mind. In any case, the contemporary ideal is very different from the farm family in rural America of a few generations ago. While our understanding of a good marriage has changed over time, nevertheless the concept of marriage has remained. Couples still bind themselves to each other, have children, and raise them in the best way possible. There is little today's parents want more than the very best for their children.

Gustafson names several ideal types or models for marriage but rejects them all as irrelevant for Christian ethics. Not surprisingly, he wishes to replace the old, moral logic by moving away from the standard approach that argues from the ideal to the real; the theocentric approach asks how we should respond so as to respond to God. In other words, he exploits the model he has learned from Niebuhr and one that follows directly from his own work. How does this help us in thinking through the morality of marriage and family?

He begins by suggesting that marriage and family are signs and evidence of God's ordering of life in the world.[66] Yet there is no absolute ordering that pertains to the pattern of marriage that is somehow derived from the mind of God. For example, monogamy is with us because there is an approximate 1:1 ratio of male and female in our species. If this ratio were otherwise, monogamy would not have the moral status that it has. In other words, our pattern of monogamous marriage is not derived from an "outside" principle but from culture and nature. Society is properly ordered when it leads to a human and cultural flourishing—one that "works" properly and takes into account what we need and who we are.[67] Hence,

> [M]arriage and family are grounded in the biological function of species survival: this is the function of sexuality at the most basic biological level. This function we share with most living species, both animals and plants. Hence, marriage and family are social institutions grounded in our nature as individuals and as moral beings.[68]

---

[64] For an interesting essay on this topic, see Stephen G. Post, "Marriage and Family," in *Christian Ethics: Problems and Prospects*, ed. Lisa Sowle Cahill and James F. Childress (Cleveland: Pilgrim Press, 1996), 265–83. This volume, a *Festschrift* for Gustafson, contains essays on several other ethical topics that pertain to Gustafson's work.

[65] Gustafson, *Theocentric Perspective*, 2:153.

[66] See Gustafson, *Theocentric Perspective*, 2:153.

[67] Gustafson is sometimes called a pragmatist and a utilitarian; neither are terms he quarrels with, although he does not conscientiously develop his approach under either label.   [68] Gustafson, *Theocentric Perspective*, 2:160.

It is important to Gustafson to speak about such natural and social functions as marriage in terms of how we see ourselves as responsible under God. After all, "God is both the ordering power that preserves and sustains the well-being of the creation and the power that creates new possibilities for well-being in events of nature and history."[69] So marriage and family are best seen as gifts and tasks. They are gifts in the sense that enormous joy and personal fulfillment can come from them and simultaneously tasks in that to produce well-being, both personal and social, they require great effort. In his words:

> [T]hey are signs both of the "grace" of God and of the "law" of God given through nature. . . . God is enabling and requiring us, as participants in the interdependence of marriage and family to be stewards, deputies, or custodians of one another and of life itself. We are agents of the divine ordering and empowering of human life in the world.[70]

The notion of steward is far-reaching for Gustafson. For example, in addition to stewardship of our material resources, time, and talents, we are also stewards of our gene pool and of our species, and here science and technology have enabled us to be better stewards today than we were in the past. Our families are also stewards of culture. "Social, moral, and aesthetic values and other aspects of culture are carried to some extent from generation to generation through the medium of family life."[71]

All of this relates to the claim that marriage and family are a school for piety and morality. Children are imitative beings and learn through copying behavior from elders, especially parents. They share this trait with other animals. Hence, it is especially important for there to be a comfortable context, like the monogamous family, in which children can

learn. Parents are by definition role models; the only question is whether they are good or bad ones. Nurturing children into moral responsibility under God's ordering and enabling power is important not only for the well-being of our children but also for the flourishing of community and culture.

There is also an important justice principle at play here, one that governs the well-being of marriage and family, especially in relation to the treatment of children. This concept can be challenging because each child is different, and hence learning the skills to do this is fraught with ambiguity. But for Gustafson, risk and improvisation are fundamental to how ethics works. There are no absolute rules or principles on the theocentric model, since the path toward which ethics moves is always determined by the contingencies of human and cultural realities.

Gustafson argues for an open debate within larger society about how to provide conditions for the well-being of family life and to name those that are harmful. In his discussion, he is openly opposed to the influence of the "Moral Majority"[72] in America, which sought to monopolize and define the institution of marriage and family life in accordance with abstract principles derived from ancient beliefs and not from the language of current, cultural sustainability. His specific criticism on this front is that leaders like Jerry Falwell are claiming the moral high ground when in fact there are important arguments to be made against his claims.

In addition to stewardship, Gustafson also emphasizes the importance of commitment and vocation in marriage. Both are needed to foster the stability and continuity necessary for the moral formation for children. For Gustafson, family is not an independent moral unit but one that participates in,

---

[69] James Gustafson, *The Contribution of Theology to Medical Ethics* (Milwaukee: Marquette University Press, 1975), 19.

[70] Gustafson, *Theocentric Perspective*, 2:164.

[71] Gustafson, *Theocentric Perspective*, 2:166.

[72] The Moral Majority was begun by Jerry Falwell in the mid–1970s for the purpose of giving voice to the moral views of ordinary American people. Among their emphases were support for family values and the traditional view of family, opposition to abortion and homosexuality, and so on.

indeed shapes and sustains the social reality of, every culture. In this sense, marriage is not a private act but a public one.

It is therefore not surprising to see Gustafson address the significance of the religious and moral wisdom of the marriage act. He argues that it is important in any ordered society like America for marriage to be performed in the church and be seen as ordained by God. Not only is it a public act, but it is also a religious one. He identifies with the traditional three characteristics of marriage. First, it has to do with the procreation of children. For children to be brought up in the "fear and nurture of the Lord," they need to be raised in the charge of caretakers who will nurture their spiritual and moral welfare. This is a socialization process that requires the learning of language and moral skills. It does not happen by itself on the basis of intuition or conscience; it requires the cohesive social reality of family.

Second, marriage is ordained by God for the remedy of sin. In other words, marriage is an ordering of sexual activity. The power of this normal sex drive should not be left without ordering, or it will turn from being a gift intended to beautify to a curse threatening the destruction of relationships. Hence, "Sexual intercourse is a moral matter; conditions of moral responsibility must be met."[73]

The third way marriage is seen as ordained by God is that it is for the purpose of providing comfort and mutuality of relationships for all aspects of life both in prosperity and adversity. This is in harmony with what God wills for the world. Marriage becomes the context in which love flourishes. Hence, he concludes by saying about the traditional "Solemnization of Matrimony" that

> [I]ts religious and moral wisdom is deep and well-grounded, and that is no doubt why it has become traditional. It is not archaic but timely, and is backed by the theocentric perspective and the ethics following from it which we have developed in this book.[74]

For Gustafson, marriage is not an end in itself; its *telos* is found in the well-being of the social order sustained by a God who wishes to preserve the goodness, beauty, and justice of society. This is not an "orders of creation" theology because, as he sees it, there is no ideal form of the family toward which we should strive. The form is determined by a kind of striving; the bringing to bear well-being, flourishing, care, and justice for all of society. These are God's goals for creation; these should be our goals as we seek to be responsible to God's enabling power upon us. For God works through nature—meaning that God works through those who are open to the ends of God's rule.

CONCLUSION

Gustafson's theocentric approach to ethics seeks to make compelling what H. Richard Niebuhr first envisioned. Niebuhr brought two important notions together: radical monotheism and responsibility. For him, the logic of Christian ethics went like this: first we seek to determine what God is doing in this world and then the ethical task is to pattern our lives in such a manner as to respond to, or to fit into, God's actions. Hence, Niebuhr's approach necessitated the crucial theological task of discerning God's activities in the world.

Gustafson accepted only part of the Niebuhr approach. He states his limited acceptance of his mentor's ethics as follows:

> I think I nowhere say that we discern what God is doing. That is what my mentor, H. Richard Niebuhr, said, that he could discern what God is doing. I think that I have always been very careful to say that we do not discern what God is doing. What I said is that we seek to discern what God is enabling and requiring us to be and to do.[75]

---

[73] Gustafson, *Theocentric Perspective*, 2:179.

[74] Gustafson, *Theocentric Perspective*, 2:184.

[75] In a panel discussion in *James M. Gustafson's Theocentric Ethics*, ed. Beckley and Swezey, 226.

This language leaves Gustafson rather vulnerable. It is difficult to see how to determine "what God requires or enables of us" if we cannot know what God is doing. It seems that Gustafson can say little more than that we ought to do whatever moves society in the direction of well-being. Admittedly, we can discern this from a God who is said to be Creator and Sustainer. But is this all that can be said for Christian ethics? Certainly it leaves some ethicists to wonder.

Stanley Hauerwas wonders whether this limitation stems from the agenda that was set by Walter Rauschenbusch in seeking to Christianize the social order. He suggests that once the task of Christian ethics becomes that of making all of society Christian the question that follows is how ethics can be Christian.[76] And insofar as that question can be answered affirmatively, it can do so only by the most general appeal to God. Yet Gustafson's general appeal to God does not mean it lacks passion. And the affirmation of human moral agency is just as strong. Certainly Gustafson has pushed his readers to improvise, to be creative, to take the moral charge in improving the world, and so on.[77] He has an indefatigable belief that God wills that this world be a better place and that the call to the moral responsibility of human beings is toward that goal. Hence, his concluding words in *Ethics from a Theocentric Perspective* make a fitting conclusion to this chapter; "God does not exist simply for the service of human beings. Human beings exist for the service of God."[78]

[76] Stanley Hauerwas, "On Keeping Theological Ethics Theological," in *The Hauerwas Reader*, ed. John Berkman and Michael Cartwright (Durham, N.C.: Duke University Press, 2001), 51.

[77] See esp. Albert R. Jonsen, "The Ethicist as Improvisationist," in *Christian Ethics*, ed. Cahill and Childress, 218–34.

[78] Gustafson, *Theocentric Perspective*, 2:322.

Excursus

PART III-B

Whereas the European group of early twentieth-century theologians presented in the previous section were heavy on theology and not that explicit in their ethics (with the exception perhaps of Bonhoeffer and Sölle), the American early twentieth-century theologians presented in this section are much more explicit in their ethics and not that demanding in their theology. It is interesting that Bonhoeffer, after spending time at Union Theological Seminary in New York, expresses similar sentiments about the shallowness of theological engagement in the American context. He was unimpressed with both students and professors but impressed with what was happening in the African American church.

The six scholars presented in this section are diverse, North American voices on what it means to live as Christians. All have been deeply influenced by and some formally educated in the European liberal tradition. Most of them read Troeltsch, Barth, and Bonhoeffer. All struggled with issues of peace and justice.

By far the most important theological force in North America during this time was the rereading of the gospel teaching on the kingdom of God. This led directly to the Social Gospel, which in many ways revolutionized the reading of the gospel itself. Although they embraced the social interpretation of the gospel in very different ways, after Walter Rauschenbusch all North American Christian ethicists had to come to terms with its impact.

SOCIAL GOSPEL

It is interesting to see how the Social Gospel gets narrated by Rauschenbusch. There was no doubt in his mind that the old language of the kingdom of God—that it was a spiritual kingdom, and hence politically irrelevant—was a false reading of the Gospels. Clearly, the new kingdom was social-political; hence just as God, through the teachings and life of Jesus, was building a kingdom of peace and justice on earth, so God wills to work through every faithful Christian in America. Hence, poverty, meaningful employment, racism, capitalism, and social inequities of every kind were to be brought under the scrutiny of Jesus' teaching of the kingdom. And the flourishing spirit of democracy in America made it the perfect setting for this new, gospel message. No one needed to be convinced of the importance of freedom, peace, and justice—it was all already there. What was required was for the churches to get on board and see the social revolution as the message of the gospel. So evangelism needed to be reconceived.

It did not seem to occur to Rauschenbusch that not only was there a new message of social justice not noticed in the gospel before, but that the way God's kingdom was being realized, as was seen through the telling of the biblical stories, was also new. That the slaves in Egypt were liberated by the miraculous hand of God and that Jesus died in the process of "establishing" the new kingdom and was resurrected by an act of divine grace, never made it into the discussion of how

413

the new kingdom was to be brought about in America. In fact, he openly advocated the old rule of continuity—causal power relations—employed by established political and social structures. The old philosophy of history—how history changes—was not rethought.

The Social Gospel logic of social change seemed to be borrowed from the liberal philosophers and went something like this: the important aspect of Jesus' teaching on the kingdom was what he was *pointing to*. It was not *how* Jesus was doing what he did, or why, that really mattered; it was rather what he was seeking to achieve that mattered. The ethic derived, therefore, looked as follows: for Jesus to be our moral guide meant that we, like him, were mandated to establish the kingdom of God on earth, a goal that was also his but one which he was not able to fully realize. Given Jesus' failure, we should perhaps even question his strategies. Although it was never said explicitly, the language sometimes suggests that twentieth-century North America had a better chance at success than a first-century Palestinian rabbi because the conditions were more favorable now—democracy, better-educated public, high moral standards, and so on.

This made for easy (tempting) connections with the dominant, liberal notions of the day, like the inevitability of progress driven by technology and education and the assumption of the essential goodness of human beings. It also meant that Rauschenbusch and J. S. Woodsworth were set up for personal failure and disappointment. Perhaps this is more evident with Woodsworth than with Rauschenbusch, and perhaps it is because in Canada the Social Gospel revolution for a while looked more promising. Woodsworth was able to make several important changes to social legislation through government power structures, which Rauschenbusch was not. But when he sought to make Canada (and even his own political party) pacifist, he failed.

What is interesting in Woodsworth's case is that he claims he needed to give up on both the church and the state to remain a Social Gospel pacifist. That might well be a commentary on the failure of the church, and it certainly speaks to the strength of Woodsworth's theological convictions. The church as he saw it had accommodated to the cultural logic of the inevitability of war as the way to deal with social-political conflict without the benefit of the Christian vision to which he so passionately held.

Both Rauschenbusch and Woodsworth seem to stand outside the church in ways that appears somewhat tragic in the sense that they received so little theological and spiritual support from their church community. Moreover, neither spent much time developing a theology of church other than to see it as an agent of social change. Of course that is not wrong, but it is the nature of this agency that requires careful nuance if it is to be faithful to the biblical call of the Social Gospel. In other words, can one really understand Social Gospel change in terms of continuity, or does the story of Jesus teach us the importance of being open to *discontinuity*, that is, the reality that God is acting in the very arena of history in which we are called to act? In other words, how do we place ourselves ethically into God's miracle? This is a strange ethic indeed but it seems to be what is called for if we take the cross-resurrection story seriously. And it calls for the kind of ecclesiology that works at making meaningful a language of the Christian community entering into participation with the divine.

CHRIST AND CULTURE

The issue of "participation in the divine" leads directly to the dispute about whether God still acts in history. This debate took place between the Niebuhr brothers and later involved James Gustafson as well. It is directly related to the issue of divine and human agency. If resurrection is at all morally relevant for us today, we are required to make intelligible an apocalyptic view of history that Rauschenbusch and Woodsworth were unable to empower.

What is at stake here is clearly articulated by contemporary theologian Graham Ward in his book, *Christ and Culture*. In reflecting on the words of Thomas Aquinas, "God is not known to us in His nature, but is made known to us from his operations,"[1] Ward says:

> Taking our cue from this statement by Aquinas, the Christological question begins not with *who* is the Christ or *what* is the Christ; it begins with *where* is the Christ. The Christological enquiry therefore does not begin with the identity of the Christ, what in dogmatics is the nature as distinct from the work of Christ; it begins with an analysis of the operations whereby Christ is made known to us. And in being made known we participate in him.[2]

Ward's work attempts to evaluate what went wrong in the American discussion on the relation of Christ and culture. As a corrective, he suggests a renewed emphasis on body. As we see from the words above, they connect Christology with the body of Christ. In other words, Christ is made known to us in the embodiment of Christ, that is, as we participate in the body of Christ. This suggests that Barth and Bonhoeffer were on the right track in their association of Christology with ecclesiology. Yet Bonhoeffer went much further and somewhat in the direction that Ward suggests and, it seems, that the American Social Gospel ethicists did not pick up on.

The unresolved debate of the six theologians presented in this section, according to the work of scholars like Ward, sets up a false agenda. For the logical binary (a false binary) names the distinction between Christ and culture by lifting Christ out of culture—making him someone else than a first-century Palestinian Jew—that is, he is de-bodied. Although H. Richard Niebuhr fought valiantly to retain the notion that God acts in history, the Christ-culture dualism made that very difficult. Hence in his "Christ as Transformer of Culture" model, he is unable to bring to bear a view of history and philosophy of social change that was different from that of

Rauschenbusch. In the end, it differed very little from the model of "Christianizing the social order."

The Christ and culture dichotomy as Niebuhr viewed it still has currency in many circles; in particular it appeals to the Protestant churches in North America. But there are at least two problems with this language: one is that Christ is not appropriately named in opposition to culture since he was a first-century Palestinian Jew, that is, fully encultured. And the second issue is whether we know what culture really names since cultures are contingent and vary from place to place. It is in this regard that it becomes important to notice the differences in reception between Rauschenbusch's and Woodsworth's work. We saw within Canada, through the work of Woodsworth, that the Social Gospel was received in the shaping of national politics in ways that it was not in the United States. In other words, the embodiment of Christ's message is a contingent matter, and just because the receptivity to the politics of Jesus in the United States was what it was, does not mean that it needs to be that way in all places. For the expression of human sin and the propensity for violence by human beings are also culturally contingent; yet this is where God acts and this is also where we are invited to act. Not only that, God is in charge of the development of history, which means that we can neither understand it fully nor can we control its movement.

So then if the "Christ and culture" language gets us off course, where can we look to see the alternative of a participation model at work? Perhaps the answer is in the work of Martin Luther King Jr. Clearly he did not develop an American version of incarnation theology, but in many ways he expressed it. And perhaps he learned this approach from his years of worship in the African American church, where he experienced the immediacy of encountering Jesus. For when Jesus is

---

[1] Thomas Aquinas, *Summa Theologica* I, Q. 13. Art. 1.8.
[2] Graham Ward, *Christ and Culture* (Oxford: Blackwell, 2005), 1.

present, then all that is required is to speak the truth of the pains of the world so that the inflictors of such pain can hear it. For Jesus promises to heal. Perhaps it is also this simple reality that struck the young Bonhoeffer when he worshipped with the black community, and explains why that experience led him to name black worship as the most important locus of American theology.

PART IV

CRITICAL RESPONSES TO TWENTIETH-CENTURY
CHRISTIAN ETHICS

•

Section A
Christian Social Philosophers

Chapter Twenty-Four

GEORGE PARKIN GRANT
(1918–1988)

George Grant came from a distinguished, Canadian family with roots in Great Britain. His parents were William Grant and Maude Parkin; both were from prominent families dedicated to scholarship and the development of the new country of Canada in the early twentieth century.[1] William was born in 1872 and Maude in 1880. Maude attended McGill University at the turn of the century. After graduation she became the dean of women in a residence at the University of Manchester in England. During this time, William was studying at Oxford University and the Parkin family lived in the same region since Maude's father, George, set up and then administered the world-renowned Rhodes Scholarship. The close proximity with the Parkin family made it relatively easy for William and Maude to meet and come to like each other.

They were married before they left for Canada in 1911, where William had a new job as history professor at Queen's University in Kingston, Ontario. They would have three girls, Margaret, Charity, and Alison, before George was born in Toronto on November 13, 1918.

William was fortunate to be well-connected socially and politically. When Upper Canada College[2] (UCC) was experiencing low enrollment, the trustees cast around for advice for new leadership. Two influential figures were consulted: the former headmaster of the college, who was Maude's father, George Parkin, and William's brother-in-law, Vincent Massey, an influential businessman in the region.[3] Both recommended that William become principal, and so he was appointed to the position in 1917. This is how it came about that the Grant children grew up in the elite surroundings of UCC. The family resided at the college, which proved to deeply shape young George's life, until William's death in 1935.

HIS EARLY LIFE

While his sisters contest the claim, Grant often spoke of having had an unhappy childhood.[4] It is certainly true that he was driven to succeed, especially by his extremely ambitious mother, who reminded him over and over that he was George Parkin's grandson.[5] There was a great deal of class consciousness in the family. All the women in the family

---

[1] The biographical information is taken largely from William Christian, *George Grant: A Biography* (Toronto: University of Toronto Press, 1994).

[2] Upper Canada College was established in 1829 and was modeled after the prestigious Eton College in England. It is located in Toronto, Ontario. It was intended as a prep school, especially for King's University (now University of Toronto).

[3] Vincent Massey, George Grant's uncle (married to Maude's sister Alice in 1915), was head of the family-owned agricultural equipment company, Massey-Harris, and he later became a prominent Canadian dignitary. He was appointed Canada's High Commissioner in London in 1935 and was the first Canadian-born governor general of Canada from 1952 to 1959.

[4] Christian, *George Grant*, 15.

[5] Christian, *George Grant*, 36.

were powerful personalities, single-minded and determined. This extended from his sisters, who were all older, to his mother, his grandmother, and even to the parlor maid.[6]

Whatever the personality dynamics in Grant's extended family, his was a life of privilege. He had all the great world literature and art at his disposal; access to the best schools; opportunities for travel, recreation, and sports; occasions to meet important political leaders and more—that is, all the benefits of an upper-class lifestyle.

By the time Grant enrolled as a student at UCC, where his father was principal, he was quite familiar with the school. This may have given him an advantage; in any event, he was a first-rate student. He was known as Willie's boy and excelled, especially in literature, history, art, and politics, but not in sports.

At the time, UCC was a Christian school. This is where Grant heard his father give daily chapel services. Religion in the Grant household was not of the evangelical variety. Biographer William Christian tells the story of mother Maude's encounter with the American evangelist, John R. Mott. After he had finished preaching, "Maude was so disgusted by Mott's attempt to link the spread of the Gospel with the world-wide triumph of the English-speaking peoples that, according to George [Grant] in an interview with his Uncle Raleigh in 1972, she walked out and said she 'would never have anything to do with organized religion again.'"[7] Grant suggests that his mother was not particularly devout, even though the family regularly attended church. Christian faith and the church were simply givens that were not challenged but, especially in his mother's case, held in check. This did not mean that faith was unimportant, certainly not for Grant of whom it was said that, as a schoolboy, he was a "deeply religious person."[8]

Later in life, he became part of the Anglican church.

Faith was never merely a matter of subjective piety for Grant; it led directly to public stances on social issues. For example, the story is told about how he became convinced of pacifism while at UCC. The school required boys to join the cadet corps when they entered high school. Grant's close friend, Michael Gelber, had already protested this requirement at the school he attended prior to coming to UCC, and now he sought to do the same here. So he had his mother write a note to the principal asking to be excused. Biographer Christian reports, "He was summoned to the principal's office and asked why he had come to the school if he were not prepared to abide by its regulations."[9] Yet Gelber was granted the exemption in due course. Since Grant's father was the principal, it was more difficult for Grant to ask his parents to intercede on his behalf, and so he never escaped the requirement, although he wished he had. However, he remained zealous in his effort to convince fellow students to become pacifists. One such effort involved reading a book called *Cry Havoc*.[10] Although this book was negatively reviewed in the school paper, *College Times*, its antiwar perspective affected many students, including Grant. It clinched his convictions that war was senseless and evil.

Although Grant did not at this time link his pacifism explicitly with his Christian convictions, his politics in general clearly arose out of his thinking as a Christian. This he learned from his father who, for example, saw it as a Christian priority to promote the League of Nations at the school. This new forum for international debate held out the promise that peace could indeed be the conclusion of rational discourse with enemies. This led Grant to become a member of the

---

[6] See Christian, *George Grant*, 12–15.

[7] Christian, *George Grant*, 29.

[8] Christian, *George Grant*, 29.

[9] Christian, *George Grant*, 27.

[10] Beverley Nichols, *Cry Havoc* (Toronto, Ontario: Doubleday, Doran, 1933).

League of Nations club. He often heard his father describe the Great War, which he knew from first-hand experience, as a time when "the best young English-speaking Canadians went away to be slaughtered in an absolutely senseless war."[11] Yet Grant's stance on war was only the beginning of a career of struggle with how to live, think, and speak in a society that was drifting away from an embrace of the giftedness of truth, beauty, and goodness.

Since William married when he was thirty-eight years old and Grant was the youngest of four children, and because William died in 1935 at age sixty-three, Grant was left fatherless when he was only seventeen. This created considerable stress on both him and his mother, and even between them. As he said later, "My mother programmed me for ambition"[12] and his father was no longer there to intervene when the pressure became unbearable for Grant. Grant and his mother were emotionally very close, yet life without William was a new reality for both of them. For the first time in her life, at age fifty-seven, his mother needed to work to earn money and so became the dean of women at the Royal Victoria College at McGill University in Montreal.[13] Among other things, this meant that she and George were now separated.

Grant went off to Queen's University in Kingston after graduating from UCC in 1936. This was both freeing and very lonely for him. He craved his mother's love desperately. But there was work to be done. The enormous pressure to succeed pushed him into his studies.

In his undergraduate program, Grant was interested in history and international affairs. He was a good student and won several scholarships. Already here Grant was concerned with the public role of the university. When a prominent businessman, Sir Edward Wentworth Beatty, the president of Canadian Pacific Railway, came to Queen's to address

a group of students, Grant became appalled at the close relationship between big business and the university. He sarcastically described what he heard as, "We have the money and if you university professors don't do and say what we want, out you get."[14] Since Beatty was also chancellor of McGill, Grant even sought to persuade his mother to resign in protest from her position as dean of women at McGill.

While a student at Queen's, Grant wrote a short essay on "Art and Propaganda." His thoughts on aesthetics, morality, and society anticipate his later, more refined thinking. But already here he claimed that "Propaganda, far more effective and far more insidious than physical force, becomes the means whereby civilization may lose its finer instincts and political freedom may become the despised product of a past age."[15] Throughout his entire career, he struggled with permitting beauty and truth to be themselves in shaping human consciousness.

In 1938, on the advice of the principal of Queen's, Grant applied for a Rhodes Scholarship. Contrary to his own expectations, he was successful in obtaining it. Yet his departure for Oxford would need to wait until his work for the Bachelor of Arts degree from Queen's was done.

This was a very tumultuous time for everyone, let alone those, like Grant, who were interested in international affairs. In 1939 war appeared more and more likely. How would he respond if war should break out? Would he join the army? One hears his struggle in correspondence with his mother.

If one is a Christian one must be forced back without doubt that one can never fight. Force cannot vie with force. Christ could have called on the angels to tear the temporal power of Jerusalem into ten billion fragments but he didn't because he realised that by passive resistance he won in the long run because he realised that if he let tyranny, stupidity & foolishness be destroyed they would

[11] Christian, *George Grant*, 30.
[12] Christian, *George Grant*, 39–40.
[13] Christian, *George Grant*, 37.
[14] Christian, *George Grant*, 43.
[15] Christian, *George Grant*, 46.

crop up again. . . . Therefore if one is a Christian one cannot fight. Of course if one isn't there is no reason in the world why one shouldn't fight. . . . But of course when war comes one must not say "I won't fight; I won't fight." One must [propagate pacifism] so that other people won't fight. I don't think it is nearly enough to just sit still and be killed. Of course again if you say that Christ was not divine then the whole argument is broken through. All I say is that if Christ was right & inspired then one is breaking divine law if one fights *however* just one's cause is. Because Christ's cause was just and still he wouldn't fight force by force. Of course this does not mean that you cannot fight with word & deed reaction & oppression, that you cannot even risk your life under the dictatorship for the sake of asserting your cause.[16]

Britain entered the war on September 3, 1939, and Canada followed a week later. Grant was now faced with another immediate question. Should he go to England to study or should he defer like so many other young Canadian Rhodes scholars were doing? He decided to go, and in early October he, with only one other Canadian Rhodes scholar, left for a new experience on the now dangerous seas.

In Oxford he studied law which, he admitted, was notoriously difficult. There was much that he missed about Queen's, but he soon made several good friends, one of whom was Peter Clarke. Clarke was also a pacifist, as were about 15 percent of the students at Balliol College, where Grant was studying.[17] To be a pacifist in England during wartime was no simple matter. But the students had some help from A. D. Lindsay, who was a Scot "teaching and writing" at Balliol. He was married to a Quebec Quaker and freely presented his pacifist convictions in chapel sermons, as well as in a booklet called *Pacifism as a Principle & Pacifism as a Dogma*.[18] This

helped the young aspiring scholars to think carefully about how resistance to war could be justified theologically.

Resisting war in wartime is no theoretical matter. A disturbing experience for Grant involved his friend Peter Clarke, who applied for conscientious objector (CO) status and was denied. How wrong it seemed to Grant for a society to waste a brilliant person's contribution for refusing to do what was wrong. It affected him deeply.

The war also affected Grant personally. His studies were interrupted when the university had to close. The question he faced was whether to return to Canada. This was difficult for him because there was no assurance that he would receive CO status back home. He was not a member of an Historic Peace Church,[19] and so exemption from military service would need to be sought on the basis of individual conscience. And experience had shown that that was difficult. For advice, he went to the Canadian High Commission in London, where he had family friends, Mike and Marion Pearson.[20] This was in the summer of 1940; in June, France was overrun by the German army. It was also the time when the Oxford COs under the leadership of a prominent pacifist, Vaughan Williams, set up a medical response service called the University Ambulance Unit. Grant decided to volunteer and train for work in that unit.

In September Grant experienced the London Blitz with bombing raids continuing for eight months. During this time, Grant had a job as a warden for the Air Raid Precautions unit, an experience that affected him deeply.

Toward the end of the summer, Grant was restless and torn. He became ever more conscious that he was a Parkin, meaning he was born to serve king and country. Was he really doing that? Quite suddenly and somewhat

---

[16] Christian, *George Grant*, 54 (emphasis and square brackets in original).

[17] See Christian, *George Grant*, 59.

[18] A. D. Lindsay, *Pacifism as a Principle & Pacifism as a Dogma* (London: SCM Press, 1939).

[19] The Historic Peace Churches, Mennonites, Amish, Hutterites, Quakers, and Church of the Brethren, had an agreement with the Canadian government to permit members in these groups to receive exemption from military service.

[20] Lester B. (Mike) Pearson was then a senior diplomat at the Canadian High Commission and later became the Prime Minister of Canada (1963–1968). Christian, *George Grant*, 63.

out of character, he decided to "join the navy." He writes, "I am going to try to get into the navy or the merchant marine next week even though I think it is one of the stupidest, most useless, basest actions I have done. But people expect it so there one goes . . ."[21] He went through the entry process, including a medical examination which he failed because "the x-ray revealed a tubercular lesion."[22] This discovery sent him into a panic because he feared the worst when he heard the word "tuberculosis." So after some time of aimless wandering in Great Britain, with virtually no contact with family and friends, he returned to Canada in 1942. His friends and family were surprised at his poor health when they finally saw him, and his doctors ordered him to rest. Tuberculosis was not making him sick, because his lesions were inactive, but he was emotionally run down. It took until the fall of 1942 before his spirits began to recover.

During his convalescence, Grant read many of the classics, like Dostoevsky and Tolstoy, and learned especially about the patience of God. He reflects on this notion thus:

> God sees the truth but waits. Personally it is a great emotional discovery of God, the first glimpse of that reality . . . but so beyond our comprehension that the mere glimpse is more than we can bear. God not as the optimist, nor as the non-mover, but God *who sees the truth but waits.* . . . For me it must always be *credo ut intelligam.* The opposite of that is incomprehensible.[23]

Grant had become a kind of medievalist in his thinking. *Credo ut intelligam* (I believe in order to understand) was the twelfth-century Anselmic maxim that gave priority to faith as the framework which alone makes the world intelligible. In other words, reality is not comprehensible in its own terms. To know the world truthfully is to know it in relation to God. This was the conviction of the medieval theologians, which they learned from Augustine, who got it from Jesus and Socrates.

It was not until February 1943 that Grant began to work again, taking a job with the Canadian Association of Adult Education. During this time, he published two pamphlets; one was called *Canada: An Introduction to a Nation*, and the other *Empire: Yes or No?* On May 8, 1945, the European war ended, and many people celebrated. But he could not. He said, "I felt very lonely in Toronto that day."[24] For how can one celebrate after the death of so many people? War is evil and after evil comes repentance, not celebration.

Now that the war was over, he received permission from Oxford University to resume his scholarship. At Oxford, he was advised to enter a doctoral program that brought together the study of law and theology. He was surprised by this counsel but took it, even though he had no clear focus or interest to guide his research. He gradually became convinced that he should write on the Scottish theologian John Oman, and he threw himself into his studies.

The two years at Oxford were rich in many ways. He came to love engaging with C. S. Lewis, who ran the Socratic Club. He found him to be clear, lucid, and profound in his views on how Plato could illuminate Christian apologetics. It was also at these meetings that he met a special person, Sheila Allen, who was an English reader at Oxford. Like Grant she was a pacifist and had spent the war years working in hospitals taking care of the wounded. They quickly discovered that they had much in common.

During the fall of 1946, Grant received a letter from Hart House at the University of Toronto (U of T) inviting him to consider becoming its warden (dean of the men's residence). After careful consideration, he accepted the invitation. Shortly after he had agreed, however, he was informed that the invitation had been withdrawn because the board of directors had ruled that his "war record as a pacifist would make it difficult to deal with the many returning servicemen

---

[21] Christian, *George Grant*, 82.
[22] Christian, *George Grant*, 84.

[23] Christian, *George Grant*, 93 (emphasis in original).
[24] Christian, *George Grant*, 106.

who had enrolled at U of T."[25] He was beginning to discover the costs of putting himself against the mainstream.

But all was not lost. Not long after the withdrawal from Hart House, he received an invitation from Dalhousie University in Halifax to teach philosophy. Philosophy was not what Grant had prepared for, but he was intrigued and took the job. So, well before his doctoral work was finished, he had accepted a teaching post, even though his teaching would not begin until September 1947, giving him a full year to write and attend to some unfinished business in England.

Sheila Allen and Grant had become quite fond of each other. One day he phoned her and asked her to come to see him. When she arrived at his house, the landlord handed her a letter which she read, but it was written in such convoluted style that she could not be sure whether he was asking her to marry him. So she listened for clues in their subsequent discussions and concluded that he had. When they went to her mother's house to share the good news, Shelia's mother responded in shock and horror, with the words, "I wish I were dead."[26] She had just lost her husband, and the thought of losing her daughter to a man from Canada was unbearable. Whenever Grant told the story in later years, he usually added that from then on the relationship between him and Sheila's mother only got worse. Although they had initially planned to marry a year later, after Sheila had finished her studies, they now decided to make arrangements for her to write the examinations early, and they married before they departed for Canada.

In September 1947, Grant began to teach philosophy at Dalhousie. He was now a married man with a job but an unfinished doctorate. Children soon arrived, six in all: Rachel, William, Robert, Catherine, Isabel, and David. Life was full and rich.

In 1950 Grant returned to Oxford to receive his D.Phil. for a dissertation titled "The Concept of Nature and Supernature in the Theology of John Oman." He was now set to be an academic in Canada, and indeed, he had thirty-nine years of fruitful teaching and writing and continued to write until one year before his death.

From 1947 to 1960, Grant was a professor—and for many of those years—head of the department of philosophy at Dalhousie University. He left Dalhousie for York University in Toronto but resigned in protest almost as soon as he got there. After a year as a consultant at the Institute for Philosophical Research, he went to the Department of Religion at McMaster University, where he taught until 1980 before returning to Dalhousie for the last eight years of his career.

WRITINGS AND THEMES

When Grant began to teach, he clearly had an agenda. His overall concern was that modern schools were producing generations of students who do not know how to think. He did not wish to contribute to this unfortunate turn. It had nothing to do with the quality of students; it had something to do with the teachers, although even more basic, it had to do with what we moderns have come to believe about what is real, what is thinking, and what is knowledge. That, in turn, has affected how we have structured our universities and their academic programs. Our university curricula reflect that it is more important for students to learn to become "doers," that is, technicians, than it is for them to become knowers of the truth. It should not be surprising, therefore, that students turn out the way they do—their first concern being what they will achieve in life—for that is what we have taught them.

Early in his teaching career, in 1951, Grant was asked by the Massey Royal Commission of the Arts to write an essay on the state of philosophy in Canada. The purpose of the Commission was to make recommendations regarding the state and future of Canadian

[25] Christian, *George Grant*, 126.

[26] Christian, *George Grant*, 131.

culture. Grant's essay aroused deep anger among fellow Canadian philosophers, especially Fulton Anderson, who was then the head of the philosophy department at the University of Toronto; this would come back to haunt Grant later. He was accused of wanting to "turn back the clock" to an earlier understanding of philosophy. The issue had to do with the effects of modernity on Canadian culture, and specifically, whether philosophy was an inherently secular enterprise or not. These two notions are, according to Grant, directly related. In an interview with biographer Christian shortly before Grant's death, he was asked to reflect on what he had learned from the strong, negative reaction to his essay. As Arthur Davis summarizes, Grant said he accommodated to this negative reception of his views only "to teach and write indirectly about the figures he chiefly admired, Socrates and Christ."[27] Sheila Grant's reflections on this event are poignant: "I do remember that this article . . . shocked the philosophic community to the core. He had criticized the teaching of philosophy in Canada for completely ignoring the Christian tradition. This may have prevented him from ever being offered a job at the University of Toronto."[28] I have chosen to present the argument of this essay here in some detail because it is basic to everything else Grant wrote.

The essay begins with a bold statement: "The study of philosophy is the analysis of the traditions of our society and the judgment of those traditions against our varying intuitions of the Perfection of God."[29] Lamenting that in Canadian universities philosophy is seen too narrowly, Grant's intent is to give philosophy the broadest possible definition so that it cannot be hoarded by specialists in philosophy departments. He asks, "Why do our universities fail to provide a place where young Canadians are encouraged to think about their world in the broadest and deepest way?"[30] The lament goes even deeper; our universities concentrate far too much on training technicians. For they turn out doctors, physicists, lawyers, psychologists, and sociologists, all important doers and therefore technicians, but they do not turn out people who know how to think about what is true, beautiful, and good. And this is where philosophy can help because "philosophy is not in essence a technique."[31] The purpose of philosophy is "to relate and see in unity all techniques, so that the physicist for instance can relate his activity to the fact of moral freedom, the economist see the productive capacity of his nation to the love of God."[32]

Grant postulates that it may be that Canada is too young to afford this kind of reflection. After all, a pioneering society needs people who are good at developing and building up the general infrastructure, which requires a set of technological skills. But Grant does not believe that this is the reason for the ghettoization of philosophy, which has largely become a service subject and thereby been redefined as something other than it truly is. Philosophy should never be made to serve the interests of technology or the sciences. This is precisely what has happened with Canadian philosophy departments. "Philosophy [is] thought of as a secular study to suit the modern world and the secular university."[33] Philosophy is no longer free to pursue the *love of wisdom*.

Our universities need to remember that historically they were grounded in the church. Grant argues that the Catholic Church has demonstrated a better memory here than the Protestants. Catholic universities have insisted on grounding their students in the tradition of scholastic philosophy, particularly the thought of Thomas

---

[27] Arthur Davis, ed., *Collected Works of George Grant*, vol. 2, *1951–1959* (Toronto: University of Toronto Press, 2002), 3.

[28] Davis, *Collected Works*, 4.

[29] William Christian and Sheila Grant, eds., *The George Grant Reader* (Toronto, Ontario: University of Toronto, 1998), 157.

[30] Christian and Grant, *George Grant Reader*, 158.

[31] Christian and Grant, *George Grant Reader*, 159.

[32] Christian and Grant, *George Grant Reader*, 159.

[33] Christian and Grant, *George Grant Reader*, 161.

Aquinas. In Aquinas we have a presentation of a world seen through truth and goodness. Hence, we have here the capacity for judgment. Protestant institutions have fared less well, partly because of Martin Luther's doctrine of *sola scriptura* and his accompanying scorn for Thomism. Reading the Scripture alone is not enough, according to Grant, because Scripture does not yet show us how it ought to be read nor how its reading is related to the reading of the world. In fact, Luther's kind of exclusive "dualistic" scriptural emphasis has participated in the "freeing of philosophy from a dependence upon faith, even in those very institutions founded and supported by the men of Protestant faith."[34] So Grant concludes that "Philosophy has been, by and large, taught in the universities of non-Catholic Canada as a secular study not necessarily connected with the progress of faith."[35] And this he laments!

Grant singles out several individual scholars as examples of doing philosophy in the manner he is suggesting: people like literary critic Northrop Frye, English professor A. S. P. Woodhouse, and political economist Harold Innis. Yet most of his examples were not teaching in Canadian philosophy departments.[36] The reason he lauds these scholars is because each sees his discipline of study as occupying space within a larger domain of truth. And when you remove the larger context, you become a technician because your inquiry is guided by a very narrow goal. Our university curriculum rests upon a tragic split between activists and people of contemplation. Lawyers, economists, medical doctors, and engineers don't think; and thinkers are given a narrow arena of reflection and hence are impractical.

What Grant is calling for is a "more unified conception of education."[37] This is directly related to how a curriculum is structured. He is less critical of an undergraduate curriculum than a graduate one, because "advanced degrees [should] not be granted unless the student shows some grip of the tradition."[38] He singles out the Pontifical Institute of Medieval Studies in Toronto as a model in bringing together history, theology, art, and literature. Here an overarching goal of truth and its understanding are the driving force.

Grant's understanding of the world is in direct contrast with what is happening in our society. "Our society is being challenged to defend itself against a barbaric empire that puts faith in salvation by the machine."[39] The promise of today's machines is enormous, partly because machines are immediately at hand; they can be purchased and they can be used. But of course, machines cannot save us; they cannot even give us real quality of human existence. Philosophy ought to be telling us about such false soteriologies and why they are false. Grant concludes this essay, "The practice of philosophy . . . will depend on a prior condition—namely the intensity and concentration of our faith in God. . . . without such faith it will be vain to expect any . . . flowering of our culture in general and of our philosophy in particular."[40]

This early essay is seminal in many ways. One finds here a unique style of philosophy characterized by lament; life-long themes such as the university, technology, nature, and freedom; one also sees a nod to the thinkers of the past, whose thoughts he seeks to rethink in a time very different from theirs. Each of these topics warrants further discussion.

Lament

Lament is not a common philosophical or theological posture. Grant argues that this

---

[34] Christian and Grant, *George Grant Reader*, 163.
[35] Christian and Grant, *George Grant Reader*, 163.
[36] Grant cites only two Canadian philosophy professors: John Watson (1847–1939) who taught at Queen's University and George S. Brett (1879–1944) who was a classics professor in the philosophy department at the University of Toronto. Christian and Grant, *George Grant Reader*, 164–65.
[37] Christian and Grant, *George Grant Reader*, 169.
[38] Christian and Grant, *George Grant Reader*, 170.
[39] Christian and Grant, *George Grant Reader*, 172.
[40] Christian and Grant, *George Grant Reader*, 173.

is no accident, for if we don't like the way the world is we change it. Hence, wishing it were otherwise and throwing ourselves into the process of making it so is what drives us. Lament, on the other hand, names a mode of inquiry that begins by placing ourselves differently into a reality we know could be otherwise. Lamenters believe that changing the world is not simply dependent on the employment of the right technique. Change is in fact not the first act to consider; understanding is. Moreover, lament names the stance of being firmly convinced that not all important matter is knowable and not all is within our capacity to change. We are subject to some fundamental limitations, such as sin and tradition. The mode of lament is therefore the very opposite of the popular mantra, "we can fix it; we have the technology."[41] Hence, in important ways, lament names not only the demeanor, style, and posture of Grant's approach, but his ethics. Although lament as a mode of inquiry is careful and thoughtful, it is not passive and inactive; it measures why something is not as it ought to be by embracing the conviction that there is a way it could be, and the first order of inquiry is taking the steps to unveil that way.

Lament is closely related to the notion of irony in the classical sense, that is, in being simultaneously inside and outside of Plato's cave.[42] Human responsibility demands that one always stretch whatever is given by the good which is not perfectly attainable. Grant quotes Thomas More, saying, "When you can't make the good happen, prevent the very worst from happening."[43] The only way to get to goodness is from the less than good place one currently occupies. Hence, it need not be dishonest or hypocritical to speak up for justice from a place of injustice, or to speak against technology while using a computer, or to advocate for Christianity within a secular university, or to yearn for holiness in a less-than-faithful church.

An important book written in this genre is *Lament for a Nation*.[44] Grant was a conservative in more than just the philosophical sense. Not only did he wish to revive the thought of Plato and other ancient thinkers, he was also a political conservative, arguing that the political vision of leaders like John Diefenbaker[45] was vastly superior to the liberals, who seemed to advocate unfettered progress. Grant's views were not rooted simply in stubborn resistance to change; they were the conclusion of a political philosophy and theology. None of this should be surprising because Grant held Plato in high esteem and "In the ambiguous heart of Plato's dialogues, philosophy included political philosophy."[46]

In this ninety-seven page booklet, by far his most popular work, he presents the thesis that the political philosophy of Canada rested on a notion of progress inherent in a technological society. He contrasted this with a view of a nation where goodness, beauty, and truth were important virtues. The latter was part of an earlier Canadian vision. So he laments the loss of this tradition, "the dying of something loved." He continues, "This lament mourns the end of Canada as a sovereign state. Political laments are not usual in the age of progress, because most people think that society always moves forward to better things."[47] Grant firmly believed that Canada's death as a sovereign state was imminent.

---

[41] The 1970s' TV series "The Six Million Dollar Man" opened each show with the fictional story of astronaut Steve Austin, whose body was virtually destroyed in an accident and an announcer stating confidently, "Gentlemen, we can rebuild him; we have the technology." This series, based on the novel *Cyborg* by Martin Caidin (Westminster, Md.: Arbor House, 1972), was the inspiration for several movies and other series as well.

[42] See chap. 1 above.

[43] Larry Schmidt, ed., *George Grant in Process: Essays and Conversations* (Toronto: House of Anansi Press, 1978), 19.

[44] George Grant, *Lament for a Nation: The Defeat of Canadian Nationalism* (Toronto: McClelland & Stewart, 1965).

[45] John Diefenbaker (1895–1979) was leader of the Conservative Party of Canada (1957–1967) and prime minister of Canada (1957–1963). See Christian and Grant, *George Grant Reader*, 76.

[46] Christian and Grant, *George Grant Reader*, 433.   [47] Christian and Grant, *George Grant Reader*, 77.

Grant upheld a particular view of Canada. In his 1945 work *The Empire: Yes or No?* he states the alternative views sharply.

> One is that it is only an unfortunate accident that we were ever created and that the sooner we join the United States the better. The other (and what seems to the present writer a much nobler version) is the vision of Macdonald, Laurier, and Borden, that on the northern half of this continent has been created a nation, raised in a different tradition from the U.S.A. and dedicated to the extension of certain different political and social concepts.[48]

These political and social concepts arise first of all out of a Canadian self-understanding as a *community* of different people.

Obviously, many factors and ideas come together in the writing of his lament for Canada, and one of them arises from his views on pacifism.[49] Grant was morally outraged that Canada's political leaders offered no resistance to the "hideous manifestations of technological destructiveness"[50] that was being offered in the name of security. When asked later in life why he wrote this book, he said "He was driven by sheer anger that Lester Pearson's Liberals had brought down Diefenbaker's government so that they could yield to American pressure and bring nuclear arms into Canada."[51] As Grant saw it, this was an abomination.

For Grant, peace and justice named not a state of being or a goal but a process. Basic to his lament, therefore, was the loss of public debate of what Canada is and how French and English communities could come together to live just lives. The logic of a technological society is to make everyone the same in the enterprise of progress. Canada has two founding cultures, one English-speaking and hence sharing the language of the United States, and the other French-speaking, which in Grant's day included only six million people. He often uses the expression, "This is six million people in a sea of 250 million English-speakers."[52] And it is important to remember that the French imagination was grounded in Roman Catholicism, in which justice is a virtue defining us; we do not define it.

The culture of a technological society pushes to universalize, and hence cannot appreciate difference. The way it eradicates difference is by privatizing the individual, and particularizing truth and goodness, thereby destroying communal and national identities. Here, what binds everyone together is not the notion of a good and just society but aimless progress. And combining aimless progress with the power of empire is dangerous indeed.

Technology and Progress

As we have already seen, Grant's lament about the loss of Canadian nationalism is connected to a more general lament regarding technology and progress. In 1966 Grant wrote a review of French political philosopher Jacques Ellul's massive book, *The Technological Society*.[53] He acknowledged that this book had a huge impact on his understanding of how a society dominated by technique thinks and acts. The most important insight for Grant was Ellul's account of how technique has become autonomous. Says Grant, "What [Ellul] means by autonomous is that technique is not limited by anything external to itself. It is not limited by any goals beyond itself. It is autonomous with respect to the areas of economics and politics—indeed, throughout society as a whole. It is the creator of its own morality."[54]

Grant came to believe that technology had become so dominant that it had indeed become a mode of being; that is, it had

---

[48] Christian and Grant, *George Grant Reader*, 48.

[49] See Christian, *George Grant*, 245.

[50] Christian, *George Grant*, 244.

[51] As reported by Christian and Grant in *George Grant Reader*, 76.

[52] Schmidt, *Grant in Process*, 17.

[53] Jacques Ellul, *The Technological Society*, trans. John Wilkinson (New York: Vintage 1964).

[54] Christian and Grant, *George Grant Reader*, 395.

redefined us ontologically.[55] It used to be that technology was under the dominion of human will; it now is the other way around—we are under the thumb of technology. Or, it could be said, we too are technique, for we are what we do. Saying it this way is important, not that it helps us in overcoming technology's power, but, as he says in his essay on computers, in the acknowledgment alone "lies the hope of taking a first step: to bring the darkness into light as darkness."[56]

But where did this kind of "technical reason" come from? Of course it has been a long time coming, but it was Karl Marx (1818–1883) who has perhaps stated it most clearly. Grant references Marx's famous dictum, "Philosophers have only interpreted the world in various ways; the point, however, is to change it."[57] Notice how aptly this describes what Grant vehemently opposes. He wants to return to the agenda of interpreting the world truthfully. The implication of Marx's statement is that this quest is futile.

Another philosopher Grant was enamored with was Jean-Paul Sartre (1905–1980). In 1955 Grant wrote an essay praising Sartre as "a maker of the modern mind."[58] Although his praise was not unconditional, he clearly lauded Sartre for offering important insight in illuminating twentieth-century thought. The limitations of Sartre's thought are nuanced in Grant's concluding sentences:

> It is said of existentialism that it takes one to Golgotha to find there only two thieves dying on their crosses. Certainly I would not be content with such a vision of what happened there. Nevertheless to be at Golgotha, in despair and without vision, is better than not to be there.[59]

Thirty years later, in 1985, Grant wrote a strong retraction to this essay, in which he wonders, "How could I have ever taken Sartre's thought seriously?"[60] Grant does not answer his own question explicitly, but it is clear that near the end of his life he saw Sartre's thought as the antithesis of his own. For anyone who argues, as Sartre does, that human beings define themselves fully by how they act, that is, "existence comes before essence," is stating precisely what Grant holds to be the heresy of contemporary thought.

Grant points out that it is not by accident that Marx, Sartre, and one could add Friedrich Nietzsche (1844–1900), all found it necessary to reject God. For God inhibits our freedom. If God exists, then God determines us. If God exists, history is not ours to define. If God exists, technology has limits. If God exists, unlimited human freedom and progress are heresies.

Somehow American society has found it possible to make Christianity compatible with technological progressivism. In Grant's analysis, Christianity in North America looks a lot like the atheism of Marx, Nietzsche, and Sartre. The language of God and technology are made compatible when both can underwrite the way of progress. In other places Grant has labeled this marriage of technique with Christianity as secularized Christianity. He identifies especially the liberal, Protestant theologians of the late nineteenth- and twentieth-centuries as being able to present a theology in which God has no role. And in North America, he names the pragmatists, of whom he says, "The nearest we have come to the systematic presentation of the secularized Protestant moral language is in pragmatism—the philosophy of William James and John Dewey . . ."[61] And the reason for the success of American-style pragmatism is that it

---

[55] See Christian and Grant, *George Grant Reader*, 417ff.

[56] From his essay, "The Computer Does Not Impose on Us the Ways It Should Be Used," in Christian and Grant, *George Grant Reader*, 434.

[57] See his article, "Karl Marx," in Christian and Grant, *George Grant Reader*, 229. The quote comes from Karl Marx in his *Theses on Feuerbach*, Thesis XI.

[58] George Grant, "Jean-Paul Sartre," in Davis, *Collected Works of George Grant*, 2:124.

[59] Grant, "Jean-Paul Sartre," 133.

[60] Grant, "Jean-Paul Sartre," 133.

[61] George Grant, *Philosophy in the Mass Age*, in Davis, *Collected Works*, 373.

associates truth with expedience, the kin of progress.

Grant makes the point that if anything at all guides technology, it is progress. But progress has no moral compass outside of itself. The "better" that is identified as the judge of progress is not a moral better, but something else that masquerades as morality. This is confirmed by researchers who answer the question of why they invented certain things like cloning or atomic weapons with the answer: because it was possible. As Ellul suggests, the logic of technology implies that the possible is necessary. This simply means that, although technology was once thought of as a tool that was neutral, it is not; it is its own morality.

Grant relates technical reason to the idea of history. In 1969 he gave the Canadian Broadcasting Corporation Massey lectures titled, *Time as History*.[62] In these lectures, he discussed the impact of making "history" a central category of modern thought. This approach is also known as historicism, and today dominates our approach to knowledge. Marx, Nietzsche, and Sartre have all contributed to making it popular. In this approach, time becomes the key symbol of self-understanding. We believe, for example, that we can only understand ourselves properly when we see ourselves as twenty-first-century people. We are different from people of other generations—we know much more, we see more clearly now, and we have far more control of things. The implication of these observations is that who we are is largely determined by the "time" in which we live.

The Greek view of human nature is a contrast to this approach, and one which Grant prefers. Plato understood human nature in terms of timeless essences. In this model, we do not define ourselves along the way; rather, our task is to understand who we are as having been defined. It is a matter of "getting out of the cave" in order to come to know

our true selves. This world of metaphysical givens which in the past gave the anchors for all knowledge is gone; it no longer exists.

We now think of ourselves as creators of our own worlds. The way we are taught to read history is that all there is and all we can know is relative to some time when people of their own volition interpreted the world differently. But this has grave consequences. Says Grant:

> Nietzsche affirms that once we know that horizons are relative and man-made, their power to sustain us is blighted. Once we know them to be relative, they no longer horizon us. We cannot live in an horizon when we know it to be one. When the historical sense teaches us that our values are not sustained in the nature of things, impotence descends. Nietzsche's most famous aphorism, "God is Dead", implies that God was once alive. He was alive in the sense that he was the horizon from which many could know what was worth doing and therefore be sustained in the resolute doing of it.[63]

It does not follow from this that we no longer talk about morality; what follows is that the language of morality has changed. We do not talk about right or wrong, good or bad—these terms have lost their meaning. We now talk about "values." Values are those subjective qualities we project onto things which we hold to be important. If it is of "value" for us, we create it, provided that it is possible to create. If it is not possible to create it, we make it possible, since being able to bring about what we value is itself a basic value. This is how our technology and our morality have merged.

Grant reflects on this state of affairs as follows:

> What is comic about the present use of "values," and the distinction of them from "facts," is not that it is employed by modern men who know what is entailed in so doing; but that it is used also by "religious" believers who are unaware that in its employment they are contradicting the very possibility of the reverence they believe they are espousing in its use.[64]

[62] George Grant, *Time as History* (Toronto: University of Toronto Press, 1995).
[63] Grant, *Time as History*, 40.
[64] Grant, *Time as History*, 58. See also George Grant, "The Good or Values," in Davis, *Collected Works*, 2:387ff.

Values are always time and person relative. We speak about our values, my values, your values. Values imply valuers. Values are contrasted with facts; facts exist independently of human beings; values only have subjective existence. What is worth teaching, therefore, is only in the realm of facts, that is, science. This realm holds the promise of truth. Moreover, science enables progress, and progress names our highest value. He summarizes the entrenchment of this way of thinking in our education system as follows:

> Every literate high-school student would take a simple statement of this historicism for granted. We are taught early to use the language of values, to say that our values are dependent on our historical situation, and that this generalization proceeds from any objective study of the past. Civilizations and individuals have lived by different values. As there is no way of judging between the values of these values, we are taught early a very simple historical relativism. As we go farther in our education, we are taught to express that historicism with greater sophistication. However, the almost universal acceptance of this relativism by even the semi-literate in our society is very recent. The belief that men are enfolded in their historicity, and the consequent historical relativism with its use of the word "values," only began to be popular vocabulary in this century. Nietzsche is the first thinker who shows how this historicity is to be recognized in the full light of its consequences, in every realm of existence.[65]

As Grant saw it, the consequences of the contemporary commitment to technology and progress were staggering. And one of the reasons for a whole civilization to have taken this turn hinges on the rejection of natural law and a redefinition of human freedom.

Freedom and Natural Law

The common assumption of modern, Western thought is that we are, or ought to be, free in an unfettered way. Grant describes this as "the ability to make an unambiguous choice between open possibilities."[66] Yet this is in error; we are not free in this way. We are much more bound than we think. Most of our actions arise in the context of outside determinations which are so subtle we are not even able to articulate them clearly. Grant believes what constitutes the good life has little to do with freedom; that is, it is not a matter of being unbound but rather of being bound to the right things.

Think about the following example: just because we are not free to jump fifty feet into the air does not mean that we think of ourselves as unfree. Being bound by the laws of nature may restrict us, but why does this not inhibit our freedom? The answer is that we know them to be restricting only when we desire to overcome their power over us toward some "better" end. That is, only when we fail to understand the ways in which they make our lives good do we wish it to be otherwise. Similarly, just because the moral law prevents us from taking what is not ours, or from killing other people, or from speaking falsehoods, does not mean that we are unfree. In fact, it is precisely our acceptance of these laws, both moral and natural, which makes freedom an intelligible notion. When we violate these laws, we discover our unfreedom. Hence, we might say that freedom entails living an ordered existence under the rubric of the laws that make the good life possible. In other words, true freedom means being determined by moral law.

Grant was quite open about the notion of freedom being a philosophical conundrum that was difficult to state correctly, but he was convinced that the modern notion was deeply flawed. And he connects his critique of freedom closely to what he calls "natural law," which he learned from Thomas Aquinas. Natural law in this sense names a moral order which we can discover through reason. He describes it thus:

> By [natural] law is meant not something simply human, which we make. It is that which at every point makes the universe what it is. It is that reason which is common to God and to men. The

---

[65] Grant, *Time as History*, 36.

[66] George Grant, "Natural Law," in *Philosophy in the Mass Age*, in Davis, *Collected Works*, 2:339.

universe is a great system of beings, all moved by law and ultimately governed by the divine mind. . . . Aristotle once said that the belief that there was a moral law depended ultimately on how we interpreted the movements of the stars. What he meant by this is that if we come to deny that the planets in their motion can be finally caused, we will eventually, if we are consistent, deny that there is any purpose or law governing human life. If we deny that, we are denying that there is such a thing as human morality.[67]

All of this means that there is a givenness to human nature which we are not at liberty to create, but which we can understand. And herein lies the greatest tension within modern thought. On the one hand, we believe we alone are the determiners of our nature—this is what Grant calls existentialism or historicism—and on the other hand, there is the view that our nature has been given and the good life entails the discovery of what that is through reason. The latter, of course, is Grant's view.

These two different approaches—natural law and the freedom of history—give rise to two very different ways of viewing Christian ethics.

> On [the natural law] model we are called to fit into what God has ordered as good. Goodness is given through the structure of being itself and is not created by us; nor is it shown to us by way of God's special acts in history. On this view God's freedom and creativity are seen in God's detachedness from the physical order, since goodness has its source in the non-physical. Our freedom and creativity are seen as secondary categories to discipline and training. We are called to act not on the basis of our own ingenuity, but in keeping with what we have come to see as real. Our task is directed at getting ourselves to understand being and then "ordering" our actions and character into this understanding.
>
> On the [freedom] of history model, the task of ethical construction is quite different. Here action determines being. God is what God does, and we are what we do. Since God is seen primarily as one who acts in history, we as moral beings

must somehow relate ourselves to these acts. What God does and has done becomes normative for our actions. As God is free, so we are free. As God is moving history to its completion in time, so we are called to participate in this process which may be understood as liberation, humanization, democratization, or obedience. Our ethical self-understanding is grounded on the *Imago Dei* and demands that we collaborate in the process of moving history toward the goal as we come to see it. In doing this we see ourselves as participating in God's history.[68]

These fundamentally different ways of understanding Christian ethics derive from very different worldviews. For Grant, the historical model is thoroughly flawed yet is uncritically normative in North American society. His quest is to educate his generation in critical thought so that they can begin to emerge from "the cave."

University

Throughout Grant's writing we see his critique of the modern university. We saw this already in his article "Philosophy" in 1951. The longer he worked within the university, the more he became convinced that it was no longer a place where the pursuit of knowledge and wisdom was the primary preoccupation. Instead universities were being driven by progress, technique, and the myth of neutrality. Not only did this pertain to the new programs like computer science, but it also engulfed the entire education system, including the long-standing faculties like arts and humanities—after all, the dominant ideologies here are Marxism, pragmatism, and utilitarianism.[69] These were indeed times of lament for Grant, for he saw the proper task of university education to entail the search for a truthful understanding of reality.

In 1959, after twelve years of teaching at Dalhousie, Grant received the offer of a lifetime. He was asked to head up and develop the philosophy department at a new

---

[67] Grant, "Natural Law," 2:332–33.

[68] Harry Huebner, "Christian Pacifism and the Character of God," in *The Church as Theological Community: Essays in Honour of David Schroeder*, ed. Harry Huebner (Winnipeg, Manitoba: CMBC Publications, 1990), 251–52.

[69] See Davis, *Collected Works*, 2:101.

university in Toronto: York University. Not many professors have such an opportunity. And given his critique of established universities, he was determined to make this one more faithfully truth-seeking.

Little did Grant know that the die had already been cast. Although York was a new university, it was closely affiliated with the University of Toronto, and the curriculum at York was under the supervision of the University of Toronto. In other words, it was simply more of the same. Grant intended to teach Plato's *Republic* to first-year students, but it was not permitted by the University of Toronto. Fulton Anderson, who in 1951 had taken issue with Grant's essay on "Philosophy," again proved to be his nemesis. On this occasion, the conflict generated into an all-out battle over the nature of philosophy and the relationship between philosophy and religion. Grant appealed to the university president on the grounds that academic freedom permitted a professor to determine the nature of a course, but to no avail. He drafted a long letter of resignation delineating his view of the nature of philosophy. His resignation was promptly accepted. So he left York without ever teaching a course there. Within a year, he was teaching in the department of religion at McMaster University in Hamilton.

Perhaps this transition could be seen as a sign of destiny. As a student, Grant had never imagined himself teaching in a philosophy department; now, after twelve years of teaching philosophy, he moved to a religion department, again not as he planned it. Yet the issues he pursued remained substantially unchanged. And certainly his critique of the university did not abate.

There were two closely related criticisms that Grant made of the university: one was that it had become a "multiversity," and the other that it was being monopolized by scientific research that was fostering an approach to education in tension with the best in the humanities. Regarding the first criticism,

Grant believed that the original understanding of a university was that its *telos* was to bring all aspects of knowledge under the dominion of a single, universal truth. Not surprisingly, this too harkens back to Plato and the issue of "the one and the many." As Plato had taught, although there is diversity, there is not only diversity. Ultimately, there is oneness in which each particular thing participates. This view of the world is only possible under the belief that everything participates in the universal which, for Grant, was the "perfection of God." As Grant has emphasized over and over, a proper philosophy of education entails a well-worked-out doctrine of metaphysical knowledge. In our day, the fact-value dichotomy has so firmly taken hold of the minds of intellectuals that it has succeeded in convincing them of the total separation of empirical reality and goodness.[70] Hence, we now have multiversities, meaning that it is no longer possible to embark on the search for the unity of truth because there is no such thing. All we have left are competing departments engaged in empirical investigation of facts in the name of neutrality, that is, without any value commitments like ethics or religion. Insofar as ethics and religion are taught at universities at all, they are supposed to be departments of empirical investigation, not inquiries into the nature of goodness, justice, and God.

Hence, every area of study is its own master. Each does its own thing without the possibility of having one discipline critique another or to be judged by anything outside of itself. Each discipline is autonomous. The traditional notion of wisdom, which was to bring diversity under the domain of truth, is gone.

His second criticism focused on the preoccupation of scientific research in universities. Of course, the two criticisms are closely related. The less room there is for the pursuit of truth, beauty, and justice, the more room is made for the investigation of "facts." And for this, huge amounts of money are made available. After all, it enhances progress.

---

[70] See George Grant, "The University Curriculum," (1975) in Davis, *Collected Works*, esp. 194–95.

In 1980, at the age of sixty-two, Grant again resigned his teaching post in protest, this time from McMaster University. He was sick and tired of seeing the nod given to scientific and technological research, instead of to teaching in general and to the arts and humanities in particular. He penned an article in a Toronto newspaper, *The Globe and Mail*, explaining why he had resigned, and it set off a kind of national debate over the issue of research-driven universities in Canada.[71] In the article, he begins by highlighting "the amazing achievements of research." He continues by naming progress in medicine, food production, and modern warfare. Then, he reflects on the role of research in universities thus:

> If one ever has doubts about the goodness of many of its achievements, it is well to remind oneself of penicillin. It is the method of scientific research that had made Western civilization a world civilization. . . . Yet there are great questions which present themselves to all thinking human beings and which cannot be answered by the method of research. What is justice? How can we come to know what is truly beautiful? Where do we stand towards the divine? Are there things that can be done that should not be done? One just has to formulate these questions to see they cannot be answered by research. Yet thinking people need to be clear about such questions and therefore they cannot be excluded from the university.[72]

Early in his teaching career, in the 1950s, Grant gave a lecture titled, "What's an Arts Faculty for?"[73] In it he emphasized that it is not that research is not important within the arts and humanities, but the chief concern here is not to manipulate the objective world; it is rather to understand and learn to see the world aright. Reason and imagination are two important skills of training. Grant is not the one who wants to make the distinction between doers and thinkers, but that is the distinction that is today imposed upon university education. This is another lament.

Justice

As is readily apparent, justice was Grant's concern from the very beginning of his career. It is anything but a narrow topic for him; it encompasses all of life: view of nation, structure of university, health-care, concept of life, personal life, social life, death, everything. In working out his thoughts on justice, he was helped by an amazing array of philosophers; obviously the ancients like Plato, Aristotle, Augustine, and Thomas Aquinas, but also contemporaries like Friedrich Nietzsche, Martin Heidegger, Leo Strauss, and especially Simone Weil. He admired her more than any other thinker because she was able to articulate with such clarity and poignancy the givenness and character of God, beauty, and truth. Grant relied on the contemporaries to teach him how deeply the empire of technology and freedom had taken hold of us, and, ironically perhaps, he needed the ancients to remind him how human beings can be rescued from this fallenness and how we can still be trained for justice.

Specifically, his concern was about North American liberalism and how it had brought about a moral tyranny that he likened to Nazism. Nowhere did the logic of this approach surface more starkly than in the Canadian abortion debate.[74] Abortion was, of course, a legitimate issue in itself but for Grant it represented more. This issue went to the very core of modernity.

In 1988, the year of his death, he responded to the latest act of the Canadian court in an article called "The Triumph of the Will."[75]

---

[71] George Grant, "The Battle between Teaching and Research," in *The Globe and Mail*, 28 April 1980, 7. This article is reprinted in Davis, *Collected Works*, 2:200–203.

[72] Grant, "Battle," 201.

[73] George Grant, "What's an Arts Faculty for?" in Davis, *Collected Works*, 2:437–40.

[74] On January 28, 1988, shortly before Grant died, the Supreme Court of Canada struck down Canada's existing abortion law, making abortions available like any other medical procedure.

[75] George Grant, "The Triumph of the Will," in *The Issue Is Life: A Christian Response to Abortion in Canada*, ed. Denyse O'Leary (Burlington, Ontario: Welsh 1988). It is reprinted in Christian and Grant, *George Grant Reader*. Subsequent references are to the latter.

Grant's words are stark: "The decision of the Supreme Court concerning abortion could be seen as comedy—if it did not concern the slaughter of the young."[76] This comment should be read against the knowledge that "The Triumph of the Will" was also the title of Leni Riefenstahl's documentary of the National Socialist Party convention at Nuremburg in 1934. The connection to Nazism here is deliberate and deeply serious. He says, "In the film, Hitler is seen, not as the liberator of his own will, but as a man who through his own liberation can make possible the liberation of each individual will in his nation."[77] In other words, it takes a dictator to convince the people that their wills are "free." And what were they free to think? That the Jews were expendable because they were not truly human.

The "triumph of the will" in the abortion debate is possible precisely because the courts have ruled that fetuses are not persons.[78] This leads Grant to agree with the saying, "When fascism comes to America it will come in the name of democracy."[79]

The logic of American political liberalism, which underwrites this "moral tyranny," is worked out in 1974 in the Josiah Wood Lectures delivered at Mount Allison University in Sackville, New Brunswick. He called these lectures "English-Speaking Justice," and they were published under the same name.[80] In negotiating the focus of these lectures, Grant wrote the following: "I would like to write-out . . . the reason why the 'contractualism' which lies at the basis of English-speaking liberal moral philosophy seems to me a failure and why one must try

and understand morality as *natural* rather than *contractual*."[81]

The lectures were delivered a year after "Roe v. Wade" in which Justice Harry A. Blackmun wrote the majority decision of the U. S. Supreme Court. In his statement, he "virtually legalized abortion on demand."[82] Grant analyzes the ruling carefully. He states that Blackmun interprets the American Constitution as being concerned about fairly adjudicating between the rights of persons and other legal entities. Hence, the abortion issue is set up in terms of the mother's rights and the rights of the fetus. The dilemma then is that granting the fetus the right of birth infringes on the right of the mother to control her own body. Hence, "[Blackmun] states that the foetuses up to six months are not persons, and as non-persons can have no status in the litigation."[83] This reasoning is a form of "pure contractualism" where "rights [are] prior to good."[84] And for Grant, unless goodness and truth are prior to rights, rights cannot adjudicate morally,

Yet Blackmun is merely saying what North American political liberals have come to believe. Contractualism is what has survived into modernity. Grant puts it thus: "There are the intellectual democrats who adopt modern thought while picking and choosing among the ethical 'norms' from a dead past. Justice as equality and fairness is that bit of Christian instinct which survives the death of God."[85] But how can fairness and equality be moral if they are not derived from outside of themselves?

Contractualism and its concomitant principles of justice as equality and fairness are

---

[76] Grant, "Triumph," 142.

[77] Grant, "Triumph," 144–45.

[78] Already in "Roe v. Wade" in 1973 "the American Supreme Court ruled by a 7–2 majority that women have a constitutional right to abortion and that the foetus is not a person within the meaning of the American constitution." Grant, "Triumph," 108n.†.

[79] Grant, "Triumph," 142.

[80] George Grant, *English-Speaking Justice* (Sackville, New Brunswick: Mount Allison University, 1974).

[81] In correspondence with Alex Colville, May 24, 1973, in Christian and Grant, *George Grant Reader*, 108 (emphasis added).

[82] Christian and Grant, *George Grant Reader*, 108.

[83] Christian and Grant, *George Grant Reader*, 109.

[84] Christian and Grant, *George Grant Reader*, 109.

[85] Christian and Grant, *George Grant Reader*, 114.

developed by the scholar John Rawls in his book, *A Theory of Justice*.[86] Rawls argues that justice must be defined in terms of contract, where the wills and responsibilities of the parties are clarified. This alone can give us rights because such an agreement determines what I can rightfully demand which cannot rightfully be withheld by the other; and this alone can determine what the other can rightfully demand which cannot be withheld by me. In other words, without the notions of human commitments to each other, there cannot be a functional understanding of justice, fairness, and rights. Grant's chief criticism of Rawls' theory of justice is that it presupposed there was no natural morality. Justice can only be derived by agreement and agreement is possible because of human freedom. Hence, whatever people agree to makes it just. This is the triumph of the will and, although it provides the logic for rights, it is nevertheless bad news for minorities like the Jews in Nuremburg and the unborn in North America. In Rawls' world, there cannot be justice in the "natural" sense because there is no allowance for the possibility of the good. This means that there is nothing that can ensure that agreements themselves are just. The air of lament is again thick!

The underlying logic of contractual liberalism and technology cannot give us a reason to believe justice and freedom is due all human beings. This leads Grant to say, "How, in modern thought, can we find positive answers to the questions: (i) what is it about human beings that makes liberty and equality their due? (ii) why is justice what we are fitted for, when it is not convenient? Why is it our

good? The inability of contractual liberals (or indeed Marxists) to answer these questions is the terrifying darkness which has fallen upon modern justice."[87]

CONCLUSION

According to Grant, one of the failures of Christianity in general and Christian ethics in particular is that it "scorns the discipline of philosophy." He saw this particularly in the work of Jacques Ellul and why he was unable to answer the important questions about technology he was raising, and he saw it in theologians generally. The intellectual community has forgotten that there is a very close relation between love and reason. For if we do not love the other, we cannot think and understand the world aright.[88]

Grant remained a passionate Christian philosopher till the end, even in his own death. When his doctors could no longer treat his pancreatic cancer, he was placed on life support and in a state of unconsciousness. After two unsuccessful surgeries, his wife asked that the machines be disconnected. She knew that this too would be his wish. For as biographer Christian summarizes Grant's thoughts on death, "what is due a dying man is death,"[89] not the prolongation of artificial existence. Everyone knew, that in holding before his students the lives of Socrates and Jesus Christ, Grant had taught about the art of dying well. So the doctors absolved themselves of legal responsibility by having Sheila sign the necessary documents, and the machines were turned off. Eleven hours later he died.

---

[86] John Rawls, *A Theory of Justice* (Cambridge, Mass.: Harvard University Press, 1971).

[87] Rawls, *Theory of Justice*, 119.

[88] The comments in this paragraph are gleaned from Grant's remarks in a conversation recorded in Schmidt, *Grant in Process*, 146–47.

[89] Christian, *George Grant*, 370.

Chapter Twenty-Five

ALASDAIR CHALMERS MACINTYRE
(1929–)

Alasdair MacIntyre began publishing books at a very young age. His first book, *Marxism: An Interpretation*, appeared in 1953 when he was only twenty-four years old. Since then he has written numerous books and articles, too many to list here; and he is still writing and lecturing.[1]

MacIntyre is a prominent international philosopher who has done groundbreaking work in the areas of political and moral philosophy and has helped give a philosophical account of the nature of theological ethics. Although he has treated many subjects of philosophy and theology and reinterpreted many scholars of the past, his most widely recognized contribution to scholarship has been in the area of virtue ethics. In large part he has been responsible not only for bringing back to respectability the classical view of Aristotelian ethics, he has argued that unless we find ways to reappropriate Aristotle's thought, the discipline of studies called ethics remains philosophical nonsense.

MacIntyre's project has affinities with that of George Grant. Both see the Enlightenment as having been not so enlightening. Both present a philosophy of repair; both see pre-Enlightenment philosophers as the resource from which to draw. Yet Grant reaches back to the thoughts of Plato, while MacIntyre sees the best promise in the philosophy of Aristotle and Thomas Aquinas. This choice makes the analysis of the problem as well as the details of the solution quite different. Moreover, MacIntyre came from the tradition of analytic philosophy with a Marxist turn, and Grant had no use for either. Grant is a self-confessed conservative, and MacIntyre is neither conservative nor liberal.

BEGINNINGS

MacIntyre was born in Glasgow, Scotland, to John and Emily (Chalmers) MacIntyre. Very little has been written about his early life. As a young adult, he attended the University of London, the University of Manchester, and Oxford University. In 1991, in an interview with Italian philosopher Giovanna Borradori, he gave us a brief glimpse into his youth. He said that when he was still young he had the "philosophical good fortune" to be shaped in two different ways. One influence came from the "Gaelic oral culture of farmers and fishermen, poets and storytellers," and the other came from older people who told him that immersing himself fully into this culture was "a waste of time for someone whose education was designed to enable him to pass those examinations that are the threshold of bourgeois life in the modern world."[2] What was the

---

[1] For a selection of MacIntyre's publications up to 1993, see "Selected Bibliography of the Publications of Alasdair MacIntyre," in *After MacIntyre: Critical Perspectives on the Work of Alasdair MacIntyre*, ed. John Horton and Susan Mendus (Notre Dame, Ind.: University of Notre Dame, 1994), 305–18.

[2] "An interview with Giovanna Borradori," in *The MacIntyre Reader*, ed. Kelvin Knight (Notre Dame, Ind.: University of Notre Dame, 1998), 255.

modern world? "A culture of theories rather than stories."[3] This dualistic pull remained at the center of MacIntyre's early life.

MacIntyre believed philosophy could not help in reconciling these two worlds because philosophy taught that holding contradictory beliefs was indeed irrational. Logically, the affirmation of a contradiction implies anything whatsoever. In school, he studied "Latin and Greek—literature, philosophy, and history."[4] But in his mind the tension of coherence and incoherence was not easily resolved. Sometimes he would think of justice from the standpoint of Aristotle and Aquinas, and other times he would find himself thinking about justice from the standpoint of modern liberalism.

In response to a question about the influence of Christianity in his early life, MacIntyre said he initially sought to "fence off" religious belief and practice from the rest of life. But he became convinced through reading Wittgenstein, especially his view on "forms of life," and Hans Urs von Balthasar's critique of Karl Barth that this separation could not be done. Through these scholars, he came to see that religious thought and practice are inseparable from larger metaphysical, scientific, and moral claims. But were Barth and von Balthasar indeed right about their religious claims? Alas, MacIntyre thought not and so, as he puts it, he "mistakenly rejected the Christian religion" despite keeping much of Aquinas' thought.[5] Later, in the early 1980s, he would embrace the Christian religion via the thought of Thomas Aquinas and Roman Catholicism.

At age twenty-two, MacIntyre began his teaching career. His first job was at Manchester University, and he taught at Leeds,

Essex, and Oxford before moving to America in 1969. Here he has had no fewer than nine teaching positions, the most recent of which were at Duke University and the University of Notre Dame. He has held several prominent research posts, received many prizes, and been president of the American Philosophical Association.

MacIntyre has been married three times: from 1953 to1963 to Ann Peri, with whom he had two daughters; from 1963 to1977 to Susan Willans, with whom he had a son and daughter; and since 1977 to Lynn Joy, who is also a philosopher teaching at Notre Dame.[6]

In another interview, when asked to give account of the development of his thought, MacIntyre speaks about three stages.[7] The first began in his graduate student days (1949–1971), during which he wrote several works he later characterized as "badly organized, sometimes fragmented and often frustrating and messy enquiries, from which nonetheless in the end I learned a lot."[8] The time from 1971 to 1977, following his arrival in the United States, he describes as an "interim period,"[9] characterized by critical reflections on moral philosophy and attempts to come to terms with the many different perspectives in the field. Finally, he has been engaged since 1977 in a single, constructive project that he says some scholars have described as *An Interminably Long History of Ethics*.[10]

This self-described three-stage development makes it somewhat difficult to know how to best present MacIntyre's thought. I cannot in this short essay do justice to subtleties of his arguments nor get involved in the debate over interpretation that his writings have spawned. Instead, I will attempt a brief summary of a part of the last

---

[3] "Interview with Giovanna Borradori," in Knight, *MacIntyre Reader*, 255.

[4] "Interview with Giovanna Borradori," in Knight, *MacIntyre Reader*, 256.

[5] See "Interview with Giovanna Borradori," in Knight, *MacIntyre Reader*, 256.

[6] From "Alasdair MacIntyre," *Wikipedia*, last modified April 8, 2011, http://en.wikipedia.org/wiki/Alasdair_Macintyre.

[7] See "An Interview for *Cogito*," in *The MacIntyre Reader*, ed. Kelvin Knight (Notre Dame, Ind.: University of Notre Dame, 1998), 267–75.

[8] "Interview for *Cogito*," in Knight, *MacIntyre Reader*, 268.

[9] "Interview for *Cogito*," in Knight, *MacIntyre Reader*, 268.

[10] "Interview for *Cogito*," in Knight, *MacIntyre Reader*, 269 (emphasis in original).

stage of his still-developing thought. This runs a particular risk which I want to name in an attempt to avoid: the danger of seeing MacIntyre narrowly as an epistemologist. If one were to concentrate properly on the development of his thought, one could not help but realize how his Marxist convictions have remained and how political theory permeates his thought to the last stages of his writings. To read him merely as a critic of Enlightenment *philosophy* within a narrow intellectual tradition is to miss his critique of North American culture's hidden enslavements to capitalist practices and capitalistic ways of knowing. We need to caution against misreading MacIntyre's work precisely at this point since it is his intent to frustrate the distinction between epistemology and politics. Having said that, I will nevertheless focus on the third stage of his thought, specifically on his three works, sometimes referred to as his moral trilogy: *After Virtue*; *Whose Justice? Which Rationality?*; and *Three Rival Versions of Moral Enquiry*.

AFTER VIRTUE

In *After Virtue*,[11] first published in 1981 and revised in 1984, MacIntyre is not merely critical of certain aspects of Enlightenment thought but argues that the whole project, which puts forward a way of understanding the world, rationality, and human existence, has failed. More importantly, it had to fail. And the consequences of this failure are huge. For the past three hundred years we have been seduced into believing a conception of rationality exists that is universal and independent of history and tradition, in other words, that epistemology is separable from ethics and politics. And this belief has succeeded in making our moral life unintelligible. The only way to escape from the ongoing consequences of this failure is to develop an alternative view of rationality which is, contrary to the modern understanding, able to make sense of our moral commitments and practices. This in turn will permit us to develop a defensible view of morality commensurate with reason. To pull this off will require not a minor tinkering and fixing but a wholesale rejection—a starting over, as it were.

The book is an analysis of this failure—its extent and its consequences. And it seeks to point toward a way out. As he says in the last sentence of the book, "We are waiting not for a Godot, but for another—doubtless very different—St. Benedict."[12] As this sentence suggests, this study is not yet the full answer to the problems he identifies, but it does set a direction.

Our Predicament

MacIntyre begins with a "disquieting suggestion" that there is no coherence to our current moral practices and commitments.[13] All we possess are remnants of an earlier language and imagination. He puts it as follows "we possess . . . fragments of a conceptual scheme, parts which now lack those contexts from which their significance derived. We possess indeed simulacra of morality, we continue to use many of the key expressions. But we have—very largely, if not entirely—lost our comprehension, both theoretical and practical, or [*sic*] morality."[14]

MacIntyre suggests that the current moral imagination is governed by emotivism.[15]

---

[11] Alasdair MacIntyre, *After Virtue: A Study in Moral Theory*, 2nd ed. (Notre Dame, Ind.: University of Notre Dame, 1984).

[12] MacIntyre, *After Virtue*, 263.

[13] See chap. 7 above for a fuller citation of MacIntyre's "disquieting suggestion." In his "allegory," he asks readers to imagine that a natural catastrophe has turned people against natural science. They riot and destroy society's entire scientific infrastructure—from books to labs. Later, when remnants of a world past are discovered—mere fragments—the people take these to be the real thing. No doubt this allegory conjures up images of Plato's cave or indeed of scenes from Walter Miller, *A Canticle for Leibowitz: A Novel* (Philadelphia: Lippencott, 1959), although neither are explicitly mentioned in MacIntyre's account.

[14] MacIntyre, *After Virtue*, 2.

[15] MacIntyre's succinct definition of emotivism is as follows: "Emotivism is the doctrine that all evaluative judgments and

Why? Because moral language in today's society does not name anything objective. The term "emotivism" comes from the logical positivists, and it holds that moral language is not cognitively meaningful, that is, not capable of being either true or false.[16] Hence, moral language functions merely to express the feelings or attitudes of the speaker. In this model, the role of moral language is quite different from factual language. Disputes about facts are, in principle at least, resolvable, whereas moral disputes are in principle not resolvable. The latter are subjective and hence admit no common rationality to which appeal may be made for resolution.

Emotivism rests upon a dichotomy going back to Enlightenment philosopher David Hume, and the distinction he proposed between facts and values, or "is" and "ought" statements. This distinction relegates morality to the realm of values, which of necessity makes them subjective, that is, lodged within the human emotive capacity.

Hence, we face an oddity in today's language of morality; we participate in moral debates in ways that assume we are speaking rationally and therefore in ways we believe can lead toward resolution. In other words, we engage in moral discourse on the supposition that the pursuit is about truth or goodness. Yet the disagreements are interminable. There seems to be no truth or goodness that can settle moral disputes. Not only do we argue endlessly about important social issues like war, euthanasia, and homosexuality, more fundamentally, we have abandoned the bases upon which such arguments could be resolved. Societies that have adapted to emotivism have resorted to conducting public opinion polls to resolve moral issues because such polls give people an opportunity to express their opinions. And public speakers, especially politicians, seek to convince, not by rational arguments, but with language and images that appeal to the emotions. The more graphic the imagery, the more convincing the rhetoric. This is the crisis MacIntyre identifies, analyzes, and seeks to remedy.

This is, however, far from a narrow intellectual matter. MacIntyre is interested in what the *social world* looks like with emotivist eyes. He refers to Henry James' novel, *The Portrait of a Lady*,[17] in which James (1843–1916) seeks to understand the "rich aesthete" when the distinction between manipulative and nonmanipulative social relationships has been obliterated, moral instrumentalism has triumphed, and the metaphor of consumption rules.[18] These insights are not so different from those of Denis Diderot (1713–1784) and Søren Kierkegaard (1813–1855), who have also spoken of "those who see in the social world nothing but a meeting place of individual wills, each with its own set of attitudes and preferences and who understand that world solely as an arena for the achievement of their own satisfaction, who interpret reality as a series of opportunities for their own enjoyment and for whom the last enemy is boredom."[19] MacIntyre concludes that, in the emotivist world, one of the "model characters"[20] is the *aesthete*.

Another social context MacIntyre addresses are organizations such as private institutions and government bureaucracies. Organizations structure relationships and determine much of the lives of ordinary

---

as they are moral or evaluative in character." *After Virtue*, 11–12 (emphasis in original).

[16] See chap. 9 above for a full discussion of "emotivism" and "logical positivism."

[17] Henry James, *The Portrait of a Lady* (Boston: Houghton Mifflin, 1963).

[18] See MacIntyre, *After Virtue*, 24–25.

[19] MacIntyre, *After Virtue*, 25.

[20] MacIntyre defines "character" to mean a "social role that places certain kinds of moral constraint on the personality of those who inhabit them in a way in which many other social roles do not" (*After Virtue*, 27). He emphasizes that this entails a fusion of role and personality and in this way a "*character* morally legitimates a mode of social existence" (*After Virtue*, 29) (emphasis in original).

citizens. And while the metaphor of the rich aesthete does not neatly apply here, since organizations are engaged in "a competitive struggle for scarce resources,"[21] nevertheless, the logic of emotivism has just as thoroughly infiltrated this social realm. This is borne out especially by the work of Max Weber (1864–1920), the social scientist who defines "bureaucratic authority" in equally emotivist terms making the "aesthete" and the "manager" look like close first cousins.

Weber's language is that of values, which, as we have seen, rest on the subject. In fact, MacIntyre suggests that Weber derives his view of values from Nietzsche, where "the choice of any one particular evaluative stance or commitment can be no more rational than that of any other."[22] In Weber's model, "no type of authority can appeal to rational criteria to vindicate itself except that type of bureaucratic authority which appeals precisely to its own *effectiveness*."[23] Hence the distinction between authority and power is eradicated, and there is no moral basis other than subjective values for evaluating either.

This conclusion, which is but the natural outgrowth of embodied emotivism, is very different from a view that sees authority as giving someone the *moral right* as well as the *moral parameters* to exercise power to bring about moral ends. The latter requires a social context or a tradition that makes intelligible and justifiable the ends toward which authority and power are to be used. In other words, it requires a moral framework for the understanding of the relation of means to ends. In Weber's obsession with a value-free social science, casting the structure of authority in terms of "managers" who are assigned particular roles and given the power to make decisions to bring about particular ends has become the governing logic of organizations. MacIntyre concludes that *managers* are the second example of model characters.

The third model character is the *therapist*. Like the manager, the therapist treats ends as given from the outside, for which no accountability is assumed. Also, like the manager, the concern of the therapist is only with technique, not with good. "Neither manager nor therapist, in their role as manager or therapist, do or are able to engage in moral debate."[24] Their sole aim is to bring about the goal which they have been given either by their superior or by their profession.

In summary then, MacIntyre identifies these three model characters, all of which arise out of emotivism: the aesthete, the manager, and the therapist. Essentially he points out that an emotivist view of the self (the view most common in our day) cannot be associated with a moral point of view because it lacks all rational criteria. Everything can be engaged and responded to from any standpoint whatsoever. Even the choice of standpoint is without criteria. Moral agency is therefore characterized by the notion of *choice*, that is, criteria-less decision-making. This means that the "emotive-self" can have no *social* or *moral* identity and admits of no collective content. This is why there are debates which go nowhere and, when decisions need to be made, the only option available is imposition of a will by a higher authority or through the democratization of attitudes and feelings, (public opinion polls or elections) to see which emotions are most prevalent.

How Did We Get Here?

Before MacIntyre speaks about getting out of the current predicament, he asks how we got into this state of moral degeneration. He does this by showing in reverse chronological order how the following philosophers built upon their immediate predecessor's socially embodied logic: the Danish thinker Søren Kierkegaard, the German philosopher Immanuel Kant (1724–1804), the Scottish philosopher David Hume (1711–1776), and the French philosopher Denis Diderot. It is in response to this deconstruction of the intelligibility of moral language that the

---

[21] MacIntyre, *After Virtue*, 29.
[22] MacIntyre, *After Virtue*, 26.

[23] MacIntyre, *After Virtue*, 26 (emphasis in original).
[24] MacIntyre, *After Virtue*, 30.

predicament of our own culture must be seen.

Kierkegaard has taught us that the key to human existence is choice. He meant by this not only the choice between various potential moral options—that is, whether war, for example, is ever justifiable or not, but also the choice of whether to be moral or not—in other words, whether to treat something (or anything) as a moral issue or not. To ask on what rational basis choices are made is to ask a question that Kierkegaard cannot answer. Why not? Because rational discernment has been replaced with criterion-less choice.

It is, however, impossible to understand Kierkegaard without the work of Immanuel Kant, because Kierkegaard is an extension of Kant's thinking and also because Kierkegaard attempts a corrective reconstruction of him. For Kant, the alternatives for moral justification common in his day were desire and religion. Morality cannot be based on our desires like happiness since it is easily conceivable that there are acts that make us happy that are not right. Moreover, religious belief cannot be the basis of morality either, since to say that we should do what God commands requires that we answer the question of why God's commanding something makes it right.

One can see some ready similarities here with Kierkegaard's logic, yet the difference is profound in that Kierkegaard sees *choice* as the basis of ethics and Kant sees *reason* as basic. Moreover, Kant understands reason in a particular way. It is *sui generis* and admits of no content from experience. Consider MacIntyre's summary of Kant: "it is of the essence of reason that it lays down principles which are universal, categorical and internally consistent."[25] In other words, Kant presupposes an equivalence between universalizability and rationality. Therefore, the test of a moral act or principle for Kant is whether it can be consistently willed for everyone.

Kant's categorical imperative[26] is purely formal and has no moral content. But clearly Kant had moral content in mind, which is evident from his reformulation of the categorical imperative as "Always act so as to treat humanity, whether in your person or in that of others, as an end, and not as a means."[27] But nowhere does he state what the end of person is. Regardless of its formulation, the categorical imperative is a way of saying that one should always do what can be rationally willed, and what that forbids is the imposition upon another of one's own or another's will. It is fair to ask why this should be convincing to us. What reason would compel us to will like this? Here Kant seems not to have a ready answer.

It turns out that Kant's attempt to found morality on *reason* fails just as surely as Kierkegaard's attempt to ground it on *choice*. Moreover, the two failures are not that different. Kierkegaard realized that Kant could not consistently defend reason as a basis for morality, and therefore invoked choice where reason failed. Just as Kierkegaard attempted to repair the errors of Kant, so Kant responded to the failures of the Scottish philosopher David Hume and the French philosopher Denis Diderot, for they had attempted to ground morality on desire and passion, which Kant held to be intolerable.

Hume, an empiricist, recognized that passion moves us to action, and hence moral judgments are properly considered expressions of our passions. But what accounts for the discrimination among the passions? Here Hume's answer is "sympathy."[28] How does this work? He sees the moral act as involving three characters: the agent, the receiver, and the observer. And it is the interplay among them that constitutes the justification of the moral act. An agent acts from a passion rooted in a character trait, either virtuous or vicious. For example, if you do a good deed such as helping a needy person, then your action

---

[25] MacIntyre, *After Virtue*, 45.

[26] One of the ways Kant states the categorical imperative is: "Act only according to that maxim whereby you can at the same time will that it should become a universal law."

[27] MacIntyre, *After Virtue*, 46.

[28] MacIntyre, *After Virtue*, 49.

is virtuous. And a virtuous act like this will sympathetically affect an observer, who will experience an agreeable passion, and hence approve of the agent's action—*mutatis mutandis* for vicious actions like robbing a bank.

This then is MacIntyre's summary of why emotivism is so prevalent today. Hume's attempts to ground ethics in passion and desire, Kant's recourse to reason, and Kierkegaard's emphasis on choice all fail to provide a rationale that makes ethics intelligible. Yet his argument goes deeper than merely citing the litany of contingent, historical failures that help us understand the contemporary cultural malaise. He points out that not only *did* the Enlightenment project fail, but *it had to* fail. It had to fail because shared characteristics derived from the deconstruction of the predecessor's culture were inherently flawed. What are those characteristics?

Why the Enlightenment Had to Fail

It is interesting that from Hume to Kierkegaard all were moral conservatives. Promise-keeping, justice, and institutions like marriage were all upheld without critique. Yet their rationale changed from those in the Middle Ages. MacIntyre is specifically interested in what changes took place in both the recasting of human nature as well as the logical movement from human nature to moral rules and precepts.

He spells this out as follows: in the Aristotelian tradition, which dominated the Middle Ages up to the Enlightenment period, the logic of ethics was built upon a threefold scheme. First, human-nature-as-it-happened-to-be (if you like, human nature in its untutored state); second, human-nature-as-it-could-be-if-it-realized-its-*telos* (that is, if the full potential of human nature were reached); and third, the precepts or rationale for moving from the first to the second (if you like, how to move from the potentiality to act).[29] The change that took place

during the Enlightenment was first of all with respect to an understanding of human nature. The Enlightenment scholars rejected "any teleological view of human nature, any view of man as having an essence which defines his true end. But to understand this is to understand why their project of finding a basis for morality had to fail."[30]

The argument here is not that for the Enlightenment philosophers human nature did not figure in their moral logic. It did, only it is not a teleological view of human nature. This meant they could no longer speak of moral injunctions in terms of precepts that guided the movement from human-nature-as-it-happened-to-be to human-nature-as-it-could-be-if-it-realized-its-*telos*. This meant further that the inherited moral language of the predecessor's culture became meaningless, with mere moral fragments from a forgotten past, since words like virtues and vices were meant to guide the movement from untutored to tutored human nature.

In fact, the whole logical move from *what is* to *what ought to be* (or if one likes, the logical continuity of facts and values) became suspect not as a mere neglected deference to the past but as a perceived problem of logic; that is, the logical movement from "is" to "ought" was seen as an error in thinking. Yet the traditional flow of thought had not considered this logical movement to be a problem since it was common to go from what a person or thing *is* to what that person or thing *ought* to do. For example, if one is a farmer, one could conclude what one ought to do, since in the farmer lies the *telos* of farming. Similarly, one could conclude that a watch *ought* to tell time. Good watches tell time well just as good farmers do the job of farming well. Bad watches and bad farmers do not express their ends well. Hence, to call something good is to make both an evaluative as well as a factual statement.[31] It also follows that on this basis moral statements can be called true or false,

---

[29] See MacIntyre, *After Virtue*, 52–53.
[30] MacIntyre, *After Virtue*, 54.

[31] See MacIntyre, *After Virtue*, 58–59.

just like factual statements. This is the very thing that emotivists deny, and their denial is premised upon their rejection by earlier habits of the mind. And this is why the Enlightenment project had to fail.

Yet the Enlightenment thinkers did not consider their discovery of the is/ought dichotomy as a loss. Instead it was heralded as an achievement of the free and autonomous self, one no longer tied to extraneous and imposed definition. We are now free to define ourselves in terms of our own values and interests, not in relation to a given *telos*. The emotivist self is then an individual very different from a self who affirms the distinction between a tutored and untutored person. The emotivist self is a self-defined individual in a way that the pre-modern self could not be. Hence, MacIntyre can say, "when the distinctively modern self was invented, its invention required not only a largely new social setting, but one defined by a variety of not always coherent beliefs and concepts. What was then invented was the *individual*. . . ."[32]

Consequences of the Failure

MacIntyre rehearses several "moral fictions" that are the consequences of the failure of the Enlightenment project. He uses the term moral fictions to mean contemporary theories disguised as moral frameworks seeking to provide guidance for a way of life, which in fact are morally vacuous. Based on the culture of emotivism, they provide the type of sanctions for behavior and relationships between individuals that are coercive and manipulative. In other words, since there is no moral or rational ground that can be appealed to for settling disputes, there is only the authority and power of one will (emotion or opinion) over the other.

MacIntyre names two such moral fictions: utilitarianism and human rights. It is quite apparent that J. S. Mill's notion of "the greatest happiness for the greatest number" has no moral content. As such, this notion can easily justify the most extreme, immoral actions if they make the majority of people happy. This is the defense that can justify the murder of millions of unwanted people. It is therefore a *moral* fiction, even though it may serve to make an entire society feel justified for their actions.

The second popular moral fiction, also rooted in contemporary emotivist culture, is rights language. This is today by far the most common "moral" appeal; we speak of natural rights, the "rights of man," human rights, and so on. Although slightly different in meaning, all have in common the idea that human beings, simply by virtue of being human, have something due to them, which, when withheld, constitutes a moral breach.

MacIntyre gives an analysis of the rights argument as developed in the work of Alan Gewirth (1912–2004).[33] He points out that Gewirth's effort to underwrite morality with the language of human rights commits him, whether he likes it or not, to a concept of "the good" which alone can make it *moral*. Otherwise, we could give each other entitlements of the most bizarre and immoral kind, such as to kill people we don't like. Surely the mere extension of such rights would not make it moral. Thus Gewirth, in order to make his system of human rights work as a moral theory, "has illicitly smuggled into his argument a conception which does not in any way belong, as [he] must do if his case is to succeed. . . ."[34] For there simply are no "moral" rights that are not derived on some notion of goodness.

MacIntyre argues that it is very odd to think of rights as somehow naturally "attached" to human beings. It is noteworthy that before the fifteenth century, nothing in classical or medieval literature—religious or otherwise—hinted at the notion of rights, even during times when the works spoke of morality in terms of natural law. Rights

---

[32] MacIntyre, *After Virtue*, 61 (emphasis in original).

[33] MacIntyre, *After Virtue*, 66–69. See Alan Gewirth, *Reason and Morality* (Chicago: University of Chicago, 1978).

[34] MacIntyre, *After Virtue*, 67–68.

language is the product of an emotivist invention of the self, through which desires and wills are given maximum liberties. But can it be accepted as a truthful description of the human condition? MacIntyre says "no" rather bluntly, "the plain truth is; there are no such rights, and belief in them is one with belief in witches and the unicorns."[35] That is, the imaginations that have their roots in human rights and utilitarianism are moral fictions.

In summary, MacIntyre has argued that given the notion of the emotivist self and the emotivist account of human existence in today's world, our model characters,—the aesthete, the therapist, and the manager—guided by the moral illusion of rights and the utility principle cannot give us an adequate account of the moral life. Such a project not only has failed, but it must fail.

Nietzsche or Aristotle

MacIntyre's master argument is that once one recognizes the Enlightenment had to fail, there remain few options available in reconstructing the good life. Once we conclude, as MacIntyre thinks we must, that Nietzsche is right and there is no universal rationality that can ground our morality, then there are only two options left: either we accept the Nietzschean proposal to substitute will for reason or we reassess a view of the world where human *telos* defines us and we do not define ourselves. In other words, it is a choice between Nietzsche and Aristotle.

MacIntyre believes that "Nietzsche is *the* moral philosopher of the present age."[36] More than any other contemporary thinker, Nietzsche understood the reality of emotivism and the consequences of freeing the subjective will. The brilliance of Nietzsche made visible the absurdity of Humean moral sentiment and the Kantian categorical imperative. MacIntyre summarized the structure of Nietzsche's argument thus:

If there is nothing to morality but expressions of will, my morality can only be what my will creates. There can be no place for such fictions as natural rights, utility, the greatest happiness of the greatest number. I myself must now bring into existence "new tables of what is good." "We, however, *want to become those we are*—human beings who are new, unique, incomparable, who give themselves laws, who create themselves" [quoted from Nietzsche, *The Gay Science*]. The rational and rationally justified autonomous moral subject of the eighteenth century is a fiction, an illusion; so, Nietzsche resolves, let will replace reason and let us make ourselves into autonomous moral subjects by some gigantic and heroic act of the will, an act of the will that by its quality may remind us of that archaic aristocratic self-assertiveness which preceded what Nietzsche took to be the disaster of slave-morality and which by its effectiveness may be the prophetic precursor of a new era. The problem then is how to construct in an entirely original way, how to invent a new table of what is good and a law, a problem which arises for each individual.[37]

Hence, according to MacIntyre, Nietzsche sees insightfully the implications of the Enlightenment project, thereby explaining why emotivism has so dominated contemporary Western thought, both in the social sciences and in the humanities. His "prophetic irrationalism" is displayed in today's model characters of the aesthete, the therapist, and the manager. But MacIntyre finds Nietzsche's alternative unconvincing.

It is not as though MacIntyre arbitrarily chose Aristotle as the "new" intellectual power with a stronger moral arsenal than Nietzsche and his disciples. It is rather that Aristotle's view of the world is precisely what was systematically dismantled by the Enlightenment project. That is, Nietzsche is not the real issue here; the Enlightenment is. The question, therefore is, "can Aristotle's ethics, or something very like it, *after all* be vindicated."[38] In other words, it is not that the alternatives—Nietzsche or Aristotle—remain the options for rational people to choose

---

[35] MacIntyre, *After Virtue*, 69.
[36] MacIntyre, *After Virtue*, 114.

[37] MacIntyre, *After Virtue*, 113–14 (emphasis in original).
[38] MacIntyre, *After Virtue*, 118 (emphasis added).

between; to defend Aristotle, according to MacIntyre, is to argue that the emotivists are wrong; for the basis of their project (the Enlightenment) has not succeeded. To say this differently, we need to remember that MacIntyre's reading of Aristotle is an historicist reading,[39] and so the question is how Aristotle fits into a tradition and ultimately whether today Aristotle gives us a better account of the moral life than Nietzsche.

The difference between Nietzsche and Aristotle is stark. And while MacIntyre spends the next several books developing and refining the work of Aristotle, he begins with a fundamental contrast. Nietzsche rejects, while Aristotle affirms, the notion of a human *telos*. To say this differently, for Aristotle there is an answer to the question, "what sort of person am I to become"; for Nietzsche there is not. By contrast, with the eradication of Aristotelian teleology, the question in an emotivist society is "what rules ought we to follow."[40] In this approach, we need to determine what the rules are and why they should be binding on us. In the Aristotelian approach, we need to ask what view of human nature do we accept and what are the virtues that guide us in getting there.[41] These are fundamentally different approaches rooted in different moral imaginations. As we have already seen, Aristotle presents a teleological view of human nature in a threefold manner: humans as they are empirically (actuality), humans as they could be if they were fully human (*telos* or potentiality), and the virtues that get us from the first to the second.

Virtues

The ancient rendition of the virtues has not remained unchanged. MacIntyre spends five chapters[42] tracing the historical development of the virtues from classical times to medieval times. But he begins with Aristotle because Aristotle best represents the virtue tradition.

Aristotle gives a somewhat different account of the virtues than Plato, seeking to correct what Plato got wrong. For Aristotle, the perfection of an object was an extension of the object itself and did not reside in an other-worldly realm as Plato taught. For human beings, this means that we understand ourselves properly when we understand ourselves as teleological beings, that is, beings moving toward a *telos*. MacIntyre puts it thus: "Every activity, every enquiry, every practice aims at some good; for by 'the good' or 'a good' we mean that at which human beings characteristically aim."[43] According to Aristotle, human beings, like all animals, have a specific nature. This nature is best understood in terms of an end or a goal toward which it naturally tends.

Virtues are the skills or qualities that make possible the attainment of the human *telos*. To say this differently, virtues are habits that nurture the excellence of our being. There are, of course, many different kinds of virtues and which virtues are cultivated will be commensurate with the *telos*. For example, just habits make just people. Aristotle goes out of his way to show that the human *telos* cannot be money, or honor, or pleasure. After some searching, he states that the human *telos* is *eudaimonia*, which is hard to translate but is often presented as blessedness, happiness, or prosperity.[44] MacIntyre describes it as follows: "It is the state of well being and doing well in well being, of a man's being well-favored himself and in relation to the divine."[45] This description enables MacIntyre to restate what the virtues are: "The virtues are precisely those qualities the possession of which will

---

[39] MacIntyre acknowledges that a historicist reading of Aristotle is something Aristotle would not understand. He says, "to treat Aristotle as part of a tradition, even as its greatest representative, is a very unAristotelian thing to do" (MacIntyre, *After Virtue*, 146).

[40] See MacIntyre, *After Virtue*, 118–19.

[41] It should be noted here that in his next book, *Whose Justice? Which Rationality?* (Notre Dame, Ind.: University of Notre Dame Press, 1988), MacIntyre admits to having overstated the contrast between an ethic of virtues and an ethic of rules.

[42] See chaps. 10–14 in MacIntyre, *After Virtue*.

[43] MacIntyre, *After Virtue*, 148.

[44] See MacIntyre, *After Virtue*, 148.

[45] MacIntyre, *After Virtue*, 148.

enable an individual to achieve *eudaimonia* and the lack of which will frustrate his movement toward that *telos*."[46]

An important feature in Aristotle's view of human nature is reason. He distinguishes human beings from the other animals in that humans have the unique capacity of reflecting, projecting, contemplating, and evaluating, and on this basis they make choices that, to some extent, determine outcome, both internal and external to the person. Hence for Aristotle, excellence of character and excellence of intelligence are inseparable. The moral life requires both intellectual virtues and virtues of character. MacIntyre summarizes: "Intellectual virtues are acquired through teaching, the virtues of character from habitual exercise. We become just or courageous by performing just or courageous acts; we become theoretically or practically wise as a result of systematic instruction. Nonetheless these two kinds of moral education are intimately related."[47]

A key virtue in Aristotle's ethics is *phronêsis*, sometimes translated as prudence or practical wisdom. "*Phronêsis* in an intellectual virtue" which "characterizes someone who knows what is due to him."[48] What this means is that this virtue is required in order for all the other virtues to be exercised properly. After all, for Aristotle, virtue is the mean between two vices; for example, courage is the virtue between rashness and timidity, and so discerning the proper balance requires the wisdom of practical reason.

Other aspects of Aristotle's ethics are friendship and the polis. Aristotle's polis is a kind of political community that is constituted by a bond between citizens who share common goods and virtues. "That bond is the bond of friendship and friendship is itself a virtue."[49] The kind of friendship Aristotle is identifying here is the bond that is necessary in order for a political community to exist; for it trains one to exist as if others mattered

because they are of ultimate importance in sustaining the body in which one's own goodness is nurtured. This is difficult for contemporary emotivists to comprehend. Aristotle is envisioning a polis where the bond that binds the political community together is friendship—that is, grounded in the concern for common well-being, common disciplines of goodness, common virtues, and common cultivation of *phronêsis*. Without friendship, the bond that holds a group together is coercive. We are used to seeing political communities constituted by an aggregate of strangers forced into obedience and submission to a sovereign state which has authority backed by threat of death to limit and control behavior. This is said to be for our mutual protection. Hence, friendship, in our society, becomes a kind of emotional state between individuals and is not thought of as a type of political relationship.[50] For Aristotle, friendship sustains the polis because it supports the cultivation of the virtues through which alone we can attain *eudaimonia*.

Practices, Narratives, Traditions

The concluding chapters in *After Virtue* develop three concepts that lie at the center of MacIntyre's moral theory: practices, narratives, and traditions. Combined with his view of the virtues, these three notions form the basis of his proposal for a post-emotivist morality.

In seeking to make intelligible the sense in which the moral life can again become meaningful, MacIntyre is rather careful in describing the components of his proposal. In what context do the virtues function? How is the moral self to be understood? His answers to these questions are somewhat difficult to understand because the language is new to contemporary, emotivist ears.

MacIntyre begins with the explanation of how virtues function within the context of practices. This is after all their proper home.

---

[46] MacIntyre, *After Virtue*, 148 (emphasis in original).
[47] MacIntyre, *After Virtue*, 154.
[48] MacIntyre, *After Virtue*, 154.
[49] MacIntyre, *After Virtue*, 155.
[50] MacIntyre, *After Virtue*, 156.

But what are practices? He gives a rather obtuse and convoluted definition saying:

> By a "practice" I am going to mean any coherent and complex form of socially established cooperative human activity through which goods internal to that form of activity are realized in the course of trying to achieve those standards of excellence which are appropriate to, and partially definitive of, that form of activity, with the result that human powers to achieve excellence, and human conceptions of the ends and goods involved, are systematically extended.[51]

What is important to note here is that practices are human activities which bring about goods internal to these activities. This means that they *are good for* the people engaged in the practice. Moreover, these goods are realized in the process of engaging in the activity. Also, such practices, if engaged in over time, will have a progressive excellence-making effect; as he says it, they are systematically extended. For example, today's hockey players have appropriated skills from past hockey players and have thereby become better at what they do and have improved the game of hockey.

With this definition, he gives a list of examples of human activities that are and are not practices. He says, "Tic-tac-toe is not an example of a practice in this sense, nor is throwing a football with skill; but the game of football is, and so is chess. Bricklaying is not a practice; architecture is. Planting turnips is not a practice; farming is."[52] That is, practices are cooperative social activities and not just the exercising of individual skills.

Life obviously consists of many practices, among which MacIntyre lists: "arts, sciences, games, politics in the Aristotelian sense, the making and sustaining of family life."[53] Practices and virtues are, of course, intimately related, for practices are shaped by the virtues. As MacIntyre puts it, "without justice, courage and truthfulness, practices could not resist the corrupting power of institutions."[54]

So while practices need virtues to guide and shape them, their meaning is derived only in relation to practices.

With a clear definition of a practice then, MacIntyre can more precisely define the concept of virtue.

> A virtue is an acquired human quality the possession and exercise of which tends to enable us to achieve those goods which are internal to practices and the lack of which effectively prevents us from achieving any such goods.[55]

Practices and virtues alone do not make a well-formed, moral life. To begin with, they presuppose a nonmodern view of the self and how the self negotiates history and tradition. MacIntyre points out that the common notions of self as decision-maker or as one who chooses among available options are antagonistic to virtue ethics. Aristotle has taught him to see the self as a participant in a narrative. The most basic moral question, therefore, is not how to decide or choose, but rather who am I and how ought I to participate in the stories that shape me. He says:

> [M]an is in his actions and practice, as well as in his fictions, essentially a story-telling animal. He is not essentially, but becomes through his history, a teller of stories that aspire to truth. But the key question for men is not about their own authorship; I can only answer the question "What am I to do?" if I can answer the prior question "Of what story or stories do I find myself a part?" We enter human society, that is, with one or more imputed characters—roles into which we have been drafted—and we have to learn what they are in order to be able to understand how others respond to us and how our responses to them are apt to be construed.[56]

Hence, for us to understand what we ought to do requires that we seek to understand ourselves in relation to the stories and the history of these stories that shape us. Not only that, it requires that we learn to place ourselves into these stories in a particular

---

[51] MacIntyre, *After Virtue*, 187.
[52] MacIntyre, *After Virtue*, 187.
[53] MacIntyre, *After Virtue*, 187.
[54] MacIntyre, *After Virtue*, 194.
[55] MacIntyre, *After Virtue*, 191 (emphasis in original).
[56] MacIntyre, *After Virtue*, 216.

way. There are two dynamics to this process. One is that the stories in which we find ourselves are not of our own choosing; they represent long traditions of families, cultures, place, and so on. Second, we participate in many narratives. We are part of a biological family, geographical community, a nation, a religion, an education or lack of one, and so on. How can life have unity of character throughout all these narratives? That is the inescapable, narrative quest; for anyone to give a true account of self requires a weaving into a single strand of the many narratives of which one is a part.

This leads to the last theme of *After Virtue*, namely, tradition, which becomes the central focus of MacIntyre's writings following *After Virtue*. Once he has made the point that the moral life is only intelligible in relation to "the unity of a narrative quest"[57] the question naturally arises as to whether there are better or worse narratives. To state this differently, if what I ought to do is derivative of who I am, and if who I am is determined by the stories that are given to me which I must seek to own, and if these stories are rooted within larger traditions like the Western tradition, or the Eastern tradition, or the Christian tradition, or the modern tradition, can anything be said about the evaluation of these traditions? Indeed, can one be better than the other? These are some of the questions that MacIntyre addresses in his subsequent writings, especially, *Whose Justice? Which Rationality?*, and *Three Rival Versions of Moral Enquiry*.

Notice here that the moral concern, namely, what the good life is and what we ought to do, and the epistemological concern, namely, how we can know, or better stated, how we can convince other people what to do, are not separable questions. In effect, this is of one concern with the assertion that facts are not separated from values. "Ought conclusions" indeed follow logically from factual premises. The analysis of the interrelationship of

morality and epistemology characterizes much of his post *After Virtue* works.

Before I turn to this next focus of his work, a brief summation of the argument of *After Virtue* is in order. First, he claims that emotivism dominates in contemporary, Western societies—making moral statements mere expressions of emotions and moral disputes unresolvable. Second, ethical theories like utilitarianism and human rights theories that seek to repair the damage remain "moral fictions" because they are unable to name a good with moral content. Third, the Enlightenment fails and must fail because it severed facts from values. With that dichotomy, made popular by David Hume, goes the possibility of a teleological account of human nature because the possibility of a relation between human beings as they are (*fact*) and human beings as they could be if they were fully good (as they *ought* to be) has been eliminated. Fourth, given that the Enlightenment's success was premised on the overcoming of classical philosophy, its failure implied that classical philosophy was not overcome. Hence, MacIntyre argues that Aristotle did not need to be rejected, even though he needed some repair. Nietzsche is only necessary if Aristotle is untenable. For certainly the Enlightenment is indefensible, and if the options were between Nietzsche and the Enlightenment, the former may well be preferred. Fifth, MacIntyre's proposal is therefore an ethic of virtue grounded in a teleological view of human nature and the cultivation of virtues. What is required here is the justification of the Aristotelian tradition.

In *After Virtue* MacIntyre does not give an explicitly Christian account of virtue ethics; that comes later when he becomes a Roman Catholic and sees more clearly how Aquinas was able to weave the philosophy of Augustine and Aristotle together. But there are many Christian ethicists who believe that his virtue theory is paradigmatic for understanding the Christian narrative.[58]

---

[57] MacIntyre, *After Virtue*, 219.
[58] See, e.g., Nancey Murphy, Brad J. Kallenberg, and Mark Thiessen Nation, eds., *Virtues and Practices in the Christian*

For to overcome the fact that value dichotomy requires many of the same moves is to overcome the oft-named Christian tension between nature and grace.

JUSTICE AND RATIONALITY

If the task of *After Virtue* was to set out a trajectory to vindicate Aristotle over Nietzsche and thereby expose the sorry moral condition of modernity, the task of *Whose Justice? Which Rationality?* was to move further on that same trajectory. In this work, MacIntyre's focus is less on Nietzsche and more on the philosophy of the Enlightenment which Nietzsche was reacting to. In this work, David Hume serves as the poster boy for what is wrong with the Enlightenment. MacIntyre pits the two competing modes of rational inquiry—Aristotle and Hume—against each other and asks how to decide which one ought to be followed.

MacIntyre realized that this way of putting it would sound strange to modern emotivists. To begin with, the very notion that there can be a rational justification for acting in a particular manner is suspect. It is even a greater problem to contend on rational grounds that one *ought* to follow one rational tradition over another. He states his objective as follows:

> I promised a book in which I should attempt to say both what makes it rational to act in one way rather than another and what makes it rational to advance and defend one conception of practical rationality rather than another. Here it is."[59]

In effect, this project requires an analysis of the way of reasoning itself since modern reason says that no "ought" statement can be the conclusion to an argument. Of course, the challenge of convincing someone from within a particular rational perspective that that framework of thought is irrational is fraught with difficulties. Where can one stand to make the case? Moreover, how can

the case be made that there even is a genuine and viable alternative to Hume and his admirers, given that this is the mode of thought that has trained us and has done so in a manner making it impossible to see what we have lost? MacIntyre asks it as follows:

> Is there, then, such an alternative mode of understanding? Of what did the Enlightenment deprive us? What the Enlightenment made us for the most part blind to and what we now need to recover is, so I shall argue, a conception of rational enquiry as embodied in a tradition, a conception according to which the standards of rational justification themselves emerge from and are part of a history in which they are vindicated by the way in which they transcend the limitations of and provide remedies for the defects of their predecessors within the history of that same tradition.[60]

To make his case, one of the things MacIntyre established was that the two approaches to justice and rationality represented by Aristotle and Hume were radically different and incommensurate. After this, he discussed the question of how to adjudicate between them. In an effort to be clear, MacIntyre goes to great lengths to describe rationality. He does this by way of four points:

1. The concept of rational justification is itself a historical concept. This means that "To justify is to narrate how the argument has gone so far."[61]
2. Not only is how something is justified different from the Enlightenment mode of doing this, but what must be justified is also different. That is, not only form, but form and content are different; actually, the form/content distinction as it has been cast by the liberal tradition is altogether suspect.
3. "[R]ationality itself, whether theoretical or practical, is a concept with a history: indeed, since there are a diversity of traditions of inquiry, with histories, there are, so it turns out, rationalities rather than rationality, just as it will also turn out there are justices rather than justice."[62] Moreover, there are also better and

---

Tradition: Christian Ethics after MacIntyre (Harrisburg, Penn.: Trinity, 1997); and Joseph J. Kotva, *The Christian Case for Virtue Ethics* (Washington, D.C.: Georgetown University Press, 1996).

[59] MacIntyre, *Whose Justice?*, ix.
[60] MacIntyre, *Whose Justice?*, 7.
[61] MacIntyre, *Whose Justice?*, 8.
[62] MacIntyre, *Whose Justice?*, 9.

worse explanations or accounts of the diversity of traditions.

4. "[T]he concept of tradition-constituted and tradition-constitutive rational enquiry cannot be elucidated apart from its exemplification. . . ."[63] In other words, tradition-constituted rationality cannot be purely abstract but is always embodied within social life forms.

We see from this account that MacIntyre's representation of rationality cannot make sense apart from a carefully articulated view of tradition. He defines it thus:

> A tradition is an argument extended through time in which certain fundamental agreements are defined and redefined in terms of two kinds of conflicts: those with critics and enemies external to the tradition who reject all or at least key parts of those fundamental agreements, and those internal, interpretive debates through which the meaning and rationale of the fundamental agreements come to be expressed and by whose progress a tradition is constituted.[64]

For MacIntyre, the debate about justice cannot make any sense apart from the debate within a particular tradition as well as about which tradition is best able to negotiate the complexities of life.

Hence, he undertakes an extensive and multifaceted analysis of four traditions: Aristotle and the ancient Greek tradition, Augustine and the early Christian tradition, Thomas Aquinas and the medieval tradition, and David Hume and the Scottish Enlightenment tradition. The narration of these traditions has two distinct purposes: first, they show how the different accounts of justice and rationality are embodied within each tradition; and second, they show how conflict within or between traditions can be negotiated. Most fundamentally, they provide examples of what a socially embodied tradition of rational inquiry is.[65] This leads MacIntyre to conclude: first, there is no universal rationality that is independent

of tradition; second, understanding the views of one tradition within another tradition, while difficult, is possible; third, rival traditions have rival rationalities, but this does not lead to relativism; and fourth, although he does his own analysis from the standpoint of Thomist Aristotelianism, this means neither that truth is relative nor that it is inconsistent to make universal claims from the standpoint of a particular tradition.

As has become quite clear throughout this discussion, the hero for MacIntyre is Thomas Aquinas, partly because he was successful in synthesizing the Aristotelian standpoint with the Augustinian Christian approach. And so it turns out that there is really one sustained tradition of rational inquiry from the Greek to the medieval period, which is able to overcome internal debates. Clearly the villain is Enlightenment liberalism, as we see with Hume and Kant because it assumes a position of antagonism to all traditions. This is very odd and inconsistent since it too is a tradition. But because of its false dichotomy (facts and values) it assumes that there is a value-free inquiry into an understanding of the world.

In the end, according to MacIntyre, it turns out that there are three main, rival versions of moral inquiry: the socially embodied, tradition-based mode of rational inquiry (the one MacIntyre defends and proposes); the universal non-tradition-based mode of rational inquiry (the Enlightenment approach, as developed by Hume and Kant); and the Nietzschean nihilistic approach. He discusses these in his next book, *Three Rival Versions of Moral Enquiry*.[66]

In this study, originally the 1988 Gifford Lectures at the University of Edinburgh, he analyzes the successful integration of Aristotle and Augustine in the work of Thomas

---

[63] MacIntyre, *Whose Justice?*, 10.

[64] MacIntyre, *Whose Justice?*, 12.

[65] See Alasdair MacIntyre, "Précis of *Whose Justice? Which Rationality?*" in *The MacIntyre Reader*, ed. Kelvin Knight (Notre Dame, Ind.: University of Notre Dame, 1998), 107.

[66] Alasdair MacIntyre, *Three Rival Versions of Moral Enquiry: Encyclopaedia, Genealogy, and Tradition* (Notre Dame, Ind.: University of Notre Dame Press, 1990).

Aquinas and shows how the encyclopedist's position (Enlightenment liberals) fell with the genealogist's (Nietzschean) critique and how the genealogical framework could not be sustained in light of the Thomistic critique. Hence, he concludes that the Thomist synthesis is vindicated as the best account of moral inquiry so far.

It is important not to push MacIntyre to over-conclude. He is not suggesting that his approach cannot be improved upon or that in principle it could not be proven false. Fallibilism[67] is what a socially embodied tradition of moral inquiry must remain open to. Hence, his conclusions must always carry the caveat "so far."

The concluding chapter of *Three Rival Versions of Moral Enquiry* explores the topic of reconceiving the university. This is again reminiscent of George Grant. Yet the argument here is quite different. Grant attempts to reconceive the university via Plato and Augustine and MacIntyre via Thomas Aquinas' synthesis of Aristotle and Augustine. Hence, one gets different results. For example, with Grant's account, there is less awareness that the liberal university is operating on a different rationality than a tradition-based university might. Moreover, technique and technology play significantly different roles on the two accounts. For MacIntyre:

> [I]t was not merely that academic enquiry increasingly became professionalized and specialized and that formal education correspondingly became a preparation for and initiation into professionalization and specialization but that, for the most part and increasingly, moral and theological truth ceased to be recognized as objects of substantive enquiry and instead were relegated to the realm of privatized belief.[68]

This has come to mean that religion and morality can be studied only as meta-disciplines, that is, the objects of inquiry by history, psychology, and sociology. But themselves they are not given academic credence.

MacIntyre conceives a change in the very nature of the university, a change that would permit open attention to the conflicts of traditions—where the university would admit challenges by Nietzschean genealogy and the Thomistic tradition. It is because the liberal university has enforced agreements or structured uniformity that it has felt it needed to reject moral and religious notions. What alternative is possible according to MacIntyre? Here is his answer:

> [T]he university as a place of constrained disagreement, of imposed participation in conflict, in which a central responsibility of higher education would be to initiate students into conflict.[69]

In other words, real debate is envisioned where representatives of live traditions would represent their own standpoints as well as remain open to hearing other standpoints. But MacIntyre goes further:

> [E]ach of us would also have to play a second role, that not of a partisan, but of someone concerned to uphold and to order the ongoing conflicts, to provide and sustain institutionalized means for their expression, to negotiate the modes of encounter between opponents, to ensure that rival voices were not illegitimately suppressed, to sustain the university—not as an arena of neutral objectivity, as in the liberal university, since each of the contending standpoints would be advancing its own partisan accounts of the nature and function of objectivity—but as an arena of conflict in which the most fundamental type of moral and theological disagreement was accorded recognition.[70]

In response to the obvious retort that this is a pure fantasy alternative to the well-established, liberal university, MacIntyre says, to the contrary, it has happened in the past and could happen again.[71] For MacIntyre, this is

---

[67] Fallibilism is the philosophical thesis that all claims of knowledge can in principle be wrong.

[68] MacIntyre, *Three Rival Versions*, 217.

[69] MacIntyre, *Three Rival Versions*, 230–31.

[70] MacIntyre, *Three Rival Versions*, 231.

[71] He cites the thirteenth-century University of Paris as the place where the "Augustinians and Aristotelians each conducted their own systematic enquiries while at the same time engaging in systematic controversy" (MacIntyre, *Three Rival Versions*, 232).

not only a real possibility but an urgent necessity. After all, an alternative view of rationality requires an alternative mode of inquiry into truth and goodness; hence, an alternative mode of education and learning is key.

CONCLUSION

Lest we forget that in *After Virtue* MacIntyre emphasized the importance of Aristotle's view of the polis, I conclude with a few comments on the notion of the community of virtue, which can be upheld only by a context of debate in which "ought conclusions" can indeed follow from factual premises. As we have said, the Aristotelian polis was the community where the habituation of virtues was made possible on the grounds of friendship. With the liberal universities relegating moral and theological matters to the private realm, and the larger public learning well from this teaching, we are left at the mercy of the nation state which is very different from Aristotle's polis. According to MacIntyre, this entity is ill-equipped and morally inept in the task of habituating us into a life of virtues since it seeks only the obedience and allegiance of its citizens in gratitude for the goods and services it renders. MacIntyre says it thus:

> The modern nations-state, in whatever guise, is a dangerous and unmanageable institution, presenting itself on the one hand as a bureaucratic supplier of goods and services, which is always about to, but never actually does, give its clients value for money, and on the other as a repository of sacred values, which from time to time invites one to lay down one's life on its behalf. As I have remarked elsewhere . . . it is like being asked to die for the telephone company.[72]

In other words, in the absence of a set of practices that can shape us into good people, we are set adrift by whatever will has authority. The connection between the standard emotivist account of morality and the evils of our society like racism and war should be readily apparent. Sadly, they are not.

MacIntyre is dead serious in his challenge to students, scholars, and all people around the world duped by the liberal imagination to join in the debate of re-envisioning the good life, not merely to repeat what Aquinas has already said, but nevertheless in the Thomistic style. He knows all too well that this will go against the stream of prevailing forces, but then "to unfit our students for the contemporary world ought in any case to be one of our educational aims."[73]

---

[72] Alasdair MacIntyre, "A Partial Response to My Critics," in *After MacIntyre*, ed. John Horton and Susan Mendus, 303.
[73] "An Interview for *Cogito*," in Knight, *MacIntyre Reader*, 275.

PART IV-A

The chapters on George Grant and Alasdair MacIntyre are profound and important for the discussion of Christian ethics. Not only do they lift out for further discussion many germane topics like technology, notion of the university, abortion and human life issues, politics, pacifism, human rights, the notions of goodness and beauty, and what it means to be human, but they also offer a profound critique of modernity and the impact of the Enlightenment on today's way of seeing the world.

Each author has a unique perspective on the problems and the solutions: the manner in which Grant reads the "fall" of modernity prompts him to lament the rejection of "nature" in favor of "history" as a paradigm through which to read the world. This leads him to critique the prevalence of historicism as a mode of inquiry, a technique made popular especially by Hegel and Marx. Hence, Grant is an advocate of a return to the realism of Plato, which he believes helps us to an understanding of Christianity not unlike we see in Augustine. The reason for his position is clear; he believes that unless we ground goodness, truth, and beauty in something given, that is, in something outside the human subject and outside history, there can be no stability and base for knowledge and we are left with merely the human will (Nietzsche). The result is, as we see everywhere around us, that goodness and truth swim off the charts of relevance and into the oblivion of an unusable past. The implication is that we moderns can "know"

only insofar as we "know how" to realize our aspirations and goals (knowledge defined by technology), but we can "know" precious little about what there really is (knowledge defined by truth). Hence, as moderns, we manipulate our environment to suit our needs and desires, for there is nothing to place ourselves under—nothing to open ourselves up to—that can form us. We shape everything; nothing shapes us! Hence his lament.

MacIntyre represents a somewhat different approach to philosophy, and yet he shares many of Grant's concerns. Perhaps the difference can be accounted for by MacIntyre's reliance on Aristotle rather than Plato for his reconstruction of the post-Enlightenment debacle. But he uses Aristotle in a unique way. He develops an Aristotelian historicism (admittedly an odd combo), which he reads through the theology-philosophy of Thomas Aquinas. This, of course, has a strong flavor of "natural law," just like Grant advocates, only for MacIntyre it is not outside but within history. For MacIntyre, the dichotomy between history and nature is not as categorical as Grant supposed. In fact, as he sees it, the acceptance of the absoluteness of this dichotomy is itself part of the negative Enlightenment legacy.

For MacIntyre, then, there are competing rationalities (liberal universal, Nietzschean relativism, tradition-based) whose conflicting interpretations of reality must be freely admitted. Each of these is born in history and must remain in history. This is different from Grant, for whom there is but one ahistorical reason properly presented by Plato and corrupted by modernity. The difference here affects their *solutions* to the problems of modernity; with respect to the *problems* much is shared.

THE ENLIGHTENMENT

Both philosophers have named the Enlightenment as the locus of a profound shift in thinking that has made ethics impossible for moderns. Both have named the fact-value distinction as the fatal blow because it makes the notion of "the good" unintelligible for moderns. It does this by convincing moderns that all ethics are private matters over which disagreements cannot be resolved in principle. Hence, when it comes to ethical theory, we are stuck with emotivism. Since there are no "goods" outside of the human will, we are left with human desires that parade as moral qualities called values. This move is made possible because modernity has made matters of both ethics and religion private and personal. The result is that the notion is gone of a human nature that can guide us into what we might become if we were to become fully human.

Some might argue that their lament is premature or misplaced since the Enlightenment is more gain than loss. After all, it has brought us "human rights," which we should herald as a great step forward in making the language of ethics intelligible and internationally useable. Both philosophers argue that the problem with human-rights language rests on the absence of a *moral good* which could serve as its ground. In the absence of such, the only basis for human rights is agreement, covenant, or imposition, and that often eliminates or diminishes the well-being of minorities and the powerless.

VIRTUES AND THE GOOD LIFE

On the question of the nature of the good life, our two authors take somewhat different turns. They both ask a key question, "What are we for?" which is but to highlight that

human beings have a nature. And both argue that, once human nature is identified, it is possible to name the virtues (skills, habits) that might get us there. For MacIntyre, however, it gets more complex when he introduces notions like traditions, narratives, and practices into the mix. Here is where the differences between the two philosophers become apparent. Because MacIntyre employs a tradition-based rationality, he also has a tradition-based view of the good. That is, for him, goodness is supplied by the narratives and practices within specific traditions. For Grant, on the other hand, the good emerges from a synthesis of Plato's cave and the ethic of Jesus. From Jesus we can see what is good, which gives us a place from which we can critique and overcome modern historical relativity.

UNIVERSITY

The notion of the university is important for both philosophers. For how do we educate our youth when the assumptions that underwrite our Western university systems are not credible? While both address this question, their answers diverge.

Grant emphasizes a return to the classics and especially philosophy, which holds before us the pursuit of knowledge guided by the virtue of wisdom. He laments that the university has been hijacked by the "know how" view of knowledge that teaches students to become doers at the expense of becoming thinkers. Further, he points to the tragedy of the autonomy of the disciplines and suggests that the notion of university is itself a misnomer because they have become "multiveristies." He therefore advocates substantial curriculum change that would find ways of binding all knowledge together under a common domain of truth in pursuit of wisdom.

MacIntyre's vision for the university, while different in content, stems from a similar concern—that religion and ethics have lost their rightful place in the university because they have been relegated to the private, personal sphere. Like Grant, he laments that the modern university is not open to challenges from outside the liberal tradition itself. In its place, MacIntyre advocates an open debate among the competing traditions of rationality, where students would be initiated into and tutored in the conflict and debates of the different perspectives, rather than being given only the Enlightenment perspective of a single, universal rationality.

It is interesting to observe that both philosophers have injected the nature of the university as itself an important, ethical issue. It is not often that this question enters the realm of relevance for moral debate. But surely it is a matter of great importance to inquire how we teach and what we teach our young people; for there is perhaps nothing more important than how we train our youth to see the world. The philosophers are concerned that to teach young people that religious and ethical matters belong to the private and personal realm, off the map of intellectual scrutiny, is to teach them the very impossibility of ethics. And to place these matters on the agenda of rational scrutiny is to give them their rightful place.

THEOLOGY

Perhaps it is to be expected that philosophers would be somewhat weak on theology. But it could make a significant difference to have a thicker read of theology than either Grant of MacIntyre provide. Without a more carefully nuanced Christology and ecclesiology, the notion of Christian truth is conceived too easily only in terms of theories and abstract principles. The temptation of philosophers is to corral truth; to control the terms in which truth and goodness get narrated; to place faith in rationality over against faith in Jesus. The "I am the truth" in the Gospel of John names an important process, one which invites participation of both body and mind. Here, the process entrenches openness to the other that a mere rationale process can easily foreclose.

It is important to remember that the effort to out-narrate or out-compete in philosophical debate is a war by another name, which can have casualties. The most frequent casualties in such a conflict are those with a weaker voice, not necessarily those who lack the capacity to give voice to the truth—the powerless ones or the conquered ones. And surely whatever goes by the name of Christian ethics should place special emphasis on hospitality for the stranger.

There can be no doubt that these two social philosophers have offered a prophetic voice that helps us to see deeply into the structures of society. The implications and warnings that stem from the Enlightenment calamity should not be underestimated. At the same time, a thicker reading of theological ethics reaching back to the story of Jesus, especially to the cross and resurrection, could have helped in giving a more nuanced account of how to embody the debate over truth.

PART IV

CRITICAL RESPONSES TO TWENTIETH-CENTURY
CHRISTIAN ETHICS

•

Section B
Liberation Theologians

Chapter Twenty-Six

GUSTAVO GUTIÉRREZ
(1928–)

Liberation theology has a distinct connection with Christian ethics because it is a theological response to injustice and oppression. Yet, clearly, liberation theology does not name a single theology; there are many. It therefore becomes challenging to precisely identify liberation theology. Virtually every oppressed group has a liberation theology—North American aboriginals, North American blacks, Asians, Africans, Latin Americans, Palestinians, women, and many others.[1] While they all have the theme of liberation in common, they differ markedly as far in their struggle for overcoming oppression because the injustices causing the oppression differ.

Readers will notice that there are two other chapters in this section on liberation theology, one that focuses on the struggle of North American blacks and another that deals with North American aboriginal liberation. And while there is also diversity within each of these groups, I will focus on only one theologian from each group. In this chapter, I discuss Latin American liberation theology and specifically the work of Gustavo Gutiérrez.

It is important to note that Gutiérrez has a special place within the history of liberation theology because he was the first to use the phrase. Hence, he is often called the father of liberation theology. Yet Gutiérrez cautions against an exaggerated sense of its importance when he says, "I was a Christian long before liberation theology and I will be a Christian long after liberation theology."[2]

Liberation theology usually has its roots in specific church denominations, and the Gutiérrez variety comes out of the Roman Catholic Church. This produces its own set of dynamics. At first, the Church hierarchy was quite skeptical of his approach, partially because of its affinity with Marxism and partially because it raised questions about the theology of the church hierarchy. Yet within twenty years, the church spoke quite differently. For example, in 1986 Pope John Paul II addressed the Bishops of Brazil saying:

> Liberation theology is not only timely but useful and necessary. It should be seen as a new stage, closely connected with earlier ones, in the theological reflection that began with the apostolic tradition and has continued in the great fathers and doctors, the ordinary and the extraordinary exercise of the church's teaching office, and more recently, the rich patrimony of the church's social teaching as set forth in documents from *Rerum Novarum* to *Laborem Exercens*.[3]

---

[1] There are also Jewish liberation theologies, e.g., Marc H. Ellis, *Toward a Jewish Theology of Liberation: The Challenge of the 21st Century*, 3rd expanded ed. (Waco, Tex.: Baylor University Press, 2004); and Muslim liberation theologies, such as, Hamid Dabashi, *Islamic Liberation Theology: Resisting the Empire* (New York: Routledge, 2008).

[2] Quoted from Robert McAfee Brown, *Gustavo Gutiérrez: An Introduction to Liberation Theology* (Maryknoll, N.Y.: Orbis, 1990), 22. Comments on Gutiérrez's life draw heavily from this work.

[3] Quoted from Gustavo Gutiérrez, *A Theology of Liberation: History, Politics, and Salvation*, trans. Sister Caridad Inda and John Eagleson (Maryknoll, N.Y.: Orbis, 1988), xliv.

This statement is testimony of how deeply Latin American liberation theology, especially as articulated by Gustavo Gutiérrez, has affected and changed the face of Catholic theology. Perhaps it is as Pope John XXIII said in a different context some years before Gutiérrez's book was written, "It is not that the Gospel has changed: it is that we have begun to understand it better."[4]

GUTIÉRREZ'S LIFE

Gutiérrez was born in "Old Lima," Peru, on June 8, 1928. This was not an affluent part of town. Moreover, he was a *mestizo*, which means "half-breed," part Hispanic and part Quechuan Indian. So, from the beginning of his life he was acquainted with the conditions of poverty and structured oppression. His family was relatively small—he had only two sisters—and he speaks of his family fondly as a context of love and affection. The early years of his life were fraught with "economic difficulties," and when he was still quite young, the family moved to Rimac and then to Barranco on the outskirts of the large city of Lima.[5]

As the only boy in the family, he felt pressure on him to help his family out of poverty. But at an early age, he developed an interest in reading that was not exactly considered an asset for this familial calling. Moreover, at the age of twelve he was struck with a severe case of osteomyelitis[6] and was confined to a bed and later a wheelchair for a period of six years. This disease left him with a permanent limp. During his illness, when the pain permitted it, he engaged in reading, visiting, and playing table games. He speaks about his illness and its effects thus:

There was physical pain although I must say that the strong bonds of friendship that I formed in those years compensated greatly for my physical

limitations. During the years I was sick my house became a regular center for meetings, conversations, games. I developed a real passion for chess and one of my frustrations as an adult is not having time to play.[7]

As a young adult, he began university studies at the San Marcos University in Lima. Perhaps it was his physical illness that motivated him to study medicine, but his first degree was a Bachelor of Science in medicine and literature. He went on to the National University in Lima to study philosophy, and then to Santiago, Chile, to study theology. He studied philosophy and psychology at the Catholic University in Louvain, Belgium, from 1951 to 1955, and here wrote a master's thesis on "The Psychic Conflict in Freud." From 1955 to 1959, he studied in a theology program at the Catholic University of Lyons, France, from where he eventually received his doctorate in 1985.[8] In addition to these schools, Gutiérrez studied at the Gregorian University in Rome, at the University of Nijmegen in the Netherlands, and at the University of Tübingen in Germany. Whatever might be the larger benefit from attending such a smorgasbord of theological schools, one tangible gain for him was that he became fluent in French, German, and English, in addition to his native Spanish and Quechua.

During the time of his university studies, especially at Lima, he became involved in political activities. Soon he was thoroughly convinced of the Christian calling to make every effort to challenge unjust practices and change unjust structures. It was never a question of whether to be politically active, only how. The two ways open to him were to become overtly active through secular channels or alternatively to work at the same issues through the Church. In 1959 he made that choice when he was ordained as a Catholic

---

[4] Gutiérrez, *Theology of Liberation*, xiv.

[5] See Brown, *Gustavo Gutiérrez*, 24.

[6] Osteomyelitis is a severe infection of the bones that often leaves its victims crippled.

[7] Brown, *Gustavo Gutiérrez*, 24.

[8] See Gustavo Gutiérrez, *The Truth Shall Make You Free: Confrontations*, trans. Matthew J. O'Connell (Maryknoll, N.Y.: Orbis, 1990) for a "Presentation of the Dissertation" followed by a discussion.

priest. That did not settle everything, but it meant that from now on both the impetus for his work and its focus would be determined by his reading of Jesus' social teachings. It meant further that he would pick up the challenge of rethinking for Latin America the concrete social-political ramifications of his European educators—scholars like Henri de Lubac, Jean Daniélou, Yves Congar, Karl Rahner, Edward Schillebeeckx, Maurice Blondel, and Gerhard von Rad. This would prove to call for wisdom beyond what he had anticipated.

When he returned to Lima in 1960, he began teaching part-time at the Catholic University there. Immediately he sought to embody his decade-long, rich, theological learning in a "foreign" land. What was the "meaning of human existence and presence of God in the world"[9] in the barrios of Lima, Peru? We notice here that Gutiérrez was a contextual theologian from the start. He explains: "This led me to confront Christian faith with thinkers like Albert Camus, Karl Marx, and others, as well as film directors like Luis Buñuel and Ingmar Bergman, and writers like José María Arguedas or poets like our César Vallejo."[10] He believed it important to be in dialogue not just with aspects of culture that supported Christianity but especially with aspects of culture that were critical of Christianity. For Christianity is an embodied religion, and when Christ's grace is concretely experienced by the poor, it will be received as good news. When it is not, it ought to be critiqued.

This approach would soon lead Gutiérrez to wonder about the adequacy of the theology he had learned in his training. He became more and more aware that the questions and issues that shaped this approach were not the questions and issues that arose from a culture of poverty and oppression.

Biographer Brown identifies three thinkers who were especially influential in shaping Gutiérrez's theological struggle during this time.[11] First, Bishop Bartolomé de Las Casas, whose theology, both method and content, made a deep impression because it was indigenous to Latin America and eminently faithful to Jesus' teaching. Gutiérrez later explored his social teaching extensively in a major study.[12] Second, the Peruvian sociologist José Carlos Mariátegui influenced Gutiérrez greatly. He believed that Mariátegui's Marxist analysis of social reality, especially his understanding of class struggle and the unity of theory and praxis, could be made compatible with Christian theology. And third, the novelist José María Arguedas, who was able to highlight the violence done to the poor so as to lift out dynamics of poverty not ordinarily seen.

Influences like these pushed Gutiérrez ever further in the direction of exploring new, indigenous forms of theology. He became more and more overwhelmed by the claim Christ had on him and by the idea that Christ's call to love neighbor could not remain abstract but required the concrete response of going to the neighbor and seeking liberation for the neighbor. Later, he described this stage of life in terms of three important discoveries: the first had to do with discovering that poverty is destructive; the second that poverty is not accidental but structural; and the third that the poor are themselves a social class. Brown says, "As a result of these three discoveries, Gutiérrez concluded that in order to serve the poor one must move into political action."[13]

What does political action mean for a Catholic priest in Latin America? A friend of Gutiérrez, a fellow priest named Camilo Torres, by taking a very different road, inadvertently helped him sort this out.[14] The

---

[9] Brown, *Gustavo Gutiérrez*, 25.

[10] Brown, *Gustavo Gutiérrez*, 25.

[11] See Brown, *Gustavo Gutiérrez*, 26–31.

[12] See Gustavo Gutiérrez, *Las Casas: In Search of the Poor of Jesus Christ*, trans. Robert R. Barr (Maryknoll, N.Y.: Orbis, 1993).

[13] Brown, *Gustavo Gutiérrez*, 32.

[14] Camilo Torres (1929–1966) was a Catholic priest from Bogota, Colombia, who believed it was incumbent upon him

two had become friends in Louvain, where they studied together. Upon their return to Latin America, both were concerned with how the church could become more involved in changing the unjust status quo that was underwriting poverty. In autumn of 1962, along with many other church leaders, they were invited by the Bishop of Chile to a conference to discuss the work of the church in Latin America. Here a rift developed between the two revolutionary priests. Brown describes it thus: "Gustavo wanted to explore 'a specifically Christian form of radicalism that did not simply follow the Marxist current,' while Camilo felt that this was an abstraction and that since Marxists were the ones who were fighting for a new society, Christians should work openly with them."[15] Gutiérrez argued that whatever might be the role of the layperson in political struggle, priests should not engage in such secular work.[16] After Torres left the priesthood to join the liberation movement, he exclaimed that he would "not celebrate the eucharist again until there was justice in the world." Gutiérrez is reported to have replied, "If we can't celebrate the eucharist until we have attained a perfect society, then we will have to wait until we get to heaven, in which case the eucharist is superfluous."[17]

During the 1960s, Gutiérrez worked as a parish priest in the slum barrio of Rimac in Lima. But more and more he realized that his training as a theologian gave him neither the resources nor the tools to be a faithful church worker in this setting. He was completely convinced that his priestly call was to live with and help the poor overcome their poverty. Torres and other Marxist-inspired theologians were right in contending that the

system needed to change. But the answer to how to conceive of that change and then how to engage in it should come from theology. He realized that his training had not prepared him to be *theologically* present to poor people in Rimac. Small wonder that people like Torres felt they had to leave the priesthood in order to do Christ's work. He began to see how desperately the church needed a new theology to help direct the Christ-inspired passion to overcome poverty in the right direction. This would require a rethinking and, sadly, also a clash with the theology of the church.

It was not as though Gutiérrez was without resources in this project of re-imagining theology. In addition to the Spanish writer already identified, he found other European theologians such as Dietrich Bonhoeffer, Johann Baptist Metz, Hans Küng, and Jürgen Moltmann to be very helpful. Among this group, perhaps especially significant, was the thought of the Protestant Bonhoeffer, who wrote about the dispossessed in ways Gutiérrez calls "a beautiful text of Bonhoeffer." He quotes him as follows:

> We have learned to see the great events of the history of the world from beneath—from the viewpoint of the useless, the suspect, the abused, the powerless, the oppressed, the despised. In a word, from the viewpoint of the suffering.[18]

Gutiérrez saw here the makings of an indigenous theology of the poor. Bonhoeffer came to this view of theology not in the context of poverty but in the context of a different form of power abuse. In many ways, Bonhoeffer still represented the voice of mainline theology, but there were here the beginnings of something new.

---

as a Christian to use guerrilla warfare to overthrow unjust structures in society. He once said, "If Jesus were alive today He would be a *guerrillero*." Torres died in his first battle shortly after joining the liberation movement. For a study of the thought and life of Torres in comparison with another Latin American theologian, Dom Hélder Câmara, see Titus Guenther, *Torres and Câmara: Violence and Nonviolence from a Mennonite Perspective* (unpublished M.A. thesis, University of St. Michael's College, Toronto, Ontario, 1977).

[15] Brown, *Gustavo Gutiérrez*, 34.

[16] This was on the verge of Vatican II, when the distinction between religious and secular work was strongly maintained. For more on this topic, see the discussion on von Balthasar's struggles in chap. 16 above.

[17] Quoted from Brown, *Gustavo Gutiérrez*, 34.

[18] Gustavo Gutiérrez, *The Power of the Poor in History*, trans. Robert R. Barr (Maryknoll, N.Y.: Orbis, 1983), 203.

Much of Gutiérrez's later life revolves around writing books, and so it becomes intelligible only in the context of discussing his work. Yet he remains active in Rimac at the Bartolomé de Las Casas Center while also traveling all over the world. He is in much demand for his ideas and his passion for the poor. Since 2001 he has been the John Cardinal O'Hara Professor in Theology at the University of Notre Dame. and he also continues to teach occasionally at the Pontifical Catholic University of Peru. He holds honorary degrees from some twenty universities around the world.[19]

In 1998, fairly late in his life, Gutiérrez joined the Dominican Order. Although this took some time, he says the step came quite naturally to him. Many of his teachers in France—Yves Congar, Marie-Dominique Chenu, and Edward Schillebeeckx—were Dominicans. He says, "I was attracted to their profound understanding of the intimate relationship that should exist between theology, spirituality and the actual preaching of the Gospel. Liberation theology shares that conviction."[20] Gutiérrez remains active as a theologian, a preacher, and a priest; in all that he says and does, his love for Christ and his devotion to the poor are what drive him.

BIRTHING LIBERATION THEOLOGY

The year 1971 was an important one for Latin American liberation theology, as it was the year Gutiérrez published his first book, *Teología de la liberación, Perspectivas*. Two years later it was translated into English as *A Theology of Liberation*.[21] This was the first time that the phrase "liberation theology" appeared with such prominence.[22] And it stuck!

Gutiérrez was of course not the only Latin American theologian at work crafting a new approach to theology. Leonardo Boff of Brazil and Juan Luis Segundo of Uruguay were writing their own versions of liberation theology.[23] Yet Gutiérrez was key in working out a theology that, although it affirmed much of the tradition, wished to set itself apart from what is sometimes called "dominant theology."

Brown contrasts dominant theology (DT) and liberation theology (LT) as follows:

DT: responds to *nonbeliever* whose faith is threatened by modernity;

LT: responds to the *nonperson* whose faith is threatened by forces of destruction;

DT: begins with the world of modernity and remains thought-oriented;

LT: begins with the world of oppression and becomes action-oriented;

DT: is developed "from above"—from the position of the privileged, the affluent, the bourgeois;

LT: is developed "from below"—from the "underside of history," the position of the oppressed, the marginated, the exploited;

DT: largely written by "those with white hands," the "winners";

LT: only beginning to be written; must be articulated by those with darkskinned, gnarled hands, the "losers";

DT: focuses attention on a "religious" world that needs to be reinforced;

LT: focuses attention on a political world that needs to be replaced;

DT: linked to Western culture, the white race, the male sex, the bourgeois class;

LT: linked to "the wretched of the earth," the marginated races, despised cultures and sex, the exploited classes;

---

[19] See the faculty website at the University of Notre Dame, http://theology.nd.edu/people/all/gutierrez-gustavo/index.shtml, accessed May 11, 2011.

[20] From Daniel Hartnett, "Remembering the Poor: An Interview with Gustavo Gutiérrez," *America: The National Catholic Weekly* (February 3, 2003).

[21] Gustavo Gutiérrez, *A Theology of Liberation: History, Politics, and Salvation*, trans. Sister Caridad Inda and John Eagleson (Maryknoll, N.Y.: Orbis, 1973). The citations in this chapter are to the 1988 revised edition already cited.

[22] Gutiérrez had given a paper by this title in Chimbote, Peru, in 1968. He said this is when he believes "theology of liberation" was born. See Brown, *Gustavo Gutiérrez*, 35.

[23] For a summary of the development of liberation theology in Latin America, see Phillip Berryman, *Liberation Theology: Essential Facts about the Revolutionary Movement in Latin America—and Beyond* (New York: Pantheon, 1987).

DT: affirms the achievements of culture—individualism, rationalism, capitalism, the bourgeois spirit;

LT: insists that the "achievements" of culture have been used to exploit the poor;

DT: wants to work gradually, reforming the existing structures by "supervision";

LT: demands to work rapidly through liberation from existing structures by "subversion."[24]

Although a helpful heuristic schema, even Brown admits to oversimplification in setting up the two approaches this way. For what here is called "dominant theology" does not fully characterize Roman Catholic theology, and the liberation theology is much more nuanced than this contrast suggests. Moreover, it should be remembered that Gutiérrez was thoroughly committed to the theology of the Catholic Church, even though he found himself pushing in a direction of conscientiously developing a theology from the standpoint of the poor, a direction that should not be that foreign to the church's theology to begin with.

Three more factors should be kept in mind in seeking to understand the birthing of liberation theology.

Impact of Second Vatican Council

First, the Second Vatican Council (1962–1965) was influential in making liberation theology possible. This council had the effect of giving more people a voice in shaping the theology of the church. One example of this was that the Catholic Latin American bishops met in Medellín, Colombia, in 1968 to discuss and accept important statements, several of which Gutiérrez had a direct hand in writing. Among them was a statement in which they agreed that it was acceptable and indeed important for the church to speak of "institutional violence."

Why was this important? Because it implied that the very structure of society was violent and that the church must separate itself from such a society in order to become a force of liberation—a force opposed to the violence wrought by social structures perpetuating poverty. Such seemingly innocent changes have significant, theological implications. For example, sin is no longer understood merely as a human act but is also seen as a problem for institutions, which also need to repent and be "saved." Even more important, the church must not participate, sanction, or baptize violent social structures but must find ways to join the forces seeking to change such structures. Hence, the church's acceptance of the language of institutional violence was seen as a great victory for people like Gutiérrez because it pushed the church to underwrite the liberation movement.

The Medellín conference was a significant milestone for liberation theology. In fact, the implications of this event were so powerful for the thinking and practice of the people in the region that many bishops got cold feet after the event. What kind of power had they really unleashed? By 1979 another conference was called by the bishops in order to undo "the damage" of Medellín. This time they were to meet in Puebla, Mexico. A "Preliminary Document" was circulated, written from the "European perspective," in an effort to tone down the revolutionary reading of Medellín. This did not sit well with Latin American leaders like Gutiérrez. Says Brown:

> Objections by the planeload made their way to Rome and to the various episcopal centers in Latin America, and not a few Latin American bishops were among the most vocal opponents . . . The result of the ferment was that the Preliminary Document had to be virtually scrapped and a brand new text hammered out during the Puebla meetings themselves.[25]

The story of the Puebla conference is worth telling in greater detail. The leaders had decided not to invite Gutiérrez and

---

[24] Brown, *Gustavo Gutiérrez*, 91 (emphasis in original).

[25] From Robert McAfee Brown, preface to *The Power of the Poor in History*, by Gustavo Gutiérrez, trans. Robert R. Barr (Maryknoll, N.Y.: Orbis, 1983), ix.

his fellow liberation theologians, who were seen as the problems of Medellín, but while they could not attend the proceedings, they nevertheless could not be kept out of the city of Puebla. So they gathered in a rented house as close as possible to the compound, where they wrote their own documents. Although they were not permitted entry, sympathetic bishops attending the conference could visit them. Hence, via the "friendly bishops," they were able to get their drafts into the sessions for debate and as a result the conference was another huge success for liberation theology. The Latin American bishops managed to re-instate all that Medellín had given, plus the bishops committed themselves to a "prefer-ential option for the poor." An official Puebla document reads:

> The poor merit preferential attention, whatever may be the moral or spiritual situation in which they find themselves. Made in the image and likeness of God to be his children, this image is dimmed and even defiled. That is why God takes on their defense and loves them.[26]

The concept of the preferential option for the poor is at least as important as the recog-nition that violence can be structural. In fact, structural violence and poverty are really of one piece. After all, it is the system that in many cases makes people poor. Gutiérrez says, "The poverty to which the option re-fers is material poverty. Material poverty means premature and unjust death. The poor person is someone who is treated as a non-person, someone who is considered insignifi-cant from an economic, political and cultural point of view."[27] And the term "preferential" should not be read to mean that God does not love the non-poor. There is no inconsistency in saying there are special needs in the king-dom that deserve special attention.

Medellín and Puebla had profound effects in changing the direction not only of Latin American theology but of Roman Catholic theology as a whole. Given that Second Vati-can Council had already loosened the theo-logical grip that Rome had on the churches of developing regions, a new spirituality was given wings, which fostered the formulation of a theology written from the underside of history. Thinkers like Gutiérrez have been foremost among them.

What did it mean to write a theology from the standpoint of the poor? It changed a lot. The rich of the northern hemisphere have a different set of questions they ask of theol-ogy than the poor have. The rich have the luxury of being concerned about intellec-tual sense-making, whereas the poor ask about what measures can be implored from God to change their condition of social and economic misery. For the wealthy post-En-lightenment world, the most important theo-logical issue is a crisis of belief in the face of the critical theories emanating from modern science. For the poor, the most important theological matter is a crisis of existence in hopelessness and what theology can provide for changing this reality.

It is important to remember that Gutiérrez's theology did not have its roots merely in the social condition of poor people but reached back directly to what he discovered in the Scriptures as he read and reread them. After all, both tenets—structural violence and the "preferential option for the poor"— Gutiérrez argued, were thoroughly biblical concepts. The poor and the dispossessed were given special status in God's kingdom; they were the ones who seemed to be able to understand the meaning of the gospel best. These insights gave Gutiérrez new hope that the biblical message held out the possibil-ity of liberation from poverty. However, at the same time it fostered a "hermeneutic of suspicion" about what he had been taught. In much of the teaching of Jesus, the dom-inant theology and culture are the objects

---

[26] Quoted from Gustavo Gutiérrez, *On Job: God-Talk and the Suffering of the Innocent*, trans. Matthew J. O'Connell (Maryknoll, N.Y.: Orbis, 1987), xiii.
[27] From Hartnett, "Remembering the Poor."

of ridicule and critique. And for Gutiérrez, Jesus Christ is the hermeneutical principle.[28] How can dominant theology today be the source of our knowledge of God? Wealthy and powerful people find it very difficult to train their eyes, ears, and minds to behold what the gospel really teaches about the human stance of openness to God.

Church in Latin America

A second factor in understanding the birthing of liberation theology, and one that follows directly from the first, focuses on the nature of the church among the Latin American Christians. One of the documents discussed at Medellín was called "Poverty of the Church." It distinguished three meanings of poverty: "real poverty as an evil—that is something that God does not want; spiritual poverty, in the sense of a readiness to do God's will; and solidarity with the poor, along with protest against the conditions under which they suffer."[29] There is, then, a biblical call both to embrace poverty and to overcome poverty; to acknowledge our sinfulness before God at the same time as we open ourselves to God and work at overcoming the conditions of poverty and the pain of the poor. But there can be no justification of material poverty.

Doing theology from the standpoint of poverty requires that the poor be brought into the very process. That is, the church, including the poor, is not only the recipient of theology from a hierarchical structure but theology also emerges from the church at work itself. Liberation theology therefore requires a renewed view of the church. Theology now gets shaped by a people who read the Bible and believe that what is written there is about them. This is a concrete manifestation of the claim that for theology to be liberating it must come from the bottom up (the underside of history) and not from the top down. The church in the liberation struggle is therefore reshaped into groups called *comunidades de base* (base communities). These communities meet to bring their lives into interaction with the world of the Bible.

It is not hard to imagine that this approach would have serious implications for the established Church. In some regions, people attended Mass much less frequently preferring the "church" of the base communities. This was, of course, a factor in the bishop's concern with liberation theology. The people, on the other hand, saw it as part of Church renewal. They believed that the Church ought to be a community of people struggling together to overcome oppressions, rather than an institution doing little more than administering the sacraments. They looked at the New Testament church and saw there the kind of community they were attempting to emulate.[30]

Nature of Theology

A third factor in understanding liberation theology relates to the nature of theology itself, both its method and content. Prior to Vatican II, classical theology taught the importance of the universality of the Christian faith; that is, it was the same in Latin America as it was in Europe. Hence, it got formulated in doctrinal creeds, often to combat false philosophies of the day. Natural theology was prominent, and natural reason was the route to get to theological truth. This approach was inadequate for theologians like Gutiérrez because it was possible from this standpoint to legitimate oppression. The resistance to poverty and injustice needed to be part of theology itself.

---

[28] See Gutiérrez, *Power of the Poor*, 60f. Here he says, "The great hermeneutical principle of faith, and hence the basis and foundation of all theological reasoning, is Jesus Christ," 61.

[29] Gutiérrez, *Theology of Liberation*, xxv.

[30] Latin American liberation theology's spawning of *comunidades de base* suggests an ecclesiology with affinities in several other Christian denominations. One such example is LaVerne A. Rutschman, "Latin American Liberation Theology and Radical Anabaptism," in *Journal of Ecumenical Studies* 19, no. 1 (1982): 38–56.

Gutiérrez sets out to change all this. This change is outlined in *A Theology of Liberation*,[31] but later he says:

> From the beginning, the theology of liberation posited that the first act is involvement in the liberation process, and that theology comes afterward, as a second act. The theological moment is one of critical reflection from within, and upon, concrete historical praxis, in confrontation with the Lord as lived and accepted in faith—a faith that comes to us through manifold, and sometimes ambiguous, historical mediations, but which we are daily remaking and repairing.[32]

This is not so much an epistemological formula as it is a simple recognition that you cannot do theology from a place of neutrality or from anywhere. You must stand somewhere, in a particular place, in order to be able to see God's work of the kingdom. Where one stands makes an important difference. Gutiérrez's claim is that unless one stands with the poor—where God is at work—one cannot think right theologically.

What does it mean for theology to be a second act? It certainly did not mean, for Gutiérrez, that theology was insignificant. Liberation theology is *theology*, both a method and a content. As a method, it is an inquiry that begins in solidarity with the poor; as content it works every bit as hard as any other theology at understanding God, Jesus Christ, the church, sin, salvation, and so on. But it does so with its feet squarely planted with the poor and powerless. The two acts—solidarity with the poor and theological reflection—must always be held together. Understanding comes through action, and action is made intelligible only through the study of the Scriptures.

EXPLORING KEY THEMES

Not being able to address all the important themes that Gutiérrez develops, I have selected five for further exploration, to most of which I have already alluded.

Role of the Bible

The first is about reading the Bible. The Bible is important to Gutiérrez, but it plays a somewhat unique role in his theology.

We have seen that for Gutiérrez Jesus Christ is "the hermeneutical principle of faith." He explains further, "Jesus is the irruption into history of the one by whom everything was made and everything was saved. This, then, is the fundamental hermeneutical circle: from humanity to God and from God to humanity, from history to faith and from faith to history. . . ."[33] We have here another way of saying that Christ is the ultimate liberator. Yet this is not merely another kind of foundationalism. For Gutiérrez overtly embraces the classical theology of Anselm's *credo ut intellegam* (I believe in order to understand).[34] Gutiérrez works hard at not giving "liberation" a *sui generis* understanding; rather he attempts to understand it through the eyes of Jesus and the biblical story. The reader may well find this puzzling because of Gutiérrez's critical stance toward the theological tradition. But what he is seeking to do here is espouse an experientially based theology in the way he sees it operative in the biblical narratives. And it is Anselm's approach of faith seeking understanding that permits him to do so.

Gutiérrez highlights some startling biblical insights about the saved life that are not as the tradition has given them to us. For example, sin and salvation have been defined primarily in terms pertaining to the individual. Yet one of the biblical words for salvation is *liberation*, and a word for sin is *oppression*, and these are political terms. In other words, in the Bible, both sin and salvation have important social and political allusions.

---

[31] See Gutiérrez, *Theology of Liberation*, chap. 1.
[32] Gutiérrez, *Power of the Poor*, 200.
[33] Gutiérrez, *Power of the Poor*, 61.
[34] See Gutiérrez, *Power of the Poor*, 50ff., and also Gutiérrez, *Theology of Liberation*, xxxiii.

Moreover, a most important story in the Bible is the exodus of the Israelite slaves from Egypt.[35] It is the story around which the entire Israelite experience is interpreted; it is therefore a *paradigmatic* event. And, of course, this is a story of the salvation of a people from slavery and poverty. This story becomes the "creed" of the Bible. The prophets remind the readers of it constantly, and the master, biblical narrative would be meaningless without it. The writers of the Bible clearly want the readers to understand that the God of the Bible acts in saving people from oppression. Hence, sin equals oppression and salvation equals liberation! And that is why justice and judgment are so pivotal. Says Gutiérrez, "The God of Israel makes justice and judgment the foundation of the divine reign."[36]

Not only the Old Testament but also the New Testament portrays God as the liberator. Jesus is the liberator of the poor, the sick, and the weak. He is seen as the new Moses. And the Apostle Paul proclaims a message of liberation—"For freedom Christ has set us free" (Gal 5:1). What Paul names here is "liberation from sin." But what is sin? Gutiérrez says, "To sin is to refuse to love one's neighbor, and, therefore, the Lord himself. Sin—a breach of friendship with God and others—is according to the Bible the ultimate cause of poverty, injustice, and the oppression in which persons live."[37]

Perhaps the most significant and unique hermeneutical twist that Gutiérrez makes is that the Bible is not to be read as an ancient source book but instead as an account of the activities of God into which we are drafted. We can only come to know God in God's operations in history (as Aquinas has taught us), but we live in the same history that the Bible recounts. That is, God is not an abstract idea knowable through speculation but one who becomes knowable by being present where God is at work. Hence, the Bible invites us into its arena of activity in contemporary time and place. God is always—then and now—active in moving history in the direction of liberation. To remain uninvolved or worse, to participate in oppression, is sin.

Mistakes of Theological Tradition

The second topic I want to highlight involves Gutiérrez's beliefs about where and how the theological tradition went wrong. He argues that the plague suffered by much of dominant theology is that it has not been able to extricate itself from the false dualisms of thought.[38] The early church was born into an intellectual world which had its origins in Greek philosophy, and the modern church lives in the environment of Enlightenment thought. The Greeks had a tendency to draw a sharp line between the spiritual (mind) and the physical (body); the Enlightenment philosophers distinguished between facts and values, and contemporary theologians are inclined to distinguish between nature and grace. The result has been that we are constantly tempted to conceive life through an imagination of realms and operations that are judged to be either sacred or secular. Gutiérrez believes that one consequence of this is that questions often get raised which cannot admit of faithful answers because of the false dualistic assumptions behind them. Examples of such false dualisms are:

theory	practice
liturgy/ritual	ordinary life
thinking	doing
sacred	secular
individual	social
nature	grace
clerical	lay
doctrine	story
objective	subjective

---

[35] Gutiérrez makes frequent reference to the exodus event. See, e.g., *Theology of Liberation*, 87ff.; and *The God of Life*, trans. Matthew J. O'Connell (Maryknoll, N.Y.: Orbis, 1991), 3ff.

[36] Gutiérrez, *God of Life*, 20.

[37] Gutiérrez, *Theology of Liberation*, 24.

[38] Gutiérrez speaks of this problem in several places. Two examples are *Theology of Liberation*, 83ff.; and *Truth Shall Set You Free*, 39ff.

mind/soul	body
heavenly	earthly
spirituality	ethics
prayer	action

Gutiérrez notes that when we examine these dualisms we find that God resides in the realms designated by the left column, and social oppression occurs on the other side. God, according to this way of thinking, is disinterested in physical suffering and ordinary life, or, we could say, God has no interest in earthly existence. However, Gutiérrez has already pointed out that this is thoroughly unbiblical. In the Bible, God acts *in history* to establish a kingdom on "*earth as in heaven*"—messing up the neat dichotomies. Moreover, Jesus related to ordinary people and was deeply concerned about their bodies.[39] He called them to pray *and* to act. The spirituality of Jesus was his ethic. And so on! To break apart what was held in unity in the biblical presentation of the kingdom puts much of the theological tradition at odds with the biblical world.

From the biblical vantage point, salvation is both personal and social; contemplation and action are not separable, and liberation from social bondage (enslavement) is the mandate of the gospel. Physical oppression—keeping people hungry, poor, weak, and sick—is sin and evidence of the poverty of the spirit. The body and the spirit ought not to be broken apart in the way the tradition has taught us. Salvation is whole; *shalom* names the well-being of the entire community.

Articulation of Theology

The third topic I will explore further is Gutiérrez's articulation of a *liberation* theology in which these dualisms can be overcome. As he sees it, the task here is to re-imagine both theology and reality because it has to do with a new way of seeing the world in holistic terms. To know God means that we must concentrate on: liturgy in ordinary life and there develop life-sustaining rituals/habits; how doctrine helps us to tell untold stories and not assume that we can come to know them without the eyes of faith; and how action becomes embodied prayer. But it is not as if each dualism is a unique challenge, for there is an underlying challenge here, namely, to find a way to overcome the dichotomy of theory and practice. Everything hinges on not succumbing to the traditional casting of getting theory right in order to "apply" it in practice. His emphasis on the first and second act of theology is premised upon this overcoming.

Key to this triumph is Gutiérrez's notion of praxis. On the one hand, praxis simply names the "active presence in history" of the people of God.[40] Yet by the time he is done it turns out that it means much more. He says:

> The praxis on which liberation theology reflects is a praxis of solidarity in the interests of liberation and is inspired by the gospel. It is the activity of "peacemakers"—that is, those who are forging shalom. Western languages translate this Hebrew word as "peace" but in doing so, they diminish its meaning. Shalom in fact refers to the whole of life and, as part of this, to the need to establish peace and justice.[41]

Praxis then defies every theory and every narrowly defined practice because it is the embodiment of the reign of God's love within social reality. Such a thing can never be contained by theory, and its practice is always open for renewal and change. Furthermore, it is also more than a mere social phenomenon since "[t]he complexity of the world of the poor and lowly compels us to attend to other dimensions of Christian practice if it is to meet the requirement of a total love of God."[42] This means, among other things, that the interplay between thinking and doing is creatively interactive, driven by the Holy Spirit. And hence, one cannot happen without the

---

[39] The Gospels record bodily healing stories in almost every chapter.

[40] Gutiérrez, *Theology of Liberation*, 6.

[41] From "Introduction," to *Theology of Liberation*, xxx.

[42] Gutiérrez, "Introduction," *Theology of Liberation*, xxx.

other, and where the dynamic between them will lead is not known in advance.

Although Gutiérrez does not spend much time developing a theology of the incarnation, he does allude to it as the basis for the overcoming of the dichotomies. After all, Christ was the God-man, the unity of nature and grace, the embodiment of the Spirit. Gutiérrez puts it this way:

> Christ not only announces a prayer "in spirit and in truth" which will have no need for a material temple (John 4:21-23), but he presents himself as the temple of God: "Destroy this temple . . . and in three days I will raise it again." And John specifies: "The temple he was speaking of was his body" (John 2:19, 20). And Paul tells us: "It is in Christ that the complete being of the Godhead dwells embodied" (Col. 2:9; Eph. 2:20-22; 1 Pet. 2:2-8). God is manifested visibly in the humanity of Christ, the God-man, irreversibly committed to human history.[43]

In other words, in Christ the spirit of God is fully embodied, providing the bridge of every dichotomy. Moreover, that embodiment shows itself in a preferential option for the poor.

Gutiérrez argues that God of the Bible does not admit of theoretical comprehension because God *acts* in history and invites all who are followers also to act in concrete, social history. Hence, God is known to us through God's and our own actions. Since God is in the slums of our cities, God is encountered (known) there as we, with God, work to overcome the misery of those caught in the evils of poverty. This knowledge is not available through doctrine alone; learning this concept must include encounter with life.

These comments offer some challenges for a theology that is concerned only about *orthodoxy* (right thinking about God). Gutiérrez argues that it is helpful only insofar as it is held in check with "*orthopraxis*" (proper living). Notice that he does not reject the importance of orthodoxy, but he says, "orthopraxis and orthodoxy need one another, and

each is adversely affected when sight is lost of the other."[44] In fact, we can only think straight when we act straight; we can only know the truth when we do the truth. Unless doing and thinking, ethics and spirituality, are thoroughly interrelated, religious knowledge cannot be knowledge of the Christian God.

Gutiérrez offers a critique of the theological tradition at another level. The church has it wrong when it seeks to think *for everyone*. It cannot. It must be partial in its own logic, that is, it must think from the place of its action: the locus of the poor and the oppressed. Why? Because this is the way the God of the Bible is revealed to us. Jesus was on the side of the poor. Christians are called to be partisan and partial, not impartial and seeking to speak for everyone. Christians speak for Christ, who speaks for the poor. The notion of being on the side of everyone is developed by the Western, liberal tradition, which believes that this can be a strategy for peace. But it has a false view of peace; its peace seeks to make the powerful majority happy. This means that the poor are excluded. Solidarity with the poor creates conflict as it did with Jesus—it brings not peace but the sword (Matt 10:34)—but therein lies the hope of true peace and justice because it points to the beauty of a holistic peace, one where the cause of conflict has been eliminated.

Gutiérrez's emphasis on the particularity of the church of course is in some tension with the notion of a "*universal* church" as understood by the traditional Roman Catholic Church. He does not wish to reject the concept of the universal church entirely and accepts the more relaxed interpretation of universality as viewed by Vatican II, but still he warns of the temptation to abstract Christianity from the local congregation of faithful worshippers. How can Christianity possibly find expression the same way in all parts of the world? There are linguistic, cultural, social, economic, and other important

---

[43] Gutiérrez, *Theology of Liberation*, 108–9.
[44] Gutiérrez, "Introduction," *Theology of Liberation*, xxxiv.

differences which will give a different expression to faithful, Christian witness in each region. The rich Christians of the north must come to grips with their complicity in injustice in a different way than the Christians of his own region. Although we may all worship the same Lord, we do so in different way because we inhabit different spaces.

Views on Marxist Theology

The fourth theme I explore further is Gutiérrez's affinities with Marxist ideology and his views on a "theology of social change." It is important to understand the role of Marxism in Gutiérrez's thought.[45] Two very general comments need to be made: first, Gutiérrez shares many of the same concerns as did Marx—poverty, praxis, the relation of thought and action, the power of superstructures, and the philosophy of history, but he addresses these concerns in profoundly different ways than did Marx and his followers: for Gutiérrez seeks to give *Christian* answers to all of them, and Marx did not. Second, it so happens that much of what Marx wrote about—and much of what Marxists uphold in their liberation struggle—is a true and necessary critique of establishment Christianity. It is not difficult to see the similarities between the Marxist revolution and the revolution called for by Gutiérrez. This has made liberation theology generally, and Gutiérrez in particular, easy targets for criticism. It is therefore not hard to understand why some of Gutiérrez's comments on the subject of Marxism sound reactionary. For example, in response to criticism for his Marxist leanings that he received from the church hierarchy, he says:

> The accusations have come from those who see any denunciation of the *fact* of misery and exploitation as motivated by *ideology*. They would have liked to see preparation for Puebla take the form of an ideological dispute. They were crestfallen

when it dealt instead with the massive facts. "How wonderful things would be," someone has ironically claimed they said, "if it weren't for reality."[46]

Yet not all of Gutiérrez's comments on Marxism are reactions to criticisms. In 1984 he wrote an essay in which he developed his view of the relation of theology and the social sciences.[47] In this essay, he argues that it is not Marxism that is important for liberation theology, but the contribution of social science in general, of which Marxism is a part. He is adamant here that theology needs the social sciences in order to understand the world politically. He says: "It is not possible to deduce political programs or actions from the gospel or from reflections on the gospel. It is not possible, nor should we attempt it; the political sphere is something entirely different."[48] This comment may sound odd in light of his earlier critique of the dualisms since he seems to assume here a distinction of realms between theology and politics which one thought he was rejecting in the dualism discussion. But this is no mere slip of inconsistency. He says further, quoting his earlier work:

> It is not the function of liberation theology "to offer strategic solutions or specifically political alternatives. . . . In my opinion the 'theology of revolution' set out on that path, but it seems to me that it was not a theologically sound course to follow; in addition it ended up 'baptizing' revolution—that is, it did not acknowledge the autonomy proper to the political sphere."[49]

This leaves Gutiérrez at a rather peculiar place. He seems to have forfeited the basis on which to comment on the *theological* ethics of social change. In other words, that there should be change from poverty to justice is clear, but how that change should happen seems to be relegated to the political realm, and hence is outside of the theological sphere.

---

[45] On the relationship between Marxism and liberation theology in general, there is much discussion and debate. Some liberation theologians are more inclined than others to rely on Marx for an analysis of society's ills. I am not able to enter into the general debate here but will focus only on Gutiérrez's views.

[46] Gutiérrez, *Power of the Poor*, 156 (emphasis in original).

[47] See Gustavo Gutiérrez, "Theology and the Social Sciences (1984)," in *Truth Shall Make You Free*, 53–84.

[48] Gutiérrez, "Theology and the Social Sciences," 64.

[49] Gutiérrez, "Theology and the Social Sciences," 65.

His comments here are directly relevant to the matter of whether there is within his liberation theology an overt theology of social change. And it specifically raises the question of violence as a legitimate means of change. There is a great deal of discussion on the topic of violence and liberation theology, but much of it is misguided. There is no question here about whether Gutiérrez is guilty of the charge of glorifying violence. He is not! Nor is he a pacifist. His view on the use of violence for social change falls somewhere in between these two, and hence in this respect, his views are not different from mainline, Western theology. He speaks directly to the issue of the use of violence by distinguishing among three different kinds of violence. He says:

> In Latin America, we have three types of violence. The first is the *institutionalized violence* of the present social order; the second, the *repressive violence* which defends the first, keeping in power the ruling regimes; and the third, *counter-violence*. To me, counter-violence is the least of the evils.[50]

It seems that his position on the use of violence in the social revolution is consistent with that of the Catholic Church. Violence could be used, but only as a last resort since clearly the path of nonviolence should be pursued as long as possible. It is important to remember that he rejected the route of fellow priest Camilo Torres; yet neither did he follow the route of some other liberation theologians, for example, the pacifist, Brazilian priest Dom Hélder Câmara.[51] Insofar as there is a theology of social change at work in Gutiérrez's theology, it would seem to go something like this: the theologian's and church's task is to hold before the people and the entire world the sinfulness of poverty and its structures which are held in place through unjust and violent means. All are called to do whatever they are able to, peacefully if possible, violently if absolutely necessary, to radically change both the structures and the social reality.

In all of this, Gutiérrez is quite aware that human problems cannot be solved by economic and political changes only. More is required, which he names as a relationship with God. In fact, it has been the breaking of this primary relationship that is the cause of the economic and political problems to begin with, and ultimately it is only the mending of this relationship that can fix social problems.

View of God

The fifth and last theme in Gutiérrez's work that I will address has to do with his view of God. He points out that the dominant theologies of the Western world view God as one who rules with power from on high. God is omnipotent and omniscient and does whatever God does through wisdom that is not ours to own. It is easy to see how church structures emulate this model of authority. But in the incarnation of Jesus Christ—God becoming human—the barriers which are set up with such a perceived hierarchy are broken down. This calls for a review of the nature of God.

Gutiérrez refers to the debate between Dietrich Bonhoeffer and Karl Barth on this issue. Of course, Bonhoeffer is deeply indebted to Barth, but in the end he rejects the terms of the debate as Barth sets it up. For Barth it is a matter of whether religion is a way of controlling God or whether it is a way of understanding how God controls us. For Bonhoeffer both paths are problematic.

With Bonhoeffer, Gutiérrez suggests that if we take the incarnation seriously we must conclude that God does not save us by controlling us, or ruling over us, but by becoming present with us. After all, "God is the God of Jesus Christ."[52] Hence, God is more accurately understood through categories of weakness than through categories of power. God is present among those who are oppressed to empower them toward liberation, exactly as the children of Israel experienced

---

[50] Quoted from Robert McAfee Brown, *Makers of Contemporary Theology: Gustavo Gutiérrez* (Atlanta: John Knox, 1980), 39 (emphasis in original).

[51] See Guenther, *Torres and Câmara*.

[52] Gutiérrez, *Power of the Poor*, 230.

his presence while in Egypt and the wilderness. This is the view of God that Gutiérrez's liberation theology presupposes.

Gutiérrez makes the point poignantly when he contrasts Bonhoeffer's view of God with the "imperialistic theology" of Barth. I quote him at some length:

> God is a God who saves us not through his domination but through his suffering. Here we have Bonhoeffer's famous thesis of *God's weakness* (Bonhoeffer, *Letters and Papers*). It will make its mark in theology after he is gone. It is of this God, and only of this God, that the Bible tells us. And it is thus that the cross acquires its tremendous revelatory potential with respect to God's weakness as an expression of his love for a world come of age.
>
> Here is a concept charged with force and power. "It is not the religious act that makes the Christian, but participation in the sufferings of God in the secular life" (Bonhoeffer, *Letters and Papers*). This is conversion. This is what it is to believe in the gospel. What makes a Christian a Christian is "being caught up into the messianic sufferings of God in Jesus Christ" (Bonhoeffer, *Letters and Papers*).
>
> ... God in Christ is a God suffering, and to share in his weakness is to believe in him. This is what it means to be a Christian.[53]

These are powerful words, and they summarize well Gutiérrez's entire theology. To learn to see the world from beneath, from the standpoint of the despised and useless is, perhaps ironically, to learn to see the world as Christ taught his disciples. This is in the end what discipleship means for Gutiérrez—letting yourself be led into the innermost parts of life's struggle in deficiencies, solidarity with the oppressed. This is the meaning of Jesus' call to his disciples to "take up their cross daily and follow me" (Luke 9:23b).

CONCLUSION

A Protestant liberation theologian from Argentina writes:

> Gustavo Gutiérrez has lucidly described his own experience recounting how, from the common Christian and Catholic instruction to help the poor, he was led to understand Christian commitment as solidarity with the struggle of the poor for their liberation.[54]

This is a rather modest assessment of Gutiérrez's work. But I think it is true! Gutiérrez often has remarked that in his home country he is known as an activist priest, although he is viewed in the rest of the world as a theologian. That is no accident, for he is an activist priest before he is a theologian. However, the practice of his faith has made him see that there is something lacking in the theology of the West, of which he was a student. And what is lacking is that it teaches the faith in such a way that it renders its students useless for Christian practice. It suggests that the real issues of theology are in the mind and not in the world of people who are hurting. How can that be the faith to which Jesus calls us? Students of the Christian faith need to learn to see the world from the standpoint of solidarity with the poor, the place where Christ is at work, in order to learn to see who God is in Jesus Christ.

I suspect that most who read these words will be students in the "rich" world. What does the liberation theology of Gutiérrez have to say to us? Perhaps three things: first, we too desire to be faithful Christians. Hence, the reality that Gutiérrez names should not be ignored. His challenge is for us to take stock of our complicity in violence and injustice that are simply part of our lifestyles and to repent and renew our commitment to follow the Jesus of the biblical story. Second, Gutiérrez also challenges us to do our part to change the policies of our own countries, recognizing that the good news of the gospel may well be bad news for the rich before it becomes good news for them. And third, solidarity with the poor, as Gutiérrez has narrated the issues, implies ecclesiological solidarity. It is a sincere call to celebrate our oneness in Christ. We are one body, however diverse, and the riches of God's grace are extended to us all.

---

[53] Gutiérrez, *Power of the Poor*, 230 (emphasis in original).
[54] José Míguez Bonino, *Doing Theology in a Revolutionary Situation* (Philadelphia: Fortress, 1975), 157.

Chapter Twenty-Seven

JAMES HAL CONE
(1938–)

James Cone is sometimes called the father of black theology in America. But what is black theology, and why does the Christian church need a theology called black? Is it not the case that calling for a black theology is divisive and the church's call is for unity? There are many similarities between Latin American liberation theology and black liberation theology, but one important difference is that the former designates a geographical region while the latter names a race. The region of black theology is coextensive with that of the white church. This heightens the intensity of why a black theology might be necessary. And if so, that necessity speaks to a deep divide between white and black Christians; to say this differently, black theology is only necessary if Christian racism is prevalent. This was the clear conviction of James Cone.

It could also be asked why we need black theology when we have Martin Luther King Jr. or why there should be a chapter in this book on Cone when we have one on King. Two responses: first, who is the "we" asking the question? I suspect most whites would be perfectly happy with King and the current status quo because it does not seriously threaten the structures of racism. Simply stated, King never forced us to confront the racism within white Christianity in the way that black theology does. And second, the issue here goes to the very heart of theology itself and asks whether the way it has been handed down through the white tradition is consistent with the biblical call of Jesus to his disciples. And since that is the issue here, Cone's goal is to give an account of black theology that grows out of the American black experience of oppression and to show how it can offer a gospel of liberation and justice.

We will notice obvious affinities of black theology with Latin American liberation theology, for black theology too is a praxis. Moreover, it is a theology rooted in a Christology, a way of interpreting who Jesus was and to what he calls his followers. Both see the work of Jesus Christ as essentially a work of liberation. What is different between black theology and Latin American liberation theology is social location. And this is not insignificant. It means that the oppression is different, the source and history of the oppression is different, and the vision for its overcoming in most cases is different.

As with Latin American liberation theology, black theology is not the domain of one writer. Moreover, there is vigorous debate among the different theologians. Two volumes of essays have been collected under the label of black theology, and they illustrate that there is a community of scholars working at articulating the nuances of this theological approach.[1] And a third one is

---

[1] James H. Cone and Gayraud S. Wilmore, *Black Theology: A Documentary History*, vol. 1, *1966–1979*: vol. 2, *1980–1992* (Maryknoll, N.Y.: Orbis, 1993).

planned.[2] Yet, as with Latin American liberation theology, I will deal with only one representative of black theology in this chapter.

CONE'S LIFE STORY

Cone was born in Fordyce, Arkansas, approximately sixty miles southwest of Little Rock. His parents, Lucy and Charlie Cone, were both active in resisting segregation. For example, his father was involved in a lawsuit seeking to desegregate a school. His mother was a gifted orator, a skill much appreciated in her church. She embodied a generous spirituality, typical of black women in that setting. Cone says, "My mother was one of the pillars of Macedonia [local church], and a firm believer in God's justice. Since my father joined the church because of the pressure that my mother applied before their marriage, he sometimes had to be reminded by her that God alone is the supreme judge of all things."[3] Thus, Cone and his two brothers, Charles and Cecil, grew up in a family where racism, justice, and Jesus were intentionally brought into one mode of thought and practice.

In 1948, when Cone was ten, the family moved to a segregated town named Beardon not far from Fordyce. Beardon was a small community with a population of twelve hundred, two-thirds white and one-third black. Cone says that here "two important realities shaped my consciousness: the black Church experience and the sociopolitical significance of the white people."[4]

Cone attended his family's church, Macedonia African Methodist Episcopal Church, where on Sunday morning one could hear powerful spirituals, passionate prayers, and fiery preaching. He remembers the oft-repeated theme of heaven as the home where oppressed people will someday find refuge. "Home was that eschatological reality where the oppressed would 'lay down that heavy load,' singing and shouting because 'there would be nobody there to turn [them] out.'"[5]

At age ten, Cone became a church member, and at age sixteen he became a minister in his home church. He speaks of this time positively although he acknowledges that in the black secular world what he was doing would be called the "art of survival" while in the black church it was called "the grace of God." "It is called *survival* because it is a way of remaining physically alive in a situation of oppression without losing one's dignity. We call it *grace* because we know it to be an unearned gift from him who is the giver of 'every good and perfect gift.'"[6]

There was also a white community in Beardon that did everything in its power to define the black community as other. "They tried to make us believe that God created black people to be white people's servants."[7] That was, after all, the black people's place. But it was a very terrible place, because it meant that they were often beaten by cops and sent to jail and kept poor and ghettoized, not only geographically but also intellectually and spiritually. This "place" meant separate schools, designated seating areas in movies, and separate "colored" drinking fountains. It was not that the white folks thought of themselves as bad people. They went to church, and in Beardon they did not rape or lynch the black folks. They were Christ followers, but the black folks were not like them, and the assumption of difference made it impossible for them to see their own social location as one of privilege. Cone says he and his brother were often tempted to attend a white church service on Sunday morning just to make the worshippers say that they were not welcome there. But they were afraid that that might provoke a beating.

---

[2] For a promise of a third volume see Cone and Wilmore, *Black Theology*, 2:3.

[3] James H. Cone, *My Soul Looks Back* (Nashville: Abingdon, 1982), 22.

[4] James H. Cone, *God of the Oppressed* (New York: Seabury, 1975), 1.

[5] Cone, *God of the Oppressed*, 1.

[6] Cone, *God of the Oppressed*, 2 (emphasis in original).

[7] Cone, *God of the Oppressed*, 2.

"Because I lived in Beardon" is a frequent refrain in Cone's life, and it is also a silent echo in his theology. Beardon determines much. How could he respect Christianity, given what he experienced from white Christians? Had the whites not been Christian, it might have been a different matter, but precisely because they were Christian, it meant that blacks who wished to be followers of Christ had to go by a different name. And Cone became critical even of the theology of his own church. There he heard repeated expressions of gratitude to God for the small scraps they were given and the beatings they were spared. But this is the language of a slave religion and not the Christianity born from the liberating gospel of Jesus Christ.

Cone was an avid follower of the civil rights movement in its early years. He heard the speeches of Martin Luther King Jr. and of the Muslim leader Malcolm X. He was a devoted advocate of King's love ethic and his nonviolent campaign for social change. Yet it was not difficult for him to see why Malcolm X had so many followers. There was a consistency within Islam that was not apparent in the white, Christian world. Christians seemed to have a Sunday faith and a week-day faith and the two were different. This was less so among the Muslims. Theirs was a disciplined faith, habituated by daily prayers and conscientious efforts to integrate their conviction of the justice of God into every aspect of life. For them, all of life was under Allah's rule. Their religious zeal was attractive to Cone and many others. When he heard Malcolm X proclaim that Christianity was a white man's religion, he began to understand himself not merely as a Christian but as a *black* Christian. When he heard civil rights activists Willie Ricks and Stokely Carmichael[8] speak of "black power," black began

to designate a reality that went far beyond a mere adjective describing his race. He began to see black as a social and political identity that named a struggle of the oppressed people of America—a struggle for liberation that was far greater than the personal quest for serenity with things not being as bad as they could be.[9]

During the 1950s, Cone began university studies, which would eventually lead him to theology—white theology (that is all there was)—Karl Barth, Emil Brunner, Rudolf Bultmann, Paul Tillich, and so on. He began college after graduating from high school in 1954. His first stop was a small, unaccredited college called Shorter College of the African Methodist Episcopal Church in North Little Rock, Arkansas. After two years of study there, he transferred to a somewhat larger, accredited college, Philander Smith College, from which he graduated in 1958. These were impressionable years for young Cone, and some of his experiences with racism left deep scars.

Cone tells the story of riding a public bus during this time when buses were still legally segregated. He says he and his brother never observed that rule.[10] So one day when he entered the bus, he chose to sit beside "an elderly, churchly looking white woman who seemed so serious and pious."[11] But this did not turn out well.

> She quickly got up, uttering angry expletives at me. I went over to her, with a smile on my face so as to calm her down. I said: "Madam, you look like a Christian, and that was why I sat down by you. How could you say the things you said to me when Jesus said that what you do to the least you do to him?" "You are not Jesus," she replied with hate and violence in her eyes. "Get the hell out of my face, you nigger!"[12]

Such experiences were often repeated, sometimes several times a week.

---

[8] Both Willie Ricks (also known as Mukasa Dada) and Stokely Carmichael (1941–1998, also known as Kwame Ture) were civil rights activists in the 1960s.

[9] See esp. his first book, James H. Cone, *Black Theology and Black Power* (New York: Seabury, 1969).

[10] Cone, *My Soul Looks Back*, 26.

[11] Cone, *My Soul Looks Back*, 26.

[12] Cone, *My Soul Looks Back*, 26.

In his undergraduate studies, Cone majored in religion and philosophy, although black history was what he considered his most interesting subject. He developed oratory skills and loved to preach and debate. He was academically a strong student.

In 1958, he enrolled in the Garrett Biblical Institute (now Garrett-Evangelical Theological Seminary) in Evanston, Illinois. He eagerly anticipated moving "up north" (from Little Rock to Chicago) because his northern relatives led him to believe that blacks were free up there. That turned out to be false! Not only did he experience racism in public places (for example, he was told upon entering a local barbershop that "We don't cut niggers' hair in this place,"[13]) but he also discovered that racism extended to the classrooms in Garrett as well. The first experience was not that surprising, the second was. He discovered that professors treated black students as if they were dumb, and they did not expect black students to receive grades higher than C. So Cone went from being an A student to being a C student. This was deeply humiliating.

Cone was committed to proving his professors wrong. So he reduced his course load, worked very hard, and in his second quarter managed to get two Bs. This boosted his confidence and convinced him that he could do even better. There were also some professors who gave him honest evaluations. He mentions especially William Hordern, who was a systematic theologian at Garrett at the time. Hordern even encouraged him to seek admission into a Ph.D. program and promised to be his advisor if he got accepted.

Gradually Cone developed the courage to explore possibilities of doctoral studies and spoke to the graduate advisor at Garrett, who, at the time, was also the ethics professor. He was told that he did not have a chance of getting accepted into the graduate program because the competition was simply too stiff. When Cone relayed this information to Hordern, he was furious and said, "Jim, you go right ahead and apply, and if you are not accepted then I will quit."[14] Cone took the advice and was accepted, first into a master's and then later into a Ph.D. program.

Cone reflects on his theological education in some detail.[15] He realized rather early in his graduate program that this was no place for open discussion on the topic of racism as a theological and ethical problem. He was convinced that the ethics professor was himself racist, and so Cone decided on the safer route of writing a dissertation on Barth's theological anthropology. He graduated in 1965.

Cone was the first black, doctoral student to graduate from Garrett, and in his class there were five graduates. He tells the story of his ethics professor coming through the receiving line on graduation day. Cone was standing in the middle of the group of five and the professor "congratulated the first two doctoral students, shaking their hands; then he skipped me as I extended my hand, and went to the next two, congratulating them for their outstanding achievement. I could not believe that he could continue to be so obvious with his racism. But I smiled and said to myself: 'Racism runs deep even among seminary professors.'"[16]

After graduation, Cone took a teaching position at Philander Smith College, his alma mater. Here he discovered rather quickly that his knowledge of Barth, Tillich, and Brunner had little appeal to his students. They were interested in justice questions, and those were not questions addressed by these theologians.

Two years later, in 1966, it was made known to Cone by the school administration

---

[13] Cone, *My Soul Looks Back*, 30.
[14] Cone, *My Soul Looks Back*, 34.
[15] See esp. "From Beardon to Adrian," in Cone, *My Soul Looks Back*, chap. 1.
[16] Cone, *My Soul Looks Back*, 38.

that "his departure would be welcome." It was becoming increasingly clear that his strident critique of the racist status quo was making some colleagues and board members uncomfortable. And so he left to teach at another Methodist school, Adrian College in Adrian, Michigan.

There is no doubt that the summer of 1967 was a pivotal year for Cone, and one event that made it so was the uprising that took place in Detroit, Michigan.[17] He saw in this a glimpse of the battles that were to come. The issue for him was the question of how to relate such events to the fundamental reality of Jesus Christ. Empathetic white Christians, that is, the "supportive" ones, were saying, "We deplore the riots but we sympathize with the reason for the riots."[18] But Cone knew instinctively that there was something wrong with this expression of Christian solidarity. It was like saying:

> Of course we rape your women, lynch your men, and ghettoize the minds of your children and you have the right to be upset; but that is no reason for you to burn our buildings. If you people keep acting like that, we will never give you your freedom.[19]

This patronizing demeanor was far from the theology practiced by the wandering Galilean, who fed the poor, healed the sick, preached freedom for the oppressed, and died for and in poverty. But it was the reality of the Christian culture in America, and it was in this culture where black liberation must be sought.

The next year, 1968, King was assassinated. Another extreme shock to Cone! It was not as though it was disconfirmation of King's approach to racism, but the event did lead Cone to begin to raise critical questions. King's death was part of the impetus that inspired this thirty-year-old, black theologian to write his own books and to think carefully about black liberation. Certainly King was right in much of what he represented and taught, but he was also wrong.

As he wrote, Cone quickly became convinced that universal theological discourse, standard fare among white, European, and North American theologians, was at most half the story. If white theology were to represent all of Christian theology, it would require black people to underwrite their own oppression. Universal theology is dangerous if it is not balanced with particular theology. This is so because Christian theology is embodied faith and therefore always both universal and particular, always liberating theology. Jesus practiced this when he placed himself in critique of the Pharisees. Properly rendered Christian theology is about exploring the liberating activity of God; particular theology conducts the test of whether a given theology is truly liberating.

Cone has written many books, some of which I will examine imminently, but before I do, a brief comment on his latest project. He is examining the relationship between the cross of Christ and the lynching tree. On this topic, one cannot help but hear the echoes of Elie Wiesel's account of a child witnessing the hanging of another child in a Nazi concentration camp. When someone in the crowd shouted, "For God's sake, where is God?" Wiesel said that a voice from within answered, "Where He is? This is where—hanging here from this gallows."[20] Cone makes the point that the lynching of blacks must be understood in the same way. God is present in that black body, just like God was present in the body of Jesus Christ.[21]

There are white people who will think the analogy between the cross and the lynching tree is inappropriate, but Cone believes

---

[17] From July 23 to July 27, 1967, Detroit saw one of the deadliest racial riots of all time. Forty-three people died, hundreds were injured, and over seven thousand were arrested. In addition more than two thousand buildings were destroyed.

[18] Cone, *God of the Oppressed*, 6.

[19] Cone, *God of the Oppressed*, 6.

[20] Elie Wiesel, *Night*, rev. ed. (New York: Hill & Wang, 2006), xx.

[21] I am drawing here on comments made by James Cone in an interview with Bill Moyers available at http://www.pbs.org/moyers/journal/11232007/watch.html, accessed May 14, 2001.

that this is because, while they might want to speak of mercy and forgiveness, they don't want to address issues of justice and reparations. That is too costly. Hence, they resist the implication that they are today's crucifiers of Christ. But Cone insists that, as with the disciples of old, the only way we can call ourselves followers of Christ is to take up our crosses and follow him daily (Luke 9:23). Such a radical call means full identification with the Christ of the cross. In America, this would have Christians give up the power of oppression and become one with the victims. Such identification is no abstraction, for it leads to repentance and from there to reparations. This is the starting point for the flourishing of the beloved community of which King spoke. Cone sees talk about the cross and the lynching tree as opening up a conversation in which blacks and whites can be frank about American history and a dialogue that invites repentance and forgiveness, and seeks to build toward a community of justice. This is Cone's ultimate goal in all of his writings.

Cone is actively engaged in teaching, lecturing, and writing. He is the Charles A. Briggs Distinguished Professor of Systematic Theology at Union Theological Seminary in New York City and has received many awards and eight honorary doctorates. In 2006 he was to receive an honorary degree from Turner Theological Seminary in Atlanta, Georgia, but he turned it down "because the speaker at the graduation was a 'prosperity gospel' preacher."[22]

Regarding his family life, Cone was married to a woman named Rose (now deceased), with whom he had two children, Michael and Charles. He is now married to Sandra.

THE LOGIC OF BLACK THEOLOGY

As we have seen, the details of Cone's life cannot be told without telling part of the story of black theology. And yet there is much that is not included in what has been said so far.

Black Power

Cone's first book is about black theology and black power.[23] Here he begins with a definition of black power. He says that whenever the words "black power" are used by its advocates, "it means *complete emancipation of black people from white oppression by whatever means black people deem necessary.*[24] We should notice here how different this way of speaking is from the language of King. Cone spells out his idea of black power by suggesting that it means black freedom and black self-determination. He reaches back to the French existentialist, Albert Camus (1913–1960), whose "rebel" says both "no" and "yes" to life; no to the conditions of oppression and yes to the rebellion that can overcome it. He quotes Camus as saying, "*Better to die on one's feet, than to live on one's knees.*"[25]

Cone relies on people like Camus because racism is an existential issue. Black oppression in America is a result of white culture seeking to define blacks as non-persons. Hence, life becomes absurd—another theme in Camus' writings.[26] The only way to cope with life's absurdity is through rebellion. While Cone does not go all the way with Camus' view of rebellion, he refers to his writings to show the depth of the human struggle for meaning in a world that seeks to deny it.

In the 1960s, *integration* was the new craze intended to overcome black oppression. This was also central to King's campaign. Cone opposed the "integration strategy" because

---

[22] From the Union Theological Seminary faculty website at http://www.utsnyc.edu//Page.aspx?pid=353, accessed May 14, 2011.

[23] Cone, *Black Theology and Black Power* (New York: Seabury, 1969).

[24] Cone, *Black Theology and Black Power*, 6 (emphasis in original).

[25] Cone, *Black Theology and Black Power*, 7 (emphasis in original). See also Albert Camus, *The Rebel*, trans. Anthony Bower (Harmondsworth, U.K.: Penguin, 1962), 15.

[26] See Albert Camus, *The Stranger*, trans. Stuart Gilbert (New York: Vintage, 1946); and *The Myth of Sisyphus and Other Essays*, trans. Justin O'Brien (New York: Vintage, 1955).

it did not address the roots of racism. Integration forced blacks to accept the structures that white society had to offer them. The freedom that blacks were seeking was not a freedom derived from being given something from the whites; rather it was the freedom of self-determination which required full participation in the decision-making processes that affected black people and American society in general. So he says, "What is needed, then, is not 'integration' but a sense of worth in being black, and only black people can teach that. Black consciousness is the key to the black man's emancipation from his distorted self-image."[27]

There are both red-neck, conservative racists and bleeding-heart, liberal racists, and Cone's attack is often focused on the liberals because their form of racism is subtle. Speaking of the hypocrisy in the liberal's effort to be nice, he says that the white person's

> [F]avorite question when backed against the wall is "What can I do?" One is tempted to reply, as Malcolm X did to the white girl who asked the same question, "Nothing." What the liberal really means is, "What can I do and still receive the same privileges as other whites *and*—this is the key—be liked by Negroes?" Indeed the only answer is "Nothing." However, there are places in the Black Power picture for "radicals," that is, for men, white or black, who are prepared to risk life for freedom.[28]

It may be difficult for white people to understand this rather harsh response, but that is because liberal whites especially find it impossible to accept that there is a problem in the world that they cannot fix. And it is fundamentally this issue that Cone is lifting out here. Liberal whites are not the only moral agents in this world.

Black Power and the Gospel

As a theologian, Cone derives both his personal and theological resources from the gospel of Jesus Christ. He asks what it might mean for black people to find their freedom from white Christian oppression by appealing to the gospel. After all, freedom is what Jesus offers all his followers. The Apostle Paul knew that when he said, "For freedom, Christ has set us free" (Gal 5:1). But Cone is careful in defining the freedom of which he speaks. He says that the freedom which blacks seek is not a freedom to do what we will, but a freedom to become what we should be. "*A man is free when he sees clearly the fulfillment of his being and is thus capable of making the envisioned self a reality.*"[29]

Cone laments the fate of history that Christianity came to black people through white oppressors who expected them to accept the whiteness of the Christian faith. Fortunately, black people also have the capacity to come to know Jesus—his life, death, and resurrection.

When Cone unveils his understanding of Jesus' message, he begins with Jesus reading from Isaiah 61 as recorded in the gospel of Luke:

> The Spirit of the Lord is upon me, because he has anointed me to bring good news to the poor. He has sent me to proclaim release to the captives and recovery of sight to the blind, to let the oppressed go free, to proclaim the year of the Lord's favor. (Luke 4:18-19)

He concludes from these words that Jesus is here proclaiming to all who are willing to hear that the movement he is inaugurating is a liberation movement. And the manner of this announcement is important; it is not proclaimed from a distance but in immediate presence with the oppressed. In effect, Jesus so completely identified with the poor that he himself became a slave and in so doing opened up an entirely new reality of who God is—one not seen before. God in Christ became not only human but, "one of the least of these" (Matt 25) in order to lift the oppressed up to God. Clearly, to be a worshipper of the God of Jesus Christ, we too must, like Jesus,

---

[27] Cone, *Black Theology and Black Power*, 19.

[28] Cone, *Black Theology and Black Power*, 28 (emphasis in original).

[29] Cone, *Black Theology and Black Power*, 39 (emphasis in original).

identify with the dispossessed. What we see here is that in Christ God enters time-space history and what God does in history is take sides with the poor. Their suffering becomes God's suffering, their pain God's pain, their struggle God's struggle.

When black people hear this message, they quickly recognize its political overtones. If the gospel is a gospel of liberation, then Jesus becomes a contemporary for blacks in America and the head of their liberation movement. Hence, "Christianity is not alien to Black Power; it is Black Power."[30] And the demand of justice implies a demand of faithfulness to the cause of Jesus Christ, both for white and black Christians.

Cone is not suggesting that all black power advocates are Christian. But he is suggesting that there is a way of understanding black power that is consistent with understanding the gospel of Jesus Christ. And to do that, black power messages must be reconciled with the Christian message to love.[31] Thus, it is impossible to speak of black power without also speaking of Christian love. Yet it could be asked whether black power as Cone has defined it is inconsistent with the Christian call to love the enemy. In other words, is the quest for self-determination using any means necessary, including violence, consistent with the message of Jesus? King argued no and Cone argues yes! The hermeneutical move Cone makes here in order to get out from the pacifist demands of Jesus' call to love enemies is both typical of mainline American Christian ethicists and unique. He says:

> [W]e must remember that it is most difficult to make first-century New Testament language relevant to a contemporary "world come of age." Jesus did not give us a blueprint for identifying God and his work or for relevant human involvement in the world. But this is the never ending task of theology and the church.[32]

In other words, like most liberal American ethicists, Cone suggests that Jesus points us in a general direction but leaves the details of how to attain his goals for us to determine.

Yet he also says more than this. He argues that the big issue for the Christian church and New Testament ethics is the failure of mainline theologians to read Jesus as the liberator of the powerless. In other words, the mistake is on the white oppressor's side of the violence ledger. The point is not *how* liberation should be brought about; it is *that* it should happen. And liberals fail on the second score.

This does not mean, however, that New Testament language is no longer useful for the process of black liberation in America. Cone affirms the biblical teaching of the Great Commandment to love God and neighbor. But he also emphasizes the teaching of God's grace which sets people free; that is, free to respond creatively to God's actions upon us. Grace helps us to better understand what it means for black people to love their neighbors. He explains:

> [W]hat does it mean for a black man to love the neighbor, especially the white neighbor? To love the white man means that the black man *confronts* him as a Thou without any intention of giving ground by becoming an It. Though the white man is accustomed to addressing an It, in the new black man he meets a Thou. The black man must, if he is not to lose sight of his new-found identity in Christ, be prepared for conflict, for a radical confrontation. As one black man put it: "Profound love can only exist between two equals." The new black man refuses to assume the It-role which whites expect, but addresses them as an equal. This is when the conflict arises.[33]

In other words, love cannot be measured exclusively by the standard of nonviolence, nor can nonviolence be measured by Christian love.[34] That is, you can be nonviolent without love and you can love and still

---

[30] Cone, *Black Theology and Black Power*, 38.

[31] See Cone, *Black Theology and Black Power*, 48–49.

[32] Cone, *Black Theology and Black Power*, 49.

[33] Cone, *Black Theology and Black Power*, 53 (emphasis in original). Cone is here reaching back to the language of Jewish scholar Martin Buber, *I and Thou*, trans. Walter Kaufmann (New York: Scribner, 1970).

[34] See Cone, *Black Theology and Black Power*, 55.

be violent. The two are not essentially connected. For Cone, love is the more important of the two. For to love as Jesus did implies hating injustice; whereas whites can advocate love and nonviolence and at the same time participate in violent and unjust systems. To forswear violence as Christian pacifists do because the price of change is too high means accepting injustice. For Cone, social revolution simply requires violence since without it revolutions could not address injustice all the way down.

Revolution, Violence, and Jesus

The revolution that Cone endorses calls for radical social and political change employing whatever effective power is necessary to bring it about. He quotes from C. Eric Lincoln: "Revolution is more than protest. Protest merely calls attention to injustice. . . . [Revolution] is an act of defiance against what is conceived to be an established evil. It is the refusal to be silent in the presence of wrong to which others are accommodated."[35] The "more" of revolution is radical change. Protest may point to the problem, but revolution is the engine that corrects the problem.

Cone links this notion of revolution with biblical theology and the absolute sovereignty of God over creation. He explains it this way:

> [B]lack people must be taught not to be disturbed about revolution or civil disobedience if the law violates God's purpose for man. The Christian man is obligated by a freedom grounded in the Creator to break all laws which contradict human dignity. Through disobedience to the state, he affirms his allegiance to God as Creator and his willingness to behave as if he believes it. Civil disobedience is a duty in a racist society. That is why Camilo Torres said, "Revolutionary action is a Christian, a priestly struggle."[36]

In the absence of any qualification, the reader is left to assume that Cone fully endorses Torres' style of guerilla warfare, even though he himself does not "revolt" in this manner. We should note that in this stance Cone differentiates himself from both King and Gustavo Gutiérrez.[37]

The stated intent of Cone's analysis here is to get theologians to speak honestly about the issues of violence and racism in America. The discussion is too easily dismissed by saying that because Jesus never resorted to violence oppressed people of America should not either. Fundamentally, the question is not whether or not to use violence, because that overlooks the basic reality that violence already exists; it is a given, and to ignore its givenness is to live in an unreal world. In Cone's words:

> The Christian does not decide between violence and nonviolence, evil and good. He decides between the less [sic] and the greater evil. He must ponder whether revolutionary violence is less or more deplorable than the violence perpetuated by the system. There are no absolute rules which can decide the answer with certainty. But he must make a choice. If he decides to take the "nonviolent" way, then he is saying that revolutionary violence is more detrimental to man in the long run than systemic violence. But if the system is evil, then revolutionary violence is both justified and necessary.[38]

His defense of revolutionary violence is unequivocal. From these words, it is not hard to detect a Marxist reading of revolution. He also uses Marx in other ways. He says the Marxist critique of religion applies well to the white churches because their religion is a kind of drug that allows the people to cover up and justify social oppression. But this is not the way religion functions within the black community; there religion serves to expose injustice and to empower the people to overcome it.

Cone's ethic of revolution is spelled out further in his later writings. As we have already

---

[35] Cone, *Black Theology and Black Power*, 136. Quoted from C. Eric Lincoln, "The Black Revolution in Cultural Perspective," *Union Seminary Quarterly Review* 23, no. 3 (1968): 221.

[36] Cone, *Black Theology and Black Power*, 137.

[37] See chaps. 22 and 26 above.

[38] Cone, *Black Theology and Black Power*, 143.

seen, he is adamant that black Christians should not let white rhetoric about nonviolence confuse them. Under the heading "Ethics, Violence, and Jesus Christ," he further addresses the question of why violence is essential for his view of revolution. He presents three arguments.

First, violence is not primarily what black people threaten white people with; it is what white people have done for centuries and continue to do by creating and maintaining violent structures of society. Violence in American is a fundamental given; that is, "Violence is American as cherry pie."[39] Hiroshima and Nagasaki are not the first American crimes against humanity; the first were committed by slave owners named George Washington and Thomas Jefferson.[40] To suddenly call blacks to nonviolence is merely an attempt to hoodwink them into accepting the violent status quo in which they are the victims.

Second, since violence is a fundamental American reality, the distinction between violence and nonviolence is illusory and the insistence of its importance is a deliberate political strategy by whites. But this is hypocritical! Whites have always accepted that the proper way of thinking about violence is in terms of being either justified or unjustified. Why is that prerogative not extended to blacks? The implied answer seems to be that it would give them too much power. This is why whites are elated with a Martin Luther King Jr. This is also why Cone disagrees with King on this point. He says:

> [King's] dependence on the analysis of love found in liberal theology and his confidence that "the universe is on the side of justice" seem not to take seriously white violence in America. I disagree with his conceptual analysis of violence versus

nonviolence, because his distinctions between these terms did not appear to face head-on the historical and sociological complexities of human existence in a racist society.[41]

Although there is much about King's revolution that Cone admires,[42] he objects to King's legacy, which seems to leave the impression that in order to attain their freedom, black Americans must use only nonviolent means. Here, King and his supporters have fallen victim to the subtle politics of white liberalism that will keep black people exactly where whites want them—poor and powerless.

Third, since the issue of Christian ethics is not violence versus nonviolence, Cone believes that the real issue can finally be named—"the creation of a new humanity."[43] In other words, the issue is how Jesus is morally relevant for black, Christian ethics. Again, the issue is not about whether Jesus committed violent acts; nor is it even about whether love is compatible with violence. Cone is emphatic and passionate in speaking about the role of Jesus in Christian ethics. He says:

> We repeat: the question is not what Jesus *did*, as if his behavior in first-century Palestine were the infallible ethical guide for our actions today. We must ask not what he did, but what he is *doing*—and what he did becomes important only insofar as it points to his activity today. To use the Jesus of history as an absolute ethical guide for people today is to become enslaved to the past, foreclosing God's eschatological future and its judgment on the present. It removes the element of risk in ethical decisions and makes people slaves to principles. But the gospel of Jesus means liberation; and one essential element of that liberation is the existential burden of making decisions about human liberation without being completely sure about what Jesus did or would do. This is the risk of faith.[44]

---

[39] Quoted in Cone, *God of the Oppressed*, 218. It was said by Rap Brown (1943–) who was an active civil rights worker and a prominent member of the Black Panther Movement.

[40] Cone, *God of the Oppressed*, 218.

[41] Cone, *God of the Oppressed*, 221.

[42] In James H. Cone, *Risks of Faith: The Emergence of a Black Theology of Liberation, 1968–1998* (Boston: Beacon, 1999), 72. Cone says that there are good reasons why King should be considered the most outstanding American theologian.

[43] Cone, *God of the Oppressed*, 222.

[44] Cone, *God of the Oppressed*, 222 (emphasis in original).

These are obviously important words for Cone since he repeats them verbatim twenty-four years later in another book.[45] But what do these words imply for how to live now? He is not saying that Jesus is irrelevant for Christian ethics. For Cone, Jesus is not merely a historical figure; he is a resurrected and present figure. Moreover, "the resurrected Christ is not bound by first-century possibilities. Though the Jesus of yesterday is important for our ethical decisions today, we must be careful where we locate that importance. It is not found in following in his steps, slavishly imitating his behavior in Palestine. Rather, we must regard his past activity as a *pointer* to what he is doing now."[46]

Cone's emphasis on the resurrected Christ makes it possible for him to claim a revolutionary process in which Christ becomes inseparably bound to the black struggle for liberation. Hence, he speaks of Christ's blackness in both literal and symbolic terms. Christ is black in that he takes the suffering of the blacks into his own being and suffering. "If Christ is not black, the gospel is not good news to the oppressed."[47] And his logic extends: since Jesus is good news to the oppressed, his blackness should not be overlooked.

Cone gets exasperated with what he calls "favorite white questions." As he sees it, white theologians are not concerned with violence in general, but only when they are the victims of violence. He says, "As long as blacks are beaten and shot, they are strangely silent, as if they are unaware of the inhumanity committed against the black community."[48] He says further: "When I hear questions about violence and love coming from the children of slave masters whose identity with Jesus extends no further than that weekly Sunday service, then I can understand why many black brothers and sisters say that Christianity is the white man's religion, and it must be destroyed along with white oppressors."[49]

White questions about violence are deeply insulting to the black community. Cone says, "When whites ask me, 'Are you for violence?' my rejoinder is: '*Whose* violence?'"[50] He says that the reason he devotes as much attention to the issue of violence is that he hopes to "lay to rest once and for all white people's obscene questions about whether we blacks ought to be violent in the attainment of our freedom."[51]

In summary, Cone sees the revolution that will overcome the oppression of black people as firmly rooted in the resurrected Christ, through whom liberating God continues to redeem those who are oppressed. To name in advance *how* liberation will occur is to tie the hands of the one whose hands cannot be tied.

Cone on Other Ethicists

Besides engaging the writings of Martin Luther King Jr., Cone relates his approach specifically to several other American ethicists presented in this book—Reinhold Niebuhr, H. Richard Niebuhr, and James Gustafson. He refers to these ethicists particularly in relation to Marxism and the issue of ideology, which he suggests black theologians must face head-on. "Unless we black theologians can make an adequate distinction between divine revelation and human aspirations, there is nothing to keep Black Theology from identifying God's will with anything black people should decide to do at any given historical moment."[52] In other words, how can we adequately distinguish between "our words" and "God's Word?" After all, unless theological discourse is capable of being received as the Word from the Lord, it is heresy.

---

[45] See Cone, *Risks of Faith*, 36–37. In fact, all three points about violence are repeated here.
[46] Cone, *God of the Oppressed*, 223–24 (emphasis in original).
[47] Cone, *God of the Oppressed*, 136.
[48] Cone, *God of the Oppressed*, 196.
[49] Cone, *God of the Oppressed*, 196.
[50] Cone, *God of the Oppressed*, 196 (emphasis in original).
[51] Cone, *God of the Oppressed*, 196.
[52] Cone, *God of the Oppressed*, 84–85.

In showing how his theology is able to avoid that charge, Cone refers to H. Richard Niebuhr's work in *Christ and Culture*. As we have seen, Niebuhr works precisely at the question of how we fit into what God is already doing in this world.[53] Yet Cone is critical of how he sets up the issue using the Christ-culture binary. He raises two basic objections; the first has to do with Niebuhr's understanding of Christ, and the second with his understanding of culture. For Cone, both are abstractions and do not take into account what Christ is doing in American culture today, or in any other culture, for that matter.

On the definition of Christ, he begins by saying that "No theologian can define Jesus Christ's essence once and for all time, for Jesus is not a category but the divine event in history who is not subject to the limitations of human concepts."[54] While Cone recognizes that this point also applies to his own rendering of Jesus, nevertheless, he argues that Niebuhr does not go far enough in his interpretation of who Christ is. Nowhere in Niebuhr's work is there the recognition of "Jesus' identity with the little ones and his proclamation that God wills their freedom."[55] In other words, by ignoring the historically verifiable picture of Jesus as the liberator of the oppressed, Niebuhr presents a view of Christ that is stilted at best and just plain false at worst.

The second critique deals with Niebuhr's view of culture, which he defined in terms of language, habits, customs, technical processes, values, and so on. This, like the definition of Christ, is simply inadequate. Cone wonders how it is possible for Niebuhr to ignore all references to social oppression and exclude all social problems from the definition of culture. This is especially surprising since the binary of Christ and culture is to set up the basis for a *Christian* ethic, which must in some way reach back to the Christ event.

As Cone says it, "Christ's relation to culture is not defined in cultural generalities but in terms of the concreteness of human pain and suffering."[56] Hence, Cone finds in Niebuhr's approach an ethic so general that it cannot possibly be relevant to real people in hurting situations.

Cone reminds the reader that there is not just one culture but many, even in a given society. And Christ's attitude was different, depending on which cultural segments were under consideration. Says Cone, "Therefore, if we are to understand Christ's relation to culture, we had better be clear about whose human striving we speak of, the oppressed or the oppressors [*sic*]."[57]

Cone's point is that there is within Niebuhr's analysis, as there is so often when white men write ethical analyses, an "ideological distortion," meaning that he forgets the gospel is about the liberation of the "slaves" of every culture. The God of Jesus Christ stands against the culture of oppression, and therefore calls the rich ruler to "Sell all that you own and distribute the money to the poor, and you will have treasure in heaven; then come, follow me" (Luke 18:22b). This message would never be given in a culture of poverty. Black theology seeks to name the partiality evident in the gospel; in order for liberation and justice to occur, the message to the rich and the poor must be different. And unless that is acknowledged, Christian ethics cannot be an ethic grounded in the God of Jesus Christ. Martin Luther King Jr. realized this, and that realization—not his race—is why King is the most important Christian theologian in America.[58] He just got the gospel right. Very few white ethicists realize this point, and that is why their approaches are inadequate—it is not because they are white.

Indeed, there are also black ethicists who do ethics badly, according to Cone. He names Preston Williams who, in response to

---

[53] See chap. 21 above.
[54] Cone, *God of the Oppressed*, 89.
[55] Cone, *God of the Oppressed*, 89.
[56] Cone, *God of the Oppressed*, 90.
[57] Cone, *God of the Oppressed*, 91.
[58] See Cone, *Risks of Faith*, xvii.

Cone's work, pleads for "rationality in ethics."[59] Williams argues that Cone's approach represents a kind of fideism, meaning that he only "makes sense" once you adopt his perspective; otherwise his approach is not rational. Cone quotes Williams' proposal as:

> Our alternative relies upon beliefs and values associated with the Christian faith and American constitutional principles. . . . [It] is determined by reliance upon some prima-facie duties acknowledged by the generality of mankind.[60]

It is not difficult to see why Cone's approach lies in sharp contrast to Williams'. The appeal to rationality in general is anathema for Cone. It is precisely such an appeal that makes it possible to avoid the call of Jesus to liberate the oppressed. Cone accuses Williams of relying on "white theological irrationality."[61] He suggests that Williams has permitted white theologians, like James Gustafson and the Niebuhrs, to set the terms in which ethics is to be discussed. But this kind of ethic is precisely why America is in the sad moral state it is in, why oppression is so rampant and tolerated, even defended. In response to Williams, Cone says, "I contend that the black Christian ethic must start with Scripture and the black experience. We must read each in light of the other, and then ask, 'What am I to do?'"[62]

The challenge that Cone presents to Christians is unequivocal: be liberators for Christ. He suggests that just as the Jewish Holocaust has forced Christian theologians to reconsider the depths of Christian theology's entanglement with anti-Semitism,[63] no less should be expected of Christian theology in the face of black racism. For this to occur, the theology that emerges from Jesus of Nazareth should not be seen as abstract but as fundamentally concrete. And it is the nature of concrete theologies that they disrupt. Cone's analysis of race deeply disrupts because via his reading of Jesus he refuses to permit an inclusion of the other into merely a general account of being. Yet only in this way can the issues of racism be properly addressed.[64]

CONCLUSION

Cone is a controversial theologian-ethicist because he names a racism that makes white people squirm, perhaps precisely because he is so convincing. He truly makes the good news of the gospel bad news for many of us. Yet Cone did not mean to suggest that black racism was the only form of oppression in America.[65] Says Rufus Burrow:

> Cone was primarily concerned with white racism and its brutalizing effects on black life-chances in a racist-capitalist system. Yet he was from the beginning aware that there were other serious forms of oppression in the United States which dehumanized and crushed other groups. He did not name these, but there is evidence that he knew that racism was not the only major social problem.[66]

Moreover, Cone also realized in his later years that he had some blind spots. He especially "confessed" his blinders regarding his use of sexist language in his earlier writings.[67]

Cone is hard on white theology and its proponents. This does not mean that he believes

---

[59] See Preston Williams, "James Cone and the Problem of a Black Ethic," *Harvard Theological Review* 65, no. 4 (1972).

[60] Quoted in Cone, *God of the Oppressed*, 203 (emphasis in original).

[61] Cone, *God of the Oppressed*, 203 (emphasis in original).

[62] Cone, *God of the Oppressed*, 205.

[63] See Cone, *Risks of Faith*, 134. We notice again that Cone makes connections between black racism and anti-Semitism. See the earlier reference to Elie Wiesel's story at the beginning of this chapter.

[64] For a further discussion of this theme, see J. Kameron Carter, "James H. Cone, Liberation, and the Theological Meaning of Blackness," in his book, *Race: A Theological Account* (New York: Oxford University Press, 2008).

[65] See James H. Cone, *Speaking the Truth: Ecumenism, Liberation, and Black Theology* (Maryknoll, N.Y.: Orbis, 1999), 77. Here he argues that blacks should not be selective in the forms of violence and oppression they oppose and lists racism, sexism, classism, militarism, and neocolonialism.

[66] Rufus Burrow Jr., *James H. Cone and Black Liberation Theology* (Jefferson, N.C.: McFarland, 1994), xviii.

[67] Cone, *Risks of Faith*, xxv.

that "whites by nature are more sinful than other people. They just have more power."[68] Nor would he argue that the only form of racism is black racism. But he does argue relentlessly that unless racism is named as a key issue of Christian theology, it cannot be *Christian* theology. And he warns that the struggle is against powers and principalities and without the help of almighty God, victory will not be ours.

---

[68] Cone, *Risks of Faith*, xxvi.

Chapter Twenty-Eight

GEORGE E. "TINK" TINKER

George "Tink" Tinker is an Osage American Indian theologian who has spent his entire writing and teaching career searching for ways to help people hear the voices of aboriginal peoples. He is the Clifford Baldridge Professor of American Indian Cultures and Religious Traditions at Iliff School of Theology in Denver, Colorado, where he has taught since 1985. He lectures and writes in the area of religion and social change.

In an established Euro–American seminary, Tinker says that he teaches from an American Indian Osage perspective, meaning he does theological reflection in a counter-narrative way. In other words, he presents constructive and challenging ways of looking at the world based on American Indian traditions, ways that do not frame reality with the customary Euro-American assumptions.[1]

Tinker teaches courses in justice and peace studies as well as in American Indian spirituality. He explains that the reason for calling his area of teaching "American Indian Cultures and Religious Traditions" is that American Indians do not have religions as such. This is partly why his teaching is "counter-narrative"—traditional language simply does not work to get at what is at stake here. The word "religion" is much too Euro–Western and does not adequately describe American Indian spirituality. One is here reminded of a pre-Enlightenment notion of "religion" that is far more holistic than the post-Enlightenment concept, which is able to separate religion from cultural life. Tinker emphasizes that everything about traditional American Indian life has both religious and cultural overtones; faith is always embodied in a culture, and the two are simply so intertwined that they cannot be separated. Hence, to unpack American Indian theology, one has to find ways of speaking about the unity of culture and religious traditions.

Of course, Tinker does not stand alone as an American Indian intellectual challenging the hegemony of the Western intellectual tradition. People such as Vine Deloria Jr., who brought us best-sellers like *Custer Died for Your Sins* and *God is Red*,[2] have gone before him. Indeed, Deloria is an important mentor for Tinker, especially in his challenge to Euro–American modes of thought as shaped by temporality and offering an alternative spatiality mode of seeing the world. As in other liberation theology groups, it is important to point out that there are many scholars to choose from within American Indian theology. Yet we will analyze the thought not of the movement at large with its many twists and turns but of a particular scholar's work.

---

[1] From "Meet Dr. Tinker" biographical video available on his faculty web page ("George E. 'Tink' Tinker," *Iliff School of Theology*, http://www.iliff.edu/index/learn/your-faculty/george-e-tink-tinker/, accessed April 19, 2011).

[2] Vine Deloria Jr., *Custer Died for Your Sins: An Indian Manifesto* (New York: Macmillan, 1969); and *God Is Red: A Native View of Religion* (New York: Putnam, 1973).

HIS LIFE

Not much public information is available on Tinker's personal life: his date of birth, his early years of school, or his childhood community. We know that his parents were George Edward Tinker III and Carol Wicks Tinker, and that he is married to Dr. Loring Abeyta, whom he describes as a "Chicana indigenous person."[3] Among other roles, she is an adjunct professor at Iliff School of Theology, where she co-teaches a course with Tinker on race, gender, and class.

Tinker also tells us about his "adopted" brother, emphasizing that "adoptive relationships in the American Indian world are considered closer than blood in terms of their enduring importance."[4] In 1995 his brother committed suicide, an event that shook Tinker to the core of his being. He had known and shared some of his brother's pain and been the beneficiary of his extraordinary mechanical skills and selfless friendship. Tinker's brother was a wonderful friend but one with deep scars. By the time his brother was six years old, he had been physically and emotionally abused by his parents. At that age he was "taken away" from the reservation to a church mission school where the priest "baptized him" into the evils of white, Christian domination. Tinker gives us a brief glimpse into his brother's life:

> Having introduced the youngster to a forced intimacy that had been completely unknown to him before, this priest proceeded to demonstrate his extraordinary virility that same night by transferring his affection to his roommate, Clifford. He then left after threatening both boys with physical punishment and eternal perdition should they reveal anything of what had transpired. Then . . . these two little boys were left to wonder aloud what had happened to them and to ask each other, "Did it hurt?" As is the case with an inordinate

number of Indian youth (up to ten times the average for all U.S. teenagers), Clifford committed suicide at age seventeen, leaving my brother with a deep, enduring sense of responsibility not only for his own shame but for the death of his young friend. He always felt, he said, that he should have done *something* to help Clifford, however irrational that may seem to us in hindsight.[5]

There is no doubt that both the beautiful and the ugly experiences Tinker had with his brother, ending in his suicide, colored the lens through which he saw the "message of salvation" offered by white missionaries and teachers.

Perhaps it is no accident that we know so little about Tinker's personal life, for his way of viewing human existence is from the standpoint of the community, not the individual. This is a concept Euro–Americans have trouble understanding and what Tinker's American Indian theology is built on.

Tinker provides us with plenty of information about the history of his American Indian family—the Osage Nation (*Wazhazhe*). He introduces himself as an "enrolled member of the Osage Nation," and while the Osage prefer to be called *Ni-u-kon-ska-wa-zha-zha*, he says that government officials cannot pronounce this name and so have settled on Osage. Among the Osage, he is a member of the Bald Eagle clan.[6]

Tinker says he is of mixed blood. "I am an American Indian on my father's side and an ordained Lutheran minister on my mother's side. My mother hates it when I introduce myself that way, but being Lutheran is an ethnic identity in the United States. Lutherans in North America are not just Amer–European. They are Amer–Northern European—Germans and Scandinavians."[7]

He is an ordained minister in the Lutheran Church and has served as pastor of the

---

[3] George E. "Tink" Tinker, *American Indian Liberation: A Theology of Sovereignty* (Maryknoll, N.Y.: Orbis, 2008), 1.
[4] Tinker, *American Indian Liberation*, 152n14.
[5] Tinker, *American Indian Liberation*, 153 (emphasis in original).
[6] See George "Tink" Tinker, "Dreaming a New Dream: Cowboys, Indians, Global Violence and the Gospel," 1. This was a plenary address at a Call to Action Conference in Milwaukee, Wisconsin, on November 5, 2000. It is a *Spirituality and Justice Reprint* available at http://www.cta-usa.org/reprint11-00/dreaming.html, accessed May 14, 2011, 1.
[7] Tinker, "Dreaming a New Dream," 1.

Living Waters Episcopal-Lutheran Indian Ministry in Denver. Yet he confesses that he does not function well as a Lutheran minister anymore because he has claimed his father's side of culture identity and has found that American Indian and Lutheran spirituality do not mix well.

Tinker is active as a volunteer, especially in urban communities. He works both with the liberation of American Indian peoples from their oppression as the colonized *and* with the liberation of white Americans as the colonizers. He is the director of Four Winds American Indian Survival Project in Denver and as such is a traditional American Indian spiritual leader.[8] His community involvement is much more than a mere tangential interest, since, as a scholar for indigenous peoples, he is naturally drawn into their political and social lives. His scholarship is embodied in his people in two ways: how he thinks comes from his people and what he thinks is expressible by his people.

As a member of the American Indian Movement, Tinker is involved in drawing attention to political prisoners in the United States. He states that American prisons are filled with political prisoners, especially blacks, Latinos, and Indians. The United States imprisons more people per capita than any other country in the world. Says Tinker, "and we call this a free country."[9] Americans have created an intensely violent society, and the challenge is to re-imagine ways in which this can be undone.

Tinker's brief history of the Osage Nation goes as follows: in the early 1800s the Osage controlled "most of Missouri, a big chunk of Kansas, and a little of Arkansas and northeastern Oklahoma—everything west of the Mississippi, north of Arkansas, south of the Missouri Rivers."[10] In 1803 the Osage land was purchased from France by the U. S. government. He admits that his people still do not understand this transaction. How could France sell their land to the U. S. government? But it did and it "enabled [U. S. President] Jefferson to double the size of his country overnight."[11] It was called the Louisiana Purchase, and this act of "unprecedented generosity," he opines sarcastically, permitted the U. S. government to give it to the Lutherans for refugees to settle.

Tinker was educated in America's white schools. He holds a bachelor's degree from New Mexico Highland University; a Master's in Divinity from Pacific Lutheran Theological Seminary in Berkeley, California; and a Ph.D. from Graduate Theological Union, also in Berkeley, which he received in 1983. His doctoral dissertation was in biblical studies.

Teaching and writing have been Tinker's preoccupation since 1985. He has authored or co-authored four books, and co-edited two.[12] In addition, he has contributed many articles to journals. His writings address a variety of concerns but always are rooted in one overriding goal, namely, to articulate an American Indian liberation theology of place. Such a theology insists on the unity of thought and practice, and hence cannot be separated from his Osage tradition. An overarching objective is to give an account of Christian theology that finds ways of bringing together an account of creation and Christology in such a manner that "lordship" language does not trump the sacredness of God's earth. In other words, conquering

---

[8] From "George E. 'Tink' Tinker," *Iliff School of Theology* faculty website.

[9] Tinker, "Dreaming a New Dream," 2.

[10] Tinker, "Dreaming a New Dream," 1.

[11] George E. "Tink" Tinker, *Spirit and Resistance: Political Theology and American Indian Liberation* (Minneapolis: Fortress, 2004), ix.

[12] George Tinker, *American Indian Liberation*; *Spirit and Resistance*; *Missionary Conquest: The Gospel and Native American Genocide* (Minneapolis: Fortress, 1993); George Tinker, Clara Sue Kidwell, and Homer Noley, *A Native American Theology* (Maryknoll, N.Y.: Orbis, 2001); George Tinker, Richard A. Grounds, and David E. Wilkens, eds., *Native Voices: American Indian Identity and Resistance* (Lawrence: University Press of Kansas, 2003); and George Tinker, Curtiss Paul Deyoung, Wilda C. Gafney, Leticia Guardiola-Saenz, and Frank M. Yomada, eds., *The People's Bible* (Minneapolis: Fortress, 2008).

metaphors are appropriate to neither Christ-ology nor creation theology.

THEOLOGICAL ORIENTATION

From the foregoing, it is not surprising to learn that a key emphasis in Tinker's theology has to do with challenging the notions of human dominance and control. The problem, as he sees it, is anthropocentrism in Euro–American thought; that is, the centrality of the place of human beings in determining what can be known and the insistence on the right to set the terms of human actions for everyone. Such a theology could be contrasted with his own stance of receptivity to what has been given in creation. An illustration of the problematic anthropocentric theology is the common distinctions between the sacred and secular realms. In this view, God is in charge of the sacred and humans of the secular. Hence, whatever human beings decide in their realm—about the environment or the natural order—goes. The receptivity model, on the other hand, requires openness to reach beyond one's own understanding of things, listening to what can speak—the tradition, the human community, the Spirit—and to what can "speak" in other ways—in nature, such as trees and stones. For all the world is "worded."

This alternative view of theology stands in contrast to much of Euro–American theology. Tinker's theology of liberation emphasizes the importance of place rather than history, of space rather than time. Hence, not only is it different from Western theology but it is also different from much of Third World liberation theology.

Tinker is a member of the Ecumenical Association of Third World Theologians (EATWOT), yet he continues to speak of the indigenous people as part of the Fourth World. While the Third and Fourth "worlds" share many problems, like hunger, poverty, and oppression by colonialists, there are also distinct differences. In a speech delivered at the General Assembly of EATWOT in Nairobi, Kenya, in 1992, he argues that Third World liberation theologies are themselves derived from the Western imagination against which indigenous peoples have struggled for centuries.[13] Their reliance on a Marxist analysis is testimony to this, for Marxist views on development and modernization have been instrumental in inflicting spiritual genocide on Fourth World peoples.[14]

Tinker differentiates his view of liberation from the Latin American variety presented by Gustavo Gutiérrez.[15] He argues that a Third World liberation theology's model of social change is not applicable to indigenous people. This is so in part because Native peoples' spirituality is different from that of Latin Americans, but even more fundamentally for other reasons, like having a different view of what it means to be a person, a different view of revelation, a different understanding of revolution, and a different view of praxis.[16]

Tinker begins with Gutiérrez's analysis of personhood. Gutiérrez states that Western theology focuses on the challenge of the non-believer, whereas Latin American liberation theology focuses on the status of a non-person. What he means is that Western dominant theology dehumanizes people in the very process of wanting to make them believers. Much of this analysis Tinker affirms, but given the Marxist undercurrent of revolution and the class struggle to overcome poverty, it overlooks the indigenous peoples' view of "personhood in terms of their relationship to the land."[17]

[13] Tinker, "Spirituality, Native American Personhood, Sovereignty, and Solidarity," in *Native and Christian: Indigenous Voices on Religious Identity in the United States and Canada*, ed. James Treat (New York: Routledge, 1996), 116. For a slightly revised version of this article under the same title, see George Tinker, *Spirit and Resistance*, 100–115.

[14] Tinker, "Spirituality, Native American Personhood," 116.

[15] See chap. 26 above for a summary of Gustavo Gutiérrez's thought.

[16] Tinker, "Spirituality, Native American Personhood," 116.

[17] Tinker, "Spirituality, Native American Personhood," 117.

The concept of class struggle is altogether foreign and inappropriate for the indigenous people because they are not a class. Even though the majority of them may be poor, the overcoming of their poverty would not change their reality of being colonized. Since being part of an oppressed class is not the issue, labor analysis cannot solve their problems; only landedness can. And if landedness is the issue, it follows that sovereignty also is key.[18]

The failure of the Euro–American missionaries to see that their gospel is inseparably linked to a certain view of "civilization" requires that indigenous theologians need to start over with a new theology of land and sovereignty. A Marxist political analysis has not been helpful because cultural diversity is no more tolerated in that process than in a capitalist system. Tinker cites the Miskito situation in Nicaragua as an example of the oppression of a native people under a Marxist government.[19]

The American Indian understanding of how we come to know God is also different from Latin American liberation theology. Gutiérrez assumes, along with dominant Western theology, that God is revealed in history, but Tinker argues that while that may be true in part, the primary revelation of God comes through creation. The debate over whether revelation comes via history or creation is, of course, not new in the West. Tinker gives this discussion a particular twist by arguing against the destructive, time-oriented, Western theology in favor of a space-oriented, Indian theology.[20]

The time/space distinction is important to Tinker. Temporality is the metaphor necessary to make conquest decisive. The notion of revolution, whether violent or nonviolent, is rooted in the metaphor of temporality. Moreover, with revolution comes the idea of dominance and control. Hence, in this model, there is little room for people of difference; all are subject to the movement of time. Here, capitalism and socialism are identical, and the war between them is a war waged for supremacy, to have difference dissolved in the name of a common goal.

The American Indian imagination of spatiality differs. Says Tinker, "This is perhaps the most dramatic (and largely unnoticed) cultural difference between Native American thought processes and the Western intellectual tradition."[21] Tinker does not mean to suggest that time and space are categorical opposites, but rather the question is which metaphor dominates. He says, "progress, history, development, evolution and process become key notions that invade all academic discourse in the West, from science and economics to philosophy and theology. History, thus, becomes the quintessential Western intellectual device and gives rise to structures of cognition and modes of discourse that pay dutiful homage to temporality."[22]

It is relatively easy to get from the spatiality metaphor to the significance of land. Says Tinker:

> If the primary metaphor of existence for Native Americans is spatial and not temporal, this goes a long way towards explaining what nearly everyone already knows, that American Indian spirituality

[18] Tinker's emphasis on land and sovereignty relates to other liberation theologians like Palestinian authors. See, e.g., Naim Stifan Ateek, *Justice, and Only Justice: A Palestinian Theology of Liberation* (Maryknoll, N.Y.: Orbis, 1989) who argues that Palestinian liberation is essentially linked to the self-determination of a people. Similarly, Tinker says, "we do not just want existence, that is, life in the sense of mere biological survivability. What we want is life in the sense of self-sufficient, cultural, spiritual, political, and economic sustainability—on our own terms" (*American Indian Liberation*, 81).

[19] The Miskito Indian population of about 200,000 centers in Nicaragua and Honduras. In Nicaragua they have had an ongoing battle with the Sandinistas as well as with other governments over economic and land rights. In 2009, they declared their independence, but the Nicaraguan government has not responded to that declaration.

[20] Different versions of this issue are evident in the Karl Barth/historicism and the George Grant/historicism debates. This is also a debate internal to Roman Catholic theology. Alasdair MacIntyre, it could be argued, seeks to resolve the history/nature distinction in his writings.

[21] Tinker, "Spirituality, Native American Personhood," 121.

[22] Tinker, "Spirituality, Native American Personhood," 121.

and American Indian existence in general is deeply rooted in the land. It explains why the history of our conquest and removal from our lands was so culturally and genocidally destructive to our tribes.[23]

While land (and sovereignty) is a special symbol of liberation theology for Native Americans, it is not the primary one; for it is "the circle" that best represents the spiritual meaning of American Indian life. The circle offers a metaphor that connects family, clan, tribe, and eventually all of creation. It is itself a creation symbol. It has no beginning, no end, and no hierarchy. All elements within it are equal; all are included. All are relatives: animals, people, vegetation and other life forms, even inanimate objects. The circle is the medicine wheel with two lines forming a cross in both horizontal and vertical directions. "those four directions symbolize the four cardinal virtues of a tribe [bravery, generosity, humility, and honesty], the four sacred colors of ceremonial life, the sacred powers of four animal nations, and the four nations of Two-leggeds that walk on earth (Black, Red, Yellow and White). That is, in our conception of the universe, all human beings walk ideally in egalitarian balance."[24] Spatiality functions as the category of egalitarianism. He says further, "If temporality and historicity lend themselves implicitly to hierarchical structures because someone with a greater investment of time may know more of the body of temporally codified knowledge, spatiality lends itself to the egalitarian. All have relatively similar access to the immediacy of the spatially present."[25]

Tinker is a biblical scholar and so relates his view of spatiality to the biblical teaching of the *basileia tou theou* (kingdom of God). He reminds the reader that the kingdom question for Jesus was not "when" but "where"; "in Luke 17:20 Jesus instructs the Pharisees that the *basileia* is 'in your midst' (*entos humas*), that is, already spatially present."[26] Hence, faithfulness has to do primarily with a way of "seeing what is there" before it has to do with a way of acting and bringing about something new. The notion of the presence of the kingdom has specific implications for the Gospel writers. In Mark 1:15, for example, Jesus tells his audience that because the kingdom is present, they are to "repent and believe in the good news."

Tinker uses this language of the presence of the kingdom to flesh out his own theology. First, American Indian spirituality emphasizes harmony and balance in all of creation. God is mysteriously present among us in all that is, and human beings are fully part of creation and not apart from creation. We participate in maintaining the balance and harmony of creation. He sees a difference between this approach and Western theology, where transcendence from creation is the platform from which to act. This he says "has been recklessly imposed on the rest of us in the name of development."[27] In the Western model, the people are in charge; in Tinker's model, God is in charge.

Second, the stance of repentance and believing in the givenness of the new community becomes the impetus for justice and for peace. He says:

> What I am arguing is not some value-neutral creation theology of Matthew Fox, some new-age spirituality of feel-good individualism. Rather, it is an ultimate expression of a "theology of community" that must generate a consistent interest in justice and peace. Namely, if I imagine myself as a vital part of a community, indeed as a part of many communities, it becomes more difficult

---

[23] Tinker, "Spirituality, Native American Personhood," 122.

[24] Tinker, "Spirituality, Native American Personhood," 123 (square brackets insert added).

[25] Tinker, "Spirituality, Native American Personhood," 123. See also *American Indian Liberation*, 70–74, for Tinker's discussion on spatiality.

[26] Tinker, "Spirituality, Native American Personhood," 126. For a further discussion of the concepts of spatiality and *basileia*, see the chapter titled "Indian Culture and Interpreting the Christian Bible," in *Spirit and Resistance*, 93ff.

[27] Tinker, "Spirituality, Native American Personhood," 126. For other critical comments on the Western notion of "development" see *American Indian Liberation*, 77f., and *Spirit and Resistance*, 9ff.

for me to act in ways that are destructive of the community.[28]

Third, it is because God is among us that American Indian theology speaks about creation as sacred; it is because God is in creation that the earth is the source of life. This notion goes far beyond the concern of environmentalists, like those in Greenpeace and the Sierra Club, who are able to do some good but do it in the name of placing themselves above creation—thereby claiming the same posture of mastery over the environment as those they accuse of destroying it. Hence, there is a clash of power but no potential moral basis for resolving it. This power clash is undermined by the American Indian notion of spirituality, in which justice and peace are rooted in a view of inclusiveness of all human beings and all creation, a view that can speak of the earth as good.

The remainder of this chapter will explore four main areas of Tinker's work as it further explores his theological orientation: the big lie, spirituality and violence, creation and ecojustice, and a new imagination. These are not mere academic topics for Tinker; they are at the very center of faithful, Christian practice. If Christian faith is embodied (or housed) in a specific culture, that is to say, if an enculturated Christianity is an oxymoron, how can Christian faith be communicated cross-culturally without doing violence to the very nature of Christianity on the one hand and the people whose lives are given social and personal meanings by a given culture on the other? To ask it differently, can two profoundly different cultures both "house" the same Christian faith? These are extremely important questions for the Christian faith generally and for Christian ethics and native spirituality particularly.

Tinker does not answer these questions simply, but his writings explore them in sharp ways, and he often suggests avenues of resolution. Throughout his writings, he raises

the issue of whether Christianity, which is a "Good News" religion, needs to "violate" a person's traditional context of meaning and significance in order to effect salvation. In the final analysis, the question is, what does it mean to be "born anew" (John 3:3)?

THE LIE

Tinker is among a handful of North American theologians who have engaged in critical analysis of Euro–American evangelization of the American Indian people. His critique is sharp but particularly important for those who, like Christian ethicists must, ask what it means to live in faithful response to the call of the gospel.

Tinker refers to Leslie Silko's 1977 novel *Ceremony*[29] to give content to the grand illusion perpetrated upon all North Americans, both immigrants and natives. Through his protagonist Tayo, who finds himself cutting fences to release cattle, itself a symbol of the internal struggle, Silko contemplates the personal upheaval produced by centuries of propaganda by prophets of untruth.

> The lie. He cut into the wires as if cutting away at the lie inside himself. The liars had fooled everyone, white people and Indians alike; as long as people believed the lies, they would never be able to see what had been done to them or what they were doing to each other. . . . If the white people never looked beyond the lie, to see that theirs was a nation built on stolen land, then they would never be able to understand how they had been used by the witchery; they would never know that they were still being manipulated by those who knew how to stir the ingredients together: white thievery and injustice boiling up the anger and hatred that would finally destroy the world: the starving against the fat, the colored against the white. The destroyers had only to set it into motion and sit back to count the casualties. But it was more than a body count: the lie devoured white hearts, and for more than two hundred years white people had worked to fill their emptiness; they tried to glut the hollowness with patriotic wars and with great technology and the wealth it brought. And

---

28 Tinker, "Spirituality, Native American Personhood," 127.
29 Leslie Marmon Silko, *Ceremony* (New York: Penguin, 1977).

always they had been fooling themselves, and they knew it.[30]

It is particularly hard to hear that those who have been caught by the gospel message of "you will know the truth, and the truth will make you free" (John 8:32) should be accused of lies. When this happens it calls for very careful listening.

Tinker summarizes his own understanding of "the lie" as follows: "[A] self-serving illusion of white superiority . . . an illusion that damages the health and well-being of both white and Indian peoples. The truth is, however, that Indian people have internalized this illusion just as deeply as white Americans have, and as a result we discover from time to time just how fully we participate today in our own oppression."[31] This is the diabolical work of lies. No untruth is dangerous unless it convinces people. Tinker suggests that the lie of white superiority has convinced everyone, and just as it destroys the oppressed, it also destroys the oppressors, albeit in different ways.

When Tinker narrates the cultural genocide of the Native Americans, the first missionaries play a dominant role in the story. Had there been a distinction made between the political goals and the Christian message, it might have been different, but the two were entirely collusive from the beginning. Yet it is important to understand Tinker on this point. He is not accusing Euro–American missionaries of intentional deception; that is, of willfully presenting the untruth, knowing it to be so. On the contrary, they believed their message to be true. The problem is that they lived in an illusory world. They were caught up in their own lie.

Despite the illusions, Tinker does not exonerate those early missionaries from responsibility. The ideology of white superiority was ingrained in the Christian message itself, and hence the missionaries, as emissaries of the "gospel," were party to the church-state strategy of subjugation. The missionaries, on behalf of the church, simply collaborated with governments, colonization and settlement organizations, land purchasers, and banks. History shows the devastating effects of the Euro–American strategy of conquest, including an intellectual conquest, in which the missionaries were fully implicated. Says Tinker, "The American Indians continue to suffer from the effects of the conquest by European immigrants over the past five centuries. We live with the ongoing stigma of defeated peoples who have endured genocide; the intentional dismantling of cultural values; forced confinement on less desirable lands called reservations; intentionally nurtured dependency on the federal government; and conversion by missionaries who imposed a new culture on us."[32]

The effects of the colonialist policies on American Indians are easy to document. Consider, for example, that they "suffer the lowest per capita income of any ethnic group in the United States, the highest teenage suicide rate, a sixty percent unemployment rate nationally, and a scandalously low longevity that remains below sixty years for both men and women."[33] Tinker suggests that it should not be any wonder that the "gospel" as proclaimed, which, in part at least, is responsible for such pathetic social reality, has itself become suspect. And if the "gospel" has not lost its credibility, then at the very least the white church, which has paraded as its representative, has.

Tinker traces the history of "missionary violence," from the very beginning, especially its view of intellectual and cultural superiority. Even before the missionaries came, there was Christopher Columbus (1451–1506), who got things going. Tinker quotes his diary entry reflecting his perspective of domination toward the natives of the "new land."

---

[30] Tinker, *Missionary Conquest*, 2.
[31] Tinker, *Missionary Conquest*, 2.
[32] George Tinker, "The Integrity of Creation: Restoring Trinitarian Balance," *Ecumenical Review* 41 (October 1989): 531.
[33] Tinker, *Missionary Conquest*, 3.

[October 12, 1492] They ought to make good and skilled servants, for they repeat very quickly whatever we say to them. I think they can easily be made Christians, for they seem to have no religion. If it pleases Our Lord, I will take six of them to Your Highnesses when I depart. . . . [October 14] . . . these people are very unskilled in arms. Your Highnesses will see this for yourselves when I bring to you the seven that I have taken. After they learn our language I shall return them, unless Your Highnesses order that the entire population be taken to Castile, or held captive here. With 50 men you could subject everyone and make them do what you wished.[34]

Columbus was not a missionary in the official sense, yet his racist perspective seems to have set the tone for the missionaries of the church who followed. Tinker analyzes the work and writings of four prominent missionaries in order to show their complicity in the process of American Indian cultural genocide.

First, Tinker considers the work of John Eliot (1604–1690), longtime Puritan missionary to the American Indian peoples in Massachusetts. It seems that Eliot may have been a well-intentioned "preacher of the gospel," but he certainly did not hesitate to use the full force of the law and political powers to have his way with American Indians. He felt pity for them, saying: "As for these poore Indians, they have no principles of their own, nor yet wisdome of their own. (I mean as other Nations have)."[35] The accounts are mixed about his intentions, but there is little doubt about the effects of his work. It was devastating for the American Indian people of New England because they lost their power of self-determination—from freedom to practice their own rituals and ceremonies to control over their land. Their independence was simply swindled away from them, and they were made dependent upon the Puritan politics of white foreigners.

In Tinker's account of Eliot's work, he tells the story of his first effort to "preach the gospel" to the American Indians in Massachusetts. When he ventured into their territory, he was not well received; there was open resistance from their leader, and Eliot was heckled by the people.[36] This was an embarrassment for him, and when he reported his poor reception to the political authorities, they responded by "passing legislation to ensure a gentler, more submissive response to Eliot's preaching."[37] The new law actually did much more; it also made blasphemy a capital crime and outlawed traditional American Indian practices like powwows and the worshipping of "false gods." And, of course, the law was interpreted by a white court system. This was but the beginning of a process that would lead to complete subjugation of the American Indian people.

As Eliot traveled from place to place, often accompanied by civil servant Daniel Gookin, (testimony to his collusion with government), he established "praying towns." By 1660 Eliot had established seven such towns. Praying towns were for converted American Indians, who were taken out of the general American Indian population in order to become "good Christians." They were known as "praying Indians." Here they were "civilized," and asked to give up their old ways of life. This meant that they had to leave behind their traditional clothing, their hunting-gathering lifestyles, their rituals and ceremonies—everything that the Puritans considered "savage." This practice had a profoundly negative effect on the American Indian economy, their social interaction, their sense of peoplehood, and in many other ways; for it divided the people in two. On the other hand, it assisted in the Puritan economy because it brought in cheap labor.[38]

This genocidal process took place at the intellectual and theological levels as well. It is striking that the confessional statements made by American Indians who became church members completely and utterly

[34] Tinker, *Missionary Conquest*, 8.
[35] Quoted in Tinker, *Missionary Conquest*, 21.
[36] See Tinker, *Missionary Conquest*, 29.
[37] Tinker, *Missionary Conquest*, 29.
[38] See Tinker, *Missionary Conquest*, 32f.

denounced as evil all their old ways. Their life before they became Christians was fully rejected; their life now was of God. What was named and cast off included powwows, lust, gaming, lying, adultery, and so on. Tinker records one convert as saying: "Before I prayed to God, I committed all sins; and serving many gods. I much despised praying unto God, for I beleeved the Devil."[39] This, says Tinker, is indicative of the racism that underwrote the white view of Christianity and the relentless assault on the American Indian peoples' way of life. It represents an absolute dichotomy between the Euro–American culture and the American Indian culture; at the same time, it shows the complete assimilation of the gospel of Jesus Christ with white culture.

Tinker discusses the work of three other early missionaries, Junípero Serra (1713–1784), a Franciscan priest originally from Spain who was involved in mission work in Mexico and California; Pierre-Jean De Smet (1801–1873), a Jesuit missionary from Belgium working in the western United States; and Henry Benjamin Whipple (1822–1901), born in New York and a bishop in the Episcopal Church in Minnesota. Space does not permit to tell the stories of their work in detail, but Tinker's thesis is that each contributed to "the lie" of white superiority and the destruction of the culture that sustained the American Indian people. Whether through the violent tactics of forcing potential converts into submission with the use of shackles and stocks (Serra),[40] or economic exploitation of American Indian peoples by being functionaries of the government's interest to "domesticate" a people (De Smet), or as willing agents of one-sided assimilation (Whipple); all, according to Tinker, failed to see American Indians as a people with a unique and life-sustaining culture. Hence, in their effort to "preach the gospel of Jesus Christ" they, in effect, preached the gospel of cultural superiority, the consequences of which have decimated a people.

SPIRITUALITY AND VIOLENCE

Tinker suggests that the spirituality of America is repeatedly cast in language of violence. It began five hundred years ago with Cristóbal Colón, commonly known as Christopher Columbus[41] reaching the Americas in 1492. And in relation to the Indian people it has not changed. America was born in violence, and violence has come to define its spirit.

We have seen, via Columbus' diary, that his stance was one of total dominance toward the native people. This same spirit was perpetuated by the early Christian missionaries and by the settlers, then through the formation of the United States, the purchase of the Louisiana Territory by President Jefferson, through the Lewis and Clark expedition as they explored the western frontier, and perhaps most definitively, with the massacres of the American Indian people.

Of course, Tinker acknowledges that violence against the native people in America is not unique; it also extends to the abuse of women and children. Moreover, violence gets expressed in a different form in relation to other nations, in the globalization of capital, and the U.S. involvement in the School of the Americas. The spirituality of white, American society is defined by violence.

It is important to note that Tinker believes that *things could be otherwise*. America is the way it is not because it must be this way, but because it has been imagined into this form of existence. America is the product of a limited, human imagination. In other words, the white man's spirit need not be violent. To

---

[39] Tinker, *Missionary Conquest*, 39.

[40] Tinker, *Missionary Conquest*, 56.

[41] Christopher Columbus was born in Genoa, Italy, and according to tradition was given the name, Cristoforo Colombo. It is thought that he changed his name to Cristóbal Colón when he moved to Spain. Several websites narrate the story of his name, e.g., http://en.wikipedia.org/wiki/Christopher_Columbus, accessed May 14, 2011. In English, Christopher Columbus has stuck.

say it this way implies something about how Tinker sees history and creation. He says, "I want to suggest that we begin to create our own world anew, to think it anew, to dream it anew, and to dream out of existence the violence, the globalization, the World Bank and the International Monetary Fund, and the School of Americas, to re-imagine out of our world the abuse and the subjection of women, and the racialization of blacks and whites, yellows, browns and reds."[42] To say that it could be otherwise is to make a profound claim about ethics—*what we do matters*. It also means that he holds the white man responsible for the failure of imagination.

To say that our actions matter does not imply, for Tinker, that violence is best understood as a set of individual acts, for violence is also a system, and as a system it is a way of habituating and a way of thinking. It is a system that legitimates taking away property from another person or people simply because you can; you belong to a system that will defend you if you do it because you have status in that system. That is why a violent system functions best with religion as a legitimation force. For example, the structures of the World Bank and the International Monetary Fund are undergirded by the churches, especially through what the churches call development.[43] "Our churches are part of this new religious movement called the globalization of capital,"[44] and when we make poor people and nations dependent on global economic structures, we participate in the violence of subjugation. Any re-imagination of this violent world calls for resistance, and as Tinker reminds us, when people act in resistance to systemic violence they act against themselves on behalf of the exploited.

We have already seen that when the first Europeans came to the Americas they came in an imagination of violence; that is, they came with the view that it was legitimate to enter a foreign territory to conquer its people—to set the terms in which their life was to be meaningful. They came with the arrogance of cultural superiority, that is, the assumption of violence. But violence is by nature unnatural, and hence, the only way for humans to live with violence without going insane is to find justification for it. That is why elaborate, rational systems are necessary for violent societies to live "normal" lives.

Tinker suggests that violence has become a key American value. It is part of what we call "family values" because we teach it to our children through Hollywood productions, children's stories, and cartoons. For example, TV shows for children, although they do not show people being killed because parents would not like this, can be extremely violent; thus, the message is learned at a very young age: "As long as you think you are right, you can engage in an act of violence on behalf of justice and righteousness as you define it."[45] Moreover, children watch their parents as they conduct their businesses. It is not enough to have a market for our products; we need to "corner the market," "outcompete," and to make it impossible for a competitor to survive. That is how capitalism works; it is a way of violence.[46]

Because of the violent nature of American spirituality, Tinker does not find tragedies like the one at the Columbine High School in 1999 to be a surprise.[47] He hears people say: "these were two sick young boys,"[48] but thinks this is a self-deceptive way of excusing ourselves from having taught them (the

---

[42] Tinker, "Dreaming a New Dream," 3.

[43] For Tinker's critique of Western notions of development, see "Liberation and Sustainability: Prolegomena to an American Indian Theology," in *Spirit and Resistance*. See esp. the sections "'Sustainable Development': An Oxymoron?" and "Sustainable Development or Mal Development?" 9ff.

[44] Tinker, "Dreaming a New Dream," 3.

[45] Tinker, "Dreaming a New Dream," 4–5.

[46] Tinker, "Dreaming a New Dream," 5.

[47] On April 20, 1999, at Columbine High School in Columbine, Colorado, two senior students killed twelve students and one teacher. They also injured twenty-four other students. Then the two committed suicide.

[48] Tinker, "Dreaming a New Dream," 5.

murderers) how to do what they did. We say that the children in our city gangs have failed to understand the American value system, but the truth is the opposite—they have understood it all too well and are trying to employ it the best way they can.

An insidious quality of violence is that it eventually becomes habitual and addictive; it is very hard to get out of it. And we know from other contexts that if an addicted person does not get help, eventually the person dies. The violence in North America is eating away at the spiritual and emotional core of our collective being. Tinker demonstrates the habituation of violence by referring to Columbus Day. This is an explicit celebration of violence because Columbus was a slave trader and a murderer. It is an established, historical fact that Columbus was responsible for the deaths of two million to three million people between the years 1492 and 1500.[49] How offensive might it be for there to be a national holiday in Germany called Hitler Day! Yet the most serious problem in celebrating Columbus Day is what in addiction therapy is called denial. Denial easily transforms into self-righteous justification of whites in North America. It is an act of defending white privileges; the rights of the whites to impose upon society in general, and indeed the world at large, the terms of economic progress, development, security, and dominance.

The systemic nature of violence in North America is incredibly complex. We are all addicted, and hence our default reactions tend to be violent. We are also all victims. Even our gospel is read through violence, as a banner in a Columbus parade suggests: "Columbus brought Christ to the Americas." "The problem is so systemic that no one can rise to the top without committing to the violence of the system."[50] It therefore makes little difference who our leaders are or who we vote for because whenever we vote, we support the perpetuation of violence. Social Christianity of the past has found it impossible to eradicate this kind of violence and hence has accommodated itself to it. But we all know that this is not the gospel of Jesus Christ.

Tinker advocates a particular kind of liberation theology that might help us take some small steps out of our dilemma of violence. However, the liberation theology that can help us must go beyond Latin American, African, and Asian varieties. Yes, we need a preferential option for the poor, but we also need to talk about how we can become free. American Indian people will never be free unless white Americans also are free. We need to be freed from our commitment to sexism and systemic violence. And the only way to do that is to dream a new dream, to reimagine ourselves and begin to tell a different story to our grandchildren than the one we get from Hollywood. Hollywood gives us "Dances with Wolves," where another white, Christ-figure, this time via Kevin Costner, tries to save the good American Indian from the savages. Tinker suggests that this is liberal Hollywood at its best.

Tinker's call is for a return to an earlier view of Christianity, where the story of Jesus was read from the margins. When Christianity was commandeered by Constantine and married to imperial and militaristic power, it became heretical; for it made violence its *modus operandi*, Only from the standpoint of a pre-Constantinian, Christian imagination can we understand what it means to pray for healing and to receive it as a gift. This is the stance that is opened up through Indian ceremonies, sun dances, and sweat lodges; this is the spirit of peace and inclusivity.

---

[49] Tinker, "Dreaming a New Dream," 6.

[50] Tinker, "Dreaming a New Dream," 7.

[51] See, e.g., George Tinker, "The Integrity of Creation: Restoring Trinitarian Balance," *The Ecumenical Review* 41, no. 4 (1989); "Spirituality, Native American Personhood," several chapters in *American Indian Liberation;* and one chapter in *Native American Theology.*

CREATION AND ECOJUSTICE

Tinker discusses creation and the environment in at least half a dozen essays and book chapters.[51] Creation is fundamental to an American Indian perspective on existence. A key essay here is "The Integrity of Creation," which he opens with the following words:

> We live in a crazy and dangerous time. We are destroying God's creation at such an alarming rate, polluting the earth's waters and air, and at the same time inventing ever new and ever more brutal ways to oppress greater and greater portions of the earth's human population, ways more devastating than ever known before. We are told that ten percent of the world's rain forest is being destroyed, cut, cleared every year. Within fifteen years this regenerative source of the earth's oxygen supply will be completely destroyed.[52]

Tinker comments that this craziness has precipitated human oppression of the American Indian people in North America, as it has in the jungles of Brazil. The "integrity of creation" and notions of peace and justice are one seamless issue. The church cannot afford to be protective or defensive on these matters; it must find new ways of opening itself to God's grace and proclaiming God's cry for justice and the reign of peace. We need to engage in a "reassessment of our theological reflections on creation."[53]

In all of his writings on these topics, Tinker argues that the theological lacuna here is due to a lack of Trinitarian balance in Euro–American theology. The restoration of this balance requires a return to a theology of nature, by which he means an affirmation of the sacredness of the entire world. "If we can affirm the sacredness of the natural world, if we can begin to live our affirmation, if we begin to experience the world, including one another, as sacred, then God's demand for justice must become a vital and consuming concern."[54] There are obvious echoes here of the pre-Enlightenment doctrine of natural

theology, and the affirmation of the *analogia entis*,[55] in the theology of Thomas Aquinas. However, there is no reference to any of this in Tinker's writings, nor is he saying the same thing as Thomas Aquinas says.

Tinker suggests that as we embark on a process of theological rediscovery we need to learn from each other; the West from the East and the North from the South. We should especially learn from the marginalized people, those who are the poorest of the poor—the Fourth World people. And it is especially the American Indian peoples' view of the sacredness of the earth that can help us appreciate a Christian doctrine of creation with a potential to serve as the ground for justice.

What has hindered Christian theology in developing a proper view of creation is an overemphasis on Christology. "Christomonism" is what Tinker calls this heresy. He refers to his own denomination, the Evangelical Lutheran Church in America, as a case in point. When this church recently wrote a statement of purpose, it began with the following declaration: "The purpose of the church shall be: To proclaim God's reconciling act in Jesus Christ."[56] Tinker states that there are few churches in the world that would disagree with this statement, and yet he wants to raise the question of whether it is an appropriate starting place for the church's theological affirmation. He suggests that "Any structuring of theology that *begins* with 'God's reconciling act in Jesus Christ' violates the traditional Trinitarian confession of Christianity and hence tones down the significance of the doctrine of creation."[57]

Tinker's point here is that to begin with Jesus Christ is to prioritize fall and redemption language. And that is profoundly different from beginning with creation. With the prominence of fall and redemption, the church has given priority to human agency. He puts it this way: "My Native American

---

[51] Tinker, "Integrity of Creation," 527.
[52] Tinker, "Integrity of Creation," 527.
[53] Tinker, "Integrity of Creation," 527–28.
[55] See chaps. 14 and 16 above.
[56] Tinker, "Integrity of Creation," 529.
[57] Tinker, "Integrity of Creation," 530 (emphasis in original).

ancestors had a relationship with God as Creator that was healthy and responsible long before they heard of God's reconciling act in Jesus Christ. To make fall/redemption the beginning point in theological proclamation generates traumatic experiences of spirituality and emotional dislocation for American Indians which some people survive and many do not."[58]

What Tinker is arguing is that the notion of fall/redemption suggests a dichotomy between the created order, which is fallen and therefore not of God, and the redeemed order, which only those who are emissaries of Jesus Christ know about and thus on which they are able to enlighten the "pagans." This is what he calls Christomonism and it is oppressive to aboriginal peoples. But when fall and redemption are put in the context of creation, the Christian message can actually be healing for American Indians.

Tinker argues for two ways in which a strong creation theology can help us: first, to begin Christian theology with creation makes it possible for there to be an appreciation and value of the gifts of culture that indigenous people bring to Christianity, a base upon which peace and justice can be pursued. And second, a strong respect for creation can help us with a proper theological understanding of peace and justice.

An important goal in developing a viable Christian theology of creation is for human beings to learn to live in spiritual "harmony with nature," rather than to see nature as something that needs to be conquered. He says:

> Life as a gift is more than just my life or even human life in general, but every rock and every tree and every stream is a part of life and has life itself. And all these things participate, along with human beings in a spiritual harmony—a perception of the world which is much closer to Paul, where he talks about the whole of creation groaning in

the pains of childbirth (Rom. 8:22) than anything represented by modern industrial Christianity.[59]

In his view, one sees the interrelatedness of all of creation; we are relatives with the buffalos and the eagles and the trees and the rocks and the mountains and the lakes.[60] This counter-dominance model of human relationship with nature puts the matter of hunting and killing animals for food in a unique perspective. Tinker refers to the traditional stories where different forms of animal life debate about who has the right to eat whom. "In many of these stories, the four-legged and winged exchange in long debate which concludes with a consensus to permit hunting two-leggeds—for their good, that is, survival—but establishes certain parameters which will always ensure respect for the sacredness of all life."[61]

Tinker suggests that this is different from the concern that Greenpeace expresses over seal-hunts. The American Indian concern embraces all of life, "from trees and animals to international relations."[62] Theirs is a concern for justice and fairness for all of creation—a witness offered to the civilized world. Says Tinker, "Indian life as a gift from God will survive only if Indian peoples are free to choose Indian lives, that is, to be *uncivilized*."[63] This also applies to American Indian Christianity; it will survive only if it can do so with some degree of independence of the dominant, Christian church culture.

Tinker's theology of the land is far from mere romanticism. It draws on a theological understanding of nature, illuminated through parabolic storytelling, to show that everything in nature is related: animate, inanimate, local communities, larger communities, and international communities. He tells the story of "Corn Mother" who emerges from the sacrificial death of "First Mother" in order to provide for the harvest of all her children. In her death and return

---

[58] Tinker, "Integrity of Creation," 530.
[59] Tinker, "Integrity of Creation," 532.
[60] Tinker, "Integrity of Creation," 532.

[61] Tinker, "Integrity of Creation," 532.
[62] Tinker, "Integrity of Creation," 532.
[63] Tinker, "Integrity of Creation," 532 (emphasis in original).

to the earth, Corn Mother breathes into the earth the very capacity for bountiful harvest in order to sustain her people. For earth itself is our Mother![64]

If the earth is Mother, the sweat lodge is the womb of the earth. To enter into the sweat lodge is not only to purify body and spirit but to be "born again." Thus participants emerge with "cries" of "new-birth" as they re-receive life from Mother Earth (Corn Mother). The ceremony symbolizes the interrelatedness of all of life and hence, the participation in the balance and harmony that life demands in order for it to be life-giving. Says Tinker, "Acts of violence against any relative disrupt the balance and are inexcusable—even those that become necessary."[65] Hence, the need for rebirth for when the balance gets broken; it can be restored, but only if the proper boundaries are respected. For example, animals can be killed for food and shelter but only under the appropriate rituals and ceremonies, which remind us that all of life participates in a balance. For in killing an animal for food, we kill part of ourselves, only to be able to live again.

Tinker gives another example of necessary rituals, this time in cases of war: ". . . most tribes engage in elaborate rituals before going to war with another tribe. Even one's enemies must be respected. No killing was to be random. A tribe's survival or territorial integrity could be at risk. Nevertheless, maintaining balance, respect for all one's relatives, meant that four days of ceremony might be necessary before battle could be engaged."[66]

Similar respect is due a tree before it is cut down. Rituals involving words spoken to the tree explaining why this act of violence is necessary must take place before a tree is cut down. "Only then can balance be maintained when the tree is cut down, always in a ritual, sacred way."[67] Even though violence cannot always be avoided, nevertheless sacredness and interrelatedness with all creation governed the way of peace and justice.

Tinker goes on to say that when American Indian people look at the ways of the modern, military-industrial complex and the creation of ever-new luxuries, they see disrespect for the earth. They see the same disrespect of the people that were behind the European invasion and found it impossible within themselves to see the American Indian tribes as part of their community. And even today they notice a spirituality of control and dominance in "the ways our oppressors pray."[68] The spirituality of a people is seen in how they live with others and with nature. "If we rape the earth, then we will rape each other as well."[69]

In Tinker's calls for a re-imagining of a theology of creation, he calls for a reorientation of ourselves, "especially our bodies ecclesia" in order to have anything to say to the social institutions of our world.[70] And that can come only as we re-imagine creation. "Thus a theology of creation is not merely a justice (ecology) concern to be set alongside other justice concerns. But it is a fundamental theology of self-understanding out of which justice, and then peace, will flow naturally and necessarily."[71]

Tinker suggests that Christian peace advocates in North America have not done a good job of holding the many peace concerns together precisely because they have no theology of Trinity. They tend to focus on ecology, as if it is a separate issue from the larger creation, or on war, or on racism, or on something else. Tinker claims that, "If our theology—and hence our human communities—can begin to wrestle seriously with the necessity of balance and harmony in all of creation, then our self-image as a part of creation must also be deeply affected."[72]

---

[64] See Tinker, "Integrity of Creation," 533.

[65] Tinker, "Integrity of Creation," 533.

[66] Tinker, "Integrity of Creation," 534.

[67] Tinker, "Integrity of Creation," 534.

[68] Tinker, "Integrity of Creation," 534.

[69] Tinker, "Integrity of Creation," 534.

[70] See Tinker, "Integrity of Creation," 535.

[71] Tinker, "Integrity of Creation," 535.

[72] Tinker, "Integrity of Creation," 536.

A NEW IMAGINATION

Tinker's project begs for a constructive alternative to the mainline theology he critiques. He says that he is sometimes pushed to move beyond mere critique and offer solutions.[73] In his *American Indian Liberation* (2008), he points to several new, imaginative proposals. I will present only two: first, a new kind of evangelism, and second, a new vision for constructive, social change. Both arise out of his comprehensive critique of colonial Christianity.

New Evangelism

First, Tinker summarizes his view of the new evangelism as, "Be Jesus. Don't preach Jesus."[74] We have already seen his critique of what he calls "Christomonism." His point here is similar. Evangelism has to do with communication, and cross-cultural (often cross-religious) communication is very difficult. Tinker gives the example of speaking with American Indians about God. The assumption is that what "God" names in English will also be named by the translation of that term in another language. So when we find the word for "God" in another language, we believe the job is done. But it is far more complicated than that.

Tinker gives an example of this difficulty by introducing the reader to a rich description of of *"Wako"da,"* often used as the translation of God. He says:

> *Wako"da* who is ultimately an unknowable mystery that is knowable only in particular manifestations, makes itself manifest first of all, but not exclusively, as Above and Below, *wako"da mo"shita* and *wako"da udseta*, symbolized as Sky and Earth, and called upon as Grandfather and Grandmother, he and she. *Wako"da*, which has no inherent or ultimate gender, is knowable only in the necessary reciprocal dualism of male and female.[75]

When Christian evangelists speak of God as the Father of our Lord Jesus Christ, and then add that all other views of God are heretical, it is utterly and needlessly confusing to American Indians. It has been the assumption that the language of the gospel is universal, and hence the "negotiations" necessary to make particular speech meaningful across cultures has not been given sufficient heed.[76]

Evangelism is normally understood as proclamation of the good news of Jesus Christ. The evangelism of the early American missionaries and subsequent preachers has in fact not proven to be good news for many American Indians. Hence, Tinker suggests boldly that, "it is time for amer–european Christians to declare a moratorium on twentieth-century style evangelism. To put it bluntly: just say no to preaching Jesus."[77] These are provocative words for the church, but Tinker is making a particular point. Christians, especially after so many destructive and genocidal effects, should stop telling the world *about* Jesus and simply *be* Jesus to the world. And this includes "Stop worrying about purity of doctrine."[78] If the love of God in Jesus Christ is important to spread, it must be spread by expression in action and not preaching a message that destroys a culture and violates a people. For that is not the Word Jesus Christ made flesh.

The evangelism that Tinker is proposing should take the form of a critical analysis of the world power structures; it should be the proclamation of a gospel which is the very opposite of the colonial Jesus. But this gospel will require deep wisdom in order to see the complicity with violence and evil of so many of society's structures. Hence, repentance will be key; repentance focused first on the church and its own complicity in violence. Tinker says, "Real evangelism means an

[73] Tinker, *American Indian Liberation*, 160.
[74] Tinker, *American Indian Liberation*, 122.
[75] Tinker, *American Indian Liberation*, 64.
[76] See the section "No Other Name: Colonizer's Claim to Universal Truth," in Tinker, *American Indian Liberation*, 98ff.
[77] Tinker, *American Indian Liberation*, 124.	[78] Tinker, *American Indian Liberation*, 124.

active struggle to facilitate social, economic, and political transformation for justice, peace, and the integrity of creation."[79]

Social Change

The second act of imagination has to do with articulating constructive steps which might be taken jointly by whites and American Indians toward a less violent world. One cannot help but sense an ambivalence here as Tinker speaks about "solutions." The colonial or even the post-colonial logic of, "fix it—it's broken," arises from the imagination, not of gift and receptivity, but of controlling the forces that move life forward. This itself characterizes the Euro-American disposition, not the American Indian's way of seeing the world. The metaphor of healing is different, and more appropriate in the context of centuries of abuse, for it does not foreclose possibilities that do not come from our own capacities to fix things. After all, healing happens!

There is a similar reticence in his later writings to embrace the language of liberation theology since that too may still share too much with the imagination of colonialism. Yet the quest for freedom and overcoming dislocation remain fundamental.[80]

Nevertheless, Tinker offers nine steps that the white and American Indian peoples could begin to take together as we move out of a world of violence and into a balance of creation. First, a move must be made on the part of the white people to own their violent past. This means collective and corporate acts of confession and repentance. This also means, second, that together we identify "systemic structures of oppression" and begin the process of dismantling. Third, there needs to be a willingness to take the risks that will come with the dismantling efforts; risks to our comfortable lifestyles and

our economic well-being. Fourth, we need to reduce our consumption and find alternative energy resources without reducing our food supply and harming the environment. Fifth, we must learn cross-cultural ways of relating to one another, ways that are grounded in genuine respect for one another. Sixth, the respect of another culture can only happen when we understand and respect our own identities well. This means that just as American Indians must learn to understand their American Indian-ness, white Americans must understand their whiteness. Seventh, whites need to learn from indigenous peoples that all things—living and non-living—are interrelated and that nothing exists only in relation to itself. Eighth, we must move beyond the liberalism of our culture, both in our need for knowledge as well as in our consumption patterns. Ninth, we must learn to dream together in ways that are not merely romantic.[81]

The world has changed. Tinker sees opportunities today that could be taken. The colonial world is no longer what it was, although its effects and its logic linger. This is evident even in the postcolonial writers like Michael Hardt and Antonio Negri,[82] who give a commendable critique of the globalization movement, yet their solution falls short, according to Tinker. They "want a Marxist international system . . . to impose a new socialist order."[83] Hence, the logic is the same old logic— what is the best structure to *impose* upon all people? This is borrowed directly from the colonialist! The colonialist imagination runs very deep. It will take much wisdom, generosity, and humility to move beyond it.

CONCLUSION

Tinker has issued a serious challenge to mainline, Euro–American theology. Its stance of superiority and imposition is not

---

[79] Tinker, *American Indian Liberation*, 124.
[80] Tinker, *American Indian Liberation*, 150.
[81] See Tinker, *American Indian Liberation*, 160ff.
[82] See Michael Hardt and Antonio Negri, *Empire* (Cambridge, Mass.: Harvard University Press, 2000).
[83] Tinker, *American Indian Liberation*, 159n25.

only un-Indian but unchristian. The message spoken and portrayed as receptivity, gift, and witness is so integral to the story of Jesus Christ that to have found ways of connecting it with the colonial politics of imperial powers has undermined its integrity. As Tinker puts it, "being Jesus means the church must sacrifice any arrogant ambition of being Herod or Pilate or Caesar or even archbishop."[84] The church must decide whom to serve, and with that comes the question of identification: the poor and powerless or the rich and powerful. The temptation of the church was the temptation of Christ; only Christ rejected it, and the church is still struggling.

Tinker's challenge in general is to hold colonizer Christians to their own best theology and moral views. In particular it becomes poignant and immediate when he asks: "Will american Christians continue to act both implicitly and explicitly as religious validations for existing power structures, or will they join their voices with Jesus, calling for a real evangelization that recognizes the *basileia* (kingdom, queendom, reign, realm) of God that Jesus proclaimed as near or in our midst? The well-being of the world, the lives of people around the globe, hang in the balance."[85]

---

[84] Tinker, *American Indian Liberation*, 125.

[85] Tinker, *American Indian Liberation*, 125.

Excursus

PART IV-B

Liberation theology, perhaps more than any other theology, names the failure of contemporary, Christian ethics. All three authors presented in this study hold as central to the gospel of Jesus Christ the Pauline text: "For freedom Christ has set us free. Stand firm, therefore, and do not submit again to a yoke of slavery" (Gal 5:1). While all advocate the centrality of freedom for Christian ethics, they portray "unfreedom" in different ways. Freedom is correlative with oppression; oppression is caused by systems or groups of people lording it over others. This lording can be inadvertent by individuals participating in structures they did not create, or it can be direct, intentional, and overt for reasons of security, fear, or simply the desire to dominate.

Regardless of how it is cast, the quest for liberation is obviously significant for Christian ethics because it is the pursuit of justice and a deep concern for the entire biblical narrative. For ethicists to attune their ears to freedom and oppression is an extremely important discipline since many forms of subjugation are hidden from oppressors because of their inability to see properly. Hence, liberation theology in its most profound contribution is an effort to help people—not only people of the church but *also* people of the church—*to see* what they are doing.

THE FAILURE OF THE CHURCH

Besides the theme of liberation itself, there are few topics more prominent in the writings of liberation theologians than the failure of the church to be faithful to the biblical call. Their challenge is to ask how the church could have missed it: that God is a liberating God, that the call of Jesus Christ is a call to revolution—changing the unjust status quo—and that the call of the New Testament church is to break down walls of separation as it seeks to build up a new reconciling body—*ecclesia*. Church renewal is therefore the message, whether by Gutiérrez toward the Catholic Church, Cone to the American church more generally, or Tinker to the ecumenical church. One hears here a profound cry to let the church be the church.

Part of this challenge is to rethink the nature of Christian theology as such. Liberation theologians are right in pointing out that theology (indeed knowledge generally) and power are intertwined. The dominant, developed world has sought, whether intentionally or not, to name the terms of a universal theology. This alignment between theology writing and economic power is problematic, especially in a church that confesses the spirit of truth works through all people and that revelations and insights often come from the least likely voices. Although the critique gets expressed differently in Gutiérrez's work toward the Catholic Church than it does in the writings of Cone and Tinker, the point remains the same: no one has the right to control the manner in which theology must be done, especially not the theology of a liberating God calling all people out of bondage into freedom in

509

Christ. Liberation theologians have argued the theology developed by those who have assumed that right has not only been found to be inadequate when measured against the canons of Scripture but has also been the source for underwriting oppression for millions of people all over the world, among them those who are also part of the church. This is a tragedy of the most grievous kind.

This failure of the church to be the church calls for a stance of acknowledgment, confession, and repentance, not retrenchment and defensiveness. Unless there can be healthy engagement within the church between the rich and the poor, the powerful and the weak, even the theologians and the ordinary, it is hard to see how the church can be the body that Paul calls forth in his writings, especially in 1 Corinthians 12 and 13.

But the church has been a failure in another way: not only has it failed in relation to others in the church, it has done so in relation to the world around it. The oppression experienced by those represented by our three authors comes from both inside and outside the church. The church has failed by not modeling proper alternatives challenging evident racism and by presenting patterns of thought and life that have underwritten oppression. That is, the failure of the church is both a theological failure as well as one of praxis.

PRAXIS

The idea of praxis is an enormous contribution to contemporary, theological discussion. Liberation theologians are right that much of traditional theology has emphasized orthodoxy at the expense of orthopraxis. It is an interesting exercise to wonder what might have been the impact on Christian ethics and theology had there been as much effort exerted on getting right the *practices* of the church as there was on getting right the theology at the early church councils. Indeed, this is not that farfetched. The early church father Origen (185–254), at his Catechetical School of Alexandria, sought to foster precisely such a process. Alexandria was a training base for learning what disciples must believe in order to live as Jesus called them to live. For the teachers and students at this school, theology did not make only speculative sense but also as a way of thinking required to sustain a particular kind of life. Hence, what liberation theologians are identifying here is as old as the church itself and offers an enormously important contemporary corrective.

Gutiérrez names two implications of the affirmation to keep theology and ethics in close unity: first, there is no ethics for everyone; it is always specific to theology. Second, theology is not a first act but a second act. The first move is another way of saying that what the Enlightenment has taught us is wrong. But it is also a somewhat precarious move in that liberation theologians repeat the idea that there is not one universal theology—there is a black theology, an American Indian theology, and so on. Does it therefore follow that there are also several different, Christian ethics? But if so, how then is it possible to hold dominant, Western Christianity to the standards of a liberation ethic? Can there not be a *Christian* theology-ethic? This question should not be seen to undermine the important claim of holding theology and ethics together; it only means that more work needs to be done in sorting out how.

The second implication is perhaps more contentious. Liberation theologians tend to agree that the first act for Christians is an act of solidarity with the liberation movement, and the second act of theology follows later. This seems different from Origen's claim that following Jesus comes first, followed by asking what we must believe in order to make this commitment intelligible. Origen believed that you cannot know God unless you follow Christ! It is easy to agree with the intent that ethics cannot be the conclusion that follows from a nicely worked-out theology, but unless the relationship is stated in a somewhat more dialectical way, what could compel us to identify with the liberation movement as a starter? And why would anyone make the second move to a Christian theology after joining the revolution?

GOSPEL AS LIBERATION

Another major contribution of liberation theology is the affirmation that the gospel of Jesus Christ is a gospel of *liberation*. It is impossible to read Luke 4 without concluding that Jesus was proclaiming a revolution of liberation and justice for all people—Jews and Gentiles. And it is further impossible to read about letting the "oppressed go free" (Luke 4:18b) without connecting his message with the exodus story. The liberating message of Jesus and the exodus story are two compelling sources of liberation theology.

In terms of biblical hermeneutical warrant, however, questions arise that complexify the gospel of liberation. Are there not two models of liberation in the biblical canon that, when pulled apart, render a truncated gospel? In the history of Israel, the two models go by the name of the exodus and the exile; in the Christian narrative, they go by the cross and resurrection.

In the story recorded in Jeremiah 28–29, the very question of how to understand liberation is debated between Jeremiah and Hananiah. Hananiah promises to liberate the exiles from Babylon at any cost; Jeremiah says the exiles should stay put and make a life for themselves in Babylon: plant gardens, marry, raise families, and generally "seek the welfare of the city where [God has] sent you into exile" (Jer 29:7a). Jeremiah's suggestion that liberation should not always be sought makes things much more difficult and calls for careful discrimination. And of course, it raises a serious problem: who is able to judge when exiles should end? And how should they end? And this is not yet to address the conundrum of how to deal with the claim in the text that sometimes God places people in exile.

Liberation theologians draw almost exclusively on the paradigm of exodus, making this the dominant metaphor through which liberation is understood. Yet in the story of Jeremiah, we hear it is possible to live "liberated lives" in Babylonian exile. This has prompted some writers to wonder whether there are not two models of liberation in the biblical literature.[1] In fact, there are those who wonder whether, in the post-Christian world, living in exile has not become the norm, for there is so little that is "home" or "promised land" about the world around us.

The New Testament dialectic between cross and resurrection raises similar questions. In Luke 9, the story of Jesus' instruction to his disciples echoes the Jeremiah story. When Jesus inquires about whether his disciples understand who he is, Peter answers: "The Messiah of God" (Luke 9:20b). Jesus accepts the answer and then maps out the path of liberation as one of great suffering and even death. To his disciples, he says, "If any want to become my followers, let them deny themselves and take up their cross daily and follow me" (Luke 9:23).

Both the Jeremiah and Luke stories suggest that liberation has to do with more than being in a state of exodus—freedom. One can also be liberated while on the way to the "promised land" or even when there is little of it in sight.

Toward what end does any of this matter? It matters not because it suggests that these accounts lessen the concern for liberation. It matters instead because it can instruct us on how we might get from oppression to liberation. The quickest and most direct route may not always be the faithful route. Hence, it matters because it helps to tease out further a biblical model of an ethic of social change.

AN ETHIC OF SOCIAL CHANGE

An important issue here has to do with the biblical story itself. As it is told, resurrection and exodus are both gifts from God. This raises the question of how to construct an ethic of social change on a model where God is a primary actor liberating an enslaved

---

[1] See, e.g., John H. Yoder, "Exodus and Exile: The Two Faces of Liberation," *Cross Currents* (Fall 1973): 298–309; and Daniel L. Smith, *The Religion of the Landless: The Social Context of the Babylonian Exile* (Bloomington, Ind.: Meyer, Stone, 1989).

people when Moses does little more than tell Pharaoh that this is going to happen. Can we think of liberation theologians speaking as did Moses—"let my people go?" Perhaps!

The Moses story points to a new vision for social change not heard of earlier by the protectors of empire, who thought of themselves as indomitable to the threat that came from a "powerless" Moses. Might there be a strategy here that is not fully exploited, even by liberation theologians who seek to embrace this metaphor of social change? For the ways of empire are as seductive today as they were in the time of Moses and Jesus.

The question I am raising is whether it is possible to see both Jesus' move through cross and resurrection and the move of Moses and the slaves in Egypt to the Promised Land as moves of social revolution operating with a similar logic (strategy) that in effect is no logic (strategy) at all? If so, we have here a profound disruption of the old social space, the old empire logic, that questions whether history can only be moved forward through the power of the mighty.

The problem named by each of our authors is the problem of the "white masculine" who has been a master at perfecting the colonial past—a model of control and manipulation. But it is not at all clear whether the post-colonial ways operate by a different social logic. And how do we get out of merely replaying the white game which has so defined the rules that outcome is already determined? Is not the invention of an alternative theology with a black or red god only to compete with the rules that have been stacked by the masters of the past? And is not the message of the gospel of liberation one that invites us to consider a change to these very rules? Gospel

rules are about giving up on winning strategies; finding new ways of pointing to the beyond, the good, the beautiful, the all-too-human, through participation in new signs of *koinonia*. Racism will not likely be overcome by *imposing* an alternative theology on the Christian church. But saying this should not be taken to imply a defense of the old theology that has underwritten an oppressive, colonial ethic. But if the church can give up its control of the one whom it worships already and learn to see with transformed eyes the one new humanity made possible in such worship, which means giving up on the eyes of empire, then there may well be new hope.

The word that was made flesh in Jesus Christ surely speaks profound condemnation upon racism, but racism can be fostered in many ways. The breakthrough grounded in a theological vision of cross and resurrection requires a fundamentally new way of seeing the possibilities. For as Christians, we dare not make the mistake of assuming that we are alone; that earth, the social, the political, are all knowable on the basis of what we have already seen; or that we know in advance what can and cannot happen. For this is the very logic that resurrection and exodus shatters.

There are signs of this "strategy" of overcoming in each of the three authors' works, and it is in the cultivation of these signs wherein the hope lies for the future. We do well to remind ourselves of how much we have inadvertently absorbed from the colonial approach to make history move in the right (white) direction and how little we know of the Messiah's way of the cross in which he was willing to give up all handles to history—and was liberated.

PART IV

CRITICAL RESPONSES TO TWENTIETH-CENTURY
CHRISTIAN ETHICS

•

Section C
Feminist Theologians

Chapter Twenty-Nine

ROSEMARY RADFORD RUETHER
(1936–)

This chapter begins another face of liberation theology—feminism. There is no single, uniform view of feminism just as there is no one Latin American, black, or American Indian form of liberation theology. In the end, it is important to remember that each theologian, or each subgroup of theologians, speaks out of a specific context and from a unique set of convictions and experiences.

The theologians highlighted in the previous three chapters have all sought liberation from oppressive forces supported by the white power establishment with its intellectual, political, and social controls. As a general category of oppressors this, of course, includes white, North American women. Yet feminists address many of these same issues; they just name the "oppressing forces" somewhat differently. This should remind us that just as there is no uniform "liberation theology," there is also no homogenous oppressor-group. Even theologians who consider themselves feminists come from a wide range of backgrounds: white, North American, middle-class, African American, Latin American, African, Asian, Middle Eastern—literally from every part of the world. And many of them suffer double and triple forms of oppression.

Of course, not all feminists are Christian; but some are. Feminism has a long history, usually thought of as beginning in the eighteenth century with women seeking to rectify official inequities like discrimination in politics, education, health-care, the workplace, and so on. Here, the efforts of British philosopher Mary Wollstonecraft (1759–1797), American social activist Lucy Stone (1818–1893), and Canadian political activist Nellie McClung (1873–1951), among many others, are extremely important, and their work has resulted in significant political, social, and legal changes for women, including the right to vote. These efforts are sometimes called "first-wave" (or "first-stage") feminism; it is "first-wave" because, clearly, not all was accomplished with formal changes to the law.

What is called "second-wave" feminism focuses more on unofficial inequities, and hence, it is much broader in scope than "first-wave" feminism. This movement got its major impetus in North America in 1963 with Betty Friedan's book, *The Feminine Mystique*.[1] Although Friedan (1921–2006) does not deal seriously with religion in this book, she does point out that churches are as seriously implicated in maintaining closed and oppressive structures and attitudes as are other institutions of society.

"Third-wave" feminism, thought to have started in the 1980s, is seen as a response (sometimes called a backlash) to "second-wave" feminism. One important author in this movement is Rebecca Walker, born in

---

[1] Betty Friedan, *The Feminine Mystique* (New York: Norton, 1963). Friedan also writes a book called, *The Second Stage* (New York: Summit, 1981).

1969 and daughter of famed author Alice Walker, from whom we have *The Color Purple*.[2] "Third-wave" feminists question the assumptions around the somewhat rigid understanding of femininity common to many "second-wave" thinkers. Hence, today there is a greater range of feminist literature, as women feel free to imagine femininity in a variety of new ways.

However, the focus of this chapter is not feminism in general but feminist *theology*. Mary Daly (1928–2010) in her book, *Beyond God the Father*,[3] which appeared in 1973, brings the issue of feminism squarely into theology and the church. Trained as a philosopher and theologian, and coming from the Catholic Church, Daly believed that Christian theology and the church represented a sacred edifice that has served to justify the oppression of women. Despite her critique of the church, she taught for thirty-three years at Boston College, a Jesuit school, retiring in 1999 amid controversy.[4] She describes herself as a "radical lesbian feminist"[5] and makes it clear in her writing that no male figure, either a male god or Jesus, can rescue women from the oppression caused by patriarchy. In other words, a male savior cannot save women![6] And certainly the hierarchal church cannot offer liberation to women.

By the mid-1970s Daly had already become "convinced that not only Christianity, but all patriarchal cultures, as these had ruled the world from the time of an archaic overthrow of women-centered cultures, must be rejected."[7] The role of feminism, argued Daly, was now to chronicle the oppression and evils of the patriarchal systems. She did not refer to herself as either Christian or theologian during the last thirty years of her life because both carried the stigma of oppression which she sought to overcome.

Naturally, there are less radical feminist voices critiquing theology and the church. Letty Russell (1929–2007) emphasized the importance of hospitality in a world of difference, a skill, she says, the church has not practiced well. Moreover, the traditional structures of domination and control should be replaced with models of partnership—signs of God's peace on earth.[8]

Rosemary Radford Ruether began to write in the early 1970s in the context of this vibrant debate. She continues to be a powerful voice in the liberation movement in general and in Christian feminism in particular. She is every bit as critical of the history of sexism as any other feminist, even those who have rejected the church, but for her this does not imply the abolition of either Christian theology or the church. It does, however, imply the reimagination and deconstruction of both.

AN OVERVIEW OF HER LIFE

Ruether was born in 1936 in St. Paul, Minnesota,[9] to Rebecca Cresap Orb and Robert Armstrong Radford. She describes her family as follows:

> My family was religiously ecumenical and included a Catholic mother, an Episcopalian father, and

---

[2] Alice Walker, *The Color Purple* (New York: Pocket Books, 1982). "The Color Purple" was also made into a popular movie in 1985.

[3] Mary Daly, *Beyond God the Father: Toward a Philosophy of Women's Liberation* (Boston: Beacon, 1973).

[4] In 1998 a male student sought admission to Daly's advanced "women's only" course and was denied permission from her. She suggested that he could take the course from her privately. This resulted in a dispute which ended in her losing her tenured position at the college. Daly argued that to have men in her class would inhibit frank discussion. Eventually an out-of-court settlement was reached, and she agreed to retire. See Margalit Fox, "Mary Daly, a Leader in Feminist Theology, Dies at 81," *New York Times*, January 10, 2010.

[5] Fox, "Mary Daly."

[6] See Daly, *Beyond God the Father*, 96f.

[7] Rosemary Radford Ruether, *Women and Redemption: A Theological History* (Minneapolis: Fortress, 1998), 217.

[8] See Letty Russell, *Just Hospitality: God's Welcome in a World of Difference*, ed. J. Shannon Clarkson and Kate M. Ott (Louisville, Ky.: Westminster John Knox, 2009).

[9] There is a discrepancy in the public literature on Ruether's place of birth. She has personally confirmed to the author that she was born in St. Paul, Minnesota, and not in Georgetown, Texas.

a Jewish favorite uncle. My mother was serious and free-thinking in her spiritual life, in a way that suggested that there were both valuable and questionable aspects of Catholicism.[10]

Both her parents were from English stock, but their families had lived in the United States for a few generations before Ruether was born. As she has stated, religiously, her parents were quite different. Her father, an Anglican who was not overly religious, came from Washington, D.C., and worked for the U. S. government as an engineer. Her mother grew up in California and spoke Spanish and French. She was devoutly Catholic but not of the narrow and doctrinaire variety. Both were proud of their British heritage.

Early in her life, Ruether attended a Catholic girl's school. In elementary and high school, she spent much time reading and painting, and as a child dreamed of becoming an artist. But later in college the world of intellectual and social history would change all that.

When Ruether was eleven and twelve years old, the family lived in Greece, where her father worked as an engineer. Here she cultivated her artistic interests by sketching buildings of antiquity. She was also a student at a French Ursuline convent where she learned some modern Greek.[11] While living in Greece, her father died "from pneumonia contracted during his years in France during the war."[12] Ruether was alone with her father at the time of his brief illness and fairly sudden death. Facing mortality in this unusual way was naturally traumatic for her and caused her to reflect seriously on the meaning of life and death.

Four years after her father's death, Ruether and her mother moved to La Jolla, California, close to where her mother had grown up. Here, breaking with the pattern of attending Catholic schools, Ruether enrolled in a public school, where she became the editor of the school paper. At this time she had no particular interest in theology, yet already she was thinking critically of practices like Christmas, even writing a short essay in the school paper on the "vulgarization of Christmas." Other faith matters, like the creeds and the problem of evil, also began to preoccupy her thoughts. She was becoming theologically interested.

Her final year of high school was in a Catholic institution in Washington, D. C. Here she met a history teacher who made her aware of the problems of racism in America. She suddenly discovered how racist her own father's family was, their racism masked by "southern gentility."[13] This alerted her to the reality that many of our own deeply held prejudices are hidden and not apparent even to those of us who hold them. Hence, it often takes outside observers to tell us what we actually believe.

In 1954, after graduating from high school, Ruether enrolled in Scripps College, a women's college, in Claremont, California. She graduated with a Bachelor of Arts degree in philosophy and history in 1958. As is so often the case, the direction for a future career is set by a charismatic professor. We have already seen the influence of her history teacher in high school; at Scripps it was Robert Palmer, her classics and ancient history teacher. What made him so impressive was his ability to embody what he taught. In doing so, he was able to make the "dead bones" of history come alive and even become "things of beauty."[14] Thus she became forever hooked on the world of origins and symbols: how religions came to be, how they developed, how they took hold of a people and became embodied in concrete narratives.

Reading the Bible from the background of ancient history proved both powerful and

---

[10] Ruether, *Women and Redemption*, 221.

[11] The source for much of this biographical information is Rosemary Radford Ruether, "Beginnings: An Intellectual Autobiography," in *Journeys: The Impact of Personal Experience on Religious Thought*, ed. Gregory Baum (New York: Paulist, 1975).

[12] Ruether, "Beginnings," 38.

[13] Ruether, "Beginnings," 40.

[14] Ruether, "Beginnings," 40–41.

controversial for Ruether. As she transposed herself into the ancient world, she could not help but ask questions that seemed to have been definitively settled by the Christian theological tradition; questions that pushed at a dichotomous imagination she found difficult to accept. For example, were the Ba'al worshippers really as categorically evil as the tradition has insisted? After all, she thought, "Ba'al was a real god" and "there was more to him than 'sex.'"[15] Moreover, Yahweh has demonstrated extreme violence, and Yahweh worshippers have perpetrated much evil through events like the Crusades and the pogroms. She found herself unable to accept the standard version of a story which she wanted to embrace, albeit differently. This got her to become a dialectical thinker, even before she encountered Hegel. That is, she began to hold in tension two views ostensibly at odds with one another, which, when brought into interaction, could dissolve difference into something new and better. Theologically stated, she could no longer believe in a god who favored one people over others. True God would lead diverse traditions and peoples into one humanity, not without difference but in transcendent unity, because True God is the "ground of all being."

It was becoming clear that Ruether had serious tensions with her Catholicism roots. The hierarchy was simply not open to new formulations of theology and resisted reform in the church; tradition remained firm, closed, and normative. Fortunately, the spirit of the Second Vatican Council (1962–1965) was beginning to move, and gradually the questions she was asking seemed more "askable." This did not yet mean her questions were dealt with satisfactorily, but at least asking them was not immediately branded as

heresy. Hence, the alternatives of "capitulation or leaving the church" were no longer as exclusive as they had been. In other words, a middle path of reform was becoming imaginable, as the church gradually entertained the possibilities of a new future.

Ruether speaks of the guilt she struggled with in relation to her critique of the church, much like the guilt that pushes a child to seek "reconciliation with the parent."[16] But gradually she came to believe that the problems were more appropriately located with the church leaders than with her. She thought this not because she was stubbornly sure of her own convictions but because her convictions were confirmed by so many other seriously committed church theologians—men and women alike—making it impossible to hold back on a "truth force" that had taken hold of her.

During the time that she was a student at Scripps, at age twenty-one, she married Herman J. Ruether, who became a political scientist and cultural historian. Although they had separate academic careers, he had an enormous influence on her; he helped to pull her beyond the world of the fifth century into current, political reality.[17] Later they even collaborated on projects of mutual interest.[18] All three of their children, Rebecca, David, and Mimi, were born during their parents' graduate school days.[19]

Upon graduating from Scripps College in 1958, having written an honors thesis on apocalypticism, she enrolled in an M.A. program in ancient history at Claremont Graduate School. Two years later, she began doctoral studies at the same school in classics and patristics. In 1965 Ruether received her Ph.D. from Claremont, having written a dissertation titled "Gregory Nazianzus Rhetor

---

[15] Ruether, "Beginnings," 43.

[16] Ruether, "Beginnings," 46.

[17] Ruether, "Beginnings," 51.

[18] See, e.g., Rosemary Radford Ruether and Herman J. Ruether, *The Wrath of Jonah: The Crisis of Religious Nationalism in the Israeli-Palestinian Conflict* (New York: Harper & Row, 1989).

[19] Ruether has written an account of her son's struggle with mental illness. See Rosemary Radford Ruether (with David Ruether), *Many Forms of Madness: A Family's Struggle with Mental Illness and the Mental Health System* (Minneapolis Fortress, 2010).

and Philosopher."[20] Her formal studies were now complete, and so she could look for a teaching job.

In 1966 the Ruethers, with their three children, moved from Claremont, California, to Washington, D.C., where Ruether initially had part-time teaching positions at George Washington University and at Howard University School of Religion. Howard University is historically an African-American school and was actively involved in the civil rights movement in the 1960s. Ruether's teaching there was a perfect match, for she too had been involved in the civil rights movement, having just spent a summer working for the cause in Mississippi. She saw racism as one of the biggest evils in North America and thought of Martin Luther King Jr. as "the most skilled exponent in recent American history (perhaps all of American history) of American civil religion in prophetic criticism and liberation."[21] So during this time, she participated in many demonstrations, especially against the war in Vietnam (1955–1975) and even spent nights in jail after being arrested at peace demonstrations. She had become a social activist, a long way from library research on medieval thought. The synthesis of ideas she had insisted upon in her reading of ancient history had now become a synthesis of academics with social practice, something of which the academy was skeptical. This bridging approach to learning would stay with her for the rest of her life.

Ruether ended up teaching at Howard University for ten years, leaving in 1976 to go to Garrett-Evangelical Seminary in Evanston, Illinois. From 1976 to 2000, she was the Georgia Harkness Professor of Theology at Garrett. Since 2000 she has been the Carpenter Professor of Feminist Theology at the Graduate Theological Union in Berkeley, California. She is also adjunct professor at the Claremont School of Theology and Claremont Graduate University.

Although Ruether's primary area of writing and research was in feminism and liberation theology, an overarching preoccupation has been to critique theology and the church where they pay insufficient attention to their own complicity in sexism, racism, patriarchy, violence, and hierarchy—in general, where they express and practice a theology of control. In an article written in 1986, she says that Catholicism faces three major challenges, which she identifies as democratic values and human rights within the church, feminism and sexual morality within church and its teachings, and Third World liberation movements. She notes: "How the Catholic community responds to these three challenges will determine in large part whether Catholicism will be able to use its enormous human resources as a witness for truth and justice in this critical period of human history or whether it will lose its creative leadership and its opportunity for both its own renewal and its witness to the world."[22]

For Ruether, feminism is not only about gender; it is about race, class, marginality, and injustices of all kinds. This distinguishes her from some other North American feminists and makes it possible for her to relate closely to many other issues and discussions. Hence, she is involved in areas like ecology, the Israel-Palestine conflict, Third World liberation, ecumenical work, militarism, and so on. Her passion for the church is reflected by her friend, Susan Brooks Thistlethwaite, former president of and current professor at the Chicago Theological Seminary, who suggests in a foreword to one of Ruether's recent

---

[20] Ruether's dissertation was published as *Gregory of Nazianzus: Rhetor and Philosopher* (Oxford: Oxford University Press, 1969).

[21] Quoted from William Ramsay, "Rosemary Radford Ruether and Feminist Theology," in *Four Modern Prophets: Walter Rauschenbusch, Martin Luther King, Jr., Gustavo Gutiérrez, Rosemary Radford Ruether* (Atlanta: John Knox, 1986), 74.

[22] Rosemary Radford Ruether, "Crises and Challenges of Catholicism Today," *America: The National Catholic Weekly* (March 1, 1986), 152.

books, "In a truly just world, Rosemary Radford Ruether would be Pope."[23]

A unique feature of Ruether's work is that she writes not only for herself but on behalf of friends and communities. Sometimes she even collaborates with other theologians (as she has with her husband Herman), such as Canadian theologian Douglas John Hall, Jewish scholar Marc Ellis, Palestinian theologian Naim Ateek, and feminist Eleanor McLaughlin. Says Rosalind Hinton: "Each book of Rosemary's represents personal friendships, an activist front and a feminist community engaged in bettering their world whether in Africa, Palestine, the Philippines or Latin America. She digs deeply into the world around her and uses her relationships as the wellspring of her inspiration and a vital source of knowledge."[24]

Ruether is the author or editor of more than thirty-five books and hundreds of articles. She holds more than ten honorary doctorates, has lectured in at least twenty-five countries, and at seventy-five years of age continues to teach and write.

THEOLOGICAL ORIENTATION

In 1998 Ruether wrote a brief article situating her own thought in relation to other feminists.[25] By this time, she had adopted a thoroughly sociological reading of history, and so she naturally resisted rising above the contingencies of the actual by imposing upon them an abstract, intellectual structure, an approach she attributes to Mary Daly. Hence, we do not get from Ruether a definitive or purist view of Christianity; rather we get a mixture of the positive and the negative aspects of Jewish, Christian, and pagan traditions interacting with each other.

Ruether's approach has her read history from "the underside," that is, from the standpoint of the victim. She has this in common with other liberation theologians. She hastens to add, however, that victims are not always right, and that some would be as ruthless as their oppressors if they were given an opportunity. Nevertheless, there is an implicit assumption within her work that unless Christianity can address the plight of the oppressed and the marginalized it loses integrity. For she shares with Letty Russell the approach of beginning from "the other end," and with Mary Daly an approach that has her looking at "an ontology of primal 'origins.'"[26]

In the essay about herself, Ruether explains how her theology and ethics come together. She says, "God is not a 'being' removed from creation, ruling it from outside in the manner of a patriarchal ruler; God is the source of being that underlies creation and grounds its nature and future potential for continual transformative renewal in biophilic mutuality."[27] In other words, God cannot be understood apart from the natural order, as on the outside looking in. God is fully present here and now, within nature.

It is because she sees God as the ground of being that the concept of "biophilic mutuality" is so important for Ruether, for it describes how we ought to live on this earth. It ties the human way of life directly to divine reality. It names an interdependence found in all of creation, one that has its ground in Creator God and as such is a model for how we ought to embrace each other and the earth. She says:

> Only when we act in this manner of biophilic mutuality with one another (across not only gender, class, and race, but also species lines) is there well-being, while the exploitative domination of some by others violates this ontological ground and leads to violence, hate, escalating oppression, misuse of the earth, and eventually a social system

---

[23] Susan Brooks Thistlethwaite, Foreword to *Catholic Does Not Equal the Vatican: A Vision for Progressive Catholicism*, by Rosemary Radford Ruether (New York: New Press, 2008), x.

[24] Rosalind Hinton, "A Legacy of Inclusion: An Interview with Rosemary Radford Ruether," in *Cross Currents* 52 (2002). Quoted from internet version, at http://www.crosscurrents.org/Ruetherspring2002.htm, accessed May 14, 2011, 1–2.

[25] "Rosemary Ruether," in Ruether, *Women and Redemption*, 221–24.

[26] "Rosemary Ruether," in Ruether, *Women and Redemption*, 223.

[27] "Rosemary Ruether," in Ruether, *Women and Redemption*, 223.

that will destroy itself. Even though such systems may be able to survive by force for some time, the longer they survive in this way the more destructive they become.[28]

In other words, only that which itself is firmly grounded in the very source of life will survive in the long run, and since all of reality is so grounded, there can be no de-valuation of any part of reality.

"Biophilic mutuality" is not something that is foreign to us as human beings or as creatures, for it is our essence. Interdependence is natural and can be found in the plant and animal worlds, which have their own systems of checks and balances that ensure ongoing existence. However, when human control and domination take over, the result is slavery, hierarchy, sexism, and the idea of property and possession, which divide and alienate. Patriarchy stands at the center of this insistence on dominance and control. This is not only a matter of ethics but of survival, for unless we learn new ways of understanding ourselves under the concept of biophilic mutuality, we will destroy ourselves and much of the earth with us.

The concept of biophilic mutuality also produces a unique view of authority, for God is not in charge of this world in the sense of intervening "to save us despite ourselves and bring in a reign of God from the sky. Rather, the deep ontological structures that dictate biophilic mutuality as the only way to generate well-being give us the potential for making a new future, but one we could miss through our greed, hatred, and delusions."[29]

Clearly, the verdict is not yet in on whether humankind will make the change necessary to avert the inevitable destruction that will follow from dominating systems that act in contradiction with our ontological ground. Whether or not we will be saved from this destruction is a contingent matter, not one that has been determined one way or the other. That is, while both failure and redemption are possible, neither is necessary or fated. This understanding of reality forms the basis of her ecological liberation theology.

It is a daunting challenge to do justice to the massive corpus of written material Ruether has produced. The following is but a representation of a few key themes. I have chosen three general categories under which to summarize her ideas: feminist theology, ecojustice and ecofeminism, and political theology.

FEMINIST THEOLOGY

It would be unfair to suggest that Ruether's work comes in packages of "feminist" and other aspects of theology like ecology and politics. Her writings are much too integrated for that. In 1972 she wrote her first major book on liberation theology, and it is interesting to note the breadth of the subject; she covers Christian origins, ecclesiology, eschatology, anti-Semitism, Zionism, feminism, ecology, black theology, Latin American liberation theology, and political theology. Each of these themes gets the attention of separate studies later in her work.[30] Just as all of life is interconnected through the concept of biophilic mutuality, so, she would argue, theology, properly understood, is of one piece. In fact, her point is that it is precisely the fracturing of theology by the diminution of the feminine that makes traditional theology untenable. And it needs to be made whole! It would be equally unfair to her thought, however, if we did not identify the important themes in her seminal book, *Sexism and God-Talk*,[31] which she subtitles, "Toward a Feminist Theology." Here, in 1983, she lays the groundwork for her feminist thought.

Ruether identifies the critical principle of feminist theology as "the promotion of the

---

[28] "Rosemary Ruether," in Ruether, *Women and Redemption*, 223.

[29] "Rosemary Ruether," in Ruether, *Women and Redemption*, 224.

[30] See Rosemary Radford Ruether, *Liberation Theology: Human Hope Confronts Christian History and American Power* (New York: Paulist, 1972).

[31] Rosemary Radford Ruether, *Sexism and God-Talk: Toward a Feminist Theology* (Boston: Beacon, 1983).

full humanity of women. Whatever denies, diminishes, or distorts the full humanity of women is, therefore, appraised as not redemptive."[32] Moreover, whatever excludes women does not reflect authentic relations to the divine or the nature of things. I have chosen four themes to explain her elaboration of this principle: God/ess, Christology, Mariology, and the new world.

God/ess

Ruether gives a thick description of the history-sociology of sexism and its linkage with divine imagery and language (God-talk). In other words, she traces the development of how we got to where we are today by asking whether God has always been seen as male. And if not, what has happened that has made Christian theology so patriarchal?

In answering this question, Ruether begins with ancient, Near Eastern mythology. Here she notes the prevalence of Goddess imagery and language, which, although not exclusive of male images, are at least as prominent. Moreover, she points out that there was a mutuality or duality to divine reality, yet explicitly not a complementarity. Goddess and God are equivalent and equal images of the divine and not dependent on one another.

This equality was threatened with the advent of monotheism, both within the Hebrew tradition and in Plato's creation account in the *Timaeus*. Here a hierarchy developed; a hierarchy of God-male-female, where the woman was seen as distant, and even as negative, in relation to the divine. Ruether says:

> Whereas the male is seen essentially as the image of the male transcendent ego or God, woman is seen as the image of the lower, material nature. Although both are seen as "mixed natures," the male identity points "above" and the female "below." Gender becomes the primary symbol for the dualism of transcendence and immanence, spirit and matter.[33]

In other words, monotheism, in an effort to overcome polytheism, moved, unnecessarily,

Ruether would claim, to a singularity of gender, and that gender was male. Yet there is nothing about monotheism that necessitates gender singularity.

The image of the Goddess is not lost entirely in Judeo-Christian monotheism, even though the female Goddess is reduced to a servant of God. Ruether makes the point that the Yahwist tradition did not at first exclude Goddess imagery. "Yahweh simply replaced Baal as the husband of the Goddess."[34] Hence, in the ancient graves we find Yahwist and Goddess symbols appearing together. The male symbol for Yahweh seems to have been too limited for a people for whom fertility and procreation were paramount in understanding human existence. Hence, the maternal, creative, and "womblike" qualities such as birthing and rebirthing were essentially tied to biblical divinity. Feminine imagery simply could not be easily expunged from biblical God-talk. Ruether cites Isaiah as an example of language that reaches for the feminine to describe Yahweh.

> For a long time I have held my peace,
> I have kept still and restrained myself,
> Now I will cry out like a woman in travail,
> I will gasp and pant . . .
>
> These things I will do and I will not forsake them,
> They shall be turned back and utterly put to shame,
> who trust in graven things.(Isa 42:14, 16b-17)[35]

As the text suggests, the issue here is trusting in "graven things," and this clearly does not include feminine attributes since there is not only no warning against female divine qualities but they are explicitly included, and hence, acceptable. In other words, monotheistic language does not require gender singularity.

In the wisdom tradition, *Sophia* (Wisdom) participates with God in the creation of the world. Says Ruether, "In the Wisdom tradition the female image appears as a secondary persona of God, mediating the work

---

[32] Ruether, *Sexism and God-Talk*, 18–19.
[33] Ruether, *Sexism and God-Talk*, 54.
[34] Ruether, *Sexism and God-Talk*, 56.
[35] Quoted from Ruether, *Sexism and God-Talk*, 57.

and will of God to creation."[36] But in later Hebrew thought, the view of wisdom as a female manifestation of the divine changed to become an expression of the transcendent male; and hence God and femaleness gradually became separated.

In the early Christian writings, especially in the Epistle to the Hebrews and in the Pauline literature, wisdom is associated with *logos* and becomes identified as the son of God. Yet the Holy Spirit remained female for a considerable time. There was even debate around the language of the Virgin Mary becoming impregnated by the Holy Spirit. Ruether quotes the Gospel of Philip as follows: "Some said: 'Mary conceived by the Holy Spirit.' They are in error. They do not know what they are saying. When did a woman ever conceive by a woman?"[37] While Gnosticism sustained the view of the femininity of the Holy Spirit for some time, Greco–Roman Christianity gradually repressed it.

Ruether also identifies several forces of critique of patriarchalism within the biblical literature to counter the argument that the Bible presents an inherently hierarchical male theology. She mentions the prophetic tradition, the liberating sovereign theme, the proscription of idolatry, which is a warning against literal ascription of attributes to God, and the inclusion of both male and female images in God—especially in the seeking of the lost. Clearly then, the biblical push toward monotheism and the efforts to narrate the salvation that comes through the male Messiah Jesus do not entirely remove the feminine from the imagination of the divine.

With this as background, Ruether presents the feminist understanding of God/ess as a more inclusive and salvific image of the divine. God/ess is not the same as Goddess; in fact, it is intended to point to a gender mutuality which neither God nor Goddess alone is able to do. "God/ess" is not a sayable term and cannot be used in worship. That is in part its value—it is intended as an unsayable construct, in this way similar to the Hebrew tetragrammaton, YHWH. Ruether puts it forward as the way to imagine God which does not slip easily into patriarchy and other forms of idolatry. She says: "We have no adequate name for the true God/ess, the 'I am who I shall become.' Intimation of Her/His name will appear as we emerge from false naming of God/ess modeled on patriarchal alienation."[38]

Ruether suggests several reasons for her choice of God/ess as the divine designation. First, she relies on the ancient, Catholic tradition of appealing to analogy for God-language. Literal attribution to God is idolatry. This prohibition then means that "male language for the divine must lose its privileged place."[39] Second, God/ess is the One who can liberate us from the existing, hierarchical, social order, not the one who defends and entrenches it. Third, the image of God/ess must be drawn from all levels of the social order, the lowly and the powerful, men and women, and so on. Images of God/ess must be transformative "pointing us back to our authentic potential and forward to new redeemed possibilities."[40] Fourth, to simply add male and female images together is not sufficient. Nor is it helpful to resort to abstract gender-neutral images like parent. Rather, we should "start with language for the Divine as redeemer, as liberator, as one who fosters full personhood and, in that context, speak of God/ess as creator, as source of being."[41] Fifth, most liberation theologies are not adequate here because they mistakenly identify the ground of creation with the foundations of the existing social order. Hence, they still operate within the matter-spirit and nature-transcendence paradigms, which is the legacy of a past male-dominated theology and one in which women are relegated to the lower rungs of being. Sixth, feminist theology rejects these dualistic paradigms and

---

[36] Ruether, *Sexism and God-Talk*, 57.
[37] Quoted from Ruether, *Sexism and God-Talk*, 59.
[38] Ruether, *Sexism and God-Talk*, 71.

[39] Ruether, *Sexism and God-Talk*, 68–69.
[40] Ruether, *Sexism and God-Talk*, 69.
[41] Ruether, *Sexism and God-Talk*, 70.

moves to "the converted center, the harmonization of self and body, self and other, self and world. It is the *Shalom* of our being."[42] On this model, a true encounter with God is possible because such an encounter does not imply a denial of the self, either female or male, but permits the alienated self to be resurrected into the authentic self.

God/ess imagery is Ruether's attempt to reject, and offer a credible replacement for, a theology rooted in the devaluation and exclusion of women. A theology that is grounded in a bias against half of humanity cannot be a Christian theology that flows from the one who desires to create peace through the formation of "one new humanity" (Eph 2:15).

Christology

Ruether boldly addresses the challenges of the radical feminists, for she too asks, "Can a Male Savior Save Women?"[43] Although she takes their questions with utmost seriousness, she does so with the faith that the church and theology reimagined can find answers to these difficult questions, albeit they will need to let go of their patriarchal past.

Ruether begins this essay by suggesting that the Council of Chalcedon (451) is not the result of a Hebraic understanding of the Messiah. Important theological shifts had taken place by that time. In tracing the history of these shifts, she notes that the Ancient Near Eastern roots of Christianity brought together two ideas: the messianic king and divine wisdom. The figure of divine wisdom is represented by the Goddess Sophia. In the New Testament, however, divine wisdom becomes *logos*, or *Son* of God, that is, male. And then the maleness of *logos* gets connected with the maleness of Jesus. Hence the female figure of divine wisdom is displaced from the Trinity.

Also, in the biblical narrative, the reign of God and prophecy both undergo transformations. Initially, the hope was stated in terms of plenty of food, peace, security, and justice in human relations; in other words, human well-being was closely associated with the agricultural cycle. However, this hope soon took on a larger historical perspective. Yet, it remained lodged in the notion of a sovereign king—God directing history toward an irenic and just end. The idea of the coming Messiah embodied the hope in a new form of the reign of God, and as "God's anointed," the Messiah would be an instrument of the people's salvation. And this would have to do with delivering the people from bondage—from their enemies—and restoring Israel as an autonomous power. This coming "Davidic King" was, however, not seen as an incarnation of the divine, as we see later in the Christian tradition. The Messiah was expected to win the battle against the enemies—not to suffer and die as a redemptive self-sacrifice. Hence, because of the association with military prowess, the only way of imagining such a messiah was as a male.

In the story of Jesus, a radicalization of the hope for God's reign took place. In particular, there was a renewed emphasis on including not only what we might receive, like food and security, but also what each ought to give to those in need. Hence, Jesus was especially critical of the religious authorities—those who had the power to effect change—for excluding the little ones from the hope of redemption. Jesus' vision for the kingdom was neither nationalistic nor otherworldly; the new reign which Jesus proclaimed was expected to happen on this earth with great revolution in human affairs, all of which must begin with human repentance.

The new reign in Jesus did not have to do with Israel defeating its enemies and being installed as the great power. In fact, the priority of Israel under God was itself partly undone with the opening of the covenant

---

[42] Ruether, *Sexism and God-Talk*, 71 (emphasis in original).

[43] See Rosemary Ruether, "Christology: Can a Male Savior Save Women?" in *Sexism and God-Talk*. An earlier version of an article by a similar title, "Christology and Feminism: Can a Male Saviour Save Women?" appeared in *To Change the World: Christology and Cultural Criticism* (New York: Crossroads, 1981).

to include the Gentiles. Even the notion of kingship was turned upside down with the announcement that the king would become a servant and not the dominator of others. In addition, servant language goes through a change, as the people became servants of God, freed from earthly masters. The God of Israel was suddenly no longer one who *had* acted in the past but one who *was* acting in the present. Ruether says, "To encapsulate Jesus himself as God's 'last word' and 'once-for-all' disclosure of God, located in a remote past and institutionalized in a cast of Christian teachers, is to repudiate the spirit of Jesus and to recapitulate the position against which he himself protests."[44]

All of this sounds like the context for radical inclusion; so how did the patriarchalization of Christianity come about? This process takes place over five centuries, during which time the Christian church seeks to understand what to do with Jesus. Of course, it begins with the shock of the crucifixion. It now becomes utterly impossible to think that Jesus is the new king who will set up the new political rule of Israel. And so the understanding of Jesus gets interpreted in terms of the atonement for Israel's sin. Jesus is resurrected by God and given ongoing life. The risen Lord now lives in their midst. The messianic community begins to understand itself apocalyptically—that is, living in the end of time, anticipating the intervention of God. They themselves will be taken up with God and identify with Jesus.

In the Gospel of Luke, Christology gets de-eschatologized. Ruether means by this that Christ becomes the center of history; Christ is a timeless revelation, a timeless perfection. Fear of distorting the image of Christ begins to arise, and a strategy of protectionism and control takes over. She summarizes, "Access to Christ is now through the official line of apostolic teaching. Only males can occupy the apostolic teaching office and thus represent Christ. Women are to keep silent."[45]

The most significant step in the patriarchalization of Christianity, however, came when the church aligned itself with the Roman Empire, whereby the state became religious and the church became political. With Constantine and his Christian eulogist Eusebius, we now see a reinterpretation of messianism which aligns the rule of God with the rule of the emperor. It now works something like this: *Logos* and *Nous* (mind) of God govern the cosmos, the empire and the church govern the political universe, the masters govern slaves, and men govern women.[46] In this model, women are unable to represent Christ because Christ is "the male disclosure of a male God."[47] Salvation is now understood in imperial terms, and the cross becomes an instrument of power and war. This is seen as the way of God, who is the ultimate (male) warrior and whose wars men must fight. Hence, as Ruether says, "Women's inability to represent Christ in the priesthood becomes an unchangeable 'mystery' that lies on a sacramental and metaphysical plane."[48]

These are the roots of a very long patriarchal tradition that are reflected even in recent church theology. Ruether quotes the Vatican Declaration of 1976, which says, "there must be a physical resemblance between the priest and Christ."[49] She summarizes this Christology by saying: "The possession of male genitalia becomes the essential prerequisite for representing Christ, who is the disclosure of the male God."[50]

But there are other Christologies around. Ruether explores two which she calls "androgynous christologies" and "spirit christologies." Both are ways of trying to understand how Christ redeems humans—men and women. Androgynous Christologies tend to be rooted in the Pauline language that we are neither "male nor female, we are all one in

---

[44] Ruether, *Sexism and God-Talk*, 122.
[45] Ruether, *Sexism and God-Talk*, 124.
[46] Ruether, *Sexism and God-Talk*, 125.
[47] Ruether, *Sexism and God-Talk*, 125.

[48] Ruether, *Sexism and God-Talk*, 126.
[49] Ruether, *Sexism and God-Talk*, 126.
[50] Ruether, *Sexism and God-Talk*, 126.

Christ" (Gal 3:28). They seek to bring male and female into gender unity under Christ. However, it is almost always the case that women somehow end up receiving their identity through the male. Androgynous Christologies never seem to be able to grant to the woman full, human status on her own. Says Ruether, "As long as Christ is still presumed to be, normatively, a male person, androgynous Christologies will carry an androcentric bias."[51]

The biblical roots of spirit Christologies go back to the story of Pentecost in Acts 2, where the presence of the resurrected Lord is proclaimed in spiritual form. From this, the conclusion is drawn that the past is not normative, and that the ever-present resurrected Christ moves in new ways not confined to patterns of the past. Ruether says that this Christology "sees Christ as a power that continues to be revealed in persons, both male and female, in the present."[52] This notion grants opportunities for all forms of creative, new innovations and liberating models.

Ruether finds both of these Christologies less than adequate and offers what she sees as a more authentically theological-biblical take that is centered in "the Jesus of the synoptic Gospels."[53] Her claim is that the church needs to go no further than to the proper reading of the Jesus story to see the errors of sexism and patriarchy. She says, "Once the mythology about Jesus as the Messiah or Divine *Logos*, with its traditional masculine imagery, is stripped off, the Jesus of the synoptic Gospels can be recognized as a figure remarkably compatible with feminism."[54] In other words, she argues that Jesus' criticism of the hierarchy is remarkably similar to the criticisms she wants to give as a feminist. Jesus carries forward the prophetic mode of

denouncing hierarchical structures, whether they be religious or social, and lifts up the marginalized and the outcasts of society. And in this context, he continually promotes and teaches liberation: the overcoming of all oppressive powers. Women are often identified among the oppressed, whether the Samaritan woman, widows, or prostitutes; these women are named as among those who will be first in the kingdom of God.

Ruether concludes from this that "Theologically speaking, then, we might say that the maleness of Jesus has no ultimate significance."[55] She explains this further by saying, "Christ is not necessarily male, nor is the redeemed community only women, but a new humanity, female and male."[56] Jesus Christ saves women and men because of the social revolution promised in his ministry, for which the maleness of Jesus is theologically irrelevant.

Mariology

Ruether suggests that the most important theological symbol of the feminine is the church herself. In her 1977 booklet, *Mary— The Feminine Face of the Church*,[57] she says that in late medieval theology, "Mary is the personification of the church, the New Israel, the hope of humankind."[58] The biblical warrant for this view of Mary and the church is found in the Pauline language of the messianic bride of Christ (Eph 5:25-27), and the apocalyptic image of the ecclesial bride being joined in marriage to the messianic king (Rev 21:2).[59] But these images have a rather colorful history that Ruether believes is itself in need of redemption.

In tracing the historical understanding of Mariology, Ruether reminds us that the debates over Mary, both as the mother of the

---

[51] Ruether, *Sexism and God-Talk*, 130.
[52] Ruether, *Sexism and God-Talk*, 131.
[53] Ruether, *Sexism and God-Talk*, 135.
[54] Ruether, *Sexism and God-Talk*, 135.
[55] Ruether, *Sexism and God-Talk*, 137.
[56] Ruether, *Sexism and God-Talk*, 138.
[57] Rosemary Radford Ruether, *Mary—The Feminine Face of the Church* (Philadelphia: Westminster, 1977).
[58] Ruether, *Mary*, 68.   [59] Ruether, *Mary*, 44.

church and the mother of Christ, had every-thing to do with fleshliness, sexuality, pur-ity, and holiness. Virginity became known as godliness because it symbolized purity, in the sense that it had not been tainted with the flesh. This negative view of the body was dif-ficult to expunge from both Christology and ecclesiology.

In medieval thought, Mary *as virgin* comes to represent the pure humanity in its original goodness, that is, the virgin Mary becomes the new symbol for the fallen Eve. Says Ru-ether: "As the representative of humanity in its original goodness, [Mary] becomes the anticipation of its restoration and fulfillment at the end of history."[60] As Eve sinned in her acquiescence to fleshly desires, so Mary re-tains her purity through her perpetual virgin-ity.[61] Hence, goodness and godliness became inextricably associated with a spirituality not tainted by the flesh.

In this theology, virginity and sexual ab-stinence became the model calling for Chris-tians, and hence there followed a kind of devaluation not only of Christian marriage but of physicality itself. This was part of the debate during the Reformation period when the Reformers offered a new theology of marriage as a kind of Christian vocation. Yet given Protestant biblicism, a strict reading of Paul led them to a view that made the hus-band the head of the house and through the husband the lordship of Christ was exercised over the wife.

Hence, after the sixteenth century, there were two theologies to choose from: one where woman as woman is seen as virginal and sin is rooted in participation in the flesh; or where woman as woman is placed under the authority of the husband who repre-sents Christ to her. Both, of course, devalue women.

Ruether makes the point that, traditionally, the fear of sexuality and the association of

virginity with purity had a negative effect on women because it required them to be what they could not be. Moreover, this fear of the flesh is rooted in a profound misreading of the story of Jesus. In the first place, Jesus too was "in the flesh." His "purity" was not root-ed in his escape from physicality, but in his unique participation in it. Second, Jesus in-sisted on the reciprocity between the love of God and the love of brothers and sisters. They were *like* each other, not different. "Those who love God must love their brothers and sisters also" (1 John 4:21b). Third, Jesus was constantly critical of hierarchal leadership calling the "greatest" to become "servants" (Matt 23:11; 20:26). Fourth, Ruether cites the story of Mary and Martha (Luke 10:38-42), where Jesus calls Mary out of her traditional role into the circle of disciples, to sit at the Lord's feet and listen to his teaching. In other words, no husband is required to represent Christ to her. Says Ruether:

> If Christ represents the emptying out of a divine power that puts itself at the service of others, then Mary, or the church, represents liberated human-ity. Mary represents the *person of the church* from the perspective of the conversion that has to go on in history, and between people, to overcome de-humanizing power and suppressed personhood. From the perspective of final salvation, the new humanity is neither male nor female, neither slave nor free, neither Jew nor Greek, neither black nor white (see Gal 3:28).[62]

Yet Ruether warns that we should be care-ful when giving Mary the exalted status that she has held in Catholic theology, since there are many Marys. That is, Mary is not signifi-cant because of her essence—her perpetual virginity. Her exalted (model) status lies in her openness and readiness to serve God. When she says: "Here am I, the servant of the Lord; let it be with me according to your word" (Luke 1:38), she is speaking the words of faithfulness for every disciple of Jesus.

[60] Ruether, *Mary*, 68.
[61] For a discussion of the doctrine of the "perpetual virginity" of Mary, which arose in the second century and argued that Mary retained her virginity even after the birth of Christ, see Ruether, *Mary*, 54–55.
[62] Ruether, *Mary*, 86 (italics in source).

Ruether suggests that the doctrine of Mary's Immaculate Conception, especially when it is connected with the "lost alternative before the Fall,"[63] has not served women well. This is the male view of the feminine because it represents the traditional dualism of matter and spirit. It presupposes an association of perfection with virginity and the absence of fleshly contamination; and an association of sinfulness and mortality with the flesh. But Ruether says, "This very effort to sunder us from our mortal bodies and to scapegoat women as cause of mortality and sin is the real sin. This sin has alienated us from that fruitful unity of mind and body that we have lost and that we seek in our redemptive quest."[64]

Ruether argues that God's entry into history through Christ and through Mary's obedience was not to redeem us from matter and physicality into an impossible and false spirituality, but rather "to effect a liberating revolution in human relationships. Mary is exalted because, through her, God will work this revolution in history."[65] Mary herself was the lowly one who was lifted up and became the symbol of salvation because of her obedience and openness to God. In this way the redemptive power of God could work through her body. Hence, Mary represents God's "preferential option for the poor."[66] And to think of the church as feminine is precisely to proclaim in the church the liberating power that can transform the reality of oppression and sexism into one of hope for liberation.

New World

Ruether works at the task of constructing a new reality of inclusion and mutuality. She points out how diabolical it is that women are excluded from being ministers—preachers and priests—within the body of Christ whose explicit raison d'être it is to break down walls of division (Eph 2:14). For a church to be freed from sexism, it must be freed from the imagination and practice of patriarchy.

The new world imagined through the feminist challenge is one grounded in the unity of creation and redemption. Ruether says:

> The God/ess who underlies creation and redemption is One. We cannot split a spiritual, antisocial redemption from the human self as a social being, embedded in sociopolitical and ecological systems. We must recognize sin precisely in this splitting and deformation of our true relationships to creation and to our neighbor and find liberation in an authentic harmony with all that is incarnate in our social, historical being. Socioeconomic humanization is indeed the outward manifestation of redemption.[67]

The failure to hold a theology of creation and redemption together results in a justification of sexism and exploitation. Here is how the logic works: if creation is all about matter coming into existence and redemption is about the spirit transcending the evils of matter, then body loses out. If salvation is a flight from nature, then body and sexuality are on the wrong side of the ledger. And it becomes easy to associate women with this side. Ruether seeks to overcome this theology. As she sees it, the redemption offered in Jesus Christ is not at odds with the original intent of creation. Christ is the new Adam, not in showing us what the old Adam could not be because of his essence, but in showing us what Adam could have been—in the flesh—had he been obedient to God's call. Likewise, Mary is the new Eve, not in showing us what the old Eve could not be because of her essence but in showing us what she could have been—in the flesh—had she been obedient to God's call.

Ruether's proposed feminist vision for an integrated theology seeks to go beyond other views of feminism because other views tend to make definitive claims that encapsulate themselves within their own systems.[68] Ruether maintains that unless feminism

---

[63] Ruether, *Sexism and God-Talk*, 151.
[64] Ruether, *Sexism and God-Talk*, 152.
[65] Ruether, *Sexism and God-Talk*, 155.
[66] Ruether, *Sexism and God-Talk*, 157.
[67] Ruether, *Sexism and God-Talk*, 215–16.
[68] Ruether, *Sexism and God-Talk*, 232.

remains open in principle to a newness not yet known, it becomes the very opposite of what it espouses. The new world of openness, equality, and justice is sadly not yet here, not because it cannot be imagined, but "because of the insufficient collective power of those already converted to an alternative vision. The powers and principalities are still very much in control of most of the world. The nucleus of the alternative world remains, like the Church (theologically, *as* the Church), harbingers and experimenters with new human possibilities within the womb of the old."[69] The new world is coming, but alas it is not yet here, not because of an inherent flaw in the old system, but because of the failure of the collective human will.

ECOJUSTICE AND ECOFEMINISM

The connection between the poverty of the land and the poverty of women is an obvious one for Ruether; both have their roots in a dualistic imagination of nature and history.[70] In her 1981 booklet, *To Change the World*, she addressed the issue of ecology and human liberation, and makes the point that the modern, romantic return to nature does not help us because it fails to challenge the history-nature dichotomy.

Ruether tackles the crisis of ecology in relation to the way the dominant world understands development and industrialization. We tend to believe that if Western industrialization were expanded into the underdeveloped countries it would destroy the ecological systems. As for population growth, we believe there must be a campaign for birth control in Third World countries or we will run out of food. But both views arise from the assumption of the right to social domination by the West. Both are deeply entrenched systemic matters. She says:

The environmental crisis is basically insoluble as long as a system of social domination remains intact that allows the owners and decision-makers to maintain high profits for the few by passing on the costs to the many in the form of low wages, high prices, bad working conditions and toxic side effects of the techniques of extraction.[71]

Social domination, according to Ruether, is firmly rooted in another related dualism of the mind (spirit) and the body. Here is how the logic goes: the mind (the educated and wealthy) should have control over an unruly body, to purge it of its natural (sinful) tendencies. Earth, body, women, workers, and so on, in different ways, all defile the spirit—pull it down from its pure state. She summarizes the argument as follows: "The domination of the body, nature and woman turns into a flight from the body, nature and woman. For at least 1300 years Western civilization became obsessed with this world-fleeing agenda and shaped its ethics, religion and cultural institutions around it."[72] In this view, nature is seen as fallen and in the realm of sinfulness, and to redeem it requires that it be made into something other than it is. Of course, only God can do that. Humans can only *subdue* its sinful tendencies. Conclusion: since nature is sinful, history must control it.

Ruether develops a view of ecojustice which seeks to bring history and nature into unity. As we have already seen with her concept of biophilic mutuality, her concern for interdependence is paramount. Ecojustice names a reality of interconnection. The hierarchical model, where one part of creation controls another part, leads ultimately to nature's destruction. This is so between nations, with development practices, relations to the earth, gender relations, and so on. The only sustainable option is "ecological" mutuality, which she draws, in part, from the prophet

---

[69] Ruether, *Sexism and God-Talk*, 233–34 (emphasis in original).

[70] We have encountered the theme of ecojustice earlier with George Tinker's theology (see chap. 28 above). Ruether's thought has more similarities to Tinker's thought, like the critique of the history-nature and other dichotomies. Although she does not cite Tinker's work, she does refer to his mentor, Vine Deloria Jr., *God Is Red: A Native View of Religion* (Golden, Colo.: Fulcrum, 1973). See Ruether, *Sexism and God-Talk*, 250ff.

[71] Ruether, *To Change the World*, 59.   [72] Ruether, *To Change the World*, 61.

Isaiah's vision for the year of Jubilee (Isa 61:1-2) and Jesus' reference to releasing captives, remitting debts, and so on (Luke 4:18-19). The way she sees it, ecojustice does not reach to either a historical beginning point (nature in its pure form) or end point (*telos*) for normativity, but to the center of existence that brings history and nature together. She says that ecojustice calls for a

> conversion back to the centre, rather than to a beginning or end-point in history. . . . I suggest that we think of the messianic hope towards which Jesus points us, not as the eschatological endpoint of history or as transcendence of death, but rather as the Shalom of God which remains the true connecting point of all our existences, even when we violate and forget it.[73]

In another book on the subject, *Gaia and God*,[74] Ruether explores further the interrelatedness of ecojustice and spirituality toward a view of healing what is broken in this world. She offers this description of what this book seeks to do:

> I juxtapose the terms *Gaia* and *God* in the title of this book because all the issues that I wish to explore finally pose the question of the relationship between the living planet, earth, and the concept of God as it has been shaped in the Western religious traditions. *Gaia* is the word for the Greek Earth Goddess, and it is also a term adopted by a group of planetary biologists . . . to refer to their thesis that the entire planet is a living system, behaving as a unified organism.[75]

It is important to understand what Ruether is getting at here. This is not part of the old discussion of bringing "man and nature" into unity, because neither pole here names the reality properly. For obvious reasons, "man" is problematic, and "nature" is problematic, precisely because here it is juxtaposed with living human beings. Her point is that humans are part of nature. We are interconnected within a living web we call the natural world. The dichotomies of the academy, like mind and body, fact and value, heaven and earth, are all more problematic than helpful in the quest for interconnectedness. Ruether's images of Gaia and God are intended to provide the lens for this quest.

The Christian tradition has perpetuated a model of ethics that has a voice thundering down commandments for human beings to act against our *natural* inclinations, as if we could be lifted up out of our natural state. But Ruether identifies another voice, "one that speaks from the intimate heart of matter. It has long been silenced by the masculine voice, but today is finding again her own voice. This is the voice of Gaia. Her voice does not translate into laws or intellectual knowledge, but beckons us into communion."[76] These two voices can speak in harmony if we permit them to.

To develop such a viable "harmonious" ethic of ecology, Ruether contends, requires that we set up the issues properly—begin with the right questions. And this means redefining good and evil themselves. Good is not a flight from nature, and evil is not being natural. In other words, it is not that we are natural that makes us sinful but how we are in nature that counts. Hence, goodness invites us into a reorientation of being in this world, not a flight from it; that is, goodness invites us into a mode of biophilic mutuality—a way of living that acknowledges our interconnectedness.

All of this opens up many opportunities for relating to others—animals, nature, other human beings—not in negation or opposition but in mutuality. Perpetual technological fixes will not save us because they arise out of the view that we can (and indeed must) domesticate a hostile world; but mutuality can save us because it links our own well-being to all of nature. Hence, it is not about changing the world to satisfy our own goals but allowing the goals of the world to change us. Therefore, we must change our

---

[73] Ruether, *To Change the World*, 69.

[74] Rosemary Radford Ruether, *Gaia and God: An Ecofeminist Theology of Earth Healing* (San Francisco: HarperCollins, 1992).

[75] Ruether, *Gaia and God*, 4 (emphasis in original).

[76] Ruether, *Gaia and God*, 254.

own practices, reducing harmful emissions through new transportation systems, utilizing better insulation in our buildings, eating lower on the food chain, reducing reliance on fossil fuel, and so on. All are ways of re-orienting ourselves to the earth in biophilic mutuality.

History is replete with a male "dominance" style of relating and thinking. This is borne out in political structures and military ways of resolving conflict. Mutuality is an alternative to dominance and control. Politics—the master model of control—too is a spirituality, and Ruether's proposal calls for the spirituality of politics to be grounded in biophilic mutuality and not the logic of the greatest might.

POLITICAL THEOLOGY

We have seen that Ruether's feminist theology is a lens through which she analyzes the whole world, and hence, she speaks to many social issues one may not immediately associate with feminism. Many of her feminist colleagues begin with gender and more or less stay with gender issues. Ruether does not. Her awareness of gender injustice spills over into many other issues of injustice, especially race, ecology, militarism, poverty, and international relations. In this last section, I will briefly highlight a few aspects of her work in areas political.

Her first foray into critiquing politics with theology came early in life by the sheer fact of living in Washington, D.C., during the Vietnam War era. But her connections with the civil rights movement and her tenure at Howard University gave that a particular turn. Being part of the North American peace movement during the 1960s and 1970s naturally placed her into a dialogue about social justice in the company of voices for socialism. So as she searched for an alternative

to American politics, it was natural for her to look to the left. However, she was as afraid of the left as she was of the right. Socialism as a political philosophy has as great a problem with corruption, violence, hierarchy, and dominance, as does any other form of government. Socialism is neither desirable nor possible in the United States unless it is democratic, American, nonsectarian, and openly political.[77] But then, socialism is merely another name for a just society.

Ruether sees peace and justice for North America as rooted in the larger vision of liberation theology.[78] To read the Bible correctly, she maintains, is to read it as advocating a "preferential option for the poor" and as empowering the marginalized. Liberation theology is biblical because at the center of its message is the view that God is present among us redeeming what is broken through faithful participation in the coming of the kingdom of God. To understand Jesus properly is to understand him as embodying the hope of a just and peaceable kingdom. Hence, followers of Christ are called to move society closer to the goals of peace, justice, and mutuality. Here she agrees with Gustavo Gutiérrez, that "For Latin American Christians, it becomes evident that the real denial of God is not atheism, but idolatry. Many who think they deny the existence of God do so because they reject the abuses of religion. The ones who really deny God are the ones who use God's name to justify evil."[79]

There are, of course, many different ways, both political and theological, of justifying evil. One way that concerns Ruether is related to the theology of the cross. Too often, Christians have seen the cross and the sufferings of Christ as a legal transaction with God paying for the sins of humanity.[80] But this is inconsistent with her view of God as the ground of being. Ruether argues that in

[77] See Rosemary Radford Ruether, *Disputed Questions: On Being a Christian* (Maryknoll, N.Y.: Orbis, 1989), 86ff.

[78] See, e.g., Rosemary Radford Ruether, "The Crisis of Liberation Theology: Does God Opt for the Poor?" in *God and the Nations*, by Douglas John Hall and Rosemary Radford Ruether (Minneapolis: Fortress, 1995).

[79] Ruether, *Disputed Questions*, 103. For a discussion of Gustavo Gutiérrez's thought, see chap. 26 above.

[80] Ruether, *Disputed Questions*, 103.

Christ we encounter the One who delivers us from all evil, not one who uses suffering for some higher purpose. The instrumental use of suffering, which is the ground of virtually every act of violence and war perpetrated by the state, is itself renounced as evil in the story of Jesus' death and resurrection.

The relationship between the cross and resurrection of Christ is not such that we should take from it a simplistic resolution of suffering; that is, resurrection is not a mere good news story for sufferers. This cheapens both the resurrection and the cross. Rather, it is a story of how Jesus identifies with the victims in real history and responds by truly abandoning the standard forms of imperial power. The cross and resurrection story suggests that God has indeed become part of the struggle of life against death and that God does not bless the principalities and powers in the struggle for liberation but blesses those who are powerless to change their lot. Hence, for the body of Christ to take up the "cross and follow" (Luke 9:23) implies picking up the same cause of liberating the suffering ones; namely, identification with the powerless. As Ruether puts it, "The Christian should be with those who suffer rather than with those who inflict suffering."[81]

Ruether does not take this logic in the direction of pacifism because of the complexities of political contexts. While nonviolence is always preferable to violence as a way of resolving disputes and nonviolent methods are clearly not sufficiently utilized, nevertheless, there is simply no way to keep our hands clean in this messy world. She agrees with the Latin American liberation theologians, who argue that the givenness of structural violence places the onus on its employment, not in their hands, but in the hands of the oppressors.[82]

One of the areas in which Ruether has worked out her political theology is in relation to the Israeli-Palestinian conflict. In the book she co-authored with Douglas John Hall, *God and the Nations*, she raises the question of how to understand God's presence in history.

In response to Hall's chapter in the book on what it means to be the church in a post-Constantinian world, Ruether disentangles the contentious matter of God's elect, and whether the Christian church can be said to be God's only elect and "chosen to discern God's truth and life in the midst of human contradictions."[83] This is a primary issue in the Israel-Palestine discussion because this is the locus of three religious groups, Jews, Christians, and Muslims, each of which claim primacy as God's chosen people. Although Ruether raises these as questions, it is clear that her own leaning is to say that since God is the ground of being, the notion of God's elect is altogether problematic and unhelpful language.

Ruether has written or edited at least three books addressing the Israeli-Palestinian conflict: one with her husband;[84] one with a Jewish liberation theologian;[85] and one with a Jewish and a Palestinian liberation theologian.[86] In these books, she expresses a passion for mutuality and justice that grows out of deep roots and friendships in the region.[87] As outsiders to the conflict, Ruether and her husband are naturally reluctant to

---

[81] Ruether, *Disputed Questions*, 106.

[82] See Ruether, *Disputed Questions*, 106.

[83] Hall and Ruether, *God and the Nations*, 65.

[84] See Rosemary Radford Ruether and Herman J. Ruether, *The Wrath of Jonah: The Crisis of Religious Nationalism in the Israeli-Palestinian Conflict*, 2nd ed. (Minneapolis: Fortress, 2002).

[85] Rosemary Radford Ruether and Marc H. Ellis, eds., *Beyond Occupation: American Jewish, Christian, and Palestinian Voices for Peace* (Boston: Beacon, 1990). See also her seminal study on anti-Semitism, Rosemary Radford Ruether, *Faith and Fratricide: The Theological Roots of Anti-Semitism* (New York: Seabury, 1974).

[86] Naim Ateek, Marc H. Ellis, and Rosemary Radford Ruether, eds., *Faith and the Intifada: Palestinian Christian Voices* (Maryknoll, N.Y.: Orbis, 1992).

[87] Two of her friends have helped Ruether to "see" the conflict and the region. Kathy Bergen, to whom *The Wrath of Jonah* is dedicated, has spent many years working for peace and justice with Israelis and Palestinians and is currently working

"pronounce" solutions to the conflict, nevertheless, drawing on their knowledge of the region and commitment to a political theology of mutuality, they venture the following comments about resolution in the preface to the second edition (2002) of *The Wrath of Jonah*:

> It lies finally, we believe, in the hands of Israeli Jews themselves, who have to decide that Palestinians cannot be "removed." They are their neighbors, and they have to live, not just alongside them but with them as fellow humans, neighbors, and finally extended family. We put the onus on the Israeli side because they have overwhelmingly been the aggressors. Palestinians have offered their concessions (the two-state solution within the 1967 borders). A genuine response by Israel must be based on a recognition of just coexistence as the minimal condition for "peace" and "security" for both peoples in relation to each other.[88]

The focus of Ruether's political critique is not only on conflicts in other parts of the world. In *America, Amerikkka*,[89] she examines the idolatry of the conviction that America is God's elect nation. The views of God and of the messianic hope that lie behind such a claim are the same as those of Hitler's Germany. And it behooves the church to rise up and denounce such claims wherever they are made.

For Ruether, the church is a counter political body, not in a narrow or partisan sense, but in the broadest way possible. Her 2008 booklet, *Catholic Does Not Equal the Vatican*, shows her passion for the church—not a blind passion that overlooks its fractured existence, but one that holds the possibility of speaking the truth of a justice that can heal and sustain life. This passion for the church is not new or recent in her life; it permeates her entire work, from her earlier books like *The Church Against Itself* and *Women-Church*[90] to her most recent writings. But she also issues a challenge to the church to work at the task of remaining faithful; to write ever-new "Barmen Confessions"[91] to keep it from being seduced by the ever-present powers and principalities that seek to commandeer the church into their own self-serving agenda.

CONCLUSION

For Ruether, the powers of a lost history are lodged not in their romantic appeal but in their ability to save us. We have inherited a distorted view of goodness, beauty, and salvation. We need to look again at what there is for us to see; we need to look deeply to the very ground of being, and we will see there not only otherness but connectedness. And this in turn can help us see the present differently—the earth, our neighbors, ourselves—for in them we may behold the very icons of the Divine.

In a postscript to her *Sexism and God-Talk*, Ruether writes:

> Layer by layer we must strip off the false consciousness that alienates us from our bodies, from our roots in the earth, sky, and water. Layer by layer we expose the twisted consciousness that has distorted our relationships and turned them to their opposite. But in so doing we discover that the Big Lie has limited power. Earth is not mocked. She brings her judgment, and this judgment can no longer be confined to the ghettos and the reservations of the poor.[92]

Life cannot be made whole and good "once and for all," but it can be made whole again and again, day after day, season after season. For this to occur, there must be commitment, not only to the cause of healing itself, but also to the vision of healing rooted in the very ground of being, a ground that knows body, nature, and earth.

---

with the Quakers in Ramallah. Jean Zaru, a Quaker writer and public speaker, also from Ramallah, has written her own book, *Occupied with Nonviolence: A Palestinian Woman Speaks*, ed. Diana L. Eck and Maria Schrader (Minneapolis: Fortress, 2008).

[88] Rosemary Radford Ruether and Herman J. Ruether, *Wrath of Jonah*, 2nd ed., xvi.

[89] Rosemary Radford Ruether, *America, Amerikkka: Elect Nation and Imperial Violence* (Oakville, Conn.: Equinox, 2007).

[90] Rosemary Radford Ruether, *The Church Against Itself: An Inquiry into the Conditions of Historical Existence for the Eschatological Community* (New York: Herder & Herder, 1967); and *Women-Church: Theology and Practice of Feminist Liturgical Communities* (San Francisco: Harper & Row, 1985).

[91] See 248ff. above.   [92] Ruether, *Sexism and God-Talk*, 259.

Chapter Thirty

SHARON D. WELCH

What does it mean to be a Christian theologian in contemporary times? Sharon Welch suggests that whatever it might be, theology today cannot be determined by abstract, theoretical reason. This is because theologians are always called upon to reflect on Christian faith from the standpoint of given social and political locations and assumptions. Hence, she says two factors in particular have compelled her to move beyond the traditional approaches to theology characterized by an emphasis on metaphysics, reason, and anthropology. They are "my desire to be faithful to the radical moral challenge and new political complexion of liberation faith, and my conclusion that there are fundamental distortions in the categories of Western thought."[1]

Welch is creative and bold in her challenge of tradition, both the tradition of modernity and postmodernity. Perhaps even more so, she challenges the tradition of Christian theology. She becomes increasingly less comfortable with the language of *theological* ethics as she moves ever further in the direction of spirituality and humanism. In part, this is due to the concern that violence is all too often perpetrated by adherents to closed and exclusive systems of thought. The history of religions is rife with such violence. Western Christian theology, even peace theology, embraces divisions and absolutes that contradict the very morality they purport to embrace. Her lifelong goal is to name these distortions and propose alternatives.

HER LIFE

There is little biographical information available in the public domain about Welch's early life—when she was born, about her elementary and high school education, or her community. We know that she has a sister and a brother and that her parents were James Welch and Reta Graef Welch and that she has two daughters, Zoe and Hannah. She is married to Jon Poses.

In her book *After Empire*,[2] Welch reflects briefly on her background. She says, "I was raised in a small farming community in West Texas. My grandparents and parents were farmers and ranchers who embodied a profound Christian faith, one that focused on living life fully and well. The main point of their daily prayers was an invocation to be mindful of the needs of other people."[3]

Welch casts her parents' faith in terms of their concern and service for others. They worked on school boards and hospital boards and were active in addressing and volunteering for social organizations in the local community and church. Both her father and mother were ordained ministers in

---

[1] Sharon D. Welch, *Communities of Resistance and Solidarity: A Feminist Theology of Liberation* (Maryknoll, N.Y.: Orbis, 1985), 8.

[2] Sharon D. Welch, *After Empire: The Art and Ethos of Enduring Peace* (Minneapolis: Fortress, 2004), 1–11.

[3] Welch, *After Empire*, 2.

the church (she does not say which church) and actively supported the families of gays, lesbians, and bisexuals, and defended their rights. She says that "their ministry was pastoral and political. . . . The variant of Christianity that they followed rejected the division of sacred and profane and claimed that all is spiritual. The heart of their life and work was clear: building the kingdom of God on earth."[4] She says she could not have had better role models.

The way Welch narrates her story is interesting because she intersperses her academic work and political activities with short vignettes of caring for her children and beholding the wonder and awe of new life in the face of society's injustices and violence. For both exist—the beautiful and the immoral. She would confess later that she was initially outraged when she discovered that Jacques Derrida, in response to the violence of apartheid in South Africa, had said the only real basis of political critique was aesthetics. She thought this was a blatant, moral disregard for the evils of racism. But after rereading scholars like Dietrich Bonhoeffer, she became more sympathetic to Derrida's position and realized that "[a]esthetics is a key component of ethics."[5] Perhaps it was Derrida's insight that helped her narrate her own life as shaped by a tension between academic, moral reflections on the one hand and the coos of her baby girls on the other.

Welch has been a social and political activist all her life, for which she credits her parents. But activism is also rooted in her view of spirituality. Although her ethic is lodged within the Christian tradition, it is at the same time shaped by the following three forces: African American Christianity and humanism, Native American traditions, and Buddhism.[6] Yet she is careful about claiming and embracing identity with traditions in which she is not at home. The only way this is

responsible, she claims, is to see in the tradition of another something that already exists in the very core of your own being. And this is what she identifies as having learned from her parents, who did not sacrifice themselves for the sake of the other, but were able to celebrate and relish larger selves in which all could flourish.

In the 1970s and 1980s Welch, was involved in protesting the nuclear arms race. In this process, she gradually began to see ethics in a new light. It was not as though ethics was all about setting a goal of peace and then developing a strategy for how to bring it about; for example, how to put an end to racism, militarism, class exploitation, and sexism. She learned, especially from African American ethicists, poets, and novelists, that an ethic of control lay at the roots of most Western ethical thought, and hence could not possibly be part of the solution. The alternative was an ethic of risk; and risk had to do with giving up control and being able to live comfortably in ambiguity. And here she found moral courage from unusual sources, like jazz.

We have already seen that ethics of liberation, from Gustavo Gutiérrez to Rosemary Radford Ruether, have sought to overcome the traditional structures of binary thought—sacred/profane, history/nature, fact/value, and so on. Welch is no exception, although perhaps she is more radical in her rejection of binary thought structures. For she also finds notions like true/false, good/bad, right/wrong, to be unhelpful, because they are too judgmental and hence too exclusive. We will see later that this will have implications for how she conceives of the project of peacemaking itself.

Her own "political location" has connected her with peace and women's groups at universities, both while she was a student and after she became a teacher. She was involved

---

[4] Welch, *After Empire*, 2–3.
[5] Sharon D. Welch, *Sweet Dreams in America: Making Ethics and Spirituality Work* (New York: Routledge, 1999), 119. Welch cites Jacques Derrida, "Racism's Last Word," *Critical Inquiry* 12, no. 1 (1985): 290–99.
[6] See Welch, *After Empire*, 4.

in women's communities at Vanderbilt University and Harvard Divinity School, as well as with the peace communities there. In addition, she was active in the Memphis Nuclear Weapons Freeze Campaign while she was a student at Vanderbilt.

Welch did her graduate studies at Vanderbilt University in Nashville, Tennessee, where she earned both M.A. and Ph.D. degrees. She has held several academic teaching posts, including assistant and later associate professor of theology and religion and society at Harvard Divinity School from 1982 to 1991. From 1991 to 2007, she served as director and professor of women's and gender studies and professor and chair of religious studies at the University of Missouri, and since 2007 she has been provost and professor of religion and society at Meadville Lombard Theological School (Unitarian Universalist) in Chicago.[7]

Welch has written five books and many articles and received many awards, including an honorary degree of doctor of sacred theology from Starr King School of Ministry in 2007. She is considered a mentor to many, especially many younger, American feminists.

THEOLOGICAL ORIENTATION

Welch's thought goes through stages of development, especially as she continues to explore the aesthetic and literary traditions alongside her political and ethical research. She is conscious of the moral failings in history, many of which implicate her own nation. She mentions five historical events that have been significant to her as she is pushed to move ever further from a "Pax American" to a "Pax Humana."[8]

The five events that demonstrate her claim that humanity has inherited a shameful history are:

1. The bombings of Hiroshima and Nagasaki, Japan, and the killings of two hundred thousand people without warning and for which the Americans were responsible;

2. The complicity as "bystanders" to the Jewish Holocaust, which was the stance of many nations, including the United States, during the Second World War;

3. The genocide of the American Indians by the American government and many other American institutions, including the churches;

4. The horrors of the socialist regimes with leaders such as Vladimir Lenin (1870–1924), Joseph Stalin (1878–1953), and Mao Tse-tung (1893–1976);

5. The abuses of power in an effort to bring about social change, even among feminists and pacifists.

These five events are constant reminders of the dangers of intolerance and the need for people and groups to learn how to deal justly with difference and disagreements as well as how to embody our own ideals.

As general guiding principles that she says have governed her life's work in an effort to live justly and joyously with difference and seek to avoid the tragedies of history, she states two absolutes. The first is as follows: *"under conditions of even a modicum of justice, life is wondrous, rich, and profoundly meaningful, a glorious gift to be celebrated and cherished."*[9] Her second absolute is: *"I and every person, movement, group, and institution that I trust can be deeply, profoundly, tragically wrong. Not only can we be wrong in minor ways, but our best ideals can be used to justify cruelty and violence."*[10] She notes that the first absolute speaks of wonder and beauty and the second warns of horrific brutality. Hence two poles—aesthetics and politics-ethics—need each other and are at work throughout Welch's writings.

Welch's early work sets out a trajectory for her larger project. She says the West faces a "fundamental crisis in Christian theology," both a moral and an intellectual crisis. Intellectually, the "masters of suspicion,"

---

[7] From the Meadville Lombard Theological School website, http://meadville.edu/Ab_Fac_Welch.htm, accessed May 2011.

[8] Welch entitles the Preface to her *After Empire*, "Pax Americana, Pax Humana," suggesting a peace that is "for" only one nation cannot be a just peace.

[9] Welch, *After Empire*, 7 (emphasis in original).

[10] Welch, *After Empire*, 10–11 (emphasis in original).

[11] Welch, *Communities of Resistance*, 2.

Friedrich Nietzsche, Karl Marx, Sigmund Freud, and Ludwig Feuerbach, have raised for us the doubts about a real referent to theological language. Welch adds another suspicionist, the radical feminist, Mary Daly, whom she quotes as saying "patriarchy is the prevailing religion of the entire planet and its essential message is necrophilia."[11] In other words, as Daly and Welch see it, Christianity has become escapist and is more interested in a "dead" transcendence ("necrophilia" literally means "love of corpse") than in the real lives of people in this world. Try as they might, modern, liberal theologians have not been able to mount a successful refutation of Feuerbach's view that religion is projection and not based in the real world. Hence, the conceptual crisis.

However, the moral crisis of the Christian faith is even more dangerous than the conceptual one. Drawing on the work of Paul Johnson, she says, "The atrocities of the Inquisition, the witchburnings, the Crusades, the justification of imperialism and colonialism, the perpetuation of sexism, racism, and anti-Semitism, the silence of most churches in the face of the horrors of war and the Nazi holocaust should cause even the most committed Christian to question the truth of Christianity's claims."[12] Hence, her point of departure is the belief that in the modern world both the Christian faith and its practice are in serious peril.

Yet all is not lost. Welch believes that "feminist liberation theology" is a way out of this crisis, because it offers a critique of liberal theology at both the conceptual and moral levels. Its approach to theology emphasizes "practice," and more particularly the practice of liberation.

The feminism Welch embraces is distinct. All liberation theologians speak of a "liberating God." Yet they do not all do so in the same way. Some emphasize "God" when using this phrase and others emphasize "liberation." It is with the latter liberationists that Welch identifies. She makes her point by referring to the Salvadoran theologian, Jon Sobrino.[13] Sobrino was once asked whether the persecuted people of El Salvador ever questioned the existence of God. He replied that they did not. They knew that the God of liberation existed, in the same way that they knew of the existence of other gods—the god of capitalism and the god of the state security system. These gods required the sacrifice of real lives. The important question for the poor people of El Salvador was whether the God of liberation would be given the power to save the people from death or whether the worship of "false" gods would continue, and thereby continue the suffering and sacrifice of innocent lives.

Welch points out that this way of speaking about God is characteristically different from the way it was traditionally done. Sobrino speaks of the "'gods' in terms of their function in people's lives, not in terms of their correspondence to something about the divine nature in itself."[14] This is the way she speaks of God.

Welch reads liberation theology largely through two additional forces: feminist spirituality and the writings of two philosophers, Michel Foucault (1926–1984) and Jürgen Habermas (b. 1929). She states that although feminist spirituality does not engage in explicit God-talk, it is nevertheless religious because "it does refer to dimensions of ultimacy."[15] What she especially likes about the language of feminist spirituality is that it is concerned about actual, historical processes of liberation and resistance. Here it is Foucault who has influenced her most.

With Foucault, Welch discovers ways of speaking about an *epistemic* shift—a shift in the account of how we come to know things—that has radically questioned the tradition of Western thought. Foucault offers us an explanation "of the collapse of the

---

[12] Welch, *Communities of Resistance*, 4.
[13] Welch, *Communities of Resistance*, 7.

[14] Welch, *Communities of Resistance*, 7–8.
[15] Welch, *Communities of Resistance*, 8.

meaning of language, and of its relation to reality."[16] What is this account?

Foucault argues, in his *The Order of Things*,[17] that the very structure of knowledge which was thought to be reliable in the past actually consists of a constantly shifting set of factors involving political, self-interested, and other tradition-based authorities. Hence, our claims to knowledge are in fact quite different from what we have taken them to be. They are not at all rooted in an ontologically given reality as the tradition has led us to believe. We have been taught that truth and knowledge are politically neutral. This is not so, says Foucault. Truth is concretely historical, self-interested, and political. Welch summarizes him, saying, "In his work, truth is removed from the realm of the absolute and is thoroughly historicized."[18]

The import of this language of truth is profound. We can no longer speak of "discovering truth," we must instead speak of the practice of truth. In the past, we believed that we changed our behavior as we came to know new things. Now, according to Foucault, we come to see things in new and different ways when we adopt new practices of behavior. How truth is determined and who determines it are what govern the power sufficient to accept something as true.

Welch, with Foucault, accepts a kind of epistemological relativism which embraces order only insofar as it is rooted in the experience of order we impose upon reality. We can no longer believe in a universal system which orders our experiences. In other words, since systems are made by us, they must serve us, not we them. This experience of order is not static and therefore not a secure basis for thought and action. "It is rather a seething mass of contradictions, and as more definitively pointed out in his later works, it is an arena of conflict between different powers, a literal struggle not only of knowledge per se, but also a struggle that determines who will live and how, and a struggle that determines who will die, and for what 'grand cause.'"[19]

Jürgen Habermas, the German social philosopher, is the other philosopher upon whom Welch draws. She argues that Habermas is right in combining both pluralism and social responsibility.[20] That is, Habermas reminds us of the important pedagogical utility of encountering other moral communities. In this regard, Welch prefers Habermas to Alasdair MacIntyre, whom she takes to defend the adequacy of a particular community-tradition like the Aristotelian polis over against others. In MacIntyre's system, Welch fears, difference is a problem because it must eventually be absorbed or out-narrated. Habermas, on the other hand, gives a more helpful account of the systematic distortion of communication within liberal society. Nevertheless, when all is said and done, Habermas does not develop an adequate strategy for the emancipation of subjugated knowledges.[21] In the end, Welch prefers Foucault's approach over Habermas'.

LIBERATION THEOLOGY

Sharon Welch calls herself a "feminist, white, middle-class, American Christian theologian."[22] This self-location determines much of what she has to say about the nature of theology. Her starting point is the confession that theology is political and that therefore theologians must take into account the notions of politics, such as power, ideology, biased rationalities, struggle, solidarity, and

---

[16] Welch, *Communities of Resistance*, 9.

[17] Michel Foucault, *The Order of Things: An Archaeology of Knowing and the Discourse on Language* (New York: Vintage, 1973).

[18] Welch, *Communities of Resistance*, 10.

[19] Welch, *Communities of Resistance*, 13.

[20] See Sharon Welch, "A Genealogy of the Logic of Deterrence: Habermas, Foucault and a Feminist Ethic of Risk," *Union Seminary Quarterly Review* 41, no. 2 (1987): 13–32; and also Sharon D. Welch, *A Feminist Ethic of Risk* (Minneapolis: Fortress, 1990), 127ff.   [22] Welch, *Communities of Resistance*, ix.

[21] Welch, *Feminist Ethic of Risk*, 131.

strategy. This leads her to struggle with several tensions, the most basic of which is that of power and knowledge. She questions the "Western form of the will to know" especially its "correlation with elitism and oppression."[23] In so doing, she develops a "theology of resistance." It is here that the work of Foucault and her view of liberation theology converge.[24] Foucault helps Welch to see how one can be a liberation theologian and at the same time white, middle class, and from the Northern hemisphere. The solution for the tricky union of the theologies of the North and the South is found in the articulation of a new epistemology. As Welch puts it, "The warrants and truth-claims of these theologies diverge sharply from those of traditional theology."[25]

To give account of this "new way of doing theology," she appeals to Gustavo Gutiérrez, Jon Sobrino, and Dorothee Sölle. Like all liberation theologians, these three speak of the shift in theological adjudication that has taken place from theory to practice. This means that if theology is not sound "praxis," it is not sound theology. Quoting Sölle, Welch says, "The truth of Christ exists only as concrete realization, which means: the verification principle of every theological statement is the praxis that it enables for the future. Theological statements contain as much truth as they deliver practically in transforming reality."[26]

We should note that with this new point of departure, we encounter some stark implications for theological grounding. A concern for practice has superseded all quests for theoretical clarity and universal truth seeking, whether ontological, metaphysical, anthropological, or whatever. In addition,

Welch draws the following conclusions regarding the traditional sources of theology:

> To use scripture and the person and work of Jesus as criteria for faith and theological reflection, while definitely more particular than to use ontological structures as points of evaluation, is still to avoid the costs and risks of history. I will not ground a feminist theology of liberation in either scripture or in the person and work of Jesus. To do either would be to abdicate liberation theology's uniqueness. . . .[27]

It is clear from this account of the agenda of liberation theology that the traditional anchors of theology have been discarded in favor of autonomous praxis. There is nothing that defines liberation theology; it gets defined in the struggle for the "battle of truth." And in this, Welch goes considerably further than the Latin Americans—Gutiérrez and Sobrino—whom she quotes. Their claim is that it is the right understanding of the biblical canon, and especially of Jesus Christ, that enables them to arrive at the tenets of liberation theology. She is suggesting that it is liberation theology that allows her to assess the value of the canon and the work of Jesus. And since there are no nonexperiential bases for theology, there is no surety in Welch's program; it remains a radical theology of risk.

On this model, there is, properly speaking, not just one liberation theology, but many, each with its own grounding in the solidarity experiences of specific oppressions and the liberation struggles peculiar to a specific solidarity group. Hence she says, "Feminist theology is grounded in the liberating experience of sisterhood, in the process of liberation from sexism; Latin American theologies of liberation are grounded in the resistance

---

[23] Welch, *Communities of Resistance*, 21.

[24] Welch says, "Foucault's work complements that done by liberation theologians in two ways. First, Foucault is aware of the representative role of ostensibly liberating forms of discourse. . . . Second, Foucault is committed to challenging oppression (he writes of the insurrection of subjugated knowledges) and is thoroughly self-critical" (*Communities of Resistance*, 23).

[25] Welch, *Communities of Resistance*, 24.

[26] Welch, *Communities of Resistance*, 25. Quoted from Dorothee Soelle, *Political Theology*, trans. John Shelley (Philadelphia: Fortress, 1974), 76.   [27] Welch, *Communities of Resistance*, 25.

and solidarity within base Christian communities."[28] The only defining characteristic of a liberation theology is the a priori commitment to the overcoming of a particular oppression. Social and political emancipation are the sole criteria of truth.

Welch's articulation of the grounding of liberation theology offers a profound critique of traditional theology. The most powerful perhaps is the failure of traditional theology to recognize that it too is political. Its embrace of theology-as-universal-discourse is itself a political act—intentional or not—resulting in untold oppression of those whom it excludes. Since it claims universality. it should include all; since it does not include all, those who are excluded are theologically dispossessed. It is this practice of oppression that has falsified theology, and it is this falsification Welch seeks to correct.

Welch suggests that the temptation to universal discourse lies behind every theology—even liberation theology. One of the most tantalizing "perils of theological discourse" stems from the failure to recognize the transitory nature of theological language itself. Just because one way of speaking may produce liberation does not mean it always will. Language must adapt itself to current oppression and its real resolution.

Welch's brand of liberation theology demands a sensitivity to the political use and abuse of theological discourse through the memory of past oppressions. And this injects two fundamental categories into her approach to theology—skepticism and risk. It is impossible to trust even one's own certainties "once basic myths and ideals have been exposed as illusory and ideological."[29] Hence, suspicion becomes the methodology of liberation theology rooted in an ever-present consciousness of a memory of past oppressions.

Liberation theology's new criterion of truth—practice—also points to the roots of the failure of traditional theology. Welch argues that Christianity did not fail because it could not handle the intellectual debates generated by the Enlightenment. Here it was quite successful. Quoting from Johann Baptist Metz, she states that, "The failure of Christianity is the failure of practice, a failure to transform the corruption and inhumanity of the world. The failure of Christendom is not a failure of intellectual understanding, but a failure to establish in practice its vision of the human community."[30] The challenge that this acknowledgement provides is the reinterpretation of all theology within a new political matrix of liberation. This means locating the very source of theology within the communities of resistance—a resistance fostered by "dangerous memories."

A dangerous memory is guided by both hope and suffering. Welch cites James Cone as an example of what she means. Cone identifies racism as the sin of the church in the sense that it makes a mockery of the very notion of church. She quotes him as saying "racism implies the absence of fellowship and service, which are primary qualities, indispensable marks of the church. To be racist is to fall outside the definition of the church."[31] Wherein does hope lie? According to Cone, "with the One who is the Author of black faith and existence."[32] That is, oppressed black Christians can find hope as they live in resistance to their poverty and oppression; as they remember that the story of the Egyptian slaves, who were miraculously liberated, is in fact their story. Hope lies in their solidarity of refusal to accept as inevitable and natural the oppression that is currently theirs through no choice of their own. Their memory of the actuality of

[28] Welch, *Communities of Resistance*, 25.
[29] Welch, *Communities of Resistance*, 30.
[30] Welch, *Communities of Resistance*, 33.
[31] Welch, *Communities of Resistance*, 36. Taken from James Cone, *Black Theology and Black Power* (New York: Seabury, 1969), 73. For a further discussion of the writings of James Cone, see chap. 27 above.
[32] Welch, *Communities of Resistance*, 41.

liberations past is the basis of both their current hope and resistance.

According to Welch, resistance is rooted in what Foucault calls "the insurrection of subjugated knowledges." Foucault's genealogy is committed to emancipating "historical knowledges from that subjection, to render them, that is, capable of opposition and of struggle against the coercion of a theoretical, unitary, formal and scientific discourse."[33] In other words, the very idea of resistance is premised upon the development of a language and memory housed in an alternative, strategic knowledge which alone can sustain it. Conversely, the very roots of oppression lie within a universal discourse and a "scientific" knowledge which seeks to subjugate minority knowledges. In the process, there is little regard for the "primacy of the particular,"[34] allowing for the unchecked exercise of power. Power and knowledge are, in fact, not separable, as the scientific tradition would like us to believe. Foucault says, "The exercise of power perpetually creates knowledge and, conversely, knowledge constantly induces effects of power."[35] And so Welch says, "My critique [of traditional epistemologies] focuses on the particular result of a given apparatus of power/knowledge and not the relation of power/knowledge per se."[36] And the particular power she advocates is the "power of relatedness." She issues no call for justice in general, but only the concrete embodiment of particular, just, social structures. Justice, like ethics, is practice.

THE PRACTICE OF ETHICS

It would be unfair to Welch's work on ethics if we did not present its practical import. Although it is true that Welch remains an intellectual even as she calls for the practical—the nemesis of all academic ethicists—she nevertheless addresses many social issues. The issue which preoccupies her most is the nuclear arms race and its interconnections with sexism.

Welch wrote two essays on this topic. In 1985 she wrote that "the nuclear arms race is a test of faith."[37] She argues persuasively that although the arms race is a problem for all people, it is a special kind of problem for Christians. It is a "test of faith" not in the sense that it forces us to ask, "Are we true to the Christian tradition?" This is not the real challenge of truth since the Christian tradition itself has been an accomplice to the war-rationalizing imagination in history. Instead, the important question is, "Is the Christian tradition true itself?"[38] That is, is the rationality and practice of the Christian faith in fact sustainable; or even, what is this rationality and practice?

Welch points out that the arms race is not merely the product of an idea rooted in the mind of politicians or even in the collective mind of government; it is a "particular type of rationality and sociality"[39] embodied by an entire people. It is a comprehensive way of thinking and being, and the question is whether it can sustain life. She speaks of an alternative: "I find in sisterhood, in the peace movement, and in some religious communities an 'insurrection of subjugated knowledges' (to use the phrasing of Foucault), a type of knowing and being that challenges not only the nuclear arms race, but stands in opposition to the entire apparatus, the system of rationality and sociality, that makes nuclear war and the moral and economic costs of an escalating arms race possible."[40] What is at stake here is not just a decision of whether one is for or against war, but an alternative way of thinking and living.

---

[33] Welch, *Communities of Resistance*, 55.

[34] Welch, *Communities of Resistance*, 75.

[35] Welch, *Communities of Resistance*, 63.

[36] Welch, *Communities of Resistance*, 64.

[37] Sharon Welch, "The Nuclear Arms Race as a Test of Faith," *Union Seminary Quarterly Review* 40, no. 1–2 (1985): 37–46.

[38] Welch, "Nuclear Arms Race," 37.

[39] Welch, "Nuclear Arms Race," 38.

[40] Welch, "Nuclear Arms Race," 38.

The rationality of the arms race is rooted in an understanding and exercise of power not unrelated to the imagination of sexism. In her 1987 essay, she spells out the "logic of deterrence,"[41] and offers a feminist critique. Drawing upon the work of other feminists like Carol Gilligan, Mary Daly, Beverly Harrison, Simone de Beauvoir, Rosemary Radford Ruether, and Carter Heyward, Welch contrasts the values of feminism and masculinism. Women are "concerned with responsibilities to others and to self, in contrast to a masculine preoccupation with rights as the measure of ethical obligation."[42] They are drawn to "an ethic of care and connectedness." Hence, feminists critique patriarchal forms of power as control and domination. As an alternative, they advocate power "as the ability to persuade, to enable others to act creatively, being able to exist in a mutually reciprocal relationship with the rest of the world."[43]

In explicating the meaning of power within Western society, she relies, not surprisingly by now, on Foucault's work. He has argued that in the West we understand power primarily as "disciplinary" and no longer in its classical form as "deduction." In his book, *Power/Knowledge*, he describes this transition in terms of a move to associate power with the quest for the normal, for the universal, for control and the management of the forces around us.[44] This has brought with it a shift in the understanding of the enemy. No longer do we see a sovereign of a particular state as the enemy, but an entire people as the enemy; that is, a people other than us. In parallel logic, no longer is only the king in need of subjugation and destruction, but the entire system that supports an enemy people: the economic, social, political, and educational infrastructures. Our way of life is threatened by a rival way of life, because it has become unimaginable that another way of life could possibly be worth living. Universal logic prohibits this. This type of rationality, Welch argues, characterizes the language of the "cold war."

How did we in the West come to think and live this way? Welch suggests that we have come to accept as good a way of life that can only be sustained with a view of power as domination. Since our lifestyle demands the use of a disproportionate amount of the earth's resources, it can only be sustained by a disproportionate amount of power. Having what does not belong to us cannot forever be sustained by the good will of those who suffer from our greed. It can only be sustained by power as domination. Hence, for the West, security and domination have become inextricably linked.

Welch argues that the linkage of power and domination leads directly to the notion of "total security." Moreover, when universality is the language of truth, the assurance of total security can only be guaranteed through the threat of total war. This is why the doctrine of Mutually Assured Destruction (MAD) is the logical outcome of such rationality, and why disarmament is literally inconceivable. On this model, disarmament produces insecurity and the likelihood of destruction, whereas the threat of total war produces security and a lesser probability of war.

A major problem with this logic, according to Welch, is the assumption of the possibility of total security. It is itself a grand illusion, albeit inevitable in a "disciplinary society."[45] Not surprisingly, an illusory aim of this nature requires what Habermas calls "systematically distorted communication" by the institutions which promote it. Welch puts it this way, "Not only do we have the pursuit of an illusory aim—total security—but this aim is pursued by a policy of deliberate deception."[46]

---

[41] Welch, "A Genealogy," 13–32.
[42] Welch, "A Genealogy," 15.
[43] Welch, "A Genealogy," 15.
[44] Welch, "A Genealogy," 16. Also see Michel Foucault, *Power/Knowledge: Selected Interviews and Other Writings 1972–1977* (New York: Pantheon, 1980), 104–8.
[45] Welch, "A Genealogy," 22.
[46] Welch, "A Genealogy," 22.

Deception here functions on two levels, according to Welch. First, we must create the "perception of readiness" by giving the impression that we are ready to use nuclear weapons in a wide variety of ways and not just in a full-scale nuclear war. This might be called a strategy of deception, and in fact has proved to be one of the most destabilizing factors in the whole arms race. Second, there is the moral deception. "To protect our highest moral values, we contemplate the most immoral act in history—the slaughter of all human life. Merely to analyze the policy of deterrence without naming this horror—this intent to kill the innocent, to destroy life on the planet—is to perpetuate the horror, and is to participate in its condition of possibility."[47] This form of rationality requires us to think and behave as if we are willing to destroy all life on this earth. This is the very antithesis of morality, and yet it gets paraded as the moral equivalence of goodness because it is put forward as a policy of security and life's protection.

It should not be surprising that there are many additional deceptive arguments such as the winnability of a limited nuclear war, or that it is better to lose twenty-five million lives than two hundred and fifteen lives, or that it is better to be dead than red.[48] Deception is simply a required practice for the sustaining of an illusory reality. Moreover, for power to be most effective, it must be masked.[49]

Welch identifies two benefits of this kind of analysis. First, to unmask that which is hidden is always better than to keep it disguised because it can then be seen for what it really is. Second, since, according to Foucault, we best recognize a "system of logic" when it is

not our own, it is important to expose it. In naming it, it becomes objectified and thereby enables the overcoming of a subjective (blind) attachment. Yet the most important reason for naming the "logic of deterrence" is to advocate an alternative which Welch calls a "feminist ethic of risk."[50] Feminists are especially well suited to analyze and reject this approach because it is not theirs. Deterrence logic is the logic of patriarchy. "To describe this as patriarchal does not only mean that it is men who execute these policies, but that the power exercised is of a particular sort: the aim is total control; part of the motivation is fear of finitude, of relatedness, of vulnerability."[51] Hence "risk" is the alternative.

A FEMINIST ETHIC OF RISK

One of the myths Welch seeks to debunk is that "there are things worth dying for." Actually, the military uses this slogan deceptively to suggest that there are things worth killing millions of people for; perhaps the whole human race. She says, "[f]rom a feminist perspective, the ethic of 'things worth dying for' appears as an ethic of cowardice, as the choice of killing over the challenge of sustained resistance to oppression."[52] The moral question, she maintains, is whether "there are things worth *living* for." She is careful not to appear to be arguing for the absolute prevention of nuclear war, or any other morally lofty end for that matter. This is not the primary drive of a feminist ethic since such strategies could only emanate from an ethic of control; she advocates an ethic of risk.

An "ethic of risk" is rooted in "sheer holy boldness."[53] This means that the moral strategy of action does not entail a step-by-step projection, assurance, or even an

---

[47] Welch, "A Genealogy," 23.

[48] See Welch, "A Genealogy," 24; and "Nuclear Arms Race," 39.

[49] Welch, "A Genealogy," 24.

[50] Welch, "A Genealogy," 25.

[51] Welch, "A Genealogy," 24.

[52] Welch, "A Genealogy," 25.

[53] Welch borrows the phrase "sheer holy boldness" from Toni Cade Bambara, *The Salt Eaters* (New York: Random House, 1980). See Welch, "A Genealogy," 26.

understanding, of how, or whether, victory will be achieved. Action is rather rooted in the conviction that resistance to evil is necessary, since the only alternative is to capitulate to it. "To stop resisting, even if success is unimaginable, is to die."[54] Responsible action is rooted in a community of resistance, driven by the strategy of risk-taking, in order to expose and overcome oppression. From this she concludes, "The aim is simple; given that we cannot guarantee an end to racism nor nuclear war, we *can* prevent our own capitulation to structured evil."[55] And again, "We cannot determine the shape of the future; we can only do our part to make it possible for there to *be* a future by refusing to act as the agents of nuclear annihilation. We can only do our part to provide models of responsible action and restraint."[56] The modern craze of needing-to-*do*-something, and the simultaneous realization that there is nothing that we can do to ensure a permanent state of peace and justice, fuels a culture of despair far too evident in our society, particularly among the middle class. What is needed is an alternative view of moral agency.

Welch positions herself in relation to other theologians of this century. She is critical of both the liberal and postliberal theologians. She applauds the liberals for their inherent theological skepticism and their critique of "conservative" theologies, especially those which rest upon Scripture, doctrine, and tradition. She also lauds liberals for their responsiveness to human suffering.[57] Yet she would like to see them be as critical regarding their anthropology as they are regarding their theology. Their failure to be self-critical at this point permits them to sneak in universal assumptions about human nature which are not warranted and which foster oppression.

Postliberal theologians fare only slightly better. Relying upon George Lindbeck's *The Nature of Doctrine*,[58] she suggests that postliberals are right in rejecting the liberal's supposition that religion can be understood on the basis of a universally common experience. Nevertheless, Lindbeck's proposal that religion and theology function as a cultural-linguistic enterprise has two fatal flaws: it does not take into account the "theologian's own social and political location within this cultural-linguistic matrix" nor does it take seriously enough "the possibility that the 'grammar of faith' is itself oppressive."[59] Hence, whatever values there may be with Lindbeck's project, according to Welch, it is unable to ensure liberation.

Yet the strongest criticisms of liberalism appear when Welch discusses the enslavement of Western thought generally to the "erotics of domination."[60] "A theology that valorizes absolute power through its concept of an omnipotent God is dangerous for middle-class people."[61] Although the *conceptual* impact of the doctrine of the sovereignty (omnipotence) of God is to relativize human power, its *political* effect is to glorify and even absolutize it, especially for those who are already the powerful ones. Welch cites in her defense the great process philosopher/theologian Alfred North Whitehead, who considers the notion of absolute power an evil rather than a good, a notion the ancients adopted when fashioning an understanding of God's power after that of the ancient, imperial kings. Absolute power is evil because it assumes that to act apart from connectedness and community, that is, with disregard for the other, is good, when in fact it is deeply dehumanizing and hence evil. Absolute power not only idealizes exclusivity; it also

---

[54] Welch, "A Genealogy," 26.

[55] Welch, "A Genealogy," 29 (emphasis in original).

[56] Welch, *Feminist Ethic of Risk*, 26–27 (emphasis in original).

[57] She cites the following liberal theologians, Edward Farley, David Tracy, and Gordon Kaufman (Welch, *Feminist Ethic of Risk*, 105).

[58] George A. Lindbeck, *The Nature of Doctrine: Religion and Theology in a Postliberal Age* (Philadelphia: Westminster, 1984).

[59] Welch, *Feminist Ethic of Risk*, 106.

[60] Welch, *Feminist Ethic of Risk*, 111ff.

[61] Welch, *Feminist Ethic of Risk*, 111.

legitimate submission and domination of others.

Welch draws on an essay by Elaine Pagels (b. 1943) contrasting John Chrysostom's and Augustine's exegesis of Genesis 1–3 to argue that the modern view of power-as-domination has its roots in Augustine's writings.[62] According to Pagels, for Augustine the effects of the "fall of Adam" were so drastic that a government's use of violence was indispensable in order to defend against the impact of human evil, even if that government were tyrannical. Says Pagels, "[l]ater in his life Augustine came to endorse, for the Church as well as the state, the whole arsenal of secular government that Chrysostom had repudiated—commands, threats, coercion, penalties, and even physical force."[63] According to both Welch and Pagels, this led Augustine not only to advocate the use of coercive powers against dissenting Christians, but also to use the language of power-as-domination to explicate the very core of the Christian faith; both in defining the character of God as well as speaking of our salvation in terms of our submissiveness to the absolute power of God. Hence, it is not surprising that the association of human bondage and salvation became definitive for orthodoxy. Says Welch, "[i]t is a view of human weakness and divine power that has had disastrous effects in Western history."[64] Rather than being an agent of liberation, the church has come to see its task as similar to that of the state, namely, to *control* (that is, not liberate) sinful human beings.

With very few exceptions, most notably Dietrich Bonhoeffer, mainline theologians, along with states like the Third Reich and the American government, have accepted this view of power. Welch singles out three such theologians: Paul Tillich, Karl Barth, and H. Richard Niebuhr. All of them explicitly attempt to show how we can be saved by God's

power and our submission. Each endeavors to identify a domain of power proper to God and proper to humans. Evil is then viewed in terms of stepping outside of this domain, for example, when human beings do that which belongs to God. Each has proper power in separate domains—God in the spiritual realm and humans in the social-political realm. Yet this way of thinking about God and ourselves fails because it is rooted in the "valorization of absolute power" model. It ultimately projects a view of moral agency premised on the belief that on earth everything depends on us. Unless we are given unlimited powers to implement our "program of justice," our submission (defense) of almighty God is not adequate. Being just on the small scale is of little value on this model. The alternative model Welch suggests is called an ethic of "solidarity and difference," which she develops further in her subsequent writings.

PEACE AND JUSTICE MAKING

Welch's thought goes through a process of refinement as she continues to explore the aesthetic and literary traditions alongside her political and ethical agenda. We need only to note her recent titles, and especially the subtitles of her books, to observe these themes: *Sweet Dreams in America: Making Ethics and Spirituality* Work (1999); *After Empire: The Art and Ethics of Enduring Peace* (2004); and, *Real Peace, Real Security: The Challenges of Global Citizenship* (2007).

The strategy in Welch's mature work is to develop the imagination of hope that takes seriously that we have some power in the moral chaos around us and that some change is possible in the midst of contingency. This calls for more than mere resistance, which is the limitation of many peace movements; it calls for the developing of new coalitions and for building new institutions without falling into the pitfalls of an ethic of control. She

---

[62] Welch, *Feminist Ethic of Risk*, 112ff. See also Elaine Pagels, "The Politics of Paradise: Augustine's Exegesis of Genesis 1–3 versus That of John Chrysostom," *Harvard Theological Review* 78, no. 1–2 (1985): 67–99.

[63] Welch, *Feminist Ethic of Risk*, 112–13. From Elaine Pagels, "The Politics of Paradise," 89.

[64] Welch, *Feminist Ethic of Risk*, 113.

reflects on what happened in South Africa. It was not enough that the apartheid regime was overthrown through massive world protest and that the key figure of the resistance— Nelson Mandela—became its president. The really important challenge was to determine what kind of president he ought to be in order to establish South Africa as a just and peaceful nation. It was not as though South Africa had suddenly become an undivided nation free from conflict. The real test of responsible peace-building has to do with understanding difference, negotiating its tensions, and permitting its full expression without violence. She notes that difference is not the same as tolerance; it is instead serious engagement with the other as other. This is not an easy skill to learn and requires what she calls "diversity training." Such training is especially important in democracies; in fact, it is the very ground of democracy.

Welch admits that she has been influenced by jazz in her understanding of ethics. She finds here an aesthetic style characterized by ambiguity and improvisation. Social ethics is like that, and hence, diversity training is all the more important and goes beyond the notion of "safe space" which has sometimes been advocated by feminists. The idea of a "safe space" for women was intended to encourage women to be genuinely open in a protected place. The problem Welch identifies, however, is that "safety is predicated on uniformity,"[65] and diversity presupposes risk, and democracies must value diversity.

Welch identifies five assumptions that underlie diversity training within a democracy.

1. Democracy is a goal that is both worthwhile and difficult to achieve. 2. Bias, exclusion, discrimination, exploitation, and oppression are pervasive and hurt everyone. 3. People and institutions do grow and change. 4. What motivates change is

accountability, not guilt. 5. Establishing justice and practicing democracy is a lifelong process.[66]

Welch calls us to learn to "see simultaneously yet differently." She says:

The ability to see and value difference is often misunderstood by those who focus on foundations of common ground, shared ideals, and same values. The ability to see simultaneously yet differently is better served by an acknowledgment of the relativism of our understandings of truth, justice, and beauty. Multicultural education helps us understand difference: it is the epistemology and pedagogy of politically engaged and politically accountable relativism.[67]

While relativism is often seen as a bad thing, Welch believes it is not. It is simply the acknowledgment that truth, value, goodness, and hope can only be known in relation to past and present contexts and future possibilities. We can know only in relation to contingent historical notions, and communities—sustainable people relations—can happen only in the contingency of time. To say this differently, communities are not created by uniformity or by the imposition of moral absolutes but by openness and appreciation of stories that can be told and heard because there is an appreciation of difference.

Welch resorts again to the work of Bonhoeffer to spell out the moral implications of her thoughts on seeing simultaneously yet differently. Bonhoeffer was able to act in a morally responsible manner precisely because he was able to overcome the fear of moral ambiguity. He realized that the reason that so many Germans were unable to do the right thing was because of their fear of moral ambiguity. Welch says, "resisting fascism required acting in ways that were themselves immoral. To be moral, to save Jews, required lying and deception, it required breaking the law; it might even lead, as it did in the case of Bonhoeffer, to the plan to murder Hitler."[68]

---

[65] Welch, *Sweet Dreams in America*, 84.
[66] Welch, *Sweet Dreams in America*, 85.
[67] Welch, *Sweet Dreams in America*, 62–63. She borrows the phrase "simultaneously yet differently" from Patricia J. Williams, *Alchemy of Race and Rights: Diary of a Law Professor* (Cambridge, Mass.: Harvard University Press, 1991).
[68] Welch, *Sweet Dreams in America*, 123.

In order to embrace the "art of ambiguity," Welch invites the reader into an "ethic without virtue." It may be tempting to read her view of moral and political ambiguity to be simply the arbitrary exercise of creativity and political power. But she is imagining something quite different. While this means that there is no foundation to moral action, or as she puts it, "[t]here are no principles, no rules, no authorities that can insure that genocide will be stopped, that the abuse of children will end, that men will stop raping and exploiting women,"[69] nevertheless, there are many times when we observe the decency of people. She continues:

> At times, we act with courage and compassion. We take risks, we learn from our mistakes, we respond appropriately to the needs of others. The alternative to fanaticism is simple: gratitude for joy and pleasure, mourning, rage, and resilience in the face of life's horrors. The mystery of human evil lies in peoples' attempts to hold on to the fragile gift of goodness; we try to make it binding, eternal, and absolute.[70]

There are those who will be unhappy with the vagueness and lack of content to Welch's ethic. Yet she freely acknowledges her commitment to a Kantian formalism here. She says that she is engaged in

> [A]n examination of what it means to live out Kantian ethical expectations in a world of continental limits. That is, we are still shaped by expectations of the categorical imperative ("Act only on that maxim through which you can at the same time will that it should become a universal law") and yet our very ability to act, the extent to which we are in any sense individuals, is itself historically and culturally constructed, malleable, and contested.[71]

She says it in another way as well: "How about a postmodern answer to Kant's three questions: What can I know? What may I hope? What must I do?"[72] Her answers to these questions are brief and interesting. Of course, in our postmodern world, the information explosion is such that we know more and more all the time, but we trust it less and less. Our hope is for resilience, endurance, companionship, respect, and celebrating life in the company of friends and colleagues.[73]

And what must we do? She says the following: "Here the postmodern ethos is clear, offering an image of power and chaos, of vitality and humor, as we learn to live fully and act creatively in the midst of a world we can never control and can only partially understand."[74]

In *After Empire*, Welch develops the "peace mandate" further by presenting a transformed view of political activism and an alternative political vision. The categories that guide her through this process are: laughter, virtuosity, respect, ceremony, audacity, and again risk.

Welch points out that the current American understanding of the social contract is inadequate because it is not based on the history and wisdom of all American peoples, particularly Native American history which is excluded from this account. Americans have much to learn from the notions of tribal sovereignty, sacred places, land, and especially about community. Communities cannot exist without ceremonies which heighten awareness and respect. "Ceremonies bring a people into honest and grateful connection."[75]

Welch relies on the poetry of Carol Lee Sanchez and Jace Weaver to bring out the disrespect of the American culture of greed and brutality that has been perpetrated upon American Native peoples. Both authors are careful in how they present the aboriginal story. They oppose beginning with the available atrocities committed against them because this suggests that "real" Indians have all been slaughtered and their cultures have been destroyed. They begin instead with the

---

[69] Welch, *Sweet Dreams in America*, 132.
[70] Welch, *Sweet Dreams in America*, 133.
[71] Welch, *Sweet Dreams in America*, xxi (in Preface).
[72] Welch, *Sweet Dreams in America*, 51.

[73] See Welch, *Sweet Dreams in America*, 51.
[74] Welch, *Sweet Dreams in America*, 51.
[75] Welch, *After Empire*, 54.

power of the culture that has continued to survive. There is power in aboriginal cultures that a militarized and controlling culture of America needs to hear.

Welch speaks of having encountered Buddhist monks in the mid-1980s when she was demonstrating against nuclear armament, but she confesses that it was only twenty years later that she began to understand and appreciate their witness. She says, "The presence of those gracious, calm, joyful monks was as much a challenge and gift to us angry peace demonstrators as they were to those who created and supported the creation of nuclear weapons. It is surprising that it has taken me so long to recognize this challenge and this gift."[76] She relies particularly on the work of Thich Nhat Hanh and Massao Abe for understanding of Buddhist peace protests. She opens herself to the challenge of Thich Nhat Hanh, who writes about American peacemakers as follows: "In the [American] peace movement there is a lot of anger, frustration, and misunderstanding. . . . The way you speak, the kind of understanding, the kind of language you use should not turn people off. The President is a person like any of us."[77]

Buddhism can offer this critique of American peacemakers because they do not share the American dualisms of good and evil, right and wrong. They are able to experience transcendence of the ordinary while remaining in it. They can be involved in political engagement with compassion and joy, not anger and hatred. It is possible for them to adopt this stance because they have overcome the dichotomy between us and them. So Welch can say that, for Buddhists, "Ethical action or compassion and wisdom do not spring primarily from the will or the intellect but from a changed perception of self and others."[78] As a summary of her thoughts, she says the model of political action she is proposing is neither "the ringing judgment of the prophet nor the confident witness of the martyr. Our model is, rather, the ironic vitality of the trickster, the audacity and connection of the artist, and the virtuosity of the jazz musician, playing with skill and verve the rhythms and risks of life."[79]

In the last chapter of *After Empire*, Welch returns to risk. This is a dominant theme in all of her writings. Risk is required to oppose war. The standard Western responses to the brutality of war have been the just-war tradition and pacifism. And while we desperately need both, she says that "Without other actions, however—without sustained, concerted attempt, to institutionalize means of preventing war—I question our creativity and wisdom."[80]

Contemporary peacemaking is an art form and not a science, not even a political science. She lauds the Global Action to Prevent War program and identifies its top two concerns: instead of waging war against an elusive enemy like al-Qaeda, they suggest that U.N. member nations should conduct international tribunals of al-Qaeda leaders for crimes against humanity. The other immediate action that they call for is for the United States to work with European and Muslim states to prepare proposals for the settlement of the Israeli-Palestinian conflict.

In order to make peace today, the world, and especially the United States, needs to be open to the risks of international cooperation. Of course, this is threatening to the current understanding of sovereignty, but this should not deter us. Why should our current definitions be normative for all time? She says, "Instead of asking, 'Are we so naïve as to think a Pax Humana, an international rule of law, is realistic?' let us ask, 'Are we daring enough and creative enough to find the political, cultural, and ethical resources to make it real?'"[81]

---

[76] Welch, *After Empire*, 133.
[77] Welch, *After Empire*, 134.
[78] Welch, *After Empire*, 149.

[79] Welch, *After Empire*, 157.
[80] Welch, *After Empire*, 161.
[81] Welch, *After Empire*, 172.

Welch argues that her way of thinking will lead us to see "the folly of empire."[82] For military and economic coercion are not the only powers that can bring about peace. She argues that when we call instead for many different forms of cooperative powers, the prospects of peace are infinitely enhanced. The kind of ethic that underlies this form of cooperative power she calls, via Danilo Perez, "an improvisational ethic." The process of improvising an alternative to empire requires the empowerment of the qualities of beauty, irony, suffering, and joy in the continued challenges of life.[83]

CONCLUSION

In 2009 Welch wrote a kind of overview article of her approach to social ethics in the Jewish magazine *Tikkun*. She says: "We are in the midst of a momentous paradigm shift in making peace and waging war. While there is widespread international support for multilateral armed intervention to protect peoples from genocide and crimes against humanity, there is equally widespread dissatisfaction with the legitimacy, morality, and even efficacy of traditional military intervention."[84] This is a hopeful sign. She notes that there are now mainstream political theorists who are questioning the power of violence. She says, "They challenge us to take seriously the limits of force to either maintain security or ensure compliance with cherished values, ideals, and institutions."[85]

She believes there is considerable political momentum supporting the idea of global citizenship. This would mean that conflict would be responded to through a threefold strategy of peacekeeping: early intervention to stop escalation, bringing hostile parties to the negotiating table, and creating structures for redressing injustices and resolving ongoing conflict. This "third way" entails a limited use of force to bring about peace. But just because it legitimates some force does not mean legitimating the use of violence as such. In fact, it is a critical stance toward the just-war theory and to holy war. For, she argues, "the value of peacekeeping is not in resolving a conflict, but in providing the space in which enduring security and sustainable peace may be created through the long-term nonviolent work of obtaining comprehensive political assent and participation."

This third way, as Welch sees it, is one between "waging war and nonviolent resistance." While it may well be difficult to figure out what this means in particular instances, it commits peacemakers to the ongoing process of envisioning new ideas, forming new coalitions, and to the activity of creative institution-building. This alone is a hopeful commitment to peace.

---

[82] Welch, *After Empire*, 172.
[83] See Welch, *After Empire*, 184.
[84] Sharon Welch, "Sharon D. Welch on the Path to Sustainable Peace," *Tikkun* (January 2009): 1.
[85] Welch, "Welch on the Path," 1.

Chapter Thirty-One

MERCY AMBA ODUYOYE
(1933–)

Mercy Oduyoye is often regarded as the most outstanding woman theologian in Africa. Of course, she comes from a particular part of Africa, the country of Ghana, in western Africa, and does not presume to speak as an African in general. She locates herself within the Akan community, itself consisting of several ethnic groups. The Akan comprise about two-fifths of Ghana's population and divide into two major groups, the Twi and the Fantse. The Asante, which are part of the Twi, form the cultural locus for Oduyoye's work. She says: "I cannot pretend to write about all of Africa, West Africa, or even Ghana. The living center of my study is the Akan of Ghana, and specifically the Asante, one of three major streams of Akan life. . . . But the sisterhood that has nourished [my work] spans the face of Africa."[1]

This geographical and cultural location of Oduyoye's work is important because it reminds us that Africa is a diverse place. It is not uncommon for Westerners to think of Africans as people with a uniform culture. But this is a relic of the colonial imagination.

A few words must be said about the African, colonial experience and the neocolonial reality (some speak of postcolonialism) out of which theologians like Oduyoye write. The era of colonialism dominated the region not only politically and economically but in virtually every other way as well. The terms in which knowledge was crafted, the way in which theology was written, thought, and practiced, even the ways in which art and images were validated, all were determined by the culture and imagination of the colonial powers.[2] Racism, sexism, and other forms of exploitation were rampant during this era and, from the colonialist viewpoint, normal. The colonial reality therefore left virtually no room for indigenous voices that did not speak to or out of this "foreign" context. None of this is to suggest that the cultural disrespect of colonialism is history. While post-apartheid reality in South Africa has changed some things for Africa, even today the colonial past and new forms of colonial practices shape much of the exchange—cultural, economic, political, and religious—with the Western world.

African feminists generally, and Oduyoye in particular, work within this neocolonial context and here address the long legacy of sexism, hierarchy, and racism they have inherited. In doing so, they butt up against many forces. Oduyoye highlights three in particular: sexism within their own traditions, the legacy of the racial and sexist policies and practices of colonialism in general, and the power of "colonial feminism."[3]

---

[1] Mercy Amba Oduyoye, *Daughters of Anowa: African Women and Patriarchy* (Maryknoll, N.Y.: Orbis, 1995), 6.

[2] See, e.g., Kwok Pui-Lan, "Mercy Amba Oduyoye and African Women's Theology," *Journal of Feminist Studies in Religion* 20 (22 March 2004), who relies on Edward W. Said, *Orientalism* (New York: Vintage, 1994) for an account of the philosophy and effects of colonialism on Africa.

[3] The term "colonial feminism" names the inclination to have feminists from foreign cultures set, for African feminists,

It becomes clear in her work that liberation from gender oppression is not an abstract social science but a struggle to find culturally embodied practices of liberation and justice. While this means that African feminists address practices particular to their culture, which include "women's roles and sexuality, such as polygamy, child marriage, veiling, female circumcision, and widowhood,"[4] it also means that the failure to appreciate the traditions and mythologies out of which these practices emerge, while simultaneously embodying life-giving qualities, can easily become counter-liberating.

The *theological* challenge for African feminist theologians is acute. Modern, Western missionaries have so confused the Christian gospel with Western culture that they have communicated "that the African woman needed to be domesticated: washed, clothed in garments that concealed her body, trained to work in the kitchen and become a housemaid in the European manner."[5] Moreover, women have typically not been invited into the same education and development opportunities as men. This has meant that women need to exert enormous energies and personal initiatives to become involved in writing theology.

The church scene in Africa is complex. The continent has been seen by Western churches as the place to spread the gospel. This in itself should sound odd because the church existed in Africa long before any of the missionary churches did.[6] Nevertheless, many Western churches have been established on the continent. Most of these churches have men, often foreign men, in leadership positions.

Since the 1920s, indigenous "independent churches" have emerged. These are referred to as Spirit, or Prophet, or Praying churches. Here women have been more involved than in the missionary churches, but even so they are normally not in primary leadership positions.

Perhaps more than anything else, the organization called "The Circle of Concerned African Women Theologians" (The Circle) has been the catalyst for women doing theology in Africa. Certainly it has been so for Oduyoye. In describing its history and accomplishments, "The Circle" lists the following: it was inaugurated in 1989 in Accra, Ghana, by seventy African women; its raison d'être is the promotion of research and writing in light of the dearth of literature by African women; it boasts fifteen chapters in thirteen countries in addition to small, working groups in several other countries; "The Circle" also has "diaspora" chapters in Europe and North America and solidarity chapters at Yale University in New Haven, Connecticut. It lists the following accomplishments: it has published thirty-one books by group authorship and several by single authors; it has established a center for women, religion, and culture in Accra; and it runs a women's resource center in Limuru, Kenya.[7] In merely twenty years, "The Circle" has produced a brave, new reality for theology in Africa generally and for women's theology in particular. African children now have books to read that are rooted in indigenous cultures, written in a voice that has until now largely been silent. It has created a new reality which "The Circle" describes as follows:

---

the terms of women's liberation, and is used by Kwok Pui-Lan in "Mercy Amba Oduyoye," 1 (website version at http://www.accessmylibrary.com/article-1G1-139172134/mercy-amba-oduyoye-and.html, accessed May 14, 2011).

[4] Pui-Lan, "Mercy Amba Oduyoye," 1.

[5] From Tumani Mutasa Nyajeka, *The Meeting of Two Female Worlds: American Women Missionaries and Shona Women at Old Mutare and the Founding of Rukwadzano* (Ph.D. diss., Northwestern University, 1996), and quoted from Rosemary Radford Ruether, *Women and Redemption: A Theological History* (Minneapolis: Fortress, 1998), 255.

[6] We need to remember that Augustine was the bishop of a Christian church in Hippo, North Africa, in the fifth century. The church has always existed in Africa. For a helpful study of the church in Africa, see Bengt Sundkler and Christopher Steed, *A History of the Church in Africa* (New York: Cambridge University Press, 2000).

[7] See the website, "The Circle of Concerned African Women Theologians," http://www.thecirclecawt.org/newsletter5855.html?mode=content&id=17270&refto=2564, accessed May 14, 2011, from which this history and list of accomplishments are drawn.

The determination by African women to address the dearth of theological writings by women from the continent has given birth to Women's Communal Theology. It has given birth to solidarity of African women with us and with our global sisters. The most important learning is that the motivation for Africa [sic] women's commitment to doing theology comes as a result of the inner conversion by concerned women theologians. It is not motivated by a need to confront, impress or even wins [sic] the church or other religious institutions. If this were the case, we would give up because many do not read our works. Our goal is to make Theology in Africa fly by equipping it with the missing wing. A bird with one wing does not fly.[8]

As this description testifies, there is a unique sense of identity at work here; one that cannot be caught with typical, Western notions of the individual. As we will see later, there is also a unique sense of time and place. History has voices with which one can be in dialogue.

OVERVIEW OF HER LIFE

Oduyoye was born on October 21, 1933,[9] in Asamankee, Ghana. Her mother was Mercy Dakwaa Yamoah, and her father was Charles Kwaw, a Methodist minister. Oduyoye describes the Akan culture into which she was born as a matrilineal society. She says:

> I define myself politically by my mother, as do the majority of Akans. The same is true of my brothers. Akan women are the center of the kinship unit and girls are brought up to feel the weight of this responsibility. Without women "a lineage is finished," the Akan say. So I grew up with a keen sense of my own importance and the necessity to play my role faultlessly.[10]

The nation of Ghana has about one hundred ethnic groups, each with its own language and culture. English is the official language of Ghana, but almost half of the population speaks the Akan language. Religiously, thirty-eight percent of the population practices traditional, African religions; thirty percent are Muslim; and twenty-four percent are Christian. Oduyoye's Methodist preacher father served several missionary churches in the Akan communities, and so from a young age she was nurtured into the Methodist church.

When Oduyoye was young she "absorbed" a particular view of womanhood. She explains it thus:

> All the women I knew worked: farming, trading, or processing and selling food and other daily necessities. Marriage did not change women's economic involvement. Only two of the women I knew were exclusively homemakers, although one of them had previously been my mother's teacher. Marriage, therefore, only added responsibilities to these women's lives. It seemed to me, however, that the more these women made others comfortable and dependent upon them, the more they felt alive. I absorbed all of this.[11]

Whenever the family met in the Akan community, it included both women and men. "Women's concerns" were dealt with through a decision-making process that culminated in the "Queen Mother" who, she says, "is in fact senior" to the king in the hierarchy.[12] This did not mean that Oduyoye was entirely comfortable with the complementarity between men and women in her community, although she did not feel restrained. She felt free to be and become what she wished.

Oduyoye had the shock of her life, however, when she encountered the "patriarchal-patrilineal Yoruba of western Nigeria,"[13] the region and culture from which her husband comes. Here, the wife is expected to work in her husband's house but not be party to any of

[8] "Circle of Concerned African Women Theologians," 1.

[9] Oduyoye's birth date requires comment. Public literature states she was born in 1934, but in a personal interview with Christina Landman from the Research Institute for Theology and Religion, University of South Africa, Pretoria, Oduyoye corrected that date to be October 21, 1933. See Christina Landman, "Mercy Amba Ewudziwa Oduyoye: Mother of Our Stories," *Studia Historiae Ecclesiasticae* 33, no. 2. Available on the Internet at http://www.christina-landman.co.za/mercy.htm, accessed May 14, 2011.

[10] Oduyoye, *Daughters of Anowa*, 6–7.

[11] Oduyoye, *Daughters of Anowa*, 7.

[12] Oduyoye, *Daughters of Anowa*, 7.

[13] Oduyoye, *Daughters of Anowa*, 7.

the family decisions. Not only that, there was here an acceptance of a "British style patriarchy"[14] which affected everything: church, university, government, economic development, and family. When she saw these two very different forms of gender roles, she began to wonder what her own role should be: was it to adopt the new, modern, British model, or her inherited, mother-centered world? She found the sexism of the Nigerian-British culture intolerable, but perhaps it was somehow better. After all, it came from the West.

Out of this struggle came the overwhelming conviction that social and gender relationships are not divinely given but created on the basis of convictions and myths. And if that is the case, then we have both the responsibility and the power to create them justly, in a manner that could be affirming of all of humanity. So she devoted her life to the search for developing this new kind of world, especially for the African people over whom she had some influence.

Oduyoye was already a keen student in elementary and high school. She says that she went through school "like any boy."[15] She completed high school in 1952 at the Achimota School in Accra, Ghana, and from there went to study education at the University of Kumasi, in Kumasi, Ghana. Her childhood dreams of being a teacher were gradually realized, and after graduation she spent the next twenty years teaching in secondary schools in Ghana and Nigeria.[16]

From 1959–1963 Oduyoye studied religion at the University of Ghana in Legon. After receiving a bachelor of arts degree, she embarked on a bold move to England, where she enrolled in the University of Cambridge for graduate studies in theology. Says Landman, "It was during her studies at these two universities that she was influenced towards the de-dogmatising and re-storying of Christian beliefs."[17] Here she learned to contextualize

both Christian history and dogma. She came to see that doctrines were human constructs, and hence not themselves sacred. And unless doctrine meets life, it cannot offer theological knowledge or insight about the divine. However, when doctrine does meet life, there is a story to tell. Stories are unique, utterly particular, and concrete. In other words, whereas doctrine pretends to be universal, when it is embodied in real-life experiences, its universality becomes shattered by the concreteness of history. This means that the study of theology is more akin to a search or struggle than it is like the scientific discovery of truth.

While at Cambridge, she became more and more interested in ecumenism because she found interesting the stories of the way others practiced their faith. She became involved in the Student Christian Movement (SCM), which would have major career-shaping influence in her life. SCM later brought her to Geneva, Switzerland, as the Deputy General Secretary of the World Council of Churches (WCC), and it also led her to the man who would become her husband, Adedoyin Modupe Oduyoye, the Nigerian SCM General Secretary.

In 1969 she was awarded an M.A. degree from Cambridge. The next phase of Oduyoye's life was preoccupied with teaching in universities. In 1974 she began teaching at the University of Ibadan in Ibadan, Nigeria, and taught there for thirteen years. This is where she came into her own as a scholar, researcher, writer, and lecturer. In 1987 she was invited to the position of Deputy General Secretary of the WCC. She held that post for seven years.[18] Since 1994 she has lectured in many settings and in many countries. Most recently she was appointed Director of the Institute of African Women in Religion and Culture at Trinity Theological Seminary, Legon, Ghana.

She has received honorary doctorate degrees from several universities, including

[14] Oduyoye, *Daughters of Anowa*, 8.
[15] Oduyoye, *Daughters of Anowa*, 7.
[16] Landman, "Mother of Our Stories," 2.
[17] Landman, "Mother of Our Stories," 2.
[18] Landman, "Mother of Our Stories," 3.

Yale University and the University of Amsterdam, and was awarded the E. H. Johnson Award in 2008 from the Presbyterian Church in Canada, an award given to someone "on the cutting edge of mission."[19] She has written several books and many articles, served as president of the Ecumenical Association of Third World Theologians (EATWOT) and the Ecumenical Association of African Theologians (EAAT), and became the first African woman member of the WCC Commission on Faith and Order. While we do not know much about her family, we do know that she and her husband, Adedoyin Modupe Oduyoye, have raised five foster children.[20]

RE-STORYING HISTORY

Oduyoye is keenly aware that life is a process, a movement into which we are placed due to circumstances beyond our control. Our own spirits can shape this process, but only in part. We are located in a particular place—in her case, Africa—and we are given a particular history. Both place and history are alive and teeming with possibilities, as well as with obstacles and difficulties. Histories and cultures, therefore, must be constantly reinvigorated and renewed, that is, they must be re-storied.

In 1999 Oduyoye presented a paper at the fiftieth anniversary of the WCC Assembly in Harare, Zimbabwe. In it, she traces the struggle of the African people—past and present. She does this in a unique way—through dialogue with her ancestors, some of whom were living as recently as the previous WCC assembly. She begins by speaking to both the audience and to her ancestors thus: "Today, as I pour these words to you like a libation, my heart and soul are full of grief and hope . . ."[21] History is personal and immediate for her, as she speaks of "reliving in my bones and hearing in my ears the voices of the pain." This personal passion continues as she addresses her ancestors, who live deep within her being:

[W]e yearn to be authentic, we yearn to discover the strength with which you [ancestors] resisted total obliteration of what you had received from your forbearers and indeed of the total annihilation of our kind from this soil. We yearn to rediscover your wisdom, for who knows but that we may glean insights and inspiration for our contemporary struggles and dilemmas for we too resist total absorption into an euro-centered global culture we have not helped to shape. We know that you have something to say to us.[22]

I make two general observations about the way Oduyoye approaches the matter of liberating history through re-storying. I mention these because everything she writes depends on her distinctive view of time and culture.

First is her view of time. Time and history are so much more than a chronology of events which would put her at great distance from her ancestors. Like George Tinker and Rosemary Ruether, she rejects the Western time/space dichotomy.[23] For her, the past lives in present spaces. The ancestors have left a living legacy, not one which we can merely analyze, study, and reflect upon from a distance; ancestors are among us and we can commune with them. They can still dispense wisdom and speak the truth, and they must be interrogated. Their voices can be empowered, enlivened, and reinvigorated.

The second observation relates to Oduyoye's view of culture. Culture is what sustains daily living: habits, practices, rituals, liturgies, myths, imaginations, the way we search for meaning, and the ways we debate the truth. Life without culture is dead. We

---

[19] From a news release by the Presbyterian Church in Canada, Toronto, Ontario, October 1, 2007, available on their website at http://www.presbyterian.ca/community/newsandevents/2100, accessed May 14, 2011.

[20] Erika A. Kuhlman, *A to Z of Women in World History* (New York: Infobase, 2002), 224.

[21] Mercy Amba Oduyoye, "From Cover to Core: A Letter to My Ancestors," 1. This paper was presented to the Eighth Assembly of the WCC, in Harare, Zimbabwe, December 3–14, 1998. It is available on the WCC website, http://www.wcc-coe.org/wcc/assembly/or-mo-e.html, accessed May 14, 2011.

[22] Oduyoye, "From Cover to Core," 1.

[23] See chaps. 28 and 29 above.

are in it and view the entire world through it. To seek to escape it is to seek death. Culture is also given by our ancestors, not in a "take it or leave it" manner, but as a gift through life-sustaining habits, which we adopt and adapt. Sometimes, of course, these habits are not life-sustaining, and then they need to be redeemed. In any case, all cultures must be interrogated. The reality in Africa is that colonialism has left a legacy that is profoundly dehumanizing because it disrespects culture in the name of abstract (that is, transcultural) truth-claims stripped of the powers to sustain life.

Oduyoye reaches back to the struggle her ancestors faced in embodying their religion in an African culture. She says their search was led by the Spirit of the Creator because that is how the Spirit works—through time and open human spirits. Some held on tenaciously, even to their death, to a pristine version of their faith, and many enhanced their faith with tenets from Christianity and Islam.

Oduyoye issues an apology to her ancestors for a promise unfulfilled. Two thousand years ago the Christian "spiritual ancestor" (Jesus) offered his followers peace and fullness of life if they would accept his "Way." Unfortunately, the world has known little of this peace because those who proclaimed the "Way" did not understand it. The peace Africans have seen has been an imposed peace and has come at the price of dehumanization. This false peace is present to this day, and she hears Anowa saying, "Enough is enough."[24] Oduyoye sees Jesus weep because we do not know what makes for peace; we have refused to "stay under his motherly wings."[25] We have instead created "better" worldviews, ones that justified our own superiority and lined

our own pockets. While she apologizes, she also asks for wisdom from the ancestors to help lead the world out of these exploitative and fractious ideologies and practices.

In her work, Oduyoye names several avenues through which, by listening to our ancestors, we can learn to see beyond the current state of unpeace. First, as we have already seen, the past is rich with resources, and it has something to tell us. Unlike many other liberationists, she sees history not only as oppressive but as containing the seeds of liberation and justice. While the past can liberate us if we listen aright, "the past has nothing to *impose*."[26] Present experience shows us that there is an unhealthy Christianity in Africa. Insufficient attention has been paid to oppression, structural injustice, and violence, and privatized economic systems have divided people against each other. By opening ourselves to becoming storied, Jesus people, we can be initiated into practices and structures that can sustain beautiful lives and honest and just relationships.

Second, our ancestors challenge us to be open and honest with them and with one another because only then will we see how we today continue to violate the humanity of each other; and only then can we become open to new possibilities. They call us to hear the voices and cries of the marginalized. And when we hear and obey these voices, we begin to embody the promise of the church. For Oduyoye, the church is central to everything! Jesus prayed that we might become one body, that the rich and the poor might be one in spirit and body. Herein lies our new hope, yet in reality even the church is divided. And there are reasons for this! We need to resist "confessional fundamentalisms" and

---

[24] Oduyoye, *Daughters of Anowa*, 1. The figure of Anowa is important in Oduyoye's work. Anowa is the feminine form of a popular name in Ghana (the male form is Anoo), and it is a name with a story. The story was made popular through a drama, Ama Ata Aidoo, *Anowa* (London: Harlow, 1970). In it, Anowa was to be a priestess but never became one. In another African epic, Ayi Kwei Armah, *Two Thousand Seasons* (Nairobi, Kenya: East Africa Publishing House, 1973), Anoa, a variant of Anowa, was the central figure. She was a prophetess in the Sahara before the patriarchal ideology gained hold, that is, before slavery and sexism. Anoa's people were peaceful, not looking for self-glorification, but living a life in which everyone—women, men, and children—participated in life-sustaining practices. Oduyoye seeks to empower this character as a model for African Christians today. See Oduyoye, *Daughters of Anowa*, 6–7n6.

[25] Oduyoye, *Daughters of Anowa*, 1.   [26] Oduyoye, *Daughters of Anowa*, 2 (emphasis added).

empower the ecumenical spirit through companionship and conversation with each other, similar to that modeled by Jesus and the disciples on the Emmaus road (Luke 24:13ff.). Such conversations—which are ways of re-storying the past into which we may place ourselves (see Luke 24:27)—can help us *see* a whole new world; a whole new way in which death (cross) can become life (resurrection).

Third, our ancestors challenge the church to be faithful. Although the early church had a presence in Northern Africa, Africa is certainly no leader in the Christian world today. In fact, the indigenous church is weak. The Christianity of Africa has been shaped by missionaries from colonial countries who have kept their power to themselves. Indeed, Africa is weak economically, politically, and intellectually, and this is not unrelated to the weakness of the church. But what is the church to do with this? Oduyoye hears the voice of ancestors saying that the church can exploit its "counter power,"[27] which is the power of weakness. But it is difficult to see how this "power" is to be used. This can only happen when Christians remember that the gospel of Jesus is inherently political; when they recall that it speaks of liberating the poor, and the ones held captive, and it denounces the ones who abuse power. Western missionaries forgot about this political form of the gospel because they believed that Christianity could be made into an abstract set of ideas. At the same time, they paid insufficient attention to their own complicity in politics and thus corrupted the "good news" with heresies like the gospel of prosperity and military might. This false political gospel is all over the West for everyone to see. The dilemmas of speaking the "power of weakness" into this scene are extremely difficult to overcome and require a radical re-storying of history in openness to the politics of Jesus.

Fourth, given the unity of body and soul, and hence the impossibility of an uncultured religion, Oduyoye acknowledges that, through her ancestors, Africans have a responsibility to embody Christianity into their own cultures. No less can be authentically Christian. She laments the extent to which Africa has become Euro-centric, through the imposition of Western laws, language, science, and technology. The time has come to make Africa African again. South Africa is an example here. It was able to begin reversing the harm done by a foreign power in a manner that other parts of Africa can emulate, and it was done under indigenous, Christian leadership who listened to the voices of the ancestors.[28] Yet Oduyoye seeks not to be provincial here. That is, it is not a matter of freeing one part of Africa, or even one part of the world—Africa. It is not women against men; it is about humanity. The ancestors expect this of us because they warned us about developing the power of one region over another; their view was to sustain the quality of life on the entire planet.

History can be re-storied, in fact, it *must* be re-storied; there are resources in the past and in the present for this to happen. The vision for a just humanity is everywhere to be found, especially in the story of Jesus. What is required is not a new vision but a new form of embodiment; a new practical theology.

THEOLOGY AND ETHICS

Since theology is always dressed in cultural garb, for Oduyoye, all theology is practical theology. To say this differently, there can be no theology apart from ethics. This is so because of who we are as human beings. We are particulars, meaning, we exist in a particular time and place, in families, and nations. Just as we do not merely speak or think but do so in a specific language, so we do not merely

---

[27] Oduyoye, *Daughters of Anowa*, 3.

[28] Bishop Desmond Tutu (1931–) from South Africa was actively involved in leadership of the resistance movement that eventually led to the dismantling of the apartheid regime in 1994. See his sermons and peace speeches in Desmond Tutu, *Crying in the Wilderness: The Struggle for Justice in South Africa*, ed. John Webster (Grand Rapids: Eerdmans, 1990).

act, but act in Winnipeg or Washington or Asamankee or Tehran.

Although we are particular beings, still all human beings have a built-in desire to know what lies beyond life and death and what makes existence meaningful and beautiful. Oduyoye traces this universal quest back to Abraham, who was called to walk in openness to God to a new place. Moses was called to liberate a people from a specific place of slavery to a new place of freedom and plenty. So it was with Jesus and Paul, who drew heavily on their knowledge of history and culture in giving expression to faithfulness in the present. So it has been in Africa.

When the missionaries came to Africa after the Protestant Reformation, their theology arose out of the same culture that brought them steam and gunpowder. And this made a difference. Says Oduyoye:

> This theology clashed with African culture, which was pious in its own right but had no steam engines and rifles and was by no stretch of imagination evangelical in the sense of going out to tell its own good news to other nations. The missionaries reflected their culture in the symbols they brought along and in their telling of the story of salvation.[29]

The theme of indigenization is extremely important to Oduyoye because it is the way in which theology is made practical in her homeland and that is the only theology worth calling Christian. However, when the modern Africans began to indigenize Christianity their way, the foreign Christian leaders began to scrutinize them and to offer criticism. This was made even more painful when it was learned that the Western churches—Anglicans, Methodists, and Presbyterians—were exempt from this faith test.

Oduyoye roots her understanding of indigenization in the Gospel of John, where we read, "And the Word became flesh and lived among us, and we have seen his glory, the glory as of the father's only son, full of grace and truth" (John 1:14). She asks, "How should we understand the manner of Jesus living among us?"[30] Notice that for her Jesus too is alive in Africa, teaching, healing, and encouraging. She suggests further, "Some of us involved in this search find that we have to look again at all that we have been taught by our parents, pastors, and professors concerning the incarnation and its meaning in Christianity."[31] There is a hermeneutic of suspicion at work in her writings that she does not officially name but nevertheless utilizes.

For Oduyoye, the incarnation is the center of evangelism, in that the spreading of the gospel is never a "naked" affair; it is always clothed in culture. To pretend that this is not so is to do violence both to the gospel and to the people to whom it is preached. The Word must become flesh for it to be the Word from God! This makes communicating the gospel across cultures extremely challenging.

She uses two words to talk about indigenization: acculturation and inculturation. By acculturation she means, "the efforts of Africans to use things African in their practice of Christianity."[32] By inculturation she means "the manifestation of changes that have come into the African way of life as a result of the Christian faith."[33] In other words, this is a distinction between Africanizing Christianity (acculturation) and christianizing Africa (inculturation). Both are inevitable, and in fact essential, in the process of evangelization.

To illustrate the dynamics of indigenizing the gospel, Oduyoye tells the story of her music teacher, Owura Ephriam Amu, who was the only teacher who retained his Ghanaian title, "Owura," which means "Master." All other teachers were called "Mister." He also insisted on wearing African clothes instead of Western clothes. He taught students Western music, piano, violin, and oboe, composers like Handel, Bach, Beethoven, and Tchaikovsky, but he was most appreciated

---

[29] Mercy Amba Oduyoye, *Hearing and Knowing: Theological Reflections on Christianity in Africa* (Maryknoll, N.Y.: Orbis, 1986), 68.

[30] Oduyoye, *Hearing and Knowing*, 69.

[31] Oduyoye, *Hearing and Knowing*, 69.

[32] Oduyoye, *Hearing and Knowing*, 69.

[33] Oduyoye, *Hearing and Knowing*, 69.

when he taught them how to sing Ghanaian songs and make music with drums, rattles, gongs, and dances. He was an educated African Christian and was able to communicate to his students that God was among them, and that God had been there before the white man came.

Owura Amu was not always received well by the Western churches because he was seen as being too African to be Christian. Oduyoye speaks about such cultural arrogance and its effects as follows:

> Owura Amu was once refused the pulpit of the Presbyterians (then Basel Mission) because he went to his appointment wearing the Ghanaian toga. I hasten to add that this contempt for African traditional clothing, even when modified by European fashions, was found not only in the church but also among the anglicized Ghanaians, especially those on the coast. My mother remembers a lawyer, who seeing his daughter wearing African traditional dress, exploded: "Off you go and get dressed. I thought you were one of these *adesefo* [villagers] who come [*sic*] here to sell *dokon* [a wrapped dumpling of corn dough].[34]

Oduyoye notes that the Roman Catholic Church is more open to acculturation than the Protestant churches. Drums and dances ceased being symbols of paganism after the Second Vatican Council. Although on the Eucharist they were less generous; it required wine made from grapes and bread made from wheat, neither of which were indigenous to the region.

Inculturation, which has to do with changes to the African way of life as a result of the Christian faith, has its own challenges. It is equally important, however, since Oduyoye acknowledges that not all African ways are Christian. Moreover, foreign Christians also bring insights of the Spirit. Hence, the question, "How can one be African and Christian at the same time?"[35] ought not to be left only to the African Christians to determine.

Discerning what it means to "be in Christ in Africa" calls for careful, ecumenical listening. Oduyoye reaches back to the story of Pentecost in Acts 2 to frame this process. This story is not about every Christian who is filled with the Spirit speaking the same language, but rather about the Spirit giving utterance in different tongues which can be understood by speakers of other tongues. It suggests that the gospel spoken by foreigners can be heard *in the language of the indigenous peoples* if it is both spoken and heard through the Spirit.

All of this has significant implications for doing theology in Africa. For Africans too have a voice to bring to the discussion. Oduyoye puts it this way: "those who were for a long time content to be consumers of theology have begun to be producers of theology, and it is Christian theology. They are widening the panorama of symbols, heightening the colors of issues, and demanding commitment and action."[36] This new, African "theology from the underside of history" is what African Christians bring to the ecumenical table of theological discussion. And as Christians speak to each other in the ecumenical family, we need to pay careful attention by honing the skill of listening. Here Oduyoye issues a caution: to treat the African voices as "exotic additions would be to sin against the Holy Spirit, and *that* would be heresy. We have to do theology, believing that when our honest labors are offered to God, God's holiness burns away the dross and allows the purity of the gold to shine, leading those who live in darkness to see a Great Light."[37] This is ecumenical theology at work.

Trinity, Community, and Church

Oduyoye distinguishes two ways of doing theology, one called dogmatics and the other problematics. Dogmatics begins with the

---

[34] Oduyoye, *Hearing and Knowing*, 71.

[35] Oduyoye, *Hearing and Knowing*, 73.

[36] Oduyoye, *Hearing and Knowing*, 76.

[37] Oduyoye, *Hearing and Knowing*, 76 (emphasis in original).

creeds and focuses on the essential tenets of Christianity. Problematics is different. She relies on philosopher of religion John Hick to describe problematics, which he says is concerned with rewriting theology in light of changed times.[38] Here, theology is placed within the tension of either the past and present, a conviction and challenge, or another form of the new meeting the old. This is reminiscent of several other liberation theologians, where experienced insensitivity to culture led to a skepticism of systematic theology.

We have already seen Oduyoye's interest in the incarnation, where God bridged the gap between the divine and the human. This helps her to see in Christ the approximation of human actions with the ways of God. And so in her comments about what it means to be the church, she speaks about "living out the Trinitarian life."[39]

Oduyoye roots her understanding of the Christian life in the story of Jesus. Jesus had a particular way of viewing the world; he believed that the ultimate reality *in this world* is God.[40] Hence, all efforts of seeking to secure ourselves through material means and other forms of control are atheistic and sinful. It should not be a surprise, therefore, that Jesus spoke of "losing yourself" as the way of authentic existence (Matt 16:24-26). Jesus' language here comes out of a new vision and calls for a "new creation" involving healing and restoration of broken creation.[41] This new creation is the focal point for Oduyoye's casting of the ethical life for Christians, and this is also what she sees as the participation in the Trinitarian life.

Oduyoye believes that this view of the Christian life requires a reassessment of the notion of salvation, especially as it has been taught by the missionaries. Contrary to what Africans were told, salvation is not first and foremost an individual matter. for in losing oneself, one gives up any attempts to secure one's own status. Hence, Christian salvation requires knowing oneself in community. In fact, she argues, you can know neither truth nor salvation in advance of living with others. She says, "The truth of what Jesus has said about the world and about God is not something you can expect others to accept simply because you have taught them. They will only come to know as they begin to walk along the Way. Our relation to truth cannot be theoretical."[42]

Even though her language may sound like it here, Oduyoye is not interested in postmodern epistemology; she is interested in the notion of church and community. And she catches it by listening to the voice of Jesus. The specific ground for her claims is the Trinity, where the mode of existence is not "individuality in relationship" but rather individuality mirroring plurality. That is, the three persons of the Trinity are not independent individuals, but each carries the identity of the others within their own identity. Oduyoye suggests that this is the model for true self-understanding, as well as the ground for understanding Christian salvation.

Such a view of existence has profound implications for how we understand not only ourselves but also corporate reality—institutions, nations, families, and church. She summarizes: "One could say that it is only in community that our humanity means anything. Experiencing Jesus was for the disciples an experience of God's self-revelation, and the Spirit that guided their lives they described as the Spirit of God."[43] The church, called the body of Christ, embodies this form of communitarian existence and as such models all other forms of corporate identity, even though adaptations will make them look quite different.

---

[38] See esp. John Hick, *God Has Many Names* (London: Macmillan, 1980).

[39] Oduyoye, *Hearing and Knowing*, 139. Oduyoye's language around Trinitarian living is reminiscent of the language of "participating in the Trinity" used by Hans Urs von Balthasar. See chap. 16 above.

[40] See Oduyoye, *Hearing and Knowing*, 139.

[41] See Oduyoye, *Hearing and Knowing*, 140.

[42] Oduyoye, *Hearing and Knowing*, 140.

[43] Oduyoye, *Hearing and Knowing*, 141.

Oduyoye contrasts the Trinitarian model community with the polytheistic model. In the latter model, emphasis is placed "on the units that make up the community rather than on the whole."[44] This generates a way of life based on the individual's rights, needs, and powers. But eventually, such a community will lead to anarchy because as each individual becomes more and more separated from others, the only way to rule such a society is with a supreme authority that keeps some semblance of order and peace through absolute, dictatorial power. She also speaks of a deistic model, which initially might look like an alternative to the polytheism model, but in fact, it merely underwrites absolute authority right from the outset.

In contrast to these two forms of political community, she says, "The trinitarian model is full of vitality, and its energy is generated by love, participation, and sharing. It is a model that gives unique meaning to our being created in the image of God."[45] As she sees it, the Trinity models human relationships of every kind. The worth and value of one human being, including one's own, cannot be abstracted from the worth and value of others. Putting it this way undermines the justification of superiority and dislodges the logic of all racisms and sexisms. Furthermore, it justifies the dignity of every individual. but only in community with others. Human relationships are healthy and godly only when each individual is strong and mirrors the dignity of all others.

The Trinity, for Oduyoye, is not merely a model for human and social relationships; it is also a model for the empowering of our own being through a "vertical relationship" with God. Under the general heading of "The Trinity and the Sacraments," she says that when Christian believers are baptized into the name of the Trinity, it enlists them in participation in the Trinity, where they are brought into a "sharing of power and responsibilities" with God. She recognizes that this is a somewhat dangerous claim because it could lead to versions of "seizing godlikeness." To protect herself from this implication she refers to (but does not elaborate) the Catholic doctrine of the principle of analogy.[46]

Our baptism into the name of the Trinity also enlists us in Jesus' openness to the world, to sinners, and to suffering. To be baptized is to be passionate about the salvation of the entire world, and it simultaneously invites us into a celebration of the Eucharist, through which we give thanks for God's grace and pray for the entire world which God is seeking to reconcile. Says Oduyoye, "In the Eucharist we demonstrate our faith in the unity and diversity that is God."[47] Therefore, the church must be both united and diverse and should be careful never to emphasize uniformity at the expense of diversity. While the Eucharist is a profound demonstration that "the world is the church's business,"[48] it is that uniquely as a witness to wholeness of a kind that the world does not know—one rich with diversity and colorful expression.

All of this has important implications for the oneness of the church. Oduyoye reminds us that the WCC and the Vatican have now agreed with what the Eastern Orthodox Churches have always said, namely, that the ground of the church is the blessed Trinity. In accepting this, we are now able to speak of the unity of the church in a new way. Unity does not mean organizational unity but organic unity. She asks, "Should the organic unity of the Trinity which we confess (although we do not fully understand it) not make us tolerant of the idea of organic unity of the church?"[49] While diversity within the church body remains evident, she wants to claim a kind of eschatological unity in which the diverse enculturated church bodies can all participate.

[44] Oduyoye, *Hearing and Knowing*, 141.
[45] Oduyoye, *Hearing and Knowing*, 142.
[46] For a fuller discussion of the analogy of being, also called the *analogia entis*, see chaps. 14 and 16 above.
[47] Oduyoye, *Hearing and Knowing*, 143.
[48] Oduyoye, *Hearing and Knowing*, 143.
[49] Oduyoye, *Hearing and Knowing*, 144–45.

The church and society today seem not to be ready for the implications of the underlying Trinitarian structure of reality. But if the church is able to allow itself to be formed by this reality which it confesses, it will model a form of reconciliation and redemption for all of humanity. And this can hardly go unnoticed.

FEMINISM

Like many feminists, Oduyoye does not focus narrowly on women's issues. In *Daughters of Anowa*, she raises the question: "Why respond to feminism?" Her answer is straightforward: feminism, as she sees it, provides a vision for Africa that is unique and holistic. She describes how she has found herself at a critical juncture; behind her was a world that she wanted to run away from, and in front of her was a "global patriarchy" which also needed to be rejected. In facing these impossible options, she developed a third. She says:

> This book describes why I have come to see that situation as a false dilemma and how, instead, I have come to realize that by looking more critically around us, as well as deeper into our history, we can be motivated and empowered to create structures that obviate all that we have denounced in patriarchy."[50]

In other words, in order to be faithful to the voices of those offering her wisdom, she felt the need to envision and help realize a new humanity which affirmed peace and justice for all. And for this, history requires a rereading from the standpoint that the future is not inevitable; it can be shaped.

To keep this project from slipping into pure, idealistic romanticism, she reminds herself that the imagination of colonialism has so infiltrated the minds and voices of Christianity that the task of listening again to the voices of the past will not be easy. The challenge to Christianity in Africa is huge and beyond challenges related to sexism and the self-image of the African woman. Yet the liberation of African women is key to the redemption of the Christian church in Africa.

Many in Africa say that "our women are not oppressed."[51] Oduyoye suggests that this is an effort to make feminism a non-issue, and in effect it is male propaganda, an effort to keep women oppressed. The same, latent sexism lies behind calling African women to be African; that call normally comes with the assumption of submissiveness. There is a crisis of definition in Africa, not only of what it means to be woman, but also what it means to be African.

It is tempting to think that the important issue here is "who has the right to define what it means to be African or woman?" Yet Oduyoye is quick to point out that, while important, the quest for definition is unhelpful because not all Africans are alike and certainly not all women are alike.[52] Hence, part of the task of feminism is to free not only women, but men as well, from an imagination that is enslaved to the generic. That is, the issue is not what it means to be African or woman, the issue is how we can learn to become full human beings. And in order for that to happen, we need to shed the quest for control by definition. The goal of women in Africa, therefore, is to initiate new meanings of life into a larger community of meaning. She says it this way:

> As women we affirm our being and we begin to weave a new pattern of womanhood from the threads in which we feel comfortable. Through the telling of our stories, I attempt to demonstrate the political nature of gender hierarchy and its effects on man-woman relations. This is the life-giving center of my story-telling venture, my belief that human nature, though complex, is one. Our dreams become a new cloth with an African pattern that fits into the global women's *asaasaa*. All must be open and flexible, a style of being that is the antithesis of death-dealing patriarchy.[53]

---

[50] Oduyoye, *Daughters of Anowa*, 8.
[51] Oduyoye, *Daughters of Anowa*, 13.
[52] See Oduyoye, *Daughters of Anowa*, 13.
[53] Oduyoye, *Daughters of Anowa*, 16 (emphasis in original).

The *asaasaa* is an important symbol for Oduyoye. It is a practice similar to what in North America is known as quilting, but in Ghana it has special political meaning. She says, "In Ghana this patchwork cloth represents the creativity born out of poverty. The poor clothed themselves by piecing together the surpluses from the rich, who invariably bought more fabric than was needed for their garments. The feminist *asaasaa* will be a new creation from a world torn to shreds by patriarchy."[54] Part of the challenge to patriarchy is the new way of viewing humanity, that is, the diversity of individuals linked together in one cloth. Of course, this is but another expression of Trinitarian community.

Oduyoye's book *Daughters of Anowa* is presented in three cycles: language, culture, and dreams. This tripartite unity is indicative of how she thinks; we are storied, linguistic people with an imagination to dream of possibilities that are not yet, but through which we can be re-storied. In the dreaming section, she has a chapter titled "Acting as Women." It might seem surprising to see a title that could suggest that there is after all a generic view of woman, but that is not what she says here. Rather she is giving expression to the *asaasaa*, the patchwork body of diverse people, women among them, that makes up the church. She encourages each woman to accept her humanity under God and thus respond to God within the larger body of the church. Anything less than that, she says, dehumanizes both women and men and makes the church something other than the body of Christ.

The African church must remember that although the colonial, Western missionaries have taught them to read the Bible—indeed a wonderful gift—they have taught them to read it in a particular way. And especially the proof-texting approach of the Pauline texts on women has been harmful to women. Such readings of the Bible lack contextual interpretation, and as such often misinterpret

passages like Genesis 3 and Pauline pronouncements on women. Moreover, even what Paul says about women must be placed within his own cultural context, and hence is not necessarily transculturally usable. She says, "Paul's words on women are not necessarily a direct message from God to the church. Similarly, problems of same-sex love, which made Paul clamp down on women's freedom in Christ, were also discussed by contemporary Jews, Greeks, and Romans."[55]

It is important to note, Oduyoye argues, that writers like Paul often make general, liberating announcements that "all are free in Christ" (Gal 3:28), and then, on the other hand, speak the language of subordination to women (Eph 5:22ff.). These notions are hard to bring together. And the tendency of patriarchy has been to ignore the liberating comment and affirm the subordinate language.

Oduyoye argues that unless women become involved in reading, translating, and interpreting the Bible, these patterns of interpretation will continue. She says:

> [M]ost important of all, we must begin to question and to do our own thinking. Each of us has a duty to contribute to theological thinking. Leaving theology in the hands of an all-male caste whose pronouncements on the Bible are hardly ever questioned—not by men, and certainly not by us women—is to be content to respond to God through others.[56]

Hence, women must reread the Bible and learn how to listen to God and discern where God is working in the world today.

Underneath Oduyoye's claims lies a distinct view of hermeneutics. The Bible never just says something in the abstract; it speaks into particular experiences. It can only be God's word if it has something to say to the living. Hence, women's experiences cannot be written out of the context into which God's voice speaks. There needs to be an ongoing synthesis of discerning the word that involves reading both the Bible and the context into which it speaks. So she says:

---

[54] Oduyoye, *Daughters of Anowa*, 16n13.
[55] Oduyoye, *Daughters of Anowa*, 190.

[56] Oduyoye, *Daughters of Anowa*, 191.

[I]f women appropriate both our Christian and African heritages, we can be social commentators on behalf of justice and true religion as well as cultic functionaries. We can be prophets in our churches like Anna, who saw in the baby Jesus the vision of a New World (Luke 2:36–38), as well as prophets like the *Ahemaa* and the *Iyalode* who stood for social justice and women's participation in political decisions.[57]

Rituals are important for Oduyoye, and they can be both liberating and oppressing.[58] She is critical of rituals in the church that have been dehumanizing for women. For example, pregnant or menstruating women have been refused presence at the communion table. She asks why birth and pregnancy—important life-giving events—cannot be celebrated in the church. African women ought to question these restrictions. There is a false identification here of maleness and spirituality. She appeals to Jesus who denounces religious authorities for seeking to keep people—men or women, clean or unclean—from gaining access to God.

The Christian missionaries have brought a perverse notion of purity and impurity to the continent. Impurity and earthiness have become synonymous. But this is rank heresy because it questions God's choice of the creative process on earth. Impurity should not have to do with the fact that women menstruate, have babies and sex, but rather with how these natural phenomena are practiced, such that they can be liberating for all. If impurity is associated with earthiness, then Jesus could not have been pure. The doctrine of the incarnation should fundamentally destroy such notions of impurity.

Although Oduyoye is adamant that theological language is important, she says that "the gender of God is not the heart of the matter."[59] For Jesus to call God Father was not a mistake; the mistake was the subsequent inference of male authority and control. The locus of authority is not maleness, but God; and God liberates.

Oduyoye discusses the complicated dynamic of the Christian call: on the one hand we are called to give up power over others; on the other hand, she is calling women to take charge of their own lives in the face of the patriarchal-colonial heresy. This problem is made complex with an overlay of gender roles. For example, in Africa the "abdication of autonomy" is often heralded as the hallmark of "the virtuous woman."[60] But why should this Christian virtue be linked to gender? She says, "we should still question why gender is the ultimate distinction between human beings? Other qualities—those that determine how we interact with other human beings and with our environment—seem far more significant."[61] And it is not as though African women are unaccustomed to using power; they are in fact quite adept at it. Moreover, like men, they often misuse it. She says, speaking of African women:

> We desecrate our life-giving function if our kitchens with their pots and pans or our sexuality become areas for exercising control over others, rather than ways of sharing and participating in life. Instead of prostituting our kitchens or profaning our bodies, church women would do well to loosen our tongues and raise our voices telling aloud our real hurts and seeking redress. Using the kitchen or the bedroom is simply playing the man's game. When market women have been really pushed by unrealistic taxation or pricecontrol, they have taken to the streets in protest. We must ask, though, why women were not present in the first place when these decisions were being made.[62]

In other words, the issue is not women or men, using power or giving it up, it is rather a matter of being the kind of people who by their character commit to building structures of peace and justice within the community.

---

[57] Oduyoye, *Daughters of Anowa*, 192.

[58] See esp. Mercy Oduyoye, "Women and Ritual in Africa," in *The Will to Arise: Women, Tradition, and the Church in Africa*, ed. Mercy Amba Oduyoye and Musimbi R. A. Kanyoro (Maryknoll, N.Y.: Orbis, 1992).

[59] Oduyoye, *Daughters of Anowa*, 194.

[60] Oduyoye, *Daughters of Anowa*, 196.

[61] Oduyoye, *Daughters of Anowa*, 196.

[62] Oduyoye, *Daughters of Anowa*, 196.

Virtues do not come in male and female varieties; virtues predicate human beings. A specific example Oduyoye mentions is that since women have excelled in the art of caring—being loving mothers and giving generously of themselves—there is the tendency to think, even gloatingly (by women), that caring is a woman's virtue. Oduyoye asks sarcastically, "Why . . . do we seem to enjoy a perverse kind of power? Has our monopoly of caring turned it into a tool for seeking power?"[63] Moreover, once both men and women acquiesced to the notion that the quality of caring is relegated to one-half of the human race—women—we have forgotten what it means to listen to the voice of Jesus. This does not mean that women should stop caring; it only means that caring is not based in gender. She says:

> We create a situation of conflict if we do not see that the woman with one child on her back and perhaps another in tow as she peddles tomatoes and peppers throughout the day is also doing her duty. We Christian women, and particularly those of us who are part of the educated urban elite, might be creating a new African woman who will end up carrying the burdens of the Western woman on top of her traditional ones. As we re-imagine our womanness, we must remember that women need to stand by women and that, contrary to our proverbial sayings, all women are not the same. Celebrating both unity and diversity, women can stand together.[64]

Oduyoye believes that women can be models of how to overcome oppression and sometimes this will even be a challenge to their own women's organizations. For example, some women's groups forget that not all women are married with children; they exclude single and childless women. She warns against borrowing from the model of exclusion that has been fostered by missionary churches that have marginalized women. Healthy, human relationships require openness and inclusion. For a model of inclusiveness, she reaches back to the biblical story of Mary and Elizabeth. She says, "The bonding of Mary and Elizabeth was so liberative that it enabled a virgin with child to put away fear and shame to declare that God had done great things to her. Their bond of solidarity becomes ours."[65]

None of this should suggest that for Oduyoye gender does not matter. Gender binds together, and in its binding, it liberates. There are, after all, stigmas around sexuality, pregnancy, and childlessness which are unique to women in a society where the value of women is measured through their offspring. As she puts it, "Womanhood in Africa is almost synonymous with motherhood."[66] Hence, the importance of solidarity among women cannot easily be overstated in the process of both naming oppressions and also seeking ways to overcome them. She says:

> The most difficult part of re-imagining ourselves and affirming our experience is to articulate our oppression. Our inhibitions are valid because we have been brought up to smile—even when suffering. Any collective hurts we identify are immediately personalized and particularized. We must, therefore, find ways of acting not just as individuals but collectively.[67]

Not only is this the way of healing for women, it is also the way of healing for the nations. In summary then, Oduyoye suggests that women can model a move to liberation and justice in two ways. First, in letting go of the quality exclusively assigned to women and extending them to all human beings. She says: "Our desire to make a home is positive. The problem with our homemaking is the unilateral way in which we women appropriate the process, shielding men and male children from learning self-giving."[68]

The second act of modeling moves beyond the individual and family context and extends to all communities, even the state, as the voice of women is heard. She explains:

[63] Oduyoye, *Daughters of Anowa*, 197n13.
[64] Oduyoye, *Daughters of Anowa*, 197–98.
[65] Oduyoye, *Daughters of Anowa*, 199.
[66] Oduyoye, *Daughters of Anowa*, 202.
[67] Oduyoye, *Daughters of Anowa*, 204.
[68] Oduyoye, *Daughters of Anowa*, 205.

Women's demand for fuller participation is therefore not a self-serving call. Our accumulated wisdom of mothering can serve the nation by community building. What African woman, having a chance to run from disaster, would leave children and relatives behind? If forced to do so, what African woman would not look back on the disaster? For women the figure of Lot's wife is a portrait of the cost of compassion, not the punishment for disobedience of a patriarchal injunction.[69]

Healing women can heal an entire nation. As African women create more and more structures of compassion, solidarity, caring, and community, they will create structures of justice both for themselves and for the nations. This models an entirely new way of making ethical decisions—issues like abortion, same-sex love, female prostitution, male prostitution, child abuse, and child care will then not be responded to with abstract pronouncements but with people of compassion, love, and caring. This may well result in variety rather than uniformity, but then the Spirit cannot be tamed.

CONCLUSION

Oduyoye's rebellion against the Western imagination of power and control is evident throughout her writing. She rejects the right of the West to set the terms in which theology is written and practiced or the right for anyone to define what it means to be human and liberated; and this goes all the way down the cultural divide, whether it is the church, the academy, Western women, or other nations. This is but to say that place matters, and it matters in particular ways. It matters because the Spirit has worked and continues to work in places like Africa, and therefore there is wisdom there; and it matters because how we hear the Spirit is colored by the place from which it is heard. The oneness of the church, therefore, requires that we are able to hear multiple voices in harmony or even sometimes in a cacophony of irreconcilable voices. For dissonance and struggle are not evil!

Oduyoye is a poet and although I have not given voice to much of her poetry, it is fitting that I end this chapter with words that highlight what she says throughout her theology, namely that place matters.

> Where is the way forward
> When we do not want to know where we are
> When we do not care where we've come from
> When we refuse to talk about where we would like
>   to be or where we want to head for?
> How do we know which is the way forward?[70]

---

[69] Oduyoye, *Daughters of Anowa*, 206.
[70] Mercy Amba Oduyoye, *Introducing African Women's Theology* (Cleveland: Pilgrim Press, 2001), 120.

PART IV-C

The chapters in this section focus on issues in feminist theological ethics. It is clear from the three writers that feminism does not admit of a single approach to Christian ethics nor one set of issues. This is so in three ways: first, oppression is not understood in the same way; second, liberation admits of no uniform definition; and third, the role of the church, Jesus, and God vary vastly in crafting models of justice. This variety has to do in part with different cultural settings and in part with the matter of how the qualifier "Christian" shapes feminism. Indeed, it raises the question of whether there can be feminism in general or whether it is always embodied within a culture-religion-tradition. Of course, this is but a variant of the question of Christian ethics in general: can Christian ethics be conceived in such a manner as to provide ethical answers and guidance for everyone? Or is ethics, and by implication feminism, somehow bound by a qualifier? For feminists, this is an especially sensitive question because "exclusion" lies at the heart of so much of what they oppose due to the history of marginalization of women in the church.

Christian feminism seems to insist on a theological culling of sorts: what must go and what can remain of the theological tradition? Can the notion of biblical authority survive? The authority of Jesus? Classical theology? The church? Even Christianity as an intellectual construct is suspect since some feel it inhibits free thinking and practice. And among the three scholars there are different answers to these questions.

SOURCES

The question of legitimate sources for doing theology is important to all three authors. All seek to broaden the theological canon to include nontraditional voices. Ruether gleans the wisdom of ancient myths in helping us see what Christianity needlessly discarded and what it might profitably reclaim; Welch wants to add to Christian history the traditions of Buddhism and the insights of humanism and aboriginal spirituality; and Oduyoye endeavors to bring into harmony with Christianity the practices of African traditions, which, as she sees it, can illuminate the Christian faith.

Although all three move beyond a narrow casting of normative Christian sources, there are clear differences among them. Ruether and Oduyoye insist on reclaiming the Christian tradition in ways that Welch does not. Welch is unable to give moral authority to anything in history, including the historical figure of Jesus, the Bible as authoritative source, and the theology of the church. She resorts instead to a spirituality without God and an ethic without virtues. Ruether wishes to reclaim Jesus and biblical authority, but only after showing that the maleness of Jesus has no theological significance and the biblical story is subjected to hermeneutical critique. Oduyoye is less bothered by these theological issues and seeks instead to help Africans open themselves to the voice of Jesus without closing themselves to the voices of African ancestors. Her concern is that too much Western culture has come firmly attached to the gospel preached by the missionaries.

HISTORY

The category of history functions differently in their respective theologies. It is a problem for Welch in a way not shared by Ruether or Oduyoye. All agree that history is replete with practices of oppression, especially for women. And yet for Ruether and Oduyoye, history also carries much of the wisdom for overcoming oppression in ways that it does not for Welch. For Welch the promise of overcoming lies in the power of the human imagination directed toward *future* possibilities in the hope of disclosing new models and new practices of liberation, guided not by past theological constants but by a creative human spirit. In other words, Welch's history is more radically problematic than it is for either Ruether or Oduyoye, and her future more radically open.

HUMAN FREEDOM

A related issue in these chapters is the matter of human freedom. All three agree that the way things currently stand is not the way they need to be. "Things could be otherwise" is an underlying mantra for all liberation theologians and especially for feminists. This means that structurally their ethic is eschatological, but not in the sense that the future is already known. The future must remain open; hence the "now" cannot be measured by a known "end of history." Therefore all three emphasize *process* rather than *telos*. And this process is guided by free, human agents. Ruether names this process "biophilic mutuality," which ties all of reality together under God; for Welch it is human decency in openness to the checks and balances of public debate and the quest for human liberation, all under the umbrella of free democratic exchange; and for Oduyoye it is the incarnation, learning

to hear Jesus in discussion, as did the early disciples on the Emmaus road. That is, all three lodge ethics in a "dialogue" on the way rather than in rules or principles. Ethics is less about right and wrong and more about struggle, listening, and discerning together. What *is* wrong, however, is the curtailment of an open process by imposed closure of any sort.

CONTROL/POWER

All three are adamant about the evils of an ethic of control. The use of power by a few to determine the manner in which life ought to move—whether that is done politically, morally, religiously, intellectually, or relationally—is hubris and hence undermines all efforts to articulate a defensible view of the Christian life. This has them all denouncing militarism, sexism, racism, statism, poverty, and so on. All are structured forms of violence that deny some people the freedom to be full human beings and its leaders the capacity to recognize their own sin. It is, therefore, not surprising that we find most feminists horrified by war as a means of resolving disputes and engaged in the avid search for alternatives. And it should not escape our notice that all three have been active members of the peace movement in their respective locations and aggressive in naming injustices around the world and rallying support for just alternatives.

While each feminist argues the evils of control in general, each also names a special locus of concern particular to her own context. For Ruether, an especially troublesome control is found in the Catholic Church hierarchy; for Oduyoye, it is with colonialism in general and the missionary church specifically; and for Welch, it exists with the very notion of moral authority as such. It must be said that a major contribution of feminists in general and the three presented in particular lies in naming the insidious effects of power abuse, especially in its camouflaged and hidden forms. It can be found everywhere, in well-intentioned people, in churches, social and political structures, in the peace movements, in language—religious, ethical, political—thought patterns, habits, and so on. In their writings they seek to reconceive both the meaning and use of power. None argue that power is inherently evil; all advocate that power be lodged in relationality and dialogue rather than in hierarchical structures or abstract systems of thought.

PEACE

The issue of power has direct connections with peacemaking. None of the three feminists presented takes a strong position for pacifism. Welch explicitly rejects it, because she believes that sometimes violence is required to bring about a just peace, and yet she is perhaps the most active in the American peace movement. Ruether, while lauding Martin Luther King Jr. and commending a theology of "letting go," nevertheless remains aloof on the matter of pacifism. And Oduyoye is difficult to assess on this issue because she has no interest is discussing "isms." Actually, the approach is common to all three: once ethics is placed into the space of relationality and dialogic exchange, pacifism is far too abstract to be considered morally relevant.

There are, however, questions related to peacemaking that persist. How are readers to understand their incisive critique of the "valorization of power" and "the ethic of control," on the one hand, and, on the other hand, a justification for minimal violence when done in the right way? It sounds as if the issue is less the imposition of power and use of violence and more a matter of who is using it. Does this mean that when placed in the right hands limited violence is justifiable after all? While these questions are clearly more apropos to Welch than to Ruether and Oduyoye, nevertheless, it is not clear from the writings of any of the three under what conditions, if any, violence may be considered permissible in the quest to bring about peace and justice.

It is noteworthy that both American feminists link their thought to issues discussed by aboriginal writers. Ruether engages the work of Vine Deloria Jr. in *God Is Red*, and echoes his concern for the ecological crisis in her proposal of ecofeminism and ecojustice. Welch draws on the writings of Carol Lee Sanchez and Jace Weaver in her own work, especially their thoughts on native spirituality. It should not be surprising to find affinity between Native and feminist concerns because they clearly share common forms of oppression. One sees fewer appeals from the aboriginal side, however. Perhaps this is true because the liberation issue for American Indians is closely tied to nationhood and especially to land. It is harder to find common ground with American feminists on this issue.

There are also other important topics that our three authors have placed on the ethical agenda: sexuality, marriage, abortion, female circumcision, same-sex love, mental illness, and male/female existence. In each case the matter is not raised to be resolved by rules, or goals, or by a different authority. Rather, resolution is lodged within an embodied community, which for Ruether and Oduyoye is the church and for Welch is open democratic exchange. In other words, the question is how loving, open, and compassionate persons can be a community of support for the resolution of these matters; how can they help in naming what is at stake and how can they provide support and healing to those who are hurting?

It should not be surprising that an American Catholic, a Unitarian, and an African Methodist would not agree on the details of the parameters for Christian ethics; perhaps what is surprising is that these scholars agree on so much of what is wrong with the world—militarism, sexism, racism, colonialism, patriarchalism, hierarchalism, cultural arrogance—in general, the erotics of domination.

Yet agreement on the problems does not lead them in the same direction regarding the church and theology. Ruether and Oduyoye remain committed to the church—Ruether to an open Catholicism and Oduyoye to ecumenism. For Welch the church, and to a large degree theology, seem to have become relics of history because they are themselves inherently oppressive. Both church and Christian theology are simply too exclusive for Welch to see them as agents of liberation. For Ruether and Oduyoye, although in different manners, the church holds the possibility of bringing together in Christ what has been broken apart through human sin. For them there is nothing definitionally exclusive about the church as such. That being said, the reader detects within the voices of both Ruether and Oduyoye a lament; neither are able to celebrate the reality of structures and embodied communities of Christians who are able to participate in their own quest of developing the skills necessary to read the world and the Christian faith aright.

Welch and Ruether also have different visions for how to live responsibly in America. And it has to do with risk-taking. Clearly, both are critical of the quest for global dominance that has characterized so much of American history; both hold before the American people a model of cooperative power that seeks justice on the basis of an exchange with people of difference rather than protection on the basis of superior might. Nevertheless, Ruether's vision for America is one that, although not clearly defined, participates in a reign that was inaugurated with Jesus Christ. Hence, her vision for peace and justice in America and in the world has ontological roots, which Welch is unable to embrace. For Welch, the risk is much more absolute. "Pax Humana" rests in the human spirit and the challenges of global citizenship, and not in God's gracious, redemptive, and agential love. For Ruether and Oduyoye, that risk is too great, all the more so because it is a needless one. For them, God is the peacemaker under whose care, empowerment, and wisdom it becomes possible for us to be agents of peace. And in the end, might this not be the greater risk; for it is the risk of faith that there is more to the real world than is empirically given.

PART IV

CRITICAL RESPONSES TO TWENTIETH-CENTURY
CHRISTIAN ETHICS

•

Section D
Peace Theologians

Chapter Thirty-Two

JOHN HOWARD YODER
(1927–1997)

This study has already made several references to the theological ethics of John Howard Yoder. While Yoder was not a mainstream American ethicist like the Niebuhr brothers, for example, his influence on the American ethical discussion is significant. He was able to inject into that discussion the rather obvious, but highly controversial, claim that Christian ethics should be about Jesus Christ.

Twentieth-century, post-Troeltschean thought had found it necessary to think of ethics only by denying the relevance of Jesus. Jesus was thought to be too radical in his demands. References like the following were cited as proof: "But if anyone strikes you on the right cheek, turn the other also; and if anyone wants to sue you and take your coat, give your cloak as well; and if anyone forces you to go one mile, go also the second mile" (Matt 5:39b-41); and "Sell all that you own and distribute the money to the poor, and you will have treasures in heaven; then come, follow me" (Luke 18:22b).

The point is then made that a discipleship (following-after) ethic is not possible; a responsible, social-economic ethic and even accountable, interpersonal ethic can be constructed on the basis of Jesus' demands. Reinhold Niebuhr, for example, concludes that Jesus represents an "impossible ideal"

which, while still relevant generally, nevertheless simply cannot be practiced in today's society. Major reconstruction is required from the standpoint of assumptions that we must be realistic about our claims of social responsibility because Christianity is meant to be practiced *in this world*.[1] The issues of mainstream ethics consequently get framed under the rubric of the tension between the real (social reality) and the ideal (the teaching of Jesus).

One way Niebuhr negotiates the real/ ideal tension is by invoking the distinction between the morality of individuals who are able to live according to the principle of love versus the much more-restricted morality of corporate identities like societies or organizations which are not.[2] For the latter, he reserves the language of justice, and here Jesus is not very helpful. In a parallel way, his brother H. Richard Niebuhr makes the distinction between Christ and culture, suggesting that Christ stands outside of culture, wishing to "transform" it.[3] In other words, Christ is the ideal and functions as a general critique of "real" culture.

With the Niebuhrian critique of pacifism, the idea of Christian nonviolence lost credibility in the twentieth century. Yoder set out to change that. He showed that the common Nieburian approach to Christian ethics

---

[1] See esp. Reinhold Niebuhr, *An Interpretation of Christian Ethics* (San Francisco: HarperCollins, 1987). See also chap. 20 above.

[2] See Reinhold Niebuhr, *Moral Man and Immoral Society* (New York: Charles Scribner's Sons, 1932). See also chap. 20 above.

[3] H. Richard Niebuhr, *Christ and Culture* (New York: Harper & Row, 1951). See also chap. 21 above.

was the wrong way to start. To suggest that Jesus is an ideal which must be made realistic or that his teachings must be domesticated by the givenness of a particular culture is already to misunderstand Jesus. Jesus was enculturated in first-century, Palestinian Jewish tradition, and he invited his hearers to see the world from a standpoint other than the status quo politics. In other words, Jesus advocated a "counterculture." But to call this idealism is to prejudge the possibilities of worlds other than the one we inhabit. The issue is not a choice between the real and the ideal or between Christ and culture. The issue is about seeing the world and being in it differently—that is, the issue is about competing imaginations.

Yoder sought a way out from under the Niebuhrian dualisms, and he found it in Jesus. He suggests that Jesus was painting a picture not of unreality or ideality but of the world as imagined in the Judeo-Christian tradition, namely, created good, fallen, and being restored by the redeeming activities of God. Hence, Jesus is seen as presenting an alternative (or counter) politics, advocated not because Jesus was under the illusion of an imminent end to the world (as modern theology since Troeltsch has commonly assumed) and therefore could afford to be radical but because it was the way of the kingdom that he was announcing to be at hand.

HIS LIFE

John Howard Yoder was born into a Mennonite family in Smithville, Ohio, on December 29, 1927, to parents Ethel Good and Howard C. Yoder. He had a brother who died as a child and a younger sister, Mary Ellen. Growing up in the ways of a Mennonite family, and training in the Oak Grove Mennonite Church in his hometown, allowed

him to own the faith of his people without needing to prove his independence from it, he says. "[M]y choice to stay within [the faith of the church family] . . . was by no means a matter of bowing to superior pressure but was rather a willing choice made in small stages in young adulthood."[4] As a child, he attended public schools; at one point, he hoped to enter a special accelerated program at either the University of Chicago or St. John's College in Annapolis, Maryland. Instead, at his parents' urging, he enrolled in the fall of 1945 in a Mennonite denominational school, Goshen College in Indiana, where he majored in Bible and completed the four-year B.A. in two years.

At Goshen, he encountered two influential teachers—Harold S. Bender and Guy F. Hershberger. Both were in their prime teaching years, and both had just completed seminal studies which attempted to show the relevance of sixteenth-century Anabaptism for twentieth-century Christians.[5] Yoder was especially fascinated with Bender's work, partly because "he gave Mennonites a 'usable past.'"[6] This was the beginning of what was to become his relentless effort to reconstruct for the Christian world a dynamic faith from a rich tradition that stretched over several millennia.

Upon graduating from Goshen College in 1947, Yoder began working on a farm doing research in plant nutrition. After a year, he was able to travel to many Mennonite churches and camps to speak about the Mennonite peace teaching. He applied during this time to serve under Mennonite Central Committee (MCC) in Europe and took courses in religious studies and Hebrew while waiting for his assignment to be processed.

In 1949 MCC sent Yoder to France to work in "homes for stranded children." For the next

[4] Quoted in Mark Thiessen Nation, "John H. Yoder, Ecumenical Neo-Anabaptist: A Biographical Sketch," in *The Wisdom of the Cross: Essays in Honor of John Howard Yoder*, ed. Stanley Hauerwas, Chris K. Huebner, Harry J. Huebner, and Mark Thiessen Nation (Grand Rapids: Eerdmans, 1999), 7. The following comments about Yoder's life rely upon Nation's work.

[5] See Guy F. Hershberger, *War, Peace, and Nonresistance* (Scottdale, Penn.: Herald, 1944); and Harold S. Bender, "The Anabaptist Vision," *Church History* 13 (1944): 3–24.

[6] Mark Thiessen Nation, *John Howard Yoder: Mennonite Patience, Evangelical Witness, Catholic Convictions* (Grand Rapids: Eerdmans, 2006), 15.

five years, he supervised several such homes, making sure the children were well-fed and housed while also taking every opportunity to get into venues where he could teach about peace. While on assignment, he met a fellow worker, a French Mennonite named Anne Marie Guth. They married on July 12, 1952. They would have seven children, six of whom survived: Rebecca, Martha, Elisabeth, Esther, Daniel, and John-David.[7]

While in Europe, Yoder also began graduate studies at the University of Basel, where he received his doctorate in theology in 1962. Here, he studied with well-known scholars like Walter Eichrodt, Oscar Cullmann, Karl Jaspers, and Karl Barth. It was in Europe that he began his lifelong commitment to an ecumenical conversation on Christian theology and especially pacifism and the Christian view of peace and justice. He believed that if you were a follower of Jesus, you had no option but to be committed to pacifism. The story is told that in 1962, shortly before his dissertation defense, he handed Karl Barth a fifty-page critique of Barth's views on pacifism. The move came just a few days before Barth was to sit on Yoder's defense committee. This style of bold proclamation of how he saw the gospel of Jesus Christ characterized all Yoder's ecumenical work, as well as his teaching.

After returning from Europe, he began a long teaching career—first at Goshen College, his alma mater, and then from 1965 to 1984 at Goshen Biblical Seminary, which became Associated Mennonite Biblical Seminary (AMBS) when it joined Mennonite Biblical Seminary in Elkhart, Indiana. Here, he taught theology, church history, Christian ethics, and peace studies, and from 1970 to 1973, also served as president of the seminary. While he was teaching at AMBS, he also taught courses at the University of Notre Dame in South Bend, Indiana. He valued the Catholic setting and felt privileged to be able to teach peace theology in places other than Mennonite institutions. After 1984 he taught full-time at Notre Dame as a professor of Christian ethics in the theology department and at the Joan B. Kroc Institute for International Peace Studies.

Yoder's scope of writing and research is extremely broad, and not all of his work has been published. He wrote on the relation of church and state; Christian ethics; pacifism; ecclesiology; Christology; church discipline; marriage, divorce, and sexuality; war and peace; Constantinianism; Jewish-Christian schism; just-war theory; and so on. There is probably no other Christian ethicist who has insisted more strongly on the central place for church in defining the meaning of Christian ethics. For him, church was the disciplined community without which there can be no moral accountability. This is perhaps nowhere more poignantly stated than in his booklet *Body Politics.*[8]

His emphasis on church discipline, especially on "binding and loosing" (Matt 18:15-20), makes it important to note that Yoder had his own "discipline" issues with the church. In 1991–1992 he was confronted by his home congregation, Prairie Street Mennonite Church, when several women came forward to report Yoder's inappropriate sexualizing of his relationship with them over a period of years. These charges were believed by the church leaders, both in the local church and in the regional conference. In June 1992, Yoder's ministerial credentials were suspended followed by a process of confrontation, confession, forgiveness, and restoration. In June 1996, this formal process came to an end with a statement from the conference leadership reporting that they saw sufficient change in Yoder's beliefs and behaviors to encourage the churches to again "use his gifts of writing and teaching."[9] By

---

[7] See Nation, "Ecumenical Neo-Anabaptist," 15.

[8] John Howard Yoder, *Body Politics: Five Practices of the Christian Community Before the Watching World* (Nashville: Discipleship Resources, 1992).

[9] From "Disciplinary Process with Yoder Concludes," *Gospel Herald* (June 18, 1996): 11.

mutual agreement his ministerial credentials were not reinstated. Throughout this process, his marriage to Annie survived.

Yoder continued to write and teach until December 30, 1997, when, in his office at the University of Notre Dame, he died suddenly of an aortic aneurysm. To illustrate the shock of his death for his colleagues, allow me a personal anecdote. On that day, I received a phone call from Stanley Hauerwas—an event that does not happen often—who, after introducing himself, simply said, "John is dead!" Hauerwas was stunned, for the impact of Yoder's work on his was immeasurable.

HIS EARLY WRITING

This chapter will focus primarily on Yoder's 1972 book, *The Politics of Jesus*, not because it is the only important book he wrote—perhaps in the long run it will not even prove to be his most important work—but because it played such an important role in shaping some American Christian ethicists, most notably perhaps, Stanley Hauerwas and James William McClendon Jr. In addition, *The Politics of Jesus* is not easy to summarize briefly because it is one, long, sustained argument. Hence, I have decided to give it its due in this chapter.

This should not cloud the fact that Yoder wrote many other books, essays, and pamphlets, both before and after 1972. He began writing in Europe as a student, especially with the "Concern" group, seven Mennonite men doing graduate studies at the time.[10] All were inspired by writers like Harold S. Bender and were seeking in their own way to recover the Anabaptist vision. An important essay that comes from Yoder at this time is "Peace without Eschatology?"[11] in which he questions the thinking of those who believe that peace is within human reach and, given

the faith in human progress, may be just around the corner.

In 1964 Yoder wrote *The Christian Witness to the State*,[12] in which he articulates at once a separation of church and state and an engagement model. During this time, he also wrote short pamphlets in critical engagement on the topic of pacifism with prominent scholars like Karl Barth and Reinhold Niebuhr. Then in 1971, two books explicitly on pacifism: *Nevertheless*, and *The Original Revolution*.[13] Although there are many other essays and pamphlets during this time, in 1972 he published *The Politics of Jesus*.

THE POLITICS OF JESUS

The most general way to state the thesis of this study is to say Yoder wants to question the notion that the only way of getting from the gospel story to ethics is to leave the story behind. He claims he is not doing original, exegetical, or textual explanation but is pushing a single question of whether a persistent and clear political/social ethic exists in the story of Jesus. This is an important matter to test because of the predominant, negative answer to the question provided by contemporary Christian ethicists.

In order to set the stage for his argument, Yoder lists the six most common ways contemporary ethicists reject Jesus as relevant for social ethics.

1. The ethic that Jesus advocates is meant for an "interim" which Jesus thought would be brief.[14] This view suggests Jesus was quite unconcerned about lasting social structures because he believed that the world would soon pass away. So at the point where ethicists are to give guidance on responsible, survivable, social structures, Jesus cannot be of any help.
2. Jesus was a simple, rural figure who may have had some insights into a village sociology, but he knew nothing about large, social

---

[10] See Nation, *John Howard Yoder*, 19ff. for more on the Concern group.

[11] "Peace without Eschatology," is reprinted in John Howard Yoder, *The Royal Priesthood: Essays, Ecclesiological and Ecumenical*, ed. Michael G. Cartwright (Grand Rapids: Eerdmans, 1994), 143–67.

[12] John Howard Yoder, *The Christian Witness to the State* (North Newton, Kan.: Faith & Life, 1964).

[13] John Howard Yoder, *Nevertheless: A Meditation on the Varieties and Shortcomings of Religious Pacifism* (Scottdale, Penn.: Herald, 1971); and *The Original Revolution: Essays on Christian* Pacifism (Scottdale, Penn.: Herald, 1971).

[14] John Howard Yoder, *The Politics of Jesus: Vicit Agnus Noster*, 2nd ed. (Grand Rapids: Eerdmans, 1994), 5.

organizations like multi-national corporations. In fact, the argument goes, he seemed altogether naïve about social power dynamics.

3. Jesus lived in a world over which he had no control, but we live in a democracy where we are to exercise responsible judgment. Jesus simply never had to face the kinds of complex, practical problems that we do because in his day he was not permitted to make a political difference. We are!

4. The message of Jesus was in principle not about social and political matters but about the individual or about the inwardness of faith. In other words, he was speaking to spiritual and not social matters.

5. Jesus was a "radical monotheist," which is language used by H. Richard Niebuhr.[15] In this model, all values are relativized under God's commands, and the call to faithfulness is to remain open to God to hear what should be done. This means what Jesus did can be an example only in a formal way (being open to God as he was) but not in a material way.

6. Jesus came to deal with the sins of humanity. That is, his mission focused on atonement not ethics. Hence, to use his life as a model for ethics is to simply misunderstand the work of Christ and to mistakenly assume he was modeling faithfulness for his followers.

The dismissal argument does not end with the (mis)reading of the Jesus story. It is followed by a larger reconstruction. It is said that the Apostle Paul realized that the significance of Jesus was not ethics but grace and points out that an emphasis on ethics leads to a works righteousness, which is antithetical to salvation. Paul could therefore continue to support institutions like slavery, the subordination of women, and tyrannical governments—that is, he was unconcerned about social ethics. And when it came to give moral counsel, he turned to other sources like Stoicism since Jesus had so little to contribute on the subject.

Yoder explicitly challenges these common (mis)readings of the Jesus (biblical) story. He does this first on the basis of New Testament interpretation, then on theological grounds

such as the meaning of the incarnation and Trinity, and finally on the basis of the inner consistency of Christian ethics itself. He sets out to argue that a careful reading of the biblical text requires one to conclude that Jesus is relevant for social ethics—and not only relevant but normative.

The basis of Yoder's (re)reading of the Jesus story is the Gospel of Luke. He begins with the prebirth narrative to disclose the kind of birth that is being expected. For example, he refers to the Magnificat (Luke 1:46-55) and, relying upon recent biblical scholarship, suggests that it should be read as a Maccabean battle song. More particularly, the birth of the one who is being announced in this "song of praise" is expected to be "an agent of radical social change."[16] He is to bring good news to the people. Moreover, this good news, in the words of Zechariah includes "being saved from the enemy,"[17] and cannot be dismissed simply as something to be "taken spiritually." Whatever the misunderstanding may have been about Jesus, it could not have been that Jesus intended a spiritual message while the hearers hoped for real, social/political change. If that were the issue, surely the story would have had to start differently. In other words, the people were *entitled* to hope for real, social, and political change in the coming of Jesus, even though this change would happen in ways that defy conventional imaginations of how it should occur.

The Temptations

When Luke moves on to the stories of the temptations and the baptism of Jesus, we see the beginnings of the outline of the task to which Jesus is summoned. Yoder points out that the words which "came from heaven" (Luke 3:22), "You are my Son, the Beloved; with you I am well pleased," have a double biblical allusion, one to enthronement (Ps 2:7) and the other to the suffering servant (Isa 42:1b). The theme therefore emerges at the very beginning that Jesus is being enthroned

---

[15] H. Richard Niebuhr, *Radical Monotheism and Western Culture* (New York: Harper, 1960).
[16] Yoder, *Politics of Jesus*, 22.   [17] Yoder, *Politics of Jesus*, 22.

as a new king whose reign will be character-ized by suffering servanthood. So when the devil begins his temptations with the words, "If you are the Son of God, then . . ." the issue is the nature of his kingship, for the "Son of God" in Psalms 2:7 is the king.[18] Hence, each of the temptation accounts, according to Yoder, are ways of cracking the messianic son/servant union of the heavenly call.

Luke's first temptation is about turning stones into bread. Yoder calls this the eco-nomic option. Feed the crowds, and they will make you king. In the second tempta-tion, Jesus is shown "all the kingdoms of the world" and told they can all be his if he will worship the devil. Yoder suggests that Jesus is here tempted by the "idolatrous character of political power hunger and nationalism."[19] The third temptation takes Jesus to the "pin-nacle of the temple," where he is told to throw himself down and allow the angels to come and save him from harm. Following Niels Hyldahl's work, Yoder suggests two possible interpretations: since the prescribed penalty for blasphemy was being thrown into the Kidron Valley from the temple tower, Jesus would here be tempted to avoid the conse-quences of his claim to divine authority, that is, avoid the way of the cross. Alternatively, if he were to throw himself into the temple court, he would be the heavenly messenger injected into history to miraculously set things right.[20] Both have political import. Jesus rejects all of these ways of being king.

Jesus' Ministry

The Lukan introduction of Jesus' Galilean ministry begins far more modestly than the grandiose options would have the reader anticipate. The text simply says he began to teach in their synagogues. Luke, at the start, leaves off the content of Jesus' teaching, while

Matthew and Mark speak immediately of his proclamation of the kingdom of God (heav-en), which is distinctly political language. A kingdom requires a king and a people over whom the king reigns. When Luke later re-fers to the nature of his teaching in the syna-gogues, he uses similar political language, speaking of proclaiming the good news of the *kingdom of God* (Luke 4:43).

Instead of *describing* the nature of Jesus' teaching, Luke begins with a specific example at Nazareth. In the synagogue, Jesus reads from Isaiah 61, stating that "He has anointed me to preach good news to the poor . . . re-lease to the captives . . . sight to the blind . . . liberty to the oppressed, to proclaim *the ac-ceptable year of the Lord*."[21] Then when Jesus sits down, he says, "Today this scripture has been fulfilled in your hearing" (Luke 4:21b).

Yoder suggests that the reference to "the acceptable year of the Lord" is the Jubilee year, that old tradition of the Sabbath year when the tenets of equalizing justice were put in practice. Here he relies upon the work of André Trocmé, who elaborates the provi-sions of the Sabbath year as they are record-ed in Leviticus 25. The point Yoder makes is simple: Jesus' teaching in the Nazareth synagogue had the effect of "announcing the imminent implementation of a new regime whose marks would be that the rich would give to the poor, the captives would be freed, and the hearers would have a new mentality (*metanoia*), if they believed this news."[22]

A second theme in the Nazareth story is the tension between the hearers and Jesus. At first, Jesus is highly regarded for his mes-sage. Words of justice are always good news to the oppressed! Then when Jesus extends this good news to others "outside the fold" by telling the stories of the widow at Zarephath in Sidon and Naaman the Syrian (that is,

---

[18] Yoder, *Politics of Jesus*, 25.

[19] Yoder, *Politics of Jesus*, 27.

[20] Yoder, *Politics of Jesus*, 27.

[21] See Yoder, *Politics of Jesus*, 29 (emphasis added). A word of explanation is in order about biblical translations used. Whenever I cite Yoder's work, I will use his translation, which does not follow a consistent version; when I cite the biblical text directly, it is from the NRSV.   [22] Yoder, *Politics of Jesus*, 32 (emphasis in original).

Gentiles) and how they too are considered part of the new kingdom, the hearers are deeply upset. The point is clear: the kingdom which is being proclaimed here includes both Jews and Gentiles.

A new teaching is of little threat as long as the teacher acts and teaches alone. But once there is an organization and a following, things change. It then becomes a movement and potentially a social alternative. And clearly the naming of the twelve disciples is more than the mere multiplication of manpower. It is a symbolic proclamation indicated by the number twelve, namely, they are the first fruits of a restored Israel.

The invitation to the Twelve and other disciples into the teaching and healing mission extends not only to Judea and Jerusalem but also to people from the coast of Tyre and Sidon—again, the Gentiles (Luke 6:17). And the content of the teaching (the "Sermon") and healing (in this case the centurion's servant) is again given by the modeling example of Jesus. Blessings are extended to the poor, the hungry, the weeping, and the hated; and woes are issued to the rich, the satiated, the laughing, and those who are spoken well of. In other words, with Jesus there is a great reversal coming, where the lives of the followers will be characterized by love of enemies, generosity, and mercy, and the commonly accepted standards and structures of justice will change.

According to Yoder's reading of Luke, the *path* of this reversal is far from typical, and consequently the disciples have a hard time understanding it.[23] Yet in order to be disciples, it is precisely this path that must become clear. In chapter 9, Luke attempts to define the nature of this path from injustice to justice with the aid of three stories/events: the mission of the Twelve, the feeding of the five thousand, and the confession of Peter.

The mission to the disciples is simple and clear, namely, do as Jesus does: "proclaim the kingdom of God and heal" (Luke 9:2). The feeding of the five thousand, as the devil had predicted, was a popular event with the crowds. What is equally clear is Jesus' discomfort with the evident misunderstanding that was taking place about his ministry, mission, and identity. So the time had come to make clear what the nature of his kingship was (and hence what it would mean to follow him) if he were to be more than a welfare king.

The question of Jesus' identity is addressed squarely when he asks what people (and the disciples) are saying about who he is. In spelling out Peter's answer that he is the "Messiah of God" (Luke 9:20) Jesus speaks of suffering and the cross as the way of the kingdom. Furthermore, this "way" exists for both himself as well as those who follow after him. Hence, peculiarly perhaps, the strategy of "bringing in" the new kingdom ends up being no strategy at all. Rather, it consists of that "style of life of which the cross is the culmination."[24] Or, as Yoder says, "the cross is beginning to loom not as a ritually prescribed instrument of propitiation but as the political alternative to both insurrection and quietism."[25] This is the culmination and the conclusion of his Galilean ministry. After this he "sets his face to go to Jerusalem" (Luke 9:51).

Jesus' Last Days in Jerusalem

We have here a clear foreshadowing of the nature of the king who is welcomed in Jerusalem in the Palm Sunday parade, in which the masses shout: "Blessed is the king who comes in the name of the Lord" (Luke 19:28). The character of this king, as introduced so far and as Jesus is to confirm explicitly later (Luke 22:25-27), is marked by service and not lordship—peace, not manipulation and violence. This prompts Yoder to say that in the ministry of Jesus we see that, "the alternative to how the kings of the earth rule is not 'spirituality' but servanthood."[26]

---

[23] Yoder, *Politics of Jesus*, 34ff.
[24] Yoder, *Politics of Jesus*, 38.
[25] Yoder, *Politics of Jesus*, 36.
[26] Yoder, *Politics of Jesus*, 39.

Not surprisingly, the events in Jerusalem prove confrontational. Jesus' first encounter is in the temple. Even before this, as he was descending from the Mount of Olives overlooking the city, he wept because the people did not recognize the things that made for peace (Luke 19:42). And now in the temple, he faced a situation that deeply distressed him and he proceeded to "cleanse" it (Luke 19:45-47).

This story is sometimes used to point out that even Jesus resorted to justified violence when the situation called for it. Yet Yoder makes the point, derived from the work of biblical translators, that the whip used in the temple was to drive out the animals and was not used on people. This is an act of authority, not violence.

By establishing his authority over the temple, Jesus is now in control of the religious establishment and it remains for him, at least as the crowds saw it, to establish control over the military power—the Roman fortress next door. It is clear, however, that there is no way Jesus could bring about this feat without recourse to violence. And while he may be interested in the same changes as the people around him, namely, the overthrow of the old order, his way was different from the old ways.

There is, therefore, clearly a clash between two regimes. The old regime entails taking matters into one's own hands and defeating the enemy by whatever means necessary, and the new regime which Jesus was inaugurating did not. Yoder makes the point that these regimes are not in different arenas, the one political and the other spiritual, which is a common view—although in the same arena the politics is profoundly different.

Yoder deals next with the story of Jesus in the garden of Gethsemane. He asks what it might have meant for the petition to "remove this cup from me" (Luke 22:42) to be answered. That is, what option was Jesus actually struggling with? Yoder puts it as follows: "The only imaginable real option in terms of historical seriousness, and the only one with even a slim basis in the text, is the hypothesis that Jesus was drawn, at this very last moment of temptation, to think once again of the messianic violence with which he had been tempted since the beginning. Now is finally the time for holy war."[27]

For the third time now, Jesus rejects the opportunity for violent takeover—he could have done so after the feeding of the multitudes, he had the chance after the entry into the temple, and now finally he could have "appealed to [the] father and he would [have] sent [him] more than twelve legions of angels" (Matt 26:53). But at each point, he rejected the option in favor of an alternative route characterized by refusing violent takeover and culminating in the cross.

Although Jesus was not violent, he clearly exercised a lot of power. And the power that he did wield bothered the authorities "to the point of their resorting to irregular procedures to counter it."[28] Yoder considers this "proof of the political relevance of nonviolent tactics, not a proof that Pilate and Caiaphas were exceptionally dull or dishonorable men."[29]

Yoder sees the matter of nonviolence lodged right at the very heart of Jesus' ministry. It is not derived from a few of Jesus' sayings. Moreover, there is in the ministry of Jesus a consistent theme of politics and social relevance, even though the path to overcome injustice is neither popular nor easy. The cross is at the very center of the politics of Jesus. As Yoder puts it:

> Here at the cross is the man who loves his enemies, the man whose righteousness is greater than that of the Pharisees, who being rich became poor, who gave his robe to those who took his cloak, who prays for those who despitefully use him. The cross is not a detour or a hurdle on the way to the kingdom, nor is it even the way to the kingdom; it is the kingdom come.[30]

[27] Yoder, *Politics of Jesus*, 46.
[28] Yoder, *Politics of Jesus*, 49.
[29] Yoder, *Politics of Jesus*, 49.
[30] Yoder, *Politics of Jesus*, 51.

Later, Yoder spells out in greater detail the social character of the cross. Clearly, the notion of the cross is related to suffering, yet the suffering of the cross is not any kind of suffering. It is specifically the "price of social nonconformity."[31] The biggest temptation that Jesus faced was not the temptation to withdraw from social responsibility or the conservative approach of the "Sadducean establishment"[32] but rather the temptation to exercise responsibility through violence. As Yoder puts it, "we understand Jesus only if we can empathize with this threefold rejection: the self-evident axiomatic, sweeping rejection of both quietism and establishment responsibility, and the difficult, constantly reopened, attractive option of the crusade."[33]

The Year of Jubilee

Jesus' emphasis on the year of Jubilee in the Isaiah 61 passage is significant for the theme of social ethics, but if it were merely mentioned once and then forgotten it could hardly be claimed as a serious invitation to social revolution. Hence, Yoder devotes an entire chapter to asking whether in fact the Gospels contain other allusions to the four principles of the Jubilee year. These principles, according to Leviticus 25, are: leaving the soil fallow every seven years, remitting debts every seven years, liberating the slaves every seven years, and returning the property back to its original owners every seven times seven years, namely, every fiftieth year.

It is important to understand the notion of the Sabbath (the symbol of the seventh year) as an invitation to live by the grace of God. In other words, we are invited to consider life as a gift rather than a possession. Jubilee justice is based on the notion that land and people should not be treated as possessions. The four provisions are really variations on this theme. And Yoder argues that these themes appear again and again throughout the Gospels, proving that Jesus was serious about his proclamation of the Jubilee year. For example, "Do not keep striving for what you are to eat and what you are to drink, and do not keep worrying. For it is the nations of the world that strive after all these things, and your Father knows that you need them. Instead, strive for his kingdom, and these things will be given to you as well" (Luke 12:29-31). The Lord's Prayer, "remit us our debts" is really a jubilary prayer. He cites two parables, the parable of the merciless servant (Matt 18:23-35), which emphasizes that there is no grace for someone who is not gracious, and the parable of the unfaithful steward (Luke 16:1-13), which highlights the connection between salvation and the remission of debts. Both stress that in the kingdom which Jesus is announcing "the practice of such a jubilee was not optional."[34] Yoder cites the story of the widow's mite (Luke 21:1-4) and the repeated chiding of the rich (Luke 11:42ff.) as instances of Jesus' emphasis on the fourth provision of the Jubilee, namely the redistribution of capital. All of these stories point out that Jesus' ministry was essentially tied up with the passion to restore a traditional structure of justice which had Sabbath grace as its foundation.

Old Testament Wars

One of the challenges in arguing for a pacifist reading of the Jesus story concerns the multiple war stories in the Old Testament. Yoder says it is hardly convincing to say that the Old Testament account of these wars, often as commanded by God, is due to the fact that the people then did not understand the will of God, whereas Jesus does. In other words, to attempt to settle the argument with the generalization "war is always contrary to the will of God" is not to the point. Yoder suggests that while this may indeed be our concern—ever pushing for a foundational truth—it was not the matter around which the hearers of Jesus constructed their past.

---

[31] Yoder, *Politics of Jesus*, 96.
[32] Yoder, *Politics of Jesus*, 97.
[33] Yoder, *Politics of Jesus*, 97.
[34] Yoder, *Politics of Jesus*, 68.

The quest Yoder sets for himself is an attempt to answer the question of how the listeners of Jesus heard what he said in light of the Old Testament war stories. And as he points out, "one of the traits of the Old Testament story, sometimes linked with bloody battles but also sometimes notably free of violence, is the identification of YHWH as the God who saves his people without their need to act."[35]

Yoder divides the discussion regarding the Old Testament war stories into three parts: the exodus, the kingdoms, and the period after the exile. In the exodus account, it is clear that the "Israelites did nothing to bring about the destruction of the Egyptians."[36] All they did was to believe and obey. In fact the Exodus text is quite clear on what they were to do: "Fear not, stand firm, and see the salvation of the Lord, which he will work for you today; for the Egyptians whom you see today, you shall never see again. The Lord will fight for you and you have only to be still" (Exod 14:13).[37]

The theme of dependence upon the Lord for the salvation of the people finds expression in a multitude of ways during the exodus period. One example is the encounter of the Israelites with Amalek. The story has Moses and Joshua initiate their own battle in this case, but they prevail only when Moses raises the "staff of God" (Exod 17:11). When he lowers it, they lose the battle, so that when Moses is utterly exhausted, his attendants are forced to prop up his arms in order for the Israelites to obtain a victory. The point, of course, is that even when the Israelites initiate their own battle, their victory is credited to God and not to their own might. Hence, for them to "believe" is "to trust God for their survival as a people."[38]

This theme of "reliance upon the Lord" (2 Chron 14:11) also carries through into the kingdoms era and beyond. Repeatedly, Israel is chided for not relying upon the Lord for its security. For example, when the Israelites choose their own king and want to become like other nations relying upon their own military, there is reluctant divine concession (1 Sam 8:1-18), and when they make an alliance with another nation, victory is withheld: "Because you relied on the King of Aram, and *did not rely on the Lord your God*, the army of the King of Aram has escaped you" (2 Chron 16:17b). The recurring motif in these stories encouraging the Israelites to "fear not, stand firm, and see the salvation of the Lord" and reminding them that the Lord will fight for them, was well within the collective memory of the hearers of Jesus. They knew God could act in their midst, bringing about amazing changes.

Such a listening stance makes a profound difference for how Jesus is heard. Yoder makes the point that "for Jesus' listeners . . . as believing Jews, the question of possibility was not allowed to get in the way of hearing the promise. They therefore did not prejudice their sense of what might happen by knowing ahead of time what Jesus could not mean."[39] Reading the Jesus story in this way is then a direct challenge to the "interim ethics" thesis. Yoder makes the point that the reason the hearers of Jesus rejected his message, was "*not* because they thought it could not happen but because they feared it might, and that it would bring down judgment on them."[40] In other words, they feared God's justice in the present.

Yoder recites some rather unusual events of divine intervention that would have been current in Jesus' time yet are not recorded in the Gospels.[41] These stories make the point that the fact of nonviolent resistance as an alternative to the standard, violent approaches usually employed to address issues of justice was not at all unknown to the Jews of the day. Relying especially on Josephus, the Jewish historian, Yoder relates three stories of nonviolent

---

[35] Yoder, *Politics of Jesus*, 76.
[36] Yoder, *Politics of Jesus*, 77.
[37] Yoder, *Politics of Jesus*, 77.
[38] Yoder, *Politics of Jesus*, 79.
[39] Yoder, *Politics of Jesus*, 85.
[40] Yoder, *Politics of Jesus*, 85 (emphasis in original).
[41] Yoder, *Politics of Jesus*, 89–92.

confrontation of the authorities by ordinary people. These stories do not set up re-useable, foolproof patterns of nonviolent resolution to matters of injustice, but they do "suffice nonetheless to negate the sweeping assumption that in rejecting the Zealot option Jesus' only other conceivable alternative would have been the end of the world or retreat to the desert; in other words to reject the responsible sword is to withdraw from history."[42]

This, then, is Yoder's counterargument for how the Jesus of the Gospels provides us with a basis for social ethics. Clearly, Jesus was not interested merely in an individual ethic, but he invited his hearers into an alternative, social reconstruction requiring both a new envisioning and a new performing.

From Jesus to Paul

We must remember, however, that the argument put forward contending the irrelevance of Jesus for social ethics deals not only with the Jesus of the Gospels but also with how the early church read the Jesus story. That is, in the move from Luke to Paul, the contention is that everything changes because Paul already knew Jesus could not be a basis for a realistic social ethic and hence had to go elsewhere to construct one, namely to Stoicism.

Of course, Yoder thoroughly rejects this argument and contends that Paul displays no moral distancing from Jesus. Paul, for example, repeatedly emphasizes that he himself is sharing in the dying and rising of Jesus Christ (2 Cor 4:10-11; Col 1:24). And in his ministry and counsel to the early Christians, Paul calls upon them to imitate Christ and participate in his life and especially in the way of the cross.[43] This is the language of Jesus when he invites his disciples to take up the cross and to follow daily (Luke 9:23).

In giving this alternative reading of Jesus, Yoder is sometimes charged with being sectarian and even heretical. Yet he claims

theological orthodoxy on his side of the debate. He seeks to avoid both ebionitic (Jesus is human but not divine) and docetic (Jesus is divine but not human) reductionisms by affirming the Nicene and Chalcedonian doctrine of the two natures of Jesus Christ. This affirmation permits him to claim that we are able to follow Jesus *because he is human* and that he has the authority to call us to follow him *because he is divine*. His orthodoxy also allows him to avoid the conclusions of a Trinitarian logic which insists on a distinction between the ethic of the son and the father,[44] and a view of the incarnation as God's approval of human nature as it was. The claim of the normativity of Jesus is the basis for saying that Creator God as well as human nature is most definitively known in Jesus Christ. Moreover, Yoder claims that this is also the faith that gets unpacked in the subsequent epistles and apocalyptic literature. But in order to understand this Jesus "as Messiah" we are required to rethink many of the traditionally formulated, theological dichotomies, like the distinction between the individual and the social, the Jesus of history and the Jesus of dogma, the prophet and the institution, the catastrophic and the inner kingdom, and the political and the sectarian.

When Yoder reads the early church (biblical) literature in light of the questions regarding the normativity of Jesus, he speaks to the following themes: how the early Christians understood their relationship to Christ, how the notion of power was cast in relation to the work of Christ, justification by grace through faith, and the concept of history. I will deal with each of these topics briefly.

Early Christian Discipleship: What language did the apostolic tradition use when speaking of the important relationship between the believers and Jesus Christ? This question matters because it helps to clarify whether the early Christians believed they

---

[42] Yoder, *Politics of Jesus*, 92.

[43] Yoder, *Politics of Jesus*, 95.

[44] This logic is developed by H. Richard Niebuhr in an article which first appeared as "Doctrine of the Trinity and the Unity of the Church," in *Theology Today* 3, no. 3 (1946): 37ff.

had to go elsewhere for their ethical guidance or whether they found adequate moral direction in Jesus Christ.

Yoder amasses a large number of biblical references to show that discipleship, or "following after," is the key concept connecting the early believers to Jesus. This gets expressed with variations of the imitation and participation theme, but the concept is simple; early believers saw their own faithfulness as Christians to *do as Jesus did.* The language is sometimes general as in "to be as he is" (1 John 4:17), or "holy as God is holy" (1 Pet 1:15-16), and at other times more specific, as in forgiving as God forgives, or loving as God or Christ loves. But always the language is imitation. The linkage to Jesus is to walk the path which he walked. The early Christians felt called to serve as Christ served, or to give their lives, or suffer, or die as he did. That is, they took seriously what Jesus said to the first disciples, "take up the cross and follow me daily."

The path that the early Christians saw for themselves was the path that led Jesus to the cross. This leads Yoder to conclude the following characterization of how the early believers understood their connection to Jesus: "There is thus but one realm in which the concept of imitation holds. . . . This is at the point of the concrete social meaning of the cross in its relation to enmity and power. Servanthood replaces dominion, forgiveness absorbs hostility. Thus—and only thus—are we bound by New Testament thought to 'be like Jesus.'"[45]

The Powers: Yoder addresses a misconception which he describes as follows: "that the primary message of Jesus was a call most properly perceived by an individual, asking the hearer for something that can be done most genuinely by an individual standing alone."[46] This view leads to the conviction that the message of Jesus has nothing to do with the structures of society. Again, this is

a crucial point since it becomes justification for the position that in the fourth century, when Christians first found themselves in positions of social responsibility, they had to turn elsewhere for moral guidance because Jesus had nothing to say about social ethics.

Yoder contends that this individualistic reading of the gospel was foreign to the apostolic tradition, which provides a consistent and clear teaching about how to view structures of society and how to live in society without being seduced by the forces that attempt to draw us away from the love of God in Jesus Christ. Hence, relying especially on the work of Hendrikus Berkof and G. B. Caird,[47] he develops a step-by-step refutation of this individualistic (mis)reading of the apostolic writers.

Yoder begins the deconstruction process with a clarification of Paul's language of "principalities and powers" and "thrones and dominions." The apostle also uses cosmological language like "angels and archangel," "elements," "heights and depths." Yoder suggests that the closest English concept for what Paul is talking about here is power structure. The word "structure," he says, "functions to point to the patterns or regularity that transcend or precede or condition the individual phenomena we can immediately perceive."[48] Structures are therefore powers insofar as they are vehicles for making things happen. For example, a university is "a power" in that it trains its students how to conceive the world. The issue Yoder examines is the moral counsel that Paul gives to the early believers about living amidst the complexities of "principalities and powers." And in the process, he discovers that the apostle speaks to precisely the kinds of social questions we were told by contemporary ethicists neither Paul nor the Gospels speak to.

Yoder reminds us that the Apostle Paul states that the powers are created and

---

[45] Yoder, *Politics of Jesus*, 131.
[46] Yoder, *Politics of Jesus*, 134.
[47] See Hendrikus Berkof, *Christ and the Powers* (Scottdale, Penn.: Herald, 1962); and G. B. Caird, *Principalities and Powers* (Oxford: Clarendon, 1956).   [48] Yoder, *Politics of Jesus*, 138.

ordered by God. "in him were created all things, those in heaven and those on earth, visible and invisible; whether thrones or dominions or principalities or powers; all was created through him and by him. And he is before all things and all things subsist in him" (Col 1:16-17).[49] Yoder suggests that the word "subsists" implies that everything is *systematized*, or held together, in Christ. In other words, the world is given to us by God as ordered—structured—and that is good.

Yet it is equally important to note Paul's insistence that the structures of the world are fallen. This means we have no empirical access to the good creation of God; we are unable to see the powers other than in their fallen state. Being fallen, whatever good, orderly function they may still serve, they nevertheless are also self-serving; and they attempt to "separate us from the love of God" (Rom 8:38), and hold us under their tutelage, vying for our loyalty.

Three affirmations then, according to Yoder, summarize Paul's teachings on the reality of the powers: they were created by God, they have rebelled and are fallen, and despite their fallen state they are still under the sovereignty of God.[50]

Yoder examines how Paul speaks about the work of Christ in relation to the powers. Since it is in ordering ourselves under these powers that we are human, we cannot simply set the powers aside or seek to destroy them. How could we even imagine a universe without structures? Being saved *in our humanity* therefore requires something else.[51]

To answer the question of what else is required, Yoder relies on Berkhof, who unpacks the passage from Colossians which speaks to what Christ did with the powers in the cross event: "He disarmed the principalities and powers and made a public example of them, triumphing over them in him" (Col 2:15).

Berkhof shows how the true nature of the powers comes to light in the crucifixion. The "thrones and dominions" are the "gods of the world." They are afforded almost ultimate power; they are even worshipped. Yet when God appears on earth in Christ, it is quickly apparent that these powers tend to overreach their own sense of importance. They can do some things but not everything. As the religious and political powers encounter God in Christ, they are "unmasked as false gods . . . they are made a public spectacle."[52] Their power is shown to be limited. To put it differently, while they could kill Jesus they could not keep him dead.

In this way, God in Christ "triumphed over the powers." In other words, there is a higher authority to which all powers are subject. In not being able to keep Jesus dead, the earthly powers lost out. The one who is the creator of life itself wins. God is ultimate; the earthly powers are not.

The powers, properly speaking, were therefore disarmed. They are able to overextend their authority only insofar as they are successful in convincing the masses of their false dominion. That fiction has now been removed, and hence the powers have lost their illusory hold on people. The cross-resurrection event points out that the powers, insofar as they are prone to promise more than they can deliver, are dishonest and vainglorious. Only God in Christ can deliver, ultimately, because only Creator God has an arsenal that includes the power of the resurrection from the dead. That alone sets God's power apart from all earthly powers. *Hence in Christ the sovereignty of the powers has been broken.*[53] This is not to suggest that the powers have been removed, or should be ignored—they still have enormous power—but rather that in the cross they have been put in their place, under the sovereignty of the living creating God.

Yoder points out that the Apostle Paul is concerned about more than the work of Christ and the powers. His central concern

---

[49] See Yoder, *Politics of Jesus*, 140.
[50] Yoder, *Politics of Jesus*, 142.
[51] See, Yoder, *Politics of Jesus*, 144.

[52] Yoder, *Politics of Jesus*, 146.
[53] See Yoder, *Politics of Jesus*, 144.

is really the church and what, in light of the work of Christ, the church ought to see as its task. Yoder summarizes Paul's "task of the church" in the words of Berkhof: "This is what the church announces to the Powers. The very existence of the church, in which Gentiles and Jews . . . live together in Christ's fellowship, is itself a proclamation, a sign, a token to the Powers that their unbroken dominion has come to an end."[54] The new humanity that is created by the cross and not the sword—the church—is that social body which by her "otherness" declares victory over the powers that divide people against each other: slaves against free, men against women, Jews against Gentiles, and so on. In the body of Christ, all are free; all are united in love, forgiveness, and freedom.

So how then should the church understand its place within society? Yoder summarizes Paul's answer as follows: "The church does not attack the powers; this Christ has done. The church concentrates upon not being seduced by them."[55] This is what gives rise to the call to "let the church be the church."

This way of speaking about the church evokes a significantly different characterization than its oft-stated role of teaching its members to be responsible citizens, namely to assist the structures in their tasks. Instead, the task of the church is to make known to the powers that Jesus Christ is Lord. This declaration is a challenge to the powers not in that it threatens their existence, but in that it recasts the manner in which their authority is conceived.

Yet the very nature of a social structure is that it has people under its rule, or it has people who are subject to it. Since it is therefore impossible to live in a society without powers, it is also impossible to live outside of the domain of subjection. Hence, it is never a matter of whether we are subject to the powers or not; that is a given! The question for Christians is rather how subjection is to be understood.

Yoder argues that the New Testament witnesses rely upon the example of Christ in understanding subjection. And in Christ's life, we see the rather complicated discernment of on the one hand, remaining subject to the religious and political authorities in that he allowed them to exercise their authority over him, and on the other hand, obeying only God. And with his obedience to God, he relativizes the power of the powers. This, then, is the model for his followers.

Yoder shows at some length how the New Testament writers argue for an embodiment of this way of the cross in their explication of living faithfully in relation to social structures. Insofar as he is successful in showing this, he will have advanced his thesis that, far from ignoring Jesus and resorting to other sources for the development of their ethics, the New Testament writers instead were quite explicit in demonstrating what it meant for the early Christians to take up the cross and follow after him daily.

Yoder focuses on two social structures to make the point: the Household Codes and the state, and his argument is that the logic here is the same. The two texts in question are from Ephesians 5:21 and following, which begins "Be subject to one another out of reverence for Christ. Wives, be subject to your husbands as you are to the Lord"; and Romans 13:1 and following, which begins: "Let every person be subject to the governing authorities." Notice that the phrase "be subject" is used in both cases.

The traditional reading of these texts is that they represent a borrowing from the Stoics because Paul could find no social ethic in Jesus' teachings. Yoder challenges that view and argues that that these are precisely the outworking of what it means to take up the cross of Christ and follow after him. The cross of Christ is an act of subordination to the powers without doing what they say.

Yoder explains his use of subordination carefully. He defines it as follows:

---

[54] Yoder, *Politics of Jesus*, 147–48.

[55] Yoder, *Politics of Jesus*, 150.

"Sub*ord*ination means the acceptance of an *order* as it exists but with the new meaning given to it by the fact that one's acceptance of it is willing and meaningfully motivated."[56] It is in this manner of subordination that the biblical text invited the early Christians to relate to all social structures. And it is no accident that this is also how Jesus related to the powers in the way of the cross.

Voluntary subordination to the powers is not the same as obedience. Obedience means doing what the powers tell us to do, but subordination is recognizing the power of the powers, even to kill, but doing what God asks us to do. This, of course, is reminiscent of Jesus' struggle in the garden of Gethsemane, where he asked that the consequences of the powers' destructive force be removed, yet that God's will be done. It also connects to the general stance of servanthood which Jesus advocates repeatedly in place of dominion and violence.

Yoder makes the point that the logic of subordination applies not only to "household practices" and to the state, but as is stated in 1 Peter 2, "subordinate yourself for the sake of the Lord to every human institution." But it is Paul's analysis of the state that is of particular interest to Yoder and is of special significance for social ethics.

Yoder suggests that Paul is arguing in Romans 13 that the state, like all powers, has a legitimate and God-given mandate, and hence believers are subject to its power; yet the call of the disciple is to "obey" only God as modeled in the life of Jesus Christ. After all, powers like the state are fallen, and hence tend to go beyond God's call by accruing loyalty to themselves. He cautions against two potential misreadings of the Romans text: a positivistic interpretation, that is, whatever government you have in power is the will of God; and a normative interpretation, namely, that what is ordained is the notion of proper government. Instead,

he suggests that the text puts the state in its proper place under the sovereignty of God. He says, "What the text says is that [God] orders [the powers that be], brings them into line, that by his permissive government he lines them up with his purpose."[57] Hence, followers of Jesus are called not to revolt against or overthrow disobedient states but to represent in their presence the notion that Jesus is Lord, which means nonviolently speaking the truth of God's justice to them.

Yoder points out that Christians in Rome were not called to military or police service. This indeed would be a strange reading of the text since they had no voice in matters of government and would not have been permitted any such involvement even if they had desired it. Yoder concludes that the early Christians were not called to "obey" the state in its demands of its citizens to participate in its killing function, nor is the call to revolution. Instead, as elsewhere, the call here is to take up the cross, meaning subordinate yourselves to the powers by recognizing their power over you; but obey only God.

Justification by Grace through Faith: Yoder also addresses the common (mis)reading of Paul which suggests that his primary message nevertheless was that a person is "made righteous before God only on the grounds of faith, with no correlation to his keeping of the law."[58] That is, salvation comes to the individual via grace given freely with no regard for works. If this is a correct reading of Paul, it seriously undercuts the call to radical social/political discipleship. With his reliance on New Testament scholars like Krister Stendahl and Markus Barth, Yoder shows that this was not Paul's concern.

However much it may have been the concerns of Augustine and Luther, there is no evidence that Paul was preoccupied with guilt and personal self-acceptance. And faith for him was not the subjective movement from self-doubt to belief in God. Paul, as a

---

[56] Yoder, *Politics of Jesus*, 172 (emphasis in original).
[57] Yoder, *Politics of Jesus*, 201–2.
[58] Yoder, *Politics of Jesus*, 212–13.

Jew, already believed in God. The question of faith was squarely grounded in the affirmation "that in Jesus of Nazareth the Messiah had come."[59] Paul knew that what he needed to do to become a Christian did not focus first on his own depravity but it focused on who Jesus was. And now that Messiah had come, the covenant was opened to include the Gentiles. This was the Jesus issue for Paul. In other words, "the fundamental issue was the social form of the church."[60]

To be justified by grace through belief that Jesus is the Messiah therefore takes on particular meaning. It means "making peace" or "breaking down walls of hostility." Quoting Markus Barth, Yoder says, "Justification is thus not an individual miracle happening to this person or that person, which each may seek or possess for himself. Rather justification by grace is a joining together of this person and that person, of the near and far . . . it is a social event."[61]

Hence, contrary to the nonsocial misreading of this text which, if true, could undermine Yoder's work on the powers, his reliance on current New Testament scholars vindicates even the concept of justification as a social phenomenon.[62]

The Meaning of History: Yoder observes that in our day we "are obsessed with the meaning and direction of history."[63] What he means is that contemporary, social ethics is preoccupied with moving history in the right direction. In other words, the quest is to find the right "handle" that will help us move history in the direction we believe it ought to go. And each social movement has its own favorite handle. For example, there are those who believe education is such a handle. Here the argument is that future justice depends upon proper education of the masses today. Others will promote economic development; those of Marxist persuasion will see the motor of history in the proletariat. Conservative evangelicals will emphasize the importance of changing the hearts of individuals, especially those in powerful, public office. The logic is that once we have identified the proper handle, everything else gets sacrificed to this central cause.

Yoder raises three questions about this logic. First, this way of thinking about history assumes there is a visible, understandable, and manageable relationship of cause and effect in history.[64] Second, it assumes that "we are adequately informed to be able to set for ourselves and all of society the goals in which we seek to move it."[65] And third, it assumes that effectiveness is itself a moral yardstick.[66]

Yoder questions all of these assumptions via the reading of Revelation 4 and 5. He sees these texts being about the meaningfulness of history. The phrase "the lamb that was slain is worthy to receive power" is an answer to the question of the meaningfulness of history. He says, "John is here saying not as an inscrutable paradox but as a meaningful affirmation, that the cross and not the sword, suffering and not brute power determines the meaning of history."[67] Hence, once again, it is the cross of Jesus Christ that is at the center of the determination of social ethics. And this means that "the key to the obedience of God's people is not their effectiveness but their patience."[68]

Yoder deserves to be quoted at greater length here. He says:

> The triumph of the right is assured not by the might that comes to the aid of the right, which is of course the justification of the use of violence and other kinds of power in every human conflict. The triumph of the right, although it is assured, is sure because of the power of the resurrection and not because of any calculation of causes and effects, nor because of the inherently greater strength of the good guys. The relationship between the obedience of God's people and the triumph of

---

[59] Yoder, *Politics of Jesus*, 216.
[60] Yoder, *Politics of Jesus*, 216.
[61] Yoder, *Politics of Jesus*, 220–21.
[62] Yoder, *Politics of Jesus*, 224.
[63] Yoder, *Politics of Jesus*, 228.

[64] Yoder, *Politics of Jesus*, 229.
[65] Yoder, *Politics of Jesus*, 229–30.
[66] Yoder, *Politics of Jesus*, 232.
[67] Yoder, *Politics of Jesus*, 232.
[68] Yoder, *Politics of Jesus*, 232.

God's cause is not a relationship of cause and effect but one of cross and resurrection.[69]

The reading of history in relation to the cross-resurrection helps Yoder define his view of pacifism. He does not find in the Jesus story a view of pacifism that suggests there are nonviolent techniques available to us so we can "obtain without killing everything [we] really want or have a right to ask for."[70] Such a view is still well within the obsession to control historical outcome. What Jesus did in accepting the cross was give up the need to govern and ensure results. God's outcome is not first of all dependent on our power to bring about our best goals; our efforts are rather dependent upon God's blessing, or if you like, resurrection. The way of the cross relinquishes not so much violence as the need to control. God controls; we obey. Hence, Yoder can say, "That Christian pacifism which has a theological basis in the character of God and the work of Jesus Christ is one in which the calculating link between our obedience and ultimate efficacy has been broken, since the triumph of God comes through resurrection and not through effective sovereignty or assured survival."[71]

OTHER WRITINGS AND THEMES

Having devoted so much space to presenting Yoder's *The Politics of Jesus* leaves little room for presenting his many other themes. I must, however, mention three: the nature of ethics, the church, and Constantinianism.

The Nature of Ethics

Yoder spends no time writing about ethical methodology—what is commonly called meta-ethics—other than disparagingly. For example, he asks,

Is Christian ethics deontological . . . Is it characterial . . . Is it teleological . . . Or do Christians evaluate only the heart? . . . My response at this point must be twofold. As an ethicist, I am not convinced that these categories are helpful for anyone in any tradition. They almost necessarily suggest that it would be possible to do ethics with one of these dimensions at the cost of all others. I doubt that this is true in logic or in real human moral experience.[72]

Instead, he argues that each ecclesiological (moral) tradition has its own distinct teleology, deontology, and so on. While it is important to recognize that there are different moral reasoning patterns, one should not reduce the complexities of the moral life to merely one such pattern of logic. One is and ought always to be reasoning from more than one moral idiom.

Yoder prefers to speak of ethics in a different mode than the traditional ones. He says that, "What is of interest is far less the question of how ethical obligation is to be formulated and far more the question of whether or not one is going to obey the Lord who commands."[73] Peculiarly, Yoder suggests, the recent ethical debate has been about whether, in spite of knowing what Jesus commands, we should do that or something else which can be more readily justified. In other words, the issue is *whether* Jesus is Lord. For Yoder, that is not in dispute. What is of concern is how we can become the kind of people who are able to do what Jesus commands. And that is not possible without the church.

The Church

What Yoder says about the church cannot be easily separated from his comments on Constantinianism. Nor is it neatly derived from a single essay or section of a book. It permeates his entire work. Yet there are two or three formative essays in which much of what he says about church is rooted, namely, "The

---

[69] Yoder, *Politics of Jesus*, 232.

[70] Yoder, *Politics of Jesus*, 236–37.

[71] Yoder, *Politics of Jesus*, 239.

[72] John Howard Yoder, "Radical Reformation Ethics in Ecumenical Perspective," in *The Priestly Kingdom: Social Ethics as Gospel* (Notre Dame, Ind.: University of Notre Dame Press, 1984), 114.

[73] Yoder, "Radical Reformation Ethics," 109.

Otherness of the Church," "Let the Church be the Church," and "Why Ecclesiology Is Social Ethics."[74]

To emphasize the otherness of the church is to stress the church as a visible community in the world. This is important since in the early church, "church" and "world" were clearly distinct, and the "Constantinian transformation" (by which, as we will see, he means much more than an historical event) has changed all this. What matters most about this shift, according to Yoder, is that "the two visible realities, church and world, were fused. There is no longer anything to call 'world'; state, economy, art, rhetoric, superstition, and war have all been baptized."[75] Since it is absurd to any thinking Christian that suddenly all people could, by fiat, be Christian, scholars like Augustine were forced to distinguish between the true church (believers), which is invisible, and the formal, visible church. Says Yoder, "Previously Christians had known as a fact of experience that the church existed but had to believe against appearances that Christ ruled over the world. After Constantine one knew as a fact of experience that Christ was ruling over the world but had to believe against the evidence that there existed 'a believing church.'"[76]

Yoder identifies two "scandalous conclusions" that follow from a non-Constantinian view of the church. First, "that Christian ethics is for Christians."[77] That is, it undercuts the Kantian categorical imperative, which asks, "What would happen if we were all pacifists?" Such logic, of course, undermines the lordship of Christ, since it is unimaginable for structured unbelief to live by messianic faith and it would be inappropriate to impose the ethic of Jesus on everyone. The second scandalous conclusion is that there may well be functions in society which are considered necessary that Christians nevertheless cannot participate in. This is scandalous because of the usual assumptions about citizenry, namely, citizens must obey the state in all its requests. Yoder's approach requires the language of tension between church and nation which Constantinianism finds intolerable.

When God in Christ came among us, many common practices were denounced. When Abraham received the call from on high he left Chaldea, a great nation, to become a nomad. Israel, a small minority, was called *out of* Egypt, a large nation. Yoder emphasizes that the incarnation does not mean that God has sanctified human society, but rather it means that in Christ we are shown what to do and what to leave behind. "God's pattern of incarnation is that of Abraham and not of Constantine."[78] That is, the invitation of Christ is not to "Christianize" society, but to sort out faithfulness from unfaithfulness. And the reading of God's acts in history is therefore not done by rehearsing the great events of nations but by observing the faithful events of the believing community.[79] As Yoder puts it, "the meaning of history is carried first of all, and on behalf of all others, by the believing community." This basic biblical theme has been made heretical after Constantine.

Constantinianism

According to Yoder, Constantine is not merely a historical figure, although he was clearly that as well. His name has come to designate a way of thinking that undermines the church, and hence Christian ethics. As such, it "stands for a new era in the history of Christianity."[80] What Constantinian logic

---

[74] These essays are reprinted in Yoder, *Royal Priesthood.*

[75] Yoder, "The Otherness of the Church," in *Royal Priesthood,* 57.

[76] Yoder, "The Otherness of the Church," in *Royal Priesthood,* 57.

[77] Yoder, "The Otherness of the Church," in *Royal Priesthood,* 62.

[78] John Howard Yoder, "Let the Church Be the Church," in *Royal Priesthood,* 172.

[79] John Howard Yoder, "Why Ecclesiology Is Social Ethics: Gospel Ethics versus the Wider Wisdom," in *Royal Priesthood,* 118.

[80] John Howard Yoder, "The Constantinian Sources of Western Social Ethics," in *Priestly Kingdom,* 135.

then produces is a reconstruction of the traditional, theological tenets of faith.

Yoder identifies several such reconstructions. We have already referred to a new ecclesiology, namely the view of an invisible church and a new eschatology which made the emperor and the nation the primary locus of God's activity. There is also a new way of testing faithfulness, or right action. Whatever advances the national cause is good. What fails to effect change is irrelevant. As Yoder puts it, Constantine wedded "piety with power."[81] Another reconstruction is a new metaphysic. Not only is there the division of the church as visible and invisible, but there is a division between the real and the ideal, and with respect to persons, the inner and the outer. All of these distinctions aided in making credible and sustaining the new, Constantinian logic.

One of the great reversals that comes with Constantinianism is the control shift from God to the people. And this is manifested everywhere: we attempt to control history, control our own lives; we develop structures of mastery and control in matters of establishing justice, peace, and even in matters of inquiry. A Constantinian consciousness expects that there will be one dominant theory or idiom that will disclose truth. A diversity or minority which intends to open up previously concealed views cannot be tolerated.

This prompts Yoder to say that what Constantinianism accepts, Jesus rejected, namely, "seizing godlikeness"[82] or seeing history as though it can be "handled"—moved in a direction under our lordship. It is a temptation that Yoder suggests we need to repent of, and only when we do are we able to know what it means to let Jesus be Lord. Yet "unhandling history" is extremely challenging because it requires a "letting go" that is best understood through the cross and resurrection; a view of history foreign to most dominant "theories" of history.

CONCLUSION

There are those who criticize Yoder's Christian pacifism by saying that Christians sometimes must resort to violence because worse consequences could follow if they did not do so. Yoder's response to this charge is simply that, on the basis of his reading of the Christian story, Christians are not charged with the task of making the world come out right. Our charge is rather to give faithful witness to the one we call Messiah, who himself was killed because he gave up on control, only to be resurrected by the one who is in charge of making history come out right. Here, Yoder agrees with the critique offered by feminists and other liberation theologians: that Christian ethics must challenge the dominant ethic of control, even though Yoder's lodgment of that challenge is made intelligible by the cross of Jesus, hence the redemptive role of suffering which liberation theologians find difficult to accept.

Yoder's critique of control, and his call for a new sense of political-social existence, has fostered many, perhaps unexpected (to him), connections from diverse places. There are currently studies that bring Yoder's work into dialogue with the likes of Michel Foucault, Jacques Derrida, Paul Virilio, and Edward Said, to name only a few.[83] In some ways, Yoder may have been ahead of his time. Whether his works will continue to be read depends on those who see in them the promise of a usable peace open to the wisdom heard in other voices, who likewise lament the dehumanizing effects of destructive powers.

---

[81] Yoder, "Constantinian Sources," in *Priestly Kingdom*, 140.
[82] Yoder, "Constantinian Sources," in *Priestly Kingdom*, 145.
[83] See, e.g., Peter Dula and Chris K. Huebner, *The New Yoder* (Eugene, Ore.: Cascade, 2010).

Chapter Thirty-Three

JAMES WILLIAM MCCLENDON JR.
(1924–2000)

James William McClendon Jr. is variously introduced as a theologian in the Anabaptist tradition, or a small "b" baptist, or a nonfoundational, or narrative theologian. Peculiarly, all of these descriptions fit, which is probably why McClendon is not easily pegged into an established theological slot. Not unlike John Howard Yoder,[1] he spends much of his theological energies debunking popular ways of conceiving of theology and the Christian life. However, not until he was fifty years old did he read Yoder, and when he did, he found him compelling and at once a theological kinship developed.

Modern theologians have taught us to think that theology is a philosophical system of ideas and its task is to provide persuasive reasons for believing in concepts like God, the soul, and life after death. Moreover, if these reasons are developed carefully enough—without any mistakes—they should be convincing to any clear-thinking person. On this model, the same conclusions about the nature of Christian ethics emerges in theology as in philosophy generally, namely, ethics is noncognitive and, hence, private and subjective. In effect, this means there is no essential connection between theology and ethics. McClendon

challenges this whole package—both what it suggests about the nature of theology as well as what it says about ethics. For that matter, he challenges the basic assumptions around foundationalism as such. Relying on Ludwig Wittgenstein (1889–1951) and J. L. Austin (1911–1960),[2] McClendon asks how theology and ethics might be reconstructed when the insights of the postmodern critique of foundationalism are taken seriously.

The task here is instructive: rather than asking how to ground theology in a sure and solid knowledge base (a foundation), McClendon postulates the idea that Christian theology emerges from the conviction that Jesus is Messiah—really not such a novel idea for Christians since it has been around only from the time of the Apostle Paul! But it has enormous implications for how to think about theology and especially how to think about the connections between ethics and theology.

In 1994 a group of scholars honored McClendon with a Festschrift titled *Theology without Foundations*.[3] In the introduction, the point is made that the Enlightenment quest for certainty on the basis of neutrality has served neither theology nor the church well. Both liberals and conservatives have

---

[1] See chap. 32 above.

[2] For a brief introduction to the thought of Ludwig Wittgenstein, see 151f. above. J. L. Austin was a British philosopher of language, influenced by Wittgenstein, who argued that speech is best understood as a form of action, hence the term "speech acts." In other words, speech does not merely describe reality passively but acts upon reality and changes it. Language performs, making the relationship between language and the world much more complex than we usually think.

[3] Stanley Hauerwas, Nancey Murphy, and Mark Nation, eds., *Theology Without Foundations: Religious Practice and the Future of Theological Truth* (Nashville: Abingdon, 1994).

[4] Cited in Hauerwas, Murphy and Nation, *Theology Without Foundations*, 16, from Jeffrey Stout, *The Flight From*

been seduced into believing that theology and Christian faith could benefit from this approach by using it to convince others of the truth of their faith, not to mention assuring Christians of their convictions. McClendon takes a very different stance: instead of asking how we can say something religious that could be convincing to every rational person, he asks, what if there is no neutral place to stand; what then can one say as a Christian? It turns out that this sets the theologian free to give the Christian faith its full due. If there is indeed no neutral place to stand, then it is not a matter of how we get there that counts, but what can be said on the way after departure. Or, it is not what justifies the perspective from which one sees, speaks, and writes, but what one's perspective reveals about the world, about the meaning of human lives, and how to live with others.

American religious pragmatist Jeffrey Stout believes moves like those made by McClendon have led theologians of like approach to "endless methodological foreplay."[4] Truth be told, it is people like McClendon and those who, like him, reject the foundationalism of the Enlightenment, who are tired of the methodological discussion. Here, theologians like Karl Barth and John Howard Yoder are clear examples of scholars who want to get on with the task of doing Christian theology.[5] Neither have any patience with method, precisely because they have come to see the errors of the Enlightenment brand of foundationalism, which assumes it is actually possible to start from scratch. McClendon dedicated his career to working at what theology (and ethics) without foundations might look like.

HIS LIFE AND EARLY WRITINGS

McClendon was born in Louisiana and raised there by a Methodist father, James McClendon Sr., and a Southern Baptist mother, Mary Drake. It would be his mother's church tradition that would sway him most; hence he was baptized at age ten or eleven in her Baptist home church. Part of the influence to become a Baptist came from a black, Baptist maid in the McClendon home whose piety made a great impression on him. Later in life, he would be ordained as a minister in the Southern Baptist Church.[6]

In high school, McClendon enrolled as a matter of course in the Reserve Officers' Training Corps. Then, when he was a college freshman in 1941, Japan attacked Pearl Harbor. After that, it was not a question of whether to participate in the defense of his country, it was only one of which service to enlist in. So he joined the Naval Reserve and was sent him to study electronics. He studied at Harvard and MIT and graduated just as World War II ended and so never saw active combat. He did, however, travel with the Navy after the war, first to Honolulu and from there to Japan, where he was able to see the effects of the war. In his autobiography, he describes the effects of the "fire-bombing" in Tokyo that his guide Mr. Saito showed him. "[Fire-bombing] involved creating a heat so intense that high winds rushed in to make an entire city a holocaust of unquenchable fire."[7] When he narrates the story, as if standing before the scorched area of the city, he "focuses" on what is not there—gone—the children on tricycles, housewives washing clothes, and students doing homework. These images would have a lingering impact on his life as

---

Authority (Notre Dame, Ind.: University of Notre Dame Press, 1981), 147.

[5] See Harry Huebner, "The Christian Life as Gift and Patience: Why Yoder Has Trouble with Method," *A Mind Patient and Untamed: Assessing John Howard Yoder's Contributions to Theology, Ethics, and Peacemaking*, ed. Ben C. Ollenburger and Gayle Gerber Koontz (Scottdale, Penn.: Herald, 2004), 23–38.

[6] Shortly before his death, McClendon wrote an autobiographical essay which I will draw on in my biographical comments. See James William McClendon Jr., "The Radical Road One Baptist Took," *Mennonite Quarterly Review* 74, no. 4 (2000): 503–10.

[7] McClendon, "Radical Road," 505.

[8] Much of this biographical information is taken from the Levellers Blog under "Mentor #5 James Wm. McClendon, Jr.,"

he gradually came to see war as completely incompatible with a biblical ethic.

After his stint in the military, McClendon enrolled in the University of Texas, where he received a second undergraduate degree, which gave him the prerequisites to enter seminary studies. Upon graduating he began theological studies at the Southwestern Baptist Theological Seminary in Fort Worth, Texas. Here he received a bachelor of divinity degree and then was accepted into Princeton Theological Seminary in Princeton, New Jersey, where he earned a master of theology degree. It was clear at this time in his life that McClendon wanted to do doctoral work, but it was not clear where or under whom he would study. Not finding the right mentor at Princeton, he returned to Southwestern Baptist to work with the great, systematic theologian, Walter Thomas Conner, only to see him die in 1952 after McClendon had barely begun his doctoral program.[8]

In summary, McClendon was fascinated with the big-name theologians like Karl Barth, Reinhold Niebuhr, and Paul Tillich. They raised the big and right questions—only not all of them. None adequately addressed the matter of Christian perfectionism. He chose this theme for his dissertation topic and suggests that if he had named it properly it would have been called "The Doctrine of Perfection in I John and Its Reflection in Modern Christianity."[9] It is evident that McClendon at this point in his life already saw a major lacuna in the American theologians, namely, their failure to pay attention to the biblical view of the Christian life.

After graduating with his doctor of theology degree from Southwestern Baptist Theological Seminary, he spent a few years as a pastor. But it was evident he would become a theology professor. In 1954 he was named professor of theology and philosophy at the Golden Gate Baptist Theological Seminary in Mill Valley, California, just north of San Francisco. At first it seemed that this was where he belonged: in a Southern Baptist Seminary. He was firmly committed to the project of training young men and women to become theologically literate and faithful for the church. He got involved in the civil rights movement in the early 1960s because he believed this to be an act of Christian faithfulness. He supported and helped students attend Martin Luther King Jr.'s rallies and became increasingly critical of the Vietnam War. His peace activities produced tensions at the seminary, and he decided in 1966 to leave.

To leave a denominational college in this way made it difficult for him to find teaching employment in other church institutions. Fortunately, McClendon had good, ecumenical friends across the country who helped him find teaching jobs. Because these were term appointments, his family stayed in San Francisco, and after a short time, he was hired at the University of San Francisco, a Catholic university run by the Jesuits. It was highly unusual for Catholics in the 1960s to hire a Baptist professor. In fact, his appointment was the first of its kind in the United States.[10] But sadly, this was not to last, either. In the mid-1960s, the Vietnam War was in full swing, and McClendon's two sons, Will and Thom, were faced with whether to resist the draft or enlist. He puts it personally when he says that for him, "Vietnam changed things. I stood by my elder son while he resisted the draft; at least one of my graduate students was jailed for a still livelier resistance. . . ."[11] As is evident from these words, McClendon was opposed to the war and supported the resistance movement wherever he could. He publicly criticized it on just-war logic, joined

posted by Michael Westmoreland-White. It is available at http://levellers.wordpress.com/2006/12/07/mentors-5-james-wm-mcclendon-jr/, accessed May 15, 2011.

[9] McClendon, "Radical Road," 506.

[10] McClendon, "Radical Road," 507.

[11] James William McClendon Jr., *Biography as Theology: How Life Stories Can Remake Today's Theology*, new ed. (Philadelphia: Trinity, 1990), v.

[12] Westmoreland-White, "Mentor #5," 2.

student protests, and supported and encouraged individual resisters. All of this led the university to ask him to leave his teaching post; this time he was at odds with a Catholic institution. The peace advocacy activities of a Baptist theologian were simply too much for the institution to take. So in 1965 he was without a job again, and it was all because of his moral convictions about war and peace. It is important to note that at this stage in his life, McClendon was not a pacifist; in his critique of the Vietnam War, his argument was based on the just-war theory, which is the official Catholic position.

To be pushed out of his teaching job twice in a few years was extremely difficult for him and his family. Not only did this mean moving to another location, but it would be difficult for him to get hired at any institution, even though his students rated him as an exceptionally gifted teacher. But he did find temporary work.

McClendon says that while he was teaching a sessional course at an eastern U.S. university, he suddenly realized that he was not only opposed just to the war in southeast Asia, he was opposed to all wars. He had in fact become a pacifist. Not until 1971 did he find another tenure-track teaching position, this time at the Church Divinity School of the Pacific (CDSP), which is an Episcopal Church Seminary and part of the Graduate Theological Union (GTU) in Berkeley, California. Although McClendon was now a pacifist, Michael Westmoreland-White says, "he was yet to discover what that meant theologically."[12] That discovery was to come after he read John Howard Yoder's *The Politics of Jesus*. And GTU was the setting for him to work this out.

Just as his teaching career was gaining some footing, tensions in his marriage became apparent. He had married Marie in the mid-1940s and now, some thirty years later, after their two sons were adults, she divorced him. While this was personally devastating

for him, it also threatened his career once again. Divorce was not acceptable within the Southern Baptist Church and even less so for clergy. But it turned out that his marriage failure did not force him into another search for new employment.

Some years later, McClendon married Nancey Murphy, a former Catholic and ordained minister in the Church of the Brethren, which is part of the Historic Peace Church family. She had completed a Ph.D. in the philosophy of science and was enrolled in a doctor of theology program at GTU, where McClendon was teaching. They became theological soulmates although she was roughly half his age. After retirement from GTU in 1990, McClendon became a Distinguished Scholar-in-Residence at Fuller Theological Seminary in Pasadena, California, where his wife was teaching. He taught some courses but primarily worked on writing his three-volume *magnum opus* in systematic theology. The third volume came out shortly before his death on October 30, 2000.

Not much written work came from McClendon during his early years of teaching—the 1960s and early 1970s. These were the years when he was moving from one teaching post to another, a schedule that is not conducive to research. (This is why universities have tenure—to secure space for faculty members to write.) However, in 1962, McClendon wrote a sixty-eight-page, theology booklet, his first publication. This was published before his work on narrative theology, but his thought here already points in that direction. In it, he presents the thought of nine theologians; he calls it "a kind of theological appetizer."[13] It is instructive in two ways: first, it is written in a style that suggests students should learn both the thought and lives of scholars—a thesis embraced in this study as well. While McClendon was still more enamored with theology as an intellectual discipline than as an ethical one, the seeds of his later approach are

---

[13] James William McClendon, *Pacemakers of Christian Thought* (Nashville: Broadman, 1962), v.

[14] His list of theologians includes Karl Barth, Reinhold Niebuhr, William Temple, E. J. Carnell, Emil Brunner, Paul

evident already in this project. Second, it is noteworthy who is not included in this list of theologians, most notably, perhaps, Dietrich Bonhoeffer.[14] Bonhoeffer would become important to him later, but at this stage in his life, Bonhoeffer and King were probably too radical for this relatively conservative Baptist theologian.

BIOGRAPHY AS THEOLOGY

In 1974 McClendon published *Biography as Theology*. He was becoming ever more convinced that our convictions (our theology) shapes our lives, that is, our characters. This, of course, has as much to do with how we preach in our churches as with how we teach students and write books. Who people are and how theological convictions can shape real lives is the subject matter of this book.

The book has no ordinary structure. It intersperses stories of interesting characters throughout while it engages in theological reflection. The four characters whose stories are told are: Dag Hammarskjöld (1905–1961), Martin Luther King Jr. (1929–1968), Clarence Jordan (1912–1969), and Charles Ives (1874–1954). In his chapter on Hammarskjöld, McClendon asks why a person like him should be included in his study. After all, he, was not a university professor or a leader of the church as the other three were.[15] McClendon's answer is that he is not interested in discovering what Hammarskjöld believed religiously in order to suggest that we all believe the same. "*That* is not what biography as theology means." He continues:

A partial explanation of the choices made [of characters in his book] is that theology is intended *for* someone: it has an assumed audience, a presupposed set of hearers. In some degree, I regard my subjects as representative of the audience for which present-day American theology must be undertaken. To dramatize this, suppose yourself a pastor who knows that your congregation includes the likes of a Dag Hammarskjöld, or the likes of a Martin King. Given such a fact, what form must your own theologizing take? It is not that you must think as they think, or say what they say. It is rather that *your theology must be adequate to lives such as these lives*. So far as it has attended to the modern world, theology has too often grown dilute because it has attended mainly to the thinnest strains in modern life (for example, to the most boring secularism). Let us rather seek to shape in our times a faith adequate to the intensity and the spiritual seriousness of such as these. If that is a fair theological goal, then what is first required is to attend carefully to these representative (though certainly not average) parishioners.[16]

In order to understand the significance of biography as theology, McClendon argues, it is essential that we understand the notion of an *ethic* of character and beyond that a *theology* of character.

It is therefore not surprising that the first essay in *Biography as Theology* is titled "In Search of an Ethic of Character." McClendon is suggesting, in 1974, that the world of Christian ethics (ethics in general actually) is at the cusp of something new. It is interesting that his essay came out the same year as Stanley Hauerwas' *Vision and Virtue*,[17] in which he has an essay titled "Toward an Ethic of Character," which had been published separately two years earlier.[18] So within two years we have two theologians from quite different backgrounds, one Baptist and the other Methodist (although in dialogue with each other), arguing that there is a new way of conceiving ethics (which actually turns out to be a very old way), that has more potential than the available options.

Tillich, Rudolf Bultmann, W. T. Conner, and Austin Farrer.

[15] Dag Hammarskjöld was a Swedish diplomat who was the second Secretary General of the United Nations, from 1953 to 1961. His personal diary, *Markings*, trans. Leif Sjöberg (London: Farber & Farber, 1964), was discovered after his mysterious death in a plane crash and revealed him to be a deeply spiritual and thoughtful person.

[16] McClendon, *Biography as Theology*, 25 (emphasis in original).

[17] Stanley Hauerwas, *Vision and Virtue: Essays in Christian Ethical Reflection* (Notre Dame, Ind.: University of Notre Dame Press, 1974). See also chap. 34 below.

[18] Stanley Hauerwas, "Toward an Ethic of Character," *Theological Studies* 33 (1972): 698-715.

[19] See chap. 20 above.

McClendon points out that there is a growing consensus around the demise of utilitarianism and along with it a fading trust in Reinhold Niebuhr's Christian realism[19] and Joseph Fletcher's situation ethics. As part of the fading package, he includes decisionism and quandary ethics.[20] He relies on John C. Raines to show that first, Christian realism has no ethic of the common good; second, it is not realistic enough in that it offers no virtues for everyday life; and third, it views God as "beyond history" and so cannot comfort living human beings in history.[21]

Character ethics, according to McClendon, is a replacement for decisionism and Christian realism. Character ethics is best seen as "the ethics of character-in-community," because it presupposes a distinct view of the self. He reaches back to H. Richard Niebuhr's *The Responsible Self*[22] in making this point. Niebuhr's view of the self is unintelligible without placement within a community and under God. Both of these notions are central to a view of self necessary for character ethics, yet Niebuhr fails to develop them adequately.

The notion of character is perhaps best understood via the common genre of the novel. Characters get shaped in novels as the author weaves them in and out of interaction with other characters and in communities. Hence, by the end of the novel, readers know the character and are surprised (or not) when the character acts in unexpected (or expected) ways. But the very capacity to judge "unusual behavior" is because someone has become a character. Every novel molds characters in a way to produce a sense of unity to the person's actions, why a person does what he or she does.

Hence, McClendon is able to say:

> To have character, then, is to enter at a new level the realm of morality, the level at which one's person, with its continuities, its interconnections, its integrity, is intimately involved in one's deeds. By being the persons we are, we are able to do what we do, and conversely, by those very deeds we form or re-form our own characters. Only a woman of (some) generosity will act generously, as a general rule; but also as a general rule the woman who acts generously on this occasion is shaping herself along generous lines. Thus, character is paradoxically both the cause and consequence of what we do.[23]

McClendon suggests that New Testament ethics is best understood via character ethics. New Testament writers are concerned about the nature of the person "in Christ."[24] And one of the factors important in developing "character in Christ" is "putting on" protective gear to help us not to stray from a particular character. In other words, there are forces that seek to pull us away from being in Christ and forces that can help us remain in character.

Speaking this way, of course, makes it plain that one cannot talk of Christian character ethics without also talking of theological convictions. McClendon says, "Convictions may be distinguished from principles, in that the latter are the product of reflective thinking, have often a rather academic flavor, and are perhaps more often weapons for attacking others than guides for ourselves (most of us have at some time served on committees with 'men of principle'); while convictions are very often particular and immediate in form and may not be consciously formulated by their holders at all, yet when we do find our convictions, we find the best clue to

---

[20] See Joseph F. Fletcher, *Situation Ethics: The New Morality* (Philadelphia: Westminster, 1966). For an analysis and critique of decisionism, McClendon refers to Edmund Pincoffs, "Quandary Ethics," *Mind* (October 1971): 552-71.

[21] See McClendon, *Biography as Theology*, 13. The John C. Raines reference is to "Theodicy and Politics," *Worldview* (April 1973): 46.

[22] H. Richard Niebuhr, *The Responsible Self: An Essay in Christian Moral Philosophy* (New York: Harper & Row, 1963). See also chap. 21 above.

[23] McClendon, *Biography as Theology*, 16.

[24] McClendon cites the following references: Gal 5:19-24; Rom 1:28-31; Eph 5:3-5; Phil 4:8; Col 3:5-15; 1 Tim 3:2-13; James 3:13-18; and 1 Pet 3:8-13. See McClendon, *Biography as Theology*, 18.

[25] McClendon, *Biography as Theology*, 19–20.

ourselves."[25] Therefore, an ethics of character is not possible without convictions. In other words, putting on the Christian character requires the conviction that our faith and trust in God makes a difference for how we live. Convictions are not propositions but forces that shape our actual behavior and existence. Hence, what we believe can often be seen from how we live, not only from how we speak. If you like, *"Biography at its best will be theology."*[26] This is why theology makes sense only through embodied, Christian convictions.

McClendon wrote a book with James M. Smith called *Understanding Religious Convictions*. This is an important book in two ways; first, it is co-authored by an unusual team: an ordained Baptist minister-theologian—that is, one who holds tightly to and seeks conscientiously to live by, his Christian convictions—and "a social philosopher who long ago gave up the foolishness of Christian faith and would appear on census as a secular atheist."[27] And second, locating this difference in conviction could easily lead readers to assume that the path they will follow in discussing religious convictions will be a typical foundational approach asking what they have in common that both might affirm. In other words, what are we left with when we bracket out faith's nonessentials like social, cultural, and personal factors. But this is precisely what does *not* characterize the authors' approach. An alternative approach might be a perspectivism which frees persons with different convictions to believe whatever they want. McClendon and Smith reject that approach as well. But what options are left?

The tragedy of American theology is that students have been trained to choose between these two options. The value of the work of McClendon and Smith is that they seriously explored the possibility of a nonfoundational alternative when that was not yet in vogue.[28] What is at stake here is the nature of theology itself; but, perhaps even more important, the question of what does theology have to do with how we live? For if theological convictions are best understood as intellectual data, there is no necessary connection with ethics. And if theology (our convictions about God) merely describes a reality from a distance, then the power of theology will not likely long be sustainable. If, however, as McClendon and Smith argue, "Convictions are the beliefs which make people what they are,"[29] then in order to take them seriously, we must take their convictions, and the stories that house them, seriously.

This is but another way of attending carefully to how language functions. McClendon and Smith have learned from Wittgenstein and Austin that language has a performative function—we *do* things with words.[30] That is, to see language as "speech acts" helps us to understand our conviction. So when we confess a creed by saying, "I believe in God, the Father almighty . . ." we are not merely stating a proposition that we hold to be true but are performing an action that commits us to a way of life.

This logic is perhaps best illustrated in another project McClendon was involved in—an edited book, *Is God GOD?*[31] This book arises out of a concern that the "Death of God Theology," prominent in the 1970s, was confused about how religious language functions. The terms of the question inquiring about the concept of God are often set up in such a way as to guarantee a negative

---

[26] McClendon, *Biography as Theology*, 22 (emphasis in original).

[27] From the preface in James William McClendon Jr. and James M. Smith, *Understanding Religious Convictions* (Notre Dame, Ind.: University of Notre Dame Press, 1975), vii.

[28] E.g., Hans Frei's book, *The Eclipse of Narrative* (New Haven: Yale University Press, 1974) had come out just a year earlier, and George Lindbeck's, *The Nature of Doctrine: Religion and Theology in a Postliberal Age* (Philadelphia: Westminster, 1984) would not appear until a decade later.

[29] McClendon and Smith, *Understanding Religious Convictions*, 8.

[30] See J. L. Austin, *How to Do Things with Words* (New York: Oxford University Press, 1962).

[31] Axel D. Steuer and James William McClendon Jr., *Is God GOD?* (Nashville: Abingdon, 1981).

[32] Steuer and McClendon, *Is God GOD?*, 9.

answer. "Are we talking about something or someone other than ourselves and our own constructed world of thoughts and ideas? Is there really a God? Is God God?"[32] This language, argues McClendon, is deceiving because it suggests that it is meaningful outside of all contexts. And the importance of context, and communities called "forms of life," which for McClendon is the church, is what philosophers like Wittgenstein help us to understand.

McClendon relies on this background for his two-decade project of writing a systematic theology with a difference. Since he has come to believe that we cannot know Christ unless we follow him, following is the first step and knowing is the second. Hence, his systematic theology begins with ethics—a rather unusual way to begin. Readers may see affinity here with the liberation theology of Gustavo Gutiérrez, and the first and second act of theology; while that affinity exists, McClendon's approach is still quite different.

ETHICS AS THEOLOGY

McClendon's life took several twists and turns. At age fifty it was about to take another; he read John Howard Yoder's *The Politics of Jesus*.[33] During this time, he was teaching at an Episcopal Seminary at GTU in Berkeley. He says of reading Yoder's work:

> That book changed my life. Implicit in it I found all the old awareness of being part of a Christianity somehow unlike the standard-account sort I had worked so hard to learn and to teach, yet somehow like what I had known as a youth growing up Baptist. Night and day I read through the *Politics*, and by the time I had finished, I had undergone a second conversion, not as at my baptism merely to follow Jesus, but now to follow Jesus understood this way—Jesus interpreted by John Yoder's scornful passion to overcome standard-account thinking, Jesus who (among other things) rejected the Zealot option, Jesus who would not do harm even in the best of causes, even in his own.[34]

At last, McClendon had found a theology for his pacifism. But what did this do to the insights he had gained from Wittgenstein and Austin? Remarkably, he found resonance with their approach and Yoder's theology. So McClendon's resolve to write a unique systematic theology only strengthened, and he began volume one—*Ethics*. Beginning this way does not mean that for him theology is determined by ethics, but it does mean a rethinking of what theology is and certainly a rejection of an Enlightenment foundational epistemology.

McClendon begins by observing that the sixteenth-century Anabaptists, who formed the background to McClendon's own baptist vision, were regarded as dangerous. They were dangerous to society, to politics, and to the religious fabric of Europe, but at the same time they were pacifists and largely people of good character. Why then were they dangerous? Because they refused to underwrite the politics of their day—claiming instead that Christians must follow Jesus. Hence, the state and other institutions had no way to shape their behavior such that they would become "good" citizens, doing the bidding of the state.

In challenging the traditional order of doing theology—beginning with method, then doing theology, and leaving ethics to the end—McClendon realizes the enormity of the task. He asks:

> Is it not worth considering . . . how different might have been the history of Christianity if after the accession of the emperor Constantine the church's leaders had met at Nicaea, not to anathematize others' inadequate Christological metaphysics, but to devise a strategy by which the church might remain the church in light of the fateful political shift—to secure Christian social ethics before refining Christian dogma?[35]

Yet McClendon reaches back to the early church fathers like Origen to define theology. He notes that Origen did not teach

---

[33] John Howard Yoder, *The Politics of Jesus*: Vicit Agnus Noster, 2nd ed. (Grand Rapids: Eerdmans, 1994).

[34] McClendon, "Radical Road," 507–8.

[35] James William McClendon Jr., *Ethics: Systematic Theology* (Nashville: Abingdon, 1986), 42.

[36] McClendon, *Ethics: Systematic Theology*, 43–44.

theology to his students as though it was a set of ideas and concepts independent of life. He summarizes:

> If we recall that Origen had been chief teacher in the catechetical school at Alexandria, the earliest Christian "theological seminary" we know about, it appears that we have here a clue to the character of Christian theology at the time of its beginning. Alexandria's School was not at heart the home of flighty speculation in philosophy. It was no "university of antiquity." It was rather a training ground for Christianity, where spiritual and moral instruction necessarily took first place since only upon such a basis could the further reaches of Christian knowledge ever be understood. Not only in the hands of Origen, but of his predecessors Pantaenus and Clement of Alexandria, it was "a school for training in virtue," whose goal was to form the lives of its students "in light of the ideal set forth in the Scriptures and imaged in Christ."[36]

He also cites Radical Reformer Menno Simons, from the sixteenth century, as an example of a writer who had "so interwoven ethics and doctrine that the seam between the two cannot be found."[37]

Not only is theology reconceived, but so is ethics. As we have seen, he rejects decisionism, along with the utilitarianism of the Jeremy Bentham and John Stuart Mill variety; and he rejects the Kantian deontological (theory of duty) approach to ethics. Not surprisingly, in keeping with the novel genre, he affirms narrative ethics. His narrative approach, however, is not one that reduces the Christian story to a single-strand story. Christian ethics must be Christian in the sense that it is deeply rooted in the story of Jesus Christ; and it must be ethics in that it helps us understand how it is that we can live in today's complex world. In order to get to the complexity of the Christian moral life, McClendon seeks to develop three strands which form the basic outline of his book on ethics. He calls these strands (or spheres) the organic, the communal, and the anastatic. But these strands ought to be seen as

intimately interconnected so that they can help us to empower the multiple dynamics of the Christian life.

He speaks of the interrelationship of the three strands via the image of a rope, an image he borrows from Wittgenstein. McClendon says, "consider a rope with (at least) three strands. Such a rope has no single strand that *is* the rope, or around which the others are formed—and there is no central, invisible core, either. The whole rope is nothing but the strands, yet none of them alone can do what the rope does. My proposal is that biblical morality be viewed as such a multi-stranded rope."[38] McClendon also identifies these strands by other names: human nature, culture, and God's kingdom. Or still differently, the body, the social, and the resurrection. All three are ways of relating to God: we are created as natural beings, our life can find fulfillment only as social persons, and we are witness to the resurrection of Jesus Christ in which we ourselves can participate. Remember, these three strands are one rope and cannot be broken apart without destroying the rope.

Body Ethics

McClendon begins by identifying two ways that the body is a problem for Christian ethics. On the one hand, Christians have become accustomed to thinking that ethics has little to do with our bodies; the body is often seen as the enemy for Christian ethics. Living in the spirit then becomes the model, and that means denying the body. On the other hand, in modern times there is a deification of nature—what is natural is right and denying fulfillment of the body is wrong. He identifies both options as problematic and points to biblical morality with its emphasis on the well-being of the body—Jesus' many healings of the body and his concern for the body in his parables. And although the Apostle Paul speaks negatively of the flesh, he calls the

---

[37] McClendon, *Ethics: Systematic Theology*, 44.
[38] McClendon, *Ethics: Systematic Theology*, 64 (emphasis in original).
[39] See McClendon, *Ethics: Systematic Theology*, 83.

church the *body* of Christ and emphasizes the incarnation and the resurrection of the body.

McClendon refers to African American religion to show especially powerful ways of accounting for the suffering of the body. Black Christianity narrates this experience in connection with the suffering of Jesus. "Were you there when they crucified my Lord?" The question raised by the spiritual is answered: "Yes, we were; for we too have been crucified with Christ."[39] This leads McClendon to identify two important aspects of black theology: "that it is irreducibly narrative in form, and that the story *now* echoes the story *then*. . . ."[40] In other words, their bodies participate in the body of Jesus; their suffering is the suffering of Jesus. "Nobody knows de trouble I see, Nobody knows *but Jesus*."[41]

In his section on body ethics, McClendon refers to Dietrich Bonhoeffer, who speaks of the sphere of the natural (body), and in so doing makes the distinction between penultimate and ultimate acts. The penultimate act, like giving the hungry bread, is a way of participating in, or preparing for, the ultimate act, but it is not yet there. This ties the body to the divine, in that there is no way to exclude suffering on earth from the realm of divine grace, meaning that hope can be found by placing our suffering in Christ's suffering (at the foot of the cross).[42]

Bodies have needs that are universal. The biblical narrative speaks of these in several ways. One is through a gospel parable told by Jesus: "I was hungry and you gave me food, I was thirsty and you gave me something to drink, I was a stranger and you welcomed me, I was naked and you gave me clothing, I was sick and you took care of me, I was in prison and you visited me" (Matt 25:35-36).[43] Responding to these needs of the body has

much to do with Christian ethics. This has gotten some ethicists to invoke the language of human rights. McClendon believes this is a mistake: "the notion that there are 'human rights' to which persons *qua* persons are entitled, confuses the idea of social rights (those that arise within a particular social structure) with the idea of basic human needs. The best picture of human rights is as a metaphor, sometimes politically (because rhetorically) effective, but not addressed to the more basic moral issues we are concerned with here."[44]

Clearly, not all bodily needs are such that they ought to be met. We have stories that illustrate this in the biblical narrative, namely, the sexual needs of King David, in 2 Samuel 11. David's troops are off in battle, during which time he beholds a beautiful woman—Bathsheba—lies with her and gets her pregnant. The actions of David, in response, are hardly laudable. He sinned once by indulging his sexual needs, he sins again by indulging his need to protect his reputation. (McClendon also analyzes the needs of Uriah and Bathsheba, but I will forego those here for sake of brevity.)[45]

McClendon acknowledges that human beings are blessed with some degree of "natural moral equipment," such as natural delight and horror at certain actions; shame, blame, and guilt; and of course, conscience. But these are hardly enough for biblical morality. He also speaks about embodied virtues: skills and habits that train the body to act in a particular manner. But which virtues should we cultivate? And how should a virtue be understood? For virtues need a narrative context to have meaning—Jesus had *courage* in a very different way than a soldier has courage.

In each of the three sections in his book, McClendon inserts a story of real people.

---

[40] McClendon, *Ethics: Systematic Theology*, 83–84 (emphasis in original).

[41] McClendon, *Ethics: Systematic Theology*, 84 (emphasis in original).

[42] See McClendon, *Ethics: Systematic Theology*, 84. See also 272ff. above for a fuller discussion of Bonhoeffer's distinction of penultimate and ultimate.

[43] See McClendon, *Ethics: Systematic Theology*, 95.

[44] McClendon, *Ethics: Systematic Theology*, 95.

[45] See McClendon, *Ethics: Systematic Theology*, 95ff. for McClendon's story of David, Uriah, and Bathsheba.

[46] Jonathan Edwards was one of the great early American theologians, preachers, and missionaries. He played an

In this section, he tells the story of Sarah (1710–1758) and Jonathan (1703–1758) Edwards.[46] Jonathan was involved in preaching and writing theology; Sarah tended to their eleven children. They were lovers and life was beautiful; they lived in a time of hardship and there were many stresses, but they shared a life together.

McClendon ends the section on body ethics with reflections on sexual love. Sex is a natural, human drive, and as we have already seen in the story of David, it is not always embraced with moral integrity. Learning how to do that requires the moral training and cultivation of the virtue of love.

McClendon characterizes sexual love in three ways.[47] First, love is a feeling. Such a feeling ought not to be denied, but we need to train ourselves in the expression of our feelings appropriate to who we are in Christ. Second, love is a virtue. Feelings come and go; virtues are skills that shape a pattern of expressing our feelings that create a character. Third, love is a gift. To say that love is a gift has us reflect back on the giver—God. Hence, when we love, we express the gift we have been given; and so we abide in God and God in us (1 John 4:16). Nevertheless, as McClendon sees it, the best training for body ethics is to recognize it as but a strand of a three-stranded rope to which it adds moral wholeness but also receives moral guidance.

Social Ethics

Social ethics is embodied in the community. McClendon says:

> My claim is that for Christians the connecting link between body ethics and social ethics, between the moral self and the morals of society, is to be found in the body of Christ that is the gathered church. The place where conscience comes to light in a baptist ethic is not in solitary or Kierkegaardian introspection, nor is it in the social concerns of individual private citizens who happen to be Christians as well (not even in their widely held

and in that sense "common" concerns). Rather the link is found in congregational reflection, discernment, discipline, and action, whose model is nearer to the Wesleyan class meeting or the Anabaptist *Gemeinde* than to the denominational social action lobby agency or the mass membership churches of today's suburban society.[48]

McClendon begins by discussing the possibility of social ethics. He acknowledges that the world is filled with forces and temptations that compete with Christian faithfulness. Given this reality, he suggests that the history of Christian thought has not been helpful in providing models of Christian living. From Augustine to Reinhold Niebuhr, social ethicists have rightly emphasized the importance of the fall, original sin, and the power of sin, but their conclusions for ethics have been less helpful. One conclusion is that we ought to be careful about how good we think we can be because our best efforts are always tainted by sin; and the other conclusion is that because of the power of sin on earth, redemption is only possible beyond history. This approach then emphasizes the importance of being realistic, that is, on not overreaching our human capacities. McClendon argues that this approach overlooks the biblical teaching of the church—new life in Christ on earth.[49] After all, Jesus lived, and called his disciples to follow him, *in history*.

McClendon points to Jacques Ellul (1912–1994) and John Howard Yoder as offering an alternative. This alternative is rooted in a biblical understanding of the church and the principalities and powers—fallen social structures. Taking the biblical language seriously here, McClendon says: "Defeated by Christ's cross and his resurrection, these powers were perceived as lingering on, beaten yet dangerous still, lurking at the margins of life."[50]

How is it then that Christians can live faithfully? McClendon relies on Alasdair MacIntyre's work on practices and games to

---

important role in the "Great Awakening" that swept across the United States in the 1730s.

[47] See McClendon, *Ethics: Systematic Theology*, 154–55.

[48] McClendon, *Ethics: Systematic Theology*, 210–11.

[49] McClendon, *Ethics: Systematic Theology*, 161.

[50] McClendon, *Ethics: Systematic Theology*, 161.

[51] See chap. 25 above.

answer this question.[51] A game is governed by rules, goals, practices, and skills, and in order to play a game well, these four qualities must come together. Skill alone will not do it, and playing by the rules alone will not do it either. Since practices are cooperative human activities and are connected with the virtues, the moral life must take a narrative form. This is why the Christian moral life cannot exist apart from the Christian moral community called church. But for McClendon, the church is understood in a particular way.

The church is the body that can proclaim the victory of Christ over the principalities and powers. Here, McClendon relies on Yoder's and Berkof's reading of Paul, who says that in Christ's death and resurrection God "disarmed the rulers and authorities and made a public example of them, triumphing over them in it" (Col 2:15). McClendon concludes:

> Wherever Christ's victory is proclaimed, the corrupted reign of the powers is challenged, and yet the powers remain in being. They are neither destroyed nor abolished, but dethroned. So in the time between the resurrection and the final coming of Christ, they remain in an ambiguous state, and thus they delimit and define the social morality of Jesus' followers, who will have to encounter in the form of these powers crosses of their own.[52]

Those who live in the body of Christ know that the ambiguous state of the powers will not last and will ultimately be abolished in Christ's victory. Hence, it is not a matter of living outside of the powers, even if corrupted, or seeing redemption only beyond history, but rather it is a matter of what kinds of powers can be embodied that already participate in the victory of the resurrection that is to come. In other words, the beyond of history has become historical in Christ. This, then, is McClendon's answer to the Augustines and the Niebuhrs.

McClendon argues that the structure of ethics we see in the biblical view of the church is the way the entire biblical story ought to be understood. In other words, he stresses continuity between the structure of ethics in the Old Testament Decalogue (Ten Commandments) and the structure of ethics found in the Sermon on the Mount in the Gospel of Matthew. The Ten Commandments were guides that shaped people to see and understand that God was working among them. In other words, the Decalogue ought not to be understood on a simple, divine-command–human obedience model.[53] McClendon argues that the Ten Commandments are ways that make "possible an understanding of law that is not 'legalistic,' but which demands of lawkeepers the recovery of the narrative structure of Israel's faith."[54] His point here is that the commandments are misunderstood on the model of decisionism and are best understood on the model of narrative and virtue ethics similar to Paul's view of the church. They characterize a community and summarize "the way" of a people, which offers a measure for determining those who are missing the way; the children of Israel, as also the disciples of Jesus, were invited to walk with God.

As in the section on body ethics, McClendon's section on social ethics also narrates the life of a prominent Christian, this time, Dietrich Bonhoeffer. After telling his story, McClendon focuses on his involvement in the plot to kill Hitler. He asks the question of how someone who was so dedicated to understanding the life of Christ, himself a sincere disciple of Christ, could become involved in such a thing. Indeed this is a tragedy. But for McClendon, it is a tragedy of a particular kind, directly related to the second strand of ethics—the church. He says:

> My thesis, then, is that Bonhoeffer's grisly death was part and parcel of the tragic dimension of his life, and that in turn but an element in the greater tragedy of the Christian community of Germany. Put in the briefest terms, it was that they had no effective strand-two moral structure in the church that was adequate to the crucial need of

---

[52] McClendon, *Ethics: Systematic Theology*, 175.
[53] See McClendon, *Ethics: Systematic Theology*, 180.
[54] McClendon, *Ethics: Systematic Theology*, 182.
[55] McClendon, *Ethics: Systematic Theology*, 207.

church and German people alike (to say nothing of the need of Jewish people; to say nothing of the world's people). No structures, no practices, no skills of political life existed that were capable of resisting, christianly resisting, the totalitarianism of the times. The tragedy is the more intense because of all Christians in Germany Dietrich Bonhoeffer was perhaps the one who came nearest to displaying exactly those skills and to developing exactly those practices. But it is a shared tragedy, for he could not in any case have met the need alone. And finally it is an instructive tragedy, for there is considerable evidence that the Christian church in the world, not least in America, faces again at the end of our century the same qualities of intrusive government, ideological warfare, and coopted religion that so readily deceived the Germans half a century ago.[55]

In exploring further what it might mean to see the gathered church as the form of the moral life for Christians, McClendon does so under three headings: discipleship and community; forgiveness; and the church in the world. He relies on the Gospel of Matthew to present each of these characteristics of the church.

Discipleship and Community: Matthew has a distinct way of speaking about the disciples. They were people who were "with Jesus." The characteristic language of Jesus' call was "Come, follow me" (e.g., Matt 19:21). It was an invitation, and the response indicated a willing participation of the follower. McClendon says, "Discipleship meant following Jesus, each disciple a follower, each follower 'with Jesus,' if and only if a disciple."[56] The disciples of Jesus came from different backgrounds—Jews and Gentiles—and what they had in common was their solidarity with Jesus. This solidarity was expressed in a "follow me obedience." Says McClendon: "Discipleship meant . . . obedience; it also meant *solidarity with one another.* Matthew would have his Syrian readers understand that, voluntarily linking their lives to Jesus, they have

linked them to each other as well. These ties override the existing links of kinship and of household."[57]

The act of solidarity with Jesus and with each other is expressed in the covenant meal in Matthew 26:26-29. McClendon picks up two themes from Matthew's simple account of the disciples eating with Jesus: one is that of solidarity—reference to body, blood, and covenant—and the other is forgiveness. He looks to 1 Corinthians 10–12 for an interpretation of the covenant meal. Here, he finds Paul identify the gathered Corinthian "disciples"—the church—as the "body of Christ" (1 Cor 12:27). The conclusion McClendon draws by bringing these two texts together is that the covenant meal is in fact a profound, moral rite. He says that this rite is "aimed at shaping the common life of Christian community. . . . The meal is part and parcel of a *practice* which we might roughly name the practice of *establishing and maintaining Christian community.*"[58] The implication, as McClendon sees it, is that the activities of the disciples in Corinth and today—following Jesus, being in solidarity with each other, eating together—is the shaping of the social, moral body.

Here McClendon issues a warning: as a set of practices and as a social structure, the church too is a *power,* and hence like other powerful practices, it can rebel, and enslave people and persecute them. Indeed, we know all too well the many examples of such practices. The church's provision for this, especially when the cultivation of the virtues fails, is the practice of forgiveness.

Forgiveness: McClendon sees the Christian community as "*exactly one in which forgiveness not punishment is the norm.*"[59] But forgiveness must be understood properly. He says, "Forgiving is not forgetting, for we can repress the memory and still be at enmity

---

[56] McClendon, *Ethics: Systematic Theology,* 214.

[57] McClendon, *Ethics: Systematic Theology,* 214 (emphasis in original).

[58] McClendon, *Ethics: Systematic Theology,* 216 (emphasis in original).

[59] McClendon, *Ethics: Systematic Theology,* 224 (emphasis in original).

[60] McClendon, *Ethics: Systematic Theology,* 225.

with one an other [sic]; for Christians, forgiving is rather remembering under the aspect of membership in the body of Christ: it is knowing that he who is our body and we, forgiven and forgiver, are all one."[60] Forgiveness is what makes it possible for sinners to live as one wholesome and life-giving body. One could perhaps say that the church is sinners living in the body of Christ. Indeed, this is the language of Paul to the Christian community at Ephesus. "Be kind to one another, tenderhearted, forgiving one another, as God in Christ has forgiven you" (Eph 4:32).

McClendon says of forgiveness in community that:

> It is exactly this skill of forgiveness that is the divine gift enabling disciple communities to cope with the looming power of their own practice of community, otherwise so oppressive, so centripetally destructive. Without forgiveness, the social power of a closed circle may crush its members, soil itself, and sour its social world. Examples of such soured communitarianism litter the pages of every honest church history. But with forgiveness controlling everything, the closed circle is opened, the forgiving forgivers' practice of community is redeemed and becomes positively redemptive; thus this powerful practice renders obedience to the law of the Lord Jesus.[61]

The Church's Presence in the World: McClendon believes that we have been all too easily captivated by H. Richard Niebuhr's Christ and culture binary model. It has taught us to feel responsible for—in charge of—the world, at the expense of losing the claim of the lordship of Jesus Christ. Instead, he draws in Karl Barth's theme of "exemplary witness" through being the new community and Stanley Hauerwas' emphasis on the church being the only body that can help us to see the world *as world.* However, for his primary resource, he turns again to Matthew's Gospel.

There is a specific form that engagement with the world takes in Matthew. For example:

> Now the eleven disciples went to Galilee, to the mountain to which Jesus had directed them. When they saw him, they worshiped him; but some doubted. And Jesus came and said to them, "All authority on heaven and on earth has been given to me. Go therefore and make disciples of all nations, baptizing them in the name of the Father and of the Son and of the Holy Spirit, and teaching them to obey everything that I have commanded you. And remember, I am with you always, to the end of the age." (Matt 28:16-20)

McClendon summarizes that the task of the disciples is to make disciples: to go into the nations and there baptize and teach.[62]

The early disciples, and disciples throughout history, faced two kinds of challenges: the ones that came from outside, like temptations to avoid the cross for other options of faithful living, in other words, the lure of the good life the world had to offer; and the challenge that came from inside, like temptations to status, unwillingness to forgive, the lure of power and wealth within the church. In other words, the temptations throughout the history of the church have been to give up on the church *being the church* distinct from the world.

How then can the church be faithful both in relation to itself and in relation to the world around it? McClendon speaks of the tension thus: on the one hand, the church is a haven, an escape from the evils of the powers; on the other hand, it engages the powers, it seeks ways of responding to the crosses of life—the sins of the world. As a haven, it seeks a healthy balance of body, mind, and spirit. The body desires *stability*—economic, political, and social order; the mind seeks *integrity*—opportunities for education, truth-telling friendships, truth-seeking debates; and the spirit seeks *liberty*—the freedom to soar, worship, praise, and lament. McClendon also adds a fourth quality, *plurality*—the human race is not just one body but consists of many and diverse groups of people and nations. We must be careful not to seek unity

---

[61] McClendon, *Ethics: Systematic Theology,* 229–30.
[62] See McClendon, *Ethics: Systematic Theology,* 233.
[63] McClendon, *Ethics: Systematic Theology,* 247.

at all costs; we must find ways of seeing the beauty, color, and complementarity within plurality without relinquishing the claim that Jesus is Lord.

Then there are the crosses of life: the tragedies, social evils, wars, racisms, sexism, and hatreds of every kind imaginable. The church cannot hide from these; yet how do we respond? Surely to engage evil with hatred, anger, and violence is but to do so on the world's terms. The body of Christ, if it is of Christ, engages evil with forgiveness, truth, love, and the peace of Christ. This is no less challenging than to respond to evil with violence; perhaps it is even more challenging. It is certainly no less engaging. However, it is the more radical because it arises out of the conviction that before God we are all sinners, and the only match for sin in this world is God's gracious redemption. For the only difference among us is that those who live in Christ know themselves to be forgiven and are called to give witness to the one who makes peace through the cross and the resurrection.

Resurrection Ethics

The third strand of ethics is the resurrection strand. We need to remind ourselves that the three strands rely on each other to be the rope that Christian ethics is for McClendon. Resurrection ethics is what makes forgiveness, love, and truthfulness possible. But still we must ask what kind of social strategy it presupposes. How are we to understand social change from violence to peace, or from injustice to justice? The resurrection strand provides the answer!

The resurrection event is both a historical event and more than that. The bodily resurrection of Jesus is important for the moral life in that "[i]f it did not happen, Christian life is false and the Christian faith lives out a lie; since it did happen, all our standards of judgment, and we ourselves, are profoundly

called into question, but Christ is fully alive, and there is hope also for us who can wonder, doubt—and believe."[63] Notice here how the resurrection of Christ relativizes us and even our ethics.

McClendon describes resurrection ethics under three headings.

"The Vindication of Justice"[64]: By what right can the Christian moral community make its claim about the possibility of justice in the world? Given the sin around us, the important question is not the age-old question of theodicy—how can we believe in God—but rather how can we believe in justice in our world? McClendon lets the Apostle Paul answer: "[Jesus] was handed over to death for our trespasses and was raised for our *justification*" (Rom 4:25).[65] The resurrection of Jesus was the "speech-act" that God is in charge; in charge not only from a distance but immediately in ordinary life. And with God, life wins. The "body of Christ" is therefore to live this life victoriously, not because *we* can but because the resurrection lives in us.

"A New Way of Construing the World"[66]: On the basis of Jesus who "died and *was raised*," the Apostle Paul says that "if anyone is in Christ, there is a new creation; everything old has passed away; see, everything has become new!" (2 Cor 5:17). The resurrection inaugurated a new age, one in which a new rule has begun even if not yet fully realized.

We tend to think of the natural world as being governed entirely by the necessity of natural law. The resurrection event announces that the world as it appears is not all there is. For the very hand of the one who created the natural order has acted in resurrecting Christ from death—an order of necessity. Hence, we need to be cautious about acting out of what our scientific-technological world tells us is necessary, or for that matter, what our social-political world tells us is

---

[64] McClendon, *Ethics: Systematic Theology*, 248.
[65] See McClendon, *Ethics: Systematic Theology*, 248 (emphasis added).
[66] McClendon, *Ethics: Systematic Theology*, 249.
[67] McClendon, *Ethics: Systematic Theology*, 252.

necessary. Resurrection ethics asks us to re-conceive the world as if God is acting in it.

"A Transformation of Human Life"[67]: The new life in Christ is characterized by new birth and conversion—transformation. This means that the new, moral life is of a distinct kind: one marked by a specific view of change, both in the self and in society. In the Christ story, the cross was followed by resurrection, not out of any natural necessity, but out of God's graciousness. So McClendon says, "the resurrection strand makes it inescapably clear that the story is to be marked with incalculable surprises, and that our lives belong to Christ just in terms of the surprise endings and turns that mark the resurrection Way."[68]

Baptism is the event in the life of a Christian that signifies the moral meaning of the resurrection because in baptism the confession is made that the story of Jesus is to become the story of the Christian. As McClendon puts it, "Here, then, the baptist vision is at work: 'this is that'—our baptisms recapitulate and so claim his resurrection in our own lives afresh."[69]

Since resurrection names the strategy of social change, we do well to recognize the implications for social ethics. McClendon contrasts his approach with the ethics of Paul Lehmann's contextual ethics and that of most liberation theologians.[70] The problem with these approaches is the assumption that revolution and change can themselves name the terms of ethics. The three-strand-approach points to why this is problematic. We cannot control the means of change, nor can we know what it means to be human on our own. Resurrection ethics confesses that since God is in charge of directing the affairs of history, faithful Christian followers must open themselves to God's guidance through the story of Jesus Christ. Unless we do so, we will forever be stuck both

with limited vision and with limited capacity for change, and our strategies for change will inevitably draw on violence.

McClendon narrates the faith story of Dorothy Day (1897–1980) as, "a Christianity that in obedience to Jesus Christ would be consistently nonviolent, refusing violence on the side of revolution, but also refusing it on the side of establishment and oppression."[71] Day was a Catholic who started *The Catholic Worker*, a newspaper and a movement in 1933, which had as its goal the Catholic support for the working poor. He says she came by her pacifism because she had read the Greek New Testament—particularly the Sermon on the Mount—already in high school. It was here that she learned the call of Jesus to love enemies rather than kill them. She was not shy about speaking this finding into the public arena, even during the Second World War when the Japanese attacked America at Pearl Harbor.

PEACE AND ESCHATOLOGY

One of the impressive features of Day's pacifism, according to McClendon, is that because it was grounded on the Sermon on the Mount, she got right an important aspect that so many other ethicists miss. You cannot talk of biblical pacifism without a discourse of participation in something that is still to come. In other words, biblical pacifism requires a Christian eschatology. This is what Reinhold Niebuhr's Christian realism gets wrong. For him, since the love of enemy is not able to dissolve the reality of sin—egoism, pride, greed, power abuse—pacifism must be socially and politically irrelevant. The biblical alternative is that love of enemy can open possibilities for God to transform even the most heinous evils and so offers the possibility of human participation without being in charge.

---

[68] McClendon, *Ethics: Systematic Theology*, 254.
[69] McClendon, *Ethics: Systematic Theology*, 257.
[70] McClendon refers to Paul Lehmann, *Ethics in a Christian Context* (New York: Harper & Row, 1963).
[71] McClendon, *Ethics: Systematic Theology*, 295.
[72] Yoder's "Peace without Eschatology," is reprinted in John Howard Yoder, *The Royal Priesthood: Essays, Ecclesiological*

McClendon recalls John Howard Yoder's 1954 essay, "Peace without Eschatology?"[72] to develop this idea further. Yoder was especially concerned with those who believed that there must be an immediate connection between our witness to peace and the coming of a peaceful world. He argues that even though there is not an immediate connection, there is a connection nevertheless. This is the model of Jesus' own actions—participating in something that is still on its way. If one does not see Christian peacemaking in this manner, then one must either declare Christian peacemaking politically irrelevant and resort to violent alternatives (Niebuhr) or withdraw from society. Jesus had both options available to him—the Zealots and the Essenes—and he rejected them both. The alternative was for him to live boldly (speech acts) the love of enemies, in the presence of the powers of Pilate and Herod—and indeed the religious establishment—which resulted in his eventual death. But these powers, even the power of death, were no match for the resurrection power of God. The future of peace, like salvation, is also not in human hands, but in the hands of resurrecting God. The Christian model of pacifism then is rooted in a participation in what is not yet here—the resurrection. Of course it is not ours to claim; yet it is ours to hope for. "For in hope we were saved" (Rom 8:24a).

CONCLUSION

Ethics is not the last book McClendon wrote. There were two more in his *magnum opus*. In *Doctrine*,[73] he explores what the church must teach in order to be the church that fosters the Christian life as characterized by the three strands of ethics. His last book, *Witness*,[74] published just before his death in 2000, shows how the church has conversations with other aspects of society and culture like the arts, science, music, philosophy.

McClendon's contribution to the discussion of Christian ethics is significant. He had greater concern than Yoder did in providing a systematic whole to the theology of pacifism, and he certainly found more room than Yoder for the contributions of contemporary philosophers. But his passions were the same: fidelity to the biblical narrative, discipleship of Jesus, and a commitment to the gathered community as the locus for faithful Christian living. Christian ethics and theology are rooted in struggle, and, as he states in his opening page of *Ethics*: "The struggle begins with the humble fact that the church is not the world."[75]

and Ecumenical, ed. Michael G. Cartwright (Grand Rapids: Eerdmans, 1994), 143–67.
   [73] James William McClendon Jr., *Doctrine: Systematic Theology*, vol. 2 (Nashville: Abingdon, 1994).
   [74] James William McClendon Jr., *Witness: Systematic Theology*, vol. 3 (Nashville: Abingdon, 2000).
   [75] McClendon, *Ethics: Systematic Theology*, 17.

Chapter Thirty-Four

STANLEY HAUERWAS
(1940–)

Perhaps more than any other contemporary, Christian ethicist, Stanley Hauerwas has injected into the current debate the voice of a radical, Christian ethic that is "radical" only because dominant, American Christianity has become so enamored with American culture. One might say that the Social Gospel approach to ethics has worked all too well; only the gospel has been Americanized instead of the social order being Christianized. Hauerwas has often said that if the goal is to Christianize the social order (as Walter Rauschenbusch has claimed), you end up asking whether ethics can be Christian (as James Gustafson asks).[1]

Hauerwas believes that it is important to question the dominant metaphors of Christian ethics—whether that is Christian realism made popular by the Niebuhrs and their disciples, the metaphor of command-obedience of Karl Barth and Rudolf Bultmann,[2] or the decision metaphor of Joseph Fletcher's situation ethics.[3] Not denying their valid insights, he nevertheless wishes to empower the ancient language of character, which "does not exclude the language of command but only places it in a larger framework of moral experience."[4] It is important to point out here that Hauerwas is much more supportive of Karl Barth's approach to theology in general than he is critical of it, but in Hauerwas' early work, he believes that a corrective is in order.

My focus in this chapter is fourfold: first, I will give a general overview of Hauerwas' life and thought made possible by his recent memoir; second, ask why Hauerwas is critical of the contemporary metaphors of Christian ethics; third, analyze the nature and implications of his replacement metaphors of character, narrative, vision, and virtues; and fourth, explore what his approach to ethics contributes to the overall understanding of Christian ethics.

HIS STORY

Of course, one cannot tell the story of a person, especially not a theologian's story, and even more especially not Stanley Hauerwas' story, without talking about what that person thought, believed, and why. In Hauerwas' recent memoir,[5] we find an extraordinary story of a life richly lived with pain and happiness, deep friendships and conflicts, teaching and interacting with colleagues and students. Not only do we see in

---

[1] This chapter is a reworked version of an earlier essay, "An Ethic of Character," that appeared in *Essays on Peace Theology and Witness*, ed. Willard Swartley, , Occasional Papers no. 2 (Elkhart, Ind.: Institute of Mennonite Studies, 1988).

[2] See esp., Stanley Hauerwas, *Character and the Christian Life: A Study in Theological Ethics* (San Antonio, Tex.: Trinity University Press, 1975).

[3] See Stanley Hauerwas, "Situation Ethics, Moral Notions, and Moral Theology," in *Vision and Virtue: Essays in Christian Ethical Reflection* (Notre Dame, Ind.: University of Notre Dame Press, 1974.) See also his *Character and the Christian Life*, 177–78.

[4] Hauerwas, *Character and the Christian Life*, 3.

[5] Stanley Hauerwas, *Hannah's Child: A Theologian's Memoir* (Grand Rapids: Eerdmans, 2010).

this book his view of the Christian life but we also see how he thinks about how he thinks and lives. To say it another way, not only do we discover how he thinks and lives we discover why—who his friends were that shaped his theology and ethics.

In 2001 Hauerwas was named "best theologian in America" by *Time* magazine. This was altogether puzzling to him because he did not understand how secular magazine writers and editors could possess sufficient theological wisdom to determine such a thing. When he was told of this honor, Hauerwas quipped, " 'Best' is not a theological category."[6] This remark tells us much about him; it was not an effort to be ungrateful or disrespectful, but all his life he had emphasized that the church's task was to help the world see itself as world, and now the world was bestowing on him accolades with categories he held suspect.

Hauerwas does not see the Christian faith primarily as a belief structure; God is not a hypothesis in which to believe. Rather, being a Christian is all about being a particular kind of person; that is, being open to God figuring in one's story.

He begins his memoir with a chapter on "Being Saved." He struggled with this notion. It was not as though he resisted it, but so little was happening that was giving it sense! He tells his mother's version of his birth:

> My mother and father had married "late." My mother desperately wanted children. She had a child that was stillborn—something I learned when I was looking through her "effects" after she had died. It was then that I discovered my original birth certificate, which indicated the previous birth. But my indomitable mother was not deterred by the loss of child. She had heard the story of Hannah praying to God to give her a son, whom she would dedicate to God. Hannah's prayer was answered, and she named her son Samuel. My mother prayed a similar prayer. I am the result. But I was named Stanley because the week before I was born my mother and father saw a movie—*Stanley and Livingstone*.[7]

He confesses that he is certainly not a Samuel, but there are some who might say he has played a Samuel-like role in challenging the religious establishment. He admits that he has certainly tried to warn Christians that having a king is not the best idea in the world, at least if you think that the king is going to save you. But he never tried to be a Samuel.[8]

Hauerwas grew up in Pleasant Grove, Texas, which is just outside of downtown Dallas. He begins his story with the Pleasant Mound Methodist Church and says he became a theologian because he could not get himself "saved" in his church. He tells it this way, "I'm not sure how old I was when I began to worry about being saved, but it was some time in my early teens. I had begun to date a young woman who also went to Pleasant Mound, which meant I was beginning to sin. I was pretty sure I needed saving, but I just did not think that I should try to force God's hand. All this was complicated for me because the church was at the center of my family's life."[9]

He dedicated his life to the Lord one day as he went to the altar and told Brother Zimmerman, the pastor, that this was his wish. But he said that he surely knew that he did not know what he was doing; he thought he was acting freely, but, of course, he could not have been because of the story his mother told him. He was deeply confused.

Hauerwas came from a bricklaying family; his father was a bricklayer, and his father's five brothers were all bricklayers. He too helped in the bricklaying business for a while. His father was named Coffee, his mother's maiden name, and Hauerwas' mother was Joanna. His father, a Methodist, died in 1992; and his mother, a Baptist, died in 2006. Although she could be tiring because she talked so much, she had an enormous influence on Hauerwas. He also had an adopted brother, Johnny. He speaks of his parental influence positively especially in teaching him to be truthful: "I do not know whence it came, but

---

[6] Hauerwas, *Hannah's Child*, ix.
[7] Hauerwas, *Hannah's Child*, 3.
[8] See Hauerwas, *Hannah's Child*, 4.
[9] Hauerwas, *Hannah's Child*, 1–2.

I have a passion for truth. I do not want to lie to others or myself. I want to know the truth about the way things are. I hope I am a Christian because what we believe as Christians forces an unrelenting engagement with reality. That my parents let me go is a testimony to the truthfulness of their lives. Without lives like theirs, the life I have led, a life shaped by books, is threatened by unreality. I try to remember where I came from."[10]

In 1958 he began college studies at Southwestern University in Georgetown, Texas, a United Methodist school. When he graduated, he knew he wanted to go to graduate school but struggled with where. He decided on Yale University in New Haven, Connecticut. This would prove to be a mind-stretching experience for him.

Hauerwas says he had assumed that Divinity School at Yale would be a place to determine whether the stuff that Christians say is true is in fact true. Then he continues: "I did not understand that Yale University itself had no use for Christianity, which is to say that theology was not a legitimate subject in the university. I had thought I had come to Yale University to study theology. I had a lot to learn."[11]

While at Yale, he took courses from many well-known theologians such as Hans Frei, Brevard Childs, Walter Zimmerli, and Paul Meyer. H. Richard Niebuhr and Roland Bainton had left Yale by that time, and George Lindbeck was on leave. He read Barth and Bonhoeffer in Julian Hartt's course. He also discovered Wittgenstein and Kierkegaard, which alerted him to the tension between the how of Christianity and the what. He discovered another important truth about himself—namely, that he loved theology. That love would never leave him.

On December 29, 1962, he married Anne Harley, whom he had been dating for several years. The way Hauerwas tells the story, the marriage was not a good one from the start.

He had not known that he was marrying a mentally ill person; although he tried his best, he could not make her happy. He soon noticed that she had a disdain for Christianity and that this was personified in him. She grew increasingly unhappy with him and the marriage.

During his second year at Yale, he took a course from James Gustafson in Christian ethics. Gustafson was an H. Richard Niebuhr disciple.[12] It turned out that Hauerwas was attracted more to Barth than to Niebuhr, and Gustafson helped in that process. He puts it way: "There is a 'no bullshit' quality to Barth's thought that appealed to a bricklayer from Texas, and that seemed to me the kind of straightforwardness Christian claims require."[13] But even so, Hauerwas does not like being either a Barthian, or Tillichian, or any other "ian," for he believes such positions are overrated. Even being a pacifist is not a position. He says: "Positions too easily tempt us to think that we Christians need a theory. I am not a pacifist because of a theory. I am a pacifist because John Howard Yoder convinced me that nonviolence and Christianity are inseparable."[14] To say this another way, theology is best understood not as a system of thought but as a way of speaking about the Christian life.

Hauerwas stayed at Yale to work on his Ph.D. During this time, he broadened his studies somewhat to include both sociology of religion through reading Max Weber, Ernst Troeltsch, Talcott Parsons, and Emile Durkheim, and philosophy by reading scholars like Alasdair MacIntyre. But his special interest remained Christian ethics. He ended up writing a dissertation under Eugene TeSelle on the topic of "Character and the Christian Life."

It was during his doctoral studies at Yale, in 1968, that his son, Adam, was born. This introduced a whole new and exciting dynamic into life. Adam would turn out to be of

[10] Hauerwas, *Hannah's Child*, 44–45.
[11] Hauerwas, *Hannah's Child*, 48.
[12] See chap. 2 above.
[13] Hauerwas, *Hannah's Child*, 59.
[14] Hauerwas, *Hannah's Child*, 60.

crucial emotional significance to Hauerwas, especially given his wife's illness. But he had work to do: finish his dissertation and get a job. He was fortunate that before he even began looking for a job he was hired at the Lutheran Augustana College in Rock Island, Illinois.

Hauerwas says that one of his qualities that has a way of getting him into trouble is speaking the truth. While at Augustana, he complained that the college had no African American faculty and suggested that rectifying this become a goal. His complaints and other political activities, such as participating in African American protest marches, made him unpopular with administrators. While Hauerwas enjoyed teaching Bible, Christianity, and ethics, and found his engagement with the English department stimulating, he struggled with the lack of openness in the administration. It was clear he would not be able to stay at Augustana long, and so he welcomed the opportunity when Jim Burtchaell, the chair of the department of theology at the University of Notre Dame, called him for a job interview. Thus in 1970, he and his family moved to South Bend, Indiana, and into the Catholic world at Notre Dame.

Catholicism was a new world for Hauerwas. He drank deeply from the rich resources of Catholic theology and says that it was in this process that he slowly became a Christian. This fourteen-year process had more to do with putting on a discipline of a liturgical life of prayer, Mass, worship, and so on than with getting his mind straight on things. And most important in this process were a group of dear friends who cared deeply for him.

Hauerwas came to Notre Dame at the height of the U.S. resistance to the Vietnam War. Just prior to his arrival, several students had been suspended from Notre Dame for protesting the war and refusing to disperse upon the university president's orders. Jim Douglass, the author of *The Non-Violent Cross*,[15] had been hired as a peace witness at Notre Dame but was soon fired by President Theodore Hesburgh.

Hauerwas loved Notre Dame; he loved the diversity of students, the engaging faculty, and the interaction with philosophy through colleagues like David Burrell. He enjoyed participating in the Mass and says: "That is how I became a Catholic at Notre Dame. Of course, only a Protestant could be that kind of Catholic."[16] What he liked most of all was the dynamic of the theology faculty under the leadership of Burrell, who thought of it "[n]ot as a Catholic department but as a theology department in a Catholic context."[17] This made it possible to have non-Catholics and even non-Christians, teaching in the department. But it also required that there be a discipline of collective thinking. Under Burrell's leadership, the faculty would regularly read a book together at retreats. Later they would discuss strategies for excellence.

At Notre Dame, Hauerwas began to write seriously. He received inspiration from many sources, including unlikely ones like Sargent and Eunice Kennedy Shriver,[18] who funded one of his sabbaticals because they were interested in his work on medical ethics.

Not long after Hauerwas came to Notre Dame, he decided to pay a visit to John Howard Yoder at Associated Mennonite Biblical Seminary in Elkhart, Indiana, which was not far from South Bend. He went to Yoder's office and discovered that "[c]harm and John Howard Yoder were antithetical."[19] Yoder lacked the ordinary social graces that we tend to take for granted, like hospitality and engagement and offering responses to questions. Hauerwas discovered him to be incredibly shy. But he discovered something even more surprising. Yoder was a prolific writer

---

[15] See James W. Douglass, *The Non-Violent Cross: A Theology of Revolution and Peace* (New York: Macmillan, 1968).

[16] Hauerwas, *Hannah's Child*, 105.

[17] Hauerwas, *Hannah's Child*, 107.

[18] Sargent Shriver (1915–2011) was an American statesman who served under Presidents John F. Kennedy and Lyndon B. Johnson. He headed up the U.S. Peace Corps under President Johnson. His wife, Eunice, was Kennedy's sister.

[19] Hauerwas, *Hannah's Child*, 117.

on Christian ethics and was approaching the subject in ways that were completely different than what Hauerwas had studied at Yale. He began to read Yoder's work and quickly discovered that scholars at Yale and Notre Dame, where the assumption was that Jesus was too radical to be relevant for social ethics, were wrong. Yoder changed Hauerwas' life because his work challenged everything that he had been taught about Christian ethics. Once Hauerwas made this discovery, he knew that "this was not going to be easy,"[20] for backing this approach would make him extremely unpopular as a Christian ethicist. He had to become a pacifist, but his whole training as a Christian ethicist had been on the basis that pacifism was a Christian heresy.[21]

About the same time, the illness of his wife was becoming more and more severe, although her problem was hard to diagnose. It was clear that she was having psychotic breaks of some kind—detachments from reality—and this would express itself in her hearing religious voices and secret messages and falling in obsessive love with other men, especially Hauerwas' colleagues, not secretly but overtly. And she made it clear that she wanted Hauerwas to disappear. She would have several episodes per year and was hospitalized several times, which made life very difficult for the family. Still, Hauerwas did everything he could to be a good husband and good father to Adam.

During this time. he threw himself into his writing and teaching. One of Hauerwas' gifts, an enormous asset in his teaching, was his sense of humor. He says, "I love to laugh, and I love to laugh with people. I do not necessarily try to be funny, but I would like to think that my gift with 'one-liners' is correlative with how I think."[22] He teaches to *engage* students, not so much to offer them a position, as to help them see Jesus in a world

that thinks he is irrelevant. But that seeing is not done only through the mind but through the way that bodies encounter one another. He says, "I believe that through the cross and resurrection of Jesus of Nazareth we live in a new age, and that is why theologians do not have a position. Rather our task is to have the church know what it has been given. But I was beginning to sense that I had quite a particular take on that 'given.'"[23] This meant that students sometimes thought of him as having a "wholly different Christianity."[24] But really he did not, even though he had a way of saying it that sounded strange given our assumption about our own world.

During this time, he also wanted to become a Catholic but Anne vetoed that idea, and so he became a member of the Broadway United Methodist Church in 1980. He also began to jog while at Notre Dame. Jogging was more than exercising the body; it was also therapeutic and it helped him to think.

In his writings, he began to place stress on Christians needing a narrative because life is contingent. Just because Christians do not have positions does not mean they do not have a story. This does not mean that there is no need for a metaphysic; it only means that Christians should try to avoid metaphysical reductionism. That is, the Christian life is about people and how they live and how they worship and what they believe and how their beliefs shape them. They need a story. Hauerwas sees this as but a restatement of Barth's theology. Barth had a way of letting theology be theology because he believed that the church should be the church. Says Hauerwas:

> My claim, so offensive to some, that the first task of the church is to make the world the world, not to make the world more just, is a correlative of this theological metaphysics. The world simply cannot be narrated—the world cannot have a story—unless a people exist who make the world the world. That is an eschatological claim that presupposes

---

[20] Hauerwas, *Hannah's Child*, 117.
[21] See Reinhold Niebuhr, "Why the Christian Church is not Pacifist," in *Christianity and Power Politics* (New York: Charles Scribner's Sons, 1940).
[22] Hauerwas, *Hannah's Child*, 133.
[23] Hauerwas, *Hannah's Child*, 134.
[24] Hauerwas, *Hannah's Child*, 135.

we know there was a beginning only because we have seen the end. That something had to start it all is not what Christians mean by creation. Creation is not "back there," although there is a "back there" quality to creation. Rather, creation names God's continuing action, God's unrelenting desire for us to want to be loved by that love manifest in Christ's life, death, and resurrection.[25]

During his time at Notre Dame, he also met Alasdair MacIntyre,[26] the philosopher, although their teaching time did not overlap. He got to know him better later at Duke and says of MacIntyre that he was one of the smartest people in the world, intimidating, yet very helpful in having him understand what a narrative understanding of Christianity might look like. MacIntyre's work proved invaluable in shaping his own.

Hauerwas taught at Notre Dame until the department had a new chair who saw it as his passion to "Americanize Rome." Hauerwas felt this was a killing of a dream that had become part of Notre Dame. He was no longer permitted to teach undergraduates, which devastated him; David Burrell was sent to Jerusalem to help set up Tantur, the ecumenical school there. These were two big losses for him.

Shortly after returning to Notre Dame after a year in London, Hauerwas received an offer from Duke University in Durham, North Carolina, which he accepted. It was both a new challenge and a way of getting out of a difficult situation at Notre Dame. He relates the tender story of telling Yoder that he was leaving. "He told me he would miss me, and his eyes misted. He even gave me a hug when I left the office. I had not anticipated that he would respond that way, but neither was I surprised."[27]

Hauerwas was forty-four years old when he arrived in Durham in 1984. Although he had difficulty finding a church ithere, he immediately fell in love with baseball. Baseball and theology were inseparable for him in Durham. He loved the Durham Bulls, a minor-league baseball team. He went to every home game with Adam and sometimes with colleagues. Durham was an opportunity for him to make new friends. As he says so many times, friends sustained him, friends helped him write, and friends helped him be a Christian. As he puts it: "I assume it is obvious by now that I cannot separate what I think from who I know. People make all the difference."[28]

Anne's bipolar disease and her delusional episodes were getting worse. One day in 1986, shortly after they had arrived in Durham, she told Hauerwas she was leaving him and wanted a divorce. He decided there was nothing he could do. Once she left, he broke down in tears because of the sadness of it all. She would never return. After twenty-four years of marriage, he was alone with his cat. It was not long after this that he learned Anne had made an unsuccessful suicide attempt. Several years later, she died of congestive heart failure.

Hauerwas' single status would soon change. He fell in love with Paula Gilbert who was twelve years younger. She was also working at Duke, and they were attending the same church. They had their first date in April 1987.

Paula and Hauerwas were different; she was contemplative and he was not; she was quiet and he was loud; she was patient and he was not. But they shared a love for the church and each other. She was an ordained United Methodist Church Minister, and had a Ph.D. from Duke, and had written her dissertation on Georgia Harkness. For over a year he sought to convince her to marry him; just as he was about to give up she said yes. On May 18, 1989, they were married in the Duke chapel.

Hauerwas has directed over fifty dissertations in his life, written almost as many books, and been a tour de force in helping his students think that the Christian life can be based on the life and teaching of Jesus.

---

[25] Hauerwas, *Hannah's Child*, 158.
[26] See chap. 25 above.
[27] Hauerwas, *Hannah's Child*, 177.
[28] Hauerwas, *Hannah's Child*, 196.

One of the key qualities that his story demonstrates so vividly is friendship. His passion for friendship is not only his personality; it is his theology. He says, "I sometimes worry that my hunger for friendship may be pathological. During the years with Anne, I could not have survived without friends. Moreover, I depend on friends to help me think and write."[29] No doubt, Paula has added an important, new friend-force to his life, but without the broader family called church, Hauerwas and his theology simply could not survive. Most recently, he and Paula are members in an Episcopalian church.

THE FAILURE OF CONTEMPORARY CHRISTIAN ETHICS

After this long account of Hauerwas' journey, we need to explore his writings more carefully. It is impossible to do justice to his many books, so I will endeavor to give the reader a glimpse into the early formation of his approach to Christian ethics on the assumption that the rest of his work builds on that. Hauerwas is still writing at an aggressive pace, and much of his later work is interesting precisely because it is a nuanced struggle with what a difference it makes to claim that Jesus is Lord in a variety of settings.

Hauerwas begins his writing in a critical posture toward both classical Protestantism and Catholicism. Both have a tendency to embrace moralities alien to the gospel, both confuse apologetics with ethics, and both reduce ethics to pastoral-psychological concerns.[30] For mainline Protestantism, ethics is an altogether dubious enterprise in any event since it is but a disguised way of substituting works for grace. "Indeed some go as far as to suggest that ethics is sin insofar as it tries to anticipate God's will."[31]

Given the strikingly negative disposition toward ethics within classical Protestantism, one might expect Hauerwas to adopt a more Catholic approach. Insofar as he speaks favorably of such classic Aristotelian/Thomistic notions as character and virtues, this expectation is indeed fulfilled. Nevertheless, rather than employing traditional, natural law ethics or a philosophy of essences, he emphasizes story, history, and narrative.[32]

It is difficult to understand Hauerwas' contribution to Christian ethics unless one first sees his view of the failure of the ethic of modernity, a failure that has both philosophical and theological dimensions. The following are some key problems he identifies.

Freedom and Self

First, he argues that modern Christian ethics has a problematic understanding of freedom and the self.[33] The combined impact of Protestantism's emphasis on the individual plus the Enlightenment's emphases on rationality and individual happiness have led to a contemporary conception of freedom as an end in itself. It is this presumption, according to Hauerwas, that underlies the moral view of America's political liberalism that "unlike other societies, we are not creatures of history, but that we have the possibility of a new beginning. We are thus able to form our government on the basis of principle rather than the arbitrary elements of tradition."[34]

Moreover, the modern understanding of freedom is almost entirely associated with the individual. "We have made 'freedom of the individual' an end in itself and have

---

[29] Hauerwas, *Hannah's Child*, 247.

[30] See Hauerwas, *Vision and Virtue*, 97.

[31] Stanley Hauerwas, *The Peaceable Kingdom: A Primer in Christian Ethics* (Notre Dame, Ind.: University of Notre Dame Press, 1983), 52. Elsewhere, Hauerwas says "Barth, for example, goes as far as to say that any 'general conception of ethics coincides exactly with the conception of sin,' since any such conception necessarily replaces God's command with man's" (*Character and the Christian Life*, 131).

[32] "Theology has no essence, but rather is the imaginative endeavor to explicate the stories of God by showing how one claim illuminates another" (Hauerwas, *Peaceable Kingdom*, 62).

[33] See Hauerwas, *Peaceable Kingdom*, 37–46.

[34] Stanley Hauerwas, *A Community of Character: Toward A Constructive Christian Social Ethic* (Notre Dame, Ind.: University of Notre Dame Press, 1981), 78.

ignored the fact that most of us do not have the slightest idea of what we should do with our freedom."[35] It is because of freedom that we can fight, and it is freedom that we fight for. This is true for both the selfish among us and also the altruists, except that "the idealists among us are reduced to fighting for the 'freedom' or 'right' of others to realize their self-interests more fully."[36]

Hauerwas' critical reference to "rights" in connection with freedom is instructive. He argues that our interpretation of rights in relation to freedom and the individual has made it an extremely problematic concept. We should pay more attention to the fact that the notion of rights is itself an outgrowth of enlightenment thinking, where the "autonomous person" is the starting point of morality. Hauerwas comes close to suggesting that what we call a moral right today is but the moralization of desire. "Desire" which once was a vice has now become a virtue.[37] He emphasizes that rights language, at least as it is used in North America today, is in tension with the notion of community. In fact, it is a threat to all corporate, social realities because it perceives the individual and the corporate to be in moral conflict. This is why

[T]he family has always been an anomaly for the liberal tradition. Only if human beings can be separated in a substantial degree from kinship can they be free individuals subject to egalitarian policies. Thus we assume—and this is an assumption shared by political conservatives and activists— that it is more important to be an "autonomous person" than to be a "Hauerwas," or a "Polaski," or a "Smith." For example, the Supreme Court recently held in Planned Parenthood vs Danforth that a husband has no rights if his wife wishes an abortion, because "abortion is a purely personal

right of the woman, and the status of marriage can place no limitations on personal rights."[38]

This way of thinking has made modern ethics unintelligible, according to Hauerwas. On this model, we exist first of all as individuals who are free to have our desires fulfilled. And all desires are equal before the bar of justice. Hence, freedom is seen as both the foundation and the goal of morality. Yet the freer we become, the more desperately we search for community. Somehow, intuitively and existentially, we know that a freedom which has nothing to say about how it ought to be used cannot be a freedom that lends truth to our moral experience.

Haucrwas points out several unfortunate implications of this perspective on ethics. First, it has led us to do ethics from the standpoint of moral quandaries,[39] where the question, "What would I (you) do in a given situation?" is paramount. Second, the ethic of modernity is the ethic of choice (existentialism). We are constantly called upon to make decisions,[40] and we believe them to be moral insofar as they are products and protectors of our freedom. Third, ethics has become abstract and unqualified.[41] The assumption is that we are moral beings insofar as we are individual human beings. Hence, moral authority is autonomous. All specific (concrete) heteronymous authorities, for example, family, tradition, Christianity, and Judaism, are morally irrelevant.

View of Ethics

The second limitation of modern, Christian ethics is that it believes ethics must be either teleological or deontological. There is no other model available.[42] Teleological theorists

[35] Hauerwas, *Community of Character*, 80.
[36] Hauerwas, *Community of Character*, 80.
[37] "The genius of liberalism was to make what had always been considered a vice, namely unlimited desire, a virtue" (Hauerwas, *Community of Character*, 72).
[38] Hauerwas, *Community of Character*, 81.
[39] Hauerwas makes extensive use of the following very interesting article: Edmund Pincoffs, "Quandary Ethics," in *Revisions: Changing Perspectives in Moral Philosophy*, ed. Stanley Hauerwas and Alasdair MacIntyre (Notre Dame, Ind.: University of Notre Dame Press, 1983).
[40] See Hauerwas, *Peaceable Kingdom*, particularly the section, "Decisions, Decisions, Decisions," 121.
[41] See Hauerwas, *Peaceable Kingdom*, 17–23.   [42] Hauerwas, *Peaceable Kingdom*, 17–24.

claim that moral rightness and wrongness, goodness and badness, can be determined by the nonmoral value, such as happiness, pleasure, and self-realization, that is brought into being. Deontological theorists deny this. They argue that rightness and wrongness are determined on the basis of something inherent in the object of moral judgment. For example, it simply is our duty to tell the truth, even though telling a lie may produce more happiness than telling the truth.

Hauerwas rejects this distinction because he argues that the imagination out of which it flows sees rules and obligations as the paradigmatic components of morality. While rules play a very important role in our society, focusing on them as our moral starting point, as both deontologists and teleologists do, is to misunderstand the complexity of moral experience. Both incorrectly assume that the primary element of morality consists in being confronted with a given situation and being called upon to make a decision on how to act in that situation. It assumes that the situation as well as the moral notions are givens, when in fact they can only arise out of communal perception and intelligible meanings grounded in tradition.[43]

Furthermore, to see our morality from the standpoint of obligations and rules, "also has the effect of distorting our moral psychology by separating our actions from our agency."[44] It is dangerous to understand our moral selves as an unconnected series of moral actions that do not have continuity and unity. The only way that a connection can be maintained is on the view of a moral self-understanding that arises out of community. "Communities teach us what kind of intentions are appropriate if we are to be the kind of person appropriate to living among these people."[45] Consequently, it is much more important that we know what we ought to be as moral people so we may strive to become that, than that we know what we ought to do on the basis of certain "justified" rules and obligations.

The problem here, says Hauerwas, is not that an "ethic of virtue" comes prior to an "ethic of obligation" but that to focus on the latter does not emphasize sufficiently the importance of community out of which our moral training arises, that is, out of which comes the appropriation of virtues that are needed in order for us to live by moral rules. This, he argues, is sorely needed in our society today, particularly as we face the growing threat of violence. Hence, "[T]he kind of pacifism I defend does not neatly fit into the current philosophical options for understanding normative ethics. That is, it is neither consequential nor deontological even though it may well involve aspects of both. For the emphasis is not on decision or even a set of decisions and their justification."[46]

The general difficulty which Hauerwas sees with the teleological and deontological models is that their emphasis on rules, laws, and ideals cannot deal with the constant temptation to be separated from the moral source that sustains Christian life. For this, ethics must be grounded in a personal relationship with the source. This Barth and Bultmann have attempted to do, but they have not been entirely successful.

Failure of Barth and Bultmann

The third aspect of the failure of contemporary, Christian ethics then focuses on Barth and Bultmann.[47] Hauerwas has an ambivalent relationship to these two theologians. Both appropriately emphasize the utter sinfulness of humanity and our resultant, unmitigated dependency on God for our salvation. It is

---

[43] "No account is given for why and how we have come to describe a certain set of circumstances as abortion, or adultery, or murder, and so on" (Hauerwas, *Peaceable Kingdom*, 21).

[44] Hauerwas, *Peaceable Kingdom*, 21.

[45] Hauerwas, *Peaceable Kingdom*, 21.

[46] Stanley Hauerwas, "Pacifism: Some Philosophical Considerations," *Faith and Philosophy* (April 1985): 101.

[47] Hauerwas, *Character and the Christian Life*, 131–78.

this affirmation that guides them to the insight that the paradigm for the Christian life is that of relationship—as opposed to rules and principles—between us and God.[48] With this emphasis, Hauerwas readily agrees. At the same time, they "refuse to translate their theological insights into discernible forms for the moral life."[49] The reason that they fail at this point, says Hauerwas, is that their "ethics is associated primarily with the language of decision—ethics is concerned with what we do rather than what we are."[50] Hence, "neither Bultmann nor Barth found a completely adequate means to suggest how the believer's actual moral self is determined in Christ."[51]

Hauerwas believes both Barth and Bultmann "fail to exploit the language of growth and character."[52] This naturally involves him in the details of each theologian's thought. Here, he makes several points.

He begins by criticizing Bultmann, whose denial of ethics is grounded in his view of the nature of the ethical task. If one means by ethics, "any intelligible theory valid for all human behavior"[53] then, Bultmann maintains, Jesus in fact taught no ethics, because through Christ we have been set free from the need to justify ourselves. This latter need is what ethics has traditionally engaged in. Bultmann's view of self is intimately associated with history. We cannot understand ourselves apart from our acts and our decisions. Hauerwas quotes Bultmann as follows: "what man has done and does—his decisions—constitute him in his true nature, that he is essentially a temporal being."[54] Hence, we are always in the process of choosing who

we are. Given this view of what it means to be human, the notion of character becomes a problem. It is in tension with our freedom to create ourselves, especially since Bultmann wants to claim that it is the grace of God that saves us from ourselves in that we are set free from the past and are opened to the future.

It is Bultmann's notion of radical freedom that Hauerwas objects to most. The radical discontinuity of the past, as well as the failure to take account of the social determination of the self, makes freedom impossible. This is the way of allowing oneself to be determined by the immediate situation. "Rather than an ethic of openness, Bultmann's analysis is a stultifying limitation of man's potentiality to confront his future with the kind of hope and openness that the Gospel claims is possible for us as men."[55]

His criticism of Barth is no less pointed. Barth's basis for the rejection of ethics is theological rather than ethical. It is because of who God is that we are not able to work out a proper view of Christian ethics. God's demand of grace is such that each action is but a response to God. Ethics means obedience to the command of God. This is not to suggest that the command of God is capricious; in fact, God's command is absolutely consistent. Yet since our decision to obey must be constantly repeated, it is the command of God and not our character that determines our moral actions.

For Barth, human agency is at the center of understanding the self. Hauerwas quotes Barth as follows: "the being of a person is a being in act," since "to exist as a man means

[48] "In summary, clearly I am in sympathy with Barth and Bultmann's attempt to describe the Christian life in terms of the fundamental relationship of the self to God. They rightly reject as inadequate the attempt to understand the Christian life solely in terms of obedience to laws, rules, ideals, etc. They have both perceived that when Christian ethics is so developed the constant temptation is for it to become separated from the source that sustains it" (Hauerwas, *Character and the Christian Life*, 176).
[49] Hauerwas, *Character and the Christian Life*, 177.
[50] Hauerwas, *Character and the Christian Life*, 177.
[51] Hauerwas, *Character and the Christian Life*, 176.
[52] Hauerwas, *Character and the Christian Life*, 177.
[53] Hauerwas, *Character and the Christian Life*, 132.
[54] Hauerwas, *Character and the Christian Life*, 147 (emphasis in original).
[55] Hauerwas, *Character and the Christian Life*, 166.

to act. And action means choosing, deciding. What is the right choice? What ought I to do? What ought we to do? This is the question before which every man is placed."[56]

The major difficulty Hauerwas has with Barth's ethics then, is that throughout his discussion on ethics and sanctification, his emphasis is far more on the one in whom we are already justified and sanctified than on the believer. God's grace can never be a possession of ours. And while true, it is exactly because of the distance that remains between God's behavior and ours that it is unclear how the sanctification of God can be embodied in human self-agency. Moreover, the only continuity of which Barth can speak is the continuity of God's grace. This, according to Hauerwas, makes it extremely difficult to speak about the significance of character for ethics. Hence, Hauerwas concludes "the agonizing thing about Barth's ethics therefore, is not that he failed to appreciate the idea of character, but that he really does not integrate it into the main images he uses to explicate the nature of the Christian life."[57]

In summary, Barth and Bultmann rightly reject the view that the fundamental paradigm of ethics is that of rules and ideals. Nevertheless, they fail to establish an adequate metaphor beyond command-obedience which can do justice to our own moral determination in relation to the reality of God. In the final analysis, to talk only about the character of God is insufficient. Eventually, Christian ethics must become concrete, meaning we must talk about our being in this world and our moral experience.

Situation ethics is one attempt to concretize Christian ethic. Yet it is also inadequate.[58] Hauerwas suggests that the basic contribution Joseph Fletcher makes in his *Situation Ethics*[59] is that he brings to the attention of the reader the fundamental concreteness of Christian ethics. To put it another way, for the ethical enterprise to be involved purely with the contemplation of the Absolute and the subsumption of individual situations under its domain is inadequate. With this, Hauerwas is in agreement. In fact, it provides for him the excuse for a critical comment on Barth's ethical approach.[60]

However, Hauerwas is far more critical of Fletcher than he is positive. Fletcher's mistake stems from his agreement with Barth and Bultmann that the primary ethical question focuses on decision. Fletcher does not seem to realize that "prior to decision must come the idea of our moral notions."[61] Hauerwas' basic critique of Fletcher is that he fails to understand moral notions. Relying on Julius Kovesi for an explication of moral notions, he argues that "we do not come to know the world by perceiving it, but we come to know the world as we learn to use our language."[62] The implication is that there can be no such thing as uninterpreted facts and raw values. "We never simply know facts, but we know them for some reason."[63] Hence, a notion—moral or otherwise—"is like a bag by which we group together some of the significant and recurring configuration of relevant facts in our lives."[64] Moral notions, consequently, always contain both evaluative and descriptive aspects. Consequently, we have notions

---

[56] Hauerwas, *Character and the Christian Life*, 151f. Hauerwas further quotes Barth as saying "for it is as he acts that man exists as a person. Therefore the question of the goodmen, and value and rightness of the genuine continuity of his activity, the ethical question, is no more and no less than the question about the goodmen, value, rightmen, and genuine continuity of his existence of himself" (*Character and the Christian Life*, 155n.).

[57] Hauerwas, *Character and the Christian Life*, 176.

[58] See Hauerwas, "Situation Ethics." See also his *Character and the Christian Life*, 177f.

[59] See Joseph Fletcher, *Situation Ethics: The New Morality* (Philadelphia: Westminster, 1966).

[60] "In this context Barth's claim that the ethical good is determined solely from the command of God is simply fantastic. Ethics is fundamentally reflection on our received human experience as to what is good and bad, right and wrong. It cannot escape from that experience to the realm where the good or right can be known with more exactness" (Hauerwas, *Vision and Virtue*, 28).

[61] Hauerwas, *Vision and Virtue*, 12.

[62] Hauerwas, *Vision and Virtue*, 17.

[63] Hauerwas, *Vision and Virtue*, 16.

[64] Hauerwas, *Vision and Virtue*, 16.

[65] Hauerwas, *Vision and Virtue*, 17.

only "insofar as we are rule-following rational beings."[65]

The problem of ethical living is therefore not a problem of decision in relation to the factual situation but a problem of vision.[66] To say this in another way, the moral task is not properly defined as bringing the situation together with the rule, rather as the task of how we create proper moral notions on the experience of everyday life. Hauerwas argues that Fletcher fails in his understanding of the phenomenology of moral experience. The reason that we resort to "It depends" when asked the question "Is it wrong to tell a lie?" is not because the moral notion of lying lacks normativity, and hence we substitute in its stead the situation itself, but because the notion of lying is not a complete, moral notion. It is open. Just because we are not clear on what acts can all be subsumed under lying does not imply the moral irrelevance of the notion.[67] Hence, Hauerwas concludes that "the problem with our moral notions is not necessarily the role they play in our common sense; it arises when we try to make them do more than their formal element was intended to do."[68]

Fletcher may well have done us a service in identifying for ethical thinking the limitations of the traditional usage of moral notions. Nevertheless, he "fails to appreciate the fact that moral notions are not atomistic ideas separated from actual life, but rather gain their position because they play a part in the whole way of life. To deny their significance in the name of the situation in the way that Fletcher does is not only to question them but to deny there can be such a thing as a moral way of life."[69] Moral notions are in fact not abstractions from our moral experience, rather they are moral notions precisely to the extent that they help us in the task of sorting out how it is that we ought to live together. On this basis, the Christian, moral notion can only derive from the Christian vision itself. "The moral life is therefore not just the life of decision but the life of vision—that is, it involves how we see the world. Such seeing does not come from just perceiving 'facts,' but rather we must learn how the world is to be properly 'seen' or better known."[70]

This "seeing the world" is the task of the Christian who is called to live the life of one worthy of that name. "To be a Christian in effect is learning to see the world in a certain way and thus become as we see. The task of contemporary, theological ethics is to state the language of faith in terms of the Christian responsibility to be formed in the likeness of Christ."[71]

THE NATURE OF CHRISTIAN ETHICS

Hauerwas identifies as significant the fact that the early Christians did not have an ethic. For them it was unnecessary to engage in ethics as an explicit task. The reason for this is that the early church understood itself as a community whose task it was to live the new reality begun by Jesus Christ. Hauerwas spells out this way of understanding ethics as follows.

Ethic of Character

First, he identifies this approach as an ethic of character. We have already seen that Hauerwas holds the modern view of ethics to be

---

[66] "The moral life is therefore not just the life of decision but the life of vision—that is, it involves how we see the world. Such 'seeing' does not come from just perceiving 'facts,' but rather we must learn how the world is to be properly 'seen' or better known. Such learning takes place by learning the language that intends the world and our behavior as it ought to be that the good may be achieved. The moral life is a struggle and training in how to see" (Hauerwas, *Vision and Virtue*, 20).

[67] Hauerwas attempts to make this point clear with the following: "Suppose, however, that instances of intentionally deceiving someone else to save the life of another were so common in our experience that we had a notion for it, for example, 'saving deceit.' Moreover, this notion was not even associated with lying but instead had an entirely commendatory connotation. If this were the case then we might be much more willing to say that lying is always wrong because in such a circumstance the formal element of lying would be much more complete" (*Vision and Virtue*, 21).

[68] Hauerwas, *Vision and Virtue*, 22.

[69] Hauerwas, *Vision and Virtue*, 23.

[70] Hauerwas, *Vision and Virtue*, 20.

[71] Hauerwas, *Vision and Virtue*, 29.

problematic because it confuses the order of two very important ethical questions: "What ought I to be?" and "What ought I to do?" Most ethicists since Kant have argued the priority of the latter over the former. Hauerwas, however, argues that "the question 'What ought I to be?' precedes 'What ought I to do?'"[72] To understand ethics on this basis necessitates a rethinking of the central ethical metaphor, which for him is *character*.

He defines character "as the qualification of our agency."[73] That is, character "is the very reality of who we are as self-determining agents."[74] We form or mold our character by appropriating certain intentions, beliefs, and virtues and not others. Hauerwas does not wish to suggest that we are in an unlimited way our own self-choosing. To emphasize the self-determining nature of our character does not negate the fact that much of what we are happens to us.[75] Nevertheless, "our character is our deliberate disposition to use a certain range of reasons for our actions rather than others. . . ."[76]

Hauerwas' notion of character is dynamic rather than static. "To have character is necessarily to engage in discovery."[77] Character provides for the possibility of connecting our past to our future.[78] We can never face the future as nobodies. We therefore do not come to it in an unconditional manner. Rather, we see the future through our character; we act in the future out of our character so that its impact is always only in elastic tension with the past out of which it is formed. Nevertheless, in the final analysis, we are responsible for our character.[79] "For it is through consciousness (intentionality) that we shape ourselves and our actions."[80]

Hauerwas analyzes the ethic of character with the help of several categories. First, he talks of the relationship between character and freedom. As we have seen above, his major criticism of the "freedom" of modernity is that it is understood primarily in relation to choice. "Put simply, we assume that only if we have a choice are we free."[81] But freedom does not necessarily consist in having a choice. In fact, his notion of character implies that a well-formed character is not free to make certain choices. For example, a committed pacifist is not free to make a decision to use violence. In such a case, the behavior that flows from "who we are" excludes certain actions from the realm of consideration and possibility. In fact, this is what he argues is the true nature of our freedom. "Our 'freedom' in regard to our decision depends exactly on not having to accept the determinism of those who would encourage us to assume that we have to 'make' a 'decision' because 'this is the way things are.'"[82] Our "freedom" is therefore not properly defined as our ability to make choices.[83] Nor is it related to our self-awareness. Rather it depends on the kind of character we have appropriated and by the virtues we have embraced as we live out our story. In the end, he says, "our

---

[72] Hauerwas, *Peaceable Kingdom*, 116.

[73] Hauerwas, "Toward an Ethic of Character," in *Vision and Virtue*, 61.

[74] Hauerwas, "Toward an Ethic of Character," 59.

[75] See Hauerwas, "Toward an Ethic of Character," 61.

[76] Hauerwas, "Toward an Ethic of Character," 59.

[77] Hauerwas, "Toward an Ethic of Character," 63.

[78] "Character is morally significant because, if rightly formed, it provides a proper transition from our past to our future; for the task of this transition is not to accept the future unconditionally, but to respond and remake the future in the right kind of way" (Hauerwas, "Toward an Ethic of Character," 64).

[79] See Hauerwas, *Community of Character*, 139. On this point, Hauerwas relies heavily on Aristotle and Aquinas who suggest that we have character precisely insofar as we have the ability to make our actions our own. This means that what we do arises out of the virtues we have appropriated.

[80] Hauerwas, *Vision and Virtue*, 66.

[81] Hauerwas, *Peaceable Kingdom*, 37.

[82] Hauerwas, *Peaceable Kingdom*, 125.

[83] "To use an extreme example, I may be free to choose to die by starvation or torture, but that is hardly to be free" (Hauerwas, *Peaceable Kingdom*, 37).

freedom is dependent on our having a narrative that gives us skills of interpretation sufficient to allow us to make our past our own through incorporation into our ongoing history."[84] Hence, narrative, and not freedom, is the precondition for Christian ethics.

Character and Narrative

The second element of character ethics Hauerwas spells out is the way character is related to narrative. Hauerwas argues that the quest for objectivity in ethics has led us to view ethics as a science. In the process, we have emphasized the importance of logical rules and principles.[85] But such a syllogistic way of dealing with ethics has severe limitations. In fact, ethics can be much better understood on the model of rational narrative than on syllogistic logic. "What we demand of a narrative is that it display how occurrences are actions. Intentional behavior is purposeful but not necessary."[86] The narrative understanding of events and actions relies on the contingent connection inherent in such events and actions. It is devoid of logical necessity but not of rationality.

Moreover, narrative understanding is understanding in the temporal mode. It raises the question of the connection between different events-actions-realities in time. Hence, Hauerwas contends that the narrative mode is appropriate to the understanding of Christian existence because we must see ourselves as contingent beings and as historical beings. It is within this understanding of ourselves that we can best see the form of God's salvation. "Christian ethics, therefore, is not first of all concerned with 'Thou shalt' or 'Thou shalt not.' Its first task is to help us to rightly envision the world. Christian ethics is specifically formed by a very definite story with determinative content."[87] Learning to be

disciples is learning to shape our story on the theme of God's kingdom.

Character and Virtue

The third element of character is discussed in relation to concepts like virtues and vision. For the Greeks and the early Christians, virtue (*arete*) was the key moral concept. When the question was raised about what individuals should be, the ancients gave the answer in terms of certain qualities or habits (virtues) that they should possess. Plato, for example, argues for the virtues of courage, temperance, wisdom, and justice. Why? Because he had a particular vision of the "good person." The nature of the Republic, since it was a moral community, could not become real unless the functions which these virtues determined would be realized by its citizens.

Hauerwas argues that there is no one set of natural virtues which can be shown to be universally applicable. This is so because there is no one vision or narrative which is acceptable to everyone. Nevertheless, when we talk about a particular narrative, like the Christian church, then we can talk about virtues that are appropriate to it. Then it is not only possible, but it becomes necessary to identify the vision and the functions which claim to bring about this vision. This makes ethics fundamentally concrete; that is, it is always rooted in a specific narrative. And this is why Hauerwas can claim that ethics without a qualifier is an oxymoron.[88]

Moral communities or individuals therefore require training to become virtuous. Hauerwas talks of virtues as skills. "To be a person of virtue, therefore, involves acquiring the linguistic, emotional and rational skills that give us the strength to make our decisions in our life our own."[89] Moreover, the "capacity to be virtuous depends on the

---

[84] Hauerwas, *Community of Character*, 147.

[85] See Stanley Hauerwas, "From System to Story: An Alternative Pattern for Rationality in Ethics," in *Truthfulness and Tragedy: Further Investigations in Christian Ethics* (Notre Dame, Ind.: University of Notre Dame Press, 1977).

[86] Hauerwas, "From System to Story," 28.

[87] Hauerwas, *Peaceable Kingdom*, 29.

[88] See Hauerwas, *Peaceable Kingdom*, 17–24.

[89] Hauerwas, *Community of Character*, 115.

existence of communities which have been formed by narratives faithful to the character of reality."[90]

Hauerwas discusses several Christian virtues, and especially two—hope and patience. He argues that they are important for Christians. Because we participate in so many different communities all at the same time, each of which constitutes its own vision, and hence has its own account of what it means to be virtuous, we would despair without hope. And "patience is training in how to wait when there seems no way to resolve our moral conflicts or even when we see no clear way to go on."[91] We must train ourselves to hope even when there is no empirical basis for it. We must train ourselves to be patient when almost everything we see around us is unjust. This however, "does not mean that we do not plan and/or seek to find the means to promote justice in the world, but that such planning is not done under the illusion of omnipotence. We can take the risk of planning that does not make effectiveness our primary goal, but faithfulness to God's kingdom."[92]

THE TASK OF CHRISTIAN ETHICS

For Hauerwas, the task of Christian ethics is identical with the task of being the church. Hence, it is not the task of any one ethicist or scholar to present the ethical wisdom sufficient for the new life in the church. Whenever ethics is done as an abstract, independent discipline concerned primarily with ideas, it need not have much to do with being Christian. Moreover Christian ethics also ought not properly to be seen as a subdiscipline of theology but rather "Christian ethics is theology."[93] Christian ethics is "at the heart of the theological task. For theology is a practical activity concerned to display how Christian convictions construe the self and the world."[94] The church is first and foremost to be the people of God whose purpose it is to allow God to create their community into a "people capable of witnessing in the world to the kingdom."[95] Hence the church, for Hauerwas, is a training base where we are molded into the kind of people that reflect the true character of God. "The task of Christian ethics is imaginatively to help us understand the implications of that kingdom . . . [it] imaginatively tests the images most appropriate to orchestrate the Christian life in accordance with the central conviction that the world has been redeemed by the work of Jesus Christ."[96]

For Hauerwas the church does not really *have* a social ethic at all; it *is* the social ethic. Hence, it must concentrate on keeping itself holy, not in the sense of disassociating itself from the world, but in the sense that it concentrates on shaping its character after the being of God. This it does by "imitating" God.[97] How specifically? Not by mimicking every action of Jesus, but rather, by being like Jesus in living a particular way such that we would accept death rather than abandon the truth. "Thus to be like Jesus is to join him in the journey through which we are trained to be a people capable of claiming citizenship in God's kingdom of non-violent love—a love that would overcome the powers of this world, not through coercion and force, but through the power of this one man's death."[98]

The pacifism of Hauerwas is not based on any assumption about human nature or the possibilities of good in society. Nor is it based upon any prudential calculations of success

---

[90] Hauerwas, *Community of Character*, 116.
[91] Hauerwas, *Community of Character*, 127.
[92] Hauerwas, *Peaceable Kingdom*, 105.
[93] Hauerwas, *Peaceable Kingdom*, 105.
[94] Hauerwas, *Peaceable Kingdom*, 55.
[95] Hauerwas, *Peaceable Kingdom*, 69.
[96] Hauerwas, *Peaceable Kingdom*, 69.
[97] For a discussion on Hauerwas' understanding of the "imitation of God," see *Peaceable Kingdom*, 76–81.
[98] Hauerwas, *Peaceable Kingdom*, 76.

in changing violent structure in our society. Rather, nonviolence has its basis in an understanding and character of the church.

The nature of the church for Hauerwas is defined by the event of Christ. In this sense, it sets itself apart from mainline society. It is a holy nation, a sanctified body. Hauerwas, relying heavily on Yoder, argues that this way of defining the church does not imply withdrawal from the world. Rather, it means that "the first duty of the church for society is to be the church, i.e., the body of people who insist on the primacy of faith by refusing to accept obligations that might lead them to treat in an unbrotherly way an 'enemy' of the state."[99] In other words, the church is the body of Christ—the *autobasileia*.[100] We are the ones to witness to the meaning of love in social relations. "The crucial question is not whether the church should or should not be responsible for society, but rather what that responsibility is. . . . The church cannot attempt to become another power group among others in society that seek to dominate in the name of the good."[101]

Yet the church is a political body both like and unlike other political bodies. It is like them in that it is based on a political platform. "Christians are engaged in politics but it is a politics of the kingdom that reveals the insufficiency of all politics based on coercion and falsehood and finds the true source of power in servanthood rather than dominion."[102] On the other hand, it is "unlike any other insofar as it is informed by a people who have no reason to fear the truth. They are able to exist in the world without resorting to coercion to maintain their presence."[103] Hence, the church can best be understood as "a community which tries to develop the resources to stand within the world witnessing to the peaceable kingdom and thus rightly understanding the world."[104] It is a "community of character" and a "community of virtues."

The church is best characterized, according to Hauerwas, by three New Testament concepts, namely, *forgiveness*, the *cross*, and the *resurrection*. Regarding forgiveness, it is possible for the church to live peaceably only because it is a forgiven people. In fact, says Hauerwas, "we must remember that our first task is not to forgive, but to learn to be forgiven."[105] Why? Because to be a forgiven people means that we live by trust and not by control. The Christ-like nature of the church teaches us to learn to trust other people as we have learned to trust God. It is in this sense that we can become a whole, and indeed a holy, people.[106] Regarding the cross, he says that peaceable people are people of the cross. But the cross is much more than merely a symbol of self-sacrifice. "The cross is Jesus' ultimate dispossession through which God has conquered the powers of this world. The cross is not just a symbol of God's kingdom; it is that kingdom come."[107] To be a people of the cross, therefore, means that we are people in training to become dispossessed.[108] As people of the cross, we commit ourselves to relinquish all power over the lives of others; in fact we are people who seek to live "out of control" and in the control of God alone. It also means we do not see it as

---

[99] Stanley Hauerwas, "The Non-Resistant Church: The Theological Ethics of John Howard Yoder," in *Vision and Virtue*, 211.

[100] See Hauerwas, *Community of Character*, 44ff.

[101] Hauerwas, *Community of Character*, 44ff.

[102] Hauerwas, *Peaceable Kingdom*, 102.

[103] Hauerwas, *Peaceable Kingdom*, 102.

[104] Hauerwas, *Peaceable Kingdom*, 102.

[105] Hauerwas, *Peaceable Kingdom*, 89.

[106] "But because we have learned to live as forgiven people, as people no longer in control, we also find we can become a whole people" (Hauerwas, *Peaceable Kingdom*, 89).

[107] Hauerwas, *Peaceable Kingdom*, 87. See also John Howard Yoder, *The Politics of Jesus*: Vicit Agnus Noster, 2nd ed. (Grand Rapids: Eerdmans, 1972), 51.

[108] "Discipleship is quite simply extended training in being dispossessed" (Hauerwas, *Peaceable Kingdom*, 86).

our goal to make history come out right; we give up the quest to place handles on history. As Christians, we live in the resurrection. He says, "through Jesus' resurrection we see God's peace as present reality."[109] To be a church characterized by resurrection is to be one that believes in the transforming power of love—a love which is "the non-violent apprehension of the other as other. But to see the other as other is frightening, because to the extent others are other they challenge my way of being. Only when my self—my character—has been formed by God's love, do I know I have no reason to fear the other."[110]

CONCLUSION

In his memoir, Hauerwas says, especially about *The Peaceable Kingdom*, "I suspect it is all there. Most of what I have said since I said there. But if so, then everything remains to be done, insofar as everything is projected toward the future."[111] It is of course not true that it is *all* there; there is much nuance and substance that is missing in *The Peaceable Kingdom* that he fills in with books such as *Resident Aliens*, *With the Grain of the Universe*, and *Living Gently in a Violent World*. But the hope is that the reader may be enticed into further explorations.

The Christian ethic of Hauerwas is squarely rooted in ecclesiology, and to be Christian is to be engaged in the enterprise of peacemaking. He says, "Christian pacifism is not based on any claims about the proximate or ultimate success of non-violent strategies, though we certainly do not try to fail as if failure in and of itself is an indication of the truthfulness of our position. Faithfulness, rather than effectiveness, is the ultimate test of Christian pacifism."[112] Nevertheless, the pacifist church is not called to be passive in the face of injustice. For that was certainly not the way of Jesus. And "the pacifist is no less obligated to resist injustice, for not to resist means we abandon our brother or sister to injustice. Pacifists, however, contend the crucial question is how we are to resist."[113] And this "how" can only be given shape by the true character of the church of Jesus Christ.

I conclude in summarizing Hauerwas' argument thus. Really he has no argument at all; he is calling for witnesses. And yet to juxtapose argument and witness is a precarious matter. He puts it well when he says:

I have said that without witness, there is no argument. But it does not follow that arguments always accompany witness. Sometimes witnesses are all Christians have to offer, and sometimes witnesses are enough; for what could be more powerful than the discovery that human beings have been made part of God's care of creation through the cross and resurrection of Jesus of Nazareth.[114]

---

[109] Hauerwas, *Peaceable Kingdom*, 88.
[110] Hauerwas, *Peaceable Kingdom*, 91.
[111] Hauerwas, *Hannah's Child*, 136.
[112] Stanley Hauerwas, "Pacifism: Some Philosophical Considerations," *Faith and Philosophy* (April 1985): 99f.
[113] Hauerwas, "Pacifism," 100.
[114] Stanley Hauerwas, *With the Grain of the Universe* (Grand Rapids: Brazos, 2001), 241.

PART IV-D

The chapters in this section demonstrate the impact of John Howard Yoder's work in setting the theological tone of the Christian peace witness. In the mid-1940s Reinhold Niebuhr spoke of pacifism as a heresy, but he exempted the Mennonites of the Radical Reformation because he said that they kept their pacifism to themselves. Mennonite theologians have sometimes taken this as a compliment to have a major American ethicist give them a place in the tradition. But for Yoder it was anything but that because, while it may have gotten the theology of some Mennonites right, it certainly did not get Jesus right. For the logic that produced Niebuhr's conclusion was born out of a dichotomy which suggested that you either adopt a perfectionist ethic of pacifism and live away from the imperfections and power politics of this world or you remain in the world doing battle with evil in the most responsible way possible. Yoder's simple point is that Jesus was also presented with these options and chose to follow neither. Hence, to be serious about following him means that both options are also inadequate for his disciples today and that a third way must be carefully crafted.

Yoder's approach, therefore, portrays a view of Christian pacifism quite different from a withdrawn quietism, on the one hand, and a nonviolent activism, on the other hand, which believes that nonviolent strategies can resolve all conflicts nonviolently. His view places Christians into a middle: a place of witness that at once has the possibility of effecting the most profound change imaginable (resurrection); but whether it does or not is out of our hands. Hence, while effectiveness cannot itself be a "moral yardstick," no Christian should underestimate the power of a faithful peace witness. In the pacifism that Yoder suggests is biblical, one cannot dismiss the agency of Creator/re-Creator God, who commands an "arsenal of power" in which resurrection functions. Of course, this makes things messier than we might like if we assume that human beings alone are in charge, but this messiness is what disciples of Jesus are invited into.

While Yoder's ethic has not been overwhelmingly popular within mainline Christian ethics, it has nonetheless generated a healthy debate. The recurrent fear has been that unless we hold the trump card of violence in our back pockets, we surrender too much to a power beyond our control. Hence, it remains a risk not many are willing to take, or, to say it differently, a faith few can live by.

In this section, I presented two ethicists who have taken up Yoder's charge—McClendon, a Baptist, "evangelical" theologian, and Hauerwas, a Methodist turned Episcopalian. Both speak of the radical change and cost in their own lives and careers in letting Yoder convince them of the relevance of Jesus. I will briefly identify several of the key differences it makes, according to McClendon and Hauerwas, to claim Jesus as Lord for Christian ethics.

CONTROL

To critique the human desire to take charge is not new with Yoder. We have heard this in the writings of Martin Luther King Jr. and especially with the liberation theologians and feminists. For example, no one has emphasized radical risk-taking more than Sharon Welch. But often, one senses a subtext in these voices that suggests that it is not really control that is the issue but *who* has the control; the wrong people—bad people and/or systems—are in charge. What is radical about the peace theologians is that they read Scripture to say that control itself is the issue; for God is in charge of history—really! Even Jesus gave up controlling outcome in his willingness to die in the face of no other redemptive options. This means that all efforts to seek to make history come out right are in need of judgment; all are asked to give up seeking handles on history. Moreover, since this is the way of the Son of God, it is in tune with the "grain of the universe."

LOGIC OF PACIFISM

According to Yoder, McClendon, and Hauerwas, the pacifism that is born out of the story of Jesus is intelligible in ways that challenge our rational categories. We have heard theologians like Bonhoeffer and Balthasar say that they cannot submit their lives to rules or systems that would calculate ways to act in advance of real-life social contexts. Christian pacifism, as our authors in this section have presented it, is rooted in the *person* and *life* of Jesus, not in rules or theories. They can say it this way because Jesus too had concerns with the legalism of the Pharisees. When he speaks of the rules of the tradition, he suggests that all rules, properly understood, point beyond themselves to God, in whom we are to find our allegiance and obedience. This requires nuanced openness and awareness that all people are God's and that God is already actively redeeming evil in every situation long before we get there. The pacifism that finds lodgment in the Jesus narrative is concerned neither with controlling outcome through systems of logic and rules of conduct, nor with protecting a perfectionism; rather it lives in the midst of the village, making connections with people and finding small ways to participate with them in the presence of God's redeeming work.

CHURCH

The church is integral to this way of peacemaking. We see the issue of church and peacemaking highlighted in the lives of J. S. Woodsworth and Dietrich Bonhoeffer. Both were involved in community peace-building efforts at the grass roots level as well as at the structural levels, seeking to change unjust governments. While the tragedy of their lives is quite different for the two of them, there is a common theme—neither found a church that could help them sustain their passion for peace-building. Woodsworth's church was not pacifist, and so he held merely to his conviction of a literal reading of the injunction of Jesus to love enemies. But he found no way to convince the power structures, not even his own party. So he had to withdraw from political life because he could not give up his pacifist conviction. Bonhoeffer's case is different. He could not embrace the naïve view of pacifism represented by views like Woodsworth's, nor could he get himself to withdraw from politics. And so he modified or gave up his pacifism—depending on how one reads his story. The tragedy for both is that there was no church to sustain them in their convictions and assist them in the reading of the Jesus story. The biblical pacifism of the three authors in this section requires regular worship of opening ourselves to God's grace, healing, and power. Christian pacifism is unintelligible without patience and hope, without creative, prayerful, and nuance, discerning how to place ourselves into God's redeeming activities. And seeking to do this alone, outside the gathering, praying, discerning community is extremely difficult.

METHOD

We have heard Hauerwas say over and over that he cannot have "positions" because worshipping the God of Jesus Christ whose own faithfulness brought him to the cross and who was resurrected by Creator God, cannot be reduced to or encompassed by the surety of a theory or system. The life of faithfulness to Jesus is one of radical openness to which an imposition of a theoretical framework normally does violence. Jesus wants not only our minds but our bodies. But this does not mean Christians should give up thinking. It just challenges the way we should think.

McClendon addresses this very point in the writing of his *magnum opus* on systematic theology. He argues that a discipleship ethic does not imply a softening on systematic theology; it redefines how systematic theology is done. The guiding questions change completely. Traditional systematic theology asks the ethical question this way: what must we do once we know how to think properly about theological matters? He suggests that it should be asked another way: how must we think in order to be faithful to Jesus Christ? This is in fact the way the early church did theology. And it is not by accident that, as Hauerwas reminds us, the early church had no ethic; they were a people living their faith.

It should also be said here that all three peace theologians argue that they are not writing a new theology. They are merely giving expression in a new way to a classical theology of the creeds. Yoder makes this point most directly when he says that the traditional affirmation at Nicaea and Chalcedon of the full humanity and divinity of Jesus Christ underlies all his thought. For if Jesus were not fully divine, why would anyone want to follow him? If he were not fully human, how could anyone follow him?

PEDAGOGY

How then do we teach when theories and systems will not get us there? To say this differently, how do we teach when we affirm Jesus as Lord? The first thing that must be said is that there can be no theory or method of teaching (pedagogy) that will help us.

We notice that all three theologians speak to the matter of Christian teaching. Hauerwas writes several books on the subject. It should not be surprising that this topic gets special billing with peace theologians. For how do we teach to communicate beyond the cuteness of the moment the suggestion that Jesus wants our bodies? To ask it differently, how do we develop both rituals of the mind and rituals of the body? Perhaps that is even the wrong way to ask it! Instead, we may ask, how do we learn to develop rituals in faithfulness to the Jesus narrative that do not make the modern distinction of the mind and the body? It is no easy task to learn from the Apostle Paul when he says: "I appeal to you therefore, brothers and sisters, by the mercies of God, to present your bodies as a living sacrifice, holy and acceptable to God, which is your spiritual worship. Do not be conformed to this world, but be transformed by the renewing of your minds, so that you may discern what is the will of God—what is good and acceptable and perfect" (Rom 12:1-2).

This mode of teaching is no doubt challenging but necessary for the church to be the church. It calls upon a creativity to tease out connections of difference; it calls for a listening to the learning of others from diverse places, other voices within the church and voices outside the church. Learning the liturgy of openness to others is part of the same practice as learning the liturgy of openness to God.

Conclusion

ON PUTTING CHRISTIAN ETHICS IN ITS PLACE

*Do not be conformed to this world, but be transformed by the renewing of
your minds, so that you may discern what is the will of
God—what is good and acceptable and perfect. (Rom 12:2)*

*Then turning to the disciples, Jesus said to them privately, "Blessed are
the eyes that see what you see." (Luke 10:23)*

"Someone touched me . . ." (Luke 8:46a)

Now you are the body of Christ. . . . (1 Cor 12:27a)

Extra ecclesiam nula salus. (Cyprian of Carthage)

This chapter should not be seen as a final summation that brings this book all together. The study does not admit of such a wrapping up. Rather, I reflect briefly on the nature of Christian ethics from the standpoint of my own learnings gleaned from the many stories in the entire study. I find it important to admit that, after the many presenters have been given voice, many questions still remain. And perhaps that is the first learning; questions remain! But then do all questions need to have answers? It strikes me that the quest for clear answers to all questions is itself an ethical issue, for such a drive often determines the nature of the queries we permit. If the stance toward moral questioning is itself a moral matter, then it follows that morality precedes epistemology. We must admit that, in our hurry to reach for theories, principles, or tradition to find quick answers, we often fail to exercise the patience necessary for our answers to be truthful. Discerning the faithful, Christian life takes time. The common linkage of speed with politics is hardly a model for Christian faithfulness.[1]

What then are we to do when theories and the need to have all our questions answered are not desirable? After all, we still want to live well and meaningfully. The alternative is openness to other minds to interact with, other spirits to be inspired by, and other bodies to encounter and build with, not so that these can provide easier answers but that they may help us live faithfully while we search for answers. The shorthand name for this alternative is that we need a Christian community for Christian ethics.

A fellow ethics teacher looked at the table of contents of this book and said it was easy to see where it was all going since it concluded with a section on peace theologians. My response was that I was less interested in convincing university students

---

[1] See Paul Virilio, *Speed and Politics: An Essay on Dromology*, trans. Mark Polizzotti (New York: Semiotext(e), 1986); and *Desert Screen: War at the Speed of Light*, trans. Michael Degener (New York: Continuum, 2002).

to adopt a peace position, for that is easy. If anything, I wanted to convince them that Christian ethics is impossible without the church; and that is difficult. Why? Because today we tend to want answers to questions about war, homosexuality, euthanasia, technology, and ecology quickly and definitively. Any suggestion that we embark on a process of study, discernment, prayer, search for wisdom from the traditions, serious listening to people we disagree with, and so on, is met with resistance.

One strand of ethical thought has taught us to believe that Christian ethics is all about how we place ourselves under God's reign. And, of course, it is! This is why H. Richard Niebuhr is so compelling in his *The Responsible Self*,[2] where he suggests that in every situation we should respond to God who is already active there. The problem is: why would we want to do so? Who is the self that would be driven to live that way? As we have seen, Descartes' move from the metaphysical understanding of the self, where persons were characters that were shaped by other characters, to the epistemological view of the autonomous thinking subject, has so changed the view of the self that it has made ethics itself unintelligible. We saw this especially clearly as this view made it through the philosophy of Hume and Kant.[3] The assumption that has become dominant in our day is that the self is an essential given as a subject knowing objects. But this is extremely problematic, especially for Christian ethics, because we know the self too to be formed in its relation with other subjects. Hence, who I know changes me! My family and friends shape me. In other words, we are social selves, molded in interaction with others. But who or what social forces should shape

the self? If left to the forces in society at large, whatever characters will emerge from that will not bear much resemblance to the ethics of Christ followers.

By putting ethics in its place—the church—I do not mean that it can be neatly tucked into a secure space. I rather mean that Christian ethics only becomes intelligible in a place that has the resources to disclose what it means to be a person—as individual, as social being, as child of God—so that we are able to act in response to Christ's call to "take up [our] cross daily and follow [him]" (Luke 9:23). Such an understanding cannot be resourced by an individual self or a set of intellectual ideas; for as selves we are more than minds, we are also bodies and spirits.

The argument that Christian ethics is ecclesiology is certainly not new; in some ways it is as old as the church itself. However, especially in the North American mainstream, the connection between church and Christian ethics is not at the forefront. Perhaps this is because another connection—between ethics and biblical theological reflection—has been weakened. There are, of course, clear counter-examples.[4]

If ethics were an entirely rational discipline that could be figured out intellectually, it would not need a church. But it is not.[5] Hence it requires a discerning community; a rational, political body. Only in this way can we answer questions of where the needs are, where the pain is, who the outsiders are, where the injustice is, how to train its people to see, read, be patient, and sensitive.

This chapter will not make the argument that ecclesiology is Christian ethics; that argument has been made and is here presupposed. Rather, it will build on what others have already said on what it might look like

---

[2] H. Richard Niebuhr, *The Responsible Self: An Essay in Christian Moral Philosophy* (New York: Harper & Row, 1963).

[3] See chap. 7 above.

[4] See John Howard Yoder, "Why Ecclesiology Is Social Ethics: Gospel Ethics versus the Wider Wisdom," in *The Royal Priesthood: Essays Ecclesiological and Ecumenical*, ed. Michael G. Cartwright (Grand Rapids: Eerdmans, 1994), 102–26.

[5] This is not the same argument as was made by David Hume in saying that "ought" cannot be rationally derived from "is." Alasdair MacIntyre has made clear that just because Hume may be right on the basis of a universal logic (which MacIntyre doubts exists), he is wrong in the context of tradition-based rationalities. See chap. 25 above.

if the church does not have an ethic but is an ethic.[6] It will do this under three headings: body, teaching and learning, and witness.

BODY

Given the renewed interest in the theological study of body, the face of Christian ethics also has changed.[7] Of course bodies are important for ethics because bodies act. There would be no ethics if it were not for bodies. Perhaps it is not an overstatement to say that ethics is but a way of learning how to negotiate bodies.

No one will disagree that the church is a moral community. Many ethicists, from Ernst Troeltsch onward, have viewed it as a primary agent of social change. Of course this can hardly be opposed, but what does it mean? Does this mean that the church is tasked with the role of making society Christian? This has been the dominant emphasis of the Social Gospel Movement. Richard Hays has suggested a more nuanced language. He speaks of the church as an "embodied metaphor."[8] Metaphors point beyond themselves to something else. Hence, on this model, the church in its very being points beyond itself to Christ. In a sense, it is not itself but opens itself to being shaped by another.

The Body of Christ

The New Testament church is spoken of as a body. For example, "For as in one body we have many members, and not all members have the same function, so we, who are many, are one body in Christ, and individually we are members one of another" (Rom 12:4-5). Similar language is found in 1 Corinthians 12:12, 13, 27; Ephesians 4:4, 12; Colossians 1:18. The image of the body is used to speak

of how the one and the many are understood, the multiple functions of the church work as one, and how the behavior of its members is shaped.

The church as "body of Christ" is a powerful image and lends itself to easy abuse. It can easily overreach itself and control the terms of God's activity. After all, the church, too, is a fallen power and hence is not above emboldening itself rather than pointing to the one who alone makes it what it is. This is seen in many different forms: participation in violence, abuse of its own power, and failing to speak up for those most in need of a voice.

The church is a body in a particular sense. It is a social-political entity, visible through its activities and operations; it is a community of people who are said to be "members one of another." This is indeed a strange notion and should give moderns pause. It suggests that we are not understandable in relation to ourselves alone. In other words, we are to see ourselves as being made whole by others. This picks up Alvin Dueck's theme of "the self as a plurality;"[9] that we are many selves all wrapped together, so that when others act I act and that when I act others act; when one suffers all suffer, when one rejoices all rejoice. This peculiar body of bodies, where people are not themselves in two ways—they participate in each other and in Christ—gathers to discern and to worship. But we need to add other levels of complexity here, for the church is not only gathered, it is also scattered. In its scatteredness it teaches and witnesses, thinks and acts, envisions and builds. Moreover, the church is not only particular, but universal; and we have seen, especially with theologians like Bonhoeffer, the importance of the witness of an ecumenical church.

---

[6] I am thinking here especially of what Stanley Hauerwas has said. See chap. 34 above.

[7] See, e.g., Graham Ward, *Christ and Culture* (Malden, Mass.: Blackwell, 2005). I will draw esp. on his chapter "The Body of Christ and Its Erotic Politics," 92–110.

[8] See 42ff. above.

[9] See chap. 11 above, esp. 191ff.

The Romans 12 image that church members inhabit space in the being of others needs further comment. This is a profoundly countercultural image of both personal identity and ecclesial identity. It is a rejection of Descartes' emphasis on the *epistemological* subject and a return to an emphasis on the *metaphysical*. It emphasizes that we are bodies and know each other as bodies through bodily encounter. It gives a nod to knowing the truth as bodies know it, through touch. This is different from knowing by gathering information.[10]

In the *body* of Christ, the knowledge we open ourselves to is driven by the desire of the body. Aristotle has made the point that only living things with the capacity for tactile sensation can know desire. But the desire of the body of Christ is to know God, that is, the desire to touch God—to see, hear, smell, and even taste God. (John 6:52-58 talks about Christ being the living bread.) To understand this is to orient the body in a way that draws it into the very body of Christ. The original body of Christ bridged the world by being the wholly other in a particular space. (Again this sounds like an oxymoron to modern ears!) To be drawn into that body is to be simultaneously in Christ and in the world, in nature and in grace.

It is important to ask what "being in Christ" meant for the early church. For the Apostle Paul, it meant being tied together in Christ, to become one body despite differences. It also meant taking on the ways of Christ and being clothed with the virtues of Christ. The assumption is that, in Christ, God was at work and that creation was being made complete. Hence, there is a whole new world in Christ. Paul says it thus: "So if anyone is in Christ, there is a new creation; everything old has passed away; see, everything has become new" (2 Cor 5:17). The salvation that is made possible in Christ is at the same time personal and universal. Since in Christ God was (re)creating, we as followers of Christ are drawn into the work of God, being re-created ourselves, in our relationships, and in our environment.

The ecclesial body is essentially formation in Christ. To share in his body is to share in his desire, which is the unity and peace of all creation: fundamentally the desire to live in harmony with God and all the earth. To be in Christ, then, names the desire to touch God; that is, to be in a radical way open to the other.

Openness

Openness is the fundamental stance of the body of Christ because its gaze is receptivity. Given that we know ourselves as participants in the other, we must open ourselves to reciprocal giving and receiving. This is but another way of saying that life is best seen as gift. By placing ourselves into the body of Christ, we open ourselves to receiving the gift of full humanity.

Openness is defined by openness to Jesus Christ, not a general openness to a beyond or to some other body or state of being. For example, the body called church is not modeled after a community of moral perfection like the original state of creation—the garden of Eden. The restoration of the garden belongs to the consummation of all of history envisioned in Revelation 22. The body of Christ is resident in a post-sin and a pre-fall redemption community—that is, one fully enmeshed in the project of the redemption of the world.[11] To say this another way, the church is situated between the first and second coming of Christ. It is important not to lose our place.

The church as the body of Christ therefore makes no sense outside the theology of the

---

[10] For a development of the notion of truth and touch in Aquinas, see John Milbank and Catherine Pickstock, *Truth and Aquinas* (New York: Routledge, 2001), esp. the chapter, "Truth and Touch," 60–87.

[11] I owe this insight to Dietrich Bonhoeffer, Sanctorum Communio: *A Theological Study of the Sociology of the Church*, trans. Reinhard Krauss and Nancy Lukens (Minneapolis: Fortress, 2009), esp. chap. 3, "The Primal State and the Problem of Community," 58–106.

fallenness of the created order. Christ came into the world to redeem the world of sin. Hence, the church cannot be intended to emulate the perfection of "the garden," for it knew no sin. The church is rather the body that is lifted into the reality of the grace of God despite the reality of sin. For it, too, is fallen and in constant need of God's grace. It therefore regularly confesses its own sins before God. To fail to do this would be to wander astray.

Christian worship is the paradigmatic act of openness to God through Christ. Worship is the act of being drawn into openness to a beyond in like manner to Christ; namely, to God, to the world, and to the other. Each stance is interrelated with the others.

First, openness to God means that who we are and how we can live abundantly is not given to us from within ourselves, nor from others, nor from this world; it is given to us from revelation of the Creator of the universe. For we are not our own, and who we are is defined by whose we are! In other words, what it means for us to be fully human is found in the one who is the incarnate body of the divine. For in Christ, "created Adam" is seen in all his glory—complete and whole. Hence, to be drawn into Christ is to be drawn into our own true selves.

Karl Barth was right when he emphasized that we can only know God when we open ourselves to *receiving* from beyond ourselves, and we can only know ourselves fully when we know God. This does not mean that culture, the social and behavioral sciences, cannot teach us anything about ourselves, but unless we are open to receiving from the one who created us and seeks to redeem us, we will not know ourselves fully in Christ.

Second, openness to the world is an important stance for Christ followers because God created and loves the world. So the world confronts us in both its beauty and its fallenness. Christians share a fundamental

truth with all earthly reality in that we are all part of the fallen order. Hence, we all see dimly. In seeing Jesus, we look at all of creation with different eyes, yet much of what the world gives us is beautiful and sometimes even morally superior to what we behold. We should not dismiss lightly Jesus' hard sayings about some who, although clearly considered outsiders, are nevertheless exemplary in his eyes over those who were religious insiders. What this means is that the body of Christ is not easily tamed by clearly defined borders.

Moreover, the world is not homogeneous. Social and political reality in Crystal City, Manitoba, is not the same as it is in Washington, D.C. So how to be open to the world may vary widely. This does not suggest that all that the world teaches is of Christ; careful discernment must take place. But the discernment itself should be guided by the spirit of Christ and not by a "false spirit" driven by a legalism that shuns for the sake of secure, moral borders. Shunning may be an important church practice, but it should be guided by the spirit of Christ—both Christ's truth and his love.

Third, openness to the other is premised on the assumption that others too are given life and insight by Creator God. It is an amazing thought to suggest, as the Apostle Paul does, that we are the other and the other is us. It suggests two obvious implications: a stance of listening to the other and the realization that as individuals we do not have controls on the truth. These two notions actually merge into one since truth is known through the body—the corporate body participates in the body of the one who says "I am the truth."

If Paul claims a metaphysical intersubjectivity of human beings as a basic insight, then it could extend even beyond the church.[12] The borders again become porous. Then the other as non-church member, or non-Christian, or even nonreligious person, affects my being as well; I may receive insights from

---

[12] For helpful insights on the Christian concept of person see Bonhoeffer, Sanctorum Communio, esp. chap. 2, "The Christian Concept of Person and Concepts of Social Basic-Relations," 34–57, where he discusses the intersubjectivity of the I-You relationship.

strangers on what it means to live under God. This can be a deeply troubling thought, especially if we believe we are responsible for (in charge of) keeping things neat and tidy. But truth be told, there are many hints of exactly this kind of teaching in the parables and sayings of Jesus in holding up some fairly shady characters as sources of insight. Truth in openness is precarious.

Politics

The stance of openness should not lead us to believe that the body of Christ lacks a distinct political identity. John Howard Yoder's *Body Politics*[13] presents an overview of what it means to talk of the politics of the church. He begins by showing that the difference between the church and other political bodies like the state, "is not that one is political and the other is not, but that they are political in different ways."[14] It is also not the case that some churches are political and others are not. They are all political by definition of being a body. Politics is a way of dealing with money, power, relationships, justice; it has practices, strategies, goals, liturgies, and so on. Hence, the church, interested in all these matters, is political by virtue of what it is. But the politics of church is distinct and should be seen as a counter-politics, and as such, of course, it invites its community into a counter-ethic.

Yoder identifies five practices of the church which define its politics. Remember that in this model, the church does not have an ethic—it is an ethic. So knowing what Christian ethics is implies understanding what the church is and does.

The five practices are as follows:

1. Binding and loosing. This means the church names the destructive forces of sin and practices forgiveness.

2. Breaking bread together. This practice trains disciples to learn to receive and give thanks for daily bread (Eucharist means "giving thanks"). Disciples live by the gift and grace of God; therefore, they are the kind of people who make food available to those who are hungry.

3. Baptism. This ceremony of induction would be unnecessary if the church were not a counter-politic—with a distinct identity as the new humanity. The Apostle Paul's model of church is not a *Gesellschaft* in the Ferdinand Tönnies sense, but a *Gemeinschaft*, uniting impossible differences under one spirit.[15] Members are inducted into an openness of spirit given in Christ. Paul says, "For in one spirit we were all baptized into one body—Jews or Greeks, slaves or free—and we were all made to drink of one Spirit" (1 Cor 12:13).

4. The fullness of Christ. Yoder draws this image from Paul in Ephesians 4:11-13 where he speaks of the many roles within the one body. The emphasis is on the celebration of the diversity of gifts united in Christ's body.

5. Freedom to speak. This is the rule of Paul which refers to Corinthians 12 and Paul's instruction on how meetings are to be conducted. All should be allowed to speak because in the body of Christ the Spirit works in unpredictable ways. We never know from where the insights may come.

Each of these practices is both a discipling activity as well as a modeling activity. As discipling activities, they function in much the same way as do sports camps or military training camps. They are drills that are repeated as liturgies intended to make habitual practices of forgiveness, generosity, humility, openness, kindness, and all the other Christian virtues listed in places like Galatians 5:22. In other words, they are identity-forming activities, acknowledging that being a body in Christ is a specific kind of body.

William Cavanaugh, in a book called *Torture and Eucharist*,[16] contrasts two competing

---

[13] John Howard Yoder, *Body Politics: Five Practices of the Christian Community before the Watching World* (Nashville: Discipleship Resources, 1992).

[14] Yoder, *Body Politics*, ix.

[15] For a discussion of Ferdinand Tönnies' *Gemeinschaft* and *Gesellschaft*, see chap. 10 above.

[16] William T. Cavanaugh, *Torture and Eucharist: Theology, Politics, and the Body of Christ* (Malden, Mass.: Blackwell, 1998).

ways to shape communities. The Chilean state's liturgical practice sought to tame a community of conflict with torture and by instilling fear into the people. The church's liturgy is the Eucharist, which seeks to bring people of difference into one body in Christ. These are two profoundly different, political practices requiring two different disciplines to sustain them; that is, they are two fundamentally different ways of conceiving of ethics. And they become intermingled when those who are doing the state's business of torture are also members of the body of Christ, where difference is dissolved in the Eucharist.

The liturgies of the church are also modeling activities for social bodies outside itself. In other words, the separation of the two politics is not always neat, as the Chilean example suggests. They are constantly intertwined. Unless we assign the two to separate realms, one political and the other not, which of course is intolerable and unchristian, the church cannot rely on the state and its institutions to do the justice of Christ. Nor can the church simply make all other bodies Christian. But if it takes itself seriously as a political body, the church must create spaces where its politics can be practiced outside of its own Christian communities: in grassroots communities, in businesses, in schools, community clubs, in prisons and correctional structures, in governments, in families, and so on. And it can speak and name the injustices that it sees and offer alternatives.

It is important to remember that the politics of the Christian community are the politics of Jesus. And the politics of Jesus are for this world. While the world may not know this, or may think such a politic to be impractical, the church offers models, alternative ways of living in peace and justice with one another. This does not assume easy

continuity between the politics of church and world, nor does it let us off the hook of honest engagement.

The politics of the church is also its soteriology. God wills to save humanity by inviting it to inhabit an ethical space of forgiveness, hospitality, love, and a willingness to suffer rather than harm anyone. That is, God wills to save humanity by bringing them together under Christ. The miracle of salvation is possible, where difference can be celebrated in Christ. In this way, it is fundamentally at odds with the politics and salvation plan of the modern state, which is all about how we might protect ourselves from the powers of differences that threaten us.

TEACHING AND LEARNING

The church as the body of Christ does not accept the common belief that ethics and religion are private matters. Therefore, it is actively engaged in and teaches about both, but in distinct ways. An important way of learning for the body of Christ is by being drawn into a shared space of peace and justice. This means "knowing that" is only part of what defines knowing; "knowing how" is equally important. Gathering information, analyzing what is real, learning how to think, learning what to do, learning the story, are all important guides in the pursuit of wisdom. Openness to receiving insight from outside of our own mind, spirit, and body shapes this quest in a special way.

A Jewish rabbi, Michael Goldberg, speaks of discipleship learning in an article, "Discipleship: Basing One Life on Another—It's Not What You Know, It's Who You Know."[17] In it, he contrasts the modern view of pedagogy made popular by Max Weber, where Weber makes fun of teachers who permit their political biases to affect the teaching of their academic discipline.[18] Goldberg contrasts this

---

[17] Michael Goldberg, "Discipleship: Basing One Life on Another—It's Not What You Know, It's Who You Know," in *Theology Without Foundations: Religious Practice and the Future of Theological Truth*, ed., Stanley Hauerwas, Nancey Murphy, and Mark Nation (Nashville: Abingdon, 1994), 289–304.

[18] See Max Weber, "Science as a Vocation," in *From Max Weber: Essays in Sociology*, ed. H. H. Gerth and C. Wright Mills (New York: Oxford University Press, 1946), 129–56.

disciplined teaching mode with a *discipleship* teaching mode. The latter describes the rabbinic approach to learning in which, he says, "a disciple entered into the rabbis' community of practice with an eye towards extending the rabbis' practice(s) throughout the whole community of Israel. The rabbis had in principle a specific educational goal: to make every Jew a rabbi."[19] This does not mean that teaching was done on the basis of authority avoiding careful, intellectual inquiry. In other words, while it trained its students in the art of negotiating bodies—how to live in relation to others—the approach also taught students how to negotiate minds and spirits, that is, how to think and how to worship God. And it did this by emphasizing that knowledge is not abstract, ideational content but is always mediated through a person—an embodied soul/mind. Knowledge is embodied (enmattered) just like the soul and mind are embodied. Goldberg quotes from Rabbi Nachman of Bratslav:

> There is a difference between learning from a book and hearing the word of Torah from a teacher. The book contains words that are unattached to any human spirit; they are like notes of music silently written on a sheet of paper. Teachings from the mouth of the sage have a spirit and a life, so that one who hears them feels immediately tied to the soul of the sage who speaks these words, just as an audience becomes attached to the one who sings the notes of music.[20]

This form of teaching and learning is in some tension with the model of pedagogy in most modern universities. And it is not surprising that so many of the ethicists in our study offered critiques and reflections that sought to reconceive the university in its present, Western form. This is not the place to enter into that debate; instead I offer qualities of learning and teaching that are especially important for disciples who inhabit a world in which we can expect more than is possible; that is, in a world where the God who raised Jesus from the dead is at work among us to bring creation to completion.

Seeing and Touching

One of the most powerful parables of Jesus (and disturbing because it entails judgment which we think we can avoid) is found in Matthew 25. Here, seeing and touching are linked to faithfulness in the kingdom, and the harshest judgment is in store for those who do not see and touch according to kingdom standards. The scene is set by the Son of Man gathering the nations before the throne of judgment. The king praises and rewards those at his right hand for the good they have done to the poor, the hungry, the stranger, and so on, because they have acted in ways that have met their needs. The text then continues:

> Then the righteous will answer him, "Lord, when was it that it that we saw you hungry and gave you food, or thirsty and gave you something to drink? And when was it that we saw you a stranger and welcomed you, or naked and gave you clothing? And when was it that we saw you sick or in prison and visited you?" And the king will answer them, "Truly I tell you, just as you did it to one of the least of these who are members of my family, you did it to me." (Matt 25:37-40)

It is interesting to note that when you see and touch the family of the king you see and touch the king, and vice versa. One might say that God has only one family—children—and when we are in Christ, we are in God's family doing Christ-like acts.

This story is an example of the co-extensiveness of nature and grace; for touching the earth (nature) aright is but to participate in heavenly grace in earthly form. This is itself the symbol of the incarnation; God touched the earth with divine grace in Jesus Christ, and that brings new hope for its healing and perfecting. As we embody Christ (are the church), we touch the pain of the world; which is but to touch Christ. Worshipping God through Christ, therefore, is not an act of separation from the pain of the world; it is only an act of orienting ourselves to that pain. This is a profoundly different way of conceiving our being in the world

---

[19] Goldberg, "Discipleship," 293.

[20] Goldberg, "Discipleship," 295.

than relativizing love to the extent possible in a sinful earth.

The act of learning to see and touch has another dimension as well. To behold the world is not merely to see what is wrong with it. The world we inhabit is simultaneously fallen and in the state of being redeemed; it is therefore mixed with both the beautiful and the ugly, the good and the evil. Hence, we should train ourselves to see the world as mixed. There is incredible beauty in this world, beauty that inspires awe and wonder. One cannot be in Christ and cease celebrating the beauty of the birth of a new infant because there are starving children in this world. But neither can one ignore the starving children. The challenge is to do this in right proportion and at right times. But there is no formula for this, and no method that determines universal answers to the mixed reality of good and evil. Jesus' comment "for you always have the poor with you" (Matt 26:11a) was not meant to communicate that there is no need to be concerned about the poor; rather, it was intended to hush those voices who say that in this broken world we should not celebrate the time of God's visitation of beauty and truth. This discernment of how to place ourselves into a world of the dialectic of beauty and sin requires the wisdom of the body of Christ.

Letting Go as Being Responsible

Placing ourselves into the life of Christ is in itself a statement on who is in charge. Not only that, the one into whose life we place our own is the one who himself refused to take charge over affairs such that it would move history in the right direction.

Training ourselves in the art of letting go is not easy, especially in an age of technology where we are taught that unless we are in control we are being irresponsible. In other words, we tend to believe that a responsible ethic demands taking charge. To train ourselves to see ethics differently requires careful thought. We have seen several ethicists in our study address the issue of domination and control, which speaks to its importance.[21]

We need to be clear on what is not being said here. Christian ethics is not about withdrawing and letting things happen without our involvement. The Christian life is not a spectator sport! Rather, it points to a way of being involved by giving up on a compulsiveness that attempts to ensure that the outcome will be according to our liking. While such an approach may be futile in any case, the problem is that it invites strategies that sacrifice expedience for effectiveness. The metaphor of letting go that I am suggesting here comes from Hans Urs von Balthasar's idea of drama.[22] The church should think of itself as placed into a drama in which Jesus Christ is the director. We are the actors invited to use our creative gifts to imaginatively embody a specific role. We are asked to "lose ourselves" in a script already written.

Such a "placement move" requires several distinct disciplines. First, the place of the drama performance is in the space occupied by the cross and resurrection. It has not been customary to think of the cross and resurrection of Jesus Christ as a model for Christian ethics.[23] Yet it is a profound display of the placement of one will into the other. We see in the "thy will be done" prayer of Jesus that God is directing the affair and Jesus struggles with how to fit into the larger drama. Clearly there is resistance on his part (a struggle of wills) and even lament, but also there is openness and willingness to go with the script.

Second, and closely related to the first, letting go means giving up handling history. How do we live when we do not think of ourselves as wanting to move history in the right direction? It does not mean that one ignores

[21] See especially the chapters above on the liberation theologians and the feminists.

[22] See chap. 16 above.

[23] Bonhoeffer was prominent in contemporary thought to do so, and it has been the language of all three of the "peace theologians" in this book. Martin Luther King Jr. and James Cone do so as well. John Howard Yoder and Stanley Hauerwas are further examples.

or is uninterested in outcome; it means instead an acknowledgment that outcome cannot be fully known, and that it therefore cannot alone determine means. This awareness actually frees us to a smaller agenda; more grassroots justice-making. But even more important, it acknowledges that one simply cannot know in advance all the forces and agents that will move a good idea or act forward. Creativity often provides its own momentum—generates new ideas and possibilities that could not be envisioned or imagined in advance. To actively wait and see, to pray and remain open to God's redemption, to praise God for both the small and the large acts of grace, are all part of the "unhandling" stance. That is why the alternative is sometimes called a doxological view of history.

Third, this mode of understanding ethics requires lament and forbearance. What do we do when the right does not happen; or when we are not even able to envision what is right? The answer in the drama that is written and directed by Creator God is that we wait, pray, and yield not to temptation. We lament because what we have been promised and fairly expect to receive has not yet arrived. The stance of lament retains hope that it will come; we expect it, we hope for it, but it is not yet here. Lament has meaning only when we believe that we are not the only moral agents changing things. Jesus' words, "Thy will be done," acknowledge that there is a will other than our own at work. This means that, just because we cannot think of anything redemptive to do, does not mean that nothing redemptive is being done. Lament is an expression of our pain in not being able to see God's redemptive activities; forbearance is the act of waiting in faith and not yielding to unfaithful means. People who give up on lament and forbearance resort to taking matters into their own limited hands, which is but another way of saying, "we can't wait for God."

The virtues of lament and forbearance have relevance as well for how we quarrel over important, ethical matters in the church. Debates over issues like homosexuality, euthanasia, and war, to name only a few, often result in failure to come to agreement. And this matters because real people are negatively impacted by the lack of moral agreement. Lament and forbearance can help us in our failure. The stance of waiting—lament and forbearance—should never be excuses to avoid difficult decisions. However, it simply must be acknowledged that we do not always know enough or see clearly enough or are open enough to come to agreement. Epistemological and ethical humility are important, Christian qualities precisely because neither truth nor goodness is a possession. Without active forbearance in prayer and hope, the body of Christ too may succumb to hostile division.

In all of this, we should remember that both patience and impatience are moral qualities. There are some things we should be impatient about and seek to change as soon as possible; there are some things over which we should be patient. Yet there is no formula that tells us which is which; for that we need the discerning body.

WITNESS

The alternative to being in control is witness. But witness can be both close at hand and far off. Withdrawal from society, as we see in some Christian groups like the Amish and some Catholic orders, should not be judged as irresponsible because their witness is from a distance. Their legitimacy is not derived, as Reinhold Niebuhr argued,[24] from their belief that the Christian life is apolitical; for they do not believe that. Nor is their separation justified by their insight that the ethics of Jesus will not make sense to the secular world. For all Christians know that; whether they witness from afar or in the face of injustice close at hand. It is rather a difference in the stance of witness—from near at hand or from a distance; in either case, the point is

---

[24] See Reinhold Niebuhr, "Why the Christian Church Is not Pacifist," in *Christianity and Power Politics* (New York: Charles Scribner's Sons, 1940), 1–32.

that the church's politics are distinct from the politics of the world. And that message can be spoken from several different poses.

We do well to remind ourselves that the word witness means martyr. Stephen is referred to as a witness in Acts 22:20 and Revelation 2:13; 17:6. At the beginning of this book, I told the story of Polycarp, one of the early Christian martyrs.[25] Polycarp knew whose he was and never wavered from that conviction. And when he was threatened with death if he did not renounce his faith in Christ, he refused. He did not threaten in return; he died loving the enemies that killed him, that is, in Christ. In the process, he taught volumes; nothing propositionally, but much about the one who sustained him—he bore witness.

Martyrdom is witness because it is the ultimate form of letting go. It is a way of saying that, although I am not in charge, someone into whose hands I place my life and my trust, is. And the charge taken by my tormenters is but temporary; the one into whose hands I commit my life is able to sustain "life," even if in a transformed state. This gives meaning to "taking up the cross and following."

How Then Shall We Live?

Much has already been said about the posture that the church should take in engaging the world which houses it.[26] Here I will state four stances of witness as the church seeks to be faithful to its calling to be the body of Christ.

First, learning how to resist as disciples of Christ. The Apostle Paul talks about being clothed in protective gear to resist the "powers and principalities, thrones and dominions" that threaten seduction into unfaithfulness. We tend not to believe in "powers and principalities," but these are the very powers of social and political ways of

setting the options that exist for us. So the first act of resistance is the refusal to allow alternative body politics to set the terms in which we must think and act. This requires a conscientious effort of analyzing and naming what is going on and, perhaps even more important, a clear view of the identity of the alternative politics of the church.

There are other ways we should learn to resist; some may even be in tension with the resistance of seduction. Because the body of Christ is open to the other, it is crucial to resist closure. We face many temptations to closure: like knowing precisely what a biblical text says (one might call this "resisting closure of meaning"); knowing exactly what is right and what is wrong; knowing who is "in" and who is not; and so on. These forms of closure bespeak an arrogance of spirit that inhibits the free movement of the Holy Spirit; it suggests that truth is a possession and that it can be owned. As such, these are forms of control and manipulation. The truth of Christ needs no defense. In the body of Christ, truth is seen as a person and not an object of knowledge; it asks to be embodied, not imposed.

Second, learning to listen. If Christian morality does not come from rules or principles but is lodged in the person Jesus Christ, then to know what the spirit of Christ is saying requires a posture of listening. Jesus reinterpreted the law; he challenged the ways of tradition; and he heard the pleas of the sick and the poor. To listen as Jesus did is to train ourselves in the art of hearing the Spirit, the text, and the other. And hearing commits one to action. In this way, listening is the initial step toward the faithful life.

Third, learning hospitality to the stranger. One of the powerful parables of Jesus is of the Good Samaritan (Luke 10:25-37). The story is a gloss on the moral injunction, "You shall

---

[25] See 50ff. above.

[26] In an earlier essay I identified four "strategies" of the church in engaging other political bodies like the state. They were: modeling; demythologizing especially the state since it is constantly overreaching its significance; ad hoc partnering; and repenting and re-reading our own stories. See Harry J. Huebner, "The Church Made Strange for the Nations," in *Echoes of the Word: Theological Ethics as Rhetorical Practice* (Waterloo, Ont.: Pandora, 2005), 84–106.

love the Lord your God with all your heart, and with all your soul, and with all your strength, and with all your mind; and your neighbor as yourself" (Luke 10:27). Given that the Jews hated Samaritans, Jesus tells a parable about what it means to be neighbor. His main character—the Samaritan—was himself viewed as "stranger" by the hearers of the parable; yet he is the one who showed hospitality to a man attacked by thieves. There is no doubt lots going on in this story, but a central theme is that representatives of the religious establishment—the priest and the Levite—used their piety to prevent them from practicing hospitality. The story condemns such action.

Jesus is radical in his demand to love not only the stranger but also the enemy. For enemies and strangers too are God's children and cannot be placed outside of God's grace. The Christ of the body we inhabit is the one who died loving his enemies.

Fourth, learning to love the world. One of the most commonly cited Bible verses is "For God so loved the world that he gave his only Son, so that everyone who believes in him may not perish but may have eternal life" (John 3:16). What is interesting here is that God's love for the world precipitated another gift—Jesus Christ. The church embodies this gift and is thereby initiated into the concern for the world that it may not perish. Much could no doubt be said about what is intended with the phrase "believes in him," but whatever it is, it is an attachment that has eternal implications. The assumption here is that only the person and message of Jesus Christ can save the world.

Love for the world implies a passion to save it from destruction. To show such love commits disciples to naming the structures of violence that threaten to destroy the world. This is no easy task, for many such forces are subtle and insidious. Some are obvious, like oppressive political structures and international structures of economic control,

but many are less transparent, like the structure of thought, knowledge, language, or the practices of open democracies. The challenge is to name them, speak Christ's sovereignty in their presence, and point to life-sustaining alternatives where possible. As John Howard Yoder has reminded us, however, it is not our task to destroy these powers for their sovereignty has already been broken by what Christ has done on the cross (Col 2:14-15); our task is to concentrate on not being seduced by them.[27] Naming them and offering alternatives is the liturgy that concretizes that task.

Peace of Christ

Jesus Christ is savior of the world and not merely a model for how his followers are to live. To say this, however, is not to say, as some have, that he is irrelevant for Christian ethics.

A longstanding debate in Christian thought is over the relationship of grace and good works. That is, how can the peace of Christ be both a gift given by Christ and an invitation for us to participate in? The Apostle Paul, in his famous passage of grace and good works, brings the two notions together in an interesting way. He says:

> For by grace you have been saved through faith, and this is not of your own doing: it is the gift of God—not the result of works, so that no one may boast. For we are what he has made us, created in Christ Jesus for good works, which God prepared beforehand to be our way of life. (Eph 2:8-10)

Reinhold Niebuhr is right that the good news of the gospel is not a new law of love brought by Jesus, for that was known before him. Rather, the good news is that salvation is possible despite human sin; it comes via grace, not by our good works. But he was wrong in under-reading the significance of the newness in Christ; the salvation of the world too comes by the grace of Jesus Christ. Niebuhr's "Christian realism" fails to claim the power and hope resident in the

---

[27] See John Howard Yoder, *The Politics of Jesus: Vicit Agnus Noster*, 2nd ed. (Grand Rapids: Eerdmans, 1994), chap. titled "Christ and Power," 134–61.

affirmation of God's miracle in history—then and now. If God no longer acts in history, then we are all damned; but if, as the New Testament writers declare, God continues to act through Christ and through those whom he has "created in Christ Jesus for good works," then we may dare to claim the hope of salvation that comes through God's grace.

When the Apostle Paul declares, "For [Christ] is our peace" (Eph 2:14), he does so alleging a new humanity that is possible in Christ—one where radical difference and conflict can be overcome. This is different from saying that the new humanity can only be made real through our efforts to have all people attain human justice and freedom. But this is also different from saying that the freedom and justice of all people is not a central, Christian concern. To accept that Christ is our peace is to claim a unique space between the cross and resurrection, a place where we express as we can a peace that passes human understanding and opens up hope for God's redemption. This is ethics in openness to miracle. "For in hope we were saved . . . we wait for it with patience" (Rom 8:24-25).

CONCLUSION

Finding our identity in the body of Christ rules out a one-dimensional view of the world, for there is much that cannot be seen (or claimed) from only one dimension. "But we do see Jesus" (Heb 2:9a), and that orients our sight and touch in a world that thinks it knows its true essence on its own terms.

Father Zosima's speech in Fyodor Dostoevsky's novel *The Brothers Karamazov*, reflects on his own fragile hope in the midst of Christian affirmation:

> But on earth we are indeed wandering, as it were, and did we not have the precious image of Christ before us, we would perish and be altogether lost, like the race of men before the flood. Much on earth is concealed from us, but in place of it we have been granted a secret, mysterious sense of our

living bond with the other world, with the higher heavenly world, and the roots of our thoughts and feelings are not here but in other worlds. That is why philosophers say it is impossible on earth to conceive the essence of things. God took seeds from other worlds and sowed them on this earth, and raised up his garden; and everything that could sprout sprouted, but it lives and grows only thorough its sense of being in touch with other mysterious worlds; if this sense is weakened or destroyed in you, that which has grown up in you dies. Then you become indifferent to life, and even come to hate it. So I think.[28]

To place ourselves into a world between worlds, as does the church as body of Christ, means much that we do will best be viewed as metaphor or sign—that is, pointing beyond itself and finding lodgment somewhere between the cross and the resurrection, whether that is befriending the stranger; serving those in need; beholding beauty; worshipping God; speaking truth and justice to power; addressing issues like ecology, human sexuality, economics, and so on; or resisting evil. This is not to suggest a lack of concern for concrete actions, but only that their meaning may not be fully understood, even by those of us who believe we are following Christ. Nevertheless, as signs that point to Christ's redemptive work in the world, they may well have a power far beyond our ability to imagine.

Dostoevsky seems to have understood the power of signs: for when Jesus, after having been maligned by the Grand Inquisitor, reaches over and kisses him on the lips, an act that crosses all lines of ordinary sense-making, no one really knew what happened. Yet something out of the ordinary did. Later when Alyosha does the same to Ivan, after Ivan tells him that he sides with the Grand Inquisitor, Ivan protests slightly and says, "That's plagiarism . . . Thank you though." Ironically, "plagiarism"—that word that is so laden with negative moral freight in academic circles—may not be such a bad metaphor for discipleship. For if we can claim with

---

[28] Fyodor Dostoevsky, *The Brothers Karamazov*, trans. Richard Pevear and Larissa Volokhonsky (New York: Farrar, Straus & Giroux, 1990), 320.

John the abstract affirmation that "in the beginning was the Word" (John 1:1a), and if we can model ourselves after Mary's concrete commitment, "May it be with me according to your word" (Luke 1:38), then repetition and imitation of the Word embodied here and there, all over the world (kissing the devil), can be seen as but other names for faithfulness. Perhaps even the "teacher" was reaching for something similar when he said, "there is nothing new under the sun" (Eccl 1:9b).

Pax Christi vobiscum!
(The peace of Christ be with you all!)

SCRIPTURE INDEX

INDEX OF NAMES

SUBJECT INDEX